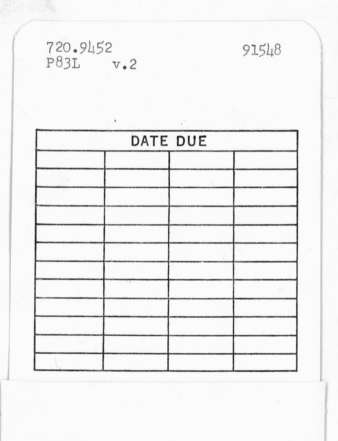

LOMBARD ARCHITECTURE

MONUMENTS
ABBAZIA DI ALBINO—MILAN

Lombard Architecture

By

ARTHUR KINGSLEY PORTER

VOLUME II—MONUMENTS

ABBAZIA DI ALBINO—MILAN

REPRINTED BY

HACKER ART BOOKS

NEW YORK

1967

First Published

1917

PRINTED IN UNITED STATES OF AMERICA

LOMBARD ARCHITECTURE

ABBAZIA DI ALBINO,[1] S. BENEDETTO

(Plate 1, Fig. 1, 2)

I.   The ancient abbey of S. Benedetto, or Vall'Alta (Vallis Alta), lies in the valley of the Luglio some kilometres above the town of Albino, from which it may be reached by a good carriage road.   The monument, although of the greatest historical and artistic importance, is still entirely unknown, having escaped the attention, not only of Enlart, but also of the numerous other writers who have occupied themselves with the question of Cistercian architecture in Italy.

The history of the monastery is but little better known than the church itself.   The archives, which must have been exceedingly rich, were dispersed when the abbey was suppressed at the end of the XVIII century.   A great number of documents found their way to the Archivio dello Stato at Milan;[2] others are preserved in the Biblioteca Civica at Bergamo.   There is a persistent tradition that still others are extant in the Ambrosiana and Castello at Milan,

---

[1] (Bergamo).

[2] These are gathered together in a parcel supplied with the provisional number Fondo di Religione 16/82-87 and labelled "Pergamene di San Benedetto di Vall'Alta, Bergamo."   The bundle is divided into smaller packages disposed as follows:

Package No. 81,	16	documents,	1240-1300
do No. 82,	32	do	1371-1380
do No. 83,	36	do	1331-1340
do No. 84,	10	do	1321-1330
do No. 85,	12	do	XVI century
do No. 86,	27	do	1421-1480
do No. 87,	17	do	1361-1370

1

but my efforts to trace them in both of those localities have been without success.[3] Some documents were copied and published by Lupi in the XVIII century, and the archives were seen and studied in their entirety by Pietro Gatti, priest at Abbazia, who published in 1853 a history of the abbey. In this the author promised to continue his researches with the publication of a *Codice dei Diplomi*, but he died in 1867 without having produced this work.[4] It may be conjectured that the documents which Gatti evidently had in his hands, and which have now disappeared, have passed into the hands of private individuals either at Vall'Alta or at Borgo S. Caterina, whither Gatti subsequently removed.[5] Until they be found, the little book of Gatti is the most important source for the history of the monument. An inscription in the church, placed there at the time of the restoration of 1843, and probably composed by the same Gatti, was, when I saw the church in July, 1913, almost illegible, and has doubtless since entirely disappeared. Gatti, however, gives a copy of it. The present priest, Sacerdote Mayer, possesses a photograph showing the Empire façade built in 1843 and replaced in 1913 by a new construction in the Romanesque style.

II. Although Gatti held in his hand a plentiful supply of original documents, his work leaves us somewhat in doubt as to the year of the actual foundation of the abbey.[6] In one place,[7] he states that it was founded in 1133, by Gregorio, bishop of Bergamo, but this notice is difficult to accept, since

---

[3] Other important sources for the history of the abbey are: *Libri Censuum* in the Archivio della Curia Vescovile at Bergamo; Celestino.—*Del matrimonio e verginità di San Grata,* and *Relazioni su diversi monasteri*—two manuscripts which passed from the possession of Cavagnis to the Biblioteca Civica of Bergamo, where they are at present preserved, Nos. λ 1.12 and ψ 2.35. Part of the second manuscript, dealing with the abbey of Pontida, was published in 1876, by Alessandri.

[4] *Elogio funebre del Sacerdote Pietro Gatti letto dal Sacerdote G. C. Sirani, nel trigesimo celebrato nella chiesa parrochiale di Borgo Santa Caterina in Bergamo, il 28 Maggio, 1867.* Bergamo, Natali, 1867.

[5] The present priest of the church, Sac. Raimondo Mayer, told me that he had knowledge of certain documents relating to the abbey in the hands of private individuals of the place, and promised to obtain for me at least a copy of the same, but the promise was never kept.

[6] It is quite impossible to connect our abbey with the basilica of S. Daniele, founded in 928, by Adelperto, bishop of Bergamo, as is evident from the following passages of the will of this prelate: In nomine Domini nostri Iesu Christi. Regnante domno nostro Hugo rex in Italia anno tercio mense november, indictione secunda. Adelbertus sancte pergamensis ecclesie episcopus. . . . Casis denique et rebus seu familiis juris mei, quas habere visus sum in vico et fundo qui dicitur Albinies, statuo et judico, ut presenti post meum discessum usque in perpetuum habeat presbyter et custos ille, qui pro tempore custos et officialis fuerit in capella et basilica illa, que est constructa in curte illa, que dicitur Albine, quam ego in honorem beati sancti Danielis consecravi. . . . (*Hist. Pat. Mon.,* XIII, 899).

[7] 4.

Gregorio did not become bishop until the following year, 1134.[8]   It is, moreover, certain that the abbey was really founded by this bishop, who had been a monk of the Cistercian order, since Gatti cites a document of April, 1136, fourteenth indiction, in which Bishop Gregorio, *indignus monachus et Sancte Pergamensis ecclesiae humilis episcopus,* invests the monks sent him by St. Bernard with a good part of the lands which he possessed in Vall'Alta.[9]   The bishop goes on to state: *ecclesiam edificavi, fratresque meos sub monastica regula victuros constitui.*   This document implies that the abbey was founded by Gregorio and that the church had already been at least partly constructed in April, 1136.   It therefore follows that the foundation must have taken place immediately after the accession of the bishop to the episcopal throne in 1134, since it is inconceivable that the many formalities connected with the foundation and the obtaining of monks from St. Bernard could have been arranged in less than two years.[10]   In 1138 the pope, Innocent II, confirmed, with a bull dated May 5, all of their possessions to Oprando, abbot of Vall'Alta, and his monks.[11]

The church, although it is spoken of as built in 1136, could then have been only partially completed, since the edifice was not consecrated until May 24, 1142.   This function was celebrated by the bishop Gregorio, assisted by Magnifredo, bishop of Brescia, and Giovanni, bishop of Lodi.[12]   The consecration of 1142 is also recorded in the inscription on the west wall of the church, thus given by Gatti:[13]

[8] According to Vincenzo Coronelli, *Rerum et Temporum Ecclesiae Bergomensis Synopsis,* ed. Graevius et Burmannus, *Thesaurus Antiquitatum et historiarum Italiae,* Vol. IX, pt. 7, p. 15, Gregorio succeeded Agino, suspected of simony, in the early part of 1134.   He came in personal contact with St. Bernard at the council of Pisa, June 19, 1134.

[9] A few days afterwards the bishop made another donation to the monastery.

[10] Gatti, 4-5.

[11] *Ibid.,* 5.

[12] Condotta poi al suo termine la chiesa di S. Benedetto, il vescovo Gregorio assistito dagli onorevoli vescovi Magnifredo di Brescia e Giovanni di Lodi, col consenso ed autorità del sommo pontefice Innocenzo, ne fece la solenne dedicazione nel mese (ai 24) di Maggio del 1142.   Ed avendosi dato principio in nome della Santissima Trinità ai venerabili offizii della consecrazione, e fattosi discorso della dote della medesima chiesa, senza la quale, giusta i canoni, non si può celebrare la dedicazione, e tenendo tutti volti gli occhi al venerabile vescovo di Bergamo, a cui quel luogo specialmente s'apparteneva, egli col consiglio dei canonici e dei nobili uomini, ponendo sopra l'altare un legno che teneva nella sua mano, *per lignum quod in sua tenebat manu, super altare ejusdem ecclesiae positum,* etc., fece alla chiesa investitura di donazione di altre possessioni, cioè del versante di nord del Monte Pelsino (Pizzo), serbato però a se il diritto di tagliarne legna a' propri usi, e della Valle Altina.   L'istromento si legge al foglio 142 del libro vescovile *Censuum tempore R. R. D. D. Joannis Barotii episcopi, qui profecto fuit magni ingenii vir.*   (Gatti, 5-6).

[13] 49.

3

LOMBARD ARCHITECTURE

CON SANTO PENSIERO

L'ANNO 1136

IL VESCOVO GREGORIO DI BERGAMO

FONDAVA

L'ANNO 1142

I VESCOVI

GREGORIO DI BERGAMO, MANFREDO DI BRESCIA E GIOVANNI DI LODI

CONSACRAVANO

PEI MONACI CISTERCENSI DI S. BENEDETTO

QUI CONVENUTI A SALMEGGIARE

L'ETERNO

QUESTO TEMPIO

CUI NEL VOLGENTE ANNO

1850

IL DEVOTO POPOLO

COL SUDORE DEL SUO FRONTE

AMPLIANDO ADORNAVA

AD ONORE DI S. BENEDETTO

ED ALLA MASSIMA GLORIA

DI DIO

Notwithstanding the donations of the bishop Gregorio, the monastery seems always to have been poor, and several donations of the XII and XIII centuries refer to the fact that the monks did not have sufficient revenues on which to live.[14] Moreover, as time went on, the prosperity of the monastery and the number of monks seem to have diminished, as is shown by the following table deduced by Gatti from various documents seen by him:

1220, 15th December	The Abbot, 6 monks, 16 lay-brothers.
1289, 12th October	The Abbot, 5 monks, 9 lay-brothers.
1325, 19th May	The Abbot, 8 monks, 12 lay-brothers.
1351, 30th May	The Abbot, 4 monks, 6 lay-brothers.
1387, 14th June	The Abbot, 2 monks, 1 lay-brother. (2 lay-brothers absent).
1408	The Abbot, 2 monks and 1 lay-brother.
1472	Two monks.
1518	A single monk.

In the XV century the monastery, following the lot of many of its prosperous contemporaries, passed into commendam, and in the XVI, XVII and

[14] Gatti, 15-16.

4

XVIII centuries it fell into the state of decay usual in those times. Nevertheless, in 1772 the church was entirely repainted with frescos. In the Revolution the abbey was finally suppressed, and in 1813 a parish was established in the church. The growth of the latter necessitated in 1843 the enlargement of the church. A radical transformation was undertaken and the work was carried to completion only in 1850. Two new side aisles were added to the nave, originally of a single aisle. A new façade was erected, and the whole church baroccoized.[15]

When I visited the church in July, 1913, a new and even more radical reconstruction was in progress. The façade was being rebuilt on pseudo-Lombard lines, the barocco stucco and plaster had been removed from the interior, and the whole church was being restored in a style which the architect doubtless intended as Romanesque. It is unfortunate that the new side aisles added in 1843 were also being made over so as to appear integral parts of the ancient structure.

III. The church at present consists of a nave three bays long, two side aisles, a choir of a single bay also flanked by side aisles (these side aisles are now walled off), an apse, a southern absidiole, a modern chapel replacing the old northern absidiole, and a campanile to the south of the choir. As we have seen, the side aisles of the nave are a modern addition, and, except in the choir, the edifice originally had only a single aisle. The choir is covered by a rib vault, of which the broad rectangular diagonals, some half a metre in width, are slightly segmental in elevation. The vault surface is, nevertheless, highly domed. There are no wall ribs, and the wall arches are approximately semicircular. It is a singular fact that this vault is pierced by two square-headed windows, apparently original. It is plain from the stereotomy of the intersection that one diagonal was completed first and the other subsequently added against it. The remainder of the nave is also covered with rib vaults, but of a very different character, since the diagonals have a torus section and the intersection is formed by a regular keystone which completes both arches

[15] The church as thus made over is described by Gatti in the following words: Pilastri di ordine composito con basamenti e capitelli semplici reggono le volte del vasto tempio. Il volto che si alza sopra la navata di mezzo, si sfoggia a padiglioni, ciascuno diviso in lunette da lunghi filoni, che salgono dal suolo co' pilastri e si incrocicchiano nel centro delle arcate. .... Nell'alto e sulle pareti, sugli scomparti e ne' frontoni sono dipinte figure di Santi, gloriette, rappresentazioni storiate, simboli religiosi e diversi ornati e festoni di finti stucchi e bassi rilievi benissimo sfoggiati e disposti con dolcezza di tocchi, con grazia di chiaro oscuro, e con vaghezza e varietà di pensiero e si bene rispondenti alle varie parti d'architettura, etc. The church as it was before the restoration he describes on page 5, as follows: La chiesa era ad una nave colle mura schiette e liscie ma tutte di vive pietre senza intonaco nè dentro nè fuori; le volte pure di pietre erano sostenute da forti pilastri, che sporgevansi nell' interno e nell' esterno delle pareti; e la maniera di costruzione è precisamente secondo il gusto di quel secolo.

at the same time. The southern side aisle of the choir has an undomed groin vault. The two western vaults of the nave are modern and have been entirely rebuilt. In the east wall the choir vault is carried on corbels, but elsewhere there is a logical and continuous system consisting of three members, of which the central one is rectangular and the two outer ones are torical. In the choir, uncarved and characterless capitals serve to adjust the rectangular load of the ribs to the shafts, but in the nave the shafts are continued to form ribs, and no capitals are interposed.

The masonry consists of rough ashlar, of which the stones are often not square and are separated by wide mortar-beds. The horizontal courses are frequently broken. The windows, widely splayed, were evidently intended to serve without glass. Above the heavy domes of the apses there is apparently laid solid masonry, so as to produce a conical form externally; there are, however, and probably always have been, wooden roofs over the main vaults, although it is evident that the eastern wall of the church has been raised.

IV. The edifice is notable for the absence of decoration. The apse and southern absidiole are not supplied with either arched corbel-tables or pilaster strips, and the cornices are formed of a single moulding of the simplest character. In the interior there is a similar absence of all decoration and carved ornament. There are no bases; capitals are either omitted altogether, or are replaced by imposts of the simplest description.

V. It is evident from the edifice itself that the church consists of two distinct periods of construction. To the first belongs the choir, with its side aisles and apses. It was evidently intended to construct a church of three aisles which should be entirely vaulted, the side aisles by groin vaults, the nave by rib vaults of thoroughly Lombard type, with broad, rectangular diagonals. This plan was subsequently changed. A single-aisled nave was erected, and was covered with rib vaults, of which the diagonals had a torus section. The two epochs of construction differ so slightly from each other that it is not possible that they are separated by a great interval of time. The story told by the stones coincides perfectly with the documentary evidence, and it seems certain that the choir, its side aisles and apse, were erected 1134-1136, and formed the church which Bishop Gregorio in 1136 speaks of as constructed. Owing probably to lack of funds the work was temporarily suspended, and resumed in a somewhat less ambitious manner. In 1142 the entire edifice was finished and consecrated. The abbey of Albino, thus authentically dated, is a most important monument. Not only is it one of the earliest Cistercian abbeys in Italy, but it also furnishes the earliest example of a profiled rib vault south of the Alps.

6

ABBAZIA DI SESTO CALENDE, S. DONATO

ABBAZIA[1] DI SESTO CALENDE,[2] S. DONATO

(Plate 1, Fig. 3, 4, 6)

I.   The frazione of Abbazia, in which is situated the ancient abbey church of S. Donato, lies about a kilometre distant from the commune of Sesto Calende.   De Dartein[3] has studied and illustrated the architecture of the church.   The history of the abbey has been made the object of a special monograph by Spinelli in a work which is a serious contribution to the local history of Sesto Calende.   The historians Robolini, Giulini,[4] Bescapè and Ughelli have all treated of the history of the monastery.

II.   The exact year of the foundation of S. Donato is unknown. Ughelli has published a bull of Pope John VIII, dated 874, in favour of Giovanni, bishop of Pavia, in which, among other goods, are confirmed to the latter "the monastery of S. Donato founded by your predecessor Bishop Luitprando, in the place which is called Scozzola."[5]   This bull, which is very badly printed by Ughelli, offers several difficulties.   According to Ughelli, Bishop Luitprando or Liutardo died in 830,[6] but whence this information is derived I do not know, and I suspect that it is incorrect, since a Bishop Liutardo of Pavia is mentioned by Anastasius Bibliothecarius[7] as a contemporary of Pope Nicholas I (858-867), and of the archbishop Giovanni of Ravenna.   On the basis of this evidence historians have been divided as to what year and even as to what time the foundation should be ascribed, and have assigned it anywhere from 822 to 860.   At any event, it is certain the foundation must have taken place in the second or third quarter of the IX century.

1 This frazione was formerly known as Scozzola.

2 (Milano).

3 383.

4 I, 274.

5 JOANNES EPISCOPUS *Servus servorum Dei.   Reverendiss.* Joanni S. Ticinensis Ecclesiæ, &c. in perpetuum. . . . Igitur postulante à nobis tua reverentia quantum ea, quæ ad stabilitatis integritatem, & ad profectum honoris sanctæ tuæ pertinere noscuntur Ecclesiæ . . . confirmamus, tibi, successoribusque tuis; . . . harumque tenore præcipienies [*sic* = praecipientes], ut Monasterium S. Dorati [*sic*] fundatum à Luitprando Epis. decessore tuo in loco, qui dicitur Scogialo, cum omnibus rebus mobilibus, & immobilibus secundùm testamenti sui seriem collatis . . . te, successoresque tuos perpetuis temporibus jurisdictionem tenere, habereque decernimus. . . . Datum est hoc nono Kal. Septembris, per manum Leonis Episcopi missi, & Apocrisarii S. Sedis Apostolicæ, imperante Dom. Carolo coronato magno imperatore.   Et ut certius appareat hoc nostrum Privilegium, & inconcussum permaneat, sigillo nostro jussimus insigniri. Anno II. & post consulatum eius anno II. indict. XI. (Ughelli, I, 1085-1086).   This bull has been reprinted in the *Hist. Pat. Mon.*, XIII, 463.

6 *Ibid.*, 1084.

7 *De vitis Roman. Pontif.*, ed. Muratori, R. I. S., III, 255.

The monastery, although outside of the diocese of Pavia, depended upon the bishops of that city. In 1105 it is mentioned among the possessions confirmed to the bishop Guido by Pope Paschal II.[8]

The subsequent history of the abbey, so far as it is known, is of minor importance for the study of the architecture. In 1509 the monastery passed into commendam,[9] and in 1533 the commendam was given to the Ospedale Maggiore of Milan.[10] Subsequently Olivetani monks were introduced. From a passage of the acts of the pastoral visits of the bishops of Pavia, Spinelli[11] has deduced that in 1566 the sacristy was placed at the east end of the south side aisle and was vaulted. The church was whitewashed between 1607 and 1613, but the final baroccoization did not take place until after 1616. It was, I presume, at the end of the XVIII century that the monks were suppressed and a parish established in the church, although I have found no explicit mention of the fact. In 1816 the church was removed from the jurisdiction of the diocese of Pavia and placed under that of Milan.[12]

III. The edifice consists of two distinct parts, a church and a narthex. The church comprises a nave four bays long, two side aisles, a raised choir flanked by side aisles, three apses and a crypt of three aisles four or five bays long. The narthex, of about the same width as the church, consists of two bays divided into three equal aisles, which do not correspond to those of the basilica. The campanile rises to the north of the choir.

The narthex is covered with groin vaults, oblong in plan, highly domed and provided with transverse arches of which the extrados is so much loaded as to form a pointed curve. These vaults are provided with wall ribs, also with loaded extrados. The free-standing supports are columns notable for their rather exaggerated entasis. The responds comprise five members, of which the central one is semicircular or semioctagonal.

The nave has been covered internally and externally with barocco stuccos, which make it exceedingly difficult to trace the original forms. The rectangular piers show a very pronounced entasis or inward lean on the side of the nave as well as on that of the side aisles.

The crypt retains to a much larger extent its original character. The groin vaults are not so highly domed as those of the narthex, but have similar disappearing transverse arches.

The façade of the narthex and part of the side walls of the same are constructed of large and carefully wrought blocks of ashlar somewhat crudely laid in courses frequently broken and separated by thick beds of mortar; in parts of the narthex, however, much cruder masonry, hardly superior to rubble, is introduced. The campanile and the remainder of the basilica

---

[8] Monasterium S. Donati à Ticinensi quondam Episcopo in Scovilla fundatum. . . . (Ughelli, I, 1085).

[9] Spinelli, 47.   [10] *Ibid.*, 228.   [11] 111.   [12] Spinelli, 111.

(where the latter has not been remade in the period of the Renaissance) are constructed of very much smaller stones—in the apse many bricks are introduced—for the most part uncut, rather carelessly laid in a manner which suggests rubble construction. In addition to scaffolding holes, there are numerous scaffolding brackets. A distinct break in the masonry of the exterior walls makes it evident that the narthex was added after the nave had been completely finished.

IV. The capitals of the narthex are of a curious type, without, so far as I am aware, analogy in Lombardy.[13] The coarse carving possesses a certain barocco quality that recalls the capitals of S. Giorgio in Palazzo at Milan.[14] The design is confused, and one hardly knows whether one is looking at leaves, interlaces or an all-over pattern. The execution is mechanical, and undercutting is avoided, yet the character of the leaf-forms seems rather advanced. One of the capitals[15] of the free-standing columns has a row of uncarved acanthus leaves surmounted by two sets of volutes—a motive Carlovingian in origin, but here treated in the dry manner of the capitals of Fontanella al Monte.[16] The abacus of this capital has a scale ornament, other abaci are decorated with rinceaux, or similar motives. Some of the bases are of Attic character and supplied with griffes. Others have a profile consisting of two square fillets separated by a scotia, in the centre of which is a torus. The capitals of the crypt, on the other hand, are uncarved or merely with corners splayed in the form of a leaf; the monolithic shafts are without bases.

The campanile is decorated with arched corbel-tables grouped three and three resting òn pilaster strips. On the west face these pilaster strips are grouped two and two, but here, like the belfry itself, they appear to have been rebuilt.

The central apse is adorned with a cornice of blind niches in two orders. In two orders also are the windows. The north absidiole, still preserved, has a cornice of arched corbel-tables and small, widely splayed windows. Imbedded in the apse as second-hand material are several bits of Carlovingian carving.

V. The narthex, as proved by its ashlar masonry and by the capitals analogous to those of S. Giorgio in Palazzo at Milan (1129) and Fontanella al Monte (c. 1130), is certainly a construction of the XII century, and may be ascribed with confidence to c. 1130. Of the remainder of the edifice, which appears homogeneous, in so far as it has not been remade in the barocco period, it is more difficult to determine the epoch. There is, it has been seen, conclusive internal proof that the nave is earlier than the narthex, that is to say, earlier than c. 1130. The masonry is precisely analogous to that of the

[13] Plate 1, Figs. 3, 4.   [14] Plate 128, Fig. 5.   [15] Plate 1, Fig. 3.
[16] Plate 93, Fig. 2.

neighbouring church of S. Vincenzo, consecrated in 1102. I therefore assign this portion of the edifice to c. 1100, with the exception of the columns and capitals of the crypt, which are probably taken from an earlier building. I experience, I confess, considerable reluctance in ascribing an edifice in many ways so primitive to so late a date, but the close analogy of the masonry to that of S. Vincenzo seems to leave no other alternative. The singular crudeness of the masonry and the numerous primitive features of the edifice must be ascribed to extraordinary haste and carelessness on the part of the builders.

ABBAZIA DI SESTO CALENDE, S. VINCENZO

(Plate 2, Fig. 1)

I. Spinelli is the only author who has noticed the existence of this monument, which lies in the fields a short distance from the abbey of S. Donato.

II. In the acts of the pastoral visit of the bishop of Pavia of 1595, Spinelli found and quotes a passage which proves that this church was formerly a convent of nuns.[1] In 1595 it had already ceased to have a separate existence owing to the calamities it had suffered in the wars, and its goods were given to the abbey of S. Donato. The church, however, continued to be officiated as a dependence of S. Donato until 1780, when it was finally suppressed.

In the Ambrosiana at Milan, in that very valuable transcript of ancient documents known as the *Codice della Croce,* I had the good fortune to find an inedited document which throws light upon the early history of the convent, and happily gives us the year (1102) in which the church was consecrated.[2] It may, consequently, be assumed that the abbey was founded somewhat before this date.

The edifice appears to have been made over and baroccoized in the early XVIII century. On the wall is a destroyed inscription of 1729, and the altar bears the date of 1732.

[1] Ad quam [ecclesiam sub titulo sancti Vincentii] et monasterium quodam ut dicitur ibi ad eamdem ecclesiam . . . . . constructum permanebant moniales et iterum visa fuerunt quedam vestigia et fundamenta monasterii et ut item dicunt fuit monasterium. . . . tempore bellorum vastatum fuit. (Spinelli, 145).

[2] I transcribe the most important part of this document: Anno ab incarnacione domini nostri Ihesu Christi milleximo centeximo secundo mense iulii indicione decima. Dum in Dei nomine intra clausa modoeciensis ecclesie bernardus romane ecclexie insignis cardinalis atque legatus domni apostolici pascalis, nec non et grosolanus uenerabilis archiepiscopus ecclexie mediolanensis honeste tractarent de diuinis et humanis aduenerunt legati ermeline abbatisse sestensi monasterii suplicantes exconsecrationem prefati monasterii. (*Codice della Croce,* MS. Amb., D. S. IV, Vol. V, f. 20).

ACQUANEGRA SUL CHIESE, S. TOMMASO

III.   The edifice is extremely simple in character, and consists of a single-aisled nave and an apse.   The upper part of the nave walls has been rebuilt in the barocco period, but with the exception of the apse, the church has evidently always been roofed in wood.   Like the nave, the apse was somewhat raised in the barocco period.   This apse, however, is the best preserved part of the edifice, and still retains its widely splayed windows, albeit walled up.

The masonry is extremely rough, and recalls that of the choir of S. Donato. Uncut bits of stone, pebbles, bricks and a few roughly squared blocks of stone are crudely laid in courses, frequently broken and deviating widely from the horizontal.   The mortar-beds are extremely wide, and there are numerous scaffolding holes.   The herring-bone masonry of the nave is the result of late alterations.

IV.   The apse is decorated externally with arched corbel-tables supported on pilaster strips.   The interior possesses fine frescos of the XVI century, one of which bears the date 1516.

V.   The documentary evidence seems conclusive that this church was consecrated in 1102.   It is true that the masonry is singularly crude to have been executed at this epoch, and I confess that I have long debated whether it be not necessary to assume that the apse is the remains of an earlier chapel preserved in the church reconstructed in 1102.   However, having observed that in the narthex of S. Donato, an edifice evidently constructed c. 1130, there is some masonry almost as crude as that of S. Vincenzo, I am forced to the conclusion that the masons of Sesto Calende were singularly careless and slipshod in their work.   They were, perhaps, forced to this by the lack of good stone or brick for building.   It therefore seems necessary to accept S. Vincenzo as an authentically dated monument of 1102.

ACQUANEGRA SUL CHIESE,[1] S. TOMMASO

I.   The mosaic pavement of Acquanegra has been illustrated by Matteucci and Venturi.[2]   For the history of the monastery the little book of Casnighi is of great value, and some important notices are contained in the inexact publication of Lucchini.

II.   The earliest known document relating to this monastery dates from November 9, 1101, and is a deed of Adalperono, bishop of Trent, investing the abbot of Acquanegra with the abbey of S. Maria della Gironda of Bozzolo.[3]   Since in this document the choir of the church is very precisely

---

[1] (Mantova).   [2] III, 436.

[3] In nomine Domini Dei eterni.   Die Sabati nono intrante mese novembris.   Dum in Dei nomine dominus Adalperonus Dei gratia Tribentinus adesset episcopus in

11

mentioned, it is evident that the edifice must have been constructed and in use at this period.   Lucchini states[4] that after examining fifty-two documents contained in the *Libro dei Privilegii del comune di Acquanegra e Mosio* he reached the conclusion that the monks had been put under the jurisdiction of Trent by the emperor (Barbarossa ?), who was favourable to them, and that they were subsequently spoiled and plundered by the papal party.   A document of 1104 referred to, but not published, by Casnighi[5] makes it evident that at that epoch the monastery had already been in existence for some time.   The same author also cites numerous other documents which prove the continued existence of a monastery of Benedictines at Acquanegra in the XII century.[6]

In the first half of the XV century the abbey passed into commendam,[7] and in 1562 a *vicaria perpetua* was erected in the church,[8] which in 1802 was reduced to the rank of a simple parish.   In 1898 an act of atrocious barbarism was committed when the fine old Lombard basilica[9] was torn down and replaced by the existing modern edifice.   At this time was discovered the mosaic pavement which is now all that remains of the ancient monastery.

III.   Of the ancient church as it was before 1898, there is extant not even a description or a photograph.

IV.   The ancient mosaic pavement is preserved under the wooden floor of the new church, and can only be seen when the planks above have been specially removed—a fatiguing piece of work which requires much time. The ancient pavement covered an area at least as great as that of the existing church.   It is in very unequal preservation, some parts being in good condition while others are much damaged.   In the northern side aisle there was probably a representation of the signs of the zodiac—at least a crab, a ram and a capricorn are extant in part, and it is reasonable to suppose the other signs were placed in the remaining squares into which the pavement was divided. Other fragments of the northern side-aisle pavement show animals which I believe to be purely fanciful.   At the west end of the northern side aisle is one of the most interesting representations of the entire pavement.   On an excellently drawn stallion rides the figure of a horseman apparently nude. In his left hand he holds the reins, and his right hard is placed against his cheek with a gesture that seems to indicate thought.   From his head flutters in the breeze what I take to be the crest of a helmet, but the pavement is so much damaged that it may be in reality long hair.   The inscription SINON is clearly legible and complete.   Venturi[10] calls this figure "Sidone sul cavallo," and says that it is a representation taken from the Æneid.   He means to identify the horseman, I presume, with the Sinon of wooden-horse fame.[11]   I

Ecclesia S. Thome apost. de Acquanigra.   Ibi in choro ejusdem ecclesie etc. . . . . Factum est hoc anno Domini Millesimo C. primo Indictione nona . . . (Lucchini, 95).
    [4] 96.   [5] 23.   [6] *Ibid.*, 26-27.   [7] *Ibid.*, 30.   [8] *Ibid.*, 31.   [9] *Ibid.*, 36.
    [10] III, 436.   [11] *Æneid*, II, line 77 f.

confess, however, this identification seems to me to offer several insurmountable difficulties. In the first place, the horse in the mosaic, far from being of wood, is extremely realistic. Secondly, it does not appear from Vergil's account that Sinon ever rode upon the wooden horse. Finally, in all mediæval church art I know of no other representation of a subject taken from Vergil. I consider it much more likely that we have here a fragment of a representation of a scene from the Maccabees, such as Lombard artists loved to represent, and executed, for example, in the pavements at Casale Monferrato and Bobbio. Simon, the second son of Mattathias, called also Thassi, is a prominent character in the first book of Maccabees, and upon the death of Jonathan became the head of the nation, both as captain and high priest. During his brilliant reign he took part in many warlike enterprises.[12] Our pavement doubtless represents a fragment of a scene from one of these battles.

Near the figure of Sinon are placed various animals of a veritable zoölogical garden. Particularly well drawn is what looks like a kangaroo. Below is an immense dog. The fore parts, including the long ears, pointed nose and eyes, neck and forelegs, are seen in plan from above. The hind parts, the leg with claws and the skinny tail, are, on the contrary, shown in elevation. Below is the inscription [CER]BERVS. At the extreme western end of the side aisle and, in fact, under the door, may be read the inscription IDRA. The figure of the hydra herself is broken, but one of the dog-heads can still be clearly seen.

The extant fragments of the pavement of the southern side aisle show a great deal of conventional ornament. The patterns here, as throughout the entire pavement, are most varied and interesting, and consist of rinceaux, Greek frets, or a sort of "T"-formed pattern, guilloches, parallel lines, and numerous other motives. Many of these ornaments are extremely similar to those found in the mosaic of the Campo Santo at Cremona. The pavement of the southern side aisle, in addition to these purely ornamental forms, shows also several animals. In one medallion is a fox looking at a chicken placed in the neighbouring medallion, as if Reynard saw with considerable enthusiasm a prospective dinner. We apparently have here a version of one of the folk stories which later took form in the *Roman de Renart*. Below is seen another episode of the same cycle, a fox hunting a hare. A fragment showing part of a goose may also have belonged to the same epic. Another scene represents two birds, perhaps geese, and two animals I am unable to identify, placed on the four sides of a large diamond, the interior of which has been destroyed.

In the nave, the extant fragments represent interlaces of circles in the centre of which are seen two birds drinking out of a bowl, after the manner of the early Christian frescos in the catacombs;[13] an animal which I am unable to identify, and numerous bits of other destroyed subjects.

---

12 I *Maccabees*, passim.
13 This fragment has been illustrated by Venturi.

Technically this mosaic is excellent, and represents a great advance over that of Pieve Terzagni, in that much green is used in addition to black, white, yellow and red. The colouring of the pavement in the nave is particularly fine and delicate, perhaps the daintiest and most charming I have ever seen in a Romanesque mosaic. All crudeness has disappeared alike from the colour and the drawing, and the design is as exquisite as is the colour.

V. The excellent technical quality of the mosaic at Acquanegra gives reason to believe, notwithstanding the naïveté of the subjects, that we have here not a particularly early work. Numerous of the conventional figures show great analogy with the mosaic of the Campo Santo at Cremona, which was executed 1106-1117. There is documentary evidence that the church was in use in 1104, and it is probable that the edifice had been constructed not long before this. We may, therefore, ascribe the pavement of Acquanegra to c. 1100.

ACQUI,[1] CATHEDRAL

(Plate 2, Fig. 2, 3, 4, 5, 6; Plate 3, Fig. 1; 3, 4, 5; Plate 4, Fig. 1, 4)

I. Although an extremely important monument of Lombard art, the cathedral of Acqui remained completely unknown, save for a passing reference of Pellate,[2] until I published an account of it in the *American Architect* in 1913. Only the mosaics, carried away to Turin in the middle of the last century, had attracted some notice. Aus'm Weerth[3] published a drawing of them made by Vico when they were still in their original position in the crypt, and before they had been broken in pieces for transportation. This drawing is, therefore, of great value. The study of Fabretti is also of some help in interpreting the inscription. For the history of the cathedral of Acqui, the same writers—Savio, Moriondo, Biorci, Lavezzari and Blesi—are to be consulted as for the history of the church of S. Pietro.[4]

II. In the account of the early documents regarding the cathedral of Acqui, cited below in connection with the history of S. Pietro, it will appear there is every reason to believe that until 1023 the cathedral of Acqui was situated in the church of S. Pietro. In view of the serious documents which prove this, there is no reason to give heed to the late and unreliable chronicler, Fra Jacopo, when he tells us that Lodovico Pio (†840)[5] was buried in the existing cathedral.

---

[1] (Alessandria).   [2] 423.   [3] 18.   [4] See below, p. 25.

[5] Facta strage Sarracenorum. predictus imperator Ludovicus Pius de Roma venit in Lombardiam. et in civitate Aquis Lombardie infirmatur et moritur. et in capitulo ecclesie sancte Marie Maioris sepellitur. ubi stat ipsius sepulcrum. (Frate Jacopo da Acqui, *Chronicon Imaginis Mundi,* ed. *Hist. Pat. Mon.,* V, 1524). In alia autem Ecclesia

The bishop Primo (989-1018) began the construction of the new cathedral church of Acqui on its present site.[6] This church, continued by Primo's successor, Brunengo, must have been sufficiently advanced in 1023 so that services could be held in it, for the bishop Dudone in that year transferred to the new cathedral the canons from the old cathedral of S. Pietro, and began to celebrate mass in the new edifice.[7] In 1034 Dudone was succeeded by S. Guido. A document of 1042 speaks of the canonica of S. Maria at Acqui as already constructed.[8] S. Guido embraced the task of completing the cathedral with such enthusiasm that in after times he came to be considered as its sole builder. A pious reverence for the saint has doubtless played its part in somewhat exaggerating his rôle. None the less it is certain that he made very large donations to the diocese, and there is still extant the confirmation of one of these donations, made by the emperor Henry III, in 1040.[9]

In 1067 S. Guido consecrated his cathedral. The most authentic source for this fact is an inscription in the contemporary mosaic discovered in the crypt of the cathedral at Acqui and now in the basement of the Museo Civico di Arte Applicata ad Industria at Turin.[10] Although sadly mutilated, enough of the inscription is extant to leave no doubt as to its significance. According to Durand there was in his time a portion of this inscription still to be seen in its original position in the crypt; but, if so, it has since disappeared.[11]

The fact that S. Guido completed the cathedral in 1067 is confirmed by a number of other sources. The most ancient of these is the sculpture of the XII century now in the façade of the arcade of the episcopal palace facing the Piazza del Duomo, in which is shown a bishop, evidently S. Guido, holding a model of the church in his hand. In the life of S. Guido written by Lorenzo Calceato about 1260, the consecration of the cathedral by S. Guido in 1067

S. Mariæ majoris est corpus Ludovici pii Imperatoris. (*Chronica* Fr. Jacobi de Aquis, ed. Moriondo, II, 135). As a matter of fact, Lodovico Pio died on an island in the Rhine near Mainz.

6 See text cited below, p. 26.

7 See text cited below, p. 27.

8 . . . . . canonica sanctæ Mariæ quæ est constructa intra civitatem Aquensem. (Moriondo, I, 30). Cf. Biorci, II, 286.

9 Biorci, I, 189-190.

10

. . . . . DNO WIDONE PONTIFICE VIR[O] PRVDENTISSIMO C[PLETVM

EST . . . . . W]

IDONE [PER] OMIA LAVDABILI ET OBTO [observantissimo] O . . . . .

[ANNO AB INCARNATIONE DNI NRI]

IHV X[PI ML]XMO VII. INDICE V . . . . .

11 Un petit fragment est seul visible; il contient deux mots latins qui seraient les noms d'un évêque d'Acqui du XII siècle.

is very explicitly recorded,[12] although the author makes two mistakes in his chronological notes, giving the sixth, instead of the fifth, indiction, and the emperor as Henry III instead of Henry IV. Calceato says nothing about the cathedral having been begun by Guido's predecessors, and although it is not stated that S. Guido began the construction, the text might be construed to imply it, and it probably was so interpreted by later authors. Calceato gives us two new details touching the consecration: (1) that S. Guido was assisted by the bishops Pietro of Tortona and Oberto of Genoa; and (2) that the consecration took place on November 13. The first detail is certainly correct.[13] The second item appears to be also accurate, since the day of the consecration is given as the thirteenth of November in an ancient parchment missal cited by Biorci.[14] It is therefore probable that later texts which give the date of the consecration as the eleventh of November are erroneous.

The longer life of S. Guido, edited by the Bollandists and written long after the death of the saint,[15] repeats the notice of the consecration in 1067 with the same chronological errors, and states that S. Guido transferred the cathedral from the church of S. Pietro to a loftier situation, built it from its foundations, gave it the new name of the Assunta, and provided it with a chapter of canons.[16] It is evident that the pious author, in his religious zeal,

[12] Divinæ namque providentiæ nutu, qua Christi miles diregebatur in omnibus, nobilissimam Christi matrem, ac reverentissimam suis expensis ædificavit ecclesiam, in qua nunc sedes Episcopalis est, & illam fecit solemniter consecrari a venerabilibus Episcopis Petro Terdonensi viro per omnia laudabili, & Alberto Januensi tertio idus novembris anno incarnationis Jesu Christi millesimo sexagesimo septimo inditione sexta domino Henrico III. Imperatore regnante. . . . (*Vita B. Guidoni Aquensis Episcopi* auctore Laurentio Calceato Aq. circa an. 1260 conscripta., Cap. XVI, ed. Moriondo, II, 99).

[13] It is known that Pietro I was bishop of Tortona 1022-1068. See Moriondo, II, 100. Oberto, not Alberto, was bishop of Genoa in 1067. (Ughelli, IV, 844).

[14] . . . idibus hoc fit officium consecrationis hujusce Ecclesiæ majoris . . . (Biorci, I, 189-190).

[15] This fact is witnessed by such passages as: . . . hæc omnia approbante Imperatore Longobardorum, anno ab Incarnatione Christi millesimo sexagesimo quinto, constantibus de hisce omnibus etiam hodie privilegiis et scripturis authenticis. . . . Corpore ipsius . . . marmoreaque hic in arca usque in præsens recondito, meritissime veneratur.

[16] Suscepto igitur Pastorali regimine, quod mira devotione simul et auctoritate regebat . . . universo patrimonio, quod habebat, Cathedralem imprimis ecclesiam, ante sub titulo S. Petri in dicta civitate nimis antiquatam, et æris intemperie fere inhabilem, eminentiori dictæ civitatis loco, ampliorem et ornatiorem sub invocatione Assumptionis Beatæ Virginis, quam Advocatam excorde gerebat, ab imis fundamentis instituit proprio ære; illamque Archidiaconatu, Præpositura, Archipresbyteratu, et Canonicatibus duodecim exornavit et auxit, prout hodie adhuc cernitur: accersitisque una Reverendissimis Dominis Episcopo Dertonensi et Oberto Episcopo Januensi, viris undequaque laudabilibus et dignissimis, eam devote consecrarunt, anno a Nativitate Domini millesimo sexagesimo septimo; Indictione sexta, Henrico Imperatore tertio. (*Vita S. Guidonis*, ed. Jean de Bolland, *Acta Sanctorum*, Junii die secunda, I, 224). Cf. also Moriondo, II, 110.

has attributed to S. Guido certain acts really performed by his predecessors, Primo and Dudone.

The office for the feast of S. Guido in the church of Acqui contains three different references to the construction of the church by the saint.[17] Similar notices, derived from one of the lives of the saint, are repeated by the late and inaccurate Fra Jacopo da Acqui.[18]

In later times the tradition that S. Guido constructed the cathedral was universally accepted. It is, for example, recorded on two inscriptions on the western portal added to the cathedral in 1481.[19] Similarly in an inscription of 1655 in the choir, S. Guido is referred to as the founder of this basilica,[20] and in an inscription in the episcopal palace, I know not of what time, but evidently late, he is said to have built the cathedral at his own expense.[21]

About 1177 the diocese of Acqui suffered a severe blow when, at its expense, was created the new see of Alessandria. A long struggle ensued between the rival cities. A bull of Innocent III of 1198, which ordered that

---

[17] Ecce Sacerdos magnus, qui in diebus suis ædificavit domum, & exaltavit templum sacrum Domino paratum in gloria sempiterna. (*Officium in festo B. Guidonis Aquensis Episcopi*, ed. Moriondo, II, 104). Templum fecit templi cultor honoris eximii quo completo fine lœto cursum hujus seculi consummavit, & intravit in gaudia Domini (*Ibid.*, 107). Ecce Sacerdos magnus, qui in vita sua suffulsit domum, & in diebus suis corroboravit templum &c. (*Ibid.*, 108). Cf. Eccli., 1, 1.

[18] [sanctus Guido] facit suis expensis et Ecclesie [*sic*] ecclesiam maiorem sancte Marie matris Dei quam mirifice ornavit. clericis officio libris divinis et paramentis. ecclesia quasi completa . . . ad extremam horam devenit. Et . . . spiritum suum suo tradidit Salvatori. in ecclesia sua quam edificavit. in archa marmorea collocatur ubi devotis cottidie crebra fiunt miracula de quibus plenam fidem invenies in legenda sua que servatur in sacristia ecclesie predicte aquensis civitatis. (Frate Jacopo da Acqui, *Chronicon Imaginis Mundi*, ed. *Hist. Pat. Mon.*, V, 1548). Cf. also Moriondo, II, 142.

[19]   HOC T̄EPL̄V . ASS̄VPTE . C̄OSTRVXIT . WIDO . M̂ARIE

       WIDO . VENₗₗₛ
       COMES . AQ
       SANE . ET
       AQVN . ĒPS .
       H̄AC . PROP̂IO
       ERE . C̄oŜTRVXIT .
       ET . DOTAVIT .
       ECCLEXIAM
       ȦD . H̄OR̄EM .
       VIRGINIS .
       ET . IN . EA .
       REQUIESCIT
       . V . F . Aº . D̂I   (= viri facti anno domini)
       M . L X VII

the episcopal seat of Acqui should be transferred to Alessandria, precipitated a war between the two towns.[22]   In 1202 Innocent III settled the dispute by uniting Alessandria and Acqui in a single diocese, of which Alessandria was the primary seat and Acqui the second.   The bishop resided six months alternately in each,[23] but in 1405 the two dioceses were again separated and Acqui regained the rank of an episcopal city, albeit with sadly diminished prestige.

In 1479 the bells of the cathedral were transferred from the old to the new campanile.[24] From this fact it may be inferred that the old Romanesque campanile was destroyed about this time, and that the new campanile, which still exists, was finished in the year 1479. Two years later the existing western portal was erected by Giovanni da Pillacorte, son of Antonio of Val Cavargna, Lugano.[25] Pillacorte is possibly the name of the native town of Giovanni, but where it is I have not been able to discover. Still another inscription records that the same portal was made in the time of Tommaso de Regibus, of Alba, bishop of Acqui, who also caused the adjoining episcopal palace to

[20]
D.O.M

CIVITATI . IMMINENTIBVS . IAM . BELLORVM . PERICVLIS .
S . GVIDO . EPISCOPVS . HVIVS . BASILICÆ . FVNDATOR
NATALIV̄ . NOBILITATE . INSIGNIS . PIETATE . CONSPICVVS .
INC̄OPARABILI . CHARITATE . EXITIA . CÆDESQ . AVERTIT .
VOVIT . VNIVERSVS . POPVLVS . AQVENSIS .
NOVISSIME . TANTVM . INVOCAVIT .
ALLOBROGES . INTERCESSOR . RETRAXIT .
ITALOS . TEVTONES . ET . IBEROS . E . MVRIS . PROTECTOR .
DEIECIT
RARI . CIVES . IN . PVGNA . OMNES . INCOLVMNES .
ORNATIORI . ARA . PRÆSTANTIORI . VRNA .
VOTVM . EXOLVERVNT .
MDCLV .

[21]
S . WIDO . DOMO . AQVESANA
TEMPLVM . MAXIMVM . B . V . ASSVMPTÆ . AERE . SVO
CONSTRVXIT .   (Biorci, I, 191).

[22] G. Schiavinae, *Annales Alexandrini*, ed. *Hist. Pat. Mon.*, XI, 92.
[23] Lavezzari, 43, 45.
[24] Eo anno [1479] die prima septembris presbiteri majores Aquensis Ecclesiæ permutaverunt campanas de campanili veteri super novo luna existente in oppositione cum sole & sequenti die Bartolomeus . . . . . Carpentarius, qui dictas campanas collocavit in dicto campanili novo, cecidit, & mortuus est. (Notae historicae repertae in quodam antiquo Codice Can. Gabrielis Chiabreræ Præpositi Capituli Aquensis, ed. Moriondo, II, 265).

be erected. This is entirely consistent with the preceding inscription, since it is known that Tommaso de Regibus died in 1484. The Maggiorino, who is invoked with S. Guido in the first part of the inscription, is reputed the first bishop of Acqui, and is revered as a saint. His statue and that of S. Guido are placed in relief on either side of the portal and distinguished by the inscriptions S. MAIORINVS and S. WIDO.[26]

In the west gallery of the cloister on the second floor is an inscription which states that Costantino Marenco[27] built from the foundations the houses of the canons at his expense, March 24, 1495.[28] On the west side of the

[25]
MCCCCLXXXI
HOC.OP' IM
PRESSIT DE PIL
LACVRTE.IOHA.
NES.QVE.TV
LIT.ANTONIV'
VALIS.CAROA
LVGANI.

[26]
MAIORINE
PSVL.POPVLO
QVOQ'.GRAT
AQVESI.NVC.
CV.VVIDONE
SALVA COGE
DO.NOCETES.
HEc.PORTA.
FACTA.TPR.D.
TOME.DE.REGI
BV' DE.ALBA.EPI
AQN.QVI.PALA
CIV'.VNA.CV
DOMO.[CON]TIGVA
FIERI.FECIT

[27] For an account of this bishop, see Lavezzari, 91.

[28]
✠CONSTANTINVS.MARENCVS.IS
TIVS.AQVENSIS.ECCLEXIE.PASTOR.
RESTORATORQ'.HAS.CHANONICH
ALES.MANSIONES.SVO.ERRE.A.FON
DAMENTIS.ERRESIT.
.SVB.DOMINI.1.4.9.5.DIE.24.MARCII

canons' house is another inscription from which it appears that Costantino Marenco reconstructed not only the houses of the canons, but also the cloister.[29]

At the close of the Cinquecento began the baroccoization of the church. Francesco dei Conti di S. Giorgio e Biandrate, bishop of Acqui (1585-1600), was the first who seriously undertook to change the church "da spelonca di ladri in casa di Dio."[30] His principal achievement appears to have been the whitewashing of the nave.[31] His successor, Camillo Beccio, added the western portal in front of the cathedral and the graceful colonnade of the episcopal palace. A manuscript of Blesi, written about 1614, but containing several later annotations and additions, gives an interesting description of the church as it emerged from these alterations.[32] In 1618 the body of S. Guido was translated

[29]   R' D' IN . X̄P̄O . D̄N̄S .
CONSTĀTIN' . MARENCHVS .
CIVIS ET . ĒP̄S . AQV̄ĒN . AC CŌĒS . HAS
EDES . CV̄ CLAVSTRO P[ER] CANONICOR[VM]
ALIOR[VM]Q[VE] HVI' ECCLIE SACERDOT̄V
RESIDENTIA . SVA IMPENSA .
A FŌD̄AMĒTIS ERREXIT
MCCCCLXXXXV

[30] Biorci, I, 233-234.
[31] Lavezzari, 255.
[32] [La Cattedrale] quale fu fatta fabbricare dalla Santa memoria del Beato Guido vescovo e prottettore della medma Città, con bellissima regola d'architettura, e giusta proporzione, tutta di pietre forti piccate a scalpello, e che la rendevano magnifica, e riguardevole, e sebbene fù bonissima l'intenzione di Monsignor Ilͫo S. Giorgio vescovo di far imbiancar dᵃ Chiesa le ha nondimeno scemato assai d'onorevolezza, et antichità che dimostrava. Rende però riguardevole La medma Chiesa una piazza detta del Duomo. . . . E nella medma Chiesa un oratorio ossia Confessione, ovvero il Scurolo, il più bello, e meglio disposto, e proporzionato, che io abbia a quest'ora visto in altra Città e talmente assicurato sopra una quantità di collonne di Pietra, che è molto lodato da chi giudiciosame lo considera. Ha di più la Cattedrale preda la canonica congionta ad essa con Claustri, e stanze comode alli Sigʳⁱ Cannonici, che quelle servono anco tal volta a Cittadini Privati di molta conversazione [sic, considerazione]. Aggiongono poi molto di magnificenza a qᵗᵃ Chiesa due scale commodissime, una nell'entrare che resta sulla detta piazza del Duomo, e l'altra che separa il Coro et Altare maggiore con l'ala a traverso del Corpo più grande d'essa Chiesa. La quale fù dedicata dall'istesso Beato Guido alla Assonzione della Gloriosissima vergine Maria Nostra Signora, et in dᵃ Chiesa oltre i corpi del Beato Guido sud. e del Beato Majorino, sono altre relliquie. . . . Addizione.—Questa piazza che dice il nostro autore esser di competente grandezza, al presente si trova poco meno che del tutto occupato da un antiporto fatto fare, e solame principiato avanti detta Chiesa dal medmo Revmo vescovo della Città. Li claustri, e Canonica furono fatti edificare da Monsig. Costantino Marenco, Vescovo della Città, ad effetto che li Sgⁱ Canonici dovessero in quelle Stanze far residenza . . . ma di presente ne restano esclusi. . . . La Seguente memoria di Monsige Bicuti, è stata ritrovata in un manuscritto. Monsige vescovo Gio' Ambroggio Bicuti, ha primierame fatto lastricare

from the crypt into the upper church.[33]   From 1644 to 1655 was erected a new chapel of S. Guido in accordance with the vow made by the citizens thirty years before.[34]   The bishop Giovanni Ambrogio di Bicuti (1647-1675) at his own expense raised the pavement of the choir and lateral chapels, and adorned the choir with stuccos and paintings.   He also remodelled the dome over the crossing.[35]   In 1709 the chapel of S. Guido was repaired.

In 1845, in the course of restorations in the choir, there came to light in the crypt a mosaic pavement.   The chapter of Acqui, moved by loyalty rather than by good judgment, tore up this mosaic from the spot in which it had been discovered, and sent it as a gift to the king at Turin, where for a long time it was stored away in the cellar of the royal palace.   The project of Promis, who wished to place it in the library of the University of Turin, happily came to nought, for had he done so it would doubtless have perished with the other treasures of that institution in the lamentable fire.   Recently the mosaic has been placed in the basement of the Museo Civico di Arte Applicata ad Industria.

The cathedral of Acqui has suffered severely in the loss of its precious mosaic and in the barocco restorations of which it has been the unfortunate victim.   However, it has had the rare good fortune to escape a modern restoration, and the Romanesque structure wherever it appears is still genuine and unfalsified.

III.   The edifice consisted originally of a nave six bays long, two side aisles, projecting transepts with eastern absidioles, a choir flanked by side aisles, three apses and a crypt extending beneath the transepts and choir. Numerous alterations have, however, somewhat modified this plan.   The western bay of the southern side aisle has been blocked up by the walls of the XV century campanile.[36]   A complete set of side chapels was added to the church in the time of the Renaissance, destroying the old side-aisle walls, of which, however, some bits, with fragments of their corbel-tables, are still

di Chiapponi quadrati L'Antiporto, et con sassi, e suoi cordoni fatto far fuori, et intorno di esso con bella architettura una cordonata, ossia Lastricatura, et indi ha fatto adornare di stucco, e Pitture il coro di essa Chiesa Cattedle nell'anno 1668, et fatto fare due Cantorie corrisponti et accomodar la Camera sopra la Capella della Ssma Annunciata.

[33] 1618.   Corpo del nostro Protettore S. Guido si colloca nella Cappella maggiore della Confessione del Duomo.   Convocati 27 Maggio, e 5 Giugno 1618.   Il sito è umido, si trasporta al disopra nella Cappella detta de' Santi.   (Extract from the Municipal Archives, cit. Biorci, I, 203).

[34] Biorci, I, 203.

[35] *Ibid.*, II, 257.

[36] The upper part of this campanile rests on the top of the clearstory wall.   S. Guido's masonry must have been very substantial to enable it to bear all this extra weight.

preserved under the aisle roofs. Finally, the absidioles of the transepts have been destroyed. The fact that they formerly existed is proved only by the lower story still preserved in the crypt.

The nave has been entirely covered with stucco, so that it is exceedingly difficult to trace the original dispositions. However, parts of the bases of the original piers, still visible here and there, prove that the latter had a compound section consisting of a rectangular pilaster strip towards the nave, two half columns to the east and west, and a half column engaged on a pilaster strip towards the side aisles. In all probability the pilaster strip towards the nave did not support a system, but the second order of the archivolts, as at S. Maria Canale, Tortona (Plate 211, Fig. 5). The piers of the crossing had a similar section, but were heavier and had some extra members. The responds of the side aisles probably consisted of a simple pilaster strip, but this point cannot be definitely determined.

The side aisles were doubtless covered with groin vaults. The existing vaults of the side aisles show great variation of form and perhaps—even probably—some of the original ones still survive, but so thick is the coating of intonaco that it is impossible to be certain. The transverse arches of the side aisles were, I believe, in one order. The nave was not vaulted, but roofed in wood. The ancient clearstory walls are still perfectly preserved above the modern vaults which cut across the old clearstory windows. These clearstory windows are peculiarly spaced, in that there are only three on each side, corresponding to six bays. Above the modern vaults the wall of the nave on the interior shows no signs of a system or of vaults, a clear indication that no vaults were ever erected.

It is evident that the wall of the south transept has been raised. Externally there are two rows of arched corbel-tables (Plate 2, Fig. 5), of which the lower one corresponds to the symmetrical arched corbel-table of the other transept. Under the roof may still be seen the old arched corbel-tables of the south wall of the crossing, which originally were visible above the transept roof. The wall above and the second arched corbel-table are of inferior masonry. It is evident that the wall was raised at the time the barocco vaults of the transepts were erected. There is nothing to prove that the transepts were originally vaulted, and nothing to indicate how the crossing was treated, but it may be conjectured that the latter was surmounted by an octagonal cloistered vault. The choir vaults appear to be modern, but it is not improbable that they replace similar barrel vaults of the ancient edifice. The crypt still retains its original groin vaults, although the greater number of them have been made over or at least covered with intonaco. Especially under the north transept the original forms of the crypt vault may still be traced. It is evident that the vaults were not domed, but formed of bricks laid in courses generally approximately regular and separated by wide mortar-beds. The masonry is nevertheless very crude. There were disappearing transverse arches but apparently no wall ribs. The church possessed no buttresses.

The campanile, Gothic in style, is evidently later than the church. A proof of this, were other needed besides the style of the architecture and the character of the masonry, is to be found in the fact that the arched corbel-tables which originally crowned the south clearstory wall are still visible inside the campanile.

The masonry throughout consists of crudely shaped pieces of stone of about the size of bricks, with an occasional brick (bricks are used especially in the archivolts and the upper portions of the edifice), laid in thick beds of mortar. The courses are in general horizontal but often are irregular. There are numerous square scaffolding holes.

To the south of the cathedral are the graceful cloisters (Plate 3, Fig. 3), entirely rebuilt in 1495, but in part with the ancient columns and capitals of S. Guido.

IV. The capitals of the nave piers have, for the most part, been so denatured in the barocco period that it is impossible to judge of their original style, though from the stunted proportions of some of them it is possible to infer that they were of the same type as the capitals of the upper gallery of the cloister. In the two western piers of the crossing, however, the old Lombard capitals are still preserved above the new stucco capitals of the Renaissance, having been spared because they were hidden by the gallery which runs around the church on top of the cornice. They are of a rudimentary bell type, with the angles slightly indented or foliated. The capitals of the crypt are all alike and of a similar type, but somewhat shallower. More interesting are the capitals of the cloister (Plate 3, Fig. 3). Those of the upper story recall the capitals of Lodi Vecchio, and are characterized by shallow, plain abaci, with grotesque heads or leaves in the angles, and some-times a rosette in the centre of each face. One is a crude imitation of the classical Ionic. Those of the lower story and of the west gallery of the second story have broad, flat leaves, volutes in the angles, acanthus leaves stiffly carved under the volutes and a bulbous projection in the middle of each face, something between a volute and a leaf. They are evidently of the XV century (Plate 3, Fig. 4). In the west gallery of the cloister in the lower story are gathered together several carved fragments of interest. One is a capital like those of the upper story of the cloister (Plate 4, Fig. 1); another is a capital carved with a representation of the Resurrection (Plate 3, Fig. 5). At one angle is seen St. Peter with a key and a book. In the centre of the front face Christ rises from the tomb, naked, and with an inscribed halo. The haloed and draped figure to His right with clasped hands must be the Virgin. To the left stands the Magdalen carrying a vase. These rough figures must have belonged to a capital of the cloister of S. Guido of 1067, and are of great interest as the first extant serious figure sculptures in stone of an iconographic subject made in northern Italy after the famous altar (744-749) of Ratchis at Cividale (Plate 3, Fig. 2). However crude, these sculptures, therefore, mark a new era in plastic art.

The central apse (Plate 2, Fig. 5; Plate 3, Fig. 1) possesses a cornice formed of arched corbel-tables in two orders and surmounted by an ornament consisting of a saw tooth and two rows of zigzags like those of Fontanella and S. Pietro in Vallate. In the principal apse the pilaster strips are in two orders. Elsewhere the edifice is crowned by cornices consisting of arched corbel-tables rising from pilaster strips and surmounted by saw teeth. In the absidioles the arched corbel-tables are grouped two and two (Plate 2, Fig. 6), but elsewhere the pilaster strips are placed at much rarer intervals (Plate 2, Fig. 5; Plate 3, Fig. 1; Plate 4, Fig. 4).

In the façade of the arcade of the episcopal palace facing the Piazza del Duomo are several fragmentary reliefs. One represents St. Lawrence with his grill, another St. Stephen, distinguished by a palm and a book, a third S. Guido in episcopal robes and holding a model of the church, the others St. Paul, St. Peter and St. Bartholomew—the latter, however, represented with a hatchet instead of with a knife. These sculptures appear to be of the XII century.

The mosaic in the Turin museum is finely executed in black and white. The designs are for the most part conventional or grotesque, such as birds, fishes, a devil, an archer shooting a camel with an arrow, and a dragon. The only biblical subject is Jonah and the whale, represented in the early Christian manner, the whale being a winged and footed dragon, who holds Jonah's foot in his mouth.[37] Curious above all is the representation of the flight of Icarus. Icarus with his hair arranged in a manner that recalls a cock's comb, and with a strange wing, is seen falling. Below is the inscription [V]OL[ITVS]: ICAR.[38] It is noticeable that these mosaics are more evenly executed than the neighbouring ones coming from the church of S. Salutore.

V.   As an authentically dated edifice begun before 1018 and consecrated in 1067, the cathedral of Acqui is a most important monument of Lombard architecture.

---

[37] Compare the relief in the cathedral of Verona (Plate 216, Fig. 5).

[38] Fabretti saw in this mosaic the letters MID, of which I can discover no trace. He also made out a ship which he said was misunderstood as a dead panther by Aus'm Weerth.

ACQUI,[1] S. PIETRO

(Plate 4, Fig. 2, 3, 5; Plate 5, Fig. 1)

I.   With the exception of a very brief reference in an article by Pellate, the architecture of the church of S. Pietro at Acqui had never been referred to in print until I published, in 1913, a short account in the *American Architect*. For the history of the edifice the classic work of Moriondo is indispensable, and the historians of Acqui, Biorci and Lavezzari, have also contributed much that is important.   Savio, with his fine scholarship and extraordinary perspicacity, has solved several puzzles of ecclesiastical history bearing directly upon the vicissitudes of S. Pietro.   Finally I found much valuable information in the book of Blesi, a manuscript copy of which was shown me by Canonico Vincenzo Macciò.[2]

II.   Although one may feel some hesitation in following Biorci[3] in believing that the diocese of Acqui was founded as early as the III century, there is still reason to suppose that it dates from a venerable antiquity.   In the cemetery of S. Pietro was found a Christian inscription of the year 432,[4] which probably indicates that the cathedral church existed on the site of S. Pietro as early as the V century.   Savio states that before 1023 the bishops of Acqui were buried at S. Pietro.[5]   This assertion is perhaps a little sweeping, but it is certain that at S. Pietro were buried many of the early bishops, including the first three, Maggiorino, Massimo and Severo;[6] the problematical bishop Tito;[7] Ditario († 488);[8] Gotofredo, the eleventh, and Arnaldo, the thirteenth, bishops of Acqui.[9]   In the time of Pedrocca there were to be seen in S. Pietro statues of SS. Maggiorino and Tito.[10]   It is, moreover, clear that before 1023 the cathedral was known as S. Pietro, for it is cited under this title in three documents of 891, 978 and 996.[11]   The conclusion is therefore justified that until the year 1023 the cathedral was situated at S. Pietro.

---

1 (Alessandria).

2 To the latter I am indebted also for the use of his unique library during the three weeks that I was at Acqui, as well as for much valuable information and innumerable acts of courtesy and kindness.

3 I, 91.

4 *Ibid.*, I, 107-108.

5 Savio, 27-28.

6 *Catalogue* of Pedrocca, ed. Savio, 10.

7 His epitaph was found in 1753 at S. Pietro.   (Biorci, I, 95).

8 Biorci, I, 111.

9 Pedrocca, ed. Savio, 10; see also Lavezzari, 254-255.

10 Savio, 17.

11 . . . . . in Episcopatu Aquensi, videlicet in honorem D. Petri Apostolorum principis dedicato . . . (Diploma of Wido, 891, ed. Moriondo, I, 2). . . . . jam dicto Episcopo in honorem S. Petri dicato. . . . (Diploma of Otto II, 978, *ibid.*, 7).   The same phrase occurs in a diploma of Otto III of 996, *ibid.*, 15.

The statement in certain old chroniclers that the monastery of S. Pietro was founded in the time of the Lombard kings merits no faith, and probably originated in a tradition of a reconstruction of the cathedral church in the VI or VII century. This notice is first given by the fabulous chronicler Jacopo da Acqui, who assigns the reconstruction to about 595 A. D. and states that the altar was consecrated by angels.[12] This is doubtless the ancient manuscript from which Della Chiesa derived his information[13] and from which the tradition has been spread by numerous other writers. It deserves no greater belief than many of the other fabulous accounts of the uncritical Fra Jacopo.

From the ancient catalogue of the bishops of Acqui written by Pedrocca early in the XI century and published by Savio,[14] we learn that Bishop Primo built a cathedral church; that he first established a canonica in it and that he built another church of S. Pietro without the walls of the city. It appears furthermore that this bishop was the first of all the bishops of Acqui to be buried at S. Maria Maggiore.[15] Now Primo occupied the episcopal throne of Acqui, according to Savio, from 989-1018. It seems probable, therefore, that what happened was this. Primo commenced to build a new cathedral on a new site, that is to say, the cathedral of Acqui as it stands to-day. Not only did he move the cathedral from S. Pietro to the new church, but he reformed his clergy as well, and established for the first time in the diocese of Acqui a chapter of canons regular. He also rebuilt the old cathedral church of S. Pietro, doubtless with the idea of founding there a new monastery.

The extraordinary building activity of Primo may be best understood in the light of the history of the see of Acqui at the end of the X century. Acqui had been one of the few dioceses of northern Italy which had remained faithful to the emperor, Henry II, throughout the long period of wars which closed in 1014. This fidelity was richly rewarded. In a diploma of 1014 granted by Henry II in favour of the bishop of Acqui, there is omitted the clause almost constantly used in the earlier diplomas in favour of the diocese, referring to

[12] In civitate Aquis de Lombardia est factum monasterium monachorum sancti Petri cum maxima et honorabili devotione in suburbio civitatis. et habetur ibi. quod maius altare illius ecclesie fuit ab angelis consecratum. et ibi multa iacent corpora Sanctorum. (Frate Jacopo da Acqui, *Chronicon Imaginis Mundi*, ed. *Hist. Pat. Mon.*, V, 1449). Published also by Moriondo, II, 134.

[13] Noi habbiamo ritrovato in alcuni libri antichissimi, scritti à penna da i sudetti Rè [lombardi] esser stati fondati in essa Provincia molti monasterij in honore di S. Pietro: tra gl'altri il Monasterio di Acqui . . . (Della Chiesa, 52).

[14] 10.

[15] Primus vener. Epus qui sedit ann. XXVIII M III. et D. XVI. Θ. X Kal. aprilis et cessavit episcopatus M. III et dies VI. Hic Ecclesiam episcopalem funditus edificavit et Canonicam primum constituit, et aliam foris muros in honorem Apostolorum Principis, Aquensis Episcopii defensoris, doctoris et magistri. Hic etiam Heribertum Mediolanensis Ecclê. Episcopum consecravit. Requiescit ad S. Mariam Maiorem. . . . (Ed. Savio, 10).

the poverty of the church of Acqui. It appears that, thanks to the donations, not only of the emperors, but also of other pious persons (such as, for example, the marchese Guglielmo and Riprando, who in 999 made notable gifts to the diocese of Acqui), the bishops found themselves in conditions of extraordinary financial prosperity. Hence it was that a remarkable series of building enterprises was undertaken.[16] The tradition that the church of S. Pietro was begun by Primo was recorded in an inscription in the episcopal palace seen and cited by Biorci.[17] Primo was succeeded by the bishop Brunengo, who occupied the episcopal throne for the brief space of four years (1018-1022), and by Dudone (1023-1033). The catalogue of Pedrocca says of the latter bishop that he was the first to celebrate mass at S. Maria, the new cathedral church, that he transferred thither the canons of S. Pietro and that he established a monastery in the latter church[18]—all this at Christmas, presumably in the first year of his episcopate. The catalogue of Pedrocca is confirmed in regard to the foundation of the monastery at S. Pietro by Dudone by a document of S. Guido of 1041, which explicitly mentions that the monastery of S. Pietro was founded by Dudone.[19] It is still further confirmed by a legal document of 1224 in regard to a lawsuit over the parish rights of S. Pietro, claimed by both the canons of the cathedral and the Benedictine monks of S. Pietro. The lawyer of the monks asserted that in the church of S. Pietro there had anciently been secular canons and not monks, and his adversary replied denying that there had been canons two hundred years before, but admitting that there had been two hundred and twenty years before; that is to say, he claimed that the monastery of S. Pietro was established between 1004 and 1024, which coincides perfectly with the date of foundation (1023) given by Pedrocca in his catalogue.[20] Still further confirmation, were any

[16] Biorci, I, 177.

[17] *Ibid.*

[18] Dudo qui et Petrus bonae memoriae Episcopus. . . . Nativitatis Domini primam ad S. Mariam, antiquitus episcopalem ecclesiam, missam celebrare, Sanctique Petri Ecclesiae Canonicos ad istam transvexit, et de illa Monasterium fecit. (Cit. Savio, 10).

[19] In nomine Domini Dei nostri & Salvatoris Jesu Christi. Wido favente divina clementia sanctæ Aquensis Sedis Episcopus. . . . Sit ergo notum omnibus Ecclesiis Dei, omnique Lajcorum fidelium conventui, quod Monasterium sancti Petri, quod in suburbio civitatis Aquensis, in qua auctore Deo sedem Pontificalem, quamvis indigne habemus, situm scilicet a D. Dudone bonæ memoriæ antecessore nostro Episcopo, in primis aliquid de rebus etc. . . . Actum anno incarnationis Domini Nostri Jesu Christi millesimo quadragesimo primo, indictione secunda [*sic*]; Enrico regnante anno ejus secundo. . . . (Ed. Moriondo, I, 28).

[20] Exposuit Magister Otto Sindicus, & procurator monasterii S. Petri Aquis . . . quod prædictum monasterium est circumdatum habitationibus hominum undique. . . . Item ponit, quod in Ecclesia S. Petri fuerunt canonici seculares, & non monaci. Ad quod respondet, quod non concedit a ducentis annis infra, sed a ducentis viginti annis infra concedit. . . . Item ponit, quod ipse Episcopus [Dudo] jacet ad prædictum monasterium. (Moriondo, I, 177).

needed, is given by the fact that Dudone was buried at S. Pietro, that is, in the church of the monastery he had founded.[21] The cathedral chapter and monks of S. Pietro, thus closely associated in origin, had many rights which were not clearly defined, and which resulted in subsequent times in endless litigation. As early as 1108 these lawsuits were in full progress.[22]

The subsequent history of the abbey was comparatively uneventful, and the documents seem to indicate that the monastery enjoyed for some centuries a prosperous and tranquil life. The commendam was established sometime after 1415.[23] In 1663 the episcopal visitor seems to have been little edified with the condition in which he found the monastery, to judge from the inedited acts of the proceedings.[24] The bishop Carlo Antonio Gozzani (1625-1721) dispersed the monks entirely and divided the church into two parts, one of which he desecrated and the other of which he dedicated to S. Maria Vergine Addolorata, after redecorating it in the barocco style.[25] It is in this condition that the edifice has come down to our own time, having had the rare good fortune to escape modern restoration.

III. The church originally consisted of a nave, two side aisles, a choir flanked by side aisles, three apses (Plate 4, Fig. 2), a crypt and an octagonal campanile (Plate 5, Fig. 1) rising over the southern side aisle of the choir.

---

[21] In the face of all this trustworthy evidence it is impossible to lend faith to the rather vague tradition that the cathedral was built by S. Guido. The work of S. Guido must have been merely to complete and consecrate it. See above, pp. 16-17.

[22] Moriondo, I, 45. Cf. ibid., 72, 89, 90.

[23] Lavezzari, 255.

[24] Delli disciplini di S. Pietro del dᵒ luogo. Si prouedino qto pra tosto quelli fratelli della loro regola di Milano, et procurino ad ogni suo puotere di ben essiguirla, et agiutino il Rettore della Chiesa la festa in insegnare la vita Christiana.

Non si facciano più bacanali dell'entrate o elemosine della Compania di San Spirito ma li diuidano a poueri conforme al decreto gnale di qsta visita. (Visita Apostolica, inedited document of 1663).

[25] Blesi's description of this church is not without interest: La chiesa di S. Pietro è posta nel Borgo maggiore della Città, qual dall'istessa Chiesa, si chiama Borgo di S. Pietro, è molto antica, e tengo che sii la più antica Fabbrica che si trovi oggidi nella Città, et a vederla solame ne può restar certo chi si voglia. Fu fatta fabbricare dal re de' Longobardi, et con la Chiesa maggiore, et Cattedrale, et dalli medmi Re fu data, et assegnata entrata di qualità. Dopo che dal Beato Guido per accrescimento del culto Divino, et maggior comodità de' Cittadini et onorevolezza della Città fu fatta edificare l'altra della quale abbiamo detto di sopra, fù data alla Religione de' Padri di S. Benedetto, con l'entrata, e Titolo d'Abbazia, ma essendo anco dai Padri lasciata è stata conferta a diversi Abbati Secolari. Finalme essendo vaccata nel tempo che monsigᵉ Costacciara era vescovo della nostra Città, procurò Egli come desiderossissimo di augmentare l'entrate del vescovato d'unirla a quello, et per effettuare tale unione, fidendo molto più nell'amicizia del Sig. Francesco. . . . In questa Chiesa si vedono alcune pietre antiche di marmi, e d'altra sorte con i nomi di quelli antichi Romani. Avanti l'ultima amplificazione della Città, che seguì del 1400, restava detta Chiesa fuori delle mura, ma ora resta nella Città. . . .

The edifice has, however, been much changed. The barocco church of the Addolorata has been built in the western bays of the old nave, and the rest of the building has been transformed into houses, warerooms and stores (Plate 4, Fig. 5). The ancient architecture is best preserved in the three apses and in the clearstory walls of the flanks (Plate 4, Fig. 2, 5). The choir, which was lower than the nave, must have been vaulted;—in fact, some traces of the groin vault which covered the north side aisle of the choir were still extant when I studied the church. The nave was not vaulted, as may be clearly seen from the ancient walls still preserved above the vaults of the existing church, and it is evident also that there was no system in the nave. It is possible that the side aisles in the nave may have been vaulted, but I believe that they were not. The piers were octagonal, with plain, square capitals, and apparently no bases (at least none are visible). Several of these piers are still to be seen in the north arcade. Of the ancient crypt nothing is extant save some few fragments of old masonry sufficient to prove its existence. Otherwise the cellars under the church are entirely modern. The clearstory (Plate 4, Fig. 5) had large, round-headed windows, doubtless glazed. They were placed at great intervals, as in the cathedral. A curious feature of the church is the polygonal form given externally to the absidioles (Plate 4, Fig. 2; Plate 5, Fig. 1). With the exceptions of the apses of VI century churches in Ravenna and of the sacristy of SS. Felice e Fortunato at Vicenza I know of no other example of a similar construction in northern Italy.

The masonry is formed of uncut brick-shaped stones, with a few bricks roughly laid in thick beds of mortar (Plate 4, Fig. 3). Some attempt is made to keep the courses horizontal. In the clearstory the masonry is even rougher than in the apses. Horizontal courses are abandoned, and the wall is frankly rubble.

IV. The nave piers are without capitals, and the octagonal supporting member slides into the rectangular load merely with a sort of bevel. The clearstory walls are decorated with arched corbel-tables grouped two and two (Plate 4, Fig. 5), and the side-aisle walls had also the same decoration, as may be seen from the few fragments which still survive in the south wall near the campanile (Plate 4, Fig. 5). The absidioles were decorated with blind arches resting on a podium (Plate 4, Fig. 2, 3), but in the central apse (Plate 4, Fig. 2) the pilaster strips separating the arches were in three cases interrupted by windows, thus forming arched corbel-tables grouped two and two. The existing cornice of the central apse (Plate 4, Fig. 2), formed of flat corbel-tables, dentils and saw teeth, is obviously an addition of the XIII century. The original cornice of the absidioles, however, consisting of a single cavea, is preserved. The clearstory walls are, and perhaps always have been, without a cornice. The campanile (Plate 5, Fig. 1) has pilaster strips at the angles, rising from a podium crowned by a string-course of saw teeth. The buttress that marks the end of the south wall is decorated with an ornament consisting of two vertical zigzags (Plate 5, Fig. 1).

V. The primitive style of the architecture is completely in accord with the documentary evidence that the church was begun by Primo between 989 and 1018, probably c. 1015, and was already finished when Dudone established the monastery in 1023.

AGLIATE DI CARATE BRIANZA,[1] BATTISTERO

(Plate 5, Fig. 5, 6; Plate 6; Plate 7)

I. Practically all the works mentioned below in connection with S. Pietro of Agliate treat also of the baptistery, which forms an interesting complement and almost a part of the church itself.

II. There are no historical documents which throw light upon the archæology of the baptistery, besides those already mentioned below in connection with the basilica. The baptistery, however, enjoys one great advantage over the church in that it escaped restoration in the fatal campaign of 1890-1895. We here find ourselves, therefore, face to face with a document, mutilated, it is true, and much consumed by age, but without the modern falsifications which so largely destroy the scientific value of S. Pietro.

III. The baptistery is a severely simple but irregular structure, in plan (Plate 6) a nine-sided polygon, two of whose sides have been replaced in the lower story by an apse. The walls are of enormous thickness (Plate 6; Plate 7), and the edifice displays surprising asymmetries in the placing of its windows (Plate 6) and other details. It is covered at present by a cloistered vault, but this has been remade, as is shown by the character of the masonry, after the original construction of the church and probably in the XII century. The monument suffered in the restoration of the XVIII century, when the windows were walled up, the west wall in part rebuilt, the doorways altered and the interior covered with intonaco.

The walls, like those of the basilica, are constructed of rubble (Plate 5, Fig. 5), consisting of stones, pebbles and pieces of brick laid loosely in a mass of mortar. However, this masonry is more advanced than that of the church (Plate 5, Fig. 7). The stones are laid more carefully, there is more of an approximation towards horizontal courses, and the mortar-beds are narrower. The masonry of the upper part of the exterior wall above the arched corbel-table is better and later than that below (Plate 5, Fig. 6). Here, the horizontal courses are distinctly maintained, and the stones are carefully fitted

---

[1] (Milano).

together (Plate 5, Fig. 5). This masonry, executed in imitation of the earlier masonry below, doubtless belongs to a restoration of the XII century.

IV. The ornament of the church consists merely of the cornice. Above, there is a row of semicircular niches, precisely like those of the basilica, except that there are no pilaster strips (Plate 5, Fig. 5). It is singular that below this is placed a row of arched corbel-tables (Plate 5, Fig. 6). These arched corbel-tables are supported on terra-cotta brackets (Plate 5, Fig. 6) of a type characteristic of the XII century. Moreover, arched corbel-tables of this form were not used in Lombardy before c. 1035. The explanation is that in the XII century the vault was restored, and that in consequence the exterior cornice was also repaired, the old semicircular niches being retained, but built over, and an arched corbel-table being added below them.

V. The baptistery is usually believed to be contemporary with the church, that is, of the third quarter of the IX century.[2] However, as has been seen, notwithstanding strong analogies of style which prove that the two buildings can not be separated by any great interval of time, the masonry clearly indicates that the baptistery is somewhat later than the church. The baptistery may therefore be assigned to c. 900.

AGLIATE DI CARATE BRIANZA,[1] S. PIETRO

(Plate 5, Fig. 2, 3, 4, 7; Plate 8; Plate 9)

I. The ancient basilica of S. Pietro at Agliate is deservedly one of the best known monuments of Brianza, and, indeed, of Lombardy. Although situated in a small and remote village, the basilica early attracted the attention of archæologists. De Dartein, who was the first to study the edifice seriously, completely misunderstood its chronology. In 1874 appeared the study of Mongeri with valuable historical notices. To Cattaneo[2] belongs the credit of having pointed out the significance of the basilica as a dated example of the Lombard style of the IX century. The notices of Mongeri, Landriani and various other writers who have referred to the monument incidentally, have added little that was new. In 1895 appeared the monograph of Corbella, a work of real value, notwithstanding certain errors of chronology. In recent years the church has been studied by Rivoira.[3] Most of the authors who have written upon the monument have illustrated it with drawings for the most part not of unimpeachable accuracy.

II. The little that is known of the history of the church has been given

---

[2] De Dartein, I think, is the only archæologist who has assigned the baptistery and basilica of Agliate to a period subsequent to the year 1000.

[1] (Milano).   [2] 218.   [3] 196.

careful attention by Corbella, and may hence be summarized briefly here. To judge from certain early Christian epitaphs,[4] a church existed at Agliate at least as early as the middle of the VI century. At all events, there is excellent reason to believe that a chapter of canons was established in the church in the IX century by the famous Ansperto, archbishop of Milan (868-881).[5]

The style of the architecture fully justifies the conclusion that the existing church was built at the time the chapter was founded.

During the Middle Ages the pieve of Agliate acquired considerable importance. In the XIII century, according to a manuscript of Goffredo da Bussero cited by Corbella,[6] S. Pietro of Agliate enjoyed jurisdiction over fifty-seven churches and seventy-one altars. Its importance must have begun to decline soon after, for in a sort of tax-list of 1398, published by Magistretti, mention is made of this church as being officiated by eleven canons, but as having only twenty-two dependent chapels. In 1568 S. Carlo Borromeo contemplated removing the prepositura of Agliate to Carate.[7] The church was at this time in bad physical and financial condition, as is known from a passage in the 'Acts' of Federigo Borromeo.[8] A certain Marchese Guido Cusani and a certain Don Pietro Tonsi offered to restore the church,[9] but that such a restoration was ever actually executed, or that it affected the architectural forms of the monument, there is no evidence. At any event, Federigo Borromeo in 1619[10] deliberated anew upon remaking the church in better form, and upon suppressing the canons. Fortunately this unhappy idea was never put into execution, and the mutilations perpetrated upon the monument at this epoch appear to have been confined to the destruction of the ancient stone ambo, which was supplanted by a new one in wood.[11]

Until the second quarter of the XVIII century the church seems to have escaped restoration, but at length the inevitable happened. The edifice was made over in the barocco style by the prevosto Curioni, and the consecration was solemnly celebrated in 1731.[12] A new pulpit and a new ambo were made, the roofs of the nave and side aisles were rebuilt, the sacristy between the church and the baptistery was erected, a new balustrade and stairway in the barocco style were provided for the choir, the pavement was raised half a metre, the old windows were walled up and new ones opened, and the walls covered with intonaco. Fortunately the evident antiquity of the monument seems to have secured for it a certain amount of respect even in the XVIII

[4] Corbella, 30-31.

[5] This notice is preserved by Giulini, I, 330-331: Uno scrittore delle vite de' nostri arcivescovi, la di cui opera da me si conserva manoscritta, narra che la canonica di san Pietro nel luogo d'Aliate capo di una delle nostre pievi, è stata fondata da Ansperto medesimo. Io non so a qual fondamento egli abbia appoggiato la sua asserzione; nondimeno, poichè quell'autore è antico già di tre secoli, non è da sprezzarsi tal notizia in una cosa, la quale per se non patisce alcuna difficoltà.

[6] 46.   [7] Corbella, 58.   [8] Ibid., 59.   [9] Ibid.   [10] Ibid., 60.   [11] Ibid., 64.
[12] Ibid., 63-65.

century, and it was spared the complete devastation which fell to the lot of so many Lombard monuments of the Middle Ages.

In 1838 the church lost the dignity of pieve[13] to become a simple parish. In 1874 the agitation for the restoration of the monument began. An ambitious project was drawn up which provided for (1) the demolition of the campanile and the construction of a new one; (2) the remaking of the roofs of the church throughout; (3) the cleansing of the walls from intonaco; (4) the reopening of the ancient windows looking from the crypt into the church and the closing of the windows added in the XVIII century; (5) the removing of the barocco balustrades and church-furniture from the choir; (6) the lowering of the pavement to the original level; (7) the restoration of the two absidioles and their altars.[14] In 1875, however, but few of these projected changes were carried out, and the activity of the restorers was limited to executing merely the most urgent repairs to the exterior of the apses. In that same year, 1875, the church was declared a national monument. In 1893 the restoration was seriously taken in hand under the direction of the architects Luca Beltrami, Gaetano Moretti and Luigi Perrone. The actual work executed followed closely the project of 1874. In 1893-1894 the portal on the south side of the basilica was reopened; the roofs were entirely remade; the windows on the north side of the nave were reopened and restored, and an attempt was made to replace their ancient painted decorations. The roof of the northern absidiole was lowered; the southern portal of the façade was restored and a symmetrical one opened in the north side aisle. The entire lower wall of the façade was restored, and a new central portal erected. The most mischievous act of the restoration was the placing of two columns in the middle of the eastern intercolumniation on either side of the nave, in the mistaken belief that two such columns had been removed in the XVIII century. In 1894 the frescos of the triumphal arch and the choir vault and those on the north wall of the nave came to light, beneath the intonaco.[15] In 1896 the old campanile had already been destroyed, and plans for a new one were under discussion. This has since been completed and is a peculiarly offensive example of what modern restoration can do at its worst. An inscription within the church records the lamentable restoration in these pompous words:

L'AUGUSTO DESIDERIO QUI MANIFESTATO
DA UMBERTO I E MARGHERITA DI SAVOIA
DI RITORNARE QUESTA VETUSTA BASILICA
ALLE PRISTINE FORME DALLE SECOLARI VICENDE
MANOMESSE FU ESAUDITO COL CONCORSO
DEL GOVERNO, DEL COMUNE, DEI TERRIERI
E COLLA DIREZIONE DELL'UFFICIO REGIONALE
PEI MONUMENTI DELLA LOMBARDIA
DALL'ANNO MDCCCXC AL MDCCCXCV.

13 *Ibid.*, 68.   14 *Ibid.*, 70.   15 *Arch. Stor. Lom.*, 1894, 241.

In 1895 the restoration proceeded with the total reconstruction of the north wall and the north absidiole—a piece of sheer vandalism which nearly destroyed the archæological importance of the monument. The bifora of the crypt opening into the church were remade, and the new choir-rail, stairway and ambo were added, as well as a new altar in the northern absidiole and the rail of the same chapel.

III. The church consists of a nave seven bays long, two side aisles, a crypt (Plate 9), a choir and three apses (Plate 8). The apses are surmounted by half domes, the choir is covered by a barrel vault, the two compartments of the side aisles preceding the absidioles have groin vaults (Plate 5, Fig. 2), and the crypt is also groin-vaulted. The nave and side aisles have been supplied with a modern roof, presumably an imitation of the ancient one, traces of which were found during the recent restoration.[16]

The archivolts are in a single order and unmoulded. The voussoirs are alternately stones and bricks, a mannerism which recalls Roman technique. The columns and capitals are formed of a heterogeneous collection of pilfered material, mostly Roman fragments, several with inscriptions. The groin vaults of the side aisles of the choir (Plate 5, Fig. 2) have wall ribs and are very slightly domed. Although daubed over with modern plaster, they were not, I believe, actually rebuilt in the restoration. The vaults of the crypt are similarly slightly domed and supplied with disappearing transverse arches.

The masonry has been completely covered on the interior by a coat of modern plaster. On the exterior, however, it can still be studied. It consists of a mass of pebbles and bricks laid irregularly in a heavy mass of mortar (Plate 5, Fig. 3). There are no cut stones. In the original parts of the edifice little attempt is made to place the stones and bricks in horizontal courses. The north wall, where this is done, is modern. In the façade and in the eastern gable are placed two windows in the form of a Greek cross, perhaps the earliest example of this characteristically Lombard feature. Below the Greek cross window in the façade are still clearly visible the remains of a large semicircular arch. It has been supposed by Sant'Ambrogio that this opened originally into a western apse, similar to the one at S. Giorgio of Valpollicella. Unfortunately, the restoration has so denatured the façade that it is impossible now to say for what this arch served. However, from a drawing made before the restoration and published by Corbella,[17] it seems probable that this was merely a great lunette like the two at the sides, introduced in the XVIII century to lighten the church.

The windows of the apse and clearstory are all large, like those of S. Vincenzo of Milan (Plate 135, Fig. 2). They were doubtless originally filled, in the early Christian manner, with stone tracery.

[16] Corbella, 65.
[17] 71.

IV. There is but little original ornament in the church. The most important and characteristic decorative feature is the cornice of the main apse (Plate 5, Fig. 7). A series of semicircular niches is constructed below the eaves of the roof in the wall, where this is thickened by the springing of the half dome internally. These niches are separated into groups of three or two by shallow pilaster strips, which rise from the ground to the roof. This cornice is without analogy. The niches, it is true, are found at S. Ambrogio (Plate 117, Fig. 5), S. Eustorgio (Plate 127, Fig. 4) and S. Vincenzo in Prato at Milan (Plate 137, Fig. 4), but in these cases the pilaster strips support what looks very much like an arched corbel-table, encircling the niches. It is altogether probable that at Agliate similar corbel-tables would have been added had not the crude quality of the materials employed in the masonry made such a construction exceedingly difficult. The absidioles are without decoration of any kind.

The capitals of the crypt are extremely crude in character (Plate 5, Fig. 4), but seem to have been undoubtedly sculptured for their present position.

V. Until 1890 S. Pietro of Agliate was a well preserved, homogeneous and extremely important example of the style of the third quarter of the IX century, and as such has been recognized by all archæologists with the single exception of De Dartein. Although nearly everything possible was done to destroy the archæological value of the monument in the restoration, the church still retains enough of its original form to make it of no little significance for the history of Carlovingian architecture in Lombardy.

AGRATE CONTURBIA,[1] BATTISTERO

(Plate 10, Fig. 3, 5)

I. Agrate Conturbia, a little hamlet at the foot of the Alps, has attracted the attention of several students of Lombard antiquities because of the notable baptistery there preserved. To the indefatigable Mella belongs the credit of first having called it to the attention of archæologists. De Dartein[2] subsequently studied it, and the monument has since been mentioned incidentally by several other writers. In the Museo Civico at Novara there is a drawing which shows the monument as it was before restoration. Before the southern portal stood a Renaissance portico which has now disappeared, and the north side of the baptistery was entirely masked by houses built against it.

II. The baptistery belonged to the neighbouring church of S. Vittore, a fact which justifies the conclusion that the latter once enjoyed the rank of

1 (Novara).   2 401.

pieve. In a diploma of 976,[3] the basilica *Sancti Victoris constructa infra Castro agregade* is mentioned as *sub regimine et potestatem* of the episcopal church of Novara. In the early XVII century the fortunes of the church of S. Vittore must have fallen to a low ebb, since the bishop Bescapè mentions that he restored it to the rank of parish.[4]

III. The plan of the edifice is very irregular, doubtless owing to the fact that parts of an earlier building were retained. In general it forms an octagon, on each of whose sides in the lower story are built out, in the thickness of the wall, niches rectangular in plan, except that the two adjoining the entrance on the east side (Plate 10, Fig. 3) are approximately elliptical. Externally the wall of the lower story is almost circular. The structure is covered with an octagonal cloistered vault. In the centre of the interior is the depressed octagonal font to which three steps descend. All the windows were evidently intended to serve without glass.

The masonry of the exterior walls belongs to two distinct epochs. In the lower story, on the north and west sides, there is preserved a piece of wall in rubble masonry (Plate 10, Fig. 5). Pebbles of irregular size are laid in courses more or less horizontal and embedded in a thick mass of mortar. It is evident that this wall once formed part of a circular edifice. It is broken at present by a pilaster strip of brick and stone, and is crowned by a cornice, but both of these features are additions of the XII century. The masonry of the remainder of the edifice is somewhat irregular ashlar with cut stones of widely varying sizes, rather carelessly fitted together, the interstices being often filled up with bricks (Plate 10, Fig. 5). Bricks are also in many cases employed to form the archivolts of the upper gallery and the arched corbel-tables. This masonry shows much variation in character and is often little better than rubble, but is always different from the more ancient rubble masonry, being of better quality and formed of stones angular rather than round. Scaffolding holes are numerous, large and prominent.

IV. The decoration is simple and characteristic. The cornices of the two eastern niches (Plate 10, Fig. 3) are formed of arched corbel-tables supported by slender pilaster strips. The cupola, on the other hand, has a cornice consisting of simple arched corbel-tables without pilaster strips (Plate 10, Fig. 3). Below this there is inserted on each face of the octagon a group of three blind arches supported on columns (Plate 10, Fig. 3). The capitals are formed of blocks running back into the wall and carved into a bracket-like form. Such blind galleries are characteristic of the Lombard style of the XII century and are found in numerous churches of Milan, Pavia,

---

[3] *Hist. Pat. Mon.,* I, 246.

[4] Agratum . . . a nobis parochia erecta est: licet iam ibi rotundum templum esset pro baptisterio plebano nescio quo modo paratum. (Bescapè, 108).

etc. The doorway (Plate 10, Fig. 3) is a severely plain rectangle, surmounted by a simple lunette.

V. The edifice possesses so little architectural character, in both its earlier and later portions, that we have no guide other than the masonry itself for assigning it a date. The rubble masonry of the earlier part of the edifice (Plate 10, Fig. 5) is evidently later than that of the basilica (Plate 5, Fig. 3) or baptistery (Plate 5, Fig. 5, 6) of Agliate, since the courses are more horizontal, the stones better laid, the mortar-beds thinner. On the other hand, it is distinctly less advanced than that of S. Vincenzo of Galliano (Plate 99, Fig. 1), where a certain number of rectangular blocks are introduced among the pebbles, where the horizontal courses are even better maintained, where the stones are more skilfully fitted together, and where the mortar-beds are thinner. It is evident, therefore, that the older part of the baptistery of Agrate Conturbia is later than c. 900, the probable date of the baptistery of Agliate, and earlier than 1007, when S. Vincenzo of Galliano was consecrated. Since, however, the character of the masonry approaches that of Agliate more closely than that of S. Vincenzo, we may assign the earlier portions of Agrate Conturbia to c. 930.

The later portions are undoubtedly of the XII century, as is shown by the character of the ornament. All the motives here used, however, persisted for a considerable period, and hence offer no criterion for determining the date with precision. The masonry in its mixture of ashlar and rubble, offers striking analogy with that of the not distant narthex of S. Donato at Abbazia di Sesto Calende, an edifice there is reason to believe was erected c. 1130. Since, therefore, the masonry at Agrate Conturbia is very similar, but slightly more primitive, we may assign the XII century portions of the latter edifice to c. 1125.

ALBUGNANO,[1] S. PIETRO AL CIMITERO

(Plate 10, Fig. 2)

I. The position of the little town of Albugnano, perched on one of the loftiest crests of the Monferrato, and to be reached only by an extremely difficult carriage road leading from Castelnuovo d'Asti, is so inaccessible that, notwithstanding its proximity to the well known and much visited abbey of Vezzolano, the charming little church of S. Pietro, when I found it in 1910, was still entirely unknown. In 1911, however, a photograph of it was published by Bevilacqua-Lazise.[2]

II. I know of no documents which throw light on the history of the church.

1 (Alessandria).   2 42.

III.   The edifice consists of a nave of a single aisle, and an apse. The nave is roofed in wood, and the interior is without interest. The masonry is formed partly of ashlar of rather indifferent quality, and partly of bricks incised and of regular size, laid in horizontal beds. The mortar-joints average about fifteen centimetres in width. A curious feature is a cross-hatching on certain of the stones.

IV.   The decoration is in flat and double arched corbel-tables, with shafts and pilaster strips. The apse cornice is carved with an interlace, and the cornice on the south wall is in part decorated with a rinceau. The apse windows (Plate 10, Fig. 2) are in three unmoulded orders. The great interest of the building, however, lies in the fact that one of these windows still retains its original perforated stone tracery (Plate 10, Fig. 2). This is one of the few extant instances in Lombardy of a form of decoration which was once undoubtedly common. Analogous tracery is found in Apulia, at S. Gregorio of Bari (Plate 10, Fig. 1), in the cathedrals of Barletta and Ruvo (Plate 10, Fig. 4) and also at S. Maria in Cosmedin at Rome.

V.   The church of S. Pietro, both in its masonry and in its decoration, is strikingly similar to the neighbouring abbey of Vezzolano, by which it appears to have been influenced. The construction may, therefore, be assigned to c. 1185.

ALMENNO S. BARTOLOMEO,[1] S. TOMMASO

(Plate 10, Fig. 6, 7; Plate 11, Fig. 1, 2, 3)

I.   The circular church of S. Tommaso in Limine, locally known as S. Tomè, lies in the fields about a kilometre from the present town of Almenno S. Bartolomeo, and about the same distance from the church of S. Giorgio of Almenno S. Salvatore. It is one of the most discussed of all Lombard monuments. In the third quarter of the XVIII century Lupi,[2] the venerable historian of Bergamo, described the church at length and published accurate drawings on a large scale, including an elevation, plan and section. So excellent are these engravings that they are still of the greatest value as showing the form of the church in the XVIII century, before it had suffered from modern restorations. The ancient cupola and other features which have since disappeared are clearly shown. In 1828 the church was discussed at length by the Sacchi brothers.[3] The historian Ronchetti,[4] who wrote in the first half of the XIX century, has contributed several historical notices of value. In 1823 Séroux d'Agincourt[5] published small-scale drawings of the

[1] (Bergamo).   [2] I, 209.   [3] 36.   [4] V, 89.   [5] IV, Plate 24, Fig. 16-18.

church. The large-scale plan, section and elevation of Knight[6] appeared in 1843. These drawings show the cupola crowned by a pseudo-Lombard ædicule. Of great value also are the large-scale plan, section, elevation and plate of details published by Osten,[7] from which it is evident that in the middle of the XIX century the inscriptions of 1704 and 1752 were still in place in the portal. In 1866 more drawings of the church were issued by Hübsch.[8] Locatelli published in 1879 a description which supplements all these drawings and gives precise information as to the condition of the church as it was before the recent restoration. A new plan and section were published in the *Grande Illustrazione*,[9] and still others by De Dartein. The little monograph of Fornoni, which appeared in 1896, is a convenient résumé of what had before been written relating to the monument.

II. Nothing is known of the early history of S. Tommaso. Two documents of 1346 and 1347, cited by Ronchetti,[10] refer to two episcopal visits made to the nuns of S. Tommaso of Almenno. It is therefore evident that the church belonged to a convent, but of this convent nothing further is known.[11] In 1403 certain Ghibellines took refuge in the church, but were besieged and driven out by fire. Fornoni[12] conjectures that in consequence of this the edifice was abandoned. At all events it appears to have been in bad condition in 1672. According to an inscription formerly in the portal, but now placed inside the church, the edifice was struck by lightning in 1704 and subsequently restored. According to a second inscription, now also removed from its position and placed inside the church, another restoration was carried out in 1753.[13] The unfortunate edifice was again struck by lightning in 1885, and sustained damage which either necessitated or formed a pretext for the restoration begun in 1892, the hardest blow which the monument has had to suffer. At this time the church had long been closed for worship, and had been used as a store-room for agricultural implements. The project of restoration included the remaking of the pavement and the lantern, and the replacing of the tiles on the roof by slates. Actually the works executed under the sanction of the Minister of Public Instruction (for the edifice is a national monument) were considerably more extensive. In 1892-1893 two bases and a capital were removed from the lower story and replaced by new ones, and the exterior walls were thoroughly restored. In 1893-1894 the lantern was rebuilt on the authority of two colonnettes and a portion of the old cornice discovered in the course of the restoration, and in the gallery in the interior three columns, one base and two capitals were made anew. The

---

[6] I, Plate XVII.   [7] Plates XLIII, XLIV, XLV, XLVI.
[8] Plate LIV, Fig. 6-13.   [9] V, 984.   [10] V, 89.   [11] *Ibid.*, I, 58.   [12] 13.

[13] These inscriptions have been published by Locatelli (III, 186). The last time I visited the church (1913), one was leaning against the north wall near the stairway, and the other, upside down and only partly legible, served as a doorstep.

groin vaults were patched up where they were cracked, as was also the dome. The southern portal and two columns of the lower story were restored. In 1895 the western portal was renovated.[14] During the restoration, I know not in what year, the intonaco was stripped off the walls of the interior.[15]

It has been supposed by some authorities that the church of S. Tomè is the baptistery of a destroyed basilica, but such is manifestly not the case. In addition to the fact that it is known that the church belonged to a convent, Lupi[16] has published a document which proves that it was only in 1175 that the bishop and canons of Bergamo ceded to the inhabitants of Limine the right of administering baptism. The Duomo Vecchio of Brescia proves that a circular church need not necessarily be a baptistery.

III. The church consists of two parts: an octagonal nave, surrounded by a side aisle, which is surmounted by a gallery; and a rectangular choir terminating in an apse (Plate 11, Fig. 1). The apse has a half dome; the choir, side aisles and gallery are groin-vaulted, while the nave is surmounted by a dome. The groin vaults of the side aisles and gallery have much depressed wall ribs (Plate 10, Fig. 7; Plate 11, Fig. 2). While the arches in the main arcade are stilted, as are also the transverse arches, the groins are depressed in elevation and sometimes curved in plan; moreover, they do not intersect in the middle of the compartments. The line of the groins is worked to a sharp point towards the springing. These vaults are constructed of rubble and were erected with the aid of a solid centering in wood. This is proved by the fact that their soffit still bears the traces of the boards of the centering impressed on the plaster (Plate 10, Fig. 7). The groin vaults of the gallery, instead of being horizontal, lean against the nave, being in this respect analogous to those of S. Fedele at Como. This inclination, given them partly to buttress the dome, partly to avoid raising the roof so high as would other-wise have been necessary, gives rise in the actual construction to several distortions. The capitals of the responds are placed at a lower level than those of the columns separating the gallery from the nave, and consequently the transverse arches springing from a higher level on one side than on the other, produce a singular curve in elevation, the irregularity of which is increased by the fact that its highest point is thrown nearer the outer than the inner wall. The resulting distortion in the vault surface itself is somewhat minimized by the loading of the transverse arches. The wall ribs are very much depressed in elevation, so that their crowns rise to a height much lower than that of the transverse and arcade arches. The groins, though broken, tend to intersect at a point which is nearer the inner than the outer edge of the vault. The transverse arches thus seem to sink into the surface of the

[14] *Arch. Stor. Lomb.*, anno 1894, 254.
[15] *Arte e Storia*, I Ottobre, 1894.
[16] II, 1281.

wall on the outer side, and would be totally submerged were not the surface hollowed out, as it were, to receive them.

The groin vault of the choir is approximately square in plan. The groins are somewhat depressed in elevation, the other arches are semicircular; nevertheless, there is considerable doming, and traces of the solid board centering are evident.

The walls of the rotunda are enormously thick (c. 1.15 metres), and the two stairways giving access to the galleries, and the six semicircular niches of the ground floor are merely voids in this mass of solid masonry. The technique of the construction recalls that of Roman buildings, a core of well laid rubble being faced on both sides with a coating of ashlar masonry (Plate 11, Fig 1). This masonry is formed of rather roughly dressed blocks showing great variation in size, but skilfully laid in courses in which the horizontal direction is generally well maintained. Scaffolding holes, penetrating sometimes the entire thickness of the wall, occur at frequent intervals.

Above the gallery arcade is a row of segmental relieving arches, an unusual feature in Lombard construction. A small clearstory, consisting of windows in the form of a Greek cross alternating with oculi, is pierced in the dome (Plate 11, Fig. 1). In the north wall a graceful triforium window lightens the gallery (Plate 11, Fig. 1).

IV. S. Tommaso presents decorative features of extraordinary interest. The capitals are evidently of two distinct epochs. Most of those of the ground story (Plate 11, Fig. 3), together with their columns, have evidently been pilfered from an earlier edifice. This is clear not only from their style, earlier than that of those of the gallery, but from the fact that inverted capitals are used as bases, and a base with griffes in one instance is used as a capital. It is clear that the old columns were a little too short for the position in which the builders wished to use them. They were accordingly pieced out by a variety of expedients. New abaci were inserted above the inverted base already mentioned, and above one of the capitals; fragments of columns were placed under the inverted capitals which served as bases. Of the aisle responds, some of the capitals and bases are pilfered, others are original. The half columns form an integral part of the masonry of the walls (Plate 11, Fig. 3). The pilfered capitals are of several types. Four are cubic (one was carved at a subsequent epoch with an interlace), nine are of a curious type, somewhat resembling a cubic capital, in which the curve of the outer edge is concave instead of convex (Plate 11, Fig. 3), and with four simple flat leaves incised on each corner. One has eagles, the earliest and crudest example of this motive that I have seen; one has sirens; one is ornamented with a double row of crude uncarved acanthus leaves, which recall the capitals of Caen, and one has a kind of interlace. The bases are of Attic type with griffes; the shafts have a marked entasis (Plate 11, Fig. 3), and one is octagonal.

41

Besides these capitals there are several more or less fragmentary capitals and bases lying about the building, for the most part the originals of those replaced by the restorers. Two now placed on either side of the altar in the gallery I suppose to have been those of the lantern found during the restoration. They are distinctly crude, rather than primitive, in style. Another capital of broad-leaved Corinthianesque type in the gallery has been placed in the wall near the restored capital which replaces it, and a third capital with ram's head is also near the modern copy. A fourth capital, now in a niche on the ground floor, is a copy of one of the ancient ones in the gallery, and the original base of this column is near its original position. These fragments were all made for the existing edifice, *i.e.*, are not pilfered.

The capitals of the gallery (Plate 11, Fig. 2) also were undoubtedly made for their present position, and are superb examples of Lombard decorative art. With a single exception they are of the Corinthianesque type. In one the volutes are replaced by rams' heads, in another by the figures of the Evangelists.[17] The exception is the one sculptured with what I take to be scenes from the history of Tobit (Plate 10, Fig. 7). On one corner we have the figure of Tobit, the blind old man, with a long beard and patriarchal garments. To the left Raphael, the archangel, with staff in his hand, leads back to his father Tobias, whom the sculptor has represented not as a boy but as a bearded man.[18] On the other faces are depicted the husband of Sara, killed by the evil spirit[19] Asmodæus, in the form of two dragons, and finally a scene which probably represents the union of Tobias and Sara.[20] Tobias here is shown as a boy, very small, beardless and with long hair, who seems to cling to his powerful bride. One of these gallery capitals of block Corinthian type is unfinished.

The exterior of the edifice is characterized by small, arched corbel-tables surmounted by flat corbel-tables and supported on pilaster strips, or on shafts which terminate in capitals, cubic or of interlaced or broad-leaved type (Plate 11, Fig. 1). The principal portal, which has been restored, is in many orders, as is the window above it. The impost of the portal is adorned with crude and much broken figure sculptures. Of the subjects I can recognize only St. Bartholomew, characterized by his knife. By the same hand is the relief of a monk bearing a candle over the lunette of the southern portal. The rectangular choir and the apse, obviously later than the main body of the edifice, are adorned with a very rich cornice of brackets, saw teeth, and double arched corbel-tables (Plate 10, Fig. 6). The latter motive also recurs over the little doorway (now walled up) in the south wall (Plate 10, Fig. 6). In the church are two inferior frescos of the XV century.

[17] This capital and the one with scenes from Tobit appear to be by the same hand as the ambo of the Madonna del Castello.

[18] Tob., xi.   [19] Tob., iii.   [20] Tob., vii.

V. It is evident that we have in S. Tommaso three distinct eras of construction: first, the pilfered capitals and bases coming from an earlier building, not improbably on the same site; second, the rotunda itself; and third, the choir, added subsequently. It is to the main structure of the building that it is easiest to assign a date. The vaults of the gallery are less finely executed than those of S. Fedele at Como (Plate 64, Fig. 2), an edifice of c. 1115. They are, however, of a more advanced type. The builders have attempted a more difficult experiment than those of S. Fedele dared to undertake, for they have renounced the easy expedient of doubling the number of supports in the outer perimeter of the annular gallery which was to be vaulted. Notwithstanding the complex problem they thus set themselves, they carried the execution through with great skill and mastery of the technical obstacles to be overcome. Such vaults could not have been erected before the year 1125. On the other hand, they still contain distortions and crudities which do not allow us to place them later than the year 1150. The style of the capitals is advanced. The two with figure sculptures are by the same sculptor who executed the ambo at the Madonna del Castello (c. 1130). Moreover, the masonry is much better than that of the church of S. Giorgio, erected c. 1120, and the rich mouldings of the western doorway and window betray a late date. We may therefore conclude that the present rotunda was erected about the year 1140.

The pilfered capitals must consequently be somewhat earlier than this. They are all contemporary with each other, and were doubtless taken from some one single building. The cubic capitals are of the type familiar at S. Abondio of Como and other edifices of the XI century. The grotesques also are crudely executed and appear to be not later than the year 1100. On the other hand, the capitals with leaves cannot be earlier than this epoch, so that the pilfered materials may be with confidence ascribed to c. 1100. As for the choir, the cornice is evidently of c. 1180, a date which agrees with the details of the other parts of the structure.

ALMENNO S. SALVATORE,[1] MADONNA DEL CASTELLO

(Plate 11, Fig. 4, 6)

I. Some distance beyond the church of S. Giorgio lies a curious monument known as the Madonna del Castello. It has been published by De Dartein[2] and more recently has been made the subject of a little monograph by Fornoni. For the history of the monument the historians of Bergamo, Calvi[3] and Ronchetti[4] as well as Lupi,[5] should be consulted.

[1] (Bergamo).   [2] 61.   [3] I, 33; II, 264.   [4] II, 169; IV, 34.   [5] II, 327, 653.

II. The will of the priest Giovanni, dated April 9, 975, mentions the priests, deacons, subdeacons and officials of the church of S. Maria and S. Salvatore near the castle at Limine.[6]   It is, therefore, evident that at the end of the X century the church enjoyed considerable importance and was officiated by a chapter.   Another document of 1058, cited by Ronchetti[7] and Lupi,[8] shows that at this date the church belonged to the jurisdiction of the bishop of Bergamo, but in 1169 it was given to the cathedral chapter[9] by the bishop Guala.   Other documents of 1073[10] and 1228[11] mention the priest of this church as being appointed by the chapter of Bergamo.

On the western portal of the church is the date 1578, which doubtless records the epoch in which the western, or ante-church, was added.   But the construction probably occupied twelve years, for according to Calvi[12] the consecration was not celebrated until June 4, 1590.   Calvi also relates[13] that in 1613 a miraculous image was translated into the church, and he intimates that the edifice was at this time again enlarged.   This statement, however, is in contradiction with his own assertion of a consecration in 1590, and with the date of 1578 over the portal of the church.   Moreover, his sources for the date of 1613 are contradictory, and one inscription, he says, places it in 1611. It therefore seems probable that there is an error in this second part of his account, and that the enlargement of the church between 1578 and 1590 was really made to accommodate the image which was translated then, and not in 1613.

The campanile was restored in 1894, as is evident from the inscription which it bears: R 1894.

III.   The singular plan comprises a modern ante-church, a nave of two bays covered with a modern barrel vault (Plate 11, Fig. 4), two side aisles, also with modern barrel vaults, a groin-vaulted choir (Plate 11, Fig. 4) of a single double bay terminating in a square east end and flanked by two side aisles, and a crypt.   Heavy rectangular piers (Plate 11, Fig. 4) separate the nave and side aisles, but these were made over in the time of the Renaissance. They are ornamented with a simple moulding forming the impost of the rectangular archivolt (Plate 11, Fig. 4).   The choir is sharply deflected, and indeed the whole monument abounds in irregularities of every description. The groin vault of the choir (Plate 11, Fig. 4) is not domed, but is supplied with wall ribs, of which the lower parts were cut away when a sort of screen-wall carried on an architrave and Ionic columns set transversely was added in the XVI century (Plate 11, Fig. 4).   These Ionic columns, which are so disposed that the central one on each side comes squarely on axis, have been

---

[6] . . . presbyteris diaconis vel subdiaconis & officiales Ecclesie Sancte Dei Genetricis Marie & Domini Salvatoris que est edificata intus castro eodem Lemenne . . . (Lupi, II, 327).

[7] II, 169.   [8] II, 653.   [9] Ronchetti, IV, 34.   See text cited below, p. 46.
[10] Ronchetti, II, 183.   [11] *Ibid.*, IV, 34.   [12] II, 264.   [13] I, 33.

mistaken by archæologists for part of the original construction. At the east end of the side aisles are flat niches in the thickness of the wall. The crypt is covered by groin vaults with transverse ribs, which disappear towards the springing. It is greatly to be regretted that the walls internally and externally have been covered with a thick smudging of intonaco so that it is absolutely impossible to determine the character of the masonry (Plate 11, Fig. 4).

IV. The capitals of the crypt are of the style of the Roman decadence, probably of the IV century, and are pilfered.

In the north side aisle there is an ambo (Plate 11, Fig. 6) supported on four stump columns with capitals of Corinthianesque design. The sculptures, representing the emblems of the four Evangelists, are heavy and ponderous, similar to, but evidently more advanced than, those of S. Giacomo of Bellagio (Plate 22, Fig. 1, 2). The wings are awkward, and lack grace of line. The eagle has an unduly prominent breast and a widely spread tail; the lion is quaintly drawn and represented as roaring. In the curls of the angel and other details the influence of Guglielmo da Modena is evident. These sculptures are like those of Bellagio in that the animals seem to be suspended in mid air, and the feet hang limply down, supporting no weight. At Almenno, however, the sculptor appears to have tried to represent flight, whereas at Bellagio the wings are folded. The Almenno sculptures are, moreover, superior in the details of the technique, the general animation of the figures, and in the composition.

V. So few fragments of the ancient church remain—really only the vaults of the crypt and choir—that it is almost impossible to ascribe a date, especially since the masonry can not be examined. The choir vault, however, is of a type which suggests the XII century; and the conjecture is, therefore, permissible that the remains of the ancient edifice are contemporary with the ambo. The latter, from the style of its capitals and sculptures, more advanced than those of S. Giacomo at Bellagio (c. 1115) and showing the influence of Guglielmo da Modena, must have been executed about the year 1130.

ALMENNO S. SALVATORE,[1] S. GIORGIO

(Plate 11, Fig. 5, 7, 8, 9)

I. About a kilometre from the village of Almenno lies the notable church of S. Giorgio. The architecture has been described and illustrated by Osten[2] and by De Dartein.[3]

II. Lupi has printed a document from which it appears that the bishop Guala, in 1169, gave to the chapter of S. Alessandro at Bergamo the Madonna

[1] (Bergamo).   [2] XLVII, XLVIII.   [3] 393.

del Castello and the church of S. *Gregorio* at Almenno. I believe that the venerable historian of Bergamo has here made a mistake, or else his manuscript has been misprinted, and that it was a question, not of the church of S. Gregorio, but of S. Giorgio.[4] Certain it is, in any event, that our church has been called S. Giorgio at least since the XIV century, since at that epoch it was adorned with frescos of the titular saint.[5]

On the west porch is the inscription ANNO 1774, which doubtless indicates the epoch in which this feature was added to the church, and the upper part of the façade remade.

III. The church consists of a nave (Plate 11, Fig. 8) three bays long, with wooden roof; two side aisles, also with wooden roof; a rib-vaulted choir (Plate 11, Fig. 9) of a single bay, flanked by two groin-vaulted side aisles now walled off, and a single apse (Plate 11, Fig. 7). Over the eastern end of the northern side aisle rises a Renaissance campanile (Plate 11, Fig. 7).

The nave (Plate 11, Fig. 8) is separated from the side aisles by rectangular piers with no capitals or bases, and only a very simple moulding at the impost, to mark the springing of the arches. The archivolts are in a single unmoulded order, but of light and graceful construction.

The rib vault of the choir (Plate 11, Fig. 9) has diagonals of rectangular profile about half a metre in width. They describe in elevation, not a semicircle, but a segment of a circle; the wall ribs describe in elevation an egg-shaped curve. However, the vault itself is somewhat domed, and the ribs are allowed to project from its surface much more at their crown than at their springing. We have here, evidently, a very interesting experiment in the

---

[4] . . . Ea propter ego Guala Dei Gratia Sancte Pergamensis Ecclesie Episcopus dono cedo atque per hanc presentis privilegii paginam confirmo ut a presenti die & hora deveniat in jure & potestate Ecclesie Beati Alexandri que constructa est extra prope civitatem Pergami ubi ejus sanctum requiescit corpus videlicet capellam unam cum parochia sua que constructa est infra villam de Lemine ad honorem Dei & Beate Virginis Marie. Et aliam Ecclesiam que constructa ex extra predictam villam in salecto [= salicto] ipsius loci ad honorem Dei & Sancti Gregorii. . . . (Lupi, II, 1254). The chronological notes of this document are erroneous. January 3 fell on a Wednesday in the year 1168, which would seem to be indicated by the year of the Incarnation 1169. There is a further confusion in the indiction which, in 1168, would be the first, not the second. The year 1170, on which the third of January fell on a Friday, corresponds neither with the year nor with the indiction.

[5] Above the fine figure of S. GOTÃRDV' on the second pier from the west of the southern arcade is an inscription giving the date of the fresco:

.DIS' LVIN' DE CAROLIS DE LEMEN.

VI

FECIT.FIERI.HOC.OPVS.M.C.C.C.L.X.X.X.I.I.

On the west respond of the same arcade is a similar inscription of the same date, now in part illegible.

construction of rib vaults and one full of significance for the history of architecture. The builders, for æsthetic reasons, wished to avoid excessive doming of the vault. Not being able, however, to obviate this entirely in a vault constructed without solid centering, they minimized its effect by depressing the intrados of the diagonals into a curve more segmental than that of the vault itself.

Since the vault is erected over an area nearly square in plan (6.39 x 5.90 metres), the wall ribs project but slightly, and like the diagonals are loaded at the crowns. The vault is probably constructed of ashlar, but is covered with intonaco, so that the stereotomy can not be studied. The stone courses of the diagonals, however, can still be seen, and it is evident from the arrangement of the stones at the intersections, that one diagonal was erected first as a complete and self-sustaining arch, and that against this were later placed the two half arches of the second diagonal. Shafts are provided for the diagonals in the eastern piers, but on the west side they are carried on corbels.

The side aisles of the choir have been walled off to form separate rooms, but the ancient groin vaults are still intact. These vaults were very oblong in plan, and are so highly domed that they look more like longitudinal barrel vaults than groin vaults. They were undoubtedly erected with solid centering, since the imprint of the boards of the centering is still clearly visible in the plaster. These vaults are constructed of rubble. The piers separating nave and choir have systems consisting each of a broad pilaster strip (Plate 11, Fig. 8). The pavement slopes sharply towards the west.

The masonry of the church is most peculiar. The lower part of the side-aisle walls and the nave piers and arches (Plate 11, Fig. 8) are constructed of ashlar. In the piers this ashlar is smooth and well laid, but in the side-aisle walls, even internally, it is somewhat rough, and externally it is decidedly rough, the blocks being unsmoothed and treated almost like rusticated work. It is probable that it was the intention of the builders to polish off these blocks, but that for some reason the walls were left unfinished. The choir (Plate 11, Fig. 7) and the east bay of the nave (Plate 11, Fig. 5) on the south side are constructed of smooth blocks, but this ashlar is somewhat crude and has irregular courses and wide joints. The clearstory walls of the nave (Plate 11, Fig. 5) and the upper part of the side-aisle walls (Plate 11, Fig. 5) are of rubble in which herring-bone pebbles are much used. This rubble masonry can not be altogether the result of later rebuilding, since it is quite mediæval in character, and in the nave XIII century frescos are placed upon the rubble wall (Plate 11, Fig. 8).

IV. The supports of the choir are Lombard compound piers (Plate 11, Fig. 8), of which the bases have, for the most part, been covered up, leaving only a few mouldings visible, not enough really to determine their character. The capitals are of Corinthian type, with a single row of uncarved leaves, or of broad-leaved type, or with curious handle-like volutes, and show very skilful execution. They are quite analogous to those of S. Fedele at Como (Plate 63, Fig. 6, 7; Plate 64, Fig. 5). The apse (Plate 11, Fig. 7) is adorned with a row of blind arches supported on pilaster strips, with engaged shafts. Above is a cornice ornamented with a saw tooth, and there may well have been originally a row of arched corbel-tables above this, for the apse roof has been lowered in modern times. The few windows are widely splayed, and evidently never had glass. The nave imposts are without capitals (Plate 11, Fig. 8); in the west wall, however, are two responds which have capitals, one of which is cubic, the other of the curious wreath variety familiar at Fontanella al Monte.

Without doubt the interior walls were anciently covered entirely with frescos, of which many notable fragments are still extant. These fragments comprise at least three layers, of which the latest is dated 1388 by two inscriptions. It is to be regretted that no critical study of these important monuments of pictorial art has yet been made. There are clear traces of frescos also on the exterior walls.

V. Although there appears to be a distinct break in the masonry between the nave and the choir, the style of the two portions of the edifice is so similar that the former can not be more than a year or so later than the latter. The severe, almost bare character of the nave is extraordinary, and suggests the XI century. The character of the two capitals in the west wall, however, the lightness of the arches, and the skilful stereotomy, show that it could not have been erected before the XII century. Moreover, the rib vault of the choir is obviously not an early experiment, since it shows refinements which the builders could have introduced only at a period when they had thorough mastery of the technique of construction. This vault is less highly domed and more skilfully executed than the vaults of S. Savino at Piacenza (Plate 186, Fig. 1), a church consecrated in 1107. The capitals present analogies with those of S. Fedele at Como (c. 1115). Finally, the masonry in its mixture of rubble and ashlar recalls the narthex of Abbazia di Sesto Calende (c. 1135). We may, therefore, conclude that the monument is essentially a homogeneous structure of c. 1120.

AOSTA,[1] CATHEDRAL

(Plate 12, Fig. 1, 2, 4, 5)

I. The literature of the cathedral of Aosta is more conspicuous for quantity than quality. The church as a monument of architecture was first studied by De Lasteyrie in 1854 in a work hardly worthy of the famous archæologist's reputation. In 1857 Aubert published an article upon the

[1] (Torino).

mosaics, and in 1860 a large illustrated work on the valley of Aosta, which included a sumptuous illustration of the cathedral pavement. In 1873 the mosaics were further studied by Aus'm Weerth,[2] and in 1880 Berard returned to the thesis of Aubert that the pavement was a work of the XV century, bringing forward new documents of some importance. This thesis was in 1891 again reaffirmed by Duc, who incidentally published several new texts. The article of Leclère on the Challant family, which appeared in 1907, contains some important notices bearing upon the cathedral. In 1911 Toesca published, under the auspices of the Italian government, a catalogue of the works of art of Aosta. The publication is pretentious and contains numerous half-tones of great value. The text, however, is perfunctory and disappointing. In the same year Monneret de Villard published a little handbook on Aosta in the Bonomi series, containing excellent half-tones of the mosaics. Finally should be mentioned the study of the architecture by Commendatore Rivoira.[3]

II. Berard has published a notice taken from an ancient martyrology of the cathedral, which speaks of Gontran († 593), king of the Franks, as the restorer of the cathedral.[4] Berard says that Gontran was a king of Burgundy in the middle of the VI century, but with evident error, since Godomar, the last king of the first kingdom of Burgundy, fell in 534, and no Burgundian king of the name of Gontran is known to history.[5] The restorer of the cathedral of Aosta must be Gontran, the pious grandson of Clovis, renowned for his orthodoxy and mild character.

The documents of the Middle Ages are silent in regard to the history of the monument, and it is only in the XV century that we begin to have notices of the changes and alterations made in the cathedral. The keystones of the vaults of the nave are sculptured with the coat of arms of the family of Challant. De Lasteyrie[6] has conjectured that these escutcheons belong to François I, who died in 1421 and was buried in the cathedral. Leclère,[7] on the other hand, assigns the vaults of the nave to Georges de Challant, who became a canon of the cathedral chapter in 1460. As a matter of fact, the shields prove only that the vaults must have been erected in the XV century by some member of the Challant family. There is extant a notice of the consecration of the church on August 24,[8] but the year, unfortunately, is not

---

[2] 17.　　[3] 230.

[4] 　　　　　QVINTO KL' APRILIS. . . . .

EODEM DIE APVD CABILONE CIVITATE
GALLIARV DEPOSITIO BTI GONTRANNI REGIS
FRANCORUM INSTRAVRATORIS HVI ECCLIE　　(Berard, 146).

[5] Lavisse, *Histoire de France*, Paris, Hachette, 1903, II, pt. 1, pp. 121 f., 138, 146. Lavisse et Rambaud, *Histoire Générale*, Paris, Colin, 1905, I, 100.

[6] 7.　　[7] 137.

[8] *Extractus Anniversariorum ecclesiae Augustae*, ed. *Hist. Pat. Mon.*, V, 648: Augustus 24. Bartholomei apostoli et dedicatio ecclesie cathedralis Auguste.

given. It is possible this consecration may have been that solemnized after the vaults had been erected, or it may refer to one of the consecrations which must have taken place in the XI and XII centuries.

François de Challant, whom De Lasteyrie suspects of having vaulted the nave, was buried in the cathedral. The tomb, which was placed in the choir, was of great magnificence and its construction was the occasion for erecting in the choir a *solanum*.[9] The misinterpretation of this word *solanum* as referring to the mosaic pavement of the choir has misled several archæologists into assigning the latter to the XV century, whereas the style clearly shows the pavement must be of the XII century. Just what *solanum* means is not clear; it may refer to the vaults, to the ambulatory or to a raised platform for the tomb. The word, so far as has been shown, does not occur elsewhere in mediæval Latin.

In 1460 the cloisters were begun by Georges de Challant,[10] whose name appears with those of the other donors sculptured in relief on the capitals of the arcade. On June 5, 1518, the campanile was struck by lightning. It must have been old at this time, since it had been previously restored by one of the canons who was also master of the *fabbrica*.[11] The atrium was adorned with frescos by Giovanni Goubaudelli, who died in 1525 apparently, although he is recorded as having made a bequest to the church dated 1535.[12] Besides this we know that an important reliquary was donated by François de Challant.[13]

The necrologies of the cathedral[14] abound in records relating to the various

[9] Pro Magistro imaginum. In nomine Domini, Amen. Per hoc praesens publicum instrumentum ad universorum notionem deducatur quod cum illustris et magnificus Dominus Franciscus Comes Challandi, nuper ordinaverit et proposuerit fieri facere in ecclesia Augustense, auxilio divino mediante, quoddam magnificum opus valde sumptuosum videlicet eius sepulcrum et solanum chori dictae ecclesiae, et ipsius magnifici operis onus fiendi in se suscepit discretus vir magister Stephanus Mossettaz, burgensis Augustae, hinc est quod constituti in capitulo praedictae ecclesiae . . . venerabilis viri, etc. . . . die vigesima prima mensis ianuarii, anno Domini millesimo quatercentesimo vigesimo nono etc. (Duc, 6-7).

Anno Domini millesimo quatercentesimo trigesimo quarto, die decima octava mensis iulii . . . magister Stephanus Mossettaz confessus fuit habuisse a Domino Comite Challandi plenam solutionem de septem centum et quinquaginta florenis parvi ponderis in deductionem operis solani ecclesiae et suae sepulturae . . . (Duc, 9).

Item fecit fieri suis expensis solanum supra chorum. Jacet in confessione. . . . (Duc, 10).

[10] The inscription has been published by Aubert, 216.

[11] Venerabilis domini Hugoni Ferrenchi de Curia maiori canonici Auguste, magisti fabrice huius ecclesie, qui reparauit aulam nostram capitularem et campanille, ante consumationem fulguris que euenit. 1518. die 5a iunii. (*Hist. Pat. Mon.*, V, 645).

[12] Venerabilis dominus Iohannes Goubaudelli de Liniaco in ducatu Barri, Tulensis diocesis, canonicus Auguste, et magister fabrices benemeritus . . . ornauit atrium ecclesie nostre picturis variis, sumptibus propriis. (*Ibid.*, 631-632).

[13] *Ibid.*, 640.   [14] *Ibid.*

chapels, at least thirty-one in number. The notices are strikingly confused and contradictory, but it appears that the earliest of these chapels of which the date can be established were those of S. Tommaso and S. Maria Magdalena, founded by the bishop Nicolao (1281-1300).[15]

The western portal was rebuilt 1522-1526, and in 1848 the façade was adorned with mediocre statues.

III. The church has been almost entirely modernized and retains of its original architecture, at least that is visible, only the crypt (Plate 12, Fig. 2), the campaniles (Plate 12, Fig. 4), three capitals of the ambulatory, and the mosaic pavement. These fragments, however, are sufficient to show that the monument in the Romanesque period possessed remarkable architectural forms. The ambulatory (Plate 12, Fig. 5) and the twin towers flanking the choir (Plate 12, Fig. 4) savour of dispositions common enough in ultramontane churches but rare in Italy. The ambulatory at present (Plate 12, Fig. 5) presents superficially all the characteristics of the Gothic style of the XV century. It is evident that it is not part of the original construction, for the crypt stops with the wall of the choir, and does not extend beneath the ambulatory. The crypt was enlarged in the XII century, and it is probable that at this time the ambulatory was added. The irregularity of the existing soffits gives some reason to suppose that in the XII century the ambulatory was covered with compartments of wedge-shaped transverse ribs almost like triangular barrel vaults and with trapezoidal groin vaults (Plate 12, Fig. 5). I can find no evidence that the radiating chapels (Plate 12, Fig. 5) are ancient, or that the Romanesque edifice was supplied with any such absidioles. In fact, it is impossible to prove absolutely that the vaults, and, indeed, the whole ambulatory, be not of the XV century, since modern plaster completely covers the masonry. It seems, therefore, that Commendatore Rivoira ventured a somewhat hazardous conjecture when he brought this church forward as an important example of a Romanesque ambulatory.

The crypt (Plate 12, Fig. 2) is covered with groin vaults with transverse ribs which disappear towards their springing. The western bay of this crypt is obviously later than the eastern bays, since not only the capitals differ, but the structure of the vault itself is different. In the eastern part the vaults (Plate 12, Fig. 2) are undomed and have transverse arches which completely disappear at the springing, but are loaded in a very exaggerated way at the crowns. One which I measured projects 60 centimetres (Plate 12, Fig. 2). In the side walls the wall ribs were in two orders, and the responds appear to have consisted of five rectangular members without capitals. The traces

---

[15] *Selecta e libro anniversariorum ecclesiae cathedralis Augustanae*, ed. *Hist. Pat. Mon.*, V, 548. Compare, however, *ibid.*, 627. A great wealth of perplexing details in regard to the chapels of the cathedral is supplied in the records published in the *Hist. Pat. Mon.*, V.

of the solid board centering are still preserved in one vault. The masonry is rubble of the roughest kind, only the responds and the ribs being executed in a crude sort of ashlar of stone or brick. The western part of the crypt, on the other hand, has groin vaults similarly undomed and with transverse ribs, but these transverse ribs do not die away altogether at the springing and are but slightly loaded at the crown. Moreover, the vaults themselves are far better executed than those of the eastern part of the crypt.

The campaniles are of widely different design (Plate 12, Fig. 4). The southernmost is unbroken by windows, save bifora in the face of the two upper stories. Below are arched corbel-tables grouped two and two by pilaster strips. The northern campanile, on the other hand, has two sets of bifora in its three or four upper stories, and is adorned with arched corbel-tables of the customary type. Both campaniles are crowned by pinnacles and turrets evidently later than the towers themselves.

The southern campanile is supplied with an eastern apse, and it is evident that the northern campanile as well must originally have had a similar excrescence. The undomed groin vaults of the lower stories of the campaniles are the original ones of the XI century. They had continuous responds consisting of three rectangular members (three have been made over), and were characterized by loaded wall ribs and much depressed diagonals. It is clear that the church must originally have had five apses, three aisles and no transepts.[16]

The piers of the nave, rectangular in section, may be the original ones, and original also appears to be the south side-aisle wall, with pilaster strips so disposed as to suggest that the arched corbel-tables were grouped two and two. The north side-aisle wall and clearstory, on the other hand, appear modern. The ambulatory is supplied with flamboyant buttresses, doubtless added when the vaults were remade in the XV century.

North of the church are the lovely flamboyant cloisters, unfortunately in part destroyed to make room for a modern chapel.

IV. The ornamental details of the church, like those of most of the monuments of the Val d'Aosta, are singularly lacking in character. The cubic capitals of the ambulatory appear to be of the usual Lombard type. Since, however, similar capitals were added to the choir in the XV century, it is, in the present state of the edifice, impossible to be certain that the whole ambulatory does not date from this time. The capitals of the campanile are similarly completely without architectural character. The capitals of the eastern portion of the crypt are formed of ancient bases, uncarved blocks of stone, etc. (Plate 12, Fig. 2). Among the pilfered materials are notable two fine Roman Ionic capitals (Plate 12, Fig. 2). Only one capital is original, and this has chamfered corners adjusting the rectangular load to an octagonal

16 Toesca (7) is wrong in saying that the Romanesque church had transepts.

shaft. It is exactly analogous to the capitals of the piers of S. Pietro at Acqui. The capitals of the later, western portion of the crypt, on the other hand, are of Corinthianesque type, or else are adorned with string patterns and are skilfully executed in fine marble with sure technique and deep undercutting.

The absidiole of the southern campanile is adorned with blind niches.

The mosaic of the choir is the decorative feature of the church which commands the greatest interest. The subject recalls that of the mosaic pavement of S. Savino at Piacenza. In the centre is the Year, ANNVS, haloed—significant detail—bearing in his hands the Sun, SOL, and the Moon, LVNA. About him is a circle formed by medallions with the works of the twelve months. January, IAN . . . . . with two heads, stands between two doors, the one open, the other closed. February, FEBRV|ARIVS, warms himself at the fire; March, MARCIVS, prunes a tree; April, APRILIS, is represented holding a flower in either hand and with a bird's nest; May, MAIVS, is on horse-back; June, IVNIVS, mows; July, IVLIVS, binds the grain in sheaves; August, AVGVSTVS, threshes it; September, SEP|TEMB|ER, treads the grapes; October, OCTO|BER, sows; November, NOV, carries·a load of wood on his back; December, DECEMBER, slaughters the swine. At the angles of the quadrangle are four figures pouring water from jars, representing the four rivers of Paradise. The inscriptions naming two of them, FIZON, GION, are still extant, but those of the other two, Euphrates and Tigris, if they ever existed, have disappeared. I suspect, however, that they were not repeated, since already represented in the upper mosaic. Here we see first EVFRA|TES represented as a nude woman pouring water from a jar. The head of the bull of St. Luke placed near this figure tells us that in the thought of the artist these four rivers signified the four Evangelists. Then follows the TIGRI|S, near which may be seen part of the lion of St. Mark. This mosaic contains other grotesques and symbolic figures; among the former an elephant, ELEFANS, and a CHIMERA with two heads (both, however, possibly have reference to the bestiaries); among the latter three of the symbols of the Evangelists, but a unicorn is substituted for the fourth (St. Matthew).

In the cloisters is a carved plaque (Plate 12, Fig. 1) which probably belonged to some of the church-furniture. The central motive is a whirl which has a Carlovingian look, although it must be remembered that similar whirls persisted at Pieve Trebbio until the XII century. Around the outer border of the whirl is a row of crockets, and in the outer corners were four animals. The two uppermost, of which one has been almost entirely destroyed, were lambs of God, holding each a cross. The two lower ones represented stags taking the poison from serpents, according to the bestiary story. These animals are drawn in excellent proportion, but the details, such as the eyes and mouth, are very crude.

V. The core of the campaniles, with their absidioles, the bays of the side aisle adjoining them, the choir and the eastern part of the crypt, the piers of the nave and parts of the southern wall are undoubtedly fragments of a basilica of the early part of the XI century. The only original capital of the crypt is perfectly analogous to the capitals of the piers of the nave of S. Pietro at Acqui, a dated monument of c. 1015-1023. The blind niches of the absidiole of the southern campanile recall those of the same church of S. Pietro at Acqui, and those of S. Vincenzo at Galliano, a surely dated monument of 1007. The rectangular piers also recall those at Galliano. The southern wall was probably adorned with arched corbel-tables grouped two and two, like those of S. Pietro at Acqui and other churches of the early part of the XI century. This portion of the cathedral of Aosta may, therefore, be assigned with great confidence to c. 1010. I do not hesitate to ascribe to the same epoch the carved plaque of the cloisters, which probably belonged to the church-furniture made for the XI century basilica. The motives, it is true, are still Carlovingian, but there is a largeness in the design, a freedom in the execution, and a certain verve in the technique which announce the transition towards the developed Lombard forms. This is apparent upon comparing it, for example, with the carved archivolt from the cathedral of Ferentino (Plate 12, Fig. 3). Moreover, the introduction of a bestiary story is without analogy in Carlovingian work, and is one of the earliest examples of a subject of definite iconographic purport in Lombard art. About a century later the crypt was extended to the westward, the mosaics of the choir executed, and possibly the ambulatory added. The mosaic is very analogous to that of S. Savino at Piacenza, which is known to date from 1107. We may, therefore, with confidence ascribe the Aosta mosaic to c. 1110, a date which accords well with the style of the capitals of the western bays of the crypt. The northern campanile entire and the upper part of the southern have been much made over and restored in the XIII and succeeding centuries. But the lower part of the southern tower with its arched corbel-tables grouped two and two appears to preserve essentially unaltered its XI century form.

AOSTA,[1] S. ORSO

(Plate 12, Fig. 6; Plate 13, Fig. 1, 2, 3; Plate 14, Fig. 1, 2, 3; Plate 15, Fig. 1, 3)

I. The collegiate church of S. Orso, although it has been mentioned incidentally by a number of writers upon Lombard antiquities, has never been given the careful study which this really very important monument deserves. As early as 1860, Aubert[2] described the cloisters and published an engraving

[1] (Torino).   [2] 225.

which shows the monument as it was before the existing ugly grill was erected. The history of Duc, the publication of which was begun in 1901, contains some historical notices of value, especially in regard to the pastoral visits to the church. Ten years before, Ceradini had published a little book in which he undertook to give the subjects of the cloister sculptures. His work is not altogether successful, for many subjects are passed over in silence and others are misidentified. However, as a first attempt at this difficult task, the book merits praise, and is far superior to the iconographic study of Venturi,[3] which is well illustrated but abounds in mistakes and inaccuracies. Equally unsatisfactory, except for the illustrations, is the pretentious but inaccurate catalogue compiled by Toesca under the auspices of the Italian government, and published in 1911. The little handbook of Monneret de Villard, also published in 1911, contains excellent half-tones. Sumptuous photographs have been published by Martin. The architecture of the church has been touched upon by Commendatore Rivoira.[4]

II. According to the *Vita Sancti Ursi* our church was in existence during the lifetime of the saint, or about the middle of the VI century.[5] This life, it is true, is not of great weight as an historical source. Internal evidence shows that it was written by a monk of Aosta who lived long after the death of the saint. The writer shows himself perfectly familiar with the local geography, but his only sources for the events which he narrates seem to have been vague traditions of the place passed down by word of mouth. His scant matter is padded out with texts from the Scriptures and platitudes upon the virtues of the saint.[6] Nevertheless the tradition that S. Orso was a priest in the church

---

[3] III, 72.   [4] 231-232.   [5] Savio, 84.

[6] I transcribe from the Bollandists those passages of the life of the saint which seem to bear upon the history of the church or the sculptures of the cloister: In nomine sanctæ & indiuiduæ Trinitatis, hic subter insertū est, qualiter beatissimus Vrsus Confessor Christi, & Sacerdos Dei excelsi, natione Scotus, Patronus contitularis Ecclesiæ, ciuitatis & burgi Augustæ, nocte ac die Christo famulans, curam gerebat officij sui in Ecclesiâ, quæ in honore S. Petri Principis Apostolorum ædificata, & dedicata est, extra ciuitatem quæ nuncupatur Augusta. . . . Fuitque in illo tempore in eadem vrbe Præsul quidam, nomine Ploceanus: sed, vt res gesta apertissime probat, & illius loci ciues asserrunt, ob perfidiam suam nimiamque crudelitatem, non Pōtifex pastoralis curæ, sed sub veste ouis lupus rapax, & crudelissimus inuasor, atque tyrannus potius extitit, quam Pontifex vel pastor. . . . Circa ecclesiam verò S. Petri, vbi vir Dei Vrsus fungebatur officio, tanta inundatio fuit, vt nullus eam ingredi, aut egredi valeret. . . . Restat autem adhuc & aliud miraculum, quod per ipsum Domini virtus operatur est, quod mihi visum est non prætermittere, quod tamen hominibus loci illius notissimum est. . . . Cumque aues superiùs nominatas aleret, & resideret ante ianuam ecclesiæ, vbi sedulò Deo seruiebat; aspiciens vidit iuuenem quemdam equum domini sui equitantem, & amarissime flentem: qui cum assidue hic idem custos equorum ante iam dictum templum transiret, numquam tamen ad orationem descendit, nec caput suum Sanctorum reliquiis inclinauit. Tunc beatissimus Vrsus hæc intuens frequenter agentem, vocauit eum ad se, cui & dixit: Dic, inquit, mi fili . . . & omnia secreta tua mihi fac manifesta. Tunc ejulans

of S. Pietro, which was subsequently renamed in his honour, merits faith, and the life of the saint, dubious as it is as an historical source, still gives sufficient reason to believe that the church of S. Pietro existed as early as the VI century.

According to Duc,[7] S. Orso was a collegiate church from the earliest times. It is evident, however, that the historian of Aosta has here made an

ille, ait ad virum Dei: Heu mihi, Domine, hodie cum transirem per hanc viam, ablatus est a me equus domini mei optimus, quem nimio diligebat amore, unde nimio coarctor timore: quid faciam nescio. Unde non aliud peto, nisi tuam beatissimam orationem pariter et consolationem. Tunc idem vir Dei in Domino confisus, cum magna fiducia dixit adolescenti: Vade, fili mi, ingredere, in hanc domum Domini, in qua antea non fuisti: flagita misericordissimum et amatorem omnium benignissimum Deum de salute tua: postea vero venies ad me, et quicquid necessarium fuerit pandam. Quibus ille jussis libentissime obediens, ad virum Dei concito gradu reversus est. Dixit ad eum S. Ursus: Dic mihi juvenis, quanti tibi in custodiendo, curam gerendo, commendati sunt equi? Respondit: Sex. Dicit ei S. Ursus: Quantos ad pabula dimisisti, quando hunc, quem quærere cœpisti? Aut quis tibi talem dedit equum tam pulchrum, tamque formosum et honestum? Tunc pavefactus puer ille, videns se captum in interrogationibus S. Ursi, prosternens se ad pedes ejus cum lacrymis dixit: Miser ego, ipsum, quem equito, et quæro lugens, ipsum sedeo. . . . Tunc demum castigavit eum S. Ursus. . . . Eodem tempore . . . Ploceanus, ut dictum est, in eadem urbe Pontifex esse videbatur. Contigit autem ejusdem Ploceani ministerialem quemdam incurisse crimen. Unde valde pertimescens, præsidium fugefecit ad ecclesiam S. Petri, ubi S. Ursus custos erat. Cumque more solito in ecclesiam fuisset ingressus, vidit eum juxta altare stantem, cui et dixit: Quidnam, inquit, peccasti, fili? Cumque puer singulas retulisset admissionis suæ culpas, cœpit eum rogare, ut apud dominum suum pro se intercederet. Egrediensque S. Ursus venit ad Episcopum in civitatem, et prosternens se ad pedes ejus dixit: Mi domine Pater, quidam ex pueris vestris sciens se graviter deliquisse in vos, confugium fecit ad S. Petrum: unde peto, ut in ejus amore, ad quem confugit, absolutionem criminis ei concedatis, et vestræ domesticitatis concessionem. Ploceanus vero fallens in virum Dei dixit: Vade, frater, dic ei, ut securus cum gratia veniat ad præsentiam nostram, nulla pertimescens mala. Tunc vir Dei ad puerum reversus, dixit: Vade fili mi, quia ex hac re impedimentum tibi nullum erit. Ploceanus enim Episcopus clam quibusdam sibi astantibus dixit: Nisi eum, cum exierit de ipsa ecclesia, in qua nunc latitat, mihi vinctum præsentaveritis, ejus sententiæ vos subjacebitis. Qui jussa complentes, ante eum adductus est. Qui frendens et tabescens in eum, tanquam crudelissima bestia, tamdiu a dorso et ventre flagellatus est, quousque expirare crederetur. Tunc capite ejus tonso, jussit tyrannus viscosum bitumen super illum fundi, ut vix evaderet usque ad virum Dei morte vicina . . . cui et dixit: Quid, inquit, facere in me voluisti, Pater mi, ut me . . . egredi de hac domo Dei juberes? . . . Tunc beatissimus Ursus . . . dixit . . . Vade cito fili mi, dic Ploceano: Notum tibi sit, quia post paucos dies tolletur anima tua a te, et a dæmonibus, ut dignus es, strangulaberis, et a tetris spiritibus susceptus sepelieris in infernum; ut quibus nunc usque servire studuisti, ab his recipias meritum servitutis. . . . Tu ergo, fili mi, præpara iter tuum, quia et tu migrabis cito de hoc mundo pergens altercaturus cum eo. Ego autem subsequens ero iter vestrum, ut sim audientiæ vestræ assistens, cum in ratione steteritis ante tribunal Judicis magni. Mira res, ac verissima, quia quicquid in illa hora prædixit, in utroque postea rei probavit eventus. Eadem vero nocte, in qua migraturum Episcopum prædixit, projectus est de stratu suo a dæmonibus in humum, et sic miserabiliter expiravit. (*Vita S. Ursi*, ed. Jean de Bolland, *Acta Sanctorum*, Februarius, I, 946).

[7] I, 225.

error, for there is extant a charter of the bishop Anselmo of 923, establishing a chapter of canons in the church.[8] It is therefore certain that before 923 no canons existed. The chronological notes of this charter offer some difficulty, for while the eleventh indiction corresponds to the year 923, Rodolfo did not become king until 924. However, the fact that the chapter was founded by Anselmo is not open to question,[9] since it is confirmed by a passage in the necrology of the chapter[10] and by a martyrology cited in the acts of the pastoral visit of 1419.[11]

In 1032 one of the canons made a donation to the chapter, from which we learn that the latter must have consisted of at least six members, since so many are mentioned individually by name.[12] Another donation of 1040, made by Conte Umberto I to the canons of S. Orso, has been published by Carutti.[13] It seems to have been a vague tradition of this donation which inspired a curiously erroneous passage in a XVI century necrology of the cathedral, in which the Marchesi of Monferrato are named as founders of the monastery or priory of SS. Pietro e Orso.[14]

In 1132 at the prayer of the bishop of Aosta, Ariberto, Pope Innocent II reformed the chapter and established canons regular of the order of St. Augustine at S. Orso. The papal bull on this subject is still extant.[15] On the capital of the cloister of the church (Plate 14, Fig. 2), moreover, there is an

[8] Quapropter ego anselmus largiente diuina clementia episcopus augustensis ecclesie et comes. Notum esse uolo omnibus sub Xp̄o principe militantibus, quod anno ab incarnatione domini nostri Ihū Xp̄i DCCCCXXIII, indictione XI, pro amore Dei et remedio anime mee et animarum parentum meorum et item pro remedio anime domni regis Rodulfi. dono donatumque esse in perpetuum uolo ecclesie sancte Marie et sancti Iohannis sanctique Ursi ad communem uictum suorum canonicorum predicto rege Rodulfo laudente . . . hoc est quasdam terras, etc. (*Hist. Pat. Mon.*, VI, 28).

[9] See, however, Savio, 84.

[10] XVII kal. Febr. Ob. Anselmus Episcopus Augustensis qui nostram construxit ecclesiam. (*Necrologium insignis collegii canonicorum Sancti Petri et Ursi*, ed. *Hist. Pat. Mon.*, V, 519).

[11] . . . Interogati . . . . . quis fundauit ipsum prioratum, Responderunt unamiter quod bone memorie dnus Anselmus quondam episcopus augustensis, quia ita describitur in eorum libro vocato martiligio [= Martyrologio] ligato cum cathena ferrea in pulpito in medio dicti capituli. (Duc, 113).

[12] *Hist. Pat. Mon.*, I, 497.

[13] *Archivio Storico Italiano, Anno* 1878, quarta serie, II, 348.

[14] . . . anno 1040, sedente in cathedra Beati Grati felicis recordationis Arnulpho episcopo, necnon regnante et principiante in valle nostra Auguste Sallassorum Humberto primo comite Maurianensi, filio illustris Beroldi de Saxonia, qui Humbertus eodem anno legauit capitulo nostro dominium loci Derbie pro duabus partibus, legata alia tertia parte cenobio seu priori Sanctorum Petri et Vrsi, quod dudum fondauerunt, et dotauerunt bone memorie Marchiones Montisferrati . . . (*Extractus Anniversariorum ecclesiae cathedralis Augustae*, 1 Nov., ed. *Hist. Pat. Mon.*, V, 656).

[15] *Hist. Pat. Mon.*, I, 769. The bull is dated: Datum Placentie XIII kalendas decembris indictione X. Incarnationis Dominice anno MCXXXIII. Pontificatus Domni

inscription recording this same fact.[16] This inscription has been interpreted by Venturi[17] to indicate that the cloisters were erected in 1133, and by Toesca to prove that they were erected before 1133. As a matter of fact, it does neither the one nor the other. Since the inscription is manifestly contemporary with the other inscriptions in the cloister, which were evidently part of the original construction, it proves that the cloisters were erected after 1132.

On another capital of the cloister is a sculptured representation of the foundation of the chapter of canons regular. On one face St. Augustine, SCS. AVGVSTINVS| EPISCOPVS, with crosier, gives his blessing to the reverencing figure of Arnolfo, the first prior, ARNVLFVS. PRIMV'. PIOR.,[18] who is presented by S. Orso, QVI REDDIT . SCS . VRSVS. On the other side the bishop Ariberto, ARBERTVS . EPS., approaches St. Augustine and gives his blessing and approbation to the new order, as is evident by the inscription on the book:

BENE

DICIT.

PRIORS

As an historical source this sculpture has considerable importance. It confirms, in the first place, by a nearly contemporary document, the fact that the chapter of canons regular was founded in 1132. In the second place, it demonstrates that the cloister was erected soon after this foundation, for the capital formed an integral part of the construction of the cloister, and it is inconceivable that it could have been sculptured and added after the construction of the latter. The cloister must, therefore, have been built after 1132. Nevertheless, the fact that the foundation of the chapter was given so prominent a pictorial representation gives great plausibility to the conjecture that the cloister was erected immediately after and in connection with that foundation.

That the bishop Ariberto played a prominent part in the foundation of the new chapter is also indicated by the fact that he was buried at S. Orso when he died in 1139.[19]

Innocentii Pape II. anno III. This date has been interpreted 1133 by the editors of the *Hist. Pat. Mon.*, erroneously. Savio (90) has shown that it should be interpreted November 19, 1132.

[16] ANNO. AB INCARNATIOE . DNI M. C. XXX. III. IN H. CLAUSTRO. REGVLARS VITA INCEPTA. EST

[17] III, 71.

[18] That Arnolfo was the first prior of the reformed chapter is known also from a passage in the necrology of the chapter: prid. idus Aug. Ob. Arnulfus primus prior S. Ursi et Episcopus Augustensis (*Necrologium insignis collegii canonicorum Sancti Petri et Ursi*, ed. *Hist. Pat. Mon.*, V, 531).

[19] Duc, I, 15 f.

According to a tradition handed down by the historians of Aosta, there was an inscription above the vaults of the existing church which stated that the campanile was built in 1151.[20] The style of the tower gives reason to suppose that this tradition is correct, rather than that other which assigns the construction of the campanile to Goutier d'Ayme, and to the year 1131.[21]

The reformed chapter of S. Orso speedily acquired importance and wealth. Rich donations were made to the canons in 1136 by Guido, bishop of Ivrea.[22] These were followed by a bull of privileges and immunities of Innocent II in 1136,[23] and by other bulls of indulgence of Innocent II in 1142,[24] and of Lucius II in 1144.[25] In 1146 another donation was made to the chapter,[26] and in the same year Eugenius III granted the canons a bull of privileges.[27] Other papal bulls in favour of the monastery were granted by Adrian IV, c. 1159,[28] by Alexander III in 1161,[29] and two by Lucius IV in 1164.[30] In addition, there are extant two donations in favour of the church, without date, but doubtless of c. 1134.[31]

A curious feature of the internal discipline of the chapter was the presence of many female conversae, frequently mentioned in the necrology. In 1400 the chapel of S. Erasmo was founded by the canon Oddo.[32]

In the pastoral visit of 1419 it was ordered that the roof of the church should be repaired, since it menaced ruin.[33] It was doubtless at this epoch that the existing vaults were erected. In the same pastoral visit complaint was made of the condition of the cloister, and it was ordered that here, too, a new roof should be erected.[34] Apparently, however, this order was not carried out, since it was repeated in 1427.[35] This order must have occasioned the reconstruction of the cloister in its present form.

With the exception of the addition of the modern grill, which greatly impedes the enjoyment of the beauty of the cloister, the monument has happily escaped modern restoration.

III. The edifice, although considerably altered, evidently possessed originally a nave (Plate 13, Fig. 2) of seven bays flanked by two side aisles.

---

[20] Toesca, 119.   [21] Ibid.   [22] Hist. Pat. Mon., I, 773, 774.   [23] Ibid., 776.
[24] Ibid., 784.   [25] Ibid., 785.   [26] Ibid., 789.   [27] Ibid., 790.   [28] Ibid., 819.
[29] Ibid., 822.   [30] Ibid., 930, 933.   [31] Ibid., VI, 218, 219.

[32] III nonas Iunii. Ob. venerabilis Oddo canonicus, qui fundauit capellam S. Erasmi 1400 . . . (Necrologium insignis collegii canonicorum Sancti Petri et Ursi, ed. Hist. Pat. Mon., V, 526).

[33] . . . reformetur solare desuper per longitudinem ecclesie quia in pluribus locis minatur ruynam. (Duc, 113).

[34] Subsequenter accessimus ad claustrum quod reperimus de novo fuisse coopertum. Ordinavimus tamen reparari et bituminari in ipso clsustro et in capitulo in locis caducis et ruinosis. (Ibid., 122).

[35] Et item coopertura claustri [reparerentur] ejusdem prioratus secundem exigentiam defectus quia propter hujusmodi defectum perspeximus picturas ejusdem claustri de vita sancti ursi esse deletas (Ibid., 148).

The crypt (Plate 15, Fig. 1) is placed only under the choir, and does not extend beneath the side aisles. The original piers were probably rectangular, but the rectangular section of the existing piers (Plate 13, Fig. 2) is evidently the result of alterations executed in the XV century, when new masonry was built around the original supports so as to strengthen them to bear the weight of the new vaults. The segmental curve of the arches of the main arcade (Plate 13, Fig. 2) shows that such an alteration has been made.[36] Superficially, the edifice with its Gothic vaulting and flamboyant choir-screen, appears to have been entirely rebuilt in the XV century. As a matter of fact, however, in addition to the crypt, the core of the old X century basilica is still extant, although covered by intonaco. Above the Gothic vaults are still preserved the old clearstory walls constructed of rubble, in which large, round stones are laid in thick beds of very poor mortar. The large, round-headed clearstory windows are of the type of those of S. Vincenzo at Milan. Upon the walls are still to be seen notable remains of frescos which I take to be the original ones of the X century.

The crypt (Plate 15, Fig. 1) is covered by very crude groin vaults, which are for the most part original, although repaired in the XVIII century. There are no capitals, and the transverse ribs die away towards the springing. The vaults are not domed. The supports consist of crudely hewn monoliths, square or cylindrical in section.

To the south of the church lie the beautiful cloisters (Plate 12, Fig. 6), the arcades of which on three sides still retain their original columns of the XII century. The archivolts and bases, however, were made over in the XV century, as was the entire eastern gallery, and in the same epoch were added the rib vaults resting on corbels, which cover the ambulatory.

The imposing campanile is a characteristic monument of the local style of the Val d'Aosta. It is constructed of rough ashlar masonry, and is evidently a homogeneous work of about the middle of the XII century. It terminates in an octagonal spire with four angle turrets, a motive which shows the influence of the transitional clochers of the Île-de-France.

IV. None of the ornament—if any ever existed—of the XI century basilica is extant with the exception of the frescos of the clearstory walls preserved above the existing vaults.[37] Among the subjects represented are Elijah, the apostles Andrew and John, the cities of Patras and Ephesus, angels, soldiers, etc. Above runs a Greek fret like that of Spignò, in which birds are represented at intervals. The technique of these frescos, with their broad strokes of black, is extremely similar to that of the frescos of Spignò.

It has frequently been written that the cloisters are Provençal in style.

---

[36] The tradition current at Aosta that the side aisles were added in the XV century is disproved by a study of the masonry. (Duc, I, 225).

[37] These frescos have been illustrated by Toesca, 88.

As a matter of fact, the sculptures are thoroughly Lombard and were, as will be seen, executed by a Lombard master. The archivolts of the arcade, which are the only part of the cloister which really shows Provençal influence, are of the XV century. A peculiarity of the style is the fact that many of the shafts of the colonnettes are square or polygonal.

The capitals, especially those which are sculptured, form a most interesting study. Since the subjects of many of them have never been explained, I shall give a list of them in order, beginning at the north-west angle and proceeding systematically to the south and east around the cloister.

(1) The north-west angle capital is ornamented with broad leaves and has no figure sculptures (Plate 12, Fig. 6).

(2) Coupled capitals, the inner one of which shows the birth of Jacob and Esau (Plate 13, Fig. 3). In a bed with many turned knobs (a most interesting representation for the history of furniture) lies REBECCA. By her side, with folded hands, sits a midwife, OBSTETRIX. From Rebekah emerge two twins, first ESAV and then IACOB, the latter holding his brother's heel (Gen., xxv, 25). The outer capital represents the deception of Isaac. On a similar bed lies the patriarch YSAAC, who feels IACOB, on whose hands and about the smooth of whose neck is the goatskin, while REBE|CCA brings savoury meat, two good kids, on a platter. Meanwhile ESAV shoots a stag with his cross-bow (Gen., xxvii, 1-29).

(3) (Plate 15, Fig. 3) IACOB lies on the ground, or, rather, is on all-fours, face downward, asleep; with his left hand he supports a ladder, SCALA, on which are seen two angels, ANGLI, ascending and descending; to the left is the Lord, DNS (Gen., xxviii, 11-16). On the west face of the same capital IACOB is seen seated. He holds in his lap an object difficult to identify, but which is perhaps intended to be a bag of money, symbolizing the wealth he has accumulated with Laban. On the south face REBECCA is seen seated.[38] On the east face is a seated male figure, with beard, holding in his hand a sort of fleur-de-lis. There is no inscription, but there can be no doubt that the sculptor here wished to represent Jesse and his rod, the fruit of the union of Jacob and Rebekah.

(4) Leah, LIA, and Rachel, RACHEL, are seen seated. The latter is decidedly the younger and better looking, and is characterized by long, flowing hair. Next to Rachel is seen Jacob, IA[COB], who is engaged in lifting the great stone, which looks like a cover, from the well, PVTEVS (Gen., xxix, 2-10). On the other faces of the capital are represented the flocks of Laban, swine, sheep, a camel, calves. The outer capital is entirely occupied with similar flocks, goats, swine, sheep and cattle.[39]

[38] Illustrated by Venturi, III, Fig. 62.
[39] Illustrated by Venturi, III, Fig. 60.

(5) The meeting of IACOB and ESAV, who are seen embracing each other (Gen., xxxiii, 4). Beyond Jacob are LIA and RACHEL and three sons of Jacob, FILII (Gen., xxxiii, 1-3), whom the sculptor has put to symbolize twelve, owing to lack of space. On the other side of Esau are his handmaidens and household, ANCILLE . FAMILIA ESAV, all moving to the left and apparently all girded together by ropes. Then the household of Jacob, FAMILIA IACOB, similarly with rope girdles, and holding whips or flails in their hands. In both households the beardless figures have longer shirts and are perhaps intended to represent women. Jacob's household is preceded by camels and sheep, TVRMA CAMELORVM; GREX. PECORVM (Gen., xxxiii, 1-16).

(6) The outer capital shows LABA[N] who comes to the tent and draws aside the curtains. Within sits RACHEL, feigning that it is with her after the custom of women. Below emerges the head of the image, I|DO|LŪ (Gen., xxxi, 33-35). Next is represented LIA sitting bolt upright, her hands crossed upon her lap. On the east face of this capital is one of the male children of Jacob, clothed in a curious woolen cloak, which the sculptor seems to have adopted to indicate the twelve sons of Israel. On the inner capital are three similar figures, doubtless other sons of Jacob, and on the west face of this capital is the figure of a woman, unnamed, who may be either Rachel or Dinah, Jacob's daughter (Gen., xxx, 21).[40]

(7) IACOB is seen wrestling with the angel, ANGS (Gen., xxxii, 24). On the other face is seen Jacob, now called by his new name, ISRAHEL (Gen., xxxii, 28), holding a staff, and accompanied by LIA and RACHEL.

(8) On the inner and outer capitals are eight more sons of Israel, which, with the four shown in No. 6, make twelve altogether. The four on the outer capital are distinguished by the inscriptions, SIMEON, IVDAS, IOSEP (this Joseph carries his coat of many colours hung from a pole across his shoulders) and RVBEN.

(9) The south-west angle capital is decorated with broad leaves, but has no figure sculptures.

(10) Four birds of no iconographic significance.

(11) Capital ornamented with interlaces and grotesque goats' heads. On the abacus is the inscription in rhyming hexameters:

MARMORIBVS — VARIIS . HEC . EST . DISTINCTA . DECENTER:
FABRICA . NEC . MINVS . EST . DISPOSITA . CONVENIENTER .

(12) On each angle is depicted the figure of a seated man with close-fitting shirt and short skirt. Two of the figures are beardless, two have beards.

[40] This capital is illustrated by Venturi, III, Fig. 58.

Each man takes hold with either hand of plants that grow from pots placed in the centre of each face.[41] This capital has no iconographic significance.

The five following capitals are all symmetrical, and have on each face a medallion with the bust of a prophet, who is haloed and holds a scroll:

(13) On the west face, ✛ ZACHARIAS, with the inscription which overruns the scroll, IRATVS . E . DNS|POPVLO SVO (Zechariah, i, 2). On the north face, Haggai, AGGEVS, with the inscription which overruns the scroll, EGO MOVEBO . CELVM (Haggai, ii, 21, 22, in Vulgate). On the east face, SOPHONIAS, with the inscription which overruns the scroll, LAVDA . FILIA SYON (Zephaniah, iii, 14). On the south face, MALACHIAS, with the inscription that overruns the scroll, MALEDICTVS . DOLOSVS (Malachi, i, 14).

(14) On the south face, ✛ YSAYAS, with the inscription EGREDIETUR (Isaiah, xi, 1). On the west face, DANIHEL, with the inscription which overruns the scroll, ASPICIEBAM . IN VISV NOCTIS . (Dan., vii, 13). On the north face, ✛ IEZECHIEL, with the inscription, PATRES . COME-DERVNT . VVAM . ACERBAM (Ezekiel, xviii, 2). On the east face, ✛ HIEREMIAS, with the inscription which overruns the scroll, HIC : EST : DEVS : NOS (Baruch, iii, 36-37).

(15) On the west face, NAVM, with the scroll, SOL . ORTVS . E . (Nahum, iii, 17). On the north face, MICHEAS, with the inscription which overruns the scroll, PERIIT . SCS . DE TERRA (Micah, vii, 2). On the east face, IONAS, with the inscription which overruns the scroll, DE . VENTRE . INFERI: (Jonah, ii, 2). On the south face, ABACVC, with the inscription that overruns the scroll, VE . QVI . POTV' . DAT AMICO . SVO (Habakkuk, ii, 15).

(16) On the south face, ✛ OSEE, with the inscription that overruns the scroll, ET . ERIT . QVASI OLYUA . GL[ORI]A . EIVS (Hosea, xiv, 6; in Vulgate xiv, 7). On the west face, ✛ ABDIAS, with the inscription that overruns the scroll, P[ER]DA . SAPIENTES . DE |EDVMEA (Obadiah, 8). On the north face (Plate 14, Fig. 1), ✛ AMMOS, with the inscription that overruns the scroll, DNS . DE SYON . RVGIET (Amos, i, 2). On the east face, Joel, ✛ IOEL, with the inscription, . PLANGE . QVASI . UIRGO (Joel, i, 8).

(17) On the west face, BALAAM, with the inscription that overruns the scroll, MORIATVR . ANIMA| MEA . MORTE . IVSTORVM (Numbers, xxiii, 10). On the north face, NATAN, with the inscription that overruns the scroll, DNS . TRANSTVLIT . |PECCATVM . TVVM . N . MORIERIS

41 Venturi, III, Fig. 57; Toesca, 117.

(II Samuel, xii, 13). On the east face Moses, MOYSES, with the inscription that overruns the scroll, CANTEMVS . DO|MINO (Exodus, xv, 1). On the south face, HELYAS, with the inscription that overruns the scroll, FACIAMVS HIC . TRIA TABERNACVLA (Matt., xvii, 4).

(18) This capital represents the life of S. Orso (Plate 14, Fig. 3). First, on the west face, is seen the saint, S[ANCTVS] VRSVS, giving alms to the poor, PAVP[ER]ES, who kneel naked before him. Above their heads hangs a great stone with a ring in it, possibly intended to signify the privations under which they suffer. The sculptor has followed a different legend of the saint from the one that has come down to us,[42] and there are several details of this capital which it is impossible to interpret. In the next scene we see the saint, S[ANCTVS] VR|SVS, who strikes with his cane a fountain, FONS, from which emerge three streams of water. Above is the church, ECCL[ESI]A, subsequently erected to commemorate the miracle. Finally, we see the saint, S[ANCTVS] VR|SVS, seated and holding a book in his right hand, his left hand raised in exhortation. He is approached by a servant of the wicked bishop, Ploceano, riding upon the horse he has stolen, ARMIGER . ERRANS| EPI . |CV . PALAFREDO. The saint receives the confession of the penitent transgressor, and, after having imposed a penance upon him, goes to the bishop to implore the latter to forgive his servant. In the following scene the wicked bishop is shown seated on his throne and holding a crosier. The saint, holding his cane, kneels before him, S[ANCTVS] VR|SVS| RO|GANS| P[RO] ARMIGERO . |EPM . PLOCEANVM. The bishop feigns to grant the saint's prayers, and the servant joyfully leaves his sanctuary, only to be taken by the underlings of the bishop and cruelly tortured. The saint, in consequence, pronounces a curse against the wicked bishop. In fulfilment of the saint's prayers, that very night the bishop, EPISCOPVS, was cruelly tormented in his bed by devils, DIABOLI. Near by are two crows, CORVI, who are present at his agony as birds of ill omen. Finally, his throat is cut by the demons, a scene with which terminate the sculptures of the capital, HIC . IUGVLATVR. On the abacus of the capital is inscribed in rhymed hexameters an invective against the wicked bishop, which is a delightful example of the forcefulness of mediæval Latin:

✝ ECCE . DI [= diem] . SCM . Q[I]A . FALLERE . N . TIMVISTI .
DEMONIIS . ES . PDA . MISER . Q[I]A SIC . MERVISTI;
PRESVLIS . EXEMPLO . SVBEANT . NIGRA . TARTARA . LVSI;
QVI . NOS . I [= item] . PVGNANT . CECA . FORMIDINE . FVSI .

(19) The raising of Lazarus.[43] Above is an inscription, much defaced,

---

[42] Quoted above, pp. 55-56.
[43] Illustrated by Toesca, 117.

which appears to be a paraphrase of John, xi, 39.[44] ' Christ between the Alpha and Omega, touches the tomb and commands Lazarus to come forth: LAZARE . VENI . FO|RAS . DE SEPVLCRO: (John, xi, 43). Lazarus is seen awakening in the tomb, behind which are Mary and Martha and three other persons (John, xi). On the south and east faces of this capital are represented two apostles, SCS SYMON and S ANDREA.

(20) Christ, IHC NAZARE|NVS, a fine figure, although unfortunately broken, occupies the most prominent position in this capital. His feet are anointed by MARIA MAGDALENA, whom MARTA tries to restrain (John, xii, 3). On the north and east faces are IACOBVS . ALFEI and BARTOLOMEVS.

(21) This is a capital representing the foundation of the chapter regular described above.[45] On the north face is shown SCS . PETRVS . AP[OSTO]L[V]S, with two keys.

(22) See Plate 14, Fig. 2. This is a capital with a conventional anthemion ornament of the Modenese type. On the abacus is the inscription recording the foundation of the chapter regular cited above.[46]

(23) The capital at the south-east angle has broad leaves of purely conventional type.

(24), (25), (26) These three capitals, with purely conventional ornament, were made when the cloister was reconstructed in the XV century, more or less in imitation of the XII century capitals. They are much larger than the others.

(27) The north-east angle capital is ornamented with grotesques.

(28) On this capital are seen the three children of Israel in the smoking, fiery furnace. The fire is being poked by an executioner, and an angel flies above. On another face is the image which Nebuchadnezzar, the king, had set up, and the king himself, with effeminate, beardless face, holding his sceptre languidly in his hands (Daniel, iii).

(29) The Annunciation. The Virgin is seated and holds a distaff in her hand. Curiously enough she is crowned. By this detail the sculptor doubtless wished to recall her royal lineage, since, on the other face, he has placed two of her ancestors. The one who plays the violin is undoubtedly David, the other, who holds in either hand a lily, is possibly Jesse.

(30) The Nativity. Mary lies in a bed like those already described. A woman holds the curtains. Joseph, seated, puts his hands to his face. The child is seen in the manger with the ox and the ass.

(31) The three Magi, all crowned and bearing vases, stand before Herod, who is also crowned and holds a sceptre.

[44] I believed that I could read the letters DIX . EI . IHC . . . . . M . ET MARTA IASSO . . . . . NARINV and above in smaller letters: DVS . . . . . V DEI SALVE but I am unable to explain them.

[45] p. 58.   [46] p. 58.

(32) Joseph, in bed, asleep, is warned by the angel to fly.[47] There follows the flight into Egypt.

(33) A capital of conventional Corinthianesque pattern.

(34) This capital, which has been strangely misunderstood, represents the stoning of Stephen. Stephen, tonsured and naked, is being stoned, and sees in his vision the glory of God represented by an angel and a ladder (Acts, vii, 55-60). Saul, tonsured and with characteristic features, is seated and holds a pile of stones in his lap. Beside him stands another person. Both Saul and his companion are casting stones at Stephen.

(35) This capital seems to represent a simple genre scene of monastic life. All the figures are tonsured and evidently represent canons of S. Orso, with the exception of one who is bearded, and hence is doubtless a lay brother. The latter draws water from a well. The two canons prepare the repast, bringing both jugs of wine and platters.

(36) This capital represents four grotesque birds, with human heads.

(37) This capital represents the fable of the crane and the fox.[48] The crane, having invited the fox to dine, provides for the repast a narrow-mouthed jar. The fox, returning the compliment, invites the crane to dine out of a shallow dish.

(38) and (39) are both conventional.

In addition to these capitals there are in the cellar of the Museo Civico di Arte Applicata ad Industria at Turin three capitals which evidently came from the cloister. The first, which bears the number 2609, is of the same type as the one with the inscription described above (22).[49] The second, without any number, is sculptured with representations of Adam and Eve and the serpent.[50] The third capital, No. 2608, appears to represent the expulsion from Paradise.[51] Adam and Eve are dressed as peasants with pointed hoods. Adam is bearded and bare-footed. He carries a cane, or, perhaps, an instrument of agriculture, in his left hand. He appears to be standing still, and to expostulate with the angel, pointing at Eve as the guilty one. The angel gestures with his left hand. Eve wears shoes and anklets. On the other faces of the capital are a goat and two sheep, representing the flocks of Adam and Eve.

From the style of the sculptures of the S. Orso cloister, it is evident that the latter are closely related to the work of the sculptor who executed the pulpit at Isola S. Giulio. This is clear from numerous analogies. In both we find the same massive, impassive faces, with the same heavy lower jaw; in both the use of the same hard marble; in both the same superlative skill

[47] Toesca, 118, illustrates this capital.
[48] Illustrated by Venturi, III, Fig. 59.
[49] Illustrated by Venturi, III, Fig. 81.
[50] Illustrated by Venturi, III, Fig. 63.
[51] Illustrated by Venturi, III, Fig. 64.

in conventional ornament; and in both the same curious draperies, which, in some cases, look as though they were made of leather. S. Giulio and S. Orso both carry the same peculiar kind of cane. The feathers of the birds are treated exactly alike. Many of the shafts at Aosta are covered with flutings in diapered patterns, precisely as at Isola. However, the work at Isola is finer, and appears to be the prototype of that at Aosta. The numerous analogies of the Aosta cloisters with the Milan-Pavia-Lodi school, and with that of Guglielmo da Modena, appear to be the result, not of direct influence, but of influence exerted through the medium of the sculptures at Isola. It is therefore entirely probable that the sculptor at Aosta, if not a pupil of the Isola sculptor, was at least strongly influenced by him.

V.   The architectural character of the crypt and of the core of the church leave no doubt that in them we have relics of the church of 923. The cloister was erected in the years immediately following 1133. The style of the campanile confirms the tradition that it was erected in 1151.

ARSAGO,[1] BATTISTERO

(Plate 15, Fig. 4, 5)

I.   The baptistery of Arsago has been published and illustrated by De Dartein,[2] and by Pareto. The recent notice by Serafino Ricci contains a list of the authors who have referred to the monument incidentally.

II.   With the exception of an inscription recording a restoration in 1874, now preserved inside the baptistery, there are no historical documents relating to the monument. When I visited Arsago in 1909, I found the interior of the baptistery completely blocked up by scaffolding, as shown in the photograph (Plate 15, Fig. 4), but the restoration was not in active progress. When I returned in July, 1913, however, work had long been finished. The campanaio told me that the restoration lasted from c. 1900 to 1911.

III.   The plan of the baptistery of Arsago is peculiar, and, I believe, without analogy in northern Italy. The edifice (Plate 15, Fig. 5) is octagonal, with walls of enormous thickness, but lightened in the ground floor by a series of niches (Plate 15, Fig. 4), all rectangular except the easternmost, which is semicircular. These niches open off the interior of the nave, but are not expressed externally, being merely constructed in the thickness of the wall. In the second story the walls are lightened by a gallery (Plate 15, Fig. 4) covered with groin vaults, and by an eastern niche, all carried in the thickness of the walls.

1 (Milano).   2 395.

The central area is surmounted by a sixteen-sided cloistered vault, which has almost the character of a dome. The octagon is worked to a sixteen-sided plan by means of arched squinches in two orders placed just above the gallery, and in the vault itself the re-entrant angles are smoothed out so that the plan becomes almost circular. There is a system in each angle (Plate 15, Fig. 4) supporting corbel-tables at the level of the gallery. Above the gallery and below the vault is a small clearstory (Plate 15, Fig. 5) of oculi and windows in the form of a Greek cross, or round-arched. Apparently no timber is used in the construction of the roof, which is formed of stones laid directly upon the extrados of the vaults (Plate 15, Fig. 5). In the middle of the central area is a depressed font with two steps. The vaults of the gallery, trapezoidal in plan, and with low transverse arches, are so highly domed that they resemble barrel, rather than groin, vaults. There are no wall ribs, but the wall arches, though depressed, rise to a much higher level than the main-arcade arches. Unfortunately these vaults were all remade in the recent restoration.

The masonry (Plate 15, Fig. 5) is quite different from that of the church and consists of large, rectangular blocks, laid, however, in courses of which the horizontality is not infrequently broken. The mortar-beds are about 15 centimetres in breadth.

IV. The capitals of the main arcade of the gallery are small uncarved blocks; those of the system and gallery responds are without abaci, and sculptured with grotesques or simple leaf patterns. The clearstory is ornamented externally with a series of semicircular blind arches of a simple character. The cornices are formed of the usual corbel-tables without pilaster strips.

V. The baptistery is nearly contemporary with the church (c. 1120), as is shown by the character of its capitals and arched corbel-tables. The masonry, however, is quite different, in that much larger blocks are employed (Plate 15, Fig. 5; Plate 16, Fig. 1). The explanation of this is undoubtedly partly to be found in the fact that the baptistery was a vaulted edifice, where greater strength was required in the walls than in the wooden-roofed basilica. Nevertheless it is reasonable to suppose that the church, the more essential edifice, was erected somewhat before the baptistery. The latter, therefore, may be assigned to c. 1130.

ARSAGO,[1] S. VITTORE

(Plate 15, Fig. 2; Plate 16, Fig. 1)

I. The first author to call the attention of archæologists to the pieve of Arsago was Giulini,[2] who printed a brief description of the church (which he

[1] (Milano).   [2] I, 358.

called S. Maria del Monticello) in connection with the historical events of the year 892. The monument was subsequently studied and illustrated by De Dartein.

II. Of the history of the church nothing is known. The earliest notice of it which I find is in a sort of tax-list of 1398, published by Magistretti. From this we learn that the church was officiated by a chapter of eight canons, and enjoyed jurisdiction over sixteen chapels.

III. The edifice consists of a nave (Plate 15, Fig. 2) of four double bays, two side aisles and three apses. The wooden porch which De Dartein mentions as preceding the façade has disappeared, doubtless in the restoration of 1892. The building is a simple basilica without vaults save for the half domes of the apses. The supports are alternately columns and square piers (Plate 15, Fig. 2), and there is no system. The side aisles are much higher than the level of the crowns of the arches of the main arcade. The triforium space becomes therefore disproportionately lofty (Plate 15, Fig. 2). The clearstory (Plate 16, Fig. 1) is formed of good-sized, round-arched windows, which, like the other windows of the church, were evidently glazed. The masonry (Plate 16, Fig. 1) consists of small, brick-shaped stones of irregular shapes and unsquared, laid in courses for the most part horizontal, an occasional large block being inserted usually to form a sort of quoin at the angles. The mortar-joints vary from 1 to 4 centimetres in thickness.

The campanile (Plate 16, Fig. 1) rises to the north of the church, and is so placed that its southern wall corresponds with the northern wall of the side aisle. It leans violently to the north in its lower stories, but returns towards the vertical in its upper part. It is illuminated by oculi, rather irregularly placed. The masonry, like that of the church with which it is contemporary, is supplied with numerous scaffolding holes. The stonework of the belfry is obviously somewhat later than that of the rest of the structure, and it is evident that the original belfry has been walled up. It is possible that there were originally two stories of bifora. The bells have recently been removed from the belfry and placed on top of the tower.

IV. The interior of the edifice (Plate 15, Fig. 2) preserves nothing of its ancient ornament except the capitals, the walls having been covered with plaster and painted with modern frescos of the most deplorable taste. The two eastern capitals have been restored. The second pair are of a curious Corinthianesque type, which recalls more strongly the capitals in the crypt of the cathedral at La Scala (Salerno) than anything I have seen in northern Italy. The northern capital of the second bay from the west is of a more usual Corinthianesque type with uncarved acanthus leaves, closely imitated from the antique. The remaining capitals are pilfered Roman. The bases are at present covered by the pavement. The archivolts are of a single order, unmoulded, and the piers are without so much as an impost moulding.

69

Externally the edifice and campanile are adorned with the usual cornices of arched corbel-tables and saw teeth (Plate 16, Fig. 1), but for the most part are severely simple. The capitals of the upper story of the campanile seem to be contemporary with those of the church, and were doubtless retained when the belfry was rebuilt.

V. The architectural forms and the plan of the church recall strongly the basilicas of Verona erected during the XII century, such as S. Giovanni in Valle, S. Pietro in Castello, etc. S. Giovanni in Valle (Plate 218, Fig. 4), which was rebuilt after the earthquake of 1117, has not only a plan which is nearly identical with that of the pieve of Arsago, but has several capitals which present the closest analogy with those of our monument. Moreover, the masonry at Arsago, while crude, is still much superior to that of S. Vincenzo at Abbazia di Sesto Calende (1102). The use of arched corbel-tables without pilaster strips except at the angles also accords well with the style of the first quarter of the XII century. We may, therefore, with considerable confidence, ascribe the pieve of Arsago to c. 1120, with the exception of the belfry, which has been remade, perhaps in the XVIII century.

ASTI,[1] S. ANASTASIO

I. In the cellar of the existing Collegio Nuovo at Asti are the remains of the convent of S. Anastasio. The church itself, a structure of the XVI century, was recently destroyed to make room for the new school buildings, but the fragments of ancient architecture extant in its crypt were scrupulously preserved. These remains, which have been carefully studied by Brayda and Bevilacqua-Lazise in a monograph on the crypts of Asti, are of considerable importance for the history of art. The handbook of Bevilacqua-Lazise in the Bonomi series contains excellent half-tones of the capitals of S. Anastasio. Several notices important for the history of the convent have been contributed by Savio.

II. The church was in existence as early as 792, since it is mentioned in a permutation of that year.[2] According to a catalogue of the bishops of Asti, written in 1605, but containing notices of much earlier date, Alderico, bishop of Asti, who founded in 1027 the monastery of S. Giusto at Susa, made a donation to the nuns of S. Anastasio.[3] According to Savio, who edited this text, the donation in question was made in 1029. The convent must,

---

[1] (Alessandria).   [2] Gabotto, *Asti*, 3.

[3] Aldericus ep. ast. Manfredi comitis Sabaudiae et Secusiae marchionis frater sub Io. XX, 1027, inter cetera pietatis officia monasterium S. Iusti Secusiae fundavit et dotavit. Monalibus S. Anastasij civitatis Astens. bona S. Cristophori etc. (Ed. Savio, *Vescovi*, 111).

therefore, have been already in existence in the second quarter of the XI century. The same catalogue further informs us that Pietro I, bishop of Asti, in 1042 made a further donation to the nuns of S. Anastasio, and reformed them according to the rule of St. Benedict.[4] The catalogue attributes further donations in this same year to Bishop Odo I,[5] but Savio omits Odo I from his list of the bishops of Asti and assigns the donation to Pietro II and the year 1043.[6] Further donations were made to the convent, one by Bishop Anselmo I in 1068, another in 1096 by Odo III.[7]

In 1070 Asti fell into the hands of the contessa Alaxia, who in 1091 burned the city to the ground.[8] It is probable that the church of S. Anastasio was destroyed by this fire and rebuilt immediately afterwards, since the style of the later portions of the edifice is that of the last years of the XI century. Other fires occurred in Asti in 1145 and 1155, but appear not to have injured our monument. In the XVII century the church of S. Anastasio was reconstructed, with reversed orientation, in the barocco style. The ancient crypt, however, remained accessible. When, about 1907, the barocco church made way for the existing school, the foundations of an earlier church of the XI century came to light, and these, together with the crypt, have, as has been said, been carefully preserved.[9] In addition to the foundations already mentioned, three capitals belonging to the Lombard edifice came to light during the destruction of the XVII century church, and are preserved in the courtyard of the neighbouring Museo Alfieri.

III. From the fragments which remain of the Romanesque church it is evident that the monument consisted of a nave of three double bays, two side aisles, of which the northern was much wider than the southern, a choir, probably separated from the side aisles by a solid wall, three apses and a crypt. The system of the church was alternate, like that of S. Savino at Piacenza (Plate 183). From the section of the piers it is clear that the nave was covered with rib vaults, since the system must have consisted of at least three shafts. The intermediate piers were quatrefoiled, and the aisle responds comprised five members.

---

[4] Petrus I ep. ast. sub eodem Benedicto [VIII], 1042, . . . partem castri Bradolensis, multaque alia Monialibus S. Anastasij contulit, easdemque ad regularem observantiam B. Benedicti redegit. Sedit menses octo. (*Catalogue of Bishops of Asti of 1605*, ed. Savio, *Vescovi*, 111).

[5] Otho I. ep. ast. sub eodem Benedicto, 1042, Monasterio S. Anastasii donationibus apud Valpianum et Montanarium ac Vafenaria a suis predecessoribus factis multas et copiosissimas adiecit. . . . Sedit annum. (*Ibid.*, 112).

[6] Savio, 137.

[7] See text cited below, p. 73. A document of 1182 relating to the church has been published by Gabotto e Gabiani, 71.

[8] . . . ab. ea tota succensa fuit. (*Chronicon Astense*, ed. Muratori, R. I. S., XI, 141).

[9] *Bolletino d'Arte*, II, 1908, 232.

LOMBARD ARCHITECTURE

The crypt, which terminated in a polygonal east end, and was divided into three aisles by two rows of seven columns, extended not only under the choir but into the first bay of the nave. It shows two distinct eras of construction. The three middle pairs of columns are Carlovingian and doubtless the remnant of an earlier church which terminated in an apse placed much to the westward of the later eastern limit of the church. In the XI century the crypt was much extended by the addition of three bays to the eastward and three to the westward. This crypt is now entirely covered by domed groin vaults with disappearing transverse arches. The Carlovingian vaults are less domed and rise to a lower level than do those of the XI century. It is evident also that the level of the pavement of the crypt in the Carlovingian epoch was lower than that of the Lombard pavement, for the bases of the Carlovingian columns are buried.

IV. The six capitals of the Carlovingian epoch in the crypt have been studied and carefully illustrated by Bevilacqua-Lazise. Two, numbered 1 and 4 in Bevilacqua-Lazise's monograph, and illustrated on page 17 of his handbook, are evidently pilfered and taken from some earlier edifice. No. 1 is a typical work of the Roman decadence, and may be assigned to the IV century. No. 4 shows Byzantine tendencies in the bulge of the bell and in the crisp, sharp form of some of the acanthus leaves, and may be assigned to the early V century. The other four were evidently worked for their present position. No. 5, illustrated on page 18 of the handbook, is very similar to a capital at S. Vincenzo in Prato at Milan (Plate 137, Fig. 3), and is characterized by volutes and a single row of Byzantinesque acanthus leaves. No. 3, also illustrated on page 18, shows strong points of contact with another capital of S. Vincenzo (Plate 137, Fig. 1). Capital No. 2, illustrated on page 19, is so similar to a capital of the crypt of S. Giovanni at Asti (Plate 16, Fig. 3) that it must be by the same hand. The capitals of the Lombard period in the crypt are strikingly similar to those of the crypt of Modena, being characterized by graceful swirls of foliage, intermingled with grotesque motives, or by volutes and uncarved acanthus leaves. Those of the upper church, now in the Museo Alfieri, are adorned with birds, grotesque animals grouped two and two by a single head which forms the volute, rinceaux and anthemia. They show very close analogy with the capitals of S. Savino at Piacenza.

V. Bevilacqua-Lazise has assigned the crypt of S. Anastasio to between 770 and 793. The style of the capitals, however, indicates a somewhat later epoch. One, as has been seen, shows strong points of contact with the capitals of the crypt of S. Vincenzo in Prato at Milan, an edifice of c. 830, and another appears to be by the same hand as the capital in the crypt of S. Giovanni at Asti, which is authentically dated 885. We may, therefore, assign this portion of the crypt to c. 860. As for the later portion of the edifice, the analogy of the capitals of the crypt with those of the crypt of the cathedral of Modena

(1099-1106) and that of the capitals of the upper church with those of
S. Savino at Piacenza, a monument consecrated in 1107, justifies the conclusion
that the edifice was rebuilt after the fire of 1091.

ASTI,[1] S. GIOVANNI

(Plate 16, Fig. 3)

I.   The interesting but fragmentary remains of the crypt of the church
of S. Giovanni, which serves at present as baptistery to the cathedral of Asti,
have been called to the attention of archæologists and admirably published by
Bevilacqua-Lazise.   The little handbook of the same author in the Bonomi
series contains half-tones of the capitals even better than those in the more
elaborate monograph.

II.   The history of the church of S. Giovanni is wrapped in considerable
obscurity.   Bevilacqua-Lazise plausibly conjectures that the Carlovingian
remains which at present exist did not originally, as to-day, form a crypt, but
were part of a basilica which was, indeed, at one time the cathedral of Asti.
Of the early history of the cathedral building of Asti little that is definite is
known, despite numerous documents which refer to the material possessions
of the episcopal see.   According to Bevilacqua-Lazise, the cathedral has been
placed in its present site since c. 800.[2]

A diploma of January 11, 885, mentions that the episcopal archives at
Asti had been destroyed by fire.[3]   This fire is mentioned also in the catalogue

---

[1] (Alessandria).

[2] Little faith is merited by the statement of the catalogue of the bishops of Asti of
1605, that in 1090 the cathedral was entitled S. Aniano: Oddo II ep. ast. sub eod.
Urbano, 1090.   Privilegia et donationes monialium S. Anastasij ast. diplomate confirmavit
in castro veteri ipsius episcopi, ubi tunc erat ecclesia cathedralis sub invocatione S.
Aniani martyr. dicata, cuius sacrae reliquiae in basilica S. Sixti hodie asservantur.
(Ed. Savio, 112).   According to Savio (143) it was Ottone III, not Odo II (1008-1098)
who made, not in 1090, but in 1096, the donation in question to S. Anastasio.

[3] Jn nomine. sancte et indiuidue trinitatis Karolus diuina fauente Clemencia
Jmperator Augustus. . . . Reuerentissimus Episcopus et Archicancellarius noster nostre
innotuit celsitudine quod peccatis exigentibus. casu inprouiso accidente thesaurum sancte
Astensis Ecclesie cui ioseph episcopus preesse dignoscitur igne crematum fuerat in quo
uaria. Jnstrumenta cartarum oblationes uidelicet et donationes imperatorum ducum
Comitum aliorumque sancte ecclesie fidelium que pro diuini cultus amore. eidem
Ecclesie contulerunt eedem igne combuste sunt Super quo idem lituardus. venerabilis
Episcopus summusque consiliarius noster sumissis petitionibus nostram exorauit magni-
tudinem quatinus pro dei amore et remedio anime nostre seu coniugis ac prolis necnon
pro debita ueneratione eiusdem Ecclesie que constructa est in honore sancte marie
semper uirginis et sancti Secundi ubi eius humatum corpus quiescit nostre Auctoritatis
munificentia omnia uariarum instrumenta cartarum eiusdem ecclesie confirmare

of the bishops, where it is stated that the bishop Lituardo reconstructed the church.[4] The text of the catalogue implies that there had been a previous fire of the cathedral of Asti and this Savio places—I know not on what authority— in 820. The text is erroneous in assigning the reconstruction of the cathedral to the bishop Lituardo who, according to Savio,[5] never existed. There can, however, be no doubt that in 884 the cathedral was destroyed by fire. Its reconstruction was doubtless terminated in 894, when the construction of the cloister was begun by Staurace (892-899). The catalogue of the bishops,[6] indeed, credits Audace with this work, but, according to Savio, the bishop Audace sat 904-926, so that there is evidently a confusion of name. In 899 the same bishop Staurace, or Stauracio, instituted a chapter of thirty canons regular,[7] supplanting the fourteen *sacerdotes qui sunt Custodes* mentioned as officiating the church in 876.[8] In 909, under Audace, the cloister was finished.[9] It is probable that the cathedral, as rebuilt c. 885, continued in use until the present imposing structure was erected in the Gothic period. The old building was then turned into a baptistery, and in the XV century was rebuilt at a higher level, some fragments of the old church being preserved in the crypt.

III. From the scant fragments that remain it is impossible to determine the plan of the ancient church. The four extant columns, placed in a sort of rectangle, may well have belonged to the arcades. The groin vaults which the columns at present support, notwithstanding their crudity, are modern, and were probably erected when the church was made over in the XV century.

IV. Of the capitals, one is of Byzantine Corinthian type and is undoubtedly taken from an earlier edifice of the VI century. The other two (Plate 16, Fig. 3) are of a formal voluted type. The volutes are stiff and angular; a single flat leaf, on which the veins are incised, is placed under each angle, and on each face is a medallion. On one of the capitals two of these medallions show, crudely sculptured, the heads of saints. (It may be con- jectured that these saints are S. Secondo and S. Maria, the patrons of the

dignaremur . . . Datum III idus ianuarij Anno incarnationis domini nostri yhesu xpisti. D.CCCLXXXIIII Jndicione tercia. Anno imperij Jmperatoris Karoli IIII. (Ed. Assandria, II, 175).

[4] Lytuardus ep. ast. sub Hadriano III ann. sal. 884 Imperatoris Caroli III archicancellarius cathedralem ecclesiam, denuo incendium passam, pro viribus instauravit, ad pietatem pluraque alia praestans. Sedit an V. (*Catalogue of Bishops of Asti of 1605*, ed. Savio, *Vescovi*, 110).

[5] 126.

[6] Audax ep. ast. sub Leone V. an. sal. 894 regularis observantiae studiosiss. claustra eccl. cathedralis extruenda curavit. . . . Sedit ann. IV. (*Ibid.*, 110).

[7] Gabotto, *Asti*, 47.

[8] *Ibid.*, 14.

[9] Stauratus ep. ast. sub Sergio III, 909, canonicorum claustris supremam addidit manum. (*Catalogue*, ed. Savio, 110).

cathedral). Since few other sculptured capitals of the Carlovingian period are extant, this capital is of great importance for the history of art.

V. As for the date of the capitals, it is not possible to doubt that they were executed in the last quarter of the IX century. It is, therefore, entirely probable that they formed part of the edifice rebuilt after the fire of c. 885. Bevilacqua-Lazise, it is true, assigns them to the VIII century, but with evident error, since they are without analogy to authentic capitals of this epoch, such as those of S. Salvatore at Brescia (Plate 35, Fig. 1, 2, 3, 4; Plate 36, Fig. 2, 5), S. Pietro in Ciel d'Oro at Pavia (Plate 177, Fig. 2), and S. Giorgio at Valpollicella (Plate 198, Fig. 4).[10] On the other hand, the S. Giovanni capitals show close relationship in design with a capital of S. Satiro of Milan (Plate 132, Fig. 5), executed c. 875, and in the technique of the veining of the leaves with two capitals of 903 in the crypt of S. Savino at Piacenza (Plate 186, Fig. 2, 3) and with a capital of the crypt of Agliate (Plate 5, Fig. 4) of c. 875. We may therefore accept with confidence the capitals of the crypt of S. Giovanni as authentically dated monuments of c. 885.

ASTI,[1] S. PIETRO

(Plate 16, Fig. 4)

I. The baptistery of S. Pietro at Asti, although illustrated by Osten,[2] has remained comparatively little known. The recent study of Cipolla[3] is singularly unsatisfactory, and quite unworthy of the great archæologist.

II. In 806 S. Pietro was already a pieve, and was donated to the episcopal church of Asti.[4] In a diploma of 886 mention is made of a certain *petrus ar[c]hipresbiter Custus et rector AeCClesie sanCtj petrj sita Cjujtate aste.*[5] Nothing further is known of the history of the edifice.

III. The baptistery lies to the south of, and adjoining, the Renaissance church of S. Pietro, and is a simple octagonal structure with a side aisle. The nave (Plate 16, Fig. 4) is surmounted by a dome in which a clearstory was originally pierced. The side aisles have groin vaults (Plate 16, Fig. 4) reinforced externally by vigorous buttresses. These groin vaults have been apparently much restored, but originally appear to have had disappearing

---

[10] Notwithstanding a certain resemblance in the tufts introduced in the middle of the leaves in both cases.

[1] (Alessandria).

[2] Plates V, VI. Osten's drawings show two grotesque reliefs which have now disappeared.

[3] *Appunti*, 54.   [4] Assandria, II, 222.   [5] Gabotto, *Asti*, 22.

transverse arches. They are distinctly trapezoidal in plan. The masonry is rather rough, and consists of bricks, of irregular lengths, laid in horizontal courses separated by thick mortar-beds.

IV. The capitals in the interior (Plate 16, Fig. 4) are all of a ponderous and heavy cubic type, roughly blocked out and obviously unfinished. The neckings were for the most part intended to have bead-mouldings, but these in many cases were never finished. The bases (Plate 16, Fig. 4) are without griffes in the columns of the arcades, but are supplied with griffes in some of the responds. Those of the main arcade have a plain Attic profile (Plate 16, Fig. 4). The plinths, originally square, have been cut down to an octagonal form in certain cases (Plate 16, Fig. 4). The archivolts of the main arcade are ornamented with a roll-moulding (Plate 16, Fig. 4), an extraordinary thing in Italy. Decorative use is made of the banding of red bricks and white stone in the supports (Plate 16, Fig. 4). The exterior is ornamented with an arched corbel-table on the cupola, but the side-aisle walls were bare. The sculptures of the Madonna (Plate 16, Fig. 4) and St. Catherine on two of the capitals of the interior are a later addition, as is also the relief of Christ surrounded by the four Evangelists and by eight saints, at present inserted in the wall.

V. From the heavy proportions of the capitals, the mouldings of the archivolts and the polychromatic masonry (Plate 16, Fig. 4), it is evident that we have here a monument of the last half of the XII century. However, the original vaults appear to have been similar to those of S. Tommaso at Almenno, and probably not much more advanced. We may therefore assign the edifice to c. 1160.

ASTI,[1] S. SECONDO

I. The church of S. Secondo has been published and illustrated by Bevilacqua-Lazise in his study of the crypts of Asti, and also by the same author in a handbook on Asti in the Bonomi series. The church itself is entirely Gothic, but the Carlovingian crypt is of some importance for the history of Romanesque art.

II. Of the early history of the building practically nothing is known. There is a tradition, apparently authentic, that the church was erected on the site where the saint suffered martyrdom, doubtless at a very early epoch. From a series of rather confusing documents it is deduced that until about the year 800, the cathedral was situated at S. Secondo.[2] In a document of 1202 there is mention of a priest and canon of S. Secondo,[3] and canons are

---

[1] (Alessandria).   [2] Bevilacqua-Lazise, 16.   [3] Gabotto e Gabiani, 164.

mentioned again in another document of 1214.[4] It is therefore certain that in the XIII century there was a chapter of canons connected with the church.

III. In the crypt are preserved four extremely interesting capitals of the VIII century. The vaults have been entirely remade, and indeed the church preserves nothing else of interest for the history of Lombard architecture.

IV, V. The capitals of the crypt are even cruder than the crudest fragments ("B") of the Chiesa d'Aurona at Milan (Plate 114, Fig. 1), which date from c. 950, the lowest point of the decadence of the X century. They are evidently very much cruder than capitals of the third quarter of the VIII century, such as those of S. Salvatore at Brescia (Plate 35, Fig. 2, 3, 4; Plate 36, Fig. 5), or of the crypt of the Rotonda in the same city (Plate 31, Fig. 1, 2, 3, 4). Bevilacqua-Lazise assigns them to the VII century. In view, however, of their relationship with the capitals of the Chiesa d'Aurona and of the total lack of Byzantine feeling which they display, I should consider it more likely that they were executed c. 950.

AVERSA,[1] CATHEDRAL

(Plate 16, Fig. 2; Plate 17, Fig. 1, 2, 3, 4)

I. The cathedral of S. Paolo at Aversa has attracted the attention of several general historians of Italian architecture, but has been given careful study only by Schultz[2] and Rivoira.[3] For historical notices the work of Parente should be consulted.

II. The cathedral was not founded earlier than the XI century; for, although the city of Atella existed on the site of the ancient Aversa from an early period, it was without great importance until given new life by the Normans. An inscription of late date formerly in the campanile and quoted by Parente,[4] states that the city was founded by the prince Rainolfo who, according to Parente,[5] ruled from 1030 to 1047. It was the third successor of Rainolfo, Riccardo I, who, according to Parente, founded the episcopal see of Aversa, in 1053. According to others, the foundation took place in 1047. The point is much controverted.[6] Riccardo I ruled from 1051 to 1078, and was succeeded by his son, Giordano I (1078-1090). A contemporary inscription still extant over the now walled-up northern portal (Plate 17, Fig. 3)

---

[4] *Ibid.*, 219.

[1] (Caserta).   [2] II, 189.   [3] 274-276.   [4] I, 253.   [5] I, 118.

[6] See Parente, I, 57. Cappelletti, XXI, 434, assigns the foundation of the new see to 1049.

proves that the actual construction of the cathedral was begun by Riccardo I, and completed by Giordano I:

.PRINCEPS IORDAN' RICHARDO PRINCIPE NATVS.
QVAE PAT INCAEPIT.PVS HAEC.IMPLENDARE CAEPIT.

Exactly what it was that the father, Riccardo, began between 1051 and 1078 and that the son, Giordano, completed between 1078 and 1090 is not stated in the inscription, but there can be little doubt that it refers to the building itself and not merely to the portal. The latter is a simple construction without great adornment, and it is inconceivable that the liberality of two princes could have been expended on merely this comparatively insignificant doorway.

The historian Summonte, whose work was published in 1601, records that he saw over the great western portal (*sù la porta maggiore*) of the cathedral of Aversa the following inscription:

Vultu iocundo Roberto dante secundo
Pulchra fit hæc extra satis intus & ampla fenestra.[7]

The inscription itself implies that it was originally placed in a window, so that it is probable that at the end of the XVI century it had already been displaced from its original position, and it doubtless disappeared entirely soon afterwards in the reconstruction of the edifice undertaken about this period. The inscription is nevertheless very important documentary evidence, for it proves that a window of the church was constructed by Roberto II, who ruled from 1127 to about 1135. This fact in turn implies that the cathedral, finished before 1090, was reconstructed in the early years of the XII century. Such a reconstruction so soon after the completion of the edifice could only have been occasioned by a disaster, and it is in fact known that in 1134 or 1135 the city of Aversa was burned.[8] The conclusion is therefore justified that the cathedral, finished before 1090, was destroyed by fire in 1134, and was subsequently restored by Roberto II. This conclusion is further confirmed by the internal evidence of the building itself, which gives clear indications of a reconstruction in the XII century. How radical was the rebuilding undertaken in 1134 is proved by the fact that the restoration was not finished until 1160, when the relics of the saints were translated back into the church.[9] In 1255 we hear of a solemn consecration of the cathedral, which implies that a new disaster and a new restoration must have overtaken the edifice in the course of 95 years.[10] In 1349 the building was much damaged by an earthquake and

---

[7] Summonte, I, 490.

[8] Rivoira, 274.

[9] Nella chiesa maggiore di Aversa vi sono infinite reliquie de' santi trasferiti l'anno 1160. (MS. del Calefati, f. 411, cit. Parente, II, 436).

[10] In nomine Domini amen. amen. Anno ab incarnatione Domini millesimo ducentesimo quinquagesimo quinto die Jovis tertio mensis Junij quintae decimae

was subsequently restored.[11]   That the damage was serious is proved by the
fact that Innocent VI, in 1352, granted an indulgence to all those who should
aid in the reparation of the edifice.[12]   The condition of the building as it was
in 1468 is shown by a painting of that date in the church of S. Sebastiano al
Duomo.   Parente,[13] who has studied this fresco, states that the cupola and
campanile of the Duomo are clearly shown as they were before being transformed.   In 1592 the altar of the church was remade.[14]   The edifice suffered
severely in the numerous earthquakes with which this unhappy region has
always been afflicted.[15]   In 1694 the cupola was ruined by one of these shocks.[16]
The worst blow to the church, however, was the baroccoization begun 1703-
1715[17] and completed in 1857.[18]

III.   The cathedral of Aversa at first gives the impression of being an
entirely barocco edifice, but on close examination it becomes evident that the
northern portal (Plate 17, Fig. 3), the ambulatory (Plate 17, Fig. 1, 2) and
some portions of the central tower are mediæval, although the whole is so
covered with intonaco that it is exceedingly difficult to study the original
forms.   The ambulatory (Plate 17, Fig. 1, 2), which is of very large size,
being about twenty feet wide, includes two rectangular and five trapezoidal
bays as well as three eastern absidioles.   It is entirely vaulted, the semicircular
absidioles with half domes, the ambulatory itself with rib vaults which are
among the most extraordinary extant in Italy (Plate 17, Fig. 1, 2).   The profile
of the ribs of these vaults is rectangular, and the construction is extremely
massive and ponderous.   The diagonal ribs spring from capitals placed at a

Indictionis, Pontificatus SSmi. in Xpo. Patris Domini Alexandri Papae quarti, anno
primo, dictus Dominus Alexander Papa veniens Aversam, assistentibus sibi undecim
cardinalibus, Domino Joanne Caietano Cardinali, Matheo Archiepiscopo in Tronti,
Episcopo Placentano [*sic*], Episcopo Morbonensis [*sic*], Episcopo beatae memoriae [*sic*],
ad reverentiam Dei et beatissimae semper Virginis et Beatorum Apostolorum Petri et
Pauli, consegravit altare, quod est in pede crucis, et concessit talem indulgentiam, ut
omni anno in die consegrationis et omnibus advenientibus inibi de aliquibus bonis
offerentibus, unum annum 50 dies de iniuncta salutari poenitentia relaxavit; . . . item
ex speciali gratia concessit et statuit, ut circa ipsam ecclesiam S. Pauli omni anno fiat
mercatum de festo Apostolorum Petri et Pauli usque ad octavas eorumdem. . . . item
omnibus qui benefecerint opibus Ecclesiae S. Pauli qualibet die, hinc ad V. annos
centum de iniuncta sibi poenitentia relaxavit; item in die consegrationis predictae
omnibus euntibus ibi vere poenitentibus et confessis et benefacientibus ab ipso die usque
ad octavas Apostolorum Petri et Pauli praedictorum, illam dedit indulgentiam, quae
datur euntibus ultra mare. Deo gratias. (Parente, I, 375-376, publishes from a late
and obviously incorrect copy).

11 Parente, II, 425.

12 (indulgentias trium annorum cuicumque ex universitate civitatis Aversae, qui
eleemosinam erogaverit ad reparationem ecclesiae civitatis ejusdem a terremotus
concussione pro majori parte subversa funditus, et diruta).

13 II, 80.   14 Parente, II, 438.   15 *Ibid.*, II, 425.   16 *Ibid.*, II, 428.

17 *Ibid.*, II, 429.   18 *Ibid.*, II, 439.

lower level than those of the wall arches at their outer perimeter, and the transverse arches from capitals at a level higher than that of the capitals of the outer wall arches, while the arcade arches spring from the highest level of all. The vaults are not excessively domed, but the diagonals intersect far from the centre of the compartment, since they are straight in plan. They are somewhat distorted in elevation but not sufficiently so to bring the crowns to coincide with the point of intersection. Of the actual construction of the vault surface itself, the thick coating of intonaco makes it impossible to speak. A curious expedient is a wedge-shaped form given the transverse arches (Plate 17, Fig. 1), which are made much wider at the outside than at the inside edge. The excessively trapezoidal shape of the ambulatory compartment is thus somewhat reduced. The piers, of enormous solidity, are supplied with separate members for each of the ribs and the two orders of the arcade arches.

The central cupola appears to be a Gothic structure of 1349, since it is adorned with an appliqué decoration of trilobed and pointed arches. Commendatore Rivoira states that it bears the traces of the fire of 1134, but if he saw such traces they have since disappeared.

IV. The decoration of the church, like the structure, is sadly mutilated. Enough remains, however, to leave no doubt that in the cathedral of Aversa we have two distinct eras of construction.[19] To the earlier belongs the northern portal (Plate 17, Fig. 3), the windows of the absidioles, a doorway in the south ambulatory (Plate 17, Fig. 2) and four windows of the central tower. All these fragments are marked by common characteristics,—hood-mouldings of very classic character usually adorned with egg-and-dart, bead or rope motives, the frequent use of consoles and brackets, spiral-fluted columns, capitals of distinctly Corinthianesque form, though executed with a certain stiffness and dryness that savours almost of the X century (Plate 17, Fig. 4), flat mouldings, and the use of marble. In this earlier edifice were also employed pilfered Roman capitals, one of which is now imbedded in the exterior of the north absidiole.

This decoration, thoroughly Neapolitan in its character, is in such strong contrast to the style of the capitals used in the ambulatory, that it evidently must be pilfered material used second-hand in the new edifice. Thus the old portal was used to form a new northern entrance; old windows were utilized in the absidioles and central tower; an old doorway was placed in the southern ambulatory, and even certain old capitals were used in the ambulatory. This old material, however, was pieced out with new material which shows an entirely different style of decoration. The new capitals of the ambulatory are Norman in character, though somewhat influenced, it is true, by Lombard and

[19] According to Parente (II, 439), fragments belonging to the cathedral of Aversa are now preserved at Naples in the Biblioteca Borbonica, the Chiesa dell'Immacolata, etc.

southern Italian models. They are executed in stone, not marble. Some are very spare in their ornament, a characteristic which recalls the Norman style. Others have monsters coupled together with a single head which forms a volute, and below one or more rows of very stiff acanthus leaves (Plate 16, Fig. 2).[20] Others are covered with scales.

The arches opening into the absidioles are in two orders, and in two orders apparently were the arches of the choir arcade. The apses externally are adorned with arched corbel-tables. The bases are now for the most part hidden, but enough remains visible to make it clear that they were so deeply undercut as to have an almost Gothic character. Probably they were also supplied with griffes.

V. The date of the earlier part of the church is determined approximately by the inscription on the portal. It was begun by Riccardo after he founded the episcopal see in 1053 and before he died in 1078. It was completed by his son, Giordano, before 1090. We therefore know that it was begun after 1053, that it was in construction in 1078 and was presumably finished before 1090. Indeed, the style is precisely such as we might expect to find in Campania at this epoch. This early church, like others of the same time and in the same region, was doubtless a wooden-roofed basilica.

When, however, this edifice was burned in 1134, it was rebuilt, 1134-1160, in an entirely new style, not improbably by Apulian workmen. A rib-vaulted ambulatory was introduced, an extraordinary feature in Italy. The structure of the vaults themselves is nevertheless Italian rather than French, for precisely similar vaults are found in the slightly earlier church of S. Flaviano at Montefiascone (Plate 151, Fig. 5). The capitals recall, for the most part, Norman models, although one of them is almost precisely similar to a capital

[20] Rivoira has pointed out the strong technical resemblance of this capital of the ambulatory with one of the Badia of Venosa, in the province of Potenza. In view of the fact that Venosa, Acerenza and Aversa are almost unique among Italian churches in being supplied with an ambulatory and radiating chapels, there can be no doubt of the very close relationship of the three buildings. This relationship has been used by Rivoira as an argument for assigning Aversa to 1080, but his argument remains without force until the date of the abbey of Venosa is demonstrated. True it is that Venosa was founded by Robert Guiscard, who was there buried in 1085: [Robertus Wiscardi] sepultus est apud Venusiam in Coenobio Monachorum, quod ibidem ipse adhuc vivens construxerat. (Richardi Cluniacensis *Chronicon*, ed. Muratori, A. I. M. E., ed. A., XII, 109). But what proves that the existing church of La Trinità is the edifice erected by Robert and not a reconstruction of the XII century? Venturi (III, 504) inclines to the belief that such was the case. Schultz (I, 321-322) cites verbatim, and Lenormant (34) and Enlart refer to an extant inscription recording a consecration by the pope Nicolas II in 1159. The point can not be decided until an exhaustive study has been made, not only of the abbey of Venosa, but of the Romanesque architecture of the Basilicata, and as yet neither the one nor the other has been given serious attention. Notwithstanding the studies of Schultz (I, 317) and Lenormant (51 f.), the chronology of the cathedral of Acerenza remains likewise entirely uncertain.

of the XII century in the Palazzo Arcivescovile of Verona. There is, therefore, good reason to believe that in the cathedral of Aversa we have a monument
of 1134-1160, in which are used many fragments of an older building of the
second half of the XI century.

BADIA DI VERTEMATE,[1] S. GIOVANNI

(Plate 18, Fig. 1)

I.   The desecrated priory of S. Giovanni is situated about a kilometre
from the commune of Vertemate, in the frazione known as Badia or Abbadia.
The monument was known to Barelli,[2] who published a plan, and to De
Dartein, who studied and sumptuously illustrated it.[3]   Sant'Ambrogio has
contributed observations on the history of the edifice,[4] and historical notices
of value may be found in the works of Giovio, Tatti and Giulini.

II.   The XVI century historian of Como, Giovio, has left us a long and
detailed account of the foundation of the monastery, which he says was of
the Cluniac order and had already been given in commendam long before his
time.   "It was founded by a certain Milanese, Gerardo, a noble, who, together
with his friends Lanfranco and Amizone, had been received as a monk in the
abbey of Cluny in France, by the abbot Hugo.   In the course of time a certain
prior of that order, whose name was David, head of the oratory of S. Paolo in
Lombardy by permission of the abbot, Hugo, brought Gerardo back with him
from France to Italy.   Now it so happened that Gerardo, on his way to
Milan, turned aside to Vertemate, where at that time lived certain noble
knights by whom he was hospitably received as a guest.   Gerardo noticed that
to the east of Vertemarte there was a great solitary plain, and conceived the
idea of founding there a monastery.   Therefore he laid bare his project to
his friends, and obtained from them a place to found the monastery, and
immediately built amongst the brambles a little edifice supported on poles
and covered with straw.   Not long afterwards when he chanced to be wandering about that solitude he found at the corner of a certain hill the ruins of
an old castle and fortification.   This place also was given to him by the same
knights in the year of our Lord 1084, in the month of April, in order that a
monastery of the Cluniac order and a basilica of S. Giovanni Battista might
there be founded.   To this Rainaldo, at that time bishop of Como, gave his
formal consent, for that place was in his diocese.   Soon afterwards Anselmo
and Pietro, a subdeacon of the church of Como, joined Gerardo and aided in
no mean fashion in the construction of the monastery.   At the same time

[1] (Como).   [2] *Not. Arch.,* 22.   [3] 337.
[4] *Archivio Storico Lombardo,* 1905, 217.

BADIA DI VERTEMATE, S. GIOVANNI

Gerardo founded a convent for nuns at Cantù, in honour of S. Maria, and he summoned afterwards from Cluny his companion Amizone. Soon afterwards he died having chosen Pietro as his successor, a choice which was approved by the abbot of Cluny. The new church had not yet been dedicated because Pietro preferred to wait, inasmuch as many bishops were at that time infected with the taint of simony which was rife under the emperor Henry IV. At length the pope Urban II in the year of our Lord 1095 set out for France and held a council at Piacenza, in which there was much deliberation concerning those who had bought ecclesiastical dignities, and those who had been ordained in the Gibertine schism. For Giberto, archbishop of Ravenna, was antipope under the name of Clement, having been created head of the schism against Gregory VII by the emperor Henry. When he left Piacenza, Urban came to Milan, and there Pietro, prior of Vertemate, obtained from the pope permission that Odone, bishop of Imola, might consecrate the church; and Odone dedicated with due rites the new basilica of S. Giovanni Battista at Vertemate, on the thirtieth day of December of the same year. There were present at the dedication a great number of clergy and laity of the city and diocese of Como. Landolfo of Carcano, who had recently usurped the episcopal throne of Como by a decree of the emperor Henry, was not present, however, since he had been anathematized by Pope Urban, after due trial. Beside this the pope granted privileges to the monastery of Vertemate in which the enemies of that institution are anathematized and indulgences granted to those who should aid and reverence the priory. When this monastery was later destroyed by the Comaschi, the prior Giorgio da Alzati commenced to restore it before the year 1480, but he died before he was able to finish the work; for that good man had planned to restore the abbey (which was almost deserted) to prosperity and to reform the discipline. Immediately after his death, however, it was given in commendam to a secular clerk who took no pains to finish that which had been begun."[5]

[5] Monasterium S. Ioannis Baptistæ apud Vertemate Ordinis Cluniacensis, iam diu commendatum, a quodam Gerardo mediolanensi, nobili equitum genere nato, fundatum fuit, qui cum sociis Lafrancho et Amizone in gallico cluniacensi cœnobio ab Ugone abbate in monachum receptus est. Procedente vero tempore, quidem eius Ordinis prior, cellæ D. Pauli in Lombardia præfectus, cui nomen erat David, Gerardum e Gallia in Italiam reduxit, Ugone ipso abbate permittente. Forte vero Gerardus, cum mediolanensem regionem peteret, Vertemate divertit, ubi tum nobilissimi quidam equites habitabant, a quibus hospitio benigne susceptus est. Porro Gerardus, animadvertens vertematense territorium ad orientem plagam vasta solitudine protendi, de condendo ibi monasterio cogitavit. Quare, consilio suo equitibus suis exposito, fundandi cœnobii locum impetravit, ac statim inter vepres tuguriolum perticis suffultum et paleis opertum extruxit. Haud ita multo post, solitudinis illius cuncta perlustrans, in collis cuiusdam angulo veteris arcis, munitionisque vestigium reperit. Hunc itaque locum ab equitibus ipsis pariter accepit, anno Domini octogesimo quarto supra millesimum, mense aprili, ut ibidem Cluniacensis Ordinis monasterium cum basilica D. Ioannis Baptistæ fundaretur,

Hitherto nothing further has been known of the foundation of the priory of Vertemate beyond what is contained in this passage of Giovio. Tatti[6] conjectured rightly that the historian wrote having under his eye authentic documents, but notes that the date for the foundation of the priory, April, 1084, is erroneous, since the bishop Rainaldo died in the preceding January. I am glad to be the first to point out that in the collection of the documents of Cluny published by Bernard is contained an incorrect copy of the deed of foundation which proves that Tatti's conjecture is correct, and that the foundation really took place in 1083. This document bears the date of the year of the Incarnation 1084, which corresponds to 1083. The seventh indiction, however, is erroneously given for the sixth.[7]

cui rei Rainaldus tunc comensis episcopus, quod hic locus in eius erat diocesi, assensum præstitit. Deinde Gerardo additus est Anselmus et Petrus comensis ecclesiæ subdiaconus, qui novi monasterii fabricam haud medriociter adiuverunt. Per idem tempus Gerardus ipse muliebre cœnobium apud Canturium honori D. Mariæ condidit, evocavitque post-modum e gallico cluniacensi monasterio contubernalem suum Amizonem, ac paulo post moriens prædictum Petrum successorem elegit, quod et cluniacensis abbas approbavit. Nondum autem nova dedicata erat ecclesia, quod, ut canonice fieret, idem Petrus solerter intendebat, quando simoniaca labe non pauci episcopi eo tempore infecti erant, Henrico IV imperatore sacerdotia venundante. Tunc Urbanus II pontifex maximus, vergente anno Domini nonagesimo quinto supra millesimum, in Galliam proficiscens, concilium apud Placentiam habuit, in quo magna consultatio facta est de his, qui sacerdotia emerant, quique in schismate Gibertino ordinati fuerant. Fuit autem Gibertus Ravennas archiepiscopus antipapa, nomine Clemens, quem prædictus Henricus contra Gregorium VII creaverat huius schismatis caput. Placentia discedens Urbanus Medio-lanum devenit, ubi Petrus ipse vertematensis prior a pontifice quendam Oddonem imolensem antistitem suscepit, qui Vertemate profectus novam basilicam D. Ioanni Baptistæ de more dedicavit, tertio calendas ianuarias eiusdem anni. Interfuere dedica-tioni innumeri civitatis et diœcesis comensis clerici ac laici. Abfuit unus Landulfus de Carchano, qui nuper comensem episcopatum sibi ab Henrico imperatore decretum invaserat, quem ideo pontifex Urbanus, audita causa, damnavit. Cæterum vertematense monasterium privilegiis munivit et ornavit, quibus in primis eius adversariis execrationem interminatus est; eidem vero obsequium præstantibus delictorum veniam dedit. Hoc cœnobium, a Comensibus olim dirutum, novissimus prior Georgius de Alzate restituere inceperat, ante annum Domini millesimum quadragentesimum octuagesimum [MS. V. MCCCCXXX]; sed, cum morte præventus fuisset, tantum opus imperfectum mansit. Nam cœnobium ipsum, monachis rarum, frequentem reddere et ad regularem observan-tiam reducere vir bonus cogitaverat, quod statim post eius obitum seculari clerico commendatum fuit, qui nihil minus quam inchoatum opus perficere curavit. (Giovio, 223-225).

[6] II, 258.

[7] Anno ab incarnatione Domini nostri Jesu Christi millesimo octogesimo quarto, mense aprili, inditione septima. Ecclesie et monasterio quod est constructum in honore beatissimorum Petri et Pauli, in loco qui dicitur Cluniacus, nos in Dei nomine Otto et Vuazo . . . offerimus predicte ecclesie Sancti Petri Cluniacensis, id est castrum unum juris nostri, quod est in predicto loco et fundo Vertemate, ad locum qui dicitur Castrum Vetus, cum propinquiore fossato usque in medium fundum ubi monasterium est constructum in honore Sancte Crucis [sic]. . . . (Bernard, IV, 765).

BADIA DI VERTEMATE, S. GIOVANNI

The high reputation enjoyed by the new priory is witnessed by an undated letter assigned by Bernard[8] to c. 1070, but which must, in reality, be later than 1083, in which Oberto, count of the Canevese, and Ardicio, baron of Castelletto, complain of the disorders occasioned by the base character of the prior of Castelletto, and request his removal and the substitution of Garnerio, prior of Vertemate. The abbey of Vertemate is included among the possessions confirmed to the abbey of Cluny by Urban II, in 1095,[9] but, oddly enough, is not mentioned in a bull of the same pope of 1088.[10] A prior of Vertemate appears in a Cluniac document of c. 1150, published by Bernard,[11] and the priory is mentioned in an unpublished document of 1136.[12]

In the year 1125 the town of Vertemate was destroyed by the Comaschi. "While the Comaschi were returning to their city by the public highway the Vertematensi came upon them hurling javelins and insulting them with opprobrious epithets, and strove with all their might to prevent the Comaschi from passing through their territory. The entire army of the Comaschi noted all this in secret, but they said little, and bode their time to take vengeance with deeds not words, and resolved that the Vertematensi should pay the penalty and rue their act within a month. The latter kept on insulting and the former continued to mutter between their teeth. After a few days the Comaschi returned over the same road and came to the same spot. There the Vertematense infantry was standing on the road, and hurled spears and javelins and shot arrows. Thus they prevented the Comaschi from passing. The Vertematense troops, armed in proof, prepare to fight hand to hand, sword against hard iron. The foot-soldiers on both sides began the fray. The Comaschi cavalry saw this, unfurled their banner, shouted, and rushed to the battle. They compelled their adversaries to give ground, and hurled many back on their fortifications. The Vertematensi then fled in fear and took refuge in the town near the castle. They fought from the town and sought to defend it. Then the Comaschi foot-soldiers overthrew the defenders of the gate. Then they sought fire and tried to burn the town, and they succeeded in kindling a conflagration. The entire castle and town were burned and many cattle perished. The Comaschi killed with the sword the foot-soldiers, the cavalry, the women, the strong, the weak, the young and the old together. But even more perished in the fire. Then the Comaschi cavalry were touched with pity at the death of so many, and kept circling about the walls of the castle, and drew out their enemies from the flames, and saved as well as they were able the Vertematensi themselves and their household possessions. One

8 IV, 540.
9 Tomassetti, II, 158.
10 *Ibid.*, 121.
11 V, 505.
12 Bonomi, *Dip. Sti. Ben.*, Brera MS. AE, XV, 33, f. 34.

hundred and twenty in all were killed by the sword but many more perished in the fire."[13]

It has been supposed by certain writers that the basilica of S. Giovanni was destroyed in this sack of Vertemate by the Comaschi. It is certain, however, that such could not have been the case. Not only is the architectural style of the church of the XI and not of the XII century, but the anonymous poet in his detailed description of the destruction of the town would not have failed to record any damage to the priory of S. Giovanni, had such been done. Moreover, it is expressly stated by Giovio that the abbey had been built on the site of a ruined castle some distance from the town of Vertemate, and to this day S. Giovanni lies a good kilometre from that commune, which there is no reason to suppose has ever changed location. In the deed of foundation

[13]   Dumque iter ad Cumas illis via publica donat,
Inque revertentes simul adsunt Vertematenses,
Jactantes jaculos, & turpia verba ferentes,
Transitus hinc illis ne sit, pro posse laborant.
Denotat hic illos clam tunc exercitus omnes,
Pauca tamen dicunt, ad jurgia verba rimittunt:
Pœnam solvetis sed in isto mense gemetis.
Tunc insultabant, illi post terga fremebant.
Postque dies paucos semitam redeunt per eandem,
Ad loca quæ dudum fuerant disposita tendunt,
Inque via pedites tunc stabant Vertematenses,
Et jaciunt hastas, jaculos, funduntque sagittas:
Sic iter impediunt, nequeunt transire volentes.
Vertematensis miles protectus in armis,
Cominus ense parat duro contendere ferro.
Committunt bellum pedites communiter omnes:
Hæc equites cernunt, continuò signa resolvunt,
Voces emittunt, sic ad certamina tendunt,
Obstantes pellunt, vallo pluresque revolvunt.
Dant trepidi tergum, stant in villa prope castrum,
De villa certant, illam defendere temptant.
Tunc validi pedites sternunt in limine stantes,
Inde petunt ignem, certant succendere villam,
Acceduntque rogum; comburitur igne peremptum
Castrum cum villa, nec non animalia multa.
Et pedites, equitesque simul, pariter mulieres,
Fortes, infirmi, juvenes simul, & seniores,
Ferro mactantur, sed plures igne cremantur.
Tunc equites flentes tantorum morte dolentes,
Continuò circùm discurrunt undique castrum,
Ardentes retrahunt, illos & ab igne tuentur,
Illis & vitam conservant, & suppellectilem.
Centum viginti (sunt plures igne cremati)
Sunt interfecti, sed sunt magìs igne cremati.

(*Mediolanensium in Comenses Bellum,* ed. Muratori, R. I. S., V, 439).

the monastery is said to be not in the castle of Vertemate but in the old castle— *Castrum Vetus.* The abbey would therefore have been well out of harm's way when the town was burned. Even churches situated within the walls of cities were customarily spared in times of pillage, and in this case the quarrel of the Comaschi was with the Vertematensi and not with the monks.

The same considerations give reason to believe that the monastery escaped also when the town of Vertemate was destroyed by Barbarossa in 1162,[14] and by the Comaschi a second time, c. 1260.[15] About 1287 it is true the abbey was destroyed, but it is explicitly stated by Giovio that the church itself escaped destruction. "At that time . . . the Comaschi completely destroyed the famous monastery of S. Giovanni Battista near Vertemate, except the basilica."[16]

About 1404 the town of Vertemate was again burned,[17] but the monastery was not injured. In 1480, as has been seen, the abbey was given in commendam.

The description of the church in the 'Acts' of the visits of the bishop Ninguarda is as follows: "On Monday, the thirteenth of July, the most reverend bishop of Como, pursuing his general visitation, came in person to the church of S. Giovanni Battista, called a priory, near the town of Vertemate. This church is preceded by an atrium which is almost entirely ruined, and, though ancient, the structure retains a certain air of elegance. Within there are three aisles, that is a nave and two side aisles, all in good condition. The side aisles have sixteen canopies with altars beneath them."[18]

In the Cluniac catalogue of Marrier, published in 1614, we read: "The priory of S. Giovanni of Vertemate is united with the priory of Cernobbio. According to the definition of 1367, there ought to be here a prior and six monks and alms are given to all those who ask them."[19]

---

[14] Galvanei Flammae, *Manipulus Florum,* CLXXXVII, ed. Muratori, R. I. S., XI, 641.

[15] Giovio, 48-49.

[16] Per ea tempora Lutherio Ruscha comensis populi et Bonacursio e Vicedominis a Monticulo Communis prætoribus, Comenses insigne D. Ioannis Baptistæ cœnobium apud Vertemate, Ordinis cluniacensis, salva basilica, funditus everterunt, quod eius loci monachi in eorum perniciem cum hostibus, superiore vigente bello, conspirassent. (Giovio, 55).

[17] Giovio, 80.

[18] Die Lunæ 13 mens. Iulij R.mus DD. Episcopus Comensis Visitationem generalem prossequendo, accessit personaliter ad Ecclesiam S.cti Io: Baptistæ prope pagum Vertemati, prioratum nuncupatam. Quæ habet atrium ante pene dirutum et redolet antiquitate elegantis structuræ; intus habet tres naves, mediam et duas laterales omnes convenientes, in quibus lateralibus sunt sexdecim fornices cum infradicendis altaribus. (Ninguarda, ed. Monti, II, 18).

[19] Prioratus S. Ioannis de Vercemate, qui est vnitus Prioratui de Cernobio, vbi debent esse iuxta diffinitionem anni 1367. cum Priore sex Monachi, & fit eleemosyna omnibus petentibus. (Marrier, 1746).

In 1621 the Cluniac monks were supplanted by *Frati Minimi* of the order of S. Francesco da Paola. The last of the commendatary abbots died in 1788, and soon after the monastery passed into secular hands. It is at present used as a barn.

III.   The church consisted originally of a nave four bays long (Plate 18, Fig. 1), non-projecting transepts, a choir of a single bay flanked by side aisles, and three apses, of which the central one was preceded by a barrel-vaulted compartment; but the southern side aisle of the choir and its absidiole have been destroyed, and the transepts have been walled off from the nave. The nave is at present covered with groin vaults supported on a clumsy alternate system (Plate 18, Fig. 1), but both vaults and system are modern, and the nave was without doubt originally roofed in timber. The cloistered vault that covers the crossing is also modern and supplants the original Lombard cupola. The slightly domed groin vaults of the side aisles are original, however, and are supplied with loaded transverse arches but have no wall ribs. Original, too, are the barrel vaults of the transepts, and of the choir.

The piers of the crossing are cruciform in section, but those of the nave were originally all cylindrical (Plate 18, Fig. 1). The side-aisle responds are rectangular in section and comprise one or three members. The north wall is reinforced externally by vigorous buttresses.

The masonry consists of stone ashlar, on the whole fairly well laid, although the stones vary extremely in size and the courses are frequently broken. The church has unfortunately been covered internally and externally with intonaco, which makes it extremely difficult to study the structure of the walls.

IV.   The basilica is characterized by the restraint, one might almost say the absence, of decoration. The piers of the nave are crowned by cubic capitals of fully developed type. The aisle responds and the imposts of the choir and transepts (Plate 18, Fig. 1) are crowned by simple impost mouldings. Most of the bases are at present not visible, but I believe that they were all of a similar character and consisted of a simple bulging torus surmounted by a fillet. The unmoulded archivolts are in a single order.

The exterior, though much modernized, retains in the façade traces of its ancient cornice of arched corbel-tables. In the central apse the arched corbel-tables are well preserved and are supported on shafts.

The edifice contains notable frescos of different ages.

V.   The priory of Vertemate is an authentically dated monument of 1083-1095.

BARDOLINO,[1] S. SEVERO

(Plate 19, Fig. 4)

I.   The church of S. Severo at Bardolino has been mentioned by Melani,[2] and has been studied by Cipolla.   Crosatti has made a careful search for documents relating to the history of the edifice.

II.   Since S. Severo is mentioned in a diploma of Berengario of 893,[3] Crosatti is doubtless correct in assuming that our monument was the early parish church of Bardolino.   Cipolla tried to interpret a monogram on one of the columns as signifying: O[BIIT] M[ENSE] AVGO? . . . . . MCIX, but I confess that to me this reading seems very imaginative and the meaning of the monogram in question quite enigmatical.[4]   The church is mentioned for the second time in a document of 1186.[5]

In 1349[6] and in 1398[7] bequests were made to the *laborerio* for the construction of the church.   In 1415 and 1416 other legacies were left for the reparation of the church.   It is strange, however, that the existing edifice shows no signs of alterations executed at this time.   I therefore suspect that the contemplated reconstruction of S. Severo was never executed and that a new church (S. Nicolò) was erected instead.   Confirmation is lent to this hypothesis by the fact that as early as 1447 the new church of S. Nicolò had supplanted S. Severo as the parish church of Bardolino.[8]   In 1530 S. Severo was abandoned, but was subsequently reopened for worship.[9]   In 1574 the edifice menaced ruin.[10]   About this time the church became the chapel of the cemetery.   In 1750 the old apse was replaced by a new choir.[11]   In the XIX century the church was quite abandoned again, and was used as a powder-magazine by the Austrians.   In 1869 it was in a ruinous condition, and in 1872 the campanile was mutilated.[12]   To-day the edifice serves as a concert hall for the band locally known as the Società Filarmonica of Bardolino.

III.   The edifice consists of a nave (Plate 19, Fig. 4) five bays long, two side aisles, a modern choir and a modern campanile.   Test excavations have, however, revealed the fact that there was anciently a crypt.   The building is at present entirely roofed in timber (Plate 19, Fig. 4), but it is probable that the side aisles were originally vaulted.   The southern side-aisle wall has been entirely reconstructed in modern times, but the north side-aisle wall, which is original, is divided into bays by colonnettes engaged on

---

1 (Verona).   2 215.   3 Crosatti, 130.   4 Crosatti, 130-131.   5 *Ibid.*, 131.
6 . . . relinquo laborerio ecclesie sancti severij de bardolino decem soldos . . . (*Ibid.*, 132).
7 . . . pro fabricatione ecclesie s. seuerij de bardol.   (*Ibid.*, 132).
8 Crosatti, 134.   9 *Ibid.*, 134, 135.   10 *Ibid.*, 137.   11 *Ibid.*, 139.
12 *Ibid.*, 141-142.

pilaster strips. The colonnettes end in inconsequential capitals which support nothing, but the pilaster strips are continued along the wall surface as blind arches. These arches, executed in plaster, are evidently a modern makeshift to disguise the amortizements of the vault. The supports of the nave are cylindrical piers (Plate 19, Fig. 4), the bases of which are now buried. The ancient windows were very small, widely splayed and intended to serve without glass. The existing windows are of the Renaissance, but one or two of the ancient ones are still extant in the north wall, although walled up.

The masonry consists of unhewn stones of rectangular form, laid in courses approximately horizontal, and separated by thick mortar-beds. The masonry of the piers, on the other hand, is formed of roughly hewn stones separated at intervals by bands of brick. This masonry is thus crudely polychromatic. The piers have a very decided entasis, or rather, inward slope.

IV. The capitals of the responds of the north side aisle are of a high cubic variety, with chamfered edges. The capitals of the main piers (Plate 19, Fig. 4) are also cubic, but the proportions are low. The angular cushion does not recede, that is, the piers have the same diameter as their load, and the office of the capital is merely to form a transition from the cylindrical support to the rectangular archivolt. On the abaci of these capitals are carved, or rather crudely scratched, rosettes, clover leaves, interlaces, zigzags, a head, a monogram, and similar motives. All these ornaments and the capitals themselves recall Stradella (Plate 210). The archivolts are in a single unmoulded order (Plate 19, Fig. 4). The exterior is decorated with arched corbel-tables resting on pilaster strips only at the angles. The expanse of the wall is unbroken even by buttresses.

V. The capitals of the main arcade recall those of Stradella, which date from c. 1035. Those of the north side-aisle responds, however, are of a somewhat more advanced character. Also the character of the masonry and of the arched corbel-tables indicates that the edifice was constructed in the second, rather than in the first, half of the XI century. We may, therefore, assign it to c. 1050.

BARDOLINO,[1] S. ZENO

(Plate 19, Fig. 1, 3)

I. Crosatti has made a conscientious study of the local archives for documents referring to this church, which has also been described by Cipolla.

II. According to Biancolini,[2] the church of S. Zeno at Bardolino was given to the abbey of S. Zeno of Verona by Pepin by a diploma of 807. The

[1] (Verona).   [2] I, 44.

diploma itself is lost, and we have knowledge of it only from Biancolini's reference. That the notice is authentic, however, is confirmed by the fact that Bardolino is confirmed to S. Zeno in a diploma of 847[3] and in others of 1014,[4] 1027, 1163 and 1186.[5] In many other documents as well our church appears as a dependency of the Veronese monastery.

In 1529 the church of S. Zeno at Bardolino was abandoned and in a ruinous condition.[6] In 1541 it was desecrated. In 1697 it was reopened for worship, and a radical restoration undertaken.[7] At the time of the Revolution the edifice was again desecrated, but was restored and consecrated anew in 1863.[8]

III. The edifice consists of a single-aisled nave with projecting transepts and a square apse. Over the crossing rises a lantern covered with an undomed groin vault. The rest of the edifice is spanned by barrel vaults. The walls are covered internally and externally with plaster and intonaco, so it is impossible to see the masonry except in a few scattered spots. To judge from these the church is built of rubble of many different qualities, and it is probable that the walls and vaults also have been many times made over and repaired in the various restorations to which the church has been subjected. It appears, however, that the original Carlovingian dispositions are still, in the main, preserved.

IV. The nave walls are decorated internally with two blind arches on either side, supported on two free-standing columns and corbels in the west wall. In the angle of the apse and transepts are inserted two free-standing columns.

The original capitals are of a thoroughly Carlovingian type. One is an imitation of the Ionic, with angle volutes (Plate 19, Fig. 3). It has a bead-moulding on the necking and eggs and darts on the echinus. The abacus is surmounted by a high stilt-block, decorated with a peculiar crocket-like ornament. Two capitals (Plate 19, Fig. 1) are of a Corinthianesque type, with a single row of thick, stiffly carved leaves, except under the volutes, where an extra leaf is inserted. The veins on the leaves are indicated by incised lines which, however, are scratched rather deeply. On the centre of each face is a rosette, and on the front of the stilt-block are two rosettes and a Greek cross. The volutes are rather crudely executed, and have a sagging curve, or else are continued to the lower row of leaves. On certain faces the stilt-blocks are ornamented with the same crocket-like motive as the Ionic capital. The fourth capital is pilfered Roman Ionic, with carved angle volutes, and seems to have been the model from which the first capital was copied. The bases

3 Crosatti, 166.

4 *Historia di Verona*, MS. of 1587-1597, No. 1968/Storia/90.5 of the Biblioteca Comunale of Verona, Libro Sesto, f. 13, sotto anno 1014. See also Biancolini, I, 48.

5 Crosatti, 166-167.   6 *Ibid.*, 171.   7 *Ibid.*, 172, 173, 287.   8 *Ibid.*, 174.

show considerable variation, but approach more or less closely to the Roman Doric type, with a single torus and a plinth. The exterior of the church is absolutely without ornament.

V. The capital (Plate 19, Fig. 1) shows strong analogies with the capital of S. Satiro at Milan (Plate 132, Fig. 5), an authentic monument of 875, in the carving of the Greek cross and in the technique of the leaves and volutes. Moreover, the plan of S. Zeno at Bardolino is analogous to that of S. Satiro, in that it consists of a central vaulted area with four arms, also vaulted. This type of plan is exceedingly common in IX century churches and therefore in itself is not sufficient to fix with precision the date of our monument. When taken, however, in connection with the capital, the analogy to S. Satiro at Milan is so striking that we may assign this edifice to the same date, c. 875.

BARDONE,[1] S. MARIA ASSUNTA

I. The little church of Bardone, hidden away in the wilds of the Apennines, lies a half hour's walk from the highway. The sculptures have been described and in part illustrated by Venturi.[2]

II. According to a memorial composed by the late priest and now preserved in the sacristy, the church is mentioned in a document of 1004, and has always enjoyed the rank of a pieve. A vague tradition[3] that the basilica was reconstructed by the countess Matilda appears to be confirmed by no trustworthy evidence. On one of the piers is a painted inscription of 1514, referring doubtless to frescos executed at that epoch.

III. The edifice has been entirely rebuilt in the Renaissance period, and of the old Romanesque edifice there remain visible only two piers and numerous fragments of sculpture.

IV. In a store-room to the north of the church, near the stairway which formerly led to the houses of the canons, there are several sculptured fragments,—a St. Peter dressed in episcopal robes and holding the keys, a nice head, probably of a caryatid figure, and several capitals of the XIII century.

The altar of S. Antonio, the second from the west on the north side of the church, contains in its principal face a carved Romanesque slab representing Christ in glory. In the centre is Christ with an inscribed halo and an aureole in the form of the figure eight, supported by the symbols of the four Evangelists. To the right of Christ stands a female figure with hands

[1] Frazione di Lesignano Palma (Parma).
[2] III, 134, Fig. 114, 116.
[3] Molossi, 13.

raised in adoration, doubtless the Virgin. About are seven angels flying or standing, holding scrolls, candles, censers. One hands a crown to Christ.

Opposite this altar, in another, dedicated to the Angelo Custode, there is a companion relief, representing the Deposition. Christ's right hand has been loosened from the cross, and is held by the Virgin. Nicodemus puts his arms around Christ's waist to support the body, while Joseph of Arimathea, on a ladder, pulls the nail out of the left-hand palm with a pair of pincers. Behind the Virgin stand the two other Marys; an angel flies above their heads. Beyond Nicodemus an angel with bared sword drives Adam and Eve, naked except for fig-leaves, from the Garden of Eden.

The holy-water basin is supported by a female caryatid with finely folded drapery. Over the northern portal is a weakly composed lunette showing a seated Madonna with Child, and a kneeling, beardless saint with a book, probably St. John. At the west portal are two caryatids and two lions, which formerly supported the columns of the Lombard porch. The lions hold between their paws animals the species of which it is now impossible to determine. Over a gateway east of the church, leading to the canonica, are grotesque figures, representing a hunting scene. This arch, cusped, crocketed and finely moulded, is evidently of the XIV century, although it has been taken by Venturi to be contemporary with the other sculptures. The latter, with the exception of the lunette of the portal, a contemporary, but far inferior work, are all by the same hand, and that hand must have been that of a local sculptor, strongly under the influence of Benedetto. The style is coarse and crude, and possesses something of the vigour and roughness of the mountain region in which the church is placed. Numerous details prove the influence of Benedetto, and especially of the works of his earliest period: the angels flying in a horizontal position in the relief of Christ in glory, recall the similar figures in the Deposition of the cathedral of Parma (Plate 165, Fig. 4) and in the northern lunette of the baptistery (Plate 164, Fig. 1). The figure of the angel in the lower plane to the right of Christ is inclined in a straight, oblique line, precisely like that of the Church in the Parma Deposition. The very subject of the Deposition in the other altar front recalls the plaque of the Parma cathedral, and the details of the iconography are not only identical in the two compositions, but also unique in the field of Lombard plastic art. The cross in the Bardone plaque is covered with little knots precisely as in the Parma composition. The rosettes at Bardone around the edges of the relief are evidently merely crude copies of Benedetto's originals. Numerous other details, such as the treatment of the hair, the drapery and the composition, complete the proof that the Bardone sculptor closely imitated Benedetto.

V. The fact that the sculptures at Bardone show very strongly the influence of the Deposition of Benedetto executed in 1178, and but faintly, if at all, that of the same sculptor's later works at the baptistery of Parma—all of which are later than 1196—gives reason to believe that the Bardone works were executed at a time when the more mature works of Benedetto had not yet become generally known. The Bardone sculptures may, therefore, be assigned to the very last years of the XII century, or to c. 1200.

BARZANÒ,[1] S. SALVATORE

(Plate 19, Fig. 2; Plate 20, Fig. 1, 2; Plate 21, Fig. 1, 2)

I. The unpretending little church of S. Salvatore, commonly called Chiesetta della Canonica, at Barzanò, has frequently been referred to by writers on Lombard antiquities. The indefatigable Mella[2] illustrated the portal. Barelli[3] studied the architecture, which has also been called to notice by Malvezzi,[4] Monti[5] and Melani. The little monograph of Mantovani contains, amid many inaccuracies, some notices of great value, and the same may be said of the historical compilation of Dozio. Of all the authors who have written on the church, however, not one has appreciated its archæological significance.

II. According to Mantovani[6] the church is nothing less than the temple which Novelliano, according to an inscription, erected to all the pagan gods and goddesses. This Novelliano, he believes, lived at the end of the IV century. About the year 700 (always according to our author), the pagan shrine was remade as a Christian church. A mere inspection of the building, however, suffices to show that there is in the present structure nothing Roman. That the church was built by the early Lombard kings, on the other hand, and more particularly by the famous queen, Teodolinda (who lived about 590), is a constant local tradition at Barzanò.[7] Such traditions are common in Lombardy, and especially in Brianza, and this would merit no faith were it not for the circumstance that in this case the tradition is in some degree confirmed by the style of the monument.

The villa of Barzanò is mentioned in a document of October, 1015,[8] but nothing is said of the church. At any event, it is certain that the latter, after the XIII century, enjoyed the rank of pieve.[9] In fact, the existing edifice was merely the baptistery of a basilica which has disappeared. This is clear from the existence of a baptismal font at least as old as the XIII century, still preserved in the centre of the nave. I conjecture that S. Salvatore was originally erected, not as a baptistery, but as a church; that at the end of the

---

[1] (Como).　　[2] *Elementi*, T. V.　　[3] *Not. Arch.*, 29.　　[4] 6.　　[5] 483.　　[6] 7.
[7] See Barelli; Malvezzi, 6, etc.　　[8] Dozio, 55.
[9] *Chronicon Mediolanense*, ed. Cinquini, 17.

XII century, a new and more imposing structure was built for the use of the lately established canons, and that in the XIII century the old church was remade as a baptistery.

An inscription, formerly near the church, but which has now disappeared, and is preserved only in a copy of Bombognini,[10] states that the basilica was erected by Galdino Pirovano, archbishop of Milan.[11] This inscription, however, offers some difficulty, because S. Galdino, archbishop of Milan from 1166 to 1176, did not belong to the Pirovano family as did his predecessor Oberto (1146-1166) and his successor Algisio (1176-1185). It therefore seems probable that Bombognini's copy is incorrect. There are grounds for believing that the church and castle belonged to the Pirovano family, and that the chapter, consisting of a prevosto and five canons, was established by the archbishop Algisio Pirovano.[12] I therefore conjecture that it was not S. Galdino but Algisio Pirovano who constructed the church c. 1180, and that the church he constructed was not the existing church of S. Salvatore, but the basilica served by a chapter of five canons, for which S. Salvatore was merely a baptistery.

On the archivolt of the portal, beneath the gable, may still be seen the remains of an inscription painted in Gothic letters, all but a few of which are now illegible, but the first part of which, in Barelli's time, could still be read, and was thus transcribed by that author:

Anno dominice incarnationis millesimo ducentesimo [?] *trigesimo primo*

On the keystone is the incised inscription:

Q[VI] FECIT HOC OPUS APELLATUR SERIN PETRVS

Even in the time of Barelli the date was not easily decipherable, and that archæologist expresses considerable doubt as to the exactness of his reading. Furthermore, the inscription seen by Barelli was not the original inscription, but a copy of it made in 1611, at the order of Federigo Borromeo, to replace the original inscription, which had become in part effaced.[13] We have, therefore, a copy of a copy of the original inscription. The inexact manner in which mediæval inscriptions were renovated in the XVII century is so notorious that it is needless to insist upon the fact that no faith can be placed in them. However, the main facts recorded in this inscription offer no difficulty. The style of the portal, as indeed that of the entire western bay of the nave, is

10 168.

11 GALDINVS.PIROVANVS.ARCHIE.MEDIOL.
BASILICAM.HANC.CONSTRVXIT.

12 Mantovani, 26.

13 Litteræ ostio ecclesiæ inscriptæ, quibus tempus constructionis ecclesiæ demonstratur, renoventur qua parte corrosæ sunt, nihil immutata figura sive charactere. (*Acts of Pastoral Visit of 1611*, cit. Mantovani, 15).

that of the second quarter of the XIII century. Moreover, we have seen that there is reason to believe that a chapter had been erected and the main basilica rebuilt in the last years of the XII century. It is therefore natural that the restoration of the baptistery should be next undertaken. Finally, the castle of Barzanò was ruined, probably in 1222, an event which may well have necessitated a restoration of the ecclesiastical buildings.[14]

When S. Carlo Borromeo visited the church in 1583, the basilica had already been abandoned, since he prescribed that the baptismal font should be taken away from S. Salvatore.[15] This order, however, appears never to have been carried out. In 1611 the archbishop Federigo Borromeo, in his pastoral visit, found the church abandoned and in ruin, *collapso etiam tecto,* and ordered that it should be restored in its original form. The sacristy and *ossario* (Plate 20, Fig. 2), at a lower level, were added at this epoch. Subsequently the *ossario* was converted into a second sacristy. In 1858 the church was restored. In the course of the works the break in the masonry between the newer western bay and the older eastern parts of the church was laid bare.[16]

III. The edifice consists of three distinct parts or bays (Plate 20, Fig. 1); the easternmost, a sort of square apse, is covered with a barrel vault; the next, half occupied by the nave, half by the choir, is surmounted, not by a cloistered vault, but by a true dome carried on arched squinches (Plate 19, Fig. 2). This dome is supported on arches in the wall, as in Byzantine architecture, the arches being filled in by thin screen walls, leaving deep reveals (Plate 19, Fig. 2). The westernmost bay has a timber roof (Plate 20, Fig. 1). In the middle of the nave is an octagonal immersion font, not sunk below the level of the floor but approached by a step and in turn depressed two steps (Plate 20, Fig. 2). Beneath the choir extends the crypt (Plate 21, Fig. 1), which is at present somewhat irregularly divided into a series of compartments covered with barrel vaults. The eastern of these compartments is covered by a transverse barrel vault extending the whole width of the church, with axis perpendicular to that of the edifice. The western part of the crypt is covered by two barrel vaults parallel to each other and to the church, but perpendicular to the axis of the barrel vault of the eastern part. Originally the crypt and the choir occupied only the eastern bay of the church, but they have been prolonged in modern times to occupy also half of the centre bay, and this portion of the crypt is not vaulted but covered with a wooden roof. The walls, constructed of coarse rubble, are enormously heavy, averaging about 1.75 metre in thickness.

IV. The church is singularly destitute of ornament. It contains two ancient Roman pedestals, one of which is placed in the nave and serves as a holy-water basin, the other in the crypt. Beneath the intonaco with which

---

[14] Mantovani, 18.   [15] *Ibid.*   [16] Mantovani.

the walls are covered are visible many traces of frescos. The font and the doorway are of the XIII century.

V. It is evident that notwithstanding later restorations the body of the edifice is much older than the year 1231, when the portal and font were added. Indeed, the vast thickness of the walls, the complete absence of decoration, and the use of a dome make it certain that S. Salvatore is not only anterior to the year 1000, but one of the very earliest monuments extant in Lombardy. The structure of the building shows close relationship with the Byzantine style in the use of heavy relieving arches filled in by screen walls, in the spherical dome, and in the arched squinches. Moreover, the very plan of the edifice, departing widely from the basilican and circular types, recalls edifices of Greece or Constantinople, and their imitations of the V century in the Occident, such as the basilica of Fausta at Milan. There is extant in Lombardy no edifice erected after the VI century in which there is a dome carried on squinches and supported on arches which are closed by screen walls. This construction is thoroughly Byzantine. On the other hand, the crudeness of the masonry and the enormous thickness of the wall force us to recognize in the church at Barzanò an edifice erected in the period of the greatest decadence in the arts, when the technique of construction had sunk to its lowest depths. The crudeness of this construction compared, for example, with the neat brickwork of the basilica of Fausta, prove that Barzanò must be much later than the latter edifice. We have therefore in this church architectural forms familiar in edifices of the V century combined with the technique of construction that savours of the VII. These facts lead me to assign S. Salvatore of Barzanò to the VI century, and more precisely to the end of that century. Since there is no other monument of this period extant, it would be exceedingly difficult to fix the date more exactly, were it not for the tradition that the church was erected by Queen Teodolinda. This tradition is not unworthy of belief when it is confirmed by the style of the architecture, and I therefore assign this edifice to c. 590. If this ascription be correct, S. Salvatore must be considered the only extant monument in Lombardy of the style of architecture used during the domination of the early Lombard kings.

BEDERO VALTRAVAGLIA,[1] S. VITTORE

I. The basilica of S. Vittore at Bedero has been described by Barelli[2] and by Monti.[3]

II. Nothing is known of the history of this church. Since the XVI century it has enjoyed the rank of piéve, this dignity having been transferred

1 (Como).   2 *Not. Arch.*   3 483.

from the neighbouring church of Domo, where the old baptistery still exists. It is probable that at about this time the edifice was baroccoized. In the latter part of the XIX century a restoration in the taste of the epoch was carried out.

III.   The edifice consisted originally of a nave six bays long, two side aisles and three apses, but the eastern and western bays of the side aisles have been walled off.   The existing vaults are modern, and the edifice was originally covered with timber.   The piers, which are rectangular, without bases, and with simple impost mouldings, are original, as is evident in the walled-off portions of the side aisles of the choir.   The only really well preserved parts of the edifice are the side-aisle walls and the apses.   The former are constructed of ashlar, consisting of fine large blocks which, however, are not brought to a smooth surface, but are laid in courses, frequently broken and often deviating from the horizontal.   The mortar-beds, of moderate thickness, have been smudged over with modern plaster, and the ancient windows, widely splayed and with arcuated lintels, were intended to serve without glass.   Two are still extant in the southern side-aisle wall, but have been walled up.   The existing square windows are modern.   The wall of the clearstory, unlike that of the side aisles, is built of smooth stones laid in courses roughly horizontal.   Two of the old windows extant on the southern side are like those already described, but have true arches.   Most of the windows, however, are great half lunettes of the Renaissance.

IV.   The interior of the church, restored in the worst possible taste, is of interest chiefly for the XV century frescos of the apse.   The modern façade is a masterpiece of ugliness.   The clearstory wall has at present no arched corbel-tables, and those of the side-aisle walls have been entirely remade in the recent restoration.   Those of the apse, on the other hand, are original and supported on shafts.

V.   The apse cornice, analogous to that of the baptistery of Arsago, gives sufficient reason for assigning the Romanesque portions of the edifice to c. 1130.

BELLAGIO,[1] S. GIACOMO

(Plate 22, Fig. 1, 2)

I.   The church of S. Giacomo of Bellagio, as is natural in the case of a striking monument of mediæval art situated in a great tourist centre, has been frequently referred to by various authors.   Barelli[2] was the first to call attention to it, and in recent years have appeared, in addition to many notices of slight archæological importance, monographs by Grandi and Perrone.

---

[1] (Como).   [2] *Not. Arch.*, 21.

II. Of the history of the church in the mediæval period nothing is known. The earliest notice in regard to it is a description of the XVI century made by the bishop Ninguarda,[3] which, although it furnishes us with no data for the early history of the church, at least gives an accurate account of the condition of the building in 1593. "Visitata la chiesa di santo Iacomo nel borgo di belasio membro dell'arcipretato, et lontana più d'un miglio. È fatta in tre navi, ma non ci è volta alcuna, se non alle capelle maggiore et laterali in fronte. . . . Vi si ascende per andare alla capella magiore et altri doi altari otto gradi. . . . Ha due porte, una nella nave di mezzo nel frontispicio, et l'altra nella nave laterale dalla parte dell'epistola. . . . Ha campanile con due campane et orologio." The edifice did not long maintain its mediæval forms as described by Ninguarda. In 1628 the duke Ercole Sfrondrato commenced the baroccoizing of the edifice by tearing down the two upper stories of the campanile which he planned to replace by a loftier structure in the barocco style. He also covered the lower part of the façade with intonaco, but did not live to complete the new campanile, which was finished by his grand-nephew, Giuseppe Valeriano. In 1657 S. Giacomo was raised to the rank of *parrocchia prepositurale,* a circumstance which seems to have provoked a complete restoration of the edifice in the style of the times. The wooden roof was replaced by a heavy vault. New barocco windows were opened—two circular ones in the sides of the choir, rectangular ones in the side wall, and a great lunette in the façade.[4] The pavement of the church was raised, hiding the bases of the columns. Finally, the walls and columns were covered with a thick coating of intonaco.[5] In 1690 the ancient apse was destroyed together with the ancient sacristy, and a new choir, much larger than the old one, erected.[6] About the same time the façade was remade and a new central portal erected. In 1721 the chapels of the Vergine delle Grazie and of the Addolorata were added. These chapels were placed on ground which had formerly belonged to the cemetery. The disinterred bones were gathered together and placed in a chapel built to receive them alongside of the campanile. Throughout the XVIII and most of the XIX century, restorations continued to be executed in the church, always to the detriment of the mediæval architecture.[7] In 1884 the choir was repaved and various minor works executed.[8]

In 1902 the project of completely restoring the church in the mediæval style began to be agitated; this restoration, carried out under the direction of the architect Luigi Perrone, was completed in 1907. The barocco intonaco was stripped from the walls, the barocco vaults destroyed, a new roof added, the ancient windows reopened, and the XVIII century ones closed. In addition the barocco choir was torn down and replaced by a new apse in the

[3] *Atti di Visita,* ed. Monti, II, 115.   [4] Grandi, 82, 88-89.   [5] *Ibid.,* 90.
[6] *Ibid.*   [7] *Ibid.,* 95-96.   [8] *Ibid.,* 96.

Lombard style. Fragments of the ancient ambo were removed from the campanile where they had been placed in the XVIII century, and with them was remade a new ambo. This ambo is supported by four capitals which had formerly been employed upside down as supports for the barocco baldacchino. It was a disappointment that no ancient frescos were discovered under the barocco intonaco, and the absence of such old paintings is scarcely compensated for by the modern frescos added in the restoration, although the latter, however unsatisfactory, are still not as bad as those that have been generally added to Lombard edifices in recent restorations. In 1908 the south wall was restored. It is at present planned to "restore" the campanile by replacing the barocco upper stories with a structure of pseudo-Lombard design. It is a great pity that the restorers should find it necessary to destroy the barocco campanile, a work of distinct architectural merit, and still more a pity that they should think of substituting for it a colourless structure which can only very dimly suggest the style of the XII century.

III. The edifice consists of a nave four bays long, two side aisles, a highly raised choir of one bay flanked by side aisles, and three apses. The nave and side aisles are roofed in wood, but the choir and its side aisles are covered by groin vaults, and the three apses by half domes. There is no crypt, but since the church is placed on the side of a hill, the elevation of the choir corresponds to the natural configuration of the land, and the pavement of the nave slopes sharply towards the west. The nave at present has a clearstory of square windows, which, however, are not the original ones. The soffits of the choir vault have been remade, but their structure seems to be ancient. The vault of the nave is approximately square in plan, while those of the side aisles are distinctly oblong. All are slightly domed and are supplied with wall ribs. The piers separating nave and choir are cruciform, the groins and wall ribs of the choir vaults being carried on corbels. The other piers are all cylindrical. The choir vaults are reinforced externally by vigorous buttresses.

IV. The capitals of the nave are all of cubic type, but are singular in that, instead of being formed of a single block of stone, they are constructed of small masonry like the piers themselves. They are unusually shallow, but supplied with a necking. The Attic bases without griffes are also worked in masonry. The piers of the choir have no capitals other than a simple impost moulding. The archivolts are of a single order unmoulded.

The exterior of the church is severely plain. An arched corbel-table adorns the gable of the west façade, but the walls of the nave are without any decoration. Of the three apses the two lateral ones are ancient: that to the south is adorned with arched corbel-tables in two orders supported on pilaster strips with engaged shafts; that to the north has plain corbel-tables; both have a saw-tooth cornice. The central apse has been reconstructed on traces of the original one which came to light during the restoration. The arched corbel-tables in two orders are grouped two and two and supported on pilaster strips. The windows of the apses, as indeed of all the church, were widely splayed and narrow, being evidently intended to serve without glass.

The sculptures of the ambo (Plate 22, Fig. 1, 2) are among the most notable examples of the plastic art of the XII century extant in the diocese of Como. The symbols of the four Evangelists are sculptured in white marble, with a finesse which we look for in vain in other contemporary sculptures of this region. Yet the crude drawing betrays an inexperienced age, and these sculptures are not later than those of S. Fedele at Como. The four capitals of the present ambo are of a curious type which approaches the Corin-thianesque, and may well be approximately contemporary with the sculptures.

V. The masonry of the church, consisting of small but well laid blocks of Moltrasian stone, seems about contemporary with that of S. Abondio at Como, as do also the cubic capitals. We may therefore assign the monument to c. 1095. The sculptures of the ambo, however, not earlier than the portal of S. Fedele, must be somewhat later, or of c. 1115.

BERCETO,[1] S. REMIGIO (S. ABONDIO)

(Plate 22, Fig. 3, 4)

I. The town of Berceto lies in one of the wildest portions of the Appennini Parmigiani, near the summit of the Bardone pass which leads from Parma to Tuscany. In mediæval times, this route used to be one of the most travelled between southern Italy and northern Europe. In modern times, however, the Bardone has been supplanted by easier or more direct passes, and the town of Berceto, with its interesting church, has remained almost unknown. For historical notices, the works of Affò and Molossi should be consulted.

II. A monastery was founded in Berceto by Luitprando (712-743). The best source for this fact is the brief statement of Paolo Diacono.[2] The notice of the chronicler is confirmed by the epitaph of Luitprando formerly preserved at S. Pietro in Ciel d'Oro at Pavia, which contains a distinct refer-ence to the foundation of the monastery of Berceto,[3] and by the legend of S. Moderanno narrated by Flodoard of Reims. According to the latter, in the time of Chilpéric II (fl. c. 716), king of Neustria, S. Moderanno, bishop

---

[1] (Parma).

[2] In summa quoque Bardonis Alpe monasterium quod Bercetum dicitur aedificavit [Liuprandus]. (Pauli Diaconi, *Hist. Long.*, VI, 58, ed. Waitz, 240).

[3] See below, Vol. III, under *Pavia, S. Pietro in Ciel d'Oro*, Section II.

of Rennes, set out on a pilgrimage to St. Peter's in Rome, but turned aside upon his way to visit the monastery of St.-Remi at Reims. There he obtained from the monks certain relics of the saint, which he carried away with him on his journey to Italy. While he was crossing the Bardone pass, he slept on a certain night by the wayside and hung the relics on the branch of a tree. In the morning, on resuming his journey, he forgot the relics, which he remembered only after he had proceeded some distance. He sent back a clerk to fetch them, but the messenger was unable to accomplish his mission, since, just as he was about to grasp the relics, they were miraculously lifted aloft. The bishop, when he heard of this miracle, returned and pitched his tent at the spot, nor was he able to lay hold of the relics until he had vowed to leave a part of them in the neighbouring monastery of S. Abondio at Berceto. Having done this, he resumed his journey. He was soon met by Luitprando, king of Italy, who, having heard of the miracle, immediately understood the virtue of the relics, and moved by love of St. Remi, gave to him the monastery of Berceto, with all its possessions. S. Moderanno returned from Rome and went again to the venerable tomb of St. Remi and laid at the feet of the saint the donation which he had received from the king. Then, having returned again to his own city, he appointed his successor, and, bidding farewell to his flock, returned to the monastery of Berceto, where he finished his days in the year 730.[4] The legend as told by Flodoard does not explicitly state

[4] Temporibus Chilperici Francorum regis extitisse fertur Moderamnus Redonensis ecclesiae presul, vir nobili prosapia oriundus. Qui per licentiam predicti regis limina sancti Petri adire disponens, divertit in monasterium beati Remigii situm in suburbio Remensis urbis. Ubi liberaliter a fratribus eiusdem loci susceptus, impetravit a Bernehardo sacrorum custode reliquias de stola, cilicio atque sudario sancti Remigii. Quibus gratanter acceptis, iter inceptum laetus agens, dum permeat Italiam, in monte Bardonum quadam nocte metatum habens, memoratas in ilicis ramo suspendit reliquias. Cumque diluculo surgens iter coeptum arriperet inmemor horum, nutu, ceu creditur, divino haec ibidem remansere pignera. Procedente vero aliquanto longius episcopo, ubi relictarum memor fit reliquiarum, suum statim ad has recipiendum dirigit clericum nomine Vulfadum. Quo ad has perveniente, nullo valet eas ingenio contingere, dum mirabili signo, ut eas attingere vellet, elevarentur in sublime. Hoc prefatus episcopus audito miraculo regrediens, in eodem loco fixit tentorium; sed relicta pignera eadem nocte minime valuit recipere, donec facto mane in monasterio quod vocatur Bercetum, in honore sancti Abundii martiris inibi constructum, missam celebrans, predictorum partem munerum devoveret ibidem se relicturum. Sicque rapta sibi recipiens, impleto venerabiliter voto, coeptum repetit iter. Cui obvius factus Liutbrandus Italorum rex strenuus, qui hanc auditu iam compererat sacrorum virtutem, amore beati Remigii ductus, idem monasterium, Bercetum scilicet, cum omnibus adiacentiis omnique abbatia, mansos octingentos, ut tradunt, continenti, prefato presuli Moderamno delegavit eique in presentia fidelium suorum legali de more vestituram ex ea et cartam fecit. Remeans autem ab urbe Roma memoratus presul, accessit ad venerandum beati Remigii sepulchrum, atque, sicut illi premissus rex hanc terram tradidit, ita nihilominus ille sancto Remigio eandem contulit. Sicque prospere in suum reversus episcopium, successorem sibi ordinari fecit, et valefaciens filiis suis, Bercetum monasterium repetiit et usque ad

that the monastery had been founded by Luitprando, but this is perhaps implied, since otherwise the monarch would not have had the power to place the abbey under the jurisdiction of St.-Remi of Reims. That the monastery was erected by Luitprando is confirmed finally by a diploma of Ugo, of 927.[5]

According to the legend of S. Abondio published by the Bollandists, in the time of the emperors Lodovico II and Lotario I (849-855), Tiberio, abbot of Berceto, enlarged the church of the monastery and prepared a place under the principal altar for the body of S. Moderanno, which hitherto had been buried to the left of the altar. The saint, however, appeared to the abbot in a dream and warned him that the new tomb was destined for Abondio. Years afterwards the abbot chanced to go to a council in Pavia, where he learned that the body of S. Abondio rested at Foligno. The pious abbot immediately went thither and obtained by prayers the gift of the body, which he translated to Berceto in the year 850.[6] This legend says nothing about the collapse of the mountain and the consequent removal of the monastery about this time, but implies, on the contrary, that the church remained always on the same spot, and was merely enlarged. The tradition of the collapse of the mountain is, however, constant among the historians of Parma.[7]

Affò[8] has conjectured that in the time of Pope Benedict III (855-858) the church was officiated no longer by monks but by canons, and that this change of clergy was occasioned by the disaster of c. 850. Since a diploma of Ugo of 927 mentions that the church was officiated by canons, and yet calls it a monastery, no disproof of Affò's hypothesis is furnished by the fact that the church continued still to be known as an abbey, and as such was given to the bishop of Parma by Carlomanno in 879,[9] and that in 922 Rodolfo, king of Italy, confirmed to the bishop of Parma: *abbatiam de Berceto, in honore*

---

obitus sui diem in loco illo moderate et honeste ut servus Dei conversatus vixit. (Flodoardi, *Historia Remensis Ecclesiae*, I, 20, ed. Heller et Waitz, M. G. H. Scrip., XIII, 443). Mabillon, *Ann. Ben.*, II, 51, ascribes the first visit of the saint to Berceto to the year 718 and the death of the saint to 730.

[5] See text cited below, p. 104.

[6] Temporibus invictissimorum Imperatorum Ludovici et Lotharii . . . hic [Tyberius abbas monasterii Berceti, quod est situm in cacumine montis, cui nomen est Bardo] cum sui cœnobii ecclesiam, justa quod necessitas commissæ sibi congregationis exigebat, aliquantulum in longum porrexisset, quæ prius erat modica, vel vix capiens fratrum collectam; placuit, ut sub altari ejusdem basilicæ, pararet congruum locum quo poneretur corpus S. Moderanni, quod istic ad lævam altaris jacet humatum. (*Acta Translationis S. Abundii*, ed. Boll., *Acta Sanct.*, Julii I, 40).

[7] See Affò, I, 163, who quotes Angeli to the following effect: Hebbe questo Castello suo cominciamento dalle ruine di Bercè monastero fabbricato nell'alpe di Bardone da Luitprando Re de' Longobardi et donato dopo a San Moderanno, il quale cominciando a ruinare per le mosse de' monti fu trasportato in questo luogo.

[8] *Ibid.* The basis for this conjecture is a sentence in the diploma of Ugo cited below.

[9] Affò, I, 294; Molossi, 17.

Sancti Remigii constructam in comitatu Parmensi.[10]   In 913 the bishop Elbunco of Parma left a sum of money to restore the apse.[11]

Affò has published an important document of King Ugo, of 927, in which the monarch laments that the canons of Berceto, of the monastery of S. Remigio founded by King Luitprando, were reduced to great poverty, and suffered from lack of food and clothing, and to remedy this condition, he grants them certain lands.[12]   Three years later the same Ugo confirmed to the bishop of Parma: *Abbaciam scilicet de Bercetum in honore Sancti Remigii extructam in integrum* etc.[13]   In 1007 the bishop of Parma, Sigifredo II, granted part of the oblations of Berceto to the canons of his cathedral church,[14] and the oblations of the altars of S. Remigio and S. Moderanno at Berceto were ceded by Ugo, bishop of Parma, to the same canons, in 1035.

From this time the importance of the chapter of Berceto appears to have steadily declined.   In 1313 the church was pillaged,[15] a misfortune from which the canons never entirely recovered.   In the XIX century S. Remigio became the parish church of Berceto.   In 1845 the monument received a heavy blow in the shape of a quasi-archæological restoration, which completely denatured the ancient architecture.[16]   At this epoch were added the chapels constructed, in part, of old materials.   The northern transept and the upper part of the northern side-aisle walls were completely rebuilt.   The existing façade seems to date almost entirely from this period, but here again old materials were employed in the new construction.   The old clearstory disappeared behind the new side-aisle vaults.

III.   The edifice consists of a nave four bays long, two side aisles, modern chapels, projecting transepts, a tower rising over the crossing, and three apses, of which the two minor ones are semicircular, the central one square externally, but irregularly oblong internally.   The nave is at present roofed in wood.   The side aisles have undomed groin vaults, which, however, appear to have been added in 1845 and replace the original wooden roofs. It is probable, however, that the undomed groin vaults of the transepts are original, and the highly domed rib vault of the crossing (Plate 22, Fig. 4) is

[10]Muratori, A. I. M. A., ed. A., XIV, 721.

[11] See text cited below under Borgo S. Donnino, p. 171.

[12] In nomine Domini Dei æterni. Hugo gratia Dei Rex . . . Adelbertus venerabilis Episcopus nostri per omnia fidelissimus . . . retulit nobis inter cætera qualiter canonici de Bercedo monasterio Sancti Remigii, quod Luitprandus Rex a fundamentis ædificavit, subjecitque eum, ut sub sacri Palatii tutela esset, murmurarent, atque non haberent ad ciborum seu vestimentorum necessitatem, qualiter in ipso sancto loco deservire possent . . . ut imperium nostrum inviolabile perseveret, nec non auctoritatem Apostolicæ Sedis, quam venerabilis Papa Benedictus de eisdem rebus illis fecit. . . . . Data anno Dominicæ Incarnationis 927. 13. Kal. Martii indictione 15. anno vero Domini Hugonis gloriosissimi Regis primo. (Affò, I, 335).

[13] Muratori, A. I. M. A., ed. A., VI, 320.   [14] Affò, I, 383.   [15] Molossi, 17.

[16] This restoration is recorded by an inscription in the façade.

certainly ancient. The diagonals, rectangular in section, are pointed in elevation. There are no wall ribs; the wall arches are approximately semicircular in elevation, except one, which is very slightly pointed. The diagonals, heavily loaded at the groins, are carried on corbels. The doming of this vault is most exaggerated. The arches of the crossing are pointed, as are those of the main arcade. The other arches of the church are all semicircular.

IV. The capitals of the church are of Romanesque style, but they were so much restored and made over in 1845 as to be quite misleading. The arched portal of the façade is in seven orders, and is adorned with zigzag and spiral shafts and with a sculptured lunette and architrave (Plate 22, Fig. 3). The influence of Benedetto is evident in the capitals, which have a continuous straight abacus, as in the cathedral of Borgo S. Donnino (Plate 27, Fig. 3).

Particularly interesting is the subject of the architrave sculptures (Plate 22, Fig. 3) which appear to be a sort of parody of the Dance of David as represented by Benedetto in the Parma baptistery (Plate 163, Fig. 3). In the centre an animal (which I take to be an ass) strums a harp which is of the triangular form, symbolical of the Trinity. To the left are four animals, apparently symbolical of the four Evangelists, although for the bull and the angel are substituted curiously grotesque forms. All these animals are dancing to the music of the ass, and there is also a group of three human figures on the right-hand side of the lintel. These consist of a man holding a staff or a sword in his hand and a woman, dancing hand-in-hand. Between them is a short third figure, perhaps that of a child. The lintel is completed with the figure of a grotesque animal, a knight riding a stallion and a centaur shooting a bow. Above the centaur is a rosette, clearly showing the influence of Benedetto. The sacrilegious character of this relief, in which, apparently, Christ is depicted as an ass, is most amazing, and can only be explained by the hypothesis that some rebellious and cynical sculptor of this wild mountain region imposed upon the ignorance of his patrons to place over the portal of the church a shocking blasphemy.

Equally irreligious is the relief of the Crucifixion above. Christ is depicted fastened on the cross by four nails. His head, with inscribed halo, is held upright. At the ends of the arms of the cross are sculptured two figures, probably Mary and John. This entire motive is a new one in Romanesque sculpture, and undoubtedly shows the influence of painting. In the XIII century painted wooden crucifixes were common, in which the figure of Christ was shown precisely as in these sculptures, fastened to the cross by four nails, and with painted scenes at the ends of the arms of the cross. Above the cross on either side are shown two angels flying in a horizontal position, crude imitations of the style of Benedetto. To the right of Christ are shown Mary and Joseph of Arimathea, both holding their left hands to their faces in anguish. The darkest hour of the Dark Ages never produced in Italy works more crude, less life-like and more grotesque than these, and one feels that the sculptor took a certain malicious joy in making the figures as ridiculous as possible. Behind Joseph of Arimathea, squeezed into the curving angle of the lunette, is the figure of St. Remi dressed in archiepiscopal robes, with a mitre and crosier. To the left of Christ is a figure holding an enormous wine jar in which he catches the blood that flows from the wound inflicted by the centurion's spear. This wound, contrary to tradition, is placed in Christ's left side, and the large size of the wine jar in which the blood is being caught suggests again the satiric, irreverent feeling for which these reliefs are notable. At the extreme edge of the lunette are four soldiers with helmets and swords, all treated in a grotesque manner.

V. The sculptures of Berceto, since they show imitation, or, rather, burlesquing, of the sculptures of Benedetto, can hardly be earlier than c. 1220. They are somewhat less crude than those of Bardone (c. 1200), and must be somewhat later, since they show the influence, not only of the earliest manner of Benedetto, but of his more mature works in the baptistery of Parma and in the cathedral of Borgo S. Donnino. There is nothing to indicate that the rib vault of the crossing is earlier. As far as can be judged from the present mutilated condition of the edifice, the building was a homogeneous structure until marred by Renaissance alterations and modern restorations. The existence of a rib vault of purely Lombard type at such a late date is indeed extraordinary, but must be explained by the fact that Berceto is placed in a remote mountain district where artistic forms developed somewhat tardily. Moreover, the vault of Berceto was placed beneath a tower where, as I have shown,[17] the rib vault offers peculiar constructive advantages. The date of 1220 is, moreover, in perfect accord with the fact that pointed arches are freely used in the edifice.

BERGAMO, S. MARIA MAGGIORE

(Plate 22, Fig. 5, 6, 7; Plate 23, Fig. 1, 2, 4)

I. Although situated in an important city, and one frequently visited by tourists, the notable fragments of XII century architecture preserved in S. Maria Maggiore at Bergamo have been strangely neglected by archæologists. The first to describe the church were the brothers Sacchi,[1] who wrote in the early part of the XIX century. They were followed about the middle of the century by Osten,[2] who published a large engraving of the apse. In 1880

[17] *Construction of Lombard and Gothic Vaults,* 12.
[1] 38.   [2] Plate XXXVI.

appeared the monograph of Fornoni, a sumptuous publication, lavishly illustrated with large-scale drawings. Unfortunately in this work the citations of historical authorities are not always exact, and there are numerous errors in the measurements and restorations. In the Museo Civico at Bergamo are numerous old drawings of the church, but none which throw real light upon its history. The historians of Bergamo have all treated at length of the historical problems which the church presents. Among them should be consulted especially Pellegrini, who wrote in 1553, Calvi, who wrote in 1676, the classical work of Lupi, and the modern publications of Ronchetti (1807), and Locatelli (1879). Finally should be mentioned the little study in the compilation of Strafforello.[3]

II. It is usually stated that the church of S. Maria Maggiore was founded in 1137, but such cannot be the case, since it is mentioned in a document of 774.[4] The campanile is again referred to in 928.[5]

From these documents it results that the church must have been not founded, but reconstructed, in 1137. The principal source for this fact is an inscription on the archivolt of the southern portal. This inscription was originally painted in Gothic letters, but at some unknown time the painted inscription was replaced by an incised inscription, doubtless because the original was becoming so effaced as to be illegible. When I first visited the church in 1910, some traces of the ancient letters still existed, but unfortunately not enough to make it possible to control the reading made by the person who cut the incised inscription, and when I returned to the monument three years later, the painted letters had almost entirely disappeared. The inscription in substance records that on the upper lintel of the church of S. Maria Maggiore of Bergamo, there existed an inscription to the effect that the church was founded in the year 1137, in the time of Pope Innocent II, and King Lothair, and Roger, bishop of Bergamo. The name of the master-builder, Maestro Fredi, is also given:

✠ . IN . XPI . NOMINE . AMEN . IN . LIMINE . SVPERIORI . ECCLESIE . BEATE . MARIE . VIRGINIS . CIVI . TATIS . PERGAMI . CONTINEBA . TVR . QVCCL . DICTA . ECCLESIA . FONDATA . FVIT . ANNO . DOMI- NICE . INCARNATIONIS . MILLESIMO . CENTESIMO| TREGESIMO . SEPTIMO . SVB . DOMINO . PAPPA . INNOCENTIO . SECONDO SVB . EPISCOPO . ROGERIO . REGNANTE . REGE . LOTERIO . PER . MAGIS- TRVM . FREDVM.

This inscription is not without its difficulties. The monstrous word *qvccl* is written for *quod,* as I am fortunately able to attest from traces of the

[3] *Bergamo,* 34.
[4] See text cited below under S. Giulia di Bonate, p. 162.
[5] *Hist. Pat. Mon.,* XIII, 897.

painted inscription visible in 1910.   But what are we to say of Roger, bishop
of Bergamo, when it is known that in 1137 Gregorio was bishop?   And what
of the *King* Lothair, when Lothair II was at this time really emperor?   Are
these mistakes of the master-builder of the XIV century, who misread the
original XII century inscription which he undertook to preserve, or are they
the errors of the modern restorer, who replaced the painted letters by an
incised inscription?   There can be little doubt that the former is the case.
In the historians of Bergamo we have preserved a series of transcriptions of
the inscription, which goes back to the XVII century, and hence must contain
some copies made before the restoration of the inscription.   In all these
transcriptions, despite numerous copyists' errors, it is evident that the original
inscription was always essentially the same.[6]

In addition to the inscription there were apparently documents still
extant in the XVI century regarding the construction of the church in 1137
that are now lost.   The existence of these is recorded by Pellegrini, who,
however, probably in carelessness, ascribes to the year 1137, not the foundation, but the consecration of the church.[7]   Giovanni Filippo assigns the
foundation of the church to the year 1135, and says it was begun by the

---

[6] The earliest of these copies is that of Celestino, who wrote in 1617 (II, pt.
2, p. 297): M . CCC . LX . magister Iohannes f. q. Domni Iohannis de Cāpellio fecit
hoc opus in Christi nomine. amen.   In limine superiori Ecclesiæ B. Mariæ Virginis
Ciuitatis Pergami, quæ olim dicta Ecclesia fundata fuit anno Dominicæ Incarnationis
millesimo trigesimo septimo sub Domno Papa Innocentio secundo, sub Episcopo Rogerio,
regnante rege Lothario per magistrum Fredum.   Calvi (III, 296) read the inscription
as follows: *MCCCLD* [*sic*] *Mag. Ioannes f. q. D. Ioannis de Campellio fecit hoc opus
in Christi nomine amen.   In limine superiori Ecclesiæ S. Mariæ Virg. Ciuitatis Pergami
continebatur, quod olim dicta Ecclesia fundata fuit anno Dominicæ Incarn. 1037.
Sub Domino Papa Innocentio II. Sub Episcopo Rogerio regnante Rege Lhotario per
Magistrum Fredum;* but appears to have taken it not from the original but from
Celestino's copy.   Ronchetti's version (III, 66), published in 1807, is as follows: In
Christi nomine amen.   In Limine superiori Beatæ Mariæ Virginis Civitatis Pergomi
continebatur quod dicta Ecclesia fundata fuit anno Dominice Incarnationis millesimo
centesimo III gesimo septimo sub dom. Papa Innocentio II. sub Episcopo Rogerio
Regnante Rege Lothario per magistrum Fredum.   In 1880, Fornoni published the
inscription with new variations: *In limine superiori ecclesiæ B. Mariæ Virginis
civitatis Pergomi continebatur quod dicta ecclesia fundata fuit anno dominicæ incoronationis MCXXXVII sub domino Papa Innocentio II sub episcopo Rogerio regnante
rege Lothario per magistrum Fredum.*   His version appears to have been taken verbatim
from that of Locatelli (III, 195), with which it is identical, even to the italics used,
except that in Locatelli we read *eclesia* for *ecclesia*, *incarnationis* for the monstrous
incoronationis, *Rugerio* for *Rogerio*, and *MAGISTRUM FREDUM.*   The little founded
conjecture of Osten that *magistrum Fredum* is a copyist's error for *magistrum Alfredum*
is hardly worth discussion, since *Fredi*, or *Fredo*, is a common Italian name, whereas
the Saxon, *Alfred*, is almost unknown south of the Alps.

[7] [Gregorius Episcopus] anno sequenti videlicet 1137. templum maius in vrbis
nostræ medio ad honorem beatissimæ virginis Mariæ dedicauit, & anno. 1144. die 19.
Iunii occubuit. . . . Hæc ex annalibus, & diurnalibus prædictæ Abbatiæ s. Sepulchri,

citizens *ex voto* because of a great famine and plague.[8]   The same tradition appears in an inscription of the XVIII century, now over the choir[9] and is also related by Bartolomeo Farina.[10]   It is, moreover, confirmed by a number of documents of the ancient archives now preserved in the Biblioteca Municipale at Bergamo.   These documents, when I had access to them, were only in part classified, but from those which I examined it was evident that S. Maria Maggiore has always stood in a peculiar relationship to the commune of Bergamo,[11] and was not, as has been asserted, co-cathedral with S. Vincenzo,[12] notwithstanding the fact that in 1340 a baptistery was erected in the church.   S. Maria Maggiore, as the most conspicuous church of Bergamo, has served as a burial place for illustrious citizens, such as Colleoni, Donizetti, Mayr, etc.

In an unpublished document of the archives, dated 1195, is cited an earlier document of 1170, which is dated "under the porch" (*sub porticu*) of S. Maria Maggiore.   This proves that in 1170 the construction of the church, if not completed, was at least far advanced, since the portal had been erected.[13]

& ex chronicis domini Bartholomæi de ossa Bergomatis parte 5, lib. 16, cap. 47. (Pellegrini, 7).

[8] Templum maius quod misericordiæ dicitur eam ob re[m] hac nostra in urbe Bergomo in honorem beatissimæ uirginis Mariæ in medio urbis fere iuxta cathedralem basilica indicibili prope: tu impesa: tu artis elegantia: ex lapidibus quadratis & sectis a conciuibus nostris ob misericordia[m] ipius dei genitricis Mariæ hoc aestuati tp[or]e implorada hoc anno [1135] ceptu est. Atq[ue] inde p[er] tempora eximia pulchritudine cum capanaria pulcherrima atq[ue] sublimi cosumatu fuit.   Eo naq[ue] tempore Bergomates nri fundato [ut ita dixerim] misericordiæ templo cu multi fame et peste laborarent: et misericordiæ loca plurima ad elemosinas clamet ap[er]te paup[er]ibus errogandas in urbe & extra instituere: quæ usq[ue] in præsens tanta cu religione & pietate in unu collectæ excreuit.   Vt in tota italia eidem non inueniatur consimilis. (Giovanni Filippo sotto anno 1135).

[9]   DEO OPT' MAX'
          MARIÆ VIRG' MATRI
          CIVITAS EXSTR' AN' MCXXXVII

[10] Refert *Forestus,* in supplemento, anno MCXXXIII, Bergomi & in Lombardia calores tam intensos fuisse, ut fruges exsiccarent, indeque annonæ caritas inaudita prorsus profecta, eamque pestis immanis insecuta fuerit, ob quas calamitates, ad intercessionem B. V. Civitas confugiens, in honorem ejus fabricandum curavit sumptuosissimum illud Templum *S. Mariæ Majoris,* urbis Cathedrale.   (Bartholomæus Farina, *De Bergomi Origine et Fatis,* ed. Graevius et Burmannus, *Thesaurus Antiquitatum et Historiarum Italiae,* IX, pt. 7, p. 10).

[11] In documents of 1170 and 1195, cited below, *ministri* are seen to be in charge of the church of S. Maria Maggiore, and these are not canons of the cathedral.

[12] In Lombard cities there were frequently two cathedrals, one of which was used for service during the summer, the other during the winter.

[13] Vna die que e in mse aug. . . . Arnaldus d[e] corterezze [et] lafracus d

Ronchetti, who wrote in 1807, saw in the archives of the cathedral chapter documents pertaining to a lawsuit of 1187, in which witnesses testified that about this time the church of S. Maria Maggiore was enlarged and embellished.[14] These appear to have been known also by Fornoni, who wrote in 1880, since in speaking of them he adds certain details which could not have been derived from Ronchetti.[15]

In an ancient calendar[16] of the church of Bergamo published by Finazzi, there is recorded a consecration of the altar of S. Maria Vetera in 1185. Since the indiction corresponds in this notice with the year, it is to be preferred

gastaldio ministri eccl[esi]e sce marie. . . . factū e hoc. anno dnice incarnatiois. millo centesimo septuagimo. Indjoe sexta [*sic*]

Die decimo intnte mense decembr. Jn ciuitate bgami sub porticu sce marie. maioris. Presentib; infra scriptis testib' Ottacius fili' [quon]dā pet' de pappa. q[ui] p[ro]fessus est lege uive longobar. Fecit datū uendit' noe. ad p[er]petatem. Jn manib; lanf de sca maria [et] petri redulfi [et] magri zaboni missor[um] eccle sce marie maioris vice [et] noe illi' eccle. . . . Factum est hoc anno dni millo cento nonago q[ui]nto. indjone triadecima. Similar phrases are contained in another parchment in the same writing, dated 1195: Scd'o die intate mense febr. Jn civit' b[er]gi sub porticu sce marie maioris. Presentia infra scriptor[um] testiu. Maginfredus filius [quon]da albti de lalio q[ui] p[ro]fessus e lege vive longobar. Fecit datum venditionis noe ad p[er]petatem. Jn manib; lanf d' sca maria petri redulfi [et] magistri zaboni ministor[um] eccle sce marie maioris noe [et] uice illi' eccle. Nominatim de quada petia tre vidate. iuris sue qua habe visus e foris civit b[er]gi no m[ul]tu longe . . . pdictis lanf petro. [et] magistro zabono. noe et vice pfate eccle [et] eo[rum] succes-sorib; . . . lanf d' sca maria [et] petri [et] mgist' zaboni . . . Factum est hoc anno dni millo cento nonago q[ui]nto. indjone triadecima. (Pergamene in Biblioteca Civica of Bergamo, Collezione Congregazione di Carità).

[14] Ciò che dunque rileviamo da giurati testimonianze dell'anno 1187. esistenti nell'archivio capitolare si è, che circa questo tempo detta chiesa di S. Maria fu ampliata, e resa più bella, il che però non si eseguì, che nel corso di molti anni non essendo per anco nel detto anno 1187. terminata; che dopo essersi cominciato tale rifacimento continuava il clero di S. Vincenzo ad officiarvi nelle feste della Beata Vergiue [*sic*], e nella quaresima vi si cantava dal medesimo la messa dopo nona; che la collazione de' suoi beneficj facevasi per libera elezione del capitolo; che il vescovo col clero nel Sabbato santo vi celebrava l'officio, e andava processionalmente a benedire il fonte, e ad amministrare il battesimo, trovanosi [*sic*] sino da' tempi antichi in quella chiesa il fonte battesimale, che era l'unico in tutto l'ampio circondario della città e de' borghi, e continuò ad esservi sino al secolo decimo settimo, nel quale fu trasportato in S. Vincenzo.

[15] Un documento poi che si rinvenne nell'archivio del Capitolo giustifica anche il resto della lapide; poichè in esso certo Lanfranco Mazocchi nell'anno 1187 con dichiarazione giurata attesta che le fabbriche, le quali si innalzavano in quella località, vennero completamente distrutte per ampliare e rendere piu bella una Chiesa dedicata a Maria, che ivi sorgeva. (9).

[16] V K. [Decembr.] Consecratum est altare sce Marie veteris, M C octuagesimo quinto, Ind. tertia. (Finazzi, 415).

to another similar notice in another calendar[17] published by the same authority in which the consecration is referred to 1184. In view of the other documents just noted, which prove that shortly before 1187 the church was in construction, I have no hesitation in referring these texts to S. Maria Maggiore, although I know of no other case in which the church is called *vetus* or *antica*. It seems clear, therefore, that in 1185 the construction, if not finished, was at least sufficiently far advanced to admit of the consecration of the altar.

Two inedited documents of 1211 and 1235 respectively make it evident that in the early part of the XIII century the church of S. Maria Maggiore was still officiated by a clergy entirely separate from that of the cathedral, but yet subordinate to the latter.[18]

According to Pellegrini, the church was consecrated in 1273. This historian, who wrote in the middle of the XVI century, assures us that he derived this information from documents of the archives,[19] but the notice is unknown to all the other historians of Bergamo, and is unconfirmed by any documents which have come down to our day. Moreover, in the church itself it is possible to find no evidence of any additions or embellishments made at this time, and it is almost inconceivable that changes sufficiently radical to necessitate a consecration could have been made without leaving some trace in the monument as we have it to-day.[20] I am, therefore, inclined to believe that the date 1273 of Pellegrini, owing to a misprint, or other mistake, is erroneous, and that the consecration really was celebrated after the completion of the works which were in progress in 1187.

In 1351 the northern portal was added to the church according to an

---

17 V. K. [Decembris]. Consecratum est Altare Sc̄e Marie veteris millesimo centesimo octuagesimo quarto. Indict. prima. (Finazzi, 407).

18 Die t̄tio intrante sept̄. Jn civit poī [= Bergami]. sub porticu cupticelle ecc̄lie maioris sc̄e marie. . . . Feceru' datū [et] car̄ dati noīe vendiciois ad p[er]petāte [et] iure p[er]petatio. dn̄o petro redulfi. [et] dn̄o mar. [et] ioh̄i frib̄ [et] concis [et] ministris illi' ecc̄lie. vice ac noīe illi' ecc̄lie. d' qd̄a dn̄r ficto. q. habebat. . . . Factu est hoc an̄o dn̄i mīllo ducentoe vndecimo, indictj̄oe qartadecima. . . . (Pergamene in Biblioteca Civica, Bergamo, Collezione Congregazione di Carità).

Die mcurii nono int̄nte novembri [the chapter of S. Vincenzo authorizes] dn̄o Giufredo archipsbro d'pagano psb̄ro ecc̄lie maioris sc̄e marie ciuite p[er]ḡi. comutandi [et] in causam comutationis dandi noīe ip̄i' ecc̄lie sc̄e marie [et] p[er] ea om̄es tras [et] possessiones ip̄i' ecc̄lie sc̄e marie etc. . . . Factum est hoc anno dn̄i mīlle ducent'o trig'o nono (*Ibid.*).

19 Hic [Suardus episcopus] ecclesiam sanctæ Mariæ Matris Domini dedicauit, anno Christi. 1273. & episcopatus eius primo, & concessit omnibus visitantibus ea in illa die dedicationis videlicet. 25 martii dies quadraginta. Hæc ex dicto memoriali, & antiquis scripturis ipsius monasterii, & ex nostro Kalendario. (Pellegrini, 9).

20 Unless, indeed, the changes were confined to the clearstory and vaults of the nave, which have disappeared, or to the addition of frescos which have been covered with intonaco.

inscription originally painted and now preserved in an incised copy.[21] The portal was finished probably in 1355[22] and in 1360 the southern porch was erected by the same master-builder, according to the existing incised inscription,[23] or by his son, according to old copies which probably reproduce more faithfully the original painted inscription.[24] The northern portal of the choir was added in 1367, as is evident from the fact that the date M.CCC.LX.VII. is incised on the lintel. According to Locatelli[25] the sculptures of God and the Annunciation were completed in 1403, and were the work of Antonio de Alemania.

In 1449 the care of the church was ceded by the city to the Misericordia,[26] which subsequently became the Congregazione di Carità, to which corporation it still belongs. Four years later the building was exempted from the jurisdiction of the bishop.[27]

The church must have been restored in the XV century since in the gallery of the eastern absidiole of the southern transept there are numerous indications of alterations executed at this epoch, among others a capital of the early Renaissance style.

A description of the church, written in 1516, by Antonio Michele, gives a picture of the edifice as it was in the early part of the XVI century, shortly after the addition of the Colleoni chapel, but before the building had been baroccoized.[28] In 1647 the church was much damaged by lightning,[29] an

[21]   ➕ M . CCC . LI . MAGISTER .
IOHĀNES .
DE .
CAMPLEONO
CIVIS .
PGAMI .
FECIT .
HOC .
OPVS .

[22] Merzario, I, 138.

[23]   ➕ . M . CCC . LX .
MAGISTER . IOHAN
ES . FILIVS C[= cuiusdam or quondam?] . DN̄I .
VGI . DE . CAMPILIO .
FECIT . HOC OPVS

[24] See above, p. 108.
[25] III, 205.
[26] Calvi, I, 291, and II, 343.
[27] *Ibid.*, I, 292.
[28] Contra vero D. Mariæ ædes neque tam [as S. Vicenzo] vetustæ dicationis, utpote ducentesimo circiter ab hinc anno ædificari inchoata, neque sacerdotii dignitate par, ob operantium tamen sanctitatem & frequentiam ita à populo visitur, ut nulla sit in urbe ædes celebrior. Ejus longitudo secus areolam quam dixi ab ortu ad occasum patet, forma extra quadrata est, intus christiano ritu Crucis figuram præsefert. Aræ

event which probably provoked a restoration in the barocco style, for in 1651 Calvi makes a reference to the preparations in progress for covering the interior with stucco.[30]

In 1655 a new misfortune befell the edifice. The lights hung in the campanile to celebrate the accession to the pontifical throne of Alexander VII, set fire to the church, and the conflagration was checked only after all the lead with which the cupola was covered had been destroyed.[31] In 1660 the baptistery was removed from the church.[32] From the description of Calvi, written in 1676, it is evident that at this date[33] the baroccoization of the church had been almost completed.

In 1771 the wooden doors of the southern portal were added.[34]

The monument has been happy in escaping a modern restoration, and still preserves its barocco interior, with all the gilt and restless over-decoration. Veritable oases in the desert of stucco angels and barocco curves are the lovely Renaissance tapestries and intarsia choir-stalls.

maximæ (quæ ad ortum spectat) fornicatum tribunal circumagitur, cui duo alia minora tribunalia unum à dextra, alterum à læva adhærent, pro his tribunalibus transversa ambulatio patet, per cujus utrumque cornu in ædem est ingressus: reliquum ædes quod ad occasum extenditur duabus cellis [= side aisles], una hinc, altera illinc, mediaque ambulatione [= nave] constat, è cellis illa quæ est à meridie à tergo parietem in hemicycli formam ductum habet, à fronte (qua transversam ambulationem spectat) tota patet: altera vero quæ est à septentrione in sacellum est versa in quod temere non datur ingressus, utpote ara & *Bartholomæi Colleonis* monumento religiosum. (M. Antonii Michaelis, *Agri et urbis Bergomatis descriptio*, anno MDXVI, ed. Graevius et Burmannus, *Thesaurus Antiquitatum et Historiarum Italiae*, IX, pt. 7, p. 31).

29 1647. Piombò di mattina a buon hora la saetta in Santa Maria Maggiore, entrò nel campanile, passò per l'organo, trascorse gl'altari, cagiando moltissimi danni. (Calvi, II, 539).

30 1651. In S. Maria Maggiore cauandosi verso la parte Orientale la terra, à fine di piantar li ponti per la stuccatura, si faceua in quella parte del tempio. . . . (*Ibid.*, II, 420).

31 1655. Solennizandosi con ogni dimostrazione d'allegrezza l'assontione al Pontificato d'Alessandro Papa VII dalla moltitudine di luminari posti nella sommità del Campanile di S. Maria Maggiore acceso il fuoco consumò in puoco tempo, & distrusse il piombo tutto [*sic*] di cui era la cupola ricoperta. Danno, che non si potè riparare se non con la spesa di mille scudi per rifarla di nuovo. *Diar. Par.* (Calvi, II, 91).

32 Genaio XV, 1660. A fine di render più spatiosa, e vaga la Chiesa di S. Maria Maggiore souerchiamēte dal recinto dell'antico Battisterio in essa riposto occupata, diede in questo giorno la Città nel pieno maggior Consiglio a Presidente della Misericordia licenza, di poterlo far demolire, come poi fù esseguito nel venturo Febraio. *Ex. lib. Cons. Ciuit.* 1660. (Calvi, I, 93).

33 È disposta la nobil Chiesa a forma di Croce, con sublime non meno che vaghissima cupola nel mezzo tutta a stucco, & oro di pieno rilieuo, come è anco il rimanente della Chiesa, leuata vna parte verso il Vescouato, non ancor terminata. (*Ibid.*, 290). . . . Tutta la Chiesa si è posta a stucco l'anno 1670. (*Ibid.*, 355).

34 They bear the inscription:

ANNO DOMINI MDCCLXXI.

III. Beneath the accumulated additions of later centuries, the church still preserves almost intact the original Lombard structure, and is, indeed, notwithstanding the tasteless modern decorations, one of the very finest XII century edifices of all Italy. It consists of a nave two bays long, two side aisles, projecting transepts with eastern absidioles (the southern transept has also a western absidiole) (Plate 23, Fig. 2), a choir of a single bay, flanked by side aisles, and an apse. The bays of the nave are slightly oblong, those of the transepts very oblong. It is probable that the nave was originally spanned by a single transverse arch, supporting a wooden roof, but in the present condition of the church it is impossible to be certain, for the nave walls have been rebuilt in their upper portions and in their lower portions covered with intonaco. The system of the choir was evidently alternate, a single bay of the nave embracing two of the side aisles. The existing groin vault of the choir, I believe, is not original, but was reconstructed in the XVI century. The octagonal cloistered vault over the crossing was probably originally carried on arched squinches, but this part of the edifice also has been entirely made over, so that it is impossible to be certain of the original dispositions. The upper portions of the north and south transept have similarly been entirely rebuilt, and, like the nave, are now supplied with a roof carried on modern transverse arches. The side-aisle vaults, which are not domed, have probably been rebuilt or at least denatured.

Over the side aisles of the nave and choir there existed in the Lombard basilica a high gallery, which is still extant, although walled off. These galleries are among the best preserved parts of the Lombard edifice (Plate 23, Fig. 1). They are covered by groin vaults, of which the transverse and wall arches disappear towards the springing. The original vaults are highly domed. The diagonal ribs of the vaults of the gallery of the choir must be barocco additions, and the vaults of the north gallery of the choir, which are not domed, have evidently been entirely made over. In the choir the galleries opened upon the nave by means of bifora, but in the main body of the edifice by grouped triforia (Plate 23, Fig. 1), of which the central arch was pointed.

At present the galleries and nave are covered by a roof of continuous slope, and although the upper part of the edifice has obviously been remade, it is probable that there never was a clearstory. The lower story of the campanile cuts across the southern absidiole, and therefore must be later than it.

An inspection of the masonry is sufficient to show that there are in the church two distinct eras of construction. To the later belong the upper part of the southern transept, the entire west wall of the southern transept, with its absidiole (Plate 23, Fig. 2), the south wall of the nave (Plate 23, Fig. 2), the north wall of the nave, and the west façade. These portions are constructed of rough ashlar, with small stones of irregular shape and horizontal courses frequently broken. This masonry contrasts strongly with the careful ashlar of the rest of the edifice (Plate 23, Fig. 4). Strangely enough, however, the rougher ashlar is of a later epoch than the smoother. This will be demonstrated below in studying the ornament of the two portions of the edifice. It is, however, shown also by a careful study of the masonry itself, for the inside of the nave gallery (Plate 23, Fig. 1), belonging to the second epoch of construction, is finished with ashlar even finer than that of the first epoch. It is evident that the work of constructing the church was suspended for a considerable time and that, when it was resumed, for reasons of economy, inferior masonry was employed.

The existing cupola is a curious mixture of old and new fragments. The masonry is covered with plaster and the Gothic capitals are modern. It appears to preserve very little of its original character.

IV. The capitals of the church form an interesting study, and confirm the fact already indicated by the masonry that the church belongs to two distinct eras of construction. In the gallery of the choir the capitals are foliated, with broad, flat leaves, or are of the wreathed type familiar at Fontanella al Monte. In the exterior galleries of the eastern absidioles is a remarkable series of capitals showing a great variety of design. Some are of Corinthianesque type, with feathery acanthus leaves (Plate 22, Fig. 6); several have well sculptured eagles (Plate 22, Fig. 7); some are adorned with grotesques and one has sculptures representing the four archangels blowing trumpets. These capitals are very similar to those of S. Fedele at Como (Plate 63, Fig. 1, 8) although evidently somewhat more advanced in style. To the second era of construction belong the capitals of the nave gallery, of Corinthian type, with broad, uncarved leaves (Plate 23, Fig. 1) and those of the western absidiole of the southern transept of a high bell type somewhat Gothic in character (Plate 23, Fig. 2). The apses and absidioles are decorated with practicable galleries (Plate 22, Fig. 5; Plate 23, Fig. 2). In the portions of the edifice belonging to the first era of construction, beneath the galleries are placed a row of blind arches finely moulded and supported on shafts engaged on pilaster strips (Plate 22, Fig. 5). These arches recall those of the cathedral of Parma. In those belonging to the second era of construction (Plate 23, Fig. 2), there are simply arched corbel-tables supported on pilaster strips. In the southern absidiole is an elaborate cornice and a string-course adorned with a guilloche in which are sprinkled grotesques. The north absidiole is elaborately ornamented with moulded ornaments in both string-course and cornice (Plate 22, Fig. 5), and the same motives are repeated in the central apse. The mouldings are numerous and fine.

The triforium, both in the choir and in the nave, is lighted by bifora, with broad-leaved capitals (Plate 23, Fig. 2).

In the eastern absidioles of the southern transept, there is a sculptured capital, unfortunately broken. On one side is represented the sacrifice of

Isaac by Abraham, with the angel and ram (Gen., xxii, 11, 13), on the other
the angel appearing to Abraham (Gen., xxii, 15). Notwithstanding a certain
crudity in the details of the faces, feet, etc., these figures are very fine. The
technique is excellent, as witnessed by the deep undercutting, the composition
superb and splendidly architectural. By the same hand appears to be the
southern portal (Plate 23, Fig. 4), which is part of the original basilica, and
antedates the Lombard porch which was merely added on at a subsequent
epoch. This portal is in many orders, very elaborately shafted and moulded,
and ornamented with spirals, interlaces, bead-mouldings, etc. In more than
one detail it recalls the portal at Borgo S. Donnino (Plate 27, Fig. 3). The
capitals of the western jamb are adorned with feathery, finely carved acanthus
leaves. On the eastern jamb the capitals are replaced by a frieze with figure
reliefs. To the left is shown the Visitation, with the singular detail that two
handmaidens on either side hold the cloaks of Mary and Elizabeth. Elizabeth's
handmaiden is apparently naked to the waist. The sculptor has succeeded
in elegantly expressing by means of the flying draperies the motion of Mary
and her handmaiden, who appear fairly to rush towards Elizabeth. There
follows the apparition of the angel to Joseph. Joseph holds a cane in his
right hand, the angel grasps his left arm with a firmness that suggests coercion
rather than moral suasion. The last scene represents the Presentation. The
Virgin offers the Christ-Child to Simeon, who stands behind an altar. Back
of Simeon is seen a handmaiden bearing two turtle doves. The draperies
in these sculptures are treated in broad masses, a little differently from those
of the capital of the absidiole. On the other hand numerous details, such as
the curious zigzags at the bottom of the garments, the enormous hands and
the crudity in the treatment of the faces and details of the anatomy, combined
with the architectural feeling and excellent composition common to the two
works, leave no doubt that they are by the same hand.

The southern porch is, from many points of view, a most interesting
monument (Plate 23, Fig. 4). As is evident from the inscription already
cited, it was added to the church in 1360. A close study of the structure,
however, gives reason to believe that the attic was built subsequently, and,
as the style would seem to indicate, in the early part of the XV century.
Now, we have already seen that the statues of Christ and the Annunciation
over this southern portal were added in 1403; it is therefore altogether
probable that the attic is of the same epoch. This attic is a most important
monument of mediæval archæology because of the reliefs with which it is
sculptured. Those on the south and west faces representing Christ, the
twelve apostles and five saints, among whom figure SS. Lawrence and Anthony,
need concern us little. Not so, however, those on the east face, which show
four genre scenes representing the life and activities of mediæval builders.
In the great dearth of documents referring to the building trades in the
Middle Ages, these reliefs, which have never before been published, nor, I

believe, even noticed, assume the greatest importance. In the first relief is shown a man seated at a desk and drawing with a pair of compasses. He has a curious skull cap which covers his ears and neck, and wears a sort of jerkin, apparently of leather, whose sleeves are fastened with buttons or thongs on the lower edge. Behind him is what looks like a pine-apple, but which is probably merely an ornament of the bench on which he is seated. This figure is probably intended to represent the head master-builder. His bench is more elaborate than that of the others, all of whom face him, and he is distinguished from them by his head-dress. Below is the inscription [SCV]LTORETVS, exceedingly difficult to interpret, but which is probably a latinization of the diminutive of the Italian word, *scultore*. In the second relief is shown a builder engaged in working a capital, like the similar figures in the Porta dei Principi of Modena cathedral (Plate 142, Fig. 4) and in the bronze doors of S. Zeno at Verona (Plate 234, Fig. 1). He has a head-dress of cloth caught back of his ear and allowed to flow behind, leaving the neck and ear uncovered. He appears to have a leathern jerkin like the head master-builder. He is seated on a stool and is working at a capital, which is held inverted, perhaps on a stand before him. Below is the inscription ARISTATIVS. This word, so far as I have been able to discover, is not found elsewhere in mediæval Latin, but is doubtless a technical term to indicate one of the grades in the profession of builder. The root must be identical with that of *aristato*, also a word of obscure meaning, but which is believed to have reference to a wooden structure erected on tombs.[35] The third relief shows a builder, clothed precisely like the second, but holding a chisel in his left hand and a hammer with a stone head in his right, and engaged in chiseling the neck of a capital after it has been placed in position. Taken in connection with the second relief, this shows that the mediæval builders blocked out roughly their capitals before placing them in position, but finished them afterwards. Below is the inscription PIS[C]HOMASTIVS, another word which does not occur elsewhere in mediæval Latin, but which it is natural to connect with the Italian verbs *pizzare* and *pizzicare*. The fourth scene represents a builder with a curious Oriental cap, gathered in a tuft at the top and with a flat band below. He is engaged in hollowing out with a stone hammer the inside of an object the precise nature of which it is impossible to determine, but which looks as though it might be a capital in its first stage of manufacture. Below is the inscription GRECHVS, which gives rise to many conjectures upon the extent of Byzantine influence over the mediæval building trades. From these reliefs it may be adduced that c. 1400 the head master-builder at Bergamo was known as a *scultoretus*, who occupied himself chiefly with making drawings, and that he had under him three grades of assistants, known respectively as *grechus*, *pischomastius* and

[35] See Du Cange. Cf. the Greek word ἀριστεύω.

117

aristatius, the first of whom cut out roughly the capital or stone to be sculptured, the second of whom blocked it out and the third of whom put on the finishing touches after it had been placed in position.

The northern portal of the choir is interesting, not only because it is a surely dated monument of 1367, but because it is one of the very few thoroughly flamboyant architectural works which exist in Italy. It is adorned with sculptures: above, the Crucifixion and two angels; on the pinnacles, Mary and John. In the lunette is depicted the birth of the Virgin: Joachim, S[ANCTVS] IOAHAN, stands back of the bed on which is seen S[ANCTA] . ANNA sitting upright. By the side of the latter is seen S[ANCTA] ILIZEBETH and S[ANCTA] SOSANA, the latter with her hands pressed together in the attitude of prayer. The new-born child is being washed by St. Luke, the physician, S[ANCTVS] LVC[A], and by S[ANCTA] . NESTSIA and in a half-open door to the extreme left stands Simeon, S[ANCTVS] SIMIIO. The inscriptions are all incised and evidently bad copies of the original painted ones. The northern transept portal is a fine example of the decorative art of the XIV century.

In the galleries of the church are preserved the remains of leaded glass undoubtedly ancient.

V. It has been seen that the choir of the church and the transepts in part are shown by internal evidence to be the earliest portions of the edifice.[36] The style of the architecture of the eastern portions of the edifice is completely in accord with the documentary evidence that the church was begun in 1137, and may be accepted as a certainly dated monument of that time. After the completion of the choir, works must have been suspended for a considerable period. They were resumed in 1187, in a style materially different. At this time the transepts were finished and the nave added. The southern portal (Plate 23, Fig. 4), showing a close analogy to the sculptures of Borgo S. Donnino (Plate 27, Fig. 3), can hardly be earlier than c. 1210, and indicates that the second period of construction covered a considerable period of years. Finally, the Lombard porches were added in 1351 and 1360, and the northern portal of the choir in 1367.

[36] The western absidiole of the south transept (Plate 23, Fig. 2) is shown to belong to the second era of construction by its masonry and the character of its capitals, and the upper portion of the northern transept belongs to the same period, as is shown by the character of its masonry, executed in a stone different from that of the first period. The cornices of both transepts, decorated with arched corbel-tables almost Gothic in character, belong to the second period.

BIELLA,[1] BATTISTERO

(Plate 24, Fig. 2)

I. The interesting baptistery of Biella stands in the main piazza of the city, adjoining the cathedral. A brief description of the edifice was published by Mullatera in 1778, but the earliest publication of any adequacy was that of Mella, which appeared in 1873. The monument was subsequently studied from an archæological standpoint by De Dartein, Cattaneo, and by Commendatore Rivoira.[2] The plans and photographs in the local publication of Roccavilla are of value, and for the history of the monument the work of Schiaparelli should be consulted. In the Museo Civico di Belle Arti at Turin there is preserved a water-colour drawing of the baptistery made by Cav. G. B. Degubernatis (1773-1837). This sketch is important because it shows the baptistery as it was before restoration, when it was still surrounded by other edifices.

II. The baptistery at present belongs to the cathedral church of S. Maria and S. Stefano, but formerly belonged to the collegiate church of S. Stefano, which was demolished in 1872. S. Stefano was the oldest and most venerable church of Biella, but nothing is known of its origin.[3] The earliest reference to it in historical documents is in a deed of 1027, where the church appears as a pieve supplied with a chapter of canons.[4] It is not known when this chapter was instituted, but it must have been of great dignity, since in the XII century it comprised twenty canons and twelve chaplains.[5] In 1772 the diocese of Biella was founded, and the church of S. Maria Maggiore, an edifice of the XV century, became the cathedral. When the church of S. Stefano was torn down its title was added to that of the church of S. Maria.[6] About 1880 the church underwent a radical restoration, of which no exact account has been preserved. From ancient descriptions, however, and the data referred to above, it is possible to form some idea of the changes wrought in the edifice at this time. That the works were undertaken in a very radical spirit is sufficiently indicated in the monograph of Mella, who pleads for the preservation of the monument, which one party in the commune was desirous of destroying. He proposed as an alternative solution that it should be bodily transported into the piazza! This project, happily, was never executed. But the building, freed from the various edifices which had been built around it, was deprived of its crypt, added in 1791, and seems to have been subjected to a general overhauling. A great many of the bifora must date from this period, since they do not appear in

[1] (Novara).   [2] 216.   [3] Mullatera, 14.
[4] Schiaparelli, 224; Gabotto, 337.   [5] Mullatera, 25.
[6] Strafforello, *Novara*, 70. For a description of S. Stefano, see Roccavilla, 21 f.

the old drawings. In recent years, and between the two visits which I made to Biella—one in 1910 and the other in 1913—the building was subjected to a further restoration. This consisted chiefly in stripping the intonaco from the interior, an operation which brought to light the remains of valuable frescos of the XIV and XV centuries.

III. The plan of this little structure is peculiar, and comprises a square central area, each side of which is occupied by a semicircular niche in the lower story. The second story externally is not square, but octagonal (Plate 24, Fig. 2), the walls of each side of the square being brought to a very obtuse angle on the axis. Internally, the dome of the nave is of an irregular oblong shape, and is carried on conical arched squinches in two orders. The lower part of the dome is pierced by a clearstory (Plate 24, Fig. 2). The entire edifice is surmounted by a little square ædicule with bifora in each face (Plate 24, Fig. 2). This ædicule is ancient, since it appears in the Turin drawing. The angles of the lower story are supplied with salient buttresses (Plate 24, Fig. 2) of about 32 centimetres projection, which evidently formed part of the original construction.

The masonry (Plate 24, Fig. 2) is extremely crude, and consists of roundish pebbles from a river bed, mixed with fragments of brick. The pebbles are laid, for the most part, at haphazard, and in thick mortar-beds, but in places there is a suggestion of horizontal coursing. The pilaster strips and buttresses are formed of bricks, which measure about $5 - 8 \times 24 - 32 \times 16 - 24$ centimetres, but are often cut. These bricks are not cross-hatched, and are laid in horizontal courses, the broad side frequently out. The mortar-beds average from 1 to 4 centimetres in thickness. In the main body of the structure herring-bone work occurs. There are numerous scaffolding holes (Plate 24, Fig. 2).

IV. Internally the edifice is without distinctive decoration, except that the apse arches are in two orders. The exterior is ornamented with cornices formed of semicircular niches, the second orders of which are carried on pilaster strips (Plate 24, Fig. 2). Before the doorways are embryonic Lombard porches.

V. The cornices (Plate 24, Fig. 2) recall those of S. Ambrogio (Plate 117, Fig. 5)—c. 940, S. Eustorgio (Plate 127, Fig. 4)—c. 1000, S. Vincenzo in Prato (Plate 135, Fig. 4)—c. 830, and S. Calimero (Plate 125, Fig. 2)—c. 995—of Milan. They are hence of a type in use throughout the IX and X centuries, and offer no very precise indication of date. The masonry, with its horizontal and herring-bone courses, is more advanced than that of Galliano (Plate 99, Fig. 1)—1007, though inferior to that of S. Nazzaro Sesia (Plate 201, Fig. 5)—1040, and even Lomello (Plate 111, Fig. 3)—c. 1025. Commendatore Rivoira believed he recognized in the squinches of the dome a type of construction more primitive than that of Galliano, but as a matter of fact the reverse is the case, for at Biella the squinches are double instead of single, and some attempt is made to round the angles of the dome. The baptistery of Biella shows, moreover, a remarkably advanced construction in the use of salient buttresses, a constructive expedient already known to the Romans, it is true,[7] but unpractised during the Carlovingian epoch, and even little used by Lombard builders before the very end of the XI century. At Lomello (Plate 106)—c. 1025, and Sannazzaro Sesia (Plate 200)—1040, it is entirely lacking. It was, however, known to the builders of the first half of the XI century, and occasionally used by them.[8] The use of these buttresses at Biella gives reason for assigning the structure to the very latest epoch allowed by the character of the masonry, that is, to c. 1040. This ascription of date is confirmed by the observation that the masonry of the baptistery at Biella is almost identical with that of the neighbouring campanile, the only surviving work of the destroyed church of S. Stefano. This campanile, as shown by the use of arched corbel-tables and by other characteristics, can not be earlier than 1040.

BOLOGNA, SS. NABORRE E FELICE

(Plate 26, Fig. 4)

I. The crypt of S. Zama is situated beneath the present military hospital, which was formerly a convent, but which has been transformed into a chapel dependent upon the neighbouring church of S. Nicolò. The latter in turn depends upon S. Maria della Carità. The monument has been the object of a monograph by my friend, Mgr. Belvideri.

II. The history of the crypt of S. Zama presents peculiar obscurity, and it is necessary to choose one side of an awkward dilemma. One must accept either the unauthenticated local tradition or the equally unfounded conjectures of modern criticism. According to Alberti,[1] S. Zama and his successor, S. Faustiniano, were buried in the church of S. Felice, which previously had been known as S. Pietro, and which had been founded by S. Zama as the cathedral of Bologna.[2] Mgr. Belvideri, however, finds reason to believe that the cathedral of Bologna has always been situated where it now is, and that our edifice was founded by S. Felice, the predecessor of S. Petronio. Lanzoni[3] calls attention to the fact that the early bishops, Zama, Faustiniano, Partenio,

---

[7] See my *Construction of Lombard and Gothic Vaults*, 5.

[8] Witness Stradella (Plate 208)—c. 1035, and Calvenzano (Plate 38)—c. 1040.

[1] 37; lib. II, an. 270.

[2] See also *ibid.*, lib. III, end. Cf. Pullieni, 39.   [3] 295.

Giocondo, Tertulliano and Felice, according to a tradition of the XIII and XIV centuries, were all buried at SS. Naborre e Felice. The church, therefore, in early times, if it was not the cathedral of Bologna, at least enjoyed considerable importance.

About the year 1100 Benedictine monks were established in the church,[4] but in 1686 these had been supplanted by nuns of the same order.[5] According to Alberti the church was at one period held by Franciscan nuns. In 1911 the crypt, which is the only part of the old basilica extant, was restored.

III, IV. In plan the crypt is somewhat irregular, and consists of five aisles of four bays each, terminating to the eastward and to the westward in three apses of which in each case the central one corresponds to one of the three central aisles. In the north and south outer rows the supports of the second and third free-standing piers from the west are of disproportionate size. Although built of old bricks I do not believe that these piers formed part of the original construction. They were probably here introduced instead of the colonnettes employed elsewhere in order to provide support for the piers of the upper church when these were rebuilt in the Renaissance epoch. Heavy as they are, they were, nevertheless, insufficient for the enormous weight imposed upon them, since a much heavier rectangular pier was introduced at a later epoch, blocking up entirely the space between the piers above described and the colonnettes adjoining to the west. The entire crypt was very much built over at the time these piers were added, and the vaults, walls and piers all seem to be essentially a work of the Renaissance, although constructed of old materials. Only in the southern absidiole is a portion of the original wall and vault still extant. The masonry consists of large bricks of irregular shape, separated by thick beds of mortar and laid in horizontal courses. The bricks are so rough and so much damaged that it is impossible to say whether they were originally cross-hatched. The vault of this absidiole is peculiar because, instead of being a half dome, it consists of an irregular groin vault with wall ribs. It has been much repaired, but may retain its original form. The windows, widely splayed, and intended to serve without glass, are still preserved in this absidiole, although walled up. One is still in perfect preservation, and parts of two others may be seen. Many of the colonnettes are evidently pilfered, and consist of monoliths characterized by mouldings which are cut down within the surface of the shafts. Some are upside down and pieced out with bricks, an arrangement which, however, probably does not antedate the Renaissance construction. Two other colonnettes are octagonal, with octagonal capitals, precisely like those of S. Pietro at Acqui (1023). Several of the capitals in stone are of the block type, as are all those executed in brick. Four capitals are of the type of the one illustrated in Plate 26,

[4] Belvideri, 4.
[5] Mabillon, *Museum Italicum*, I, 198.

Fig. 4.[6] Although of the Corinthianesque type, which suggests the developed Lombard style, the volutes are merely scratched on the surface in a manner which is entirely Carlovingian. Another capital, with a single leaf scratched on each corner, and a spiral-fluted ornament in the middle of each face, recalls the capitals of 903 in the crypt of S. Savino at Piacenza (Plate 186, Fig. 2, 3), but is much better executed.

V. The similarity of certain piers of this church with those of S. Pietro at Acqui of 1023 give reason to believe that the Romanesque fragments date from c. 1020. The capital illustrated in Plate 26, Fig. 4, although of a type not precisely paralleled in other edifices of the time, on the whole accords well with this date, which explains the union, which we there find, of Carlovingian technique and more developed Lombard forms. The capitals of the crypt of S. Vincenzo at Galliano (Plate 96, Fig. 2) show that in 1107 the Lombard builders were capable of executing capitals with quite as great a degree of technical skill as is shown in these capitals of S. Zama. In fact, there are numerous close analogies of technique between the capitals of S. Zama and those of Galliano. On the other hand, the persistence of Carlovingian tradition, as witnessed by the survival at S. Zama of certain capitals resembling, although more advanced than, those executed at S. Savino at Piacenza in 903, can be well understood in an edifice of the transition from the Carlovingian to the Lombard manner. I have, therefore, no hesitation in assigning the Romanesque fragments of S. Zama to the year 1020.[7]

[6] I can not agree with Mgr. Belvideri either that these capitals are of the IX century or that they belonged to a ciborio.

[7] In connection with the crypt at S. Zama should be mentioned the similar but less interesting crypt of SS. Vitale e Agricola in the same city. This edifice is characterized by slightly domed vaults with disappearing ribs, by apse vaults similar to those at S. Zama but restored, by uncarved capitals and by square colonnettes. The upper church, some fragments of which are preserved in the back yard of the existing edifice, had piers which consisted of four shafts separated by rectangular spurs and plain cubic capitals with incised lines, like those of S. Stefano. The brickwork is not dissimilar to that of the crypt of S. Zama, and the pilaster strips of the flanks seem to indicate that the arched corbel-tables must have been grouped two and two. The church may have been of the second quarter of the XI century, and it is greatly to be regretted that more has not been preserved. According to the legend this church was founded as a convent of nuns by the mythical S. Giuliana, in 396, but greater faith is merited by an inscription of 1362 in which the consecration is referred to the year 428. The edifice was reconstructed in 1476, restored in 1603, and again reconstructed in 1641. The nuns who were there in the XVIII century were suppressed at the time of the Revolution. (*Notizie storico-artistiche della parrocchia de' santi Vitale ed Agricola in Bologna.* Bologna, Tipi. a S. Tommaso d'Aquino, 1853). The capitals of S. Zama should also be compared with the cubic and carved capitals of the crypt of S. Damiano now preserved in the Museo Civico of Bologna. (Savioli, II, pt. 2, p. 142; Patricelli, 52).

LOMBARD ARCHITECTURE

BOLOGNA, S. STEFANO

(Plate 24, Fig. 3, 4, 5, 6; Plate 25, Fig. 1, 2, 3, 4, 5, 6, 7)

I. The complex group of buildings known under the collective title of S. Stefano, comprises seven distinct edifices: the basilica of SS. Pietro e Paolo; the circular church of S. Sepolcro; a court known as the Atrio di Pilato; a group of shrines called La Trinità; a church known as the Crocefisso; the crypt of the Confessi, placed beneath this church; and, finally, the cloister of the Celestines. The whole constitutes a shrine known as Nuova Gerusalemme, symbolical of the scenes of the Passion in the Holy City, each part and detail of the Bolognese edifice being typical of some spot connected with the life of our Lord. In former times the Bolognese shrine enjoyed an enormous popularity, and even to-day is not infrequently the object of pilgrimage.

It may be said at once that learned Bologna has found in the shrine of S. Stefano an archæological puzzle which has taxed the ingenuity and cleverness of her most brilliant historians and archæologists. The edifice has been made the object of discussion by a great number of scholars, not only of Bologna, but, indeed, of the world. Of the archæologists who have studied the edifice from a purely architectural point of view, the first in point of time is Séroux d'Agincourt, who, in 1823, published a plan of the whole shrine, sections of SS. Pietro e Paolo, S. Sepolcro and the cloister of the Celestines, as well as a plate of details.[1] Although of very small scale, his drawings are to-day of value, because they show the shrine as it was in the early part of the XIX century. Even more valuable is the large view of the interior of S. Sepolcro, published by Knight[2] in 1843, and in which the old Calvary and the screen between the columns and the Renaissance responds of the side aisle are clearly shown. About the middle of the century Osten[3] published his drawings, larger and more exact than those of Séroux d'Agincourt, and similarly important because they show the condition of the building before restoration. Somewhat later appeared the sumptuous drawings of De Dartein. In 1883 De Fleury[4] studied and illustrated the Calvary. In the following year Mothes[5] published a study of the architecture in which he showed much undigested historical knowledge combined with ignorance of the science of archæology. In 1897 Zimmermann[6] contributed a critical analysis of the sculptures. From about the same time dates Professor Goodyear's observation of the curves in plan of the cloister. Corrado Ricci, in his *Guide* of Bologna, published a brief résumé of the main facts in the history of the monument, which deserves mention.

[1] IV, Plate 28, Fig. 1-14. [2] I, Plate XX. [3] Plates XXXVII-XL.
[4] Plate CXCI; Vol. III, 29. [5] I, 283. [6] 166.

124

BOLOGNA, S. STEFANO

The list of writers who have studied S. Stefano in a purely historical spirit is even longer. The first to approach the problems which the church presents, and especially the manuscript chronicle, in a truly critical manner, was Petracchi, who published in 1747 a history which is a really remarkable achievement for the age. The radical conclusions of Petracchi were sharply attacked by the conservative Formagliari, and a lively controversy ensued between the two scholars. More radical, but less scientific than Petracchi, was the work of Bianconi, published in 1772. Bianconi erroneously supposed that SS. Pietro e Paolo was the ancient cathedral of Bologna, and S. Sepolcro its baptistery. He believed that the symbolism of the New Jerusalem was given to the shrine only at the time of the Crusades. In 1784 appeared the pretentious work of Savioli, which contained the first publication of numerous documents of the utmost importance for the history of S. Stefano. The XIX century was singularly barren of contributions to the history of our monument. Passing over Melloni's[7] attempt to interpret the text of the *Passionario*, we come to the great work of Lanzoni, published in 1907, a production, in its fine critical sense and deep erudition, worthy of the best traditions of Bologna. This work contains the best critical study of the life of S. Petronio, the *Sermo* and the *Passionario*, that has yet appeared. The work of Lanzoni was continued by Testi Rasponi, who contributed new and important observations bearing upon the history of S. Stefano. Unfortunately, his work is marred by several evident errors. In reply to the radicals Lanzoni and Testi Rasponi, the conservative Mgr. Belvideri published in 1913 a study of the vase of Luitprando, in which he sought to defend the authenticity of the S. Stefano tradition.

In addition to works of archæology and history, the shrine of S. Stefano has always been the subject of numerous books of piety, intended primarily to serve as ciceroni to explain the mysteries of the place to the faithful. These books of piety are frequently also works of erudition, and may not seldom be consulted with profit for purely historical questions. Moreover, they almost all of them contain a very detailed and exact description of the edifice as it was at the time they were written, and are hence of the greatest archæological importance for determining the changes and transformations to which the shrine has been subjected. The earliest of these books of piety is that of Gargano, which was printed in 1520. It is unfortunately extremely brief, but contains some notices of great value. In 1575 appeared the more elaborate work of Patricelli, which was reprinted in 1584 and is especially valuable because it contains a corpus of the inscriptions existing in the church at the end of the XV century. Many of these inscriptions, and notably several regarding Renaissance and barocco restorations, no longer exist. In 1600 appeared the work of Pullieni, a curious production, written in dialogue, and

[7] 366 f.

notable for piety rather than erudition. The author's keen interest in relics, however, has induced him to make incidentally several remarks which are of great value archæologically as showing the state of the church in his time. In 1633 Mainardi published the earlier chronicle of Alidosi. Four years later appeared the *Nuova Gerusalemme* of Casale, the most complete and erudite of the works of piety dealing with the shrine. So well done was the work of Casale that it has served ever since, as a sort of classic, and no other book of devotion equally dignified has since been written on the church.

In the choir book, or antiphonal, No. 121, preserved in the Museo di S. Petronio, in the sacristy of that church, there is a miniature containing a view of S. Stefano from the piazza. The church of the Crocefisso appears to be in construction, since it is roofless and a ladder leans against the façade. This miniature must therefore date from the middle of the XVII century.

For an account of the restoration executed in the last quarter of the XIX century, there should be consulted the full account of Gozzadini, published in 1878, and the briefer official account of Faccioli, published in 1901.

II. The source of almost all of our knowledge of S. Stefano, and the source also, be it said, of the very grave archæological difficulties connected with the church, is a codex which formerly belonged to the monastery, and which is now preserved in the library of the University of Bologna. It is a large volume in folio and bears the number 1473.[8] Among other compositions this codex contains three of the utmost importance for our subject: the first is a history of the translation of the relics of the saints Vitale and Agricola; the second is a life of S. Petronio; and the third is a *Sermo* concerning the discovery of relics at S. Stefano, inserted in the life of the saint. The codex has been studied and its contents more than once published,[9] but the historical questions which it raises are so delicate that to discuss them adequately it is necessary to go back to the original autograph.

The date of the codex is, fortunately, not open to question. At the end of the volume[10] it is very explicitly stated that the book was finished in the year of our Lord 1180, in the eighteenth year of the abbacy of Landolfo, on Friday, which was the fourth day after the feast of St. Martin,[11] that it was

---

[8] This codex has been studied in detail by Testi Rasponi, so that a detailed analysis may here be dispensed with.

[9] The Bollandists (*Acta Sanctorum*, Octobris, Tomus II, Oct. 4, p. 466) have published the life under the title *Vita brevior Sancti Petronii Bonensis, Episcopi et Confessoris*, and at the end the *Sermo*, under the title *Inventio Reliquiarum Sancti Petronii, aliorumque sanctorum*. The best edition, however, is that of Lanzoni, p. 218 f. Copious extracts are to be found in many of the historians and books of piety cited above.

[10] Folio 331.

[11] The feast of St. Martin (the eleventh of November) fell upon a Tuesday in the year 1180, so that the fourth day following would have been a Saturday, not a Friday, unless—as was probably the case—Tuesday itself was counted as the first day.

written in the monastery of S. Stefano of Bologna, which is called Jerusalem; and that it had been placed in the archives of the monastery. The writer also states that, since he affectionately wished the book to be at the disposal of all men, he curses anyone who shall purloin, sell or buy the book, or fraudulently receive it, and wishes that any such be damned with Lucifer and be cursed sleeping, eating, drinking, fasting, watching, lying down, standing up and sitting. He wishes that all the prayers of the saints and of the entire church of God many serve such a one only for damnation, that his children may be fatherless and his wife a widow, that the extortioner may catch all that he hath, that strangers may spoil his labour, and that, as the earth swallowed alive Korah, Dathan and Abiram, so Hell may engulf him to be tortured for all eternity.[12]

The works contained in the codex are not all by the same author, nor written at the same time.[13] However, the three which particularly concern S. Stefano appear to be all the work of the same writer and to have been composed about 1180. The *Translatio,* for example, contains the account of a miracle which took place under the abbot Landolfo who, we know from the passage cited above, became abbot in 1162,[14] and was still sitting in 1180. The writer speaks of this event in the first person as an eyewitness. In dealing with events which took place long before his time, however, the author must have had good sources for his main facts, which are narrated with a fullness of detail and an accuracy which would not have been possible were

---

[12] Anno ab incarnatione dni *mill. cent. octuagesimo* abbatiante d̄n̄o landulfo *abbate discretissimo* deo et hominib'; diligendo fama sparsim notissimo anno uidelicet abbatie eius XVIII die scilicet ueneris. qui quarto die post festum Sc̄i martini epi secutus est. completus est in monasterio beatissimi p[ro]tomartyris stephani de ciuitate bononia quod uocatur hierl̄m līb̄ iste. et thesauris armarii iam dicti monasterii aggregatus. quod utiq; ad om̄ium homin̄u noticiam uenire affectuose uolumus ab isto die in antea quicuq; molestiam aliquam prefato monastio p[ro] libro isto intulerit. uel inferre passus quoque modo auxilium dando fuerit ablator. uenditor. uel emptor extiterit. cū eo non dubitet se habiturum portionem qui rapina arbitratus est ēe [= esse] se equalem d̄o dicens. Pon̄a sedem mēa ad aq[ui]lonem. et ero similis altissimo. Sitq̄; ex uictoritate [*sic*] dei et beati stephani mar̄t et om̄ium sc̄orum dominiq; landulfi abbatis totiusq; conuentus pretaxati monasterii anathema fraudulenter accipienti. Anathema sit dormiendo, comedendo, bibendo. ieiunando. uigilando. iacendo. stando. sedendo. Om̄s orationes sanctoru totiusq; ēccle dei sint il̄li ad dampnation̄e siantq. filii eius orphani. et uxor eius uidua. Scrutetur fenerator om̄em substantīa eius. et diripiant alieni labores eius. Et sicut tr̄a [= terra] chore. dathan. et abiron absorbuit uiuos: ita infernus eum deglutiat cū anḡlo Sathane sine fine crvciandum.—Notice that the letters italicized in our copy have been retouched in the codex, and that these letters are precisely the ones which form the date 1180. For the scriptural allusions in this passage see Phili., ii, 6; Isai., xiv, 13-14; Ps., cviii, 9, 11.

[13] Lanzoni, for example, has shown that the life of S. Bononio is earlier than 1033, and later than 1026. (Lanzoni, 258).

[14] The chronology of the codex is confirmed by a document of December 15, 1162, published by Savioli (I, pt. 2, p. 267), in which Landolfo appears as abbot.

he merely expanding a vague local tradition. His work, it is true, is padded out with a certain amount of gratuitous additions of his own, such as, for example, a disquisition upon the learning of Bologna; but these digressions do not particularly detract from the authenticity of the main facts which he relates.

The life of S. Petronio, although written at the same time, that is, between 1162 and 1180, and probably by the same author as the *Translatio,* is far less trustworthy. The author appears to have had no authentic source for his life of the saint, and to have improvised freely upon local traditions.[15] The *Sermo,* on the contrary, appears to be in the main a work quite worthy of faith and to have been written or at least inspired by an eyewitness of the inventions of 1141. When, however, the author relates events that occurred long before his own time, he had recourse to no other sources than the traditions of the monastery, and fell into frequent errors.

Of the three works the *Sermo* is undoubtedly the most important for the history of S. Stefano, and it will be well to take up its text in some detail. The book opens with the statement that S. Stefano of Bologna was first founded by S. Petronio, bishop of Bologna, and was by him called Jerusalem.[16] These opening words of the chronicler have given rise to much discussion. Undoubtedly, the monk is writing at the end of the XII century, of events of the V century, of which he had no very exact knowledge. Nevertheless, the tradition that S. Petronio founded S. Stefano is very strong. It is found in three documents earlier than the *Sermo* and dating from 1074, 1114 and 1144,[17] and is repeated by a chronicle of Bologna.[18] It is, moreover, a well known fact that S. Petronio was buried at S. Stefano and the author of the *Vita* implies that this was because he had built that basilica.[19] According to this same authority S. Petronio founded not only the church but the monastery as well.[20] The later life of the saint edited by the Bollandists, however, states that the saint founded the shrine of S. Stefano with its

---

[15] See the critical studies of Lanzoni and Testi Rasponi.

[16] Sermo de inuentione scar[um] reliq[u]arū. Cum omnis eloquentie preclara urbs bononia doctrinis inter ceteras mirifice splenderet uariis. et altiuidi in ōmib' honoris deferret eminentiā inclitam sci stephani eccl[esi]am a beatissimo olim petronio sce bononiensis eccle epo aprimeuo edificatam: et ierlm typice uocatam. diuina pietas uisitare dignata est.

[17] Lanzoni, 96.

[18] Hoc tempore beatus Petronius Bononiensis episcopus construxit in civitate Bononie templum miro opere constructum in honorem sancti Stefani protomartiris. (*Cronaca A, Corpus Chronicorum Bononiensium,* Raccolta Muritoriana, ed. Carducci, XVIII, 270).

[19] Et sepultus [Sanctus Petronius] est in basilica sci. stephani. quam ipse a fundamentis construxit. (f. 266).

[20] Monasterium quoque extra ciuitatem in uia que uergit ad orientem: in honore sci stephani p[ro]tomartyris. a fundamentis miro opere condidit. (f. 261).

symbolism of Jerusalem in connection with the pre-existing cathedral church of S. Pietro.[21]

The *Vita* of 1162-1180 states very clearly that S. Petronio built the shrine at Bologna to reproduce the holy spots in Jerusalem according to measurements which he himself had made on his pilgrimage to the Holy Land,[22] and such is the constant tradition at S. Stefano.[23] The critical historians have, however, shown themselves somewhat skeptical in regard to this. The earliest certain mention of a shrine of Jerusalem at S. Stefano is a document of 887.[24] It is certain, therefore, that the idea of the symbolical shrine is at least as old as the IX century. The argument of Mgr. Belvideri, who believes that the much disputed and extremely difficult inscription on the vase of Luitprando contains the name Jerusalem, and that the shrine must consequently have been known by this title from the first half of the VIII century, is to me not entirely convincing. Still more bold is the argument of Lanzoni, which seeks to establish the resemblance of the buildings of S. Stefano to those at Jerusalem destroyed in 614 and described by Procopius. In view of the many changes to which the S. Stefano buildings have been subjected, and the extremely vague data available on the Jerusalem edifices, such a conclusion seems extremely hazardous.

To return to the text cited from the later life of the saint, which speaks of S. Petronio as having erected a shrine in the pre-existing cathedral church of S. Pietro, it should be noted that there is excellent historical evidence that the church of S. Pietro was erected to receive the bodies of SS. Vitale and Agricola discovered by S. Ambrogio in 393. S. Ambrogio himself, and

---

21 Ubi vero ad urbem [Bononiam Petronius] accessit . . . basilicam sancti Petri, quæ tum extra urbem sedes episcopi erat, ingressus, Deo . . . gratias egit. . . . Deinde templa Dei di·turbata atque eversa refecit, et alia item nova, quo major ad Dei cultus in dies accessio fieret, summo Bononiensium studio ædificavit. Quorum unum Bartholomæo Apostolo, alterum Marco Euangelistæ, tertium Fabiano et Sebastiano Martyribus, quartum Martino, quintum Barbatiano Confessoribus, sextum Agathæ, septimum Luciæ Virginibus et Martyribus consecravit. Quin etiam templa duo, non longo inter se intervallo disjuncta, magnis rerum divinarum significationibus dedicavit, unum Stephano Protomartyri, alterum Joanni Euangelistæ. . . . In illo, quod sancto Stephano dicatum, cum ecclesia sanctorum Petri et Pauli, a beato Ambrosio consecrata, conjunxit, diligenter expressit imaginem, et montis, ubi in ara Crucis Dominus sanguinem pro generis humani salute effudit, et sepulchri, in quo idem mortuus conditus est. Quæ vero inter hæc duo templa planities loco submissiore intercedit, ejus, situ celebrem illam, quæ Josaphat vocatur, vallem repræsentavit. (*Vita Brevior Sancti Petronii* auctore Galesinio, ed. Jean de Bolland, *Acta Sanctorum,* October, II, 465).

22 See text cited below, pp. 141-142.

23 This is found, for example, in the vulgar life of the saint, written between 1257 and 1372 (ed. Lanzoni, 141-142). See text cited below, p. 130. The *Vita* of 1162-1180 constantly refers to S. Stefano as the New Jerusalem, and it is evident that at this epoch the term had been accepted time out of mind. Cf., *e.g.,* f. 267: in predicta sci stephani ecclā que uocatur ierlm. . . .

24 Testi Rasponi, 163; Savioli, I, pt. 2, p. 33.

Paolino, his authentic biographer, both record this invention, which therefore undoubtedly took place.[25] The *Translatio* implies that soon after a basilica was erected on the site of the existing church of S. Pietro to contain the newly discovered bodies.[26] It is certain that the existing basilica of S. Pietro bore the title of SS. Vitale e Agricola until the bodies of the saints were translated in 1019. When the codex was written, about 1180, the church bore the title of S. Isidoro, and it was only in subsequent times, and in consequence of the relics discovered in 1141 and claimed to be those of the Prince of the Apostles, that it acquired the present name of S. Pietro. It is also certain, not only from the *Translatio* but from the sarcophagi still preserved in the basilica, that the bodies of the saints Vitale and Agricola until 1019 reposed in the church now known as S. Pietro. It is, therefore, entirely probable that at least this portion of S. Stefano antedates the time of S. Petronio. This conclusion is confirmed by the fact that the discovery of numerous early Christian epitaphs[27] proves that at the end of the IV century there was already a cemetery about the church, for it is a well known fact that the early Christians always sought to lay their dead near the shrines of martyrs.

That, however, this pre-existing church of SS. Vitale e Agricola was a cathedral there is nothing to show except the assertions of later historians.[28] The hypothesis that the circular church of S. Sepolcro was originally a baptistery and was subsequently remade and given a new symbolism, is ingenious and plausible, but remains a mere conjecture, unsupported by historical evidence. It is, therefore, unproved that the cathedral of Bologna was ever placed in the church of SS. Vitale e Agricola.

Connected with the fact, undoubtedly historical, that the church of SS. Vitale e Agricola was founded by S. Ambrogio, is the legend that a certain widow, S. Giuliana, gave her substance to erect a church for the martyrs. The earliest full version of this legend occurs in the vulgar life of S. Petronio, written between 1257 and 1392, and probably in the XIV century.[29] In the

---

[25] Testi Rasponi, 139-140.

[26] [Ambrosius] bononīa adire festinauit . . . et eor[um] [Sanctorum Vitalis et Agricolae] corpora in loco sibi a d̄o reuelato: religioso studio sepulture commisit. (f. 327).

[27] One of these epitaphs dates either from 394, 396 or 402.

[28] See, for example, Bianconi, 5; Casale, 159-160; Ricci, 123.

[29] Et mentre che S. Petronio facea edificare questa sante opere una nobile et riccha donna bolognese, chiamata Giuliana, vedova, et serva di Dio, dispensando lhaver suo, fece edificare la chiesa di san Piero di consentimento et licentia di san Petronio. Et lì dove a laltare de la Trinitade in santo Stephano, dal sepulcro andando innanzi quel luoco fe fare san Petronio a similitudine del monte Calvario. Et di quelle due croce, che furono mettute in quel luoco, luna fe mettere a similitudine di quella, dove fu crucifisso il Figliolo de Dio (e questa e ne piu ne manco grande in longhezza et larghezza quanto fu quella assagiada per messer san Petronio). Et fe mettere li appresso quella pilla grande et quel predon grosso a similitudine di quella pila, in la

vulgar legend and the later *Vita,* it is true, S. Petronio is substituted for S. Ambrogio, but this is an evident error, since it was S. Ambrogio, not S. Petronio, who discovered the bodies of the martyrs. Although not related in detail by the chronicler of 1180, the legend of S. Giuliana was known to him, and the *Vita* distinctly refers to it in connection with the discovery of the bodies of SS. Vitale and Agricola by S. Ambrogio.[30]

This legend has given rise to a vast amount of discussion among the historians of Bologna. Bianconi[31] was the first to point out the similarity between the Bolognese legend and that of the good widow Giuliana of Florence, who, according to authentic documents, built a church for S. Ambrogio in the Tuscan city. Lanzoni[32] has reinforced by his successful historical criticism the thesis of Bianconi, proving that the legend of S. Giuliana originated in the misreading of the text of Ambrogio, and that it is due to two pseudo-Ambrogian documents earlier than the IX century, the *Epistula Sancto Ambrosio attributa de Martyrio Sanctorum Agricolae et Vitalis,* and the *Passio Sanctorum Agricolae et Vitalis.* The misidentification of S. Giuliana with the church of S. Stefano was doubtless furthered by the fact that a widow named Giulia actually was buried at S. Stefano. This tomb came to light in 1566, but was closed up again.[33] In 1913 it was again discovered by Mgr. Belvideri in S. Trinità. The early Christian epitaph of the VI century records a certain Giulia who lived for twenty-eight years and died survived by her husband. The entire legend therefore falls to the ground, and the supposed relics of S. Giuliana preserved in the church must be spurious.

To sum up, therefore, we must conclude that from all this mass of early legends, we can accept as historical only the fact that the church of SS. Vitale e Agricola was built at the end of the IV century in honour of the bodies of the saints discovered by S. Ambrogio. It remains to be determined exactly what changes and innovations S. Petronio wrought in the edifice.

We may at once reject any attempt at reconciling the legends by making Ambrogio and Petronio contemporaries. The result of the latest critical studies places the invention of the relics in 393, and Petronio's ministry from 432 to 450.[34] According to the *Vita* of 1162-1180, S. Petronio restored the churches of Bologna, among which the writer doubtless intends to include

quale Pilato se lavo le mani. (Ed. Lanzoni, 141-142). Compare with the later *Vita:* Quin etiam rogatu sanctæ Julianæ viduæ ecclesiam sanctis Vitali et Agricolæ consecravit; quam exædificandam eo loco pecunia sua curarat, ubi illi martyres excruciati fuerat. . . .

[30] Seu et sc̅e iuliane uenerabile corp'. quam beatus ambrosius mediolanensis ciuitatis archieps. cum reuelaret corpora sc̅orum uitalis et agricole. ore p[ro]prio collaudans: ita ait. Ea uero est sc̅a iuliana: que dn̅o templum optulit: atq' parauit. (f. 266r).

[31] 24.　　[32] 266.　　[33] Patricelli, 22.

[34] Lanzoni, 29. Petracchi (28) places the death of S. Petronio in 449.

SS. Vitale e Agricola, after the destruction by Theodosius.[35]   Authentic historical documents, however, prove that Bologna was never destroyed by Theodosius, and this whole passage must, therefore, be set aside as apocryphal. Attempts have been made to save the authenticity of the *Vita* by supposing a destruction of the city, not by Theodosius, but by Radagasso or Alaric.[36] Such hypotheses, however, rest upon mere conjecture.

In the *Vita Sancti Petronii*[37] is a privilege purporting to be of S. Ambrogio in favour of S. Stefano, but it is so obviously false that it may be passed by with a mere reference.   Similarly spurious is a bull of indulgence purporting to be of Celestine I and which seems to have been fabricated to stimulate the devotion of the faithful towards S. Stefano.   It is notable, however, that this bull must have been forged before 1476, since in that year it was confirmed by Sixtus IV in a bull published by Patricelli.[38]   The false bull, therefore, is of some historical value as evidence of the mediæval tradition of the foundation of S. Stefano.[39]

The statement of the chronicler that S. Petronio established a monastery at S. Stefano has caused much difficulty to the defenders of the authenticity of the legend, because it is known that at the time of the saint there were no monks in western Europe.   Sigonio tried to solve the difficulty by assuming that the monks were imported from Egypt.   Although accepted by numerous pious authors, this conjecture merits no faith.   The writer of 1180 had scant sources for the events of the early centuries which he narrates, and here, as elsewhere, fell into error.

What was it, then, that S. Petronio did to S. Stefano?   The fact that he was buried in the church, and that the venerable legend of fifteen centuries constantly links his name with that of the New Jerusalem, justifies the conviction that he must have restored, or enlarged, or altered in some way the pre-existing church of SS. Vitale e Agricola.   More than this it would be dangerous to say.   The tradition that he founded the New Jerusalem is neither contradicted nor confirmed by historical criticism.

---

[35] Cumq[ue]; uenerandus p̄at [Petronius] in throno pontificali resideret: primum quidem suarum uirtutum spūale iecit fundamentum. laborando scilicet ad reparationem ecclarum. theodosica uastatione dirutarum. ibidem quam plurimas reparauit.   (f. 261).

[36] Petracchi, 19-28.   [37] Folio 268 of the codex.

[38] Sanè dudum fœlicis recordationis Celestinus Papæ primus prędecessor noster, omnibus Christi fidelibus . . . ad ecclesiā sancti Stephani Bononien. Hierusalem nuncupatam per sanctę memoriæ Petronium Episcopum Bononiensem, ad instar Sepulcri Dominici erectam, & constructam, etc.   (65).

[39] Cum itaq[ue] in templo gloriosi prothomartiris Stephani, quod dicitur Hierusalem de Bononia, quod Seruus Dei Petronius eiusdem Ciuitatis Episcopus, instar Sepulchri Domini nostri Iesu Christi in Hierusalem erexit, & construxit.   (Patricelli, 62).   Attempts to save the authenticity of this bull by ascribing it to Clement I or to Clement III instead of to Celestine are wholly unsuccessful.   The document is obviously false.   It has been published also by Pullieni (221).

Gregory of Tours, who died in 594, is extremely interested in the saints Vitale and Agricola because certain of their relics had been translated to Clermont-Ferrand.[40] He relates in considerable detail a miracle of the saints which took place in his time at Bologna. From his account we learn that in the VI century the bodies of the martyrs were placed above ground, doubtless in the church of S. Pietro, as it is now known. It is notable that Gregory of Tours says nothing of the church being called by another name than that of the saints, which would tend to lead us to minimize the changes wrought there by S. Petronio.[41]

According to the *Sermo* it was S. Petronio who hid in various parts of the edifice of S. Stefano the relics of the saints which were discovered in the XII century.[42] It is evident, however, that this is a mere conjecture of the chronicler. The relics were found in the edifice, and who could have put them there if not S. Petronio, the founder of the same? But it is far more likely that they were hidden at a subsequent time when the church was imminently threatened with the danger of sack and pillage. In the Middle Ages it was the custom to secrete relics when danger of their being carried off as booty was impending. Now, we know that S. Stefano was placed without the walls of Bologna, and that in the early part of the X century it not only was threatened with pillage, but actually was sacked by the Hungarians. It is, therefore, entirely probable that the relics were hidden at about this epoch.

In the VIII century, or, more precisely, about 741, the king Luitprando gave to the church the large vase which, it appears, served for the distribution of consecrated hosts to the faithful on Holy Thursday, and which is now preserved in the Atrio di Pilato.[43]

The *Sermo* relates that S. Stefano was pillaged by the Hungarians, who

---

[40] *Historia Francorum,* lib. II, cap. 16, ed. M. G. H., *SS. Rerum Mer.,* I, 83.

[41] Agricola et Vitalis apud Bononiam Italiae urbem pro Christi nomine crucifixi sunt, quorum sepulchra, ut per revelationem fidelium cognovimus, quia nondum ad nos historia passionis advenit, super terram sunt collocata. Quae cum a multis, ut fit, vel tangeretur manu vel ore oscularentur, admonitus est aedituus templi, ut inmundi ab his arcerentur. Quidam audax atque facinorosus operturium unius tumuli removet, ut scilicet aliquid de sacris auferret cineribus; missoque introrsum capite, obpraessus ab eo, vix ab aliis liberatus, confusus abscessit; nec accipere meruit, quod temerario ausu praesumpsit, sed cum maiori deinceps reverentia sanctorum adivit sepulcra. (Gregorii Episcopi Turonensis *Liber in Gloria Martyrum,* cap. 43, ed. M. G. H., *SS. Rer. Mer.,* I, 517).

[42] Quam quidem idem reuerentissimus preclaris decorauerat honoribus. et plurimorum pretiosissimis scorum ditauerat reliquiis; Easq[ue], ne p[er]fidis inquam aliq[uis] subripiendi crudelissima: aut uiolenter auferendi: quandoq[ue] panderetur audacia: diuersis ocultandi tumulis exhibere curauit solertiā. (f. 267).

[43] This is not the place to enter upon a discussion of the many complex and much-discussed questions regarding this vase and its inscription. The recent monograph of Mgr. Belvideri contains full bibliographical references for those desiring to pursue the question further.

attempted to burn the cross in S. Croce, but in vain, since the cross miraculously resisted the flames. It does not appear whether the edifice itself was destroyed or not, although presumably such was the case.[44] This destruction by the Hungarians must have taken place in 903, when it is known that these barbarians descended on northern Italy and burned churches and monasteries in all directions. After this destruction the buildings of S. Stefano appear to have lain in ruin for a long period of years, and it is to the destruction of the barbarians rather than to the cooling of ardour in the faithful (to which the author of the *Sermo* ascribes it), that was due the wretched state of the shrine during the X century.[45]

In 887 S. Stefano had passed into the dependence of the bishop of Parma, in whose hands it remained until 973, when it was returned to the jurisdiction of the bishop of Bologna.[46] In the document as published by Affò, it is true, it is not clearly stated what the bishop of Parma renounced in return for the church of S. Maria of Monteveglio, which he acquired, but the whole tenor of the document implies that the exchange was an advantageous one for the

[44] post longa aute annorum curricula. seua gens ungaro[rum] cum plurima uastitate inuaserunt totam p[ro]uinciam. una pars que crudelior fuerat: intuens tam mirificu opus uidit crucem ibi posita. cupiens delere: ut a xpicolis deinceps non adoraretur. lignis ac paleis repleuit illud omne edificium. ignemq[ue] pariter succendit: ut cruce comburere. et tantu decus preclari op[er]is ruere in precipitium. Non meritis ullius: sed diuina clementia actu est. quod sca crux: a nefandorum feritate inlesa p[er]mansit: sicut et est hodie. et precipuum opus edificii: a ualido calore ignis inustum p[er] uirtutem sce crucis extitit.

[45] . . . frequentia. uirorum ac mulieru. sine intmissione cucurrit ad eande ecclam. ubi eoru [Sanctorum Agricolae et Vitalis] corpora marmoreis tegebantur sepulchris. que scilicet eccla sita e iuxta ecclam beatissimi martyris stephani. in qua monasteriu constitutu e in honore ei'de beati stephani. in qua etiam similitudo sepulchri dni nri ihu xpi. miro ordine constituta: refulget. Et du uirtutib' miraculoru gaudebant ppli: eccle illius parietes et tecta. aut edificabant nouiter: aut refarciebant uetusta: si qua patebat ibi ruina. Sed cu ex uirtute sco[um] peccata creuerunt pplo[rum]: quasi de bono semine mala multiplicata e fruges. ut sepe sit: uirtutes eoru n ad ppli uoluntates floruerunt. quo[rum] merita ciues eiusdem ciuitatis tanto frequentius implorare debuerunt: quanto p[ro] merentib' peccatis eorum cessauere miracula. Sed magis inflati: quasi contumaciter recesserunt: nec eorum uelle se uisitare corpora musitabat. quoru n sentiebant coruscare uirtutes. Unde ipsa ea edificia inueterata corruerunt. nec recidiua surgere potuerunt. ipsarumq' culmina arcaru. ventis. pluuiis, omniaq' aeris intemperie deformata. et neglecta uidebantur. ac p[er] hoc animi abbatu qui eidem monasterio sci stephani prefuerunt iure dubitare potuerunt. utru ipsa scorum corpora ad tutiora loca transferre debuissent: an ibidem relinquerent. Relinquere ibi ea timebant. ne quasi incuriose neglecta etiam ipsis ciuib' uilescerent. Transportare formidabant: p[ro] eo qd in passione eoru legebant locum ipsum: quo iacebant diuinitus a deo demonstratu: ac designatu fore, beato ambrosio. . . . Sic quippe metu et terrore harum dubitationum. eadem scoru corpora in sarcophagis suis permanserunt. multo tpr in eadem eccla in qua ea beat' locauit ambrosius.

[46] Testi Rasponi, 165.

bishop of Bologna, and it is likely that the latter received S. Stefano.[47]   It was probably about this time that a monastery was founded in our church, since a document of 983 contains the earliest extant reference to an abbot of S. Stefano.[48]

In the early years of the XI century, the buildings of S. Stefano (which until this time apparently had still lain in the ruin into which they had fallen after the invasion of the Hungarians) were in restoration.   On July 20, 1017, a donation was made for the restoration of the church of "S. Stefano which is called Jerusalem," to Martino, abbot of that monastery, and his brethren.[49] It is stated that the restoration had been begun by the bishop Giovanni V (997-1017) and certain relatives of the donor.   This donation was doubtless applied to work upon the church of S. Giovanni which two years later (1019) was so nearly completed that the bodies of the saints Vitale and Agricola could be translated to it from S. Pietro, as is recorded in great detail by the

---

[47] In nomine sancte & individue Trinitatis anno Dominice Incarnationis DCCCCLXXIII. apostolatus domini Benedicti primo.   Imperii vero domni Othonis octavo pontificatus domini Honesti Ravennatis metropolitani III. dum ab eodem sacrosancto Honesto Archiepiscopo suisque suffraganeis . . . in loco marzalia . . . sancta Synodus de quibusdam necessariis ac utilibus regni ecclesiarum status rebus habita coleretur perventum est ut Albertus Episcopus Bononiensis in medio illorum assurgens inopiam sui Episcopii adeo conquestus est . . . inter ceteras denique sue inopie angustias quedam loca juxta bononiam sita ab Uberto Parmensi Episcopo tum temporis detenta juris sue ecclesie videlicet bononiensis esse penitus conclamabat. Cujus quidem incessabilibus querelis prelibatus D. Archiepiscopus commotus Ubertum Parmensem Episcopum omni affectione quid ad eum predicta loca pertinerent discussit. Tunc demum prefatus Ubertus Episcopus. eadem loca sue sancte Parmensis Ecclesie sibique quarumdam scriptionum titulo ex quorumdam predecessorum suorum episcopo- rum parte devenisse professus est.   Enimvero dominus Archiepisc . . . . . Uberto Episcopo suggesserunt quatenus predicti amore presentiaque domini Metropolitani . . . bononiensem episcopum non jure fori ventilaret sed potius illius episcopio diligentiam adhibens res omnes illas de quibus super eum hactenus querebatur bononiensi ecclesie ipsique Alberto Episcopo legaliter refutaret.   Et ut ille Uberto Episcopo sueque Par- mensi Ecclesie ob hoc proprietario jure plebem sancte Marie de Montebellio concederet. . . . (Affò, I, 359).

[48] Testi Rasponi, 165 f.

[49] Anno Domini millesimo septimo decimo secundum quod in Cronaca Romana inuentum est.   In nomine Domini. temporibus Domini benedicti apostolici pontificatui ejus. in Dei nomine anno quinto. sitque imperante Domino Enrigo anno quarto die uigesimo mense Julii.   Indict. quintadecima [July 20, 1017]. . . . dabo & concedo ego qui supra lamberto una pro dei timore & remedio anime mee & pro anima quondum Dn. Johanne episcopus Sancte bon. Ecclesie & de quondam parentorum meorum seu pro restaurationis Ecclesie Sancti Stephani q. u. jerusalem uobis domnus martinus presbiter monachus & Abbas ipsius Ecclesie tuisque successoribus uestrisque fratri monachi . . . idest clusure due etc. . . . omnia qualiter supra legitur a presenti die dabo & concedo sicut supra dixi pro anima mea & pro anima quondam predicto Dn. Johanne uenerabilis episcopus & de parentis meis quo ipso predicto monasterio ordinauerunt & restauraue- runt pro anima illorum . . . (Savioli, I, pt. 2, 74).

chronicler of 1180.[50] The church of S. Giovanni exists no longer, but stood on the site of the present church of the Crocefisso and contained a crypt corresponding to the modern Confessi.[51] The two churches of S. Giovanni stood until 1637, when they were replaced by the existing edifice of the Crocefisso and the Confessi, which were completed about 1640.[52]

The general overhauling of the buildings of the shrine did not terminate with the reconstruction of S. Giovanni, but continued during almost the whole of the XI and XII centuries. It was probably these building operations which led in 1141 to the search for relics, of which the author of the *Sermo* has left us a full account, extremely valuable because of references it contains to the work of reconstructing the monastery. The monk tells us that from certain writings it was known that relics were hidden somewhere in the church, but exactly where had been forgotten. The abbot and monks, therefore, determined to search for these relics, and inquired from the older inhabitants of Bologna if they remembered anything which could help in the quest. These old men replied (this was in 1141) that they remembered having seen a box hidden under the sarcophagus of S. Isidoro, when the basilica of that saint was being rebuilt.[53] Now, the basilica of S. Isidoro is none other than the

[50] Cum uero placuit diuine dispositioni ordinare eidem monasterio. Dominum Martinu abbate tpre henrici impris aperte patuit omnipotentis uolutate fauere horu scorum corporu transmutationi. . . . Hac itaq' sanctissima et euglica scrittus auctoritate: dominiq' frugerii uenerabilis eiusdem sce bononiensis eccle epi accepta licentia. canonicorumq' eiusde sacre sedis consensu uiciniq' fere omium concesso adiutorio et fauore. cu sacro ordine monachoru pmisso ieunio et oratione. eadem corpora scoru q[ui]nto nonas martii. anno ab incarnatione dni millesimo nonodecimo. Jndictione scda. predictus dominus martin' abbas transuexit ad confessione qua ipse miro labore pulcherrimo op[er]e construx. in eccla beatissimi iohis baptiste.

[51] This is proved by numerous passages in old authors: for example, in Pullieni we read: per andare alla sesta Chiesa [di S. Giovanni di sopra detta il Crocefisso] bisogna, che . . . passando per la settima porta del Sepolcro entraremo in S. Giovanni di sotto, & salendo per questa scala, la quale rappresenta la scala santa etc. (206, 207). . . . Dove hora è questa Scala santa [the window of which opened on the atrio di Pilato and symbolized Ecce Homo] prima vi era l'Altare Maggiore di questa chiesa, che fu poi trasportato nella chiesa di sopra [leg. est sotto] del Crucifisso, & però si chiama la Maddalena, ma prima si chiamaua S. Gio: Battista, quindi dal Volgo è anco detto San Giov: di sotto. (243-244). And in Gargano: Nota doue e la scala al presente doue se ascende per andare suso in sancto Iouani, era lo altare de la Magdalena. et per fare quella scala fo guasto, perche se andaua p[er] una scala doue al presente e la capella de la Madonna grauida . . . et lo altare d[e] la Magdalena fu transferito doue e al presente. (B, ii). See also the description of Patricelli, 47 and 48.

[52] Petracchi, 230, 309.

[53] Quaru [reliquiarum] uero scriptura non loca publice dumtaxat nomina posteris denotauerat. Jnuenta enim ipsa scriptura in quodam libro fuerat. que infra tres scorum pignora fuisse capsas in predicta eccla asserebat abscondita. Cum aute iam plurimis exactis teporibus obliuioni quasi ab omnib' mandarent. neq' a quolibet colerentur. quia ab omib' ignorabant. dns inquam ihs xps q[ui] ante reges et presides suu scissimu uisserat nomen a suis fidelib' presentari. eosq' fulgidis fecerat coronis decorari.

present church of S. Pietro, and the ancient SS. Vitale e Agricola which assumed the title of S. Isidoro, when the bodies of the former patron saints were translated to S. Giovanni in 1019. If, therefore, in 1141 it was only the older men who were present and saw the reconstruction of the basilica of S. Isidoro, it must be, by an obvious calculation, that the church was rebuilt somewhere between 1080 and 1100.

According to Petracchi[54] the bishop Bernardo, who died in 1104, was buried in S. Croce.

To return to the *Sermo* and the search for relics in 1141, the monk goes on to state that the indications given by the old men led to the discovery beneath the sarcophagus of S. Isidoro of another tomb which bore the inscription SYMON. The body thus found was identified as that of Simon Peter, the Apostle, and the basilica of S. Isidoro hence came to be called in later times S. Pietro. The spurious relics thus obtained brought to the shrine of S. Stefano much popularity among the credulous faithful, but in time incurred the disapproval and even anathema of the popes, who summarily repressed the presumption of Bologna in daring to dispute with Rome the possession of the body of St. Peter. The search for relics in 1141 did not stop with the discovery of the enigmatical SYMON. The tomb of S. Isidoro was next opened, and here were found the bones of numbers of the Innocents, and numerous other relics. Stimulated by their success, the monks next went to the church of S. Croce, and a place mystically called Golgotha, where still other relics came to light.[55]

---

ipso[rum] noluit memoriam ab humanis laudibus semp[er] fieri n̄tibus incognitam: uel oblita. sed ut preclaris laudib' et dignis cotidie a fidelib' celebrentur eorū merita uoluit honorib'. p[er]specta itaq' sepi' prememorata scp̄ta ab abbate monachis prefate scissime eccle p[er]lecta: inter se inuice diligenter multotiens q[uaer]ere ceperunt. et ubi prescripte latuissent capse ab antiquioribus p[er]quirere studuert. Cumq' de hoc sepissime eo[rum] animos uariis aggrauarent opinionib': ad eorum m̄tes quandam sub sc̄i ysidori arca absconditam reuocauerunt. Nec enim intueri a quolibet poterat. sed cum prefati sc̄i ysidori basilica nouit' edificaretur. antiqui qui tunc aderant ab una parte eam perspexerunt. et predicto abbati atq' monachis ea omnia multotiens retulerunt. (f. 267).

54 228.

55 Quib' itaq' omib' auditis. atq' p[er]cognitis prelibatus abbas cum domno henrico reuerentissimo sc̄e bononie eccle epo. et quibusdam monachis et sapientioribus uicinis comunicato consilio. predictam arcam inquirere ceperunt. et eam in 'qua beati ysidori corpus iacebat seorsum amouerunt. et sic demum cum magno labore uix ad predictam attingere ualuerunt. Erat quippe fortissimo muro circūclausa. et de sup[er] int. eam et superiorem terram et marmoribus ualde onerata. atq' sup[er] eam in marmore quodā insculptum nom̄ fuerat symon. Jnterea uero cum presente predicto domno epo. et abbate atq' monachis. et quam plurib' aliis qui ad hoc opus exercendum extiterant predicta aperiret. ineffabile corpus inuenert: et ab utraq' parte arce littas post positas de prefato noīe p[er]spexerunt. His itaq' omnib' ita gestis: que sc̄i ysidori etiam fuerat aperuerunt. Qua uero ap[er]ta: beatissimi corpus. aliorumq' plurimo[rum]. et precipue paruulorū ossa qui p[ro] xp̄o ab herode interempti sunt. atq'.

LOMBARD ARCHITECTURE

To Testi Rasponi belongs the merit of having recognized that the S. Croce of this text is not the existing church of S. Sepolcro, but an edifice which formerly stood on the site of the present church of La Trinità.[56] His proofs are so full and ample that it is unnecessary to repeat them here.[57] In view of this fact the interpretation of the passage immediately following in the *Sermo* becomes easy. Turning away from S. Croce, the monks went to S. Sepolcro, where were found manna and various other relics. These were discovered at the right-hand side of the entrance. On the left-hand side of the entrance was the sarcophagus with the body of S. Petronio,[58] in which came to light not only the body of the saint, but innumerable other relics. Delighted with the discovery of such treasures, the bishop proclaimed a great festival, and sent notices of the discovery throughout the diocese. All this happened, the chronicler assures us, in 1141.[59]

pulcherimam argenteam capsam: argentea catena colligata. et confixam inuenerunt. Quam uero predictus eps cum his qui secum aderant diligenter inspiciens: suisq' manib' accipiens. uix eam aperire ualuerunt. Jn qua uero copiosa multitudine sca[rum] reliquiaru intra mirificum pallium inuolutam inuenerunt. et pre tanto gaudio oms flere ceperunt. Jmpletum ergo in hoc esse intellexerunt: quod euangelicus sermo declarare uidetur dicendo. petite et accipietis. querite et inuenietis. Quib' nempe omib' ita prudenter inspectis. maximas omnipotenti do gras reddentes: de ceteris inueniendis maxima cu diligentia querere studuerunt. Cumq' de hoc inter se inuicem altercarent. ad scam crucem in loco qui a beato petronio figuraliter golgotha appellatur unanimiter p[er]uenerunt. et post ipsam in muro ipsius eccle diuino nutu cum malleis p[er]quirere ceperunt. in quo diuina fauente clementia aliam thecam pretiosis reliquiis plenam inuenert. Jntra quam: etiam capsula auream pretiosam. et alia argenteam pulcherimam perspexerunt. Jn aurea uero quandam unius claui partem: defixi in manib' uel pedibus dni: p[er]spexert. Jn argentea aut quida de sudario dni particula continetur. Sic enim et antiqua uidetur declarari scriptura. Sublata igitur omni scriptarum rerum funditus hesitatione de ceteris nempe questio int eos uehemtissime subintuit [= subintroivit]; Sed qui inter maris p[ro]cellas petri scissimi dubitatione penitus euacuauit: et potentie sue dextera erigere solet elisos, soluere compeditos. uelocissimum inueniendi quod concupierant consilium salubre impertire dignatus est.

[56] 180.

[57] I add, however, a new text from Alberti: Ordinò [S. Petronio] poi auanti detto sontuoso edificio [S. Sepolcro] un amplo atrio, o sia chiostro, circondato da due ordini di belle colone, l'uno sopra l'altro con ottimo magisterio. Seguitaua tanto eccellete ordine infino al luogo, figurato per Golgota o sia Monte Caluario oue fu piantata la Croce del nostro Redentore. (Alberti, I, V, an. 433).

[58] Compare the later *Vita:* Ejus [S. Petronii] corpus in ecclesia sancti Stephani sepultum est, quod multis post seculis, divino consilio, civitati ignotum, Innocentio secundo Pontifice, inventum est, dum sacras reliquias Henricus episcopus recenseret, quas in ea ecclesia extare, a majoribus traditum erat. (Ed. *Acta Sanctorum,* October, II, 468).

[59] Adest enim in ipsa sci stephani eccla ad instar eius in quo dns nr ihs xps positus fuerat sepulchrum a beato petronio fabricatum. Jn ingressu autem cuius a dextris marmoribus pretiosis arca pulcherima reperitur condita. in qua scs petronius manna. et uarias atq' innumerabiles scorum reliq[ui]as recondere curauit. A sinistris autem ea constructa esse uidetur. in qua beati petronii corpus scissimum requiescit.

BOLOGNA, S. STEFANO

The chronicler goes on to tell us that a very short time after this the abbot and monks took counsel and decided to reconstruct the church of S. Croce, which, as has been seen, stood on the site of the existing church of La Trinità; and that while the edifice was being destroyed to its foundations in order that it might be rebuilt, other relics were discovered beneath the pavement, and in the wall near the ground.[60] From the text it is clear that shortly after 1141—probably about 1142—the church of S. Croce was

Quam cum maximo aperuissent timore. ipsum scissimum aspexerunt. et iuxta eum aliam capsam preclaris. et innumerabilib' scorum reliquiis repletam inuenerunt. Tres quoq' uitreas fialas intra se scissima habentes dona eode in loco intuentur. P[er]spectis ergo his: atqu' percognitis a prefato domno celeberimo epo: et a nobis omnib' qui ad hoc tam sacrum spectaculum insistebamus. factum est in crastinum: gloriosissima ut huius rei fama a uenerabili epo p[er] tota urbem. immo p[er] tota terra bononiensium episcopii diuulgaretur. Oms uero uiri. et mulieres diuersa[rum] regionum coactis etiam maximis in unum turmis ad tantum mysterium cu muneribus quibus poterat uenire studuerunt. Jdem uero sacer eps p[er] omnes sui episcopii plebes sacras direxit precipiendo legationes. ut unus quisq' archipbr suis cleris: et p[o]p[u]lis hanc scissimam sollicite notificaret inuentionem. et ut oms ad tantam honofice festinanter cum p[ro]cessione et letaniis uenirent solemnitate. Jnsup[er] etiam omib' qui ad hanc deinceps uenire studuerunt festiuitatem octo diebus ante: et totidem postea. semp[er] suorum omnium peccatorum duoru annorum predictus domnus eps fecit cu omnib' suis clericis deuotissime: remissionem. Consules aut: et ciues bononienses. ante predicta ecclam iure iurando firmauerunt. ut oms qui ad hanc tam preclaram deinceps celebritate de quibuscumq' locis accesserut. ut predictu est octo diebus ante: et postea salui et securi ipsi: et eoru res semper existerent. Patrata uero sunt hec omia apud urbe bononiensium in predicta eccla sci stephani. anno dni millesimo centesimo quadragesimo primo. qrto nonas octubris in ipsa festiuitate beatissimi confessoris xpi. sci petronii. . . .

It is in error that Mainardi (109) assigns this invention to 1139: Abbatia Parochiale . . . quiui stanno Monaci della Congregatione di S. Pietro Celestino, militano sotto la Regola di San Benedetto, & offitiano alla Monastica, eccetto che nella Messa adoprano il Messale Romaoo [sic], i quali vennero [i.e., the Celestine monks] in questo luogo l'anno 1469. Questa Chiesa fù fabricata da S. Petronio, allhora Vescouo di questa Città, l'anno 434. e l'anno 1139. Enrico Fratta Vescouo, e Cittadino nostro, alli 4. d'Ottobre ritrouò in detta Chiesa il corpo di S. Petronio, che fino à quel tempo era stato occulto, e perciò si diede allhora principio a fare la sua festa in detto giorno. . . . Vi è vn Sepolcro di marmo, fatto à similitudine di quello di Nostro Signore: sotto questa parochia vi sono numero 264. anime da communione, e numero 43 putti, e putte, in tutti nu. 307 i Monaci sono nu. 30.

[60] Post aliquod itaq' paruissimum tpis cu a predicte eccle abbate et monachis initum fuisset consilium: ut Eccle sce crucis in qua golgotha a sco petnio locus appellatus fuerat: a fundamento murus undiq' destrueretur: et firmius reficeretur. Quem uero uti statuerant fodientes. in pauimento ipsius eccle pretiosas repererunt arcas. . . . Jnterea uero cum predicte eccle murus circumquaq' dirumperet; in ipso quippe muro p[ro]pe terram tres capse cypressi pulcherime pari magnitudine. eiusdemq' qualitatis separatim fuere reperte . . . Dic inquam dic queso beatissime petroni huius eccle edificator atq' constructor. si tam paruissime utilitatis. et nullius bonitatis que intra has continentur capsas intellexisti. quare eas ab humanis obtutibus subtraxisti. ? et tam latenter infra muru inclusisti. ? (f. 260).

139

completely rebuilt from its foundations. At this point the *Sermo,* the most valuable of our sources for the history of S. Stefano, terminates with a catalogue of the relics discovered.

In the life of S. Petronio contained in the same codex there occurs a most remarkable description of the monastery of S. Stefano. The author sets out to describe the buildings as they were erected by S. Petronio. It has been assumed that he really described the monastery as it was in his time, that is, about 1180, and the historians of Bologna have expended much ingenuity in trying to make his description fit those parts of the extant edifice which antedate the end of the XII century. It is evident, however, that the monk did not very exactly describe the monastery as he saw it, since at numerous points his description fails to correspond with the oldest parts of the extant edifice. Moreover, it must be remembered that he had with his own eyes seen reconstructed a large number of those buildings or knew from authentic documents that they had been rebuilt within two hundred years of his own time. There is no reason to suppose that he was so insincere that he wilfully ascribed to S. Petronio the construction of buildings which he knew had been subsequently rebuilt. In his description of the monastery the monk doubtless followed the same method of composition he employed in the rest of the *Vita.* Having no authentic documents, he simply wrote down what appeared to him most likely and probable. Believing as he did that the monastery and shrine of the New Jerusalem had been founded by S. Petronio, he naturally assumed that the general lay-out of the buildings had undergone no very radical change since the time of the saint. He did know, however, that numerous individual buildings had been reconstructed. For all details, therefore, he drew freely upon his imagination, with pious enthusiasm ascribing to the original buildings of S. Petronio all sorts of precious materials and magnificence lacking in the edifice which he saw before his eyes.

We must, therefore, realize that the description of the monk can be relied upon only to a very limited extent in reconstructing the monastery of S. Stefano as it was in the year 1180. If, nevertheless, we bear in mind that the author was trying to imagine what the buildings erected by S. Petronio must have been like on the basis of the reconstructed edifice which he saw before him, we may obtain some hints of value as to the actual appearance of the latter at the end of the XII century.

The description begins with platitudes upon the size of the monastery and the different kinds of stones used in its construction. It was all surrounded, according to the monk, by a colonnade with columns of porphyry and other precious stones of different colours, and adorned with bases and capitals on which were sculptured figures of men, animals and birds. This statement was perhaps inspired either by the cloister of S. Stefano, which was probably in course of construction at the time the monk wrote, or by some similar edifice. In the cloister there are columns of Verona marble, and some of the capitals are figured. The monk naturally argued that the buildings erected by S. Petronio must have been even more magnificent than those which were erected and aroused admiration in his own time. He goes on to refer to the church of S. Sepolcro, which, he says, S. Petronio built according to measures that he had taken at Jerusalem. The walls of this church, he says, were constructed of stones cut and squared and shining with exceeding brightness. The S. Sepolcro of the monk's time, it is true, was built of plain bricks, but the building of S. Petronio is imagined as far nobler. "There was another building there," he goes on to say, "built from its foundations with a great variety of columns surrounding an open court in the centre, and with two orders of precious columns, one placed over the other, with bases and carved capitals." No passage in the entire description has given rise to more discussion than this. Some historians have seen in it the cloister of the Celestines, which has indeed a two-story colonnade, but this interpretation offers the difficulty that the cloister must have been erected very shortly, if at all, before 1180, and the monk would have been ascribing to S. Petronio a building which he and everyone else knew had just been built. I consider it more likely that he is referring to the Atrio di Pilato. This atrium had been reconstructed in the first half of the XII century, as the monk probably knew, but he very likely never saw the older atrium which it replaced. This, constructed by S. Petronio, he assumed to have been much more beautiful than the actual building he saw, and with his usual poetic imagination he embellishes the actual building before his eyes with fancied splendours. Thus, the two orders of colonnades, one above the other, were perhaps inspired by the cloister, in whose recent construction the monk doubtless took a very lively interest. From the same source he derived the "columns of precious stones," although the actual columns he saw were of brick. The decorated capitals he imagines stood where he himself saw only plain cubic capitals. "This atrium," he goes on to tell us, "extended from S. Sepolcro to the place which was called Golgotha, or Calvary, where was the cross of Our Lord," that is, the church of S. Croce, which, it has been seen, stood on the site of the present Trinità. Recent excavations have shown that the Atrio di Pilato was not separated from S. Croce, but opened upon it by an arcade, so that it is perfectly clear why the monk speaks of the two in one breath, and almost as of one construction. He speaks of the frescos in S. Croce, some of which have recently come to light, and of the pavement inlaid with porphyry and Parian marble and various other stones. At this point the enthusiasm of the loyal monk for his monastery gains the upper hand, and he breaks off with the exclamation that the buildings of this place are all so beautiful and so splendid that anyone who has once looked upon them desires most ardently to see them again.[61]

[61] Edificia namq' euisdem monasterii spatiosa ualde. atq' sublimia sunt uariis intexta lapidibus. circundata p[er] girum plurimis columnis pretiosis de porphyretico lapide.

LOMBARD ARCHITECTURE

In the life of the saint is also related a miracle which is said to have occurred during the apochryphal reconstruction of the city of Bologna by S. Petronio. A workman engaged in placing a column in an upper colonnade, fell and was miraculously saved by the saint.[62]   In the codex there is nothing to indicate that this miracle took place at S. Stefano, but the fact that a colonnade in two stories is mentioned led to the cloister of the Celestines being identified as the site, and the very column of the miracle was in later times pointed out.   In the later *Vita* the event is explicitly stated to have taken place at S. Stefano.[63]

aliusq' lapidibus diuersi coloris. cum basibus et capitellis suis insignitis. uariis figuris hominum. quadrupedu. ac uolucrum.   Jllo plurimo labore typice gessit opus mirifice constructum. instar dnici sepulchri. scdm ordinem quem uiderat. et p[ro]uida cura: cum calamo diligenter mensus fuerat: cum esst ierosolime.   Jbi enim p[er] aliqua dierum curricula sibi fuerat. p[er] totā iudeam colligere uectigalia.   Etiam parietes sepulchri. intus. undiq' p[er] giru cum iuncturis suis sunt erecti. et lapidib' quadratis. et sectis. nimio candore pollentibus.   Aliud quoq' edificium ibiq' plurima uarietate columnarum a fundamtis edificauit cum atrio in circuitu. cum duob' ordinib' pretio-sarum columnaru: cum basibus et capitellis. suis signis multiplicibus decoratus. ita ut sup[er] inferiorem ordinem columnar[um] alius pretiosior sup[er]eminebat.   Tali modo extendebat usq' ad locum qui figurate golgotha: hoc ē caluarie nuncupatur. ubi crux in q[ua] xps p[ro] salute mundi fixus ē. posita fuit.   Jlle uero locus uariis ymaginib' diuersi coloris: depictus est.   Pauimentum aut totius operis stratum ē pario lapide. et porphyretico. et lapidib' diuerse uarietatis.   Ita pulcra: ac prelucida st cuncta loci huius edificia: ut qui semel ea p[er]spexerit: iterum uidere ardentissimo amore desiderat.   Jn eodem uero loco qui golgotha dicitur. posuit ligneam crucem. que in longitudine. et latitudine. undiqu' p[er] totum facta fuerat: instar crucis xpī. In the XII century the monastery of S. Stefano comprised gardens in addition to the various other parts of the shrine, as is clear from a phrase in the *Translatio*: monas-terii sci stephani cu suis eccliis: claustris: ortis. edificiis.

[62] Dum quadam die idem uenerabilis pater [Petronius] ingenti cura et sollicitudine sup[er] huiusscemodi op[er]is magistros assisteret. diuinitus actum est. quod quidam ex artificib', cu uellet erigere columnam in superiori ordine columnarum toto corporis nisu. iunctis brachiis. amplexus est eam in giro. ut erectam subsisteret: quo usq' ab aliis artificibus sustentaretur quibuslibet augmentis.   Sed uir ille mole tanti ponderis pregrauatus deficientibus uirib'. n̄ diu sub tam graui onere subsistere ualens cu eadē columna insertis brachiis in circuitu. celeri rotatu: de sursum ruit in terra.

[63] Ut autem solicitus Pastor gregis sui mentes vehementius etiam excitaret ad ardentem Dei caritatem, propositis, quas colerent, sacris imaginibus ad similitudinem eorum locorum, quæ ipse jam præsens Hierosolymis veneratus erat, in ecclesia S. Stephani hæc sancte exprimenda atque effingenda curavit: columnam, ad quam Christus Dominus flagellis est verberatus: Crucem, cui est affixus: triclinium, in quo idem cum discipulis discubuit: locum item, quo Petrus Apostolorum princeps, postquam se Christi discipulum esse negavit, peccati sui pœnitens secessit: et cubiculum præterea, in quo Gabriël angelus, de cœlo missus, Deiparam Virginem salutavit.   Quæ omnia sanctissimæ religionis monumenta adhuc magna Bononiensis populi pietate coluntur, augustioremque reddunt ipsam sancti Stephani ecclesiam, quam ille Hierosolymæ nomine appellavit, eamque ob causam vicus, nunc etiam eidem ecclesiae conjunctus, Hierusalem nominatur.   Dum autem ecclesia ipsa construitur, mirifice operis in Dei nomine edendi occasio est oblata.   Nam faber quidam non tam viribus corporis, quam ingenio fretus,

Of the subsequent history of the monument, but little is at present known, but in the Archivio dello Stato at Bologna are preserved numerous inedited documents of the monastery whose publication has been promised by Mgr. Belvideri, and from which it is hoped much new light will be shed. It is evident, however, that the great popularity which the monastery enjoyed during the XII century, witnessed by the bulls granted in its favour by Anastasius IV, Hadrian IV and Alexander II, as well as by the circumstance that a monk of S. Stefano was chosen to be first abbot of the new abbey of Lucedio,[64] was short-lived. With the decline in monastic discipline the orthodox character of the shrine became tainted. The growing belief that the church possessed the body of St. Peter became so strong that Pope Eugenius IV (1431-1447) tore down the roof of S. Pietro, had the edifice filled with dirt, and walled up the doors. By these drastic measures was suppressed the cult of the SYMON discovered in 1141. To still further punish the presumptuous monks, the same pope in 1447 gave the abbey in commendam.[65] According to Mainardi[66] the Celestine monks supplanted the Benedictines in 1469, and this same notice is given by Casale.[67] According to Patricelli,[68] however, the Benedictine monks were expelled in 1447, doubtless to aid in the suppression of the cult of the spurious St. Peter, and were supplanted by secular priests, who in turn yielded to the Celestines in 1469.[69] The installation of the Celestines in 1469 provoked a restoration of the monastery. On the exquisite Renaissance portal which now leads to the church of the Confessi is found the inscription:

OP'. M. EQ[VI]TIS . & . COĪTIS . D̄. NICOLAI. DE SANVTIS 1475.

This doorway originally formed part of a screen which filled the inter-columniations of S. Sepolcro, and was removed to its present position in the early part of the XIX century.[70] About this same time the Calvary was remade, the old colonnettes being replaced by new ones.[71]

obnixe columnam marmoream, operis et instrumentis adjuvantibus, erigebat: sed funibus, quibus columna tollebatur, effractis, ille repentina columnæ ruina oppressus interiit. Ea re audita, beatus Petronius accurrit, orationeque ad Deum habita, fabrum, qui mortuus jacebat, ad vitam divinitus revocavit, omnibus, qui aderant, cum rei admirabilis spectaculo obstupescentibus, tum Petronii episcopi sanctitatem certatim inter se collaudantibus. . . . Quibus reliquiis [obtained from Constantinople] mox demum inde regressus cum alia Dei templa a se constructa, tum in primis ipsam sancti Stephani ecclesiam, ac sacella ad cruces quatuor [i.e., the crosses at the four gates of the city] quas idem erexerat, collocata religiose pieque ornavit. (Op. cit., 466).

64 Casale, 157-158.   65 Patricelli, 54; Casale, 166.
66 See text cited above, p. 139.   67 168.   68 54.

69 Petracchi, on the other hand (68), says that regular priests were installed in 1469, and the Celestines in 1493. According to Casale the Celestines installed in 1469 remained only a short time but returned again in 1513.

70 [Nell'anno 1475] con un murello, e con spesse colonette sopravi una cornice ricorrente furono chiusi la maggior parte degli intercolonni del peristilio [that is, of

In 1514, the vaults of the Atrio di Pilato, which had been ruined, possibly when the basilica of S. Pietro was desecrated in 1447, were rebuilt.[72] About the same time the famous vase of Luitprando was restored by the commendatary abbot, who subsequently became Leo X. According to Patricelli[73] the vase was lying on the ground (*per terra*) and the work of Leo X consisted in placing it upon a pedestal. The pedestal still bears his arms. About this same time the chapel of the Magi was restored.[74] The existing church of La Trinità was remade in its present form in 1568, according to an inscription cited by Petracchi.[75] From certain ruins which in his time were to be seen lying to the eastward of the present church, Pullieni in 1600 conjectured that La Trinità was once larger than at present, but this conjecture has been disproved by recent excavations, and it is probable that the ruins belonged to monastic buildings. In the following year, 1569, the chapel of S. Martino was baroccoized.[76] In the first quarter of the XVII century a new restoration was carried out.[77] In 1632 was erected the picturesque well in the centre of the cloister.

The description of Patricelli, written in 1747, gives an interesting picture of S. Sepolcro as it was in the XVIII century, when the exquisite early Renaissance screen of 1475 was still in place.[78]

the main arcade] che attornia l'edicola [the Calvary], e paralleli alla fronte di essa vennero elevati e pitturati due muri ai quali furono addossati altari; onde rimase chiuso attorno lo spazio su cui prospetta l'edicola. Nell'intercolonnio di fronte, rincontro all'ingresso recente [*i.e.,* west] fu riservato il passaggio, e postovi un cancello incorniciato da pilastrate . . . e da architrave e cornice con questa inscrizione:

OP. M. EQTIS ET COITIS D. NICOLAI DE SANVTIS 1475

. . . Nel principio di questo secolo furono tolti l'incorniciatura e il cancello sopradetti e collocati nel peristilio di Pilato . . . e veniva sostituito un cancello ricco bensì di egregi bronzi figurati, ma che nulla aveva che fare col recinto. (Gozzadini).

[71] Patricelli, 38.

[72] In the time of Gargano (B, iii) the window which opened from the Scala Santa into the Atrio had already been closed by the new vault in the west bay of the southern arcade of the Atrio. This vault, therefore, must have been erected before 1520, and it is to this that Gargano refers: Item quando Papa Leone X era Cardinale, era Commendatario della abatia de Sancto Stephano, e nel año M.D.X III. fu eletto Papa, fo fatto Comendatario Inghelterra, et impetro uno perdo plenario per quindeci giorni. et de quella elemosina se fero quelle uolte existente gouernator de la ditta abbatia Messer Camillo de Mafredi el ql morì nel año. M.CCCCC.XIIII. (*Ibid.*). Compare also Patricelli (24): Nota anchora, che le Volte, quali son qui intorno a detto Atrio: Erano anchor loro per terra, & furono rifatte, di Elemosine nell'Anno 1514. Ma auanti che andassero per terra, nella muraglia di esse, nella parte di sopra in luogho eminente, vi era vna Finestra, qual rapprensentava la Finestra del Palazzo di Pilato, nella quale esso mostrò il nostro Saluatore tutto flagellato (24).

[73] 24.   [74] Petracchi, 238.   [75] 232.   [76] Petracchi, 233.   [77] *Ibid.*, 119.

[78] La più ragguardevole di queste Chiese è la presente [S. Sepolcro]. . . . Nel bel mezzo di essa, forma come un' altra Chiesetta, allontorno della quale remane un'ampio portico, tanto che da ogni parte si gira. La muraglia di questo ornata è da varie

BOLOGNA, S. STEFANO

In 1804 a disastrous restoration was carried out, especially in the church of S. Sepolcro. The screen was removed, the terra-cotta columns of the main arcade were covered with plaster painted to imitate marble, the valuable Byzantine frescos of the cupola were repainted, and the cupola itself radically restored. The damage wrought at this epoch, however, was comparatively mild compared with the havoc played by the restorers of 1876 and the following years. The project of restoration was first ventilated in 1870, but work was begun seriously only six years later, under the direction of Raffaelle Faccioli. From the account of Gozzadini it is possible to reconstruct a mental picture of the edifice as the restorers found it. In the church of S. Sepolcro the triforium had been walled up and the vault covered with barocco decorations, as shown in the old photograph reproduced in Plate 24, Fig. 6. The church of S. Pietro was covered with low Renaissance vaults. Numerous accessory structures existed to the west of the shrine. The work of restoration in S. Pietro consisted in demolishing the vaults and rebuilding them, together with the walls of the upper part of the nave; in rebuilding the side-aisle vaults with the exception of that of the easternmost bay of the northern side aisle; in carrying off to the Museo Lapidario the Roman inscription used as a lintel in the north portal of S. Pietro, and replacing it by a copy; and in removing the portico of the Cinquecento from the façade. When this portico was demolished the relief of the Evangelist, St. Luke, which had hitherto been hidden, came to light. The restorers proceeded to rebuild entirely the façade on the authority of some traces of the pilaster strips and buttresses. Before the restoration, in the interior of the church nothing ancient could be seen except the columns and piers, and even one of these had been mutilated to make room for a holy-water font. The restorers lowered the pavement 36 centimetres, and freed the walls of their intonaco and whitewash. In remaking the vaults of the nave, the trace of the curve of the ancient vaults was discovered on the interior wall of the façade. Traces of the clearstory string-course were found still preserved behind the modern vaults, although in the lunettes of the vaults the cornice had been shaved off flush with the walls. This cornice was restored. The system of both intermediate and alternate piers which had similarly been shaved flush with the walls was also restored, as were the capitals of the compound piers. The marble corbels which supported the intermediate system were similarly remade. The ancient clearstory with bull's-eye windows was destroyed and replaced by a new clearstory with windows imitated from an ancient one still preserved in the apse. Of the apse windows only one of

pitture principiate da Felini, e seguitate da altri di poco conto. Quella che dico Chiesetta, contornata è da due Colonnati, uno di Colonne alte e grosse, ma di pietra, e l'altro di Colonette di Marmo che il voto chiudono tra una Colonna, e l'altra. Vi si veggono mescolati varj frammenti antichi. Questa appunto si vuole l'antichissimo tempio d'Iside, coperta da un Catino tutto dipinto, ma rozzamente, esprimente la visione de 24 Vecchi . . . . . In capo di questo recinto si erge un Monticello (276).

the ancient ones was preserved. A few traces of a second were found, but the third or central one had been entirely destroyed to make way for the campanile of the neighbouring church of Loreto. On making over the passage-way between the church of S. Pietro and S. Sepolcro it was found that the wall of enormous thickness—nearly 2 metres—separating the two churches really consisted of two walls, the one built against the other, a fact which proved clearly that the two churches were not contemporary constructions but that S. Pietro, whose wall was carefully finished externally on the side facing S. Sepolcro, was earlier than the latter church.[79]

[79] E in fatti veggonsi demoliti e occorrerà rifabbricare nelle parti superiori i muri della navata principale, la cui volta fu poi rifatta, ma bassa, come è oggidì; le laterali ricostruite anch'esse, fuorchè nel tratto del primo intercolonnio a sinistra dell'abside, ove rimane l'antica volta a vela; e le rifece Giuliano della Rovere . . . che diventò . . . Giulio II, che vi pose il suo stemma (56). Ai guasti del tempo, degli Ungari, di Alessandro VI, di Giuliano della Rovere, altri ve seguirono via via, e le scialbature vennero ripetute più volte per fino sulle colonne di caristio; onde alla chiesa erano state tolte quasi interamente, o occultate, le sembianze antiche che etc. . . . La fronte della chiesa era stata in gran parte nascosta da un porticuccio e suo tetto addossativi nel cinquecento. Questo porticuccio, chiuso da un lato dalla capella Banzi che occupava anch'essa una porzione di fronte della chiesa . . . lasciava veder solo l'arco cieco della porta ornato d'una di quelle spirali a fogliame che ricorrono spesso nelle chiese antiche; e nell'arco quel bassorilievo [of Christ, S. Agricola, and S. Tecla] . . . Più in alto perpendicolarmente ad uno stipite della porta sporgeva un solo modiglione ornato del simbolo evangelistico dell'Angelo, abbastanza bellino e scrittovi S. MATHEVS EVG. . . . Il modiglione corrispondente con l'altro simbolo del bue alato e la scritta S. LVCAS EVG, riapparve quando fu atterrato il portichetto, essendo per buona sorte rimasto intatto dentro il peduccio della volta. Riapparve allora altresì un gran tratto superiore della facciata ch'era nascosto dal tetto ed ove alcune vestigia di timpano, di nicchia, delle lesene esterne, di due ulteriori modiglioni in cui saranno stati gli altri simboli evangelistici, ed altre tracce, nonche due pilastrate triangolari scoperte appresso, gioveranno alla perspicace valentia dell'architetto per restituire le parti ornamentali della facciata (60) . . . Nell'interno non si vedeva più di molto antico se non quattro colonne marmoree, con capitelli di diverse epoche, e alcune porzioni di architravi scolpiti, incassati presso l'abside; di meno antico e intercalate quattro colonne quadruple, laterizie con capitelli cubici. . . . Una di queste colonne quadruple era stata mutilata da cima in fondo per addossarvi una grande lastra scritta ed una grande pila per l'acqua santa, le quali sporgevano e sconciavano bruttamente; e, come tutto il resto, eran state sciabate le arcuazioni, formate di grandi cunei di gesso. . . . Della volta mediana antica, che dev'essere stata a vela, è rimasta fortunatamente la traccia della curvatura nella parete interna della facciata, onde se ne ha non solo l'elevazione, ma eziandio l'andamento ch'è semicircolare con piè dritto, e doveva produrre ottimo effetto. La volta nasceva nelle pareti laterali della nave maggiore una cornice sporgente di gesso naturale, ancora in posto in gran parte, intatta dove la nascondevano i peducci della volta moderna, scalpellata pari a muro e scialbata nei tratti che rimanevano appena sotto alle arcate della volta. Erano state parimente scalpellate e scialbate le mensolette di marmo sulle quali avevano poggiato pilastrate ora rifatte che si collegano con quelle sorgenti da sopra colonne, e che, elevandosi nel mezzo degli archi antichi della navata verticalmente alle finestre circolari, comprovano che queste furon costrutte in un ristauro, e molto probabilmente in quello di Giuliano della Rovere. Vi si dovranno

146

BOLOGNA, S. STEFANO

In the church of S. Sepolcro the barocco screen which had replaced that of the early Renaissance, with its vases and festoons, was removed. Gozzadini wearies of enumerating the many alterations, additions and changes wrought in S. Sepolcro. Before the restoration, he says, there was nothing ancient visible externally except the top of the lantern, the rest of the outside walls being hidden by the roof of the triforium. West of the edifice was a sort of passage-way belonging to the marchese Banzi, where a few decimetres of the ancient wall had been freed of the intonaco, like certain other patches in the Atrio di Pilato. To the west of the church lay not only the passage-way of the marchese Banzi, but two chapels; and the three faces of the baptistery towards the Atrio di Pilato were hidden by three arcades of Ionic columns added in the Cinquecento. The colonnade facing the Atrio di Pilato and the chapels to the west were destroyed. The intonaco was stripped off the edifice internally and externally. On the west façade came to light the amortizements of an ancient portico with three arcades on the central face, and two arcades on each of the faces joining the central one. On the central face the arcade rested on pilasters, on the others on corbels. This arcade was still visible in the middle of the XVII century, since it is clearly shown in the miniature in the choir book of S. Petronio. It was restored according to the traces discovered, and the polychromatic masonry of the walls was replaced from fragments of the original masonry which came to light here and there. The pilaster strips terminating in shafts on the angles, the bifora and the cornice of double arched corbel-tables were all restored on the authority of traces discovered, indicating that such features existed in the original edifice. The façade of S. Sepolcro facing the Atrio di Pilato was similarly restored. Of the three doors which at present open from S. Sepolcro into the Atrio, only the central one is ancient. The arcades of the Atrio were disfigured by a high modern cornice which the restorers removed. Speaking of the capitals of the side aisles of S. Sepolcro, Gozzadini states that only four are ancient. Before restoration the others had been replaced by Renaissance capitals of the Tuscan order. These Renaissance capitals were all replaced by cubic capitals. The transverse arches, freed from intonaco, reappeared in polychromatic masonry. These arches showed clear traces of having been reinforced by tie-rods, which were accordingly replaced. The biforum of the triforium opposite the western

pertanto sostituire delle finestre che armonizzino con quelle del curvo abside; una delle quali era stata per buona ventura murata, scialbata, ma non guasta, onde si è potuto riaprirla nella sua interezza. . . . Il muro ov'è questo passaggio antico è d'una grossezza enorme (m. 1.94); ma toltone l'intonaco si è veduto che tale grossezza risulta da due muri distinti l'uno addossato all'altro senza esser collegati, ond'è chiaro che le due chiese non furono costrutte simultaneamente, bensì una dopo l'altra, quantunque i grandi mattoni romani, si interi che mezzi, impiegativi e l'antica calce bianca siano uguali [sic]. Anzi il muro della cattedrale, a contatto con l'altro, è costrutto all'esterno in modo da far ritenere che originariamente era in vista. Onde l'anteriorità della cattedrale (65).

portal had been destroyed and replaced by a great arch, which in turn had been walled up before 1804. On this wall was the Byzantine fresco, probably of the Trecento, representing the Slaughter of the Innocents. In order to reopen the biforum the restorers transferred the fresco to canvas and transported it into the church of the Crocefissi, from which it was subsequently removed to the sacristy where, after much difficulty, I saw it in 1913. The restorers found the dome itself well preserved, and discovered the singular fact that it is constructed with internal chains. In the gallery came to light traces of four niches with sculptured string-courses, which were restored. The roof of the triforium was entirely remade, and the Calvary was very radically repaired.[80]

[80] Non guari prima [than 1813] furono collocati, in ogni intercolonnio, sulla cornice del recinto vasi e-festoni di stucco barocchissimi . . . che venner scacciati nei primi giorni del ristauro. Poi fu tolto tutto il recinto sanutiano essendochè non solo era un anacronismo, ma impediva la visuale e turbava l'antica semplicità e spaziosità dell'edificio. . . . Ma troppo sarebbe lungo annoverare, difficile e inutile ordinare cronologicamente, le molte altre alterazioni fatte al battistero, le aggiunte di anditi, di portici, di cappelle, di altari, di nicchie per immagini e di finestre (75). . . . Speaking of S. Sepolcro in 1876: Esternamente rimaneva solo in vista la parte più alta corniciata della lanterna dodecagona, la quale rinchiude e afforza la cupola ed è rivestita di tasselli a rombo contornati da mattoncini sottili, il cui complesso ha somiglianza coll'opus reticulatum degli antichi. Solo quella rimaneva in vista, imperciochè la parte meno alta era nascosta dal tetto spostato del triforio. Nell'andito di proprietà del Marchese Banzi erano scoperti pochi decimetri del muro di circuimento fatti da me scrostare per saggio quindici anni prima, e così due rombi, disintonacati in appresso, nel lato opposto che dà sul cortile di Pilato. I quali pezzetti di parete, mostrando il modo antico, adorno e singolare di struttura, attiravano l'occhio e la considerazione dell'osservatore. Tre facce del circuito, irregolarissimamente ottagonale, volte verso la piazza, erano occultate dall'andito e della cappella del March. Banzi non che dalle cappelle della contessa Pallavicini Nugent e dei Marchesi Malvezzi Campeggi; tre altre facce verso il cortile di Pilato nascote da un portico e dal suo tetto. (80-81). . . . Quindi coll'atterrare le cappelle Banzi, Pallavicini e Malvezzi, e l'andito Banzi, si è renduta novamente palese la parte di battistero che prospetta la piazza. . . . Ma prima togliendo l'intonaco si scoprirono avanzi appena sporgenti di tre arcate nella fronte e di due allato, le prime sostenute da pilastrate, le altre da mensole con quella alterna varietà che ha riscontro nell'interno. In fine a quell'altezza trovaronsi avanzi di un rivestimento a fasce di mattoni alternate con altre di marmo (81), e circoli a scompartimenti ornati di marmi orientali, e avanzi di pilastrini con sopra colonnette agli angoli delle facce, non che di una bifora in alto e della cornice in cima ad archetti intrecciati. Tutte le quali cose si sono potute per ciò rimettere nel pristino stato. E come giustamente s'interpretassero e si seguissero quegli avanzi dall'architetto Faccioli, fu recentemente dimostrato da una veduta esterna del battistero, miniata nel cinquecento in un libro corale di S. Petronio, la qual veduta mi venne fatta conoscere cortesemente dai signori Alvisi e Rubbiani (81) . . . Dal lato opposto del battistero, che prospetta il *cortile di Pilato* furono abbattuti tre archi d'ordine ionico addossativi nel cinquecento. . . . Queste tre facce [of S. Sepolcro], ora disgombre, hanno anch'esse sulla fascia marmorea che fa basamenti i pilastrini d'angolo, i quali in alto si mutano in colonnette, ma non han gli archi nè il rivestimento a zone del lato principale che dà sulla piazza. Invece grandi mattoni romani vi son murati diagonalmente, in guisa da

BOLOGNA, S. STEFANO

From this radical restoration the church emerged a very different structure from what it was when the restorers took it in hand, and, it may also be added, a very different structure from what it was in the Middle Ages.

S. Pietro

III. The church of S. Pietro consisted originally of a nave (Plate 25, Fig. 6) five bays long, two side aisles and three apses, but the southern apse has been walled off. The edifice is, at present, vaulted throughout—the nave (Plate 25, Fig. 6) and side aisles with groin vaults, and the apses with half domes. It has been seen, however, that all these vaults with the exception of that of the eastern bay of the northern side aisle and the half domes, are modern. There is considerable room for doubt whether the restorers were

formar l'opera spiccata degli antichi. Poi rombi suddivisi in altri piccolissimi di marmi a vari colori, poi circoli a scompartimenti con pietrazze orientali, ma tutto questo rivestimento ricco e cospicuo senza corrispondenza ornamentale simmetrica. Più in alto, e solo nella faccia di mezzo, il rivestimento è a due zone di mattonelle di forme e colori diversi, combinati a intrecciamenti, in parte geometrici, vari e leggiadri; si che l'insieme offre combinazioni lineari ricche, assai vaghe, etc. (82). . . . Nella parete della faccia a destra della mediana è un'altra bifora, anch'essa . . . era otturata. . . . grandi dischi situati allato dei pilastri che soprasstanno alle colonnette. I quali dischi avevano nel mezzo avanzi di piatti di maiolica rabescati a colori con attorno ornamenti geometrici svariati di mattoncini a rimesso, che girano eziando attorno agli archi ed han riscontro nel muro vicino del battistero. La prima arcata di ambidue i lati, che s'appoggia senza immorsarsi nè al battistero nè al resto del portico è fattura d'altro tempo (83-84). . . . Ora sono stati sostituiti [four Renaissance capitals of the side-aisle responds] da capitelli rettangolari smussati in baso, come quelli delle colonne rincontro, e gli archi nettati dall'intonaco, mostrano come in antico la costruzione cospicua di mattoni a diversi colori, alternati da cunei di pietra gallina. E come in ciascuno di questi archi si sono scoperti fori quadrangolari otturati, con dentro avanzi di travicelli di rovere che anticamente facevan l'uficio di catene, così i travicelli vi sono stati restituiti. La parete all'ingiro insudiciata da pessime pitture rifatte, è stata altresì liberata da questi sgorbi e dall'intonaco. Venne ricostruito presso la porta santa quel tratto di muro ch'era stato abbattuto a fare un ampio ingresso alla cappella Banzi, la quale scomparve com'era di ragione, trasferendone l'antico sarcofago di S. Giuliana nella chiesa vicina della Trinità. Fu veduto allora che nel lato del sarcofago addossato al muro è scolpita la seguente antica iscrizione:

✠ HIC REQVIESCIT CORPUS S. IULIANE VIDUE.

Nell'interno del sarcofago era ed è ancora una tavoletta marmorea con questa scritta: ✠ ECCE CORPUS S. IULIANE VIDUE. . . . Speaking of the triforium: Nella faccia mediana [of the east wall internally] . . . sono incavate quattro nicchie, tre delle quali attorniate da una fascia scolpita a foglie con intreccio spiraliforme di cui furono trovati alcuni pezzi tra le macerie. Una di tali nicchie, un po' più alta e assai più larga ha uno spiraglio, e forse conteneva un piccolo altare. Agli angoli sporgenti del dodecagono tra le bifore entro il triforio, s'innalzano a una data altezza pilastrate con mezze colonnette che han capitelli di mattone semplicemente smussati, sopra i quali si prolunga la mezza colonnetta (91).

correct in placing groin vaults over the nave. The nave was certainly vaulted, as was proved by traces of one of the old vaults discovered in the inner face of the west façade; but Osten, who saw the church before the restoration, has left a drawing in which he makes these vaults rib, not groin. The system is alternate (Plate 25, Fig. 6), a single bay of the nave embracing two of the side aisles, except in the westernmost bay, which is single. The system of the alternate bays has been entirely restored, and there is nothing to show that the restorers were correct in rebuilding here a single flat member instead of a group of shafts. Above the capitals of the intermediate supports rise flat pilaster strips (Plate 25, Fig. 6), similarly restored, carried on corbels. These are crowned by a cornice which is carried around the nave and supports blind arches encircling the clearstory windows (Plate 25, Fig. 6). The restorers appear to have found authority for the cornice, but the upper part of the walls with the blind arches and the clearstory windows is entirely a work of the modern imagination. The alternate piers consist of a square core, on which are engaged four half columns. The side-aisle responds consist of three rectangular members and are uniform. The modern vaults are supplied with wall and transverse ribs.

The exterior is supplied with prismatic buttresses which do not express the alternation of the system. These appear, however, to be entirely modern, and there is no proof that the restorers found indication of any such features in the original edifice.

The masonry of the building internally (Plate 25, Fig. 6) and externally has been so thoroughly remade in the restoration, that it is almost impossible to judge of its original character. At present it consists of wide bricks, some of which are extremely long, well laid in thin beds of mortar. The courses are horizontal and unbroken. Herring-bone work does not occur, but externally there is fancy inlaying in triangular patterns and polychromatic work with bits of marble. How much of all this is original there is no means of telling. The bricks are cross-hatched. Stone is used to form certain of the string-courses, archivolts and trimmings.

IV. The intermediate supports consist of monolithic columns (Plate 25, Fig. 6). Several of these columns and their capitals are formed of pilfered Roman materials. In fact, the use of pilfered materials is a remarkable feature at S. Pietro. The eastern responds of the nave arcade are formed of richly decorated Roman jambs, and a Roman inscription was employed in the northern portal. The imposts which serve as capitals appear to be Byzantine of the early V century, as is also the capital of the easternmost intermediate pier of the north arcade and the impost of the eastern respond of the south side aisle. These all probably came from earlier buildings on the same site. The capital above referred to is characterized by a single row of scrawny leaves and by very much reduced volutes. The other capital is of the Roman Ionic order, an unusual type in Lombard churches. The western intermediate piers are supplied with original capitals of Corinthianesque type, full of character and with acanthus leaves under the volutes sweeping horizontally (Plate 25, Fig. 5; Plate 24, Fig. 4). The abaci are formed of a pilfered architrave of the Carlovingian epoch, in part recarved in the XII century. The alternating piers have finely proportioned cubic capitals in which the form of the cushion is emphasized by an incised line. These capitals are precisely like those in the Atrio di Pilato. We must beware of arguing from this fact that S. Pietro is nearly contemporary with the Atrio, because these capitals of S. Pietro were entirely remade in the restoration, and I suspect that the restorers, at a loss to discover what were the original forms, simply copied the capitals of the Atrio. The alternate piers (Plate 25, Fig. 6) and the side-aisle responds are without bases, and the base of one of the intermediate piers is pilfered. Of the other bases two are of Attic type and one consists of two superimposed tori.

It is probable that the cornices of the church originally consisted of simple arched corbel-tables beneath which were inlaid bits of marble and other fragments with polychromatic effect. But the existing cornices are entirely modern, and were erected absolutely without authority. The form of the capitals of the northern portal seems to show that this was shafted and had a roll-moulding. This portal has, however, been very freely restored, and the Byzantine capital now placed beneath the other capital at the top of the shaft (Plate 25, Fig. 3), I am informed by persons who saw the restoration, was purchased at an antiquary shop in Ravenna. The principal capitals, however, are authentic, and are carved with subjects for the most part grotesque. A figure is seen standing on what is perhaps intended to be a tree (Plate 25, Fig. 3). Near by is a lion standing on his hind legs, his fore-paws resting on the unknown person's shoulders, and apparently whispering in his ear. Between the two on the ground is seen a head (Plate 25, Fig. 3). Then follows the Annunciation, a siren and two birds. The capitals of the western portal represent a naked man astride a two-headed dragon; the Visitation; a bird with its bill in the throat of an animal with a fox's head, a bird's wings and a fish's tail; twelve heads; a griffin astride another animal. Above this capital is a high abacus with anthemia and rinceaux, recalling those of S. Ambrogio. In the façade is inlaid a plaque in low relief representing Jesus Christ, I C̅R̅S, between S A|GRI|CO|LA and S. VITALIS. These sculptures are very crude. The hands are enormously large, the upper parts of the heads too small, the draperies wooden.

Of the enigmas offered by the church of S. Stefano none, perhaps, is more baffling than that of the two sarcophagi of SS. Vitale e Agricola. We have seen that the bodies of the saints were translated from S. Pietro in 1019. Now, in the church are still preserved two sarcophagi which are supposed to be those from which the bodies were taken in the early part of the XI century.

That of S. Vitale has carved upon its principal face two peacocks separated
by a Greek cross. The workmanship is undeniably crude. The type of the
design is early Christian, and the border is formed by a moulding of
undoubtedly classical character.. On the other hand, the technique of the
cutting of the peacock's tails, which are indicated by incised parallel lines,
is perfectly analogous with that of an ambo now preserved in the court-yard
of the University of Ferrara (Plate 88, Fig. 4), which is undoubtedly
Carlovingian. The other face of the sarcophagus and the ends are ornamented
with arcades resting on columns. On the face opposite the peacocks, between
the arches, is inserted a sort of heart-leaf. This face differs from the others
in being less weathered and in that the border is straighter. At the two ends
the arches break into the upper border, and the lower border is also unsymmet-
rically disposed with respect to the base of the colonnettes. The execution
of all these three faces is very crude, and some of the arches still remain
unfinished. On the end one capital is executed in the perforated technique
characteristic of the IV century. The others have leaf patterns which appear
to be of the XI, or even of the XII century. It appears to me that this
sarcophagus is an authentic work of c. 400, and was probably the tomb in
which S. Ambrogio placed the martyr S. Vitale. The sumptuous scheme of
decoration planned, however, was not finished at the time, and was carried
on with interruptions at widely different ages. I think only the general design,
the borders, the two ends and the one capital mentioned are of the IV century.
Later—perhaps about 800—the peacocks were executed, and the arcades of
the back face carved. In the XII century certain of the capitals were
restored.[81]

On the principal face of the sarcophagus of S. Agricola is an inscription
in letters of perfectly classical character but containing strange mistakes in
grammar.[82] I see no reason for doubting that this inscription is an authentic
production of the end of the IV century. A medallion in the centre of this
face and surrounded by a wreath contains a relief of an archangel represented
as haloed, with wings and holding a crosier. The figure is executed crudely,
the chin is heavy, the forehead, and especially the head, are too low, and the
proportions are stumpy. The drapery is indicated by straight lines separated
by zigzags, yet the treatment of the wings and especially of the right hand
turned upward against the body bears witness to a certain degree of technical
skill. This relief appears to be not of the IV, but of the XI century. To
the left is a stag, upon which are two birds, placed in a rather indecent
attitude. On the other side is a lion, back of him a tree, and again two birds

---

[81] The inscription BEATISSIMO MARTIRI VITALE may be of the IV century,
but the date CCCLXXXII in Gothic letters must have been added in the XIII or XIV
century.

[82] BEATISSIMUM MARTIREM AGRICOLAM HIC RIQUIESCIT| IN DEI
NOMINE

similarly in suggestive postures. These animals are very flatly executed, and with a technique obviously different from that of the angel, although the mane of the lion shows parallel incised lines which seem to have some relation with the drapery of the figure in the medallion. The eyes of the animals are very crudely indicated by a double oval and a dot. In this detail of the technique the relief is analogous to that of the carved plaque of c. 1010 in the cathedral of Aosta (Plate 12, Fig. 1), and this similarity is enhanced by the fact that the eye of the lion is much too large and that of the stag badly placed. I hence conclude that these sculptures were added to the sarcophagus at the time of the translation of the bodies of the saints in 1019. The border is formed of a heart-leaf moulding rather well imitated from the antique, and doubtless of the IV century. Above is a crudely executed anthemion, at the left side a spiral like the abaci of the columns (Plate 24, Fig. 4), and at the right a folded leaf moulding which recalls that in the Chiesa d'Aurona at Milan (c. 1099). It appears to me that this last moulding is of c. 1100, and the spiral and the anthemion of c. 800. At one end is a relief representing S. Ambrogio, S[ANCTVS] AM|BRO|SI|VS, standing between S[ANCTVS] A|GRI|CO|LA, who holds a sceptre, and S TECLA. All three figures are haloed, and the sex of Tecla is indicated by a veil. These reliefs are certainly by the same hand as the angel on the opposite face. The technique of the drapery, as shown in the garment of Agricola, is identical. There are the same heavy proportions, the chins are too long, the foreheads and the upper part of the heads too short, the eyes similarly large and staring. The drapery of the garments of S. Ambrogio is better executed than that of the others. The folds of the garments of S. Tecla are indicated by incised parallel lines. At the two sides of the top is a moulding of anthemia, alternating with eggs and darts flatly and crudely executed, and at the bottom are eggs and darts showing a similar technique. In the centre of the remaining face is the inscription

BEATISSIM. . . . .
MARTYRI
AGRICOLE

and on either side a cartouche which must certainly be modern, and which suggests that the entire sarcophagus may be a forgery. About the edge of this face is a guilloche, and at the bottom a rinceau. I believe that this face is the only modern one of the sarcophagus, and that even this must be earlier than the XVII century.

V. The documentary evidence is conclusive that the church of S. Pietro must have been erected between the years 1080 and 1100. It is clear from internal evidence that the monument must belong to the later, rather than to the earlier, part of the period allowed by the chronicler. Structurally the church seems to belong to that period of indecision which reigned in Lombardy subsequent to the construction of S. Ambrogio at Milan. There is no doubt that the edifice was entirely vaulted, but it is not clear whether it was covered with groin or rib vaults. In the two eastern bays the system was alternating, in the western bay it was uniform. Now, the earliest extant church in which the alternating system was abandoned for the uniform is S. Pietro in Ciel d'Oro at Pavia, consecrated in 1132. S. Pietro of Bologna seems to form a step intermediate between S. Ambrogio at Milan, begun c. 1070, and S. Pietro in Ciel d'Oro. The church of S. Savino at Piacenza, consecrated in 1107, shows a somewhat analogous indecision in that a single groin vault is combined with the rib vaults erected on an alternate system. Structurally, therefore, S. Pietro seems to fall about the year 1095, and this ascription of date is confirmed by the advanced character of the mouldings and the fine masonry (which savour of the XII century), while the crude sculptures show that the influence of Guglielmo da Modena (c. 1106) had not yet reached the neighbouring city of Bologna. S. Pietro, therefore, must be accepted as an authentically dated monument of c. 1095, but it must always be remembered that the original forms were much denatured in the restoration of 1880-1885.

S. SEPOLCRO

III. In plan the church of S. Sepolcro consists of an irregular octagonal outer wall, enclosing a side aisle which is separated from the circular nave by twelve supports disposed in a circle. These supports consist of seven pairs of coupled cylindrical supports and five single cylindrical piers. The coupled columns are formed in every case of a monolithic shaft and a brick pier. The reason for this singular arrangement doubtless is that the builders had available from an older building eight shafts which they wished to utilize. Seven of these shafts were employed in the main arcade, but being too slender to support the superincumbent weight were reinforced by brick piers. The eighth monolithic shaft was employed in the east side of the side aisle, and was considered symbolical of the column at which Christ was scourged.

The nave is covered by a cloistered vault, the triforium with a wooden roof, and the side aisle by groin vaults of curious form, and with many interpenetrations. These vaults (Plate 24, Fig. 3) are modern, but the very shape of the compartments proves that the ancient ones must have been quite as irregular. The arrangement of the ancient aisle responds makes it evident that originally certain triangular compartments were introduced into the vaults, although these compartments are now avoided by the expedient of supporting the vaults in part on corbels. The free-standing column in the middle aisle of the east side seems to have been introduced to simplify the construction, as well as to make it possible to cover with vaults the aisle, excessively wide at this point. The symbolism subsequently given to this column was therefore an afterthought. The original vaults of the side aisles were doubtless groined and supplied with transverse and wall arches.

A system rises from corbels placed over the capitals of the columns of the main arcade, and supports a string-course of double arched corbel-tables placed at the level of the springing of the dome (Plate 24, Fig. 5, 6). In the re-entrant angles of the gallery of the outer wall there is a system consisting of a shaft engaged on a pilaster strip, rising from bases formed of a single square block. About five feet from the ground this shaft is crowned by a cubic capital, very high in proportion to its width, and with an angular cushion. This capital, in turn, supports a single shaft continued to the roof. In the east wall of the gallery are semicircular niches.

In the time of Pullieni[83] S. Sepolcro possessed seven doors. But there are now only six, since one of those leading to S. Pietro was suppressed in the restoration.

The masonry of S. Sepolcro is superior to that of S. Pietro, as nearly as can be judged from the denatured condition of the two edifices. Well formed and regular bricks, covered on the exposed surface with cross-hatching, are laid in horizontal courses separated by thin beds of mortar. In the north wall adjoining the Crocefisso a single herring-bone course is introduced. In the exterior walls bands of marble coating are introduced, as well as geometrical and polychromatic decorative work in brick (Plate 25, Fig. 4). This has all been restored, and how much of the original character it retains it is difficult to say. The character of the masonry proves that the inner and outer walls of the gallery are contemporary.

IV.   The capitals of the main arcade, whether executed in brick or in stone, are all cubic, of very low proportions, with an angular cushion. Those of the side-aisle responds are either pilfered Roman Corinthian or cubic (Plate 24, Fig. 3), the latter having been added without authority in the restoration. The capital of the free-standing column in the east side aisle is of broad-leaved type, with a leaf under each angle and one on each face. The capitals of the triforium (Plate 25, Fig. 1) and of the system (Plate 24, Fig. 5) are ornamented with crisp acanthus leaves or with grotesques. In many cases they are surmounted by stilt-blocks with similar ornamentation. The capitals of the exterior, of similar character, are notable for the deep undercutting. The bases are Attic, but the upper member is in some cases undercut, giving a profile of Gothic character. The ornamented string-course and the corbels of the exterior have been restored, but the portal with its unusual mouldings, of definitely Gothic character, is original. The archivolts of the main arcade are in two unmoulded orders (Plate 24, Fig. 3), and the responds of the side aisles consist of three members, the central one of which is semicircular (Plate 24, Fig. 3). At each angle of the exterior is placed a pilaster strip,

[83] 143.

which, in the upper part of the wall, is replaced by a shaft supporting the double arched corbel-table of the cornice. The masking wall of the dome has on its angles shallow pilaster strips broken in the middle. These support a cornice formed of triangular arched corbel-tables, a saw tooth and a flat corbel-table. The masonry of the upper part of the church is peculiar, consisting of diagonal courses of brick, evidently so laid for decorative purposes. This striking masonry, as well as the polychromatic inlaying of the lower part of the walls, recalls similar decorative masonry in the abbey of Pomposa.

In the Calvary, which rises in the centre of the church, have been incorporated the remains of the old ambo, which includes admirable sculptures of the four Evangelists. On the scroll of the eagle of St. John are visible the remains of an inscription evidently painted twice over. It was the usual formula, *In principio erat Verbum*. The rest of the Calvary, with the sculptures of the angel, the three Marys and the sleeping guards, is a work of the Gothic period which has suffered very severely in numerous restorations.

In the sacristy is a fresco perhaps of the XIII century, representing the Slaughter of the Innocents, and other old frescos coming from S. Sepolcro are preserved in the passage-way leading to the sacristy. These poor remnants are all that is left of the painted decoration of the monument.

V. S. Sepolcro contains pilfered materials belonging to two different epochs. The Corinthian capitals and monolithic shafts are classical, and must have come originally from some Roman building. The cubic capitals in stone (many of which do not fit their shafts) must have come from an edifice erected in the first half of the XI century, since the straight cushions and low proportions recall the capitals at Sannazzaro Sesia (Plate 201, Fig. 6)—1040, Stradella (Plate 210), and many other buildings of the same period. These capitals, I therefore conjecture, must have been made in the course of some of the restorations carried out in the church in the second quarter of the XI century. They were employed as second-hand material in the present structure, and for the sake of symmetry the new capitals in brick of the main arcade were given the same form.

To determine the date of the existing edifice, it is necessary to anticipate our study of the Atrio di Pilato. It is evident that the latter is earlier than S. Sepolcro. The proof of this is, that the two western piers of the Atrio could not have been designed to stand at the angle of a court, since they are supplied with a system which would not fit in an angle (Plate 25, Fig. 4). Therefore the western bay or bays of the atrium must have been destroyed to make way for the new church of S. Sepolcro; and, in fact, the existing arches uniting the Atrio and the church are constructed of masonry distinctly different from that of the rest of the atrium.[84] Now the Atrio, we shall presently see, was constructed c. 1142. S. Sepolcro must, therefore, be later than 1142.

[84] It is true these arches have been restored.

The triangular arched corbel-tables of the upper cornice of S. Sepolcro are an extraordinary feature which recalls a similar cornice at S. Ruffillo (1178). From this it may be argued that S. Sepolcro belongs to the last half of the XII century, and in fact the flat corbels of the upper cornice can not be earlier than 1150. The masonry of S. Sepolcro is distinctly less advanced than that of S. Ruffillo (Plate 203, Fig. 3), a fact which enables us to limit the construction of S. Sepolcro to the third quarter of the XII century. The date may be still further limited by observing that the broad-leaved capital of the eastern aisle, and the uncut bases showing clearly French Gothic influence, can not be earlier than c. 1160, while the purely Lombard capitals of the shafts and triforium, ornamented with grotesques and string designs, can not be much later than that date. S. Sepolcro may, therefore, be assigned to c. 1160. The sculptures of the ambo may be supposed to have been executed soon after the completion of the church, or c. 1170.

S. Trinità and the Atrio di Pilato

III. The excavations made in the church of S. Trinità in 1913 have thrown a flood of light upon the history of S. Stefano. These excavations have not yet been published, and had only been partially completed when I was able to inspect them by the courtesy of Mgr. Belvideri; but enough had been laid bare to establish the fact that the ancient church of S. Croce and the Atrio di Pilato formed a single and homogeneous edifice. This building[85] consisted of an open court, part of which is still preserved in the Atrio, probably surrounded originally on all four sides by a colonnade. On the east side the arcade was double, and beyond the second aisle opened a group of chapels, the central one in the form of a cross, the two at the two ends square, between which and the central chapel on either side were two semicircular niches. It is possible, but not proved, that the arcade on the east side of the Atrio may have been in two stories (for the remains of monastic buildings extant above the church of S. Croce give reason to think that there may have been a loggia opening from the monastery upon the east side of the Atrio), and that it is to this that the monk refers when he speaks of the superimposed arcades of the Atrio. In the XIII century a wall was constructed which shut off the Atrio from the eastern chapels known as S. Croce. The foundations of this wall, earlier than the existing eastern wall of S. Trinità, have been discovered. Beneath the foundations of the chapels of 1141 came to light during the excavations the foundations of other chapels of earlier date, possibly of the VI century. The masonry of S. Croce is identical with that of the Atrio di Pilato, and consists of large bricks well laid in horizontal courses.

The Atrio di Pilato at present consists of a central area with porticoes on two sides. In the court stands the famous vase of Luitprando. The porticoes

---

[85] A sketch plan of the excavations has been published by Testi Rasponi, 260.

are at present covered with groin vaults of the XVI century, for the most part remade in the recent restoration (Plate 25, Fig. 4). That they were originally covered with groin vaults with wall and transverse ribs is, however, proved by the section of the piers (Plate 25, Fig. 7), which are quatrefoiled, with spurs on the inner angles.[86] The member of the piers which faces the court is surmounted by a system consisting of a stout pilaster strip which forms an effective buttress to the thrust of the vault, and terminates in an arched corbel-table. The responds have a plain rectangular section (Plate 25, Fig. 4).

It is evident that the Atrio was at one time larger than it is now. The ancient piers, as may be clearly seen, have been imbedded in the façade of S. Trinità. Moreover, as has been already pointed out, the western bays of the Atrio must have been torn down when S. Sepolcro was erected. It is worthy of observation that there could not have been a vault in a western bay of the Atrio subsequent to the construction of S. Sepolcro, for a window of S. Sepolcro, with many mouldings and in many orders, is so placed that a vault would necessarily have had to cut across it (Plate 25, Fig. 4). There must, therefore, always have been a wooden roof here from the time of the construction of S. Sepolcro to the restoration of the Atrio in the XVI century.

The masonry of the west arches of the Atrio is different alike from that of S. Sepolcro and from that of the other bays of the Atrio. These arches must have been destroyed when the Ionic portico on the east side of the Atrio was erected in the XVI century, and they were doubtless replaced by the restorers of 1880-1885. The restorers probably found traces of the old masonry which must have been like that of S. Sepolcro, but their attempts to imitate it were only very moderately successful.

IV. The capitals of the Atrio are of a developed cubic variety in which the line of the cushion is emphasized by an incised moulding (Plate 25, Fig. 7). In the excavations at S. Croce have come to light several Gothic capitals, as well as others of 1141. One of the latter, with finely executed grotesques, recalls certain capitals of S. Zeno of Verona. Another is of Corinthianesque type, with small and dry acanthus leaves, deeply undercut, and showing excellent technical execution. The bases of the piers of the Atrio are of the Renaissance, but the old bases, of brick, with Attic profile, have been laid bare in the two piers imbedded in the façade of S. Trinità. The western bay of the Atrio on the south side has on the archivolt a saw-tooth moulding which resembles the similar moulding on an archivolt of the monastery. This arch has, however, been restored, and it is impossible to know what authority there was for the presence of the ornament.[87]

[86] The supports of S. Croce were probably monolithic columns, since three shafts of Verona marble and one of green marble are still visible.

[87] I was long puzzled by observing that the cornice of the monastery, identical with that of S. Sepolcro, extends as far as the existing western façade of S. Trinità. It was

BOLOGNA, S. STEFANO

In the existing façade of S. Trinità is a portal of c. 1190, evidently not in its original position.

V. The Atrio di Pilato and S. Croce formed a homogeneous construction rebuilt, according to the testimony of the monk, c. 1142.

THE CROCEFISSO AND CONFESSI

III, IV. The ancient church of S. Giovanni has been at least twice reconstructed, once in the Gothic period (as witnessed by the character of the masonry of the south wall) and once in the middle of the XVII century. In the crypt of the Confessi are some remains of Romanesque architecture. The modern Renaissance vaults are supported on columns and piers. The eastern columns are of the Renaissance, and supplied with Doric capitals. Of the other capitals, three are of Byzantinesque-Corinthianesque type, like the capitals of S. Sepolcro. The rest, with cubic capitals having an incised line following the curve of the cushion, are precisely like those of the Atrio di Pilato. The quatrefoiled columns of the west end of the crypt also recall the Atrio.

V. Of the church of S. Giovanni, to which the bodies of the saints Agricola and Vitale were translated in the year 1019, nothing remains. The few fragments of Romanesque architecture preserved in the crypt of the Confessi, dating from c. 1150, give us reason to suppose that the church of S. Giovanni was reconstructed in the XII century after S. Croce and before S. Sepolcro.

CLOISTER OF THE CELESTINES

III. The charming cloisters (Plate 25, Fig. 2) are in two stories. In the lower story there are in each face five great round-arched openings, of which the central one forms a doorway giving access to the court. These doorways are severely plain, and have not even an impost moulding, so that the arch rests on the rectangular brick pier, without any connecting member. The two openings on either side of each doorway are grouped together and furnished with intermediate supports consisting either of four colonnettes or parts of large marble shafts. This material is all second-hand. One of the colonnettes appears to have come from a biforum of c. 1120. The columns and colonnettes have no capitals properly speaking, but merely entablature slabs. The west and north galleries of the lower story are now walled off to form chapels which connect with the Atrio di Pilato. Like the south

difficult to see how, in the XII century, this cornice could have been suspended in the air over the empty centre of the atrium. The explanation, of course, is, that this cornice of the monastery entire is an addition of the restorers of 1880-1885, who merely copied the old cornice of S. Sepolcro.

gallery they are covered with Renaissance vaults, but it is certain that the east gallery, with its plain wooden roof, more nearly reproduces the ancient dispositions. The masonry of the lower story, as far as can be judged in its present much restored state, was rough, but the bricks, without cross-hatching, were regularly shaped and laid in perfectly horizontal beds. The bits of marble and Lombard carving encrusted in the walls were probably put there by the restorers.

The upper story has in the gallery fourteen graceful arcades in two orders, carried on coupled columns, except at each corner, where there is a single heavy column. The masonry is very decorative, and consists of bricks and stones of varied tints, inlaid in geometric and polychromatic patterns.

IV. The capitals are of varied types. The prevailing type is adorned with broad leaves which betray French Gothic influence, and volutes which similarly smack of northern character. In the west gallery are many capitals sculptured with grotesques. The bases are of Attic type and supplied with griffes. Those of the coupled columns are cut from a single block and left attached. In some cases the two shafts also are left attached.

V. A study of the masonry of the north wall of the cloister adjoining the church of S. Trinità proves (1) that the lower story of the cloister is anterior to the church of S. Croce, that is, to 1142, and that the upper story is later than S. Croce, that is, than 1142. Now, while there is a difference of character in the upper and lower stories of the cloister, this difference is not sufficient to make it possible to place more than forty or fifty years at the utmost between the construction of the two parts of the edifice. We must therefore assume that the lower story was constructed only slightly before S. Croce, or c. 1135. The upper story must be of c. 1180, as is proved by its close analogy to the cloisters of S. Ruffillo.

BONATE DI SOTTO,[1] S. GIULIA

(Plate 26, Fig. 1, 3, 5)

I. The ancient basilica of S. Giulia, of which the ruins now serve as the chapel of the Campo Santo of the commune at Bonate di Sotto, has been much studied, especially by archæologists of the older school. As early as 1784, Lupi, the classic historian of Bergamo, studied and described the edifice from an archæological standpoint, and published several excellent engravings.[2] These drawings are of great value because they show the condition of the church at the end of the XVIII century when numerous portions, which have

[1] (Bergamo).   [2] I, 204 f.

since fallen into ruin, were still intact. It is evident, however, that even before the time of Lupi the edifice had been subjected to a crude restoration, for his engravings show a high wall of rubble in the choir, evidently the same wall which still stands to-day. This wall, as well as the block capitals at the north of the choir, which are also shown in the drawings, must have been added not long before the time of Lupi. His drawings show, moreover, a wall rising over the triumphal arch, with traces of a window. This must have been the remains of a belfry. The nave responds, many of which have disappeared, are shown in the drawings as being all uniform, and as consisting of five members of which the central one was a shaft, the others rectangular. The piers of the nave were uniform, and of a section identical with that of the central one, which is still extant. In Lupi's time the east gable of the church was well preserved, but the gables over the absidioles were in ruin. The church had no roof, and the nave had already been in great part destroyed. Lupi's drawings and description of the church are a most remarkable achievement for the XVIII century, and are worthy of the best archæological production of a much later period. In his drawings the irregularities of the bays and even of the piers are shown.

Lupi was followed in 1807 by Ronchetti, who included a study of S. Giulia in his history of Bergamo.[3] In 1823 Séroux d'Agincourt published important engravings of the edifice.[4] These drawings show the side-aisle walls with their responds still intact throughout the entire length of the nave, and also the base of the façade. The choir and its southern side aisle are shown without vaults, but parts of the eastern arcade of the nave appear as still standing. Like Lupi, Séroux noticed the irregularity in the length of the nave bays, but in his plan no vaults are indicated. Five years later, or in 1828, appeared the description of the Sacchi brothers.[5]

About the middle of the XIX century Osten published a plan and a section of the church.[6] His engravings show the building much more ruined than it appears in the sections of Séroux and Lupi, but are extremely important because they show clearly in the choir the amortizements of a rib vault. There can, therefore, be no doubt that Osten's plan, which shows the nave and choir entirely covered with rib vaults, is a correct restoration. The sumptuous drawings of De Dartein show the monument almost exactly in the condition that it is to-day. Some years later Mothes[7] studied the building, of which a description was also published by Locatelli, in 1879.[8] In 1888 an important study of the documentary evidence for the construction of the church was contributed by Ferroni.

II. In the early part of the XVI century Pellegrini wrote that Queen Teodolinda built the church of S. Giulia of Bonate, and cites as his authority

[3] I, 56.   [4] Vol. IV, Plate 24, Fig. 1-5; Plate 69, Fig. 17.
[5] 35.   [6] Plates XLI and XLII.   [7] I, 235.   [8] III, 189-192.

for this fact a stone found in that church by a certain Giovanni Filippo of Novara.[9] The inscription, unfortunately, has entirely disappeared, and was no longer to be seen in 1784 when Lupi first studied the edifice. That author conjectures that it disappeared when, about 1745, the nave of the church was torn down to furnish building material for the new campanile of the modern town.

Whether or not the church was founded by Teodolinda, there is no doubt that it existed from a very early epoch, since it is mentioned in a will of May, 774.[10]

This document proves that in the VIII century the town of Bonate had the same name that it has to-day. Ferroni, however, has brought forward several documents which seem to imply that in the XII century the town was known as Lesina, from the river which flows near it. Now it is known that on May 14, 1129, the church of S. Giulia at Lesina was not yet consecrated.[11] Some confirmation is lent to the view that Lesina and Bonate are one and the same place by the fact that the style of S. Giulia is precisely that of c. 1130.

III. The edifice originally consisted of a nave four bays long, two side aisles, a choir of one bay flanked by side aisles (Plate 26, Fig. 5), and three

[9] Operata est hac in Vinea beata Theodelinda longobardorū regina Vxor Agilulphi. 13 regis, quando circa hæc tempora ædificari fecit Ecclesiā ad honorem S. Iuliæ Virginis, & martyris, in territorio Bergomensi in loco de bonate, in ripa fluminis Brembi, eamq; prediis dotauit. Hæc ex quodam marmoreo quadrato lapide in eadem Ecclesia inuento a Reuerendo Dno Io. Philippo nouariensi canonico regulari. (19).

[10] Regnante domini nostri Desiderio et Adalchis viris excellentissimis reges, anno regni eorum octabo decimo et quintodecimo, mense madio, indictione duodecima. . . . Tuido gasindio domni regis filius bone memorie Teoderolfi civis Bergome dixi: . . . Primis omnium volo atque instituo habere suprascriptas sanctas basilices sanctorum Alexandri et beatissimi [Petri] ecclesia sancte Marie et sancti Vincentii curte domoculta juris mei, quam habere videor in fundo Bonnate . . . de suprascripta divisione, volo atque instituo, ut de istas suprascriptas curtis et de omnia ad eas pertinentes habeant mea portione in integrum basilicas suprascriptas inter se equaliter dividentes custodibus earum per medietatem, ut exinde de mea portione . . . . . accipiat basilica S. Alexandri et S. Petri, et reliqua medietatem accipiat ecclesia S. Marie et S. Vincentii pro missa et luminaria mea et anime mee remedium. Quidem vero de massariis de nostra curte in Bonate pertinente statuo exinde habere era una massaricia in Raudus exercente per Gundepert massario . . . volo hec omnia habere basilica beatissimi Christi martyris sancti Juliani sita Bonnate et ejus custodibus pro missa et luminaria mea. Insuper et volo ea habere orto meo in Bonnate prope era suprascripte basilice in integrum . . . Basilice beatissimi et confessoris et sacerdotis sancti [Zenonis] prope civitate veronensium, ubi ejus requiescit sanctum corpus, volo habere portionem mea de democulta in finibus veronense. . . . Basilice beatissimi S. Archangeli Michaelis intra civitate ticinensium volo ut habeat pro anima et luminaria mea ad presenti die obiti mei possessionem mea de terra massaricia super fluvio Pado, locus ubi dicitur Gravanate. . . . (*Hist. Pat. Mon.*, XIII, 97).

[11] Preteria de ecclesia de Licena nondum consecrata cum tamen nulli omnino liceat absque licentia episcopi ecclesiam construere, ecc.

apses. However, all except the three apses, the lower part of the choir, and in some places the foundations of the nave, have disappeared. The choir has been rebuilt to form a mortuary chapel (Plate 26, Fig. 5). Mothes states that the vaults were never completed. On what authority this statement rests I have never been able to discover. Certain it is, however, that the builders planned to erect a vaulted edifice. This is clear, not only from Osten's drawings mentioned above, but from the section of the compound piers on which are engaged members which could have served only for vaulting shafts (Plate 26, Fig. 1, 5). Since the system was uniform, many of the vaults must have been very oblong. The two eastern bays of the nave were about square, and the corresponding compartments of the side aisles hence oblong; the remaining bays of the nave were shorter, and in consequence the compartments of the side aisles of less extreme proportions. The fact that the system included three members (Plate 26, Fig. 1) shows that the vaults of the nave were supplied with diagonal ribs, but the side aisles were doubtless covered with groin vaults. In the south side aisle of the bay which still stands are clearly visible the remains of a wall rib. These groin vaults of the side aisles must have been very highly domed and have had almost the character of a longitudinal barrel vault, like the vaults of S. Giorgio at Almenno. This may be deduced from the placing of the window in the one bay which still stands. It is impossible to say whether there was any gallery or clearstory. The masonry was of ashlar, in which, however, the horizontal courses were frequently broken, and in places rubble was introduced, as at S. Giorgio at Almenno, S. Fermo di Sopra, etc. The exterior walls were reinforced by very heavy rectangular buttresses of almost Gothic character.

IV. The capitals (Plate 26, Fig. 1, 3) are of a grotesque or of a Byzantine-Corinthianesque type. They are executed at times somewhat crudely, but the design is refined and evidently rather advanced. There is little undercutting, the turned-over edges of the uncut acanthus leaves being hardly more than incised. These capitals are without exact analogy in Lombard art, but present points of contact with those at S. Pietro in Ciel d'Oro at Pavia. The abaci show very dry mouldings of a complicated character, and the same abundance of fine mouldings that characterizes the bases. The bases are at times Attic (Plate 26, Fig. 1), at times formed of a series of tori without any scotiæ (Plate 26, Fig. 1). There are no griffes. The archivolts were originally in two unmoulded orders. The windows are small and evidently intended to serve without glass. Those of the central apse are in three orders, and shafted. Two half columns were engaged on the façade.

The apses are adorned with small, arched corbel-tables supported on shafts. A fragment of an arched corbel-table and a shaft between the central apse and each of the absidioles seem to imply that the former was built later than the latter. There is, however, no appreciable difference in the style of the architecture, and the break of the masonry probably denotes a change of plan rather than an interruption in the construction.

V. The character of the mouldings as well as of the capitals makes it evident that S. Giulia of Bonate can not be earlier than the second quarter of the XII century. The uniform system with rib vaults recalls S. Pietro in Ciel d'Oro at Pavia, an edifice consecrated in 1132. The church may, therefore, be considered as an authentically dated monument of 1129.

BORGO S. DONNINO,[1] CATHEDRAL

(Plate 27, Fig. 3; Plate 28, Fig. 1, 2; Plate 29, Fig. 1, 2, 3, 4, 5; Plate 30, Fig. 1, 2, 3, 4, 5)

I. The cathedral of Borgo S. Donnino has attracted considerable attention among archæologists, less for its architecture,[2] remarkable as this is, than for the celebrated sculptures of the façade, which critics are almost unanimous in ascribing to Benedetto, called Antelami. Lopez was the first to call attention to these reliefs, but he has been followed by almost every subsequent writer who has treated of Italian sculpture. The study of Zimmermann is, perhaps, the keenest and most critical of any which has yet appeared. This author ascribes the sculptures of the central and southern portal to Benedetto, but considers that they belong to his latest period, that is, that they were executed in the XIII century, subsequent to that master's activity in the baptistery at Parma. The northern portal, however, with the exception of the triangular gable subsequently added, is judged by Zimmermann to be earlier, and an imitation of the work of Nicolò at Piacenza, Verona and Ferrara. The capital of the interior, the Madonna in a niche of the campanile, and the life of the saint, are all works by the hand of Benedetto himself, according to the same authority; but the reliefs in both towers and those inserted in the façade are the work of pupils. The sculptures of Enoch and Elijah, Zimmermann believes to be Benedetto's earliest work at Borgo S. Donnino, but later than his work at Parma. Less analytical is the criticism of Toschi, who merely assigns broadly the sculptures of the façade to Benedetto,[3] and believes that they were executed in the XII century, that is, before the works in the baptistery of Parma. Venturi[4] agrees with Toschi that the sculptures were all executed between the years 1178 and 1196, but

[1] (Parma).

[2] It is remarkable, however, that as early as 1843 Knight (II, Plate XIII) published an engraving of the façade.

[3] Toschi attributes to Antelami even the Hercules and the sculptures of the apse vault. The reliefs at the north end of the façade, however, he ascribes to pupils.

[4] III, 324-328.

concedes that Benedetto was aided by his pupils. Pettorelli has contributed a study of the holy-water basin without, however, arriving at any definite conclusion, either as to its date or the interpretation of its sculptures. Good photographs of the church and sculptures have been published by Martin.

An important historical source, both for the interpretation of the sculptures and the history of the church, is the life of S. Donnino, of which numerous versions are extant. An attempt (which, however, is far from being satisfactory) to collate and standardize the various manuscripts has been made by the Bollandists.[5] A close student, however, will find it necessary to consult the original codices. Of these two are preserved at Paris in the Bibliothèque Nationale,[6] both copies of the same life and the one subsequently printed by the Bollandists. A somewhat more extended life contained in a codex at Florence, which I have not seen, has been severely condemned by the Bollandists.[7] In fact, it appears that even the earlier life of the saint "was composed with greater love for S. Donnino than for the truth." This life forms, nevertheless, the sole basis for the numerous later lives, of which the longest one, written in Italian sometime before 1720, is preserved in an elaborate manuscript which I saw in the episcopal archives. The modern biographies of Giacopazzi, Farinelli, Bagattoni and the anonymous *Brevi Cenni* are all without critical value. For the history of the church, in addition to the notices contained in the classic work of Affò, should be consulted the *Ordo* of Buscarini, in which are printed valuable extracts from the *Memorie Istoriche di Borgo S. Donnino* of Pietro Granelli. The latter is a manuscript preserved in the archives at Borgo. In the same archives are also numerous other documents, of late date, it is true, but frequently of considerable value for the study of the edifice.

II. The tradition is constant that the cathedral of Borgo S. Donnino stands upon the site of the tomb of the martyr. The life of the saint merely tells us that he suffered under the emperor Maximian, but a chronicle of Piacenza places his passion very precisely in the year 289.[8] Flying from the face of the emperor in Germany over the Via Claudia towards Rome,[9] the saint was overtaken by executioners, midway between Piacenza and Parma, and decapitated. After this, having miraculously picked up his head with his

---

[5] The edition of Mombrizio, ed. 1910, I, 423, is inferior.

[6] No. Latin 5353, f. 125; and Latin 5308, f. 164.

[7] See texts cited below, pp. 168, 169-170.

[8] Anno Christi CCLXXXVIIII. tempore Diocletiani Imperatoris & Maximiani decollatus fuit S. Domninus Miles apud Flumen Sistroni inter Placentiam & Parmam. Qui postquam fuit decollatus, miraculosè caput ejus abscissum in manibus suis capiens, portavit ultra dictum Flumen Sistroni, reponendo illud in loco, ubi nunc est Ecclesia sui nominis. (Johannis de Mussis, *Chronicon Placentinum*, ed. Muratori, R. I. S., XVI, 447).

[9] The Bollandists have amply proved that the Via Emilia was known in mediæval times as the Via Claudia. (9 Oct., IV, 988).

hands, he carried it across the river Stirone, and lay down in the spot where is now the church dedicated in his honour. According to the discredited Florentine codex, the body lay in this place unknown to all for about thirty years. After this, in the time of Constantine the Great, it pleased God to manifest it to the faithful by sending upon that place a celestial light. Therefore the bishop of Parma was summoned, who, divinely instructed that the body of some holy martyr would be found there, dug into the ground to the depth of three cubits, where he found a stone tomb and in that the body of the saint, fragrant with an ineffable perfume, carrying his head in his hands, and as uncorrupted as when first laid there. The bishop, therefore, raised the body from the ground, and deposited it in a church which he built to the holy martyr, and commanded that that place should henceforth be called by the name of S. Donnino.[10] This passage is open to considerable difficulties. In the first place, as the Bollandists observe, in the time of Constantine the Great there was no bishop of Parma. Ughelli, it is true, gives a bishop of Parma who sat in 362, but critical studies have demonstrated that in point of fact the diocese of Parma was not founded until considerably later. It is, therefore, impossible that a bishop of Parma should have been present at the invention of the body of the saint about the year 314. Accordingly, the chronology of the Florentine codex has been almost unanimously abandoned by historians, and the invention of the body of the saint has been assigned to various later dates. Thus, the author of the *Brevi Cenni* ascribes it to the VII century, following in this probably the manuscript in the archives cited by Buscarini.[11] Michele, however, accepts the date 314 for the first invention and gives a new legend that the church was enlarged about 604 by the inevitable Teodolinda.[12]

[10] Jacuit eo loci [where he was martyred] sancti Martyris corpus, ut codicis Florentini Acta narrare pergunt, annis circiter triginta, omnibus ignotum: at iis evolutis, & Constantini Magni tempore illud Deo placuit, immissa illuc cælesti luce, fidelibus manifestare. Evocatus igitur fuit Parmensis episcopus (primus è Parmensibus episcopis, nomine notus, fuit Philippus, qui anno 362 sedit secundum Ughellum) qui, cum divinitus (ut aiunt iterum Acta laudata) edoctus fuisset, sancti cujusdam Martyris corpus ibidem inventum iri, effossa humo ad trium cubitorum altitudinem lapideum detexit tumulum, in eoque corpus sancti Martyris, mirabili odore fragrans, gestans in manibus caput, & adeo recens, ac situm primum Sanctus martyrium subiisset. . . . Levatum è terra cum sarcophago corpus in templo, sancto Martyri dicato, deposuit, locumque illum S. Domnini nomine, deinceps appellari voluit . . . . . Haec corporis S. Domnini inventio prima, primaque ejus nomini dedicata ecclesia. (*Acta Sanctorum*, Oct., IV, 991).

[11] Occasione primae Inventionis Corporis S. Domnini, quae probabiliter accidit vertente saeculo VII, Episcopus Dioecesanus erigere fecit aediculum in loco, ubi nocturni luminis indicio S. Martyris ossa reperta fuere. Ineunte vero saeculo IX parva illa Ecclesia collectis oblationibus ad nobiliorem formam fuit redacta. (*Mem. hist. asservat. in Episcopal. Cancellaria*).—Buscarini, 9.

[12] Quantunque si pretenda con qualche fondamento, che circa l'anno 604 da Teodolinda moglie di Agilulfo Re de' Longobardi assieme con suo Marito fosse fabbricata

BORGO S. DONNINO, CATHEDRAL

According to a tradition almost as elusive as those which surround the life of the saint, the church received notable benefactions from Charlemagne. The best source for this is the sculptures of the last years of the XII century, still extant in the tympanum of the northern portal (Plate 29, Fig. 5). These reliefs show an emperor seated on a throne, crowned, and bearing a sphere and a sceptre. Above is the inscription:

. . . . . KARVLVS IPR

This relief is placed next to another which shows the pope, Hadrian II, investing the archpriest of Borgo S. Donnino with mitre and crosier, and can only be intended to commemorate some privilege granted to the church by Charlemagne. This privilege conferred by Charlemagne is also referred to in a diploma of Frederick Barbarossa of 1162.[13] It appears, however, that modern commentators have gone too far in deducing from this diploma that the church of Borgo S. Donnino carried the title of *Ecclesia Imperialis* from the time of Charlemagne.[14] The author of the *Brevi Cenni*[15] points out that there is no evidence that Barbarossa created the office of archpriest in the church. In fact, in the absence of authentic documents it is impossible to

una Chiesa sopra il Corpo di San Donnino Martire nello stesso luogo dove oggi si trova la Cattedrale di Borgo San Donnino, qualunque però ella si fosse, in vece dell'antica capelletta, la quale eretta vi fu dai pii fedeli dopo la prima invenzione del detto Santo, che si crede avvenisse circa l'anno 314, restituita la pace alla Chiesa sotto Costantino il Grande: pure non si sa, che allora costituito vi fosse alcun Sacerdote, o Custode, il quale avesse cura di quella Chiesa ad onta che probabilmente nell'anno 777 l'Imperatore Carlo Magno la dichiarasse Chiesa Imperiale, siccome ciò si annuncia nel privilegio concesso alla detta Chiesa da Federico I. Imperatore detto Barbarossa, li 26 Luglio dell'anno millecento sessanta due. (*Memorie storiche su la Chiesa Cattedrale di Borgo San Donnino*, MS. of Giuseppe Michele, of 1837, in Archivio del Cancelliere Vescovile, Borgo S. Donnino, f. 3).

[13] In nomine sancte & individue Trinitatis Fredericus divina favente clementia Romanorum Imperator Augustus. . . . Nos divine retributionis intuitu Ecclesiam sancti Donnini Martyris de Brugo [*sic*] sicut semper fuit in tuitione Imperatorum antecessorum nostrorum ita sub nostra imperiali protectione ac defensione benigne suscepimus. Tandem est quod nostra imperiali auctoritate jubemus quatenus feuda que data erant clericis pro prebenda eorum videlicet possessiones Ecclesie a clericis alienata vel vendita vel in libellum data vel pignoribus obligata aut aliquo alio modo injuste alienata ad Ecclesiam redeant. Et liceat Archipresbitero auctoritate nostra in possessionem eorum feudorum ingredi quemadmodum laicis ex constitutione Imperatorum licet. Preterea statuentes precipimus ut de villa Furnuli que Ecclesia a Karolo Imperatore pro prebendata est . . . non Consules . . . potestatam super eos habeant. . . . Acta sunt hec anno dominice Incarnationis M. C. LXII. Indictione decima regnante Domino Federico Romanorum Imperatore victoriosissimo anni Regni ejus decimo Imperii vero octavo. Dat. in Territorio Placent. in plano Bardonese post destructum Mediolanum sexto Kalendas Augusti (Affò, II, 373).

[14] See *Memorie storiche di Borgo S. Donnino* da Sac. Pietro Granelli, MS. in archivis, f. 35; also text cited above, pp. 166-167, and Michele, MS. cit., f. 6.

[15] 113.

say how many of the privileges in the diploma of Barbarossa are new concessions and how many merely confirmations of rights long enjoyed. No more,
therefore, is certain than that in the XII century there was prevalent a
tradition that the church had been privileged by Charlemagne.

Little new light is afforded by a legend narrated in the Florentine codex
and branded as fabulous by the Bollandists. According to this source
Charlemagne, after he had conquered Desiderio, the last king of the Lombards,
was hastening towards Rome and was passing on horse-back through Borgo
S. Donnino. At that time the church of the saint had been destroyed. When
his horse came to the spot where the body of the saint lay, it remained
motionless. The king, enlightened by an angel as to the cause of the miracle,
immediately exhumed the body of the saint and placed it in a costly church
which he erected there, after which he hastened on to Rome where, by the
favour of S. Donnino, he was honourably received.[16]

The life of the saint tells us that in the course of time the miracles
performed at the tomb of the martyr gave rise to a great increase in the cult
of the saint, not only among the natives of Borgo S. Donnino, but also among
pilgrims, so that the old church became obviously incapable of holding the
worshippers. It therefore seemed good to the inhabitants of Borgo to begin
to build a larger church, but it so happened that no one knew in what part
of the old church the body of S. Donnino had been laid. Nevertheless it was
revealed repeatedly to a certain priest that it was to be found in the middle
of the church. Therefore the bishop of Parma was summoned, who began to

---

[16] . . . Ex Actis hactenus laudatis ecclesia S. Domnino extructa fuit Constantini
Magni tempore, instaurata verò & ampliata seculo XIII: at Actis Flor. ad calcem lacinia
quædam additur, valdè fabulosa, in qua Carolus Magnus novam S. Domnino ecclesiam
excitasse dicitur. Sic ferè quantum ad substantiam habet: Carolus Magnus cùm,
devicto Desiderio, Longobardorum rege, Romam properaret, transiretque Burgo S.
Domnini, equus ejus eo loco, quo S. Domnini corpus jacebat (destructa quippe tunc
erat ejus ecclesia, ut quidem ibi legitur) immobilis substitit: rex verò rei causam
ignorans ab angelo edocetur, S. Domnini corpus ibi tumulatum esse, & honorifico magis
loco reponendum esse: qua de causa Carolus, effosso S. Domnini corpori magnificam
suis sumptibus jussit condi ecclesiam: tum verò Romam progressus S. Domnini favore
honorificè fuit susceptus, auctusque jure ipsum Pontificem Romanum eligendi, &
ordinandi Apostolicam Sedem, & quidem de voluntate omnium Cardinalium & totius
concilii; & jure investituræ episcoporum & archiepiscoporum ante eorum consecrationem,
ac denique titulo imperatoris à Romanis fuisse decoratum. Sed sufficere debuerant
laciniæ hujus auctori fabulæ satis equidem multæ & palpabiles S. Domnini Actis sive
ab eodem sive ab altero jam prius intrusæ. Addit confici præterea jussisse Carolum
calicem, cui S. Domnini deus fuit insertus, eaque divinitus concessa vis, ut ex illo
bibentibus nullum sit læsionis a rabidis canibus periculum: addit denique calicem illum
à latronibus aliquando fuisse subreptum; sed ad Sisterionem fluvium, ubi occisus martyr
fuerat, nullis malleorum ictibus frangi potuisse: latrones verò corporis doloribus sibi
immissis compulsos fuisse, eò, unde illum abstulerant, reportare, quæ, si vera sunt,
doleo à magis probato auctore litteris non fuisse consignata. (*Acta Sanctorum*, Oct.,
IV, 989-991).

look for the sacred relics. The ground was dug in that place where it had been revealed to the priest that the body lay. Meanwhile, in the neighbouring church of S. Dalmazio a multitude of people prayed for the happy invention of the saint. God heard the common prayers, and the tomb of the holy martyr was discovered, and immediately the news was carried from the church of S. Donnino to that of S. Dalmazio, and excited the people assembled there to rush in haste across the river to the church of S. Donnino, over the wooden bridge which spanned the Stirone. This bridge, owing to the sudden weight, broke, and many were precipitated into the water, among them a pregnant woman whose time was almost fulfilled; but by the merits and prayers of S. Donnino it was granted that all escaped uninjured from the grave peril. After these things the bishop raised with great devotion the holy relics of the martyr, and translated them into the place in which they are now preserved, and the church of the martyr was adorned with reliefs and paintings.[17]

[17] Crescente temporum lapsu prodigiorum beneficiorumque in mortales sancti Martyris meritis et intercessione à Deo collatorum numero, crevit pariter in sanctum Martyrem cultus & veneratio, non modò indigenarum, sed & peregrè illuc venientium, ita ut antiqua S. Domnini ecclesia capiendo illuc concurrentium numero impar videretur, ut utraque Acta loquuntur. Visum itaque indigenis est ampliorem sancto Martyri ecclesiam condere: at interim tamen temporis diuturnitate contigerat, ut qua ecclesiæ veteris parte S. Domnini corpus delitesceret, dubitaretur: tandem sacerdoti cuidam iterum ac iterum revelatum fuisse aiunt, illud in media jacere ecclesia: ergò arcessitur Parmensis episcopus, qui in sacras exuvias inquirat: effoditur humus eo loci, ubi illas jacere supradictus sacerdos divinitus intellexerat, orante interim in propinqua S. Dalmatii populi multitudine pro felici inquisitionis in sacras istas reliquias successu. Audivit communes preces Deus; detectus est sancti Martyris tumulus, ac statim ejus rei fama è S. Dalmatii ad S. Domnini ecclesiam excivit multitudinem populi; quæ dum confertim per ligneum pontem, Sisterioni fluvio injectum ad S. Domnini ecclesiam properat, præ nimio pondere disrupto ponte, plurimi in præceps acti sunt, eosque inter mulier vicina partui: sed S. Domnini precibus meritisque datum est, omnes è tam grandi periculo, ne leviter quidem sauciatos, evasisse. *Post haec,* inquiunt Acta apud Gallonium & Mombritium, *episcopus magna cum devotione, elevans sacrosanctas martyris Domnini reliquias transtulit in locum, in quo nunc venerabiliter conditæ sunt. . . . Ecclesia quoque sancti Martyris amplioribus extensa spatiis, laquearibus verò & parietibus vario picturæ genere decenter ornata refulget. . . .* Quo tempore, quove Parmae (anno enim dumtaxat 1601 Burgus S. Domnini sede episcopali donatus fuit) sedente episcopo ea contigerint, silent laudata Acta: docet autem Ughellus tom. 2 Italiæ sacræ auctæ col. 174 de Opizzone, Parmensi ita scribens: *Vir fuit Opizzo eloquentissimus, in utroque jure peritissimus, & in rebus pertractandis sagax & prudens, erga divinum Sanctorumque cultum pius: corpus enim S. Domnini ann. MCC VII in oppidum Burgi solemni pompa transtulit, quod inde oppidum S. Domnini nomen accepit.* Ughello Picus, pag. 224 Theatri Sanctorum & Beatorum Parmensium consonat in Vita Italica S. Domnini, addens, S. Domnini exuvias arcæ novæ marmoreæ ab Opizzone inclusas & sub altari reædificatæ ecclesiæ anno 1207 repositas ibidem permansisse usque ad annum 1448, quo in novam arcam marmoream, priore augustiorem translatæ fuerunt . . . tum verò tractum illum, qui priùs castri veteris nomen sortitus fuerat, S. Domnini Burgum vocari cœptum ex indigenarum erga Patronum suum pietate, *ut,* inquit verbis Italicis, *fusè referunt Vitæ ejus bini scriptores, Burgi S. Domnini cives, qui annis abhinc multis,*

The date of this so-called third invention of the body of the saint has been very much disputed. Affò, the most serious of all the historians of Borgo S. Donnino, assigns this invention to the IX century,[18] chiefly because, from this time forward, the name of the saint begins to figure in martyrologies, a proof of the diffusion of his cult. In this same judgment concur Buscarini[19] and the anonymous author of the *Brevi Cenni*.[20]

Several authorities cited by the Bollandists with some skepticism ascribe on the contrary this invention to the year 1207. Ughelli also ascribes the translation of the body of the saint to this same year, and goes on to state that in consequence the town commenced to be called by the name of Borgo S. Donnino, which is obviously contrary to fact.[21] Michele cites a passage from Bordoni to the same effect.[22] In the manuscript of the archives entitled *Descrizione dei bassi e alti rilievi e delle Statue che ornano la Facciata della Cattedrale di Borgo San Donnino*, the date 1207 is given as established beyond any question, and the author of the manuscript life anterior to 1720, in the archives, gives the date April 4, 1207, *come lo rapportano gli autori*.[23] Finally, Granelli ascribes the invention to this same year, 1207.[24] Notwithstanding the great diffusion of this notice, it is extremely difficult to discover whence it came, since it cannot be traced further back than the XVI century.

stilo satis quidem bono, sed affectu majori fusè explicarunt gloriosi Martyris gesta & monumenta. Verosimiliter Picus hic auctores Actorum, quæ in codice Florentino & apud Gallonium Mombritiumque reperiuntur, indicat: unde porrò liquet, eos serò admodum, seu non ante annum 1207 suam de S. Domnino lucubrationem subinde ex affectu in sanctum Martyrem magis (quod auctori Actorum Florentinorum maximé quadrat) quàm ex rerum veritate exarasse. Burgum S. Domnini prius *castrum vetus* dictum fuisse, sit penes Picum fides: at oppido isti ab anno tantum 1207 aut serius S. Domnini nomen inditum fuisse, videtur a vero alienum . . . (*Ibid.*).

[18] I, 149. [19] 9. [20] 77.

[21] [Opizzo 1195-1224] corpus enim S. Domnini ann. 1207 in oppidum Burgi solemni pompa transtulit, quod inde oppidum S. Domnini nomen accepit. (Ughelli, ed. C., II, 174).

[22] Anno vero 1207. corpus S. Domnini, qui fuit martyr Legionis Thebanæ, solemni pompa processionaliter detulit intra oppidum, vbi nunc in Matrice Ecclesia veneratur, ab eius nomine multo tempore ante appellatum Burgum S. Domnini, vt in eius vita probaui. (MS. cit., f. 65).

[23] Furono da Dio ispirati li habitatori di Borgo di que' tempi a fabricarte [*sic*] una noua chiesa di maggior sito, di qualità piu magnifiche, e di sacra pompa piu riguardevole della prima. . . . A segno che quantunque non fosse ancor perfetta la fabrica, come haueuano dessegnato in alcune cose accidentali, l'haueuano condotta però a tal segno, che poteuano decentemente uenire alla desiderata traslatione in essa del Santo, come serano proposti diuotamente di fare. . . . Non si trouauano scritture di sorte alcuna, ò memorie, ch'insegnassero con fermezza; Se le Sacre Reliquie, ò sacro Corpo del Santo Martire Domnini . . . fossero sepolte nel mezzo d'essa, ò pure sott'al-l'Altare della Medema, onde nacque grandissima perplessità, etc., etc. (*Ibid.*, f. 1425).

[24] Ineunte sæculo XIII, post secundam Inventionem Corporis S. Domnini Martyris, quæ accidit anno 1207, verisimiliter ampliatum valde fuit Templum dicto Protectori nostro dicatum. . . . . (*Mem. hist.*, etc., 35; see also 81).

I suspect that it originated with Pico, and that the latter held in his hand an authentic document relating the consecration of the church in 1207, which he erroneously applied to the reconstruction described in the *Vita*. At any rate, it is impossible that the miracle of the Stirone could have occurred in 1207. A very evident proof of this has been pointed out by Farinelli.[25] He remarks that an account of this miracle is contained in a codex of Parma which dates from the XI century. It is, therefore, manifestly impossible that the miracle could have occurred two centuries afterwards. Furthermore, this miracle is depicted in sculptures of the façade (Plate 30, Fig. 5) which, on stylistic grounds, are evidently of the end of the XII century. It is therefore certain that the invention must be ascribed to some time before the XI century, and most probably to the IX century.

To the year 830 belongs the earliest original and authentic document relating to the church of Borgo S. Donnino.[26] In this mention is made of a certain *Ursoni Presbytero et vice Domini* of our basilica. A further evidence of the increased importance of the church in the IX century is offered by a relief in the tympanum of the northern portal (Plate 29, Fig. 5). Here we see the pope investing the archpriest of S. Donnino with the mitre and crosier. Behind stands another ecclesiastic with a mitre and stole but no crosier. The inscriptions are now so much weathered as to be practically illegible, but from documents[27] now in the Cancelleria it is possible to restore accurately the original reading, which was:

[A]RCHIPBR [BVRGI $\overline{SCI}$ DONINI]
ADRIANVS PP II

We are thus enabled to identify two of the personages in the relief. Hadrian II was pope from 867 to 872. The sculptor of the end of the XII century doubtless wished to indicate by this relief that Hadrian II had conferred upon the archpriest of Borgo S. Donnino the right to carry the crosier and wear the mitre. Although the documents have been lost, there is no reason to doubt that the tradition of the XII century was correct.

In the year 913 the bishop of Parma, Elbunco, left to the church of S. Donnino a sum of money which was to be expended for a chalice, a paten and for restoring the apse.[28] In has been conjectured that the restoration

25 26.

26 The chronological notes are: anno Imperii Dominorum nostrorum KLudovicus & HLotorij . . . septimodecimo, & vndecimo mense Martii, indictione octaba. (Campi, I, 206-207). Cf. Affò, I, 148.

27 See folio labelled "Descrizione delle figure e dei soggetti che ornano la facciata della Chiesa Cattedrale di Borgo S. Donnino."

28 In nomine Domini Dei & Salvatoris nostri Jesu Christi anno dominicæ Incarnationis DCCCCXIII & anno domni Berengarii gloriosissimi Regis vigesimo septimo mense Aprili Indic. II. Quia ego Helbuncus Sanctæ Parmensis Ecclesiæ indignus Episcopus considerans . . . caducam hujus sæculi vitam . . . dono . . . a præsenti die

may have been necessitated by the devastations of the Hungarians who, in the early years of the X century, wrought great damage to numerous churches and monasteries in the country surrounding Borgo (S. Savino at Piacenza, Nonantola, S. Stefano at Bologna, etc.). From the document it is evident that in the year 913 the bishop of Parma exercised undisputed sway at Borgo, and that the struggle of the archpriest of Borgo to free himself from the jurisdiction of the bishop had not begun, since otherwise the bishop would hardly have left a legacy to the church. In a document of 929[29] King Ugo granted a privilege to the church of Borgo freeing it from the exactions of the count. It is evident that at this time the church of Borgo had succeeded step by step in gaining for itself considerable power and importance, a conclusion confirmed by the fact that Sigefredo I, in this same year, calls himself bishop of Parma and S. Donnino.[30] Michele conjectures that between 981 and 990 the church of Borgo obtained the rank of *Diaconia* and the archpriest began to assume the title of deacon. In documents of 991[31] and 1011[32] the priest of the church of Borgo is given the title of deacon. The meaning of the term is not altogether clear, but it undoubtedly represents a step in advance in the development of the power and independence of the church of Borgo. In 1007 the church was still under the jurisdiction of the bishop of Parma, for there is extant a document of that year in which Sigefredo II, bishop of Parma, granted a part of the offerings of the church to his canons.[33]

It was probably during the struggle between the Empire and the Papacy in the third quarter of the XI century that the church of Borgo succeeded in freeing itself from the dominion of the bishop of Parma. Authentic documents are lacking, but Granelli, by a clever piece of historical induction, has succeeded in making clear the probable trend of events. In 1062 Cadolao Pallavicini, bishop of Parma, was elected antipope and assumed the title of Honorius II against the legitimate pope, Alexander II. Cadolao was excommunicated by the council at Mantua. The church of Parma thus remained until 1106, or for more than forty years, schismatic and excommunicated. In all probability this schism offered to the canons of Borgo S. Donnino the long-sought opportunity to free themselves from the jurisdiction of the bishops of Parma.[34] That Granelli's conjecture is well founded is proved by an important document in the church itself which has hitherto not been under-

per hujus judicati testamentum ipsi sanctæ Matri Parmensi ecclesiæ etc. . . . . Offero etiam sancto Domnino Martyri Christi modiolos aureos II unum ad calicem faciendum et alium ad Patenam. Ad absidam restaurandam argenti Lib. X. . . . . Ad sanctum Remigium de Bercedo ad absidam parandam Lib. X. (Affò, I, 317).

[29] *Ibid.*, 337.   [30] Michele, MS. cit., f. 4.

[31] Raimbaldus Diac. de ordine plebe sancti Domnini sito burgo territorio parmens. (Affò, I, 369).

[32] Granelli, MS. cit., f. 3.   [33] Affò, I, 383.   [34] MS. cit., f. 4 f.

stood. The holy-water basin is adorned with sculptures which have been erroneously explained by Pettorelli as having reference to the promulgation of a suppositious decree of Pope Alexander II, authorizing the use of holy water. But there is absolutely nothing to show that the use of holy water was instituted by Alexander II, and such an idea has merely been derived from a mistaken interpretation of the sculptures and of the inscription:

INSTI

TVCI

O. ALE

XAN.

DRI PP II.

As a matter of fact the word *institutio* is commonly used in mediæval Latin to denote a privilege or concession,[35] and the sculptures themselves, when carefully examined, seem to have reference not to the rites connected with holy water, but to various privileges which no doubt Alexander II (1061-1073) granted to the church of Borgo in recognition of its fidelity during the schism. There has been considerable discussion as to whether the basin was intended originally to serve for holy water or as a baptismal font. I am inclined to believe from the subject of the sculptures and from the historical connection that it was a baptismal font, although the fact that an analogous basin of the Museo Leone of Vercelli undoubtedly served for holy water lends some support to the former hypothesis.[36] On the principal front of the Borgo vessel is sculptured the figure of Pope Alexander II, distinguished by his conical papal tiara, and by the inscription, already cited, on his scroll. Behind the pope, with his hand on the latter's shoulder in an attitude of petition, stands the archpriest of Borgo wearing a mitre, but no stole, and holding in his other hand an egg-shaped object, undoubtedly an oil-stock. This scene must represent the archpriest petitioning and obtaining from the pope certain privileges. Precisely what these privileges are we could doubtless know if the original bull were preserved. In the lack of the document, however, it is possible to conjecture from similar concessions made to other churches. Thus, Calixtus II, in 1123, granted to the pieve of Carpi the right of the chrism and holy oil and of the ordination of priests and of the consecration of churches by any Catholic bishop whom the canons might select.[37] Paschal II, in 1113,

---

[35] Compare, *e.g.*, per hanc nostrae institucionis vel concessionis paginam—(Donation of the bishop Alberto of Reggio made in 1147 to the nuns of S. Tommaso, apud Muratori, A. I. M. A., Dis. 66, ed. A., XIII, 511). The same phrase is repeated below in same document, p. 512, etc., etc.

[36] This basin comes from the church of S. Lorenzo at Saluzzo. On it is sculptured a priest holding in his left hand a holy-water vessel and in his right an aspergillum with which he sprinkles one of his parishioners, a mature man, who presses the palms of his hands together as in prayer.

[37] See text cited below, p. 237.

granted the monastery of S. Silvestro at Nonatola the chrism, holy oil, the consecration of altars or basilicas and the ordination of monks and of clerics by any Catholic bishop the monks might select. These two cases are extremely analogous to that of Borgo S. Donnino, for both Carpi and Nonantola, like Borgo, eventually succeeded in becoming independent dioceses. It is evident that the right to receive the chrism, the holy oils, to consecrate altars and churches and the ordination of priests by a bishop other than that of the local see constituted an important first step by which a rising church was enabled to free itself from the jurisdiction of the superior bishop. In all three of the cases above cited this initial first step eventually led to complete exemption from the episcopal authority. I think there is no doubt that these four privileges were granted by Pope Alexander II to the church of Borgo and that this fact is commemorated in the basin. In the first scene already described we see the archpriest petitioning the pope for this privilege and holding in his hand the oil-stock symbolical of the first two most important privileges. The next scene to the left shows a bishop holding a book, and before him a monk, bare-headed and tonsured, his hands covered with a napkin. This must represent the ordination of a canon by a bishop selected by the canons themselves. The next scene shows a bishop, again undoubtedly other than the bishop of Parma. The head of this figure has unfortunately been broken. He holds a book, and his right hand is raised, palm outward. Then come two women, designated as such by their head-dresses, both carrying candles. These two figures and the two following ones, one of whom is a woman and the other a man, doubtless represent the congregation, and the scene depicts the consecration of an altar or a church. The next scene represents the churching of a woman who holds the candle, while the archpriest (the head again broken) bears in his right hand an aspergillum and raises his left hand. The final scene represents the archpriest wearing a stole, a book in his left hand, his right hand extended. A canon, bare-headed and tonsured, holds out, over a vase, a round shallow object like a plate. This scene is usually interpreted as representing the blessing of holy water and the pouring of salt into it. If this conjecture be correct it must be that the right of blessing holy water was one of those conceded to the archpriest by Alexander II.

New progress towards independence from the episcopal jurisdiction was made by the church of S. Donnino in 1086, when Urban II took the pieve under his pontifical protection. The original document is lost but is referred to in a bull of Celestine II of 1196, cited below. This privilege was doubtless a reward for the continued fidelity of the church to the papal party, while the bishops of Parma, and even of Piacenza, were schismatic. Finally, in 1100, S. Bonnizone, papal legate and bishop of Piacenza, became the *prevosto mitrato* of Borgo S. Donnino. Thus the church of Borgo was transferred from the diocese of Parma to that of Piacenza, and undoubtedly obtained additional power and privileges by the change.[38]

Michele goes on to state that in the year 1101, and doubtless in consequence of the new importance acquired during the struggle between the Empire and the Papacy, the church was enlarged.[39] The same notice is repeated on

[38] Il Vescovo di Parma perdette il dominio e la giurisdizione, che aveva sopra la chiesa Fidentina nell'anno 1062 pel scisma di Cadolao Pallavicini vescovo di quella città, che si fece eleggere Papa assumendo il nome di Onorio II contro il legittimo Pontefice Alessandro II. Il detto Cadolao venne scomnicato da un concilio di Mantova. Per tale avvenimento la Chiesa di Parma restò senza Pastore, e per conseguenza anche la Chiesa di Sandonnino. Siccome la Parmense Chiesa dovette per longo tempo rimanere in tale infelice stato, allorchè il partitante dall'Jmperatore Arrigo quarto Giberto Coreggio di Parma arcivescovo di Ravenna s'era fatto eleggere Papa contro il legitimo Romano Pontefice Gregorio VII, e quindi esso pure unitamente ad Eberardo Vescovo di Parma scismatico restò scomunicato; così con probabilità si conghiettura, che anoiata Borgo San Domnino di tale allontanamento dalla Santa Sede, no meno che del Dominio de' Vescovi di Parma, stimasse bene nell'anno 1088 di ricorrere al Sommo Pontefice Urbano II per mettersi sotto la sua protezione, e per avere da Lui un legitimo Capo. Acconsentì di fatti il Papa all'inchiesta di Borgo, e trovando nello stesso tempo, che anche la Chiesa Piacentina era priva di Vescovo, e premendogli ancora di restituire la pace alla Chiesa, & concigliarsi in questa parte gl'altri vescovi, i quali per la maggior parte seguivano il partito Jmperiale contro di Lui, si determinò d'inviare in codesti luoghi San Bonnizzone, destinandolo Legato Apostolico creandolo Vescovo di Piacenza e facendolo ancora Prevosto mitrato di Borgo S. Donnino, dignità la quale allora si erigeva in que' luoghi e pochi avevano quella distinzione. In tale maniera la Chiesa di San Donnino colle sue annese Parocchie, ossia Borgo nello spirituale fu separato dalla Diocesi di Parma ed unito a quella di Piacenza, benchè con male animo di Parmigiani. La quale conghiettura per brano ricavasi dalle circonstanze de' tempi, e da Bolle di privilegi Papali; e particolarmente dalla Bolla di Papa Celestino III che porta la data del 4 Maggio 1196. (Michele, MS. cit., f. 4 f.).

In the archives of the Cancellaria at Borgo there is a copy of the bull of Celestine in Michele's own handwriting. I transcribe the most important phrases: Celestinus Episcopus Servus Servorum Dei. Dilectis Filiis Gerardo Preposito Prepositurae Ecclesiae Sancti Domnini de Burgo eiusque Fratribus tam presentibus quam futuris canonice substituendis in perpetuum. . . . Ecclesiam Sancti Domnini de Burgo in qua divino estis obsequio mancipati ad exemplar felicis recordationis Urbani Papae Predecessoris Nostri sub Beati Petri et nostra protectione suscepimus . . . [Confirms numerous possessions]. . . . Usumque Mitrae alias antiquas ac rationabiles consuetudines dignitates libertates etiam et immunitates ab Ecclesiasticis secularibusque Personis rationabiliter vobis et ecclesiae vestrae [concessas] et hactenus observatas ratas habemus, easque perpetuis futuris temporibus illibatas decernimus permanere. . . . Datum Romae apud Sanctum Petrum . . . quarto nonas Maji, Jndictione quarta decima Jncarnationis dominicae anno MCXCVI Pontificatus autem domini Celestini Papae tertio anno sexto.

[39] In questi tempi fu dilatata la Chiesa di S. Donnino, cioè nell'anno 1101. (Ibid.). Sotto di questo prevosto e sotto l'antecedente [i.e., c. 1196-1202] si fabbricò la presente Chiesa Cattedrale, o si ristaurò; dacchè fino dal 1101 erasi incominciata ad ingrandire, riducendola alla forma che ha al presente, eccettuate però alcune piccole mutazioni che furonvi fatte dappoi. Nell'anno 1207. seguì la seconda invenzione del corpo di San Donnino Martire. (Ibid.).

a loose leaf in the hand of Pincolini, written about the middle of the XVIII century, and also preserved in the Borgo archives.[40]

These notices are in a measure confirmed by others which speak of a consecration of the basilica celebrated by Paschal II in 1106. Various sources for this consecration are cited in a note of Pincolini still preserved in the archives,[41] by Granelli[42] and by Michele.[43] The authorities vary considerably as to the day of this consecration, which Pincolini, Granelli and Michele assign to October 28, while the manuscript *Descrizione* assigns it to September 28. As early as 1590 the tradition was confused, since in that year it was decided in view of the uncertainty of the documents to celebrate the anniversary of the dedication on the first of October.[44] The tradition is, however, constant and widespread, and is confirmed by the fact that in 1106 Paschal II must have passed through Borgo S. Donnino on his way from Parma to Piacenza. The consecration in 1106 may therefore be accepted as an historical fact.

In 1152 the Parmigiani took and burned the town of Borgo S. Donnino,[45] and I suspect that at this time the church was probably destroyed or at least

[40] 1101.—10 Lug.o Liberi i Borghegiani dalla Real Residenza [of Corrado] pensarono all'esempio de' circonvicini alla Fabrica della Basilica del loro Santo Protettore Donino. . . . 1101 MSS. Pinc. Respirando Libertà il nostro Borgo dopo la morte di Corrado, inoltri pensarono a fabbricare una Chiesa degna del nostro Santo, e degna dell'onor compartito loro da Borbone [sic] e del visibile capo mitrato.

[41] 1106. 28 8bre in Lunedì giorno de' SS. Simone e Giuda Pasquale 2. consecrò la nostra Basilica dopo quella di Parma, e venne accompagnato dal Vescovo di quella Città e Cardinale Legato Bernardo Pinc. 1106. 28 8bre Pascal Secondo consacra il nostro Duomo in Lunedì presente Bernardo Vescovo di Parma. 16. xbre era ancora in Piacenza Pascale. Campi. t.2o f. B78. cola. 1a. 1106. 28 8bre in Lunedi nel giorno dedicato a due SSti Apostoli Simone, e Giuda Taddeo. Venne in Borgo S. Donnino Pasquale II. e vi consecrò anche qui il nostro Duomo, ossia la nostra Chiesa Maggiore ad onore del Nostro Santo Protettore Donnino Martire. Il Sigr. Antonio Bertolini Cancelliere dell'eccelsa Dettatura di Parma nella sua Storia manuscritta de' Vescovi di Parma così ha fatto videre a me scrittore [Prevosto Pincolini] di questi frammenti storici di Borgo S. Donnino 1752. Giacomo Gozzi Storia manuscritta di Parma anch'egli ciò conferma.

[42] Quamvis indubitanter constet de Consecratione Ecclesiæ S. Domnini, tamen non æque constat de die, in qua hæc habita fuit. Joannes Maria Gozzi, Antonius Bertolini, et Fidentinus noster Præpositus, Victorius Pincolini in codicibus eorum calamo exaratis narrant (quamvis nullis innitantur certis documentis) Summum Pontificem Paschalem II supradictam Ecclesiam die 28 Octobris anni 1106 dedicasse. (Granelli, MS. cit., f. 14).

[43] Fu consecrata la detta Chiesa di San Donnino Martire dal Papa Pasquale II. li 28 ottobre dell'anno 1106 ricorrendo la Festa de' Santi Simoni, e Giuda. (MS. cit., f. 5).

[44] Die 30 Septembris 1590 Præpositus Mitratus Carolus Sozzi una cum Capitulo statuerunt diem primam Octobris ad celebrandum imposterum quottannis Anniversarium Dedicationis Ecclesiae S. Domnini, cum valde incerta forent documenta adserentia ipsam peractam fuisse die 28 Octobris 1106. (Repert. Trecassali).—Buscarini, 33.

[45] *Chronicon Parmense*, ed. Muratori, R. I. S., IX, 760; Johannis de Mussis, *Chronicon Placentinum*, ed. Muratori, R. I. S., XVI, 453.

injured, although Granelli is of the contrary opinion.[46] In 1196 the privileges of the church were confirmed by Celestine III. The authenticity of this bull has been attacked, but it seems to me without sufficient grounds.[47] At this time there is no doubt that the church of Borgo was subject to the jurisdiction of the diocese of Parma. During the last years of the XII century the construction of the existing edifice must have been in progress, since on internal evidence the sculptures must have been nearly completed in 1196, when Benedetto was called to work upon the baptistery of Parma. In 1199 the Piacentini besieged Borgo S. Donnino, but there is no evidence that the church itself suffered any damage.[48] It has been seen above that the tradition that the third invention of the relics of the saint took place in 1207 is in all probability a mistaken conjecture, based upon the authentic fact of a consecration in that year. Undoubtedly the existing edifice was substantially completed at this time. According to a notice of Granelli, in the year 1284 the three western portals were reduced to their present condition.[49] This notice is hard to understand, and I can only conjecture that there is a mistake of a century in the date, and that for 1284 we should read 1184. This error might all the more readily have crept in because it is followed by a notice of the year 1285, recording that the two towers flanking the façade were erected in that year.[50] In 1287 the exterior cornice of the apse was completed and the nave vaults were raised.[51] In the early years of the XIV century the church was fortified, and turned into a stronghold by the exiles of Parma. In 1309 the Ghibellines of Parma captured it.[52] In 1448 the body of the saint was translated into a new sarcophagus.[53] In 1470 the tower and vaults

[46] Parmenses anno 1152 die 20 Septembris Oppidum S. Domnini igne vastarunt, sed inter flammas remansit illaesa S. Martyris Ecclesia. (Granelli, MS. cit., f. 31).

[47] *Brevi Cenni*, 114.

[48] Sicardi Episcopi *Chronicon*, ed. Muratori, R. I. S., VII, 618. Salimbene, ad. ann. 1285, ed. Parma, 1857, 343.

[49] Anno 1284 Ecclesiae S. Domnini vestibulum major Templi Porta, binaeque laterales januae ad statum in quo etiam nunc sunt perducta fuerunt. (*Mem. hist.*, etc., 62).

[50] Anno 1285 constructae fuerunt duae turres adhuc existentes ad latera frontis Ecclesiæ nostræ Cathedralis; sed anno 1512 cecidit fulmen super turrim ad sinistram positam, et ejusdem pyramidem diruit, quæ hactenus reficienda desideratur. (Granelli, 5).

[51] Anno 1287 Chorus nostri Majoris Templi extrinsecus ita perbelle crustis marmoreis obductus fuit, ut hinc transeuntes hujus modi artem callentes studiose egregium opus intuentur. Circa id tempus fornix Ecclesiæ S. Domnini ad majorem altitudinem evecta putatur. (*Ibid.*, 1863, 14).

[52] Item, durante dicto exercitu [1309], turris et ecclesia sancti Donini que munita erat per predictos extrinsecos [fuorusciti da Parma], die prima Octobris per Parmenses per fortiam prelij capta fuit: et multi de populo Parme partis ecclesie, ibi existentes super dictam turrim, ab intrinsecis Parmensibus in dicta captione occisi fuerunt. (*Chronicon Parmense* apud Muratorium, ed. Carducci, 114).

[53] See text cited above, p. 169.

were repaired.[54]   Three years later Pope Sixtus IV freed the church from the jurisdiction of Parma, as recorded in the original bull still preserved in the Archivio.   In 1490 the church was adorned with frescos.[55]   Eleven years later a bell was made for the campanile.[56]   In 1512 the northern tower of the façade was struck by lightning and ruined.   This damage, in the time of Granelli, was still unrepaired.[57]   In 1561 the lions of the central portals were restored, the choir stairway was remade, and the altar moved into the apse. Six years later the choir-stalls were built.[58]   In 1569 the existing campanile north of the choir was erected.[59]   In 1597 the door in the base of the campanile was closed and a new door opened in the south flank of the church.[60]   In 1601 the church was raised to the rank of a cathedral.[61]   This promotion, perhaps, was the cause of whitewashing the crypt in 1603, although the church itself was not whitewashed until 1689.[62]   In 1857 the whitewash was re-applied to the crypt,[63] and in this same year the holy-water basin and the lions at the western portal were restored, as is evident from the inscription: R 1857.   In 1881 was begun a restoration of the church of which some description has been left in the *Brevi Cenni*.[64]   Fortunately, the original stones removed from the apse at this period and replaced by copies have been preserved, and may still be seen in the Cancelleria.

III.   The edifice consists of a nave three double bays long, two side aisles, a choir, a crypt and an apse (Plate 30, Fig. 4).   The system of the nave is alternate, a single bay of the central aisle corresponding to two of the side aisles.   Above the side aisles is a gallery (Plate 30, Fig. 4) which opens on to the nave by means of two groups of four arches in each bay and which is covered by a wooden roof supported on heavy transverse arches. With the exception of this gallery the edifice is entirely vaulted, the side aisles with groin vaults, the nave (Plate 30, Fig. 4) and crypt with rib vaults, and the apse with a ribbed half dome (Plate 30, Fig. 4).   The diagonal ribs of the crypt have a smooth torus section, those of the nave are rectangular with chamfered corners (Plate 30, Fig. 4), while the apse ribs have a developed Gothic profile consisting of two roll-mouldings separated by a hollow fillet. From the profile of the ribs, therefore, it is evident that the crypt vaults are older than those of the nave and the apse.   The nave vaults are reinforced by transverse buttresses (Plate 29, Fig. 2) carried on the transverse arches of the side aisles, and hence practically flying buttresses.   It is evident that the

---

[54] Anno 1470 Populus et Clerus rogavit Fidentinum Municipium, ut reparare faceret Turrem Majorem et partem fornicis Ecclesiae S. Domnini minantes ruinam. Annuit libenter Communitas, et expensas sustinuit instaurationum.   (Buscarini, 1863, 14).

[55] Buscarini, 1863, 39.   [56] *Ibid.*, 43.   [57] See text cited above, p. 177.

[58] Buscarini, 1864, 5, 11, 19.   [59] *Ibid.*, 28.   [60] *Ibid.*, 42.   [61] *Ibid.*, 48.

[62] *Ibid.*, 53, 63.   [63] *Ibid.*, 39.   [64] 58 f.

edifice contains portions which date from several different epochs. To the church of c. 1135 belonged the fifth respond from the west of the southern side aisle, which is characterized by a complicated section consisting of seven members (the other side-aisle responds have only three members) and by a Corinthianesque capital of rather archaic design. Contemporary with the sculptures of Benedetto of the façade are the lower parts of the two campaniles which flank the façade, the two western responds of the main arcade, with their Corinthian capitals similar to those of the façade, the first respond from the west of the northern side aisle with a similar capital, the corresponding capital of the southern side aisle and a capital with broad, flat leaves at the north-east angle of the south aisle. The rest of the edifice all belongs to the reconstruction of the XIII century.

At the eastern end of the southern side aisle rises at present a Renaissance campanile (Plate 29, Fig. 2), but it was the original intention to erect two towers flanking the choir on either side. There must have been anciently a room for the bell-ringers on the south side of the choir adjoining the campanile, for the exterior of the south wall of the choir at present bears numerous graffiti[65] of 1441, 1519, 1520, 1529, 1538, 1548, 1751, etc. The two western piers of the nave have been deprived of their colonnettes on the inner face. Pointed arches are used only in the vaults (Plate 30, Fig. 4) and in the relieving arches of the side-aisle walls (Plate 29, Fig. 2), but owing to the erection of a complete set of chapels those in the latter position have for the most part disappeared.

IV. The ornament of the church, like the construction, shows clearly the trace of several different epochs. To c. 1135 belong the northern (Plate 29, Fig. 5) and southern (Plate 29, Fig. 4) portals and the capitals of the interior already enumerated. The capitals of the portals (Plate 29, Fig. 4, 5) are of a dry Corinthianesque type, and show strongly the influence of the sculptor Nicolò. The abacus of the capitals of the jambs is continuous. The colonnettes of the northern porch (Plate 29, Fig. 5) rest on caryatids of a type first formulated by Guglielmo da Modena, but afterwards perfected by Nicolò. The porches themselves are entirely in the style of Nicolò, and the archivolt of the northern portal (Plate 29, Fig. 5) is adorned with diamond-shaped medallions containing grotesques and conventional patterns, strikingly similar to that sculptor's works. The grotesques of the archivolt of the southern portal (Plate 29, Fig. 4) recall those of the Pontile of S. Zeno at Verona

[65] Among others:

                    1441
                    Adi 21
                    Otobre
                    Domenico e Batt Santelli
                        Campanari.

(Plate 228, Fig. 1). These portals (Plate 29, Fig. 4, 5) are in several orders, shafted and moulded. The colonnettes of the southern porch (Plate 29, Fig. 4) are carried on rams.

The central portal (Plate 27, Fig. 3) of the end of the XII century is far more developed in style. The colonnettes are carried upon lions, one of which holds in his paws a bull, and the other a dragon, both of which animals bite the lions. The richly moulded and shafted jambs (Plate 27, Fig. 3) are supplied with elaborate diaper-patterns, especially on the colonnettes. On the inner archivolt is a rinceau, and the sculptures are set in the outer edge of the voussoir of the porch in quite the French manner. Compare, for example, the southern porches of Chartres, Plate 27, Fig. 1. There is a projecting moulding of several fine members on the outer face of this archivolt (Plate 27, Fig. 3). A Greek fret, very Provençal in character, is freely used in the ornamentation of the façade and the two flanking towers (Plate 30, Fig. 1, 2). To the XIII century (and probably to the early part of that century) belong the capitals of the side aisles and also part of the piers of the nave. These capitals are all cubic (Plate 30, Fig. 4) and all uniform. They are characterized by a sort of a double cushion, whose curve is followed by an incised line. The bases, of Attic type, are supplied with griffes. Only slightly later are the fully developed Gothic capitals of the crypt, the choir, the transepts, the galleries, and the vaulting shafts of the nave. The archivolts of the main arcade are in two unmoulded orders (Plate 30, Fig. 4).

The sculptures of Borgo S. Donnino are among the finest plastic works of the Middle Ages in Italy. In the centre of the archivolt of the central Lombard porch (Plate 27, Fig. 3) of the west façade may be seen a relief of the Deity seated on a throne and holding in either hand a scroll. The scroll in his left hand bears the inscription (Bar., iii, 9):

> AV.
> DI. ISRL.
> MAN.
> DA.
> TA. VI
> TE.

which calls to mind the failure of the Jews to hear the new commandments brought into the world by our Lord. That to the right hand contains one of the beatitudes:

> BEATI
> PAUPE
> RES.
> SPIRI
> TV.[66]

[66] Matth., v, 3.

On either side of the Deity are two angels flying. Flanking the central figure
are placed on the voussoir of the archivolt a series of figures (Plate 27, Fig. 3).
To the left of the spectator, but on the right of the Deity, these are:
(1) Moses, characterized by horns[67] and dressed like a mediæval warrior,
bears a scroll, with the inscription:

> DILI
> GES
> $\overline{\text{DNM}}$ [68]

which is a commandment of the old law, but also the first and greatest
commandment of the new law.[69]   (2) A personage designated as a Hebrew
by his conical bonnet and whom the scroll[70] makes known as a personification of
the fifth commandment.[71]   (3) The personification of the sixth commandment,
an entirely similar figure bearing the scroll:

> N O N
> M E
> C A B E [R I S] [72]

(4) The personification of the seventh commandment, bearing the scroll:

> N O N
> F U R
> T V M
> F A C I E S [73]

(5) The personification of the ninth commandment, bearing the scroll:

> N O N
> C O N
> C V P I
> S C E S [74]

(6) The personification of the second commandment, bearing the scroll:

> N O N
> A S V
> M E S
> N O M E
> N D E I [75]

On the bases of the soffit of the vault are two other similar figures (Plate 27,
Fig. 3) without inscription or scroll, but which are doubtless intended to
stand for the remaining five commandments.

[67] Exod., xxxiv, 29.   [68] Deut., vi, 5.   [69] Matth., xxii, 37-38; Marc., xii, 30.

[70]
> N O N
> O C C I
> D E S

[71] Exod., xx, 13.   [72] Exod., xx, 14.   [73] Exod., xx, 15.
[74] Exod., xx, 17.   [75] Exod., xx, 7.

To the left of Christ on the archivolt (Plate 27, Fig. 3) are six haloed figures, all (with the exception of the fifth) with beards. They bear each a scroll upon which is inscribed one of the beatitudes:

(1)[76]	(2)[77]	(3)[78]	(4)[79]	(5)[80]	(6)[81]
BEATI	BEA	BEA	BEATI	BEATI	BEATI
MVNDO	TI MI	TI MI	Q[VI] LV	PAC[I]	Q[VI] $\overline{\text{NC}}$
	TES	SERI	GENT	FICI	ESVRI
		[CORDES]			TIS

These figures are not, however, mere personifications of the beatitudes, as the analogy with the commandments on the other side of the voussoirs or with the lamp at Aix-la-Chapelle[82] might lead us to suppose. The first figure carries as an attribute two keys, and hence must be the apostle St. Peter. The fifth, the only one which is beardless, must be St. John the Evangelist. A seventh figure on the inner face of the vault at the bottom, haloed and carrying a T-square and a scroll, must be St. Thomas. We have therefore the beatitudes announced by the apostles. The figures carrying the commandments consequently were, in all probability, in the mind of the artist not mere personifications, but the prophets of the Old Testament. The conception, therefore, is one full of symbolical meaning. In the place of honour in the centre, the post of greatest hieratic dignity, is placed the Saviour. On either side of Him are shown, in parallel, the prophets of the Old Testament bearing the laws of the old dispensation, and the apostles of the New Testament bearing the new laws of Christ.

The frieze on which is depicted the life of the saint begins at the left of the portal, is carried across the jambs forming the capitals of the colonnettes, and ends in the wall on the south side of the portal (Plate 27, Fig. 3). The scenes of which it is made up are as follows: (1) the emperor Maximian is seen seated on his throne, holding a sceptre and a sphere. S. Donnino, without halo and wearing a helmet, places a crown on the head of the emperor. A person to the right bears a sword, and beyond him stands a helmeted figure, both facing the emperor. In the doorway of the building to the left, stands a page. An inscription

[IMPERATO]R . A BEATO . DONNINO CORONATVR .

makes it evident that we have here a representation of the life of S. Donnino as crown-bearer to the emperor, before his conversion, although in none of the extant lives is there a description of a scene which exactly corresponds with the sculptures, or explains who may be the three unnamed personages. A comparison with the succeeding reliefs, however, shows that two of these youths are the companions of S. Donnino in the house of the emperor, who

---

[76] Matth., v, 8.　　[77] Ibid., v, 4.　　[78] Ibid., v, 7.　　[79] Ibid., v, 5.
[80] Ibid., v, 9.　　[81] Ibid., v, 6; Luc., vi, 21.
[82] Illustrated by Martin et Cahier, III, 45, Plates 4-5.

subsequently became Christians with him. (2) The emperor is seen again seated on a throne, wearing a crown and holding a sceptre and sphere. Before him stand three figures, the same as in the preceding scene. The first, with a helmet, is doubtless S. Donnino. His hands are pressed together in the attitude of prayer. The other two—one of whom is helmeted, the other without helmet—raise their hands as if seconding the prayer of the saint. The inscription

LICENCIA   ACCEPTA . DEO . SERVIRE   D   IPRE

makes it evident that the Christians are obtaining from the emperor permission to serve God according to their consciences. Here, again, it is clear that the sculptor is following a version of the life which has not come down to us. (3) The flight of Donnino and the Christians (Plate 30, Fig. 3). The emperor Maximiam, M A X I M I A N' I P[E R]R, is seated on a throne and holds a sphere. His legs are crossed, and with his right hand he strokes his beard with a gesture of thoughtful cunning. To the left is a beardless, bare-headed page holding a sword, as in the first relief. To the right, seven haloed figures seem to be going away and up. They are Donnino and his six companions leaving the emperor. The last, distinguished by a special and elaborate halo, and by the inscription, D O M N I N V S , turns, however, back towards the emperor. His left hand is raised with a gesture of decision, his right hand points towards the preceding figures. He has a beard and is bare-headed. According to the *Passionario* the emperor Maximian, while he was sojourning in Germany, undertook to persecute the Christians and to make them sacrifice to his gods. Among these Christians was Donnino, the crown-bearer of the emperor. Seeing the cruelty and ruthlessness of his master, Donnino urged several other Christians to join him in opposing the will of the emperor. The latter, in rage, killed numerous Christians, while the others flew in various directions, S. Donnino towards Rome over the Via Claudia. Notwithstanding the discrepancy between this version of the life and that followed by the sculptor, it is evident that the main outlines of the story are the same in both. (4) To the left (Plate 29, Fig. 1) is a sort of tower in four stories, in the lower of which is a bolted door. From two of the windows emerge human heads, one in each, and another head peeks over one of the balconies. This tower perhaps represents the gate of the city, for from it emerge two figures on horse-back. They are in armour, but bare-headed, and carry drawn swords. Their horses are galloping. The inscription

MISSI MAXIMIANI IP[ER]ATORIS

makes it clear that these are the messengers or executioners sent by the emperor to overtake the fleeing saint. Somewhat in front of them is seen the saint himself, S[ANCTVS] DOMNIN', on horse-back, with an elaborate halo and a cross. His horse at full gallop approaches another city like that from

183

which emerge the executioners, indicated as a tower with a closed gate in the lower story and human heads emerging from the upper windows and battlements. The inscription, CIVITAS PIACENCIA, leaves no doubt that this is the city of Piacenza. This scene corresponds more closely with the text of the Paris codex, in which the phrase *Missi Imperatoris* is used to indicate the messengers sent to pursue the saint. (5) The pursuers of the saint (Plate 29, Fig. 1) are seen emerging from the city of Piacenza. (6) The execution of the saint (Plate 29, Fig. 1). An executioner holds his drawn sword aloft after having severed the head of the martyr. The saint stands upright by a block in front of which falls his haloed head. Above the head is the inscription S[ANCTVS] DONINVS. Between the executioner and the saint is seen growing a rose, the symbol of martyrdom. Above the scene is the inscription:

ANI MA MARTIRIS DEFERT IN C[ELVM]

The soul of the saint which is borne to heaven is represented by a beardless haloed head carried upward by two angels. (7) The saint (Plate 29, Fig. 1) is seen carrying his own severed head across the river Stirone, indicated by the inscription, S I S T E R. Here for the first time the version of the life of the saint followed by the sculptor seems to be in complete accord with the text of the Paris codex.[83] (8) The saint, still bearing his bearded head in his hands, lies down under the trees on the farther side of the river: HIC IACET CORPVS MARTIRIS. (9) The church of Borgo is seen in construction. The apse of the choir has been finished, but one of the trees of the preceding scene is still growing where the new nave will be built. Before the half-finished edifice kneels a sick man who is being cured by the intercession of the saint: HIC SANATVR EGROTVS. About the tree is seen tied a hitching rope, but the horse which it tied has disappeared. The Paris codex gives us the explanation of this sculpture. The sick man's horse had been stolen while he was in the church praying to be healed by the saint.[84] (10) In this scene is shown the sequel of the theft of the horse, not altogether in accord with the Paris codex.[85] The thief is shown being brought back by the horse. He

---

[83] S̄cs uero domnin'. manib; suis app̄hendens caput suum de terra. t[ra]nsiuit fluuiū sisterionem: & q[ua]ntum iactus ē lapidis sustulit caput suū. ibiq; eum pausauit: ubi n̄c corp' eius integrum p[er]manet et inuiolatum.

[84] Post hec aūt multi egri de diuersis p[ro]uinciis audientes ei' mirabilia que faciebat: ad ei'. oraculū confluebant. Jnter quos uenit unus eger. q[ui] alligans equum suū. ing[re]ssus est ante conspectū sci domnini et lacrimabilit' cepit rogare. et beneficia eius dep[re]cari. p[ro]pter egritudinem q[ua]m habebat: ut opem sue salutis dignarē̄t tribuere. Qui mox p[ris]tinam recepit santitatē. Tunc illesus foras egressus: equum quē dimiserat n̄ inuenit. This miracle is also related in the cited manuscript life of the Archivio, f. 1415.

[85] Jterum introiuit ante conspectū p̄dicti m̄ris; et p[ro]num se iactans in terra: lacrimis cepit rogare dicens. heu s̄ce domnine. ad tua beneficia concurri. Placet t[ibi] ut hec patiar: Et eg[re]ssus foras; conspexit ad uiam publicam; et uidit illum hominē

resists in vain by grasping a tree with his left hand. His right arm is held firmly by the horse in his mouth. The position of the horse's neck and nose, both held in a horizontal position, his ears held back against his neck, his front feet braced forward and his chin in an attitude of straining, shows that he is bringing back the thief to the church against the latter's will. The reins hang loosely to the ground, the saddle is empty. The meaning of the sculpture can not be mistaken, although no light is thrown by later sources or by the simple inscription: HIC RESTITVITVR EQVS. (11) To the extreme left (Plate 30, Fig. 5) is seen the church of S. Dalmazio, to the extreme right the gate of the city of Borgo S. Donnino, within which, it must be imagined, is the sanctuary of the saint. Between the two flows the river Stirone, represented by wavy incised lines. Over the river is built a wooden bridge, which is seen to collapse under the weight of a procession, which moves from the church of S. Dalmazio to the town. This procession consists of citizens of all sorts and degrees, headed by a figure (possibly an acolyte) carrying a cross. As the bridge collapses, the planks fly in all directions, and four persons are represented as falling head foremost. In the centre, however, a bare-headed woman, whose state of pregnancy is graphically represented, continues on her way unperturbed. The persons on dry land on either side of the bridge regard the miracle with an expression of devout complacency, with the exception of one small man with a cowl, who bends almost double in his excitement. The inscription

✦SIC . SANCTIS . EXEQVIIS . CELEBRATIS . MVLIER GRAVIDA . A
RVINA . PONTIS . LIBERATVR .

and the passage cited above from the Florentine life, make it evident that this relief represents the collapse of the wooden bridge over the Stirone, which occurred when the citizens of Borgo thronged from the church of S. Dalmazio to the church of S. Donnino after the invention of the body of the saint, probably in the IX century. The miracle consisted in the fact that in the collapse of the bridge no one was injured, not even a pregnant woman who chanced to be in the middle of the disaster.[86]

On the front of the architrave of the central porch on the north side (Plate 27, Fig. 3) is seen Abraham, ABRAHAM. The patriarch is of ample and portly proportions. Seated on a throne, he holds his hands under a jupe, from which, on his knees, emerge three heads of the blessed. In a corresponding position on the south side of the porch (Plate 27, Fig. 3) is the holy man Job, SCS . VIR . IOP., who is held by the devil in what seems to be a coffin or box. On the north side, below the sculpture of Abraham, is a

q[ui] equū abstulerat, rapido cursu reuertentem. Qui reuocans eum. tradidit in manus ei' et exilivit.

[86] This miracle is recounted in the manuscript life in the Archivio, ff. 1448-1449, but the author confesses he uses the sculptures as a source.

figured capital (Plate 27, Fig. 3) representing the life of the Virgin. The first scene represents the Presentation in the Temple. On the west face (Plate 27, Fig. 3) is seen the Virgin, SCTA MARIA, holding in one hand a flower and in the other what appears to be a jar or vase. She is accompanied by St. Elisabeth, ELIZABET, holding in her hands a skein of wool, and by two other figures, one with long hair and the other carrying a flower. The inscription, VIRGINES, makes it clear that these must be virgins of the Temple. On the angle is shown a priest, bald and wearing a stole. According to the inscription he is the master of the Temple, MAG[ISTER] TENPLI. On the north face of the capital is depicted the Annunciation. The angel, GABRIHEL, with sceptre, stands to the left. The Virgin, SCA MARIA, is seated to the right. In her left hand she holds a ball of yarn and in her right a double skein of purple. On the opposite capital (Plate 27, Fig. 3) are represented the four Evangelists, depicted in an extraordinary manner. Matthew appears as an angel, but the others have the heads, wings and bodies of angels with the lower parts of the corresponding symbolic animals. Each holds a book, with an inscription from the corresponding Gospel:

John[87]	Mark[88]	Matthew[89]	Luke[90]
IN	[VOX]	LIBER	FVIT
DR [sic: PRI]	CLA	GENE	IN DI
NCI.	MAN	RACI	EBVS
PIO	[TIS]	ONIS	

In the wall to the north of the central portal are inserted numerous sculptures. These are: (1) The Epiphany. The three Magi, whose names are indicated by the inscription,

CASPAR BALTASAR MELCHIOR

are seen in the presence of the Virgin, MARIA, and Child, ... HVS. Meanwhile, the angel appears to Joseph, IOSEP., and commands him to fly to Egypt:[91] ✠ S[VR]GE . ACIPE PVERV. (2) Around the niche in which stands the large statue of David, and below the beginning of the frieze with the life of the saint, is a curious relief in which is shown an angel who shows to a family consisting of a father, mother and child, the door of the church. This relief, together with a similar one in a symmetrical position, on the other side of the portal, probably are simply meant to indicate to the citizens of Borgo that through the door of the church lies the entrance to eternal salvation. Inserted here, however, between two scenes of the early life of Christ, it may also recall the journey of Mary, Joseph and Jesus to the Temple at Jerusalem. (3) Immediately below the upper part of the niche is a relief representing

[87] Joan., i, 1.   [88] Marc., i, 3.   [89] Matth., i, 1.   [90] Luc., i, 5.
[91] Matth., ii, 13.

the Presentation in the Temple. Mary gives the Child to Simeon. Behind her a maidservant bears two turtle doves. The leonine inscription is somewhat damaged, but may be restored as follows:

DANS BLANDŪ MURMUR [PUER] RARO MUNERE [FE]R[TUR]
SUSCIPIT OBLATŪ SYMEON DE UIRGINE NATUM.

(4) In the great niche below is the statue in the round of David (Plate 28, Fig. 1), crowned and bearing a scroll, with the inscription:

DAUID

P[RO]PHA

REX

HEC

PORTA

DOMINI

IUSTI

INTRANT

PER EAM [92]

The sculptures of the wall south of the main portal represent: (1) The translation of Enoch into the earthly paradise. The prophet, whose identity is made clear by the inscription, ENOCH, wears the conical bonnet of the Jews and is seated. In his left hand he holds a fruit, probably of the tree of knowledge, the wisdom of Enoch being proverbial. To the left a bare-headed personage stands in the tree of knowledge, and plucks a branch of the fruit. To the right another man offers the prophet a cup, perhaps of the water of immortal life. Back of this figure is another tree of the terrestrial paradise.[93] (2) The ascension of Elijah, ELY.AS. (Plate 30, Fig. 5) (IV Reg., ii, 11). The prophet stands in a chariot which resembles a two-horse peasant's cart, and prepares to ascend to heaven. Elisha, ELYSEVS, stands behind, pressing his hands together in an attitude of prayer. The Lombard sculptors almost invariably represented together Enoch and Elijah, the two prophets who were translated living from the earth, and whom the church-fathers identify with the two witnesses of the Apocalypse. (3) Below the life of the saint is another scene like the one in the corresponding position already described (Plate 30, Fig. 5). An angel shows the door of the church to a father, mother and son. These are evidently working people. The father carries a staff and holds a sort of knapsack suspended on a cane held over his shoulder. The angel in this relief has also a staff, but the angel in the corresponding relief on the other side has a sceptre. It is notable that all three

[92] Psal., cxvii, 20.

[93] I am unable to find the exact source of this relief. Some light is thrown upon it by the passages in Enoch, xxv, 1; xxxii, 3-4; xlvii, 1; xlix, 1. See what has been said on the subject in Vol. I.

personages in this relief have wallets at their sides. They are perhaps pilgrims, and the family on the other side may be burgesses of Borgo S. Donnino. If this interpretation be correct, the sculptures were intended to refer to the dual character of the church of S. Donnino (a) as a parish church for Borgo, and (b) as an object of pilgrimage. (4) In the upper part of the niche in which is contained the large statue of Ezekiel (Plate 28, Fig. 2), are represented the Madonna and Child. The leonine inscription

✠ VIRGA . VIRTŪTIS . PROTV̄LIT . FRVCTŪQVE . SALVTIS
✠ VIRGA . FLOX . NAT̄US . EST . CARN̂E . DEUS . TRABEAT̄US

explains why the Virgin is represented as holding a flower in her hand, and is seated on a fruitful vine. (5) The large statue in the round (Plate 28, Fig. 2) represents Ezekiel, who wears a curious head-dress which is one of the ear-marks of the style of Benedetto. He bears the scroll:

EZECHI

EL : PRO

PHETA

VIDI

PORTAM

IN DOMO

DOMINI

CLĀUSAM [94]

On a column between the central and north portals stands a large archaic statue worked in the round. The figure (Plate 29, Fig. 5) is bare-headed and bears a scroll with the letters:

SIM̄O

AP[OSTO]L[U]S

EŪ DI

ROMA .

S̄C̄S D[E]

MON

ARAT

HĀC

VIAM

The interpretation of this inscription is exceedingly difficult. The first words make it clear that the figure must represent the apostle Simon, but the remainder I am unable to explain. It should be noted, however, that the inscription has been restored. The letters are of distinctly Gothic character

[94] Ezech., xliv, 1-2.

and are of a later epoch than the statue itself. It is probable that the inscription was originally painted and was subsequently incised by some ignorant restorer, when the letters of the original had become so effaced that they were no longer legible. The figure, with smooth face and long hair down the back, looks more like a woman than a man, but is not without analogy iconographically with the statue of the same apostle in the cloister at Moissac (Plate 142, Fig. 1).

On the capital below (Plate 29, Fig. 5) is a representation of Daniel in the den between two lions, who lay their paws on his knees. The inscription was probably originally in leonine verse, but has been badly restored. The interpolated letters I indicate by brackets:

✠ DANIEL . IVSTVS . IN LA . [EST] CV . LEONVM.

On one of the side faces of the capital is represented Habakkuk carrying the newly baked bread to the reapers in the fields. This bread is partly contained in a sack suspended from a pole carried over his right shoulder, and partly carried in his left hand. The prophet is accompanied by a boy, who also carries a staff over his shoulder. He is met by the angel, who commands him to go to Babylon.[95]

On the pinnacle of the gable of the northern portal are several sculptures (Plate 29, Fig. 5). On the west face is the standing figure of a bearded man without attributes. On the north face is a man on horse-back blowing a trumpet. This figure is beardless, but from behind emerges the head of a man with a long beard. On the south face is shown a beardless figure on horse-back, blowing a trumpet. If these sculptures have significance, I am unable to explain it. In the tympanum are the two sculptures of Charlemagne and Pope Adrian II, already described. In addition is represented the Lamb of God, and the miracle of the sick man already depicted in the life of the saint. The sick man, E.GRO.TVS., stands with bowed head and hands pressed together in prayer before the church of Borgo S. Donnino, ECLIA. Behind him may be seen his horse tied to a tree. In the lunette of this portal (Plate 29, Fig. 5) is an archaic relief representing the Madonna enthroned with the Child and on either side seven figures with curious head-dresses, their hands upraised, palms outwards. These doubtless represent donors, and from their head-dresses there can be little doubt that they are the burgesses of Borgo S. Donnino (Plate 29, Fig. 5). In the north tower are reliefs representing: (1) Herod ordering the slaughter of the Innocents. Herod, EROIDES, is seated on a throne. He is crowned, and carries a sphere and sceptre. To the left is seated Herodias, crowned, and with a cup in her hand. To the right kneels a courtier, a soldier in armour is behind, and a marshal stands in the doorway of the palace beyond. (2) The three

[95] Dan., xiv, 30-36.

Magi, CASPAR BALTASAR MELCHIOR. Caspar is beardless, the other two are bearded, and are seen riding on horse-back at full gallop.

On the pinnacle of the gable of the southern portal (Plate 29, Fig. 4) is seen the half figure of a bearded personage whose head is enveloped in a cowl. On his back is a half barrel, in his hand a staff and candle. Below is the inscription: RAIMUNDINS : VILIS : . Who Raimundino was, it is difficult to state. The sculpture is perhaps a caricature of some one at Borgo. Below in the tympanum is seen seated a bishop (Plate 29, Fig. 4) or rather, an archbishop, to judge from his stole, with crosier and mitre, his right hand raised in benediction. On the vault of the southern porch on the north side is a relief representing Hercules holding the Nemean lion by the tail. The inscription, FORTIS HERCVLES, leaves no doubt as to the identity of the figure. It is strange, however, to find this pagan subject represented on a Christian church.[96] In the tympanum (Plate 29, Fig. 4) is represented St. Michael holding a cross and trampling upon the dragon. On the abacus of the southern respond there is an inscription, much damaged, which I was unable to read. The letters as far as I could make them out, seemed to be:

. . . . . ROME . . . . . ERMO . TI DONIMI

T̂VLI

On the west and south faces of the southern door runs a sculptured frieze, the interpretation of which is exceedingly difficult. Beginning at the left we see: (1) Two animals (Plate 30, Fig. 2) followed by a man carrying a battle-ax over his shoulder and accompanied by another similar figure who carries over his shoulder an implement which is now broken away. Then follow two figures, both beardless, perhaps a youth and a maiden (since they are differently dressed), but more probably two youths, each holding the other by the ear. Then comes a girl with a long braid, holding a flower in her left hand. A youth, beardless, with sword hanging at his side, leans towards her tenderly and inserts his left hand beneath her skirt in an indecent manner. Then follows a figure of a youth holding a cross-bow, then a man standing before a lion, which tramples upon a human figure. On the southern face of the tower the frieze represents a long and continuous procession (Plate 30, Fig. 1). Beginning at the east there is: first, a man without armour riding on horse-back. He carries over his right shoulder a sword, which has been broken away. He is followed by a beardless, bare-headed man on foot, who carries his cloak over a staff suspended from his right shoulder. In his left hand he has a sort of bell or basket. Then comes a bearded man on foot, carrying a sack on his back. He had a staff in his hand, but this has been broken away. He is followed by a bearded man with his face wrapped in a cowl, his right hand under his garment, and a staff in the left hand. Then

---

[96] Can it be possible that S. Ercolano, who was a popular saint at Parma (Affò, II, 71), by confusion contributed to the popularity of Hercules in this region of Emilia?

comes a precisely similar figure except that the face is beardless. Then comes the figure of a beardless youth carrying in his left hand a water-bottle, and with his right leading a horse ridden by a dog of which the head has been broken off. Then comes another figure on foot, carrying an object so badly weathered that its nature can not be determined. Then comes a man on horse-back. His head has been broken off, and on his left arm he carries a shield. He is succeeded by a person on foot carrying a water-bottle and a cloak on a staff over his shoulder. Finally the procession ends with a bearded, bare-headed figure on horse-back, who carries a curious object which somewhat resembles an inverted pennant. On the west face of the southern door is an archaic relief (Plate 29, Fig. 3), representing a personage seated on a throne and holding in either hand widely projecting distaffs. Fastened at either side of the throne are winged griffins. It is the tradition at Borgo that this figure represents the mythical *Berta che filava*.[97]

[97] The saying, "Non sono più i tempi che Berta filava" is common in Italy, and many anecdotes and stories are related to account for the proverb. These stories, however, all appear to have been invented to explain the proverb, and none of them corresponds well with the sculpture of the cathedral. In the archives of the Cancelleria are preserved researches on the question by several local antiquaries, from which I transcribe the most interesting passages: 1102. MSS. Pinc. Parla della libertà de' Borgheggiani, e dice, che questa si raccoglie in quel quadro di marmo antico, che scolpito rozzamente ci rappresenta la Storia, o la Favola di certa Donna detta Berta, che filava a due rocche; la qual scoltura ridiccola osserviamo anche oggigiorno incastrata nella facciata del primo Torrione della facciata del nostro Duomo a mano diritta dell'ingresso in detta Chiesa. Che se vi si puon mente, è lavoro di scappello più goffo e più antico dell'altra incostratura pure di marmo più moderna e più polita. Quest'effigie è tutto il gran Palladio rappresentante la Libertà Borghigiana; attorno alla quale facevansi da nostri nella Vigilia del nostro Santo Protettore Domnino, come attorno al Caval di Troja pazze danze, vociferazioni, smorfie, e ridicole galorie. Passa indi a darci la storia di Berta, che filava a due rocche. Alla quale storia, e popolar racconto attenendosi questi di Borgo, o per far anch'essi applauso all'Augusta Madre del Re Corrado, che qui l'onorava di sua presenza, e di stanza, o per esprimergli la necessità in mistero del Paese pari a quello di quella povera donna, che avrebbe avuto bisogno di estension di territorio gli mise in faccia i di lui voti. Già filava Borgo a due mani, tenendo e dal partito del Padre Arrigo, e del Figliuolo Corrado filando e per Parma e per Piacenza, che sarà stato il misterioso simbolo della Berta filante. (Loose leaf of unknown author).

Berta che fila a due rocche, e che si vede in Basso rilievo nella facciata meridionale del nostro duomo. 1081 circa. Berta povera Montanara di Padova portò a vendere in Città certo filo sottilissimo, e non potendo vendere a quel prezzo, che aspettava, lo donò a Berta Moglie di Enrico IV. Imperadore, che in tal tempo trovauasi in Padova. Amirato il dono, ed il lavoro ordinò, che se le desse tanto terreno di pubblica ragione, quanto potesse cingere quel filo. Ella diventò di povera ricca, e la sua Famiglia è delle prime di Padova, detta Mantagnani. Vollero imitarla altre povere Donne col donar altro simile filo alla da Imperatrice, la quale a tutte rispondeva: non è più il tempo che Berta filava. Vedi Scardeon Lib. 3. *Historia Patavina.* . . . Berta. La Berta nostra in pietra non può essere che la Madre del Re Ugone, che unitamente a Lotario esso pure Re d'Italia fecero una donazione alla Chiesa di Parma nel 936. . . . Berta, a cui si facevano Palli ec.—Tutte le Città non dirò dell'Italia, ma dell'Europa intiera per tacer

LOMBARD ARCHITECTURE

In the interior of the church, on the first free-standing pier from the west of the southern arcade is a relief representing the fall of the rebellious angels. Above, the Deity is shown in an aureole,[98] and holding a scroll, with the inscription (Ps., cxviii, 121):

FECI
IVDI
CIV
M E
T IV
STI
CI
AM

On a sort of abacus are represented two good angels flying, and two bad angels in the form of monsters or devils, falling. Below, Michael, with the cross, transfixes with his spear one of the fallen angels. Beside Michael stands another angel, and beside the devil are seen two others, one flying and one standing. In the choir under the apse vaults are sculptures of Christ and symbols of the four Evangelists and of two angels. Christ has as an attribute a book, and the Evangelists have scrolls, but the inscriptions, if any existed, can not be read. The corbels which support the vaulting shafts are carved with reliefs representing the Madonna enthroned, the Annunciation, St. Joseph and grotesques.

In the buttress in the south-east angle of the choir is a stone carved to represent a face surrounded by petals. According to the local tradition at Borgo, this stone represents the sun; beneath it the Verzoli were entombed as is recorded by the neighbouring inscription:

✠CLARI : UERZOLI : Q
[CL]AVDUNTVR : SUB : PE
TRA : SOLI : ✠

delle altre parti del Mondo avevano i loro abusi col mescolare il sacro al profano. (MS. *Annotatione* in Archivio).

Il Padre Codagli nella sua storia Orceana-Brescia alla pag. 49 dice, che questo Proverbio nacque negli Orci, ed ecco in che modo. Primachè incrudelissero in questo modo le fazioni [de' Guelfi, e de' Gibellini] vogliono che negli Orci fosse una Vecchiarella per nome addimandata Berta, che solita era di star tutto il giorno su le muraglie vicino la Rocca guadagnandosi con la canocchia il vivere, laonde quella parte verso il fiume della Rocca ne acquistasse il nome di Berta e levandosi poi come di sopra le fazioni de' Guelfi, & Gibellini, per essersi distolta la vecchiarella da quel luogo ne nacesse il Proverbio *Non è più il tempo che Berta filava*. Ma la nostra Berta ha due rocche. (*Ibid.*). Too much emphasis should not be laid upon the fact that Berta has two distaffs. In the early XIII century it apparently was customary to weave with a double distaff; witness the Virgin in the Annunciation of the capital of the central portal.

[98] His halo is inscribed with the letters L V X. (MS. Zani, f. 10b, in Archivio).

BORGO S. DONNINO, CATHEDRAL

In the eastern wall of the southern side aisle is a pointed arched corbel-table (Plate 29, Fig. 2). In the rinceau above it, are represented an Annunciation and a haloed figure who holds his hand out towards a person with a spade. A grape-vine twines about. This scene recalls the reliefs of the parable of the householder and the labourers in the Parma baptistery. In the first niche of the campanile (Plate 29, Fig. 2) is a fine XIII century statue of the Madonna. In the apse are four other sculptures (Plate 29, Fig. 2), of which certainly two and possibly all belong to a cycle of the months. In the first are seen two figures, perhaps the twins, standing in a fruit-tree, and a standing figure, representing, perhaps, the month of April. Somewhat below is a relief depicting a beardless youth on horse-back, with a shield, helmet, lance and banner. This probably represents the month of May. Further on a small low relief represents a woman (Virgo?) with a hawk on her wrist, standing between a grape-vine and a fruit-tree. In the apse, March blows on a horn and is accompanied by a youth bearing a leafy branch. January, with two heads, holds in his right hand a raised cup, and in his left a loaf of bread. Sausages are hung above his head on a pole, and a kettle is suspended over a fire. Although these reliefs are all of similar style, it is by no means clear that they belong together. January and March are the only two of the same size, and the only two indubitably months.

V. Undoubtedly the earliest portions of the cathedral of Borgo S. Donnino are the lunette of the northern portal (Plate 29, Fig. 5), the relief of Berta (Plate 29, Fig. 3), and the statue of Simon the Apostle. The lunette of the northern portal and the relief of Berta are by the same hand. The bird-like faces and the sharp noses recall vividly the archivolt of the Porta della Pescheria at Modena (Plate 144, Fig. 3), with which they must be contemporary. We may, therefore, recognize in these two reliefs fragments of the church begun in 1101 and consecrated in 1106. The crude statue of Simon (Plate 29, Fig. 5), of wooden character, with long, heavy neck, a body full of angles, the arms plastered against the sides, probably also belongs to this early period, but is of a very different school from the two reliefs. These earlier fragments were incorporated by Benedetto in his reconstruction.

Somewhat later are the north and south portals (Plate 29, Fig. 4, 5), which show the very strong influence, or, rather, imitation of the work of Nicolò. The caryatids (Plate 29, Fig. 5) show the same curious treatment of the hair which is found in the work of Guglielmo da Modena, for example in the Enochs and Elijahs of Modena (Plate 142, Fig. 2) and Cremona, and in the prophets of Cremona (Plate 83, Fig. 8). This mannerism Nicolò took over when he sculptured the prophets at Ferrara (Plate 89, Fig. 4). Strikingly reminiscent of Nicolò are the grotesques in diamond-shaped panels (Plate 29, Fig. 5) of the Lombard porch, the doorway itself in four moulded orders, the capitals and the caryatids that serve for responds (Plate 29, Fig. 4, 5).

Characteristic of his style also are the capitals and the grotesques of the archivolts. The reliefs of the Hercules and the St. Michael, however, which are evidently by the same hand as the portal, show that we have here, not a genuine production of Nicolò, but an imitation of some very close follower. Both these sculptures are distinguished by a certain flabbiness of the face and a classic feeling that recalls Guglielmo da Modena. The side portals may, therefore, be assigned to c. 1135. Like the earlier fragments of 1106 they were incorporated by Benedetto in his reconstruction of the façade.

Critics are unanimous in recognizing the façade as a work of Benedetto, but there is still considerable discussion as to whether these sculptures are earlier or later than those of the Parma baptistery, and as to which ones were executed by Benedetto himself and which by pupils. For reasons of style it seems clear to me that the Borgo sculptures are earlier than those of the Parma baptistery. Now we know that Benedetto was engaged at Parma in working the Deposition of the ambo in 1178 and that he returned in 1196 to direct the baptistery. The inference is therefore justified that his work at Borgo falls between these two dates. In fact, if we are correct in ascribing to 1184 the notice of 1284 recorded above, it is probable that the work of Benedetto at Borgo was accomplished in the twelve years between 1184 and 1196. These twelve years would have been a reasonable length of time for the execution of all the works at Borgo in which the hand of Benedetto himself can be indubitably recognized. These are, in my judgment, all the reliefs of the façade (with the exception of those earlier fragments already noted), the capitals and archivolt of the central porch (Plate 27, Fig. 3) sculptured with commandments and beatitudes. The frieze of the southern campanile (Plate 30, Fig. 1, 2) was executed by a close follower of Benedetto, who must have been in some ways an even finer artist, under Benedetto's direction and inspiration, and after Benedetto had left Borgo to take charge of the construction of the baptistery at Parma. Also executed in the time of Benedetto and probably under his direct supervision are the earliest parts of the architecture of the church,—the bases of the two campaniles flanking the façade, the two western responds of the main arcade, with their Corinthianesque capitals, the westernmost responds of the side aisles, and the capitals of broad, flat leaves in the north-east angle of the southern side aisle.

In the usual Lombard fashion the construction of the church at Borgo had been begun with the reliefs of the façade, and when Benedetto left in 1196 these had in all probability been completed. His successor attacked the actual construction of the church, and in the years 1196 to 1207 the building was carried to completion. In the edifice itself, however, numerous changes of style are noticeable which give reason to suppose that Benedetto in this brief period of time had not one but two successors. To the first, who was primarily a sculptor, I assign the reliefs of the façade already mentioned as not being by the hand of Benedetto,[99] and also part of the nave and the crypt. To his second successor I ascribe the gallery of the nave and the holy-water basin, as well as the sculptures now incorporated in the apse and campanile. Not all of these sculptures were executed by the same hand, but they appear to be contemporary, and were probably the work of the different sculptors working under the direction of the second successor of Benedetto.

In 1285 the apse and vaults were rebuilt in their present form, and of that epoch are the sculptures of the interior of the choir. The exterior cornice of this apse is a reproduction of the cornice of the baptistery at Parma erected in 1270, and probably the same artist executed both.

BREBBIA,[1] SS. PIETRO E PAOLO

(Plate 30, Fig. 6)

I. The church of Brebbia, although among the more interesting of the Varesotto, has never been studied from an archæological standpoint.

II. According to the legend of the saints Giulio and Giuliano, the church of Brebbia was founded by the two confessors in the IV century, and was the scene of one of the miracles performed by them.[2]

In the year 999 the church was already a pieve and under the jurisdiction of the archbishop of Milan.[3] The church is called a pieve in other documents of 1024[4] and 1030.[5] Extant documents of 1153[6] refer to a controversy between the prevosto of Brebbia and the abbot of S. Celso at Milan. It is clear that at this time the pieve of Brebbia enjoyed considerable importance, and was officiated by a chapter of canons. In 1250 the prevosto appears contesting certain rights with the decumani of the cathedral of Milan.[7] The dignity of the church at the end of the XIII century is apparent from the catalogue of Gottofredo, who assigns to Brebbia forty-six dependent churches and fifty-five

[99] The manner in which the frieze is placed in the campanile recalls the cathedral of Benevento.

[1] (Como).

[2] Aliud quoque miraculum in loco, qui dicitur Beblas, contigit. Dum labori insisterent [upon the basilica founded by SS. Giulio and Giuliano], unus virorum incaute manum prævidens ferramento, quod vulgus dextrale appellat, pollicem amputavit, unde tantus emanans profluxit cruor, ut vir ille deciderit in dementiam. Quod idem ejusdem plebis socii S. Julio studuerunt indicare. Sanctus autem Julius ad eum illico veniens, eumdem inquisivit pollicem, dicens: Afferre digitum huc ad me, qui cum allatus fuisset, accipiens eum in locum posuit, et facto Crucis signo, restituta est, sicut antea fuerat, integra manus. Accipiensque vir Dei ferramentum dedit in manus ejus dicens, Labora et confortare in nomine Patris et Filii et Spiritus sancti. (*Vita SS. Julii et Juliani*, ed. *Acta Sanctorum*, 31 Januarii, III, 718).

[3] Giulini, I, 692.   [4] *Ibid.*, II, 141.   [5] *Ibid.*, 173.   [6] *Ibid.*, III, 390.

[7] *Ibid.*, IV, 452.

studies by Stiehl[6] and Rivoira[7] are important, but the monograph of Arcioni is of slight value.

II.   Possibly no other monument in all Lombardy offers more complex historical problems than the Rotonda of Brescia. According to tradition the church was founded by Teodolinda in 590 and was consecrated in 612.   It is a too familiar fact, however, that a very large proportion of the churches of northern Italy are accredited by tradition to the famous Lombard queen, but, in the great majority of cases, such legends appear to have no foundation in historical fact.   In the absence of confirming circumstances, it is therefore probable that this tradition of Brescia, though gravely discussed by many historians,[8] is apocryphal.   Another notice, hardly more worthy of credence, is furnished by a late chronicler who states that the church of the holy apostles Peter and Paul, meaning doubtless thereby S. Pietro in Dom, which, with the Rotonda, served as dual cathedral, was erected in a pagan temple apparently about the year 246, since he mentions this among other fabulous events of that time.[9]   The history of the monument has been greatly obscured by the forged chronicle of Rodolfo the Notary.   This appears to have been fabricated by Biemmi, who forged also two other chronicles.   The false chronicle of Rodolfo contained many confusing and conflicting notices of the churches of Brescia, but was accepted as genuine by all the local historians and even by Cattaneo.   Thus in all extant histories of the monument there is a crowd of misleading notices drawn from this false fount.

Of authentic documents relating to the history of the church there are few.   According to a catalogue of the VIII century,[10] the bishop Benedetto, who died in 774, was buried *ante regiam sce marie.*   Odorici contends that it is by no means sure that the S. Maria referred to in this notice was the church which preceded on the same site the existing edifice of S. Maria Rotonda; that in a catalogue of bishops of 1073,[11] our church is constantly distinguished from others of the same name existing in the city of Brescia by the adjective "Maggiore" (*major*), and that Ardingo (920-921) and Odorico (1031-1048) are mentioned as having been buried in the church thus specified.   Odorici, however, apparently has forgotten that in 875 our church is called, in a text

---

[6] 16.   [7] 182.   [8] See Zamboni, 105-107.

[9] Itaque diebus illis Ecclesiam Sanctorum Apostolorum Petri, & Pauli, quæ templum erat Idolorum, sicut paulò ante prædixi, taliter dedicarunt. (Jacobi Malvecii, *Chronicon,* III, 11, ed. Muratori, R. I. S., XIV, 801). Compare also: Sanè & hujus Civitatis templa ad honorem & gloriam altitonantis æterni, & gloriosissimæ Virginis, nec non Sanctorum ejus à patribus nostris opinandum est fuisse constituta, ornamentis multis atque facultatibus ditata: eosdem etiam templa ipsa à dignissimis personis ordinari voluisse, ut sublimis Deus precibus Beatissimæ Virginis, & Sanctorum, in quorum reverentiam præfatas Ecclesias construxerat, Brixiensem populum victoriosum, & ab omni adversitate securum efficeret. (*Ibid.,* 780).

[10] Published by Odorici, III, 70.   [11] Published by Odorici, IV, 106.

I shall cite below, simply S. Maria. Moreover, this adjective "Maggiore" implies a cathedral church and is constantly used in the Lombard towns to denote the cathedral. Now in early times the cathedral of Brescia was situated in the church of S. Andrea[12] but had been transferred to S. Maria before 838, as will be evident from a passage of Ramperto that I shall quote later. It is therefore just possible that the cathedral might have been transferred between 774 and 838, and that in 774 the church was not called "Maggiore" for the reason that it was at that time not a cathedral.

The connection between the Rotonda and the church of S. Pietro in Dom has much puzzled historians, but the explanation is simple. From a text of Ramperto it is evident that in 838 S. Maria was the winter cathedral, and it is safe to infer that S. Pietro was the summer cathedral. It was the common practice in Lombard towns to have thus two cathedrals in connection with each other, as, for example, was the case at Milan and Pavia. The Rotonda is still connected with the Duomo which was erected in place of S. Pietro, and throughout the Middle Ages now S. Maria, now S. Pietro is referred to as the principal church of Brescia. It is therefore clear that after the IX century there was in Brescia a dual cathedral.

Of the early history of S. Pietro in Dom, nothing is known except the vague tradition of its origin above referred to. Certain it is, however, that at the end of the X century the church was already ancient, and was restored in connection with the translation of S. Apollonio. This is known from three sources. The first is the epitaph of Landolfo II, which no longer exists, but which has been preserved by Gagliardi and published by Odorici[13] and Ughelli.[14] "This altar covers the body of the noble-born Landolfo, an illustrious bishop. He himself during his pontificate erected this so admirable altar

---

[12] Jacobi Malvecii, *Chronicon*, III, 11, ed. Muratori, R. I. S., XIV, 802; *ibid.*, IV, 3, ed. Muratori, 810.

[13] IV, 68.   [14] IV, 536, ed. C.

[15]   Ara tegit corpus clara de stirpe creatum
      Præsens Landulfi Præsulis egregii.
Hanc aram, cujus semper pia linea rexit,
      Ordine quam miro struxerat ipse potens.
Hic quoque nobilitate lucens, opibusque rifulgens,
      Omnibus ut decuit claruit ipse probus.
Alta silex ceu quam non turbidus impulit Auster
      Manserat immotus turbine flanti secli. . . .
Vitæ quietem cernens sibi valde propinquam
      Edixit fieri hoc sibi Mausoleum.
Præsulis Antonii iuxta quod pia membra quiescunt,
      Quem morum pietas vexit ad astra poli.
Omnia quæ nunc his potiora videntur in aulis
      Multiplici studio fecerat ipse pius [Ughelli reads *prius*]. . . .
                        (Ed. Odorici, IV, 68).

which he ever piously served. His life was ever noble and filled with good works. He performed with honour whatever duty imposed. Like a lofty rock undisturbed by the force of the wind, he remained staunch in the whirling hurricane of the world. . . . Perceiving that the end of his life was approaching, he caused this tomb to be prepared for himself. Near it rests the holy body of the bishop Antonio whom piety carried to the heavens. All the nobler things which are now seen in these halls he himself piously wrought in his fervent zeal."[15] The second source is a description of certain events of the last quarter of the X century. Atto, marchese of Canossa, stole by violence c. 971 the head and left arm of S. Apollonio, which he carried off to place in the basilica which he had founded in his own castle.[16] In the book *De obitu sancti*

[16] II. The castle of Canossa was founded about the middle of the X century, by Atto or Azzo, count of Parma. (Sigonio, 260-261, ad. ann. 945; Ferretti, 21; Muratori, A. I. M. A., ed. A, XIII, 657). The church of Canossa must have been founded at about the same time, since in 976 the pope, Benedict VII, issued a bull in its favour. (Tiraboschi, *Cod.*, I, 140). The church was collegiate and officiated by a chapter of twelve canons. The rich treasury of the establishment was given in 1082 by the countess Matilda to the pope, who was at that time being besieged in Rome. Twenty years before this the canons had been replaced by monks, as we learn from a passage of Donizone:

> Bina Monasteria cum qua [Mathilde] simul
> edidit ipsa [Beatrix];
> Ut tueatur eas qui Cœli ducit habenas,
> Faxinorense Monasterium primum fuit illud;
> Prædia multa satis dedit illis magna
> Beatrix;
> Esse quia Monachos plus quàm Clericos
> venerandos
> Credebant ambæ; Canusinæ quoque Sanctæ
> Ecclesiæ nomen mutaverunt & honorem
> In melius, dudum cui præpositus fuit unus,
> Usus cum Cleris non ni tantùm duodenis
> Deservire quidem, nunc Abbas servit
> ibidem
> Cum Monachis Christo multis famulantibus
> illo.

(*Vita Mathildis* a Donizone scripta, 17, ed. Muratori, R. I. S., V, 360. See also *ibid.*, 350).

The church itself must have been rebuilt, since it was consecrated by the bishop Ariberto, who held office from 1085 to 1092 (Saccani, 53). A bull of Pascal II of February 26, 1116, in favour of the monastery, has been published by Torelli. During the early years of the XII century Matilda improved and beautified her castle at Canossa, but there is no evidence that the church itself was altered. In 1187 Gregory VIII issued a bull in favour of the monastery. In 1255 the castle was destroyed by the Reggiani, but was subsequently rebuilt. In 1392 the relics which the church contained were sold in Pavia, and the celebration of mass was suspended. In 1449 the castle was purchased by Leonello d'Este, and a radical restoration was begun in 1451. In 1570, according to an

Apolonii[17] we read: "When the bishop Landolfo learned of the theft of a part of the holy body . . . he decided that what was left ought to be buried within the walls of the city . . . . . lest something similar should happen again. However, before translating the very sacred body from the place in which it had anciently been laid, he restored the choir of the basilica of St. Peter the Apostle, which was ruinous with age, and beneath the same church he dedicated a beautiful vaulted crypt entirely worthy to receive the body of the patron saint. When this had been done on a certain day he gathered together all his clergy and many of the laity . . . . . and many women and approached the venerable body; raising it from the place where it had been, he brought it to the crypt which he had constructed in connection with the cathedral. When he had thus reburied the body of Apollonio, he instituted a chapter of canons which he endowed with revenues derived from his own property, in order that by them and by their successors forever that most holy body might be served."[18] The third source is another account of the same translation in a late chronicle: "A certain very strenuous

inscription still preserved in the museum at Canossa, Alfonso II of Este gave the castle to Bonifacio Ruggieri, who again restored the fortress as a pleasure villa. It subsequently fell into ruin. About 1878 excavations were begun to explore the site of the mediæval fortress. In the local museum which has been established in a part of the old castle are preserved various objects found during the exploration of the site and showing the results of the excavations.

III. As reconstructed by the excavators, the church of S. Apollonio consisted of a nave two bays long, two very narrow side aisles terminating in absidioles preceded by a rectangular bay, a highly raised choir, and a crypt with two columns. The church was entirely roofed in wood. In the west wall were two engaged half columns serving as responds to the main arcade. According to the excavators the church was subsequently deprived of its southern side aisle by the successors of Matilda, and completely destroyed by the Estensi. Of the church there remain standing only the crypt, with its two stairs of access, two columns, and one capital. This capital is of an Ionic-like type precisely similar to another one in the museum, which consequently must also have come from this crypt. Such capitals can certainly not be of the XII century, and are more probably of the Estense period. It therefore seems clear that the excavators entirely misunderstood the edifice and that absolutely no reliance can be placed upon their reconstruction.

IV. In the museum are various fragments which presumably came from the church, though no record appears to have been kept as to where they were found. One is a crude baptismal font carved with grotesques and symbols of the Evangelists, but the eagle of St. John is lacking. There is also a capital of a large Romanesque pier carved with grotesques. The technique is similar to that of the font, and suggests the XIII century work at Toano. Four smaller capitals look as though they might come from a crypt, but it is impossible that they could have found place in the small crypt of S. Apollonio. One carved with grotesques might be of the early XIII century.

17 Ed. Odorici, IV, 98.

18 [Landulfus] postquam vero sacratissimi corporis diminuti cognovit delationem, ne quid simile iterum fieret sacratissimum corpus . . . . . infra ejusdem civitatis muros reconditum iri fore dignissimum judicavit. Prius vero quam sacratissimum corpus a

marchese, by name Atto, accompanied by a strong band of armed men, took the citizens by surprise and carried away the head and right arm of S. Apollonio. These he placed with all honour in his castle at Canossa. In consequence of this theft the venerable body of the saint was translated to the cathedral church, where it was placed with all reverence on the southern side next to the altar of the Holy Apostles Peter and Paul."[19] Putting together these three texts we see clearly that S. Pietro was rebuilt by Landolfo. The basilica was destroyed in the early XVII century to make way for the existing Duomo, but some fragments are still extant.[20]

Unfortunately the fact that the winter cathedral of S. Pietro was restored at the end of the X century throws but little light on the history of the Rotonda. It is even impossible to say which of the two churches was first founded. The earliest certain mention of S. Maria Maggiore occurs in an account of the translation of the body of S. Filastro into the crypt, in the IX century. The 'Acts' of the translation contain these words: "Thirty bishops of Brescia of whom we have record celebrated mass at the altar dedicated to S. Filastro, and placed over his head. And they all venerated the day of his death ordering the people of Brescia to abstain from all manual labour, and they honoured and revered him . . . I, Ramperto, the last in order and in merit of this number, unworthy bishop of Brescia, since due ceremony and sufficient lights were not in that venerable place in which was lying the body of Filastro of very blessed memory . . . in the year of our Lord 838, the

loco, in quo primitus fuerat positum sublevaret, tribunal basilicæ beati Petri Apostuli jam vetustate turpissimum, sui laboris novitate honestavit, atque sub eodem domum pulcherrimam absidum expolitam testudine patroni sui corpus suscipere dignissimam magnopere dedicavit. Hoc itaque facto, quadam die collectis omnibus suis clericis pluribusque laicis . . . . . muliebri etiam sexu non absente, venerabile corpus agressus est. Elevansque a priori sede ad domum, quam sibi prope sedem episcopii sui construxerat, illud adduxit. Recondito itaque beati Apollonii corpore, ibidem canonicos ordinavit, atque singulis de sua proprietate beneficia erogavit, quatenus ab ipsis, eorumve successoribus perpes famulacium sanctissimo corpori non deesset.

[19] Strenuissimus quidam vir Marchio, nomine Azzo, Caput Brachiumque dextrum ipsius Sanctissimi Apollonii armatorum comitiva valida præmunitus inopinato Civibus adventu arripuit, & ea in arce sua Canusii honorabiliter collocavit; quamobrem venerabile ejus corpus ad Cathedralem Ecclesiam translatum exstitit, ubi à Meridiana parte juxta Altare Sanctorum Apostolorum Petri, & Pauli cum ingenti exhibitione reverentiæ repositum fuit. (Jacobi Malvecii, *Chronicon*, III, 9, ed. Muratori, R. I. S., XIV, 800).

[20] Mothes, I, 243. Zamboni, 118 f., gives a description of the church as it was before its destruction. Compare also the description of the brothers Sacchi, 77-78: Di questa basilica, che era la cattedrale estiva [*sic*], unicamente sappiamo fosse a tre navi, sostenuta da venti quattro colonne di marmo, diverse di diametro, di altezza, di qualità e colore, due delle quali scanalate erano di marmo bianco, altre oscure, il maggior numero di un colore come di ferro. L'ortografia era volta ad occidente, avea una porta maggiore e un'altra laterale: non avea volte ma era coperta a travi e da quanto ne insegna Arnaldo aveva i cancelli o logge sulle navate laterali come voleano i riti del cristianisimo.

first indiction, the eighth day of April . . . sought the venerable body with
fear as it befitted that so unworthy a one should, who touched such venerable
clay, and I raised up the body, and placed it on a bier. Then on the ninth
day of April, in the presence of all the clergy and a great number of the
populace of both sexes, with the greatest respect and reverence we translated
that body to the winter cathedral of Brescia, placing it in the altar of the
blessed Mary, Mother of God, where was the seat of the above-mentioned
bishops of Brescia. There on the twelfth of May, in the presence of all the
faithful who prepared themselves by sacred functions and fastings and prayers,
with the greatest devotion we buried the body in the marble crypt, in order
that there where had formerly been the seat of the bishops should lie the body
of so great a father and patron, and that this body might endow the bishopric
with honour, the people with devotion, the clergy with judgment, by the intercession of the worthy saint and the grace of Christ . . . . . When therefore
as we have said, we gathered together a multitude of people of both sexes,
and the clergy had sanctified itself and put on sacred vestments, we opened
the very secret grave which for nearly five hundred years had hidden the
blessed body. Astonished at the revelation we bore the very holy and very
dear treasure very reverently upon the shoulders of the priests, and we came
with the greatest devotion to the church of the Blessed Virgin Mary."[21] In

21 Triginta autem Brixienses Episcopi, quos meminimus, qui in altari nomini beati
Philastrii dicato, et super caput ejusdem posito, preces Missarum celebraverunt, et
diem transitus ejus venerantes, ab omni terreno opere Brixiensem populum abstinere
jubentes, reverenter honoraverunt. . . . Quorum ordine et meritis novissimus ego
Rampertus indignus Episcopus Brixiensis sanctæ Ecclesiæ, dum officii assiduitas, et
abundantia luminaria in eo venerabili loco non essent quo beatissimæ memoriæ Philastrii corpus jacebat . . . anno Dominicæ incarnationis *octingentesimo trigesimo octavo,*
indictione prima, *sexto Idus Aprilis* . . . venerandum corpus reperiens, maximo cum
timore, ut puta tam venerabilem glebam, tam immeritus contingens, elevavi, collocans
in feretri locello. Deinde quinto Idus Aprilis, congregato clero, stipantibus utriusque
sexus immodicis catervis, maximi cum honore timoris summaque reverentia, idem corpus
transtulimus in matrem *Ecclesiam hiemalem nostram Brixiensem, penes altare sanctæ
Dei Genitricis Mariæ, ubi prescriptorum Pontificum erat sedes* . . . . . Ubi quarto Idus
Maji, coadunata Ecclesia, officiis et jejuniis cum orationibus præeuntibus, maxima cum
devotione, *in marmoreo recondentes* antro, sepelivimus: ut ubi modo Pontificum sedes
aderat, ibi tanti patris et Pontificis jaceret corpus, quo sedes honore, et populus
devotione, et clerus suffragio, ejusdem meritis intervenientibus, Christo in omnibus
favente, potiretur . . . . . Cum igitur, ut a nobis prædictum est, plurimis utriusque
sexus instructi phalangibus, prius sanctificato clero, sacrisque vestibus induto; effoso
clandestino antro, quod ferme *centum lustris* beatissimum habens *occuluit corpus;*
attoniti super revelatione, sanctissimum, carissimumque thesaurum, in sacerdotum
humeros reverenter detulissemus; ad domum sanctæ, ac semper Virginis Mariæ summa
cum devotione pervenimus. Poi narra il solenne ingresso alla Rotonda fra l'acclamante
moltitudine: poi si volge agli operati miracoli; e parla della povera donna, che al sesto
dì convalescente *erexit sese, et accepto baculo cepit huc et illuc templi ambitus testi-
tudinem ambulare. (Narratio translationis Sancti Philastri,* ed. Odorici, IV, 28).

addition to this contemporary account of the translation of S. Filastro into the crypt of S. Maria, there are two other notices not without importance. The first is in a late chronicle: "The bishop Ramperto, a man of innocent and holy life, full of good works, was in those days head of the church of Brescia. He translated the body of S. Filastro from the church of S. Andrea, where it had been buried, to the principal church of the city founded in honour of the glorious Mother of God. At that time that church was already the cathedral just as it is in our days. . . . This translation took place in the month of April, in the year of our Lord 838. Indeed the much-to-be-revered body was buried in the cathedral church with an honour which contrasts strangely with the neglect with which it is guarded in my time, for that place is so flooded with water that no one can enter the crypt, nor do the citizens take any care about this."[22] The second is a notice which Averoldi read in a manuscript chronicle to the effect that the crypt of S. Maria Maggiore was dedicated to the Redentore before the translation of the body of S. Filastro.[23]

From these notices, we may safely deduce the following facts: (1) the body of S. Filastro was translated in 838 from the church of S. Andrea to the crypt of S. Maria Maggiore; (2) S. Maria Maggiore at that time was the winter cathedral, and had been the cathedral so long that the bishop Ramperto had no knowledge that the cathedral had even been situated in any other church; (3) the crypt existed before 838, since it was not specially constructed to receive the body of the saint.

In 875 the church of S. Maria Maggiore and its crypt are again mentioned by a contemporary chronicler: "The following August [875], Lodovico [II] the Emperor, died in the territory of Brescia on the twelfth day of the month. Antonio, bishop of Brescia, took his body, and placed it in a tomb in the church of S. Maria, where rests the body of S. Filastro."[24]

The church of the IX century was a basilica of which fragments are still extant. It was replaced by the existing Rotonda later than 897, since a stone

[22] Regebat quoque diebus illis Brixiensem Ecclesiam Rampertus Episcopus vir innocentiæ & sanctitatis operibus florens. Hic corpus Beatissimi Filastri ab Ecclesia Sancti Andreæ, ubi sepultum fuerat, in Templum majus Civitatis, quod in honore Gloriosissimæ Matris Domini conditum exstat, transferri fe.it. Jam quidem diebus illis Ecclesia ista pro Episcopali Domicilio habebatur, quemadmodum in diebus nostris habetur. . . . Actum est hoc mense Aprili Anno Domini DCCCXXXVIII. Verùm quanto devotiùs id excolendissimum corpus in ipsa Cathedrali Ecclesia reconditum exstitit, tanto in diebus meis indecentiùs observatur; nam locus ipse adeò aquis demergitur, ut nullus id Oraculum ingredi possit; nec ulla est hac de re Civibus cura. (Jacobi Malvecii, *Chronicon*, V, 18, ed. Muratori, R. I. S., XIV, 860).

[23] Rosa, 164.

[24] Sequenti autem mense Augusto Hludovicus Imperator defunctus est pridie Idus Augusti in finibus Brescianis. Antonius vero Brescianus Episcopus tulit corpus ejus, et posuit eum in sepulcro in Ecclesia Sanctæ Mariæ, ubi Corpus Sancti Filastrii requiescit. (Andreæ Presbyteri, *Chronicon*, ed. Muratori, A. I. M. A., ed. A, I, 74).

with inscription of that date was used as second-hand material in the new edifice. This is still extant in the church together with two other fragmentary epitaphs.[25]

A document of 1153 records that the consecration of the church was annually celebrated on the thirtieth of July, but it is not stated in what year the original consecration took place.[26] A new choir was apparently built in the first half of the XIV century, since there is a notice of the consecration of the great altar in 1342.[27] In 1456 an additional stairway leading to the crypt was constructed.[28] In 1489 the choir was again enlarged and extensive alterations undertaken which were completed before 1493. In 1496 the frescos were finished.[29] In 1565 the old north and south doors having become inconvenient because the level of the surrounding soil had risen, a new west door was opened through the campanile. This work, finished in 1571, ultimately caused the fall of the campanile in 1708. About the same time new alterations were begun in the choir, which was deepened, and the Cappella della S. Croce was constructed. This work was finished in 1605. The chapel of S. Giustina was founded in 1579.[30] At the end of the XIX century the church was thoroughly restored. Work was finally finished in 1898, after having lasted with interruptions nearly twenty years. In the course of this restoration the intonaco was stripped off the interior, traces of the eight ancient windows of the cupola were discovered, the vaults of the side aisle were repaired and consolidated, the Gothic northern portal was renovated, the second stairway leading to the crypt was rebuilt on the traces of the ancient one, the walls were thoroughly restored, and the chapel which had been added to the Rotonda on the side towards the Vicolo del Lupo was removed. Six of the ancient piers of the nave were remade. There came to light beneath the existing pavement traces of an older edifice which was evidently a basilica. In the new pavement these traces are indicated by layers of darker marble placed over the exact spot where the ancient foundations were found. The ancient pavement was about 10 centimetres below the level of the existing pavement. Two fragments of the ancient mosaic were removed and mounted;[31] the others were left in their original position, but covered with a wooden lid which can

[25] QVI FVERAT MITIS PATIENS HVMILISQ.SACER[DOS]
    INGENIO POLLENS NOBILITATE VIGENS
VITA NAM SEMPER XPĪ SPEM RITE REGEBAT
    ILLIVS METAM NOVIMVS ESSE BONAM
TVM P[RO]PRIO REDDENS ANIMAM DE CORPORE PVLCHR[AM]
    CORPVS HVMO SEPELIT SPS ASTRA PETIT
VOS ROGO LECTORES QUI CARPITIS ACTA TAPHONIS
    IN DNO VALEAS DICITE CORDE PIO
ANNO DOMINICAE INCARNATIONIS.DCCCXCVII.IND [XV]
    III.ĪD.APRILIVM.FELICITER MIGRAVIT AD XPM

[26] Odorici, V, 103.   [27] Zamboni, 108.   [28] Odorici, II, 241.
[29] Zamboni, 109.   [30] Zamboni, 109-114.   [31] These are now in the narthex.

be removed. Between the Duomo and the Rotonda was found a fragment of an altar with a relief of S. Apollonio (Plate 31, Fig. 5), and other bits of ancient church carving.[32] The restoration was directed by the architect Archioni.[33]

III. The church consists of a western narthex, a circular nave surrounded by a side aisle (Plate 31, Fig. 7, 8), a choir of irregular shape, and a crypt. The nave is covered by a dome, the side aisle by rectangular groin vaults alternating with triangular barrel vaults (Plate 31, Fig. 6) and the crypt with groin vaults. The groin vaults of the side aisles (Plate 31, Fig. 6) are only slightly domed. The curve of the groins is depressed in elevation; the wall and transverse arches, loaded at the crown, disappear at the springing. There are no responds in the outside wall (Plate 31, Fig. 6, 8). The barrel vaults of the triangular compartments are placed much higher than are the groin vaults (Plate 31, Fig. 6). According to the drawings of Hübsch, the dome is of a most peculiar construction. At the springing it is buttressed by a little barrel vault, which rests on the walls of the drum. Archioni, who had an opportunity of observing the construction during the restoration, fails to note this peculiarity, but mentions that the dome is constructed of two different kinds of materials. Heavy blocks of stone are used in the lower portions below the springing. Above, light pieces of porous stone are employed. This vault is over a metre in thickness.

The arch which opens into the chancel at the east end of the Rotonda, is highly stilted. The existing choir is of the Gothic and Renaissance periods, but it is evident from the fact that the large eastern arch of the Rotonda is original, as well as from the crypt placed under the choir, that the Rotonda originally had an eastern channel, and was not a simple circular edifice. At the west end are two broken-off stairways which formerly led to the tower which, it will be remembered, was destroyed in 1708.[34] At the west end of the church, at the level of the nave, is the narthex, barrel- and groin-vaulted. The side aisles are carried around over this narthex.

The crypt is in basilica form, and consists of a nave four bays long, two side aisles of the same height and three apses. Its vaults appear to have been modernized, but probably preserve in part the original construction. They are much domed, and the transverse arches, loaded at the bottom, disappear at the springing.

The nave (Plate 31, Fig. 8) is separated from the aisles by eight square piers without system. The clearstory (Plate 31, Fig. 7) consists of ten small,

---

[32] These are now all preserved in the church.

[33] *Archivio Storico Lombardo*, Anno XXIII, 1896, 446; *ibid.*, 1895, 245; *ibid.*, 1899, 226; *ibid.*, 1894, 256.

[34] According to Archioni, the foundations of this tower, laid bare during the restoration, are of a masonry identical with that of the rest of the edifice. The tower, therefore, formed part of the original structure.

round-arched windows irregularly spaced; oculi are pierced in the dome; the windows are small and splayed, and they appear to have been designed to hold glass. The masonry, entirely homogeneous with the exception of those parts of the wall which were remade in the recent restoration, consists of ashlar, on the whole well laid, although the courses are often not horizontal, and the blocks are small and of different sizes (Plate 31, Fig. 7, 8). Only the exterior cornice of the clearstory is executed in bricks often laid in herring-bone courses.

Earlier than the existing Rotonda are the remains of a basilica discovered during the restoration beneath the pavement of the nave. At the time of the discovery the remains, consisting of a fragment of the wall and the mosaic pavement, were published in the *Archivio Storico Lombardo*.[35] Of this early church it is impossible to say more than that it was a wooden-roofed basilica, so scant are the vestiges that remain.

IV. The ornament of the church like the construction belongs to different epochs. Of the first are the remains of the mosaic pavement. This pavement is very simple in character and contains several inscriptions, doubtless recording the names of donors and the amount they ordered executed.[36]

The capitals of the crypt form an interesting study. The western one on the south side is pilfered Roman. The next one towards the east (Plate 31, Fig. 1) is apparently a Carlovingian imitation of a Byzantine model of the VI century. The acanthus leaves are crisp and pointed in design but flat and flaccid in execution. The crude carving of the volutes and the exaggerated quasi-classical moulding prove the unskilfulness of the Carlovingian worker. The next one is a typical Carlovingian design and is of Corinthianesque type. The next capital is evidently pilfered, being of the VI century, and is supplied with a single row of sharp, pointed acanthus leaves, vigorously executed and deeply undercut. The easternmost capital of the southern row of columns is a half capital of the VIII century, similar in type to one extant in the church of S. Salvatore. The westernmost capital of the second row is of the VI century, of Byzantinesque type and with two rows of acanthus leaves. The decadent era, however, is betrayed by the strange proportions. The next

---

[35] Anno 1895, 245.

[36]

. . . . .	
THEODO	CVM. [SVI]S FC
ET MARTA	PED . XVII
[CVM] SVIS	
FECERVN̂T PD XVII	
LIBERIVS ET	SEVLI . . . . .
PIEN?T?IA C . S .	MATR . . . . .
FC . P . XVII	C S F PD . . . . .

capital (Plate 31, Fig. 4) is of the end of the VIII century, and is one of the weakest and most decadent of all the capitals of the crypt. The next capital (Plate 31, Fig. 3), with a single row of very anthemion-like acanthus leaves, finely drawn and skilfully executed, is of a type, so far as I know, without analogy elsewhere, but must be of the VI century. The next capital (Plate 31, Fig. 2) is a Carlovingian design of the end of the VIII century. The easternmost capital of the second row is ancient Roman, as is also the westernmost capital of the third row. The next capital is Byzantine of the VI century, and has been injured by long exposure to the weather. The next one, of the VI century, has anthemion-like acanthus leaves similar to those of the third capital of the second row, already described. The next capital is an inverted base. The easternmost capital of the third row is antique. The westernmost capital of the last row is of the VI century, but more poorly executed than others of the same epoch in the crypt; the poor drawing and shallow execution of the volute bear witness to great lack of technique on the part of the sculptors. The design, however, is distinctly Carlovingian, not Byzantine. The next capital is probably of the V century. The proportions are not happy, and there is a single row of flaccid acanthus leaves. The execution of the volutes, however, is very classical. The next capital is a typical Carlovingian design of the VIII century. The next capital is of the VI century, like several already described. The next one is Carlovingian of the VIII century. Thus it will be seen that the crypt contains capitals of all epochs anterior to and including the VIII century, but none later than this date.

The Rotonda itself is characterized by the extreme simplicity of its ornament. The archivolts are in a single unmoulded order (Plate 31, Fig. 8). There are no capitals, and the impost mouldings are formed by a single simple fillet. The exterior (Plate 31, Fig. 7) is adorned with arched corbel-tables, supported on pilaster strips, which do not, however, reach below the level of the clearstory. The clearstory wall externally has blind niches in several orders, and the arched corbel-tables, in one or two orders, surmount an open-work zigzag, in places double. This zigzag recalls the similar ornament employed at Fontanella al Monte (Plate 93, Fig. 1), the Cathedral of Acqui (Plate 2, Fig. 5), and S. Pietro in Vellate. The cornice, with double saw tooth, rope-moulding and flat corbel-table, is executed in brick, and has evidently been several times retouched. The oculi externally have rope-mouldings.

At present there are placed in the church several fragments coming possibly from the destroyed basilica of S. Pietro, and discovered during the recent restoration. The most interesting is the statue of S. Apollonio, S AP[PO]LONI|VS (Plate 31, Fig. 5), which perhaps belonged to an altar and is evidently a work of the XIII century. In addition there are several fragments of Carlovingian and Roman carvings, and of ancient tracery in stone.

BRESCIA, S. MARIA DEL SOLARIO

V. The character of the names shows that the mosaic pavement must be of the IV or V century. The crypt must be older than 838, since the documentary evidence on this subject is confirmed by the style of the capitals, of which those that were executed for their present position may be assigned to c. 780.

As for the Rotonda itself, the shafts of the exterior, the construction of the aisle vault, and the character of the masonry, are all characteristic of the first quarter of the XII century. The extreme simplicity of the ornament, on the other hand, indicates a comparatively early date, and we should doubtless not be far wrong in ascribing the church to c. 1105. It may, indeed, have well been rebuilt after the fire which destroyed Brescia in 1095.

BRESCIA, S. MARIA DEL SOLARIO

(Plate 32, Fig. 1, 2, 3)

I. This interesting little chapel was for many years exceedingly difficult of access, and has hence perhaps not received the attention which it deserves from historians of art, though the notable frescos with which the interior is adorned are well known. Cursory descriptions have been given by Cummings[1] and Longfellow. The drawings of Hübsch[2] are important. The edifice is mentioned by the brothers Sacchi in 1828 as undergoing great damage from the soldiers who were then there quartered. A description of the edifice, written by Andrea Astezati, about 1730,[3] is preserved in a manuscript of the Biblioteca Quiriniana. In 1843 Knight[4] published an engraving which shows the cupola surmounted by a square Renaissance ædicule, as it was before the restoration.

II. Of the history of the edifice nothing is known except that it formed part of the neighbouring convent of S. Giulia.

III. The plan of the building is very peculiar. There are two stories, of which the lower consists of a single rectangular chamber divided into four groin-vaulted compartments (Plate 32, Fig. 1) by a single pier placed in the middle; while the upper (Plate 32, Fig. 3) has three apses worked in the thickness of the eastern wall, and was surmounted originally by a cloistered vault supported on arched squinches, but the vault was replaced by a dome in the XVI century.

[1] 143

[2] Plate LIII, Fig. 7; Plate LIV, Fig. 5.

[3] *Indice . . . dell'archivio di S. Salvatore e S^a Giulia,* MS. Codice Quirin. of c. 1730, f. 83.

[4] I, Plate XXI.

The groin vaults of the crypt (Plate 32, Fig. 1) are approximately square in plan and very highly domed. They are supplied with transverse wall arches which do not disappear. The curve of the groin is elliptical, almost pointed in elevation. These vaults are constructed of brick and stone, well laid in courses normal to the outside walls. Traces of the board centering can still clearly be seen (Plate 32, Fig. 1). The masonry of the walls themselves (Plate 32, Fig. 1, 2) is a fine ashlar, and consists of well-dressed blocks, for the most part apparently quarried from Roman ruins, since several bear fragments of inscriptions. The horizontal joints of the masonry are at times broken. The blocks are large but of varying width. There are scaffolding holes even in the interior. The windows in several orders, moulded, are widely splayed and evidently intended to serve without glass.[5] Beneath the dome of the upper church is a clearstory of oculi. The dome is masked externally by an octagonal drum (Plate 32, Fig. 2).

IV. The crypt contains little original ornament. The responds in several orders are supplied with imposts of simple mouldings. The central pier is a pilfered Roman pedestal with the inscription

DEO SOLI
RES PVBL

which may explain the name of the church. The interior of the second story has archivolts in two orders (Plate 32, Fig. 3), but is entirely covered with frescos of the XVI century, which doubtless replace earlier ones of the XII century. Externally, the building is characterized by arched corbel-tables, pilaster strips and by a gallery which runs around the wall of the drum (Plate 32, Fig. 2).

V. The simple splayed capitals of the gallery, as indeed the character of the entire edifice, is analogous to the baptistery of Agrate-Conturbia (Plate 10, Fig. 3). We may therefore assign the building to c. 1120.

BRESCIA, S. SALVATORE

(Plate 33; Plate 34, Fig. 1, 2, 3, 4; Plate 35, Fig. 1, 2, 3, 4;
Plate 36, Fig. 1, 2, 4, 5, 6, 7, 8; Plate 37, Fig. 1)

I. The church of S. Salvatore at Brescia is among the most important monuments of northern Italy anterior to the year 1000. As such, it has attracted the attention of almost every writer on the Romanesque architecture of Lombardy. Of especial value from an historical standpoint are the studies

---

[5] Those of the upper church were probably glazed, but were remade in the XVI century.

by Odorici and Rosa. Garrucci, Hübsch and De Dartein have measured and illustrated various parts of the building. The description of the brothers Sacchi, made in 1828, is unfortunately incorrect, and can not be depended upon to draw inferences as to the changes which the church has undergone in the course of the XIX century. More help is derived from the description of Andrea Astezati, written about 1730[1] and preserved in manuscript in the Biblioteca Quiriniana. To Cattaneo belongs the credit of having been the first to recognize the significance of S. Salvatore for the history of art. The recent study of Rivoira is a terse but brilliant analysis of the history of the monument and of its architectural form.

II. The history of few churches or monasteries of Europe is as abundantly illustrated with authentic documents as is that of S. Salvatore at Brescia. A ritual of 1438 records the foundation of the monastery in these words: "In the year of Our Lord, 753, our monastery was begun . . . . . and it was endowed by the most excellent queen Ansa. It was subsequently consecrated by the pope and his cardinals as is written in authentic chronicles extant in our monastery."[2] This notice is not altogether free from difficulties. It is known that Pope Stephen II passed through Lombardy in the year 753.[3] It is therefore probable that the author of the ritual confused the date, and that the monastery was consecrated in 753, but begun some time earlier. On the other hand, Ansa did not become queen until 756. It is certain, however, that the monastery was begun before Ansa and Desiderio ascended the throne, since this is explicitly stated by an early chronicle.[4]

This text states that the church (*Ecclesia*) of S. Salvatore, S. Maria and S. Michele was built by Desiderio (the husband of Ansa), and therefore implies that the monastery was founded, not in a previously existing chapel, but in a church expressly erected. The fact, however, that in the earliest times the convent was called S. Michele, a title subsequently dropped, has given rise to the conjecture, so often repeated by historians as to have acquired the currency of an indubitable fact, that the monastery was established in the pre-existing chapel of S. Michele. As for the title, that was changed subsequently at least twice, and the mere fact that S. Michele in early times was

[1] *Indice . . . dell'archivio di S. Salvatore e Sa Giulia*, MS. Codice Quirin. of c. 1730, f. 82.

[2] Anno ab Incar. Dni CCCCCCCLIIII. Inchoatum fuit monasterium nostrum . . . . . et similiter dotatum per excellentissimam dnam Ansam Reginam. Postea consecratum fuit per dominum Papam cum suis cardinalibus prout invenitur in CHRONICIS SATIS AUTENTICIS in dicto monasterio nostro. (Odorici, II, 275).

[3] Odorici, II, 275.

[4] Sed et Ecclesia ad honorem Domini Salvatoris, et Beatæ semper Virginis Mariæ, et Beati Archangeli Michaelis ædificata est ab ipso præfatus rex [Desiderius] antequam Regnum cepisset. (*Breve Chronicon Regum Longobard. et August, ab anno 568 ad a. 883* scriptum a quondam Monacho Monasterii Brixiani ad Leones. Ed. Odorici, IV, 11).

included among the patron saints does not necessarily prove that the monastery was founded in a church originally dedicated to him.

That the monastery was founded by Desiderio and Ansa is established by a host of documents. The earliest of these is a fragmentary charter of 758 in favour of the monastery which is designated by a title unfortunately in part destroyed, but which included the saints Michele and Pietro.[5] From this document we learn that not only did Desiderio and Ansa found the convent, but that their daughter Ansilperga was the first abbess. These facts are confirmed by another diploma, the date of which offers difficulties, but which probably[6] is of October 4, 760.[7] This diploma also implies that Desiderio and Ansa not only founded the monastery but erected the buildings; the title is given simply as S. Salvatore. The same title is given in another diploma of 761,[8] and in a bull,[9] apparently of 762, although the chronological notes are

[5] . . . . . Rex & gloriosa atque precelsa Ansa . . . . . Michaëlis atque Apostolorum Principis Petri, quod . . . . . intra Civitatem nostram Brixianam, & Deo dicata Ansilperga Abbatissa . . . . . Monacharum ibidem Domino servienti. . . . Mensis Januarii . . . . . nostri in Dei nomine Secundo . . . . . ne XII. . . . . . (Muratori, A. I. M. A., ed. A, XIII, 413).

[6] See Odorici, III, 34-37.

[7] Flavivs Desiderivs atque adelchis viri excellentissimi reges, atque precellentissima ansa regina monastero dni salvatoris quod nos deo auxiliante intra civitatem nostram brixianam fundavimus et ereximus et superna subveniente misericordia hedeficavimus, et sacrate deo Anselperge *abbatisse* dilecte filiæ et germane nostræ seu cuncte congregationi monacharum ibidem permanenti divina. . . . Primum omnia edificia cuncta que nobis jubentibus ibi fundata sunt seu et sacra vasa et pallia et ea omnia que ad altaris monisterium pertinent adferimus nec non aurum argentum eramenta ferramenta lignea et fictilia omnia et in omnibus mobilibus et immobilibus rebus simul cum animalibus bovibus bobulcis familiis utriusque sexus ibidem pertinentibus eidem sancto cenobio adferimus possidendum. . . . Et hoc statuimus ut amplius quadriginta monachas non ibi recipiatur, nisi tantummodo per hoc numerum ipso (*sic*) dei officio impleantur. . . . Ex dicto suprascriptorum dominorum nostrorum regum persisigno illis referentibus scripsi ego rodoald notarius dato Ticino in palacio quarto die mensis hoctobri anno felicissimi regni nostri in dei nomine quarto et secundo Indictione quintadecima feliciter. (Odorici, III, 34-37).

[8] Anselperga sacrata Deo abbatissa Monasterii Domini Salvatoris, qui fundatum est in Civitate Brixia, quam Domnus Desiderius excellentissimus Rex & Ansam precellentissimam Reginam genitores ejus ab fundamentis edificaverunt. (Muratori, A. I. M. A., ed. A, XIII, 417).

[9] Paulus episcopus servus servorum Dei Ansilpergiae religiosae abbatissae venerabilis monasterii Domini Dei et Salvatoris nostri Iesu Christi siti intra civitatem Brixiam, quod a nobis fundare visa est Ansa excellentissima regina. . . . Igitur quia postulatis a nobis quatenus venerabile monasterium Domini Salvatoris nostri Iesu Christi sito infra civitatem Brixianam, quod noviter fundare visa est Ansa excellentissima regina; privilegii sedis apostolicae insulis decoretur . . . decrevimus, ut praefatum monasterium Domini Salvatoris cunctaque monasteria cum universis basilicis ad se pertinentibus, quae a piissimae reginae Ansae iure constructa esse noscuntur, apostolicae sedis privilegii insulis . . . decoretur. . . . [consequently the convent is freed from the jurisdiction of the bishop]. Data septimo kalendas novembris imperante Domino

confused.[10] A diploma apparently of 763 states that Ansa and Desiderio built the monastery of S. Salvatore from the foundations.[11] Ansa, however, is called the founder of the convent by her son Adelchi in a diploma of 766.[12] On the other hand, in another diploma, apparently of the same year, the credit of having founded the monastery is assigned equally to Desiderio, Ansa and Adelchi.[13] But in two diplomas of 767, Desiderio only is named as founder,[14] while in two of the following year Desiderio and Ansa are said to have built the monastery from its foundations.[15] The formula is the same in still another

Augusto Constantino a Deo coronato Magno imperatore anno vigesimotertio, sed et Leone imperatore filio eius anno decimo, indictione prima. (Tomassetti, *Bullarum Romanorum*, I, 252).

10 *Hist. Pat. Mon.*, XIII, 52.

11 Flavius desiderius et Alehis viri excellentissimi reges monasterio domini et redentoris ac Salvatoris sito in brixia quod nos deo juvante una cum coniuge et genetrice nostra et (*sic*) ansa regina a fundamentis edificavimus et dicatæ deo Anselpergæ abbatissæ dilectæ filiæ et germanæ nostræ. . . . (Odorici, III, 41-42).

12 Flavius Adelchis vir excellentissimus rex. Monasterio domini et redemptoris nostri salvatoris sito intra civitatem nostram brixianam quam domna et genitrix nostra ansa regina a fundamentis edificavit et sacrate deo anselpergae abbatissae dilectae germanae nostrae. . . . Ex dicto domini regis per ansemund notarius et ex ipsius dictato scripsi ego petrus notarius. Actum *ticino in palatio,* vigesima die mensis ianuarii. Anno felicissimi regni nostri in dei nomine septimo pro indictione quarta feliciter. (*Hist. Pat. Mon.*, XIII, 58).

13 Adelchis vir excellentissimus rex monasterio dni et redemptoris ac salvatoris quam . . . . . dm et genit . . . . . desiderius piisimus rex et Ansa gloriosa regina vel nos intra civitatem brixianam a fundamentis . . . . . i sacrate deo Ans . . . . . abbatisse germane nostre vel cuncte congregationi monacharum . . . . . presentie nostre . . . . . preceptum suprascriptorum genitorum nostrorum ubi legebatur quatenus . . . . . esserant in predicto sancto cenobio. . . . Actum ticino in palatio. tercia die mensis marcii. anno felicissimi regni nostri in dei nomine septimo. per indictionem quartam feliciter. (Odorici, III, 45-48).

14 Regnantibus dd. nn. Desiderio et Adelchiso filio ejus Viris excellentissimis Regibus. Anno piissimi regni eorum in Xpi nomine XII et VIII. die XIX mensis Aprilis Indictione VI. Placuit atque bona voluntate convenit inter *Venerabilem Virum* Halanum Abbatem monasterii s. dei genitricis Marie site in Sabinis, nec non et Hisilpergam (*sic*) sacratam deo Abbatissam monasterii dni Salvatoris fundati infra muros civitatis Brixianæ constitutum a suprascripto Principe, ut etc. (*Ibid.*, 48-49).

Regnante domni nostri Desiderii et Adelchis reges, regni eorum undecimo et nono die VI de mensi decembris per indictione VI feliciter. Dilectissima nobis semper donna Anselperga a Deo dilecta abbatissa monasterii domini Salvaturi scita in civitate Brexia quam domnus Desiderius rex a fundamentis edificavit. (*Hist. Pat. Mon.*, XIII, 64).

15 Regnante domino Desiderio et Adelchis filius eius viris excellentissimi regibus, anno pietatis regni eorum in Christi nomine duodecimo et decimo, vigesimo secondo die mensis octobris, indictione septima. Vobis Ansilpergae sacrata Deo abbatissa monasterio Domini Salvatoris sito intra civitate brixiana, quae domino Desiderio et Ansa regina a fundamentis edificaverunt. (*Hist. Pat. Mon.*, XIII, 69).

Regnante Dno Desiderio et Adelchis filius eius viris excellentissimi Regibus, anno pietatis regni eorum in Xpi nomine duodecim et decem vigesimo secondo die mensis Octobris ind. septima. Vobis Ansilperge sacrata Deo Abbatissa monasterio Dni Salva-

diploma of 769[16] and in one of 771;[17] but in one of 772 Ansa is mentioned as having founded the monastery with the aid of Desiderio and Adelchi. In three other documents of the same year, 772, Ansa is designated as sole founder,[18] as also in one of 773.[19]

Ansa was buried in the monastery which she had founded. The tomb, it is true, is no longer extant, but the epitaph has been preserved in a manuscript at Leipsic, and distinctly records the foundation of the convent by the queen.[20]

In view of the abundant and authentic testimony supplied by this superb series of contemporary monuments recording the foundation of the monastery, it would perhaps be hardly worth while to consider the numerous notices in

toris sito intra civitate Brixiana que Dno Desiderio et Ansa regina a fundamentis edificaverunt. etc. (Odorici, III, 51-52).

[16] . . . à te Anselperga dicata Deo Abbatissa Monasterii Domni Salvatoris situm intra Civitatem Brixianam, & fundatum à Domno Desiderio piissimo Rege, & ab Ansa gloriosa Regina genitoribus tuis . . . (Muratori, A. I. M. A., ed. A, II, 137).

[17] Desiderius vir excellentissimus rex Monasterio domini et redemptoris nostri salvatoris sito intra civitate nostra brexiana quam nos Xpo iuvante una cum reverentissima coniuge nostra Ansa regina a fundamentis construximus, et sacrate domna (sic) Anselperge abbatisse dilecte filiæ nostræ detulisti etc. . . . Acto Brexia die mensis iulii anno felicissimi regni . . . . . XV per Indictionem VIIII feliciter. (Odorici, III, 54).

[18] Flavius Desiderius et Adelchis piissimi reges. Monasterio domini et redemptoris Salvatoris constituto intra civitatem nostram brixianam, quae regiam nostram potestatem deo auxiliante et excellentissima Ansa regina dilecta coniux et genitrix nostra a fundamentis construxit, in quo Anselperga deo dicata abbatissa dilecta filia et germana nostra. . . . Acto Ticino in palatio quartadecima die mensis iunii. Anno felicissimi regni nostri sexto decimo et tercio decimo per indictione decima feliciter. (Hist. Pat. Mon., XIII, 86).

Sigualt servus servorum Domini Patriarcha. . . . monasterium domini Salvatoris cunctaque monasteria cum universis basilicis ad se pertinentibus, quia piissimae adque tranquillissimae Ansae reginae jure constructum esse noscitur . . . Anno invictissimorum principum Desiderii et Adelgis XVI et XIV sub indictione XI. Dato Ticino in urbe regia III idus octobris. (Hist. Pat. Mon., XIII, 90).

Nec non etiam statuimus ut ipsa basilica sancte marie [ripa fluvio Ollio quam ipse Emisoind ab fundamentis edificaverat] una cum res ad eam pertinentes in potestate et defensione monasterii dni Salvatoris quod domina et genetrix nostra intra Civitatem nostram brixianam instituit, ubi et abbatissa germana nostra Anselperga esse videtur esse debeat sicut in mundio et potestate palacii nostri esse debuit. . . . Dato ticino in palacio nono kalende septembris Anno felicissimi regni nostri in Xpi nomine quartodecimo per indictionem decimam feliciter. (Odorici, III, 62). See also Hist. Pat. Mon., XIII, 89.

[19] Flavius adelchis vir excellentissimus rex. Monasterio Domini Salvatoris sito intra civitatem brexianam quod domina et precellentissima ansa regina genetrix nostra et dicate deo Anselperge abbatisse dilecte germane nostræ. . . . Quadere justum est quam ipsa precellentissima domna Ansa regina suavissima genetrix nostra in amorem domini nostri Jhesu Xpi ipso monasterio ad fundamentis construxit etc. . . . Acto civitate in Brexia undecima die mensis novembris Anno felicissimi regni nostri in dei nomine quartodecimo per indictione Xima. (Odorici, III, 64-68).

late chroniclers, were it not that several of these, together with much that is fabulous, add certain new details which merit belief. Jacopo Malvecio speaks at length of the history of S. Salvatore: "There was a mountain not far from the city and situated to the east of it, almost touching the mountain of the citadel . . . On that mountain the fountain of S. Apollonio sprang up . . . Therefore in precisely the place where the sacred waters gushed forth, the people of Brescia not long afterwards built a church and monastery in honour of the Saviour, and endowed it with many possessions and sacred ornaments. In this monastery the priests lived a life of prayer and were renowned for their strict discipline. Reverend nuns also led the religious life in the same place; but in these days the buildings of that monastery are falling into ruin."[21]

Further on in his chronicle the same writer speaks at length of the possessions of the monastery and of the relics there deposited, inveighing in his customary manner against the corruption and the lack of chastity of the nuns of his own day, and contrasting all this with the ancient strict discipline of the establishment.[22] "Ansa, the most worthy of all matrons, for the praise and glory of Almighty God, and the Blessed Virgin Mother Mary, and for the honour of S. Giulia, martyr and virgin, built a basilica outside of the walls [sic] of the city of Brescia in the year of our Lord 753. There she founded also a monastery which she wonderfully endowed with many ornaments and ample lands. . . . She made Anselperga, her daughter, first abbess. . . . There she buried the body of the holy virgin and martyr Giulia

---

20   Lactea splendifico quae fulgit tumba metallo
            Reddendum quandoque tenet laudabile corpus.
            Hic namque Ausonii coniux pulcherrima regis
            Ansa iacet. . . .
            Fortia natarum thalamis sibi pectora iunxit,
            Discissos nectens, rapidus quos Aufidus ambit,
            Pacis amore ligans, cingunt quos Renus et Hister.
            Quin etiam aeterno mansit sua portio Regi,
            Virgineo splendore micans, his dedita templis.
            Cultibus Altithroni quantas fundaverit aedes. . . .

                (Ed. Waitz, *Pauli. Hist. Long.*, 249).

21 in monte, loco, ubi nunc Sancti Florani Basilica consistit. . . . Erat autem mons ille non longè à Civitate ad Orientalem plagam situatus immo pæne Civitatis monti contiguus. . . . & Beato Apollonio fons eodem loco ortus est. . . . Igitur apud montem in ipso loco, ubi sacra unda defluxerat, post non multa tempora populus Brixiæ Ecclesiam, atque Cœnobium in honorem Salvatoris construxerunt, sed & idem multis possessionibus, & ornamentis dotaverunt, in quo sacerdotes celeberrimam vitam agentes orationibus insistebant. Venerandissimæ etiam mulieres in eodem loco sacræ religionis cultus exercebant. Verùm his diebus Cœnobii illius ædificia in ruinam abierunt. . . . (Jacobi Malvecii, *Chronicon*, III, 8, ed. Muratori, R. I. S., XIV, 797). Cf. *ibid.*, III, 11, ed. Muratori, 802.

22 *Ibid.*, IV, 87, ed. Muratori, XIV, 846-847.

of Carthage translated from the island of Corsica, in whose most worthy memory she wished to dedicate the church. . . . The body of that most serene queen Ansa also rests in the same monastery in a stone tomb near the campanile."[23]

In the *Chronicon Imaginis Mundi*[24] we read: "The wife of Desiderio, by name Ansa, when she became queen, caused the body of S. Giulia the Virgin to be brought from Sardinia [*sic*], and built a very beautiful monastery in honour of that saint and richly endowed it."[25] Another late chronicler states more simply: "Desiderio constructed the monastery of S. Giulia in the city of Brescia."[26] In a gloss of the *Codice Estense* of the chronicle of Siccardo is the following passage: "Ansa, the wife of Desiderio, a most devout queen, followed the example of her husband, and caused to be erected with her own resources an equally well endowed monastery to which she magnificently donated villas, lands, fields, mills, fountains, slaves and servants, and with possessions situated in the dioceses of Brescia, Cremona, Piacenza, Reggio and elsewhere. She also made a most generous donation to the church of the said monastery, giving it gold, silver, precious stones, censers, vials, crosses, books of the gospels, samite pallia and silk vestments, as befitted the queen of the Lombards when moved by great affection and pious devoutness. And she decreed that from those possessions which she gave to the monastery should be supported a great convent of nuns and virgins who day and night should devoutly worship the Lord. After these things the pious queen of the Lombards sent official and trusty and devout messengers to the island of Corsica to translate with all pomp the body of the blessed martyr Giulia and bring it to the monastery which she had constructed."[27] Finally in Galvaneo

---

[23] Hæc namque præstantissima matronarum [Ansa] ad laudem & gloriam Omnipotentis Dei, ac Sanctissimæ Matris Virginis Mariæ, & ad honorem Beatæ Juliæ Martyris & Virginis pretiosæ, Basilicam foràs ambitum Brixiensis Civitatis construxit, cùm jam ab Adventu nostri æterni Salvatoris anni DCCLIII essent evoluti. Illic etiam Monasterium ædificavit; ea quoque ornamentis multis mirificè decoravit, prædiisque ampliissimis. . . . Ibique Anselpergam natam suam & Desiderii, primam Abbatissam instituit. . . . Ibi enim corpus Sacræ Virginis & Martyris Juliæ Carthaginensis de Corsica insula translatum reposuit, ad cujus dignissimam memoriam Templum id ejusdem nomine voluit nuncupari. . . . Membra quoque hujus Serenissimæ Ansæ Reginæ in eodem Cœnobio apud Campanile in sepulchro lapideo sepulta fuere. (Jacobi Malvecii, *Chronicon*, IV, 87, ed. Muratori, XIV, 846-847).

[24] Ed. *Hist. Pat. Mon.*, V, 1486.

[25] Uxor autem Desiderii. quando fuit facta regina. fecit portari de Sardinia corpus sancte Iuliane virginis. et intra Brixiam regina. Anxa nomine. supradicti Desiderii uxor. in honorem sancte Iuliane pulcherrimum construxit monasterium. et illud optime dotavit.

[26] [Desiderius] Monasterium Sanctæ Juliæ in Civitate Brixiæ construxit. . . . (*Chronicon Modoetiense*, ed. Muratori, R. I. S., XII, 1076).

[27] Ansa verò uxor, ejus devotissima Regina, vestigia sequens mariti, intra Civitatem [Brescia] Monasterium æquè nobile locuples de suo peculio fecit fieri, quod dotavit

della Fiamma we read the simple notice: "Desiderio built the monastery of S. Giulia at Brescia."[28]

The Carlovingian conquest in 774 was not without effect upon the fortunes of the monastery, as was natural in the case of a convent which had been founded and flourished chiefly by the bounty of the vanquished Lombard sovereigns. The valuable possession of Sermione was alienated by Charlemagne in the very year of the conquest;[29] but this withdrawal of royal favour was only temporary. Sermione was soon restored, and the convent became the favourite charity of the Carlovingians, as it had been of the Lombard kings, overwhelmed with privileges and donations.

From the Carlovingian conquest dates the habit of bestowing the convent as a benefice upon some member of the royal family. In a diploma of 822 it appears as a benefice of the empress Judith.[30] Lothair I, in 848, bestowed the monastery upon his wife Hermingarda and his daughter Gisla.[31] In 851, on the death of Hermingarda, the emperors Lothair I and Lodovico II confirmed the monastery to Gisla,[32] and in 856 Lodovico II reconfirmed to his sister, the above-mentioned Gisla, the *monasterium quod dicitur Novum in honorem domini et salvatoris nostri fundatum atque infra muros Brixiæ situm.*[33] The title is given in almost the same words in another diploma[34] granted to the new monastery and its abbess Amalperga, at the petition of Gisla. In 861 another Gisla, daughter of Lodovico II, became a nun in the *Cenobio Domini Salvatoris intra menia civitatis Brixiæ constructum quod dicitur novum,* and upon her the emperor bestowed all the goods of the monastery, which, in the case of her death, were to revert to her mother, Angilperga.[35] Seven years later, in fact, the same emperor conceded the convent to his wife Angilperga, with the pact that on her death it should revert to his daughter Ermingarda,[36] who, indeed, later became abbess.[37] In 916 the emperor Berenger mentions in a diploma his daughter Bertha as abbess of the monastery of S. Giulia at

magnificè villis, terris, pratis, molendinis, fontibus, servis, mancipiis, tam in Episcopatu Brixiæ, quam Cremonæ, & Placentiæ, & Regii, & pluribus aliis locis. Dona etiam largissima contulit Ecclesiæ dicti Monasterii, aurum, argentum, lapides pretiosos, thuribula, phialas, cruces, textus evangelia, & alia pallia samita, & sericas vestes, sicut decebat Reginam Longobardorum, & tanto plus quanto ex magno affectu, & pia devotione hoc agebat. Et constituit, ut de his, quæ donaverat monasterio, conventus magnus haberetur Sanctimonialium, & Virginum, quæ die ac nocte devotum obsequium Domino exhiberent. Post hæc misit devota Regina gentis Longobardorum nuntios solemnes & fide dignos, ac devotos in Insulam Corsicam, & mandavit, ut Corpus Beatissimæ Martyris Juliæ cum omni sollicitudine deferretur ad Monasterium, quod ipsa construxerat, etc. (Sicardi Episcopi, *Chronicon,* ed. Muratori, R. I. S., VII, 578).

28 In Brixia fecit [Desiderius] monasterium sanct Iullie. (Galvanei Flammae, *Chron. Maius,* ed. Ceruti, 548).

29 Odorici, IV, 107.   30 Odorici, IV, 20.   31 *Ibid.,* 39.

32 *Ibid.,* 41. This diploma enumerates Sermione among the possessions of the monastery.

33 *Ibid.,* 44.   34 *Ibid.,* 46.   35 *Ibid.,* 50.   36 *Ibid.,* 54.   37 *Ibid.,* 59, 62.

Brescia.[38]   It is therefore evident that the Carlovingian emperors bestowed upon the convent the same favour which the Lombard kings had done.   Among the abbesses were many of imperial blood, and if at times the emperors exploited the monastery, treating it as their private possession to be bestowed upon some member of the royal family, they nevertheless never failed to protect it and to enrich it with new gifts and privileges.

Soon after the Carlovingian conquest the name of the convent was changed first to the New Monastery of S. Salvatore, then afterwards simply to the New Monastery.   The earliest mention of the new title is in a document of 814:   *Monasterii . . . civitatis Brixiæ . . . Domini Salvatoris . . . quod vulgo appellatur Monasterium Novum.*[39]   In another of 822 it is called: *monasterii Domini Salvatoris quod dicitur nobo,*[40] while in a diploma of 837[41] occurs the phrase: *in cenobio domini salvatoris fundatum intra muros brixie in monasterio scilicet novo.*   In 878 the convent is called . . . *monasterii Domini Salvatoris fundatum in civitate Brixia, que dicitur novo . . . ;*[42] in 879, *monasterio Domini Salvatoris in urbe Brixia quod dicitur novum;*[43] in 880, *Monasterio Domini Salvatoris in Urbe Brixia, quod dicitur Novum. . . .*[44] In 889, however, the convent is designated by the simple term *Monasterio novo.*[45]   The enormous wealth of the abbey at the beginning of the X century is evident from the inventory of its possessions assigned to 905 or 906, and which occupies ten folio pages in the *Historiæ Patriæ Monumenta.*[46]

About the first quarter of the X century, the name of the convent was changed for the third time.   In a concession of 915 it is called *monasterii sanctae Iuliae.*[47]   The reason for this change of title was probably the growing popularity of S. Giulia, whose body, according to the legend, had been transported to S. Salvatore in the VIII century.[48]   In a diploma of 916, the two titles are combined: *monasterii novi Brixiae siti, fundatum in honore beatissimae Juliae . . . ,*[49] but in another of the same year, the abbey is called *Monasterii sancte Julie.*[50]   However, the old name was not abandoned.   In a document of c. 950, we find *monasterii domni Salvatoris . . . qui dicitur novo*[51] and similar phrases occur in others of 960 and 961.[52]   In 966, however, we find *monasterio sancte Julie quod dicitur novo,*[53] and in 978 *monasterio domni Salvatoris et Sancte Iulie sito Brisia civitate.*[54]   After this date the abbey is always referred to as S. Giulia.[55]

I have mentioned all these ancient documents relating to S. Salvatore not so much to study the relatively unimportant question of the name, as to call

[38] Giulini, I, 439.   [39] Odorici, IV, 18.   [40] *Hist. Pat. Mon.,* XIII, 178.
[41] Odorici, IV, 26.   [42] *Hist. Pat. Mon.,* XIII, 471.   [43] *Ibid.,* 477.
[44] Muratori, A. I. M. A., ed. A, VIII, 377; *Hist. Pat. Mon.,* XIII, 506.
[45] *Hist. Pat. Mon.,* XIII, 574.   [46] XIII, 706.   [47] *Hist. Pat. Mon.,* XIII, 788.
[48] Sicardi Episcopi, *Chronicon,* ed. Muratori, R. I. S., VII, 578.
[49] *Hist. Pat. Mon.,* XIII, 809.   [50] *Ibid.,* 812.   [51] *Hist. Pat. Mon.,* XIII, 1016.
[52] *Ibid.,* XIII, 1104, 1107.   [53] *Hist. Pat. Mon.,* XIII, 1210.
[54] *Ibid.,* XIII, 1381.   [55] Muratori, A. I. M. A., ed. A, IX, 720, etc.

attention to the great importance of the convent, and the vast wealth of extant documents anterior to the year 1000, relating to it. In all this literature, there is not a single reference to any reconstruction or restoration of the church. Had such taken place, it is impossible to doubt that some reference to it would have crept into some one of all these numerous parchments. The style of the existing edifice precludes absolutely a reconstruction after the year 1000. It is certain, therefore, that in the Carlovingian portions of the existing church of S. Salvatore we have a part of the very church erected by Desiderio and Ansa.

The later history of the monastery it is unnecessary to study in detail. As early as the XI century it appears to have begun to lose its prestige, and it is mentioned less and less frequently in extant parchments. A document of 1153 records that the consecration of the edifice was annually celebrated on the twentieth of October.[56] At the end of the Middle Ages, to judge from the passages of the late chronicler quoted above, the discipline was much relaxed, and the establishment in decline. In the XVI century the existing vault was erected over the old church of S. Salvatore, and in the beginning of the XVIII century the capitals were covered with stucco, which was stripped off a hundred years later.[57] In 1797 the convent was suppressed and the church desecrated. Twenty-seven years later, the *Commissione Bresciana* removed from the crypt several capitals. These are at present in the Museo Civico Età Christiana, which has been installed in the new church built in the barocco period to supplement the old basilica of S. Salvatore. In 1878 part of the convent, including the basilica of S. Salvatore and the new church known as S. Giulia, were acquired by the city of Brescia, and have since been preserved with an intelligent care which it is a pleasure to record in these days of archæological vandalism.

III. The church (Plate 33) at present consists of a nave seven bays long, two side aisles, of which the southern contains in its eastern bay a curious groin-vaulted ædicule known as the Tomba d'Ermingarda, two northern chapels, a square apse, and a crypt. Such, however, were not the original dispositions. The monument was deprived of its western bay and supplied with its present ungainly west wall at the time that the upper church of S. Giulia was erected. At the same time in all probability the original horse-shoe apse, the foundations of which still survive in the crypt, was replaced by the existing rectangular choir. In the XII century, the crypt, which originally occupied only the space below the apse, was extended under a part of the nave also, and in the XVI century the chapels were added, and the existing vaults erected over nave and side aisles to replace the ancient timber roof.

The church of Desiderio and Ansa was a simple basilica, of which the columns, for the most part pilfered, supported round, unmoulded archivolts

[56] Odorici, V, 104.   [57] Rosa, 168.

(Plate 34, Fig. 1, 2, 3, 4). The choir was not raised, the crypt, or more properly the 'confessio,' being entirely underground, as in the earliest Christian basilicas. The nave is extraordinarily wide—about 7.43 metres—a characteristic which recalls S. Apollinare Nuovo and other churches at Ravenna (Plate 33). The inner perimeter of the apse was not precisely semicircular but of horseshoe form (Plate 33), and it is probable, although the scanty remains make it difficult to speak on this point, that the exterior was polygonal. Here again the edifice recalls the basilicas of Ravenna.

The masonry of the church is for the most part concealed beneath intonaco, but from what little is visible (Plate 35, Fig. 1, 3) it is evident that it has been many times restored. It is difficult to determine its original character. A large piece visible in the south wall consists of a rough sort of rubble, formed of stones of various sizes and shapes with fragments of flat Roman-like bricks laid together in rather promiscuous fashion, but with the broad surfaces of the stones always turned outward. This wall, however, must have been restored, since it contains certain bricks which are not older than the Renaissance. The mortar, of very poor quality, contains large-sized pebbles. There are many traces of breaks in the masonry and rebuilding of the walls; in the south wall is visible the arch of an ancient doorway that has been walled up (Plate 35, Fig. 2, 3). This doorway was at a level much lower than that of the existing church. Since this has obviously never been changed, we are forced to conclude that we have here a fragment of the earlier church of S. Michele. There are numerous scaffolding holes in the masonry. The walls of the side aisles, like those of the clearstory, have been so repeatedly restored and patched up that, with the exception of the piece of wall in the south side aisle already described, I have been quite unable to satisfy myself either as to the character of the original masonry, or the history of the changes it has gone through. What does appear to be certain is that some parts of the wall of the north side aisle show masonry identical in character with that of the south wall just now described; hence the church of S. Michele must have been built on approximately the same plan as the present basilica. Traces of five of the windows of this earlier church are now visible. Of entirely different character is the masonry of the clearstory wall (where it has not been made over) and of the archivolts above the columns, which are formed of a double arch of flat Roman-like bricks laid as voussoirs and surmounted by a row of bricks laid flat (Plate 35, Fig. 1). These archivolts are considerably stilted (Plate 35, Fig. 2). The clearstory wall is formed of similar bricks laid in horizontal courses (Plate 35, Fig. 1). The masonry of the crypt, to judge from the little that can be seen of it, appears to resemble that of the south side-aisle wall.

Those portions of the crypt which are under the nave are covered with groin vaults, considerably domed and with disappearing transverse ribs. The system of roofing employed in the portion of the crypt under the choir is, however, different and peculiar. The horseshoe-shaped apse is divided into three aisles (Plate 33) by two rows of two columns (these columns have been replaced by brick piers in recent times) supporting longitudinal arcades, on which were placed transverse lintels forming the pavement of the apse above (Plate 37, Fig. 1). In the middle of the side aisles, if we may call them such, was introduced on either side a square pier giving an additional point of support for the lintel (Plate 36, Fig. 1). The capitals of the four central columns are lost, and the ornaments in stucco on the archivolts of the arches are of the XII century; the two side piers, on the other hand, are of the XV century, yet that the crypt is old is proved by the character of its masonry, and the windows, traces of which still remain. In the XV century it must have been remade on practically the old lines.

IV. The decoration of the church, like the structure, belongs to several different epochs. The two westernmost capitals of the northern arcade (Plate 36, Fig. 2) are, as Cattaneo has recognized, of the basket Byzantine type of the VI century, entirely analogous to several extant at Ravenna (Plate 36, Fig. 3). They are covered with deeply undercut, crisp foliage, arranged in a conventional over-all pattern, the vines in some cases springing from vases. The next two capitals are of a different type, being Corinthianesque, with large acanthus leaves, at once flaccid and Byzantine in character and not deeply undercut. Similar capitals are not uncommon in the neighbourhood of Rome and may be seen, for example, at S. Maria in Domnica and in the cathedral of Civita Castellana. They are probably of the V century. The fifth (Plate 35, Fig. 4) and seventh capitals of the north arcade and the three easternmost of the southern arcade (Plate 35, Fig. 3) appear to me to be original works of the VIII century. They are of Corinthianesque type and show characteristic Carlovingian treatment of the volutes and acanthus leaves.[58] Unfortunately they have been for the most part much mutilated. The acanthus leaves are always uncarved and are marked by a certain stiffness analogous to the capitals of the crypt of Cimitile. The sixth capital from the west of the northern arcade is still covered with barocco stucco, and it is impossible to tell what was its original form. The two western capitals of the southern arcade are of the V century Corinthianesque type already described (Plate 35, Fig. 2). The bases and shafts appear to be antique. In the Renaissance northern chapel are two capitals evidently coming from earlier constructions, one cubic (Plate 35, Fig. 4), perhaps of the XII century, the other antique of Corinthian type, and probably of the IV century, to judge from its perforated technique.

In the XII century the archivolts of that part of the crypt (Plate 37, Fig. 1) which is beneath the apse were decorated with a leaf ornament executed in stucco quite analogous in character to similar work at Civate.

[58] Cf. the capital in the cathedral cloisters at Verona, Plate 216, Fig. 2.

This stucco ornament can not possibly be of the VIII century, as has been frequently published. A similar error has been made in regard to the piers in the side aisles of the same part of the apse, of which the capitals are not Carlovingian, but late Gothic, probably of the XV century (Plate 36, Fig. 1).

The western part of the crypt contains capitals of advanced Lombard type; two, sculptured with iconographical subjects of considerable interest, are at present in the upper church of S. Giulia, used as a museum. On the principal face of one (Plate 36, Fig. 4), is shown the crucifixion of S. Giulia dressed as a nun, who is clubbed by two executioners. About her head is a halo and from above reaches the divine hand with a dove. On another face, S. Giulia, dressed as a nun, with cross and palm, appears as the patroness of\ a queen or empress (since the figure is crowned) and of two nuns. The royal personage is doubtless an abbess or patroness of the convent, not improbably Ansa. On the third face is depicted S. Ippolito in military garb, who talks with S. Lorenzo in his prison. The scene is doubtless the conversion of his jailer by the martyr deacon. On the fourth face is the martyrdom of S. Ippolito, who is thrown into a ditch of water. On another capital (Plate 36, Fig. 6), also in the museum, is depicted S. Michele wrestling with Jacob, a scene repeated in the cathedral of Modena and typical of the strife of Faith and Infidelity or of the Church and the Synagogue. On the second face, S. Michele tramples on the dragon. In these two capitals, we have, therefore, representations of the patron saints of the convent. A third face of this same capital represents Samson and the lion. A fourth shows a bearded man (perhaps David, typical of Christ) holding a cross and engaged in strife with a lion. The man wears a Phrygian cap, and cleaves in two with his sword the head of the beast. A third capital (Plate 36, Fig. 8) has on its volutes the symbols of the four Evangelists. A capital in the crypt has a figure of S. Michele. The other capitals are decorated with purely conventional designs or grotesque figures. They are among the most beautiful and technically perfect Lombard sculptures extant, admirable alike from the point of view of design and execution. The carving is skilful, the undercutting deep.

In the museum are also many other carved fragments, chiefly of church-furniture, some of which certainly were discovered at S. Salvatore. It is most unfortunate that no record has been kept of whence these fragments were taken, and the museum authorities know no more than the vague local tradition that some of them were discovered in our church. Together with the Carlo-vingian fragments are eight capitals of c. 1160. These presumably came from the newer part of the crypt of S. Salvatore, but the capitals of only seven of the colonnettes of the crypt are lacking *in situ*. There is also a bit of rinceau of about the same date. The Carlovingian fragments (Plate 36, Fig. 5) are very numerous, and include seven capitals of different sizes, two stilt-blocks, parts of two diapered colonnettes, an octagonal colonnette, half of the gable of a ciborio (superbly sculptured with a peacock), parts of a choir-rail and of a pergola, and a great many miscellaneous fragments. These all show great variation of style, and probably come from different pieces of church-furniture executed by different hands and at different epochs of the first half of the IX century after the completion of the church. The large capital with stilt-block might be one of the four lost ones of the apse of the crypt, and would be extremely interesting if this could be proved to be the case; but the style is very lifeless and decadent, far inferior to that of the original capitals of the nave arcade. There is also a large slab of a choir-rail of Byzantine style, which almost suggests Arabic workmanship. Possibly this belonged to the pre-existing church of S. Michele, and is as early as the second half of the VI century. Two decorated fragments and a rinceau are evidently Gothic.

V. That an earlier church existed on the site where Desiderio and Ansa founded the monastery of S. Salvatore, has, as we have seen, been inferred from the documentary evidence by certain historians. Confirmation of the hypothesis may be deduced from the fact that the church contains a number of capitals of the V and VI centuries, and considerable fragments of masonry, which must be earlier than the existing basilica. These fragments, consisting of the parts of the north and south side-aisle walls and of the crypt wall, are of such crude masonry that they may be assigned tentatively to the third quarter of the VI century. At all events, of whatever date be these earlier fragments, there can be no doubt that the edifice was entirely rebuilt by Desiderio and Ansa about the year 760, and that it has preserved this form, with the exception of the later alterations already noted, to the present day. S. Salvatore is therefore the best and most complete example extant of the architecture of northern Italy in the VIII century. From the style of the capitals of the western part of the crypt it is evident that the crypt was extended to the westward in the XII century. These capitals, analogous to, although more skilfully executed than, those of S. Tommaso at Almenno, must date from c. 1160.

BRUSASCO,[1] S. PIETRO VECCHIO

(Plate 37, Fig. 2, 3, 4, 5)

I. The ancient parish church of S. Pietro is now used as the chapel of the cemetery. It has been illustrated by Venturi.[2] In the archives of the parish of Brusasco are preserved several modern manuscripts dealing with the history and antiquities of Brusasco. For the most part they are of little

---

[1] (Torino).   [2] III, 15.

value, but some information of importance is contained in one entitled *Cenni storici del comune di Brusas*.).

II.   According to this manuscript the old Roman town on the site of Brusasco was destroyed by an inundation of the Po about the XI century,[3] and the name was consequently changed.   The whole question of the name, nevertheless, is very confused.   According to the same authority, the priest of Brusasco depended upon the abbey of Lucedio.   Nothing appears to be certain, however, except that S. Pietro Vecchio was the old parish church, and continued to be such until the construction of the new church in 1753.

III.   The edifice consists at present of a nave of a single aisle (Plate 37, Fig. 2) and an apse (Plate 37, Fig. 3, 4), but originally there was a northern side aisle (which has been destroyed) and a northern absidole.   The nave was originally three bays long, but has been extended to the westward.   It is evident that there is a distinct break in the masonry at the point where the old side-aisle roof abutted against the clearstory (Plate 37, Fig. 3).   Below this point the bricks employed in the masonry are of small irregular size, laid in courses which depart freely from the horizontal.   The mortar-beds average about 2 centimetres in width, and in the construction are employed many pebbles, as well as bricks set on end.   In the archivolt of the arcade and in the capitals and piers which are visible amid the modern screen-wall are some pieces of stone (Plate 37, Fig. 2).   The masonry of the main body of the edifice, on the other hand (Plate 37, Fig. 4), is polychromatic and of good quality.   Well cut blocks of stone alternate with courses of regularly shaped bricks, cross-hatched and laid in horizontal courses.   The mortar-beds average about 1 centimetre in thickness.   The masonry of the façade and of the western parts of the church is again different, and there is noticeable a distinct break where they abut against the main portion of the edifice (Plate 37, Fig. 4). In the western parts there is no polychromatic work.   The bricks, less well formed than those of the main body of the edifice, are cross-hatched and laid in courses which frequently depart from the horizontal.   It is evident, therefore, that we have in the church of S. Pietro Vecchio three distinct epochs of construction.   To the earliest belongs the lower part of the northern wall (except the screen-walls between the arcades) and this was the side aisle of an older church of which only this portion has been preserved, and to which were added a new nave and an apse.   This nave and apse were subsequently extended to the westward.   The piers (Plate 37, Fig. 2), which all belong to the first epoch of construction, are cylindrical.

IV.   The capitals of these piers (Plate 37, Fig. 2) are bell-shaped in form and covered with primitive conventional carving (Plate 37, Fig. 5). They are of a type which recalls the capitals of Lodi Vecchio (Plate 105,

[3] 3.

Fig. 4). Of the second epoch of construction, the church contains much characteristic ornament. The string-course of the interior of the apse (Plate 37, Fig. 2) is covered with interlaces and anthemia. The north clear-story wall (Plate 37, Fig. 3) is adorned with a cornice of double arched corbel-tables unfortunately restored, but the similar cornice of the east gable is ancient (Plate 37, Fig. 3). The double arched corbel-tables of the south wall are supported on shafts with cubic or grotesque capitals (Plate 37, Fig. 4). The apse (Plate 37, Fig. 4) also has shafts and a gallery that appears never to have been finished, since the capitals are merely blocked out, and the cornice ornament has been only partially carved. The eastern oculus has tracery in the form of a Greek cross (Plate 37, Fig. 4). The little campanile that rises from the north-eastern angle of the church is modern (Plate 37, Fig. 3).

The third epoch of construction, as shown in the western portions of the edifice, is less interesting. The double arched corbel-table is continued to form the cornice (Plate 37, Fig. 4), and in the façade is a biforum. The interior of the church is adorned with frescos of the XVI century.

V. The similarity of the capitals to those of Lodi Vecchio (Plate 105, Fig. 1, 2, 4)—c. 1050, and of the masonry (Plate 37, Fig. 3) to that of Sannazzaro Sesia (Plate 201, Fig. 5)—c. 1040, forms sufficient grounds for assigning the remains of the old northern side aisle to c. 1050. The main body of the edifice must be of c. 1130, as shown by the character of the masonry, the galleries and capitals. The capital of the biforum of the façade shows that the western bay must be of c. 1200.

CALVENZANO,[1] S. MARIA

(Plate 38; Plate 39, Fig. 1, 2; Plate 40, Fig. 1, 2; Plate 41, Fig. 1, 2;
Plate 42, Fig. 1, 2, 3, 4, 7)

I. The desecrated priory of S. Maria of Calvenzano can not be said to be unknown, since it has been occasionally noticed by archæologists ever since the time of Giulini. Biraghi published a study upon the church, chiefly devoted to the development of the exceedingly dubious thesis that the edifice was erected to mark the site of the martyrdom of Boethius. He deserves great credit, however, for having recognized the subject of the sculptures of the death of Herod. In recent years, Sant'Ambrogio has sought to use the church as an argument to prove the influence of the Cluniac order upon the architecture of northern Italy, but he has completely misunderstood the

[1] Calvenzano is a frazione of the commune of Vizzolo Predabissi and is situated about a kilometre to the east of Melegnano, in the Province of Milano.

archæology of the monument. In the work of Lucchini are some extremely erroneous historical notices referring to the priory. In 1910 the church was declared a national monument.

II. The recently deceased Lucchini, who was parroco of Romprezzagno, wrote an extremely curious book which he entitled *Storia della Civiltà diffusa dai Benedettini nel Cremonese*. Lucchini seems to have been a man with a mind so curiously inexact that it amounted well-nigh to insanity. In his productions are found errors and mistakes of all sorts, inexactitudes, and confusions, such as would seem almost incredible to any one who has not seen his writings. Nevertheless, strangely enough, he seems to have been an indefatigable student of the archives, and amid all his tortuous aberrations, has occasionally preserved for us the memory of some important document which appears to be entirely authentic, and which has escaped all other historians. For all his inaccuracies, Lucchini does not appear to have been a conscious and deliberate falsifier. Now, in his history, he has printed what purports to be the act of foundation of the monastery of Calvenzano, dated 1037. The document which he gives is hopelessly wrong and confusing, and the last portion of it is evidently part of a diploma referring to S. Ambrogio at Milan, which has been tacked on to the earlier part of a document which refers to Calvenzano. Hence the author has given to the priory of Calvenzano the extraordinary title of S. Maria e S. Ambrogio.[2] There appears, however, to be some reason to think that Lucchini may really have seen in the archives of

[2] Correndo l'istesso anno 1037, nelle guerre di Calvenzano dal pio Cav. Alberico de Soresina veniva fondato un monastero Benedettino chiamandovi ad abitarlo i monaci di Cluny, sotto la giurisdizione della chiesa di S. Maria e di S. Ambrogio Arcivescovo. L'istrumento di fondazione fu steso in Milano, ed è riportato dal Sormani e dal Giulini nella loro *Storia di Milano* al Vol. IV. a pagina 203. Eccolo:

ATTO DI FONDAZIONE DEL MONASTERO DI S. MARIA E S. AMBROGIO IN CALVENZANO

1037.—In nomine Sancte et Individue Trinitatis, que in unitate colitur maiestatis, in civitate Mediolani, in Curte propria de heredibus Domini Mainfredi, multis presentibus Nobilibus quorum ad retinendum memoriam hic subter inserta est noticia.

Anselmus Vicemoes [*sic*], Albertus Alberti Advocati filius, Atto filius Aliprandi vicecomitis, Tertio filius quodam Nazarii, Ardericus Mura, Arialdus qui vocatur Crivellus, et Redaldus Boccardo. Qui convenerunt et attestaverunt quod dominus Albericus de Surexina in mentis recto statu dum persisteret, deprecatus est ipsos dicerent ac testarentur, quod medietatem de omnibus rebus in fundo Gerre, pro anime sue remedio instituerat Ecclesiam Sancti Ambrosii, ubi eius sanctum et venerabile corpus quiescit, quatenus presbyteri canonici ufficiales ipsius faciant ex fructibus quidquid voluerint in canonica vivendo comunitate.

Testimonii sottoscritti Reifredo Stampa.

Pumone Cassina, ed Arialdo da Lampugnano.

Nell'atto di fondazione citato ci appaiono innanzi i nomi di nobili personaggi milanesi di cui si deve occupare la nostra storia, perchè ebbero molta parte nelle geste cattoliche accadute in Cremona a quei tempi. L'arcivescovo Eriberto da Cantù, etc.

Cremona—with which he possessed great familiarity—the charter of foundation for the priory of Calvenzano in 1037. My chief reason for suspecting that this was the case, is the fact that a study of the architectural forms of the church shows that certain parts of it must date from precisely this epoch. I confess, however, that I have sought in vain for Lucchini's document. Perhaps some one enjoying greater facilities than myself for research in Cremona may be more successful.

Whether or not founded in 1037, the priory of Calvenzano does not appear in the list of possessions confirmed to the abbey of Cluny by Urban II, in 1088.[3] It does appear, however, in a bull promulgated by the same pope, in 1095.[4]

An extremely important document for the history of S. Maria of Calvenzano is a diploma of the archbishop Anselm, published by Baluzio[5] and reprinted by Giulini: "In the name of the Son of God, who is perfect Truth, Anselm, only by the mercy of God, archbishop of the church of Milan. It behooves our Christian office to assent with alacrity to the petitions of those who are moved by religious piety and benevolent compassion. Therefore it is the duty of our authority to love with paternal affection all the sons of our church and not to deny aid to any act of piety which they may wish to perform. Thus shall we merit the greatest reward from God, the creator of all things. Wherefore we wish it to be known to all our faithful, present and future, that while we were disputing with our cardinals in our church of Milan, concerning the safety of our souls, at the prayer of certain of our diocesans of Melegnano, to wit, Arialdo and Lanfranco, brothers, and Atone their kinsman, we conceded to the holy church of Cluny, the church of S. Maria of Calvenzano (which the above-named kinsmen had long held of our church together with the land which belonged to it), and the tithes of the land of Arialdo and Lanfranco, which they had given to S. Maria of Calvenzano, and in addition all the goods which that church at present possesses or may in the future acquire. Furthermore it is our wish and desire that if any of their heirs or any other man shall wish to give to the above-mentioned church of Cluny some church now built or to be built in their possessions, or their tithes, by the inspiration of Him who inspires men to do that which He wishes, let such a one give it with the benediction of God and this our permission. We furthermore decree that the above-mentioned church depend without condition or limitation upon the monastery of Cluny and that it shall not be subject in any manner to the authority of any other church."[6] This charter is without

---

[3] Tomassetti, II, 121.   [4] *Ibid.*, 158.

[5] VI, 483. This document has also been printed by Bernard, V, 144.

[6] In nomine filii Dei, qui est summa veritas. Anselmus sola Dei misericordia Mediolanensis Ecclesiæ Archiepiscopus. Convenit nostro Christiano moderamini pia religione, ac benivola compassione, alacri mente poscentium animis assensum impertire. Idcirco ad nostram auctoritatem pertinet cunctos nostræ Ecclesiæ Filios paterno affectu

date, but Baluzio believed that the archbishop Anselm was the fourth of that name, who held office from 1097 to 1100, and in this judgment, strangely enough, both Sant'Ambrogio and Bernard seem to concur. Giulini, however, has pointed out that the political conditions at Milan during the reign of Anselm IV make it certain that the charter must have been granted rather by Anselm III (1086-1093). The various dignitaries who signed the document might, so far as it is possible to determine, have been in office at the time of Anselm III. Giulini, in consequence, refers the document to the year 1093, but this precise date is supported by no substantial evidence.

At any rate, from this document we learn two important facts. First, that the church of S. Maria of Calvenzano was given to the abbey of Cluny in the last quarter of the XI century, and second, that the church itself had at this time been long in existence.

Calvenzano is mentioned as a priory of the Cluniac order in 1367, at which time it contained only three monks, as we learn from a notice of Marrier.[7] The monastery also appears in a sort of tax-list of 1398, published by Magistretti.[8] After this there are no documents known which throw light upon the history of the priory. In the time of Giulini it had passed out of the hands of the Cluniacs and was subject to the metropolitan chapter of Milan. The revenues had been given in 1563 to S. Giovanni in Borgo of Pavia.[9] In 1854 half of the church had already been desecrated, and the monument has continued in that condition to the present day.

III. The edifice consisted originally of a nave seven bays long, two side aisles and three apses (Plate 38); but the ancient dispositions have been

diligere, et optatæ pietatis opem non denegare. Ex hoc enim lucri potissimum præmium apud Deum omnium Conditorem promeremur. Quapropter omnibus nostris Fidelibus, tam præsentibus, quam futuris notum fieri volumus, quod Nos in nostræ Mediolanensi Ecclesia, cum nostris Cardinalibus, de nostrarum animarum salute disputantes, nostrorum Fidelium, scilicet Arialdi, et Lanfranci Fratrum, ac Atonis eorum consanguinei de Meregnano imploratu, Sancte Mariæ Ecclesiam de Calvenzano, quam ex nostra Ecclesia tenebant longo tempore, cum terra, ac eorum scilicet Arialdi, et Lanfranci propri prædii decimis, quas ad præsens concesserunt, et omnibus bonis, quae nunc habet, et in perpetuum adipisci poterit Sanctæ Cluniacensi Ecclesiæ concessimus. Insuper volumus, et laudamus, quod si quis eorum heredum vel alius quilibet homo, de Eclesiis supra eorum prædium ædificatis, vel ædificandis, aut eorum decimis, eo inspirante, qui ubi vult spirat, prætaxatæ Ecclesiæ conferre voluerit, conferat cum Dei benedictione, et hac nostras concessione: eo scilicet ordine, ut nostra præfata Ecclesia amodo sine penditio, et conditione libera Cluniacensi Cænobio deservire, et nullius alterius Ecclesiæ ditioni in aliquo per infinita sæcula subiaceat . . . (Giulini, VII, 72-73).

[7] Prioratus B. Mariæ de Caluenzano, Mediolanensis dicesis, vbi debent esse, Priore computato, iuxta diffinitionem anni 1367. tres Monachi, Eleemosyna ibidem omnibus petentibus eam tribuitur. (Marrier, 1745).

[8] Cf. *Status ecclesiae mediolani* conscriptus auctore Francesco Castello. Amb. MS. A, 112 Inf., f. 520.

[9] Giardini, 111.

greatly altered. The eastern bay of the nave has been walled off to form a choir, and the northern absidiole and the eastern bay of the north side aisle have been turned into a sacristy, while the eastern bay of the south side aisle and the southern absidiole have been destroyed. The existing church occupies only the four eastern bays of the original edifice (Plate 42, Fig. 1, 2, 3). On the ground floor of the fifth and sixth bays (Plate 42, Fig. 4) has been established a storehouse for cheeses, and the seventh bay is used as a wood-shed. These desecrated bays have moreover been divided into two stories, the upper of which serves as a granary.

The side aisles were vaulted throughout with highly domed groin vaults with transverse and wall ribs (Plate 42, Fig. 3). The nave, at present covered by a ceiling, was, I believe, originally roofed in timber. The system is alternate, the heavier piers comprising in all twelve separate members, rectangular or semicircular (Plate 38). The intermediate piers have only eight members. It is a singular fact that the number of supports is even, although the system is alternate—a circumstance which results in the two easternmost free-standing piers being heavy, whereas one would expect them to be light (Plate 38). The system of the piers is at present not continued above the impost level (Plate 42, Fig. 1, 2). The responds of the side aisles are also alternately heavy and light, and contain three or five members, rectangular and semicircular (Plate 38).

This alternation of supports and responds and the presence in the alternate piers of a system certainly never intended to end in its present unmeaning fashion, make it clear that the church originally either was, or was intended to be, supplied with transverse arches spanning the nave. In the fifth and seventh bays, now desecrated, there are traces in the masonry which give some reason to believe that the system was formerly carried up along the clearstory wall and was cut down to its present form only in the time of the Renaissance. The side-aisle vaults (Plate 42, Fig. 3) are all covered with intonaco where they have not been destroyed, so that a study of details is difficult. It is evident, however, that the vaults are supplied with transverse and wall arches, and constructed of bricks rather carelessly laid in wide beds of mortar in courses approximately normal to the walls.

The interior of the church has been entirely covered with intonaco (Plate 42, Fig. 1, 2, 3, 4); the exterior, too, has undergone grave alterations, especially on the south side (Plate 39, Fig. 2), so that it is exceedingly difficult to trace the original forms. It is evident, however, that the existing edifice represents several distinct eras of construction. To the first belongs the northern absidiole (Plate 39, Fig. 1), the greater part of the apse (Plate 40, Fig. 1), and the core of the four eastern bays. The masonry of these portions consists of small bricks which are not cross-hatched, laid almost entirely in herring-bone courses (Plate 41, Fig. 1, 2). This primitive edifice—which I believe dates from c. 1040—had probably transverse arches in two orders, springing from the alternate piers, and a simple system engaged on the intermediate piers. The side aisles were groin-vaulted and the archivolts of the main arcade in not more than two orders. At a later epoch, a radical reconstruction of the church was undertaken, when the nave was extended to the westward. Still later the central apse was supplied with two heavy buttresses, and its original simple corbel-tables were supplanted by the present cornice (Plate 40, Fig. 2)[10] which foreshadows that of S. Michele at Cremona (Plate 86, Fig. 3). The clearstory was entirely rebuilt, though in a manner which followed approximately the original lines. At the same epoch the northern wall was reinforced by a series of buttresses, which were later connected one with the other by arcades (Plate 39, Fig. 2). These arcades have been taken by Sant'Ambrogio to be part of the reconstruction of the XII century, but they can not be such, since the brickwork is of a totally different character from that of the XII century masonry to which they are appliquéd. Moreover, the cornice is clearly of the XIII century (Plate 39, Fig. 2), and in addition the arches of the arcades cut across the old windows, even in the western bays (Plate 39, Fig. 2).

The windows in the north wall are deeply splayed and served without glass (Plate 39, Fig. 2). Those of the apses were doubtless originally similar, but in the XIII century were enlarged. The enlarged windows of the XIII century were in turn walled up at the time of the Renaissance and supplanted by the present barocco apertures (Plate 39, Fig. 1). It is probable that the clearstory was originally much lower than at present and in fact hardly higher than the existing apse. The present clearstory (Plate 39, Fig. 2) contains no masonry earlier than the last quarter of the XI century. It was probably rebuilt a third time in the XIII century, for in the north wall are preserved fragments of two distinct cornices, one of double arched corbel-tables of the XIII century, the other of a simple corbel-table supported on colonnettes of the XII century (Plate 39, Fig. 2). The church was much altered in the barocco period, when new windows were opened and the capitals of the interior shaved down to their present indeterminate forms (Plate 42, Fig. 1, 2, 3). The unfortunate intonaco of the interior appears to be of even more recent date.

IV. In the ornament of the church may be traced the same series of restorations as in the structure. Of the XI century edifice survive the Attic bases of the responds with griffes, but those of the piers, if they ever existed, have been cut down (Plate 42, Fig. 3). Several cubic capitals survive in that portion of the edifice which serves as a storehouse for cheese. It is true they all belong to that part of the church which was added in the XII century, but they seem to preserve the type of the earlier (now lost) capitals of c. 1040, which in the enlargement of the primitive edifice appear to have been copied

---

[10] In the photograph the break in the masonry is clearly visible.

with remarkable fidedity. These capitals have a straight instead of a curved cushion, and are as entirely analogous to the capitals of Stradella (Plate 210)—c. 1035, as they are different from any known capitals of the XII century.

Of the reconstruction of c. 1095 survive two capitals in the present sacristy, which are of Corinthianesque type and carved with eagles. Of c. 1140 is the fragment of an arched corbel-table supported on colonnettes at the western end of the north clearstory wall (Plate 39, Fig. 2). Of the XIII century, on the other hand, are the double-arched corbel-tables of the central portion of the north wall, and the flat corbel-table which surmounts the buttress arcades of the same wall (Plate 39, Fig. 2) and the west façade.

This west façade, gravely denatured in the barocco period, contains a portal of the second era of construction, on the archivolt of which are sculptured a series of highly interesting reliefs. The subjects are, beginning at the right (Plate 42, Fig. 7): (1) The Annunciation. Mary, haloed, stands to the left. The angel Gabriel, also haloed, holds a sceptre in his left hand, while he gestures with his right. The divine Hand appears in the cloud above. (2) The Visitation. (3) The angel appears to Joseph. (4) The Nativity. Mary in the bed above, is watched over by Joseph. Below the Christ-Child is seen in the manger, with the ox and the ass. The star of Bethlehem is above to the right. (5) The shepherds and their flocks. The angel holding a sceptre in his left hand, appears to two shepherds, one of whom holds a staff, the other of whom sits on the top of a mountain above his flocks. (6) The Adoration of the Magi. The Virgin sits enthroned in an open loggia drawn with an excellence of perspective that would do credit to Ghiberti. On her lap she holds the Christ-Child. The three kings, all bearded and crowned, approach, bearing gifts on napkins. The first is already kneeling in adoration. Above him is seen the star of Bethlehem. In the background an admirable representation of a mediæval city doubtless represents the city of Bethlehem. (7) The Flight into Egypt. The Christ-Child rides upon the ass, led by the Virgin. Mary puts her right hand tenderly around the Child, to prevent him from falling. Behind the ass is seen Joseph, who carries in his left hand a stick slung over his shoulder, on which are suspended two bundles. In his right hand he holds a whip, which he vigorously applies to the ass. In the background we have again the city of Bethlehem. (8) The Slaughter of the Innocents. Herod sits on a throne, holding a sceptre. He is crowned, and watches with complacency an executioner who dismembers a naked baby with his sword. (9) The Death of Herod. According to Josephus, Herod, at the end of his life, was afflicted with horrible ailments, intestinal pains, a watery humour in his feet, and worms in his testicles. In a last desperate effort to save him, his physicians sent him to celebrated baths, where they directed that he should stand in a barrel of oil, his peculiar maladies making it impossible

for him to assume either a sitting or a lying position.[11]   In the Calvenzano
relief, we see the guilty king standing naked in a barrel of oil, attended either
by his faithful sister Salome, or by one of the physicians.

In point of style, the sculptures of Calvenzano excel for their fineness
and delicacy.   They show a mastery of technique infinitely superior to any
to be found in contemporary works in Milan and Pavia.   The execution of
the faces, the proportions of the figures, the treatment of the draperies, and
numerous other technical peculiarities, make it probable that these reliefs are
by the same sculptor who executed the tomb of S. Alberto at Pontida, soon
after 1095.   This sculptor shows certain analogies with Guglielmo da Modena
as, *e.g.*, in the treatment of the draperies in the scene of the Visitation.   The
arcades which enclose certain of the scenes of Calvenzano seem to anticipate
the similar motive adopted by Nicolò at Piacenza.   The sculptor of Calvenzano shows himself not only the forerunner of Nicolò, but his superior in
proportion, in facial expression and in delicacy of technique.   The composition
of the Calvenzano reliefs is, in general, very good.   Only in the scene of the
shepherds does the artist appear quite unable to tell his story effectively in
the awkward space which he has allotted himself.   Remarkably fine, also, is
the conventional ornament of the roll-moulding and flat band of the archivolt.
The rinceau of the latter is dainty enough to be a work of the early
Renaissance.

V.   Lucchini's citation of a document of foundation of 1037 is entirely
untrustworthy, and it is therefore necessary to depend upon internal evidence
to establish the date of the earliest portions of the church.   The masonry
(Plate 41, Fig. 2), characterized by the use of uncross-hatched bricks, and
the constant use of herring-bone courses, seems distinctly more primitive than
that of Sannazzaro Sesia (Plate 201, Fig. 5, 6)—1040.   It offers analogies
with the masonry of Stradella, especially in the pilaster strips of the absidioles,
where some very large bricks are used; but in general the more sparing use
of bricks of enormous dimensions seems to indicate that Calvenzano is later
than Stradella (c. 1035).   The arched corbel-tables of the absidiole (Plate 40,
Fig. 1) are, however, entirely analogous to those of Stradella (Plate 211,
Fig. 1), and it has been seen that there is reason to believe that the cubic
capitals of Calvenzano were similar to those at Stradella (Plate 210), except
that they had no zigzag ornament.   The bases are like those of Stradella,
except that they have griffes, which is, perhaps, an indication of slightly later
date, although this is an old Byzantine motive which goes back to remote

---

[11] Κἀνταῦθα τοῖς ἰατροῖς δοκῆσαν, ὥσε [sic] ἀναθάλπειν καθεθεὶς εἰς πύελον ἐλαίω πλέον, δόξαν
μετασάσεας ἐνεποίησεν αὐτοῖς.   (Flavius Josephus, *Antiq. Jud.*, Lib. XVII, Cap. VI, § 4).

δόξαν δ'ἐνταῦθα τοῖς ἰατροῖς ἐλαίω θερμῷ παν ἀναθαλψαι τὸ σῶμα, χαλαθὲν εἰς ἐλαίω πλήρη
πύελον, ἐκλύει δὲ τὰς ὀφθαλμὰς, καὶ ὡς τεθνεὼς ἀνέστρεψε.   (Flavius Josephus, *De Bello Jud.*,
Lib. I, Cap. XXXIII, § 4).

antiquity. The section of the piers (Plate 38) is more complicated than that of the piers at Stradella (Plate 208), and presupposes archivolts and transverse arches in two orders (the existing archivolts, in two and three orders, have been made over); but the Calvenzano piers (Plate 38) are hardly more complicated than those of Sannazzaro Sesia (Plate 200). All things considered, the edifice seems to fall midway between Stradella (c. 1035) and Sannazzaro Sesia (1040), and may therefore be attributed to c. 1040.

It is almost equally difficult to speak with certainty in regard to the various reconstructions of the church. The capitals of the sacristy, the western bays, and the sculptures of the west portal, all belong to an enlargement of the building undertaken in consequence of the foundation of the Cluniac priory, which took place certainly before 1095, and probably in 1093. As has been seen, the sculptures of the west portal are by the same artist who executed the tomb of S. Alberto at Pontida, soon after 1095. These portions of the edifice may, therefore, be ascribed to c. 1095. On the other hand, the cornices of the central apse and the buttresses (Plate 40, Fig. 2), the masonry of which consists of large, cross-hatched bricks horizontally laid with perfect technique, and separated by mortar-beds of moderate thickness—masonry entirely analogous to that of the Chiesa Rossa at Milan (Plate 115, Fig. 2), an authentically dated monument of 1133—and the fragment of cornice preserved at the northern end of the clearstory (Plate 39, Fig. 2), quite analogous to S. Lazaro at Pavia (Plate 169, Fig. 4)—1157, must date from c. 1140. Finally the arcades of the north wall, and their cornice (Plate 39, Fig. 2), are clearly of the early years of the XIII century.

CAMPO DI LENNO,[1] S. ANDREA

I. The picturesque little church of S. Andrea of Campo has been published and illustrated by Monneret de Villard in his monograph upon the Isola Comacina.[2]

II. I know no documents which throw light upon the history of the edifice.

III. The little building consists of a single-aisled nave, an apse, a modern sacristy, and a slender and picturesque campanile. The interior of the building has been completely baroccoized, as has also the upper part of the façade. The masonry consists of roughly squared stones, laid in rather regular courses, and separated by broad beds of mortar.

IV. The campanile in five stories is characterized by a graceful belfry, and by arched corbel-tables grouped two and two, and supported on pilaster

---

1 (Como).   2 124.

strips. The apse is ornamented externally with a cornice of arched corbel-tables. The side walls of the eastern gable have no corbel-tables. The deeply splayed windows were intended to serve without glass.

V. The masonry of S. Andrea of Campo is entirely similar in character to that of S. Benedetto di Lenno (Plate 102, Fig. 5), an authentically dated monument of 1083. S. Andrea may consequently be ascribed to c. 1085.

CARENO DI PELLEGRINO PARMENSE,[1] SANTUARIO DI S. MARIA ASSUNTA

I. The church of Careno has been made the object of a monograph by the local priest, Guerra.

II. In the west wall of the church north of the principal portal and back of a confessional which has to be moved to make it possible to inspect the monument, is the following inscription in letters of the XVIII century:

STEPHANVS III.

P M

IN DESIDER. LANGOB. REGE

RECTORI TEMP CARENI

DIGNITATEM

ABB. MITRATI IN PERPET.

CONTVLIT

The inscription at least proves that in the XVIII century it was believed that the sanctuary existed as early as the time of Stefano III (768-772).

Another inscription, which was visible in the church until 1710, and which has been preserved in a copy, now in the parish archives, has been published by Guerra. It seems to record a reconstruction of the church in the year 1494, by a certain Ghirardo.[2]

In the house of the parroco is preserved another stone which comes from the church, and which, like that of Stefano III, is evidently a conscious forgery of the XVIII century. It bears the false date of 1351, and seems to have been fabricated to increase the fame of the shrine for the cure of the insane:

ABBAS MITRAT[V]S

CARENI

BENEDICAT DEMENTIB[V]S

1351

---

[1] (Parma).

[2]   Mille jerant quinginta minus sex ordine messis
    Dum molem hanc fieri magne Ghirarde jubes (Guerra, 20).

CARENO DI PELLEGRINO PARMENSE

What is meant by these two references to the mitred abbot it is difficult to say, since there is no other indication that the church was ever the site of a monastery. In the early years of the XVIII century, the edifice was baroccoized.[3] In 1834 the parish was split into two parts, and Careno thus lost jurisdiction over Pellegrino.[4] The consecration of the high altar is recorded in an extant inscription of 1836. On the west façade is a modern Italian inscription by Guerra, which states that the church was founded in the X century (this notice is derived from a misinterpretation of the inscription of 1494, cited above) and commemorates its acquisition of the rank of santuario.

III. The edifice consists of a nave four bays long, two side aisles, a central apse, and a campanile which rises to the north of the apse. The interior has been entirely modernized. The groin vaults of the side aisles, and the side-aisle responds, as well as the octagonal piers of the nave, do not seem to be older than the XVIII century. The rib vaults of the nave, on the other hand, appear to be of 1494. They are about square in plan and not much domed. Both the light diagonals of rectangular profile and the wall ribs rest on corbels. The diagonals are segmental, and very regularly constructed. The rectangular transverse rib is carried on a rectangular system which rises from the abaci of the capitals and is apparently original.

The windows, widely splayed and narrow, were square or round-headed. The arcuated lintels have sometimes a stone joint at the summit of the arch. The windows of the campanile are pointed.

The church is constructed in its lower parts of ashlar masonry. Where this has not been made over—as, for example, in the apse—it is seen to be of excellent quality. The courses are horizontal and unbroken, and the mortar-beds are about 1 centimetre in thickness. In the campanile, however, the masonry is of rougher quality, and the masonry of the north side-aisle wall is even inferior, while the clearstory is built of little better than a mass of rubble.

IV. The apse has a simple cavea cornice. The side-aisle walls have large arched corbel-tables grouped three and three or two and two. The elaborate triangular arched corbel-tables of the nave clearstory were being rebuilt without authority when I visited the church on May 12, 1913. The very few of them that are old were added in the reconstruction of 1494.

V. The cavea cornice and the arcuated lintels of the windows seem to be Cluniac features, and suggest the influence of such edifices as Monastero di Capo di Ponte, and Monastero di Provaglio. The general type of the church of Careno, however, is that of the local school of Parma of the end of the XII or early XIII century. The arched corbel-tables recall S. Croce and

[3] Guerra, 66.　　[4] Ibid., 60.

S. Andrea of Parma and Vicofertile (Plate 240, Fig. 1). The masonry shows many points of contact with that of the baptistery of Serravalle (Plate 206, Fig. 1), where are also found the same arcuated lintels and a cavea cornice. The edifice may consequently be ascribed to c. 1200. In 1494 the church was almost entirely reconstructed, and the campanile erected.

CARPI,[1] S. MARIA

(Plate 42, Fig. 5, 6; Plate 43, Fig. 2, 3)

I. S. Maria of Carpi, locally known as the Sagra, is a monument of considerable interest and importance. Undoubtedly the most important publication dealing with the edifice is a volume published by the municipality under the title *Memorie istoriche di Carpi*. This contains several monographs by local antiquarians, notably Franciosi,—whose account is important although somewhat diffuse,—Sammarini and Guaitoli. The edifice has also been noticed by Stiehl[2] and Semper. For the recent restoration, the official account of Faccioli[3] should be consulted.

II. In the northern bay of the façade is an inscription which we may translate as follows: "In the year of Our Lord Jesus Christ 751, we, Aistolfo, king of the Lombards, for the remedy and salvation of our soul, erected and endowed this church in honour of the glorious Virgin Mary in this manor of our kingdom which is called Carpi, and which depends directly upon us. This when Constantine V, the son of Leo, was emperor of the Romans, and Pepin king of the Franks was reigning in Gaul."[4] We know from a letter of Alberto Pio, of January, 1514, that the present inscription was made to replace an older inscription which was destroyed at the time that the western bays of the edifice were demolished.[5] The original inscription was placed over the

---

1 (Modena).   2 23.   3 70-73.

4 ANNO . A NATIVITATE . IESV X̄P̄I . VCCLI . NOS . ASTVLFVS . LŌ
GOBARDOR . REX . PRO . REMEDIO . ET . SALVTE . ĀIĒ . N̄RE . EC
CLESIAM . ISTĀ . IN . HONORĒ . GLORIOSE . VIRGINIS . MARIE . IN
P̄DIO . HOC . REGNI . N̄R̄I . QD . CARPV̄ . DICITVR . NOBIS . SPECIALI
TER . SVBIECTO . C̄OSTRVXIMVS . ET . DOTAVIMVS . IMP[ER]ANTE
COSTĀTINO . QNTO . LEONIS . FILIO . ROMANOR[VM] . IMP[ER]ATORE
REGNĀTE . IN GALIA . PIPINO . FRANCHOR[VM] . REGE .

5 La Chiesa vecchia di Castello ormai dovete cominciar a farla distruggere . . . gli ha da restare qual è tutto quella da la Torre in dietro, al quale si faccia tirare davanti una fascia sopra in volta con un muro per serrarlo e tolgasi un estratto di quelle lettere, che sono scritte ne la porta della Chiesa verso il borgo di sotto, della dotazione e fondazione della Chiesa ed altare, se alcuna ve n'è, di memoria per rimetterle poi nell'oratorio a perpetua memoria. (*Memorie*, IV, 236).

portal of the church, and was hence probably not older than the XII century.
The XVI century transcription offers considerable difficulty, for while the
chronological notes are sufficiently exact, there is, to my knowledge, no Lombard
document which refers to the Frank kings in its chronological notes. We shall
find that in later times the pieve of Carpi was engaged in a desperate struggle
to free itself from the jurisdiction of the bishops of Modena, and I suspect
that the present inscription was forged to authenticate the claims of the pieve.
There is, however, no reason to doubt that the tradition that the church was
founded by Aistolfo is correct.

The use to which our inscription was put, may be deduced from a bull of
Callistus II, of 1123, in which the pope states that the church of Carpi is
known to have been founded by Aistolfo, and to have been exempted by him
from the jurisdiction of all episcopal authority. The pope goes on to state
that the pieve of Carpi had been taken under the apostolic protection and made
to depend directly upon the see of St. Peter, by Pope Stephen (II, 752-757).
He, Callistus II, therefore, confirms this same liberty to the church of Carpi,
and decrees that it shall be subject to no bishop except the apostolic see.
He also grants to the clergy the tithes as they had been conceded by
Gregory VII (1073-1084), Urban II (1088-1099) and Paschal II (1099-
1118). Moreover, he grants the church the right to receive the chrism, holy
oils, the ordination of clergy, and the consecration of churches from whatever
Catholic bishop the prevosto and canons prefer. He allows the prevosto,
within the limits of his parish, to ordain clerics; also to promote them at his
will, not only in the parish of Carpi itself, but in all the churches dependent
upon it. He gives him the right to reconcile penitents and impose penances for
mortal sins.[6] The privileges enumerated in this bull were reconfirmed by

[6] Calixtus Episcopus, servus servorum Dei, dilecto Filio Federico Archipresbytero,
& ceteris Canonicis Plebis Sanctae Dei Genitricis Virginis Mariae, que in Pago Carpensi
sita est, eorumque Successoribus in perpetuum. . . . Astulphus siquidem Longobardorum
Rex in Regni sui Pago, quod Carpum dicitur, Beate Marie semper Virginis Ecclesiam
construxisse dignoscitur, quam ut a vicinorum Episcoporum, in quorum confiniis idem
Pagus erat, contentionibus et molestiis omnino liberam redderet . . . Ecclesiam illam
in jure semper Sedis Apostolice permanere constituit, & libertatem ex Stephani Pape
Privilegio acquisivit. . . . Et nos ergo eamdem libertatem predicte Ecclesie per Dei
gratiam conservandum statuimus, ut nulli Episcopo . . . eadem Ecclesia subjecta sit,
nisi tantum Apostolice Sedi. . . . Decimas quoque . . . vobis, vestrisque Successoribus
firmas perpetuo munere sancimus, sicut eas Praedecessorum nostrorum Apostolice
memorie Gregorii VII & Urbani, & Pascalis II. atque aliorum concessione hactenus
habuistis. . . . De Chrismate, & Oleo Sancto atque Ordinatione vestra, sive Consecra-
tionibus Ecclesiarum, a quocumque velitis Episcopo Catholico, accipiendis licentiam
vobis liberam indulgemus, sicut a prefatis Pontificibus constat fuisse concessam. . . .
Infra eosdem quoque terminos Preposito Plebis Clericos ordinare permittimus, ad cujus
providentiam & dispositionem tam ordinationes & promotiones Clericorum, qui infra
eamdem Parochiam ordinandi vel promovendi sunt, quam etiam prelationes eorum, qui
in subditis Ecclesiis proficiendi sunt, pertinebunt. De criminalibus etiam intra supra-

237

Innocent IV, in 1250. The bull of Innocent is conceived in almost the same words as the bull of Callistus, but we learn from it that the canons of Carpi were of the order of St. Augustine. In addition to the bulls of Stephen II, Gregory VII, Urban II and Paschal II, this bull also mentions privileges granted to the church by Honorius II (1124-1130), Innocent II (1130-1143), Eugenius III (1145-1153), Hadrian IV (1154-1159), Alexander III (1159-1181), Gregory VIII (1187), Honorius III (1216-1227), and Gregory IX 1227-1240).[7] It is evident that the clergy of Carpi put to good use their claim that the church had been founded by Aistolfo. Indeed, we shall see further on that eventually the church of Carpi was successful in raising itself to the episcopal dignity. It would be claiming too much to assert that the starting point for all this ambitious climbing was the original of our inscription. Although there is no certain means of establishing at what date the letters over the western portal of the old pieve were cut, it is entirely probable that they were not anterior to the XII century. The canons of Carpi, therefore, may well have already put forth their claims of exemption from the episcopal jurisdiction of Modena some time before, and these claims were undoubtedly founded upon a tradition or upon more or less authentic documents of a foundation by Aistolfo. The forged inscription, nevertheless, was placed over the doorway in order that it might form an explicit and categorical support for the claims of the chapter.

The earliest authentic document relating to Carpi dates from 1066, and mentions an archpriest of our church.[8] It is therefore evident that at this period the church was already a pieve, and officiated by a chapter of canons.

In the west façade of the church is an inscription, like the other a copy of an early inscription and erected by Alberto Pio in 1514. In this inscription we read: "His Holiness Pope Lucius III, with seven cardinals and twelve bishops and many prelates, consecrated the pieve and church of S. Maria at Carpi, in the year 1184, on the fifteenth of June, and he granted several

dictos terminos penitentias dare, & reconciliationem facere vobis concedimus. . . . Datum Laterani . . . IV. Idus Februarii, Indictione Prima, Incarnationis Dominice Anno MCXXIII. Pontificatus autem Domni Callisti II. Pape Anno Quinto. (Ed. Muratori, A. I. M. E., Dis. 69, ed. A, XIV, 213; printed also by Tiraboschi, II, *Cod. Dip.*, 95).

[7] Innocentius Episcopus Servus Servorum Dei. Dilectis filiis Archipresbitero Plebis Sanctæ Marię, quæ in Pago Carpensi sita est Ordinis Sancti Augustini, eiusque fratribus tam præsentibus quam futuris regularem vitam professis in perpetuum. . . . quam videlicet libertatem felicis recordationis Gregorius septimus, Urbanus, Paschalis, Calistus, Honorius Secundus, Innocentius, Eugenius, Adrianus, Alexander, Gregorius octavus, Honorius tertius, & Gregorius nonus prædecessores nostri Romani Pontifices prædictę Carpensi Ecclesię servaverunt, etc. . . . Datum Lugdun. per manum Magistri Marini . . . III. Kalendas Maii, indictione VIII. Incarnationis Dominicæ anno MCCL. Pontificatus vero Domini Innocentii Papae quarti anno septimo. (Tiraboschi, V, *Cod. Dip.*, 39).

[8] *Memorie*, VII, 5.

indulgences to all those who should visit the said church on the day of its consecration and on the day of the Assumption and for the octave afterwards, provided that such were duly penitent and had confessed, and he granted that these indulgences should be renewed every year in perpetuity."[9] The chronological notes of this inscription offer some difficulty, because the year 1184 corresponds with the second, not the first, indiction. Moreover, it is known that Lucius III was at Modena on July 12, 1184,[10] and it is therefore probable that the consecration of the church of Carpi took place, not on the fifteenth of June, but on the fifteenth of July. The copyist of the XVI century doubtless misread the original inscription in these particulars.

The campanile was erected from 1217 to 1221, according to an inscription.[11] In 1344 there was in existence a portico on the north side of the church.[12] During the Middle Ages, at least seven accessory chapels were added to the edifice, but of these only that of S. Caterina, founded before 1431, is extant.[13] In 1458 the church passed into commendam.[14]

From a document of 1512, published in the *Memorie*,[15] we learn that in this year Alberto Pio petitioned the pope, Julius II, for permission to demolish partially the old pieve. Alberto recites that the church, because situated in the castle, had to be kept closed much of the time on account of wars, pestilence and other reasons, that this was a great inconvenience to the parishioners and canons who, consequently, were not able to celebrate their offices. Moreover, the church was not large enough for the parochial needs. Alberto therefore proposed to erect a new church, handsomer and more convenient, *reservato dumtaxat quodam parvo oratorio in quo quandoque missae et alia divina officia celebrari possent.* The petition of Alberto was granted by the pope, and the former proceeded to carry out his plans, as we learn from a letter of his dated January, 1514.[16] There is also extant a contract of 1515 for *facere seu construere Ecclesiam seu Oratorium situm in Civitatella Carpi, ubi alias erat S. Maria Plebis de Carpo; his pactis et conditionibus.* . . . *Item si obbliga a voltare il corpo di mezzo del detto oratorio a fascia; e fargli sotto*

9

SANCTISSIMVS . ET . BEATISSIMVS . SV̅M̅VS . PONTIFEX . PAPA . LVCIVS
TERTIVS . COM . SEPTEM . CARDINALIBVS . ET . DVODECIM . EPISCO‾
PIS . ET . MVLTIS . ECCLESIARVM . PRELATIS . CONSECRAVIT . PLEB̅E̅
ET . ECCLESIAM . SANCTE . MARIE . DE . CARPO . ANNO . MCLXXXIIII
INDICT' . PRIMA . DIE . XV . MENSIS . IVNII . ET . OMNIBVS . VISTA̅TIBVS
DICTAM . ECCLESIA̅ . IPA̅ . DIE . DICTE . CO̅SECRATIOIS . ET . IN . DIE . AS
SVMPTIONIS . P[ER] . OCTAVA̅ . VERE . PENITE̅TIBVS . ET . CO̅FESSIS . PRO
REMEDIO . ET . SALVTE . AIAR[VM] . SVAR[VM] . Q̅Z . PLVRIMAS .
INDVLGE̅TIAS
DEDIT . ET . CO̅CESSIT . IN . P[ER]PETVVM . ANNVATIM . DVRATVRAS

[10] See inscription cited below, Vol. III.　　[11] *Memorie*, IV, 116.
[12] *Ibid.*, 113.　　[13] *Ibid.*, 109-111.　　[14] *Ibid.*, VII, 7.　　[15] IV, 235.
[16] *Memorie*, IV, 236. An extract is cited above, p. 236.

il cornicione e l'architrave da due lati. Item fare le crociere degli altri lati; e murare sotto li archi e farci due uscii . . . e stabilire la facciata davanti tutta. Item si obbliga detto Mastro tagliare tutte le cornici intorno agli archi in detta Chiesa e mettere su una di quelle porte di marmo che erano di costa della Chiesa vecchia.[17] The completion of the changes executed at the initiative of Alberto Pio is recorded in an inscription still extant over the west portal.[18]

The new basilica erected by Alberto became, in fact, the cathedral of Carpi, and to this were transferred the Lateran canons who had officiated in the old pieve.[19] The pieve itself was destroyed except the two eastern bays, which were baroccoized and converted into a chapel. In this condition it continued until the restoration of 1898. From the official account of Faccioli,[20] it is possible to form a good idea of the condition of the church before its restoration. Much valuable information is also contained in the account of Sammarini.[21] The restoration, ventilated as early as 1888, was not begun until 1898, and was completed only in 1901. The changes executed at this time included: (1) The destruction of the numerous Renaissance and modern additions to the church. (2) The reconstruction of the roof of the southern side aisle on the model of the modern roof of the northern side aisle. (3) The reconstruction of the southern façade and of the base of the northern wall. The authority of certain ancient fragments is supposed to have guided this rebuilding. On both sides the bases of the columns and the cornices are new, and, in fact, of the exterior flanks of the church, only the semi-columns on the north side are original. (4) The walls which had been erected between the arcades of the interior in the XVI century were destroyed. (5) Excavations having proved the side aisles originally terminated in absidioles, the southern of these absidioles was reconstructed. (6) The southern side aisle (which had been desecrated) was restored to the church.

[17] *Memorie*, IV, 338.

[18] AEDEM VIRGINIS DEIPARAE VETUSTATE COLLABETEM
      NEC ABV̄DE CAPACEM
QVVM EX ARCE IN FORVM TRANSFERENDĀ CVRASSET
      ALBERTVS PIVS L. F. CARP CO.
AVCTA SACERDOTVM ET DIGNITATE ET VTILITATE
      NE OMNINO PRISCAE
RELIGIONIS DIVINVS INTERMITTERETVR CVLTVS
      NOC [sic] SACELLVM INSTAVRAVIT
        M.D.X.V.

[19] That the canons of the pieve were of the Lateran order is evident from an inscription in the chapel of S. Caterina:

    SACROSANCTÆ . ECCLESIÆ . LATERANENSI . AGGREGATA.

[20] 70-71.

[21] *Memorie*, VII, 5.

III. In 1877 traces of the foundations of the demolished portions of the pieve were discovered. The plan of these was published in the *Memorie*.[22] It is evident that the church was originally three double bays long, that the intermediate supports were columns, the alternate, piers. These piers are said to have had four members, two semicircular and two rectangular, but there is little authority for determining the section. Although there seem to have been found no traces of the side-aisle responds, there were probably transverse arches across the nave and side aisles, as in the cathedral of Modena. Before the recent restoration, the nave had been barrel-vaulted, and the northern side aisle had been covered with groin vaults. The southern side aisle had been divided into two stories, of which the lower was a stable; the upper, groin-vaulted, formed two rooms. The result of the excavations makes it evident that all these vaults demolished in the recent restoration were not original.

At present the church consists of a nave two bays long (Plate 42, Fig. 5), two side aisles, two apses (Plate 42, Fig. 6), and a large northern chapel. The edifice is entirely roofed in wood, and the clearstory (Plate 42, Fig. 5) has small, widely splayed windows. The masonry consists of large, well made, cross-hatched bricks laid in perfectly horizontal courses. When I visited the church in June, 1912, it was still possible to distinguish the restored from the original portions of the edifice, by the colour of the bricks. It was evident that the southern absidiole (Plate 42, Fig. 6) and the southern wall with its blind arches are modern, but that the blind arches on the north side (Plate 42, Fig. 5), which are part inside of, and a part outside of, the chapel of S. Caterina, are original.

IV. The cubic capitals, with high curved cushions, have a spur in the angle where the cushion joins the abacus. Other capitals are ornamented with grotesques, eagles, birds and animals. The original bases of the exterior shafts (Plate 42, Fig. 6), which are engaged on pilaster strips, are of Attic type, but adorned with several fillets.

The clearstory wall is ornamented with simple arched corbel-tables carried on pilaster strips (Plate 42, Fig. 5). The apse (Plate 42, Fig. 6) was externally ornamented with blind arches enclosing two arched corbel-tables, a motive reminiscent of the cathedral of Modena (Plate 140, Fig. 3), but the pilaster strips or shafts which supported the arches have disappeared. The flanks of the church were adorned with a similar motive (Plate 42, Fig. 5).

In the lunette of the western portal (Plate 43, Fig. 3) is an interesting sculpture of the Crucifixion. In the centre is seen Christ on the cross. His head inclines to the left of the spectator. To His right is the centurion who pierces His right side with a spear. To His left is a sponge-bearer, holding the sponge on a rod in one hand, a pail of vinegar in the other. Mary, who

[22] IV, 162, 184.

holds her hand to her face in grief, is at the Deity's right. John, making a similar gesture of grief, is at His left. Two small figures in the corner of the lunette at either side perhaps represent the populace. Below is the inscription

$\overline{\text{XPS}}$. PER . MORTEM . DE . MORTE . RESVSCITAT . ORBEM

The late date of this relief is shown by the technique of the draperies, the good proportions, and the knowledge of anatomy shown in the figure of Christ. It is, nevertheless, the work of an inferior artist. The faces are poor, and the composition bad. The sculptures are surrounded by an anthemion motive, and the archivolt of the portal is carved with a rinceau, exceedingly classical in character. The jambs are shafted, and the archivolt is moulded.

Of much greater importance are the sculptures of the ambo. This ambo was transported from the pieve to the cathedral, but was brought back again to its original site at the time of the restoration. It contains sculptures of the four Evangelists, of whom Matthew, Mark and Luke have books, John a scroll.[23] On another face is a superb figure of a prophet with closed eyes and far-away dreamy expression, his head resting on his left hand. The skilful treatment of the drapery and the details of the execution of the toe-nails betray an art that is no longer archaic (Plate 43, Fig. 2), but the curls of the beard and the stringy incisions of the feet recall strongly the manner of Guglielmo da Modena (compare, for example, the Enoch and Elijah of Modena, Plate 142, Fig. 2, or the prophet of Cremona, Plate 83, Fig. 8). Moreover, the diapered background shows a repetition of the same pattern as that which is used to represent water in the archivolt of the Porta della Pescheria at Modena (Plate 144, Fig. 3), in Guglielmo's relief of the ark of Noah (Plate 145, Fig. 3), and in the voyage of S. Geminiano in the archivolt of the Porta dei Principi (Plate 142, Fig. 4). The same diapering also occurs on the archivolt of the portal at Nonantola (Plate 155, Fig. 5).

The Sagra of Carpi is notable above all for its fresco decorations. In one of the clearstory windows on the southern side are remains of the original frescoing in conventional patterns. These consist of a sort of rinceau, with very thin spiral lines, painted in red on a white background, with yellow, white and red border, with wavy lines, bands of colour and triangular dots. In the apse window are remains of a frescoed rinceau with grotesques. In the apse is a fresco which evidently represented the Adoration of the Magi, two of whom are seen to the left, one to the right, of the Madonna. This

---

[23] Matthew, Mark and John have respectively the following inscriptions:

✠ LI|BER| GEN$\widehat{\text{E}}$|RA|TIO|NIS| IH$\widehat{\text{V}}$ X$\widehat{\text{I}}$ (Matth., i, 1).

VOX| CLA|MAN|TIS| IN DE|SERTO| PARA|TE V[IAM] (Marc., i, 3).

✠ IN PRINCIPIO| ERAT VERBVM| ET VERBVM ERAT| [AP]VT DE$\overline{\text{V}}$

ET $\overline{\text{DS}}$ (Joan., i, 1).

fresco is given a remarkably architectural character by the background, which represents an arcade supported on colonnettes. This same motive is used by Nicolò in his sculptured architraves of the cathedral of Piacenza (Plate 181, Fig. 1; Plate 182, Fig. 4). In the apse are also ancient graffiti. On the triumphal arch are remains of other frescos, on the southern clearstory fragments of a Slaughter of the Innocents, and on the northern clearstory portions of an Ascension. These are all part of the original decoration of the XII century. In addition, the church contains lovely examples of the pictoral art of later epochs, especially in the chapel of S. Caterina.

V. The style of the building fully confirms the documentary evidence that the pieve was erected in 1184. The sculptures of the ambo and of the western portal must be contemporary. The campanile (Plate 42, Fig. 5) is of 1221.

CARPINETI,[1] S. ANDREA DEL CASTELLO

I. The museum of Canossa contains a XVI century drawing of the castle of Carpineti, in which the church is shown. Viganò and Saccani have published the church, of which some account is also contained in the geography of Strafforello.[2]

II. Viganò states that he had seen in the Archivio Estense the original of a placito held at Carpineti by Matilda, wife of Henry V of Germany and daughter of Henry I of England, in the year 1117. In this placito figures Bonsignore, bishop of Reggio (1098-1118), who had gone to Carpineti to consecrate the church of S. Andrea.[3]

I know of no other documents which illustrate the history of the church with the exception of the inscription over the doorway: RESTAURATA ANNO 1902.

III, IV. The church has been entirely modernized. Of the Romanesque structure only the portal remains. This is very simple, but shafted and moulded. An old capital now serves for the holy-water basin. In the exterior wall are the remains of a fresco.

V. The scanty remains of this edifice are a surely dated monument of 1117.

[1] (Reggio). The church lies in the castle a half-hour's climb up the mountain from the town.

[2] Modena, 266.

[3] Viganò, 60, 207; Saccani, 56.

LOMBARD ARCHITECTURE

CASALE MONFERRATO,[1] DUOMO S. EVASIO

(Plate 43, Fig. 4, 5; Plate 44, Fig. 1, 2; Plate 45, Fig. 1, 2, 3, 4, 5, 6, 7;
Plate 46, Fig. 1, 2; Plate 47, Fig. 1, 2)

I. The ancient collegiate church of S. Evasio, at present the cathedral of Casale Monferrato, is a monument of considerable importance for the history of the Lombard style. It has, however, been but little noticed by archæologists, doubtless because of the series of unfortunate restorations which have denatured the original structure. Indeed, so thoroughly did the ancient building lose its character in the last of these reconstructions that it is necessary to have recourse to drawings made before 1860 in order to establish the ancient forms. Of such drawings the most important is an inedited plan and elevation of the façade, made for the condemnation proceedings for destroying the houses which adjoined the structure. The plan was made by Mella in 1858, and was approved and signed by Cavour on March 6, 1859, and by the Genio Civile at Casale, on September 28, 1858. These drawings, in the possession of Sig. F. Ghione at Casale, were kindly shown me by that gentleman. From them it is evident that before 1860, two large blocks of houses, one belonging to the chapter, the other to private individuals, were engaged against the façade and the narthex, so that there were visible only the main portal, the two triforia above it, the round-headed window in the gable, the top middle part of the cornice, and the two campanili. From this drawing it appears that the reconstruction followed the original lines of the edifice in the main features of the design. The principal portal was in three unmoulded orders, and surmounted by a gable as it is at present, but there was no lunette. The tympana of the triforia were pierced. On either side of the upper triforium was a statue standing, not as at present, on the capitals of the engaged columns, but on corbels. The corbel-tables of the cornice have the same curious, heavy character as now, but the drawing indicates them as being of a single order. The campaniles are shown essentially as they are at present, except that the southern one had no spire and no belfry. In the drawing only the upper arched corbel-tables of the northern campanile are shown as pointed, but this is doubtless an inaccuracy on the part of the draughtsman. The plan shows that there was authority for the design of the existing façade; at least the larger features, such as shafts and pilaster strips, were placed as at present. The campaniles each contained, as they do now, spiral stairways leading to the gallery. The plan proves that the existing western vestibule preceding the narthex is ancient and authentic.

Equally valuable are the plan (Plate 45, Fig. 7) and the details of the narthex (Plate 46, Fig. 1, 2; Plate 47, Fig. 1, 2), published by Osten.[2]

---

[1] (Alessandria).   [2] Plates II, III, IV.

Important, too, is the remark which Osten makes in his text that some of the capitals were unfinished. The drawings of Hübsch also show the edifice as it was before restoration.[3] Hübsch's drawings confirm those of Osten in all important particulars. The piers are quatrefoiled, the apse is shown with two converging ribs, the vault of the narthex is as at present, and the façade of the narthex is adorned with an intersecting Norman arcade.

Mella himself published the drawings he made of the mosaics at the time they were discovered. In these drawings are shown many details and some entire panels which have since disappeared, doubtless having been destroyed when the pavement was transported into the ambulatory. Among the lost portions are notable numerous purely ornamental motives. The little monograph of Pareto, published in 1861, contains drawings of the façade, and capitals of the interior. Aus'm Weerth described and sumptuously illustrated the mosaics. Critical studies of historical problems bearing upon the history of the edifice have been contributed by Cipolla and Savio. Almost the only archæologist who has studied the edifice is Mothes.[4]

II. In the Archivio Capitolare of Casale is a slab of lead inscribed with what purports to be a donation by Luitprando of all his rights and dominions in the city of Sedula to S. Evasio.[5] The year is illegible but the indiction is given as the thirteenth. This document offers several serious difficulties. In the first place, the story that the town of Casale was anciently called Sedula (found in several more recent chroniclers)[6] has been believed by Cipolla to be without historical foundation, and to have originated probably in a misreading of the word *senodochia*. In the second place, Luitprando was

---

[3] Plate LIII, Fig. 5; Plate LIV, Fig. 2, 3.　　[4] I, 282.

[5] ANNO AB $\overline{\text{ICARNAC}}$' DNI . NON . . . . . XI ID' XIII EGO $\overline{\text{LIPRAD}}$': $\overline{\text{GRA}}$ DI [gratia Dei] REX REGNI: ET SCE ECCL[ESI]E $\overline{\text{DEFESOR}}$ $\overline{\text{I}}$ $\overline{\text{OIB}}$ [= omnibus]: $\overline{\text{APLCE}}$ [= apostolicae] SEDIS; DO ET CONCEDO P[ER] $\overline{\text{HAC}}$ $\overline{\text{CFIRMACIOIS}}$ $\overline{\text{NRE}}$ $\overline{\text{TABVLA}}$ BEATO EVASIO QD [= quidquid] ABEO [*sic* = habeo] $\overline{\text{MO}}$ [= modo] MEO $\overline{\text{DNIO}}$ $\overline{\text{I}}$ HAC CIVITATE SEDVLE ET SVCCESSORIB; EI' $\overline{\text{I}}$ P[ER]PETV$\overline{\text{V}}$ SI$\overline{\text{C}}$ A $\overline{\text{PDECESSORIB}}$: MEIS VSQ' $\overline{\text{NC}}$ $\overline{\text{I}}$ MEA PO$\overline{\text{TESTATE}}$ ET DIC$\overline{\text{CIOE}}$ $\overline{\text{TENEO}}$ CIVITA$\overline{\text{TE}}$ $\overline{\text{CV}}$ VICLIS $\overline{\text{OIB}}$ ET $\overline{\text{TERRITORIIS}}$ EI' $\overline{\text{MOTANIS}}$ AC LITTORIB . ET $\overline{\text{PORTIB}}$. $\overline{\text{CTA}}$ TRIBVO $\overline{\text{SCO}}$ EVASIO $\overline{\text{C}}$ $\overline{\text{CVTIS}}$ HONORIB; Q [= quis] $\overline{\text{HO}}$ $\overline{\text{IFRIGERE}}$ $\overline{\text{TETAVERIT}}$ SIVE DVX . MARCHIO . SEV ALIA POT' [= potestas] SCIAT SE CPOSITVRV . C . L $\overline{\text{LIB}}$ AVRI MEDIETA$\overline{\text{TE}}$ IMP[ER]ATORIS CA$\overline{\text{MERE}}$ ET $\overline{\text{MEDIETATE}}$ ECCL[ESI]E ✠ EGO IOH[ANNE]S IVDEX SA$\overline{\text{CI}}$ PALACII $\overline{\text{HAC}}$ $\overline{\text{TABVLA}}$ SCRIPSI . F ARICO [= fuerunt Arico] [ET] NOLDEBERT COMES ET $\overline{\text{ADOIN}}$' F $\overline{\text{DS}}$ TES$\overline{\text{TES}}$

[6] *e.g.*, Fra Jacopo da Acqui, *Chronicon Imaginis Mundi*, ed. *Hist. Pat. Mon.*, V, 1475.

245

king, and not emperor. In view of these and many other considerations there can be little doubt that the leaden tablet is a forgery. This forgery, nevertheless, must have been executed before 1220, since the leaden tablet was copied in a diploma of Frederick II of that year.[7] The tablet was also copied in a necrology of the church at Casale which has been published in the *Historiae Patriae Monumenta*.[8] This necrology dates from the XII to the XV century. According to Cipolla the copy of the tablet, while found in the XVIII century copy of the necrology, of which the editors of the *Historiae Patriae Monumenta* availed themselves, was not in the original, which is now lost. However that may be, it is nevertheless certain that the leaden tablet was known to the authors of the necrology, since in another part of the same necrology occurs the following text relating to the foundation of the church of Casale by Luitprando: "August 22 . . . the discovery of the body of the most illustrious and serene king Luitprando, a most Christian man, who was buried in the city of Pavia in the church of S. Pietro in Ciel d'Oro, which he had built. Luitprando drove out Caunio, a most impious Arian, at the prayers and by the merits of S. Evasio, who appeared to him in his sleep, and ordered him to enlarge this church in his honour and to erect a wonderful structure. He endowed the church with many gifts and honours and with broad lands, and gave to it his own palace which was near it, together with all the public taxes which were derived from these possessions. The arms which he used in war he gave to the great and honourable chapter of canons, which he founded in the church, and he charged these canons in the name of the Holy Trinity that the praise of the eternal God might ever resound in that edifice, and that the memory of him, Luitprando, might live forever with the blessed. Amen. Let a procession be made about the church and the office for the dead be solemnly celebrated."[9] It is evident that the writer of this

---

[7] *Hist. Pat. Mon.,* V, 456.

[8] VI nonas Oct. . . . Memoria ut facta fuit . . . . . Ecclesia Sancti Evasii . . . . . Anno ab Incarnacione Domini . . . . . indictione XIII. Ego Liprandus gratia Dei Rex regni, et Sanctae Ecclesiae defensor in omnibus Apostolicae Sedis, do, et concedo per hanc confirmationis meae tabulam Beato Evasio quidquid nunc habeo de meo dominio in hac civitate sedule, et successoribus eius, in perpetuum, sicut a praedessoribus meis usque nunc in mea potestate, et dicione teneo . . . . . omnibus. Ita tribuo Beato Evasio cum cunctis honoribus . . . . . hoc infringere attemptaverit sive Rex, sive comes, sive potestas, sciat se compositurum centum . . . . . medietatem . . . . . Camerae, et medietatem Ecclesiae. Ego Iohannes iudex Palacii scripsi tabulam. (*Necrologium Ecclesiae Beati Evasii Casalensis,* ed. *Hist. Pat. Mon.,* V, 499).

[9] 11. kal. Sept. . . . Inventio corporis illustrissimi, et serenissimi Regis Leuprandi viri x̄pianissimi quiescentis in urbe Papiae in ecclesia Sancti Petri in coelo aureo, quam construxit, qui devicto Caunio impiissimo ariano, precibus, et meritis Beatissimi Evaxii, qui ei in somnis apparuit hanc ecclesiam in honore ipsius ampliari, et mirifice fabricari praecepit, ipsamque multis muneribus, et honoribus, atque amplissimis terris ditavit, palatiumque suum, quod ibi prope erat eidem ecclesiae cum oneribus publicis, quae illis respiciebant, donavit, et cunctis armis bellicis, quae in bello habuit, datis canonicorum

notice used the leaden tablet as a source. In still a third passage of the same
necrology we read: "February 1. Anniversary of Luitprando, most pious
king, who gave to S. Evasio the entire town of Casale, with all its dependencies,
and let a procession be made about the church as is done on the feast of All
Souls," etc.[10] Here it is absolutely clear that the authors of the necrology
knew the leaden tablet, since in the passage cited the peculiarity of the tablet
is reproduced in that the donation is said to be made to S. Evasio. Cipolla
explained this by assuming that by S. Evasio was meant the church of S. Evasio,
since he believed that the saint lived in the III century. According to the
more recent studies of Savio, however, the saint really lived in the VIII
century and was a contemporary of Luitprando. It therefore appears that
the leaden tablet was probably founded upon authentic documents of a donation
made to the church by Luitprando. The very fact that all the false documents
are attributed to Luitprando proves that the tradition of the foundation of
the church by him was strong and universally accepted in the Middle Ages.
The passages of the necrology at least prove that it was the habit of the canons
to celebrate the anniversary of Luitprando's death as that of the founder of
the church, and this custom was still observed in the XVII century.[11] A
diploma of Frederick I of 1159 refers to the church having been founded by
Luitprando.[12] Finally the tradition is said to be found in the legend of
S. Evasio, written (as Savio has shown) between 839 and 983. While
rejecting, therefore, various details of the notices of the necrology and of the
leaden tablet, we may accept as reliable the tradition that the church was
founded by Luitprando.

At what date the priests officiating in the church were regularly organized
into a chapter, it is difficult to say. In a donation of 947[13] occurs the phrase,
canonicorum caetum . . . seruentium beatissimi evasii, which seems to imply
that the chapter was already formed, and from the signatures we learn that
it contained eighteen members. In another donation of 988,[14] it is stated that
the canonica of S. Evasio was a pieve situated in the town of Casale. On the
other hand, it has been plausibly argued by Savio that the chapter was not
founded until the XI century on the ground that, in the bull of Innocent III

---

collegio, quod ibi magnum, et honorabile constituit, ipsa eis dato pretio comparavit,
ipsosque sub nomine S. Trinitatis rogavit, ut laus Dei aeterni nunquam ibi cessaret, et
memoria eius in saeculum viveret cum Beatis. Amen. Fiet processio circa ecclesiam,
et solempniter celebrabitur officium mortuorum. (*Necrologium Ecclesiae Beati Evasii
Casalensis*, ed. *Hist. Pat. Mon.*, V, 491).

[10] G. kal. Febr. Anniversarium Liutprandi piissimi Regis, qui dedit Beato Evasio
totum locum Casalis cum omnibus pertinentiis suis: et fiet processio circa ecclesiam,
sicut fit in festivitate omnium mortuorum, cantando *Libera me, Domine, de morte
aeterna*, et alia spectantia ad honorem et laudem omnium defunctorum. (*Necrologium
Ecclesiae Beati Evasii Casalensis*, apud *Hist. Pat. Mon.*, V, 456).

[11] Tatti, I, 749.   [12] *Hist. Pat. Mon.*, V, 456.
[13] Published by Gabotto e Fisso, II, 227.   [14] *Ibid.*, 228.

of 1212, there are enumerated the various popes who had confirmed the goods of the chapter, and the first of these is Pascal II (1099-1118). Savio therefore concludes that the chapter did not exist very much before this time. I have had the good fortune to have in my hands a copy of the inedited bull of Pascal II, which dates from April 21, 1115,[15] and which certainly gives the impression of having been promulgated because of the foundation of a chapter regular. From the texts of 947 and 988, however, it is evident that there was a large body of priests officiating in the church from an early date, and that these priests were called canons. It is probable, in consequence, that at the end of the XI century the chapter was merely reformed. It is hence not impossible that a chapter may have existed as early as the VIII century, and that the passage in the necrology is, after all, in this particular accurate.

The church built by Luitprando was replaced by a new structure consecrated in 1107. This is evident from a passage in a fragment of the martyrology: "January 4. On this day was celebrated the consecration of the church of S. Evasio by the pope Pascal II with several bishops in the year of the Incarnation of our Lord, 1106 (*i.e.*, 1107)."[16] Subsequently the cloister was built by Frederick I. This fact is recorded in a passage of the necrology: "June 11, in the year of our Lord 1190. Frederick of happy memory, formerly emperor of the Romans, having gone abroad to defend the land of Christ's nativity, died. Among other benefits which he bestowed upon this church, he erected the cloister at his own expense."[17] It is probable that this generosity on the part of Frederick was prompted by the act of vengeance of the Alexandrians, who in 1175 attacked Casale and burned the buildings of the canonica.[18]

Numerous documents of the XII, XIII and XIV centuries, for the most part published by Gabotto e Fisso,[19] relate to the history of the chapter rather

---

[15] *Codice della Croce*, MS. Amb., D. S. IV, Vol. V, f. 89.

[16] Ianvarii D. II. nonas Ian. Eodem die consecratio ecclesiae Beati Evasii celebrata a domino Paschale secundo Summo Pontifice cum pluribus Episcopis anno ab Incarnatione Domini nostri Ihū Xp̄ī MC. VI. (Fragmentum *Martyrologii Ecclesiae Beati Evasii Casalensis*, ed. *Hist. Pat. Mon.*, V, 445).

[17] III idus Iunii. Anno Domini MCLXXXX. Fredericus felicis memoriae quondam Romanorum Imperator peregre profectus pro defendenda Dominicae Nativitatis terra, migravit ad Dominum, qui inter multa beneficia, quae huic ecclesiae contulit claustrum suis expensis fecit. (*Necrologium Beati Evasii Casalensis*, ed. *Hist. Pat. Mon.*, V, 475).

[18] Ex hoc repentino Imperatoris discessu Alexandrini animum et spiritus sumpserunt, confestimque, ne per otium torperent, et dissolverentur, simulque ut aliquando injurias, quas insignes acceperant a Gullielmo Marchione Montisferrati, foenerato ei talione referrent, pridie kal. septem. conflato magno, validoque exercitu, Casale S. Evasii adorti sunt tanto impetu, ut illud per vim captum foedissime diripuerint, succensis Canonicorum aedibus, et oppidi magna parte. (G. Schiavinae, *Annales Alexandrini*, ed. *Hist. Pat. Mon.*, XI, 29).

[19] II, 230, 28, 104, 207, 208, 217, 220, 221, etc.

than to that of the architecture of the church. In 1266 the process of hiding the exterior walls of the edifice by the addition of various extraneous structures was begun. In the XIV century there was much dispute between the commune and the ecclesiastical authorities in regard to the superstans, who administered the *laborerium* or *fabbrica* of the church, both parties claiming the right to appoint this official. Before 1348 the chapel of S. Michele was endowed by one of the canons,[20] and on October 7, 1403, the bodies of several saints were translated into the church, probably after a restoration.[21] A curious feature of the internal discipline at this epoch was the presence of many female *conversae*. According to Pareto, the campanile was struck by lightning in 1544 or 1635. In 1720 a thorough baroccoization of the edifice was carried out which, according to Pareto, "masked, covered or destroyed all the monumental architecture of the interior of the church, and spared only the narthex." In the XIX century it was proposed to destroy the church and replace it by a modern structure. Canina pleaded that instead the old edifice be preserved, and after an unsuccessful attempt at restoration had been made, the task was confided to Conte Edoardo Mella. Under his direction the edifice was practically rebuilt in 1860-1861.[22] There is no doubt that the archæologist completely destroyed the artistic value of the monument. The extent of the damage wrought by him is, however, generally over-estimated. His restoration was hardly worse than those which are still being carried out in all mediæval edifices throughout the length and breadth of Italy. It consisted in replacing the old building by a modern copy. His copy, like those of the present-day restorers, is far from having the value of the original from any point of view, and undoubtedly, in his reconstruction, he made many errors and mistakes. A careful comparison of the old drawings with the existing edifice, however, serves to show that the main lines of the original building were generally preserved.

III. The edifice at present consists of a nave (Plate 45, Fig. 3) six bays long, double side aisles (Plate 45, Fig. 4), a complete set of chapels, a choir of a single bay, an apse, an ambulatory, and an extended narthex. Such, however, were not the original dispositions. In the first half of the XII century, the building probably consisted of a nave six bays long, double side aisles, projecting transepts, a central cupola surmounted by a tower, a choir

---

[20] XVI. kal. Oct. . . . Obiit MCCCXLVIII presbiter Iohannes de Maria, qui dotavit, et ordinavit capellam Sancti Michaelis in ista ecclesia. . . . (*Necrologium Ecclesiae Beati Evasii Casalensis*, ed. *Hist. Pat. Mon.*, V, 495).

[21] nonis Oct. MCCCCIII. Die ista, translatio corporum SS. Evaxii, Natalis, et Proiecti facta est die VII octobris per illustrissimum dominum Facinum de Canibus et egregium virum dominum Castelinum . . . . . ducta fuerunt dicta corpora in ecclesia Beati Evaxii. (*Necrologium Ecclesiae Beati Evasii Casalensis*, ed. *Hist. Pat. Mon.*, V, 500).

[22] Inscriptions in mosaic pavement and in narthex.

two bays long flanked by side aisles, three apses (the central one preceded by a rectangular bay), and a campanile with axis at about 45 degrees to that of the church, tangent to the southern absidiole. The narthex was subsequently added. At present the five aisles of the interior and the chapel are of four different heights, the edifice having thus a pyramidal section. Bits of the old cornices still in place under the roofs indicate that the section has always had this character. The old arched corbel-tables of the nave, which are still extant, show that the nave was originally lower than it is now, since these corbel-tables are hardly higher than the cornices of the inner side aisles. It is evident, therefore, that the nave did not have a high clearstory.

The fourth bay of the nave—counting from the west—is covered by an octagonal cloistered vault, with ribs and drum, and carried on arched squinches (Plate 45, Fig. 3). The upper part of the existing cupola (Plate 45, Fig. 1) is obviously modern, but the gallery appears to be ancient. It is therefore probable that the original edifice had a cloistered vault on squinches over the crossing.

At present the choir is covered by a barrel vault, the apses by a half dome, the remainder of the church by rib vaults, which are only slightly domed and distinctly oblong in plan (Plate 45, Fig. 3). Originally, however, the edifice was not entirely vaulted. From an examination of the masonry it is obvious that the existing vaults are modern, and the disposition of the transepts, taken in consideration with the levels of the cornices, justifies the inference that anciently the nave and transept were roofed with wood. The old plans show (Plate 45, Fig. 7) that the half dome of the apse had originally two ribs. On the other hand the vaults of the narthex (Plate 43, Fig. 5) are original, and of an amazing type, which is found elsewhere, so far as I know, only in the mosque of Cordoba (Plate 43, Fig. 6). This narthex consists of a nave of two bays, and two side aisles with chapels surmounted by galleries (Plate 43, Fig. 5; Plate 46, Fig. 1, 2; Plate 47, Fig. 2). The nave is spanned by two great ribs without intermediate supports, crossing it in a longitudinal direction, and by another similar one rising from a lower level, and crossing it transversely. These arches are surmounted by walls which divide the vaulting space into nine rectangular compartments covered with barrel, groin or rib vaults. The restorers have done little damage to this vault, which is still the original one, and in excellent preservation.

There can be no doubt that the transepts originally projected beyond the outer aisles, and that anciently there were no nave chapels. The transepts were hardly wider than a normal bay of the nave (Plate 45, Fig. 7), and they were separated from the crossing by a heavy transverse wall with a square window. It is entirely doubtful whether the transept arches originally were higher than they are at present. The wall with bifora in either transept, surmounting the arch which separates the inner and outer side aisles, is modern, although constructed of old materials. The transepts, although they were not vaulted, were supplied with internal pilaster strips. The end of the upper part of the north transept which evidently extended to the line of the present chapels, but which has been walled off from the church, is still extant. The southern transept is also preserved.

The two piers of the narthex have each a different section (Plate 46, Fig. 1). The northern consists of four semi-columns engaged on a rectangular core, the southern has the section of a Greek cross. The piers of the interior have been entirely denatured. Osten's plan (Plate 45, Fig. 7) shows them as having the section of a Greek cross, but it is entirely probable that they were altered beyond recognition in the barocco period.

The clearstory of the nave is at present lighted by skylights pierced in the lean-to roofs of the aisles, so that the roof of the entire edifice has a continuous slope. Nothing survives of the original clearstory of the nave but a few thin pilaster strips and some bits of wall, but it is evident that the roof anciently did not have a continuous slope. The walls of the inner and outer side aisles are also ancient.

The upper part of the campanile is of the Gothic or Renaissance period, but the lower two stories are Lombard. The construction has been much confused by the circumstance that the church has been extended underneath this tower. The façade is flanked by two towers. Of both of these the lower part is modern, and the belfry of the southern is entirely, and that of the northern in great part, new. The original forms are, however, shown in Mella's drawing. The southern end of the narthex (Plate 48, Fig. 4) is ancient, as is also the clearstory gable of the narthex on the north side.

The narthex resembles a western transept in that its nave was broader than that of the church (Plate 45, Fig. 7). This narthex is supplied with a clearstory, consisting of bifora in four unmoulded orders (Plate 48, Fig. 4). The narthex evidently possessed side aisles and chapels as at present. The existing roof cuts across the round-headed windows under the biforum of the clearstory of the south side (Plate 48, Fig. 4). This roof, consequently, must originally have had a lower slope. On the north side a similar biforum has entirely disappeared under the roof. Numerous bits of the old construction and old capitals still in place make it evident that the gallery of the narthex, with its bifora, must have existed originally.

It is evident that the narthex is later than the church. This is proved by the fact that under the roof of the church may still be seen some of the original carved decoration of the old façade, cut across and in part buried by the new narthex.

Some traces of the cloister survive, but are not older than the XVI century.

The masonry of the campanile is much rougher than that of the church. The bricks are of regular size and laid in horizontal courses, but the mortar-beds are very wide. The masonry of the church proper is polychromatic and of excellent quality. Herring-bone work occurs as well as vertical courses.

The bricks show great variation in width, and the mortar-beds are wider than those of the narthex. The masonry of the narthex is also polychromatic (Plate 43, Fig. 4). The ashlar parts are formed of very finely squared blocks, laid with exceedingly fine joints. The courses are perfectly horizontal, though occasionally interrupted. The bricks are large and cross-hatched, and the mortar-beds are not excessively wide. There are numerous scaffolding holes. The masonry of the northern tower of the façade is even better than that of the narthex.

IV. The capitals of the church itself have been entirely remade. In the gallery of the narthex are numerous fragments of ancient architecture, including several capitals of broad-leaved type, but these seem to have come from the narthex rather than from the church. The capitals of the narthex are for the most part of Corinthianesque type, with carved or uncarved acanthus leaves. A great many of them were left unfinished by the Romanesque builders, and the process of execution may be traced by comparing the different capitals in various stages of completion. The classical character of the ornamentation is extraordinary. So admirable is the imitation, that in some instances it is difficult to determine whether the capitals may not be really Roman. It is evident that many of them have been much damaged, probably from having been chipped and covered with stucco in the Renaissance period. It is not altogether easy to distinguish the original capitals from those replaced in the restoration. It is evident, however, that all those which are unfinished are ancient. In the gallery are preserved many more of the original capitals, for the most part of the uncarved Corinthian type, and very classic in character, although there are some grotesques (Plate 44, Fig. 1, 2). The ancient capitals are here to be more easily distinguished from the hard and mechanical modern reproductions. In some cases the abaci have the section of their load. The fact that certain of the Corinthian capitals have carved leaves leads to the suspicion that it was the intention of the builders to carve all the leaves, and that those which are at present broad are merely unfinished. In the north gallery there is still in place a bulbous and perfectly crocketed capital.

The bases are for the most part Attic with griffes (Plate 44, Fig. 1, 2). The side-aisle walls of the narthex have a series of bifora (Plate 43, Fig. 4). The piers separating these bifora have an engaged colonnette on the outer face, a feature which recalls S. Michele of Pieve Pelago. The smaller windows have arcuated lintels in two orders, unmoulded, or with a simple roll-moulding. The inner order is adorned in some instances with interlaces. The outer or grouping archivolt is finely moulded and adorned with leaf patterns. The cornice has very classic heart-leaf and bead-mouldings. On the southern side of the narthex, however, the cornice is adorned with anthemia.

The southern tower of the façade has simple arched corbel-tables, the northern has double arched corbel-tables. There are inlaid plaques on both the north and south façades of the narthex. The windows of the north transept have fine continuous mouldings. One has the extraordinary form of a sort of double trefoil. The south transept has round windows surmounted by square mouldings, two windows in the form of a quatrefoil, and an oculus. All these are finely moulded, and in some instances there is an ornament of heart leaves. The cornice of numerous fine mouldings of the northern transept seems to be modern.

The two lower stories of the eastern campanile are adorned with simple arched corbel-tables.

Among the ancient fragments preserved in the gallery of the narthex are the bases of two shafts upon which are engaged reliefs of lions, a feature which recalls Cemmo (Plate 51, Fig. 2). There are extant numerous of the ancient corbels, as well as the consoles of the narthex, on which are carried some of the ribs of the vaults.

On a capital of the northern gallery of the narthex is depicted a figure in armour on horse-back, carrying a mace. This is possibly intended for Luitprando, the founder of the church. On the façade, before 1860, there were statues of a king and a queen, doubtless Luitprando and his wife. These, it is true, have been replaced by modern copies, and the originals, which are still preserved in a shed back of the church, are not older than the XV century. A statue of the XII century preserved in the gallery represents a bare-headed man carrying a sceptre. This is probably also Luitprando, but it is impossible to know where it was originally placed. It is unfortunately much mutilated, but appears to be a late work of the school of Pavia.

The fragments of the mosaic pavement now disposed in the ambulatory, form the great glory of the cathedral of Casale (Plate 43, Fig. 1; Plate 45, Fig. 2, 5, 6). With the help of Mella's drawings, made before the pavement had been transported, it is possible to determine the subjects of several of the panels.

One of the most important represents the victory of Abraham over the four kings, according to Genesis, xiv, 9, 14-17 (Plate 45, Fig. 2). In the centre of the field is seen Abraham, ABRAA[M], clothed as a mediæval knight in helmet and armour, holding a shield in his left hand and a lance in his right. He is accompanied by two other unnamed knights, similarly clothed. With his lance he transfixes RE[X]| CHO|HORLAHO|MOR, also in armour and crowned. The vanquished king of Elam falls from his horse, which is represented as galloping away in full flight from Abraham. The two knights behind Abraham transfix with their lances the fallen kings T͡HADAL and

ARA͡|PHEL, who lie dead on the ground, though still wearing their crowns. The fourth king, [A]RI|[O]CH, also lies dead.

Equally important, but unfortunately not so well preserved, is the panel representing a scene from the Maccabees (Plate 45, Fig. 6). The middle part of this mosaic was destroyed when it was transported, and is preserved only in the drawing of Mella. To the left is seen the altar of the temple at Jerusalem and a curious piece of architecture which evidently represents the portico of the temple. In this gate are hung up the severed head and arm of Nicanor, both spouting blood—CAPVT| NICA|NO|RIS. In Mella's drawing we see that in the central part of the mosaic which is now missing, there was a man standing in front of the group of warriors still extant in the right-hand fragment. This man had a pointed shield with horizontal stripes, and could only have been Judas Maccabæus. Mella, therefore, must entirely have misunderstood the inscription which he transcribed IC|N|C|DE|I.[23] In the right-hand fragment are the figures of knights on foot, in armour, with long pointed shields. The first carries a lance. This is evidently the army of the Israelites, and Mella's drawing shows that in his time eleven distinct figures could be distinguished. The scene represented is evidently not that of 1 Mach., vii, 46-50, but rather that of 2 Mach., xv, 30-34. The head and hand are hung not in the gate of the city, but before the temple, which is indicated by the altar and ciborio to the left.

Another fragment of the pavement which has now entirely disappeared represents another scene from the Maccabees. According to 1 Mach., vi, 43 f., Eleazar killed in battle the elephant on which the king Antiochus was riding, and thus put to flight the Syrian army, but the elephant fell upon Eleazar and killed him. The lost panel showed the lower parts of horses mounted by men, doubtless warriors in the battle. In the centre was an elephant, and the figure of Eleazar—ELEAZAR.

Another fine panel shows the story of Jonah (Plate 45, Fig. 5). In a boat are shown three sailors. One is engaged in throwing overboard Jonah, IONAS, whom the whale approaches to swallow. Several other fish are seen swimming in the water. In Mella's drawing there are visible two wind genii who puff the sail, one at either end of the boat. Only one of these is now extant in the mosaic.

Another panel shows the beast with seven heads—SEPTEM C[A]P[I]T[A]—of Apocalypsis, xii, 3. Another figure—possibly also inspired by the Apocalypse—shows a monster with a woman's head, crowned and grinning, the body of a leopard covered with spots, the wings of a bird, and a tail like a leopard's, but with branches.

A peculiarly interesting panel shows a grotesque figure holding bow and arrow. There is no head, but the features of the face are placed upon the chest. Above is the inscription: ACEFALVS. Pliny tells us that there existed a race of men without a head, having eyes in their shoulders.[24] Isidore

---

[23] The two C's were perhaps ornaments; the N a V; the EI an AS.

[24] Idem hominum genus, qui Monocoli vocarentur, singulis cruribus, mirae pernicitatis ad saltum; eosdem Sciapodas vocari, quod in maiore aestu humi iacentes resupini umbra se pedum protegant. non longe eos a Trogodytis abesse, rursusque ab his

of Seville took over the ancient conception, called the headless men *acephali* and branded them as heretics.[25] Equally interesting is another which shows the antipodes—ANTIPODES. Antiquity was vastly interested in a fabulous race of beings who were supposed to live on the under side of the world, and walk about with their feet uppermost. The artist of Casale seems to have confused these people with the *sciapodes* who, according to Pliny in the passage just cited, were accustomed to raise their foot as a sunshade in the heat of summer, lying flat on the ground to facilitate the operation. In the mosaic we see a man holding in the air his right leg, the foot of which is enormous.

Another panel shows a man bare-headed, with short skirt and cane, carrying over his left shoulder a pole, from which is suspended on the forward end, a net, such as is still used for fishing in the Po, and at the rear end a fish, evidently intended to be of extraordinary size, since the inscription, in good Italian, tells us that it is as big as the castle of S. Evasio—QVALE| LARCA| DE SAN| VA. . . . . . Another panel shows a duel between two champions with broadswords and long shields (Plate 43, Fig. 1). It is very similar to the scene represented in the pavement of S. Maria Maggiore of Vercelli (Plate 215, Fig. 4). In Mella's drawing is shown a fragment of an inscription which no longer exists:

. . . . . TO
. . . . . SG
. . . . . A . . . . .
. . . . . NA

The fact that there was an inscription makes it probable that we have here represented some definite and particular combat, rather than one of the general scenes of duel often depicted on capitals. I confess, however, that on the basis of the few letters preserved by Mella (and which it is probable are incorrectly transcribed), I am unable to conjecture who the characters represented may be.

A panel now entirely lost, but a drawing of which has been preserved by Mella, shows apparently a bear-baiting. The two animals stand on their hind legs and hug each other. A man pricks the side of one with a spear. The inscription as copied by Mella is unintelligible:

AD . . . . . ANIS OCCVP
N . . . . . IDR PERCVTI

occidentem versus quosdam sine cervice oculos in umeris habentes. (Pliny, *Nat. Hist.*, VII, 2, § 24).

25 Acephali dicti, id est, *sine capite;* nullus eorum reperitur auctor, a quo exorti sint. Hi trium Chalcedonensium capitulorum impugnatores, duarum in Christo substantiarum proprietatem negant, et unam in ejus persona naturam prædicant. (Isidore of Seville, *Etymologiarum*, VIII, 5, ed. Migne, *Pat. Lat.*, LXXXII, 304).

Another panel of similar character still extant, shows a man who seems to be wrestling with a bear.

Still another panel, in which a man and a grotesque animal are indistinctly shown in the drawings of Mella, has entirely disappeared. Another panel shows a man who turns to look back at a great bird with long legs, long neck and long bill that marches after him and puts its claws on his ankle. The drawings of Mella show that the man carries a spear in his hand. A destroyed panel preserved in the drawings of Mella shows two grotesque griffins standing back to back in a diamond.

Technically these mosaics are perhaps the finest extant in Lombardy, with the exception of those of Bobbio. There is expression in the faces, and the artist evidently possessed considerable rough humour and power of caricature. As illustrations the compositions are excellent, and the artist also shows that he was endowed with feeling for the beauty of line and the balance of spacing. The conventional ornament is very classic in character and excellent in execution. Notable is the sparing use of grotesques, which figure so prominently in the mosaic of S. Savino of Piacenza, S. Michele of Pavia, and the cathedral of Cremona. The colours, black, white and red, are soft and dainty. Movement is capitally expressed, especially in the scene of the duel (Plate 43, Fig. 1). The artist is able to foreshorten the arm of the knight in the scene of the Maccabees, but his anatomy is weak and his horses are especially poor (Plate 45, Fig. 2).

V. The mosaic is decidedly more advanced in style than that of S. Savino at Piacenza (1107), or that of S. Michele at Pavia (c. 1100). On the other hand, it is less advanced than that of S. Maria Maggiore at Vercelli (1148). Compare, for example, the two scenes of the duel (Plate 43, Fig. 1; Plate 215, Fig. 4). At Vercelli the faces are drawn much better, the ornament is more carefully executed, and the individual pieces of stone are smaller. The two compositions are, however, amazingly similar. The mosaic of Casale therefore falls between that of S. Savino at Piacenza (1107) and that of S. Maria Maggiore at Vercelli (1148), but approaches much more closely the latter. It may consequently be ascribed to c. 1140. The slight remains of the nave of Casale still extant leave no doubt that they belong to the edifice of 1107. The combination of polychromatic and herring-bone masonry found in the transepts could only have originated at about this time. The campanile, evidently somewhat earlier, may be ascribed to c. 1090. The narthex shows points of contact with S. Maria Maggiore of Vercelli (1148) in its carved ornament, and with S. Bernardo, of the same city (Plate 215, Fig. 1)—1164, in certain of its capitals of the uncarved Corinthian type. The analogies to S. Maria Maggiore are, however, much closer, and the narthex may consequently be ascribed to c. 1150.

CASALINO, SS. PIETRO E PAOLO

CASALINO,[1] SS. PIETRO E PAOLO

(Plate 48, Fig. 1, 5)

I. The monument has never been published.

II. An inscription in the church records a restoration carried out in the year 1753. At this epoch the eastern chapels of the side aisles (Plate 48, Fig. 1) were remade, the edifice was baroccoized (Plate 48, Fig. 5) and other unfortunate changes executed.

Our monument was originally the parish church of Casalino. In more recent times it served as a cholera hospital, and now is a simple chapel.

III, IV. The edifice at present consists of a nave three bays long (it was originally four bays long, but the eastern bays have been walled off—Plate 48, Fig. 5), a choir, an apse and a southern absidiole. The northern absidiole—which doubtless originally existed—has been destroyed. The nave and the side aisles are now covered with a modern wooden ceiling, but the barrel vault of the choir (Plate 48, Fig. 5) is probably original. The piers are rectangular or sometimes (in the northern arcade) with rounded ends. They are without capitals or bases (Plate 48, Fig. 5).

A peculiarity of the church is the sharp deflection of the choir to the north.

The masonry consists of bricks without cross-hatching, of small and irregular sizes, laid in very thick beds of mortar. Herring-bone work predominates. The interior is without ornament (Plate 48, Fig. 5). The archivolts are in a single unmoulded order. The apses are ornamented externally (Plate 48, Fig. 1) with cornices of arched corbel-tables, with pilaster strips only at the extremities. The clearstory appears to have had a similar cornice. The façade and side-aisle walls, on the other hand, had arched corbel-tables, broken up into groups of three, five or seven, by pilaster strips.

The edifice contains fine frescos of the XV century.

V. The masonry (Plate 48, Fig. 1) is analogous in character to that of those portions of S. Sepolcro at Milan which date from 1030 (Plate 133, Fig. 2, 6). The arched corbel-tables, however, are more advanced than those of S. Sepolcro, in that they are not grouped two and two, but in larger numbers. The edifice, therefore, can hardly be earlier than 1040, since at this date arched corbel-tables of this more advanced type first came into use at Sannazzaro Sesia (Plate 201, Fig. 1), Piona (Plate 188, Fig. 4), S. Pietro di Civate (Plate 56, Fig. 1), etc. On the other hand, the primitive character of the masonry makes it impossible to assign the edifice to a later time. The building may consequently be ascribed to c. 1040.

[1] (Novara).

LOMBARD ARCHITECTURE

CASCINA S. TRINITÀ,[1] LA TRINITÀ

(Plate 50, Fig. 2)

I. Prigione published rather inexact drawings of the church without text. A photograph of the apse has been reproduced by Venturi.[2]

II. The edifice was baroccoized in the year 1731, as is recorded in an inscription in the choir:

TRIADI
ÆDEM HANC SACRAM
VETVSTATE COLLABENTEM
D. THOMAS MARCHIO CHILINVS
SARDINIÆ REGIS
NOBILIS A CVBICVLO
INSTAVRANDAM ET EXORNANDAM
CVRAVIT
ANNO SAL. M.D.C.C.XXXI.

III. The church at present consists of a nave three bays long, two side aisles, a choir of two bays, and an apse (Plate 50, Fig. 2). It is evident, however, that originally the western bay of the nave was flanked by side aisles and that there were two absidioles. At present the church is entirely vaulted, but the vaults, with the exception of the barrel vault in the eastern bay of the choir, are of the Renaissance. The interior has been so covered with intonaco that it is difficult to make out the original dispositions. It is clear at least that the western bay of the choir was covered either with a groin, or a rib vault. The system on the northern side at the juncture with the barrel vault of the eastern bay, still survives, and has a section consisting of a central circular member flanked by two oblique rectangular members. The eastern diagonal has no capital. The western piers of this same bay are compound, and include semicircular and rectangular members, set diagonally and square. The nave probably had originally no system. The piers now have a section which consists of two semi-columns and two rectangular pilaster strips, but it is impossible to say how much of this is old. At least the capitals of the shaft must be ancient, but there may have been no system. It is similarly impossible to determine now whether there were any side-aisle responds.

Prigione apparently found traces of the old transepts, but none are now visible. The upper part of the walls and the clearstory were remade in 1731. Only in the lower part of the façade and in the apse is the ancient masonry

[1] Frazione of Castelazzo Bormida (Alessandria), which is distant about two kilometres.
[2] III, 5.

preserved. It is evident that this (Plate 50, Fig. 2) consisted of bricks of very variable size (many are extremely narrow like Roman bricks), well laid in horizonal courses, in which are introduced at intervals polychromatic bands of herring-bone pebbles or ashlar. The bricks are not cross-hatched; the mortar-beds are broad; but the masonry, especially the ashlar work, is of superb quality. The windows of the apse are in three unmoulded orders (Plate 50, Fig. 2), and were not glazed. The central window had a circular sill (Plate 50, Fig. 2).

IV. The capitals are of unique type. The abacus is either omitted altogether, or is reduced to a very slight moulding. The necking, on the other hand, is excessively heavy, and comprises many different ornaments—always a dentil (a motive characteristic of the church and found also in the façade and apse—Plate 50, Fig. 2), which is often double; one or two rope-mouldings; sometimes an interlace, and various unornamented mouldings. The capitals themselves are very high in proportion to their diameter. They are carved with interlaces, acanthus leaves arranged in stiff rows, sirens, grotesque animals, etc. Several are of Corinthianesque type, with queer leaves. The shafts of the apse have capitals carved for the most part with unfoliated acanthus leaves (Plate 50, Fig. 2). The two capitals of the western respond of the nave are cubic, and very high in proportion to their width.

In the nave no bases are visible. The two shafts of the façade rest on corbels, and have bases of a most elaborate profile in which figure two rope-mouldings and numerous smaller members. The archivolts are in two unmoulded orders.

V. A certain coarseness in the execution of the grotesques of the capitals recalls the capitals of S. Giorgio of Milan (Plate 128, Fig. 5), a surely dated monument of 1129. The design of others recalls the capitals of Montefiascone (Plate 152, Fig. 2), a building of c. 1130. The church of Cascina S. Trinità may therefore be ascribed to c. 1130.

CASORSO,[1] MADONNA DELLE GRAZIE

I. The Madonna delle Grazie has never been published.

II. The Romanesque church of the Madonna delle Grazie is preceded by a pompous Renaissance vestibule, known as S. Giorgio, which has given its name to the whole sanctuary. In the west wall of the church of the Madonna proper is this inscription:

[1] (Alessandria).

LOMBARD ARCHITECTURE

D. O. M.
MATTHAEVS . CISALBERTVS . EX . DOMINIS . MOMBARVTII
MONTISCALVI . PLEBANVS .
ANNO . MCDVI . VERCELLENSIS . RENVNCIATVR . EPISCOPVS .
QVINQVENNIO . POST . V . IDVS . JVLII .
HANC . AEDEM . D . GEORGIO . NVNCVPATAM .
QVAE . MODO . S. MARIAE . GRATIARVM . SIBI . NOMEN . ADSCIVIT .
SACRO . INVNGIT . CHRYSMATE

The date MCDVI is obviously written by error for MDCVI. When the church of S. Giorgio was erected it is probable that the interior of the sanctuary of the Madonna was also baroccoized.

III. Externally the southern wall and apse of the Romanesque chapel are still well preserved, although the interior has quite lost its character. It is evident that the original structure was of a single aisle and roofed in wood. The masonry is ashlar of the finest quality. The widely splayed windows were intended to serve without glass. Those of the apse are in six orders and moulded.

IV. The apse and the side wall are adorned with cornices of double arched corbel-tables. Those of the apse are supported on shafts, those of the side wall on a very thin pilaster strip placed on axis. The apse cornice has saw-tooth mouldings.

V. From the style of the masonry, analogous to that of the cloisters of Voltorre (c. 1180-c. 1195), it is evident that the Madonna delle Grazie dates from c. 1180.

CASTELL'ALFERO,[1] MADONNA DELLA NEVE

I. The edifice has been illustrated by Venturi.[2]

II. In the interior of the apse is the following inscription:

TEMPLUM HOC B. V. M. DICATUM
PIORUM ELEHEMOSINIS A GUBERNIO AQUISIT[UM]
ANNO MDCCCLXVIII
RESTAURATUM FUIT ANNO MDCCCLXX

III. The edifice consists of a nave of a single aisle and an apse. The south-eastern campanile rises over a heavy, square buttress, and is awkwardly supported, partly on squinches, partly by corbels. This campanile is

---

[1] (Alessandria). The Madonna della Neve stands in the vineyards a half-hour's walk from the town on a carriage—but not an automobile—road.
[2] III, 11.

cylindrical. The barrel-vaulted nave is entirely modern. Only the apse and campanile are of interest.

The masonry is polychromatic and of good quality. The mortar-joints are of moderate thickness. The bricks are cross-hatched. On the north-eastern angle, symmetrical with the campanile, is a heavy buttress.

IV. The arched corbel-tables of the apse are supported on shafts. The campanile also has shafts, but the cornice of arched corbel-tables was never erected, since this part of the structure was left unfinished. The capitals are adorned with uncarved or perforated leaves.

The windows in several orders, shafted and moulded, were intended to serve without glass. Certain of the abaci of the shafts are circular.

V. The masonry is very analogous to that of the eastern bays of S. Zeno at Verona (Plate 224, Fig. 1) which date from c. 1150-c. 1160. Castell'Alfero may consequently be ascribed to c. 1155.

CASTELL'ARQUATO,[1] L'ASSUNZIONE

(Plate 48, Fig. 2, 8, 4; Plate 49)

I. The primary source for the history of Castell'Arquato are the rich— and as yet largely unexplored—archives of the church itself. In these are contained, not only numerous original parchments, but two valuable manuscript histories of Castell'Arquato, of which the first, written by Don Giovanni Antonio Morandi, and entitled *Antichità di Castell'Arquato,* seems to have been composed about the end of the XVII century, and the other, by the canonico Giuseppe Curati, entitled *Annali Ecclestici e secolari della terra di Castell'Arquato,* appears to be slightly earlier. Archæologically, the church is practically unexplored. The pamphlet by Zancani contains a reproduction in half-tone of the sculptures, and an accurate transcription of the inscriptions, but does not enter into a discussion of the architecture of the church. Venturi[2] dismisses the sculptures—masterpieces of XII century art—with the remark *quanto mai grossolane!* A photograph of the cloister has been published by Faccioli.[3]

II. According to Campi, the church of Castell'Arquato was built perhaps on the site of a pre-existing church, and endowed by a certain noble, Magno, in 758.[4] In support of this statement Campi cites a document in the archives

---

[1] (Piacenza).   [2] III, 140.   [3] 118.

[4] E nel Piacentino fece pure in tal tempo edificare, ò più tosto riedificare, & aggrandire vn nobile, e potente Signore de' nostri [*sic*], nomato Magno, forse in forma più bella, che dianzi non era, il luogo, ò Terra, che Castello Quadrato, od Alquadro appelauasi (hoggi Castell'Arquato, e prima del nascimento del Saluatore, Castel Torquato da C. Torquato, nobilissimo Cauaglier Romano, secondo che altroue accennai) e quiui

of the pieve. This document, however, is no longer in existence there, and it is evident that it had disappeared at least as early as the XVII century, for Morandi and Curati both cite the notice of Campi, and show that they have been unable to find the original document. Poggiali[5] also gives this notice merely on the authority of Campi.

Campi goes on to relate that in 772 Magno donated the church which he had built at Castell'Arquato to Desiderio, bishop of Piacenza, upon the condition, however, that this gift should become valid only upon his (Magno's) death.[6] Again the original in the archives of Castell'Arquato has disappeared.

Under the year 789, Campi proceeds to relate that Magno died, and, since he left no sons, the donation which he had made to the bishop Desiderio was consummated. The church of Castell'Arquato accordingly passed to the see of Piacenza, on the condition, however, that the bishop pay annually to the basilica of S. Maria of Castell'Arquato, in the fall, a certain quantity of wine, on Good Friday a certain amount of oil, and on Holy Saturday wine for sprinkling the altars, and for washing the pictures and the crosses, and in addition supply the ropes for the bells and a certain quantity of salt.[7] For a third time, the original document has disappeared, and we have only Campi's paraphrase. Confirmation of this last document, however, has been found in the archives at Castell'Arquato by Curati, who has discovered documents which prove that the payments agreed upon in 789 were continued throughout the Middle Ages.

A document of 1059, cited by Campi,[8] shows that in the XI century the

eresse ancora vna Chiesa in honore della gran Madre di Dio, la quale di molte beni dotò. In margin: *Tabulæ antiq. in Arch. Eccl. ma. Castri Arquati.* and the date *758.* (Campi, I, 193).

[5] II, 291.

[6] A cui [Stefano III] uscito di vita nel settantadue diedero per successore Adriano; sotto del quale fece donatione il pijssimo Magno nostro (ricordato di sopra) al Vescouo Desiderio non solamente della sudetta Chiesa di S. Maria da lui eretta nel luogo di Castel Quadrato, ò si voglia dir' Arquato, ma anche dello stesso Castello, ò Terra, e di tutti i suoi beni, & heredità, ch'era per lasciare, in venendo à morte, la quale indi à non molti anni seguì. (Campi, I, 194, sub anno 772. Cites in marginal reference: *Tabulæ, sup. cit.*).

[7] E l'anno, che seguì dopo questo, imperado all'hora in Oriente (così stà notato in vna scrittura di ciò antichissima Latina dell'infrascritta Chiesa) Costantino Sesto; accadette la morte di Magno Signore, e padrone di Castello Arquato, e no hauendo egli lasciati figliuoli, si effettuò la donatione fatta da lui per l'anima sua al già Desiderio Vescouo di Piacenza, di tutti i propri beni, e della stessa terra di Castello ancora; con carico però à Giuliano, & a' suoi successori, nel Vescouato, che pagar douessero ogni anno (e tanto poscia si osseruò da loro, finche godettero essi i detti beni) alla Basilica di S. Maria di quel luogo, ne' tempi delle vendemmie, tre portioni, ò fossero tre quarti d'vna veggiola di mosto per la decima del suo vino; nel Venerdì Santo vna lira d'oglio da mescolarsi con la Santa Cresima; nel Sabbato Santo vno staio di vino di spruzzare gli altari, ed da lauare le tauole, e le Croci, e darle di più le funi per le campane, e certa quantità di sale, etc., etc. (Campi, I, 198, sub anno 789).

church was a pieve. It is frequently called *plebs* in documents of the XII century, which I have inspected in the archivio. In 1319 the church had six or seven canons besides an archpriest, according to Campi,[9] and in the time of Morandi, the clergy consisted of an archpriest, eight canons, and four *mansionarii*.

Campi states that in 1122 the church was consecrated by Aldo, bishop of Piacenza, and that at this time the prevosto was given the title of archpriest.[10] This document, like all the others submitted to Campi's inspection, has disappeared, but there is no reason to doubt that the notice is authentic. Curati has conjectured that the edifice was reconstructed in consequence of having been destroyed by the earthquake of 1117.

In 1132 a donation was made to the church,[11] and in 1159 the canons obtained a papal bull aimed against the bishop of Piacenza, according to Curati. The importance of the church in the late XIII century may be gathered from the bull of Boniface VIII, of 1296, confirming its various rights and possessions.[12] In 1361 the portico was added to the north side of the church. In 1445 the chapel of S. Giuseppe was erected, according to Morandi. About the same time, the existing cloisters must have been erected, to judge from their style. The chapter was suppressed at the end of the XVIII century, since which the church has been reduced to the rank of a simple parish. When I visited the monument, in June, 1913, a disastrous restoration was in progress. The dissension between the archpriest and the governmental authorities threatened dire results to the edifice, for the local authorities were executing excavations secretly and making restorations surreptitiously in order to avoid government censure.

III. The church consisted originally of a nave (Plate 48, Fig. 2) eight bays long, two side aisles and three apses, but these dispositions have been altered. Owing to the reconstruction of the eastern portions of the edifice, the nave now embraces only six bays. During the recent restoration, there was discovered the trace of an apse to the south of the southern absidiole. This might seem to indicate that the church had originally five apses, but

---

[8] See below, note 10.   [9] III, 50.

[10] E nella Diocesi, essendosi pure in tai giorni riedificata l'antichissima Chiesa (quasi del tutto distrutta) del luogo di Castell'arquato, la consecrò co' debiti riti il Vescouo Aldo sotto il primiero titolo della gran Madre di Dio, e l'ornò anche dell'Archipresbiteral dignità, non perche ancor diäzi non fosse Pieue (dimostrandola tale la seguente memoria, che nell'Archiuio di quella Chiesa si legge: Fictum solidorum duorum, & denariorum sex, quod reddit in perpetuum Plebi Saluetus de Prato de Otesula, de omnibus illis terris positis in territorio Otesulæ, quas Plebs tenet in dicto territorio. Rolandus de Saluagno Notarius 1059 8. Martij), ma perche forse le accrebbe Aldo per maggior decenza il numero de' ministri, ò delle Chiese à lei soggette. (Campi, I, 391, sub anno 1122. Marginal reference: In Archiu. Eccle. Archipreb. Terrae Castri Arqu.).

[11] Campi, I, 403.   [12] Campi, III, 269.

such an interpretation is open to several serious difficulties. In the first place, the ancient eastern piers are still perfectly preserved, and it is evident that the eastern bay of the main arcade was no wider and no higher than the others. There could, consequently, have been no transepts, and there is no analogy for a three-aisled church without transepts terminating in five apses. Furthermore, the pavement of the fourth apse is much lower than that of the church. The suspicion therefore arises that the fourth apse did not form part of the basilica itself, but was a subsidiary structure. This suspicion became a certainty, and the purpose of the subsidiary structure was established by the discovery of a large round baptismal font and an altar.

The campanile rises over the eastern bay of the northern side aisle, but is not part of the original structure. The church is at present entirely covered with barocco stucco internally (Plate 48, Fig. 2), but is undergoing a radical restoration.

The system of the Lombard church was uniform, and the piers all had the section of a quatrefoil (Plate 48, Fig. 2, 4). The polygonal shafts of the fourth pair of piers from the west end were cut down to this form at a later time. The side-aisle responds, which at present exist, do not antedate the XV century, and were erected at the time that the chapels were added. There is no system, the shaft of the piers facing the nave ends in an unmeaning capital at the same level as the others (Plate 48, Fig. 2). The nave vault is obviously modern, as are also the vaults of the side aisles. The nave must anciently have been roofed in timber, but it is uncertain whether the side aisles were roofed in timber or groin-vaulted. Many of the ancient clearstory windows are still preserved, although walled up.

The masonry is formed of ashlar of good but not superlative quality. The courses are not always very true, the joints are frequently wide, and there are numerous square scaffolding holes.

IV. The capitals are for the most part well preserved, and very interesting (Plate 48, Fig. 2). They are ornamented chiefly with vegetable forms, in which grotesques frequently enter, but seldom play a predominating part. Among the grotesques represented are eagles, two rams with a single head—which forms the volute—griffins eating their tails, an elephant, monsters standing on their heads, etc. The vegetable ornaments include anthemia, star flowers, interlaces and acanthus leaves of the Civate type. Several capitals of a proto-Ionic form seem to have been inspired by similar capitals at S. Savino of Piacenza. Other capitals have an almost Carlovingian form, and are decorated with bunches of grapes and leaves with a row of queer, stiff, uncarved leaves below. The abaci are, as a rule, well developed. The necking consists of a heavy rope-moulding as at Cascina S. Trinità. Although the execution is good, these capitals display a certain coarseness of design which is akin to S. Giorgio of Milan (Plate 128, Fig. 5), rather than to S. Pietro in Ciel d'Oro at Pavia (Plate 178, Fig. 1). The bases are at present not visible, but the bases of the shafts of the apse are of Attic type. The capitals of these shafts have broad leaves at the angles, strangely Gothic in appearance. In one capital, grotesque heads are inserted among the volutes. The colonnettes of the gallery rest on simple blocks, and are crowned by capitals with leaves or volutes at the angles.

The exterior of the church is ornamented by simple arched corbel-tables surmounted by a saw tooth. In the façade are several windows of the form of a Greek cross. The western portal is perfectly simple. The apses were ornamented with shafts. The original windows were widely splayed, and of a single unmoulded order. Only the central apse preserves its ancient cornice, which consists of an open-work gallery, surmounted by corbel-tables.

The southern portal, in contrast to the rest of the building, is constructed of a very fine quality of stone. The stereotomy is flawless, the joints neat. The portal is in five orders, and both the jamb and the archivolts have numerous elaborate and complicated mouldings. The architrave is supported by two hunchback caryatids. The running capitals are ornamented with fan-like leaves and triangular anthemia. The voussoirs of the outer archivolt (which is flush with the wall) are sculptured. In the centre is a hand of God, with two fingers raised in benediction; on either side the busts of a man and of a woman, placed symmetrically. These figures, I think, are not significant, but are merely imitations of some Roman sepulchral monument which was reproduced also on a capital of the interior. The other voussoirs are filled with pure ornament, except that one grotesque head is inserted.

One of the capitals of the interior is adorned with figure sculptures (Plate 48, Fig. 4). On one face, two blacksmiths are seen at work, one of whom forges a chain on an anvil, while the other blows the fire with a bellows. A round object to the right is perhaps a forge. This capital was doubtless given by the blacksmiths, as several columns in the cathedral of Piacenza were given by the various corporations. On another face are represented a man and a woman. The man grasps the right hand of the woman in his right hand, his left hand is about her waist. The woman's left hand is raised almost as if she were struggling against violence. The figures appear to be nude. I think, however, that this is not a representation of the vice of Luxury, but an attempt to reproduce a Roman sepulchral monument. It may possibly be intended to represent some married couple who were donors to the edifice. Technically the execution is incredibly crude. The figures have enormous heads of curious oblong shape, and are seen only in bust. The eyes are crudely scratched on the surface. The limbs seem to be without bones and without joints, and the fingers, indicated by parallel incisions, are made to resemble claws. The whole sculpture is characterized by a certain flabbiness, for which the soft stone and weathering are only partly responsible, and it is with the greatest difficulty that the subjects can be made out.

In the tympanum of the southern portal is a lunette with an interesting relief (Plate 48, Fig. 3).[13] In the centre is seated the Madonna, who holds on her left knee the Christ-Child, designated by His inscribed halo. To the left is an angel holding a scroll, and to the right is St. Peter, holding a single key. Stylistically, this relief evidently belongs to the school of Guglielmo da Modena, and is characterized by the hardness which is so familiar in the works of that master. Yet the draperies of the sculptor of Castell'Arquato are distinctly less metallic than those of Guglielmo in the sculptures of the cathedral of Modena (Plate 142, Fig. 3). Although the folds of the drapery lack grace and possess a certain woodeny character, they are still full of dignity. The scarf of the Virgin blows in the breeze in charming and natural- istic folds. An entirely successful effort is made to imitate the form of the limbs beneath the draperies. The composition is pleasing and strongly rhythmical. Wholly delightful are the lines of the wings of the angel. Only in the faces of the angel and the Virgin, and in the anatomy of the Child is there noticeable a certain archaic stolidity and crudeness. The face of Peter, on the other hand, where the artist was helped by the presence of a beard, is fine.

On the archivolt below these sculptures is the inscription: ✠ NATA GERIT NATVM. DE SE SINE SEMINE CRETUM EST PATER IHC NATVS . NATE . DE VENTRE CREATVS. It is evident that by *nata*— "she who is born"—is meant the Virgin, and that *natus* refers to Christ. The inscription therefore means that Christ, who is of the same substance as His Father, was created without seed in the womb of Mary.

In the room adjoining the chapel of S. Caterina (the frescos of which, once lovely, have been irretrievably and forever ruined in the recent restoration) there have been lately placed the important fragments of the ancient ambo. These masterpieces of XII century sculpture were until recently inserted in the north exterior wall of the church, and above them was placed an inscription which still exists: TRANSLATA MENSE MAJO MDCCCX. These fragments include nine separate plaques as follows:

(1) The hand of God in a circle, two fingers raised in benediction. About the circle is the inscription: ✠ DEXTRA DEI CELVM TOTVM BENEDICAT ET EVVM. AMEN.—that is, the right hand of God blesses the heavens and the earth.

(2) The winged bull—evidently the Evangelist Luke—is supplied with the inscription: . FVIT IN DIEBVS| ERODIS REGIS IVDE.[14] The

---

[13] I regret exceedingly that the great height at which this lunette is placed, and the sharp fall of the ground in front of the church at this point, have made it impossible to procure a better photograph. The angle at which it was necessary to tip the camera has resulted in a distortion and elongation of the figures, and especially of their faces, so that our reproduction does scant justice to the beauty of the original.

[14] Luc., i, 5.

execution of this sculpture is fine, especially the wings. The surface of the body is subtly modelled, and affords a charming play of light and shade.

(3) This larger plaque, in higher relief, represents the lion of St. Mark. The wings have the grace and beauty which is characteristic of all these sculptures. The face is that of a lion, but the sculptor has been able to express upon it a psychology which few would have been able to impart to the human countenance. The eyes are full of an expression of wistfulness. The beast seems lost in thought and is looking into the distance far beyond the spectator. The sculptor, like the Gothic artists of northern France, seems to have succeeded in imbuing his grotesques with a certain subtle quality with which he was unable to endow his human figures. The composition of this panel is masterly, the lines rhythmical, the space well filled. The body, on the other hand, is much more crudely modelled than is the St. Luke. The idea of making a beast sit down like a man is not happy, and results in unduly elongating the upper portions of the figure. The arm seems to lack bone and muscle, the paws are neither beautiful nor naturalistic. On the scroll is the inscription: ✠ INI|TIVM| EVAN|GELII| IHV XI| FILII| DEI.[15]

(4) This smaller plaque, which doubtless served as a lectern, is sculptured with the conventional eagle of St. John. Only the exquisite grace of the wings betrays the rare genius of the sculptor. Below is the inscription: IN PRINCIPIO| ERAT VERBVM| ET VER.[16]

(5) This large plaque, symmetrical with the St. Mark, represents the winged man of St. Matthew (Plate 49), and is the most exquisite relief of all, although unfortunately much broken. Worthy of the best masterpieces of French sculpture[17] is the drawing of the wings, one of which is shown raised in a horizontal position, while the other falls in repose. The figure is full of grace, the composition singularly rhythmical and harmonious. The scarf which floats so gracefully to the left, is precisely similar to that of the Madonna in the tympanum (Plate 48, Fig. 3), and leaves no doubt that these sculptures are by the same hand. A certain clumsiness of execution and lack of technique is noticeable in the hands, feet and even in the draperies, which, while better than those of any of the other figures, are still somewhat woodeny. On the broken scroll is the inscription: [LIBER| GEN]ERA|[T]IONIS| IHV XI| FILII DA|VID FILI|I ABRAAM.[18]

(6) The Annunciation. The Virgin stands to the right, and, curiously enough, wears shoes. The sculptor has made a distinct effort to depict motion in the figure of Gabriel, and this result is achieved, although both feet of the angel are shown planted firmly on the ground. Our sculptor has a habit

---

[15] Marc., i, 1.   [16] Joan., i, 1.

[17] This sculpture in fact shows close analogies with an angel on the architrave of the portal of the cathedral of Le Mans.

[18] Matth., i, 1.

of making his figures stand on their toes, and in this case the mannerism has stood him in good stead. Gabriel's feet are crossed in full face. The legs are seen in profile, but the upper part of the figure is again in full face. All of this results in a curious distortion, which nevertheless does, somehow, suggest motion. The composition of this plaque is masterly except that the wings are less pleasantly disposed than in some of the other reliefs. The execution, on the other hand, is decidedly crude. Especially the hands are carelessly drawn and woodeny. The draperies lack grace, but a distinct effort is made to suggest the form of the body beneath the robes, particularly in the figure of Gabriel.

(7) This plaque, symmetrical with the preceding, represents the Visitation. The figures are labelled S[ANCTA]. ELISÂBET, S[ANCTA] MÂRI|A, but this means of identification was quite unnecessary. Notwithstanding the heaviness and crudeness of the faces, notwithstanding the fact that the eyes are drawn in full view, although seen in profile, notwithstanding the lack of modelling in the cheeks, the sculptor has succeeded in showing Elisabeth, clearly and distinctly, as the older woman. She stands composed and firm, while, on the other hand, the timidity and modesty of Mary are graphically indicated by the slight forward dropping of her head, and by her hands, one of which is laid upon her breast, while the other is raised from the elbow in a gesture eloquent of humility. The execution of this plaque is technically somewhat less refined than that of certain other of the reliefs, but the composition is extremely good. The relief almost suggests a Greek grave stele. Our sculptor certainly fell, either directly or indirectly, under the influence of classical models.

(8) This plaque represents Isaiah—S[ANCTVS] ESAIAS. The figure, which is a little stiff, suggests the influence of earlier Lombard models rather more strongly than do the preceding sculptures. The prophet stands squarely on both feet, which are placed rigidly parallel. The arms are glued to the body, the head is much too long and too narrow, the hair and the beard are indicated by parallel curved lines, and the drapery is but slightly modelled. Nevertheless the face does not lack a certain expression of sanctity, and is distinctly superior to the faces in the relief of the Visitation. On the scroll is the inscription: ✠ ECCE| VIRGO| CONCI|PIET| ET PA|RIET| FILIV̄.[19]

(9) This plaque, which must have formed part of the railing of the ambo, represents St. Jerome—S[ANCTUS] IERONIMÛS. It is of irregular shape, but the awkward field has been skilfully filled by the sculptor. The superb composition is somewhat marred by inferior execution. The saint, beardless and with tonsure, is seated before a lectern on which is a book with the inscription: ✠ VENI|TE FILI|I AV|DITÊ| MÊ . |TI|MO|REM| DN̄I| DO|CE|BO| VOS.[20] The face of the doctor is turned upwards in a manner

[19] Isai., vii, 14.   [20] Ps., xxxiii, 12.

which is probably intended to express inspiration. The drapery is much cruder than in the other figures, and crude, too, is the execution of the hair.

V. The church of Castell'Arquato is an authentically dated monument of 1117-1122. The sculptures of the ambo and of the southern portal are, however, a later addition. The mouldings of the southern portal show that this can not be earlier than the second half of the XII century. It is difficult to assign a date to sculptures on their style, since the greater or less skill of the individual artist frequently results in producing works either in advance of or behind their time. The sculptor of Castell'Arquato was clearly a follower of Guglielmo da Modena. On the other hand, he shows himself the superior of his master in many directions. The closest analogy that exists to the reliefs of Castell'Arquato is furnished by the ambo of Carpi (Plate 43, Fig. 2), which dates from 1184. The sculptures of Castell'Arquato may consequently be assigned to c. 1185.

CASTELLETTO D'ORBA,[1] S. INNOCENZO

I. This monument has never been published.

II. The castle of Castelletto d'Orba was destroyed by the marchese Guglielmo c. 1033,[2] but there is no evidence that the church suffered damage at this time. S. Innocenzo is now used as a chapel for the cemetery.

III. The edifice consists of a single-aisled nave and a broader choir. This choir was evidently added subsequently to the original construction of the edifice, although fragments of Romanesque architecture were used in its walls as second-hand material. It must, however, have been erected earlier than the XVI century, since it is adorned with frescos which appear to be of c. 1500. It still retains its old timber roof, lined with bricks and painted red and white with a diamond-shaped pattern.

The original masonry of the church seems to have consisted of ashlar of the finest quality, although the joints are somewhat wide. The stones are often incut, and the courses are consequently much broken. Even the walls of the nave, however, have been much made over.

IV. The windows of the flanks, widely splayed and intended to serve without glass, are in two orders unmoulded, but that of the façade is in four orders, and moulded. On the north wall is engaged a half column, which terminates brusquely without capital ten feet above the pavement.

On the lintel of the portal is a fragment of Lombard carving. In the centre is a rinceau, and on either side bits of pure ornament—an interlace and

---

[1] (Alessandria).   [2] Biorci, I, 180.

rings. To the extreme left are two cocks facing each other, separated by a vase; to the extreme right, two lions.

The holy-water basin contains a Lombard disk. The edifice is embellished with many frescos of the XV and XVI centuries.

V. The masonry is analogous to that of those portions of the church of Fontanella al Monte (Plate 93, Fig. 3) which date from c. 1130. The remains of Romanesque architecture in the edifice may consequently be ascribed to this year.

CASTELNUOVO SCRIVIA,[1] S. PIETRO

(Plate 50, Fig. 1, 4, 7)

I. The church of S. Pietro at Castelnuovo Scrivia was first described in 1816, by Millin.[2] In recent years the monument has been studied by Bertetti, whose article was plagiarized by Palenzona.

II. Over the western portal is an inscription which offers several difficulties of interpretation. In the restoration of 1588, this portal was transferred from the southern transept, and set up in the west façade. It suffered considerably in this process, and the difficulties of the inscription may be in part due to damages and restorations executed at this epoch. It is, nevertheless, evident that some of the errors are due to the XII century stone-cutter, who probably did not know Latin, and did not understand the letters he was cutting. The inscription seems to mean: "In the year of the Incarnation of our Lord Jesus Christ, 1183, in the time of the emperor, Federico, the fifteenth of October, I, master Alberto, made this portal."[3]

The church itself was probably completed in the same year, since it is mentioned in a document of 1184.[4] The church was collegiate;[5] according to Carnevale[6] there were originally five canons, but in 1621 this number was doubled by Paul V.[7] That the church was also a pieve appears from a permutation of October 9, 1244.[8] The cloister is mentioned in a document of May 14, 1301.[9] The church appears in a catalogue of the diocese of Vercelli of 1440, under the simple title *ecclesia Castrinovi*.[10] In 1558 the church was

---

[1] (Alessandria).   [2] II, 287.

[3] ✠ ⫶ ANNO AB INCARNACIONE $\overline{\text{DNI}}$. $\overline{\text{NRI}}$. $\overline{\text{IHV}}$. XPI . MC . OCTUAGE . XIMO ⫶ III $\overline{\text{INDIC}}$ PMA ⫶ $\overline{\text{I}}$ $\overline{\text{TEPORE}}$ FEDERICI IMPERATORIS ⫶ $\overline{\text{OCTOBRI}}$ [IDI]B' SUP[ER]$\overline{\text{ANTE}}$ ⫶ EGO MAGIAER [*sic*] ALB[ER]TUS FECI ⫶

[4] Jn loco castrinoui iusta ecclesiam sancti petri. . . . (Gabotto e Legé, 125).
[5] Bertetti, 156.   [6] 31.   [7] Pollini, 71.   [8] Trucco, I, 235.
[9] *Ibid.*, II, 50.   [10] Ed. Orsenigo, 404.

restored and enlarged, as is known from a consular act of November 16 of that year, paraphrased by Bertetti. In this act is contained the agreement entered into between the common council of Castelnuovo Scrivia and the bishop of Tortona for the restoration and enlargement of S. Pietro. This restoration was executed on the plans of the celebrated architect, Pellegrino Pellegrini. The contract provided for the construction of twelve columns to support the arcades of the new church, but in fact only ten of these columns were erected. A temporary façade was built, and in this was placed the Romanesque portal transferred from the southern transept.[11]

An important inscription on the west wall of the church mentions this restoration of the end of the XVI century, and goes on to state that the church was raised to the dignity of *prepositura* by Paul V (1605-1620), and again adorned by the prevosto Costa in 1623.[12] The church was consecrated on July 16, 1622, as is recorded by an inscription on the back of the high altar.[13]

The chapel of the Virgin was endowed in the year 1623, but rededicated in 1812, according to an inscription. In 1896, the church was restored under the direction of Tagliaferri. The existing façade is entirely a work of this epoch. In the north flank is the inscription: AD NOVUM REDACTA 1896.

III. Only small portions of the existing structure belong to the Romanesque period. The façade dates from 1896, and at this epoch even the portal was unfortunately in part remade, the shafts of Veronese marble being added. The nave dates from 1588, but was restored in 1622 and 1896. The ancient southern transept façade, in which was originally placed the Samson portal, has been largely denatured, but the traces of the rake of the cornice

---

[11] Bertetti, 156-161.

[12]

D. O. M.

FRIDERICO I. IMPERANTE

CONSTRVCTVM AC DICATVM TEMPLVM

NEOCASTRENSES

XVIe SALVTIS SÆCULO

VENVSTIORI STRVCTVRA REÆDIFICARVNT

INSIGNIBVS S. DESIDERII EPI ET Ms RELIQVIIS

PLACENTINAE ALLATIS EXORNARVNT

ÆRE PVBBLICO

QVOTIDIANIS STATVTIS DISTRIBVTIONIBVS

ECCLESIAM IAM A PAVLO V

PRÆPOSITVRIALI INSIGNITAM DIGNITATE

EXORNARVNT ITERVM

JVLIVS ANTONIVS COSTA PRÆPOSITVS

ANNO MDCXXIII

PERENNITATE POSVIT

[13] CONSECRATIO HUJUS ECCLESIAE ANNO 1622 DIE 16 JULII.

are still preserved, and parts of the foundation are said to be visible in the court-yard of the priest's house. The barrel vault of the northern transept is original, but that of the southern transept has been made over. The southern absidiole appears to be ancient, although the exterior can not be seen, since it is blocked up by the campanile. The lower part of this campanile contains remains of a groin vault, doubtless ancient. The masonry of the old portions of the edifice consists of cross-hatched bricks, very large in size, laid in courses perfectly horizontal, and separated by rather wide mortar-beds.

IV. It is evident that in the reconstruction of the church in 1183, fragments of an earlier building were used as second-hand material. In the pier to the north of the choir are two twin half columns, with capitals and bases (Plate 50, Fig. 7). These are pieced out with a stunted column with cubic capital and base and a high pedestal to bring them to the desired level. The base consists of low plinth, and two low tori separated by a very high and slightly incut scotia. In the angles are griffes. The capital, very crudely executed, is ornamented with grotesque figures (Plate 50, Fig. 7). The abacus is decorated with anthemia. The grotesques of this capital recall certain capitals in the cathedral of Aversa (Plate 16, Fig. 2), which are not anterior to the year 1134, but the base is analogous to those of S. Vincenzo at Gravedona, a surely dated monument of 1072. The twin columns, without analogy in Lombardy so far as I know, are paralleled at Ste.-Croix of Quimperlé (Plate 50, Fig. 3), a building with which our monument presents numerous surprising points of contact.

Of the church of 1183 there are extant three cubic capitals which are characterized by abaci with late and elaborate mouldings, much smaller in proportion to the capitals than is usual in Lombard work. The bases of these columns are of Attic type and supplied with griffes. In some cases they are finely moulded. Two other capitals in the southern transept are evidently contemporary. One is of Corinthianesque type, with a single row of acanthus leaves, very stiffly carved, as in decadent Roman work. The surfaces are flat, the incisions deep, the drawing often crude. The abacus consists of a narrow fillet and a high splayed moulding. The other capital (Plate 50, Fig. 1), with a similar abacus, is very low and decorated with a row of detached acanthus leaves and anthemia. It shows points of contact with the capitals of S. Antonio of Ranverso, Sagra S. Michele, and the Annunziata at Corneto Tarquinia (Plate 66, Fig. 3). Outside the southern portal, another capital is used as a console. The grotesque work on the head, which serves as a fleuron, is very crude, but the deeply undercut foliage, and the symmetrical, well-poised character of the design, show that it must date from 1183. The archivolt of the portal consists of a great number of fine and varied mouldings (Plate 50, Fig. 4). The southern transept façade is ornamented with simple arched corbel-tables, surmounted by dentils.

CASTEL SEPRIO, S. GIOVANNI

The sculpture of the lunette of the portal shows Samson, SANSON, astride of the lion. The hero appears to be riding the animal, and his long hair streams back in the wind. With his hands he takes hold of the lower jaw of the beast. Two animals—probably purely grotesque—complete the scene on either side. The execution is very crude. The eye of Samson is executed as though seen in full face, although the figure is really viewed in profile. The group is, nevertheless, full of movement and spirit. On the flank of the lion are incised curious scrolls. The drapery of Samson falls in heavy, fluted folds, like a spiral column. It is evident that Alberto was acquainted with the works of Nicolò. The lion recalls the lions of the Ferrara façade, and the figure of Samson seems reminiscent of the Theodoric of S. Zeno (Plate 227, Fig. 4).

The capitals on the left-hand jamb are ornamented with eagles (Plate 50, Fig. 4). On the capitals of the right-hand jamb are four figures (Plate 50, Fig. 4) the significance of which I am unable to determine. The one to the left holds a curved knife and is beardless. In his left hand he carries a round object. The next figure is bearded and holds in his hands four similar objects. Behind these two figures are wavy lines, which perhaps represent the sea. The next figure, with beard, appears to have had wings. He holds out both his hands. On the right one a bird is perched. His left hand is grasped by the next figure, more narrow-waisted than the others, and hence probably a woman. Her long hair falls over her breasts, and in her extended left hand she holds a flower.

V. The Romanesque fragments of the church of Castelnuovo Scrivia undoubtedly belong to the church for which the portal was executed in 1183. In this building, however, were contained fragments of an older structure which must have been erected c. 1100.

CASTEL SEPRIO,[1] S. GIOVANNI

I. The ruins of Castel Seprio have been referred to by various writers, especially historians, among whom Giulini, Bombognini,[2] Clericetti, Barelli and Monti are the most important.

II. In the XI and XII centuries Castel Seprio was an important town which dared at times to defy even the power of Milan. The pieve of S.

---

[1] (Como). The scanty remains of the ancient town of Castel Seprio lie in the woods about a kilometre to the north of the modern town of the same name. They are thickly overgrown with underbrush, and not easy to find or identify. Remains of four churches in all are extant, but S. Maria Secreta Fuori, known also as the Madonnetta, and the Convento de' Frati, although fairly well preserved, are without interest.

[2] 125.

Giovanni is mentioned in the *Chronicon Mediolanense*[3] and in a sentence of July, 1173.[4] A document of 1193 mentions a priest of the church.[5]

In 1287 the town fell into the hands of the Milanesi, who razed it to the ground with the exception of the churches. From this date the site ceased to be inhabited, but the churches none the less continued to be officiated and kept in repair.

S. Giovanni was an ecclesiastical establishment of considerable importance. As early as 1173 it was officiated by a chapter of canons.[6] In a sort of tax-list of 1398, published by Magistretti, the church is credited with twelve canons and twenty-three chapels, all of which, except S. Maria Fuori, were situated outside of Castel Seprio. In the index of Goffredo it is stated to have had jurisdiction over forty-eight churches and sixty altars.[7] S. Carlo, in the XVI century, transferred the canons to Carnago.[8] Since this time the church has been abandoned. Bombognini, who wrote in 1790, relates that the edifice was still in good preservation until shortly before this time, when some of the parishioners of Vico Seprio, seized with an unfortunate religious fervour one Sunday, demolished the nave to carry off the stones to use them in the construction of their new parish church.[9]

III. The main apse, one of the absidioles and parts of the walls still stand, although in a state of ruin. The masonry is formed of a rubble of large round stones, but bricks are used to form the archivolts of the windows. The walls were reinforced externally by salient pilaster strips.

IV. Of the decoration of the church nothing remains, except some traces of the intonaco with which the walls were covered, and a few fragments of frescos.

V. There is little evidence upon which to determine the date of construction. The character of the masonry in which stone rubble and brick archivolts are combined, certainly can not be later than the year 1100, and a comparison with other edifices, such as Sannazzaro Sesia (Plate 201, Fig. 5)—1040, would lead to the conclusion that it is of the third rather than of the fourth quarter of the XI century. Sannazzaro Sesia, it is true, an edifice begun in 1040, contains more brick and less rubble than S. Giovanni at Castel Seprio (Plate 201, Fig. 5). However, it must be borne in mind that stones were much more abundant in the hilly region of Castel Seprio than in the alluvial plain of the Sesia. It is therefore entirely probable that rubble might have been used at Castel Seprio much after it had been abandoned

[3] Ed. Cinquini, 18.   [4] *Codice della Croce*, MS. Amb., D. S. IV, 9/I, 9, f. 193.

[5] Petrus de Monteuariis Sacerdos et Ministeriallis Ecclesie Sancti Johannis de Castro Seprio. (*Codice della Croce*, MS. Amb., D. S. IV, 11/I, 11, f. 110).

[6] See document cited above and Giulini, VII, 136.   [7] Magistretti, *Notitia*.

[8] Bombognini, 125.   [9] *Ibid.*

in the plain. The pilaster strips of the exterior walls recall those of the basilica of Gravedona which was erected in 1072. We may therefore assign the church of S. Giovanni at Castel Seprio to c. 1070.

CASTEL SEPRIO,[1] S. PAOLO

I. All the authors who have written upon the church of S. Giovanni[2] have also described the ruins of S. Paolo, also known as the Battistero de' Pagani.

II. S. Paolo was perhaps the baptistery of S. Giovanni. Nothing is known of its history beyond what has been said above in speaking of S. Giovanni. Bombognini, who saw the church in the last part of the XVIII century, described it as being surrounded by a portico of columns in two stories.[3] In the description contained in the book entitled *Milano ed il Suo Territorio,* written in 1844, the double portico is again described, but the similarity of phrase with Bombognini is so striking that it is altogether probable that this description was copied from the earlier author, and was not founded upon independent observation of the ruins.[4] In the geography of Strafforello[5] it is stated that the columns of the portico were carried off in the XVIII century, in order to construct the cemetery of Cornago. That cemetery, however, is still in existence, and in it are to be found no traces of the columns. The truth seems to be that the whole story of the double portico and the columns is a myth generated by the excessive fondness of XVIII authors for everything classical, and their desire to discover in mediæval monuments features which would entitle them to be classed as Roman. There is no analogy among Lombard edifices for a baptistery with an exterior portico in two stories.

III. The building is very much ruined, but appears to have consisted of an hexagonal central area and an apse. Clericetti says that the central area was covered by a dome supported on true pendentives, but nothing extant in the ruins to-day would justify such a conclusion. In one of the angles are the remains of a compound respond. The loose rubble masonry is analogous to that of the church of S. Giovanni.

---

[1] See above, p. 273.   [2] See above, p. 273.

[3] Vicino a detta chiesa avvi l'avanzo d'un tempietto esagono antichissimo, con doppio ordine di porticati a colonne, inferiore e superiore, che si crede fosse un tempio dei Gentili, dedicato poscia a S. Paolo, ed indi forse il battistero plebano. (Bombognini, 125).

[4] Veggonsi in un bosco le reliquie di un tempietto esagono con doppio ordine di porticati a colonne, del coro d'una chiesa più vasta, etc.

[5] *Como,* 280.

IV. Of the ornament nothing remains.

V. The style of the masonry shows that S. Paolo is contemporary with S. Giovanni. It may therefore be ascribed to the same time, that is, to c. 1070.

CAVAGNOLO DI BRUSASCO,[1] S. FÈ AL PO

(Plate 50, Fig. 5, 6; Plate 51, Fig. 3, 4, 5)

I. The church of S. Fè was first published by Mella, who illustrated the edifice with drawings and with the scant historical notices obtainable. Other drawings were published in the *Elementi* of the same author.[2] The edifice has also been described by De Dartein[3] and by Biscarra. Illustrations of the building have also appeared in *Arte in Italia*[4] and in an article by Melani published in the *Architectural Record.*

II. Of the history of the church singularly little is known. The deed of foundation, certainly extant in comparatively recent times, since it was seen by Moriondo, has been most unfortunately lost, and no hint of what it contained has come down to us. Mella has shown[5] that the tradition that the church was founded by S. Mauro in 543 is without foundation. A *Dnus Petrus de Sancta Fide* is mentioned in documents of 1210 and 1212.[6] There is no doubt that the church was a priory, but it is by no means clear upon what monastery it depended. Mella believed that it depended upon S. Salutore of Turin. The fact, however, that no mention of Cavagnolo (except the one name *Petrus Prat de Cauagnolio*) is found among the charters of the abbey of S. Salutore, which have now been published by Cognasso, is conclusive proof that Cavagnolo did not depend upon S. Salutore. Sant'Ambrogio,[7] on the other hand, makes the statement that Cavagnolo depended upon S. Michele of Susa, probably meaning by that Sagra S. Michele. This, however, is a wild assertion, unfounded on any documents.

In 1355 the emperor Charles confirmed earlier diplomas of Frederick Barbarossa (1164) and *Conradum ellectum* in favour of the marchese Giovanni of Monferrato. Among the possessions confirmed is the castle of Cavagnolo.[8] In 1214 Cavagnolo was pledged, together with other possessions, by the marchese Guglielmo, in the controversy which had arisen between him and the Vercellesi.[9]

In the façade are several inscriptions which are puzzling. They are cut across by columns and would hence appear to be used as second-hand material

1 (Torino).   2 Tav. V.   3 448.   4 Anno II, 37.   5 684.
6 *Ibid.,* 685.   7 *Ant. Chies. Ben.,* 35.   8 Moriondo, I, 63.
9 *Ibid.,* II, 645.

CAVAGNOLO DI BRUSASCO, S. FÈ AL PO

(Plate 51, Fig. 4). Such, however, can not be the case, since the second of the inscriptions continues across several stone joints. The only explanation is that the inscriptions were cut during the construction of the edifice, after the wall had been erected, but before the column was placed against it. The inscriptions are fragmentary and can only be read in part. Two of them, however, appear to commemorate a certain Rolando, prior of the church:

✦ XI K̄L̄ NOVĒBRIS OB[IIT]
    ROLANDVS PR[IOR]

✦ DOMINVS ROLANDVS [PRIOR] HIC MERIT[I͡]S̄ VEN. . . . .
    TEMPLI

    P . . . . . S . . . . . T̄R̄O . . . T

Unfortunately nothing further is known of this Rolando.

The priory of S. Fè of Cavagnolo is included in a list of the churches of the diocese of Vercelli, of 1440.[10] An inscription in the church mentions a restoration executed by a commendatary prior about 1728.

When Mella visited the church in 1870, the edifice was used as a stable, and he states that it had served as such since 1866. The northern absidiole had been walled off, and the southern one destroyed. In 1878 Biscarra found the church used as a store-room. It has now been restored, and serves as a chapel for the adjoining seminary.

III. The church consists at present of a nave (Plate 51, Fig. 5) five bays long, two side aisles, a choir of a single bay flanked by side aisles, and an apse. There were originally non-projecting transepts, the exterior walls of which still survive (Plate 50, Fig. 5), but these have been walled off. The nave and choir are covered with barrel vaults, the transverse ribs of which are supported on a uniform system (Plate 51, Fig. 5). The crossing has a groin vault, which appears to be modern, like the square tower which surmounts it. In Mella's drawings a rib vault is shown in this position. The apse is vaulted with a half dome; the side aisles, with groin vaults, oblong in plan and highly domed, except in the two eastern bays, where the vaults have been made over. The side-aisle vaults are supplied with transverse arches and wall ribs. The capitals of the shafts supporting the transverse arches of the side-aisle vaults are set lower than those of the main arcade. Mella's drawings show the tiles laid directly upon the extrados of the vaults. The system (Plate 51, Fig. 5) is formed by a shaft engaged on a pilaster strip. The piers (Plate 51, Fig. 5) consist of a rectangular core, upon which are engaged four semi-columns, each of which is supplied with a separate capital and base. The walls are reinforced externally (Plate 50, Fig. 5) by buttresses of slight projection.

---

[10] Prioratus S. Fidei de Cavagnolio. (Ed. Orsenigo, 409).

The masonry of the exterior (that of the interior is entirely covered with intonaco) consists of a mixture of finely jointed ashlar and skilful brickwork (Plate 51, Fig. 3, 4; Plate 50, Fig. 5). The stone blocks are large and well squared. The bricks are all about the same size, and laid in horizontal courses of unimpeachable accuracy.

IV. The ornament of the church is exceedingly rich and varied. The capitals of the main portal (Plate 51, Fig. 4) are of a skilfully executed Corinthianesque type, or carved with grotesques. Those of the interior are similar (Plate 50, Fig. 6), or supplied with broad, flat, stiff leaves, and crudely executed volutes, that recall the Romanesque style of Normandy (Plate 51, Fig. 5). One such capital has distinctly Gothic crockets.

The archivolts are in two orders, and supplied with projecting mouldings, ornamented with a triple billet (Plate 51, Fig. 5), a feature paralleled in Piemonte only at Montiglio. The Attic bases have griffes and are placed on high plinths.

The main portal is in three orders, shafted and moulded (Plate 51, Fig. 4). In the tympanum is a sculpture of two angels who hold a medallion with a bust of Christ. The archivolts are adorned with rope-mouldings, interlaces, grotesques, rinceaux, bead-mouldings, guilloches and a projecting triple billet-moulding (Plate 51, Fig. 4). On the abaci of two capitals lie animals, perhaps lions, and above, at either side, are reliefs of two griffins and two grotesque gargoyle-like creatures (Plate 51, Fig. 4).

Against the façade (Plate 51, Fig. 3) are engaged two half columns which end in capitals which support nothing. Over the main portal is a biforum (Plate 51, Fig. 3), which appears to be the result of an alteration executed in modern times. In the gable is an aperture in the form of a cross (Plate 51, Fig. 3). The cornice is formed of simple arched corbel-tables (Plate 51, Fig. 3; Plate 50, Fig. 5). The buttresses (Plate 50, Fig. 5) have regularly profiled bases which rest on a podium, but no capitals.

V. The grotesques of Cavagnolo (Plate 51, Fig. 4) are executed with a coarseness which recalls those of S. Giorgio in Milan (Plate 128, Fig. 5), which date from 1129. Compared with the portal of S. Pietro in Ciel d'Oro at Pavia (Plate 177, Fig. 1), an authentically dated monument of 1132, the Cavagnolo portal is seen to be later because of the greater number and smaller size of the mouldings. Moreover, the rope-moulding appears to be the first esquisse of a motive which was destined to develop and become important in the second half of the XII century (see, for example, the portal of Borgo S. Donnino, executed between 1178 and 1196, Plate 30, Fig. 3). Cavagnolo, evidently later than S. Pietro in Ciel d'Oro, may therefore be ascribed to c. 1140. With this date agrees well the character of the masonry, which is more advanced than that of Cascina S. Trinità (Plate 50, Fig. 2), an edifice of c. 1130, in that there is no herring-bone pebble work.

CAVANA,[1] S. BASILIDE

I.   The badia of Cavana has never been published.

II.   Of the history of the edifice nothing is known beside the tradition that it was a monastery and that it was founded by St. Bernard.[2]

III.   The church itself—which consists of a single-aisled nave of three bays covered with groin vaults, barrel-vaulted transepts, a groin-vaulted crossing and an apse—has been completely modernized, and is without interest. It is, however, preceded by a narthex, which retains its original character. This narthex is at present two bays broad and one bay long. The local priest told me that this narthex was originally a bay longer, but that the western bay was destroyed, and the capitals sold. He said that he had himself discovered traces of the ancient foundations. A confirmation of the priest's statement is to be found in the façade wall of the second story, which is evidently modern.

The lower story of the narthex is covered with undomed groin vaults, of which the transverse and longitudinal ribs are semicircular in elevation and rectangular in section. In the northern wall, however, there is no wall rib. The vaults are constructed of courses which tend to radiate. These courses are somewhat roughly laid, and are separated by heavy mortar-beds. Between the ribs and the vault surface intervenes a considerable crack, proving that the ribs were constructed first, and that upon them was hung the solid centering for the vault. In the northern wall where the wall rib is omitted its place was supplied structurally by cutting the wall surface in the form of an arch.

The masonry of this part of the edifice is in the main ashlar of the finest quality. Some of the stones are cross-hatched, and the reason for this is apparent in traces of fresco still visible. The single free-standing pier and the responds are alike compound, and contain numerous polygonal or semi-circular members, with square spurs. On the west façade above the abaci rises a system which at present ends unmeaningly. The portal is placed out of axis because of the respond in two orders placed in the centre.

The ancient Romanesque windows are no longer in their original position in the church. It is evident that the body of the building has been entirely rebuilt, in part with old materials and perhaps on the old plan.

IV.   The architrave and archivolt of the portal are ornamented with interlaces and anthemia. The corner responds are either without bases, or have bases of Attic profile from which the griffes appear to have been broken

---

[1] Frazione di Lesignano de' Bagni, provincia di Parma.

[2] L'antica badia di monaci vallombrosiani fuvvi eretta per opera di S. Bernardo, sotto il titolo di S. Basilide. . . . Vi abitarono i monaci sino al secolo XV, ma poi l'abbandonarono. (Molossi, 81).

off. The capitals of the responds on either side of the portal are sculptured with the symbols of the four Evangelists. St. Mark has a book on which is inscribed:

S̄	EVAN
MA	GELI
RC	STA
VS	

St. Matthew similarly has a book on which is inscribed:

SANC̄T	EV
MAH	AN
THĒV̄	GELI
	STA

St. Luke, S̄ LVC|AS| EV̂A|GELISTA, is without attribute, but St. John, S̄. IOHS EVGE, has a book upon which is inscribed:

IN PRI	BV
NCIPIO	M E
ERAT V	RAT
ERBVM	APVT
ET VER	DEVM[3]

The other capitals are ornamented with acanthus leaves and volutes— that is to say, they are of Corinthianesque type—or with all-over patterns, formed of strings. The abaci have anthemia or rinceaux, the neckings are carved with a rope-moulding. One capital is carved with grotesques. These capitals are remarkable for the deep and skilful undercutting, and in this they differ from the S. Ambrogio type, which, nevertheless, they approach in the dry forms of the acanthus leaves and the ornamentation of the abaci. They offer even closer analogies, however, with the capitals of S. Pietro in Ciel d'Oro, and with those of the cathedral of Parma.

The sculptures, especially that of the angel, are excellent. If they be not by the hand of the master of the earlier capitals at Parma cathedral, they must be by an equally skilful and contemporary rival. The head is somewhat large for the body, and the chin is a little heavy. The hair is indicated by a series of wavy, parallel incised lines, ending straight. The stool upon which the angel is sitting is admirably executed and interesting for the history of furniture. The draperies are heavy and woodeny. The wings also are heavy and badly placed, yet they fall in graceful lines. The execution of the eyes recalls strongly the sculptures of the master of Parma, as do also the tails of the animals. That of the lion is twisted behind his hind legs, and that of the bull ends in a flourish of foliage. This sculptor, like the

[3] Joan., i, 1.

master of Parma, is at his best in the grotesques, which are executed with a verve and dash lacking in his figure subjects.

On the soffit of one of the wall ribs of the narthex are the remains of a lovely conventional pattern in fresco. This consists of a diaper of extraordinary delicacy and feeling.

V. The analogies which Cavana shows to S. Pietro in Ciel d'Oro of Pavia, an authentically dated edifice of 1132, and to those portions of the cathedral of Parma which were begun c. 1130, are sufficient to justify the ascription of our monument to c. 1130.

CAVRIANA,[1] MADONNA DELLA PIEVE

I. The pieve of Cavriana has been published by Matteucci.

II. In the exterior wall of the choir, and used as second-hand material, is the following inscription incised in Gothic characters:

FEC . FIEI   . M . CCC
BOALENTU   . XXXIJ
RIN'   hō . OP' .

There is, however, nothing to indicate to what the *hoc opus* refers. Another inscription, also in Gothic characters, and near the first, bears the legend:

. SEPVLTVRA .
D . MVRGONI .

On the roof of the nave is a modern inscription in Italian:

IN QUESTO TEMPIO
I FIGLI DI CAVRIANA
VENERANDO DEVOTI L'ANTICA E CARA
MADONNA DELLA PIEVE
NEL SOLENNE GIUBILEO
DE L'IMMACOLATA CONCEZIONE
VIII DEC. MDCDVI

III. The church consists of a nave of a single aisle roofed in wood and a groin-vaulted choir. The choir is modern, as are the northern and southern chapels, and the interior of the nave has been entirely covered with stucco. The campanile, which rises to the south-east of, and over the nave, so that the outside wall of the campanile is flush with the southern wall of the church,

---

[1] (Mantova).

is a later addition of the Gothic period. The masonry, although similar to that of the nave superficially, is, in reality, of radically different character. The upper part of the western façade, with pointed arched corbel-tables and open-work zigzags, also appears to have been remade in the Gothic era. The portal and window of the west façade are barocco.

The exterior walls of the nave are well preserved and interesting. They are constructed of odd pieces of bricks and stone, laid in courses more or less horizontal, although frequently broken. There is much herring-bone work, and many bits of broken bricks and tiles (evidently second-hand material) are laid vertically. The mortar, of excellent quality, contains large pebbles, and is laid in broad courses. Some of the stones are roughly squared, but most are round rocks taken from the river-bed. The bricks are not cross-hatched. There are numerous scaffolding holes.

The windows are perfectly plain, widely splayed and intended to serve without glass.

IV. The edifice is ornamented externally with arched corbel-tables, grouped two and two, and supported on slender pilaster strips. In the interior nothing ancient is visible except in one place, where the intonaco has been stripped away to reveal two superb frescos of the XII century.

V. The arched corbel-tables of the exterior show such close analogy with those of S. Pietro of Acqui (Plate 4, Fig. 5)—a surely dated monument of 1023—that there can be little doubt that the pieve of Cavriana dates from this same time, let us say c. 1025.

CEMMO,[1] PIEVE S. SIRO

(Plate 51, Fig. 1, 2; Plate 52, Fig. 2, 4)

I. The pieve of Cemmo was first published by Rizzi.[2] More recently Canevali has printed a description of the church illustrated with nine photographs. His account is of great value, because made before the restoration.[3] A photograph and description are also contained in Nebbia's review of Canevali's book.

[1] Frazione di Capo di Ponte (Brescia). The pieve is situated almost directly across the river from Capo di Ponte, and should not be confused with the parish church of S. Stefano at Cemmo, which contains a fragment of façade dating from the late XII century.

[2] 134.

[3] He describes the ancient roofing in the following words: . . . il soffitto delle piccole navate laterali è a volta in muratura; quello della navata grande di mezzo è invece orrizzontale in legno, assai male dipinto. (Canevali, 189).

CEMMO, PIEVE S. SIRO

II. The castle of Cemmo was probably destroyed in 1157,[4] but there is no indication that the church suffered damage at this period. Faino, who wrote in 1658, speaks of the church as the ancient parish church of Cemmo.[5]

When I visited the edifice on May 28, 1913, I found a most radical restoration in full progress. The exterior of the northern clearstory wall had been entirely made over, so that nothing ancient was left above the line of the side-aisle roof, except the arcuated lintels of the widely splayed windows, which were intended to serve without glass. The southern wall had fared somewhat better (Plate 52, Fig. 2), since some portions up to the level of the cornice were old. The masonry, however, had been entirely patched up and worked over, and had lost utterly its original character. The interior walls of the nave were ancient up to the level of the last three courses of the clearstory, but the gables of the eastern and western walls had been entirely rebuilt. The arched corbel-tables of the south clearstory (Plate 52, Fig. 2) were new, although some of the original corbels, carved in the shape of heads, had been preserved. The southern side-aisle wall (Plate 52, Fig. 2) with its superb portal (Plate 51, Fig. 2), although altered in the time of the Renaissance, was still, when I saw it, well preserved, and I trust it was not subsequently spoiled by the restorers. The carved lunette was intact in the crypt. The apses (Plate 52, Fig. 2) were still entirely undamaged. The wooden roof of the nave was new, and the vaults of the southern side aisle had been demolished (Plate 52, Fig. 4), leaving, however, the original transverse arch separating the side aisle of the choir from that of the nave still standing. It was evident, however, that the vaults of the side aisle of the nave dated from the barocco period, and that originally only the side aisle of the choir was groin-vaulted. The Renaissance vaults were still standing in the northern side aisle when I saw the edifice, as well as the groin vault in the northern side aisle of the choir (Plate 51, Fig. 1). Clearly, however, this vault was not original, but remade in the time of the Renaissance. Only the wall rib, segmental in elevation (Plate 51, Fig. 1), must have been ancient. The construction of this wall rib displayed a remarkable expedient adopted to minimize the distortion of the vaulting. Since the outer wall bends noticeably outward, the resulting vaulting compartment was decidedly trapezoidal in plan. Now the wall rib, made very thick at the eastern end, almost disappears at the western end. Thus the trapezoidal shape of the compartment is materially reduced. In the corresponding bay on the southern side, the wall rib has disappeared, but that there was one is proved by the section of the respond in one order on the west side, and in two orders on the east side, as in the opposite compartment. When I visited the church, in the northern side aisle of the choir there was visible the head of a doorway projecting perhaps

[4] Rosa, 41.

[5] Ecclesiam S. Syri, Vallis Camunicæ Apostoli, antiquam Cemmi Parochialem. (Faino, 201).

half a metre above the present floor. This doorway probably gave access to the church from the north side. It was being reopened by the restorers. The existing northern and southern doorways of the choir both seem modern. Traces of the original timbers of the side-aisle roof were still visible in 1913.

III.   The edifice consists of a nave three bays long (Plate 52, Fig. 4), two side aisles, a choir of a single bay flanked by side aisles, three apses (Plate 52, Fig. 2), a crypt, and a campanile (Plate 52, Fig. 2) rising to the west of the church, and connected with it by means of buildings of later date (Plate 52, Fig. 2).   The campanile itself does not appear to be anterior to the XVI century.

The church is perched in a cleft of the rock (Plate 52, Fig. 2) high above the rushing Olga, and surrounded by wild mountains.   The exigencies of the situation have caused several peculiarities.   The principal entrance (Plate 51, Fig. 2) is situated upon the south side of the church.   The western end of the edifice abuts against the face of the rock.   There is consequently no western façade, and the steeply sloping crag penetrates into the interior of the church at the west end, where it is cut away to form a flight of steps in the west wall. The northern side aisle of the choir is sharply bent out, to take advantage of a projecting ledge in the rock.   The exterior wall of this side aisle overhangs a precipice.   Here, therefore, decoration is spared, while on the contrary it is concentrated on the southern façade.

The bays of the nave are very irregular.   The western is short, the next two somewhat longer, while the choir is longest of all.   The supports also show considerable diversity.   The westernmost piers are rectangular.   The next pair are cylindrical, while the easternmost contain four rectangular members, except that there is a half column towards the side aisle on the northern side.   This half column, however, is a result of a barocco alteration. The eastern pier of the nave has a rectangular system (Plate 52, Fig. 4) which ends unmeaningly at about the level of the crown of the arches of the main arcade.

The choir is considerably raised above the interesting crypt.[6]   This crypt, with the exception of the portion under the northern side aisle of the choir, which is covered with a modern barrel vault, is supplied with groin vaults. These have transverse and wall ribs, highly loaded at the crowns.   The transverse ribs are much stilted.   The wall ribs, especially in the curves of

[6] With this crypt it is interesting to compare that of S. Prospero at Castellaráno (Reggio), the fragments of which were discovered between 1898 and 1901. (Faccioli, 82-83).   Maestri, who published the monument (*Rubbiano*, 24 f.), states that a collegiate church existed on the site as early as the IX century, but the earliest document relating to the church which I have been able to find dates only from 967: . . . loco & fundo qui dicitur Castro alariano cum capellis inibi habentes. (Affò, I, 354).   The church was given to the abbey of S. Benedetto Po on October 5, 1092 (Bacchini, 110), and was confirmed to that abbey by Pascal II in 1105 (Bacchini, *Ap.* 59; Viganò,

the apses, are depressed. The vaults are considerably domed. The responds are without capitals. Rectangular supports are in most cases supplied for each member of the vaults, but in some instances the groins disappear. In the central apse two free-standing columns of granite, although short and stumpy, appear to be pilfered from some Roman edifice. Pilfered Roman material was used elsewhere in the building, witness a fragment of an inscription in one of the windows of the central apse.

The masonry of the exterior (Plate 51, Fig. 2; Plate 52, Fig. 2) consists of a rough kind of ashlar. The stones, well enough squared, but of various sizes, are laid in courses, the horizontal direction of which is frequently broken. The mortar-beds are of moderate. thickness. Bits of brick are occasionally introduced. The masonry of the interior of the clearstory walls (Plate 52, Fig. 4) was probably of somewhat superior quality. Several blocks of stone in the southern wall, and many in the interior of the church, are covered with herring-bone cross-hatching, added, doubtless, to prepare the walls to receive frescos.

IV. Only the cylindrical piers of the nave have carved capitals. These are ornamented with anthemia, grotesques or palmettes. The capitals of the crypt are pilfered Roman, which were repaired in the mediæval period. The volutes and fleurons are antique, but the acanthus leaves were in part recut in the XII century.

The archivolts are in a single order, unmoulded (Plate 52, Fig. 4). The northern clearstory and side aisle and the southern side aisle are externally without cornice. The apses are ornamented with arched corbel-tables, resting on pilaster strips, which, however, are not continued to the ground, but are supported on a high podium (Plate 52, Fig. 2). There are blind niches beneath the arched corbel-tables of the central apse (Plate 52, Fig. 2).

The southern portal (Plate 51, Fig. 2) is shafted and has a roll-moulding. On either side are two half columns, ending in grotesque capitals. These have bases with griffes. The portal itself, executed largely in marble, is sumptuously adorned with grotesques, rinceaux, acanthus leaves, interlaces, etc. At the foot on either side are animals, unfortunately broken. One, apparently a lion, holds in his paws what may be a man. The other animal seems to be a ram. This ornamentation seems like a first esquisse of a Lombard portal (Plate 51, Fig. 2).[7]

46). Maestri saw in the crypt dated frescos of 1464. The extant remains consist of part of the crypt or pontile of a Lombard basilica, and may be seen beneath the pavement of the existing church. The colonnettes are cylindrical or octagonal in section. In a store-room is preserved a lunette, with two griffins, coming from the same edifice. From the style of the capitals it is evident that the remains date from c. 1105.

[7] This portal recalls that of S. Margherita, now preserved in the Museo Civico of Como. The Como portal, too, has a roll-moulding, and shafts supported on lions in relief, like the animals of Cemmo. The grotesque carvings are crude in style. One

The lunette of the southern portal, which was in the crypt when I saw the church, has carved ornament consisting of a cherub with six wings, an eagle, a string pattern, and a dragon, held in the claws of a monster with bird's head, wings and claws and a serpent's tail. The dragon itself has a bird's wings and claws, a serpent's tail, and a duck's bill. Below is the leonine inscription: HINC O̅S̅ INTRANTES . AD TE B̅N̅DIC PROPERANTES.

A large baptismal font in the church resembles a hogshead. The church contains two superb Quattrocento frescos, one of which dates from 1437.

V. The southern portal (Plate 51, Fig. 2) recalls the Porta dello Zodiaco (Plate 196A, Fig. 1, 2) at Sagra S. Michele (a monument which dates from c. 1120), in the animals depicted in relief at the base, and in many details of the ornamentation. It is, however, obviously cruder and earlier than the portal of Nicolò. The ornament of the church, especially the apse cornice and the capitals, recall so vividly S. Ambrogio of Milan, that they must have been inspired by that edifice. Cemmo was, therefore, probably erected after 1098, when S. Ambrogio was finished. Since, therefore, it is earlier than 1120 and later than 1098, we may ascribe it to c. 1110.

CERRETO,[1] S. MARIA

(Plate 52, Fig. 1, 3)

I. For the history of the abbey the various works of Agnelli should be consulted.

II. Our monastery should be carefully distinguished from the abbey of S. Michele located at Cerreto, in the province of Cremona, which is probably the modern commune of Monasterolo.[2] Our monastery bears the title of SS. Pietro, Paolo, Maria e Nicolò, and is situated in the Lodigiano.

The abbey of Cerreto was first founded as a monastery of Benedictine monks in the year 1084. The copy of the deed of foundation has been torn from the *Liber Jurium* of Lodi, so that Agnelli was able to read of it only a few lines. Its contents, however, are in part repeated in the following document, a confirmation of the deed of foundation, which has been published by Agnelli.[3]

capital recalls the apse gallery of S. Giacomo. In a room near by is a grotesque animal coming from the same church, and closely resembling those of the atrium of S. Ambrogio. The Como portal may be ascribed to c. 1100.

[1] The frazione of Cerreto, sometimes known as Abbadia, lies on the left bank of the Adda, a few kilometres below Lodi, and is best reached via Corte Palasio (Milano).

[2] See Lupi, I, 945; Giulini, I, 340; *Hist. Pat. Mon.*, XIII, 540.

[3] Carta confirmationis domini Benni filii dicti domini Alberici et uxoris ejus qui firmaverunt fondationes et donationes quas fecit pater ejus.

Anno ab incarnatione domini nostri Jeshu Xripsti MLXXXIIII. VI die mensis

CERRETO, S. MARIA

The terms of this document seen to imply clearly that a church previously existed on the site, but it is not equally clear whether or not this church was to be reconstructed in consequence of the foundation of the monastery. A document of 1087 mentions an abbot of Cerreto.[4] An important donation was made to the abbot and monks in 1095.[5] Numerous documents of the early XII century prove the power and importance of the early Benedictine abbey.[6]

It appears that the Benedictine monks took sides with the antipope Anacleto II, and for this reason they were suppressed, and supplanted by Cistercian monks. At this period Alberto Oldrato became a conspicuous benefactor of the new monastery, and finally was made first abbot of the Cistercian order. For this reason he acquired such renown that in subsequent times he came to be known as the founder.[7]

The documents which establish all this are somewhat confusing. Between 1131 and 1137, the instruments of the abbey are signed by a procurator of the abbot. The explanation doubtless is, as Agnelli has recognized, that the Benedictine abbot, while still nominally in power, was not living in the abbey, but had been forced into exile. In 1139 Innocent II gave the abbey into dependence upon Chiaravalle Milanese.[8] Galvaneo della Fiamma refers the foundation of the Cistercian monastery to the year 1136.[9]

decembris, Indictione VIII vobis Vitali et Oldoni presbiteris. Nos Benno filius Alberici ipso genitore meo mihi consentiente et subter confirmante et Melior iugales filia Pagani qui nominatur de Trexeno . . . ipso namque iugale et Mondoaldo meo mihi consentiente et subter confirmante. Presentes presentibus diximus promittimus et spondemus nos qui supra Benno et Melior iugale una cum nostris heredibus vobis qui supra presbiteris vestrisque successoribus et parti romane ecclesie hedificande in monasterium in loco Cereto in honore beatorum Petri et Pauli et sancte Virginis Marie Dei Genitricis atque sancti Nicolai; ut non habeamus licentiam nec potestatem per aliquod ingenium ullamque occasionem que fieri possit agere aut curare vel removere, nominative res illas omnes quas nos qui supra iugales et iam dictus Albericus tradidimus et concessimus in ipsa hedificatura ecclesia que esse debet monasterium. . . . res omnes quas ipsa ecclesia hedificanda in monasterium nunc habet. . . . (Agnelli, 8).

[4] Agnelli, 11.   [5] Ibid., 13.

[6] Ibid., 15 f. Ughelli, IV, 666, mentions one of these documents of 1117.

[7] See Ughelli, IV, 665-667, who cites an inscription formerly at S. Sebastiano, Rome.

[8] Innocentius episcopus servus servorum Dei dilecto filio Brunoni abbati monasterii sanctae Mariae quod in villa Balneoli [i.e., Chiaravalle] in mediolanensi territorio situm est eiusque successoribus. . . . Huius rei gratia . . . abbatiam de Cerreto. que beati Petri iuris existit. tibi tuisque successoribus apostolica dispensatione concedimus. ut videlicet per te ac fratres tuos ibidem honestas et religio reformetur. et idem locus tam temporaliter quand [sic] spiritualiter gratum incrementum suscipiens. monasterio Clarevallensi subiaceat. . . . Datum Laterani per manum Aimerici sancte romane ecclesie diaconi . . . XIIII kal. decembris indictione III. Incarnationis dominice anno MCXXXVIIII pontificatus vero domini Innocenti II pape anno decimo. (Agnelli, 25-26). This bull is also printed by Giulini, VII, 98.

[9] See text cited below under Chiaravalle, p. 296.

The possessions of the abbey were confirmed by the archbishop Robaldo in 1144.[10] A lawsuit against the bishop of Lodi ended in 1147 to the advantage of the monastery.[11] The bull of Innocent II was confirmed by Eugenius III in 1148.[12] The monastery was united with SS. Vito e Modesto in the year 1302.[13] In 1439 the abbey passed into commendam. In the wars of the XV century Cerreto was the scene of several severe battles, and was taken and retaken with considerable damage to the monastery and to the church. In 1481 Osservanti monks were established.[14] The abbey was restored by the Cardinale di Recanati, and the church was largely rebuilt by Federico Cesio, in 1541.[15] The choir-stalls were erected in 1679.[16] In 1680 the central tower was struck by lightning. When it was restored it was deprived of its crowning *guglia*. During the XVIII century the church was covered with frescos. In 1798 the monastery was suppressed.

In 1890 an archæological restoration of the church was undertaken. The roofs were all made over and the southern clearstory wall was restored.

III. The church consists of a nave (Plate 52, Fig. 3) four double bays long, two side aisles, projecting transepts (Plate 52, Fig. 1), and seven rectangular apses. Over the crossing rises an octagonal tower (Plate 52, Fig. 1), and east of the southern transept is a modern campanile (Plate 52, Fig. 1). The church is preceded by a western exterior narthex, obviously remade in the barocco period, but still preserving the original Romanesque core.

The nave and transepts are covered with square, highly domed rib vaults (Plate 52, Fig. 3). The diagonals have a torus section; the wall ribs are rectangular, and the transverse arches in two orders (Plate 52, Fig. 3). The rib vault of the crossing was probably originally of the same character, but it was remade in the Gothic period when the central tower was added. The apses are all covered with pointed barrel vaults, the only pointed arches visible in the interior of the edifice. The side aisles are covered with groin vaults. The central bay of the western narthex has a rib vault like those of the nave, except that pointed arches are used. The remaining vaults are groined like those of the side aisles.

The nave system (Plate 52, Fig. 3) is alternate, and comprises three continuous members, of which the central one is semicircular. Originally the alternate piers contained four semicircular colonnettes, separated by single spurs on the side of the side aisles, and double spurs on the side of the nave. The intermediate piers (Plate 52, Fig. 3) had only three semicircular members, a flat pilaster strip being engaged on the side of the nave to carry the second order of the archivolts. The side-aisle responds are all uniform, and consist of three members, the central one of which is semicircular.

[10] Ughelli, IV, 666.   [11] Agnelli, *Dizionario*, 3.   [12] Ughelli, IV, 666.
[13] *Ibid.;* Agnelli, *Dizionario*, 3.   [14] Agnelli, *Dizionario*, 3.
[15] *Ibid.*   [16] Agnelli, 61.

CERRETO, S. MARIA

The side-aisle walls were strengthened by vigorous rectangular buttresses. The clearstory walls were reinforced by transverse buttresses (Plate 52, Fig. 1), raised high above the aisle roofs, and applied only where needed to resist the thrust of the vaults;—that is, to every other bay.

The windows of the eastern portion of the edifice have numerous mouldings. Those of the western half of the building have been for the most part made over. These windows must have been glazed.

The masonry is very advanced in character. Large, well formed cross-hatched bricks are laid in perfectly horizontal courses, but the mortar-beds are wide.

To the south of the church are traces of the destroyed cloisters (Plate 52, Fig. 1) and uninteresting remains of other monastic buildings.

IV. The capitals are usually of the developed cubic type (Plate 52, Fig. 3), but some have angular cushions. Three are carved with broad, flat leaves of a type which somewhat recalls the French transitional style. One of c. 1085 was undoubtedly taken from the old church destroyed in the XII century. The western portal has an engaged gable, is moulded, and supplied with broad-leaved capitals of a characteristically French type.

In the choir wall is a piscina which has lost its colonnettes but still retains its broad-leaved capitals and moulded archivolts.

V. The purely Cistercian architecture of the abbey of Cerreto makes it certain that the church was entirely built after the Cistercian rule had been established in the abbey, that is to say, after c. 1136.

Compared with the church of Chiaravalle, begun in the year 1135, Cerreto appears slightly later. In both churches we find the alternate system, the same type of vaults, the same rectangular apses covered with pointed barrel vaults, the same groin-vaulted side aisles, the same torus-shaped diagonals, the same transverse arches in two orders, the same exterior ornamentation in arched corbel-tables, the same transverse buttresses, and the same western narthex. (Compare Plate 52, Fig. 1, 3, with Plate 54, Fig. 1, Plate 55, Fig. 1). The most salient differences are that at Cerreto (Plate 52, Fig. 3) the arches of the main arcade are in two orders, whereas at Chiaravalle (Plate 55, Fig. 1) they are of a single order; that at Cerreto (Plate 52, Fig. 3) the proportions are higher and loftier than at Chiaravalle (Plate 55, Fig. 1); that at Cerreto (Plate 52, Fig. 3) the adjustment of the system to the load is weaker and more awkward than at Chiaravalle (Plate 55, Fig. 1), and that at Cerreto (Plate 52, Fig. 3) the piers are compound, whereas at Chiaravalle (Plate 55, Fig. 1) they are cylindrical (although I am not certain that this was the original form of the Chiaravalle supports). As a result of this comparison, it seems evident that the church of Cerreto is slightly later than that of Chiaravalle. We may consequently assume that the construction of Cerreto began c. 1140. All the Cistercian abbeys of northern Italy with the exception of Albino were long in construction. Chiaravalle, begun in 1135, was not finished until 1221; Morimondo, commenced in 1186, was not finished until 1296; Rivolta Scrivia, begun in 1180, is still unfinished. It is therefore entirely probable that the construction of the vast church of Cerreto occupied considerable time, although the original plan was preserved without changes. The pointed arches of the narthex and the western portal with engaged archivolt and Gothic capitals show the style of c. 1200. It may, therefore, be assumed that the construction occupied the entire second half of the XII century. The central tower (Plate 52, Fig. 1) was added in the Gothic period.

CHIARAVALLE DELLA COLOMBA,[1] S. MARIA

(Plate 53, Fig. 2, 3)

I. The abbey of Chiaravalle della Colomba enjoys among all the Cistercian edifices of northern Italy the distinction (shared only by Chiaravalle Milanese) of having been known to Enlart, who has mentioned the edifice in his work upon Italian Cistercian architecture,[2] and in Michel's *Histoire de l'Art*.[3] The church has also been the subject of an excellent monograph by Bertuzzi.

II. The monastery of Chiaravalle della Colomba was founded in the fourth decade of the XII century. Ughelli has preserved an inscription which formerly existed in the church, according to which this foundation took place in the year 1135.[4] The inscription states that Arduino, bishop of Piacenza, together with his clergy and many nobles, begged S. Bernardo to found this monastery. The same facts are recapitulated in a deed of April 11, 1136, by which the bishop Arduino donated certain tithes to the monastery.[5] Ughelli

---

[1] Frazione di Alseno, provincia di Piacenza.

[2] 15, 70, 94.

[3] II, pt. I, 87.

[4] Arduinus Placentiæ Episcopus Clerus ac multi nobiles obnixe sanctum deprecantur Bernardum, ut fundo, ac aliis bonis ab eis acceptis ad divinas laudes persolvendas, Cisterciense hoc ædificet Cœnobium anno M. C. XXXV. (Ughelli, IV, 211).

[5] Arduinus sanctae Placentinæ Ecclesiæ Episcopus licet indignus.

Omnibus . . . in Christo filiis etc. . . . Ea propter nostrum charissimum in Christo fratrem Bernardum S. Clarævallensis congregationis religiosissimum Abbatem obnixis precibus deprecantes, ut religiosissimos fratres ejusdem cogregationis, atque ordinis, qui in nostro Episcopatu cœnobium fundarent, nobis concederet, & ipse nostro affectui postulationis, piæ voluntatis, ut pius pater adquievit, & religiosissimos fratres nobis concessit. Quibus supramemoratis in Christo fratribus præsentibus, atque canonice substituentibus in loco, qui olim Caretum dicebatur, nunc Columba nominatur, omnium terrarum decimas, quas propriis manibus . . . excoluerint, . . . donamus, etc.

has also printed a decree in favour of the monastery on the part of the people and clergy of Piacenza, dating from this same year (1136), the fifth day of April.[6] In 1137 Innocent II took the abbey under his protection, and among other possessions confirmed all the land which had been given by the marchese Oberto Pallavicino.[7] It is evident that the marchese Pallavicino was one of the most conspicuous benefactors of the new monastery. The *chartularium* of his donation, which dated from 1136, has been published by Ughelli,[8] and Poggiali.[9] This marchese Pallavicino died in 1147, and was buried in the narthex of the church, where his tomb is still preserved.

In the light of all these documents there can be little doubt that the actual foundation of the monastery did not take place until 1136, although the project was ventilated as early as 1133.[10] The new monastery was entitled Chiaravalle della Colomba, in consequence of which grew up the picturesque legend that the site of the abbey had been miraculously determined by a dove which transported in its beak the building materials that had been gathered together on another site.

. . . Dom. Incarn. anno 1136. Indict. 14. tertio Idus Aprilis. (Ughelli, IV, 213. Also printed by Campi, I, 537).

[6] Die Dominica, id est 5. die mensis Aprilis, inspirante divina clementia, Placent. tam clero quam populo majoribus, & minoribus Placentinæ civitatis plena, & evidente concione decretum fuit dare monasterio Clarævallis, sito in curia Basilica ducis in loco, qui dicitur sanctum Michaelem, ut quicunque habent terram ibi adjacentem, & massariam laboratæ terræ precio quinque librarum Melanensium, inculta vero, sive sit pratum, sive nemorem precio quinquaginta solidorum Melanensium, aut tantam terra, quæ possit haberi suprascripto precio. Statutum quoque est ut a villa, quæ dicitur Budiro, & a villa, quæ dicitur Senus, nullus homo masculus, seu fœmina habitaculū habeat. . . . Anno ab Incarnatione Domini nostri Jesu Christi 1136. Indict. 14. (Ughelli, IV, 212).

[7] Innocentius Episcopus, Servus servorum Dei. Charissimo in Christo filio Bernardo Clarevallensi Abbati. . . . Omnes videlicet terras illas, quas illustr. vir Pallavicinus marchio, & nobiles signifer Placentiæ civitatis, sive alii boni viri, eidem loco devotionis intuitu, contulerunt. . . . Pisis . . . 7. Id. Feb. Ind. 15. Incarn. Dom. an. 1137. Pontific. vero D. Innocentii Papæ XI. anno 7. (Ughelli, IV, 213).

[8] *Ibid.*, II, 213.

[9] IV, 134-139.

[10] Poggiali, IV, 143-144. It was in 1133 that took place the Roman expedition of the emperor Lothair, referred to in connection with the foundation of the monastery in a diploma published by Campi: In nomine Sanctæ & Indiuiduæ Trinitatis, Lotharius Tertius Dei gratia Romanorum Imperator Augustus, Bernardo Venerabili Clareuallensium Abbati. . . . Quamobrem nouerit omnium fidelium nostrorum . . . industria, quod cum in labore Romanæ expeditionis in terra Italica essemus, petitione prædicti religiosi Abbatis, cuius consilium in rebus diuinis multum valere gaudebamus, & Placentinoru Ciuium, & Consulum, plebisque voluntate concessimus Cenobium fieri in loco, qui dicitur Caretum . . . & per manum eiusdem Abbatis Fratres ibi Deo seruituros imponi, & omnem eorum ordinationem, habitum, regulam ex eius sententia constare. . . . Et . . . placuit nobis . . . vt ab hac die, & deinceps nulla sæcularis habitatio vicinior eis, quam in præsenti die, construatur. . . . Anno Incarnationis Dominicæ 1137. indictione 14. anno regni sui 12. (Campi, I, 538).

The marchese Oberto Pallavicino is mentioned in documents of 1143 and 1145.[11] In a bull of 1144, the possessions of the abbey are clearly defined.[12] Another bull in favour of the monastery was promulgated by Eugenius III,[13] and still a third by Anastasius IV in 1154.[14] In 1248 the abbey was sacked and burned.[15]

It is unnecessary here to enter into detail upon the later history of the monastery, especially since this has been excellently worked out by Bertuzzi. In 1444 the abbey was given in commendam. In 1769 the monastery was suppressed, but nine years later the monks returned. In 1768 the chapels of the transept were baroccoized, according to an inscription published by Bertuzzi.[16] In 1810 the monks were again suppressed, and the church became a simple parish. In recent years the monument has been subjected to a thorough restoration, in the course of which the barocco intonaco was stripped from the nave, and the façade and cloisters rebuilt.

III. The church consists of a nave (Plate 53, Fig. 2) four double bays long, two side aisles, transepts, and seven square apses. A Renaissance campanile replacing the original central tower rises to the north of the transept. To the west of the church is an exterior narthex (Plate 53, Fig. 3); to the south, the beautiful cloisters. About the cloisters are the remains of monastic buildings. Of especial interest is the chapter-house of the late XIII century, reconstructed in the recent restoration, according to traces of the ancient one discovered.

The nave is covered with rib vaults (Plate 53, Fig. 2), approximately square in plan and highly domed. The diagonals (which are exceedingly slender) have a torus profile. The transverse ribs are in two unmoulded orders, and the wall ribs rectangular. All the arches of these vaults seem to be semicircular, but the diagonals are perhaps slightly depressed (Plate 53, Fig. 2). The side aisles are covered with groin vaults, square in plan, and highly domed. The transverse arches are similarly in two unmoulded orders, and the wall ribs rectangular. The groins seem to be very slightly depressed.

The alternate system of the nave consists of five members, of which the central one is semicircular. The adjustment to the superincumbent load is extremely awkward (Plate 53, Fig. 2), and recalls a similar cramping of the vaults in the abbey of Cerreto (Plate 52, Fig. 3). The intermediate system, which, like the alternate, is continuous, consists of a semicircular member (sometimes engaged on a pilaster strip), terminating unmeaningly without capital below the clearstory windows, one of which was placed in each double bay (Plate 53, Fig. 2). The side-aisle responds are alternately heavier (consisting of five members, the central one of which is semicircular) and

[11] Affò, II, 353, 358, 191. [12] Poggiali, IV, 196; Bertuzzi, 16.

[13] Poggiali, IV, 139-140. [14] Pflugk-Harttung, I, 252.

[15] Bertuzzi, 50. [16] 76.

lighter (consisting of a semi-column and two spurs). The alternate piers on the side of the side aisles have a rectangular member for the groin of the vault and each order of the transverse and main-arcade arches. The intermediate piers, on the other hand, have a spur only for the groin of the vault. In the second bay from the transept, however, the intermediate piers have an extra spur introduced on the side of the side aisles.

The groin vault of the principal apse is certainly modern. Indeed, the apses have all been very much made over. Only the two southernmost ones, covered with pointed barrel vaults, still preserve something of their original character. The bays of the transepts corresponding to the side aisles of the nave are covered with very oblong groin vaults, so much domed in the transverse sense as to resemble barrel vaults. They follow the heavy transverse semicircular arches, dividing the crossing from the transepts, and rise to the level of the crowns of the transverse arches of the nave. These vaults have pointed wall ribs. The bays we have just described are separated from the projecting portion of the transepts on either side by low semicircular arches. The southern transept is covered with a pointed barrel vault. The northern transept has two groin vaults, similar to the one already described, and separated by a semicircular arch. In the south transept a broad flight of stairs led to the second story of the monastery. Originally this stairway was placed in the middle of the transept, but in the XVII century it was moved against the western wall.

The narthex (Plate 53, Fig. 3), like the transepts, has a complex series of vaults placed at different levels. In the middle over the portal is a rib vault, placed at the highest level. There are no wall ribs. The diagonals of torus profile on the side of the church rest on ill-adjusted corbels, and the mouldings of the portal are cut off. It is evident, therefore, that this vault is later than the portal. On either side are two oblong groin vaults with pointed wall ribs. The outermost bays are covered with square groin vaults, with round arches, much modernized.

Square buttresses reinforce the side-aisle walls, and the vaults of the nave are strengthened by massive transverse buttresses pierced by an arch (Plate 53, Fig. 3). Both buttresses and transverse buttresses are applied only to the alternate piers.

It is evident that the vaults and buttresses of the cloisters are a later addition to the original construction.

The nave and transepts are constructed of cross-hatched bricks of uniform character. The courses are horizontal, the mortar-beds of moderate thickness. The bricks used for the inside facing are quite different from those of the exterior facing, and much finer, being very wide, and in some cases of enormous length. Still different is the brickwork of the façade.

IV.   The capitals of the interior are chiefly (with the exception of those about the chapel of the southern aisle, remade in the barocco period) of cubic type.   An incised line following the curve of the cushion, is often introduced, or leaves or other similar motives are applied in the angles (Plate 53, Fig. 2). Those of the transepts are simplest, but the ornament becomes more and more fanciful as the west end of the church is approached.   Here, indeed, several capitals of broad-leaved type appear.   The bases, if they exist, are not visible except in the western bays of the nave, where they are of Attic type with griffes.   The archivolts are in two unmoulded orders (Plate 53, Fig. 2).   The capitals of the narthex are of broad-leaved or cubic type.

The clearstory walls are adorned externally with round arched corbel-tables, but the side aisles, transepts and apses have cornices formed of flat corbel-tables (Plate 53, Fig. 3).   The original windows of the transepts and side aisles were heavily moulded.

In the recent restoration have come to light admirable frescos of the XV century.

V.   The abbey of Chiaravalle della Colomba closely resembles Cerreto. (Compare Plate 53, Fig. 2, with Plate 52, Fig. 3).   In both edifices we find the same alternate system, compound piers of similar section, torus diagonals, transverse arches in two orders, main-arcade arches in two orders, transverse buttresses of similar character (Plate 53, Fig. 3; Plate 52, Fig. 1), simple arched corbel-tables, cubic capitals, and load ill adjusted to the system (Plate 53, Fig. 2; Plate 52, Fig. 3).   Chiaravalle della Colomba, however, appears more advanced than Cerreto, in that pointed arches are introduced in the vaults of the transept; in that the intermediate system is continued along the clearstory wall (Plate 53, Fig. 2), and in that the cubic capitals are ornamented.   We have found reason to believe that Cerreto was begun c. 1140. The advance at Chiaravalle della Colomba is sufficiently great to justify us in assigning the commencement of this abbey to c. 1145.   It is therefore probable that some ten years elapsed after the foundation of the monastery before the construction of the church was undertaken.   The west façade has been so reconstructed in the recent restoration that it is difficult to determine its date.   Assuming that the restoration has been correct in its main lines, we notice that the tracery of the rose-window resembles that which formerly existed in the north transept of Morimondo, and must consequently have been erected c. 1190.   The narthex, obviously somewhat later, may be ascribed to c. 1200.   It is probable, therefore, that the construction of the church proceeded gradually from the east end, and that the edifice was completed about the end of the XII century.   The cornice of the cloisters is like that of the apse of Borgo S. Donnino, and of the baptistery of Parma.   It must consequently date from the last quarter of the XIII century.

CHIARAVALLE MILANESE,[1] BADIA

(Plate 54, Fig. 1, 3, 4; Plate 55, Fig. 1, 2)

I. The badia of Chiaravalle is the one Cistercian edifice of northern Italy which can be said to be really well known. It has been declared a national monument, and its accessibility has brought it within the notice even of tourists. The historical documents bearing upon its history have been published by Puricelli, Ratti and Fumagalli. In the western wall of the church is a fresco by Fimenghini (Plate 54, Fig. 3), painted in the XVII century, and representing the foundation of the church. This painting is of historical value, not only for the fact of the foundation, but because the façade is shown as it was before the baroccoization. This fresco has been studied by Nebbia. An engraving of the edifice was published in 1845, by Zuccagni-Orlandini.[2] This shows, not the façade, but the north transept-end as it was before the restoration. The windows of the northern wall are shown as pointed in the clearstory, but as half lunettes in the side aisles. About the same time Knight[3] made a drawing of the east end of the edifice. In the main apse are shown three round-headed windows walled up, four oculi, and a cornice of simple arched corbel-tables. The north wall of the apse has double arched corbel-tables, as have also the absidioles. An inedited monograph of the Mellas upon the church, recently published by Beltrami, is of but little importance. The monograph of Caffi, although printed as long ago as 1842, still remains the best and most complete description of the edifice. Mongeri's study of the tower is of little value, although illustrated with two drawings. Enlart[4] studied the edifice in his work on the Cistercian monuments of Italy. Much more valuable is the archæological analysis of the architecture contributed by Stiehl.[5] In the *Archivio Storico Lombardo* for 1895 is a valuable account of the modern restoration.[6]

II. The monastery of Chiaravalle was founded on January 22, 1135. Among the many sources from which this information is derived the most important is an inscription placed in the east wall of the cloisters. This inscription also records the date of the consecration of the church, May 2, 1221.[7]

Additional details of the story of the foundation are given in a diploma which, according to Fumagalli, is a copy of an authentic original, made in the XIII century, and containing a few errors. In it we read: "When the Milanesi saw that St. Bernard was evidently inspired by God in his speech

[1] (Milano). The abbey is situated about four kilometres to the south of Milan, on the line of the railway to Pavia.
[2] I, *Lombardo-Veneto, Bassi Tempi*, I, 1.
[3] II, Plate IV.　　[4] 68.　　[5] 11-13.　　[6] 212.

and discourse and performed many miracles, they willingly promised to erect from its foundations a monastery of his order in their territory. Wherefore he sent several of his monks to Milan where they remained for several days and abode in the monastery of S. Ambrogio. . . . And they bought a certain group of huts, such as in our language are called *casine,* in a place named Rovegnano. There was constructed the monastery which they called Chiara-valle. These things were done in the year of our redemption 1135."[8]

The tradition that the monastery was founded in 1135 was widely diffused during the Middle Ages, and left its imprint in several late chronicles. Among these may be mentioned the *Chronicon Maius*[9] and the *Manipulus Florum*[10] of Galvaneo della Fiamma (the latter embellished with fabulous details), Giovanni da Musso,[11] the *Cronichetta di Daniele,*[12] the chronicle of the

---

[7] The inscription, which has been very incorrectly printed by Puricelli (629), and more exactly by Giulini (III, 224; IV, 269), is as follows:

✠ ANNO ✠ GRATIE ✠ MCXXXV ✠ XI ✠ KL' ✠

✠ FEBR ✠ CONSTRVCTV̄ ✠ Ē ✠ HOC ✠ MO

NASTERIV̄ ✠ A B̄TO ✠ B'NĀRDO ✠ ĀB̄B̄E ✠ CLАR̂E

VAL' : MCCXXI ✠ CŌSECRATA ✠ Ē ✠ ECCL'A ✠ ISTA

A D̄N̄O ✠ HENRICO ✠ MEDIOLNENSI ✠ ARCHIĒP̄O ✠ VI

NONNIS ✠ MAII ✠ Ī HONŌE . SĈE MĀIE CLAR̂EVAL' .

[8] Mediolanenses cùm vidissent, Beatum Bernardum tum sermone & verbo Dei potentem, tum signis coruscantem; vltrò polliciti sunt Cœnobium de Ordine illius in Territorio suo à fundamentis erigere. Qua de re missi ab eo ad eandem Vrbem nonnulli ex eius Monachis, & ibidem per aliquot dies moram facientes IN MONASTERIO SANCTI AMBROSII SE LOCAVERVNT. . . . emeruntquè quædam Mapalia, quæ nostri vocant Cassinas: quod tunc Ravagianum appellabatur. VBI CONSTRVCTVM EST MONASTERIVM QVOD CLARÆVALLIS NVNCVPAVERE. . . . Acta sunt hæc Redemptionis nostræ Anno Millesimo centesimo trigesimoquinto. (Puricelli, 647-649).

[9] In MCXXXV beatus Bernardus fundavit monasterium de Clarevalle iuxta Mediolanum, cuius adiutor spetialis fuit Guido ex Capitaneis porte orientalis in die sancti Vincentii, et in MCXXXVI ipse fundavit monasterium de Corredo. (Galvanei Flammae, *Chron. Maius,* ed. Ceruti, 641).

[10] Sequenti anno B. Bernardus rediit Mediolanum, Claravallem construxit, Ordinem S. Bernardi ordinavit, qui modò dicuntur Fratres de Conegio. Prima domus istorum Fratrum fuit domus Portæ Orientalis, quam Guido ex Capitaneis Portæ Orientalis construxit. Hic autem Guido vir illustris Roman ivit, & ab Innocentio Tertio in quodam prandio aquam ad manus recepit, & istum Ordinem confirmavit. Et quia iste Papa dicebatur Innocentius Tertius, ideo iste Ordo Tertius appellatus est, & exemtus est ab omnibus gravaminibus Communitatis Mediolani. Hi Fratres fundaverunt primum, & secundum Ordinem Humiliatorum, & visitabant ipsos Fratres Humiliatos. (Galvanei Flammae, *Manipulus Florum,* CLXIX, ed. Muratori, R. I. S., XI, 632).

[11] Eodem anno [1135] B. Bernardus Monasterium Claravalle Mediolanensis Diœcesis construxit, & Ordinem, qui dicitur S. Bernardi, ordinavit, qui Ordo Tertius appellatur ex confirmatione Innocentii III. Papæ. (Johannis de Mussis, *Chronicon Placentinum,* ed. Muratori, R. I. S., XVI, 452).

CHIARAVALLE MILANESE, BADIA

Biblioteca Ambrosiana, which passes under the name of Filippo da Castel Seprio but which has been published by Grazioli[13] under the name of Goffredo da Bussero,[14] another chronicle contained in the same codex[15] and the *Chronicle of the Cistercians*.[16]

An inscription of 1614, in the west wall of the church, repeats that the abbey was founded in 1135, and mentions the name of Archinti, who gave the land on which the abbey was built.[17] This inscription explains the fresco (Plate 54, Fig. 3) in which two citizens of Milan are seen presenting a model of the church and the deed of donation to S. Bernardo.

In a charter of October, 1135, the church and monastery of S. Maria of Chiaravalle appear as already in existence.[18] In 1138 the first abbot was appointed.[19] The monastery had evidently been directed during the first three years of its existence by a prior.[20] In 1196 the construction of the church must have been practically completed, for altars were then consecrated.[21] The church itself, however, was not consecrated until 1221. This fact is recorded in the inscription cited above, in the chronicle which Grazioli calls Goffredo da Bussero,[22] and in other sources.[23]

The wealth and importance of the abbey in the later Middle Ages is indicated by a tax-list of 1398 published by Magistretti. In this, Chiaravalle appears as by all odds the wealthiest monastery of the diocese, being rated

---

[12] An. MCXXXV. Edificatum fuit Monasterium Clarevallis. (Ed. Giulini, III, 223).

[13] 240.

[14] Anno d̄ni 1135 in die S. Vincentii edificatum fuit monasterium Claravallis Mediolani. (*Chronicon* detto di Filippo da Castel Seprio, MS. Amb., S. Q. + I, 12, f. 62).

[15] Anno d̄ni 1135 Beatus Bernardus et cives Mediolani construxerunt monasterium Clarevallis extra Mediolanum. (*Edificationes Ecclesiarum Mediolani, ibid.*, 70).

[16] Eodem anno [1135] vndecimo Kalendas Februarij, [fundata est] Abbatia Clarævallis Mediolanensis. (*Chronicle of the Cistercians*, cit. Manrique, I, 301). For a study of these and other minor sources see Ratti, *La Misc.*, 125.

[17] REC̅OCILIATIS EC̅C̅LIAE M̅L̅N̅S̅I̅B̅ PER D. BERNARD̅V̅ VARIISQ.
INFIRMIS

ET DÆMONIACIS CVRATIS PIETATIS ERGO AD HOC INSIGNE
CLARÆVALLIS COENOBIVM CONSTRVENDVM, LATIFVNDIO AB
ILLVST

ARCHINTIS OBLATO EVM ENIXE ROGANT. ANNO MCXXXV
R. R. ABBAS ET MONACHI IN SANCTISS. PATRIS MERITORVM ET
MEDIOLANENSIVM PIETATIS MEMORIAM P. ANNO MDCXIV

[18] Giulini, III, 243. See, however, the comments upon this charter by Bonomi, *Diplomatum . . . Claravallis*, Brera MS., AE, XV, 20, f. 132.

[19] Fumagalli, IV, 208.   [20] *Ibid.*, 205.   [21] Ratti, *La Misc.*, 134; Puricelli, 1117.

[22] Anno domini 1221 . . . mense madii consecrata fuit ecclesia Clarevallis . . . (Cronaca di Goffredo da Bussero, ed. Grazioli, 244).

[23] See Giulini, IV, 269; Ratti, *La Misc.*, 134.

at 1500 lire or more than twice as much as S. Ambrogio of Milan, its nearest competitor. On October 19, 1433, the abbey was given in commendam.[24] In 1465 the monastery was reformed and "Tuscan Brothers," *i.e.*, monks from Settimo Toscano, were introduced. In 1474, however, the Cistercians returned.[25] In 1496 the monastery was united with that of S. Ambrogio of Milan. Under the year 1501, in a Codex published by Ratti, is inserted a notice of a reparation of a portion of the campanile which cost 32 soldi, 17 denari. In 1504, 1019 lire, 17 denari and 8 soldi were spent for the same purpose. In 1528 there is record that the monastery contained nineteen monks, seven *conversi,* nine *oblati* and eleven *servitori;* it was in this same year that the monastery was sacked by the imperial troops.[26] In 1571, 3364 lire were expended to construct the 'façade of the choir' in stone 'with statues and histories in bronze,' and in 1573 the *Cappella Grande* was built at a cost of 1789 lire. In 1581, 4889 lire were expended for the three chapels of S. Michele, S. Stefano, S. Maddelena and part of the campanile. In 1596 the church was repaved, and the cloister and dormitory whitewashed.[27] The sacristy was renovated by Gaspar Novato, who died in 1635. Many works were carried out by Damianus de Porris (†1638). Bonaventura de Piolis (†1645) built the new library and restored the choir. Carolus Em. Maldura, who died in 1659, enclosed the cloister. Various pavements were executed by Damianus Latuada (†1674). Giovanni Andrea Gambarana (†1709) renovated the choir-stalls and the frescos of the church, and Innocenzo Gradignani (†1735) restored the ruined painting over the stairs of the church, and the winter choir, which in his time was almost deserted.[28]

In 1879 a restoration of the abbey was determined upon, and a contract for 3934 lire was signed on the fifth day of September with the architect Colla. This restoration has continued with interruptions up to the present time. Among other works, the masonry of the apse was restored and the houses which had been built in the one gallery of the cloister which still survives, were cleared out. The walls and vaults of the cloister were restored and covered with intonaco. The roof was completely remade. About thirty fragments of capitals and bases were excavated in an adjoining cellar. Greatly to be regretted is the demolition of the XVIII century balustrade of the campanile, which formerly lent to this part of the edifice so much of its picturesque charm.

[24] Ratti, *La Misc.,* 133.

[25] 1465 D. Ioannes Posbonellus, hoc anno facta fuit reformatio Monachorum Clarævallis et divisa bona immobilia inter Monachos Clarævallis et Ascanium Mariam Sfortiam Commendatarium, et hoc anno fratres Tusci venerunt habitare in monasterio Clarævallis et habitaverunt usque ad Annum 1474; et tunc ipsi discedentes [*sic*], nostri reversi sunt ad habitandum Monasterium Clarævallis. (Ratti, *La Misc.,* 128).

[26] *Ibid.,* 130.   [27] *Ibid., passim.*   [28] *Ibid.,* 131-132.

CHIARAVALLE MILANESE, BADIA

III.   Although the church has suffered much from barocco alterations (Plate 55, Fig. 1), the lines of the original edifice may still be clearly traced. This consisted of a nave (Plate 55, Fig. 1) of four double bays, two side aisles, transepts (Plate 54, Fig. 1; Plate 55, Fig. 2), a choir (Plate 55, Fig. 1) and seven square apses (Plate 54, Fig. 1). The six absidioles, however, have been walled off and turned into chapels. The piers are all cylindrical (Plate 55, Fig. 1).

The nave is covered with rib vaults (Plate 55, Fig. 1), considerably domed, and erected upon a plan approximately square. The diagonals have a torus section. The side aisles are covered by groin vaults with transverse arches in two orders and with wall ribs, except in the easternmost bay of the north side aisle, where there is a rib vault. This vault and the adjoining transverse arch of torus section have obviously been remade in the Gothic period. The central apse has a rib vault like that of the nave, but the absidioles have pointed barrel vaults.

Pointed arches are introduced also in the main-arcade arches of the west bay of the nave and in the windows of the second story of the northern absidioles. The other arches are all round, except in the crossing (Plate 55, Fig. 1), where later pointed arches have obviously been added to strengthen the older round ones when the campanile was erected.

The system of the nave is alternate (Plate 55, Fig. 1). The intermediate piers have no system. That of the alternate piers consists of five or seven members, which may originally have been continued to the ground. The responds of the northern side aisle are all uniform, and consist of five members, the central one of which is semicircular. Those of the southern side aisle have all been remade.

The masonry consists of large bricks, well laid in horizontal courses, but the masonry beds are wide. In the clearstory are evident two distinct breaks in the construction.

To the south of the church have been reconstructed the scant remains of the once lovely cloisters (Plate 54, Fig. 4).

The vaults of the nave are reinforced by heavy transverse buttresses, rising above the aisle roof (Plate 54, Fig. 1).

IV.   The ornament of the church is extremely simple. The capitals for the most part are cubic. Certain carved capitals, however, were drowned when the pointed arches were added in the crossing, and others in the baroccoization of the western portal. The latter have been recently uncovered, and are of the broad-leaved voluted type. The portal itself had complicated mouldings, some of which even project.

The archivolts are of a single unmoulded order, except in the three western bays of the nave, where they are in two orders. The exterior is adorned with arched corbel-tables. In the north transept (Plate 54, Fig. 1) there are two sets of these corbel-tables placed at different levels, a clear indication that the wall has been raised. This alteration perhaps was made at the epoch when the absidioles were added. The fresco of the west façade (Plate 54, Fig. 3) shows that this, as well as the narthex which once preceded it, was adorned with similar arched corbel-tables.

Test excavations have revealed the existence of a mosaic pavement which, however, had not yet been explored at the time I last visited the church (September 28, 1913).

V. A study of the edifice itself makes it evident that the construction was begun at the east end, and that first was built the apse and the transepts. This part of the edifice must have been erected in the years following 1135. It is probable that the construction had proceeded as far as the second bay of the nave when the altars were consecrated in 1196. The western bays of the nave, in which a later style of architecture appears in the pointed arches and the archivolts in two orders, must have been built between 1196 and the consecration of 1221. Soon after, the cloisters were erected. Subsequently the absidioles were added. The central tower, is, of course, a construction of the late Gothic period.

CIRIÉ,[1] S. MARTINO

(Plate 55, Fig. 4)

I. S. Martino of Cirié has, so far as I know, never been published.

II. In the interior is an inscription recording a restoration of 1754.[2]

[1] (Torino).

[2]
SACRAM HANC AEDEM OLIM PAROCCHIALEM
TITULO D. MARTINI EPISCOPI
IAM INDE SECULO XV
MAXIMA VETUSTATE COLLAPSAM
IACOBUS PHILIPPUS IOANNINI CIRIACENSIS
SUB EODEM TITULO PRIOR
ET VICARIUS FORANEUS
IN AUGUSTIOREM FORMAM RESTITUENDAM
CURABAT ANNO MDCCLIV
UT QUE SINGULIS MENSIBUS IN PERPETUUM
SECUNDA PRIMAE HEBDOMADAE FERIA
SEMEL IN EA SACRA RES FIAT
IN ANIMARUM SUAE PAROECIAE SUFFRAGIUM
QUARUM NULLA FIT SPECIALIS COMMEMORATIO
PROPRIO AERE DOTAVIT

COMO, S. ABONDIO

The church is now an oratory of the parish of S. Giuseppe, but its ancient importance is witnessed by the fact that the parish still retains also the title of S. Martino.

III, IV.   The existing edifice evidently dates chiefly from the XVIII century, when the orientation of the Romanesque basilica was reversed.   Of the ancient church there survives only the campanile (Plate 55, Fig. 4), the apse, the southern absidiole (Plate 55, Fig. 4), and part of one of the nave arcades.   It is evident that this building possessed three aisles.   The extant Romanesque remains belong to three distinct epochs, which are best described separately.   (1) The main apse, the east gable and the south side-aisle wall are constructed of rubble of the roughest kind.   The arched corbel-tables of the apse were grouped two and two.   The south side-aisle wall has been much restored, but seems to have had no corbel-tables.   (2) The campanile is constructed of rubble, but of superior quality.   There are seven stories (Plate 55, Fig. 4), each with arched corbel-tables, grouped five and five or six and six.   The openings gradually increase in size towards the top.   In the upper two stories there are bifora or trifora with capitals like those of S. Benigno.   (3) The southern absidiole is constructed of masonry of fine quality.   The incised bricks of regular size are well laid in perfectly horizontal courses and separated by mortar-beds about $1\frac{3}{4}$ centimetres in depth.   The arched corbel-tables are grouped three and three.   The deeply splayed windows of a single order were intended to serve without glass.   To this same epoch seems to belong also the one remaining arch of the southern arcade, which is of a single unmoulded order.   The cylindrical pier is constructed of brick and crowned by a cubic capital of developed type.   The short barrel vault which precedes the principal apse is possibly contemporary.

V.   The arched corbel-tables of the principal apse, grouped two and two, recall the pieve of Cavriana, which dates from c. 1025.   Since, however, the masonry is somewhat rougher than that of Cavriana, this part of the edifice may be ascribed to c. 1020.   The campanile, more advanced in style, may be ascribed to c. 1040.   The cubic capital of the arcade of the interior recalls the capitals of S. Abondio of Como (Plate 59, Fig. 1), an edifice consecrated in 1095.   The third epoch of construction may consequently be ascribed to c. 1100.

COMO, S. ABONDIO

(Plate 58, Fig. 2, 4; Plate 59, Fig. 1, 2, 4)

I.   The important abbey church of S. Abondio at Como has long been justly ranked as one of the most impressive and interesting monuments of the Lombard style.   In the XVI century it was described by Giovio and Ninguarda.   Both these descriptions are important sources for the history of the church. In the XIX century De Dartein described[1] and illustrated[2] the edifice. The monograph of Boito in its day represented an important forward step in archæological methods. In it is contained the publication of the important remains of a pre-existing basilica discovered during the restoration. Less important is the archæological study of Barelli. The Carlovingian carvings were illustrated and analyzed by Cattaneo.[3] In recent years Monti and Rivoira[4] have contributed studies upon the church which deserve mention.

II. The earliest authentic monuments which testify to the existence of the church of S. Abondio are a number of early Christian inscriptions dating from the V century, and which came to light during the restoration. These epitaphs were found in the pavement of the lower church.[5] The existence of such inscriptions is a sufficient indication that the church of S. Abondio existed as early as the V century.

It is a tradition at Como that S. Abondio was originally dedicated to SS. Pietro e Paolo, and was in early times the cathedral of Como. This, for example, is stated by Giovio, who adds that in his time there were still extant half-ruined buildings of the episcopal palace.[6] Cantù[7] states that the church was founded by S. Felice, but according to Giovio, S. Amanzio translated the relics of St. Peter and St. Paul from Rome.[8] Tatti[9] conjectures in consequence that the church was founded by S. Amanzio, and not by S. Felice. This deduction is comforted by a text in Ninguarda: "Beyond the bridge is the church of S. Abondio where Eutichio, the eighth bishop of Como, was accustomed to retire to a cave to pray, because the ancient residence of the bishops of Como was at that place, and because in it were buried and venerated by the people of Como the bodies of many holy bishops. The temple which is very large and famous was originally dedicated to the holy princes of the Apostles Peter and Paul, a part of the relics of whom S. Amanzio, third bishop of Como . . . translated from the city of Rome and placed under the high altar of the church dedicated to the same apostles. The bishops of Como had their seat here, and there was also a college of canons endowed with many privileges by Hugh and Lothair, kings of Italy, about 940."[10]

[1] 312. [2] LXXV and LXXIX. [3] 188-189. [4] 253.

[5] Boito, 314; De Rossi.

[6] Ecclesia extra urbem sita, quæ S. Abundii nuncupatur, apostolis prius Petro et Paulo consecrata fuit et hæc antiquissima est. Hic aliquando comensium episcoporum sedes fuit. Supersunt hoc etiam tempore semidiruta haud mediocris impensæ ædificia, quæ comenses antistites incolere consueverant. (Giovio, 213).

[7] I, 54.

[8] Apostolorum Petri et Pauli nonnullas corporum reliquias ex urbe Rome Comum attulit, quas in eorum templo sub altari maximo venerabundas composuit. (Giovio, 181).

[9] I, 284.

[10] . . . est ultra pontem templum Scti Abundij . . . ubi Divus Eutichius Episcopus Comensis octavus, quandoque ad speluncam orandi gratia secedere solebat, cum ob

COMO, S. ABONDIO

The very diffusion of the tradition and the fact that it contains nothing intrinsically improbable, combine to lend it a certain weight, notwithstanding the fact that it has come down to us only in documents of late date. It is therefore probably at S. Abondio that officiated the chapter of priests of the church of Como, mentioned in 803 in a privilege of Charlemagne published by Tatti.[11] The chapter of S. Abondio—although it is not clear that it was at this time a chapter regular—is explicitly mentioned in a privilege of Louis the Pious of 818, also published by Tatti.[12] This diploma is dated *Actum Cumo ad Sanctum Petrum*, which gives some reason to doubt the tradition which identifies the church of the Apostles with S. Abondio. In a privilege of Berenger I of 911,[13] S. Abondio is explicitly called a pieve. In the will of the bishop Walperto of 914,[14] it appears that the cathedral was at that time established in the church of S. Eufemia, now called S. Fidelio. It is true that in 937 the emperors Hugh and Lothair granted to the bishop of Como a privilege *ad laudem, & gloriam Omnipotentis Dei, ac Sanctae Mariae Virginis, Sanctiq: Abondij confessoris*. This does not prove, however, that the church of S. Abondio was at that time the cathedral, since S. Abondio, one of the patrons of the city, might well have been mentioned even had the seat of the bishops already been transferred to S. Eufemia.

In 1013 Alberico, bishop of Como, established a monastery of Benedictine monks in the pieve of S. Abondio. Two copies of the deed of foundation are extant. One, published by Tatti,[15] is without date, but assigned by him and by Barelli to 1010. The other, published by Barelli, bears the date 1013. In the latter, among other things, we read: "In the name of the holy and undivided Trinity. To the much revered and most blessed father and confessor Abondio, Alberico, albeit unworthy, Thy Vicar. . . . I examined the conduct and acts of the bishops who have preceded me to find out if haply by the negligence of some one of them it had come about that the monasteries of all thy churches were destitute, and when I had learned from the report of many who told me the life of my predecessors, praising the worthy deeds of one and regretting the impieties perpetrated by another, how all the monasteries had

veterem Episcoporum Comensium ressidentiam et habitationem, quæ hoc loco erat, tum propter corpora multorum Episcoporum, in eo humata et a populo Comensi sancte venerata, maxime insigne est atque illustre; fuit initio dedicatum Divis Apostolorum Principibus Petro et Paulo, quorum ex reliquijs portionem Divus Amantius tertius Episcopus Comensis . . . ex Urbe deportavit, atque honorificentissime sub maiore altari eisdem Apostolorum principibus sacrato reposuit. Habitabant hic Episcopi Comenses et Collegium Canonicorum, multis privilegijs ab Hugone et Lothario Italiæ Regibus circiter annum 940 decoratum. (Ninguarda, ed. Monti, 83).

[11] I, 945.   [12] *Ibid.*, 946.

[13] in quadam Plebe Ecclesiæ Cumanæ, quæ dicitur S. Abundij. Cuius præcibus acclinati in iam dicta Plebe ædificando, & construendo Mercatum . . . licentiam dedimus. (Tatti, II, 789).

[14] Cited below, p. 323.   [15] II, 828.

thus been destroyed, I decided in a council of the citizens and the inhabitants of the suburbs, that since it was not possible to restore all the monasteries, at least one of the many should be restored in thy name. But where should this restoration more fittingly begin than in the church where thy venerable body lies? Wherefore in the presence of the clergy and laity who encourage and approve this act, I found in thy church a congregation of monks to whom I give what is necessary for food and clothing, partly from thy goods which have been hitherto in my use, and partly from goods which I have acquired otherwise or am now acquiring. . . . Done at Aquileia on the fifth day of August in the year of the Incarnation of our Lord, 1013."[16]

The foundation by Alberico was immediately confirmed by the king, Enrico II,[17] and in 1015 the same Enrico, now emperor, made a donation to the new monastery.[18] Other donations were made in 1027 and 1063.[19]

In 1095 the church of S. Abondio was consecrated. This notice is contained in the chronicle ascribed to Filippo da Castel Seprio, but believed by Grazioli to be by Goffredo da Bussero. In this the date is imperfectly recorded, since the name of the month is omitted after the numeral three.[20] Grazioli[21] conjectures that the consecration took place on May 23, but the date of June 3, recorded by Ninguarda, accords better with the text of the chronicle. The authenticity of these faulty notices might justly be open to suspicion were it not for the circumstance that they are confirmed by several other considerations. Urban remained in Lombardy some time in the spring and summer of 1095 before proceeding to Clermont, where he arrived in August.[22] Moreover, there is extant a bull of Urban issued at Milan on the sixteenth of May, 1095, in favour of the church of S. Abondio.[23] Such bulls

---

[16] In nomine Sanctæ et Individuæ Trinitatis. Domino Sancto ac beatissimo patri et confessori Abundio. Albericus licet indignus tui vicarius. . . . Mores et acta predecessorum antistitum inquisivi. si cujus forte incuria. tuarum omnium ecclesiarum funditus forent monasteria destituta. Cumque multis referentibus vitam priorum. alterius digna facta laudantibus alterius perpetrata flagicia suspirantibus qualiter sic cuncta destructa essent didicerim. mox deo inspirante. civium et suburbanorum conscilio statui. et si omnia non possent. vel unum ex multis. in tuo nomine recuperare. Ubi tamen aptius hæc renovatio consurgeret. quam ubi tuum corpus venerabile jacet? Unde presentibus episcopii clericis et laicis. ipsique multum cogentibus atque precantibus volo et constituo in tua sancta æcclesia deinceps sub monachico jure servituros. quibus necessaria victus et vestitus distribuo. partim de tuo hactenus in meum usum sumpto. partim aliunde adquisito. vel jam nunc adquirendo. In primis igitur dono ipsos ordines etc. . . . Tempore quo linea annorum incarnationis dominicæ millesima tertiadecima computabatur acta sunt hæc aquilegiæ nonas augusti. . . . (Barelli).

[17] Diploma published by Tatti, II, 833.　　[18] Ibid., 837.　　[19] Tatti, II, 857.

[20] Anno dni 1095 . . . Papa Urbanus . . . die 3 consecravit ecclesiam S. Abundii Cumarum et habebat secum sex Cardinales et quatuor Episcopos. (Chronica detta di Filippo da Castel Seprio, MS. Amb. S. Q. + I, 12, f. 60).

[21] 238.　　[22] Giulini, II, 609.

[23] This bull has been published, though with wrong date, by Tatti, II, 864.

were habitually granted by the popes to churches which they consecrated. In this case the consecration is not mentioned in the bull, and it is probable that the usual process was reversed and the bull granted before, not after, the ceremony of dedication. The tradition that the church was consecrated by Urban II is recorded also by Ninguarda: "Some years after . . . Urban II. . . . the pope . . . on the journey which he undertook to France passed through Como with seven cardinals and four bishops, and consecrated the church under the name and title of S. Abondio in the year 1095 on the third of June; the day after he consecrated the altars of the saints Eusebio, Eupilio, Adelberto, and Rubiano in that church, and granted an indulgence for the remission of all venial sins and a third part of all mortal sins to all those who should visit the same church on the festival of its consecration and of the above-mentioned saints and each day during the octaves, and this indulgence was afterwards confirmed by Sixtus IV, with the condition that alms should be given, and it was also confirmed by Gregory XIII."[24] Giovio also states: "Eighty-two years later [*i.e.,* in 1095], the pope Urban II journeying into France with seven cardinals and four bishops turned aside at Como and dedicated the basilica anew under the name of S. Abondio."[25] There can therefore be no doubt that the church was really consecrated in 1095.

In 1180 the bishop of Como made a donation to the monastery of S. Abondio.[26] From documents of 1195 and 1205,[27] we learn of a dispute between the monks of S. Abondio and the canons of the cathedral of Como as to who should take precedence at the ordination of the bishop. From a bull of Innocent III of 1205[28] and from a similar one of the same pontiff of 1208,[29] it is clear that the monastery depended directly upon the Holy See. The abbey was given in commendam during the pontificate of Sixtus IV (1471-1483), according to Giovio,[30] or more precisely, in the year 1475, according to Ninguarda.[31]

The description of the church written by Giovio in the XVI century deserves study: "The great age of this temple is clearly shown by its form,

---

[24] Aliquot post annis . . . Urbanus II. . . . Summus Pontifex . . . ex itinere quod in Gallias instituerat, hac transiens cum septem Cardinalibus ac quatuor Episcopis, eandem Ecclesiam sub nomine et invocatione Scti. Abundij, anno 1095, tertio nonas Junij, postridieque altaria SS.orum Eusebij, Eupilij, Adelberti et Rubiani in ea erecta consecravit, cum perpetua indulgentia remissionis omnium peccatorum venialium ac tertiæ partis capitalium, visitantibus dictam Ecclesiam diebus consecrationis ipsius Ecclesiæ ac patrociniorum dictorum Sanctorum et singulis diebus inter octavas; quæ quidem indulgentia fuit deinde a Sixto quarto, anno 1475, cum conditione erogandæ eleemosynæ, et a Gregorio XIII anno . . . . . ea conditione præterita, iuxta primæ concessionis formam, confirmata. (Ninguarda, ed. Monti, 83 *seq.*).

[25] Post annos octoginta duos Urbanus II pontifex maximus in Galliam profecturus, cum septem cardinalibus et quatuor episcopis Comum divertit et basilicam ipsam sub nomine D. Abundii denuo dedicavit. (Giovio, 214).

[26] Tatti, II, 879.   [27] *Ibid.,* 889-891.   [28] *Ibid.,* 892.   [29] *Ibid.,* 897.
[30] 216.   [31] *Loc. cit.*

for a double arcade of columns supports the roof, and a narthex precedes the edifice. Many ancient blocks, columns, epistyles and epitaphs are employed in the walls of the basilica and the surrounding buildings, so that, I think, there was formerly on the site a more ancient edifice. An evidence of this is the recently discovered brick monument of Lucius Calpurnius Fabatus, with a marble base beautifully inscribed with an epitaph."[32]

Ninguarda, discoursing of the church, describes the extraordinary veneration in which S. Abondio was held, because of the indulgences of the popes, the concourse of people who flocked to the basilica, the ceremony of the mass celebrated on the anniversary of the saint—a solemnity attended officially by the city magistrates and the corporations—and the secular and religious festival of two days observed on this occasion. "Before the doors and threshold of the temple was a high portico, or rather a rectangular atrium covered with a great vault, and above the vault, another chamber of the same size and shape, which the people called the *paradiso,* where it is said the catechumens were accustomed to be gathered when the priests celebrated the divine mysteries. This seems credible, since from the *paradiso* opened a door placed directly opposite the altar of the church, and giving access to a gallery in the interior of the basilica. This gallery was at the same level as the *paradiso,* and supported upon a rectangular vault in the breadth of the central nave of the church. At either end of the gallery a door opened upon broad stone stairs which led down to the main floor of the basilica. At the west end of the gallery was an altar with a small marble receptacle containing the bodies of S. Rubiano the fourteenth, and Adilberto the fifteenth, bishop of Como, of whom I shall speak more at length below. The vault and the upper chamber which were in front of the façade of the temple had been torn down, and the atrium left open to the air by the order and decree of the illustrious cardinal, commendatary abbot of the church, who preceded the Cardinal Tolomeo Gallio, perhaps in order that the church which was very dark and obscure, might be better lighted. There are in this church two great campaniles erected at either side of the choir, of which the one which is placed towards the sacristy has long been without bells, and the other, on the side of the public street, has three great bells. Within there are four rows of columns and five aisles; and, before the church was made over in its present form, there was a transverse screen which separated the choir from the nave. A vaulted sacristy adjoins the choir on the side of the monastery. . . . The illustrious Cardinal Tolomeo Gallio in the year 1586 . . . moved by his piety and zeal towards God and the saints, felt that he must undertake and carry out a restoration of the

[32] Multa vero in ipsius basilicæ et proximarum ædium structuram antiquæ paraturæ columnæ et epistylia, tum bases et epithaphia collata sunt, ut illic existimem aliquid ipso quoque templo vetustius fuisse, quod præcipue indicat L. Calpurnii Fabati latericium monumentum cum marmorea base pulcherrimo inscripta epitaphio nuper repertum. (Giovio, 216).

church, since the latter was ruinous, dark, without vault or ceiling, except in the choir, which was already vaulted. Moreover the church was encumbered by the stairway, the gallery at the west end, and the choir-screen, while the altars were small and without images. Of the other things which were necessary, such as sacred utensils, there was almost nothing. He therefore assiduously took every care to restore the church and put it in order. He removed the stairways, the choir-screen, the gallery at the west end with its altar, and opened a semicircular window filled with glass, by which the whole edifice was bathed with light. He restored all the altars in better form and design, and one in the choir higher than the others he erected with steps and rails of variated marbles; and this we consecrated in honour of S. Abondio in the year 1592, on the seventh of June. And four other altars which were not in the central nave . . . we consecrated . . . . . in honour of the said saints. . . . He covered all the naves with vaults, he opened up several windows in suitable places to increase the light of the edifice, and furnished them with glass as a protection against the weather. He razed the atrium to the ground, and restored the entire church in better form . . . sparing no expense, so that now this basilica, renovated in every part, presents a worthier appearance and design than ever before. . . . In this church reside three chaplains and two clerks paid by the commendatary abbot. These priests recite the canonical office every day and celebrate two masses, and on all festivals they celebrate a third mass and also sing vespers."[33]

[33] Extra fores limenque templi erat excelsa porticus seu potius atrium quadratum magna fornice tectum, et supra fornicem conclave eiusdem magnitudinis et formæ, quem locum vulgus paradysum appellabat, ubi fertur Cathecumenos, quo tempore sacerdotes divinis operabantur, segregari solitos, id quod credibile videri potest, siquidem ex illo conclavi æquo et plano pavimento in templum accessus erat per ianuam directe maiori templi altari oppositam; fornix vero quadrata latitudine medianæ navi, quæ ab utroque latere ianua amplis gradibus lapideis itionem deorsum præbebat, ac sursum æqualis erat. Supra fornicem e regione cellæ maioris erant sub parvo altaris receptaculo marmoreo inclusa corpora Sanctorum Rubiani decimiquarti et Adelberti decimiquinti Episcoporum Comensium, quorum infra longior fiet mentio. Testudo et conclave, quæ ante templi fores erant, Ill.mi Domini Cardinalis Ab. Ecclesiæ proximi ante Ill.mum D.num Cardinalem Comensem commendatarij iussu et mandato deiecta atrium, sub æthere, ut iam est, reliquerunt, forte ut Ecclesia, quæ valde obscura erat et opaca, uberiori luce afflueret. Sunt in dicta Ecclesia duæ magnæ turres campanariæ in lateribus cellæ maioris constitutæ, quarum quæ versus sacrarium vergit longo iam tempore campanis caret et, altera ad viam publicam posita habet tres magnas campanas. Intus esistunt quatuor ordines columnarum et quinque naves, et priusquam restituerentur ad eam speciem, qua nunc est, habebat etiam parietem obliquum, qui claudebat chorum. . . . Cellæ maiori versus habitationes contiguum est sacrarium fornicatum. . . . Illust.mus D. Cardinalis Comensis anno 1586 . . . nisi pro pietate ac zelo suo erga Deum et Divos Ecclesiæ restaurationem prius aggrediendam sibi et absolvendam existimasset; quæ cum esset deformata, obscura, sine testudine seu tabulato, excepta cella maiore, quæ iam erat fornicata, scalis cum camera supra ianuam et muro per eam oblique ducto impedita, et altaria parva sine imaginibus, alijsque rebus ad eam neces-

Early in the XVII century Augustinian canons were installed in the monastery and remained there until suppressed in 1796.[34] In 1834 the existing seminary was established in the buildings of the old abbey. Two years later a pilaster which stood before the church, the last relic of the ancient narthex, was torn down. In 1863 a restoration of the church was begun under the direction of Balestra. The transverse wall which had been erected across the side aisles was torn down and replaced by an iron choir-screen. The XVI century vaults were removed, and a flat ceiling, instead of an open timber roof such as the church was probably originally supplied with, was erected. The western gallery was rebuilt in accordance with the description of Ninguarda and traces preserved in the masonry. The barocco windows were closed up and new windows in the style of the XI century opened in their place. Two new windows were opened in the third story of the façade, apparently without authority. The northern campanile, which had been torn down probably in the XVII century, was rebuilt. During the course of the restorations the foundations of an earlier basilica were found beneath the present pavement. The plan of this primitive church has been published by Boito, and if correctly understood by him, was most peculiar.[35] The semicircular apse was preceded by an oblong space. The nave was flanked by two oblong halls situated on either side and opening into the nave by lateral doorways. There were five doorways on each side, and the whole edifice was preceded by a narthex. The walls were covered with traces of frescos.

During the restoration many fragments of Carlovingian sculpture came to light, the finest of which, pieced out with other fragments brought from Galliano, have been used to construct the new altars in the upper church (Plate 59, Fig. 2, 4), while others, together with the early Christian inscrip-

sarijs, ac sacram supellectilem fere nullam haberet, omnem curam ad reformandam ordinandamque Ecclesiam continuo admovit, et sublatis ex ea scalis, pariete obliquo, testudine cum altari ad ianuam maiorem, quo loco ostium Cathecumenorum erat, fenestram semicircularem ac vitreatam, cuius fulgore totum templum collustratur, reposuit; altaria omnia in maiorem formam ordinemque restituit, unum in cella maiore cæteris altius extructum cum gradibus et cancellis mixti marmoris, et Divo Abundio dicatum, quod nos anno 1592 septima die mensis Iunij, quæ fuit prima dominica, . . . sacravimus, et quatuor alia extra cellam maiorem . . . quæ altaria fuerunt etiam a nobis anno 159 . . . . . in honorem dictorum Divorum sacrata . . . naves omnes fornicato opere texit, plures fenestras locis ad augendum lumen aptis induxit et vitro ab aeris incommodis munivit, atrium ante Ecclesiam æquavit et in meliorem formam redegit . . . nullos ea in re sumptus refugiens, adeo ut iam dicta Ecclesia, omni parte innovata, longe digniorem ac unquam alias habeat aspectum et formam. . . . In hac Ecclesia resident tres capellani sacerdotes et duo clerici stipendiati a commendatario, qui singulis diebus horas canonicas recitant et duas missas celebrant, festisque diebus omnibus etiam tertiam ac vesperas cantant. (Ninguarda, ed. Monti, 38 f.).

[34] Barelli.

[35] Possibly there may have been three aisles, and what the restorers took for doorways may have been merely intercolumniations.

tions found in the pavement, have been transported to the Museo Civico. The restorers indicated the foundations of the primitive basilica by lines of black marble inlaid in the pavement of the existing church. Some parts of the old foundation walls can still be seen. The restorers also discovered remains of the foundations of the jubé described by Ninguarda, and some traces of a mosaic pavement. They also found the foundations of the narthex, the three aisles of which seem to have corresponded to the three inner aisles of the nave. Boito believed that this narthex was added subsequently to the completion of the rest of the church.

III. The edifice consists of a nave six bays long, double side aisles terminating internally in absidioles which are marked externally by a flat wall, a choir of two bays, a semicircular apse (Plate 58, Fig. 4), and two campanili (Plate 58, Fig. 2) rising over the eastern bays of the inner side aisles. As is known from the descriptions of Ninguarda and Giovio cited above, the church was originally preceded by an ample narthex in two stories and supplied with a western gallery and a nave. The latter has been restored. The choir, the western bay of the nave (Plate 58, Fig. 4) and the eastern bays of the side aisles are covered with domed groin vaults, sometimes with, sometimes without, wall ribs. The absidioles have half domes, and the main apse has a half dome with ribs of rectangular section converging on a keystone of the transverse arch (Plate 58, Fig. 4). The remainder of the edifice is roofed in timber. The aisles are of three different heights (Plate 58, Fig. 2; Plate 59, Fig. 1), so that the section of the church is pyramidal. The nave is separated from the inner side aisles by massive cylindrical piers (Plate 59, Fig. 1). The inner and outer side aisles are separated by columns (Plate 59, Fig. 1). The masonry (Plate 58, Fig. 2) is a rough sort of ashlar, consisting of rectangular blocks of various sizes laid in courses which are not always horizontal. In the shafts is noticeable a tendency to place long pieces of stone of lighter colour in juxtaposition to bands of darker material. The same rudimentary attempt at polychromy may be observed in certain of the archivolts. A system of five members, the central one of which is a shaft or a pilaster, is supplied for the groin vaults of the choir, and the ribs of the half dome of the central apse are similarly carried on shafts (Plate 58, Fig. 4).

IV. The capitals of the arcades separating the nave from the inner side aisles are cubic of a fully developed type (Plate 59, Fig. 1). Those of the outer arcades are either similarly cubic or of a Corinthianesque type with carved or uncarved leaves well executed but surprisingly simple in design. In the northern absidiole and elsewhere are capitals either cubic or with carved acanthus leaves under the angles. The bases are without griffes (Plate 59, Fig. 1) and of Attic type. The unmoulded archivolts are of a single order (Plate 59, Fig. 1), although in the absidioles there are found archivolts in two orders.

The decoration of the exterior (Plate 58, Fig. 2) is rich. Arched corbel-tables are supported on shafts or on pilaster strips, or on shafts engaged upon pilaster strips. In the apse the corbel-tables are in two orders. The cornice of the apse includes a rope-moulding and a saw tooth. The saw tooth is also employed in the string-courses and cornices of the ancient campanile (Plate 58, Fig. 2). The windows of the apse are shafted, moulded, and surrounded by a band of rich decoration with rinceaux, interlaces, and other ornaments completely Lombard in character. Here, as elsewhere in the exterior, the grotesque element so strikingly absent in the interior, is given free rein. The windows of the campanile are in two orders, and in the belfry is a triforium (Plate 58, Fig. 2). The windows of the church are so large (Plate 58, Fig. 2) that it is evident they must have been filled with glass of some sort. The restorers found some fragments of blue and red glass, and have accordingly placed in the windows mosaics of colored glass separated by leading. It has been suspected that the fragments of glass found did not belong to the original construction, and, in fact, were not older than the XV century, when, as we know from Ninguarda, glass was placed in several of the windows. However, translucent mosaics of colored glass were regularly used to fill the windows of Lombard churches in the XIII century, and the chances are that we have here a correct restoration.

In the western gallery and choir are preserved fine frescos of the XIV century. Traces of the frescoed decoration with which the earlier basilica was entirely covered, were found in abundance by the restorers.

The two side altars are formed of carved fragments, some of which were found at S. Abondio, others brought from S. Vincenzo at Galliano. The front of the northern altar (Plate 59, Fig. 2) is formed of a single slab; the southern altar (Plate 59, Fig. 4), on the other hand, is formed of five separate fragments. The slab in the northern altar (Plate 59, Fig. 2) shows a certain flaccid treatment of the leaf-form, which could only have been produced at the end of the X or the beginning of the XI century. The central panel of the southern altar (Plate 59, Fig. 4) is contemporary, since it is characterized by the same graceful flow of lines and a similar technique. The movement of the spirals radiating from the centre and the circular motives of this fragment recall the slab in the cloisters of the cathedral of Aosta (Plate 12, Fig. 1), a monument which dates from c. 1010. Hence the central slab of the southern altar and the slab of the northern altar must date from the early years of the XI century. The conclusion is therefore justified that these are the fragments brought from Galliano, and they may consequently be considered as authentically dated monuments of 1007. The remaining fragments, which were doubtless found at S. Abondio, show a very different technique; the carving is much crisper, the design is less graceful but more vigorous, and there is noticeable a fondness for interlaces and animal forms. All this recalls strongly the baptistery at

Cividale (Plate 59, Fig. 3). The fragments may consequently be ascribed to c. 735.

In the Museo Civico are preserved a great quantity of Carlovingian slabs and fragments of all sizes, coming from S. Abondio.[36] They all appear to be contemporary with each other, and with the fragments of the altars we have ascribed to c. 735. The principal motives are interlaces, guilloches, square guilloches with bunches of grapes or other motives, diamond and circle ornaments, arcades with conventionalized fir-trees or crosses, etc. In addition to these there is part of an ambo of the XI century with a most interesting sculpture. S. Abondio, with bishop's crosier and robes, is represented à la St. Michael, with wings, and trampling on the dragon.[37] In the stairway is a capital said to come from S. Abondio, and very different from the others of that church. It is sculptured with the visit of the three Magi, the angel appearing to Joseph, and the Flight into Egypt. A peculiarity of the last scene is that Joseph carries the Child. This capital shows very strongly the influence of Guglielmo da Modena and also of certain of his followers, notably Nicolò and the sculptors who executed the Porta dei Principi at Modena and S. Celso at Milan. It must date, therefore, from c. 1135, and if it really came from S. Abondio, must have belonged to some later addition to the church— possibly the narthex.[38] In the Museo Civico are also preserved numerous capitals of S. Abondio replaced in the restoration.[39]

V. The remains of the primitive church discovered beneath the pavement are usually assigned to the V century. In order to be able to discuss intelligently their date, it would be necessary to study the masonry and the remains of the frescos still preserved. It would also be necessary to eliminate the doubt that the restorers may have entirely misunderstood the remains. None of this is possible in the present inaccessible condition of the ruins. It must remain, therefore, entirely uncertain whether we have here the fragments of an early Christian or of a Carlovingian edifice. The fragments of carving coming from this church seem to date, as has been seen, from about 735, but church-furniture might readily have been added to an earlier edifice or transported into a later one.

The church of S. Abondio itself was, as we have seen, consecrated in 1095. It has been almost universally supposed by all the authors who have written of the edifice that it was begun in 1013, when the monastery was established. The donations of 1027, 1063, etc., have been taken as a proof that the construction lasted during almost the entire XI century. In the deed of foundation of 1013, however, and in the subsequent acts of donation, there

---

[36] Nos. 1-9, 11, 26, 28b, 114-124, and three without number.   [37] No. 10.

[38] This capital bears the number 95. It has been illustrated by Venturi, III, 204-207.

[39] Nos. 54, 95, 96, 97, 131, 132, and four without number.

is not a word or a phrase to indicate that the construction of the new church was contemplated or in course of execution. The charter of 1013 explicitly states that there was a church already in existence on this site. It is entirely probable that the reconstruction of this church was deferred until long after the foundation of the monastery. That such was actually the case is sufficiently proved by the style of the existing edifice, which is entirely homogeneous and bears no sign of having been in construction for a period of eighty years. The character of the masonry employed in Lombardy at the beginning of the XI century was widely different from that employed at the end of that century. In the church of S. Abondio the masonry is all of homogeneous character, and is of the type that was used at the end of the XI century, as, for example, at S. Benedetto on the mountain above Lenno (Plate 102, Fig. 5), a surely dated monument of 1083. Similar observations apply to the capitals and every detail of the architecture. It is no longer possible to confuse indiscriminately monuments of the first and second halves of the XI century. S. Abondio belongs to the end of that century. So little variation in style do the different parts of the edifice show that it is only after careful and minute study that it is possible to say that the nave is probably somewhat older than the choir. The arched corbel-tables of the nave are of a fully developed type that could not have been erected before 1060. The shafts on which they are supported are found elsewhere only in edifices of the last decade of the XI century or of the XII century, and even later in style are the arched corbel-tables in two orders of the apse, and the shafts engaged upon pilaster strips of the east end of the edifice. The latter feature recalls S. Michele at Pavia (Plate 173, Fig. 5), a building erected c. 1100. The system of the choir in several orders is analogous to that of S. Ambrogio at Milan, a church begun about 1070. The ribbed half dome of the apse is a feature paralleled in Lombardy only in the church of S. Eufemia of Isola Comacina, but which is familiar in edifices of northern France of the XII century (compare St.-Remi of Bruyère-sur-Fère, Plate 58, Fig. 3), and at S. Maria di Castello of Corneto Tarquinia (Plate 77, Fig. 2), a building begun in 1122. The square profile of the ribs, however, recalls the ribs of various Lombard vaults of the second half of the XI century. The shafted, moulded windows of the choir of S. Abondio, with their rich Lombard decorations, resemble more closely S. Michele of Pavia and other edifices of c. 1100 than S. Ambrogio of Milan, a building of c. 1075. There can, therefore, be no doubt that in S. Abondio we have a monument consecrated in 1095, and erected in the years immediately preceding. Even so, the church is remarkably advanced in style for its date, and was evidently erected by the most progressive and skilful builders of the school of Como at that time. In the absence of surely dated monuments of the last quarter of the XI century in Lombardy, it furnishes us with a valuable proof of how far the art of building had progressed at that epoch.

COMO,[1] S. CARPOFORO

(Plate 60, Fig. 1, 2, 3, 4, 5)

I. S. Carpoforo attracted the attention of writers upon the antiquities of Como as early as the XVI century, when it was described by Ninguarda and Giovio. These accounts are still exceedingly valuable. Clericetti, the pioneer of modern archæology in Lombardy, made a study of the church, which, notwithstanding numerous errors, is a remarkable piece of work for the date at which it was written. Some important bits of information are given in the inexact descriptions of Hope[2] and Mothes.[3] Barelli's monograph is of especial value, because he knew the church before the modern restorations were executed. A drawing of the interior, made before the restoration, was published in the *Grande Illustratione*.[4] The drawings of De Dartein[5] show an erroneous reconstruction with transepts, but the elevation of the apse made before the restoration is of value.[6] Monti has resumed what is known of the history of the edifice, but has added little that is new. Luigi Tatti published a monograph upon the edifice illustrated with plates, the incorrectness of which was demonstrated by a critic in the *Rivista Archeologica della Provincia di Como*.[7]

II. The church of S. Carpoforo, if we are to believe tradition, was founded at a very early date. Tatti[8] brings forward the usual hypothesis that it was erected on the site of a pagan temple, which in this case he calls the temple of Mercury. The church itself was founded, he believes, in 379, by S. Felice, the first bishop of Como of whom we have record, and there is a tradition that the body of S. Carpoforo was translated into the crypt c. 380. A more probable tradition, however, is that referred to by Giovio: "S. Felice, first bishop of Como, was buried in the crypt of S. Carpoforo, and there rest also the bodies of the sainted martyrs Carpoforo, Esanto, Cassio, Licinio, Severo and Secondo. In that place, the name of which was Silvula, there was formerly a temple; and thither Carpoforo and his comrades, fearing the rage of the emperor Maximian, flew from Milan, where the emperor was sojourning at that time, and at that spot they surrendered themselves. There was in their company Fedele, who left his comrades at Silvula and went to the lake of Como, where he found a boat and hastened to Samolaco. When Maximian learned that Fedele and Carpoforo and their companions had become Christians and had taken flight, he sent executioners who found Carpoforo and his five companions at Silvula and killed them."[9] The church may then well

---

[1] The church of S. Carpoforo lies in the frazione of Camerlata, about a kilometre to the south of Como, on the mountain side above the main highway leading to Milan.

[2] 274.   [3] I, 269.   [4] III, 1063.   [5] Plate 81.   [6] 334.

[7] 1880, Fasc. 17, Giugno.   [8] I, 266.

[9] Ibi D. Felix, primus Comensium episcopus, inferiore crypta sepultus est; neque non sanctorum Carpophori, Exancti, Casii, Licinii, Severi et Secundi martyrum corpora

have been built on the site of an earlier oratory erected to commemorate the spot where the titular saint suffered martyrdom. Tradition also affirms that S. Carpoforo was the oldest church in Como, and that it at one time served as cathedral. There is, however, no documentary evidence to prove these assertions.

The church is said to have been reconstructed and endowed by Luitprando in 724. The principal document which supports this tradition is a diploma of which the original, Tatti records, was lost while it was being copied for him. He prints, however, a summary taken from Carafino, who had seen the original, since he noted in the margin: *Extat in Tabulario huius Ecclesiæ.* This summary is entitled: "Privilege of the same king Luitprando to the basilica of S. Carpoforo of Como, which was by him restored, enlarged and endowed with various revenues and possessions." Then follows an extract from the text: "In the name of the holy and undivided Trinity, I, Luitprando, by the grace of God, king of the Lombards . . . give, bequeath, and offer to the church of S. Carpoforo and his comrades, etc." There follows a list of donations, so liberal, in fact, as immediately to raise suspicion as to the authenticity of the document. The chronological notes of the date April 2, 724, are correct, but Carafino notes in parenthesis that in other copies the document is dated April 2, 800, in the first year of Luitprando (which was 712, not 800) and the tenth indiction (the eighth, not the tenth, indiction was current in 800).[10] The authenticity of this diploma has been attacked by Rovelli, Troya,[11] Monti and the editors of the *Historiae Patriae Monumenta,* and indeed bears all the ear-marks of having been fabricated by the monks to confirm their claims to certain properties. Since the original has been lost, there is no means of judging at what date the forgery was executed, but it can hardly have been later than the XIV century. What the document does prove, at all events, is that the tradition that the church of S. Carpoforo had been restored, enlarged and endowed by Luitprando, was current in the late

---

ibi condita sunt. Ei loco, ante templum extructum, nomen erat Silvula, ubi Carpophorus et socii, Maximiani imperatoris sævitiam veriti, Mediolano fugientes, ubi tunc agebat Cæsar, sese abdiderunt. Erat et in eorum comitatu Fidelis, qui, relictis in silvula sociis, ad lacum Larium deveniens, inventa navicula, Summolacum contendit. Maximianus, cum rescivisset Fidelem ac Carpophorum cum sociis christianos effectos fugæ se dedisse, percussores immisit, qui repertos in prædicto loco Carpophorum et eius quinque comites obtruncaverunt. (Giovio, 217).

[10] Priuilegio dello stesso Rè Luitprando alla Basilica di S. Carpoforo di Como, ristorata, ampliata e dotata da lui con varie rendite, e possessioni. In nomine Sanctæ, & Individuæ Trinitatis. Luitprandos Dei gratia Longobardorum Rex. . . . Dono, atquè iudico, & offro Ecclesiæ S. Carpofori, & sociorum eius . . . . . in primis aream cum ædificijs, cum vineis, brolijs, hortis etc. . . . Datum quarto nonas Aprilis anno Dominicæ Incarnationis DCCXXIV. Regni autē Domini Regis XIII. Indictione VII. (Tatti, I, 944).

[11] Troya nevertheless reprints it, III, 375.

Middle Ages. This tradition was recorded in other documents seen by Tatti
and referred to by him.[12] A passage from one of the breviaries of Como
published by Buzzetti[13] states: "The martyrs were buried in the same place
where they suffered martyrdom, and there afterwards a celebrated church in
honour of S. Carpoforo was constructed by Luitprando, king of the Lombards.
This church was afterwards called the 'Seven Orders.' There the martyr and
his comrades are still buried."[14] The lost diploma cited by Tatti and referred
to above was doubtless the source upon which Giovio drew for his notice of
the church: "There is another older church about a mile outside of the city
dedicated to S. Carpoforo. Luitprando, king of the Lombards, in the year
of our Lord 724, on the fifth of April, the thirteenth year of his reign, being
at Como, gave to this church the possessions which it holds to this day."[15]
Sigonio, however, appears to have drawn from another source when he stated
that on April 5, 718, King Luitprando dedicated the church of S. Carpoforo
outside the walls of Como.[16]

Some confirmation is lent to the Luitprando tradition by a passage from
Giovio which seems to establish that that king translated certain relics from
Rome to Como. "Behind the high altar of the cathedral are buried the
relics of the saints Proto, Giacinto and Eugenia, martyrs, translated long ago
by Luitprando, King of the Lombards, from Rome to this city and placed
in the church of S. Carpoforo, which he himself had endowed, as I deduce from
verses cited below and found in a certain breviary. Afterwards Guido Grimoldi
transferred the relics to the cathedral and placed them in the crypt, and Leone
Lambertenghi, bishop of Como, moved them to the upper church in the year
of our Lord 1317. The verses to which I referred are the following: King
Luitprando translated the holy bodies from Rome and interred them not very
far from the city of Como. Some time after Bishop Guido transferred those
bodies and placed them in the crypt of the cathedral of Como. A third
translation was made by the clergy who moved the bodies to a worthy spot."[17]

[12] I, 740, 743, 744.   [13] 124.

[14] Sepulti sunt eodem loco, et divo Carpophoro postea celebre templum, a Luitprando Langobardorum rege, constructum est, quod etiam aliquando Septem Ordinum
appellatum fuit, VBI NVNC REQUIESCIT CVM SOCIIS.

[15] Est et alia vetustior ecclesia, extra urbem ad mille passus, D. Carpophoro dicata,
quam Luitprandus Longobardorum rex Comi agens, anno Domini septingentesimo
vigesimo quarto, nonis aprilis, regni eius decimo tertio, prædiis, quæ nunc etiam possidet,
dono datis ornavit. (Giovio, 216).

[16] Sequenti [anno, 718], Nonis Aprilis Luitprandus rex ædem D. Carpophoro
extra Comi mœnia dedicauit. (Sigonio, 96).

[17] Conditæ sunt inibi post altare maximum D. Prothi, et Hyacinthi ac Eugeniæ
martyrum reliquiæ, antiquitus Roma a Luitprando Longobardorum rege ad hanc
civitatem translatæ, et in templo D. Carpophori, quod ipse ditaverat, ut de infrascriptis
versiculis in quodam breviario vetere repertis coniicio, collocatæ. Inde Guido Grimoldus
comensis episcopus eas ad hoc templum maximum deduxit et in subterranea crypta
condidit, quas Leo Rambertengus comensis episcopus ab ea in superiorem locum

A privilege of Desiderio of 762 is mentioned by Tatti[18] as having been lost at the same time as that of Luitprando, but it is not clear that it contained any mention of the church of S. Carpoforo. At all events a bishop of the VIII century seems to have been buried in the church, which consequently must have been in existence at this epoch.[19].

According to Giovio the church in early times was known by the title of the 'Seven Orders,' because, he conjectures, there were endowments for all the ecclesiastical orders.[20] In the early XI century the church was dependent upon the abbey of S. Abondio,[21] but before 1040 a monastery of Benedictine monks was established at S. Carpoforo. A curious document without date, published by Tatti,[22] doubtless refers to this foundation: "Litigerio, by the grace of God, Bishop of Como, albeit unworthy. Let our diligence be known to all those who now live and shall be hereafter. In the name of God and of the Blessed Virgin and of all the saints we excommunicate and anathematize whoever shall molest this abbey or presume to disturb its possessions. Lest the malice of the ancient enemy should instigate me who now feel such great love for this work, or any of my successors to wish to take away from the dominion and power of the abbot and monks the goods which this monastery has already acquired, or in future may acquire, with the approval of the clergy and laity we lay upon such a one our solemn curse, and if any one shall try to infringe this act and shall try to diminish or take away the goods which the abbey has acquired or shall acquire, let him be caught in the bonds of anathema, and with Judas, the betrayer of Christ, let him be damned, and let him not rise in the council of the just. And that this may more truly be believed and observed by us and by all men, we have signed this document with our own hand, and have caused our cardinals, deacons and subdeacons also to sign it."[23]

transtulit, anno Domini millesimo trecentesimo decimo septimo. Versiculi autem sunt hi:

> Rex tulit a Roma Luitprandus corpora sancta,
> Longeque Cumana non multum condidit urbe.
> Post modicum Guido deduxit episcopus ista
> Corpora, cumani templique locavit in imo.
> Tertia per clerum constat translatio facta,
> Ad partem dignam dum corpora sancta reduxit.   (Giovio, 210).

[18] I, 944.

[19] Adelongus iuxta templum Divi Carpophori conditus, ut frustra quædam lapidea litteris insculpta significant. (Giovio, 185).

[20] Ea prius erat ecclesia Septem Ordinum appellata, in qua forte omnium Ordinum ecclesiasticorum fuere præbendæ. (*Ibid.*, 217).

[21] Tatti, II, 170.   [22] II, 851.

[23] Litigerius Dei gratia Episcopus Cumanus, licet indignus. Præsentium, & futurorum omnium noscat industria. Quod nos ad Dei preces, ac Sanctæ Mariæ, & omnium Sanctorum excommunicantes anathematizamus, ne quis hanc Abbatiam molestare, aut de bonis præsumat. Verum ne liuor antiqui hostis, aut me, quem tantus amor huci operi nunc constringit, aut meos successores aliquando instiget, quò à dominio, & potestate Abbatis, & Monachorum aliquo tempore bona huius Monasterij

This document is apparently an abstract from the original deed of foundation made by Pio Rubeo and from him copied by Tatti. Many important parts, such as the chronological notes and the explicit notice of the foundation of the monastery, are omitted, but the extract given by Tatti, fragmentary as it is, is sufficient to assure us of the authenticity of the charter and of the fact that the monastery really was founded, as Tatti says, before 1040. Litigerio occupied the pontificate of Como from 1028 to 1049. Giovio apparently had seen the deed of foundation, since he states: "Litigerio, following the example of his predecessor Alberico, founded the abbey of San Carpoforo outside the city of Como;"[24] and again: "Litigerio, bishop of Como, successor of Alberico, founded an abbey at San Carpoforo and, by a confirmation of the royal donation, endowed it with the same lands which had been given to the church by Luitprando, and added other revenues in addition."[25] Barelli[26] states that among the manuscripts of the *Curia* he found a notice of the consecration of the church of S. Carpoforo on May 25, 1040, and that in the Archivio Parrochiale he had seen another notice of the same ceremony. These documents unfortunately have not been published, but are probably authentic. We must therefore conjecture that the monastery was founded by Litigerio soon after he became bishop in 1028; that the reconstruction of the church was begun at once and entirely completed in 1040.

The monastery is mentioned in documents of 1090 and 1091.[27] A document of 1204 mentions a portico of the church.[28]

Of the later history of the abbey but very little is known. In 1511 the Benedictine monks were replaced by hermits of the order of St. Jerome.[29] The

acquisitæ, vel acquirenda subtrahere velimus, Laudantibus Clericis, & Laicis maledictionem imponimus. Vt siquis hanc ordinationem infringere temptauerit, & acquisita, vel acquirenda minorare, vel tollere voluerit, Anathematis vinculis irretiatur, & cum Domini Traditore Iuda damnetur, & in Iustorum concilio non resurgat. Quod vt verius, & firmius credatur, & a nobis, & ab omni custodiatur, manus propria immissione roborantes subscripsimus, & nostros Cardinales Presbyteros, Diaconos, & Subdiaconos subscribi fecimus.

24 Is Litigerius [episcopus], Alberici prædecessoris sui imitatus exemplum, abbatiam S. Carpophori extra civitatem comensem pariter instituit. (Giovio, 189).

25 Ibi Litigerius comensis episcopus, Alberici succesor, abbatiam instituit, quam et iisdem prædiis, ceu per confirmationem regiæ donationis, additis insuper aliis redditibus, auxit. (*Ibid.*, 217).

26 *Not. Arch.*, 13.   27 Bonomi, *Dip. Scti. Ben.*, Brera MS. AE, XV, 23, f. 45, 116.

28 ad porticum seu ad ecclesiam sancti Carpofori. (Bonomi, *Dip. Sti. Bti.*, MS. cit., f. 330).

29 Hoc monasterium Scti. Carpophori, congregationi Heremitarum observantium S. Hieronymi a Iulio Secundo Pontifice Maximo anno 1511 concessum . . . (Ninguarda, ed. Monti, 164).

Cœnobium istud, cum esset commendatum, anno millesimo quingentesimo decimo primo concessum est fratribus Ordinis S. Hieronymi, extincta a pontifice maximo abbatiali dignitate, quam Litigerius cum monachis ibi victuris perpetuam decreverat. (Giovio, 217).

monastery was given in commendam, and was degraded to the rank of a simple priory. In 1530 the cloister was reconstructed. The bishop Ninguarda at the end of the XVI century caused a description of the church to be written which is of interest, because it shows the condition of the edifice at that date. It was, he states, a parish church with monastery annexed. "The church is dedicated to S. Carpoforo and has been splendidly restored. It has three vaulted naves and a choir to which lead stone stairways fittingly disposed on either side of the horns of the high altar. . . . The crypt is separated from the church by a perforated screen, and is entered by a stone stairway leading down at the right. At the left another stone stairway, somewhat narrower, ascends into the sacristy. . . . The only doorway leading outside is on the epistle side, and before the doorway is a large cemetery. . . . Another doorway opens from the choir towards the monastery and has two stairways, one of which leads to the dormitory, the other to the cloister. A large sacristy adjoins the choir on the gospel side. . . . And on the epistle side there is a square tower with three bells. The monastery has a very large cloister of quadrangular form with stone columns, from which a stairway of stone leads to the dormitory. The latter has two wings, one of which contains cells accommodating a sufficient number of monks, the other a granary. On the ground floor is the refectory, the kitchen, a cellar excavated in the rock of the mountain and a wine-press. There is the entrance to the vineyard of the monastery. There are also several rooms, nicely enough fitted up for the use of guests."[30]

In 1872 a restoration of the edifice was begun. The description of Barelli gives some indication of the state of the edifice before the radical alterations then introduced. "The choir in ancient times rose somewhat above the roof of the nave, just as it does now, but terminated in four pyramidal pediments which lent to the edifice an exceedingly picturesque aspect. The upper wall of the choir was lighted by two oculi, the one opened in the eastern wall above the apse, the other directly opposite it. All that is still indicated by traces

[30] Ecclesia Scto. Carpophoro dicata, et egregie accommodata habet tres naves fornicatas et chorum, ad quem scalis lapideis ad utrumque cornu altaris maioris apte dispositis ascenditur . . . descenditur in cryptam ostio perforato clausam gradibus lapideis ad dextram, et ad lævam alia scala lapidea angustiore in sacrarium escenditur. . . . Ianua unica est extra vergens a latere Epistolæ, et ante ianuam magnum cœmeterium. . . . Ex choro versus monasterium est alia ianua cum duabus scalis, altera ad dormitorium, et altera ad peristylium. Choro la latere Evangelij coniunctum est sacrarium amplum . . . et a latere Epistolæ turris quadrata cum tribus campanis. Monasterium habet amplissimum peristylium quadrata forma cum columnis lapideis, ex quo commoda scala lapidea ad dormitorium ducit, cuius alæ duæ cubicula monachorum sufficientem numerum capientia et granarium continent; humi refectorium, coquina, cellarium saxo arcis Baradellæ incisum, torcularium, ex quo ad vineas monasterij introitus est, et plura sunt conclavia satis eleganter accommodata pro usu hospitum. . . . (Ninguarda, ed. Monti, 164).

visible in the existing wall." He goes on to speak of the arch of triumph, "now hidden by the nave vault. Anciently the crypt was separated from the nave by an iron screen, and the entrance to the crypt was by a cork-screw stairway placed at the end of the left aisle [sic]. When, however, that aisle was walled off from the body of the church, the lateral entrance to the crypt was walled off, and the central entrance left free." He goes on to describe how the two western bays of the nave have been secularized and the building otherwise damaged "by covering the entire edifice with vaults supported on the pilasters of the transverse arches which do not belong to the primitive construction [sic] and by covering them with intonaco." It was believed by Barelli and by all the archæologists who examined the church before the restoration, that these transverse arches marked the position of a central transept which had been destroyed. Speaking of the wall of the campanile, he refers to the masonry as "a filling in of rubble, held together perhaps only by interior wooden chains like those of S. Abondio." He also refers "to the little window of the crypt which has been imprudently enlarged and of which there are preserved elsewhere the remains of the archivolt."

The restoration carried out in the years immediately following 1872, when the description of Barelli was written, included the destruction of the groin vault of the choir and the reconstruction of the roof in its present form. The vaults of the nave and side aisles were also demolished, and the barocco intonaco was removed from the walls. During the course of the restoration the architects came to the conclusion that, at the time when the vaults had been erected, the arcades of the nave had been completely made over so as to bear the additional weight, and that two bays had been substituted for the original three between the transverse arch and the choir. They were led to this opinion by the fact that there are three windows in this space in both the aisle and clearstory walls, and by traces of a smaller arch, said to have been discovered in the course of the restoration. The first of these proofs carries absolutely no weight, since in Lombard edifices windows were often spaced quite without reference to the bays. Of the second it is now impossible to judge, for no exact description of the arch said to have been discovered has been preserved. A study of the still unrestored western bay, however, is sufficient to make it certain that there could not have been three arches here. It was, therefore, singularly fortunate that for lack of funds the nave was not remade in the supposed original form, and that it still retains only two bays between the eastern transverse arch and the choir.

In the course of the restoration fragments of Carlovingian carving—I find no evidence that they belonged to an ambo—came to light. One of these is now imbedded in the south wall near the entrance, the other in the eastern respond on the south side.

In May, 1874, the roof of the western portion of the church, which had been walled off and secularized, fell in. About this period the artistic and archæological character of the building was in great measure destroyed by a new burst of activity on the part of the restorers. Especially unfortunate was the ugly intonaco smeared over the walls of the interior so as completely to conceal the masonry. The restoration was never entirely completed as originally projected. The western double bay was left still secularized, by a happy chance, since here alone the ancient architecture may yet be studied. Similarly, the remarkable pyramidal structure which it was planned to build over the choir was never erected, and the Renaissance square cupola is still to be seen externally (Plate 60, Fig. 5). Finally, the northern absidiole was never restored, and thus were preserved for posterity the ancient frescos of the north wall of the northern side aisle.

III. The church to-day consists of a nave (Plate 60, Fig. 1) of three bays, the westernmost of which is much larger than the other two, two side aisles, a raised choir, a central apse, a southern absidiole, a crypt, and a campanile (Plate 60, Fig. 5). Originally, however, the nave contained three double bays, of which the westernmost has been walled off and secularized. The intermediate piers of the middle bay have been removed.

The side aisles are covered with groin vaults with transverse arches (Plate 60, Fig. 2). These vaults have obviously been restored, except in the secularized unrestored western bay, where it is evident that the side aisles were originally roofed in wood, and had transverse arches only from the alternate piers. The groin vault under the campanile in the eastern bay of the southern side aisle is, however, probably original. The groin vault of the choir is modern. On each face of the piers inside the present church (Plate 60, Fig. 1, 2) is engaged a broad pilaster strip. On the side of the side aisles (Plate 60, Fig. 2) these support the transverse arches and the vaults of the latter. On the east and west side they support the archivolts of the main arcade (Plate 60, Fig. 1, 2). On the side of the nave, in the alternate piers, they are continued to form a system which carries a great transverse arch spanning the nave (Plate 60, Fig. 1). In the easternmost intermediate piers they end somewhat inconsequentially beneath a window of the clearstory, which is placed on the axis of the pier (Plate 60, Fig. 1, 2). The westernmost intermediate piers in the secularized western bay are rectangular in section without engaged pilaster strips. The transverse arches are slightly segmental in elevation. Very segmental are the arches of the main arcade of the western bays of the present church (Plate 60, Fig. 1), a form made necessary by the removal of the intermediate piers.

The amortizements of the clearstory wall (Plate 60, Fig. 4, 5), which the restorers thought indicated a central transept, were probably left by buttresses which reinforced the transverse arches. It is probable that there were also transverse buttresses.

The windows are widely splayed. Those of the clearstory (Plate 60,

Fig. 4, 5) were intended to be glazed. There is no western façade, as the church abuts against the mountain.

The crypt is covered with restored groin vaults, supported on columns.

North of the church are still preserved the Renaissance cloisters.

The masonry of the western parts of the church, which still retains its original character (Plate 60, Fig. 4), is rough, and consists of a mixture of uncut and very crudely squared stones, with occasionally a brick, laid in courses only approximately horizontal. The masonry of the western bays of the nave was entirely denatured in the restoration, and it is amusing to compare in the photograph (Plate 60, Fig. 5) the difference of character between the original and restored portions. The masonry of the campanile is somewhat better than that of the nave, but the blocks are very rough and small, and the courses frequently depart from the horizontal. Very fine, on the other hand, is the masonry of the apse, formed of well-shaped blocks, skilfully laid with narrow mortar-beds to form a polychromatic effect.

IV. The decoration of the church is extremely simple. The piers, as may be seen in the secularized western bay, had neither capitals nor bases of any kind, other than simple imposts. The western portions of the edifice originally were without arched corbel-tables. Those which now exist on the southern clearstory (Plate 60, Fig. 4, 5) are an incorrect restoration. The capitals of the crypt (Plate 60, Fig. 3) are supplied with broad, flat leaves, excellently executed, almost Gothic in type. The bases have griffes; the shafts are slender. The exterior of the apse is decorated with arched corbel-tables, grouped two and two and carried on engaged shafts. The campanile has developed arched corbel-tables (Plate 60, Fig. 5).

V. It is obvious that in S. Carpoforo we have three dictinct epochs of construction. To the first belongs the nave, to the second the campanile, to the third the choir and crypt. This fact was recognized by all the archæologists who saw the edifice before its restoration. Barelli speaks of a vertical break in the masonry at the point where the choir joins the nave; and even to-day the difference in character between the masonry of the nave and that of the choir is clearly visible, although the restoration has almost completely denatured the stonework. It is not difficult to establish the date of the nave, notwithstanding the unfortunate restoration. The absence of decoration, the character of the masonry and the transverse arches all indicate the first half of the XI century. The church is obviously more advanced than S. Vincenzo of Galliano, a surely dated monument of 1007 (Plate 97), in that the piers are compound and the nave is spanned by transverse arches. The structure of S. Carpoforo resembles very closely that of Lomello (Plate 106), a monument of c. 1025 (except that the side aisles were not vaulted), but is less advanced than that of S. Maria of Calvenzano (Plate 38), which dates from c. 1040. It is certain, however, that the architectural school of Como was notably behind that of

Milan in the development of the organic vaulted basilica. There can therefore be little doubt that the nave of S. Carpoforo formed part of the church begun by Litigerio soon after 1028 and consecrated in 1040. The masonry of the campanile is analogous to that of S. Vincenzo of Gravedona (Plate 100, Fig. 5), an authentically dated monument of 1072. It may, therefore, be ascribed to c. 1070. The masonry of the apse recalls that of the lower part of the campanile of Villanova (Plate 241, Fig. 3), an authentically dated monument of 1148. The S. Carpoforo choir may consequently be ascribed to c. 1145.

COMO, S. FEDELE

(Plate 61; Plate 62; Plate 63, Fig. 1, 2, 3, 4, 5, 6, 7, 8, 9;

Plate 64, Fig. 1, 2, 3, 4, 5, 6, 7)

I.   The church of S. Fedele is one of the most conspicuous and important edifices, not only of the city but of the entire province of Como, and as such has been frequently noticed by historians and archæologists. In the XVI century Giovio and Ninguarda made full descriptions of the building which to-day form valuable sources for the archæological study of the monument. Of the historians of Como who have written of the church and its history, the most important are Tatti, who in the XVIII century published, though too often inaccurately, the documents which bear upon its history, and Cantù, who in treating of this subject, as always, united a charming literary style and profound knowledge of historical documents with a complete ignorance of even the most fundamental principles of archæology. Among modern writers De Dartein is certainly entitled to first mention, for the description and the plates which he has dedicated to S. Fedele are among the most important and satisfactory parts of his monumental work. Only less sumptuous are the illustrations of Barelli. In recent years comparatively little has been written upon S. Fedele. The church has, in reality, been unusually fortunate in having escaped a modern restoration, a circumstance to which it owes the preservation of whatever of the ancient structure the barocco centuries spared; but the Renaissance stucco with which the interior is still covered has doubtless tended to discourage modern archæologists from studying the edifice. Thus it has come about that only three modern contributions have been made to the literature of the monument; one, by Monti, adds little that is new; the anonymous pamphlet entitled *La Basilica e l'urna di S. Fedele,* and the booklet of Buzzetti are of some slight historical value.

II.   The origins of S. Fedele, like those of many other mediæval churches, are lost in the mists of tradition. Before the X century the church was dedicated to S. Eufemia; and Tatti[1] conjectures in consequence that it was founded by S. Abondio c. 452, since that bishop established the cult of S. Eufemia at Como. However this may be, a will of the bishop Walperto of 914, published by Tatti, shows that at this date the church of S. Eufemia was the cathedral of Como and officiated by a chapter of priests.[2]

Ninguarda also states that the church of S. Fedele was formerly the chief one of the city, and the cathedral, and goes on to say that afterwards the canons and revenues were transferred to the existing cathedral, but S. Fedele remained a collegiate church, and had in his day a prevosto and seven canons, to whom was confided the cure of souls, and who celebrated daily the customary offices.[3]

In the X century (probably in 964), the body of S. Fedele was translated from Samolaco to the church of S. Eufemia of Como, the title of which was in consequence changed. The most authentic texts relating to this translation are an anonymous chronicle of the X century, and passages in various breviaries and in a martyrology of Como.[4] I shall, however, translate

---

[1] I, 433-434.

[2] In Christi nomine Domini Dei, et Saluatoris nostri Iesu Christi. Berengarius Diuina ordinante Prouidentia Rex anni Regni eius XXVII. Mense Maij, Indictione II. Ego in Dei nomine VValpertus Episcopus Sanctæ Comensis Ecclesia . . . dispono, & iudico, atq; ordino . . . vt habeant in perpetuis temporibus sacerdotes illi, qui pro tempore ordinati sunt in ordine Episcopatus Sanctæ Euphæmiæ quæ est ædificata infra ista Ciuitate Cume etc. . . . vt à presenti die, & hora habeant ipsi Presbyteri, vel ipsorum posteri successores, qui pro tempore in perpetuis temporibus in sempiternum fuerint in ipsa Sancta Matre Basilica Beatissimæ Euphæmiæ sunt ordinati, sicut superius legitur, ex integrum, etc. . . . esse de amodo in antea in perpetuum temporibus habendum iure proprietario nomine tantam ordinationem ipsis Presbyteris pro tempore in perpetuis tẽporibus fuerint in ipsa sancta Matre Ecclesia S. Euphæmiæ in ea ordinati nocte, & die, qui deseruierint . . . & volo, & iudico, & ordino . . . vt habeant isti Presbyteri, qui de ordine Episcopatus fuerint etc. . . . ipsos cesendeles de ipso oleo die nocteq; sempiternum luminare debeatis super sepulturum ipsius Domini VValperti Episcopi etc. . . . Quod si Pontifices, aut Vicedominus, vel Scariones, aut communes personas de parte Episcopatus S. Abundij Cumensis, etc. . . . (Tatti, II, 790).

[3] Fuit olim Civitatis primaria, et Cathedralis Ecclesia, translatis deinde Canonicatibus, et eorum præbendis ad ædem, quæ jam summa est, et in Cathedralem erecta, retinuit hæc nomen Collegia⟨.⟩ e, Præposito, qui curam animarum annexam habet, et septem alijs Canonicis in ea relictis, a quibus quotidie sacra consueta, et debita fiunt. (Ninguarda, ed. Monti, 20 f.).

[4] The texts from the anonymous chronicle and from the breviaries have been cited below, p. 478 f. That from the martyrology is as follows: Idibus Iunij. Nouocomi Translatio prima S. Fidelis Martyris ex Vico Sumolocano, in quo sexcentis sexaginta sex annis iacuerat, ad Ecclesiam Collegiatam S. Euphemiæ Virginis in Vrbe. Huius Inuentionem diuinitus reuelatam Vbaldo Episcopus Nouocomen. effusa ad sacrū pignus excipiendum ingenti populorum multitudine, summa letitiæ significatione, ac maxima solemnitate celebrauit, & in præfata Basilica ante Aram maiorem reposuit: quæ mox antiquato priori titulo, noui hospitis causa S. Fidelis denominari cœpit. (Tatti, *Martyrologium*, 130).

the account of Ninguarda: "This church was originally dedicated to S. Eufemia, virgin and martyr, in whose honour the high altar is to this day consecrated. When, however, the body of S. Fedele . . . was miraculously found and translated hither by Bishop Ubaldo, and placed in a marble sarcophagus sustained by four columns, the church was called by the name of S. Fedele."[5] Fuller details are given by Giovio: "Why this church of S. Eufemia changed its name I shall relate. In the time of the emperors Diocletian and Maximian, in whose reign there was great persecution of Christians, Fedele achieved martyrdom at Samolaco, a place situated at the upper end of the lake of Como, and his body was buried in a chapel erected in his honour. There it lay concealed until the year of our Lord 960, when Ubaldo was bishop of Como. To him came a certain woman called Dominica, and announced that it had been revealed to her in a dream that he should translate the relics of S. Fedele to the city. The bishop believed the honest woman, and went with her by boat to Samolaco, where she immediately showed him the unknown tomb of the martyr. He therefore took the relics of the saint, and translated them to the city, to the church of S. Eufemia, which in consequence was afterwards dedicated to S. Fedele."[6] The date 960 given for the translation by Giovio is probably incorrect, since the event is referred to 964 by the breviaries.[7]

The church was at first officiated by a chapter of priests referred to in documents of 1032 and 1035;[8] some time in the XI century, c. 1063, according to Cantù,[9] or c. 1070, according to Tatti,[10] but more probably later,[11] the priests were organized into a chapter of canons regular. The deed of foundation has been published by Tatti,[12] but is unfortunately without date: "Rainaldo, by the grace of God, bishop of Como. Since I desire to restore ecclesiastical affairs to their primitive condition and imitate the example of

---

[5] Erat Ecclesia hæc initio dicata S.ctae Eufemiæ Virgini et Martiri, cuius titulum adhuc retinet summum altare, deinde corpore S.cti Fidelis . . . miraculose reperto et huc per Ubaldum Episcopum translato, postque maius altare in arca marmorea quatuor columnis sustentata reposito ab eo nomen accepit. . . . (Ninguarda, ed. Monti, 20 f.).

[6] Cur autem hoc templum D. Euphemiæ nomen amiserit referam. Per tempora Diocletiani et Maximiani imperatorum, sub quibus ingens fuit Christianorum persecutio, Fidelis apud vicum Summolacum, in summo Lario situm, martyrium consummavit, eius corpus in sacello conditum fuit, ipsius nomini constructo. Delituit autem usque ad annum Domini nongentesimum et sexagesimum, quo tempore Ubaldo comensis erat episcopus, cui mulier quædam, nomine Dominica, per somnum commonita renuntiavit, uti D. Fidelis reliquias in urbem referendas curaret. Ille, probæ mulieri fide præstita, Summolacum cum illa enavigavit, quæ martyris ignotum tumulum statim ostendit. Eius inde sublatæ reliquiæ, in urbem ad ipsum D. Euphemiæ templum translatæ sunt, quod ideo postmodum Fideli ipsi dedicatum fuit. (Giovio, 213. See also ibid., 188).

[7] Tatti, II, 76.   [8] Buzzetti, 229.   [9] I, 189.   [10] II, 212.

[11] A document of 1109 implies that the canons had not been long established. (Rovelli, II, 344).

[12] II, 856. According to Gams, Rainaldo was bishop 1061-1092.

the Apostles, all of whom led a common life and who are the most notable soldiers in the army of Christ; I invest the chapter of the church of the holy martyr Fedele with the benefices formerly held by the custodi in return for their service in the church, except the first which shall be held open, because it has been given to the acolyte Vitale, but at his death, this benefice, like the others, shall pass to the chapter. But if it should happen that Vitale die before the death of the others who are now invested, let that investiture be entirely invalid. I similarly invest the chapter with the lands[13] belonging to the church after the death of the present holders. However, I make the investiture on this condition, that the cardinals live together in a house near the church and enjoy the benefices in common and according to canonical rule, and that none of them be permitted to transfer any of these ecclesiastical possessions to secular use. If any of the brethren shall presume to do otherwise, let him be deprived of all ecclesiastical revenue. We also firmly decree that the canons must perform the customary offices in the cathedral church of S. Maria and at S. Carpoforo as well as at S. Fedele, just as the custodi were accustomed to perform them. And this I have decreed, affirmed and established, affixing my hand and seal."[14]

In the early XII century, and according to Tatti in 1103, the bishop of Como attempted to intrude certain priests in the church of S. Fedele against the will of the canons. The latter appealed to the pope Pascal II, and were successful in obtaining from him two letters addressed to the bishop of Como, forbidding him to interfere with the affairs of the chapter. These letters have been published by Tatti.[15] In a document of 1151,[16] mention is made of *atrium quod dicitur de sancto Fidele* and in another of 1270[17] it appears that

---

[13] Mansum fuisse certam agri portionem, quae et coleretur, et in qua coloni aedes esset. (Du Cange).

[14] D. Rainaldus Dei gratia Cumanus Episcopus. Ecclesiasticas res cupiens in pristinum statum redigi, imitans Apostolos dicentes [*sic;* ducentes?] omnes vitam communem, maximè in Militia Dei militantes beneficia virorum Custodum S. Fidelis, quæ ipsis ad ipsius Ecclesiæ obsequium contingunt, inuestio Canonicæ ipsius Ecclesiæ S. Martyris Fidelis, præter primum, quod apertum fuerit, quod inuestitum est Vitali Acolito, quo defuncto similiter beneficium Canonicæ eueniat. Quod si contigerit ipsum Vitalem ante istorum mortem, qui modò inuestito sunt, mori, inuestitura illa irritæ sit omnino. Mansos autem ipsi Ecclesiæ pertinentes similiter eidem Canonicæ post tenentium obitum inuestio. Eo tenore hæc omnia supradicta Canonicæ inuestio, vt Cardinales ipsius Ecclesiæ ex illis beneficijs Canonicè iuxta ipsius S. Fidelis Ecclesiam communiter viuant, & nulli ex ipsis Ecclesiasticis rebus liceat aliquid in aliquem vsum secularem transferre; quod si aliquis fratrum aliter facere præsumpserit, eo ipso omni beneficio Ecclesiastico priuari statuimus. Inter omnia hæc firmiter obseruari decernimus, vt ipsi Canonici persoluant debita penditia S. Mariæ Matrici Ecclesia, quæ Custodes solebant, & Ecclesiæ S. Carpophori, & ipsius S. Fidelis. Quod ego equidem decreui, propriaq; manu subscribens, affirmaui, rectèq; ordinaui & proprium sigillum imprimens signaui. Giovio, 213, states that "Habet hæc ecclesia præpositum et canonicos cum parochia."

[15] II, 866. [16] Cited by Cantù, I, 72. [17] *Ibid.*

the campanile was already menacing ruin at that date. In 1335 the cathedral was temporarily re-established at S. Fedele pending the reconstruction of the new church of S. Maria. In 1509 the church of S. Fedele was remade in the barocco style, a vault was erected over the nave, and a rose-window and two lateral windows were opened in the façade.[18] Giovio wrote a description of the edifice as it was after the completion of these changes. "The church of S. Fedele was formerly dedicated to S. Eufemia. It is praised by architects as an antique monument, and there are some who think it was founded by the Romans. As a matter of fact, however, it is a Christian edifice, as is shown by certain sculptures, which represent Daniel in the den of lions, and the angel carrying Habakkuk by his hair. It had a very beautiful fore-court with marble columns, which was called the atrium, for by this word the Christians denoted the fore-courts of their churches, with which anciently every church was furnished. By atrium was signified that part of the house which one first entered. The atrium of S. Fedele gave its name to the neighbouring quarter of the city; indeed, the baptistery of S. Giovanni Battista and the little church of S. Pietro there situated are even to-day distinguished by the epithet *in atrio*. The basilica of S. Fedele is entirely vaulted and is disposed in the image of the human body according to the rule of the architect Vitruvius. It has a lofty lantern dome which is commonly called the *tugurio*. It has side aisles in two stories and a twelve-sided bell-tower which formerly collapsed because of its excessive height, although even now it is rather lofty. Since the church was lower than the surrounding public streets, the level of which had everywhere been raised by the accumulation of dirt during the centuries, the pavement of the church was raised to the level of the surrounding soil, by placing it upon a layer of refuse, which has hidden the bases of the columns and the ancient pavement, worked, as I have heard, in mosaic. Also the above-mentioned church of S. Giovanni Battista is at a lower level than that of the surrounding soil. That circular edifice is supported by eight columns which were taken from the atrium of which we have spoken. This is shown by the fact that one precisely like them still stands before the church of S. Fedele, but engaged in the wall of a certain private house at the north of that basilica. For the rest, these columns I believe were never executed by Christians, as is evident from their form and age and the character of their epistyles. And they are said to be of that foreign marble which is called Greek. Pliny wrote that a most splendid portico was built at Como by Calpurnius Fabatus, his wife's grandfather. It is perhaps from this that the columns in question were taken."[19] The description of Ninguarda was written some years later.

[18] Monti, 84.

[19] D. Fidelis templum primo quidem S. Euphemiæ dicatum fuit. Id ab architectis, ut antiquæ structuræ laudatur, et sunt qui putent a Gentilibus conditum, verum Christianorum opus est, ut sculptura quædam Danielis in lacu Leonum et Abacuch ab Angelo per capillos portati pernotat. Habuit propylæum e marmoreis columnis longe

COMO, S. FEDELE

"S. Fedele was a parish church placed in the centre of the city at the right
of the cathedral and not far from it. Many think that the church was erected
by Christians because the sculptures of the portals seem to represent Daniel
in the lions' den and the angel carrying Habakkuk by his hair. It is the more
common opinion, however, that it was built before the coming of Christ and
consecrated to the pagan gods. So much seems to be indicated by the character
of the edifice, which appears to be an ancient structure adapted to Christian
usage, since the altars appear to have been added to it afterwards, and do
not correspond nor accord with the other parts of the building. Formerly the
edifice stood free, but now it is adjoined on two sides by buildings, and has a
parish house, for the use of the prevosto, adjoining the entrance at the right.
Within there are vaulted side aisles in two stories. To the upper story lead
two circular stairways at the right and two others to the left, and these are
continued to the roof. The nave vault is supported on four pilasters and is
very lofty. The pavement was formerly of mosaic but is now of common
stone, and has been raised as is evident from the moulded bases of the columns
and responds now buried. The seemly exterior of the church is constructed
of polished rectangular blocks of stone. . . . The high altar is an elaborate
construction in white marble, and is placed in the choir of the canons which
is separated from the nave by a stone railing. . . . On the epistle side,
about the middle of the choir, is the door of the sacristy which at present is
not very large. . . . The apse which rises above the high altar is semicircular
and built of rectangular blocks of polished stone. Galleries with arcades of
columns well constructed ennoble the interior and exterior of this part of the
building. . . . At the left of the principal portal is the good-sized baptistery

pulcherrimum, quod Atrium appellatum fuit. Ita enim Christiani ecclesiarum anteriores
porticus vocitarunt, sine quibus antiquitus nullam construebant. Nam atrium prima
domus pars in ipso introitu nuncupatur. Atrium istud proximæ regioni nomen dedit,
ut et baptismalis D. Ioannis Baptistæ et S. Petri ædiculæ, inibi sitæ, in Atrio in
hodiernum diem appellentur. Hæc basilica tota est concamerata et ad humani corporis
effigiem iuxta Vitruvii architecti præceptum condita, pinnaculum habens in summitate
pertusum, quod vulgo Tugurium nuncupatur. Habet et cellas supernates et infernates,
neque non turrim campanariam dodecagonam, quæ olim præ nimia altitudine corruerit,
licet adhuc satis excelsa sit. Sed et viis publicis circumquaque aggesto limo celsioribus
effectis, cum depressa esset, importatis ruderibus exteriori solo adæquata est, quod
columnarum bases et vetustum stratum tessellato opere (ut accepi) elaboratum occul-
tavit. Sed et prædicta D. Ioannis Baptistæ ecclesia eo modo declivis est effecta. Ea
rotunda est et columnis octo suffulta, quæ de atrio illo, quod diximus, sumptæ fuerunt,
quod una compar ostendit, apud ipsum D. Fidelis templum adhuc stans; sed privata
quadam domuncula, quæ sita est a sinistris basilicam ipsam ingredientibus, occupata.
Cæterum columnæ istæ, quantum coniicio, nequaquam a Christianis paratæ fuerunt, si
quidem earum figuram et vetustatem ac epistyliorum artificium spectemus. Et lapicidæ
id marmor peregrinum esse affirmant, quod *græcum* appellatur. Scribit Plinius Cæcilius
speciosissimam porticum in hac urbe a Calpurnio Fabato eius prosocero fuisse
ædificatum, quæ fortasse de columnis istis consistit. (Giovio, 212-213).

327

of oval shape and made of different kinds of marble, with a rail and a suitable cover. Near the baptistery in the angle of the left side aisle is a high campanile containing three bells, two large and one small. Inside the campanile is a stone stairway by which it may be ascended easily. This campanile was formerly so high and lofty that the upper half collapsed, and in its fall drew with it a part of the nave which is now seen to be panelled. The church had . . . six conspicuous entrances, two on the side of the forum, two back of the choir and two at the side. Of these doors, that to the right gave access to the parish-house intended for the prevosto and canons, although it is now inhabited by tenants of both sexes. The door to the left has been walled up because of the buildings which have been constructed on this side of the church. . . . In this church beside the high altar there are six other altars, two on the gospel side, and four on the epistle side. On the gospel side . . . at the end of the side aisle is a vaulted chapel similar to, and corresponding with, the sacristy on the other side of the choir. This chapel is dedicated to S. Blasio. Before the façade of the temple there was formerly a portico or atrio adorned with very beautiful marble columns, which are thought to have been brought hither by the Christians from the famous portico of Calpurnius Fabatus, whose son is said to have been the father-in-law of Pliny. In this atrio was erected for the catechumens an altar dedicated to S. Giovanni Battista and called S. Giovanni in Atrio. But when at a later time the campanile fell and ruined the portico, the atrio was supplanted by a piazza, and the church of S. Giovanni Battista was built in the circular form which it still retains. The new church is still called S. Giovanni in Atrio, but the columns have been taken away from it. In the centre of this church is a fine baptistery in marble for the use of the entire city and suburbs. Here the bishop with the canons of the cathedral on holy Saturday solemnly blesses the baptismal water."[20]

[20] Ecclesia parochialis est ad S.ctum Fidelem posita in medio Civitatis, et ad dextram summæ ædis non procul ab ea, quam licet plerique existiment a Christianis extructam, propter sculpturas, quae pro foribus Danielem constitutum in lacu leonum, et Abachuc ab Angelo per crines delatum exprimere videntur, est tamen communior opinio, ante Christi adventum fuisse ædificatum et dijs gentium consecratam, ut structura ipsa ad morem veterum adaptata et altaria post adiuncta, quæ reliquis ædificijs partibus non respondent et conveniunt facere fidem videntur. Fuit aliquando extrinsecus ambitu libero, iam vero ædificijs a duabus partibus occupata, etiam ædes parochiales ad Præpositi usus in ingressu ad dextram contiguas habet. Sunt intus multæ cellæ duplicato ordine, et fornicibus interiectis, superiores cocleis duabus ad dextram, ac totidem ad sinistram, et usque ad tectum circum circa ascenditur . . . supra medium fastigium quatuor antis impositum sublime attollitur solum taxilato olim opere, iam vero communi lapide, stratum altius esse elevatum ex stylobatis et spiris columnarum sive antarum humi depressis perspici potest, exterior templi speties ex quadrato lapide et polito constituta est. . . . Summum altare est ex candido marmore egregie elaborato intra chorum Canonicorum cancellis lapideis præclusum . . . ad latus Epistolæ medio ferme choro est ianua sacrarij, non usque adeo ampla . . . cella ipsa summi altaris est forma rotunda ex quadratis lapidibus et politis fabricata, intus et foris insignem

These XVI century descriptions are particularly valuable because they prove that the church was formerly preceded by an atrium, on the western side of which was a baptistery.[21] This disposition recalls the cathedral of Novara, where the relative positions of church and baptistery have been the same since at least c. 900, although the cathedral was rebuilt in the XII century. The church of S. Giovanni in Atrio still exists, although desecrated, hidden from sight, and converted into store-rooms, cellars, dwellings and shops. The edifice is octagonal in plan, with niches alternately semicircular and rectangular, like those of the baptistery of Novara. It is covered by a dome with lantern, carried on triangular corbels, beneath which originally stood columns of the Corinthian order with monolithic shafts. These columns, which appear to be genuine Roman antiques, were carried away from S. Giovanni before the time of Tatti and placed in the portico of the Liceo, Via Cesare Cantù. The plan and position of S. Giovanni—on axis with the church of S. Fedele—are significant, since they show the extraordinary size of the ancient atrium. It is evident, however, that only the plan of S. Giovanni is ancient, and that the building was entirely reconstructed in the time of the Renaissance, as Ninguarda explicitly states.

In 1798 the chapter of S. Fedele was suppressed.[22] Not until the early years of the XIX century were the final barocco additions made to the church.

in ea prospectum reddunt ambulationes circum circa diversis columnarum ordinibus distinctæ, et diligenter accomodatæ. . . . In maiori ianuæ ingressu ad lævam est baptisterium ovali figura ex marmore vario, non mediocri magnitudine cum cancellis et decenti operculo. Prope baptisterium in angulo sinistræ navis est turris eminens et alta pro usu campanarum, quarum duæ sunt maiores, et una minor, intus habet gradus lapideos per quos commode ascenditur, erat usque adeo edita et sublimis, ut summa pars ad medium usque deciderit, et secum partem mediæ navis traxerit, quæ modo laqueata cernitur. Habet . . . sex præcipuos aditus, duos a fronte versus forum, duos circa chorum a tergo, et duos a lateribus, quorum dexter vergit ad ædes parochiales pro usu Præpositi et Canonicorum, licet iam ab utriusque sexus inquilinis habitentur, et sinister manet clausus propter ædificia templo ad ea parte coniuncta. . . . In hac Ecclesia præter summum altare, sunt alia sex altaria duo a latere Evangelij, et quatuor a latere Epistolæ. A latere Evangelij . . . ad extremum navis est sacellum fornicatum sacrario simile et respondens choro interiacente Divo Blasio sacrum. Habebat hoc templum a fronte porticum sive atrium, pulcherrimis columnis marmoreis addietis, quæ existimantur ex insigni porticu Calpurnij Fabati, cuius filius Plinij Cæcilij socer fuisse fertur, huc a Christianis translatæ. In hoc atrio fuit erectum pro Cathecumenis altare sub Divi Ioannis Bap.tae titulo, et dicebatur S.cti Ioannis in atrio. Verum cum postea turris campanaria decidisset, et porticus hæc tacta corruisset, fuit e regione foro frumentario interiecto rotunda forma ædificata Ecclesia Divi Ioannis Bap.tæ, quæ adhuc retinet nomen S.cti Ioannis in atrio, et columnas ex eo ablatas. In medio est insigne baptisterium ex marmore pro usu totius Civitatis, ac suburbiorum, ubi Episcopus ipse adiunctus sibi Canonicis Cathedralis Ecclesiæ Sabbatho Sancto solemniter benedicit aquam baptismale. (Ninguarda, ed. Monti, 20 f.).

[21] The church of S. Giovanni in Atrio is mentioned as early as 1228. (Tatti, II, 596).

[22] Buzzetti, 229; *La Basilica*, 16.

In 1806 the cupola was restored in its present form, and some years later the nave chapels were added.[23] In 1867 important restorations were executed. The pavement was lowered though not to its primitive level, but some fragments of the ancient mosaic came to light.[24] In the same year a chapel which had been built in the west end of the south side aisle was removed, and the ancient door reopened. In 1873[25] restorations were executed in the side aisles of the north transept near the rear entrance. This part of the edifice retains very little that is ancient, but in the course of the restorations indications were discovered sufficient to prove that there was here anciently a sort of vestibule, and some traces of the foundation of a pre-existing church were discovered. In 1881 the barocco windows of the apse were removed, being replaced by new windows in the style of the XII century.[26] In 1893 the western chapels were restored, and their pavement was lowered. At this time were discovered traces of two circular stairways leading to the gallery.[27]

III. The church of S. Fedele at present consists of a nave four bays long; two side aisles; broad projecting transepts ending in polygonal apses around which the side aisles are carried; a choir of a single bay flanked by side aisles; a polygonal apse with five semicircular niches; several modern chapels; a campanile rising in the westernmost bay of the northern side aisle, and a dome over the crossing (Plate 61; Plate 62). Above the side aisles were originally galleries, but in the transepts (Plate 63, Fig. 4) and part of the nave (Plate 63, Fig. 9) these have been walled off. On the east side of the northern transept are a vestibule and entrance. A similar entrance which once existed on the eastern side of the southern transept has been replaced by the modern sacristy. In plan S. Fedele is among the most grandiose and imposing edifices not only of Lombardy but of Europe, and marks perhaps the highest development of the Romanesque style. It is, I believe, the earliest church in which side aisles and galleries are carried around the transepts. The polygonal apses in which terminate the choir and transepts are features archæologically extraordinary and architecturally beautiful (Plate 61; Plate 62; Plate 63, Fig. 4).

At present the church is vaulted throughout, but such was not the original disposition. The nave was anciently spanned by three transverse arches which supported a wooden roof (Plate 62). These arches are still preserved under the roof above the existing vaults of the nave. They ended in pyramidal pediments on which the beams of the roof were laid directly. These pediments have been damaged by the opening of apertures to afford passage-way between the different bays under the roof, but there can be no doubt as to their original form. The cloistered half domes of the transept and apse have been covered

23 *La Basilica*, 21, 29, 30, 31.   24 *Ibid.*, 23.   25 Barelli.
26 *La Basilica*, 23.   27 *Ibid.*, 30-31.

with barocco plaster and frescos (Plate 63, Fig. 4, 9). I have no doubt, however, that the core is still the original vault erected in the XII century. The slabs of thin stone which form the roofing of the church are laid directly upon the extrados of these vaults, the curve of which is expressed externally, a fact which gives the building a picturesque and decidedly Byzantine aspect (Plate 61).[28] The side aisles are at present covered with groin vaults without transverse arches. These vaults in consequence must have been entirely made over, for the original ones were supplied with transverse arches, as is proved by the ancient responds, several of which are still in perfect preservation. Whether or not these vaults were originally domed it is impossible to determine with certainty in the existing condition of the edifice. I incline, however, to the belief that they were slightly domed, although the narrowness of the space between the level of the arcade arches and the gallery in certain bays throws some doubt upon this. At all events, these vaults certainly had wall ribs, since one is still preserved in the second bay from the west in the southern side aisle. This wall rib is depressed in elevation. The vaults of the side aisles of the transepts have also been entirely made over, and it is impossible to determine what was their original form except that from the position of the responds it is evident that the vaulting spaces were divided into alternately rectangular and triangular compartments like those of the gallery.

The most interesting vaults of the edifice, however, are those of the galleries of the transept (Plate 64, Fig. 2). These galleries have been walled off from the church, and it is perhaps to this circumstance that they owe their preservation. That part of the southern transept which is over the present sacristy is now used as a carpenter shop. Here the vaults have been in part destroyed, but in such a manner as to leave a section of the original structure exposed, so that the masonry may be studied. The vaulting spaces are divided into compartments alternately rectangular and triangular by heavy transverse arches (Plate 64, Fig. 2). These arches are supported in the outer perimeter on rectangular responds without bases and with a simple impost moulding taking the place of a capital. The groin vaults are erected in a curious manner. The arch which opened on to the nave rises to a much higher level than the wall arch. The vaults in consequence have a very decided inclination downwards towards the outer perimeter. The transverse arches are heavily loaded, especially towards the inside perimeter, to reach the level of the vaults. The masonry of the vaults themselves is extraordinarily thin, averaging about six inches. Originally the tiles of the roof were doubtless placed directly upon the extrados of the vault. It was a remarkably clever expedient to erect vaults thus inclined downwards towards the outer edge. In the first place, the slope made it possible to place the roofing directly upon the vaults without the use of any wood and also without weighing the vaults down with a heavy

[28] The drawing (Plate 62) is wrong in showing a wooden roof over the apse vault.

mass of masonry on their inner side, as would otherwise have been necessary. In the second place, the nave walls were relieved of the inward thrust of the vaults, which was carried instead almost entirely to the outside walls. In the third place, in the transepts these vaults acted as effective buttresses to carry the thrusts of the cloistered domes of the transept-ends to the outer walls. These vaults are probably the cleverest and most ingenious erected in Lombardy during the Romanesque period, and for subtlety and finesse rival the best constructive work of the Byzantine and French architects. The vaults of the nave gallery are similar, being sharply inclined and separated by transverse arches (Plate 61). The compartments, however, are all rectangular, there being no need to introduce triangular compartments except in the annular perimeter of the transepts.[29]

The tranverse arches spanning the nave were reinforced by heavy transverse buttresses rising over the transverse arches of the side aisles (Plate 64, Fig. 4). Several of these buttresses have been destroyed or made over, but others retain enough of the original masonry to leave no doubt as to their ancient form. They were continued to the ground in the form of rectangular pilasters projecting from the nave walls (Plate 64, Fig. 4). The piers of the interior have been to a very large extent denatured by the addition of barocco stucco (Plate 63, Fig. 9), and in some cases by the cutting down of the original stonework to Renaissance forms. Sufficient traces, however, remain to make it certain that the piers were all uniform, and consisted of a square core, on each face of which were engaged pilaster strips or semi-columns. The semi-columns and pilasters supporting the transverse arches of the side aisles and the archivolts of the main arcade received independent capitals or imposts at the level of the springing of the arches, but the pilaster strips on the side facing the nave were doubtless continued as a system to support the great transverse arches (Plate 62). They consequently could have received capitals only at the level of the clearstory. Unfortunately the systems of the nave are completely hidden by intonaco, and the original dispositions remain in doubt. The piers of the crossing are much heavier and of more complicated section than those of the nave (Plate 62). They evidently retain their original profile, since the bases are in part ancient. The responds of the side aisles consist of semi-columns engaged on pilasters (Plate 63, Fig. 6) or of simple pilasters, and in the gallery the responds are regularly pilasters.

In the western bay of the northern side aisle rises the campanile. The lower part of this leans considerably from the perpendicular. It is known that before the XVI century the upper half—which, according to Giovio, was dodecagonal—collapsed. In recent years it was believed necessary to tear down all except the lower story and replace it by the present ungainly and

[29] See my *Construction of Gothic and Lombard Vaults*, 26.

ugly structure which recalls very dimly in its details the Lombard style.[30] The original campanile was evidently older than the church. It obstructs in an awkward manner the side aisle, the masonry of which has evidently been built around the pre-existing tower. The axis of the campanile, moreover, is placed at an angle with that of the church. The settlement of the campanile has dragged with it part of the nave walls—a circumstance which explains certain of the irregularities for which this edifice is so conspicuous. Others, however, are not to be so easily explained. The two middle bays of the nave are very much wider than the two end bays (Plate 62). The level of the gallery shows remarkable variations in height, etc. But cases of constructive asymmetry are so frequent in mediæval art, and, fortunately, now so well known, as to require no discussion.

The dome has been entirely rebuilt in the barocco style. Traces of the arched squinches by which the original cloistered vault was supported still survive, and the crossing must have been anciently surmounted by a vault similar to that shown in our restoration. I believe, however, that the roofing was originally placed directly upon the extrados of the vault, as was done over the cloistered half domes of the transepts and choir. The timber roof introduced in these portions of the edifice in our drawings (Plate 62) is therefore incorrect.

Although most of the windows of the edifice have been remade in modern or barocco times, a sufficient number still retain their original form to make clear their ancient character. The niches of the apse were lighted by widely splayed oculi; the windows of the gallery were large and not widely splayed (Plate 64, Fig. 4). Those of the side aisles and clearstory, although smaller, were without doubt supplied with glazing of some sort, in all probability with a mosaic of leaded glass like that which has been restored at S. Abondio. The edifice was constructed throughout of ashlar finely laid and with very sparing use of mortar (Plate 64, Fig. 4). The horizontal courses are not always maintained; the width of the blocks as well as their length varies excessively. The stones are very skilfully fitted together, and the joints are fine. Many of the stones are so perfectly squared that they must have been pilfered from Roman edifices.

IV. Certain fragments of Carlovingian carving which come from S. Fedele are preserved in the Museo Civico, just outside the S. Abondio room, where they bear the numbers 1-14.

The ornament of the church is exceedingly rich and varied. The capitals of the system are entirely hidden. In the drawings (Plate 61; Plate 62) they have been restored as of a classic Corinthian type on the strength of certain capitals of this form preserved in the side aisles (Plate 63, Fig. 6). In these

---

[30] The design of the structure reproduces the ancient one as far as the level of the belfry.

capitals the leaves are not carved, and the execution is somewhat clumsy, owing to the stubborn nature of the stone employed. Other capitals are cubic or of a freer Corinthianesque type (Plate 64, Fig. 5), with a single row of uncut leaves. The capitals of the choir are executed in finer stone. Between the niches on the ground story are four of block Corinthian type, showing remarkable freedom of design combined with skilful execution (Plate 63, Fig. 7). Those of the apse galleries (interior and exterior) are of varied types, with rich, almost florid, acanthus leaves (Plate 64, Fig. 3), or plain, flat leaves somewhat French in character (Plate 63, Fig. 1), with proportions freely varied, double volutes, eagles (Plate 63, Fig. 8), grotesques (Plate 64, Fig. 1), etc. The galleries are all covered by transverse barrel vaults supported on lintels (Plate 64, Fig. 1, 3, 7; Plate 63, Fig. 1, 3, 8).

The bases are usually Attic in type and often supplied with griffes, though the proportions are frequently rather clumsy (Plate 64, Fig. 5, 7; Plate 63, Fig. 1, 6, 7). The mouldings of the abaci are fine and unusually elaborated for Lombard work (Plate 64, Fig. 5; Plate 63, Fig. 6, 7), and the same may be said of the impost mouldings of the pilasters. The apse is decorated, not only with practicable galleries, but with arched corbel-tables and with buttresses consisting of a shaft engaged on a pilaster strip. The transepts are supplied with a simple cornice of arched corbel-tables (Plate 61).

A most extraordinary feature is the eastern portal surmounted by an elaborate triangular arch and row of arched corbel-tables. At the sides are interesting sculptures representing Daniel in the lions' den and Habakkuk and the angel. A large figure in an adjoining panel appears to be entirely grotesque. These sculptures appear to belong to the school of Pavia and show no trace of the influence of Guglielmo. The eastern portal of S. Fedele is without analogy with any other extant in Lombardy. In the north transept is a broken sculpture representing Samson and the lion and in the interior of the edifice are preserved numerous traces of the ancient frescos, with which doubtless the walls were once entirely covered.

V. The foundations of the campanile are without question the earliest portion of the existing edifice. Although they have but little character and can with difficulty be studied, it is evident that they can not be earlier than the last years of the XI century. The Romanesque portions of the church are all homogeneous, and evidently belong to the first quarter of the XII century. Classic influence is notable in the general restraint of the ornament as well as in the character of the capitals and mouldings. Now, this classical revival which led to a reaction against the rich and barbaric ornament of the Lombard style of the XI century, hardly began to be felt before the XII century. The cathedral of Modena, begun in 1099, is the earliest dated example of it. The practicable galleries used as a decorative feature in the apse and elsewhere at S. Fedele are also a motive which is not found before the XII century. At S. Abondio of Como, consecrated in 1095, there is no trace of this feature, nor of the preliminary steps which led to its development. At S. Fedele, however, the decorative gallery is carried to a high point of perfection. Moreover, from a constructive standpoint, the vaults of S. Fedele show the highest skill and ingenuity of construction, and are analogous to those of the Rotonda of Brescia (c. 1105), but better devised and more cunningly carried out. From the style, therefore, it is evident that the church can not be earlier than c. 1115, and in view of its many points of contact with S. Maria Maggiore of Bergamo—an edifice begun in 1137—I confess I should be inclined to place it later. However, it must be remembered that in 1118 broke out the bloody and exhausting war between Milan and Como. This war ended only in 1127 with the complete destruction of the city of Como, except that the churches were spared. The city was not rebuilt until 1158. It is inconceivable that during this war, or in the years of desolation which immediately followed it, the Comaschi should have found the resources necessary to construct a church as elaborate and expensive as that of S. Fedele. The edifice must then either have been finished before 1118, or not begun until after 1158. We are, therefore, forced to conclude that S. Fedele was erected during the period of great prosperity for the commune of Como immediately preceding the outbreak of the war with Milan in 1118, and possibly in consequence of the establishment of the chapter regular. The church may therefore be assigned to c. 1115. The existing façade with its rose-window is a work of the XV century, the nave and cupola were remade or radically altered in the barocco centuries, and the campanile, except its lower story, is, as we have seen, modern.

COMO, S. GIACOMO

(Plate 64, Fig. 8)

I. The church of S. Giacomo, although formerly of large dimensions, is among the less well known religious edifices of Como. Both Giovio and Ninguarda give of it much briefer descriptions than of the other principal churches of the city. Clericetti, the pioneer of Lombard archæology, made a brief study of the building. More thorough and systematic was the analysis of De Dartein.[1] Barelli also studied the edifice and illustrated it with sumptuous drawings that are still valuable. Rivoira has published a drawing of the apse.[2]

II. Singularly little is known of the history of S. Giacomo. The church is mentioned in a document of 1144.[3] About the year 1292 the bells of the commune were removed from the campanile.[4]

[1] 340.　　[2] 296.　　[3] Barelli.　　[4] Tatti, II, 771.

The description of Giovio, written in the XVI century, is as follows: "The church of S. Giacomo is very old. The principal nave which is called the 'cappella maggiore' was formerly dedicated to S. Maurizio, because the body of the saint was there buried. This church has a fore-court or portico in the ancient manner; it also had a bell-tower, now destroyed, in which the people of Como formerly placed their bells."[5]

The description of Ninguarda was written some years later: "At the left of the cathedral is the parish church of S. Giacomo Maggiore. . . . The façade of this church was restored a few years ago. It is rather high, and is preceded by a large piazza, which extends on one side to the campanile of the cathedral and on the other to the portal of the episcopal palace. The church itself has three aisles. A sacristy adjoins the choir on the epistle side, and here there is ample space for the vestments, silver, and holy relics. There is no campanile but instead two bells have been hung over the façade. . . . The body of S. Maurizio is usually kept under the high altar, but at present is placed in the sacristy in a wooden ark pending the consecration of the temple after the new restoration. . . . In addition to the high altar this church has seven other altars."[6] It is therefore evident that in the time of Ninguarda the church was undergoing restoration. This restoration consisted not merely in remaking the interior in the barocco style, but also in destroying the western part of the nave, since in the Vidario manuscript of Giovio, which was written between 1620 and 1630, his description was supplemented by the following note: "This church has now been made smaller and restored."[7] In 1657 another restoration was carried out which, according to Barelli, was quite as radical as the first. In 1787 the parish was suppressed, and the church became a chapel of the cathedral, and has continued to serve as such until the present day.

III. S. Giacomo to-day consists of a nave three bays long, two side aisles, projecting transepts, a choir of two bays flanked by rectangular chapels, and an apse. Such, however, were not the original dispositions. The choir

[5] Ecclesia S. Iacobi et ipsa pervetusta est, cuius principalis cella, quæ Capella maior appellatur, olim S. Mauritii titulum habuit, quod ibi ipsius Sancti corpus conditum sit. Habuit hæc ædes more veteri propylæum, seu porticum; habuit et turrim campanariam, quæ modo diruta est, in qua populi comensis campana olim habebatur. (Giovio, 212).

[6] Ad lævam Cathedralis Ecclesiæ est parochia S.cti Iacobi maioris. . . . Ecclesia hæc a paucis annis restituta frontispitio, quod est satis eminens, amplam aream habet, ab uno latere ad turrim campanariam Cathedralis et ab alio ad portam palatij Episcopalis vergit, habet intus tres cellas sive naves et sacrarium choro propinquum ab Epistolæ latere, quod indumentis, argento et sacris reliquijs egregie provisum est, caret turri campanaria, cuius loco supra frontispitium duæ campanæ accommodatæ sunt. . . . Asservabatur etiam sub summo altari corpus S.cti Mauritij, quod iam in sacrario in arca lignea depositum est, quoad templum de novo restitutione consecretur. . . . Habet hæc Ecclesia septem alia altaria. (Ninguarda, ed. Monti, I, 27).

[7] Nunc haec ecclesia diminuta et instaurata est.

anciently communicated with the side aisles by an open arcade which was subsequently walled up but of which traces still remain, and these side aisles terminated in absidioles. The latter, however, like those of S. Abondio, were not expressed externally. The western bays of the nave have been destroyed, and the western narthex with its flanking campaniles has been in great part demolished, though some traces of them still exist on the other side of the piazza.

The interior of the edifice has been entirely covered with barocco intonaco, so that it is exceedingly difficult to trace the original dispositions. At present the church is vaulted throughout, but there can be no doubt that at least the nave was originally roofed in timber. It is possible that the side aisles may have been covered with groin vaults. That such was the case would seem to be indicated by the fact that at least one of the transverse ribs of the existing modern vault appears to be ancient. Although square in plan, the transepts are covered by half cloistered vaults carried on squinches, and this must have been the original disposition, since the masonry of the upper part of the exterior wall of the transepts is certainly ancient. The eastern bay of the northern side aisle of the choir preserves the original groin vault, which is undomed and without ribs. The half domes of both absidioles are likewise extant, that on the north side, above the sacristy, being especially well preserved. No indications are extant to show how the choir was originally roofed. The cloistered dome carried on squinches which rises over the crossing, is undoubtedly of the XII century, although its exterior walls have been rebuilt. The church originally possessed a high clearstory.

The supports were plain, cylindrical piers, like those of S. Abondio (Plate 59, Fig. 1), at least to judge from the single one that has been stripped of its barocco plaster (Plate 64, Fig. 8). The church had neither system nor buttresses. The bays of the clearstory—at least in the choir (which is the only portion preserved)—were marked off only by exaggerated pilaster strips.

The ashlar masonry is formed of stones of small size and varying width, but for the most part well squared and skilfully fitted together.

IV. The capitals of the great piers (to judge from the only one which is exposed—Plate 64, Fig. 8) were of developed cubic type. Cubic, too, but more archaic, are the capitals of the gallery of the apse. The windows apparently were large and not excessively splayed. They must have been supplied with glass. The bases of the piers of the interior are not at present visible. The archivolts are of a single unmoulded order. The apse is adorned externally with a very high gallery with highly stilted arches, and with a cornice formed of blind niches surmounted by an arched corbel-table. The choir externally has plain pilaster strips, but no arched corbel-tables.

V. All the archæologists who have studied S. Giacomo are unanimous in pronouncing it later than S. Abondio, an edifice which was consecrated in

1095.   The existence of the gallery in the apse is a sufficient proof of the correctness of this opinion.   The cloistered half domes over the transept-ends seem to stand midway between S. Abondio (Plate 59, Fig. 1) and S. Fedele (Plate 62), an edifice which dates from c. 1115.   Indeed, they appear to be a first esquisse of the grandiose plan of the latter edifice.   If the side aisles of S. Giacomo were vaulted, as there is reason to believe was the case, S. Giacomo was more advanced than S. Abondio in this respect also.   On the other hand, the simple piers, the cubic capitals and the absence of transverse arches, show analogies with S. Abondio rather than with S. Fedele, as does also the character of the masonry.   S. Giacomo, lying thus midway between these two edifices, may be ascribed to c. 1105.

CORNETO TARQUINIA,[1] CHIESA DELL'ANNUNZIATA

(Plate 65; Plate 66, Fig. 1, 2, 8, 4, 5, 6)

I.   In 1918 I published a monograph upon this monument in *Arte e Storia.*

II.   Nothing is known of the history of the church of the Annunziata beyond what is contained in a manuscript chronicle of Polidori, citations from which have been published by Guerri.[2]   It appears that the church was anciently of parochial rank, and bore the title of S. Pietro del Vescovo.   In the time of Polidori, who lived in the XVII century, the edifice was already closed for worship, and in a ruinous condition.   However, an old soldier, moved by veneration for an ancient image of the Madonna there preserved, caused the church to be reopened.   In consequence of this it came to be known under the title of Madonna del Soldato.   Whether or not the edifice was restored at this epoch is not clear.   At present the church serves as chapel for the nuns of S. Vincenzo di Paola, to whose care are confided the Ospedale Civico Femminile and the orphanage just across the street.

III.   The church consists of a nave of two bays, projecting transepts, and three apses (Plate 65).   There is no campanile.   With the exception of the half domes of the apses, the church is entirely roofed with rib vaults, but those of the crossing and transepts have obviously been remade in the Gothic period, when the façade was also reconstructed (Plate 66, Fig. 6).

The ancient vaults of the nave are highly domed and have rectangular diagonals (Plate 66, Fig. 2, 3).   The transverse arches in two orders are heavily loaded (Plate 66, Fig. 1), as at S. Maria di Castello.   There are no wall ribs (Plate 66, Fig. 1, 2, 3).   These vaults are almost square in plan

---

[1] (Roma).   [2] 341-342.

(Plate 65). It is impossible to study the details of the masonry, since the interior of the church is entirely masked with intonaco, and the extrados of the vaults is covered with a mass of mortar, on which are placed the tiles of the roof. The diagonal ribs rest on corbels (Plate 66, Fig. 1, 2, 3), as in the church of S. Giacomo (Plate 69); but the transverse arch is carried by a half column engaged upon a pilaster strip (Plate 66, Fig. 3).

The wooden gallery across the west end of the church is evidently modern. The lower part of the transepts (Plate 66, Fig. 4) and the core of the apses belong to the original edifice, but have been altered in later times. The half domes of the apses are without ribs.

Originally the central apse was provided with three windows, and each of the minor apses with a single window, but several of these windows were remade in the barocco period, and all except one are now walled up (Plate 66, Fig. 5).

In the XIII century the vaults of the transepts and of the crossing were remade. The section of the diagonals, although different in each of the three vaults, is always complicated and completely Gothic in character. The ribs of the vault of the northern transept are still unfinished, since the mouldings have never been added. These vaults are all without wall ribs, but pointed arches are freely used (Plate 66, Fig. 4). The mouldings, the abaci and the capitals with simple, broad leaves, are all such as might have been executed in the Île-de-France, about the year 1180.

This edifice, like all the Romanesque churches of Corneto, is built of blocks of tufo, skilfully cut and laid without mortar.

IV. The capitals of the nave (Plate 66, Fig. 2, 3) have a spur in the angles like those of Castelnuovo Scrivia (Plate 50, Fig. 1), from which, however, they differ, in that there is no foliage ornamentation. The mouldings of the abaci were probably remodelled in the Gothic period. The same may be said of the bases, which are supplied with griffes.

The apses are adorned externally with double arched corbel-tables (Plate 66, Fig. 5) of a type which is familiar in many XII century edifices of France, for example, in the church of Audrieux, Calvados. These corbel-tables were evidently added at the time when the façade and transepts were remodelled.

The façade is notable for the rose-window and the portal (Plate 66, Fig. 6), both richly adorned in the French manner. The rose-window is divided into eight parts by radiating colonnettes, and is surrounded by mouldings and zigzags. It is placed in a square field, ornamented with rosettes in relief. The portal, in two orders, is supplied with two colonnettes with bands, and is decorated with mouldings, a double zigzag, and a pyramid flower ornament. The capitals are of early Gothic type. Were it not for the zigzags—which were employed in France only in earlier times—and the rosettes, this façade might easily pass as a monument erected in France about 1150.

In the central apse is still preserved an interesting fresco.

V. It is evident that the church belongs to two distinct epochs of construction. To the first belongs the core of the edifice; to the second the vaults of the transepts, the façade, and the arched corbel-tables of the apses. The first epoch is evidently intermediate between the churches of S. Giacomo (c. 1095) and S. Maria di Castello (begun in 1121). The Annunziata is evidently later than S. Giacomo, because in it capitals, although simple and primitive, are introduced (Plate 66, Fig. 2, 3), while at S. Giacomo there are no capitals (Plate 69). Moreover, in the Annunziata, the system consists of a half column engaged on a pilaster strip (Plate 66, Fig. 2, 3), which is an evident advance over S. Giacomo (Plate 69), where the system consists merely of a pilaster strip. In the Annunziata, the transverse arches are in two orders, and are loaded at the crown (Plate 66, Fig. 1, 2), whereas at S. Giacomo (Plate 69) they are simple. Finally, the mouldings of the Annunziata are much more developed. It is clear, therefore, that the Annunziata is later than S. Giacomo. On the other hand, the Annunziata is earlier than S. Maria di Castello. The diagonals of the Annunziata are supported by corbels (Plate 66, Fig. 2, 3), whereas at S. Maria there is a logical system (Plate 75). In the Annunziata the half dome of the apse was simple, whereas at S. Maria it was supplied with ribs (Plate 74). In the Annunziata the capitals are primitive (Plate 66, Fig. 2, 3), whereas at S. Maria they are of fully developed Lombard type (Plate 77, Fig. 1, 3, 4, 5, 6). The Annunziata may therefore be ascribed to a period intermediate between that of S. Giacomo and S. Maria; or, since it resembles S. Giacomo more closely than S. Maria; to c. 1105.

It is not so easy to determine when the building was remodelled. Yet this alteration evidently took place after the vaults and dome of S. Maria were remade before the consecration of 1207. On the other hand, it took place before the west rose-window of S. Maria was rebuilt. The reconstruction may, therefore, be ascribed to c. 1225.

CORNETO TARQUINIA,[1] S. FRANCESCO

(Plate 67, Fig. 1, 2, 3, 4, 5, 6)

I. I published an article upon this church in *Arte e Storia* in 1914.

II. From the scanty historical notices upon the church of S. Francesco published by Dasti[2] and Guerri,[3] it appears that in 1487 the pope ordered

[1] (Roma).   [2] 413.   [3] 330.

the Franciscan monks who wished to abandon the church to remain in the edifice which they had inhabited *ab antiquo*. In fact, another document of 1450 mentions the *fratres S. Francisci,* and a third, of 1392, mentions the church. It is evident, therefore, that the existing monastery dates at least from the XIV century. It may have been founded in consequence of the famous miracle performed by S. Francesco at Toscanella in 1221.[4] However this may be, the church itself must antedate the monastery, since some portions of it are in the style of the XII century. It has obviously been remodelled several times. To one of these restorations probably refers an undated bequest cited by Guerri.

III. The church is one of the largest of Corneto. It consists of a nave (Plate 67, Fig. 4) five bays long, two side aisles (Plate 67, Fig. 1, 3, 5), two northern lateral chapels, five southern chapels, projecting transepts (Plate 67, Fig. 2), to the south of which has been added a great barocco chapel, and three rectangular apses. It is probable that originally the church was rib-vaulted throughout, but in the XIV century the magnificent wooden roof of the transepts (Plate 67, Fig. 2) was erected, and when the church was denatured in the barocco period, among other changes introduced, numerous groin vaults were substituted for the original rib vaults (Plate 67, Fig. 3, 4). At present, the ancient vaults are preserved in the principal apse, in the northern absidiole, throughout the northern side aisle (Plate 67, Fig. 1), in the two western bays of the nave (Plate 67, Fig. 4) and in the two western bays of the southern side aisle (Plate 67, Fig. 3, 5). The four lateral chapels on the southern side, which were probably added in the Gothic period, are also covered with rib vaults. Except in the three eastern piers (Plate 67, Fig. 4), the original shape of which has been entirely denatured, there is no difficulty in tracing the ancient form of the edifice through the veil of barocco stucco and intonaco.

At S. Francesco the system is uniform (Plate 67, Fig. 4), the vaulting compartments of the nave being about square in plan, while those of the side aisles are oblong. This disposition is obviously more advanced than the alternate system of S. Maria (Plate 75). The vaults themselves seem more advanced in style than the sexpartite vaults of S. Pancrazio (Plate 79) and one recognizes in them the sure touch of masons who had passed beyond a stage of experiment. They are much less domed than are the vaults of the other churches of the XII century at Corneto. The difficult problem of erecting rib vaults over oblong compartments is successfully resolved in the side aisles by stilting the transverse arches (Plate 67, Fig. 1, 3, 5). These arches, like those of S. Maria, are in two orders, unmoulded, as are also the arches of the main arcade (Plate 67, Fig. 4). It will be remembered that at S. Maria the piers which supported the arches in two orders were rectangular,

---

[4] Campanari, II, 34.

in consequence of which the masons had to resort to numerous expedients to hide the awkward transition (Plate 75). At S. Francesco a far better solution has been found. The piers—where they have not been remade—are given a spur or a colonnette which corresponds to each rib of the vault and to each order of the arches, or else the upper order of the arch is made to disappear.

At S. Francesco there are no pointed arches in the original portions of the edifice.

The transepts have been added or remade in the XIV century, and are fine examples of the Italian Gothic style. The beautiful wooden ceiling is supported by majestic pointed arches. The exterior of S. Francesco has suffered so severely from barocco restorations that it is impossible to determine whether or not there were buttresses. The campanile is modern. To the north of the church is the monastery, with a fine cloister, the northern gallery of which, covered with rib vaults, perhaps dates from the XIII century.

IV. The capitals are generally adorned with leaves, in which is evident a study of natural forms, combined with a certain archaic stiffness. French Gothic influence is undoubtedly present, if not yet dominant. Other capitals, on the other hand, are of purely Lombard character, and are adorned with grotesque figures or animals. The style of these capitals is analogous to that of the capitals of S. Pancrazio, and of the second chapel of S. Giovanni.

The façade (Plate 67, Fig. 6) is a typical example of the local style of Corneto, and gives an idea of what would have been the effect of that of S. Maria if it had been preserved. This façade is divided into three parts, each of which had a horizontal cornice, above which there was anciently a wall which followed the slope of the roofs. The central part, higher than the others, has been denatured. It has lost its original cornice, and the wall which crowned it, but was adorned c. 1230 with a beautiful rose-window like that of S. Maria. About the same time, the cornice of the southern bay was remade with pointed arches. The cornice of the northern bay is still well preserved. The arched corbel-tables are carried on very thin colonnettes. Two windows and the principal portal were altered in the barocco period, but above the portal is still seen an ancient pointed arch, the only one in the church which belongs to the original construction.

V. It has been seen that the structure of S. Francesco is far more advanced than that of S. Maria, begun in 1121, and somewhat more advanced than that of S. Pancrazio, an edifice which dates from c. 1160. The analogy of the capitals with those of S. Pancrazio (c. 1160), and with those of the second chapel of S. Giovanni (c. 1165) has also been pointed out. It is probable therefore that the construction of S. Francesco was begun c. 1165. Owing to the bad preservation of the edifice it is difficult to say whether work began at the east or the west end, but the fact that a pointed arch is used in the façade gives reason to believe that the usual method of construction was here followed, and that the choir was erected first. If we allow twenty years for the construction—which is not excessive for an edifice of this size— we may conclude that the building was finished c. 1185.

The great difficulty which the building presents is the fact that the apses are rectangular. This is a Cistercian characteristic, which was afterwards frequently taken over by the Franciscans. There is no other indication that the church belonged to the Cistercians before it passed to the Franciscans, and it is therefore probable that the apses may have been reconstructed at the time the monastery was founded. The pointed arches of the absidioles lend some confirmation to this view. It is strange, however, that at so late a date rectangular diagonals should have been retained. The explanation must be that the builders sought as far as possible to retain the original character of the building in adapting it to the Franciscan type.

CORNETO TARQUINIA,[1] S. GIACOMO

(Plate 68; Plate 69; Plate 70, Fig. 1, 2, 3, 5, 6)

I.   I published an article upon this church in *Arte e Storia*.

II.   According to a text cited by Guerri,[2] S. Giacomo belonged in 1291 to a convent of nuns. This convent is mentioned in other documents of 1385, 1389, and 1446. In the second half of the XVII century, the church was still possessed by Franciscan nuns of the Third Order.

In addition to these scanty notices gathered by Guerri, I find another in the history of Campanari.[3] About the year 1258, the nuns of S. Chiara, driven out from Cortona, came to settle at Toscanella. The pope Alexander IV, taking pity upon their misfortunes, suppressed the Benedictine abbey of S. Giuliano at Toscanella, and conceded it to the nuns of S. Chiara under the title of S. Maria di Cavaglione. He conceded to the same nuns, in addition, all the possessions of the suppressed monastery, among which is expressly mentioned *ecclesiam S. Iacobi de Corneto cum omnibus pertinentiis suis*. Since S. Giacomo is called simply *ecclesiam,* it is probable that at this period there was no convent annexed. The Franciscan nuns of S. Maria di Cavaglione, however, must have established a priory there soon afterwards, since nuns of S. Giacomo are mentioned as early as 1291, as we have seen. In 1464 the monastery of Cavaglione, or of S. Giuliano of Toscanella, was suppressed,[4] but the priory of S. Giacomo at Corneto continued to exist several centuries, and was perhaps finally suppressed at the end of the XVIII

---

[1] (Roma).   [2] 348.   [3] II, 38.   [4] Campanari, II, 52.

century. The monastic buildings have disappeared without leaving a trace of themselves, but the church, although closed for worship, is still perfectly preserved.

III. The building consists of a fore-court surrounded by a high wall (Plate 70, Fig. 3, 6), a single-aisled nave of two bays (Plate 70, Fig. 2, 5), projecting transepts, and an apse (Plate 68). The orientation is irregular and parallel to that of the church of S. Maria di Castello, since the principal apse is turned more nearly to the north than to the east. In the northern wall of both transepts is a niche, somewhat less than semicircular in plan (Plate 68; Plate 70, Fig. 1). Over the eastern transept rises a little bell-tower (Plate 70, Fig. 3). This is an addition of the barocco period. It is probable that the church, like S. Maria di Castello, originally possessed no campanile. The crossing is covered by an elliptical dome, supported on arched squinches (Plate 68; Plate 69). The apse is covered with a half dome, and the nave and transepts have ribbed vaults (Plate 68; Plate 69; Plate 70, Fig. 2, 5).

These rib vaults are constructed without wall ribs (Plate 68; Plate 69; Plate 70, Fig. 2, 5). Those of the nave are erected on a plan approximately square, but those of the transepts are oblong. Of the two vaults of the nave, the southernmost is much higher and much more domed than the northernmost (Plate 69). In both, the diagonal ribs are supported upon consoles, since the system consists of a single rectangular member, which carries only the transverse arch. The diagonals have a rectangular section, except in the northern bay of the nave, where they have been in part remade with a torus section (Plate 70, Fig. 2). This strange disposition is, I believe, the result of an alteration begun long after the construction of the church was finished, and never carried to completion.

At present there is a wooden roof above the vaults (Plate 69), but such was not the original disposition. The exterior wall bears clear traces of having been raised in modern times, probably in the XVIII century, in order to receive this roof (Plate 70, Fig. 3, 6). Originally the walls ended at the level of the crown of the wall arches. In fact, in the eastern wall the ancient cornice is still preserved (Plate 70, Fig. 3). Furthermore, under the existing roof, in the lower part of the cupola, there is still extant a window, adorned externally with mouldings (Plate 69). This window is placed at a level hardly above the extrados of the vault, upon which, therefore, the tiles must have been laid directly.

In elevation the cupola has an oval section (Plate 69) which facilitated construction without centering. This cupola is entirely Saracenic in type; it was probably copied from some building of Sicily. The whole church is constructed of tufo, very skilfully blocked, and laid without mortar. The extrados of the dome is exposed, and is covered neither by roof nor by tiles

CORNETO TARQUINIA, S. GIACOMO

(Plate 70, Fig. 3, 6). The half dome of the apse, on the other hand, is covered with tiles placed directly upon the masonry (Plate 69).

The two niches of the transepts appear to be semicircular, but are not so in reality. This effect is procured by cutting the stone of the half dome in false perspective (Plate 70, Fig. 1).

No attempt is made to reinforce the exterior wall with buttresses (Plate 70, Fig. 3, 6), the thin pilaster strips dividing the bays, and at the angles of the transept, being quite inadequate for this purpose. The cupola, however, is made thicker at the point where the thrust is greatest (Plate 69).

In addition to the principal portal, there is a doorway in the south wall of either transept, but these doorways have been walled up. Two other very low doors, also walled up (Plate 69), probably opened into charnel-houses which have now disappeared.

There is a single very narrow window in the east transept (Plate 70, Fig. 3), one somewhat broader in the apse (Plate 70, Fig. 5), and a third, which is modern, in the façade.

The atrium and the façade are additions of the barocco period (Plate 70, Fig. 3, 6).

IV. The church possesses practically no ornament. There are neither capitals nor arched corbel-tables. There are only a few mouldings of entirely Lombard character (Plate 69; Plate 70, Fig. 1).

V. Compared with the church of S. Maria di Castello, which was begun in 1121 (Plate 73; Plate 74; Plate 75; Plate 76; Plate 77), S. Giacomo appears singularly simple and unadorned. This contrast is not to be explained altogether by the lesser importance of S. Giacomo, for even such mouldings as exist are of a type far less developed than those of S. Maria.

In fact, it is evident that S. Giacomo is the earliest of the rib-vaulted edifices of Corneto. In the XI century the architectural style of that city had been completely Umbrian. The best example of this epoch still extant is the church of S. Martino, which is a typical columnar basilica.[5]

At S. Giacomo the masons of Corneto experimented, perhaps for the first time, with a new method of construction, which it is evident they did not yet completely understand. They borrowed from the Lombards the essential motive of the Lombard style, that is to say, the rib vault, and they undoubtedly

---

[5] The church of S. Martino existed as early as April 29, 1051, since it is mentioned in a document of this date: Anno Xpti MLI [ex registro farfensi N. 855]. Die Lunis, quae est tertio Kal. Maji infra Civitatem de Corgneto, in praesentia Domini Adelberti missi Domini Bonifacii Ducis et Marchionis, et ingelberti episcopi Bledae missi Domini Leonis Summi Pontificis, in platea, quae est iuxta Ecclesiam quae vocatur Sancti Martini in praesentia reliquorum bonorum hominum. (Aldanesi, 106). See also Pflugk-Harttung, II, 532. Guerri (20) knows a document which speaks of *rectoris ecclesie Sancti Martini veteris de Corneto.*

borrowed this because it was particularly adapted to local conditions, since it could be constructed without wood, which was, and still is, practically unobtainable at Corneto. The Corneto builders had not, however, yet learned from the Lombards how to supply a system to support the ribs, nor had they fallen under the influence of Lombard ornament, except in the mouldings. In the church of the Annunziata we observe more Lombard elements, and S. Maria di Castello is completely Lombard.

How long the masons of Corneto were in completing this evolution of their style, it is not altogether easy to determine. The *terminus ad quem* is the year 1121, in which the church of S. Maria di Castello was commenced, and when, in consequence, the style of Corneto had reached its full development. The *terminus a quo* is the epoch in which the rib vault was discovered in Lombardy. As early as 1040 rib vaults were employed at Sannazzaro Sesia, but it is exceedingly improbable that this method of construction should have been copied in a region as far distant as Corneto before it had been applied commonly to Lombard churches. This hardly took place before the rib vault was united with the alternate system, that is to say, about 1070. The church of S. Giacomo must, therefore, have been constructed between 1070 and 1120. Reflecting, on the one hand, that Lombard influence probably took no little time to travel as far as Corneto, and, on the other hand, that the masons would have need of a considerable period of experimenting in order to advance from the point of progress represented by S. Giacomo to that represented by S. Maria, we may assign the church of S. Giacomo, with considerable confidence, to c. 1095.

CORNETO TARQUINIA,[1] S. GIOVANNI GEROSOLIMITANO

(Plate 71; Plate 72, Fig. 1, 2, 3, 4, 5, 6)

I. The early Christian sarcophagus of this church has been reproduced by Garrucci,[2] and studied by De Rossi. In 1913 I published a description of the architecture of the edifice in *Arte e Storia*.

II. Dasti[3] and Guerri[4] state that the church belonged to the Knights of Malta, but cite no authorities. Perhaps the notice comes from the manuscript chronicle of Polidori. In addition, Guerri mentions a document of the Middle Ages that refers to a cloister of this church, and another which speaks of a bequest made for certain restorations. Unfortunately the date of this last document is undetermined.

III, IV. The church has obviously been many times made over, and dates from different epochs. It now consists of a nave of a single aisle flanked

---

[1] (Roma).   [2] V, Tav. 403, Fig. 2.   [3] 414.   [4] 331.

on either side by three chapels, two absidioles and a choir of a single bay, terminating in an apse (Plate 71). South of the choir is a sacristy (Plate 71). There is no campanile. It is evident that originally the church possessed a nave three bays long, and two side aisles, but in the barocco period the side aisles were transformed into chapels by the construction of transverse walls between the piers and the outer wall.

Since the church was constructed at different epochs, it will be more convenient to describe each of the periods chronologically.

The most ancient part, undoubtedly, is the easternmost chapel on the north side, which originally formed the last bay of the northern side aisle (Plate 72, Fig. 2). The rib vault is highly domed. There are neither wall ribs (Plate 72, Fig. 2) nor external buttresses (Plate 71). The diagonal ribs are of rectangular section. The system resembles that of S. Pancrazio (Plate 79) in that a separate member of the respond is provided for each rib, and the pilasters supporting the diagonals are set normal to their load.

The capitals, with the exception of two—which were remade at a later epoch—are entirely Lombard in character, being carved with grotesque figures. They seem somewhat earlier than the most ancient capitals of S. Maria di Castello, and, therefore, earlier than 1121. The absence of buttresses also indicates that this part of the church is more ancient than S. Maria, where buttresses are employed (Plate 76, Fig. 1, 6). On the other hand, the chapel seems to be later than the Annunziata (c. 1105)—Plate 66—as is proved by the character of the capitals which are of more developed type at S. Giovanni, and also by the fact that a member of the system is supplied for each rib of the vaults. This chapel may, therefore, be assigned to c. 1115.

The second chapel on the northern side (Plate 72, Fig. 3) is less ancient. In general the design of the eastern chapel has been preserved, but the capitals are of later type, being no longer adorned with grotesques and animals, but with leaves and buds evidently studied from nature, and showing clearly the influence of the French Gothic style. The vault is similar to that of the first chapel, but is loftier and less domed. The capitals, more developed than those of S. Pancrazio (c. 1160), show that this chapel was erected about the year 1165.

The last chapel on the northern side (Plate 72, Fig. 4) is furnished with capitals even more advanced than those of the second chapel, although the execution is slovenly. A pointed arch is introduced into the vault. This portion of the edifice was perhaps erected about the year 1200. The façade with its pointed portal is of the same date, with the exception of the rose-window, which seems to be of about 1210.

The diagonal ribs of the choir (Plate 72, Fig. 1) are still rectangular, but appear to have been given this profile for the sake of symmetry with the other parts of the edifice, since the wall ribs—which we here find for the first time at Corneto—have a complex section. All the arches, except the diagonals, are pointed, and the apse arch is adorned with rich zigzags. The capitals are of pure French Gothic type. This choir may be ascribed to about 1220.

In the apse every attempt to preserve the Romanesque style of the earlier portions of the edifice was abandoned, and the style is French Gothic of the purest type. No detail of capital or of moulding differentiates this apse from the monuments of the Île-de-France, erected about 1175. Both the structure—that is to say, the vaults (Plate 72, Fig. 1), the system consisting of colonnettes (Plate 72, Fig. 1), the boldly projecting buttresses (Plate 71)—and the ornament—that is, the capitals and the mouldings—are completely Gothic. The ribs of the great vault meet in a keystone sculptured with a coat of arms. The diagonal ribs are exceedingly stilted. Even the windows are pointed. The capitals, however, are not much more advanced than those of the choir. I believe, therefore, that this apse is not much later than 1225.

It is worthy of observation that the choir is deflected to the north (Plate 71). This peculiarity is common in the churches of France, but is exceedingly rare in Italy.

The last mediæval addition to the church of S. Giovanni, and also the most beautiful, are the two absidioles (Plate 72, Fig. 5, 6), gems of pure Gothic architecture. With the exception of the ribs, which are a little heavy, and a few other details which show lack of study, these two chapels might pass as examples of French Gothic architecture of the best epoch. Their character is so clearly revealed in the photographs that it is useless to describe them at length. Suffice it to say, that the exterior is as completely Gothic in character as the interior, being furnished—at least in the case of the northern absidiole—with powerful buttresses (Plate 71). I attribute these chapels to about 1230.

The nave and the southern chapels have been entirely rebuilt in the barocco period, and retain nothing of their mediæval character. The chapels are at present covered with groin vaults, but there were doubtless originally rib vaults, like those of the northern chapels. The nave at present has a heavy barrel vault (Plate 72, Fig. 1). This evidently is not the ancient disposition, but it is not easy to say how the church was originally roofed, especially because it was impossible for me to obtain access to the roof. The local priest told me that the ancient roof of wood still exists above the barocco vault. If that be true, there may have been anciently transverse arches. In any case, it is to be hoped that on the next occasion when the roof has to be opened for a restoration or for any other reason, a careful examination will be made to determine this important point.

The northern chapel contains an interesting fresco.

V. As has been seen, the easternmost of the northern chapels dates from c. 1115, the central chapel on the northern side from c. 1165, the third chapel from c. 1200, the façade from the same period (except the rose-window, which is from c. 1210), the choir from c. 1220, the apse from c. 1225, and the absidioles from c. 1230. We have, therefore, in a single monument, an epitome of the development of the local style of Corneto during a period of one hundred and twenty years.

CORNETO TARQUINIA,[1] S. MARIA DI CASTELLO

(Plate 73; Plate 74; Plate 75; Plate 76, Fig. 1, 2, 3, 4, 5, 6, 7;
Plate 77, Fig. 1, 2, 3, 4, 5, 6, 7, 8)

I. The important inscriptions of S. Maria di Castello of Corneto attracted attention as early as 1778, when Turriozzi[2] published that of 1207. The first archæologist to study the architecture was Séroux d'Agincourt, who published in 1823 several drawings of the edifice.[3] These plates are highly inaccurate. There is depicted, for example, one polygonal apse instead of the two which exist in reality, and a wooden roof is indicated over the nave, with obvious error. The drawings are, however, of great value, since they show the cupola, which has since been destroyed. This cupola appears to have been semi-spherical, surmounted by a little lantern, and raised on a drum adorned externally with arcades.[4] In 1836 Promis published a study upon the Cosmati artists, containing an important notice of S. Maria in Castello, and inexact transcriptions of several of the inscriptions. Numerous other authors have spoken of the mosaics and inscriptions of the edifice, but it is useless to repeat the long list, already published by De Rossi. There should be noticed, however, the manuscript collection of inscriptions of Suarez, preserved in the Vatican,[5] which contains important copies of the inscriptions of the church and some other notices of value. The monograph of De Rossi, published in 1874, is an important study of the early Christian inscriptions preserved in the pavement. In 1878 appeared Dasti's history of Corneto, a work characterized by lack of critical analysis, but of some value for the modern history of the monument. In 1883 Pflugk-Harttung[6] published Wüstenfeld's register of the history of Corneto, which remains undoubtedly the most valuable contribution to our knowledge of this subject. In the same

---

[1] (Roma).   [2] 49.

[3] IV, Plate 73, Fig. 48; Plate 74, Fig. 14; Plate 42, Fig. 6; Plate 70, Fig. 17; Plate 69, Fig. 9.

[4] This cupola is described (III, 72) as follows: . . . le plan inférieur est aussi légèrement elliptique et percé de six arcs, entre lesquels sont autant de pendentifs, portant une espèce de tambour de peu de hauteur, qui reçoit la coupole.

[5] Barb. Lat. 3084, f. 27 f.   [6] II, 529.

year, De Fleury[7] published the inscription of the ciborio (which he prudently refrained from interpreting), and described the cupola, which had already been demolished.[8] In 1894 Enlart[9] referred to the edifice in his work upon Cistercian architecture in Italy, but completely failed to comprehend its archæological importance. This seems to have been grasped by Professor Frothingham,[10] who nevertheless dismisses the monument with a few words. Venturi speaks of the mosaics summarily.[11] In 1905 Guerri published a study of an inedited manuscript of the archives of Corneto, in the illustration of which he had occasion to elucidate several historical questions more or less directly affecting the church of S. Maria di Castello. In 1912 I published a monograph upon the edifice in *Arte e Storia*, unfortunately marred by several misprints in the inscriptions.

II. In the Suarez collection of inscriptions in the Vatican there is record of a certain bishop of Corneto who flourished in 798.[12] The authenticity of this notice is, however, open to grave question, for Wüstenfeld mentions a bull of Leo IV of 848, in which the pope confirmed to the bishop of Toscanella both the town of Corneto itself and the pieve of S. Maria. Corneto could not, therefore, have been a bishopric.[13]

A document of 1111[14] mentions our church. Soon after was commenced a reconstruction of the edifice. An inscription still extant in the church to the north of the main entrance informs us that in the year 1121 after the birth of Christ, when Henry V was emperor and the persecuted Calixtus II was pope, the worthy, pious, honest and benign prior Guido began the construction of the church, and that nine years later he caused this metrical

---

[7] II, 31.

[8] L'ancienne coupole, malheureusement démolie, était composée de plusieurs étages avec colonettes trapues comme au ciborium de Saint-Laurent.

[9] 217.   [10] 360-362.   [11] III, 774.

[12] Ruberts de Corneto Eps. doctrina et scīīte celebris floruit ao. dn̄i. 798. (*MS. cit.*, f. 29).

[13] Eine sichere Erwähnung von Corneto ist erst in der Bulla Leo's IV für Verobonus, Bischof von Toscana, vom Jahre 848 zu sehen, aufgenommen in einer Urkunde Innocenz III. Leo bestätigt darin dem Bischofe sämmtliche Güter, unter welchen sich vallis de Corneto befindet et fundum in territorio Corgnetensi, qui est secus fluvium Martani, dann auch plebs S. Marie, posita in Tarquinii. Das Fortbestehen des alten Tarquinii in verkümmerter Gestalt noch bis zum Jahre 1300 werden wir unten bemerken. Hätte damals ein besonderes Bisthum Corneto bestanden, so wäre es undenkbar, dass Corneto selbst als einem fremden Bischofe zugehörig genannt wird. (531). The question whether or not Corneto was a bishopric previous to 1435 has been much discussed. Guerri (335) maintains that it was, and this opinion I followed in my monograph (141). The document of Wüstenfeld, however, which was not known to me at the time I wrote the monograph, seems to settle the matter in the negative.

[14] De Rossi, 113.

inscription to be sculptured.[15]   The only difficulty these Leonine verses have to offer, aside from the abbreviations and tortured construction common to their kind, is the fact that Guido is called a prior.   It is certain that S. Maria di Castello was officiated by a chapter of canons.[16]   It is therefore to be concluded that the head of the chapter was designated by the somewhat unusual title of prior.   In fact, in the neighbouring town of Toscanella, the important church of S. Maria Maggiore was officiated by a chapter of canons, whose head is constantly called a prior in the documents of the XI and XII centuries.[17]   There are numerous other examples of the same usage in northern Italy.[18]

The expenses of the construction were borne in part by the chapter, in part by citizens of Corneto.   In the pavement of the choir is inscribed the name:

MASSARIVS DONNAINCASA

It is therefore evident that S. Maria di Castello, like the great cathedrals of the North, possessed a special official, *massario*, who was charged with superintending the works of the construction.   Another inscription in the pavement, before the altar, gives the names of two donors, but no indication of their quality:

✚TACCON'. [ET] TRASTOLLENZA H[OC] OP FIERI FECER[VNT]

Another donation, made jointly by Andrea, son of Ranero, by Giovanni and Pietro, probably sons of the same father, hence Andrea's brothers, and by the consuls of Corneto, is recorded by an inscription on the disks of the portal:

SCIL[ICET] ANDREAS RANERI IOH[ANNE]S. PETRVS IDEM

CONSVQ[VE]LATVS. [*sic*] IVSSIT H[OC] AVRARI CORNETI.

[15] ✚IMP[ER]AT HENRIC' CALIXT' FIT PP[A] PETITVS
ANNO MILLENO CENTVM P[R]IMOQ[VE] VICENO
NATALIS XI' DOM' HEC PRIMORDIA FIXIT
GVIDO P[R]IOR DIGNVS. PIVS. [ET]. P[RO]B'. ATQ[VE]
                                                      BENIGNVS.
ANNV POSTQ[VAM] NV FACIT HI H[OC] SCVLP[ER]E METRVM.

[16] Guerri, 335.

[17] Campanari, II, 119 f.

[18] *Necrologium ecclesiae Beati Evasii Casatensis*, v idus Aug., ed. *Hist. Pat. Mon.*, V, 486; Kal. Oct., *ibid.*, 499; *Necrologium insignis collegii canonicorum Sancti Petri et Ursi*, nonis Febr., ed. *Hist. Pat. Mon.*, V, 520; VII Kal. Mart., *ibid.*, 521; IIII Kal. Mart., *ibid.*, 521; VII Kal. Maii, *ibid.*, 524; III Kal. Maii, *ibid.*, 524; etc.

LOMBARD ARCHITECTURE

An inscription in Leonine hexameters on the jamb of the western portal is as follows:

✠ UIR
GO
TVÂM
PRO
LĒ RO
GITA
DEPEL
LERE
MOLĒ
VULG'
UT ĤOC
LETŪ
COR
NETI
IVRE
Q[VI]ETŪ
DET
IVGIT̄
UOTŪ
VIGE
AT SIB̂I
CRIMI
NE LO
TUM
QVOD
Q[VE] TU
A LAV
DE;
TEM
PLVM
PARAT
HOC
SINE
FRAV
DE;

Since these verses offer several obscurities, I shall translate them. "Virgin, pray thy Son to speed this structure,[19] that this people of Corneto, righteously joyful and free from anxiety, may continually sing thy praises, and that this

---

[19] Unless, indeed, *depellere molem* should rather be rendered *take away the burdens of the people.*

temple, which the people, without fraud, prepare in praise of Him and thee, may flourish, washed clean of all misdeeds." Among the benefactors of the church is recorded a certain ecclesiastic named Giorgio, who also aided the prior, Panvino, in superintending the construction of the church. This Giorgio was probably one of the canons, and it is likely that he rendered services similar to those of the superstans in the church of Milan, and identical with those performed at another epoch in this same church by the massario, Donnaincasa. Indeed, if I interpret correctly the obscure inscription of the ciborio, some years later Giorgio's successor in these duties, who was also prior of the church, was openly called superintendent or superstans (*super fuit*).

Bearing in mind this fact, let us examine the difficult inscription on the architrave of the principal portal:

HIC ADITVS VALVE.MARIE VIRGINIS ALMĒ.DVM SIC SPLENDESCIT. MILLE NVT [*sic* = nunc] CIRCVLVS EXIT.ET CVM CENTENIS.TENEAS TRES BISQ[VE] VICENIS.TCQ' PRIORAT' PANVINVM [*sic*] SEDE LOCATVS. ISTE DEO CAR'.MERITIS ET NOMINE CLARVS.INSIGNIS VITE.VIXIT SINE CRIMINE RITE.AD LAUDEM XPI STVDVIT SVA MENIA SISTI. ADIUVAT * * NC FACTIS

At this point the inscription is broken off for lack of space, but is continued on the jamb, where the words of the last line are repeated:

+ADIU
VAT
HVNC
FAC
TIS.
VENE
RAN
DVS
PBR
ACTIS.
NON
PIGU
IT SEN
SVM.
GEOR
GIVS
ET DA
RE CEN
SVM.

In one of the disks of the Cosmati decoration, the last lines are repeated:

✦ VENERANDVS PBR ACTIS. N̄ PIGUIT

SENSV̄. GEORGIVS ET DARE CENSV̄.

This inscription may be translated: "This portal of the Blessed Virgin Mary was erected in the year 1143, when Panvino was prior. He, beloved of God, of eminent merits and reputation, of blameless life, lived untouched by sin. He endeavoured to erect these walls for the glory of Christ. The reverend priest, Giorgio, aided him by his deeds and acts, not slothful to give his revenue and riches."[20]

Twenty-five years later the ciborio was erected, as is recorded by the inscription carved upon its archivolt:

✦ UIRGINIS ARA PIE. SIC Ē DECORATA MARIE. QUE GENUIT XPM.

TANTO SUB TPR SCRIPTU. ANNO MILLENO CENTENO. VI. ETAGENO

OCTO SUP[ER] RURSUS. FUIT ET PRIOR OPTIMUS URSUS. CUI

XPS REGNV̄. CCEDAT HABERE SUP[ER]NU. AM.

✦ IOHS ET GUITTO MAGISTRI HOC OPVS FECERVNT

This extremely difficult and obscure inscription I translate as follows: "One thousand, one hundred and sixty- [sexetageno = et sexageno] eight years after the pious Virgin Mary had borne Christ, this, her altar, was decorated with a ciborio. Orso was the most worthy prior, and again in charge of the work. May Christ grant him everlasting life, Amen. The masters Giovanni and Guido executed this work." Over the last words may be seen upside down part of an unfinished inscription of the same tenor.

Under the altar were doubtless preserved relics of the four saints, Saturnino, Sisinnio, Timoteo and Simforiano, whose names are recorded in an inscription on the jamb of the portal:

NON

OBE

UNT

ISTI

PASSI

PRO NO

MINE. XI.

[20] In my monograph (146) I pointed out the curious error of De Rossi, who gives to the word *sensum* the unprecedented signification "il disegno e la direzione del lavoro" (114), whereas it is clear that the word is to be taken in the sense Du Cange gives it, *tributium, pensitatio ex agris et praedis,* and is here a synonym of *censum,* as *actis* is the synonym of *factis* in the preceding line.

ECCE
SATV̂RNI
N̂US
SI
SIN
NIVS
ET TI
MO
TĤE
US.
HIC
BE
NE
CV̂M
CÂRO
RE
Q[VI]E
SCV̂NT
SIM
PHO
RI
A
NO.

Other inscriptions in the church give the signatures of Cosmati artists, the genealogy of whom has been studied by De Rossi and Frothingham.[21]

[21] On the archivolt of the principal portal is inscribed:

✚ R[A]NUCII PETRVS.LA[P]IDUM N̄ [D]OGMATE MERVS
[I]STUD OPVS MIRE S[TR]UXIT QVOQ[V]E FEĈIT OPIME

In the window above is engraved:

✚ H[OC] SIGNV̄ CRVĈIS ERIT Ī CELO
CV̄ DN̄S AD IVDICANDV̄ UENERIT.

✚ NICOLAVS RANV
CII MAGISTER
ROMANVS FECIT H[OC]

One of the most important inscriptions of the church is placed in the interior wall to the north of the main portal. It is as follows:

IN NOMINE X̄P̄Ī ĀM̄.A.D.M.CC.V

III.INDICTIONE.X.TENPORIB: [sic] D̄N̄Ī INNO

CENTII.P̄P̄.III.XIII.K[A]L[END].ĪŪN̄.HOC TEMPL

VM.B.M.EST DEDICATVM.IN CŪĪVS DE

DICATIONE.X.ADFUERVNT ĒP̄Ī.P[ER]SON

ALITER.TUSCANENSIS.AMELIEN

SIS.BALNORIENSIS.CASTRENSIS.SU

ANENSIS.ORBEVETANUS.ORTA

NUS.CIVITONICUS.NEPESINVS.SU

TRINVS.SETCVM [sic] ESSENT.XII.INUITÂ

TI DVOQ[VE] UENIRE N̄ POT̂ERANT.NARNIENSIS.

ET GROSSETANUS.ASSENSV̂M REMIS

SIONIS P[ER] LITT̂ERAS DIREXERVNT.IDCIRCO

IN PRIMO ANNO UI' DEDICATIONIS.XII.ANNOS

HIS Q[VI] VENERANT REMISERUNT ANNVA

TIM UERO . . . . . DE INIUNTA PENIT̂ENTIA

IIII.ANNOS RELAXARVNT HIS Q[VI] DEUOT̂E

AD HANC DOMUM VENIENT CUM S̄P̄ALI IOC̄V̄

DATION̂E.✛.ITEM Ī ĪŌĪ [sic; perhaps for in nomine] HVI' ECCL[ESI]E
                                          UOCABVLO
VNUM ANVM [sic] [CON]DONARVNT.

    FACTA.SVNT HEC SUPRA DICTA ACTORE.[sic]

D̄N̄O P[ER] ANGELV̄ PRIOR̄E Q[VI] HVIC TVNC P̄ERAT

ECCL[ESI]E.✛

Although the sentence *item in nomine* [?] *huius ecclesiae vocabulo unum annum condonarunt* is entirely obscure, the significance of the inscription seems to be as follows: "In the name of Christ, Amen. [An inverted "R" is written for an "A"]. In the year of our Lord, 1207, during the reign of Pope Innocent III, on the twentieth day of May, this temple of the Blessed Virgin was dedicated. On the occasion of this dedication were present in person ten bishops, namely those of Toscanella, Amelia, Bagnorea, Castro, Sovanna, Orvieto, Orte, Civita,[22] Nepi and Sutri. Though twelve were invited, two—the bishops of Narni and Grosseto—could not come. They nevertheless

[22] Civita was situated in Corsica, on the site of the present town of Terranova. (Cappelletti, XIII, 164).

signified by letters their approval of the indulgences conceded. Twelve years of indulgence were granted to those who should visit the church on the first anniversary of this consecration, and every year thereafter, four years of indulgence to those who should come to the anniversary of the consecration devoutly and with spiritual joy. Likewise one year of indulgence to any one who should invoke the Virgin by the name of this church [?]. The things above recorded were done by the inspiration of the Lord, through the hand of Angelo, who was at that time prior of the church."

The following year the ambo was erected, as is recorded by the inscription carved upon it:

> ✠ [IN] NO.$\overline{\text{IE}}$.D.$\overline{\text{AM}}$.A.D.M.C.C.UIIII.I.
> D[ICT] XI.M.A.G.T.$\overline{\text{DNI}}$.INNOCEN.$\overline{\text{PP}}$.
> III.EGO ANGEL' $\widehat{\text{PIOR}}$ HUI' ECCL[ESI]E.HOC OP'.
> NITID$\overline{\text{U}}$ AURO ET MARMORE DIVERSO.F[I]ERI
> FECIT.P[ER] MANUS MAGISTRI IOH'IS GUITTONIS
> CIUIS R.M.N.

Notwithstanding the abbreviations, this time the meaning is clear: "In the name of the Lord Jesus, Amen. In the year of Our Lord 1208 in the month of August, during the pontificate of Innocent III, I, Angelo, prior of this church, caused this work, bright with gold and various marbles, to be executed by the hand of the master Giovanni, son of Guido, and a Roman citizen."

In 1435 Pope Eugenius IV removed Corneto from the jurisdiction of the see of Viterbo and Toscanella, raised it to the rank of a bishopric united with that of Montefiascone, and decreed that the church of SS. Maria e Margarita, the new cathedral, should be united with the chapter of S. Maria di Castello, which should thus cease to be a collegiate church upon the death of the existing prior.[23]

The Carmelites called in 1566 soon left, so that in 1569 the building was closed to worship. In 1585, however, the edifice was turned over to the Padri Conventuali, who, in 1642, added some—fortunately not very important—embellishments in the barocco style. All this is recorded by an inscription

---

[23] Et insuper SS. Mariæ, & Margaritæ, ac S. Mariæ de Castello Cornetanæ Collegiatæ Ecclesiæ invicem eadem auctoritate unientes, annectentes, & incorporantes, ac in eis Collegiatarum Ecclesiarum nomen hujusmodi penitùs extinguentes, & in unū corpus unumque Collegium reducentes SS. Mariæ & Margaritæ Ecclesias præfatas in Cathedralem Ecclesiam erigimus, eamque dignitatis Episcopalis titulo insignimus . . . & Apostolica authoritate decernentes, quòd in eadem erecta Ecclesia loco Præfecti, qui nunc est, Archidiaconatus . . . nuncupetur. In alia verò Ecclesia S. Mariæ de Castello, sicut præfertur unita, prima dignitas omninò cesset, cùm illa vacare contigerit per cessum, vel decessum; ambo quoque ipsarum Ecclesiarum Collegia in unum Collegium Cathedralis Ecclesię sic erectæ Capitulum facientia reducantur, singulique ipsarum Ecclesiarum Canonici, non Collegiatarum, sed Cathedralis Ecclesiæ Canonici nuncupentur. (Ughelli, I, 983; Cappelletti, V, 650; Turriozzi, 90-100).

almost as difficult and barbaric as any of the Middle Ages, still preserved over the main portal in the interior of the church:

.D.O.M.

SIXTVS.V.P.M.

A̅N̅O.P̂O.S.Pvs.EIVS.RELIGIO.IN HOC I̅CLYTO

TEMPLO.CÆPIT.DEV̅.LA̅V̂DA̅R̂E.ET.A̅N̅O

MDC.X.X.X.X.II.RESTA̅VRvm COOPER.AC ORNAT̅v̅

CV̅.SVMPT.bvs ET.LABORIBVS.RELIGIONIS.M.CON.24

On the existing doors is sculptured the coat of arms of the Franciscans.

In 1809 the building was finally desecrated. In 1819 the cupola fell in consequence of an earthquake. Used as a barracks for the French soldiers, and in other ways exposed to damage and decay, the edifice fell into such serious disrepair that in 1857 it was found necessary to begin a restoration, which was completed only in 1878. This restoration, notwithstanding its long duration, seems not to have been as disastrous as might have been feared. Whether owing to lack of funds or some other lucky accident, the church to-day still retains its original character, which the restorations appear not to have seriously affected.

III. The church consists of a nave of four double bays, two side aisles, a choir of a single double bay, also flanked by side aisles, and three apses (Plate 73). With the exception of the apses covered with half domes, and the central bay of the nave, formerly surmounted by a dome on pendentives (Plate 75), but now roofed in wood (Plate 77, Fig. 7), the church is vaulted throughout with rib vaults erected on plans approximately square. The system is alternate, so that two bays of the side aisles correspond to a single bay of the nave (Plate 73). Since there are no wall ribs, the system of three members provided in the aisle responds, on the aisle side of all the piers, and on the nave side of the heavier piers (Plate 73), is entirely logical (Plate 73; Plate 75; Plate 76, Fig. 5; Plate 77, Fig. 6, 7). On the nave side of the intermediate piers is engaged a half column which buttresses the pier against the thrust of the aisle vault (Plate 75; Plate 76, Fig. 3; Plate 77, Fig. 1, 7). This column is crowned by a capital which supports nothing. It will be recalled that half columns used as buttresses externally are common in the contemporary architecture of the Île-de-France, and are found, for example, in the church of Laffaut, Aisne.

The orientation is very irregular, having doubtless been determined by the site of the church on the edge of steep cliffs. The apse is turned towards the north and the façade towards the south. To the east of the edifice is a curious rectangular structure (Plate 73; Plate 76, Fig. 6) without door or window, and placed against the side of the church. To judge from the

24.M.CON. = minor congregatio.

masonry, this strange building seems later than the basilica itself, and I suppose it to be a sort of charnel-house or depository for bones. In the east wall, and in the thickness of the wall, which is increased to receive it—a process which causes strange distortion in the aisle vaults (Plate 73)—is a stairway leading to the aisle roof.

The half dome of the central apse is supplied with four ribs supported on colonnettes (Plate 74; Plate 75; Plate 76, Fig. 4; Plate 77, Fig. 2, 7). These vaults, like the entire church, are constructed of fine ashlar. The ribs of the half dome are round, as are those of the two eastern bays of the side aisles (Plate 76, Fig. 5; Plate 77, Fig. 6) and of the eastern and second from the west bays of the nave (Plate 77, Fig. 7). The others all have a square profile. The transverse arches of the nave and side aisles are in two unmoulded orders, as are those of the main arcade, but in a number of cases the lower courses of the arch are in a single order, on which rest the two orders of the upper part (Plate 75; Plate 76, Fig. 3; Plate 77, Fig. 2, 6). This is doubtless a device to soften the transition between the rectangular pilasters and the arches in two orders which they carry. In other instances, the same effect is produced with much greater elegance by allowing the upper order to die away somewhat as the capital is approached (Plate 77, Fig. 1). The arches of the main arcade are highly stilted (Plate 75), as are the wall arches (Plate 76, Fig. 5). The transverse arches are loaded (Plate 77, Fig. 7, 8). Thus, although the diagonal ribs are approximately semicircular, the vaults are somewhat, but not excessively, domed (Plate 77, Fig. 7, 8). The masonry courses of the vaults tend to converge towards the keystone. The side-aisle walls are supplied with buttresses (Plate 76, Fig. 1), applied equally to each bay without regard to the alternation of the system. Half columns engaged on pilaster strips reinforce the exterior wall of the central apse (Plate 76, Fig. 7). The system of buttressing employed in the clearstory walls is peculiar and irregular, and is evidently the result of alterations executed at various epochs. In the two northern bays of the west side (Plate 76, Fig. 1) are extremely salient buttresses applied to meet the thrust of the great vaults. In the third bay is a low transverse buttress (Plate 76, Fig. 1) of the familiar Lombard type, but this rests not upon the transverse arch of the side-aisle vaults, but on the vaults themselves. In the south bay, a similar buttress appears to have existed formerly, but it has been destroyed. In the northern bay on the east side (Plate 76, Fig. 6) is a high transverse buttress in part destroyed. Elsewhere the clearstory walls are flat and without buttresses of any kind. Absolutely no wood is employed in the building. The tiles are laid on mortar which rests on top of the vaults. The side-aisle roof on the west side cuts across half of the rose-window (Plate 76, Fig. 1). In the original construction, therefore, this roof must have been almost flat. The clearstory wall shows signs of having been altered in three different epochs: when the rose-windows were added early in the XIII century; when the

Renaissance windows were made over in the XVII century; and again in comparatively modern times—perhaps during the restorations of the XIX century. It is probable that there were originally no buttresses.

The ancient windows were unglazed, tall and narrow, but of varying size (Plate 75). Those of the clearstory were for the most part made over in the XVII century (Plate 76, Fig. 1).

The original edifice appears to have been without a campanile, unless this has perished without leaving a trace of itself. The austere tower which rises near the south façade (Plate 76, Fig. 6) belonged to a palace which had nothing to do with the church.

IV. A cornice of arched corbel-tables, many of which are richly carved (as in the contemporary architecture of Piemonte), marks the level of the aisle roofs (Plate 76, Fig. 1), and is carried completely around the church (Plate 76, Fig. 7) except in the central portion of the principal façade (Plate 76, Fig. 2). The western absidiole (Plate 76, Fig. 7) has a similar cornice. The western clearstory wall (Plate 76, Fig. 1) is without any cornice. The eastern clearstory wall has a cornice, but of curiously irregular form, since, instead of following the horizontal line of the present roof, it is broken up into a series of sharply inclined lines. It is evident that this is the result of clumsy restorations executed at a late epoch.

The principal façade (Plate 76, Fig. 2) is divided into three parts by pilaster strips. Originally the central part was higher than the others. It was doubtless the intention of the builders to finish all three bays with a horizontal cornice, but that of the central bay was either never executed or has been destroyed. The horizontal cornice ought to have been surmounted by a wall following the inclination of the roofs, as may still be seen in the north wall of the church (Plate 76, Fig. 7). Later, doubtless in the XVII century, the western belfry was added (Plate 76, Fig. 2), and the left-hand division of the façade thus became higher than the central division. At the same period a blank masking wall was erected over the right-hand bay (Plate 76, Fig. 2). These unfortunate additions of the barocco period have spoiled the beauty and dignity of the original design of the façade, which, notwithstanding the splendour of the Cosmati decorations, has a somewhat mean and squalid appearance.

The capitals, with the exception of those sculptured by the Cosmati artists, are purely Lombard in style (Plate 76, Fig. 3, 4, 5; Plate 77, Fig. 1, 3, 4, 5, 6). Sirens astride, holding in their hands their legs, which end in tails; eagles; two animals with a single head; grotesques; and other motives characteristic of the churches erected in the neighbourhood of Milan, but unknown in the architecture of Rome and Umbria, are found in abundance. On the other hand, the influence of Rome is felt in certain capitals with semi-classic heart-leaves (Plate 77, Fig. 1), eggs and darts (Plate 77, Fig. 1) or rinceaux (Plate 77, Fig. 3). There is, proportionately, a far greater number of capitals ornamented only with foliage than is usual in Lombardy. While certain acanthus leaves and volutes are almost identical in character with those familiar in S. Ambrogio of Milan and S. Michele of Pavia, others have a new character, without, so far as I know, analogy elsewhere. The capitals are executed in peperino, whereas the church itself is constructed of tufo. The technique of the carving of the capitals is excellent and exact. The capitals of the east end of the church (especially of the central apse) appear somewhat earlier than the others, but the difference in style is so slight as to be barely perceptible.

The bases are of Attic type (Plate 77, Fig. 8), and are generally without griffes, although griffes do occur.

The Cosmati decorations are all excellent examples of this type of ornament, but are unfortunately much mutilated. The mosaics of the main portal have been picked out, the ciborio has lost its original columns, the mosaics of the ambo have been destroyed, and the pavement is in fragments.[25]

V. From the inscriptions already cited, it is evident that the church was begun in the year 1121; that in 1143 the mosaics of the principal portal were executed, but that at this epoch the edifice was not yet completed, since divine aid was invoked to finish it; that in 1168 the ciborio was erected; that in 1207 the church was dedicated, and that in 1208 the ambo was built. A study of the monument itself establishes with equal certainty that the construction of the edifice began with the apses. The conclusion is therefore inevitable that the greater part of the structure had already been erected when the façade was built in 1143. The style of the entire edifice is so homogeneous that it is impossible to doubt that the building was practically finished within a few years after it had been begun, and in all probability under the direction of the same master-builder who had drawn the first plan. We may, therefore, conclude that the church was completed before 1150.

Some finishing touches must, however, have been lacking, and for this reason the dedication must have been delayed. It is probable that the resources of the chapter had been exhausted by the expenses of the construction. A hint of this is to be found in the prayer to the Virgin for aid to finish the building, contained in the inscription of 1143. Yet in 1168 the structure itself must have been finished for all practical purposes, since the canons, in this year, erected the costly ciborio. Until this time they had doubtless contented themselves with the church-furniture brought from the old basilica. Indeed, the ancient baptistery, never renewed, still exists in the eastern side aisle.

About the end of the XII century, and probably c. 1190, an accident befell the church. Of this disaster, which was probably caused by an earthquake,

---

[25] Durand (223) states that a piece of this pavement was in his time to be seen in the Musée de Cluny at Paris, but it can not now be found there.

no historical notices have come down to us, but the history is written in the stones of the building itself, in letters which leave no doubt upon the subject. It is evident that the vaults of three bays in the nave—the first, third and fourth from the south—and of four of the side aisles—the two southern on both sides—and the half dome of the central apse, were all reconstructed at this period. All, with the exception of the central bay of the nave, were rebuilt as they were originally, but for the rectangular diagonals there were substituted diagonals of torus section. Moreover, the new construction was added to the ancient masonry in such a way as to leave clear traces of the fact that an addition has been made in the form of a break in the masonry, which still exists. Finally, in the second bay from the south of the nave, there is introduced a coat of arms on the keystone, a motive which is without parallel among Italian vaults of the first half of the XII century.

In the central bay of the nave, the ancient rib vault was replaced by a pendentive dome carried on pointed wall arches. Beneath this and the clearstory wall on either side was pierced a rose-window, the ornament of which is entirely different in character from that of the earlier parts of the church. Indeed, this difference of ornament is so striking that it forms the most convincing argument for assigning the earlier parts of the edifice to an epoch not later than 1150. Such a complete revolution of ornamental sculpture could hardly have been accomplished in a period of less than fifty years.

Other works as well were accomplished about the same time. The two buttresses of the northern bays of the west clearstory were added, and the Cosmati pavement was executed. The latter is evidently much later than the church itself, since it cuts across the bases of the piers. Finally, in 1207, after all these repairs and changes, the church was ready for the consecration, which was celebrated with great pomp.

In the following year, 1208, the church was embellished with a new ambo. Later, in the XIII century, the western rose-window was filled with its present tracery, and the clearstory walls were reinforced, where they showed signs of yielding, by transverse buttresses.

CORNETO TARQUINIA,[1] S. PANCRAZIO

(Plate 78; Plate 79; Plate 80, Fig. 1, 3, 4, 5; Plate 81, Fig. 1, 2, 3, 4, 5)

I. I published a monograph upon this monument in *Arte e Storia* in 1913.

II. Of the history of S. Pancrazio even less is known than of the other churches of Corneto. None of the scanty historical notices gathered by

[1] (Roma).

Dasti[2] and Guerri[3] is more ancient than the XIII century. The only matter of some significance for the history of the monument to be gleaned from the accounts of these authors is the fact that there was anciently a portico before the church. This has disappeared, but traces are still visible.

III. The edifice consists of a nave of a single aisle, almost square in plan, three apses, a campanile engaged on the west façade, and two charnel-houses, one on either side of the nave (Plate 78). The orientation is irregular, since the apse is turned to the north rather than to the east. The principal portal is in the south façade; anciently there was another portal in the east wall, but this is now walled up.

The three apses are covered with half domes. These have been covered internally with intonaco and barocco ornament (Plate 80, Fig. 5; Plate 81, Fig. 3), so that it is unfortunately impossible to study the structure of the vault. However, the fact that the central apse is reinforced externally with five half columns used like buttresses (Plate 78) gives reason to suppose that there may have been internally a system of engaged colonnettes, and that these colonnettes supported ribs, as in the apse of S. Maria di Castello (Plate 77, Fig. 2).

The northern half of the church is covered by a sexpartite vault with light rectangular ribs. The length of this vault is about half of its width (Plate 78; Plate 79). The great transverse arch is pointed and in two orders (Plate 81, Fig. 3). The upper order, however, is not continued as far as the capital, since the arch is made rectangular in its lower part (Plate 79)—a mannerism which recalls S. Maria (Plate 77, Fig. 6). The vault is domed (Plate 79). Although there are no wall ribs, the wall arches are highly stilted (Plate 79). The vault surface is thus much warped. The wooden roof which covers this vault is supported upon the northern wall and upon walls erected over the two transverse arches (Plate 79). The vault, like the rest of the church, is constructed of tufo well squared and laid without mortar.

The southern bay of the church is covered by a wooden roof, supported by a transverse wall with three arches (Plate 78; Plate 79). These arches are semicircular and in two orders. The southern half of this bay is thus made to form a sort of narthex. Undoubtedly it was the original intention of the builders to cover the southern half of the church with a sexpartite vault like that erected in the northern half, and this is proved by the fact that members are provided in the central responds for the diagonals of such a vault (Plate 78). It appears, however, that the builders were not satisfied with the result of their experiment with the sexpartite vault in the northern bay, perhaps because the construction was too expensive. At all events, in the southern bay they contented themselves with a simple roof, supported

[2] 412.   [3] 339.

by a transverse wall for the sake of economy of wood. In point of fact, no more wood is employed in the southern bay than in the northern bay, although the latter is vaulted.

The walls are reinforced externally by vigorous rectangular buttresses, of which those at the angle and opposite the principal transverse arch are, as they logically should be, more powerful than the others (Plate 78; Plate 81, Fig. 5). The central respond of the interior is so heavy (Plate 78) that it forms in itself an efficient buttress, and in this recalls the responds of the cathedral of Fréjus (Plate 70, Fig. 4). These responds are formed of three rectangular members, of which the two outermost are normal to the diagonals which they carry. The other responds consist of a single pilaster strip normal to the transverse arch or the diagonal, as the case may be (Plate 78). The arches of both doors are pointed (Plate 79; Plate 81, Fig. 4). The southern door still retains some of its decoration in mosaic (Plate 81, Fig. 4). Traces of the portico which formerly existed are still visible. This portico did not form part of the original construction, since its roof cut across the rose-window of the façade (Plate 80, Fig. 4), and its southern wall was evidently built against that of the campanile after the latter had been completed.

The campanile, of two stories (Plate 80, Fig. 4; Plate 81, Fig. 5), has bifora, and terminates in a peculiar cone. This tower is evidently later than the church, since it cuts across mouldings of the façade.

IV. The rose-window has lost its radiating colonnettes (Plate 80, Fig. 4), but still preserves its mouldings, richly ornamented with leaves of rather archaic Romanesque character. The central portal (Plate 81, Fig. 4) has broad, simple mouldings and rows of stiff, rigid leaves, except in the inner jambs and architrave, in the mouldings, mosaics and sculptured lions of which it is easy to recognize the hand of Roman artists.

The capitals of the interior have been so covered with intonaco that it is difficult to study them. Some are grotesque, being sculptured with two animals having a single head (Plate 81, Fig. 1) or other motives purely Lombard in character; others are adorned with leaves which, though stiff and archaic, none the less show the influence of the Gothic style of France (Plate 81, Fig. 2); in other instances capitals are replaced by simple mouldings without any sculpture.

V. With the exception of the campanile and the alterations carried out in the barocco period, the church appears to be a homogeneous structure. In many details the style resembles that of S. Maria di Castello. We have already remarked that, in both edifices, the second order of transverse arches is suppressed near the capitals. In both churches, a separate support is supplied in the system for each rib. In both, the principal apse is supplied externally with colonnettes, and it is probable that in S. Pancrazio the central apse had internally a system and ribs like those of S. Maria. In all these peculiarities, S. Pancrazio resembles S. Maria di Castello, and differs from the more ancient churches of Corneto, such as S. Giacomo and the Annunziata. Indeed, S. Pancrazio is later than S. Maria, as may be deduced from several circumstances. The vaults of S. Pancrazio are more complicated, and show a technique more developed and more sure of itself than do those of S. Maria. The buttresses of S. Pancrazio (Plate 78) are heavier than those of S. Maria (Plate 73), and far more skilfully applied, since they are alternately heavier and lighter according to the thrust of the vaults, while those of S. Maria are all equal. At S. Pancrazio pointed arches are introduced in the vaults, and even in the portal, whereas all the arches of the first epoch of construction at S. Maria are round. The style of S. Maria (I am speaking only of the oldest portions of the edifice) is purely Lombard without any trace of French influence. At S. Pancrazio, on the other hand, French influence is most evident in the rose-window, in the mouldings, in certain capitals, and in the sexpartite vaults. (Compare, for example, Plate 80, Fig. 1, with Plate 80, Fig. 2, which shows the vaults of St.-Étienne of Caen).

The first epoch of construction at S. Maria began in 1121, and extended until about 1150. We may therefore conclude that S. Pancrazio dates from the second half of the XII century. There is, however, reason to believe that it was erected not long after 1150. It must be held in mind that the masons of S. Maria were undoubtedly deterred from changing the style of the edifice during the construction by a desire to maintain the unity of the building. The style of S. Maria, therefore, must be considered as typical of the style of Corneto in the year 1121, rather than of that of 1150. Furthermore, the style of S. Pancrazio offers close analogies with those portions of S. Maria which were erected between 1121 and 1150, but few analogies with those erected between 1190 and 1207. S. Pancrazio may, therefore, be ascribed to about 1160, and this ascription of date is confirmed by the observation that at that period all the French elements here copied had already been long in use in the Île-de-France.

The campanile, to judge by the style of the capitals, appears to be of the first quarter of the XIII century.

CORTAZZONE D'ASTI,[1] S. SECONDO

(Plate 82, Fig. 2, 3, 4; Plate 83, Fig. 2)

I. The monument was first published by Mella in one of his monographs. Several half-tones of various parts of the building have been published by Venturi.[2]

[1] The chapel of S. Secondo is placed on top of a hill about two kilometres to the north-west of the commune of Cortazzone in the Monferrato (province of Alessandria).
[2] III, 8, 14, 17, 121, 124.

LOMBARD ARCHITECTURE

II.   Of the history of the edifice nothing is known.

III.   The church consists of a nave (Plate 82, Fig. 2) five bays long, two side aisles and three apses.   There is no campanile, but a modern belfry has been erected over the gable of the west façade.   The nave and side aisles are at present covered with domical vaults, with transverse arches, which, in the nave, are pointed.   The vaults are constructed of very flat bricks, and are undoubtedly a comparatively modern addition to the edifice, since no responds are provided in either nave or side aisles (Plate 82, Fig. 2).   The original roof was doubtless of timber.   The short barrel vault which precedes the principal apse (Plate 82, Fig. 2) may, however, be original.

The supports are piers alternately of cylindrical and of fanciful sections (Plate 82, Fig. 2).   The bays are all of unequal length, but the easternmost is decidedly the longest, a mannerism which recalls Agliate and the churches of Viterbo and Toscanella.   The widely splayed windows were evidently intended to serve without glass.

The masonry has been much restored, but appears to have consisted originally of ashlar of good quality (Plate 82, Fig. 4).   At intervals poly-chromatic decoration is introduced by the inlaying of bands or triangular patterns in brick (Plate 82, Fig. 4).   The upper part of the façade is obviously modern.

IV.   The capitals are extraordinary creations, carved with wild grotesques, or strange leaf patterns, in which the exuberance of Lombard art reaches its fullest expression (Plate 83, Fig. 2).   Sirens, birds and strange figures of every kind run riot in these delightful compositions.   The exterior is lavishly adorned with arched corbel-tables (Plate 82, Fig. 3, 4), which are carved with mouldings, billets, rosettes, grotesques, leaf patterns and balls.   The corbels themselves are also adorned with carved patterns of similar character.   The pilaster strips and shafts are frequently supplied with carved capitals (Plate 82, Fig. 4).   On the southern side, the cornices are formed of multiple billets or rinceaux, and decoration in interlaces and string patterns is introduced about the clearstory windows.

The archivolts of the main arcade are given an extrados non-concentric with the intrados, a device which imparts a light appearance to the flat and unmoulded profiles.

The extraordinary character of the bases is clear in the photograph (Plate 82, Fig. 2).

V.   Both the masonry and decoration at Cortazzone d'Asti (Plate 82, Fig. 4) recall the narthex of Casale (Plate 43, Fig. 4; Plate 44, Fig. 1, 2), a monument of c. 1150.   Cortazzone may consequently be ascribed to the same period.

COSIO,[1] S. PIETRO IN VALLATE

I.   The interesting ruins of the church of S. Pietro in Vallate were first published by Damiani.   Subsequently Sant'Ambrogio wrote of the edifice in connection with the deed of foundation published by Bernard.

II.   In 1078 the construction of the church of S. Pietro in Vallate had already been begun.   This is known from a deed of that year by which Otto and his wife, of Isola Comacina, gave, at the persuasion of Rigizone, a monk of Cluny, nine pieces of land to the church of Cluny.   This land lay just above that on which had been begun the construction of our church, which is specified as belonging "to the work of Cluny."[2]

Very little is known of the subsequent history of this Cluniac priory. Its goods must eventually have passed to the abbey of S. Nicolò of Piona, since the commendatary abbots of the latter bore also the title of abbot of S. Pietro di Vallate.   In the time of Ninguarda the same priest officiated at S. Nicolò of Piona and at S. Pietro in Vallate.   It is therefore evident that the church continued to be officiated after the abbey had ceased to exist.   In 1755, however, the church had already fallen into the ruin in which it still stands.[3]

III.   The edifice appears to have consisted originally of a single-aisled nave roofed in timber, a barrel-vaulted choir, a semicircular apse covered with a half dome, and a campanile standing to the north-west of the choir.   This campanile had a groin vault in its lower story, traces of which still survive. Subsequently the church was enlarged.   A northern side aisle was erected, and the lower story of the campanile was thrown into the church.   A great arch,

---

[1] S. Pietro in Vallate lies on a spur of the mountain on the south side of the Valtellina.   It is a ten minutes' climb on foot above the Strada Provinciale, between Cosio and Morbegno (provincia di Sondrio), a kilometre, perhaps, from Cosio.   The campanile is plainly visible from the road.

[2] Anno ab incarnatione Domini nostri Jesu Christi millesimo septuagesimo octavo, mense martio, indictione prima. . . . Quapropter nos Otto, filius quondam Cunitonis, et Boniza, jugalibus, filia Bonizonis, omnes de Insula quę vocatur Cumensis . . . suadente Rigizone, presbitero atque professus Cluniacensis monasterii . . . donamus et offerimus, ad ęcclesiam Cluniensem, quę est constructa in honore sanctorum apostolorum Petri et Pauli, et per jam dictum Rigizonem, ejusdem ecclesię professum, in vesturam et cartulam traditam sacrosancto altari legamus, nominative inter campos et prata et silvas et pascualia juris nostri petie novem; et sunt omnes in episcopatu Sancti Habundii et in valle quę nominatur Vallis Telina, et sunt positę infra territorium villarum quę nominantur Cose et Roboredum.   Prima petia de terra est campus et castagnetum, et pratum et arbores nucum super ea esse videntur, et boscum cum saxo et gerbo, ubi edificium est inceptum in honore sanctorum apostolorum Petri et Pauli et sancti Maioli, et ad opus ecclesię Cluniensis, et hec petia posita est in monte de Cose, et nominatur Valaris. . . . Actum in Insula feliciter. (Bernard, IV, 641).

[3] Damiani.

which still exists in part, was cut out of the corner of the campanile, the south-western angle of which was thus left without support. To lighten the weight, the groin vault of the lower story of the campanile was destroyed. At a still later date it was found necessary to replace the part of the tower which had been cut away by a new wall. Before the addition of the northern side aisle, there appears to have been a sort of gateway or passage through the campanile. The campanile has evidently been much restored, doubtless in consequence of the settlement caused by the removal of the south-western angle. It is crowned by a hollow stone pyramid, which is evidently original.

The widely splayed windows were intended to serve without glass.

The barrel vault and half dome of the choir are constructed of uncut stones, rather carefully laid in thick beds of mortar. These vaults were obviously erected with a solid centering, since traces of the boards of this still remain in the plaster. The masonry of the church appears to be contemporary with that of the campanile. Stones of exceedingly variable size are employed, running from squared blocks of fairly Cyclopean dimensions in the south wall, to small rough stones. The builders evidently made use of what was available. Nevertheless, the workmanship is rather good. The courses tend towards the horizontal, but the joints are often very wide.

IV. The capitals of the campanile are splayed and without character. The apse is crowned by a cornice, consisting of a saw tooth and two zigzags in relief. The shafts or pilaster strips, which must have existed, have been removed, leaving a narrow scar in the wall. There were arched corbel-tables in addition to the other decorations of the apse, and the campanile is still adorned with the same ornament. The belfry of the campanile has bifora in two orders. These, and the low and broad proportions, lend to the tower a peculiar charm. The eastern pediment of the church is relieved by a window in the shape of a Greek cross.

There are numerous traces of frescos on the interior and exterior walls.

V. The campanile, the nave, and the apse may be considered an authentically dated monument of 1078. There are not sufficient data to determine when the northern side aisle and the absidiole were added.

CREMONA, BATTISTERO

(Plate 83, Fig. 6)

I. Several old drawings of the baptistery are preserved in the museum of Cremona. One of the choir-stalls of the cathedral is adorned with a XV century intarsia, depicting the piazza and the baptistery. The latter is shown without the Renaissance loggia of the upper story which now exists. Instead of this there is a blank wall, crowned by a Renaissance balustrade. The roof and lantern seem to be similar to those which exist at present. The windows are arranged somewhat differently, but this is probably due to an inaccuracy of the artist.

Important historical notices of the baptistery are contained in the works of Aglio, Torresino and Merula. The building has been the subject of two important archæological monographs, written respectively by Von Eitelberger and Spielberg. A conscientious study of the edifice is contained in Lopez' monograph upon the baptistery of Parma. The notices of the edifice by Stiehl, Mothes[1] and Melani[2] deserve mention.

II. All the documents, purporting to be earlier than the X century, which mention the baptistery of Cremona, are, so far as I know, apocryphal. It is entirely probable, however, that the edifice existed at an early period.

There is a tradition that the baptistery was erected in the year 900. This seems to have been recorded in two lost manuscript chronicles, one by Marco Girolamo Vida, and the other by Giovanni Ballestrario. Citations from these have been preserved by Torresino[3] and Merula.[4] The citations of Aglio[5] and Lopez appear to be derived from Torresino.

Whether or not it be true that the baptistery was erected in the year 900, it was undoubtedly reconstructed in the year 1167, as is recorded in the anonymous chronicle published by Muratori.[6]

According to an inscription preserved by Vairani[7] the bronze angel on top of the lantern (Plate 83, Fig. 6) was erected in 1370.

In 1489 the leaden roof was built, as is recorded by an inscription in the façade:

REGNANTE . DIVO . IO . GZ DV$\widehat{CE}$
MLI . SEXT⁰ . ET . L^{co} PATRVO
FELICISSI[M]AE GVBERNANTE I
IO. BAPTISTA . MAL$\widehat{VM}$BRA . . . . . DOCTOR
IACOBVS . TRECHVS . ET . ROBERTVS G$\widehat{VA}$
ZONVS . PATRIE . . . . . . AC FABRICE
VIRGINIS . CONSERVATORES . HOC SACRA
TISSIMVZ . BAPTISMATIS . TEMPLVM PI$\widehat{VM}$
BEO . TECMINE . ILLVSTRARVNT . $\overline{ANO}$ $\overline{XPI}$.
. M . CCCCLXXXVIIII

---

[1] I, 343.   [2] 207.

[3] De ædificatione autem Baptisterij, constat authoritate Ioannis Ballistarij, qui fuit pręceptor Blondi, vt ipse attestatur in Italia illustrata, & attestatur etiam M. Heironymus Vida in suis actionibus, verba autem Ioannis sunt hęc (Et quando populus Cremonensis construi fecit Baptisterium intra ciuitatem, super platea publica currebant anni Domini D. CCCC.). (Torresino, 3).

[4] Qvesta è vna Fabrica rottonda fatta in ottauo à simiglianza di Santa Maria della Rottonda di Roma, e fù fabricata da' Cremonesi l'anno 900. secondo Giouanni

Mothes[8] has conjectured that the Renaissance gallery of the upper story was erected by Teodosio Orlandini, who, according to a tradition recorded by Ricci, was architect of the baptistery of Cremona. This restoration was perhaps carried out in consequence of damage inflicted upon the edifice by the French in 1512.[9]

The edifice was restored again in 1625.[10] According to Mothes the roof was rebuilt in 1803.

III. The baptistery consists of a central octagonal area covered with a cloistered dome. Internally there are, on each of the eight sides, three blind arches on the ground floor, and in each of the two upper stories, passages in the thickness of the wall opening on to the nave by means of three bifora in each bay. Each story is marked by a string-course of arched corbel-tables, the lower of which is supported by pilaster strips, rising from the abaci of the engaged columns.

Six sides of the edifice are constructed of brick, two of stone (Plate 83, Fig. 6). The stonework is evidently of the Renaissance. These two walls were doubtless made over when the vault was rebuilt and the existing exterior loggia and attic added (Plate 83, Fig. 6). The exterior angles of the buildings are reinforced by triangular buttresses (Plate 83, Fig. 6).

IV. The capitals are distinctly Gothic in character, and are carved with broad, flat, naturalistic leaves. The exterior is ornamented with arched corbel-tables, at times supported on shafts (Plate 83, Fig. 6). The portal in four orders has spiral-fluted shafts and archivolt. The Lombard porch is of the Renaissance (Plate 83, Fig. 6).

V. With the exception of the portions remade in the Renaissance, the baptistery of Cremona is an authentically dated monument of 1167.

Ballistrario, e Girolamo Vida Vescouo d'Alba, mentre così scriuano. *Et quando Populus Cremonensis construi fecit Baptisterium intra Ciuitatem super Platea publica, currebant Anni Domini 900.* (Merula, 73).

[5] 31.

[6] Quando Baptisterium Cremonæ fuit incœptum, MCLXVII. de mense Martii. (*Chronicon Cremonense*, ed. Muratori, R. I. S., VII, 634).

[7] XXXVI.

[8] I, 343.

[9] [Questo fatto] viene riferito da Giacomo Gadio all'anno suddetto [1512] nella di lui Cronaca latina MS. pag. mihi 120. tergo, ecco le sue parole Galli in Castro S. Crucis Cremonæ reclusi, columnelli marmorei [*sic*] oculi majoris Ecclesiæ cum pilis ferreis ex machinis emmissis fregerunt, & parietem in superficie Baptisterii, una pila perforaverunt. (Aglio, 35).

[10] Aglio, 33.

CREMONA, CATHEDRAL

(Plate 83, Fig. 4, 7, 8; Plate 84, Fig. 1, 3; Plate 85, Fig. 1, 2)

I. The cathedral of Cremona, although one of the largest and most imposing mediæval monuments of Italy, has unfortunately never been made the subject of that detailed and painstaking study which alone can solve the problems of archæology it presents. The bibliography of the monument is nevertheless a long one. As early as 1585 Campi illustrated the architecture and studied the history of the edifice. For nearly three centuries his work remained without a rival. In 1859 appeared Cantù's *Grande Illustrazione,* in which the cathedral of Cremona received considerable notice. The sculptures of Adam and Eve, the zodiac, and the prophets were illustrated[1] as well as the cathedral itself and the baptistery.[2] The copies of the inscriptions of the scrolls of the prophets are inexact. Of great value, on the other hand, is the bibliography of ancient drawings.[3] In 1860 appeared the monograph of Von Eitelberg, illustrated with drawings which are good for the epoch. This probably still remains the best monograph which has appeared on the cathedral, and shows a careful study of the local archives. It is unfortunate, however, that the historical portions are marred by several serious blunders and careless mistakes. Von Eitelberg was the first of many Germans to study the church. He was followed in 1869 by Förster, who, in his general history, included an important study of Cremona.[4] In 1873 Aus'm Weerth inserted in his classic work upon mosaics a study of the pavement of the Cremona Campo Santo.[5] His account is important because it illustrates portions of the mosaic which have since disappeared, and also a bit of a similar mosaic pavement found under the high altar. In 1884 Mothes[6] published numerous historical references regarding the cathedral which, could they be relied upon, would be of the greatest importance. But, although this author was a diligent student of the archives, his work is marred by inexactitude and the absence of precise citations, so that it is impossible to accept his dates unless confirmed from other sources. He moreover completely misunderstood the archæology of the building. The mosaic was again illustrated in 1887 by Müntz,[7] who also published drawings. To this author is due the credit of having recognized that the subject of the mosaic is taken from Prudentius. Dehio, in 1892, touched upon the cathedral of Cremona in his large work,[8] and two years later appeared the monograph of Lucchini, a grotesquely inaccurate publication, abounding in errors of all kinds, which nevertheless bears the pretentious title of *Annali della fabbrica dedotti da documenti inediti.* In 1897 Professor Goodyear[9] published the most accurate plan of the cathedral that has yet

[1] III, 400, 406, 478.   [2] *Ibid.,* 477.   [3] *Ibid.,* 479.   [4] 241.
[5] 19, Tf. 6.   [6] I, 424-425.   [7] 17-20.   [8] Tf. 162.
[9] *Constructive Asymmetry of Mediæval Architecture,* in *Architectural Record,* VI, 1897, 400.

appeared. The analysis of the architecture published by Stiehl in 1898[10] is of critical value. The sculptures have been studied in a manner perhaps more brilliant than sound by Venturi.[11] Finally should be mentioned the little handbook of Monteverdi in the Bonomi series, notable for its excellent half-tones.

Of works of a purely historical nature dealing with the cathedral of Cremona, Ughelli, in point of chronology, merits first place. He has preserved an inscription and several important notices bearing upon the cathedral. Other notices of importance are preserved in the *Sanctuario* of Merula, published in 1627. Zaccaria, to whom we owe the preservation of so many inscriptions throughout Italy which would otherwise be lost, has rescued also an important one of the cathedral of Cremona, which he copied about the middle of the XVIII century, but which is no longer to be seen. Other inscriptions are preserved by Aglio, in a valuable work published in 1794. Two years later appeared the *Inscriptiones* of Vairani, which is an important collection. In 1814 Sanclemente published a series of the bishops of Cremona, in which are contained several important notices in regard to the cathedral. The history of Robolotti, published in 1878, contains a description of the sculptures of the zodiac[12] and of the mosaic of the Campo Santo as it was in his time.[13] In 1894 Novati published inedited documents of the archives, which contain notices of value bearing upon the later history of the monument.

There are an unusual number of old drawings and reproductions of the cathedral of Cremona. Of these the one of most interest is the intarsia of one of the choir-stalls, showing the façade of the cathedral as it was at the end of the XV century. This has been reproduced by Monteverdi.[14] In the Museo Civico of Cremona are four seals which are assigned (I know not on what authority) to the XIII or XIV century.[15] In two—evidently the earliest—the façade of the cathedral is shown with five turrets. In the later two there are only three turrets. It is easy, therefore, to draw the inference that the two intermediate turrets were destroyed, probably during the XIV century. The later seals differ from the earlier ones in that the campanile is shown, as well as the second story of the Lombard porch, and the porticoes alongside the sidewalk in front of the façade. The seal of latest date, more carefully made than the others, shows clearly two blind arches on either side of the Lombard porch of the ground story. These same arches appear also in the earliest two seals, though less distinctly. In the museum are numerous old drawings showing the façade of the cathedral at different epochs.[16] The guide-book of Corsi, written in 1819, contains the description of the cathedral

[10] 19.　　　[11] III, 182, 187, 249, 252, 313, 318.　　　[12] 34.
[13] These drawings are reproduced in Plate 85, Fig. 1, 2.
[14] 63.
[15] Two of these are reproduced by Monteverdi, 62.
[16] One of these has been published by Monteverdi, 64.

and of the Campo Santo mosaic.[17] An engraving of the façade made about the middle of the XIX century is contained in the work of Knight.[18] Photographs have been published by Martin.

II.   Passing by numerous spurious documents purporting to date from the Lombard period and derived from the collections of Dragoni and Morbio, which have, nevertheless, been widely published and accepted as authentic, even by historians of such standing as Odorici and Troya, we find that the earliest authentic reference to the cathedral of Cremona is contained in a diploma of Lothair I, dated March 12, 841.[19] In this document the church is designated by the title of S. Maria e S. Stefano, and reference is made to earlier diplomas granted by Charlemagne and Lodovico Pio. In 916 the emperor Berenger granted certain privileges to the cathedral of Cremona, in consideration of the fact that it had been recently devastated by the Hungarians. The document has been lost, but the record of it has been preserved by Sigonio.[20] This devastation by the Hungarians must have taken place in the early years of the X century, probably in 901 or 903, when it is known that these barbarians were in the neighbourhood of Cremona. The crushing blow inflicted upon the church of Cremona by this invasion is witnessed by the fact that a quarter of a century later Rodolfo, in a diploma of September 27, 924, again refers to it.[21] As the emperor implies, the recuperation of the church was doubtless very materially hindered by the bad acts of the Christians themselves.

In 1106 the body of S. Geminiano was translated into the new cathedral of Modena. It is presumable that the sculptor Guglielmo, having completed his work at Modena, was summoned to Cremona immediately afterwards, since it is easy to recognize his hand in the works of sculpture executed at Cremona in the rebuilding of the cathedral, which was undertaken in 1107.

In the sacristy of Cremona, to the west of the northern transept, is preserved a relief showing the two prophets, Enoch, ÆNOC, and Elijah, ELIA, holding, as at Modena (Plate 142, Fig. 2), an inscription between them. This inscription is:

+ A͞N͞N D͞N͞ICO INCA͞R
NACO͞ . M͞ . C͞ . VII . INDI
TIONE͞ . XV . P͞SIDE͞NTE

DOMINO PASCALE
IN ROMANA SEDE
VII . K͞L . SEPT͞B . INCEP
TA E͞ ÆDIFICARI H͞EC M͞A
IOR ÆCCL[ESI]A CREMON͞EN
SIS [QVAE] MEDIA VIDE͞T

Exactly what is meant by the phrase *quae media videtur* is not clear, but it is probable that it refers to the position of the cathedral, placed, in the XII century, between the Campo Santo to the south, and some other edifice to the north. It may therefore be inferred that the inscription was set up somewhere in the ancient façade like the similar inscription at Modena, and that it was removed when the façade was rebuilt in later times. In 1113 the city of Cremona was burned,[22] but there is no evidence that the new cathedral suffered damage at this time. If it escaped, however, it was only to be ruined four years later in the famous earthquake of 1117, which destroyed so many churches in northern Italy. This destruction is very explicitly recorded by Siccardo, and is implied by the *Chronicon Cremonense,* which states that in 1129 the body of S. Imerio was found.[23] Siccardo tells us that the body of the saint was hidden by the ruins in 1117, and long lay lost to sight until in 1129 it was found by the bishop Oberto.[24] It is evident, therefore, that twelve years after the earthquake, the ruins had not yet been cleared away.[25] Two documents of 1138[26] mention the cathedral, but from such phrases as *in platea quae est ante ecclesiam maiorem* or *juxta ecclesiam maiorem* it is too much to draw the inference that the new building was approaching completion.[27] On July 28, 1141, the bishop Oberto consecrated the altar in the chapel of S. Giovanni. The inscription formerly on the altar has been

[17] 9.   [18] II, Plate XXII.   [19] *Hist. Pat. Mon.,* XIII, 243.

[20] Postero anno Berengarius, vt ipse scribit, *regni sui vicesimo nono, Jmperij vero adhuc primo,* Papiæ cum esset, Kalendis Septembris ecclesiam Cremonensem multis ab Vngaris detrementis affectam, ac prope attritam nonnullis vectigalibus liberauit. (248).

[21] Ecclesiam [Cremonensem] a Paganis, & quod magis est dolendum, a pessimis Christianis desolatam, multisque calamitatibus & miseriis attritam . . . (Ed. Muratori, A. I. M. A., ed. A., XIV, 83).

[22] Quando Cremona fuit incensa, MCXIII, in Festo Sancti Laurentii. (*Chronicon Cremonense,* ed. Muratori, R. I. S., VII, 633).

[23] Quando fuit Terræmotus, MCXVI. in Octava Sancti Johannis Evangelistæ hora vesperarum. . . . Et eodem Anno [MCXXIX] inventum fuit Corpus Sancti Himerii in mense Madii (*Chronicon Cremonense,* ed. Muratori, R. I. S., VII, 633).

[24] Anno Domini MCXVI terræmotus magnus in Januario fuit, propter quem Ecclesia major Cremonensis corruit, & corpus Confessoris Himerii diu latuit sub ruina. (Sicardi Episcopi *Chronicon,* ed. Muratori, R. I. S., VII, 594).

Lotharii temporibus Obertus Cremonæ fuit Episcopus, qui Sancti Himerii, quod diu latuerat, corpus invenit, & Anno Domini MCXXIX in scrineo serrato recondidit. (*Ibid.,* 596).

[25] Von Eitelberg quotes a text to prove that the work of repairing the cathedral after the earthquake was begun in 1424, meaning doubtless thereby 1124, but his references are so inexact that it is impossible to verify the text.

[26] *Hist. Pat. Mon.,* II, XXI, 112.

[27] Stiehl (19) states that in a document of the *Archivio Municipale* there is a notice that Pope Innocent III [*sic*] granted permission that the cathedral be used for divine service on August 29, 1133. Stiehl's references are not explicit, and I have searched for this document in vain.

destroyed, but copies have been preserved by Ughelli,[28] Merula[29] and Vairani.[30] The three copies differ among themselves slightly in unimportant details. That of Vairani, which, although published after the inscription had disappeared, seems the most exact, is as follows:

    ✚ALTARE VERO IN EADEM CAPELLA
    CONSECRAVIT D̄N̄S OBERTVS CREMONENSIS
       EPISCOPVS V. KALENDAS AVGVSTI ANNO
    PONTIFICATVS SVI FERE XXIIII. INCARNATIONIS
       VERO DOMINICÆ ANNO MCXLI

It is evident that this inscription could only have been erected a considerable time after the consecration of the altar, since the use of the word *fere* shows that the author was uncertain as to the year of Oberto. The chapel of S. Giovanni is the present chapel of the Madonna del Popolo, that is, the first chapel north of the choir and east of the northern side aisle. That this chapel was formerly dedicated to S. Giovanni Battista is proved by the fact that it still contains numerous statues and pictures of that saint, and also by old guide-books in which it is described under the title of S. Giovanni.[31] In this same year the bishop Oberto also consecrated the altar of S. Stefano.[32] S. Stefano was the chapel of the episcopal palace which now adjoins the cathedral, but which in the XII century must have been considerably removed, since the southern transept had not then been constructed. The existing structure is entirely of the Renaissance. In 1149 another altar was consecrated, according to the inscription preserved by Sanclemente.[33] From the facts that the two altars of S. Giovanni and S. Stefano were consecrated in 1141, and the altar of SS. Cristoforo, Blasio e Floriano in 1149, it is possible

---

[28] IV, 602.   [29] 14.   [30] No. XLI.   [31] *Guida*, 232, 235.

[32] Oberto Vescouo della Città l'anno 1141. Consacrò l'altare di S. Stefano, Capella Episcopale, riponendoui molte Reliquie Sante, fra le quali sono, del legno della Croce, del Sepolcro di Nostro Signore, etc. . . . (Merula, 15-16).

    Anno 1141. Vbertus eorum Presul erecto altari diuo Stephano cum sacello die uigesima septima Iunij illud c̄osecrauit, & titulum eius Episcopatus ipsi subiecit, repositis in eius sacello constructo in parte superiori ecclesiæ cathedralis propinqua ædibus ibidem Episcopalibus reliquijs etc. (Cavitelli, 44).

[33] ANNI MILLENI CENTVM QVADRAGINTA NOVENI
SVNTQVE KALENDENNIS VNDENAE MENSE NOVEMBR.
SIC INDICTIONE DVODENNIS SI BENE QVAERIS
CONSECRAT HANC ARAM DOM. CVI NOMEN OBERTVS
IN QVA SANCTORVM REQUIESCVNT CORPORA TRIVM
CHRISTOPHORI, BLASII QVOQ. MARTYR., AC FLORIANI
PRO MERITIS QVORVM CVRANTVR CORPORA LAPSA
ERGO CVM SVMMA DONEMVS MVNERA LAVDE.   (93).

to draw the inference that in the fifth decade of the XII century the construction of the cathedral had so far advanced that not only was the building fit for the celebration of offices, but the bishop was able to divert considerable funds to the construction of accessory chapels. In 1156 Quintilius Ala was buried in the church, if his epitaph, preserved by Vairani,[34] be authentic. In 1175 the edifice was struck by lightning.[35] Five years later the first podestà of Cremona was buried in the church.[36] In this same year the archdeacon Odo left a bequest to the *laborerio S. Mariae*,[37] which implies that the construction of the church was not yet completed.

Mothes states that in 1187 the body of S. Omobono was translated. I have searched in vain for the source of this notice, which is, however, in a measure confirmed by the following inscription preserved by Zaccaria:[38]

D.O.M.

SICARDVS CASELANVS CREMONAE EPISCOPVS AD PRECES SERENISS. CONSTANTIAE TEMPLVM HOC AD HONOREM BEAT. VIRGINIS MARIAE IN COELUM ASSVMPTAE CVM SOLEMNI RITV CONSECRAVIT, PRAESENTIBVS THEOBALDO EPISCOPO PLACENTINO, ET SIGIFREDO EPISCOPO MANTVANO. AD PRAESEN-TIAM ETIAM SERENISS. HENRICI REGIS ITALIAE ET CONSTANTIAE EIVS VXORIS, ET MVLTIS ALIIS PERSONIS. ANNO AB INCARNATIONE DOMINI MCLXXXX. DIE VERO XV. MENSIS MADII INDICT. VIII. CLEMENTE III. PONTIFICE REGNANTE, ET FEDERICO I.
IMPERANTE.

By this we are informed that Siccardo, the bishop of Cremona, at the request of Constance consecrated the cathedral of Cremona in 1190, with solemn pomp and in the presence of Teobaldo, bishop of Piacenza, Sigefredo, bishop of Mantua, and Henry, king of Italy, and his wife Constance. That the inscription is not contemporary with the events it records is proved, among other things, by the fact that it begins with the formula D. O. M., which did not come into use until long after the XII century. However, the chronological notes are very exact, and all the persons mentioned were actually alive

[34] No. XLIII.

[35] Eodem anno fulgur cecidit in Ecclesia Cremonensi. (Sicardi Episcopi, *Chronicon,* ed. Muratori, R. I. S., VII, 601).

[36] Nam Girardus de Carpenta primus Potestas Cremonæ exstitit, qui naturali interitu moriens, apud Ecclesiam majorem in lavello lapideo fuit sepultus in Festo Sancti Domini Anno Domini MCLXXX. (*Chronicon Cremonense,* ed. Muratori, R. I. S., VII, 634).

[37] Hortzschansky und Perlbach, 83. This document is also referred to by Lucchini, 25.

[38] 64.

on May 15, 1190. It appears, therefore, possible that this inscription may have been derived from an earlier inscription, to replace which it was erected. It is, nevertheless, a singular fact that the bishop Siccardo, in his chronicle of Cremona, fails to mention this pompous consecration of his own cathedral church, although he records many other occurrences of much less moment.

Certain it is, at all events, that the cathedral must have been completed about this time. In 1196 the bodies of the saints Archelao and Imerio were translated with solemn pomp. This fact is recorded by the *Chronicon Cremonense*,[39] and by Siccardo himself.[40] The fact is moreover confirmed by a later inscription now lost but preserved by Sanclemente[41] and by a passage in an old catalogue of the bishops edited by Ughelli.[42]

In 1210 we hear of a new donation to the *Laborerio* of the cathedral.[43] According to the necrology, the bishop Giovanni Bono de' Giraldi (1248-1272) built a room near the great portal of the canonica, and founded the new episcopal palace.[44]

In 1274 the rose-window of the façade was executed, as is known from the inscription now placed over the west portal:

✠ M . CC . LXXIIII .
MAGISTER . IA
COBUS . PORRA
TA . D[E] . CVMIS . FE
CIT . HĀNC . ROTAM.

[39] Quorum tempore Venerabilis Sichardus Cremonensis Episcopus corpora Sanctorum Himerii & Archelai in archa lapidea ad Ecclesiam majorem consecravit, & festum magnum & gloriosum fuit factum. (*Chronicon Cremonense*, ed. Muratori, R. I. S., VII, 636).

[40] Anno Domini MCXCVI. corpora Sanctorum Martyris Archelai & Confessoris Himerii in arca lapidea posuimus, altare XVII. Kalend. Julii consecrantes, & processionem solemniter cum CXXX vexillis Ecclesiasticis facientes. (Sicardi, *op. cit.*, ed. Muratori, R. I. S., VII, 617).

[41]
Quatuor exemptis annis de mille ducentis
Fabricat hanc Arcam Praesul Sicardus, & Aram
Qui triduo tandem perfecto sacrat eamdem
Anno dotatus undeno Pontificatus. (Sanclemente, 102).

Since Siccardo was elected in the year 1185, the eleventh year of his episcopate would fall in 1196. The altar itself was therefore finished in 1193.

[42] Anno 1197 [*sic*] Corpora SS. Hynerii Episcopi, & Archelai martyris in Arca marmorea reposuit [Sicardus]. (IV, 606).

[43] Lucchini, 25.

[44] II non. . . .
Maiorem Canonice iuxta portam fecit
Fabricare cameram (nec in hoc defecit):
Palatinas condidit novas mansiones
Atque plures alias habitationes . . . . . (Novati).

On the interior wall of the north end of the north transept, between the bifora and the rose-window, is the following inscription:

✚MCCLXXX[V]III: INDICIONE SECONDA:
HOC: OPVS FACTVS: TPR:
FRATRIS : SVPERTI : MASARY : CEPI.[ET]
MASARIOR : D̄N̄I : NIGRI : D' CASAMALA
D̄N̄I NICOLAI: D' BENGARI :
D̄N̄I . ANBROSII: D' RESTALIIS :
D̄N̄I NICOLAI: D' VAGRANO.

✚HOC OPVS FECIT MAGISTER.
IACOMVS D' CARPERIO :
MAISTER MANARIE .

✚HOC OPVS FECIT MAGISTER
BERTOLINVS : BRAGERIVS:
MAGISTER MVRI :

What is meant by the phrase *hoc opus* is not clear, for it is difficult to admit that the whole transept could have been constructed in a single year. If we are to believe an authority cited by Merula, we must conclude that the transept was finished in 1288, since according to this writer it was begun in 1284, in the same year with the torrazzo.[45] According to Mothes the campanile was substantially finished in 1285, and in 1289 the cone was begun, but whence these notices are derived I do not know. Von Eitelberg, similarly without citing authority, states that in 1289 the stairway in the angle of the north wall was erected. Under the year 1307 the necrology records the death of a massaro of the *fabbrica*.[46] Twelve years later the bishop Egidio de' Madalberti invested the *Religioso viro Fratri Thome de Domo S.ti Abundii de Cremona ordinis humiliator[um]* with the *curam, et administrationem*

---

[45] Scriuono altri ancora esser stata l'istesso anno [as the campanile] edificata la Chiesa Maggiore, fra quali è l'Auttore del Supplemento delle Croniche nel libro decimoterzo mentre così scriue: M.CC.LXXXIV. Turrim celsissimam, quam Turratium vniuersi vocant, hoc anno Guelfi Cremonenses ea in vrbe, tum maximè præualentes, vna cum celeberrimo Templo in medio vrbis foro adiuuantibus alijs huius factionis Ciuitatibus ædificari cœperunt. Il che non può stare, percioché fù edificata molto prima, come dicemmo di sopra, se non vogliamo dire, che fosse ampliata quest'anno, il che pare accenar' voglia Giouanni Balistario mentre dice: Et quando Ciuitas Cremonensis incepit edificare Ecclesiam Sanctæ Mariæ de Assumptione, currebant anni M. C. VII. quæ postmodo in sequenti tempore valdè fuit ampliata, & dilatata. (19).

[46] XIII Kal. [Iunii] Obiit frater Ubertus de Placencia olim massarius fabrice majoris Ecclesie Cremone sub millesimo trecentesimo septimo, indictione quinta, die lune decimo nono mensis junii, cujus anima sit in requie. (Novati).

laborerij et fabricae of the cathedral, intimating that the management of the finances in the past had not always been honest and economical.[47]

The southern transept was finished in 1342. The long inscription giving the names of the massaro and of the two master-builders (who were clerics) has been published by Aglio.[48] This inscription is placed on the inside of the façade. I have unfortunately lost the careful copy of it which I made on the spot, and am hence unable to publish it.

An inscription under the west portico of the cathedral[49] records the first construction of a chapel of St. John the Evangelist in 1377, but it is not clear to which one of the chapels this refers. Another proof of the continuity of the building activities at Cremona in the XIV century is contained in a notice of the necrology of a certain Giovanni de' Ghiroldi, who died in 1386 and left a yearly revenue for the works of construction in the cathedral.[50] In the west wall is a modern inscription regarding the works executed in 1487, which doubtless included the construction of the Renaissance portico on the west and south sides of the church. The inscription is probably founded on an older one which has now entirely disappeared, and of which Aglio transcribed and preserved the portions still legible in his time.[51] According to Mothes the Renaissance upper portions of the façade were added in the early

[47] Sanclemente, 287.   [48] 10.

[49]
        HANC.CAPELLAM.FECIT.
        FIERI.DOMIN'.GUILIELMIN'.DE.
        SEORUBATIS.AD.HONOREM.
        DO[MIN'] SANCTI.IOHANIS APOST
        OLI ET EVANGELISTE M CCC
        LXXVII DIE.PRIMO MADII.

[50] VIII Kal. [Julii] O[biit] Iohannes filius[?] domini Federici de Ghiroldis MCCCLXXXVJ qui reliquit nostre ecclesie pro fabricandis . . . . . ordinate fieri in hac ecclesia flor. quadraginta annuos. (Novati, 255).

[51]
        . . . . . LI. VI. TE. RMO ET ILLMO
        IN X. P. D. ASCAN . . . . .
        SVB ILLMO ET EXMO
        IO. GZM. SF. VICE DVCE M . . . . .
        RE. DIGM. AC ILLMO P. D. LODOCO
        MM. SF. VICE CARDLI S. VITI HVI
        TEPLI ADMII . . . . . EQVV ET
        TEPRE COITIS RAY. PERSICI
        VICE DVCE BARI DVLI LOCV TE. ET
        GVBERNATE INCE. EST PER M.
        ALB. CARARIEN. . . . . . 1491 IA.
        CIRIE. ET FRA. FOLY. PTI
        TE. MASS. HOC ORNA. (Aglio, 12).

years of the XVI century, but the modern inscription in the façade of the cathedral assigns this part of the edifice to 1491. The door between the campanile and the church bears the date 1513. In the gable of the façade is a cartouche with the pontifical seal and the inscription:

GREGOR XIIII
CREMONENSI PONTIFICI
OPT. MAX. M D L XXXXI

This part of the façade must accordingly have been erected at the end of the XVI century. In 1592 the church was dedicated,[52] but according to Mothes the façade was retouched again in 1606, and in the same year the crypt was done over in the barocco style. The high altar was consecrated in 1718 and again in 1731.[53] In 1888 the project for isolating the cathedral, which had been agitated for thirty years, was taken up with new vigour, but was subsequently allowed to drop. The actual execution of the plan had only just been begun when I visited the church in July, 1913. The isolation bids fair not only to destroy much beautiful architecture, but also to deprive the cathedral of a great part of its charm and beauty. In 1897 the *Commissione Conservatrice* caused a restoration which had been begun in the crypt to be abandoned, and it is to be regretted that the same body has failed to rescue the building from its present danger.

III.   The edifice consists of a nave (Plate 84, Fig. 3) three bays long, two side aisles, two very widely projecting transepts three bays long supplied with side aisles, a choir of two bays flanked by side aisles, three semicircular apses and a crypt. It is vaulted throughout. The eastern bay of the choir has a barrel vault; the remainder of the nave has Gothic rib vaults, of which the transverse arches are pointed; the side aisles have domed rib vaults (Plate 84, Fig. 3); the transepts, rib vaults; their side aisles, groin vaults; and the apses, half domes. The diagonal ribs of the nave and side aisles have a semicircular profile, but the profile of the transverse ribs is rectangular, and there are no wall ribs (Plate 84, Fig. 3). The transepts are very narrow, having the width of only a single half bay of the nave. They do not open directly upon the nave, since the galleries of the latter are carried across them without interruption. It is obvious that these transepts are an addition to the structure and form no part of the original plan. A proof of this is to be found in the gallery over the southern side aisle, where the original XII century clearstory window, which is large and widely splayed, and the cornice of arched corbel-tables, are still in position over the transept. When the transept was added, the original side aisle was preserved, but the gallery over it was heightened to the level of the clearstory. The nave is supplied with a triforium gallery which, however, has been closed (Plate 84, Fig. 3). In the first, third

[52] Merula, 13.   [53] Vairani, VI.

and eighth half bays of the nave counting from the east the triforium has four arches precisely like the triforium of the cathedral of Parma (Plate 166, Fig. 1), and the same number in the first bay on the north side. In the second bay on the north side there are five arches; elsewhere there are only two (Plate 84, Fig. 3).

A mere inspection of the building is sufficient to show that its present form is the result of numerous alterations and changes of plan. It is clear that the church of 1107-1117 occupied the same site as the existing edifice, and that in the new church rebuilt after the earthquake very considerable portions of the pre-existing edifice of 1107-1117 were preserved. These include the principal apses up to the level of the exterior gallery; the main arcades of the nave (Plate 84, Fig. 3) and of the choir probably entire (at least all visible portions belong to this period, and it is probable that the piers hidden beneath the intonaco do also); the triforium of the following bays—on the south side, counting from the east, the first, third and eighth or westernmost, all with four openings; on the north the first with four openings, and the second with five openings; the figured capital of the second vaulting shaft from the east on the south side of the choir, and fragments of that of the north side; and finally the fragmentary sculptures of the façade (Plate 83, Fig. 8).

The church of 1107-1117 was built on an alternate system. The section of the intermediate piers (which are now denatured) consisted of four semi-circular members separated by spurs. The heavier piers had four heavy rectangular members separated by two minor members, one of which was a spur, the other a shaft. It was certainly the intention to erect a sexpartite vault. When the work was resumed on the ruined building in 1129, plans were radically altered. The old piers and whatever could be preserved of the old building were retained, but the design of the triforium was entirely changed, two arches being substituted for the four or five arches in the older edifice. The sexpartite vaults were discarded, and instead a wooden roof was erected supported on transverse arches which were thrown across the nave from every pier. The proof that this was the case is found in the facts that the buttresses are uniform and that beneath the roof there is still extant one transverse arch, undoubtedly ancient, which springs from intermediate supports. In this edifice of 1129-1141 the galleries of the choir were vaulted, but those of the nave were roofed in wood carried on transverse arches. Work seems to have been begun with the southern wall of the nave; the builders then proceeded to the absidioles and the north wall of the nave.

Subsequently the edifice was much denatured. At the end of the XII century the wooden roof of the nave was replaced by a rib vault. The intermediate piers in later times were reduced to a cylindrical section (Plate 84, Fig. 3). The ancient system, however, consisting of a single shaft, still rises from above these piers (Plate 84, Fig. 3). It is similarly clear that the alternate system consisted of three members which were carried through the capitals of the piers (Plate 84, Fig. 3). The crypt, with the exception of a few capitals, has been entirely modernized.

That the existing vaults, with pointed arches, are a later addition, and supplant the original timber roof, is proved by the fact that above these vaults may still be seen transverse walls which rise considerably above the level of the vaults themselves and of the clearstory walls. These transverse walls can only be a remainder of the old transverse arches spanning the nave. Above the surface of the present vaults are still extant the old clearstory walls, which are entirely smooth and give no indication that earlier vaults preceded the existing ones. It is true that the transverse walls have been much made over, but it is equally certain that parts of them are of the first half of the XII century. The eastern one of the transverse arches is still well preserved and retains two windows in the pediment above the arch. The clearstory windows, very large, were placed one in the centre of each bay, proving that the plan of erecting a sexpartite vault had been abandoned before this part of the clearstory was erected; that is to say, that this portion of the edifice is later than 1117.

Although there were no transepts in the XII century edifice, the bay corresponding to the existing crossing must have had a sort of pyramidal roof raised above the rest of the church; for, as may be seen above the vaults, the clearstory walls are here on either side raised to form a gable level with those of the transverse arches, and pierced with pointed windows. These windows are now masked by the transepts. The fact that these windows were pointed gives reason to believe that this pyramidal construction, analogous to the similar one over the crossing of the cathedral of Verona, was erected in the last years of the XII century and at the same time that the vaults were constructed. The barrel vault of the eastern bay of the choir, although entirely Romanesque in character, can not be original, since it cuts across the clearstory windows on both sides. Like the nave vaults it must, therefore, have been erected shortly before 1196. The existing side-aisle vaults (Plate 84, Fig. 3) were executed when the vaults of the nave were erected about 1196. This is proved, not only by the similar character of the diagonal ribs, but also by the fact that the old pavement of the gallery has been ripped out and the extrados of the side-aisle vaults exposed. Before the reconstruction of the end of the XII century, the galleries were in use, as is proved by the elaborate decoration of the vault which is still in place.

The southern gallery of the choir was evidently originally covered with groin vaults with wall ribs. These vaults have been destroyed, but many clear traces remain. The original round transverse arches were later replaced by pointed arches, but the superincumbent transverse buttresses were not remade. In the eastern bay of the northern gallery of the choir, the original vault is still preserved. It is a groin vault, square in plan and very highly domed, constructed of bricks laid perpendicular to the arches. Wall ribs of rectangular profile appear to have been built without centering. The galleries of the nave are at present roofed in wood, but have heavy transverse arches supporting buttresses. These arches have all been made over in the pointed form except one, which is still original and in two unmoulded orders. It is evident that the galleries of the nave were never vaulted, since the walls above them, while preserving traces of the ancient roof, show no signs of a vault. The transverse buttresses over the galleries of the nave project very slightly above the roofs. They are of the same masonry as the buttresses of the nave, and hence probably belong to the edifice of 1107-1117. In the choir, the transverse buttresses were originally pierced by arches. The buttresses of the nave are heavy and uniform, and the buttresses of the choir are entirely similar.

In the second free-standing pier from the east on the south side of the choir the original capital is still visible, and the section of the pier can be seen in part as well as the system, which is continued through the capital. The section of the original intermediate piers can be determined in the three piers from the east on the north side of the choir, where in the organ-gallery the section of the pier and the system can be made out.

A notable feature of the cathedral of Cremona is the turrets which adorn the exterior of the edifice. Two flank the choir and each transept-end, while the façade is still adorned with three (Plate 84, Fig. 1), and originally had five. The two that have been destroyed are shown in old drawings, and their remains are still clearly visible. The turrets are all circular, diamond-shaped or octagonal in plan. Two at either angle of the façade (Plate 84, Fig. 1) are adorned with arched corbel-tables and shafts, even on those portions which are now shut in by the galleries; it is evident, therefore, that they must be older than the galleries of the western part of the nave. The windows of the clearstory were glazed and large, and in the eastern gable of the choir there is a window in the shape of a Greek cross. The east end of the choir galleries contained a niche not expressed externally.

The northern absidiole is constructed of ashlar of somewhat coarser quality than that of the apse and the southern absidiole. The XII century portions of the edifice, however, are regularly constructed of brickwork. This brickwork, as seen, for example, in the transverse buttresses, is not of very high quality. The courses, it is true, are horizontal; but the bricks, although of regular shape, are small, and the mortar-beds are wide. The bricks have oblique incisions. The masonry in the clearstory of the nave is somewhat better than that in the clearstory of the choir. There is noticeable a great difference between the brickwork at the back of the exterior gallery of the north side of the choir and that of the vaults and walls above. In the former the bricks are much wider and are definitely cross-hatched. It is evident we have here the point where the construction interrupted in 1117 joins that recommenced in 1129.

IV. The interior has been so thoroughly covered with barocco intonaco and stucco that but little of the ancient ornament can be studied (Plate 84, Fig. 3). However, the original capital of the second free-standing pier from the east on the south side of the choir is still visible. This capital is characteristic in type, and shows two rams with a single head, their feet resting on a sort of stool; a siren, and dry acanthus leaves not deeply undercut. The vaulting shafts above have a row of caryatid figures which are evidently the work of Guglielmo da Modena. In the piers about the organ on the north side of the choir may be seen other remains of Romanesque capitals, all, however, either much damaged or inaccessible. Over the two arches opening from the nave into the southern transept are Romanesque sculptures of a lamb and an angel. A much ruined capital of Corinthianesque type belonging to the third pier from the east on the north side of the choir is visible in the organ-gallery. The loggia at the top of the northern turret of the choir has broad-leaved capitals which seem to date from c. 1196. The loggia of the southern turret, however, with pointed arches, was remade in the XIII century. In the niche at the eastern end of the southern gallery of the choir are cubic capitals with high angular cushions. The capitals of the exterior gallery on the north side of the nave are all of broad-leaved type, and some have leaf-forms which resemble crockets. The apse gallery is supplied not only with free-standing colonnettes but with responds as well. The capitals of the responds are cubic or adorned with simple serrated leaves or interlaces of a type which recalls the decorative work at S. Ambrogio. The capitals of the colonnettes, on the other hand, have broad leaves, but are of a composite type with great volutes. It is evident that the responds belong to the building of 1107-1117, the colonnettes to that of 1129-1141. The exterior gallery on the southern side of the choir has plain, block capitals, like those of S. Ambrogio and the churches of Pavia. The external gallery on the north side of the choir, on the other hand, has capitals of the XIII century, the epoch in which the gallery must have been remade. One or two of the old block capitals still survive, precisely similar to those of the corresponding gallery on the other side. The shafts are very bulging. In the eastern gallery of the northern transept are some broad-leaved capitals resembling those of the nave galleries, which doubtless were removed from the ancient galleries destroyed when the transepts were added. The capitals of all the galleries are surmounted by stilt-blocks either moulded or adorned with carved heads, a feature which recalls the cathedral of Piacenza.

The denatured crypt still retains coupled columns with Gothic capitals. The bases of the columns of the nave are of Attic profile and supplied with griffes.

The most characteristic decoration of the cathedral of Cremona is the lavish use of external galleries. These were employed even in the earliest parts of the reconstruction, and were retained in the various later additions, including the transepts and façade.

Arched corbel-tables are used lavishly throughout the edifice—above and below the exterior gallery on the south side of the choir, above the gallery of the absidioles, in the cornice of the gallery and clearstory of the nave, below the exterior gallery of the nave walls,[54] on the two turrets at either angle of the façade, in the cornice of the choir, on the choir turrets and below the gallery of the north side of the choir. Double arched corbel-tables are employed in the northern turret of the façade, in the cornice of the northern side-aisle wall of the choir and in the cornice of the apse. Triangular arched corbel-tables, recalling those of S. Ruffillo and S. Stefano of Bologna, are used in the northern turret of the façade. Flat corbel-tables are employed beneath the external gallery on the southern side of the nave and in a similar position on the northern side, but in the choir this feature is omitted. The corbel-tables are frequently supported on shafts. In the absidioles the shafts terminate in cubic capitals below the gallery, but in the central apse this feature is omitted. In the southern side aisle the shafts with colonnettes are placed at intervals corresponding to the bays of the interior. Shafts are also used on the turrets of the façade. No shafts are at present extant on the northern side of the choir, but it is not certain that there were none originally. In the eastern gable pilaster strips are substituted for shafts. The cornice of the gallery on the south side of the nave contains a diamond-shaped ornament inlaid in polychrome. In the southern absidiole there is a polychromatic zigzag.

The archivolts of the nave (Plate 84, Fig. 3) are in two unmoulded orders, but in the southern absidiole there is a moulded window in four orders, and another window richly decorated with an interlace.

The Lombard west porch is in its present state a work of the XIII century, but the portal contains fragments of two earlier epochs. The free-standing shaft to the left has a capital very analogous to those of the Lombard porches of Modena, and must consequently be the work of Guglielmo. The corresponding shaft on the other side, however, which is banded, has a capital obviously much later and made to match the first. The shafts are supported on caryatids which are the work of Guglielmo. It is clear that the two caryatids, the northern shaft and capital, the fragments of a rinceau now preserved under the west porch, the two roll-mouldings and the spiral moulding are all parts of the original doorway of 1107-1117. This doorway about 1180 was made over in its present form. At this epoch were added the lions, one

---

[54] On the southern side the original simple arched corbel-tables have been in part replaced and made over.

of which holds in his paws a dog with a duck in its mouth, the other a monster with animal's head, bird's wings and serpent's tail.

The cathedral of Cremona contains notable sculptures, many of which analogy of style makes it evident are the work of Guglielmo da Modena. The jambs of the western portal contain four Assyrian-like figures, very flat and wooden in appearance (Plate 83, Fig. 8). These figures, so far as I know, are the earliest example of figure subjects sculptured on the jambs of a portal, and appear to be the forerunners of the admirable sculptures at Chartres, Arles and the French cathedrals of the XIII century. To the left, above, is Jeremiah, IEREMIAS, who bears a scroll with the inscription:

HIC

EST

IN

Q[VI]T

D̄S N̄R̄ . ET N̄

ESTIMABI

T̄VR ALIVS

ABSQ . ILLO

Q[VI] IVENIT

OMN̄E VIAM

SCIENTIE

ET DEDIT E

AM IACOB

PVERO SVO

ET ISRAEL

DILECTO

SVO. 55

Below Jeremiah is another prophet, undoubtedly Isaiah (Plate 83, Fig. 8). On a pedestal may still be seen one letter, ... A . . . . . , of his name. He bears the scroll:

HEC|CE| VIR|GO| CON|CIPI|ET ET| PARI|ET FI|LIVM| ET VO|CABI|TVR NO|MEN| EIVS| EMA|NVEL.56

On the upper right-hand side is the prophet Daniel, with the inscription:

DIC S̄C̄E| DANIH̄EL| DE X̄P̄O Q̄D̄| NOSTI CVM| VEÑERIT| INQ[VI]D S̄C̄S̄| SANCTO|RVM. CES|SABIT| VNCTIO| VES|TRA

---

55 *Contra Judæos, Paganos et Arianos,* XI, ed. Migne, *Pat. Lat.,* XLII, 1123; Bar., iii, 36-37.

56 *Contra Judæos, Paganos et Arianos,* XI, ed. Migne, *Pat. Lat.,* XLII, 1123; Isai., vii, 14.

Like the inscriptions upon the scrolls of the other prophets, this verse is taken from a sermon attributed to St. Augustine and may be translated: "St. Daniel prophesy what you know concerning Christ. When, said he, the most Holy One shall come, your unction shall cease."[57] Below is the figure of Ezekiel, bearing a scroll with the familiar inscription:

✠| VI|DI| POR|TAM| IN DO|MO DO|MINI| CLAV|SAM [58]

These four impressive figures appear to have been cut out of rectangular slabs of stone, the form of which has been almost entirely preserved, only the edges being rounded (Plate 83, Fig. 8). As a consequence they have a curious flat appearance, but, so far from being a fault, this strange method of execution seems to lend to the figures a heraldic quality, that at once makes them singularly effective as architectural accessories and lends them an air of unreality and grandeur peculiarly suggestive of the mystery of the prophetic mission. There is singularly little relief. The hands, even when raised, are glued to the bodies. The bottom fringe of the draperies falls in a zigzag so even as almost to suggest an architectural ornament. The cords of the hands and feet are represented by strong lines which continue through the wrists and ankles, and seem to be the continuation of the separation between the toes or fingers. The hands are long and thin, the finger joints and anatomy of these portions of the body are conscientiously and realistically represented. The hair is depicted by means of parallel incised lines, usually straight, but in the Ezekiel waved. Ezekiel's beard is also wavy, but the other beards are indicated by straight incised lines terminating in little curls, a characteristic mannerism of Guglielmo. All four prophets have long hair which falls over their shoulders. The feet of Daniel and Ezekiel are shown in profile, although the bodies are in full face. The feet of Isaiah and Jeremiah are seen in plan from above as it were. The hair is low on the forehead. The draperies are slightly modelled, but the folds are often represented by parallel incised lines characteristic of the art of Guglielmo. The proportions are singularly good. A comparison of these sculptures with those of S. Andrea at Barletta (Plate 83, Fig. 1) is significant, both for the points of resemblance and those of difference.

Above the portal are inserted the sculptured symbols of the Evangelists John and Matthew, evidently contemporary with the prophets. Beneath the eagle of St. John is the inscription:

IN PRINCIPIO
ERAT VERBVM
ET VERBVM [59]

---

[57] *Contra Judæos, Paganos et Arianos*, XI, ed. Migne, *Pat. Lat.*, XLII, 1123; Dan., ix, 24.

[58] Ezec., xliv, 1-2.   [59] Joann., i, 1.

and Matthew, the winged man, holds a book with the inscription:

LIBER	I̅H̅V̅
GENE	XPI
RATI	FILII
ONIS	DAVID [60]

Above the jambs of the doorway itself are the other two Evangelists, the winged bull of St. Luke holding a book with the inscription:

F[V]	ERO
IT IN	DIS
DIE	RE
BVS	GIS [61]

and the lion of St. Mark with a book, the inscription of which is broken. In the second story of the portico is another set of sculptures also representing the symbols of the four Evangelists. Below the late statue of the Madonna in the centre of the loggia is a relief representing a bishop, probably S. Ilario, standing upon two lions. These sculptures are all of a much later epoch. Above the arch of the ground story of the portico on either side of the bishop are bas-reliefs depicting the works of the twelve months: (1) February is represented by the sign of the zodiac, two fish, and a man spading the earth. (2) January is indicated by the water-pourer and a man holding a cup. In the foreground is an object difficult to identify, perhaps a brazier. Behind is a stick over which are thrown some sort of viands, possibly sausages, which are cooking by the fire. (3) Next follows March, who prunes a vine. The curious animal at the left must be a ram, the corresponding sign of the zodiac. Above the capital of the pronaos is inserted the figure of a wind god blowing his horn, which may possibly have belonged with this relief. (4) Next follows the month of December, designated by a man carrying a bow, evidently the sign of the zodiac, Sagittarius. To the right a male figure dresses a swine. (5) The next month is evidently June, since above, to the right, is the sign of the zodiac, a crab. The month himself is depicted as a youthful figure carrying a pail or bucket. Behind are a tree in full foliage and a little pig. (6) September is shown plucking grapes, while to the left stands a figure holding the corresponding sign of the zodiac, the scales.

On the other side the cycle of the months is continued: (7) November is represented by a man and his wife nailing up a barrel. To the right was probably originally the sign of the zodiac, Capricornus, but this has been restored in the form of two placid-looking cows. (8) Next follows August, holding what appears to be a flail, and accompanied by the corresponding sign of the zodiac, the lion. (9) Next comes July, who is depicted as reaping.

[60] Matth., i, 1. [61] Luc., i, 5.

The sign of the zodiac, Scorpio, is above to the right. (10) May rides upon a horse, and is accompanied by the sign of the zodiac, the twins, who stand on a tree. A crescent, probably intended to denote the moon, rises in the background. (11) April holds in his hand a branch, but is accompanied by no sign of the zodiac. Above one of the capitals of the porch is another figure, perhaps also representing April. It depicts a crowned man holding in his right hand a branch with three leaves, and in his left a palm. (12) October is typified by two figures, one, apparently male, turns away, holding to his mouth what appears to be some sort of food. There is no sign of the zodiac unless the female figure be Virgo. This scene is without analogy elsewhere, so far as I know.

In style these sculptures are evidently of the XIII century, and show strongly in several parts the influence of Benedetto. Venturi, however, appears to me to have gone too far in calling this zodiac the production of Benedetto himself.[62] The Cremona zodiac is the work of one of his imitators.

In the exterior west wall of the façade, under the portico, have been walled up several important fragments of sculpture, evidently not in their original position. Two reliefs represent the expulsion of ADAM and EVA, and their temptation. The style of these reliefs makes it evident that they are the work of Guglielmo da Modena, for they are entirely similar to his signed works depicting the same subject in the cathedral of Modena (Plate 142, Fig. 3). We notice the same curious technique in the wings of the angels and the same crude treatment of the feet, which are seen in profile, although the bodies are full-face. In both series Adam scratches his ear with the same curious gesture, and in both we find the same heavy figures, the same short legs, the same treatment of the drapery, the lower fringe of the angel's dress falling in the same formal scroll, the same use of straight incised lines and the same peasant quality. Above is a rinceau very like that of the Porta dei Principi at Modena (Plate 142, Fig. 4), a work of a follower of Guglielmo and executed under Guglielmo's inspiration. In this rinceau are figured subjects which show a man picking grapes, Samson and the lion, David seated and playing the harp, while above him kneels a girl with cymbals. Below these fragments is a caryatid with the inscription

HIC PREMITVR

evidently also the work of Guglielmo.[63] By a follower of Guglielmo, however, are two other figures with inscriptions in Gothic characters, evidently added long after the completion of the statues: BERTA and IO. BALDES (Plate 83,

---

[62] III, 318.

[63] At Modena a similar caryatid is placed below the altar in the scene of the offerings of Cain and Abel (Plate 144, Fig. 2). The inscription begins with these same words, *Hic premit*. (See below, Vol. III). This caryatid may in consequence be conjectured to have come from a similar relief.

Fig. 7). The inscriptions call to mind the mythical hero of Cremona, Zanino della Pala or Giovanni Baldesio, and Berta, the wife of the emperor, Henry IV. According to the legend, about 1080 the city of Cremona succeeded in erecting a commune, thanks to these two champions. The victory was won by Giovanni Baldesio, who fought a single duel with the son of Henry and overcame him, freeing.Cremona from the tribute of a ball of gold. Berta, the wife of Henry, granted a charter to the commune.[64] It is natural to connect this figure of Berta at Cremona with the figure of Berta depicted on the façade of Borgo S. Donnino, but in both cases the popular traditions have become so confused with the passing centuries that it is impossible now to determine exactly what the sculptures were intended to represent. On the pedestal of the west side of the north transept there is a curious colossal figure very crudely executed, and which is also supposed to represent Giovanni Baldesio. In one hand he holds a sphere, perhaps symbolical of the newly acquired power of the commune of Cremona, while his foot rests upon another which may be supposed to represent either the ball of gold or the shattered authority of the Empire.

In the sacristy is a relief of the two prophets, Enoch and Elijah, supporting between themselves the inscription which has been transcribed above. These are strikingly analogous to the similar relief in the façade of the cathedral of Modena (Plate 142, Fig. 2), and are undoubtedly the work of Guglielmo. It is notable, however, that with all their points of contact the two reliefs show certain differences. At Modena the figures of the prophets are much more dignified, architectural and classical. The figures themselves stand straight, instead of having, as at Cremona, one knee bent, as it were, to support the tablet with the inscription. At Cremona the inscription is far too long for the tablet, and runs over it at the beginning and at the end. In the Cremona figures the heads are notably too large for the bodies, and the faces (especially in the case of Elijah) and the noses are so crude as to be almost caricatures, while at Modena the faces are at least dignified, if not beautiful. At Cremona the drapery falls in folds curiously elaborate at the bottom, much fussier and less classical than is the case at Modena. Nevertheless the Cremona sculptures are characteristic productions of Guglielmo. The ear-marks of his style are the curls in the beard of Elijah, the peasant-like coarseness of the faces, the folds of the drapery of the upper part of the figure indicated merely by scratched lines (compare with the caryatid under Christ in the first panel of the Modena frieze—Plate 143, Fig. 1) and the involved Latin of the inscriptions.

The archivolt of the portal of the north transept consists of a relief (Plate 83, Fig. 4) representing Christ in the midst of the twelve apostles. This architrave has evidently been taken from an earlier building, since two apostles on either hand have been half sawed off to adapt the stone to its present

[64] Robolotti, 27.

position. To the right of Christ are S[ANCTVS] PETRVS and S[ANCTVS] ANDREAS. To the left S̄C̄S PAVLVS and S[ANCTVS] IOHS. The other apostles it is impossible to identify, as the painted inscriptions have entirely disappeared. The style of these sculptures is exceedingly curious. The apostles are all represented with bent knees as if in violent motion. The heads are carefully studied. The St. Peter, for example, is well characterized, yet a certain element of caricature is always present. St. John has a monkey-like expression which is undoubtedly due to irreverence rather than lack of skill on the part of the artist. The lower line of the draperies falls in scroll-like curves, which show the influence of Guglielmo da Modena. The execution is very hard, the figures have a motley appearance, the heads are dispropor- tionately large. The Deity in the centre spreads his legs apart in a manner which is anything but divine. The cords of the fingers are continued through the back of the hand as in the sculptures of the west portal, and the pupils of the eyes are depicted by means of incised hollows. The hair, especially the beards, is well executed. The draperies seem to be drawn tightly over the limbs, which are carefully indicated beneath them, and the folds of these draperies are denoted by incised lines in the manner of Guglielmo. These sculptures must have belonged to the church finished in 1141, but are not the work of Guglielmo. They must have been executed by an artist who fell under his influence and worked probably considerably after him.

In the northern transept is a holy-water basin ornamented with grotesques and dating apparently from c. 1180. The leonine inscription

FVGAT . OMN̄ES . DEMONIS . ACTVS . HVIVS . AQVE . LACTVS (*sic = lacus*)

seems to mean that the holy-water basin repels every aggression of the devil.

Under the sacristy in the so-called Campo Santo has been excavated an important and interesting Lombard mosaic (Plate 85, Fig. 1, 2). This mosaic was first unearthed in 1770,[65] and contains some portions which are not now visible, but which appear in the drawings of Aus'm Weerth.[66] The spot on which the mosaic was discovered is traditionally known at Cremona as the Campo Santo. The term apparently was used as early as the middle of the XII century, for in a document of 1130 there is a record of the *ecclesia S. Ambrosii in cimiterio matricis ecclesiae.*[67] The mosaic is at a lower level than that of the cathedral, and must have belonged to another edifice. Perhaps in early times a Campo Santo like that at Pisa did really adjoin the cathedral, and this mosaic adorned the mortuary chapel or some other part of it. The best preserved part of the mosaic represents the strife between CRV|DE|LI|T|A|S and IM|PI|E|T|A|S (Plate 85, Fig. 1). The two Vices stand on either side of a plant and each wounds the other in the stomach with a spear. To the right F|I|D|E|S, wearing a crown, sets foot upon the kneeling form of

[65] Grasselli, 36.   [66] Taf. VI; Corsi, 9.   [67] *Hist. Pat. Mon.*, II, XXI, 113.

D|I|S|C|O|R|DIA, and transfixes her tongue with a lance. We have here evidently a scene from the Psychomachia of Prudentius. Above are shown two curious grotesque figures facing each other as if in combat. Each is supplied with a sword and shield. The one to the right has the head of an animal and is labelled CEN|TA|V|R̂VS;[68] the one to the left has pointed ears, horns and a tail and is not labelled.[69] The mosaic contains also several other grotesque figures, the most interesting of which represents a bird with a snake in its mouth. The borders, with diamonds, zigzags, interlaces and various other motives, are extraordinarily varied and beautiful (Plate 85, Fig. 1). In another fragment of the mosaic (Plate 85, Fig. 2) may be seen even stranger figures. To the left a man is accompanied apparently by a greyhound. Then follow two animals, probably dogs, standing on their hind legs, facing each other and with tails interlocked. These tails terminate in leaves. Finally two dogs are on their hind legs, back to back. A single collar encircles their necks, and the tongues projecting from their mouths terminate in leaves. Below is a camel.[70] In the portions of the mosaic not now visible were depicted elephants.

V. The documentary evidence forms conclusive proof that the cathedral of Cremona was begun in 1107; that in 1117 it was badly damaged by an earthquake; that in 1129 the ruins were cleared away; that in 1141 the edifice was finished, and that in 1196 a consecration was celebrated. The construction, therefore, lasted, with interruptions, during the entire XII century. There were three periods of building activity, the first of which extended from 1107 to 1117, the second from 1129 to 1141, and the third from an unknown date to 1196. It remains to be determined which portions of the edifice belong to each of these three epochs.

Internal evidence fortunately makes easy the solution of the question. The mosaic of the Campo Santo, analogous to that of S. Savino of Piacenza, an edifice consecrated in 1107, must belong to the first period. To this period also belong the sculptures of Guglielmo da Modena, that is to say, the prophets of the western portal, other fragments of the western portal, the reliefs of the four Evangelists, the sculptures of Enoch and Elijah in the sacristy, the reliefs of Adam and Eve, the rinceau and the caryatid under the western portico and the caryatids of the vaulting shafts of the choir. To the same period belongs also the plan of the cathedral as we have it to-day, with alternating system, but without, however, the transepts. The actual construction up to the level of the triforium, and in some places up to the clearstory, all belongs to the original building of 1107-1117.

[68] Müntz thinks that this is a mistake for Minotaurus.

[69] Isidore of Seville, *Etymologiarum*, XII, 3, ed. Migne, *Pat. Lat.*, LXXXII, 423, describes the hydra, chimæra, centaur and minotaur.

[70] *Ibid.*, XII, 4, ed. Migne, LXXXII, 429.

CREMONA, S. LORENZO

When work was resumed in 1129, the old plan was materially altered. Instead of sexpartite vaults as originally planned there was erected a wooden roof over the nave, supported on transverse arches springing from every pier. To this edifice belonged the relief now in the northern portal of the transept.

About the end of the XII century radical alterations were undertaken. The wooden roof of the nave was replaced by rib vaults with pointed transverse arches and with diagonals of toric section. Similar vaults were erected in the side aisles, and a sort of *cuba* was built over the presbytery. These alterations were completed so that the edifice as thus made over could be consecrated in 1196. In 1288 the plan of the church was radically changed by the erection of the north transept, which was balanced in 1342 by the south transept. The façade appears to date in the main from 1274, the epoch at which it is known the rose-window was executed. The western portal, however, is proved by internal evidence to have been constructed before the consecration of 1196 and was presumably adorned in the early XIII century with the zodiac sculptures. At all events these sculptures were used as second-hand material when the Lombard porch was rebuilt in the third quarter of the XIII century. The façade was further adorned and embellished in 1591, and at various later epochs.

CREMONA, S. LORENZO

(Plate 86, Fig. 1)

I. The church of S. Lorenzo has been published by Stiehl,[1] who has illustrated it with a plan and numerous drawings and photographs. Good editions of the charter of foundation and of the donation of 996 have been printed by Novati. Vairani has preserved numerous inscriptions which formerly existed in the church, but which have been destroyed in recent times.

II. The bishop Odelrico founded in the year 990 a monastery in the churches of S. Lorenzo and S. Maria, both of which that bishop had built from the foundations.[2]

---

[1] 21.

[2] Anno ab Incarnatione Domini nostri Jesu Christi Nongentesimo Nonagesimo, Pridie Kalendas Junii, Indictione Tercia. . . . Quapropter ego Odelricus Episcopus sancte Cremonensis Ecclesie . . . edificare visus sum Monasterium in honore Sancti Laurentii Martyris in area una de terra juris mei, cum duabus Ecclesiis inibi constructis, quarum una in honore Sancti Laurentii, alia in honore Sancte Marie, seu beatorum Apostolorum Philippi & Jacobi est edificata: quas ego a fundamentis noviter edificavi, que esse videntur in suburbio hujus Civitatis Cremone, non multum longe a Porta Canonicorum. . . . Et dono seu offero atque judico eidem sancto et venerabili Monasterio pro anime mee remedio, scilicet casas & omnes res etc. . . . Proinde volo & instituo, seu judico, ut sit idem Monasterium cum omni sua integritate & pertinencia

An important donation was made to the monastery in 996.[3] According to Stiehl, relics were translated into the church in the year 1071.

In the early years of the XII century, and probably in 1113, the church of S. Lorenzo was destroyed by a fire which burned a large portion of the city of Cremona.[4] Stiehl states that the bishop Bonizo was buried in the church in the year 1117, which, if true, would be an important notice proving that the church had been reconstructed immediately after the fire. I have, however, been unable to verify it.

An inscription preserved by Vairani records some work executed in 1213, but nothing indicates what it was.[5] The same may be said of another inscription of 1214, of which we have only the indication that it was in the wall, while it remains entirely uncertain what wall this was, and whether or not the inscription was there in its original position.[6]

In 1225 the campanile was erected, according to an inscription which was once in the lower part of its wall, but which Vairani saw on the ground.[7] Another inscription preserved by Vairani has reference to another unidentifiable *hoc opus* erected in 1282.[8]

sub mundio & tuitione pretaxati Episcopii sancte Cremonensis Ecclesie tantum, ad id defendendum, & Abbatem ibidem ordinandum & consecrandum, quando necesse fuerit, secundum constitucionem sanctorum Patrum ab Episcopo ejusdem Episcopii, suisque successoribus, ita ut munera nullus exinde accipiat, & prelibata Abbacia perpetuo erga cultum religionis & regulam Sancti Benedicti in sua virtute permaneat. . . . (Muratori, A. I. M. A., Dis. 22, ed. A., IV, 477). See also *Hist. Pat. Mon.*, XIII, 1501, and Astigiani, *Cod. Dip.*, I, 38.

  [3] Novati; *Hist. Pat. Mon.*, II, XXI, 40.

  [4] See texts cited below under S. Michele of Cremona, p. 398, and above, p. 374.

  [5] AN. MCCXIII. T̄P̄R̄ FREDERICI REG .
  JVSSV MARTINI ABBATIS FACTVM EST HOC OPVS (Vairani, CCVIII).

  [6]   In pariete

  ✠IMPERANTE FED̄ĪC̄O II. ROM. ĪM̄P̄R̄E
  DOMNVS LANFRANCVS DE REGONASCIS . . . . .
  H. OP. F. FEC. A. D. MCCXIV. III. ID. VI. (*Ibid.*, CCVIII).

  [7]   In imo pariete turris.

  ✠TEMPORE FREDERICI IMPERATORIS
  JVSSV DNI CREMOSIANI ABBATIS
  HOC OPVS FACTVM EST MCCXXV
      Nuper extabant humi

  [8]   Hanc habet etiam cod. Picenard. pag. 63

  ANNO DNI M̄ĪL̄L̄O DVCĒT̄O OCTV̄ĀGO SEC̄D̄O
  INDICTIONE XI. REGNANTE REGE RODVLFO
  JVSSV COMITIS DE BEZANIS ABBATIS HVJVS
  MONASTERII FACTVM EST HOC OPVS

CREMONA, S. LORENZO

In 1549 the Benedictines were supplanted by monks of Monte Oliveto.[9] The church was restored in 1629, according to an inscription preserved by Vairani.[10]

Millin,[11] who wrote in 1817, describes the church as being still open for worship. A guide-book published in 1880, however, speaks of it as having been recently reopened after having been suppressed for a considerable period. It was still open when Stiehl described it in 1898. Now, however, it has been desecrated again, and serves as a gymnasium for the Orfanotrofio Maschile, situated in the Via S. Lorenzo.

III. The edifice consists of a nave seven bays long, two side aisles, a choir of two bays, the first of which was flanked by side aisles, and an apse. The eastern bays of the side aisle and the absidioles have been walled off from the rest of the edifice. The vaults are all modern, with the exception of those of the side aisles of the choir, which are Gothic, and the three little barrel vaults which precede the three apses. The latter appear to be original; the rest of the church was originally roofed in wood. The side-aisle walls have been entirely rebuilt.

The supports of the nave are monolithic columns, crowned by capitals of broad-leaved type. The rest of the interior has been entirely denatured.

The brickwork is of a very advanced character. The bricks, incised obliquely, are laid in horizontal courses, but the mortar-beds are fairly wide.

IV. The coarse Attic bases of the interior have griffes. Externally the edifice is adorned with a cornice formed of small round-arched corbel-tables and round billets (Plate 86, Fig. 1). The apse has a cornice of long narrow slits surmounted by arched corbel-tables supported on shafts engaged upon pilaster strips (Plate 86, Fig. 1). The archivolts of the finely moulded windows are adorned with patterns inlaid in brickwork (Plate 86, Fig. 1).

V. The analogy of S. Lorenzo with S. Michele is so obvious and so striking that it is almost unnecessary to call attention to it. A comparison of two photographs (Plate 86, Fig. 1, 3) will show how strikingly similar the two edifices are, both in structure and detail. They seem almost like replicas made from the same drawing. The only notable difference is the extra string-course of arched corbel-tables with supporting shafts introduced in the lower part of the apse of S. Michele (Plate 86, Fig. 3). This additional

---

[9] Merula, 214.

[10]   **In ara d.Laurentii**

    ASSARIO MARTIRI PIO ARDENS AMORE
    ÆDIBVS INSTAVRATIS RMVS D. DOMINICVS PVERONVS
    ABBAS GENERALIS P. ANNO MDCXXIX

[11] II, 332.

elaboration and a certain extra complication in the ornaments of the windows of S. Michele give reason to suppose that the latter edifice may be somewhat later than S. Lorenzo. We have found some reason for assigning S. Michele to c. 1200. S. Lorenzo may consequently be ascribed to c. 1195. With this date agrees well the style of the capitals of the nave, which are similar to, but more advanced than, those of the baptistery of Cremona, a surely dated edifice of 1167. What were the works executed in 1213, 1214, and 1282, according to the inscriptions, can only be conjectured. Possibly the vaults of the side aisles may have been erected in 1282.

CREMONA, S. MICHELE

(Plate 86, Fig. 2, 3)

I. An old water-colour in the museum of Cremona, bearing the number 268, shows the façade of S. Michele as it was before the restoration. Instead of the two bifora which now exist in the second story of the façade (Plate 86, Fig. 2), this drawing shows a Palladian arch. The two bull's-eye windows that now exist in both side aisles are seen to be modern restorations, replacing square windows of the barocco era. The campanile is shown as much lower than at present, and as Renaissance in style. Another drawing, also in the museum, shows the old Renaissance portal as it was before the restoration. Other photographs and drawings form a valuable record of the ancient condition of the fresco in the apse.

For historical notices regarding the church of S. Michele the works of Aglio, Merula, and Hortzschansky and Perlbach should be consulted. A monograph upon the church has been published by Lucchini. Notices of some value have been contributed by Stiehl[1] and Mothes.[2] Strack[3] published a drawing of the façade, and another drawing is contained in the *Grande Illustrazione*.[4]

II. The church of S. Michele was one of the monuments particularly selected by Antonio Dragoni, about which to weave his falsified documents. These famous forgeries are preserved in a manuscript in the Cremona library.[5] Leaving them all aside as undoubtedly apocryphal, we find that the earliest mention of the church is contained in a document drawn up in the time of Landolfo, who was bishop of Cremona from 1004 (or some say 1007) to 1030. This document may be translated as follows: "Since Landolfo, most illustrious bishop of this holy church of Cremona, inspired by the will of God,

---

[1] 22.   [2] I, 235.   [3] Tafel 39.   [4] III, 512.

[5] *Antonius Dragoni.*—Codex diplomaticus capituli cremonensis, MS. Biblioteca Governativa di Cremona, Codice aa/6/2.

has filled not only the people committed to his charge, but the whole western part of Italy, with the inspiration of his doctrine and persuasive counsels, and inasmuch as he himself unceasingly strives to perform all things furthering divine worship and the maintenance of ecclesiastical decorum, as well as the unity of the faith and the bond of peace, and fails not to admonish his followers with ghostly counsel, many refreshed by the food of his holy words have, God aiding, been directed to salutary works. And so it was that moved by such admonitions of our most benign bishop, Benedetto, an archpriest of the same, came into his presence, and begged his paternity with humble prayers, to grant his assent that, in a certain church built in honour of S. Michele, and in the jurisdiction of the archpriest, he, the archpriest, might appoint two priests who should restore that church from its foundations, since it was very ruinous with age, and officiate in it daily, praying for the spiritual and temporal welfare of so good a father . . . etc. To this petition the archpriest added another: namely, that if it should please our Lord Bishop aforesaid, he should deign to grant a written deed to the priests specifying that if, for the benefit of the chapter of Cremona, or whoever might be the feudal lords of the church, they, the priests, should rebuild that church, as has been specified, then, for all the days of their life, they should enjoy the same and all its revenues, so that no man might demand of them any tithe or tax, except half of the wax, etc."[6] This document probably dates from about 1020. From it we learn

[6] Chr. Quia auctore deo sacratissimi patris nostri Landulfi, huius sancte Cremonensis ecclesie pontificis clarissimi, non solum plebs sibi commissa, set etiam universa pene occidua pars Ausonię in talis doctrinę probabilisque consilii flatu animata resultat, adeo ut cuncta, quę ad divini cultus obsequium vel ad ecclesiastici decoris statum nec non unitatis fidei pacisque vinculum proficiunt, ipsi indesinenter agere studeat et suos asseclas incessanter sacro monitu instruere non desistat, plurimi eius sacri verbi pabulo refecti ad salutaria operante domino diriguntur exercitia. Huius itaque benignissimi nostri patroni Benedictus eiusdem archipresbiter instructione intrinsecus commotus, ipsius adiit paternitatem humillimis precibus postulans, ut ei suum prebere salutiferum dignaretur assensum, quatinus in quadam ęcclesia, de suo benefitio ad honorem Sancti archangeli [Mi]chaelis constructa, duos construere possit sacerdotes, qui eam funditus, quoniam vetustate consumitur, [conser]vent et in ea cottidie divinum peragant offitium, orantes pro statu et salute tanti patris. . . . In hac igitur petitione iam dictus archipresbiter adidit, ut si bene placitum esset gloriosissimo apici prescripti nostri rectoris, huiusmodi cyrografi firmitate sacerdotes certi redderentur, ut sicut iam dictum est, si eorum labore ęcclesia renovata constiterit, omnibus diebus, quibus vixerint, aut clericis vestris quibus tenere potuerint vel clerici alicui dederint, eadem cum omnibus muneribus ibi conferendis habeant; ita ut nullus eam iam deinceps benefitio possidens de omni munere ibidem fidelium manibus offerendo aliquid ab illis exigat, preter medietatem cere, quę in festivitate Sancti Michaelis ibi collata fuerit. Hanc ergo postulationem admirabilis semperque venerabilis prefatus pater noster gratanter audiens suscepit et hanc paginulam sua sacra manu firmavit.

Chr. Ego Landulfus uoce tantum episcopus subscripsi. Ego Benedictus archipresbiter ss. Chr. Ego Ardingus archidiaconus ss. Ego Leo presbiter ss. etc. (Hortzschansky und Perlbach, 5-7). Cf. *Hist. Pat. Mon.*, II, XXI, 44.

that the church of S. Michele at this time was officiated by two priests, that it depended upon the cathedral chapter, that it was ruinous with age, and that a reconstruction was contemplated.

Lucchini believes that the basilica was restored c. 1080 by the bishop Ubaldo, but there is no evidence to support this conjecture. In the year 1113 or, according to others, in 1109 or 1111, a great part of Cremona was destroyed by fire. On this occasion twenty-nine churches, including S. Michele, were burned to the ground.[7]

In 1124 the possession of the church of S. Michele was confirmed to the bishop of Cremona,[8] but in 1132 it was confirmed among their possessions to the canons of the cathedral.[9] It is evident that it was claimed by both bishop and chapter. In 1139 the pope commanded that the church be restored to the canons by the bishop.[10]

In the year 1159 the bishop Oberto translated into the church the body of the martyr, S. Gregorio.[11] About this same time the church was united with S. Gregorio,[12] and a chapter of canons was established.[13]

[7] Nell'anno 1113. alli 13. d'Agosto auenne in questa Città vn graue accidente; percioche essendo caduto il fulmine in questa Chiesa di S. Lorenzo, vi appiccò il fuoco, il quale andò talmente crescendo, che abbrusciò gran parte della Città. Non vò lasciare di dire, che Giacomo Redenasco scriue, Cremona questo istesso giorno, & anno essere stata presa da Andrea Visconte per le discordie de' Cremonesi, & essere stata molto ruinata con l'incendio e dice, che fu in giorno di Mercordì [sic]; & al mio giudicio questa opinione è più vera, che la prima; percioche mi pare impossibile, che per vn fuoco accidentale si fosse abbrusciata così gran parte della Città, atteso che trouò essere state consumate da questo incendio 29. Chiese, cioè s. Lorenzo, s. Andrea, s. Michele, s. Nazaro, s. Mauritio, s. Sepolcro, s. Antonio, s. Martino, s. Matteo, s. Vito, s. Geruasio, s. Erasmo, s. Pantaleone, s. Donato, s. Vitale, ss. Cosmo e Damiano, s. Giorgio, s. Pietro, s. Maria Egittiaca, s. Prospero, s. Tomaso, s. Ippolito, s. Barnaba, s. Ambrosio, s. Agnese, s. Martio, s. Alessandro, s. Romano, e s. Saluatore. Le qual Chiese sendo così lontane l'vna dall'altra, come sono hora quelle, che ancor vi restano, bisognarebbe dire, che fosse arsa la maggior parte della Città, il che, quando bene tutte le habitationi fossero state di legname, non hà punto del verisimile. E per dirne liberamente il mio parere, io tengo, che l'incendio, che narrano alcuni (frà quali è il dottissimo Sigonio) esser auenuto alli 10. Agosto del 1109. sia questo stesso da Andrea Visconte Capitano de' Milanesi. (Merula, 216).

Robolotti (*Storia*, 34) places the fire in 1113, and says of it: Ignorandosene il tempo e le cagioni, nella festa di S. Lorenzo Cremona fu preda delle fiamme, le quali distrussero 29 Chiese e molte case. Si attribuì il grande disastro ad un incendio casuale, o provocato da un fulmine; ma altri cronisti lo credettero opera degli invidi Milanesi . . . che . . . l'incendiarono per ridurla sotto il loro dominio. Ma niun documento autentico rinvenni di ciò.

Cavitelli (39) says that the fire took place in 1111. See also text cited above, p. 374.

[8] *Hist. Pat. Mon.*, II, XXI, 104.   [9] *Ibid.*, 109.   [10] *Ibid.*, 113.

[11] Eodem quoque anno [1159] Obertus Cremonensis Episcopus corpus Sancti Gregorii Martyris transtulit in Ecclesiam Sancti Michaëlis. (Sicardi Episcopi *Chronicon*, ed. Muratori, R. I. S., VII, 599).

[12] *Hist. Pat. Mon.*, II, XXI, 127.   [13] *Ibid.*, 125.

In 1187 S. Michele was confirmed to the bishop Siccardo.[14]

Lucchini speaks of important donations made to the church in 1249 and 1269. The chapter is mentioned as existing in 1317.[15] A prevosto of the church is named in a deed of 1378.[16]

Lucchini states that the church was restored in 1621, and this statement is confirmed by an inscription preserved by Vairani[17] which records the reconstruction of the façade in 1622. In the time of Corsi, who wrote in 1819, the church was of parochial rank, but it does not appear whether or not there was a chapter. According to this author the wooden roof was replaced by vaults in 1792, when other alterations were also executed. Maisen, who wrote in 1866, speaks of the Gothic façade as having been recently restored on traces of the original which had escaped the alterations of the XVIII century.

III. The church consists of a nave six bays long, two side aisles, a choir of one double bay and one single bay (the double bay is supplied with a northern side aisle, but the southern side aisle has been walled off), a crypt and a central apse (Plate 86, Fig. 3). It is evident that there are two epochs of construction. The nave and side aisles, although much modernized, date from the XIII century, but the choir and apse are somewhat earlier.

Internally, the choir is without architectural character, having been remade recently in a pseudo-Romanesque style. The nave and side aisles have also been completely modernized. It is difficult to say whether the pointed arches of the main arcade belong to the original structure, or are the result of a later alteration. The supports are slender monolithic columns of marble or alabaster.

One of the original round-arched windows of the clearstory of the choir still exists on the south side, but it has been walled up and in part replaced by a crude oculus.

A most noticeable break occurs in the masonry of the clearstory on the southern side, at the point where the choir and nave adjoin.

IV. Although completely modernized, the crypt still retains five interesting capitals. They are ornamented with interlaces, volutes and leaves. The technique is characterized by the absence of undercutting.

The capitals of the nave are of a broad-leaved, French transitional type, like those of S. Lorenzo or of the baptistery, or carved with grotesques, or adorned with very unrefined Gothic leaf patterns (the leaves are twisted into whirls, forming volutes). One is carved with strange, crude figure sculptures.[18] The apse is adorned externally with small, round-arched corbel-tables and round billets (Plate 86, Fig. 3), and is supplied with an extraordinary cornice,

[14] *Ibid.*, 165. [15] *Grande Illustrazione*, III, 512. [16] Merula, 258.

[17] CCXXXXI. Vairani has also preserved numerous inscriptions referring to the chapter.

[18] The destroyed Romanesque portal has been described by Lucchini.

consisting of long, narrow slits, introduced under the arched corbel-tables (Plate 86, Fig. 3). The arched corbel-tables of the nave differ from those of the choir and apse in that they are double.

The windows of the apse are surmounted by brickwork, inlaid with fancy patterns (Plate 86, Fig. 3). Below the windows is a string-course, formed of small, round-arched corbel-tables, supported on shafts engaged upon pilaster strips (Plate 86, Fig. 3).

The round-arched and elaborately moulded clearstory windows of the nave have been walled up and replaced by pointed windows. The façade (Plate 86, Fig. 2), with its rose-window, its restored bifora and oculi (the latter entirely surrounded by double arched corbel-tables), its double arched corbel-tables and its round billets, is a typical Gothic design.

V. The capitals of the crypt may be considered dated monuments of c. 1020. The choir and apse are constructed of brick masonry of a technique so impeccable that they must date from the last quarter of the XII century. The peculiar cornice of the apse is a development and elaboration of the cornice of the apse of Calvenzano (Plate 39, Fig. 1), erected c. 1140. It is obvious, however, that considerable time must have elapsed after the cornice of Calvenzano was erected before the motive could have been brought to the splendidly developed form that we find in S. Michele of Cremona (Plate 86, Fig. 3). An intermediate step in this evolution is furnished by the apse of the church at Pizzeghettone.[19] The cornice of this apse is formed of large, arched corbel-tables, with blind niches below, while little engaged colonnettes are placed between the niches supporting the corbel-tables. The character of the masonry shows that this apse dates from c. 1170. Pizzeghettone seems to stand about midway between Calvenzano and S. Michele. The latter edifice (that is to say, its apse and choir) may consequently be ascribed to c. 1200, a date which agrees well with the style of masonry, the mouldings, and the advanced ornament. The nave and façade are of the XIII century.

CRESCENZAGO,[1] S. MARIA

(Plate 87, Fig. 2, 3)

I. The church of S. Maria of Crescenzago is mentioned in the *Grande Illustrazione*,[2] and has been described, and even illustrated after a fashion, by Visconti.

---

[19] Pizzeghettone is situated between Cremona and Codogno, province of Cremona. The apse is the only interesting portion of this edifice, the remainder of which was rebuilt in the Gothic period.

[1] Crescenzago lies about four kilometres to the eastward of Milan.   [2] I, 457.

CRESCENZAGO, S. MARIA

II.   Giulini has found some not very substantial evidence for believing that the collegiate church of Crescenzago was founded about 1140.[3]   However this may be, it is certain that it existed in November, 1143, since it is mentioned in an inedited donation of that year.[4]   It is mentioned again in a legacy of 1152.[5]   The archbishop Oberto granted a privilege to the prevosto and canons in 1154.[6]   On November 25, 1186, the pope, Urban III, gave the prepositura of Brinate into dependence upon the chapter of Crescenzago.[7]   In 1197 the church appears as a head of a special congregation of the order of St. Augustine, having under it several dependent congregations.   The constitution of this congregation was approved by the archbishop Filippo in 1197.[8]   The church was given in commendam before 1502, and in 1772 the chapter was suppressed.[9]

III.   The edifice consists of a nave (Plate 87, Fig. 3) four bays long, two side aisles, a choir flanked by side aisles, and three apses.   The side aisles are covered by groin vaults, very oblong and highly domed in a longitudinal sense.   The nave has domed rib vaults erected on a uniform system, and about square in plan (Plate 87, Fig. 3).   The diagonal ribs have a torus section (Plate 87, Fig. 3).   The eastern bay of the nave, however, has not a rib but a groin vault (Plate 87, Fig. 3).   The choir is covered by a pointed barrel vault (Plate 87, Fig. 3).

The transverse ribs of the nave and side-aisle vaults are pointed, as are also the arches of the main arcade (Plate 87, Fig. 3).   The transverse arches of the side aisles are in two orders.

The piers of the nave are cylindrical (Plate 87, Fig. 3), and from the abaci rises a system of three members.   The piers of the choir, however, are compound (Plate 87, Fig. 3), and the system is continuous.

In the interior are visible what look like clearstory windows, although they have been walled up, one placed in each bay.   It is probable, however, that these openings merely served to air the side-aisle roofs, since no traces of windows are visible externally.

The central apse is reinforced by two vigorous buttresses (Plate 87, Fig. 2), and the side-aisle walls also have similar buttresses.

Over the eastern bay of the southern side aisle rises the campanile, the lower story of which is Romanesque (Plate 87, Fig. 2).

The masonry consists of large, well squared bricks, laid in horizontal courses and separated by mortar-beds of moderate thickness.   South of the church are remains of the cloisters dating from the XVI century.

---

[3] III, 397.

[4] Ecclesiam seu canonicam sancte Marie que dicitur a Crexentiago constructa prope ipsum locum Crexentiago.   (Bononi, *Diplomatum . . . Clarevallis*, Brera MS. AE, XV, 20, f. 116).

[5] Giulini, III, 397.   [6] *Ibid.*, VII, 118.

[7] *Codice della Croce*, MS. Amb. D. S. IV, 10/I, 10, f. 193; Giulini, IV, 32.

[8] Giulini, IV, 93; VII, 146.   [9] *Grande Illustrazione*, I, 457.

IV. The capitals of the interior have all been denatured. The cylindrical piers, however, still retain their original circular imposts, which resemble those of the eastern portions of the nave of Morimondo (Plate 154, Fig. 3). The exterior (Plate 87, Fig. 2) is adorned with simple arched corbel-tables. The two absidioles have a single shaft on axis. The apse windows are moulded. The arches of the main arcade are in two unmoulded orders (Plate 87, Fig. 3).

V. It is evident that in the church of Crescenzago we have an imitation of the abbey of Morimondo. (Compare Plate 87, Fig. 3, with Plate 154, Fig. 3). From Morimondo were derived the cylindrical piers, the circular abaci, the diagonals of torus section, the pointed arches, the system, the arches of the main arcade in two orders, the simple arched corbel-tables of the exterior, the uniform system, and the general restraint and sobriety of the whole design. (Compare Plate 87, Fig. 2, with Plate 154, Fig. 4). The abbey church of Morimondo was begun in 1186. The church of Crescenzago may consequently be assigned to c. 1190.

CURREGGIO,[1] BATTISTERO

(Plate 87, Fig. 1)

I. This monument has never been published.

II. I know of no documents which throw light upon the history of the baptistery of Curreggio.

III. The building (Plate 87, Fig. 1) consists of an octagonal central area, on four sides of which are projecting absidioles in the lower story. The nave is covered by an octagonal cloistered vault, masked externally and covered by a wooden roof. The edifice bears evident traces of having been made over at different epochs. The interior is now without interest.

The masonry is very crude (Plate 87, Fig. 1). Stones very roughly (if at all) squared are laid in courses seldom horizontal. Pebbles and herring-bone brick courses are introduced. The mortar-joints are extremely wide.

IV. The absidioles were originally adorned with arched corbel-tables supported on pilaster strips and grouped four and four, but have in great part disappeared. If the cupola ever possessed a cornice, all trace of it is now lost. On the exterior walls are remains of ancient intonaco (Plate 87, Fig. 1).

[1] (Novara).

V. The masonry of the baptistery (Plate 87, Fig. 1) is analogous to that of Sasso (Plate 205, Fig. 2), an edifice which dates from c. 1050. At Curreggio, however, the stones are larger, and, on the whole, the quality of the masonry is superior to that of Sasso, notwithstanding the pebbles and herring-bone brickwork. Curreggio may consequently be ascribed to c. 1055.

DENZANO,[1] S. MARIA ASSUNTA

I. This edifice has been published by Maestri.

II. Of the history of the building nothing is known except that it was in bad condition in 1341.

III. The building has been entirely modernized, with the exception of the apse. This is constructed of ashlar of the finest quality.

IV. The corbel-tables show close imitation of the cathedral of Modena (Plate 140, Fig. 3). Large arched corbel-tables, grouped two and two, are supported on shafts. These shafts are engaged on pilaster strips that support groups of three smaller arched corbel-tables placed within each of the large ones. The capitals are adorned with grotesque heads or broad leaves, and the corbels are carved with grotesque heads. The cornice has numerous fine mouldings.

V. The corbel-tables of Denzano recall those at Carpi (Plate 42, Fig. 5), an authentically dated monument of 1184. The grotesques of the capitals, however, show a style more primitive than that of Carpi. Many of these, indeed, show analogies with the capitals of S. Sepolcro of S. Stefano of Bologna, a monument which dates from c. 1160. Denzano may consequently be ascribed to about the same time.

DONGO,[1] S. MARIA IN MARTINICO

I. This church, so far as I know, has never been published.

II. When I visited the edifice in July, 1912, it was undergoing a radical restoration conducted by the architect Frigerio of Como. This had already been in progress for three years, and was far from being completed. The Renaissance vault had been destroyed, as had also the Renaissance campanile

---

[1] Denzano, a frazione of Marano (Modena), is situated forty-five minutes' walk from the carriage-road.

[1] (Como).

and the apse. The new campanile in a pseudo-Lombard style, had just been finished, and work had been begun on the new apse, which was being constructed on some traces of the ancient one that had come to light. When the Renaissance choir was demolished, a great quantity of débris belonging to the old edifice was discovered, including many stones bearing fragments of frescos and frescoed inscriptions. The latter, unfortunately, were so broken that nothing could be made out of them.

III. The edifice consists of a nave of a single aisle. The masonry is very fine. Well smoothed and perfectly squared stones are fitted together, with very narrow mortar-joints. The windows, with the exception of one oculus, are round-headed. They are widely splayed and evidently intended to serve without glass.

IV. The exterior is characterized by a simple cornice of arched corbel-tables, placed upon the north and east walls only. These corbel-tables have some tendency towards the pointed form, and are surmounted by a saw tooth and a moulding. In the eastern wall is a fine grotesque lion. The northern portal is characterized by grotesque heads, and two capitals, one of which is of a crude Corinthian, the other of a strange block acanthus type. The bases have griffes.

There are extant many traces of the Quattrocento frescos, with which the walls were once evidently adorned, both internally and externally.

V. The masonry shows close analogy with that of the apse of S. Carpoforo at Como, which was erected c. 1145. The nave of Dongo may consequently be ascribed to the same period.

FERRARA, CATHEDRAL

(Plate 88, Fig. 1, 2, 3; Plate 89, Fig. 1, 3, 4, 5)

I. The cathedral of Ferrara, which must have been one of the most imposing mediæval structures of all Italy, has suffered heavily from barocco and Renaissance alterations. It has, consequently, been much neglected by archæologists. The most important monograph that has appeared is that of Canonici, published in 1845, and consequently now out of date in several particulars. The naïve little pamphlet of Casazza on the *Importanza Cronologica di Ferrara* endeavours to show that the cathedral is the earliest extant example of Gothic, that is, of pointed architecture, since finished in 1135. In 1891 Gruyer published a study of Ferrara in the *Revue de l'Art Chrétien*. In the following year appeared the monograph of Agnelli, a work of popular character, but of some value for its half-tones, which include a reproduction of Frizzi's section. The study of the sculptures contributed by Zimmermann[1] is perhaps the best analysis of the artistic personality of Nicolò that has yet appeared. Venturi[2] has also studied and illustrated the sculptures. This critic has identified as one the two Guglielmi who worked at Modena and S. Zeno of Verona, and has ascribed to this sculptor and his assistant Nicolò nearly all the XII century sculptures of northern Italy. The pamphlets of Pagliarini and Peruzzi are important as sources for the restoration of the edifice carried out in the early part of the XIX century.

Ferrara, as is fitting for a university town, has produced numerous historians, practically all of whom have devoted themselves with more or less assiduity to illustrating the history of the cathedral. Of these the first in point of time is Guarini, whose work was published in 1621. It is an inexact and careless publication, marred by numerous errors and misprints, but important because it contains a description of the cathedral as it was before its baroccoization. Guarini was followed in 1646 by Sardi. Baruffaldi the elder, a man of great learning, published in the early years of the XVIII century numerous notices which are of importance for the history of the cathedral. He was present at Ferrara at the time the mosaic inscription was destroyed and the Marchesella inscription discovered, and left incorrect copies of both for posterity. Borsetti, in 1735, corroborated Baruffaldi's reading of the inscriptions, and published an important description of the old cathedral, as well as a section of the nave. In 1773 Scalabrini published for the first time the correct text of the mosaic inscription, derived from a copy made before the restoration in the XVI century. The monumental history of Ferrara by Frizzi was published 1791-1801. Frizzi republished the section of the nave which had already been published by Borsetti, and added several important observations upon the history of the cathedral. The history of Manini Ferranti which appeared in 1808 is also important. A readable summary of the history of the cathedral is contained in the *Guida* of Avventi, which was published in 1838. The bibliographical notices contained on the *Indice* of Cittadella, published in 1844, deserve mention. The *Guida* of the same author, published in 1873, is in reality a later recasting of the earlier work, but is of distinctly less value. The same author's *Notizie,* published in 1864, contains new documentary sources of a certain importance.

The mosaic inscription, as one of the earliest examples of poetry in the Italian vernacular, has received from the learned more attention than the cathedral itself. Practically all the historians above mentioned have treated at great length of it and of the problems it presents. In addition should be mentioned Affò who, in his *Dizionario,*[3] gives the two versions of Baruffaldi and Scalabrini. In recent years, Cipolla made a scientific study of the two versions, based upon the character of the letters, as shown in the facsimiles.

[1] 77.   [2] III, 186, 322.   [3] 29-41.

The authenticity of the inscription was warmly attacked by Belloni in 1906. However, the following year, Bertoni definitely solved the question by the publication of new documents which conclusively prove the authenticity of the version of Scalabrini.

II.   It is a constant tradition at Ferrara that the cathedral was, until the XII century, situated on the other bank of the Po, and on the site of the existing church of S. Giorgio.[4]   According to Frizzi[5] the migration of the inhabitants of Ferrara from the right to the left bank of the river took place gradually and was not carried out on a sudden impulse, as the *Chronica Parva Ferrariensis* seems to imply.[6]

[4] Episcopalis Sedes primò fuit in Vico Aventino, qui nunc dicitur Vicoventia, secus quam olim fluvius Sandalus defluebat de Pado antiquo in Padum, qui labitur præter Argentam.   Secundò fuit apud Ecclesiam Sancti Georgii in capite Insulæ, ubi & Cives habitabant, & is locus Ferriola dicebatur à nomine patris Padi, quæ nunc dicitur Fossa.   Cùm Cives Ferrariæ tunc molesti, & invisi essent Ravennatibus, & viribus impares, consilio publico deliberatum est inde migrare cum omni re familiari, & ædificiorum materia, & sedem ultra flumen ponere eo loco, quo nunc Civitas visitur. Nomen quoque Civitati novæ dederunt, quod est Ferraria, derivando nomen hoc Ferraria à prisco nomine Ferrariola.   Hujus autem transmigrationis tempus mihi penitus est ignotum: ideo id temerè scribere non sum ausus. (*Chronica Parva Ferrariensis*, ed. Muratori, R. I. S., VIII, 478).

[Il duomo] hebbe principio . . . nel luogo detto prima Foro Alieno, Massa Babilonica, Vico Magno, e doppo Ferraruola, oltre il Pò, doue hora albergano li Monaci di Mont' Oliueto. . . . Con l'occasione poi di sottrarsi i Ferraresi dalle continoue incursioni de' Bolognesi, che con ogni lor potere carcauano di ridurgli all'vbbidienza loro, sì come haueuano fatto d'alcune Città della Romagna, col maturo consiglio di Vitaliano principalissimo Signor di Padoua, e di Acario Conte di Este (Cauelliero di gran senno e valore) passarono di quà dal Pò nella Marca Triuigiana [date 675 in margin] in luogo detto Tridente, habitato da' Cinomani, nominato hora Ferrara, oue di presente si ritruoua, rimanendo solo nel detto luogo la Chiesa [date 1620 in margin] Cathedrale, e'l Vescouo col clero fin tanto, che dal magnanimo Guglielmo Marchesella Adellardi, principalissimo Cittadino Ferrarese, venne del suo proprio, con auttorità d'Innocenzio Secondo, edificata, sopra la Piazza del Comune, la gran machina della presente Chiesa Cathedrale volta all'Occaso; hauendo i Ferraresi a questo effetto mandati Ambasciadori Rizzardo, e Rinaldo Consoli ad Anacleto Secondo, i quali per tal concessione offersero alla S. Sede ogn'anno vn Bisanzio in perpetuo, ch'era vna sorte di Moneta d'oro di Costantinopoli di valuta di cento danari di moneta antica, che constituiscono trenta tre lire della presente nostra moneta, sì come tutto si caua dal Breue sopra ciò conceduto a Landolfo nostro Vescouo, ed a' Consoli, e Popolo di Ferrara, dato in Pisa per mano di Nemerio Cardinal Diacono, e Cancelliero di Santa Chiesa 11 Kal. Octob. Della erezione di questa, la quale in capo a due anni venne ridotta a perfezione, parlano i seguenti due versi, sopra la Porta maggiore di essa registrati in lettere d'oro, etc. (Guarini, 7-8).

[5] II, 124 f.

[6] But little is known of the history of the bishopric of Ferrara before it was transferred to the left bank of the river.   Sigonio (67) states that it was established at S. Giorgio in 657.   In 1055 there were canons regular, since at this date their privileges were confirmed by the pope, Victor II.   (Tomassetti, I, 631).

FERRARA, CATHEDRAL

The cathedral was transferred from the right bank of the river to its present site in the year 1135. So much is explicitly stated by the chronicle of Este,[7] and by the *Annales Ferrarienses*,[8] as well as by an Italian chronicle cited by Citadella.[9] Although the bishop moved over to Ferrara in 1135, the canons, according to Citadella,[10] long continued at S. Giorgio of Ferrarola.

No reliable document informs us when the new cathedral was begun. It is certain, however, that the reconstruction must have been undertaken before 1135, since in that year not only did the bishop transfer his official residence into the new church, but the edifice was consecrated. It is impossible to admit that the new building could have been so nearly completed in the brief period of two years assigned by Guarini.[11] The chronicle of Este states that the body of S. Romano was translated to Ferrara in 1103,[12] but it is difficult to believe that it could have been brought into the new cathedral as early as this. It is easy, on the other hand, to accept the notice of the XIV century chronicle of Ricobaldo, which states that the new cathedral was constructed during the reign of Lothair II, before he became emperor, and consequently between 1125 and 1133.[13]

The strong probability, amounting almost to a certainty, that the cathedral was begun before 1135, causes considerable difficulty in interpreting the inscription over the western portal:

✛ ANNO MILLE [V]NOCENTENO
QUINQUE SVPERLATIS
TER QUOQUE DENO
STRVITVR DOMVS HEC PIETATIS [14]

It must be that the word *struitur*, meaning 'was built,' is here used somewhat loosely and really should be interpreted 'was finished.' If this meaning be

[7] MCXXXV. Episcopatus Ferrariæ translatus fuit, ubi est. (*Chronicon Estense*, ed. Muratori, R. I. S., XV, 299).

[8] In 1135 fuit episcopatus Ferarie translatus ibi, ubi nunc est. (*Annales Ferrarienses*, M. G. H. *Script.*, XVIII, 663). Cf. Muratori, R. I. S., IX, 760.

[9] (44). This chronicle states furthermore that the cathedral was built by Guglielmo de' Marchesella, who began to lay its foundations in 1135, the same year that the cathedral was transferred, and who completely finished the edifice before he died in 1146. The work of collecting the stones for the marble pavement, however, was not begun until 1222, and this work was finished only in 1290.

[10] *Guida*, 8.   [11] See text cited above, p. 406.

[12] MCIII. Corpus Beati Romani conductu̅ fuit Ferrariam. (*Loc. cit.*).

[13] Lothario non Augusto . . . Ecclesia maxima Ferrariensis construitur. (Ricobaldi Ferrariensis, *Compilatio Chronologica*, ed. Muratori, R. I. S., IX, 243).

[14] *Ter deno* seems to be written for *ter deni*, meaning thirty. *Superlatis* has been read by Zimmermann as *super latis* and interpreted to mean above ancient foundations. Not only is this reading grammatically and etymologically impossible, but it is at variance with known historical facts, since the cathedral of Ferrara was, as we have seen, erected on a new site. The word is doubtless the participle of *superfero*, meaning 'added to,' and forms an ablative absolute with *quinque*.

accepted, the inscription offers no difficulties. The consecration by the apostolic legate on May 8, 1135, is recorded by Guarini[15] and by Sigonio.[16] Although it is not known whence these authors derived this notice, there is no reason to doubt its authenticity, the more so since it was confirmed by a bull of Pope Innocent II, also lost, but said by Guarini[17] to have been dated in Pisa, where it is known that the pope really was at that time.[18]

In 1141 the portal of the new cathedral was finished, for a document of this year is dated *sub porticu Ecclesiae Sancti Georgii*.[19] In this same year the bishop Grafoni transferred the old archiepiscopal palace to the canons of S. Giorgio, the ex-cathedral.[20]

It is here necessary to take up the complex question of the mosaic inscription, since this forms an important source for the history of the cathedral. This inscription, which was destroyed in 1712, when the barocco-ization of the interior was undertaken, was engraved on a scroll of one of the prophets depicted in mosaic on the triumphal arch. Before it was destroyed, Baruffaldi obtained a high ladder upon which he climbed up to examine the inscription with care, wetting it with water so as to make the characters legible. He thus made a facsimile of the inscription which he transcribed:

Il mille cento trentacinque nato
Fo questo Tempio a Zorzi consecrato
Fo Nicolao Scolptore
E Glielmo fo l'Auctore.

Some years later Borsetti published the facsimile which reads:

IL MILE CENTO TR
ENTA CINQVE NATO
FO QTO TEMPLO A
GORGI CSECRATO
FO NICLAO SCOLP
TORE E GL'M
O FO LO AVC
TORE

In 1773 Scalabrini published a new version of the lost inscription taken from a manuscript of Massi and purporting to be a copy of the original inscription

---

[15] Fu ella poi consecrata da Azzo Cardinale del titolo di S. Anastasia Legato Apostolico in Bologna, l'ottauo giorno di Maggio del sudetto Anno, con la cui auttorità vi venne anche il medesimo giorno da Landolfo sopra nominato trasferita la Sede Episcopale, soggettando Innocenzio Secondo la detta Chiesa immediatamente alla Chiesa Romana . . . si come fece Adriano primo etc. (Guarini, 7-8).

[16] Ferrariæ Gulielmus Adelardus ciuitatis princeps basilicam magnifice ædificandam curauit. eaq. ab Azone cardinali iussu Innocentij pontificis consecrata est. (Sigonio, 436, ad. ann. 1135).

[17] See text cited above, p. 406.   [18] Frizzi, II, 143.   [19] Manini, II, 27.
[20] Frizzi, II, 143.

as it was before 1570. In this year the mosaics were destroyed by an earthquake and were, in consequence, badly restored in part by painting, and the last two lines radically altered. The original version, as published by Scalabrini, is:

Del Mille cento trenta cinque nato
Fo questo templo a S. Gorgio donato
Da Glielmo Ciptadin per sò amore
E ne fo l'opra Nicolao el scolptore

Affò in 1777 published a facsimile of Scalabrini's version of the inscription:

LĪ MĪLE CENTO TRENTA CENQE NATO
FO QTO TEMPLO A. S. GOGIO DONATO
DA GLELMO CIPTADIN P[ER] SO AMORE
E NEA FO LOP[ER]A NICOLAO SCOLPTORE

There ensued a great controversy as to which version was the authentic one, and it was even suspected that the inscription was entirely apocryphal. This doubt arose chiefly from a passage of the historian Guarini, who wrote in 1621 a long description of the cathedral. In this he fails to mention the mosaic inscription, although he speaks of the mosaics of the triumphal arch. Moreover, beside this description there is noted in the margin the date 1340. It was long doubted whether this date was simply a misprint or whether Guarini possessed some authentic notice, subsequently lost, that the mosaics were erected in that year. The lost source was finally found by Frizzi,[21] who discovered in the chronicle of Este a passage which does indeed state that the crossing was built in 1341, but which Guarini evidently quite mistakenly applied to the mosaic.[22] The long and difficult controversy was finally settled only in 1907, when Bertoni published an inedited letter of Scalabrini by which the authenticity of the latter's version is clearly established. This letter of Scalabrini, written in 1678, cites the manuscript of the *fabbrica* of 1572 and 1573, in which reference is made to the restoration of the mosaic, and moreover fully explains who was the Massi who gave the copy of the inscription to Orazio, the uncle of Scalabrini. The letter, besides, contains a new version of the inscription, which must be accepted as the best, unless, indeed, Bertoni's conjectured emendation of *e mea* for *e ne* in the last line be correct:

LĪ MĪLE CENTO TRENTA CENQE NATO
FO QTO TENPLO A. S. GOGIO . DONATO
DA GLELMO CIPTADIN P[ER] SO AMORE
E ÑE' FO LOP[ER]A NICOLAO SCOLPTORE

[21] II, 132.

[22] His diebus completa fuit truyna Episcopatus Sancti Georgii de Ferraria et laborerium historiæ S. Petri et pilastrum Virginis Mariæ in dicto Episcopatu.

The correct text of the inscription being thus established, we learn that in 1135 the cathedral of Ferrara was erected in honour of S. Giorgio by Guglielmo, citizen of Ferrara, and that it was the work of the sculptor Nicolò.

That the marchese Guglielmo built the cathedral is the constant tradition at Ferrara. It is recorded, for example, by Sigonio in the text cited above, as well as in the Italian chronicle cited by Cittadella.[23] In the history of Sardi, published in 1646, we read that Guglielmo died in 1196, at the age of ninety years; that he built the cathedral and caused it to be consecrated by the legate of Innocent II; and that he left as heir the daughter of his brother, Adelardo.[24] This passage, written in 1646, is in strange accord with the inscription discovered in the XVIII century, with the notable exceptions that it states that Guglielmo was buried not in the cathedral but in another church, and that he was the grandson, not the son, of Bulgaro.

It is now necessary to take up the difficult question of this epitaph. Baruffaldi states that during the restoration in the XVIII century, this inscription was found at a lower level, very much worn, and broken into fragments. At the command of the bishop he read it carefully. He prints his reading, and substantially the same version was cut on a new stone which is at present placed in the pavement of the new cathedral. Even this new stone has now become very much worn, so that Baruffaldi's printed version is useful in restoring some of the letters which have nearly disappeared. The inscription on the stone as Baruffaldi copied it in 1712, restored with the help of his printed version, is as follows:

STRENVVS HIC MILES MORES ARTVSQ SENILES
DEPOSVIT TARDVS NOSTER PRINCEPS ADELARDVS
GVILLELMVS SAEVO GENVIT QUEM BVLGARVS AEVO
QVEM PIETAS CLARVM ET BONA MVNIFICENTI[A] C[AR]VM
FECIT QVI PLENOS SEMPER MANDAVIT [EGENOS]
QVI POPVLO EXEMPLVM STRVIT HOC [DE MARMORE TEMPLV]M
CLESTINVS [= Celestinus] PLANSIT TRISTISQVE UGVC[CIO MANSIT]
[M] ARCHESILLA ORAT VIR[QVE] ATTO IN FVNE[RE PLO]RAT
[A]NNIS [M]ILLE[N]IS CENTVM SEX ET NON[AGEN]IS
[PER] MERITVM CHRISTI REQVIEM DEPOSCIM[VS ISTI]

[23] 44.

[24] Guglielmo . . . poco dopo se ne morì [date 1196 in margin] di nouanta anni: huomo nobile, ricco, valoroso, & notabile. Perche, . . . lasciò di se eterna memoria a Ferraresi, hauendo fabricato fuori . . . la chiesa di Santa Maria in Belieme, doue fu sepolto: cinta la Città verso il Borea di mura: & entro fattoui edificare il Vescouato ampio, e per li marmi soperbo: & fatto che Innocentio Secondo mandò Azzo Card. di Santa Nastagia a consecrarlo a San Georgio l'ottauo giorno di Maggio, promettendo il Vescouo Landolfo, & il popolo di pagare santa Chiesa ogni anno per tributo del suolo, doue era fabricato vn Bizantio. . . . Non hauea Guglielmo figliuoli, & eraui solo vna fanciulla di Adelardo suo fratello. Costei lasciò egli herede. (36).

FERRARA, CATHEDRAL

D. O. M.

CAROLVS FRANCISCVS MARCHESELLVS P . . . . . ITIVS

. . . . NENSIS DE STIPITE PRA . . . . . ADFI . . . . . APDI . . . . .

AN . . . . .

. . . . . EMO ET . . . . . RMO D. CARD. RVFO FERRAREN . . . . .

[EPIS]COPO . . . . . EPITAPHIVM SVPRADICTVM A VETVSTO . . . . .

TRACTO LAPIDE SEPVLCHRAM INTEGRE DESV . . . . .

NATI HVIVS ECCLESIAE FVNDATOR . . . . .

FIDELITER PE . . . . .

[M] DCC . . . . .

The version of Borsetti is substantially the same as that of Baruffaldi, with the exception of the fourth line, which reads:

Guillielmus Sævo quē genuit Bulgarus ævo.

It is entirely improbable that Borsetti saw the original inscription, and it is likely that his variant is merely due to a careless transcription from the existing stone. The same may be said of the version of Muratori,[25] of which the only notable variation is the reading of *ipse* for *iste* in the last word.

The meaning of the inscription as restored by Baruffaldi seems to be: "Here tardily cast off the habits and limbs of old age a mighty soldier, Guglielmo, Prince Adelardo, whom Bulgaro begat in a cruel age; whom piety made renowned and generosity dear, who always sent the needy away filled, and who as an example for the people built this marble church. When he died Celestine lamented and Uguccio was sad. At his funeral Azzo wept and Marchesella prayed. In the year 1196 we pray for his repose through the merits of Christ."

If we could accept the account of Guglielmo given by Sardi and cited above, the inscription would offer few difficulties. We should say that he died in 1196 at the age of ninety years, which would have made it possible for him to have constructed the cathedral of Ferrara consecrated in 1135. The Celestine who lamented his death would be the pope, third of that name, who reigned from 1191 to 1198. The Marchesella who prayed at his funeral would be his niece, who became his heir, and Azzo d'Este would be her husband. Uguccio would be the bishop of Ferrara. Unfortunately, however, other documents whose authenticity it is impossible to doubt, contradict Sardi, and the inscription as restored by Baruffaldi. Frizzi has shown[26] that Guglielmo de' Marchesella died, not in 1196 but in 1146. This must have been the man who built the cathedral. He left a widow and two minor sons, Guglielmo III and Adelardo. Guglielmo III died in 1183 after having made a will in which, among other bequests, is one to the *ecclesiae s. Georgii*. The death of Guglielmo in 1146 I find also recorded in a manuscript of the Biblioteca del-

25 A. I. M. A., Dis. 36, ed. F., VI, 120.   26 II, 150-151.

l'Università,[27] and in the genealogies of the Marchesella family as given by Manini.[28] Muratori has tried to solve these difficulties by supposing that there were three Guglielmi who died respectively in 1154 [*sic*, 1146], 1183 and 1196. This explanation seems improbable to Frizzi,[29] who thinks it more likely that the stone was placed to commemorate Guglielmo II, who died in 1146, but was erected only in 1196, and that the mourners referred to are persons who lived in 1196, and not in 1146. Scalabrini[30] believed that the epitaph referred to Adelardo, son of Guglielmo. None of these solutions is completely satisfactory, although of the three the last seems the least improbable. It is necessary to admit, however, that Baruffaldi, be it unwittingly, or be it because of a desire to flatter members of the Marchesella family still living in his time, made many errors in reading the original stone, and supplied *lacunæ* freely from the inexact notices of Sardi. As an historical source, therefore, his transcription is of very minor value. It merely serves to confirm what is already known from other sources, viz., that the cathedral was erected on the initiative and at the expense of Guglielmo.

In 1177 the cathedral was consecrated by Pope Alexander III on the eighth day of May. In the year 1727, in the course of the reconstruction of the edifice, there was found a leaden casket containing relics.[31] This casket bore two inscriptions. On one side was a list of the relics contained and on the other the inscription thus given in the letter of Scalabrini published by Bertoni:

anno MCLXXVII consecratum fuit ab Alexandro III.VIII.id. Madii.[32]

In 1393 the statue of Alberto d'Este was erected,[33] and in 1397 *una bellissima icona* with statues in relief was placed over the high altar.[34] During the course of the XIV century the upper flamboyant gallery of the south side of the cathedral was erected, according to Cittadella.[35] If this is so, we have here a remarkably early example of the flamboyant style in Italy. The campanile was begun in 1452,[36] and its construction had advanced in 1498 to such a point that the bells could be hung.[37] In the XV century the choir

[27] Box No. 960.   [28] II, 33.   [29] II, 157.   [30] Letter cited by Bertoni.

[31] Alesso 3 consacrò nel giorno di Pasqua l'altar maggiore della nostra Cattedrale; ne qual incontro fù fatta un' iscrizione che venne ritrovata nell'edificarlo di nuovo nell'anno 1727, sopra una capetta di piombo. (MS. 160, Bibl. Ferr.).

[32] (499). The manuscript we have cited from the archives states that the consecration took place on Easter day, while the inscription, as quoted by Scalabrini, gives the date as May 8. The fact that the cathedral was consecrated in 1177 by Alexander III was known even before the discovery of the casket, and is, for example, recorded by Guarini (10). It has frequently been erroneously ascribed to 1174, instead of to 1177.

[33] MS. 160, Bibl. Ferr.   [34] MS. in Box No. 960, Bibl. Ferr.

[35] 93.   [36] MS. 160, Bibl. Ferr.

[37] Canonici (21) is therefore in error in stating that the campanile was erected in 1412.

was entirely reconstructed by Ercole I, Duke of Este.[38] In 1570 the building was injured by an earthquake, and the mosaic of the triumphal arch badly restored, as has been shown above. In 1590 the old ambones were removed.[39] In 1636 the baroccoization of the nave was undertaken.[40] It is generally believed that at this time the works were interrupted before the mediæval edifice was seriously denatured. But that such was not the case is shown by the drawing of Sardi published in 1646. This work contains a bird's-eye view of the entire city of Ferrara, in which, however, the cathedral is clearly seen. This drawing shows distinctly the three barocco gables on the south side of the nave, as they exist to-day. It is evident, therefore, that at this date the nave had already largely lost its mediæval character. In 1686 the campanile was struck by lightning.[41] In 1712 a new and radical transformation of the edifice was begun. In 1718 the southern portal—the "Porta dei Mesi"—was destroyed, and in 1724 the rebuilt cathedral was solemnly consecrated. The inscription recording this consecration is placed over the western doorway:

D. O. M.
THOMAS . S. R. E. CARDINALIS RVFVS
EP. FERRARIENSIS ET LEG. BONONIAE
TEMPLVM . HOC SINGVLARI . OPERA . AR-
TIFICIOQVE . A . TADDEO . S. R. E. CARDI-
NALI . A VERME DECESSORE SVO CLE-
MENTIS . XI . P. M. SVBSIDIIS . INCOATVM
ET . AD . TERTIAM PARTEM . EXTRVCTVM
EODEM . AVSPICANTE PONTIFICE . AERE
SVO . PERFICI . VOLVIT ANNO . MDCCXXIV

The works must have continued, however, after the consecration, since the leaden casket with relics was found in 1727.

Fortunately the mediæval cathedral of Ferrara did not perish without leaving numerous memorials of itself, from which it is possible to reconstruct with considerable accuracy its original dispositions. In the archives of the Biblioteca dell'Università at Ferrara, in the box which bears the number 960, is contained the official report of the committee appointed to examine the building in 1713. This account, which is of the greatest importance, has never been published, and I am happy to be able to make it public in its entirety.[42]

---

[38] Guarini, 11.   [39] Cittadella, 45.   [40] Cittadella, 112.   [41] MS. 160, Bibl. Ferr.

[42]   1713
Relazione dello Stato, in cui si è ritrouata| La Struttura della Chiesa Catedrale di| Ferrara, nel porre mano à riparare Li| Coperti, e rifare, come si meditaua,| Li sofitti.

P°. La maggior parte de' Legnami maestri fracidi nelle teste o scompaginati senza forza di reggere più lungamte li Tetti, ed i Legni maestri de' coperti delle Naui Laterali fracidi, come sopra, e staccati dalli Muri, sostenuti solamente da Legni posticci.

From this report we learn: (1) that the nave and side aisles of the ancient cathedral were roofed in wood, and that the nave had transverse arches; (2) that the transepts were vaulted;[43] (3) that the triumphal arch was adorned with mosaics and surmounted by a high wall, that is, there was some sort of a central tower or cupola over the crossing; (4) that the choir was flanked by two turrets; (5) that the pavement of the church was notably lower than that of the surrounding soil.

Baruffaldi wrote a description of the mosaic of the triumphal arch as it was before its destruction. This mosaic represented in different square

2°. Li soffitti di Legname consumato dal tempo, e dall'acque traforati, e quasi cadenti, che stauano assicurati al coperto suddetto.

3°. L'Arco Lavorato à musaico antico sopra l'Altare maggiore del Presbitero, scrostato in diversi siti, crepato in più parti, sopra cui era fabbricato un Muraglione, con Scale ne' fianchi di Muro massiccio, pure crepato, assai pendente verso il Corpo della Chiesa, quale appoggiatosi all'osatura del Coperto della Naue di mezzo, l'aueua fatto scompaginare, e quasi rovesciare.

4°. Nelli Laterali del Presbitero erano due Torricelle alte sopra la Chiesa quarantatrè palmi, con entro scale a lumaca di pietra, e per fare due Porte nel Laterale destro fù anticamente tagliata la Colonna, e Gradini della detta Scala dalla parte di sotto, per il che restò il Cantone del medesimo laterale di grossezza solamte palmi due, e due quinti, nel stratagliare le accennate Porte, e tal Cantone sosteneua un Muraglione di considerabile altezza e grossezza, sopra cui era fondata una delle prenominate Torricelle, con Scala, e col detto Volto à musaico, di modo che erano le pietre del del [sic] medesimo cantone infrante dal graue peso, che aveva cagionate crepature da ogni parte.

5°. Nel Laturale del suddetto Presbitero era anticamente stato escauato un gran sforo per Nicchia d'un Cassone di Marmo col Deposito della sa. mem. di Papa Vrbano III. dietro al qual Nicchio fù tagliato il muro della Torricella, e del laterale stesso, per farui Armarj, sopra quali il muro era sempre più stratagliato, et indebolito, ridotto alla grossezza di tre quinti di palmo in circa, per auerui cauata una Scaletta di Legno, che ascendeua ad una Stanza, qual grossezza di muro sosteneua un Muraglione uguale all'accennato nel antecedente capo, con Torricella, Scala di pietra, e Volta à musaico.

6°. Li Archi maestri, e Volta, che serviua di Soffitta alli Cappelloni della Crociera del Presbitero, ed un'altro Arco principiato nell'imboccatura del medesimo Presbitero erano più bassi palmi sette degl'Archi, e Soffitto della Naue di mezzo della Chiesa, à cui facendosi la Volta di pietra in tal bassezza, si perderebbero le finestre di quella Naue, non essendoui altri siti da prendere il Lume.

7°. Il Pilastro destro, à piedi del Presbitero, diffettoso nel fondamento, e nella parte superiore scopertosi uno scauo l'altezza sette, in otto palmi.

8°. La Colonna susseguente scauata sopra terra, con Nicchia alta palmi cinque, e due quinti, sopra la quale si spiccaua, per cadere, parte del muro della stessa Colonna.

9°. Il Pilastro sinistro, à piedi del Presbitero infetto nel fondamento molto più del destro.

10°. La Colonna susseguente composta di più pezzi di marmo, stratagliata sino alla metà del suo Corpo, e grossezza, per farui una Scaletta à comodo della Cantoria.

11°. Il Piano della Chiesa è più basso della Piazza auanti quella tre palmi; e verso il Palazzo Vescouale [sic] è più basso palmi cinque e due quinti; verso poi il Presbitero è più basso palmi sei, e trè quarti; onde i Muri laterali, posti in Sito paludoso, sono infettati dall'Vmidità, e Salnitro.

compartments the Madonna, angels and prophets. One of these figures, believed to be that of a prophet, held the famous inscription of 1135.[44]

The description of Guarini, written in 1621, is particularly important, because made before even the reconstruction of 1636. From this we learn that the mediæval cathedral had five aisles, that the columns were of brick, but the capitals of marble; that the pavement was of coloured marble mosaic; that there were galleries; that the wooden roofs were painted blue and decorated with golden stars; that under the triumphal arch with its mosaic of the angels and prophets was a screen of marble containing three arches above which was placed a crucifix, on one side of which was the Virgin and S. Giorgio, on the other S. Giovanni and S. Maurelio, statues which were placed here by Duke Alfonso I in 1515.[45] From the description of Borsetti, published in 1735, we learn that the capitals of the nave were sculptured with figures of men, animals, birds and beasts; that the galleries had marble

12°. Il rimanente del Corpo della Chiesa con diverse Colonne fuori di perpendicolo, e molto pendenti, Archi, Soprarchi maestri, e Muri in niala positura, con diverse Crepature, che arrivano sino al Tetto, con Finestre, e Porte antiche, in buon numero murate, parte delle quali lasciate vote di dentro. Oltre di ciò si sono ritrouate varie rotture, et incaui sopra li Archi corrispondenti alla Naue di mezzo, raggiustate solamte al di fuori, e dalla parte esteriore in un' Angolo della Chiesa, verso il Campanile, quantità di marmi, che incrostauano il medesimo angolo, e serviuano d'ornamento, disuniti, e cadenti, essendo dalla rugine corrose le Chiavette, che li tenevano connessi, avendo le Acque, e le Neui liquefatte, cadute tra essi Marmi, e le Muraglie, recato grave pregiudicio alle medesime. (Box No. 960, Biblioteca dell'Università, Ferrara).

43 These vaults, however, may have been erected in 1636.

44 Il mosaico di tutto quell'arco rappresentava in varie caselle quadrate diverse figure tutte sacre, e della Religione Cristiana. Eravi l'Immagine di Maria Vergine in mezza figura nel mezzo: da i lati alcuni Angeli ben in grande, ch'io credetti piuttosto Arcangeli, per avere tutti, oltre l'aureola, lo scettro ancora nelle mani; poi in altre caselle si vedeano altre mezze figure, le quali dal cartelloccio, che teneano in mano col loro nome, ben conosceasi essere profeti. Nella mano sinistra d'una di questi apparia sostenuto, e alquanto fuori pendente del quadrato un lungo carteloccio, etc.

45 L'altare maggiore di essa venne consegrato dal Sommo Pontefice Alessandro III a otto di Maggio, mentre si ritrouaua in Ferrara di passaggio per Roma, nel suo ritorno di Francia. Ritrouasi la detta Chiesa in cinque naui distinta da grossissime colonne di mattoni cotti, con le loro basi, e capitelli di marmo in vari modi lauorati, collastricato di marmi colorati, bianchi, rossi, ed azzurri, in diuersi foggie, e di vaghi lauori accommodati, e con alcuni circoli in particolare molto belli ed artificiosi. . . . Al piè dell'vltima colonna del nouo Arco s'ascende nella Tribuna per alcuni gradi di marmo, la quale, insieme con l'altre naui, è fatta a volto di tauole di legno dipinte di color azzurro, ed ornate d'vn numero quasi infinito di stelle dorate di rilieuo dentro ad alcuni comparti quadrati, con ordine distinti, che sembra vn serenissimo Cielo, se non che l'Arco, che copre l'Altar maggiore è di pietra lauorato di musaico antico, e finissimo, con alcuni ordini d'Angeli, e di Profeti. Questo ha sotto di se tre Archi di marmo sostenuti da colonne incanellate, con vna gran cornice, sopra della quale stà vn Crocifisso tra quattro figure di bronzo, l'vna rappresentante la B. V. e l'altra S. Giouanni, con quella di S. Giorgio alla sinistra, e l'altra di S. Maurelio alla destra, iui riposte per ornamento e diuozione dal Duca Alfonso Primo (1515). (Guarini, 10-11).

columns; that there were three rows of clearstory windows, numbering sixty in all; that in addition to the painted wooden roof, and the mosaic pavement already described, there were two marble ambones on either side of the nave in the fifth bay from the west.[46] After having spoken of the mosaic of the triumphal arch, Borsetti goes on to describe the Porta dei Mesi. In the tympanum was a relief representing Christ treading on the aspic and the basilisk, with His right hand raised in benediction. About the portal were a series of reliefs depicting the history of the Old Testament, beginning with the creation of the world, and terminating with the sacrifice of Abraham, all supplied, like the figure of Christ, with appropriate metrical inscriptions.[47]

[46] Templum in quinque distinctum naves columnis quadraginta lateritiis innitebatur, itaut pulcherrimam columnarum sylvam ingredientium oculis objiceret; hæ autèm marmoreis erant basibus Epystiliisque decoratæ, epystilia verò affabræ sculpta in angulis hominum, brutorum, avium, reptiliumque imagines exhibebant; laterales magnæ Navis muri, antheridibus ad tectum usquè supereminentes xistis, qui columellis marmoreis distinguebantur erant perforati; altiùs verò, triplex fenestrarum ordo (sexaginta erant) conspiciebatur, quorum superior xistis mediantibus lumen navibus minoribus communicabat. Sublimia Templi laquearia ex ligneis tabulis ceruleo pictis, ac tesselato opere elaboratis; in tesselo autèm quolibet bracteata micabat stella, adeò ut jucundissimam serenæ noctis imaginem cernere credidisses. Lytostrotum albi, rubei, ac cyanei coloris lapides marmorei miro quoddam compacti ordine efformabant; Marmoreum quoquè pulpitum intèr utramque columnarum antheridis quintæ à dexterâ in Templum ingredientis parte protensum, anaglyptisque exornatum assurgebat; at (quòd periisse illachrymandum) in ingenti arcu Aræ majori impendente, laquearque Navis Magnæ à Chori fornice discriminante Dominicæ Incarnationis Mysterium, perantiquo musivo opere expressum cernebatur, ibique è Prophetarum cujusdam manu (eos namque Artifex unà cum Angelis mysterio famulantes effinxerat) libellus dependebat, in quo caracteribus complicatis, quemadmodùm sequens demonstrat forma, vetustissima hæc carmina, antiquissimum, pretiosissimumque Italiæ Poesis monumentum legebantur. (Borsetti, I, 356).

[47] In ejusdem verò Semicirculo Redemptoris effigies Aspidem, ac Basiliscum conculcantis, ac dexteram in benedicentis modum protendentis prominebat, his additis carminibus:

Nèc Deus est, nèc Homo præsens quam cernis imago
Sed Deus est, & Homo præsens quam signat imago.

Variæ etiam circà portam eandem Veteris Testamenti Historiæ à Mundi exordio usquè ab Abrahæ sacrificium sculptæ, & sequentibus versis, ac S. Scripturæ Sententiis animatæ:

Omne genus rerum processit sorte dierum
Adam de Limo formatur tempore primo
Viva primæva de costâ fingitur Eva
Livor Serpentis mutavit jura parentis
Ostia fert . . . . . placet is, qui detulit Agnum
Justus Abel moritur, & fratris fuste feritur

Ubi est Abel frater tuus. Numquid ego Custos ejus sum. Arcam inibl quoque Diluvii fluctibus innatantem Sculptor effinxerat, in eà verò plures fenestrarum ordines,

Cittadella adds that on either side of the portal were two statues of natural size, one representing an old man clothed in a jacket and armed with a spear, the other a youth with breast-plate and helmet, brandishing a sword, both of which figures held aloft a shield with the sign of the cross. In the second story of the portico were the two lions of red marble which are now placed before the west façade. There were two other lions in the lower story, and in Cittadella's times one of these still existed in the court back of the apse. The whole porch was surmounted by a statue of Christ in high relief, represented in the act of blessing, while on the other side of Him knelt a youth and an old man.[48] In addition to these descriptions a section made before the destruction of the cathedral has been published by Borsetti and Frizzi. The two engravings differ slightly from each other, but both appear to be on the whole faithful to the original drawing. This drawing shows the choir as having been already made over in the Renaissance style. The transepts had also—at least to some extent—lost their original character, but the mediæval nave appears almost entirely undamaged. The system of this nave was alternate. The intermediate piers were columns; from the heavier piers rose a system which carried the transverse arches. On these arches rested a timber roof, which seems to have resembled that of S. Fermo Maggiore at Verona, and was hence probably of the XIV century. The three rows of windows in the clearstory are distinctly shown. In the drawings the arches of the main arcade are unmistakably pointed and have projecting archivolts. The triforium consisted of three equally grouped arches in each bay, but the two groups of each double bay were united under another encircling arch. At the west end of the edifice was placed a single, instead of a double, bay.[49] The supports separating the side aisles were alternately heavier and lighter.

In 1829 the lower story of the western portal was entirely remade, new lions being substituted for the ancient griffins. The old griffins are now placed

è quibus specierum diversarum animalia diuturni tamquàm carceris taedio affecta, capita exerebant: aliaque id genus multa, quæ missa facimus, ut ad Historiam nostram revertamur.

[48] Sotto l'arco stava un Salvatore con la croce in atto di benedire calpestrando l'aspide e il basilisco: intorno alla porta eranvi altri scompartimenti quadrilaterali con entro alcuni bassi rilievi esprimenti alcuni fatti della Genesi; ed ai lati erano pure due statue al naturale, una di vecchio rivestito di giacco ed armato d'asta, l'altra di giovane con usbergo e con elmo in testa, e con la spada imbrandita, tenenti ambidue in alto scudo crocesegnato, forse ad accennare a que' Adelardi che militarono alle crociate. Superiormente all'arco poi erano li due leoni di marmo rosso, che sostenevano colonne aggruppate in quattro ordini; e su di esse poggiavano gli archi del coperto della porta. Sopra tutto ciò, il Redentore, quasi a pieno rilievo, benediceva il popolo, nel mentre che a' suoi fianchi stavano inginocchiati un giovane ed un vecchio coperti di antica toga nel corpo, e di una cuffia a cappuccio nella testa. (94).

[49] These and the following particulars are derived from a plan made in 1618 and described by Canonici.

on the pavement in front of the church, one at each angle of the façade. This restoration, completed in 1830, is recorded by the inscription:

FRONS . HAEC . AEVO . FATISCENS

SOLIDIVS . REFECTA . EST

FACIE . ADHVC . VETVSTA

AERE . PVBLICO . ET . SINGVLARI

OMNIVM . CAPITVLARIVM

ANNO . MDCCCXXX .

In 1832 the upper story of the porch was restored with a similar disregard for the principles of archæology, and at the same time various other mutilations were perpetrated upon the edifice. In 1888 a new restoration of the interior was in progress, and the walls were covered with frescos. This work was begun in 1888 and finished about ten years later. In 1895 the high altar was embellished.

III. Of the original XII century structure of the church but very little remains. The interior is now completely barocco in style, and its original dispositions are only known from the old drawings and descriptions mentioned above. The outer side-aisle walls and parts of the façade are the only portions of the edifice that retain their Romanesque character.

The masonry of the façade consists of fine ashlar laid in courses alternately wide and narrow, giving a distinctly decorative effect; the side-aisle walls, on the other hand, are constructed of large well shaped bricks, laid in courses quite horizontal and separated by thick mortar-beds (Plate 89, Fig. 3). The bricks are roughened but not cross-hatched.

IV. The flanks of the cathedral (Plate 89, Fig. 3) are ornamented with a motive that recalls the cathedral of Modena (Plate 140, Fig. 3). Shafts engaged on pilaster strips support blind arches, within which is the gallery of three equal arcades rising from a string-course, below which are arched corbel-tables. On the south flank the thirteen eastern bays have coupled columns in the gallery, the remaining eight, single columns. The capitals are homogeneous in type, and it is impossible to detect any stylistic difference between those of the eastern bays with single columns and those of the western bays with coupled columns, except that the stilt-blocks of the latter are higher. On the outer side only (the mouldings not being carried around), these stilt-blocks are moulded, and in the western bays the mouldings are many and fine. Many of the capitals have broad leaves like those of the capitals of S. Zeno at Verona; others are of the composite type, or ornamented with grotesques. Several particularly unpleasant ones have circular abaci and lathe-like decoration. On the northern flank the four eastern bays alone preserve the blind arches, and have single columns in the gallery, and arched corbel-tables at a higher level. The capitals are similar to those on the southern side.

Each of the old griffins removed from the central porch in the early XIX century has carved on its flank a wheel.[50] The northern one holds between his paws two oxen and a human figure with flaming hair. The southern one holds a warrior in front and a horse behind. Two smaller lions coming from the Porta dei Mesi hold between their paws animals which it is impossible to identify. At the side of one are creatures with birds' wings, serpents' tails and broken heads.

It is primarily for its sculptures that the cathedral of Ferrara takes an important place in the list of Lombard monuments. The western portal (Plate 88, Fig. 3) is among the most notable examples of the XII century plastic art extant in northern Italy. It is the work of the sculptor Nicolò, as is shown from the inscription with his familiar signature in the tympanum:

SEOCVAITFA [these unmeaning letters were apparently added later]
ARTIFICE͞ GNARV͞ Q[VI] SCVLPSERIT HE͞C NICH͞LAV͞ ✚
HVC͞ CVRRENTES LAV͞DENT P[ER] SC[V]LA GENTES.

On either side of the outer archivolt (Plate 88, Fig. 3) are figures of the two Johns, the Evangelist holding a book, the Baptist holding a scroll with the inscription: EC|CE AG|NUS| DE|I. On the lunette is a spirited relief representing St. George and the dragon (Plate 88, Fig. 1). Below on the architrave (Plate 89, Fig. 5) is a series of reliefs, representing: (1) the Visitation; (2) the Nativity; (3) the Shepherds and their flocks; (4) and (5) the Magi—one beardless, the others bearded; (6) the Presentation in the Temple—Plate 88, Fig. 1; (7) the Flight into Egypt; (8) the Baptism of Christ. In the jambs are majestic figures which resemble those of the cathedrals of Verona and Cremona not only in the technique of their execution, but in the subjects represented and even in the inscriptions on the scrolls. First, Saint Daniel, S[ANCTVS] DANIEL (Plate 89, Fig. 4), with a scroll bearing the inscription:

DIC| S[ANCTVS] DA|NIEL . DE| CRISTO| Q͞D NO|STI C͞V VE|N͞ERIT IN|
QD S͞ SCO͞|RV͞ CESSAB|[IT] HVNCCIO| VESSTRA [51]

Near Daniel is Jeremiah, GEREMIAS, with a broken scroll, of which only a fragment of the inscription survives, but enough to make it clear that it was similar to the inscription of the Jeremiah at Cremona:

✚| ECCE| INQ'D| DEVS. . . . .[52]

---

[50] Compare Ezec., i, 15.

[51] *Contra Judæos, Paganos et Arianos*, ed. Migne, *Pat. Lat.*, XLII, 1124; Dan., ix, 24.

[52] See above, p. 386. *Contra Judæos, Paganos et Arianos*, ed. Migne, *Pat. Lat.*, XLII, 1123; Bar., iii, 36-37.

The upper figure in the left jamb is Gabriel, S[ANCTVS] GABRIEL, with a scroll:

✠| A|VE MA|RIA GRA|CIA PLE|NA . DO|MINVS| TECVM| BENE|DICTA| TV IN| M͡VLIE|RIBVS

Opposite is the Virgin, S͞CAMA MARIA, with the inscription below:

ECCE A͡NCILLA D͞N͞I

The lower figure on the right-hand jamb is Isaiah, YSAIAS, who bears a scroll:

✠| EC|CE| VIR|GO C͞O|CIPI|ET ET| PARI|ET FI|LIVM| ET
VO|C͡ABITV͞R . . . . . [53]

On one of the outer jambs on the right-hand side is Ezekiel, EZEKIEL, with a scroll on which is the inscription:

✠VI|DI POR|TAM IN| DOMO| DOMI|NI CL|AVS͞A [54]

It is evident that these sculptures represent the Annunciation and the four major prophets who had foretold that event. The portal contains besides these serious figures numerous grotesques, among which one represents a wolf in a priest's cassock holding a book.[55] On the book is the satirical inscription in the vernacular, "ABC for Heaven":

ABC POR CEL

Other reliefs represent a devil sitting on a dog, a devil fiddling, and a seated person with Phrygian cap playing the harp (Plate 88, Fig. 2).

According to a manuscript of the XVIII century now preserved in the Biblioteca dell'Università at Ferrara,[56] there was formerly to be seen *sopra la porta laterale sinistra* the inscription:

Emitte manum tuam de alto, eripe me
Et libera me de Aquis multis.[57]

Stylistically Nicolò's sculptures at Ferrara present numerous points of contact with the work of Guglielmo da Modena. The similarity in the treatment of the jambs and the figures of the prophets at Cremona and Ferrara

---

[53] *Contra Judæos, Paganos et Arianos*, ed. Migne, *Pat. Lat.*, XLII, 1123; Isai., vii, 14.

[54] Ezec., xliv, 1-2.

[55] This relief is very similar to one on the jambs of the cathedral of Verona (Plate 217, Fig. 2). See below, Vol. III.

[56] No. 305, f. 1. This MS. is by Girolamo Baruffaldi, and is entitled: *Iscrizioni antiche e moderne delle Chiese di Ferrara*.

[57] Ps., cxliii, 7.

can not be coincidence. It is to be noticed, moreover, that the inscriptions borne by the prophets are generally identical. The curious treatment of the beard which falls in curls denoted by little round holes at the end, a characteristic mannerism of Guglielmo da Modena, occurs in the right-hand caryatid of the Lombard porch at Ferrara and in several figures of the reliefs, notably the Jeremiah and the Isaiah. The cords of the feet are accentuated, but not so much as in the work of Guglielmo, and not always. The draperies of the Ferrara sculptures differ from those of Guglielmo da Modena—as, indeed, they do from those of Nicolò's own earlier work at Piacenza. On the other hand, the right-hand dwarf of the Lombard porch at Ferrara, is executed with a technique very similar to that of the Fraud in the relief of Jacob and the Angel at Modena (Plate 145, Fig. 1). The work of Nicolò is characterized by a lack of undercutting which, however, is not carried to the same extent as in the work of Guglielmo. The rinceau over the lunette at Ferrara (Plate 88, Fig. 1) recalls the rinceaux of Guglielmo at Modena. Nicolò evidently knew not only the work of Guglielmo, but that of several of his followers. The diapered ornament of one of the roll-mouldings of the Ferrara archivolt is precisely like one at Nonantola (Plate 155, Fig. 5). At Ferrara, however, the columns in relief are spiral and fluted. Nicolò is the artistic descendant of Guglielmo, but his work is far superior, and is characterized by greater feeling for space, by more architectural composition, and by better proportioned heads.

Comparing Nicolò's sculptures at Ferrara with his own earlier work at Piacenza, we perceive that at Ferrara the draperies are without the Japanese wave-like effect which is characteristic of the draperies in the Piacenza sculptures. The division of the architrave by blind arches is, however, similar at Ferrara and Piacenza (compare Plate 89, Fig. 5, and Plate 182, Fig. 4). Comparing the two in detail, we notice that at Ferrara the heads are not so disproportionately large as at Piacenza, and the eye-balls are not inlaid in another material.

Nicolò's art is perhaps seen at its best in the relief of the tympanum representing St. George (Plate 88, Fig. 1). The composition of this sculpture is admirable, as is also the execution. Motion is skilfully suggested, and the whole relief is full of a verve and dash which admirably express the characteristics of the warrior saint. Of the scenes in the architrave, the Visitation and the Flight into Egypt are the best. The others tend to be crude and restless in composition.

The sculptures of the second story of the western porch representing the Last Judgment are among the finest Gothic sculptures in Italy, but they fall without the limits of this book. The same may be said of the sculptures of the zodiac which come from the destroyed Porta dei Mesi. Six are now embodied in the façade of the cathedral, and the remaining six are preserved in the botanical garden of the University.

V. The sculptures of the west portal, when compared with the other known works of Nicolò, fully accord with the documentary evidence that they are a part of the cathedral which was erected in the years immediately preceding 1135. The remaining fragments of Romanesque architecture on the flanks of the cathedral are much later in style, and must be part of the building erected before the consecration of 1177.

FONTANELLA AL MONTE,[1] S. EGIDIO

(Plate 90; Plate 91; Plate 92; Plate 93, Fig. 1, 2, 3)

I. For the history of S. Egidio should be consulted primarily the collection of the charters of Cluny, published by Bernard, under the auspices of the French government. Important notices are also contained in the works of the local historians of Bergamo, especially those of Pellegrini, Calvi, Ronchetti and Locatelli. An account of the edifice is included in the *Grande Illustrazione*.[2] In recent years the church has been made the object of monographs by Sant'Ambrogio and Bianchi. The latter is of value for the account of the recent restoration which it contains.

II. According to a donation published by Bernard, the Cluniac priory of S. Egidio had already been begun in the year 1080. This donation was made by S. Alberto for the benefit of his soul and that of Teiperge, Isengarda and Giovanni.[3] S. Alberto is, of course, well known as the founder and first prior of the neighbouring Cluniac monastery of Pontida,[4] and as the zealous promoter of the Cluniac order in Lombardy. As for the Teiperga mentioned in the document, she is undoubtedly the same as the nun Teutperga, who is recorded in an ancient calendar of the church of Bergamo, published by

---

[1] The frazione of Fontanella al Monte lies on the mountain side known as Sotto il Monte, and may be reached from Mapello by a steep road, only the first part of which is practicable for carriages. Provincia di Bergamo.

[2] V, 967.

[3] Anno ab incarnacione Domini nostri Jesu Christi millesimo octuagesimo, terciodecim[o] die mensis januarii, indictione tercia, monesterio Sancti Petri qui dicitur de Cluniaco. Ego Albertus, filius quondam Ariprandi, qui fuit de loco Presiate, qui professus sum ex nacione mea lege vivere Longobardorum, offertor et donator ipsius monasterii . . . dono et offero pro anime mee et Teiperge et Isengarde seu Johanni mercedem: hoc est pecia una de terra in qua edificium est inceptum ad monasterium faciendum, in‑honore sancti Egidii, et omnia que ad ipso monasteri pertinent juris mei, quam habere visus sum in loco Monte qui dicitur Vergese; et jacet allocus qui dicitur Fontanella. . . . Actum foris civitate Laude, infra monesterio Sancti Marci, feliciter. (Bernard, IV, 675).

[4] See below, Vol. III.

FONTANELLA AL MONTE, S. EGIDIO

Finazzi,[5] as having died on the first of October. In a document of 1308, published by Ronchetti, Teutberga (or Toperga as she is here called) is named as the foundress of the monastery, and it is stated that lamps were kept burning before her tomb.[6] In the course of time Teutperga came to be confused with the Teutperga who was the wife of Lothair II. The foundress of the monastery assumed a mythical character, and came to be revered as a saint by the monks and populace of Fontanella. This cult was suppressed by S. Carlo as idolatrous, and at his order the tomb of Teutperga was removed from the church and placed in the cloister, where it may still be seen. Modern historians, overlooking the deed of 1080 we have cited above, have puzzled much as to who was this Teutperga, and when the monastery of Fontanella was founded.[7]

The new church was consecrated in the year 1090. This is stated by Pellegrini, who merits faith in this particular, although he adds singularly confused notices in regard to Teutperga.[8] Calvi repeats that the church was consecrated in 1090, on the ninth of April, and states that he had seen a cross on one of the altars inscribed with this year.[9]

[5] Kal. Oct. Obiit Teutberga monaca. (404).

[6] Et quinque psalterios inter quos est unum qui dicitur fuisse dominæ S. Topergæ Matris nostræ et Fundatrix suprascripti Monasterii . . . . . et duos calices argenteos deauratos quos calices fecit fieri dictus D. Prior et degostaverunt libras viginti aut plus, et duo turribula . . . et apud sepulcrum Beatæ Topergæ sunt octo lampades de quibus ardent continuæ de nocte et de die duæ, et omnes ipse lampades ardent semper ad missam et ad matutinum et ad vesperas de duodecim lectionibus. . . . Et in sex festis principalibus continue semper ardent duodecim cerea . . . quid apud sepulcrum Beatæ Virginis Topergæ in missa, laudibus et vesperis. (Ronchetti, IV, 250).

In the margin of the copy in the Bergamo library is written: Questo documento trovasi ora nella civ. Bibl. tra le carte Femi, No. 63.

[7] Of all the attempts to explain Teutperga, the most grotesque is that of Lucchini (59), who fabricated an entire myth to explain her connection with the church.

[8] In huius locum ingressus est Arnulphus, qui hanc vineam Simoniace rexit annis.18.mensibus.11.diebus.16. Hic anno.Domini.1090.consecravit ecclesiam abbatiæ.s. Iacobi puntidæ ordinis. s. Benedicti, & ædem abbatiæ. s. Egidii de fontanella eiusdem ordinis, . . . Hæc ex historia dicti Concilii [of Milan], & ex antiquis libris Bergomi, & ex dicto memoriali Episcoporum Bergomensiū (Pellegrini, 7). Operatus est in hac vinea Albertus sanctissimus ciuis Bergomensis, monasterii puntide.S.Iacobi fundator, & multū hanc.vineam diuersis bonis operibus excoluit, huius teporibus diuina illa mulier Toperga nomine, Lotarii gallorū regis vxor, ex gallia Bergomum venit, allecta sanctitate ipsius San.Alberti suis exhortationibus, quæ & ipsa plurimum in vinea hac laborauit, inter cætera vero ecclesiam, & monasterium. S. Egidii de fontanella ædificari fecit, ac dotauit, & tandem anus obiit in domino anno salutis.1047.ibiq; sepulta est in claustro illius monasterii decimo Klendas augusti postquam.S.Albertus iam annosus ad cœlestia regna migrauit anno redemptionis nostræ.1095.& in monasterio diui Jacobi tumulatus est Klendis Septembris. Hæc ex analibus, & diurnalibus ipsius abbatiæ.s.Iacobi de putida, & ex eius historia ascripta in lib.4.de antiq[ui]tatibus, & gestis diuorū Berg. (Pellegrini, 20).

[9] L'antichissima Chiesa di Fontanella . . . in questo giorno rammemora ne Diuini Officij la sua dedicatione. . . . Ad vno di detti Altari è vna Croce, che tiene in vna

In 1095 Fontanella was included among the other Cluniac priories of northern Italy confirmed to the abbot of abbots by Urban II.[10] In this document the priory appears dependent upon S. Gabriele of Cremona.[11] The new priory is mentioned again in a document of 1096,[12] and in an inedited donation of 1101.[13] Still another document of 1103 contains the phrase *Ecclesie & monasterio S. Egidii que est edificata in honore ejusdem Sancti in monte qui dicitur Verzinimus ibi ubi nominatur Fontanella.*[14] Fontanella appears among the priories confirmed to Cluny by Honorius II in 1125.[15] In 1308 there were in the monastery twelve monks beside the abbot,[16] but in 1350 there were only six monks.[17]

It appears that in 1368 the cure of souls in the church depended on the chapter of Bergamo.[18] In 1472 the existing tomb of Teutperga was executed, as is indicated by this date inscribed on one of the capitals above it. The figures are quite clear, but they were misread as 1579 by Sant'Ambrogio, and as 1419 and 1479 by Locatelli.[19] In the following year, 1473, the abbey was given in commendam.[20] In 1525 the priory was united with that of S. Giacomo of Pontida.[21] In 1604 the roof was rebuilt and the windows remade. Bianchi believes that the vaults of the campanile were first erected in 1618,[22] but in this he is certainly mistaken. In 1631 it was proposed to raise the tower.

From 1910 to 1912 a restoration of the edifice was carried out under the direction of Bianchi, thanks to which the church has lost both its picturesque charm and its archæological interest. Of all the unfortunate restorations

gioia questo millesimo ICXC., & fuori della Chiesa in picciol chiostro alla stessa Chiesa congionto è vn antichissimo Sepolcro, in cui giace la Regina Teutperga, fondatrice di questa Chiesa, . . . altri due chiostri quasi distrutti sono a questo primo vniti. (Calvi, I, 414).

[10] S. Gabrielis de Cremona cum cellis suis quae sitae sunt in Castro Fontanellae, Trigulo, Grumello etc. (Tomassetti, II, 158).

[11] It appears in a document published by Bernard (IV, 596) that the priory of S. Gabriele of Cremona was founded in 1079 by *Albertus filius quondam Adami, qui dicitur de Fontanella et Imilda jugalibus.*

[12] Ronchetti, II, 229.

[13] . . . Anno dominice incar. mill. centesimo primo mense octubris indic. decima. Ego adelaxia relicta qdam arderici . . . dixi . . . ut de terra aratoria . . . reiacenti in loco et fondo garbaniate, qui est prope locum badaglum . . . deueniat in iure et proprietate ecclesiarum sancti ambrosii que dicitur ad corpus, et sancti iohannis que dicitur ad quattuor facies de ciuitate mediol. et sancti iacobi de pontida, et sancti egirii, que est aedificata in monte prope monasterium ipsius sancti iacobi. (*Codice della Croce*, MS. Amb. D. S. IV, V, f. 11).

[14] Lupi, II, 842.   [15] Tomassetti, II, 352.   [16] Ronchetti, II, 230.

[17] Prioratus S. Egidij de Fontanella, Bergomensis dioc. vbi debent esse iuxta diffinitionem anni 1350. Priore computato, sex Monachi, & fit ibi eleemosyna, & erat augmentata dicta eleemosyna anno 1321. secundum relationem Prioris & Cellerarij, de quindecim sommis bladi. (Marrier, 1745).

[18] Ronchetti, V, 89.   [19] III, 224.   [20] Bianchi, 14.   [21] Bianchi, 14.   [22] 14.

carried out in northern Italy in recent years, I know of none which has been so ill-advised, so destructive, and so barbarous as that of the church of Fontanella. Although the changes wrought were in reality comparatively slight, it is singular how the modern architect has contrived to pick out those portions of the old edifice which were most interesting artistically and archæologically, to spoil by modernization, and how he has contrived to ruin absolutely the beauty and picturesqueness of the whole. Monstrous pseudo-Romanesque altars, models of all that is ugly, have been erected so as to cover the beautiful remains of frescos in the interior. The Madonna of the priceless polyptych was completely ruined as the result of incompetent cleaning carried out during this restoration. The mediæval brick vaults of the campanile were destroyed as too heavy, and new ones erected. The cone and turrets of the campanile were restored on the basis of some fragments of the old triforia found near the church. One of the piers under the campanile was renewed, and the upper central part of the façade was entirely remade. Three windows in the south wall were remade, as well as the upper part of the side-aisle wall internally. I am happy to be able to reproduce a photograph (Plate 93, Fig. 3) which shows the beautiful old monument as it was when I first knew it, when its charm and softness were still unspoiled by the restorers.

III. The edifice consists of a nave six bays long (Plate 90; Plate 91; Plate 92; Plate 93, Fig. 2), two side aisles, a choir of one bay flanked by side aisles, three apses (Plate 93, Fig. 1), and a central tower (Plate 93, Fig. 1, 3). The four western bays of the nave and the side aisles are roofed in timber (Plate 92), but the two eastern bays of the nave beneath the central tower are covered by a single groin vault (Plate 91; Plate 92; Plate 93, Fig. 2). The choir and its side aisles are groin-vaulted, and the principal apse is preceded by a short barrel vault (Plate 92). The groin vaults are all domed. Those beneath the tower and over the choir (Plate 93, Fig. 2) are constructed without wall or transverse ribs; but those of the choir side aisles have wall ribs on three sides much loaded at the crown, but disappearing at the springing. The supports of the nave are all columns (Plate 90; Plate 92) except a pair of heavy piers introduced to support the central tower. The choir is separated from the nave by a solid wall, in which are pierced arches opening into the three aisles (Plate 91). It is much lower than the nave, and the transverse wall facing the side aisles of the nave is ornamented with arched corbel-tables (Plate 91).[23] It is evident that the choir is earlier than the remainder of the edifice, and belonged to a single-aisled church with projecting transepts and three apses.

[23] The arched corbel-tables are in two orders on the south side, in one order on the north side. These corbel-tables, as well as the arches opening into the side aisles of the choir from the nave, were completely denatured in the recent restoration, but I was fortunate in seeing the building before it had lost its original character.

The transept-ends of the old church ended in gables adorned with a raking cornice of arched corbel-tables, which still exist, though in part covered by modern constructions. The southern wall was entirely remade in the Renaissance, when it was raised. It may have been the original intention of the builders to erect a clearstory in the nave, but the masonry of the tower roof shows that the nave walls never rose higher than they do at present.

In the southern side-aisle wall and in the façade are preserved original windows which were widely splayed and intended to serve without glass. It is probably because no glass was used that windows were omitted in the northern wall and in the clearstory. The window of the southern side-aisle wall has an arcuated lintel, with a stone joint in the centre.

The masonry of the apses is ashlar rather roughly laid. The stones are of odd sizes, and the horizontal courses are not preserved (Plate 93, Fig. 1). The masonry of the nave, on the other hand, is much finer and better where the original is still preserved, that is to say, in the north and west façades and the clearstory. In the south wall a distinct break in the masonry is visible at the point where the new side-aisle walls join the old transept. Bricks are used to form the arched corbel-tables of the apse.

South of the church are the remains of the cloisters. According to Calvi there were once three different cloisters.

IV. The choir shows great poverty of ornament in the interior. There are no carved capitals, but merely imposts, for the most part of the simplest character, although on several are scratched crude patterns, scrolls, inverted letters, etc. The latter motive reappears on the archivolt of the apse externally. The exterior of the apse (Plate 93, Fig. 1) is more richly ornamented with arched corbel-tables supported on shafts, diapering or billets on or about the archivolts of the windows, and a zigzag in relief in the cornice of the east gable (Plate 93, Fig. 1). This ornament recalls the campanile of Pomposa, Cosio, and the cathedral of Acqui (Plate 2, Fig. 5).

The capitals of the nave (Plate 93, Fig. 2), on the other hand, are of advanced type, with broad flat leaves and dry volutes that savour strongly of French influence. Two of the capitals are evidently ancient Corinthian, pilfered from some Roman monument. The Attic bases are supplied with griffes. The archivolts are in a single unmoulded order. Many traces of the ancient arched corbel-tables of the side-aisle walls still exist, and some of the original corbel-tables of the façade, surmounted by a saw tooth, may be studied in the photographs (Plate 93, Fig. 3). The corbel-tables of the side aisles were carried on broad, flat pilaster strips.

The interior walls were once covered with frescos. Interesting fragments of the XV and XVI centuries still survive.

V. The choir and apses may be considered an authentically dated monument of 1080-1090. On the other hand, the vault of the choir, the campanile and the nave evidently belong to a later reconstruction of the edifice. The capital with lobes is very analogous to one at S. Giorgio of Almenno, an edifice of c. 1120. The masonry of Fontanella, however (Plate 93, Fig. 3), is more advanced than that of S. Giorgio (Plate 11, Fig. 5, 7). This and the distinctly French character of certain capitals seem to indicate a date later than 1120. The nave may therefore be ascribed to c. 1130.

FORNOVO TARO,[1] S. MARIA ASSUNTA

(Plate 94, Fig. 1, 2)

I.   The pieve or badia, as it is sometimes called, of Fornovo is known for its sculptures, which have been described by Toschi[2] and Molossi.[3]   A critical study has been contributed by Zimmermann,[4] and Venturi[5] has published excellent illustrations.

II.   The church is mentioned in 879 in a document relating to a controversy between the church and S. Pietro of Varzi.[6]   It is certain, therefore, that the church existed at least as early as the last quarter of the IX century. It is said that at one time it was officiated by Knights Templar, but authentic documents in regard to this are lacking.[7]   The Piacentini destroyed a town of Fornovo—probably Fornovo Taro—in 1151.[8]   The campanile was erected in 1303.[9]   I have been able to find no other notices which throw light upon the architectural history of the edifice.

III.   The church consists of a nave five bays long, two side aisles, an apse, and an interior narthex (Plate 94, Fig. 1) of three aisles two bays long. The side aisles are at present covered with modern groin vaults, the nave with a modern barrel vault.   The nave was probably originally much higher than it is at present, since it is obvious that the old clearstory has been rebuilt. The second story of the narthex now forms the residence of the priest.   About the church there are several chapels, a sacristy, accessory rooms, etc.   The piers of the nave are rectangular in section, with a semicircular shaft engaged to carry the second order of the archivolts.   There is no system.   The church gives the impression of being an older structure than the narthex, the aisles of which do not correspond with those of the nave.   However, the church itself is so covered with intonaco and is so denatured that it is impossible to reconstruct the ancient forms.

At first glance the suspicion arises that originally the narthex may have been exterior, not interior, since the existing façade is entirely modern, and appears to have been built between, and in front of, the old arches.   The existence of an old window in the façade, however, proves that the narthex

---

[1] (Parma).   [2] 18.   [3] 146.   [4] 158.   [5] III, 138-139.   [6] Curati.
[7] Molossi, 146.   [8] Affò, II, 204.   [9] Molossi, 146.

must always have been enclosed. The narthex is entirely covered with highly domed groin vaults erected on plans approximately square (Plate 94, Fig. 1).

IV. The capitals of the nave are cubic, with an angular cushion. Those of the narthex are more interesting. One of cubic type, with a shallow cushion and a deep bell, strongly resembles the capitals of Vicofertile. Another of Corinthianesque type with uncarved acanthus leaves is almost Norman in character (Plate 94, Fig. 1), and recalls the capitals of S. Bernardo of Vercelli (Plate 215, Fig. 2), although the execution is obviously more advanced. Still another has very naturalistic Gothic crockets. Others are figured or adorned with grotesques.

The transverse arches of the narthex are in two orders (Plate 94, Fig. 1). The apse was adorned externally with simple arched corbel-tables, some of which are still extant.

On one of the capitals of the west portal is represented a centaur shooting his bow. On the back of the centaur is seated another figure holding a bunch of arrows. On another capital a seated man grasps the hand of a seated devil. Another man seated by the first places his hand on his arm. This scene almost suggests the Faust legend. On the capitals of the interior of the narthex is shown the story of Adam and Eve. The influence of Benedetto's capitals at Parma is clearly shown in that Adam and Eve are clothed and sit on a bench beneath the tree on which coils the serpent. On another capital a donkey strums a harp, while a man plays the viol. A man and a woman dance.

At the north end of the façade are embedded two caryatids. Below are shown two men naked except for a waist-cloth, with arms about each other's necks, their heads turned away. They appear to be wrestling. On either side are suspended in mid air two strange objects, possibly torches. The significance of this strange relief entirely escapes me. On the same stone, but around the corner, are depicted two prophets, with bare feet and bearded. One holds his hand to his head in an attitude of meditation, the other holds a scroll and raises his right hand, palm outward.

In the angles of the narthex to the west, internally, are two sculptured figures. One with crown and sceptre must be David. The other must be an archbishop—S. Ambrogio?—since he is vested in mitre and pallium, and carries a crosier. This statue is placed in a niche.

A strange sculpture in the façade (Plate 94, Fig. 2) is usually said to represent the seven capital sins, but more likely is merely a representation of the torments of Hell. The relief is of a strange trapezoidal form, the reason for which is not clear. It does not appear to be in its original position, and may possibly have formed part of the altar or a tympanum of which the slab with the life of S. Margherita in the narthex was another part; but if so, it is difficult to see why it should have had a trapezoidal form or how it could have fitted in with the subjects of the other sculptures. The reliefs represent various torments of the damned. In the centre is a miser in a seated position, with three bags of gold tied about his neck. One devil pulls his teeth. Another places a heavy load in the shape of his account book on his shoulders. To the left are seen the jaws of the dragon, from which emerge the heads of sinners who are being devoured by reptiles. A flying devil brings a newly arrived soul to thrust him into the torments. To the right others of the damned are seen boiling in cauldrons. Two devils below blow the fire with bellows, and two above push the sinners down into the boiling pitch. In the extreme upper left-hand corner are seen two newly arrived souls, naked and chained together, falling down into the abyss, and awaiting attention from the devils. Both in the subject and in the treatment this relief is unlike anything I know in Lombardy, but recalls vividly the sculptures of Moissac (Plate 94, Fig. 5).

On the inside of the narthex, in the north wall, is a sculptured plaque, with the legend of S. Margherita. Molossi states[10] that these sculptures originally formed the pallio of the high altar, from which they were removed in 1831. The sculptor appears to have followed a version of the life of the saint which is unknown to me. Of the versions to which I have had access he follows most closely that published by the Bollandists, but he has shown one scene which is found only in the life published by Mombritius, and one which occurs only in the Greek apocryphal Acts, referred to by the Bollandists. The subjects begin in the upper right-hand corner, and follow first downward, then to the left. They are as follows: According to the life published by the Bollandists, S. Margherita was the daughter of a certain very powerful man, chief priest in the temple of the idols, and called Aedesio. He gave his daughter, Margherita, to be brought up by a nurse in the country outside of his city of Antioch. From the nurse Margherita learned Christianity. When Aedesio heard this, he hated his daughter and drove her away from him, but Omnipotent God, who never deserts those who hope in Him, made Margherita so pleasing in the sight of her nurse that the latter loved her almost as her own child, and Margherita, since her father had rejected her, in all ways became attached to her nurse and mistress, and even watched her sheep for her, and did not scorn to go to the pasture with the other maidens. While she was engaged in so pasturing them one day, the prefect Olibrius happened to be coming to Antioch to superintend a persecution of the Christians. As he was passing along, he saw S. Margherita walking in the pasture among the sheep.[11] In the relief is shown the saint, bare-headed and holding a staff, standing beneath a tree. On the other side of the tree are

---

[10] 146.

[11] Hæc denique Virgo erat filia cujusdam viri, nomine nominati Aedesii, admodum potentissimi. . . . Hic ita filiam suam valde diligens, dedit eam nutriendam procul a civitate sua scilicet Antiochia. . . . Insuper abominatus est eam ac repulit. Sed Dominus omnipotens, qui numquam deserit sperantes in se [Judit., xiii, 7] . . . in tantum illam amabilem fecit suæ nutrici, ut quasi uterinam filiam eam diligeret. . . . Et quoniam

her flocks, consisting of sheep and goats. Still further to the left is seen Olibrius, bare-headed, holding a sceptre, and standing in front of a throne. The latter detail shows that he is represented, not as passing by Margherita on his journey to Antioch, but as already arrived in the city and meditating upon the plans suggested him by his lust for the beautiful maiden.

The life of the Bollandists goes on to tell us that Olibrius, overcome by desire, ordered his ministers, saying: Go and seek diligently for that maiden. If she is a free woman I will very gladly marry her. If, however, she is of servile condition, I will pay a just price for her, and she shall be my concubine. The ministers, moreover, went very quickly to perform the order of their master, and they took the maiden and brought her to him.[12] The second scene to the extreme right of the lower row of reliefs represents the two messengers of the king coming to the saint. Margherita raises her hands in dismay. "When the blessed virgin was taken by the impious men, she was struck with terror and fear, and not unmindful of feminine frailty, she commenced to be greatly terrified, and especially because of the atrocious torments which at that time were being inflicted on Christians by the impious."[13]

The soldiers came with the maiden to the prefect, and as soon as they had presented themselves, said: The maiden confesses that she is a Christian. When the wicked judge heard this, he was heavy at heart, but ordered Margherita to be brought before him. When she had come into his presence, he began to speak to her and try to persuade her first by promises, and then by threats, to renounce the Christian religion.[14] The life published by the

pater suus eam exhorrens procul ejecerat, ita in omnibus suæ famulabatur nutrici, atque magistræ, ut etiam illius oviculas custodiret, et ad pascendum cum ceteris puellis educere non dedignaretur. Pascebat autem eas cum omni humilitate, et mansuetudine: sicut illa quondam Rachel, mater patriarchæ Joseph, puella humilis et decora, patris sui oves humiliter custodiebat. Interea quidem præfectus, nomine Olibrius, crudelitate et impietate tumidus, veniebat de Asia, in Antiochiam propter persecutionem Christianorum. Qui cum iter ageret, contigit, ut videret beatam Margaretam deambulantem in passu ovium.

[12] Quamobrem concupiscentia superatus præses jussit ministris suis, dicens: Ite quantocius et diligenter inquirite puellam illam. Si libera est, amantissime eam in conjugio sociabo; si autem servitutis conditione ritenetur annexa, dignum pretium pro ea tribuam; et erit in concubinali jure sociata. Illi autem celerius euntes, suique domini jussionem facientes, comprehenderunt illam, cursuque concito reversi, perduxerunt ad præsidem.

[13] Cum autem duceretur beata Virgo ab impiis, terrore et timore contrita, utpote femineæ fragilitatis non immemor, vehementissime formidare cœpit; maximeque propter atrocitatem et incendia pœnarum, quæ tunc crudeliter ab impiis ingerebatur. . . .

[14] Pervenerunt cum ea milites ad præfectum; statimque præsentati dixerunt: . . . Puella . . . Christianam se esse profitetur. . . . Quibus auditis, nequissimus judex admodum contristatus, jusit eam suo conspectui velocius præsentari. Quæ cum præsentata fuisset, ita eam alloqui cœpit: O puella, omni deposita formidine narra mihi genus tuum, et utrum ancilla, an libera fueris, manifestius pande. Ad quem sacratissma Virgo respondit: . . . Famulam autem me domini mei Jesu Christi, ore et corde

Bollandists contains a long account of how the tyrant summoned an assembly of the people in an effort to break the courage of the saint by cross-examining her in the presence of many. The life published by Mombritius, however, says little of Olibrius' attempts to persuade Margherita to give up her religion, but lays emphasis upon his efforts to seduce her virginity. The source followed by the sculptor in the third scene of the relief must have resembled the Mombritius legend. Olibrius and Margherita are shown alone together. The prefect holds a sceptre in his right hand, his left hand is raised in an amorous gesture. Margherita turns her back to him, and raises her hand in blank refusal.

The version published by the Bollandists then narrates: "When the prefect heard these things, he was furious, and ordered the saint to be hung by her head and cruelly flogged with whips. The servants, thereupon, obeying his wicked orders, so whipped her tender and holy body, that her blood like a fountain inundated the ground."[15] Here, again, it is apparent that the sculptor is following a version of the legend which is slightly different. Before the scene of the flagellation he has inserted another in which the saint is shown stripped to the waist, with her hands tied, standing before the grill of her prison, to which she seems to be fastened by a kind of cord. One of the servants of Olibrius stands before her with his hands raised in a gesture of astonishment. The scene possibly represents an unsuccessful attempt made upon the chastity of the saint while she was in prison. The scene of the flagellation follows to the left in the same row. The saint is tied, not by her head, as the life would have it, but by her two wrists to a sort of ladder. She is naked to her waist, and an executioner is engaged in flogging her with a cat-of-nine-tails. Olibrius, holding a sceptre, stands to the left, and raises his left hand with a gesture of approval.

The life of the Bollandists goes on to tell us that the angry prefect ordered the martyr to be suspended on a wooden rack, and her holy limbs to be torn with sharp hooks. The executioners carried out the orders of the tyrant, and tore her holy members until they came to the secret parts of her belly, and they laid open her intestines and they shed her blood, so that all the bystanders were shocked at the cruelty. The saint, however, counted all these torments as nothing.[16] In our relief the saint is shown entirely nude,

profiteor. . . . Hæc ubi dicta sunt, præses nimio furore accensus, Dei famulam in tenebroso concludi carcere præcepit. . . . Cum autem videret præfectus, quod nullis blandimentis, nullisque terroribus eam posset a Christi intentione revocare, cœptum iter arripiens, profectus est Antiochiam.

15 Audiens hæc præses furibundus, jussit eam a capite suspendi, et virgis crudeliter cædi. Apparitores autem nefaria jussa complentes ita tenerrimum ac sanctissimum corpus ejus verberabant, ut sanguis ejus veluti fons inundaret super terram. . . .

16 Tunc indignatus præses jussit Christi Martyrem in eculeo suspendi atque sacratissimos ejus artus acutissimis ungulis laniare. Carnifices autem tyrannica jussa

tied by her wrists to a sort of wooden scaffolding. Two executioners are tearing her belly with pronged forks.

According to the acts published by the Bollandists, S. Margherita, after these torments, was shut up in prison, where the devil attempted to terrify her by a thousand arts.[17] About this trial by the devil, however, the acts published by Mombritius are more explicit. "And behold suddenly from the corner of the prison came out a horrible dragon all gilded with many colours. . . . From his nostrils issued fire and smoke, and he panted with his tongue, and he made a stench in the prison, and then gliding into the middle of the prison he hissed, and a light was made in the prison by the fire which came out from his mouth, and after S. Margherita had prayed, the dragon opened his mouth and put it over her head, and he reached out his tongue to her feet, and with a gulp he swallowed her into his belly. But the cross of Christ which S. Margherita had made for herself broke in the mouth of the dragon and divided him into two parts, and S. Margherita came out from the belly of the dragon without having suffered any hurt."[18] The last scene of the lower row shows this the most famous episode of the life of S. Margherita. The dragon is shown simultaneously swallowing the saint, whose skirt and feet emerge from his mouth, and bursting in the middle. The saint released from his belly, kneels upon his back and clasps her hands in the attitude of prayer. To the extreme left emerges a hand holding a cross, presumably that which burst the dragon. Below is seen a devil.

The life published by Mombritius goes on to tell us: "And behold! in that very hour she looked to the left and saw another devil seated, like a

complentes, cum acerrime sancta membra laniarent pervenerunt usque ad secreta ventris, et patefactis visceribus effusoque cruore, cunctis astantibus crudelissimum videbatur. . . . Sancta autem . . . has tormentorum pœnas pro nihilo ducebat. . . .

[17] Sed paganissimi homines . . . jusserunt illam carceralibus tenebris iterum mancipari. . . . Hæc et his similia B. Margareta dum mundi Salvatorem laudans exoraret, ecce, caput nequitiæ cum mille nocendi artibus . . . illam terrificare aggressus est. Quippe in draconis specie apparens, se in diversas formas transtulit, atque ex ore simul et naribus ignem teterrimum evomens, Dei famulam vorare nitebatur. The saint thereupon puts him to flight by the sign of the cross. But the devil returns undismayed. Namque habitu calcaneo tenus criniti hominis apparens, horribilemque se præferens vultu, nova fraude terrorem ingerere conabatur. (*Acta S. Margaritae seu Marinae*, ed. *Acta Sanctorum*, V, Julii die XX, 33).

[18] Et ecce subito de angulo carceris exivit draco horribilis, totus variis coloribus deauratus: . . . de naribus ejus ignis et fumus exibat: lingua illius anhelabat . . . et fœtorem faciebat in carcere. Traxit se in medium carceris, et sibilabat fortiter: et factum est lumen in carcere ab igne, qui exibat de ore draconis. *Et postquam orantem exhibuisset nugivendulus* S. Margaritam . . . draco ore aperto posuit os suum super caput ejus, et linguam suam porrexit super calcaneum ejus, et suspirans deglutivit eam in ventrem suum; sed crux Christi, quam sibi fecerat beata Margarita, crevit in ore draconis, et in duas partes eum divisit. Beata autem Margarita exivit de utero draconis, nullum dolorem in se habens.

black man having his hands tied to his knees."[19] Then follows a long dialogue between the saint and the devil, which ends with the disappearance of the latter. The apochryphal Greek Acts cited by the Bollandists, however, state that the saint turned about and finding an iron hammer began to beat the devil, and having put her foot upon his head she flogged his head and back.[20] This gives us the key to the general meaning, though not to all the details, of the last sculpture of our relief. The devil, with horns, wings and tail, is seen bound hand and foot, and is in a standing, or rather, a squatting, position. A heavy chain around his neck seems to hold him upright. The saint is vigorously flogging him with a whip of several lashes, instead of with the iron hammer described in the legend.

All the sculptures of the church are evidently the work of a single hand, and that of a crude imitator of Benedetto. This fact has been recognized by all critics who have studied the sculptures, and it is therefore hardly necessary to insist upon proofs. Were such needed, however, the perforations of the draperies, the treatment of the beards, the clinging garments, and the rosettes around the borders would be sufficient. A fact which seems to have escaped the critics, however, is the close resemblance of these sculptures with those of the porch of Moissac (compare Plate 94, Fig. 2, with Plate 94, Fig. 5). It is improbable that the sculptor of Fornovo himself was ever in France, and he must have derived this Languedoc influence through the medium of Benedetto. The sculptures of Hell are probably a copy of some lost work of Benedetto which, were it extant, would demonstrate his indebtedness to the sculptor of Moissac.

V. It is evident that the narthex and the sculptures are contemporary. From the circumstance that the latter are under the influence of the earlier works of Benedetto—especially of the Deposition relief in the Parma cathedral, the sculptures of Borgo S. Donnino, and the capitals of the Parma museum— while, on the other hand, they show no influence of his later works in the baptistery of Parma, I think it probable that the sculptures at Fornovo were executed before those of the baptistery of Parma, or at least before that building had been completed. The baptistery of Parma, we know, was begun in 1196, and the various other works of Benedetto, the influence of which is shown at Fornovo, were executed at different times between 1178 and 1196. The narthex and sculptures of Fornovo may consequently be ascribed to c. 1200. The church itself is earlier, but the remains are insufficient to warrant an ascription of date.

[19] Et ecce ipsa hora aspexit in partem sinistram, et vidit alium diabolum sedentem, ut homo niger, habensque manus ad genua, colligatas. (Mombritius, II, f. CIIIIv; new edition, 192).

[20] Sancta vero conversa, et inveniens malleum ferreum, verberare *victum a se diabolum* cœpit, ac pede collo ejus immisso, verberabat malleo caput ipsius ac tergum. (*Acta Sanctorum*, V, Julii die XX, 33).

FRASSINORO,[1] BADIA

I.   The fragments of Frassinoro have been published by Maestri.

II.   The abbey of Frassinoro was founded by Beatrice and Matilda, as is very explicitly stated in a passage of Donizone.[2] Donizone does not say in what year the foundation took place, but it must have been in, or shortly before, 1071, when Beatrice made a donation to the new monastery.[3] The abbey is mentioned in other documents of 1130[4] and 1164.[5] The abbey had already been given in commendam in 1454, and this event possibly took place as early as 1429. The church appears to have been destroyed about this epoch by a landslip. The commendatary abbots, however, continued to exist, and the title of abbey came to be transferred to the pieve. This was reconstructed in comparatively recent times, but fragments of ancient architecture still preserved in this building, and elsewhere at Frassinoro, and other localities of the vicinity, have been conjectured by Maestri to have belonged to the destroyed abbey. The campanile of the church was demolished some eight years ago.

III, IV.   Fragments which may be assumed to have come from the ancient abbey are preserved in the church of S. Maria Assunta in Frassinoro, in the canonica of that church, and in a peasant's house at Sera di Migno. The fragments which formerly existed at Cargedolo have now disappeared, having been sold to an antiquary.

The fragments in the church of Frassinoro consist of two capitals which serve as a holy-water basin; two others supporting the pediment above the altar in the northern absidiole; another in a sort of monument in front of the church, and a fragment of carving in the first pier from the west or the south side of the basilica.

The fragments in the canonica contain all told fourteen capitals, which, like those in the church, are of white marble. There is no indication that the abbey had compound piers. The small size of the extant capitals, which are carved with grotesques or acanthus leaves, and the character of the six small marble shafts that still survive, indicate that most of these fragments belonged to a crypt. Other fragments of bases, capitals and columns, evidently of much later date, probably belonged to a cloister.

To the cloister may also have belonged the two coupled capitals of Verona marble now at Sera di Migno. The colonnette of white marble in the same locality, on the other hand, probably comes from the crypt.

1 (Modena).
2 This has been cited above, under the Duomo Vecchio of Brescia, p. 200.
3 Tiraboschi, II, *Cod.,* 52.   4 *Ibid.,* III, *Cod.,* 3.   5 *Ibid.,* 42.

GALLARATE, S. PIETRO

V. Notwithstanding the documentary evidence that the abbey was founded in 1071, the capitals of the crypt seem to be somewhat later than this date. In style, they appear more advanced than do the earliest portions of the cathedral of Modena, which were erected between 1099 and 1106. These capitals may accordingly be ascribed to c. 1110. The capitals of the cloister seem analogous with those of the upper story of the cloister of the Celestini in S. Stefano of Bologna (Plate 25, Fig. 2), which date from c. 1180. The Frassinoro fragments may, therefore, be assigned to the same epoch.

GALLARATE,[1] S. PIETRO

(Plate 94, Fig. 3, 4)

I. Gallarate has been the subject of a monograph by Serafino Ricci. This work contains a bibliography of the numerous local illustrations of the church of S. Pietro, which consequently need not be repeated here.

II. No documents are known which throw light upon the early history of the church. Witnesses swore in 1493 that the church was surrounded by a cemetery, and that it had been used as a fortress by the men of Gallarate. At this time buildings had already been erected against the southern side of the edifice.[2] In the year 1500 the citizens of Gallarate used the church for their assemblies.

S. Carlo in 1570 visited the church, and ordered important restorations, most of which were promptly executed.[3]

---

[1] (Milano).

[2] Original document cited by Ricci, 22-23.

[3] The original documents published by Ricci (23) are as follows: "L'altar maggiore si trasporti appresso il muro et se li faccia sopra un solo scalino.

"Si stopino li doi finestroli che sono un per parte della Cappella Maggiore, et se li faccino due finestre grandi alla moderna con le invetriate et ferrate.

"Si levino via tutti li merli che restano sopra li tetti della Chiesa.

"La Chiesa tutta si cuopri col suo tetto convenientemente et si soffitti levandone gli archi et metterli delli tomeri [sic].

"Si faccino tre finestre per banda della Chiesa.

"La porta maggiore si riporti nel mezzo.

"Si faccia un occhio con una finestra per banda nel frontispizio.

"Si faccia il pavimento.

"La chiesa tutta si incrosti, et quando si potrà si depinga dove farà di bisogno. et la capella maggiore si accomodi di presente, come de sopra et si orni et depinga a spese del Preposto titolare come qua abasso, come egli spontaneamente ci ha promesso.

"Il medesimo Preposto spenda de presente circa l'ornamento di detta Chiesa tutti li frutti et redditi per lui da qui indietro goduti di quella pezza di terra, campo di pertiche 8, lasciata a questa Chiesa per il quondam Bernardo Lomeno a effetto di

A document of June, 1664, says of the church: *chorus sive oratorio ipsum recentiori forma et illustri opere constructum est nuper, reliquam* (sic) *vero Ecclesiae vetustum.*[4]

In 1902 a very radical restoration of the edifice was begun.[5] The barocco campanile and apse were demolished, as were also the buildings which had been built against the south-eastern wall. The apse, the eastern portion of the south wall and the façade were rebuilt in part according to the fancy of the restorers, in part according to indications of the original forms which came to light. The vaults of the interior of the edifice were replaced by a wooden roof, and the interior completely redecorated in very poor taste. From the colour of the stone it was evident, when I saw the edifice in June, 1913, that parts of the north cornice had also been remade.

III. The edifice consists of a single-aisled nave and an apse (Plate 94, Fig. 3, 4). The masonry consists of ashlar of good, but not of superlative, quality (Plate 94, Fig. 3). Fairly well squared blocks are laid in courses of varying width, the horizontality of which is frequently broken. The mortar-beds run from 1 to 1½ centimetres in depth. The upper part of the façade in brick (Plate 94, Fig. 3) is evidently modern.

IV. The façade (Plate 94, Fig. 8) is adorned with double arched corbel-tables, every second one of which is supported on a colonnette. The motive thus forms a sort of engaged gallery, which is treated not as a cornice

impiegar l'usufrutto circa la reparatione et ornamento di questa chiesa ad arbitrio dell'herede."

In una copia antica del verbale della visita del giugno 1570, in margine a varie delle *ordinationi* soprascritte, è aggiunta la parola *esseguito,* (sic) e precisamente in margine ai capoversi seguenti:

"L'altar maggiore si trasporti;
"Si stopino li doi finestroli;"
"Si levino via tutti li merli;"
"La chiesa tutta si cuopri col suo tetto. . . ."
"La chiesa tutta si incrosti."

In un documento senza data, ma certamente del 1570, o poco dopo, si legge che molte delle cose ordinate furono eseguite sotto questa forma:

"Per l'ordinatione della chiesa di S. Pietro sono eseguite le infrascritte cose: . . .
"Si è fatto solo una finestra senza invetriata;"
"L'altar maggiore si è trasportato verso il muro;"
"Li merli sono levati;"
"La chiesa è coperta et li archi sono levati;"
"Sono fatti tre oggi (occhi, cioè finestre, aperture) grandi verso il mezzodì et uno più grande a ponente;"
"La chiesa si è incrostata tutta."

[4] Ricci, 25.

[5] The condition of the edifice before this restoration is shown by a post-card in my possession and by two photographs published by Ricci (22, 27).

but as a band of decoration introduced in the middle of the façade (Plate 94, Fig. 3). On the southern flank there is similar ornamentation, but the colonnettes are placed under each corbel-table, instead of under every other one (Plate 93, Fig. 4). The southern façade is broken up into three divisions, by shafts which rise from the ground to the corbel-tables. These shafts receive capitals larger than those of the colonnettes (Plate 94, Fig. 3, 4). Above the engaged galleries on both the west and the south sides is a carved string-course decorated with rinceaux. On the south side, a similar cornice is also introduced below the gallery. The apse is a modern reconstruction, and hence need not be studied. The eastern gable and the northern flank have a cornice formed of double arched corbel-tables, surmounted by rinceaux. The northern flank is divided into three divisions by heavy buttresses. It is probable that these were erected to reinforce the transverse arches of the nave, destroyed by order of S. Carlo.

The capitals are Corinthianesque, of a broad-leaved type, or grotesque. They are characterized by a certain crudity and coarseness of execution, and by the lack of a sense of composition. Those of the west façade, entirely geometrical in type, are simpler and more tasteful, but have been much restored.

In the west façade are introduced two diamond-shaped windows which are moulded (Plate 94, Fig. 3). The apse windows also are elaborately moulded. These, it is true, have all been restored, but some old fragments show there was authority for the profiles. They appear to have had originally leaf ornaments. The base moulding of the edifice has something of a Gothic profile. Various bits of sculpture, inlaid here and there in the church, seem to be wholly grotesque, and are very crude in style.

On the southern wall are remains of ancient frescos.

V. The intersecting gallery of Gallarate is a feature paralleled in Lombard art, so far as I know, only in the destroyed façade of the narthex of Casale (Plate 47, Fig. 1), a monument which dates from c. 1150. The masonry and capitals of Gallarate seem, however, slightly less advanced than those of Casale. Our monument may, therefore, be ascribed to c. 1145.

GALLIANO DI CANTÙ,[1] BATTISTERO

(Plate 95; Plate 96, Fig. 1)

I. Annoni was the first archæologist to study and illustrate the baptistery of Galliano. He was followed by Garavaglio, who in 1884 and 1886 wrote two articles upon the edifice, valuable chiefly because they contain

[1] (Como).

an account of the restoration executed at that epoch. The building was illustrated by De Dartein,[2] and the architecture has been studied by Rivoira.[3]

II. Of the history of the baptistery nothing is known beyond what may be inferred from what has been said of S. Vincenzo.[4] Castiglione and Rivoira believed that they could distinguish the baptistery as well as the church in the famous fresco of Ariberto. If this be so, it would furnish documentary evidence that the baptistery was erected in 1007, but I confess that it seems to me difficult to draw such a weighty conclusion from the exceedingly doubtful evidence afforded by the fresco.

An archæological restoration of the baptistery was carried out in 1886, under the direction of Mariani. Beneath the altar were found traces of a mosaic pavement "similar to that of S. Vincenzo." Unlike the church itself, the baptistery was never desecrated. It was whitewashed between 1814 and 1830. In the time of Allegranza the baptistery possessed only one fresco, and Garavaglio believed that it was never adorned with more.

Sometime before 1893, coloured glass was placed in the lower windows, being restored on the authority of fragments found in the crypt of S. Vincenzo. The portal was remade and restored at this same epoch.

III. The edifice consists (Plate 95) of a rectangular central area from which open four semicircular niches. In the corners are free-standing piers. To the west of the edifice is an exterior narthex or porch (Plate 96, Fig. 1), and a gallery is constructed over the niches and in the thickness of the wall. The nave is surmounted by an octagonal cloistered dome, masked externally, and carried on squinches. Squinches are also used externally to thicken the wall in the angles and give extra room for the galleries. The gallery is supplied with highly domed groin vaults with transverse arches. They have been much modernized, but probably still retain the original form. The narthex also has a domed groin vault, without wall ribs. The entire interior has been much modernized, and appears to have lost in great part its original character. In the drum of the dome is pierced a clearstory of plain round-arched windows, except in the west side, where there is a biforum.

It is evident that the portico to the westward (Plate 96, Fig. 1) is a later addition. The masonry, although an imitation of that of the main body of the structure, is obviously of different character. When the portico was added, the large window in the gallery and the arched corbel-tables of the west façade (Plate 96, Fig. 1) were remade.

Some of the windows of the church were obviously intended to serve without glass, but others, on the contrary, are so large that they must have been glazed. The original altar is still preserved in the eastern niche of the gallery.

[2] 408. [3] 233. [4] See below, p. 441 f.

GALLIANO DI CANTÙ, S. VINCENZO

The masonry of the baptistery (Plate 96, Fig. 1) is similar to that of the church (Plate 99, Fig. 1), but is slightly more advanced in that the courses tend to be more horizontal.

IV.   On the east façade are original arched corbel-tables grouped two and two.   Those of the west façade (Plate 96, Fig. 1) were probably also grouped two and two, until the window of the gallery was added, when they were remade in their present form.   The archivolts are in a single unmoulded order.

V.   The baptistery is more advanced than the church, because the masonry is of slightly better quality, and because the arched corbel-tables are grouped two and two, whereas S. Vincenzo was adorned with blind arches (Plate 99, Fig. 1).   Since S. Vincenzo was dedicated in 1007, the baptistery may be ascribed to c. 1015.

GALLIANO DI CANTÙ,[1] S. VINCENZO

(Plate 96, Fig. 2, 3; Plate 97; Plate 98; Plate 99, Fig. 1, 2)

I.   In 1625 Castiglione included in his work upon the antiquities of Milan a dissertation upon S. Vincenzo of Galliano, and particularly upon the relics of S. Adeodato there preserved.   It was the opinion of that author that the S. Adeodato in question was the disciple of S. Simpliciano, who was baptized by S. Ambrogio and was supposed by Castiglione to have died at Milan and to have been buried in S. Vincenzo in Prato.   The relics, he believed, were translated thence to Galliano by Ariberto.   Castiglione, unfortunately, tells us but little of the church of Galliano as it was in his time.   Happily, however, the edifice was described in 1781 by Allegranza, in a letter which has been edited by Bianchi.[2]   This accurate account of the church as it was in 1760, when Allegranza saw it, and when as yet it had not suffered from neglect and ruin, is of the utmost importance.   Allegranza speaks of the church as consisting of three aisles four bays long, so that it is evident that in his time the southern side aisle had not yet been destroyed.   He speaks of the frescos which covered the walls up to the ceiling, but complains that those of the lower portions of the church, beneath the level of the arches, had been remade in German fashion (*al gusto teutonico*).   There follows a description of the choir, its balustrade and the pulpit.   The latter had a marble lectern, on the side of which was represented an eagle.   He says that the church was built of pagan remains, and that he had himself found two epitaphs in two of the pillars.   In the south-west corner of the nave rose a lofty campanile, and in front of the western portal appeared some pieces of wall which showed

[1] (Como).   [2] 193.

the form of the ancient quadrangular vestibule.[3] He gives a long and detailed description of the frescos of the church and of one in the baptistery—the only one then there extant,—an account extremely important for the careful study of these paintings, which have since been in part damaged and destroyed. Unfortunately, they had already suffered considerably, even in the time of Allegranza. After having described the frescos on the south wall of the clearstory at its east end, he speaks especially of the portrait of Ariberto which he saw on the south side of the apse. He says that the identity of Ariberto was clearly established by an inscription, and that he was evidently presenting both the church and the baptistery.[4] Allegranza goes on to speak of two Christian epitaphs in the pavement of the church,[5] and concludes with a résumé of the historical facts which he had gleaned from the 'Acts' of the pastoral visit of Cardinal Cesare Monti, made in 1640. From this we learn that S. Vincenzo of Galliano had in former times been a pieve and officiated by a chapter of eighteen canons, but in 1574 this number was reduced to ten by S. Carlo, who ordered that both the chapter and the dignity of pieve should be transferred to Cantù,[6] as was done in 1582.

For nearly a century the church of Galliano appears to have been neglected by archæologists. Then in 1872 appeared the monograph of Annoni. At this time the edifice had already been desecrated and in large part

[3] Nella Nave destra entrando sorge presso la Porta un alta Torre e fuori della stessa porta appariscono alcuni pezzi di muro, che abbastanza dinotano l'antico vestibolo in quadratura.

[4] A sinistra v'è una figura pure in piedi, ma senza nimbo, con tonsura e dalmatica che presenta la chiesa col Battistero, e sotto vi si legge ECCLESIA. La figura ha di dietro il nome ARIBERT . . . . . , e sotto e sopra questo nome vi sono delle lettere perdute, e più basso si legge chiarissimo   SVB
D
I
A
C

Sotto queste due figure è scritto HEC EST DOMVS DEI ET PORTA CAELI. E qui pure ricorre altro meandro foglioso, intrecciato di fiori frutti e uccelli; e sotti d'esso, un inscrizione a caratteri unciali presso che intieramente perduta:

ORNAT . . . . .
NATVM QVIA TE DECET ESSE PER VSVM: VIRTVS MVLTA
DI VEL . . . . .

[5] Perhaps those recently found by Monneret de Villard.

[6] 1. Che il Capo di Pieve in tal parte della diocesi Milanese era Galliano, oggi Canturio.

2. Che tal basilica era collegiata, e dedicata a S. Vincenzo Martire.

3. Che era offiziata da XVIII Canonici, i quali vi avevano d'intorno l'abitazione.

4. Che questi furono da S. Carlo ridotti al n. di X, i quali poi nella visita personale, che ivi fece l'anno 1574, ordinò che fossero in Canturio trasferiti; il che si eseguì nel 1582.

destroyed, but it had not yet suffered from restoration, so that the description of this author is important. He speaks of the pavement of the choir as being formed of bits of marble of different shapes and colours. He speaks of a flight of seven steps leading to the choir, and of the other flights of steps on either side of this, leading down into the crypt. Over the northern of these descending flights of stairs was the pulpit, with the marble lectern, on the side of which was an eagle. He speaks of the high tower over the south-western angle of the nave, and of the remains of the foundation of the ancient vestibule.[7] This sentence appears not to be the result of his own observation, but to have been copied verbatim from the letter of Allegranza, cited above. Such verbal similarity can not be the result of coincidence. He speaks of the stairways leading to the crypt as having been recently closed. He states that the southern side aisle had in his time been already destroyed (è ora distrutta). He asserts without proof that the baptistery and church were formerly united by a portico. The work is illustrated with a rather inexact coloured drawing of the crypt, a good drawing of the altar and a drawing of the façade showing the campanile, which was adorned with arched corbel-tables in its middle story.[8] The exterior wall of the façade was reinforced by heavy buttresses applied at the north end of the nave and opposite the north end of the campanile. Traces of these buttresses are still extant on the façade (Plate 96, Fig. 3), and it would be difficult to understand them were it not for the drawing of Annoni. In his plan, a large sacrato—the vestibolo of the text— appears as extending to the westward of the nave. The work also contains a drawing of the ambo which is shown still covered with frescos.

Barelli[9] spoke of the church very briefly and very inexactly. Romussi[10] reproduced the famous portrait of Ariberto. The architecture has been studied by Rivoira.[11] The papyri found in the altar have been published by Ratti, and a drawing of the church and baptistery is contained in the Grande Illustrazione.[12]

II. Two early Christian epitaphs, dating from 485 and 486, were found in fragments and pieced together by Monneret de Villard. These probably indicate that the church of Galliano existed at least as early as the V century. The papyri published by Ratti are believed by him to be at least as old as the VII century. They were found in the altar when the latter was demolished in the year 1801.

In the church of S. Paolo of Cantù, in the back of the high altar, is

[7] Nella nave destra entrando sorge presso alla porta un alta torre e fuori della stessa porta appariscono alcuni pezzi di muro che da noi rintracciati, abbastanza chiariscono l'antico vestibolo in quadratura.

[8] Traces of these are still extant in the façade (Plate 96, Fig. 3). The upper part of the façade and the campanile were evidently later than the rest of the edifice, perhaps of c. 1035.

[9] Not. Arch., 16.   [10] 383.   [11] 232.   [12] III, 1031.

imbedded an important inscription transferred thither from Galliano. This inscription records that on July 2, 1007, the church of Galliano was dedicated, and the body of S. Adeodato translated, together with the bodies of Ecclesio, Manifredo the presbyter, and Savino the deacon, which were found near the tomb of S. Adeodato. All this was done in the time of King Henry II, and of Ariberto of Antimiano, subdeacon of the holy church of Milan, and custode of the church of Galliano.[13]

This inscription has obviously been restored in modern times, but the correctness of the reading of the present stone is confirmed by a comparison with the copies of it made by Castiglione,[14] Bianchi,[15] Allegranza,[16] Annoni,[17] Puccinelli[18] and others. The original epitaph of Adeodato is preserved at Cantù on the other side of the altar. Those of Savino and Ecclesio have been recently found by Monneret de Villard. There can be little doubt that the early Christian tombs were discovered by Ariberto at Galliano by chance, in the excavations for his new church. Castiglione is consequently in error in supposing that they were transported from S. Vincenzo in Prato at Milan.[19]

However this may be, the inscription leaves no doubt that the church of S. Vincenzo at Galliano was dedicated in the year 1007. That it was constructed by Ariberto is proved by the fresco of the apse now in the Biblioteca Ambrosiana at Milan, but seen and described by Allegranza when it was still in its original position. In this Ariberto is seen offering a model of the church, in token that it had been constructed at his expense. This Ariberto is the famous archbishop of Milan who held office from 1018 to 1045, and is

[13]
✠ VI NO . IVL . TRANSLACĪO
S̄CĪ . A̅DODATI . ET DEDĪC ISTI'
ECLĒ . ET . IBI REQ[VI] . EXCV̄N̄T
IN PACE . B̄. M̄. ECCLESIVS . ET
MANIFREDVS PB̄RI SEV
SA . VINUS . DIA̅CₒS . Q[VI] FV̄ER
IN . VENTI . IUSTA . SEPUL
HCR̄U IPSIU' S̄CĪ . ADODA
ANNI D̄NĪ . DDVII IN̄DĪ . U
TEM̄P. DOMNI ARIBERTI DE
ANTIMIANO ET SUBDIACON
S̄CĒ . MEDIOLANESIS . ECLE
ET CUSTODIS . [I]STIUS ECLE
SEU . TEM̄P HĒRICI [RE]
GIS

[14] 130.   [15] 193.   [16] *De Sepulchris Christianis*, 12.
[17] Reproduction in altas.   [18] No. 107, 26.
[19] Rotta, *Cronaca*, 68, is, however, of the opinion that Ariberto found the bodies of Adeodato, Ecclesio, Manfredo and Savino at S. Vincenzo in Prato, and translated them thence to Galliano, and cites in confirmation a *Breviario, riveduto da S. Carlo.*

one of the most striking figures of Italian history in the first half of the XI century. He was born at Intimiano, which is only two kilometres distant from Cantù. It was hence natural that he should have been custode of Galliano, the pieve of his native district, some years before he became archbishop.

In a sort of tax-list published by Magistretti and dating from 1398, it appears that at the end of the XIV century S. Vincenzo of Galliano was officiated by twenty canons. It was the head of twenty-one chapels in addition to the two in the church. In the index of Goffredo da Bussero, it is stated that it was the head of twenty-nine churches and forty-nine altars.

At the end of the XVI century, as has been seen, the church lost its chapter of canons, and its dignity of pieve. From this time its importance declined until 1801, when the relics were translated, and the edifice desecrated.[20] Peasants' houses were erected in the church. About 1835 the campanile was demolished.[21] About 1869, carved slabs and an altar were removed to S. Abondio at Como,[22] and about the same period the portrait of Ariberto was removed to Milan by Gerolamo Calvi.

An archæological restoration of the church, which is still uncompleted, was begun in 1909. I visited the edifice in October, 1909, in April, 1910, in the fall of 1912, and in the spring of 1913, and was consequently able to observe the sad and disastrous changes wrought in the monument at this period. The plan which I publish (Plate 97) was made in 1910, under circumstances of peculiar difficulty, for the engineer Annoni, in charge of the restoration, steadfastly refused to permit measurements to be taken, and was even unwilling that I should visit the edifice. On the other hand it seemed highly desirable that some record should be kept of the building as it was before the important changes which were being carried out. Signor Covini accordingly made the plan for me as best he could, obtaining the measurements surreptitiously. As a result, the plan lacks that accuracy and careful workmanship which is highly desirable, but I nevertheless publish it as a record, however imperfect, of an edifice which has now undergone a complete transformation.

One good, it is true, has been brought about by the restoration, and that is that the edifice has been cleared of the peasants' houses with which it was formerly encumbered, and which made the study of the architecture confusing and, in fact, almost impossible. It is most bitterly to be regretted that the restorers were not satisfied with making the church available for study, but proceeded to many misleading and erroneous reconstructions. The masonry throughout has been entirely denatured. Compare, for example, the photograph (Plate 99, Fig. 1) made before the restoration, with Plate 99, Fig. 2, a photograph made after it. Nothing more glaringly new or more ugly could

[20] The order of desecration has been published by Ratti.
[21] Garavaglio.   [22] Clericetti, VII.

be imagined than the roofs which have been erected. The restorers made excavations to the west of the edifice to find the foundation walls of Allegranza and Annoni, but none came to light. The traces of the foundations of the two absidioles, however, were discovered. The barocco windows were removed, new pseudo-Romanesque windows were opened, and the clearstory was worked over. From all these changes the edifice emerged (Plate 96, Fig. 3), having lost all of its artistic and most of its archæological charm.

III. At present the edifice consists of a nave four bays long (Plate 97), a northern side aisle, two apses and a crypt. The southern side aisle, which undoubtedly existed, has been destroyed. Clear traces of the foundations of both the northern and southern absidioles are extant. The crypt extends only under the choir (Plate 98), which is raised considerably above the nave. The campanile formerly rose in the south-western corner of the nave, but it has been destroyed.

The restorers discovered that the foundations of the northern absidiole cut across the powerful buttress with which the choir was reinforced. It has been widely assumed in consequence that the church originally possessed a single aisle, and that in later times side aisles were added, arcades being pierced in the old outside walls. Such an idea is, however, preposterous. The masonry of the northern side-aisle wall is identical in character with that of the apse and of the clearstory. The clearstory of the nave is still extant (Plate 96, Fig. 3), which could not have existed had the church been originally of a single aisle. In the façade no break in the masonry is evident at the point where the side aisle joins the nave (Plate 96, Fig. 3). The arches of the main arcade are not, as has been asserted, pierced in a pre-existing wall. On the northern side, where the masonry has not been ruined by bad restoration, it is evident that the archivolts were executed in brick, and that upon this was placed the rubble of the wall.[23] In some cases, it is true, the brick archivolts are not perfectly welded with the rubble, as would be natural in view of the difference of the material. The absurdity of the theory which supposes these arcades to have been subsequently cut, will be evident if one attempts to imagine the difficult engineering that would be necessary to jack up this lofty wall while new piers and archivolts were added beneath it. The explanation of the break in the masonry where the two apses adjoin is far more probably to be sought in a change of plan during the construction. The central apse with its buttress had already been erected, at least in its lower part, when it was determined to place the northern absidiole further to the east than had been planned. Part of the buttress of the apse was consequently drowned. Subsequently the southern absidiole was extended still further to the eastward, as may be seen in the plan (Plate 97). This change of plan was probably occasioned by a desire to increase the depth and importance of the absidioles.

[23] The construction at S. Salvatore of Brescia (Plate 35, Fig. 1) is analogous.

It has resulted in irregularities in the form of the church, not only in drowning the buttress of the apse but in making the two absidioles decidedly unsymmetrical (Plate 97).

The portal of the west façade (Plate 96, Fig. 3), with pointed arch, was undoubtedly remade in the Gothic period.

The supports of the nave consist either of granite pillars or of rubble piers—hence their great variation in' size (Plate 97). The crypt is covered with groin vaults with disappearing transverse arches (Plate 96, Fig. 2). The vaults are not domed. The church itself is roofed in wood.

The responds of the crypt are rectangular. The clearstory on the north side of the church (Plate 96, Fig. 3) has been restored with a blind arch placed between each pair of clearstory windows. Between each blind arch and each window is a diamond-shaped niche. On the southern side there are no triangular apertures. The windows are so large that they must have been supplied with glass.

The masonry before the restoration (Plate 99, Fig. 1) was formed of uncut stones with a few bits of brick, laid with a certain tendency towards horizontal courses.

IV. The piers of the nave are without capitals or bases. The pillars have in some cases blocks of stone in lieu of capitals. The archivolts are of a single unmoulded order.

The capitals of the crypt (Plate 96, Fig. 2) are of the uncarved Corinthian type, and are characterized by admirable execution.

The ambo is placed over the northern entrance to the crypt. It is covered with a groined vault, and supplied with a capital ornamented with a carved grotesque face and a leaf pattern. This capital is closely analogous to those of the piers engaged against the façade of S. Abondio at Como.

The apse is ornamented with a series of blind arches (Plate 99, Fig. 1).

The church still retains remarkable remains of the original decoration in fresco.

V. S. Vincenzo of Galliano is a homogeneous edifice and an authentically dated monument of 1007. The ambo was added c. 1095.

GANACETO,[1] S. GIORGIO

(Plate 99, Fig. 3)

I. This church has been published by Maestri.[2] The monograph of Grandi is important, especially for historical notices. In the local archives, preserved in the house of the priest, are several documents of some value.

[1] Frazione di Modena.   [2] *Rubbiano*, 30 f.

II. Maestri states that the church of Ganaceto is mentioned in a document of 816, but I have searched for this in vain. The church was given in 1038 to the cathedral of Modena.[3] It enjoyed the rank of pieve, and was officiated by six canons. A prevosto of the church appears in a document of 1194.[4] In the following year the pope Celestine III granted a privilege to the church. A copy of this, made in the XVII or XVIII century, is preserved in the local archives. In this document the pope confirms the privileges the canons had enjoyed for forty years, and ratifies the privileges granted them by his predecessors, Clement III (1187-1191), Gregory VIII (1187), Urban III (1185-1186) and Lucius III (1181-1185).[5]

In the modern altar is an inscription, parts of which are now hidden. The *lacunæ,* however, may be supplied from the copy of Grandi[6] made when the stone was entirely visible. When the parts now missing are thus filled out, we learn that the inscription records a consecration of the altar in the year 1256.[7]

Near the north door is another inscription which records that the baptistery was erected in 1259.[8] The baptistery here referred to has disappeared, and the inscription has nothing to do with the holy-water basin near which it is now placed.

In 1326 the town of Ganaceto was burned.[9] Grandi believes that at this time the church was half destroyed, and the canons dispersed. In 1412, however, the church must have been officiated, since a new bell was made for it at this epoch.

The duke Borso d'Este, who died in 1471, granted to the bishop of Rimini certain revenues, in order that the church of Ganaceto might be rebuilt.

---

[3] Grandi, 6.   [4] Grandi, 8.

[5] Celestinus Episcopus Servus Servorum Dei Dilectis filiis Petro praeposito ecclesiae S. Georgii de Ganaceto atque fratribus canonice substituendis in perpetuum . . . sicut a XL annis in vestra Ecclesia rationabiliter . . . praedecessorum nostrorum Lucij, Vrbani, Gregorii et Clementis accepimus . . . Data Lateranij . . . VII. Kal. Maij. Indict. XIII. Incarnationis Dominicae Anno MCXCV.

[6] 11.

[7] [✠ MCCLVI . DE . MSE . OCTUO .] XU . INTR̄ATE . |ALB'T' . EP̄S . M̄UT. SACR̄AU . H . ALTARE . AD HONOR̄E . BEATI . GEORGII . Ī Q̄O . S̄T. R[ELIQUIE] . |S̄CO[RVM] . GEOR . IO; B̄AP̄T; [BARTH . SĪV̄RI STEPH . AD̄I. ET .]| ALIO[RUM] M[U]LTO[RUM]

[8]   . M . CCLUIIII . TP̄R
                                 DN̄I MĀTHI PP̄OĪ
                                 D' PIIS FACT̄U FUIT
                                 H' BAT̄M . ✠

[9] Grandi, 13.

This church, he mentions, had been in ruin for about a hundred years.[10] The original of this document is still preserved in the local archives at Ganaceto.

In 1571 the chapter was suppressed.[11] In 1818 the church was baroccoized. The ancient frescos of the apse were destroyed in 1839,[12] and other restorations were executed in 1855.[13]

III. The main body of the church seems to date from the XV and XIX centuries. Of the Romanesque edifice there remain only the three apses and parts of the eastern bay. There was formerly a crypt, but this has been filled up. The brickwork is of advanced character, cross-hatched bricks of regular size being carefully laid in horizontal courses. The mortar-beds are thin.

IV. The archivolts of the main arcade are in two orders, with simple rectilinear mouldings. The inner order was supported on semi-columns engaged on the piers. The semi-columns had cubic capitals of a very advanced type. The absidioles are adorned externally with pilaster strips and simple arched corbel-tables (Plate 99, Fig. 3), and traces of a similar decoration are extant on the clearstory walls (Plate 99, Fig. 3). The principal apse, on the other hand, has shafts (the capitals of which have weathered away), arched corbel-tables in two orders, and a cornice in which a rope-moulding figures.

Fine frescos are extant in the southern absidiole.

V. The capitals of Ganaceto show close analogies with those of Carpi, a surely dated monument of 1184. The masonry of Ganaceto is more advanced than that of Carpi, however, and we may therefore ascribe the extant Romanesque portion of this church to c. 1200. The inscription in the altar records that this was consecrated in 1256, and another inscription commemorates the construction of the now destroyed baptistery in 1258. Since no part of the existing structure can be assigned to 1256, it is probable that the restoration of the edifice, in consequence of which this consecration was celebrated, was confined either to the western portions of the church (which have been destroyed) or to the frescos.

GARBAGNATE MONASTERO,[1] SS. NAZARO E CELSO

(Plate 99, Fig. 5)

I. This monument has been published by Baserga, and is referred to by Monti.[2]

---

[10] . . . ecclesiae S. Georgii de Ganaceto sitae in ducatu nostro mutinensi, quae cum domibus suis ab annis circa centum pene diruta et solo aequata conspicitur. (Grandi, 15).

[11] Grandi, 20.   [12] Grandi, 19.   [13] Maestri, 34.

[1] (Como).   [2] 482.

II.   Baserga states that the monks of this monastery are mentioned in a document of 1288.

The edifice was restored in 1891, as is recorded by an inscription in the interior and by Baserga. At this period the edifice was isolated, the campanile demolished, the apse and southern wall restored, the windows remade, and the altar moved. The restorers found beneath the pavement the foundations of an earlier church. This proved to have been a very small single-aisled structure, with a square apse.

III.   The edifice consists of a nave of a single aisle and an apse (Plate 99, Fig. 5). The nave is covered by a modern wooden ceiling. Indeed, the results of the restoration of 1891 are evident everywhere in the edifice, and it is clear that the reconstruction was both radical and unfortunate.

The walls are constructed of ashlar masonry, the blocks of which vary tremendously in size, some being so large as to be fairly Cyclopean, while others are very small. The masonry joints are wide, and the courses are not always horizontal (Plate 99, Fig. 5).

IV.   The apse is adorned with a cornice of arched corbel-tables (Plate 99, Fig. 5). The windows, in many orders, are moulded internally, and those of the apse are moulded externally (Plate 99, Fig. 5). The apse arch is in two orders.

V.   The masonry of Garbagnate (Plate 99, Fig. 5) seems analogous to that of the Porta dello Zodiaco at Sagra S. Michele (Plate 196a, Fig. 2), a monument which dates from c. 1120. The church of Garbagnate may consequently be ascribed to the same period.

GAZZO VERONESE,[1] S. MARIA MAGGIORE

(Plate 99, Fig. 4)

I.   This church is mentioned in the guide of Simeoni.[2]

II.   In the eastern wall of the southern side aisle of the church is the following inscription:

```
SVMV OPVS EXCELSE CRVCIS VENERABILIS ABBA
AUTBERIVS DNI F FCIT AMORE SVI
QVA DEDIC . . . . . SIMVL ET ARA
SEXTO QVO . . . . . LOTHARII
TERTIO ACB . . . . . TA K[A]L[ENDIS]
QVA CELEBI . . . . . MVI
```

[1] (Verona).   [2] 428.

The Lothair referred to can only be the emperor Lothair II (1125-1137). The abbot Autberio was presumably abbot of S. Maria in Organo of Verona, since Gazzo is known to have belonged to the jurisdiction of that monastery.[3] Just exactly what was the *summum opus excelsae crucis* it is not easy to say. Some light, however, is thrown upon the question by another inscription in the southern wall, which gives a list of the relics contained in the altar of the Cross.[4]

The church contains two other inscriptions, both so fragmentary that their significance is entirely uncertain. One is upside down in the western pier of the northern arcade (this pier was remade in the XIII century); the other—also used as second-hand material—is inserted in the façade.

III. The church consists of a nave five bays long, two side aisles, a choir and an apse, but originally the choir was one bay longer than it is at present, and there were three apses. In the Gothic period the eastern bay of the side aisles was walled off so as to form a choir. A campanile was erected over the northern absidiole (Plate 99, Fig. 4), and the southern absidiole was subsequently destroyed to make way for a sacristy. The northern absidiole still exists, and is ornamented with exquisite XIV century frescos. Two chapels were added to the church at a subsequent epoch.

The side aisles are at present covered with vaults which appear to be of the XV century. The barrel vault of the nave may be of the same epoch. The church was undoubtedly originally roofed in wood.

The piers dividing the nave from the side aisles were originally cylin-

---

[3] Simeoni, 428.

[4]
✝ RELIQ SCORV
IN ALTARE CRVCIS
DE SEPVLCHRO DNI
ET SCAE MARIAE.
PETRI : BARTHOL : AP
IOH . MARCI : EVG
ZENONIS . SYRI . CO
FILASTRII . TICIANIC
INNOCENT . VITI . M
STEFANI . ET . XL . M
FIRMI RVSTICI . M
COSME : DAMIANI M
GEORGII QVIRICI :
MENNECANTIANOR[VM]
PROTI : CRISOGONI :
[FELI]CIS . FORTVNAT[I]

drical, but the two westernmost were given a rectangular section in the Gothic period.

The original windows were very small, in several orders, and served without glass. The larger windows (Plate 99, Fig. 4) were added in the XV century. The masonry consists of well made bricks, carefully laid, but the mortar-joints are wide. The masonry of the apse is better, and here the joints are very fine.[5]

IV.   The capitals are cubic, with very narrow abaci, high, straight cushions and curved bells. The archivolts are in a single unmoulded order. The bases of the piers are not visible. There is no system.

The exterior is ornamented with simple arched corbel-tables supported at intervals by pilaster strips, with classical moulding capitals. The cornices contain a flat saw-tooth moulding, that recalls the Gothic work at S. Pietro in Valle. In the walls are inlaid many pieces of marble, and in the east wall of the sacristy is a piece of XII century carving. The pinnacles were added in the XV century.

Trial excavations have shown the existence beneath the pavement of an ancient mosaic, which is apparently in perfect preservation for its entire extent. When and if excavated, this will be one of the finest monuments of the kind in all Italy.

V.   The masonry of Gazzo is analogous to that of those portions of the cathedral of Lodi which date from c. 1190. Our monument may consequently be ascribed to that epoch.

GRAVEDONA,[1] S. MARIA DEL TIGLIO

(Plate 100, Fig. 1, 2, 3)

I.   The important and interesting church of S. Maria del Tiglio has been described by Ninguarda and Boldoni.[2]   Mella published the church twice, and Barelli wrote a monograph upon it.   De Dartein[3] studied the monument,

---

[5] The masonry of the late XII century in the province shows remarkable variation. In the church of S. Zeno at Cerea, for example, herring-bone courses in rubble are introduced. Aside from its masonry this church, which was transformed in the XIV century, and has been recently subjected to a restoration which practically amounts to a reconstruction, is without interest.

[1] (Como).

[2] Eminent in lęuo curuati littoris cornu templa duo, antiquum alterum, & ex marmore miro opificio extructum, cui octogonia turris marmorea iungitur, atque illud, quod Sacri fontis lauacro infantes ab auitâ culpâ mundari in ipso consueuere, Baptisterium dicitur.   Alterum pręclaro Garbedonensium sumptu nuper in antiquis Canonicæ parietarijs extructum. . . . (Boldoni, 125-126).

[3] 364.

which has also been noticed by Monti. For the modern restorations the brief article in the *Rivista Archeologica della Provincia di Como* of November, 1877, is of value.

II. There can be no doubt that the church of S. Maria del Tiglio is the baptistery of the adjoining basilica of S. Vincenzo. The baptismal font was seen in the church by Ninguarda at the end of the XVI century, and, in point of fact, is still there preserved. The church was anciently dedicated to S. Giovanni Battista, and frescos depicting scenes from the life of that saint may still be seen upon the walls of the eastern apse. The edifice has, however, come to assume somewhat the character of a shrine in consequence of a miracle said to have taken place in the IX century. This miracle is recorded in a continuation of the chronicle of Aimoinus, but the passage is omitted by most of the modern editors as an interpolation.[4] The same text reappears in the *Annales Einhardi*[5] and in the *Annales Bertiniani*. In the latter we read: "In this year 823 certain miracles are said to have taken place. . . . In the territory of Como, a city of Italy, in the town of Gravedona and in the church of S. Giovanni Battista, there was painted on the apse the image of the Virgin Mary holding on her lap the infant Jesus, and of the Magi, who were offering gifts. On account of its great age this picture had faded and almost disappeared, but for two days it shone with such radiance that it appeared to those who saw it to surpass in the beauty of its age every splendour of a new picture. Nevertheless, the pictures of the Magi, because of the gifts which they were offering, the radiance did not illumine."[6]

Ninguarda has left the following description of the church made in the last years of the XVI century: "Near the church last mentioned [S. Vincenzo] is another dedicated to S. Maria del Tiglio, in the middle of which a marble basin serves as baptismal font. . . . It has a fine campanile in the form of a tower, in which there are two fine, large bells which are used also for the church of S. Vincenzo. There are three doors, one opposite the high altar and the other two on the epistle side."[7]

[4] Du Breul prints the passage but marks it with an asterisk to indicate that the text has little historical value. (Aimoni, *De gestis Francorum*, Lib. IIII, Cap. CXI, ed. du Breul, 252).

[5] M. G. H., *Script. Rer. Mer. et Carl.*, I, 211.

[6] Hoc anno [823] prodigia quædam extitisse narrantur. . . . Et in territorio Cometense Italiæ ciuitatis, in vico Grabadona, in Ecclesia sancti Ioannis Baptistæ, imago sanctæ Mariæ puerum Iesum gremio continens, ac Magorum munera offerentium in absida eiusdem Ecclesiæ depicta, & ob nimiam vetustatem obscurata, & penè abolita, tanta claritate per duorum dierum spacia effulsit, vt omnem splendorem nouæ picturæ suæ vetustatis pulchritudine cernetibus penitus vincere videretur. Magorum tamen imagines propter munera quæ offerebant minimè claritas illa irradiauit. (Bertiniani, *Annales Regum Francorum*, ed. Duchesne, *Historiæ Francorum Scriptores*, Lutetiæ Parisiorum, Sebastiani Cramoisy, 1641, III, 181).

[7] Vicino alla suda chiesa ve n'è un'altra dedicata a Sta Maria de telio, nella quale in mezo vi è il vaso di marmore per il fonte baptismale con dentro l'aqua, però a basso

In 1895 a restoration was carried out with unusual intelligence. The roof was repaired, and the church was relieved of much superfluous barocco ornament.

III. The church consists of a rectangular central area, from the east, north and south sides of which open semicircular apses (Plate 100, Fig. 1), while to the west projects a rectangular vestibule surmounted by a tower (Plate 100, Fig. 3). In the thickness of the walls of the eastern apse are three semicircular niches, and two other niches in the east wall flank the same apse. There is a gallery on the north and south sides. Notwithstanding the extraordinary thickness of the walls, the church, with the exception of the half domes of the apses, the barrel vaults in the first and second stories of the campanile, and the similar vaults in the north and south galleries, is roofed in wood. The north and south walls are ornamented internally by a blind arcade supported on free-standing columns. A similar arcade is carried around the niches of the principal apse.

The masonry (Plate 100, Fig. 2) is ashlar of good quality, and formed of large, well dressed blocks, well laid in horizontal courses. There is little mortar. Bands of white marble are introduced with decorative effect at intervals amid the darker stone (Plate 100, Fig. 1, 2, 3).

IV. The capitals are for the most part cubic, or of a rather crudely executed Corinthianesque type. One, carved with eagles, closely resembles the capitals of the apse of S. Fedele at Como. The bases have griffes.

The exterior is ornamented with arched corbel-tables, supported on pilaster strips, or upon shafts engaged on pilaster strips (Plate 100, Fig. 1, 2, 3). The arched corbel-tables of the apses are in two orders (Plate 100, Fig. 1). The cornices consist of advanced mouldings and a saw tooth. The doorways (Plate 100, Fig. 2) and certain of the windows (Plate 100, Fig. 1) are richly moulded.

On the façade are inlaid several reliefs in a manner which recalls S. Michele of Pavia. The subjects represented are a centaur shooting a stag (Plate 100, Fig. 2), a snake, a head (this is probably a Roman fragment), an interlace and a star ornament.

The interior still retains frescos of various epochs, and traces of frescos may also be seen on the exterior, especially on the archivolt of the principal portal, on the south portal, and on the south wall.

V. The capitals of S. Maria del Tiglio show, in some respects, analogy with those of S. Fedele of Como, an edifice erected c. 1115. The mouldings

in modo tale che per la vicinanza del lago vi entra alcuna volta et circonda da chiesa di dentro. . . . Ha un campanile bello a forma di torre, nel quale vi sono due campane grosse et grandi, quale servono per la chiesa di Sto Vincenzo. Vi sono tre porte, una per contro l'altare magiore et l'altre due nel corno dell'episola. . . . (Ninguarda, ed. Monti, II, 159). One of these doors has since been walled up.

of S. Maria, however, are notably richer than those of S. Fedele, and the masonry differs from that of the church of Como in being polychromatic and of decidedly superior technique. Technically, the masonry of Gravedona is but little inferior to that of the apse of S. Carpoforo of Como, which there is reason for believing dates from c. 1145. S. Maria del Tiglio may therefore be ascribed to c. 1135.

GRAVEDONA,[1] S. VINCENZO

(Plate 100, Fig. 4, 5, 6, 7)

I. The description of S. Vincenzo of Gravedona, written by the bishop Ninguarda in the last years of the XVI century, is of great value, because the bishop saw the church before it had been baroccoized. Monti, in his edition of Ninguarda, has contributed an important note illustrating the history of the edifice. Barelli and De Dartein[2] have both studied the monument.

II. To judge from two inscriptions of the VI century, found in 1710, and now preserved on the north side of the choir, a church existed in very early times on the site of S. Vincenzo of Gravedona. Possibly this may have been the church of S. Salvatore which, according to Giovio, was founded by Prospero.[3] In 931 the church enjoyed the rank of pieve and was officiated by a chapter of priests.[4]

There is record of a consecration of the church in 1072. This notice is derived from a memorandum made November 25, 1593, on the occasion of the pastoral visit of the bishop Ninguarda to the church, and afterwards incorporated in the acts of the pastoral visit of the bishop Carafino made in 1627. This memorandum states that in the parish church of S. Vincenzo there were in existence manuscript psalters, one dating from 1250 and others even older. In these it was stated that the consecration of the church took place on the first Sunday in September in the year 1072.[5] In 1164 the archpriest and

---

1 (Como).

2 364.

3 Flaviano [successit] Prosper, qui sacellum S. Salvatoris Grabedonæ apud Larium condidit. 565 ?-568 ? (Giovio, 184).

4 Vgo gratia Dei Rex, Anni Regni eius in Italia quinto, Mense Maij, Indictione quarta. Delectissimis, atq; amantissimis mihi semper, Adelbertus Presbyter, Ioannes Presbyter, Ambrosius Presbyter, Ioannes Presbyter, Radanus Presbyter, 'Ioannes Presbyter, Petrus Presbyter, & alijs, & alijs Presbyteris, afq; Diaconibus, seu Clericis, aut illorum posterioribus de ista Congregacione Plebis Grabadonæ. . . . (Tatti, II, 793).

5 These important notices have been published by Monti in his edition of Ninguarda. "In un antichissimo salterio fatto a mano della nostra Canonica, prima vi si legge in

canons of the church are mentioned in a document referred to by Monti.[6] Another instrument of 1215, seen by Barelli, mentions an archpriest and eight *sacerdoti* connected with the church.

In 1593 the edifice was visited by the bishop Ninguarda, who has left us the following description: "On the first day of November, 1593, the most reverend bishop, pursuing his visits, came to the collegiate church of S. Vincenzo at Gravedona. . . . The chapel of the high altar is vaulted and half painted, but the rest of the edifice is covered by a wooden roof which is now ruinous. This church has three aisles and is much under ground. However, the half of the principal nave towards the altar is higher than the other half, so that the pavement is much higher at the east end. There are three doors, one in the west wall, one on the gospel side and the other near the choir. Under the principal nave near the afore-mentioned side door by the high altar, there is a crypt with an altar dedicated to S. Antonio, but without revenues. In this crypt there is the water of the lake. Above the principal portal there is a gallery with a little altar dedicated to S. Michele, and the school of the Holy Sacrament. . . . . . This church has many windows without glass or paper. The sacristy is near the choir on the epistle side. . . . . . There is an old pulpit on the gospel side in the middle of the church."[7]

In 1600 the church menaced ruin because of the encroachment of the water of the lake. The pavement was raised, and the edifice was transformed from a three-aisled to a single-aisled structure by tearing down the clearstory walls and raising the walls of the side aisles. A new choir was also erected. In 1627 new chapels were added, and the sacristy rebuilt. In 1726 the apse was reconstructed, and the façade and atrium (Plate 100, Fig. 6) restored in their present form.[8]

The edifice was again restored in 1889, as is recorded by an inscription

lettera majuscola: Dedicatio Ecclesiæ Sancti Vincentii MLXXIJ prima Dominica Septembris." (Ninguarda, ed. Monti, II, 154).

[6] *Ibid.*

[7] 1593 die p° mens. novemb. Rmus DD. Episcopus, prossequendo visitationem, accessit ad Ecclesiam Collegiatam et Archipresbyterialem Scti Vincentij de Grabedona. . . . La capella dell'altare magiore è mezza depinta, et voltata, et il resto sotto sofitto però tutto rovinato. . . . Questa chiesa ha tre nave et è assai sotto terra però la meta della nave di mezzo verso l'altare magiore è alta più dell'altra parte di da nave, in modo che releva assai verso l'altare magiore. Ha tre porte, l'una in fronte della capella magiore et due altre una laterale verso il corno del vangelo e l'altra vicino alla capella magiore. Sotto la nave di mezo dalla porta laterale suda avanti verso l'altare magiore vi è sotto uno scurolo con un altare in titolo Sto Antonio, consecrato, però senza dote, nello quale vi era l'aqua del lago. Al di sopra della porta magiore vi è un grò, nel quale un altare piccolo dedicato a Santo Michele et la scola del Smo Sacramento . . . . . la detta chiesa ha molte finestre senza vetri e senza impannate . . . . . la sacristia è vicina alla capella magiore nel corno dell'epistola. . . . . . Un pulpito vecchio dalla parte del vangelo a mezo la chiesa. (Ninguarda, ed. Monti, II, 154).

[8] Tatti, I, 512.

over the western arch of the atrium.[9] In 1875 traces of the foundation of the XI century apses were excavated.[10]

III. Only the lower portion of the outside walls and the crypt date from the Romanesque period. The crypt is said to extend under the entire nave, but if so its western portion has been walled off so as to be inaccessible. It is covered by groin vaults, with transverse ribs, loaded at the crown and disappearing at the springing (Plate 100, Fig. 7). The groins are sharp, there is no doming, and the construction is in rubble. The supports are columns, or cylindrical piers (Plate 100, Fig. 7), but the responds placed at the angles of the ancient apses have a compound section.

The masonry of the walls of the side aisles (Plate 100, Fig. 4, 5) and of the crypt is ashlar in which bricks are occasionally interspersed. The small, rectangular blocks of stone are roughly squared and irregularly laid. The mortar-beds are of considerable thickness.

The windows are narrow, widely splayed and intended to serve without glass (Plate 100, Fig. 5). It is evident that the crypt formerly extended much farther to the north than the present modern north wall of the church, which cuts across the old northern absidiole near its south edge.

IV. The side-aisle walls are ornamented with a cornice of arched corbel-tables supported on pilaster strips and grouped four and four in the south wall (Plate 100, Fig. 4), six and six in the north wall (Plate 100, Fig. 5). The windows are placed not in the middle of the exterior bays (Plate 100, Fig. 5).

The capitals of the crypt are of cubic type (Plate 100, Fig. 7), not so developed as those of S. Abondio of Como (Plate 59, Fig. 1), an edifice consecrated in 1095, but more advanced than those of Sannazzaro Sesia (Plate 201, Fig. 6), an edifice begun in 1040. The bases are of unusual type, having the shape of an inverted capital, or consisting of one or more tori placed above a plinth.

In the crypt are two fragments of carving—an interlace and an anthemion—doubtless coming from the destroyed Lombard church. The lower step of the stairway leading to the upper church is formed of an old jamb decorated with an interlace.

V. The style of the monument entirely agrees with the documentary evidence that it was consecrated in 1072.

[9]

D. O. M.

ET S. VINCENTIO M.

DICATUM

BENEFACTM PIETATE ORNATUM

MDCCCLXXXIX

[10] *Rivista Archeologica della Provincia di Como*, Fasc. 12, Novembre, 1877.

LOMBARD ARCHITECTURE

ISOLA COMACINA,[1] S. EUFEMIA

I. The ruins of Isola Comacina have had the rare good fortune to have been made the subject of a monograph by Monneret de Villard, which is not only a scholarly and exact illustration of the local antiquities, but an important contribution to the history of Lombard art.

There are an unusual number of inedited documents referring to the Isola Comacina. The originals of most of these are still preserved in the Archivio dello Stato at Milan. Copies are contained in the *Codice della Croce* of the Ambrosiana,[2] and in the collection of documents transcribed by Bonomi, now preserved at the Brera.[3]

The drawing of S. Eufemia in the *Grande Illustrazione*[4] was made at a time when some portions of the church which have now disappeared were still extant.

II. The bishop of Como, Agrippino, who lived perhaps about the beginning of the VII century, was buried at Isola Comacina. His epitaph is now preserved in the church of S. Eufemia at Isola on the continent, and was undoubtedly transferred thither when the island city was destroyed in 1169. This epitaph, however, does not necessarily prove that the church of S. Eufemia existed in these early times, since it might easily have been brought to that church from some other edifice, such as, for example, S. Giovanni.[5]

Similar observations apply to a donation granted to S. Eufemia in 1054, in which it is remarked that S. Abondio was accustomed to visit the island for recreation, and that in his time many relics were there buried; but no explicit statement is made that the church of S. Eufemia existed at that early time.[6]

Such observations in the donation of 1054 are copied from the charter of the foundation of the canonica, promulgated by Litigerio, bishop of Como. The chronological notes of the latter document, which has recently been edited by Monneret de Villard, are exceedingly confused. The sixth year of the emperor Corrado coincides with the year 1032, and the fourteenth indiction with the year 1031. The sixth day before the ides of July corresponds with the tenth day of the month, whereas, in the preceding sentence, the eleventh day is mentioned. The document is also dated Thursday, but in neither the year 1031 nor 1032 did either the tenth or the eleventh of July fall on a Thursday. From the document we learn that the church of S. Eufemia was the pieve of Isola and that it was already served by priests, whom the bishop merely united into a chapter.[7]

---

[1] (Como). The ruins of Isola Comacina are situated on the famous island, which may be reached by boat from Lenno or Campo.

[2] MS. D. S., IV.   [3] AE, XV, 33-35.   [4] III, 1156.

ISOLA COMACINA, S. EUFEMIA

It is evident that the chapter instituted by Litigerio did not represent a very radical change in the clergy of the church. The canons were obliged to live together only at certain periods of the year, and their number does not seem to have been increased.

In the donation of 1054 we have cited above, the poverty of the church is expressly referred to. There is therefore no reason to suppose that the church was rebuilt in 1031.

The relationship between the church of S. Eufemia and the church of S. Giovanni is very puzzling. To the north of the ruins of S. Eufemia there

5 The inscription is as follows:

DEGERE QVIS[Q]VIS AMAT VLLO SINE C . . . . .
    ANTE DIEM SEMPER LVMINA MORTIS . . . . .
ILLIVS ADVENTV SVSPECTVS RITE DICATVS
    HAGRIPINVS PRAESVL HOC FABRICAVIT OPV[S]
HIC PATRIA LINQVENS PROPRIAM LAROSQVE PAR . . . . .
    PRO SCA STVDVIT PEREGER ESSE FIDE
HIC PRO DOGMA PATRVM TANTVS TVLERARE LA[BOREM]
    NOSCITVR VT NVLLVS ORE REFERRE QVEAT
HIC HVMILIS MILITARE DO DEVOTE CVPIVI[T]
    CVM POTVIT MVNDI CELSOS HABERE GRADOS
HIC TERRENAS OPES MALVIT CONTEMNERE CVNCTAS
    VT SVMAT MELIVS PRAEMIA DIGNA POLI .
HIC SEMEL EXOSVM SAECLVM DECREVIT HABERE
    ET SOLVM DILIGET MENTIS AMORE DNO
HIC QVOQVE IVSSA SEQVES DNI LEGEMQVE TONANTIS
    PROXIMVM VT SESE GAVDET . AMARE SVVM
HVNC ET ENIM QVEM TANTAHRVM DOCVMENTA DECORANT
    ORNAT ET PRIM[A]E NOBILITATIS HONOR .
HIS AQVILHA DVCE MILLVM DISTINAVIT IN ORIS .
    VT GERAT INVICTVS PROELIAM AGNA DI
HIS CAPVT EST FACTIS SVMMVS PATRIARCA IOHANNI
    QVI PRAEDICTA TENET DIGNVS IN VRBE SEDEM
QVIS LAVDARE VALET CLERVM POPVLVMQVE COMENSE
    RECTOREM TANTVM QVI PETIERE SIBI
HI SINODOS CVNCTI VENERANTES QVATTVOR ALMAS
    CONCILIVM QVINTVM POST POSVERE MALVM
HI BELLVM OB IPSAS MVLTOS CESSERE PER ANNOS
    SED SEMPER MANSIT INSVPERATA FIDES

6 In nomine Sancte et Indiuidue Trinitatis . . . . . regnum disponente Domno Enrico imperatore iustissimo. Nostrum hoc decretum fore compositum cunctis has litteras legentibus verissime assero septima currente indictione. Illo in tempore cęlitus autem statutum affuit quod Benno Cumane ecclesie presul inclitus Cumanum hon-estissime suum regebat populum, noxia sibi plebis commissæ diluendo cunctis dans

stands a barocco chapel known as S. Giovanni, which, according to tradition, is built upon the ruins of an older church of the same name. Monneret de Villard's excavations have shown that the church of S. Eufemia and this ancient church of S. Giovanni were connected by a portico. Now, it is known that the original parish church of Isola Comacina was called S. Giovanni. It is also known that the church of S. Eufemia was pieve of Isola before the foundation of the chapter. The suspicion therefore arises that the church of S. Giovanni either changed its name to, or was supplanted by, S. Eufemia. In later times, since S. Eufemia was a pieve, a baptistery, which would

congrua, et non profutura vellendo. Cuius iamque iusticia donec vixit in seculo, floruit omnibus rectissima. Qui cum Insulam revisere plebem sibi valde carrissimam deveniret, multaque ibi omnibus patriam incolentibus congrue difiniret, in omnibus quoque his consideravit, quod Insulanorum patria quondam sanctissimo suo patrono Abundio nimis fuit dilectissima, qua dilexit, sua reparare membra. Cuius tunc temporis pignora multa ibidem habebantur condita; quæ ut dicebat a clericis sua non habebant ministeria quia infelix paupertas in illorum parvissima ea die regnabat canonica; quorum accensu dilectione. cępit animadvertere: illam quomodo canonicam posset ditevere; cuius ad presens mentem Deo disponente pro remedio suę animę molendinum quendam in Lenno positum huic Insulanę canonicę dicavit proprium; quapropter futuros successores nostros per aeterni Redemptoris amore, sanctęque Eufemię seu Sancti Abundii omniumque Sanctorum rogamus, ac firmiter absecramus ut huic canonicę si aliquid vobis placet addere, addite, si non, non sit vobis licitum ei quicquam auferre . . . (*Codice della Croce,* MS. Amb. D. S. IV, 3, f. 33).

[7] In nomine S. et individuae Trinitatis. Regnante D. Conrado piissimo Imperatore anno imperii ejus Deo propitio VI indictione XIV. Dum in Dei nomine vir venerabilis Litigerius humiliter S. Cumanae Ecclesiae Provisor juxta ecclesiasticum morem pleben suae Dioecesis visitando circuiret, corrigens errata, atque ordinans cunctis beneplacita, instituens Canonicam, . . . contigit, ut quandam suam plebem insulam devenerit, multaque ibi audita congrue deffiniret. In his quoque comperit, quod locus ille multo à suo Patrono, S. scilicet Abundio, quondam diligebatur, atque multa eius pignora ibidem condita habebantur, indoluit quod non ita, ut decebat, divino cultu colebantur; eius accensus amore, coepit corde disponere, ut si fieri posset, ad laudem Dei, et S. Abundii ibi aliquam Canonicam vellet componere, saltem duobus temporibus in anno, Adventu Domini et Quadragesima: sed quia loca illa beneficiata erant, ac milites ea tenebant, dolebat, quod ibi unde feceret, non habebat. Tamen Dominus . . . viam monstravit. . . . Sine mora ipsius plebis Clericos ad se venire fecit, quibus dulciter dulcia verba dicendo, taliter inquit: Vos fratres volo, annuente Domino, in unum congregare et instantius Domino servire et pro omnibus orare: decimam, quammodo comperi diabolica fraude teneri, vobis in integrum concedo . . . ea scilicet ratione, ut nihil inde praeter Canonicam faciatis, meliorum fratrum iudicio colligatur et custodiatur et tot fratres ibidem congregantur, quot victu sufficere possit duabus quadragesimis in anno, et si fieri posset, Dominicis, ac festivis diebus, nec ullus in ipsam Canonicam intrare praesumat sine electione fratrum. . . . Praeterea nostros futuros successores pro eterni Retributoris amore S. D. Euphemiae, seu S. Abundii amore nostri Patroni, sub quo praesulari, ac patrocinari debent, obtestamur, ac firmiter obsecramus, ut huic sancto loco si aliquid possunt addere, addant, si non, nihil minuant. . . . Litigerius episcopus scripsit et confirmavit undecimo die instante ipso mense 6 Idus ipsius mensis Iulii. Acta mense Iulio hebdomada secunda feria quinta. Cumis feliciter in ipsa nostra domo soloriata vicina lacui, leva et palam roborata firmiter. (Ed. Monneret de Villard, 221).

naturally be dedicated to S. Giovanni, was erected alongside the collegiate church. It is probably this baptistery, as Monneret conjectures, that is represented by the existing church of S. Giovanni. Some confirmation of this view is furnished by a document of 1085, from which it appears that the canons of S. Eufemia claimed certain lands which they maintained *fuisse ecclesię sancti Ihoannis quondam plebis de iam dicta Insula.* Of these lands the bishop accordingly says: *concedimus et offerimus ad ecclesiam Sante Eufemie que nunc gradum predictę ecclesię optinet predictam terram unde ipsi questi sunt.*[8]

In 1169 Isola was razed to the ground.[9] Contrary to the usual custom, the churches also were destroyed. According to Giovio, for this sacrilege the Comaschi were laid under an interdict.[10]

From a privilege of Alexander III, without date, but assigned by Tatti to 1178, it is clear that at that year it had not yet been decided whether the church of S. Eufemia should be rebuilt on the Isola Comacina or moved to another site.[11] Soon after, however, the canons must have begun to build their new church on the mainland in deference to the edict of Barbarossa, issued in 1175, which forbade the reconstruction of buildings on the Isola Comacina.[12]

In 1913 the ruins of S. Eufemia were carefully excavated by Ugo Monneret de Villard.

[8] The chronological notes of this document are: Anno Dominice Incarnationis Mil. L.X.X.X.V. mense Mar. Indictione VIII. . . . Actum mense marcio ebdomada prima feria IIII in domo denesci feliciter. (*Codice della Croce*, MS. Amb. D. S. IV, t.III, f. 59).

[9] Barelli was wrong in ascribing this event to the year 1160. The destruction of the city is recorded in the following inscription in the modern church of S. Giovanni:

M.C.DANT ANNOS.LX.Q' NOTANDOS.

INSVLA QVADO RVIT.MAGNA PESTILENTIA FVIT

DIVINO MONITV TEMPLI REPARATA VETVSTAS

GRADINE QVASSATOS SERVET SACRA DONA FERETES

LVX MAII PRINCIPIV PRIMA FINE VLTIMA DEDIT

OPERI.MILLENO ANO QVATERCENTESIMO Q'

SEX DECE ATQ' SEPTE IVGASET CVNCTI DISC[ER]|NE

[10] Comenses cum oppidum insulæ, ut ante dictum est, excinderent, sacras ædes D. Faustini et D. Euphemiæ demoliti sunt. Quocirca sacris per annos quatuordecim eis interdictum fuit; tandem impetrata venia, Gotifredus aquileiensis patriarcha Comum accedens, de consilio fratris sui Ionatæ concordiensis episcopi, interdictum sustulit et universos Comenses fidelium communioni restituit, iubens, ut similes sacras ædes abinde Comi construerent. (Giovio, 40).

[11] Adijcimus insuper, vt si Ecclesiam vestram ad locum aliquem vestræ Plebis transferri, vel in loco, vbi fuerat, reædificari contigerit, etc. (Tatti, II, 878).

[12] In the existing edifice of S. Eufemia of Isola on the mainland (frazione di Ossuccio, provincia di Como) there are still preserved Romanesque arched corbel-tables.

III.   The church consisted of a nave six bays long, two side aisles, a choir also flanked by side aisles, three apses, a crypt extending beneath the choir and central apse, a south-western campanile, and possibly a western portico.[18]   The southern absidiole, owing to the slope of the ground, was raised upon a vaulted substructure, which is still extant, but transformed into a barn.

The piers of the nave were for the most part octagonal in section, but one of those of the choir is compound (the other has been destroyed), and the fourth pair from the west consist of a rectangular core on which are engaged two semi-columns.   The side-aisle walls are without responds, so that it is certain that the nave and side aisles were covered with a timber roof.   The choir, however, with its side aisles, was covered with groin vaults. The principal apse was supplied with a system consisting of a shaft engaged upon a pilaster strip.   From this it may be deduced that the half dome was supplied with ribs like those of S. Abondio (Plate 58, Fig. 4).   The crypt vaults have been destroyed, but sufficient remains are extant to make it certain that they were not domed, and that they were supplied with ribs which were entirely detached from the massive of the vault.   The responds (consisting generally of a semi-column engaged on a pilaster strip) and the wall ribs are still extant.   The substructures of the southern absidiole are covered with undomed groin vaults, without ribs, and constructed of rubble.

The entrance to the crypt was charmingly arranged.   On either side of the nave was a biforum, one side of which served as a doorway giving access to the crypt, the other as a window.   On the northern side, the window was blocked up at a subsequent epoch by a masonry ambo built in like that of Galliano.   A peculiarity of the church was the variation in the levels of the pavement.   The side aisles were higher than the nave, and the whole church sloped upward towards the east.   The pavement of the northern absidiole was lower than that of the choir, but higher than that of the nave, which, in turn, was higher than that of the crypt.   After the construction of the church, a new pavement was laid 20 centimetres above the original ones.   These were formed of rather rough stone, with an occasional block of marble, and are poorly laid.   It is evident that there never was any mosaic.   In the northern absidiole is still preserved an original altar in masonry.

The masonry is formed of small, roughly squared blocks of stone, laid in horizontal courses with wide mortar-joints.   Very rarely bricks are inserted. In the exterior of the apse, the stones have been so disintegrated and worn by the weather that the masonry appears more primitive than it really is. It is only in the recently excavated portions of the church that its true character can be judged.

IV.   The capitals of the responds of the crypt are for the most part of a simple block type.   Several have angle spurs, like the capitals of the

[18] Monneret de Villard, 99.

Annunziata at Corneto (Plate 66, Fig. 2). A capital of marble found in the crypt undoubtedly belonged to one of the free-standing columns of this portion of the edifice. It is Corinthianesque, with a single row of acanthus leaves of Byzantine character, rather flaccidly executed. The volutes are well drawn, but are not undercut.

The apse is adorned externally with shafts engaged on pilaster strips. These undoubtedly supported arched corbel-tables, like the shafts in the apse of S. Abondio at Como. The remainder of the edifice was not adorned with pilaster strips, but it is probable that there were cornices of arched corbel-tables, since one was found in the excavations.

The débris which came to light in the excavations abundantly proved that the edifice was covered, internally and externally, with stucco and frescos.

V. The capital of the crypt is entirely analogous to a capital of the crypt of S. Vincenzo at Milan (Plate 137, Fig. 3), which dates from the second half of the VI century. It may, therefore, be conjectured that the capital of Isola comes from a church built by S. Agrippino.

The rest of S. Eufemia is evidently homogeneous. It has been assumed by Monneret de Villard that this edifice was reconstructed when the chapter was founded in 1031. There is, however, no documentary evidence that this was the case, and an inspection of the style of the architecture, in my judgment, shows that the monument dates from the last half of the XI century. If, for example, we compare the masonry with that of edifices of the first half of the XI century, such as, for instance, S. Fedelino on the Lago di Mezzola (Plate 102, Fig. 1), which dates from c. 1000, S. Vincenzo of Galliano, an authentically dated structure of 1007 (Plate 99, Fig. 1), S. Nicolò of Piona (Plate 188, Fig. 4), which dates from c. 1030, or S. Carpoforo of Como (Plate 60, Fig. 4), a surely dated monument of 1040, we see that the masonry of S. Eufemia is decidedly superior. It holds its own with the masonry of S. Vincenzo of Gravedona (Plate 100, Fig. 4), a church consecrated in 1072, with that of S. Benedetto di Lenno (Plate 102, Fig. 5), a surely dated monument of 1083, and even with that of S. Abondio of Como, a church which was consecrated in 1095 (Plate 58, Fig. 2). Moreover, I know of no example of the use of pilaster strips engaged on shafts to adorn the exterior of an apse before 1083, when this feature appears at S. Benedetto di Lenno (Plate 102, Fig. 5). The interior system of the apse is more advanced than that of S. Abondio at Como in that the shaft is engaged upon a pilaster strip (Plate 58, Fig. 4). The piers are more advanced than those of S. Benedetto di Lenno in that they are octagonal instead of square. In view of all these considerations, it seems certain that S. Eufemia of Isola Comacina is later than S. Benedetto di Lenno (1083), and contemporary with, if not later than, S. Abondio of Como (1095). The church may consequently be ascribed to c. 1095.

LOMBARD ARCHITECTURE

ISOLA COMACINA,[1] SS. FAUSTINO E GIOVITA

I.   The ruins of SS. Faustino e Giovita have been admirably studied by Monneret de Villard.[2]

II.   The church existed as early as the X century, but the monastery is first mentioned in 1101.[3]   After the destruction of Isola in 1169, the abbey was removed to S. Giovanni di Campo,[4] where it is mentioned as being located in documents of 1211,[5] 1224,[6] 1226,[7] etc.

III.   The remains of this church consist of the foundations of the apse, and a part of one side wall.   The building at present serves as a cow-stable.

The apse is peculiar.   It is polygonal externally, having four sides, so that there is an angle on axis, and is placed upon a semicircular and elaborately moulded podium.   Internally there are two twin apses, formed of niches in the thickness of the wall.   This peculiar disposition was probably adopted with a view to supplying a separate niche and a separate altar for each of the two patron saints.

It is evident that the edifice was very low, for externally some traces of the cornice are seen just above the arched corbel-tables.   It is probable that there was only a single aisle.

The masonry consists of a rubble core, coated with ashlar of the finest quality.   The mortar-joints are extremely fine.

IV.   On each angle of the apse are shafts engaged upon pilaster strips. The exterior wall is decorated with large, arched corbel-tables grouped two and two, and supported on shafts with cubic capitals.

One of the oculi of the apse survives.   The windows of the side wall were widely splayed, and evidently intended to serve without glass.

V.   The masonry of our monument is analogous to that of the façade of S. Zeno of Verona (Plate 224, Fig. 1), a surely dated monument of 1138. SS. Faustino e Giovita may consequently be ascribed to c. 1140.   This ascription of date is confirmed by a comparison of the niches of the apse with the different but somewhat analogous arrangement in the eastern apse of S. Maria del Tiglio of Gravedona, an edifice which dates from c. 1135.

---

[1] Isola Comacina, Provincia di Como, may be reached by boat from Lenno or Campo.

[2] 106 f.   [3] Monneret de Villard, 106-107.   [4] *Ibid.*, 106.

[5] Bonomi, *Dip. Sti. Bti.*, Brera MS. AE, XV, 33, f. 398.

[6] *Ibid.*, 501.   [7] *Ibid.*, 536.

ISOLA DELLA SCALA,[1] CHIESOLINA DELLA BASTIA

(Plate 101, Fig. 1)

I.   This church is mentioned in the guide of Simeoni.[2]

II.   In the façade is the following inedited inscription:

CHEBIZO

✝ A . D . M . C . XX ✝

WARIENTO

ET ANNO FECE   RVNT HOC OPVS

Who were Chebizo and Wariento I have been unable to discover, but the inscription undoubtedly preserves an authentic record of the year in which the church was built.

The rose-window was restored in 1867, as we learn from an inscription.[3]

III.   At present the edifice consists of a single-aisled nave roofed in timber, and a square apse covered with a groin vault.   This vault is not original, since the arches are pointed, but the exterior masonry shows that the plan is old.   The campanile is much more modern than the church (Plate 101, Fig. 1).   The masonry of the façade gives some reason to suppose that the edifice may originally have had three aisles, which were reduced to one, perhaps at the time the Renaissance portal was added (Plate 101, Fig. 1).

The masonry of the exterior walls has been much made over.   The southern wall is almost entirely modern (Plate 101, Fig. 1), and the others have been in large part renewed.   The ancient masonry, where it still exists, is of very variable quality.   It is formed partly of bricks, some of which are very thin, while others are of good size.   The courses are horizontal but the mortar-beds are wide.   In other places the masonry is distinctly polychromatic, and formed of bricks and ashlar, or of bricks, herring-bone rubble and ashlar. Herring-bone brick courses occur in the façade.

IV.   The interior has been so entirely covered with plaster as to be without interest.   The façade still retains some of its arched corbel-tables surmounted by a saw tooth (Plate 101, Fig. 1).

V.   The monument is an authentically dated edifice of 1120.

---

1 (Verona).

2 412.

3   REST A. D. 1867   ROSINI [A]UTORE

LOMBARD ARCHITECTURE

ISOLA S. GIULIO,[1] S. GIULIO

(Plate 100, Fig. 8, 9, 10)

I. Although the charming church of S. Giulio is an important monument of Romanesque art, and enjoys the additional advantage of being situated in one of the most romantic and picturesque spots of all Italy, it has been but very little studied by archæologists. The most important work upon the basilica is undoubtedly that of Rusconi, but for the history of the island and a critical study of the life of the saint, the work of Fusi should be consulted. This book contains a bibliography which extends over eighteen closely printed pages, but most of the works cited are only very indirectly concerned with the basilica of S. Giulio and its history. The interesting ambo has been illustrated by Venturi,[2] under the erroneous name of S. Giusto.

II. The entire rich literature of the mediæval hagiographers has produced few works so completely charming and so full of poetry as the legend of the saints Giulio and Giuliano. It seems as if the author, who was evidently one of the canons at the Isola,[3] had been inspired by the scenery with which he was surrounded to rise to exceptional heights of lyric beauty. The dreamy softness of the lake of Orta itself, where the gentleness of the Italian plain melts into the rugged grandeur of the Alps, seems reflected in his life of the saint, in which there is a distinct foreshadowing of the spirit of the *Fioretti* of St. Francis. This very spirit of gentleness, the style of the Latin in which the life is written, and the pointed reference to the martyrdom of S. Arialdo, serve to establish its date as not earlier than the XII century.

According to this legend, S. Giulio and S. Giuliano were two priests of Ægina. Driven by heretical persecution from their homes, they crossed the sea and came to the emperor Theodosius, by whom they were commissioned to make propaganda for the Christian faith. Starting from near Rome, they proceeded throughout Latium, performing miracles and constructing churches; for they had taken a vow that they would dedicate to Christ a hundred basilicas.[4] They thus proceeded northward performing good works, until they at last arrived at Gozzano, near the shores of the lake of Orta. Here they began the ninety-ninth basilica. S. Giulio left his deacon, S. Giuliano, to superintend the work upon the new church and proceeded to the lake of Orta, in the middle of which he saw an island of no great size, where no man had ever lived. As he stood looking at it, he wondered how it would be

---

[1] Lago di Orta (Novara).   [2] III, 199-200.

[3] Sed ut ad commemorationem fratrum nunc redeat stylus, nec illud sileam, quod contulit sanctissimus Julius sacra altaris ministeria, etc.

[4] Nam in totius mundi orbem longe lateque huc atque illuc pio favoris studio centum basilicas dedicaverunt, quas omnes ob sanctam Ecclesiam uni viro indissolubili vinculo Christo Domino spoponderunt.

possible for him to reach it; but the man of God, taking refuge in Christ, as usual, fell on his knees on the ground, and poured out a prayer to the Lord, saying: Lord God Omnipotent, Jesus Christ, in virtue of Thy power grant that I this day may use my cloak as a boat, and that, protected by Thy right hand, I may merit to proceed over the waves and to reach the island, in order that to the glory of Thy twelve apostles, I may found in it a basilica, since on this shore I shall never find a boat. Then the man of God, Giulio, took off his cloak and spread it over the water, and having made the sign of the cross, he mounted upon it as upon a boat, and having taken the cane with which he was accustomed to support himself, in a marvellous manner he came safely to the island, thanks to the merits of Him who made the sea support the footsteps of Peter. Now, that island was so full of serpents that no one could ever approach the rock because of the very great multitude of these reptiles. There was also on the island a cliff surrounded by undergrowth and briars, so that it seemed fitter to be the asylum of serpents rather than that of men. But the man of God, S. Giulio, armed with the sign of the holy cross, reached the island safely and sought the summit of the rock; and when he had come thither, he took a sapling; and fashioning from it a cross, he planted it in a fissure of the rock, and having called together the serpents he thus spoke to them saying: For a long time you have possessed this heap of rocks. Now, in the name of the Father and the Son and the Holy Ghost, I command you begone hence, and give to me, a servant of Christ, this place for a habitation, and I shall build a church to the twelve apostles in the name of the Lord. When the serpents heard these words, without any delay or hesitation they deserted that place as the holy man had commanded, and proceeded together to a mountain of the mainland. Then the blessed man, Giulio, began to dedicate in the island a basilica in honour of the twelve apostles. Giuliano, however, continued to labour in the church which some time before they had begun to construct at Gozzano. But the man of God, Giuliano, the deacon, when he had finished the work of construction, undertook to prepare a tomb for his saintly brother, Giulio. Meanwhile, it happened that S. Giulio came back from the island to visit the work of his brother, and thus S. Giuliano showed him the new church completely finished, saying, my Lord and brother, you see that everything is finished. Only the sepulchre is being constructed in which you shall rest when you fall asleep. To him the man of God, Giulio, replied: Finish quickly what you have begun, since you yourself must be placed in it. This the man of God said in the spirit of prophecy. Moreover, after everything was completed, which had been begun in that church, S. Giuliano passed to the Lord. The man of God, Giulio, performed over him the fitting obsequies, and placed him in the tomb at Gozzano. Then S. Giulio returned to the work which he had begun on the island, and completed it worthily, and decorated it nobly. At that time a certain man, a senator, Audenzio by name, rich, noble and magnificent, had been placed by the emperor in power over the people. When he heard the fame of S. Giulio, he said to his servants: Let us take ship, and go to the island, that we may see and know what the man of God, Giulio, hath done there. Therefore he took a boat, and he came to the island where was the man of God, and he diligently inspected all things which that holy man had there done. For the entire building had been completed, and the saint had prepared for himself a sepulchre. Then Audenzio, seeing every work which had been done by the man of God, was well pleased with it, and entered the church to pray. Moreover, he spoke to the man of God, Giulio, with sweet words, saying: Father, if there is anything which you would wish to request from us, hesitate not to ask, since I desire to fulfill according to my ability what you command. The saint, hearing these and other similar expressions of kindliness, embraced Audenzio in the impulse of gratitude, saying: Son, let us make for you a sepulchre here next to mine, in which, after your death, you shall rest. But Audenzio replied and said: You, Father, shall have your sepulchre here, but I have mine prepared at Milan. But the man of God, Giulio, replied, saying: Believe me, since so it is pleasing to me, your body shall rest next to mine in the tomb. Audenzio, therefore, took his leave and came to Milan. S. Giulio, who had long desired to be dissolved and to be with Christ, not long after passed to the Lord, and was placed in the tomb which he had prepared for himself in the church of the holy apostles.[5]

[5] Tum inde progressus venit ad locum qui appellatur Mucorus, doubus procul millibus a loco, quem paullo superius distantem diximus, prospiciensque vidit a longe insulam non adeo magnam, in qua nullus hominum inhabitans erat; ac diutius morans mente vertebat, quomodo aditus in eam ingrediendi daretur. Sed vir Domini ad consuetum se convertens consilium, genibus in terram defixis orationem fundit ad Dominum, dicens: Domine Deus omnipotens Jesu Christe, in tuae magnitudinis virtute tribue hoc operimento meo mihi hodie ad usum naviculæ uti, ut tua protectus dextera, merear super undas salvari, atque ingredi in insulam me permittas; ut ad laudem duodecim Apostolorum tuorum in ea possim fundare basilicam, quoniam in hoc littore nusquam navim reperio. Tunc vir Domini Julius exuvit se veste, quam cappam [= pallium] nominamus, eamque super aquam extendit, et facto signo Crucis super aquam ascendit; areptoque baculo, quo solebat sustentari, mirum in modum, quasi in navis soliditate confixus, et usque ad insulam, ille qui Petri calcabile plantis præbuit mare, super latices hunc deduxit incolumen. Erat autem eadem insula ita plena serpentibus, ut nec quisquam appropinquare ad ripæ accessum præ nimia multitudine serpentum posset. Saxum quoque in insula cespitibus et vepribus circumseptum ibi invenit, quod potius serpentibus quam hominibus præbebat hospitium. Sed vir Domini S. Julius signo sanctæ Crucis armatus, in eamdem insulam securus ingreditur, ac petræ appetit summitatem. At ubi rursus in petræ ascendit cacumen, accipiens rubusculum, faciensque ex eo signum crucis in petræ fissuram defixit; advocatisque ad se serpentibus, ita eos allocutus est, dicens: Jam adeo longum est tempus, quod istum acervum lapidum possedistis; nunc autem in nomine Patris et Filii et Spiritus sancti præcipio vobis ut exeatis ex hoc loco, detisque mihi locum servo Christi ad habitandum, et in nomine Domini, duodecim Apostolorum ecclesiam construendam. Qui audientes hujusmodi verba, absque ulla dilatione vel mora, eumdem locum secundum sancti viri præceptum deseruerunt, et ad montem qui Camuncinus dicitur progressi

ISOLA S. GIULIO, S. GIULIO

That SS. Giulio and Audenzio were both buried at Isola is not only related in the legend of the saints, but is the constant tradition of the church of S. Giulio, as witnessed, for example, by an inscription of the Renaissance in the choir.[6]

sunt. Tunc beatissimus vir Julius cœpit in eadem insula in duodecim Apostolorum honore basilicam dedicare. Julianus vero insistebat labori in eadem quam pridem in Gaudiano construere cœperant, laborantes ambo pariter in zelo sancti certaminis. Sed vir Domini Julianus Diaconus suæ expleto opere fabricæ tumulum sanctissimo fratri Julio præparare curavit. Interea contigit ut S. Julius ab insula remeans opera fratris visitaret. Itaque S. Julianus totam fabricam templi cunctamque consummatam ostendit structuram, dicens: Domine frater vides quod consummata sunt omnia. Sepulchrum tantum construitur, in quo dormitionis tempore requiescas. Cui vir Domini Julius, Fac, inquit, fac celeriter, quod cœpisti, quoniam tu in eodem es collocandus. Hoc nimirum vir Domini per contemplationem prophetiæ spiritus est intuitus, quod fratri disseruit, quod postmodum debuit fieri, jam pridem cognovit. Postquam autem consummata sunt omnia, quæ in eadem structura fuerant inchoata, S. Julianus migravit ad Dominum. Cui vir Domini Julius meritas exhibens exsequias, posuit eum in eodem monumento. Reversus autem ad cœptum opus Beatissimus Julius, illud digno labore ad perfectionem perduxit, ac nobili decoravit honore. Eodem tempore vir quidam Senator Audentius nomine, dives et nobilis atque magnificus, eratque constitutus ab Imperatore in populo validam habens potestatem; qui audiens Beatissimi Julii famam, ait ad sibi domesticos: Ascendamus in navim, et ingrediamur insulam, sciscitantes et investigantes, quidnam in ea vir Domini Julius fecerit. Qui profectus ascendit in navim, et ad insulam ubi vir Domini morabatur advenit, et omnia quæ in eadem vir sanctus gesserat diligenter prævidere curavit. Jam enim omnis domus constructio perfecte fuerat consummata, sepulchrum etiam in eodem templo sibi præparatum habebat. Præfatus vero Audentius cernens omne opus quod a viro Dei fuerat peractum, eidem nihilominus placuit, templumque ingressus oravit. Virum autem Dei Julium interea dulciloquio commemorans allocutus est, dicens: Domine Pater, si est aliquid, quod ex nostro velitis opportunitatis gratia suscipere adjutorio, imperare ne pigeat; qua cupio secundum vires quod jubetis implere. Hæc et his similia humanitatis ab eodem vir beatissimus audiens, cum gratiarum actione eum amplexus est, dicens: Fili, faciamus tibi hic sepulchrum juxta me, in quo post obitum requiescas. Cui Audentius, Tu, inquit, Pater hic habeas sepulchrum, ego jam Mediolani habeo præparatum. Ad quem vir Domini Julius, Crede, inquit, mihi, quia sic placet mihi, ut juxta corpus meum, tuum in sepulchro ponatur. Audentius autem licentiam postulans Mediolanum venit. Sanctus itaque Julius cupiens jam dissolvi et esse cum Christo, postmodum non multo percurso spatio felix migravit ad Dominum, depositusque in sepulchro quod quidem in ecclesia sanctorum Apostolorum sibimet præparaverat, et cum omni veneratione ac merito reclinatus est, pridie Kalend. Februarii. . . . (*Acta Sanctorum*, III, Januarii, die XXXI, 717).

[6]

HIC SVNT . CON
DITA CORPORA
SS. IVLII P̄BR̄I . ET
CONFESSORIS
DEMETRY MART.
PHILIBERTI ABBS.
AVDENTY CONFS.
ET . ELIÆ . HÆREM

467

The attempt which has been made to identify this church with the basilica of the apostles mentioned by Ennodio, is, however, without sufficient foundation.[7]

The island was twice besieged in the X century, once in 956, and again in 961. In the following year (962) Otto the Great conceded a diploma to the canons in gratitude for his victory, and donated several possessions, among others the castle of Isola S. Giulio, which had been seized by Berenger.[8] It is evident, therefore, that at this period the church was already collegiate. A document of 970 records the exchange of certain goods between the prevosto of the church of S. Giulio and the bishop of Novara.[9] In a document of February, 976,[10] it is said of the basilica of S. Giulio in *Insula sancti iulii* and the *basilica Sancti Victoris constructa infra Castro agredade* that *ambas basilicas cum omni suorum pertinencia pertinere uidetur de sub regimine et potestatem ipsius Episcopato sancte nouariensis etclesie . . .*

Odemario, bishop of Novara from 1235 to 1249, was buried in the church.[11]

In 1697 the crypt was remade, and I presume that it was about this time that the edifice was baroccoized.[12] The XIX century saw the usual barbarous restorations carried out in the basilica. Rusconi laments the destruction of the superb mosaic pavement, on which he says were represented the signs of the zodiac and the visions of St. Joseph.[13] Until 1880, the ambo had been supported by three columns and by one of the piers of the nave. The fourth column, which had been lacking for centuries, was found and replaced, but the base had to be remade.

III. The church consisted of a nave of two double bays, two side aisles, galleries, projecting transepts and an apse. There are also several chapels and twin towers (which look like campaniles, although in reality they contain the stairway leading to the galleries) flanking the façade. The interior has been much baroccoized (Plate 100, Fig. 8), and the exterior is largely masked

---

[7] Rusconi, 141-142.

[8] In nomine sancte indiuidueque trinitatis. Hotto diuinae dispositione prouidentia Imperator Augustus. . . . Quapropter notum sit . . . nos non immemores beneficiorum trinae insecabilisque maiestatis . . . misericorditer nobis uictoriam tribuens quoddam castrum uidelicet insulam sancti iulii iam dudum per berengarium regem ab episcopatu nouariensi sublatum et sibi usurpatam nec non contra nos in rebellionem positam nostrae subdiderit ditioni per nostrae imperialis auctoritatis paginam tribuisse et omnino concedisse aecclesiae in predicto castro sitae in honore uero sancti iulii confessoris X̅p̅i̅ cuius corpus humatum ibidem requiescit . . . ut nullus Episcopus praefatae nouariensis ecclesiae qui pro tempore fuerit presumat iam dictas res de uictu et stipendio canonicorum subtrahere . . . Data IIII kalend. augustas anno dominicae incarnationis DCCCCLXII. anno uero imperii domini Hottonis serenissimi augusti primo inditione quinta. Actum in uilla quae dicitur horta prope lacum eiusdem sancti iulii feliciter amen. (*Hist. Pat. Mon.*, I, 194).

[9] *Ibid.*, 225.　　[10] *Ibid.*, 246.

[11] Odemarius sedit XIII annos et m. sex et d. decem et obiit decimo Aprilis et iacet in ecclesia b. Julii de Insula. (Dittico di S. Gaudenzio, ed. Savio, *Vescovi*, 242).

[12] Rusconi, 154.　　[13] Rusconi, 154.

by the surrounding buildings; nevertheless the original forms of the architecture can still be made out. At present, the church is entirely vaulted. The groin vaults of the side aisles are in part original, in part restored on the ancient lines. They are slightly, but not excessively, domed, and are supplied with wall and transverse ribs. The vaults of the two central bays of the southern side aisle, adorned with exquisite frescos (Plate 100, Fig. 10), are ancient, but the other vaults have been, without exception, restored. The gallery vaults are of similar type, but all seem to have been restored on the original lines. Thus the original masonry of the vaults is nowhere to be seen. The nave and transept vaults appear to be modern, as does also the octagonal cloistered vault of the crossing, notwithstanding the fact that the conical squinches and the exterior are ancient.

The nave piers, except four, are compound, and have always been so, as is proved by the old capitals still preserved. The original section was the same as that of the present piers, except that the system of the nave was semicircular instead of rectangular. This is seen clearly in the second pier from the west on the north side, where part of the original system has been bared to show a fresco. The side-aisle responds (which do not alternate) have all the same section, consisting of five members, the central one of which is semicircular (Plate 100, Fig. 10). The western responds consist of a flat pilaster in two orders. The third piers from the west of the nave, and the crossing piers, are rectangular, with re-entrant angles. The responds in the north gallery are in the form of pilasters in two orders, but those in the south gallery are in three orders. Similar members are attached to the piers on the side of the gallery, but there are always three members, never five. The ancient gallery is well preserved. Of the clearstory, one of the old windows is still preserved in the west bay on the south side, and the transverse buttresses across the galleries are still in part extant, especially on the north side. The vaults of the nave and gallery are reinforced externally by vigorous buttresses.

The masonry consists in part of ashlar, large, roughly squared blocks being laid in courses for the most part fairly horizontal, and with mortar-beds varying from 1 to $3\frac{1}{2}$ centimetres in depth. In small part, however, it consists of a sort of rubble, formed of small, uncut stones, laid in courses more or less horizontal, and bound together by ashlar quoins. Bits of brick are introduced here and there, and the cornices of the apse and cupola are built of brick in which herring-bone work is chiefly used.

All the semicircular colonnettes of the responds and of the piers (five in number in each side aisle) have separate capitals. The other members have no capitals, but the groins are carried through and supported on the relative spurs (Plate 100, Fig. 10), or else crowded on the imposts of the transverse arches. The rectangular pilaster strips supporting the arches of the main arcade or the transverse ribs have simple imposts.

IV. The capitals of the side-aisle responds are evidently taken from an earlier building, and form an interesting study. They may be divided into several types, as follows: (1) The uncarved acanthus type (Plate 100, Fig. 9, 10). The dry, uncarved leaves are placed in two rows, or in a single row. The volutes are altogether omitted or simply scratched on the surface. The abacus sometimes is adorned with queer crude ornaments in the shape of rosettes. (2) The voluted type (Plate 100, Fig. 10). The large volutes scratched on the surface form the dominant motive of the decoration, and with these volutes are combined either depressed leaves, or rosette ornament without leaves. (3) This type is like the first, except the leaves have veins scratched upon them. (4) To this group belongs only one capital, which is adorned with a strange motive that seems to have been inspired by the decoration on the outside of the volutes of a classic Ionic capital.

The moulded imposts, on the other hand, were made for their present position, as is also one capital, that of the fourth respond from the west in the north side aisle. This capital, characterized by volutes, under which is a single uncarved leaf, by an acanthus-anthemion ornament, very dry and crisp, and by an interlace, shows the same admirable execution as the sculptures of the ambo.

The cupola and façade are adorned with arched corbel-tables and the cupola has also a gallery. The apse has blind niches in two orders, but, so far as I can see, no pilaster strips. The piers of the interior either have no bases or these are not visible.

The well-known ambo (Plate 100, Fig. 8) is constructed of black marble, and is supported on four columns, of which the two more slender ones are covered with all-over patterns. Of the capitals three imitate classical Roman orders: the Doric (echinus carved with an egg-and-dart, a bead-moulding below), the Composite, and the Corinthian. The latter is so splendid an imitation that it would be almost impossible to distinguish it from an original Roman work. The fourth capital (unfinished), like the two smooth shafts (doubtless also unfinished and which were intended to be covered with diapering like the others), is probably also imitated from classical types. It is of the Composite style, but grotesque heads are substituted for volutes, and there is only a single row of acanthus leaves. The bases are Attic, with griffes. The pulpit proper is adorned with a row of superb acanthus leaves, conventional foliage ornament, grotesques (among others a centaur), interlaces, etc. There are also the symbols of the four Evangelists, together with a human figure, which I take to be that of S. Giulio. It is true there is no halo, but several of the Evangelists are without this attribute. The saint is dressed in a curious sort of cloak, and in his hands he holds the cane which is frequently mentioned in the legend. His beardless face denotes his rank as priest.

The style of these sculptures is characterized by a consummate technique that betrays the sculptor into hardness. More beautiful acanthus leaves, more delicate foliage, more accurately cut feathers than those of the eagle, even Roman workmen never produced. There is, however, much more felicitous rendering of conventional ornament than of figures. As a sculptor the artist shows himself absolutely without feeling for line or composition. His faces are entirely without expression, the noses are very long, the chins heavy, the lower parts of the face much too large. His draperies are stiff and unbroken, and the whole effect is metallic. This entire extraordinary composition looks like a huge bronze casting, and even the superbly executed conventional ornament is as unyielding as adamant.

A comparison of the conventional ornament of this ambo with that of the cloister of S. Orso at Aosta (Plate 13, Fig. 3; Plate 14, Fig. 1, 2, 3; Plate 15, Fig. 3) leaves little doubt that the two are the work of very closely related artists. In both there is the same hardness, the same metallic quality, the same precision, the same mastery of conventional ornament, and the same crudity in the figure work. The figured capitals of the Aosta cloister, it is true, are more full of motion, more broken up, less stolid than those of the S. Giulio ambo; the eyes and noses are executed in an entirely different way in the two monuments; but, on the other hand, the hands are identical, and in some cases the treatment of the hair. It is notable, however, that the classical element, so strong at Isola, is lacking at Aosta. The ambo at Isola is a product of the school of Milan and Pavia. The faces, the immobility of the composition, the heaviness of the drapery, the lack of expression, the wings of the angel, all clearly recall such compositions as the Last Supper in the cathedral of Lodi, or the sculptures of S. Michele and S. Pietro in Ciel d'Oro at Pavia. The sculptor of Isola underwent, however, Emilian influence, and derived much, if not from Guglielmo da Modena directly, at least from his followers. The treatment of the boots and feet strongly recalls the sculptures at Sasso (Plate 205, Fig. 4) and Quarantoli (Plate 190, Fig. 1). Between the treatment of the faces in the sculptures of Quarantoli and Isola there is an analogy so striking that it can not be fortuitous. The Aosta sculptures, on the other hand, seem to have been derived from those of Isola, rather than to have influenced them.

V. The Carlovingian capitals of the church, which belong to what we have called the first type, show close analogy in the treatment of the leaves with certain capitals at S. Vincenzo in Prato of Milan (compare Plate 100, Fig. 9, with Plate 136, Fig. 4), a monument which dates from c. 830. Those of the second type recall Group B of the fragments of the Chiesa d'Aurona of c. 950. Those of the third group, on the other hand, have the curious scratched ornament, of which one of the earliest examples is found in the capital of Luitprando in S. Pietro in Ciel d'Oro at Pavia (Plate 177, Fig. 2), a surely dated monument of 743, but which continued in use throughout the

IX century, and occurs as late as 903 in two capitals of the crypt of S. Savino in Piacenza (Plate 186, Fig. 2, 3). The fourth capital, of more distinctive type, shows close analogy with the capitals at S. Zeno of Bardolino (Plate 19, Fig. 1, 3), both in the imitation of the Ionic forms, and in the spirit of the design. The capitals of Bardolino date from c. 875. It will be seen, therefore, that these capitals show analogies with other Carlovingian works executed all the way from 743 to 950. In this early period, the retention of archaic types frequently causes difficulty in assigning dates. The crude quality of the execution in Isola S. Giulio, however, is sufficient to show that these capitals can not possibly be of the age of Luitprando. Compared with the capital of S. Pietro in Ciel d'Oro, they are seen to be decadent. Compared even with those of early IX century at S. Vincenzo in Prato at Milan, those of Isola appear far inferior. Compare, for example, the weak drawing of the volutes in the Isola capital (Plate 100, Fig. 9) with those of the capitals of S. Vincenzo (Plate 136, Fig. 2; Plate 137, Fig. 5). The technique is even weaker than that of S. Zeno of Bardolino (c. 875), and is much more on a par with that of the crypt capitals of S. Savino at Piacenza (903). These capitals may therefore be assigned to c. 900.

The XII century church and the ambo are contemporaneous with each other as is proved by the fact that the sculptor of the ambo executed one of the capitals in the northern side aisle. We have already seen that there is reason to believe that the sculptures of Aosta, executed in 1133, were influenced by those of Isola. The ambo of Isola must consequently be earlier than 1133, and in view of its analogies with the Last Supper of Lodi (c. 1115) and the sculptures at Quarantoli (1114), may be assigned to c. 1120. This date agrees well with the architectural forms of the church. The plan of the edifice, with gallery and towers flanking the façade, strongly recalls S. Lorenzo of Verona, a building which dates from 1110.

IVREA,[1] DUOMO

(Plate 101, Fig. 2, 3, 4, 5, 6)

I. The cathedral of Ivrea has suffered so severely from modernization that it has been neglected almost entirely by archæologists. To Rivoira[2] belongs the credit of having rescued it from obscurity, and of having pointed out the significance of the remains of ancient architecture which it contains. The mosaics have been studied by Aus'm Weerth[3] and illustrated by Venturi.[4]

II. An inscription in the ambulatory, already published by Rivoira, states: "The bishop Veremondo built this temple to the Lord from its

[1] (Torino).   [2] 224 f.   [3] 21.   [4] III, 434.

foundations."[5] The letters are extremely classic in character, and the inscription is surrounded by a decorated border that makes it impossible to doubt that it really was executed in the X century. The bishop referred to must consequently be that S. Veremondo who, according to Savio,[6] was bishop in 969 and perhaps as early as 962, and died in 1001 or 1002. Cappelletti[7] tells us that S. Veremondo was bishop of Ivrea at the time the body of the martyr S. Pegalo was found and translated into the cathedral. It may have been that the discovery of the body of the saint caused S. Veremondo to rebuild the cathedral. That he restored it is, according to Rivoira, recorded in one of the breviaries of Ivrea.[8]

Little else is known in regard to the history of the monument. A prevosto is named in 1093,[9] and a donation was made to the church in the following year.[10] In 1464 a new sacristy was erected. A complete reconstruction of the edifice in the classic style was begun in the year 1761, as is recorded in an inscription in the exterior of the north wall, and in 1854 the church was extended to the west and a new façade erected, as is recorded in an inscription over the main portal.

III. The cathedral of Ivrea is a Renaissance and modern structure, which, however, retains in the ambulatory (Plate 101, Fig. 3), the crypt, the two campanili flanking the choir (Plate 101, Fig. 2, 5), the central cupola, the cloister (Plate 101, Fig. 4) and the mosaic now preserved in the Seminario (Plate 101, Fig. 6), important fragments of Romanesque architecture.

These fragments evidently date from different epochs. To the first belong five columns, with capitals, in the ambulatory. At present these are imbedded in the solid wall which separates the ambulatory from the choir, but originally they appear to have been free-standing (Plate 101, Fig. 3). They are disposed, not in the form of a semicircle, but of a half-diamond or triangle, the central column being placed on the axis of the church, and the others in straight lines diverging at an angle of approximately 45 degrees to the axis. The outer supports on the south side certainly, and probably also on the north side, were not single but coupled columns. The outer wall of the ambulatory is entirely modern, as are the vaults (Plate 101, Fig. 3). It is, therefore, impossible to determine what system of roofing was employed in the Romanesque ambulatory. This ambulatory is much raised, and

[5]
     ✠ CONDIDIT HOC
     DOMINO PRAE
     SVL VVARMVN
     DVS AB IMO

[6] *Vescovi*, 193-194.   [7] XIV, 184.
[8] Vetustam aedem Deipare sacram novis operibus auxit. . . .   [9] Durando, 11.
[10] This has been published by Carutti, *Archivio Storico Italiano*, 4 Serie, II, 1878, 353.

approached by a high flight of steps, which probably marked the limits of the original choir.

That part of the crypt which is placed beneath the ambulatory and the eastern part of the choir also belongs to the first era of construction. The groin vaults are undomed and without ribs.

Those parts of the church which belong to the second era of construction are characterized by structural forms very different from those just described. The side aisles of the choir are covered with highly domed groin vaults with transverse arches. These vaults, like the vaults in the western parts of the crypt, have probably been modernized, but it is certain that they preserve to a large extent their original form. The responds were of five members, of which the central ones were semicircular.

The campanili are of six stories (Plate 101, Fig. 2, 5), the upper ones of which are lighted by triforia and bifora. They are covered with stucco so that the masonry can not be studied.

In the garden, directly behind the apse, are notable remains of the old cloister (Plate 101, Fig. 4).

IV. The capitals of the ambulatory are either pilfered antique or formed of almost uncarved blocks of stone.

The two eras of construction of the crypt are clearly indicated by the style of the capitals. In the eastern portion, the capitals, with one exception, are formed of uncarved, unornamented blocks of stone. The exceptional capital is covered with an all-over ornament, very flatly and roundly scratched on the surface. Two blocks crowning rectangular piers have chamfered corners. The capitals of the western part of the crypt, on the other hand, are of fully developed Lombard type. Except for a few animals' heads, the grotesque element is noticeably lacking. The undercutting is very deep. In some cases the curled-over leaves and volutes resemble great handles. The Corinthianesque type prevails.

The capitals of the cloister, long and slim, appear to have been adorned with interlaces, acanthus leaves and grotesques (Plate 101, Fig. 4), but have unfortunately been much damaged.

Except in the belfries—which are obviously of the XIII century—the campanili have no carved capitals. They are, however, ornamented by arched corbel-tables carried on pilaster strips, and grouped two and two in the lower stories, in larger numbers above. The campanili are not symmetrical in design, and the construction evidently progressed very slowly. Additions seem to have been made first to the northern, then to the southern.

The capitals of the side aisles of the choir are cubic or crudely foliated.

A fragment of the ancient mosaic is preserved in the north wall of the court-yard of the Seminario, on the ground floor. It evidently represented Philosophy and the seven liberal arts (Plate 101, Fig. 6). In what was once the middle, sits P|HI|LO|SO|FI|A, crowned. With her right hand she passes a book inscribed with meaningless Greek letters to GRA|MA|TI|CA, the only figure extant on the right side of Philosophy and badly damaged. Below are some curious letters which look as if they might be Greek, disposed in a horizontal and a vertical band. The horizontal strip seems to contain the same letters in the same order, but some of them are placed upside down. In her left hand Philosophy holds a book, also with an unmeaning inscription:

E͞A͞A͞L

OMO

On the left of Philosophy sits DIALE|TIC|A, holding a book with her left hand. With her right hand she points downward with a gesture of argumentation, which is further emphasized by the word V|T͞R͞V "whether" inscribed below. Next sits G|E|O|ME|TRI|A, holding in her hands a slim rod. Finally comes the figure of ARIMETI|CA, so much ruined that it is impossible to say whether she ever held any attribute, although the position of the hands suggests that she may have had a counting-board. All the arts, with the exception of Philosophy, are bare-headed.

This mosaic is executed in black and white, but the bench, parts of the robes, and a few other details, are in red.

V. The ambulatory in the western part of the crypt seems to be Carlovingian in its very absence of architectural character, and undoubtedly belongs to the edifice erected by S. Veremondo, c. 1000. The eastern part of the crypt, the side aisles of the choir, the central tower, the cloisters, and the mosaics, are, on the other hand, much later. The interlaced ornament on certain capitals of the cloister (Plate 101, Fig. 4) seems to show the strong influence of certain capitals in the atrium of S. Ambrogio of Milan (Plate 120, Fig. 2, 4), an edifice completed before 1098. Allowing some years for the new style to travel as far as Ivrea, we may assign these portions of the cathedral to c. 1105. This date accords well with the style of the mosaic and of the capitals of the side aisles of the choir and of the western part of the crypt. The campanili, begun probably in the early years of the XI century, seem to have been completed only two hundred years later.

IVREA,[1] S. STEFANO

I. The campanile of S. Stefano has been published by Rivoira.[2] The documents of the archives have been edited by Savio and Barelli in the *Biblioteca della Società Storica Subalpina*.[3]

[1] (Torino).

[2] 226.

[3] In our bibliography this work is listed under Durando.

II. Three different charters of foundation of the abbey of S. Stefano are extant, one purporting to date from 1001, the second from 1042, and the third from 1044. The three have been printed in parallel by Savio, who has proved that the charters of 1001 and 1042 are falsifications. From the genuine charter of 1044 it is evident that at that date the bishop Enrico had already restored and consecrated the very ancient chapel of S. Stefano, and had established therein a monastery.[4]

Notwithstanding the charter of foundation of 1044, it is evident that the monastery must have been in existence somewhat before this formal endowment, since it was privileged by Henry III, in 1042.[5] According to Boggio[6] the church was consecrated in 1041, but whence this notice was derived I do not know.[7]

III. Of the ancient abbey there remains only the campanile. This is a broad structure of six stories. The openings consist of two simple windows, two bifora or a triforium in each face.

IV. The capitals are splayed. The stories are marked by string-courses of saw teeth and arched corbel-tables, simple in the two upper stories, divided into two groups of four in the lower stories.

V. The campanile of S. Stefano may be considered an authentically dated monument of c. 1041.

[4] . . . (Anno incar)nationis dominicę millesimo quadragesimo quarto. . . . Heinricus huic sanctę hyporediensi ecclesię non meis meritis superna S. Spiritus dignatione episcopus. . . . Quapropter matricis nostrę ecclesię kapellam unam antiquissimam casum minitante maceria Jn honorem salvatoris et protomartyris eius stephani dedicatam Jn meliorem statum restituimus et consacratam ad sanctę et singularis vitę normam ordinavimus et de sumptibus et redditibus nostris secundum posse donavimus. . . . Jn primis yporedię sedilia quatuor, . . . et insulam ante monasterium ipsius ecclesię . . . Hæc concedendo stabilimus et prefatę cenobitę vitę (mo)nasticę sub abbate quem consecravimus, L. et cętu monastico inviolabiliter roboramus, tam quę nunc habet, quam ea futuris temporibus a fidelibus christianis est conqui(s)itura et possessura. (Durando, ed. Savio, 254).

[5] The best edition of this document is that of Barelli. (Durando, 279).

[6] 41.

[7] The catalogue of the bishops of Asti (ed. Savio, *Vescovi*, 111) states that Guglielmo, bishop of Asti, was present at the foundation of the church of S. Stefano, in 1041. This notice is probably derived from an erroneous reading of the charter of foundation, since Guglielmo is mentioned among the bishops present in the preamble to that document.

LAGO DI MEZZOLA,[1] S. FEDELINO

(Plate 102, Fig. 1)

I.   The chapel of S. Fedelino was discovered by Buzzetti, who, between the years 1900 and 1906, wrote three different monographs upon the church and the history of the relics of S. Fedele.   In 1902 and 1903 Cavagna Sangiuliani published two monographs on the little building.   Monti has also spoken of the edifice at some length.[2]   In 1903 appeared still another monograph by Perrone.

II.   The primary source for the history of the chapel of S. Fedelino is the *Corporis Sancti Fidelis Inventio et Prima Translatio*,[3] a chronicle written at the time of the translation in the X century.   According to this chronicle, and according to the constant tradition of the church of Como, S. Fedele suffered martyrdom at a place called Samolaco or Summolago (Summus Lacus), situated at the extreme upper end of the Lake of Como. Precisely where this Samolaco stood is not known, but in view of the fact that the Lago di Mezzola in ancient times formed part of the Lake of Como, it may well have been placed at precisely the spot where now stands the little church of S. Fedelino.   The tradition further affirms that the body of the martyr was buried in the church of Samolaco, and continued to be held in great veneration until that place was destroyed by the Saracens.   Tatti,[4] it is true, has supposed that it was destroyed, not by the Saracens, but by the Lombards under Agilulfo, in 602.   Buzzetti,[5] on the other hand, has found evidence that the chronicle is exact in ascribing the destruction to the Saracens.

Now, documents speak of two other churches of S. Fedele, situated not far from the head of the Lake of Como.   One is a monastic church which stood apparently in the Valtellina, and which is mentioned in a diploma of Lothair I (820-840).[6]   The other is a pieve situated at Samolaco, and mentioned in 973.[7]   The probabilities seem to be that it was neither in the monastery of the Valtellina, nor in the pieve situated not far from Chiavenna that the body of the saint was buried.   It may therefore be conjectured—

---

[1] The chapel of S. Fedelino lies on the western shore of the lake of Mezzola, across the Mera river, and about a kilometre distant from the commune of Novate Mezzola, province of Sondrio.

[2] 469.

[3] This legend was first published in the *Analecta Bollandiana*, IX, 1890, 354 f., and has been reprinted by Buzzetti (*Memorie*).

[4] I, 655.   [5] 178 f.   [6] Tatti, I, 829.

[7] . . . ecclesie et plebis sancti Fidelis, que est posita in loco et fundo Sumnolago que plebe ipsa de sub potestate domni et episcopatu ipsius sancte comensis ecclesie. (*Hist. Pat. Mon.*, XIII, 1292).

although it has not been proved—that our chapel of S. Fedelino stands on the site of this church destroyed by the Saracens.[8]

The anonymous author of the *Translatio* tells us that after the destruction by the Saracens the church remained deserted and unofficiated. "Moved by the merit of the martyr, Almighty God cast His eyes upon that church, which had been deprived of ecclesiastical services for many years, and determined to increase the cult of His martyr—an act worthy of His merciful Heart—so that men should again by their worship give to the saint that reward for his labour which God has decreed shall be paid to martyrs, since their names should daily be upon the lips of men. Therefore, in the time of Ualdo, a bishop who was ruling over the see of Como, there was a certain woman, a religious recluse, by name Dominica, who although she lived in a narrow cell, yet by means of her constant prayers dwelt in the divine palace of the celestial Jerusalem. On a certain night the martyr Fedele appeared to her in a dream, and revealed to her the presence of his body as it had been in life. She, terrified at the vision, began to ask of the martyr who he was. The martyr immediately replied: Behold in me Fedele, a martyr of the Lord, and look upon me with joyful confidence and hear what things thou must do diligently and immediately. Know that the place in which my body is buried, although it has been long sought for by many bishops of this place, has not yet been found; for the Son of God, our Lord, wishes that by the revelation of thy speech my body be found and translated; and do thou bury it in the church of S. Eufemia the Martyr thy patron. When he had done speaking, the handmaiden of the Lord awoke, and it seemed to her that she had seen what has been related, not in a dream, but in reality. But since she knew the extent of human weakness, she did not dare to relate her vision. . . . At length she called with all haste the priest who had been in the habit of confessing her. When he came she said to him: Father, to whom I confess, and whom I have taken as intermediary between myself and God, consider and investigate diligently what I shall say, and tell everything to our bishop. And when she had told of the vision the priest went to the bishop and acquainted him with

---

[8] Tatti (I, 829) evidently knew of the existence of our monument from documentary sources, although he was unacquainted with the actual edifice. The passage from the *Translatio* is as follows:

In fine igitur Cumanum lacus quondam Christianorum habitatio fuerat; qui, divino et christiano cultui servientes, postquam venerabilis Martyris caput abscisum est, SICUT IN EIVS PASSIONE LEGITVR, sepulturæ prædictum Martyrem tradiderunt. In quo loco, ad eiusdem honorem Martyris, ecclesia fabricata est. Verum, imminente persecutione Saracenorum quæ penes per omnes Italiæ fines imminebat, eiusdem loci Christianos persecuti sunt, qui, diversis eos afflictionibus lacerantes, omnia diripientes, totum illum locellum depopulati sunt. Quorum sævitia immanitatis ita iniquitate excreverat, quod neminem christianorum superstitem ibi dimiserat. Ex quo tempore locus desertus relinquitur, ecclesiæque sancti Fidelis martyris nullum, sicut oportebat, divinum officium a sacerdotibus impendebatur. (Ed. Buzzetti, *Memorie*, 196-197).

what had been said. The bishop then went to the handmaiden of God and with great eagerness heard from her mouth what has been above related. Immediately afterwards he ordered a fast of three days to be observed throughout his diocese in order that those things which the handmaiden of God had seen in a vision might, by the aid of Divine Providence, be accomplished in reality. When the fast had been completed, the bishop went again apart to the recluse. . . . At length she embarked upon a boat . . . and with psalms and all joy they came to the place in which the holy martyr was lying; . . . and Dominica, the handmaiden of God, entered the basilica, together with all the people who followed her, and they prostrated themselves on the ground and poured forth prayers to God. . . . The saint had commanded a pit situated back of the altar of the basilica to be excavated and there beneath a stone was found a treasure which surpassed in the inestimable fragrance of its odour all perfumes. And thus all the people, stimulated by the odour, turned to rejoicing. Then the holy body was taken up and covered with the greatest veneration, and thus amid the hymns of the faithful and after a quick and prosperous voyage it arrived at Como."[9]

[9] Quam (ecclesiam) autem per multorum curricula annorum, ab ecclesiasticis servitiis semotam, per meritum iam dicti Martyris respexit omnipotens Deus, et quod dignum fuerat suæ miserationis sinu ad augendæ sanctitatis sui Martyris laborem expleverat: videlicet ut iterum humana servitiis sui laboris præmium quod ad honorem Martyris fecerat consequatur et eius memoria cottidianis usibus habeatur. Tempore itaque Waldonis antistitis, qui cathedræ Cumanæ ecclesiæ præerat, quædam reclusa, devotissima femina, nomine Dominica, fuerat; quæ inclusa in angulari adyto, creberrimis obsequis Dominico cœlestis Jerusalem commorabatur palatio. Cui quadam nocte prædictus Martyr Fidelis per visum apparuit; sui præsentiam corporis, ut olim fuerat, ei innotuit. Quæ in eiusdem visionis pavore perterrita, percunctari Martyrem cœpit quis esset. Cui protinus subinfertur: Me Fidelem Domini Martyrem intuere, alacrique vultu respice, et quæ agenda sunt diligentissimæ inquisionis [sic] actione perfice. Locum autem in quo corporis proprii cadaver reconditum est te nosse ammoneo quod a quampluribus huius loci episcopis longo tempore perquisitum est, sed a nemine illorum inventum. Vult namque Dei Filius Dominus noster, quod tuæ allocutionis revelatione meum corpus debeat inveniri et suscipi, eumque [sic] in ecclesia beatæ Eufemiæ Martyris cui famularis, reconde. Cuius eloquii sententiis finitis, pervigil Dei famula facta, quæ iam dicta sunt, non visione somnii sed certo oculorum visu visum est vidisse. Quæ, humanis infirmitatis conscia, verita est tantæ seriem visionis narrare. . . . Cum omni festinantia presbyterum qui suæ confessionis particeps habebatur convocari præcipit. Cui advenienti inquit: Pater, cui mea confiteor, quem etiam mediatorem inter me et Deum proposui, quæ dicenda sunt diligentissima investigatione considera, nostroque præsuli per omnia manifesta.

Qua visione patefacta, sacerdos episcopo dirigitur eique quæ dicta sunt innotescit. Ad Dei famulum præfatus episcopus venit; summo cum desiderio, ea quæ superius gesta sunt ab eius ore didicit. Mox vero omni gregi sibi commisso triduanum ieiunium indixit ut hæc quæ præfacta Dei ancilla viderat, divina providentia adiuvante, perfici potuissent. Quo transacto ieiunio, ad eandem iterum reclusam semotim pervenit episcopus. . . . Navim denique ingressa, . . . Psallentibus autem pariter cunctis omnique cum gaudio, ad locum in quo Dei Martyr iacebat pervenientibus. . . . Ingressa vero basilicam Dei

The translation of S. Fedele is commemorated in several of the breviaries of Como. In the *Breviario i .triarchino* of 1519[10] the story is told in the words of the anonymous chronicler. In the revised version of the same breviary issued in 1585 the language is more elegant and the Latin purer, but no new details are added.[11] The *Antica Ufficitura*[12] seems also to be derived from the anonymous chronicler.[13]

The translation of S. Fedele took place in the year 964, as has been shown above in connection with the church of S. Fedele at Como.[14] From the *Translatio* we gather that the basilica in which the body of the saint was found had already fallen into ruin, since it had not been officiated for many years. After the body of the saint had been translated to Como, it is natural that a new chapel of modest proportions should have been erected to mark the site where he had suffered martyrdom, and where his body had so long reposed, and had at last been miraculously discovered. We shall presently see that the style of the architecture gives reason to believe that the existing chapel is not earlier than the beginning of the XI century. It is therefore probable that a considerable period of time elapsed after the body of the saint was translated to Como before the new chapel was erected on the site where the body had been found.

In recent years the monument has suffered from a most unfortunate and ill-advised restoration.

III. In plan the edifice is extremely simple, since it consists merely of a rectangular nave and a semicircular apse (Plate 102, Fig. 1). The nave is covered with a slightly domed groin vault with wall ribs, the apse with a half dome. The eastern gable is surmounted by a belfry of later date which has been walled up. A door on either side of the nave gives access to the structure, and a window is pierced in the south wall and another in the apse. These windows are widely splayed but were doubtless glazed. The roofing is laid directly upon the extrados of the vaults. The masonry consists of a rough rubble of stones and brick; the mortar-beds are thick, and but little attempt is made to lay the material in horizontal courses. The stones are for the most part round or of irregular shapes. No supports are provided for the groins of the vault, which are carried on corbels.

ancilla Dominica, pariterque eam insequentes universi populi, se in terram prostraverunt precesque ad Dominum fuderunt. . . . Ilico foveam quæ post altare eiusdem basilicæ posita erat perfodi iusserat. In qua tantus thesaurus inventus est desuper posito lapide, qui omnium pigmentorum inæstimabili odore fragrantiam superavit. Universus itaque populus, hoc odore perculsus, in lætitiam est conversus. Tunc sanctum corpus suscipitur, maxima cum veneratione reconditur, et sic omni prosperitate citissimo navigii cursu, universis psallentibus, Cumas deducitur. (Ed. Buzzetti, *Memorie*, 201 *seq.*).

[10] Published by Buzzetti, 332 *seq.*   [11] *Ibid.*, 336-339.   [12] *Ibid.*, 351 *seq.*

[13] For additional sources for the history of the translation of S. Fedele, see above, pp. 323-324, and Tatti, II, 75-80.

[14] p. 324.

IV. The church was anciently ornamented internally and externally with frescos. Those of the exterior have disappeared, while those of the interior, on the other hand, are for the most part well preserved. Of architectural decoration there is almost none, with the exception of the arched corbel-tables of the apse, grouped two and two by pilaster strips.

V. The masonry of S. Fedelino (Plate 102, Fig. 1) seems to be about intermediate between that of Spignò (Plate 207, Fig. 4), a surely dated monument of 991, and S. Vincenzo of Galliano (Plate 99, Fig. 1), which was erected in 1007. The arched corbel-tables of the apse, grouped two and two, are of a type that was used in the early years of the XI century—for example, at S. Giovanni of Vigolo Marchese (Plate 240, Fig. 5), a surely dated monument of 1008. S. Fedelino may consequently be ascribed to c. 1000.

LENNO,[1] BATTISTERO

(Plate 102, Fig. 2)

I. The baptistery of Lenno adjoins the church of S. Stefano. It was described in the year 1593 by Ninguarda. Barelli has published a plan, section and elevation of the edifice, which has also been described by Monti. Three half-tones are contained in Monneret de Villard's monograph upon the Isola Comacina.[2]

II. Ninguarda described the baptistery of Lenno in these words: "Within the same cemetery is the chapel of S. Giovanni, in the centre of which there is a round vase of stone with wooden cover. This serves as a baptismal font, and here baptism is administered on holy Saturday. . . . . . The church is circular and covered with a vault. Opposite the door there is a little altar with wooden rails and a small, ancient ancona and a similar predella. . . . . . The walls of the church are very rough. About the collegiate church of S. Stefano and this chapel there is a cemetery completely surrounded by a wall."[3] In 1876 the building was intelligently restored by the engineer F. Sterza. Beneath the modern polygonal apse were found the foundations of the ancient apse, which was semicircular.

---

[1] (Como).   [2] 128, 129, 130.

[3] Dentro lo stesso cemitero ci è la capella di S.to Giovanne, in mezzo della quale ci è un vaso tondo di pietra grande, coperto d'un tavolato per il S.to batesmo et qui si fano li offitij del sacro fonte il sabbato S.to . . . . . La chiesa è circolare, involtata et di rimpetto alla porta vi è un altare picolo con canzelli di legno et un'anconetta picola vecchia con una bradella simile . . . . . le mura d'essa tutte rozze. Attorno alla detta chiesa collegiata et capelle quasi annesso vi è un cemiterio circondato di muro, quale le cinge tutte. (Ninguarda, ed. Monti, II, 237).

III. The edifice is a plain octagonal structure of a single aisle, covered by a cloistered dome. This dome is surmounted by a little square lantern (Plate 102, Fig. 2). The roofing is laid directly upon the extrados of the vault. The ashlar masonry is formed of square, hard stones of different sizes, somewhat irregularly laid but closely fitted together. The masonry beds are of moderate width. In the lantern are bifora (the colonnettes of which have been restored), and the walls are pierced by widely splayed windows, probably intended to serve without glass.

IV. The exterior is ornamented with a cornice of arched corbel-tables supported on shafts or pilaster strips (Plate 102, Fig. 2). The capitals of the shafts are cubic. The only ornamented ones are two in the arcade over the principal portal (Plate 102, Fig. 2), which are of Corinthianesque type, and decorated with a single row of acanthus leaves and parallel incised lines. The interior is without decoration of any kind.

V. The masonry of the baptistery of Lenno (Plate 102, Fig. 2) is entirely similar to that of S. Benedetto (Plate 102, Fig. 5), an authentically dated monument of 1083. The baptistery may consequently be ascribed to c. 1085.

LENNO,[1] S. STEFANO

(Plate 102, Fig. 3)

I. S. Stefano is the parish church of Lenno, a commune of some importance, which lies on the west bank of the Lake of Como, nearly opposite but somewhat below Bellagio. Numerous unpublished documents regarding this pieve may be found in the manuscript transcription of Bonomi preserved in the Brera.[2] The building was described by Ninguarda in 1593, and by Boldoni in 1616. In recent years its archæology has been studied by Barelli and by Monti. Monneret de Villard in his monograph upon the Isola Comacina[3] has contributed an important analysis of the history and of the architectural forms of the building.

II. The description of Boldoni is so singular that it merits careful consideration. He says that in his day the church was well preserved and showed the evident traces of having been formerly a temple of Diana. This statement need cause no surprise, since in the XVII century most Romanesque edifices of northern Italy were popularly believed to be Roman ruins. Proceeding with the typical erudition of the period, Boldoni assures us (citing Vitruvius) that the building was formerly completely surrounded by porticoes.

---

[1] (Como).   [2] *Dip. Sti. Bdi.,* MS. AE, XV, 33-35.   [3] 131-132.

Traces of these porticoes, which were in two stories, and supported on rectangular piers, he says were still apparent in the façade. Barbarous and ignorant posterity, however, had walled up the exterior intercolumniations, and opened an arcade in the wall, so that what had formerly been an exterior portico, became an interior side aisle.[4]

That Boldoni should have allowed a smattering of Vitruvius to run away with his imagination is not so surprising, but it is difficult to explain why Barelli should have been seduced by Boldoni's account into seeing traces of the ancient peripteros when the intonaco was stripped from the walls in 1856. There can be little doubt, however, that Monneret de Villard is perfectly right in discrediting both Boldoni and Barelli.

It is, nevertheless, certain that the church of Lenno was founded at a very early period. Many Roman fragments have been found in the neighbourhood, and beneath the church, to the south of the crypt, may still be seen the remains of an ancient heating apparatus which must have served either for a bath or for a villa. A Christian basilica certainly existed on the site as early as the VI century, since epitaphs of the years 534, 555 and 572 have been discovered in or near the church.

The description of Ninguarda of this church is as follows: "December 2, 1593. The collegiate church of S. Stefano at Lenno, which is officiated by an archpriest, was visited, and was found in the following condition: There are three aisles all without vault. At the end of the nave there is a high altar placed in an apse which is entirely covered with ancient frescos. . . . The central aisle of the choir is covered with a ceiling which has been recently constructed. The remainder of the edifice is covered by a timber roof. The choir is entirely enclosed with wooden rails, . . . and is raised about six steps above the rest of the church. On the gospel side is a door giving access to the sacristy, which is vaulted but has a wooden sub-ceiling. . . . Beneath the choir there is a vaulted crypt whose eight columns of marble support the above-mentioned choir. Two stairways descend to the crypt from the middle of the church. . . . The church has two doors, one small, giving access to

---

[4] Durat adhuc incorruptum ab omni temporis contumeliâ, nisi insulsæ hominum manus temerassent, Sacrum quondam Dianæ, vt arbitror, Templum, quod ex vetusto structuræ genere, & religionis superstitionibus conijci potest. Ratio igitur illius fani, non quæ nunc est, sed quam periti quique Architectorum fuisse coniectantur, antequàm imperitorum manibus tangeretur, illa erat, quæ Vitruuio dicitur Peripteros, & à fronte, & à tergo, & à lateribus cincta porticibus. Eę duplices erant altitudine, quadratis pilis suffultæ, & adhuc in ijs, quæ in fronte sunt templi, priscarum imaginum lineamenta potiùs, quam picturae, & quædam templorum icones, ac propylea opticâ ratione delineata, diligenter inspectantibus apparent. Sed rudis, & ignara posteritas, apertis ad latera templi parietibus, obstructisque pilarum interuallis, interiores fecit quæ priùs exteriùs sitæ erant, porticus, innummerasque ex marmore tabulas, quibus sepulchrorum epigrammata probatæ antiquitatis erant insculpta, per summam vecordiam vel erasis, vel commutatis litteris in propria epitaphia conuertit. (Boldoni, 110-111).

the house of the archpriest, and placed near the high altar, the other on the gospel side opens into the walled cemetery. Near this door is a campanile with two bells. The walls of the church are very rough."[5]

It is evident that the church has been much altered since the days of Ninguarda. An inscription of 1698 on the portal[6] probably indicates that the edifice had lost its architectural character before this date. Vaults were erected, a great portal was opened in the centre of the façade, the ancient frescos were destroyed, and the stairways giving access to the crypt closed up. Still further damage was done to the ancient building in 1790, when the old campanile was replaced by the existing one. About the middle of the XIX century, the edifice was subjected to a final disastrous restoration.

III. Of the ancient structure there remains visible to-day only the crypt (Plate 102, Fig. 3). This consists of three aisles of five bays, covered with extraordinarily light and airy groin vaults, somewhat domed, and supplied with disappearing transverse ribs (Plate 102, Fig. 3). The angles of the groins are very sharp at the springing. The crypt terminates in a trefoiled apse.

IV. The capitals (Plate 102, Fig. 3) are among the most important and interesting examples of Carlovingian art extant in Lombardy. The two westernmost of the free-standing columns and the second column of the north arcade are crowned by Byzantine capitals of the VI century, executed in marble. There is a single row of acanthus leaves, sharp and crisp, but somewhat weakly executed, while the volutes are poorly drawn, being merely scratched on the surface. Seven other capitals are characterized by very crude technique, and are ornamented with plain geometrical figures, or stiff leaves scratched on the surface. Four others have two rows of carved or uncarved acanthus leaves, scratched volutes and square fleurons (Plate 102,

---

[5] 1593 alli 2 xbre. Visitata la chiesa collegiata et archipresbiterale di S.to Steffano di Lenno, si è trovato nel modo che segue: Ha tre navi, tutte tre senza involto, in fronte di quella di mezzo v'è l'altare magiore fabricato in una nichia tutta depinta di pitture vechie. . . . La nave di mezzo è coperta, per quanto tiene la capella magiore, d'una soffitta fattagli nuovamente; il resto è sotto il tetto; tutta d.a capella magiore è serrata con cancelli di legno. . . . A d.a capella magiore si ascende dal restante del corpo della chiesa circa sei gradi. Dalla parte dell'evangelio ci è la porta, per quale si va alla sacristia, la quale è in volta ma coperta di tavolato. . . . Sotto la capella magiore ci è un scurolo in volta, che con otto colonne di marmo sostiene la d.a capella . . . si descende in d.o scurolo per due scale dal mezzo della chiesa. . . . Ha la chiesa due porte una picola, per la quale si va nella casa dell'arciprete, vicina all'altare magiore et l'altra laterale verso la parte dell'evangelio con cemitero murato. Il campanile vicino d.a porta con due campane. Le mura della chiesa sono tutte rozze. (Ninguarda, ed. Monti, II, 235-236).

[6] D. O. M. | LAPIDES TORRENTIS | ILLI DULCES | FUERUNT | ANNO DNI | 1698.

Fig. 3). The shafts and bases are obviously formed of pilfered Roman fragments.

In the apse windows are preserved the ancient tracery of perforated stone, and part of another piece of similar tracery is preserved in the north gallery leading to the church.

In a chicken-coop which at present occupies that part of the cellar of the choir which is outside of the Lombard crypt, may be seen a fragment of the exterior wall of the latter, with the remains of pilaster strips.

Remains of beautiful frescos, apparently of the XIV century, on the walls of the south stairway and at the west end of the crypt, prove that before the Renaissance reconstruction the pavement was much lower than it is now, and that the choir was raised.

V. The wall arches in two orders indicate that the crypt was rebuilt not earlier than the last quarter of the XI century, and the character of the masonry, analogous to that of the neighbouring baptistery, an edifice of c. 1085, indicates that this reconstruction took place about the year 1080. In this reconstruction were included fragments coming from earlier buildings. Certain of the capitals of the crypt, as we have seen, are a decadent Byzantine type, and appear to date from the late VI century. Others, of Corinthian type, with carved or uncarved acanthus leaves (Plate 102, Fig. 3), show the decadent art of the X century. The scratching of the volutes recalls the capitals of the Isola S. Giulio (compare Plate 102, Fig. 3, with Plate 100, Fig. 10), a monument of c. 900, or the fragments of Group B of the Chiesa d'Aurona, which date from c. 950. The strange, lifeless carving of the acanthus leaves, moreover, recalls that of the capital of SS. Felice e Fortunato at Vicenza (Plate 239, Fig. 3), an authentically dated monument of 975. Compared with the Vicenza capital those of Lenno are perhaps slightly more vigorous and less decadent, and may consequently be ascribed to c. 980. Indeed, in some of those with uncarved leaves, there is observable an evolution towards the far more developed style of capital found in the crypt of S. Vicenzo at Galliano, an authentically dated monument of 1007 (Plate 96, Fig. 2).

LODI,[1] CATHEDRAL

(Plate 104, Fig. 1)

I. Most of the authors who have studied the church of S. Bassiano at Lodi Vecchio have discussed the sculptures of the cathedral of Lodi, which are believed to have been transported from the earlier basilica. In the Museo Civico of Lodi are several old drawings of the façade of the Duomo. A

---

[1] (Milano).

description of the building was written by Millin[2] in 1817. For historical notices the work of Agnelli should be consulted.

II. When Lodi Vecchio had been destroyed on April 24, 1158,[3] the citizens of Lodi, after a period of homeless wandering, solemnly selected the site for the new city of Lodi on August 3, 1158.[4] The spot chosen was that of the ancient village of Colle Eghezzonio, and the new cathedral was established in the ancient church of S. Caterina. On August 3, 1160, the walls of the new city were begun,[5] and in March, 1161, the foundations were laid for the new palace of the emperor.[6] The taking of Milan favoured the Laudensi. "On Monday, October 29, 1163, the emperor Barbarossa returned from Germany to Lodi with Beatrice, his most serene consort, and with his chancellor, the archbishop-elect of Cologne, and with Herman, bishop of Verdun and Conrad, archbishop-elect of Mainz, who was the brother of Otto, the Count Palatine. . . . On the following Saturday, which was the second of November, Pope Victor with his cardinals came to Lodi, and on the following Monday the body of S. Bassiano, the confessor, was translated from Lodi Vecchio to the new city of Lodi with the greatest honour and with the greatest joy. The pope himself, and the illustrious emperor, and the patriarch of Aquileia, and the abbot of Cluny, and other bishops and archbishops carried upon their shoulders the precious body out of the greater church of Lodi Vecchio, and it was after that borne to the new city of Lodi by others, both clerics and laymen. And the most clement emperor offered for the construction of the church thirty imperial pounds, and his most serene consort donated five pounds to S. Bassiano."[7] Agnelli states, apparently on the authority

---

[2] II, 36 f.   [3] See below, pp. 493-494.   [4] Morena, M. G. H. *Script.*, XVIII, 604.
[5] Morena, M. G. H. *Script.*, XVIII, 625-626.

[6] Et eodem anno [1160] de mense Augusti inceptum est ad retificandum Laude iuvenis. (*Annales Mediolanenses Minores, ibid.*, 394).

[7] Die vero Lune, que fuit quarta dies ante Kalendas Novembris predicti anni [1163], reversus est de terra Theotonica christianissimus augustus in civitate Laude cum Beatrice serenissima coniuge sua et cum canzellario, electo Collonie archiepiscopo, et cum Hermano Verdensi episcopo et Conrado electo Maguntie archiepiscopo, qui frater erat Ottonis comitis palatini, et cum ipso comite palatino et cum comite Gabardo, Marcoardo et comite Conrado de Bellanuce atque cum filio ducis Guelfi et cum multis aliis principibus et baronibus Alamanie. Deinde proxima die sabbati, que fuit secunda dies mensis Novembris, venit Laude domnus papa Victor cum suis cardinalibus; et proximo die Lune fuit ductum a Laude veteri in novam civitatem Laude corpus beati Bassiani confessoris cum maximo honore maximaque letitia. Ipse enim met apostolicus, et imperator inclitus et patriarca Aquilegiensis et abbas Cluniacensis cum aliis quibusdam episcopis et archiepiscopis extra ecclesiam maiorem de Laude veteri corpus ipsum preciosum suis humeris portaverunt, et ab aliis deinde, tam cleris quam laycis, ad novum Laude translatum est. Obtulit autem ipse clementissimus imperator ad fabricationem ecclesie triginta libras denariorum imperialium, serenissima vero coniugalis ipsius obtulit ipsi beato Bassiano libras quinque. (Morena, M. G. H. *Script.*, XVIII, 642).

of documents, that the master-builder of the church was a certain Tinto Muso de Gatta of Cremona. The same author also tells us that in 1183 the western parts of the church had not been constructed above the foundation.[8]

In 1282 the statue of S. Bassiano was erected on the façade, an event which probably marks the completion of this portion of the edifice.[9] In 1506 the rose-window was opened in the façade, and in 1509 the two windows flanking the central portal. The old campanile was burned when the city was sacked by the French, the new campanile being begun in 1539. From 1570 to 1589 the church was baroccoized.[10] In the wall south of the principal portal is an inscription recording a restoration of 1596. In 1759 a new baroccoization of the church was undertaken.[11] It is doubtless to this that the inscription of 1764, placed in the south flank of the church, refers, but another line has been added to record another restoration of 1871.[12]

When I visited the church in 1913, the vaults of the nave were being redecorated.

III. The building consists of a nave five bays long, two side aisles, a choir of two bays flanked by side aisles, two absidioles, and an apse preceded by a narrow, barrel-vaulted bay. The choir is raised, and there is a spacious crypt—like the rest of the structure, however, almost entirely modernized. The portal is Romanesque; the remainder of the façade, Gothic. The interior of the nave has been entirely made over in the barocco style; the original construction is, however, preserved in the exterior walls and in the fine northern portal. The two ancient absidioles are also in part extant.

Remains of the old wall ribs above the existing vaults but below the roof, make it evident that the ancient vaults of the nave embraced two of the existing bays, and that the system was consequently alternate. The odd western bay, however, must always have had an oblong vault. It is evident that there was once a triforium with a single round-arched opening in each bay, and that there were transverse arches under the gallery roof, reinforcing the clearstory walls at every bay, although the system is alternate. These buttresses projected far above the aisle roofs, and were pierced by round-arched openings. The masonry is very late in character.

[8] Venti anni dopo, la fabbrica, almeno nella parte anteriore, era molto indietro, giacchè in un documento di quei tempi (1183) si accennano, per coerenza ad un podere, le fondamenta della cattedrale. (Compare Agnelli, *Diz.*, 146).

[9] *Ibid.*   [10] *Ibid.*   [11] *Ibid.*

[12]

D. O. M.

TEMPLVM MAXIMVM

DVODECIMO SECVLO EXTRVCTVM

JOSEPHO CALLARATO EPISCOPO

LAVDENSIVM PIETAS RESTAVRAVIT

ANNO MDCCLXIV

ANNO VERO MDCCCLXXI DECORAVIT.

IV. The side-aisle walls externally are characterized by simple arched corbel-tables supported on shafts in the angles of the heavy buttresses. The clearstory walls are ornamented externally with, arched corbel-tables in two orders, but these have been remade. Bits of polychromatic inlaying with checker-board designs are inserted at intervals in the masonry. The eastern gable, with its double arched corbel-tables, has been destroyed, but the two absidioles still retain in part their large, arched corbel-tables, grouped two and two and supported on shafts or pilaster strips; their gallery with broad-leaved capitals supported by heads (very like the galleries of the cathedral of Cremona); and their saw-tooth and diamond cornice.

The principal portal is adorned with rinceaux and diapered mouldings, which strongly recall those of the cathedral of Cremona. The capitals are characterized by whirled leaves and crockets. The Lombard porch is Gothic. The lions hold in their paws, one an animal with beast's head, bird's wings and claws and serpent's tail, the other a ram. The northern portal is ornamented with a diapered moulding like those of the west portal of the cathedral of Cremona.

In the lunette of the western portal is sculptured Christ, whose halo is inscribed with the letters, REX, and who holds a book with the legend EGO| SVM| VIA| VE|RITAS| ET VITA.[13] The Deity is placed between the figures of a kneeling and haloed bishop—doubtless S. Bassiano—and the Virgin. Below, on the jambs, are the two figures of Adam (Plate 104, Fig. 1) and Eve. Adam is half naked, Eve holds her hand to her head in an expression of grief. The sculptor has attempted to express the shame and contrition of the sinners, by giving them a contorted attitude, which is carried even to the point of crossing the legs. The Christ and S. Bassiano of the lunette are given an alert, wide-awake expression, which almost suggests trickiness. A great effort is made to show the form of the body through the draperies, and notwithstanding the contorted attitude and the poor anatomy, the sculptor succeeds in this object (Plate 104, Fig. 1). The hands and feet are given exaggerated cords, a mannerism which shows the influence of Guglielmo da Modena.

It is evident that these sculptures of Lodi are by the hand of the same sculptor who executed the Adam and Eve of the portal of S. Antonino at Piacenza (Plate 182, Fig. 1). The drawing of the lower fringe of the draperies (derived from the works of Nicolò) is the same in both. Similar is the subject, similar the drapery covering only half the figures, and this drapery is held in exactly the same manner by the two Adams. Entirely similar is the drawing of the shoulders of the two male figures. There is the same curious use of incised lines down the middle of the breast to denote ribs in the Adam of Lodi and the Eve of S. Antonino. The hair of the two Adams is represented

[13] Joan., xiv, 6.

by the same convention. The beards are very similar, and the line from the ear to the ·chin is identical in both. The working of the eyes is precisely the same, as is the treatment of the ankles. So evident is it that the Lodi sculptures and those of S. Antonino are by the same artist that it would be merely tedious to enumerate further the many analogies.

Even more significant than the points of resemblance, however, are the points of difference. The draperies of the Lodi figures (Plate 104, Fig. 1) are far lighter and more ethereal than those of the S. Antonino sculptures (Plate 182, Fig. 1). Instead of concealing the limbs they allow the anatomy to show through. The legs of the Lodi figures, instead of being set on outside the hip, like those of marionettes, are well joined to the body. The Lodi figures, instead of standing upright and rigid, are bent in a delicate "S" curve, and, most significant fact of all, the legs are crossed. It is, therefore, evident that the sculptor who executed the statues of S. Antonino in 1171, came under the influence of a powerful and extraneous art before he executed the sculptures of Lodi. That influence could only have come from the school of Languedoc. The. crossed legs—a mannerism, I believe, found elsewhere in Lombardy only at Ferrara—is a characteristic of the sculptures of Languedoc of the XII century, and is found in the well known figures of St.-Sernin at Toulouse, and in other works of the school of Languedoc throughout Spain and southern France. How exactly the "S"-shaped form of the body and the bend of the head in the jamb sculptures of Lodi is inspired by works of the same school is shown by a comparison of the two photographs in Plate 104, Figures 1 and 2, the second of which reproduces a panel from the porch of Moissac. Nor did the borrowings of our sculptor from the school of Languedoc stop here. He copied also the thin, clinging drapery revealing the form and the anatomy beneath (compare Plate 104, Fig. 1, with Plate 104, Fig. 2), and thus possibly introduced into Lombardy a new and important motive.

The antecedents of our sculptor before his journey to Languedoc may also be deduced from the style of his sculptures. The lower frieze of his draperies shows that he knew the work of Nicolò in the cathedral of Piacenza, as is natural that he should, since he himself worked at Piacenza. The cords of the hands show the influence of Guglielmo da Modena, as does also the attitude of the Adam at S. Antonino. The treatment of the hair and beard, on the other hand, the imperfect anatomy and the stiffness of the figures, he undoubtedly derived from the Last Supper of Lodi Vecchio, now preserved in the cathedral of Lodi.[14]

Above the vaults of the church are remains of ancient frescos.

V. As has been seen, the cathedral of Lodi presents numerous close points of contact with those parts of the cathedral of Cremona which were consecrated in 1196. The sculptures, we have also seen, are by the hand of an artist who

[14] For the sculptures transported from Lodi Vecchio see below, p. 498 f.

worked in 1171 at S. Antonino at Piacenza, but who underwent a strong influence from Languedoc before he executed the portal at Lodi. We have, in addition to this, documentary evidence that in the year 1183 the western portion of the cathedral of Lodi had not been built above the foundations. In view of all these considerations, the conclusion is justified that only the crypt was built in 1163, and the Romanesque parts of the cathedral may be assigned to c. 1190. It may, however, be doubted whether the portal be not somewhat earlier than this. It was the habit of Romanesque builders to execute the sculptures of the west façade before proceeding to the construction of the building as a whole. Even had the western portal been erected, the document of 1183 still might well have spoken of the foundations of the western part of the cathedral. The fact that the sculptures show absolutely no sign of the influence of Benedetto, whose earliest work at Parma was executed in 1178, makes me inclined to believe that such may have been the case. Allowing ten years for our sculptor's journey to Languedoc after he worked at S. Antonino in 1171, we may conclude that the sculptures of the portal at Lodi were erected c. 1180, or perhaps ten years before the rest of the cathedral.

LODI VECCHIO,[1] S. BASSIANO

(Plate 103; Plate 104, Fig. 3, 4, 5; Plate 105, Fig. 1, 2, 3, 4, 5)

I. Although S. Bassiano of Lodi Vecchio is one of the most interesting edifices in all Lombardy, it is but very little known to students of Italian art. As early as 1776, Molossi[2] described the sculptures of the Last Supper, in his day as now in the cathedral of Lodi. Clericetti published in 1856 a study of the church. Archæological science in that day, however, was quite unable to cope with the extremely complex problems which the church presents. The more recent study of Sant'Ambrogio, although singularly disappointing in certain directions, is nevertheless valuable for its fine illustrations and for certain original researches. For historical notices the writings of Agnelli should be consulted. Illustrations of the monument and of the sculptures at Lodi may be found in the *Grande Illustrazione*[3] and in the works of Venturi[4] and Zimmermann.[5]

II. S. Bassiano is without question the church erected by the patron saint of Lodi and dedicated by him in honour of the apostles. The circumstances of its foundation are related in a letter of S. Ambrogio: "Ambrogio to Felice, Bishop of Como. Although I was in a poor state of bodily health,

---

[1] (Milano).   [2] 34.   [3] Drawings of the façade, V, 586.
[4] III, 128, 131, 248.   [5] 69.

nevertheless when I read your heart-felt letter I received no little benefit and
was refreshed as by pennyroyal, especially since you wrote to tell me of the
approach of that day dear to both of us, in which you assumed the duties of
bishop. It happened that a moment before I had been speaking of this with
our brother Bassiano. The subject had come up in the course of a talk which
we were having concerning the dedication of a basilica which he had founded
in the name of the apostles, for he had told me that he eagerly desired the
presence of your holiness on this occasion. I therefore interwove into our
discourse the suggestion that the dedication should be celebrated on your
birthday (which is, unless I am mistaken, the now approaching first day of
November) and on the day following; and I promised that beyond this there
should be no delay. I pledged myself to be present, and took it upon me to
promise the same for you (for I felt I should not resent your doing this for
me). I assumed that you would be present, since you ought to be. Consequently my promise will not hold you more than your own character, since
it is your nature to do what you ought to do. Thus you see I made the promise
to our brother not rashly, but rather in knowledge of your character. Do
come, therefore, so as not to convict two priests, you of not being present, and
me of having too easily promised."[6] This consecration took place in the year
380, according to an inscription of no very ancient date in the choir. "This
is to record the fact that in the ancient sacristy of this church there was an
inscription to the following effect: This church was built by S. Bassiano in
the year of our Lord 380, and was consecrated by him, by S. Ambrogio and
by the bishop of Como, and was dedicated in honour of God and of the Holy
Apostles. After the death of S. Bassiano, which occurred on January 19, 413,
his most precious body was buried with solemn ceremonies in this church.
This happened in the sixth year of the pontificate of Innocent I of happy
memory and in the eighth year of the reign of Honorius the emperor [sic].
The same church by the power of God and to the astonishment of all remained

---

[6] Ambrosius Felici Comensi episcopo. Etsi habitu corporis minus ualebam, tamen
vbi sermonem unanimis mihi pectoris tui legi, non mediocrem sumpsi ad conualescendum
gratiam, quasi quodam tui alloquij pulegio refotus, simul quia celebrem utriq. nostrum
annuntiasti diem adfore, quo suscepisti gubernacula summi sacerdotij, de quo ante
momentum cum fratre nostro Bassiano loquebar. Ortus enim sermo de Basilicæ, quam
condidit Apostolorum nomine, dedicatione, dedit huic sermoni uiam. siquidem significabat
quòd sedulo tuae quæreret sanctitatis præsentiam. Tum ego nostris fabulis intexui
di͞e natalis tui, qui foret in exordio ipso kalendar͞u Nouembrium, eumq. (si non fallerer)
appropinquasse, & crastina celebrandum die; unde posthac non excusaturum promisi.
Ergo de te, quoniam & tibi id de me licet, promisi illi, exegi mihi. Præsumptum enim
habeo quòd affuturus sis, quia debes adesse. Non ergo te magis meum promissum
tenebit, quàm tuum institutum, qui id in animum induxeris, ut quod oportet facias.
Aduertis itaq. quia non tam promissi audax, quàm tui conscius fratri spopondi. Veni
igitur, ne duos sacerdotes redarguas: te, qui non adfueris: & me, qui tam facile
promiserim. (Ed. Ioannes Battista Bandinius, *Operum Sancti Ambrosii* . . . Romae,
Ex typographia Dominici Basæ, 1585. Folio. Lib. VIII, Ep. LX, V, 255).

uninjured at the time of the total destruction of this city which occurred lamentably in the year 1158."[7]

The life of S. Bassiano tells of the foundation of the church of the Apostles by the saint, and of its consecration by Bassiano, Ambrogio and Felice. It also states that S. Bassiano, at his own request, was buried in this church, which in consequence came to be called by his name, and that his body there reposed until it was translated to Lodi in 1163.[8]

On March 29, 994, the bishop Andrea made a donation to the church of S. Bassiano. From this document it is evident that S. Bassiano was outside the city, and that it was not the cathedral. The goods were given to endow in perpetuity a chapter of four priests in the basilica, and the document specifies that upon the death of a member, the surviving three should elect

[7] MEMORIA| COME NELL'ANTICA SAGRESTIA DI QUESTA CHIESA SI TROVAVANO SCOLPITE NEL MURO| LE SEGUENTI PAROLE.| QUESTA CHIESA FU FABBRICATA DA SAN BASSIANO L'ANNO DEL SIGNORE 380. E DA LUI STESSO| COME ANCO DA SANT'AMBROGIO E SAN FELICE VESCOVO DI COMO FU SUCCESSIVAMENTE CONSECRATA| E DEDICATA A ONORE DI DIO E DE' SANTI APOSTOLI. NELLA QUALE POI DOPO LA SUA MORTE| AVVENUTA IL GIORNO 19. DI GENNAIO DELL'ANNO 413, IL SUO PREGIATISSIMO CORPO VENNE CON MESTIS|SIMA POMPA SEPOLTO. IL CHE SEGUÌ L'ANNO SESTO DELLA FELICE MEMORIA D'INNOCENZO| PRIMO SOMMO PONTIFICE, E L'OTTAVO DI ONORE IMPERATORE. LA MEDESIMA CHIESA| PER DIVINA VIRTÙ RESTÒ CON MERAVIGLIA UNIVERSALE INTATTA NEL TEMPO DELLA| TOTALE DISTRUZIONE D'ESSA CITTÀ ANTICA, CHE MISERAMENTE ACCADE L'ANNO 1158.

[8] Quodam autem tempore dum animo revolveret quod Domino acceptabile munus præter solitum offeret; placuit ei in suburbio orientali, ad honorem et reverentiam Apostolorum, oratorium condere; datisque sumptibus ad fabricam perficiendam, opus quod cœperat, non multum distulit consummare. Ad cujus dedicationem Beatissimum Ambrosium Mediolanensem, et Felicem Comanum Pontificem venire persuasit: cujus dedicationis idem B. Ambrosius in libro Epistolarum suarum meminisse non præteriit. (*Vita S. Bassiani*, ed. Acta Sanctorum, II, Januarii, die XIX, 588). Qui cum in ecclesiam Apostolorum, quam Præsul Domini fundaverat, deportaretur etc. (*Ibid.*). Sanctum vero corpus ejus, sicut ipse præceperat in ecclesia Apostolorum, cum digno exequiarum honore reconditum est. (*Ibid.*, 589). . . . cumque carnis sarcinam deposuero in basilica Apostolorum, quam ipse fundavi. . . . (*Ibid.*). Basilicam in honorem duodecim Apostolorum ædificavit, quam una cum Ambrosio Mediolanensi et Felice Comensi Deo dicavit. . . . Sepultus est in basilica Apostolorum ab ejus postea nomine nuncupata. Sed Lauda veteri deinde diruta ejus corpus in urbem novam translatum, summis Prælatis et Federico Imperatore piam sarcinam vectantibus, in æde maxima collocatun est, anno salutis millesimo centesimo sexagesimo tertio, pridie Nonas Novembris (*Vitae epitome ex officio Ecclesiæ Laudensis*, ed. *Acta Sanctorum*, II, Januarii, die XIX, 590). See Tatti, I, 274.

his successor. In the document nothing is said of the members of the new chapter living in common.[9]

In 1025 the city of Lodi Vecchio was besieged.[10] It is not too much to conjecture that the church of S. Bassiano, situated in the suburbs, suffered at this time damage which necessitated its reconstruction not long afterwards.

On May 24, 1111, the city was razed to the ground by the Milanesi.[11] It is entirely probable that at this time also the church of S. Bassiano may have suffered some damage. At any rate, it is certain that the cathedral of S. Maria was destroyed. In consequence of this, the cathedral was moved from S. Maria and established in the church of S. Bassiano.[12] A restoration of S. Bassiano undoubtedly followed, and was probably undertaken partly to repair the damage done to the edifice and partly to make it more worthy of its newly acquired episcopal dignity. After the destruction of Lodi, in 1111, the inhabitants appear not to have returned to the city itself, but to have remained in the suburbs. This is clear from numerous passages of Morena.[13] The fact probably explains why S. Bassiano became the cathedral, and the centre of civic life.

The final destruction of Lodi Vecchio by the Milanesi took place in 1158. Morena relates the sad story of the exit of the inhabitants from the city in the rain and storm on the night of April 24.[14] The Milanesi, on entering the town, did not burn it. The houses were first sacked, then pulled down.[15] It is therefore entirely probable that the church of S. Bassiano escaped damage, and this, indeed, is explicitly stated in a modern inscription in the

[9] Anno ab incarnatione Domini nostri Jeshu Christi DCCCCXC quarto. quarto Kal. aprilis indictione septima. Basilica sancti Bassiani que est constructa suburbium hujus civitate Laude. Ego Andreas humilis episcopus ipsius sancte Laudensis ecclesie qui professus sum ex natione mea lege vivere Longobardorum offertor et donator ipsius Basilice presens presentibus dixi. etc. . . . Secunda pecia de terra in dicto loco sancte Marie que est iusta ecclesiam sancti Bassiani . . . coerit . . . da meridie de canonica Sancte Laudensis ecclesie. (Vignati, I, 36-37). Cf. also *Hist. Pat. Mon.*, XIII, 1561.

[10] Sant'Ambrogio, 10.

[11] Quando civitas Laudensium fuit capta, 1111 in ultima ebdomada Madii, quadam die. Mercurii. (*Annales Cremonenses*, M. G. H. *Script.*, XVIII, 800). Otto Morena makes the delegates of Lodi say to the emperor in 1153: Nos . . . conquerimur de Mediolanensibus, qui nos ac omnes cives de Laude, qui vestri eramus, olim de ipsa civitate Laudensi iniuste expulerunt ac omnes maiores nostros tam masculos quam feminas expoliaverunt et multos etiam ex ipsis interficientes, ipsam civitatem nostram penitus destruxerunt. . . . Postea vero . . . reliqui ibi remanentes extra burgos ipsius civitatis, circa ipsam civitatem in sex burgis novis habitare ceperunt. (M. G. H. *Script.*, XVIII, 588). See also Agnelli, *Cerreto*, 16; Giulini, III, 24; Sant'Ambrogio, 10.

[12] Sant'Ambrogio, 29.

[13] *E.g.*, speaking of the year 1153, he says: Barbarossa eorum [Laudensium] civitatem, quamvis destructam, in sua custodia et protectione suscepit. (M. G. H. *Script.*, XVIII, 590).

[14] *Ibid.*, 601-602.   [15] 602.

north wall of the church: "This temple dedicated to God the most Holy Supreme and S. Bassiano, bishop and patron of Lodi, was built by S. Bassiano in the year 380 and by him dedicated to the twelve Apostles. In the year 413 his sacred body was here deposited and from that time it was dedicated to him. The church was afterwards more than once added to and restored, miraculously escaped in the destruction of the old city in the year 1158, and was restored and adorned by pious generosity in the year of salvation 1829."[16]

In 1163 the body of the saint, together, it is said, with certain sculptures of the old church of S. Bassiano, was transported to the new cathedral of Lodi.[17] The translation of the saint is recorded in a modern inscription placed in the west wall of the church of Lodi Vecchio: "After Lodi Vecchio had been captured, burned and destroyed and the citizens had fled, the sacred body of S. Bassiano bishop and patron of Lodi was translated from this church to new Lodi by the emperor, bishops, princes and nobles who carried on their shoulders the sacred burden while the whole people applauded. On November 5, 1163, the body was laid with solemn pomp in a marble sarcophagus in the crypt of the cathedral. An altar was erected in honour of the saint. Here, renowned for miracles, the body holily reposes and is piously reverenced."[18] In 1320 the church was thoroughly restored, and was intrusted to the Frati Ospitalieri.[19] The restoration in fact was practically a reconstruction, and included the rebuilding of the façade and of large portions of the nave. Work must have proceeded rapidly, for the new vault was covered with frescos in 1323, as is evident from an inscription in the eastern bay of the northern side aisle.[20] This inscription is attached to a bas-relief representing a cattle-man on horse-back, driving a pair of oxen. It is evident that the restoration of the church was carried out largely at the expense of the trade corporations of Lodi. In the two western arcades on the north side are reliefs representing cobblers, and the frescos of the vault also represent corporations. The date of the inscription of the cattlemen, 1323, establishes the epoch of the reconstruction of the church.

Subsequent restorations were carried out in 1829 and 1830. These are recorded in two inscriptions, one in the west wall which has already been

[16] D O M
ET DIVO BASSIANO EPISCOPO LAVDENSI AC PATRONO
TEMPLVM HEIC A. CCCLXXX AB IPSO XII APOSTOLIS
INDE SACRO EIVS CORPORE A. CCCCXIII HVC DEPOSITO
EIDEM DEDICATVM
PLVS SEMEL REFECTVM ET AVCTVM
IN VETERIS VRBIS EXCIDIO A. MCLVIII MIRE ILLAESVM
PIIS SVMPTIBVS INSTAVRATVM ORNATVMQVE
ANNO SAL. MDCCCXXIX

[17] Zimmermann, 69. See above under Lodi, p. 486.

cited, the other in the choir: "The devotees of S. Bassiano in 1830 caused to be restored the images and symbols of Christ the Saviour, the Virgin Deipara, the twelve apostles and other saints painted in the Middle Ages upon the walls and vaults. These frescos, recalling the art of a ruder time, had been damaged and in part destroyed by age. The ancient forms have been conscientiously preserved."[21]

18

SACRVM CORPVS
DIVI BASSIANI LAVDENSIVM EPISCOPI ET PATRONI
LAVDA POMPEIA CAPTA DIRVTA EXVSTA
FVGATIS CIVIBVS
HEINC
TRANSFERRI CVRANTIBVS
AVGVSTO CAESARE
SVMMIS PRAESVLIBVS PRINCIPIBVS PATRICIIS
HVMEROS SACRO PIGNORI SVPPONENTIBVS
VNIVERSO POPVLO PLAVDENTE
LAVDAM NOVAM
ANNO MCLXIII. NON. NOVEMBR.
SOLEMNI POMPA
DELATVM
IN SVBTERRANEO MAIORIS TEMPLI
ARA EIDEM ERECTA
IN ARCA MARMOREA
REPOSITVM
CLARVM MIRACVLIS
SANCTE SERVATVR ET PIE COLITVR

19 Clericetti.

20 MCCC|XXIII| PARATICVM BOATERIO[RVM]| FECIT FIERI HOC

CELⓋ

21

CHRISTI DOMINI SALVATORIS
DEIPARAE VIRGINIS
XII APOSTOLORVM ALIORVMQ. COELITVM
IMAGINES SYMBOLA ET RELIQVA
ADFORMATVM IN PARIETIBVS ET FORNICE
MEDIO AEVO DEPICTA
SEQVIORVM TEMPORVM ARTEM REFERENTIA
VETVSTATE PARTIM CORRVPTA PARTIM DELETA
SERVATA IN OMNIBVS PRISTINA FORMA
INSTAVRARE CVRARVNT
DIVI BASSIANI CVLTORES
MDCCCXXX

495

III. The edifice consists of a nave four bays long, two side aisles, a choir, and three apses (Plate 103). The nave is covered with oblong rib vaults (Plate 104, Fig. 4; Plate 105, Fig. 5), the side aisles also with rib vaults (Plate 104, Fig. 5), the choir with a barrel vault (Plate 105, Fig. 5), and the apses with half domes (Plate 104, Fig. 5; Plate 105, Fig. 5). The edifice has obviously been rebuilt in the XIV century, but important fragments of the Romanesque building still survive. The ancient piers were evidently quatrefoiled (Plate 103; Plate 104, Fig. 4; Plate 105, Fig. 1, 2, 4, 5). In the northern arcade these piers have been in part rebuilt (Plate 105, Fig. 5), but the alterations carried out in bricks of light colour are easily distinguishable from the original masonry. In the southern arcade the original piers still survive (Plate 104, Fig. 4), although they are covered with intonaco and painted. The existing rib vaults of the nave (Plate 104, Fig. 4; Plate 105, Fig. 5) can not be earlier than the XIV century. The system consists of a single shaft (Plate 104, Fig. 4; Plate 105, Fig. 5) which, except in the west bay, retains the original capital of the XI century. The transverse arches of the nave vaults are very broad and occupy the whole of the abaci of the capitals of the system so that the diagonal and wall ribs are left without supports and have to be carried on the wall (Plate 104, Fig. 4; Plate 105, Fig. 5). The transverse arches are covered with plaster and frescos so that it is impossible to inspect the character of the masonry; I believe, however, that they are of the XI century. The Romanesque basilica was probably covered by a wooden roof supported on these transverse arches. When the church was remade in the XIV century, the old transverse arches were retained and the existing rib vaults merely built in between them. That the Romanesque church was not vaulted is proved not only by the absence of supports for ribs or groins in the system, but by the extreme thinness of the wall, which had greatly to be strengthened to support the weight of the vaults when these were added in the XIV century.

The rib vault in the eastern bay of the south side aisle (Plate 104, Fig. 5) is part of the original construction of the XI century. This vault is covered with plaster, so that the masonry can not be studied. The ribs, however, are heavy and have a rectangular section. The vault is distinctly oblong in plan; it is domed but not so highly as the other side-aisle vaults. The wall ribs and diagonals are loaded at the crowns and tend to disappear at the springing. The rib vaults of the remaining bays of the side aisles were obviously remade in the XIV century, and have diagonals of torus section. Over the archivolts of the main arcade there is at present a blind triforium (Plate 104, Fig. 4; Plate 105, Fig. 5) consisting of a biforum surmounted by a pointed arch. The pointed arch is of course of the XIV century, and was formed by cutting into the wall a second order. The ancient triforium must have served merely to ventilate the aisle roofs and can not have been a true gallery. This is evident from several considerations. The level of the aisle roofs is shown by a fragment of the ancient cornice still preserved in the west bay of the southern side aisle (Plate 105, Fig. 3), and this cornice is so low that there could not possibly have been galleries. Furthermore, the sill of the triforium is placed at a level only very slightly above the main aisles of the arcade (Plate 104, Fig. 4). Since the aisle vaults were domed (Plate 104, Fig. 5), they would inevitably have risen above the level of the gallery floor, had there been a true gallery. Finally, there would not have been room for the clearstory, traces of which still exist above the gallery roof.

The transverse buttresses of the existing edifice are of the XIV century (Plate 105, Fig. 3), though on the north side they were much enlarged in 1829. There is no evidence that the edifice of the XI century was supplied with any such buttresses.

The masonry consists entirely of brick in the XI century portions of the edifice, except that stone is introduced in the capitals and bases, and occasionally in the piers. These bricks are not cross-hatched, and are thus easily distinguished from the bricks of the XIV century, which are cross-hatched. The masonry is different in those portions of the walls which act as screens and do not support the weight of the arches or vaults, and in the piers and apse which serve as supports for the concentrated loads of the superstructure. In the former the XI century masonry, where preserved, is very rough, small bricks being employed and many herring-bone courses being inserted (Plate 105, Fig. 3). In the latter extremely large bricks, resembling those used at Stradella, are carefully laid (Plate 104, Fig. 3; Plate 105, Fig. 1, 2, 4). These bricks are roughly finished, and contain pebbles and even large-sized stones.[22]

IV. The capitals of the church are of varied types. Some have the character almost of imposts on which are incised crude and dry leaf patterns, quite Carlovingian in feeling (Plate 105, Fig. 1, 2). Others show some attempt to reproduce the acanthus form, but the leaves are unskilfully executed and have a strange dry character (Plate 105, Fig. 4). Others are ornamented with grotesques, and show two very badly executed animals having a single head which forms the volute (Plate 105, Fig. 4), or a row of stiff birds intermingled with dry leaf patterns or vines (Plate 105, Fig. 1), or a strange animal, perhaps a unicorn, galloping amid Carlovingian foliage. One of the clearstory capitals is carved with a primitive interlace. In the triforium inverted capitals are used for bases, and in some cases two capitals are placed one on top of the other; but these vagaries are probably the result of XIV century alterations. The cornice of the side-aisle walls, a portion of which is still preserved in the western bay on the south side, consisted of arched corbel-tables (Plate 105, Fig. 3). The saw-tooth moulding at present above them was apparently added in the XIV century. The apse

[22] The exposed surfaces of the bricks in the screen wall measure 4½–25 x 5–10 centimetres. Those of the structural portions measure from 11–50 x 7–10 centimetres.

cornice (Plate 104, Fig. 3) has been entirely rebuilt in the Gothic period, but the niches below it in two orders are original (Plate 104, Fig. 3). The mouldings with which some of these niches are at present supplied are the result of a restoration carried out in the XII century, so that in the XI century the niches were probably in a single order. The walls of the apse are at present broken by two broad, flat pilaster strips (Plate 104, Fig. 3). I presume that originally these supported arched corbel-tables, but of this there is no proof. The ancient windows of the clearstory were apparently large and unmoulded. They must have been supplied with glass. The window in the western bay of the southern side aisle was probably similar originally, but was made smaller and given extra orders in the XII century. The archivolts of the interior are in a single order.

The walls of the interior and exterior were covered with intonaco and frescos. The interior still retains much of its fresco decoration, though restored, but none of this appears to be earlier than the rebuilding of the XIV century. The traces of painted decoration still extant in the painted cornice of the apse (Plate 104, Fig. 3) are interesting and important, though of late date.

In the Museo Civico of Lodi (which is open on the first Sunday of each month, from noon to 2 P.M.) there are three bases which come from S. Bassiano. They are supplied with griffes, and are of the Attic type, with, however, the peculiarity that the curves of the tori are much flattened, so that the plinth hardly projects beyond the line of the pier. The museum also contains a capital entirely similar in style to those of S. Bassiano and which undoubtedly came from that church, as well as various bits of carving that may be ascribed to the same source. A sculpture of S. Bassiano shows the same technical peculiarities, and is undoubtedly by the same hand as the sculpture of the Last Supper in the cathedral of Lodi.

It is the constant tradition at Lodi that certain sculptures of the cathedral were brought thither from S. Bassiano.[23] In so far as this tradition regards the lions, the figures of the jamb and the tympanum of the portal, it is manifestly erroneous, since these sculptures, as I have shown above,[24] were executed after the cathedral had been transferred from Lodi Vecchio and were made for their present position. The bronze statue of S. Bassiano, supposed to have been brought from Lodi Vecchio in 1503, was, it is now known, in reality executed in 1283.[25] The case, however, is different in regard to the sculptures now placed in the north wall of the church, near the entrance to the crypt. An inscription around these sculptures states that they were brought from Lodi Vecchio on November 5, 1163.[26] The inscription,

---

[23] Agnelli, *Diz.*, 146; Sant'Ambrogio, 33.   [24] p. 488.   [25] Sant'Ambrogio, 33.

[26] MCLXIII NONIS 9B̄RIS| CŒTUS APOSTOLORUM A LAUDE POMPEJA DIRUTA| HUC AD HANC NOVAM TRANSLATUS

it is true, does not appear to be more ancient than the XVIII century—though it is at least as old as 1776, since it was seen in that year by Molossi—but that the fact which it records is authentic is indicated by the considerations that the sculptures are obviously fragments merely walled in to their present position, and that their style is such that they must have been executed before the foundation of the cathedral of Lodi. The upper relief represents a bishop without halo holding a book, and a deacon, haloed, with bare tonsured head, also holding a book. The bishop has a mitre and crosier, and wears the archiepiscopal pallium. It therefore probably is not a bishop of Lodi, but represents some archbishop who, after the destruction of Lodi Vecchio in 1111, aided in the embellishment of the new cathedral church of S. Bassiano. The haloed deacon is probably his patron saint, either Lawrence or Stephen.

The lower relief represents the Last Supper. Christ, with inscribed halo, is seated in the middle. To His left is John, who leans upon His breast, and whom Christ embraces. The second figure to Christ's right is Judas, the only one of the apostles without a halo. Christ passes to him a sop. The other apostles are not distinguished. On the table are represented, in conventional perspective, almost Egyptian in its naïveté, the various foods and utensils of the meal. In front of Christ an entire lamb lies in a sort of bowl. Pieces of meat are placed on the table in front of the apostles, as are also round loaves of bread, carafes of wine, and cups. About half way down the table on either side, are bowls from which two of the apostles are engaged in dipping up water to dilute their wine. Several of the apostles have knives which in general they use to cut the bread. The figures are all stiff and conventional. They all stare straight in front, with eyes that see not, except Judas, who looks at Christ. On his face hypocrisy and simpering flattery are well expressed. The pupils of the eyes are incised, and originally were filled with glass. Several of these glass balls are still preserved. The halos are still gilt. The figures are wooden and lifeless, the arms and hands seem glued to the sides of the figures or the background. The whole technique is very hard and angular; the noses come to a sharp point, the draperies seem made of adamant. Everywhere are straight lines and sharp angles. The beards and hair are represented by parallel incised lines. The figures have the immobility but also the hieratic quality of Egyptian work. Both reliefs are by the same hand, although the workmanship of the upper one is somewhat finer. In this the ornaments of the dress are sculptured with a care that recalls the figures of the haloed bishop at S. Giovanni in Borgo at Pavia (Plate 167, Fig. 2), and that there is really relationship between the Lodi reliefs and the Pavia statue is proved by the treatment of the draperies, which are represented by means of the same unusual convention, in the arms and pallium of the Pavia statue, in the sleeves of the Lodi bishop, and in the sleeves of certain of the Lodi apostles. Compared with the Pavia statue, however, the Lodi reliefs are seen to be less fine, more crude.

LOMBARD ARCHITECTURE

It is notable that the Lodi sculptures seem to have been entirely unin-fluenced by the work of Guglielmo da Modena. On the other hand, they offer close points of contact with the relief of the same subject on the ambo of S. Ambrogio at Milan.

V. The bricks of Lodi Vecchio are not cross-hatched. From this fact we may deduce that the Romanesque portion of the church is not later than the middle of the XI century, since cross-hatched bricks were introduced about 1050 and used almost constantly after this date. At Lomello (c. 1025), it is true that cross-hatched bricks are found; but at Stradella (c. 1035), Calvenzano (c. 1040), the campanile of S. Satiro at Milan (1045), and Sannazzaro Sesia (1040), the bricks are without cross-hatching. On the other hand, the use of bricks without cross-hatching after 1050 is exceedingly rare. The character of the capitals shows the transition from the style of the first half to that of the second half of the XI century. Before the year 1050, the capitals of compound piers were seldom carved. At Lomello (Plate 109, Fig. 4), at Stradella (Plate 210), at Calvenzano (Plate 42, Fig. 2), and at Sannazzaro Sesia (Plate 201, Fig. 6) they are cubic, and ornamented, if at all, merely with some simple incised geometric pattern. Carved capitals were used only for free-standing columns, as in the crypt of Galliano (1007)— Plate 96, Fig. 2. In the second half of the XI century, on the other hand, we find the fully developed Lombard capital as at S. Ambrogio of Milan (begun c. 1070)—Plate 118, Fig. 2; Plate 120, Fig. 2, 3, 4, 5; Plate 122, Fig. 2. Midway between these two types stand the capitals of Lodi Vecchio (Plate 105, Fig. 1, 2, 4). The carving is far cruder in character than that at S. Ambrogio. The animals show a technique that is almost childish, while the leaves have a completely Carlovingian character. There can be little doubt, therefore, that S. Bassiano of Lodi Vecchio was erected c. 1050, and to this epoch belong practically all the remains of Lombard architecture in the existing edifice. The building, however, was undoubtedly embellished after the cathedral was here transferred in 1111. At this epoch some of the mouldings were added, and the sculptures subsequently moved to the cathedral of Lodi were executed, since, as has been seen, their style is slightly less advanced than that of the ambo statue of S. Giovanni in Borgo of Pavia (c. 1120). In 1320-1323 the edifice was remade in the Gothic style.

LOMELLO,[1] S. MARIA MAGGIORE

(Plate 106; Plate 107; Plate 108; Plate 109, Fig. 1, 2, 3, 4;
Plate 110, Fig. 1, 2, 3, 4; Plate 111, Fig. 2, 3)

I. The church of S. Maria Maggiore of Lomello is mentioned in the official *Elenco degli Edifizi Monumentali in Italia*. Some strangely inexact

[1] (Pavia).

historical notices of the building are contained in the work of Mothes.[2] As early as 1746 Portalupi wrote an historical monograph upon Lomello, in the composition of which he appears to have been guided rather by his own exuberant imagination than by historical documents. The more recent work of Zucchi throws little new light, either upon the history or the architecture of the church. In 1911 I published a monograph upon S. Maria Maggiore in *Arte e Storia*. This article was marred by careless printing.

II. Lomello is mentioned by Paolo Diacono as the scene of the romantic betrothal of Teodolinda and Agilulfo, but the chronicler does not mention the church of S. Maria.[3] He does not even state that the marriage took place at Lomello, and in fact many modern historians believe it unlikely that so solemn a ceremony should have been celebrated in a country church, and conjecture that instead Teodolinda and Agilulfo returned to Pavia to be married at S. Michele.[4] Waitz has even doubted the truth of the whole story of Paolo, observing that according to the *Origo Gentis Langobardorum*, Agilulfo appears to have usurped the kingdom with violence.

Almost equally romantic, but equally without direct bearing upon the history of the church of S. Maria Maggiore, is the story of the imprisonment of Gundeberga at Lomello.[5]

The earliest mention of the church of S. Maria is contained in a letter of the bishop of Pavia dating from c. 1000.[6] The bishop summons his clergy

---

[2] I, 235.

[3] Reginam verò Theudelindam, quæ satis placebat Langobardis, permiserunt in regia consistere dignitate, suadentes ei, ut sibi quem voluisset ex omnibus Langobardis virum eligeret, talem scilicet, qui regnum regere utiliter posset. Illa verò consilium cum prudentibus habens, Agilulfum ducem Taurinatium, & sibi virum, & Langobardorum genti regem elegit. Erat enim isdem vir strenuus, & bellicosus, & tam forma, quam animo ad regni gubernacula coaptatus. Quem statim regina ad se venire mandavit, ipsaque ei obviam ad Laumellum oppidum properavit. Qui cùm ad eam venisset, ipsa sibi post aliquot verba vinum propinari fecit. Quæ cùm prior bibisset, residuum Agilulfo ad bibendum tribuit. Is cùm reginæ accepto poculo manum honorabiliter osculatus esset, regina cum rubore subridens, non debere sibi manum osculare ait, quem osculum sibi ad os jungere oporteret. Moxque eum ad suum basium erigens, ei de suis nuptis, deque regni dignitate aperuit. Quid plura? Celebrantur cum magna lætitia nuptiæ: suscepit Agilulfus, qui erat cognatus regis Authari, inchoante jam mense Novembris regiam dignitatem. (*De Gestis Longobardorum*, Pauli Diaconi, Lib. III, Cap. XXXIV, ed. Muratori, R. I. S., I, pt. 1, p. 453).

[4] Galvaneo della Fiamma (*Chron. Maius*, 519, ed. Ceruti) states that the marriage took place at Lomello. Robolini (I, 63) believes that it took place at Pavia, and supports himself on the opinion of Capsoni. The authoritative voice of Biscaro is in favour of Pavia. Zucchi has printed a synopsis of the opinions of the various authors who have written upon the question, and concludes that the marriage took place at Lomello.

[5] *Chronicarum quae dicuntur Fredegarii Scolastici*, Lib. IV, 51, ed. Krusch, M. G. H. *Script. Rer. Merov.*, II, 145.

[6] Pflugk-Harttung, II, 381-382.

to a synod at Pavia, and directs an unknown abbot to publish the letter *per omnes plebes subscriptas id est: Laumellum, Carium, Basserium,* etc.   The church was, therefore, at this epoch a pieve.

According to Giulini,[7] the counts palatine of Pavia, driven from that city, established themselves at Lomello about the year 1018.   These important nobles doubtless constructed, or reconstructed, the castle, and may also have caused the reconstruction of the church, since the architectural forms of the existing edifice show that it belongs precisely to this epoch.

In 1107 Paschal II passed through Lomello on his way from the Alps to Pavia.   It was doubtless on this occasion that he conceded a bull in favour of the church of S. Maria.   The document itself is unfortunately lost, but was seen by Portalupi, who has recorded some meagre indications of its contents.   From it we learn that the church of S. Maria Maggiore possessed extraordinary importance in the XII century; that it enjoyed signal privileges and favours conceded by apostolic authority; that the prevosto possessed the right to wear a mitre and carry a crosier; and that he could confer two of the minor orders.   At a later period the church was officiated by a chapter of ten canons, which was later reduced to eight.   There can be little doubt that this chapter existed long before 1107.

Some time during the XII century Lomello was destroyed by the Pavesi. This event is referred to by two authoritative chroniclers.   Ambassadors of Milan appeared before the emperor at Tortona shortly before the siege of that city, which began on February 14, 1155.   In the course of an invective against Pavia, they complained that the Pavesi had taken Lomello, a noble castle and the seat of the counts palatine, by fraud, destroyed the city, and made its defenders captive.[8]   Although the date is not mentioned, it is clearly implied

[7] II, 107.

[8]

> Quanquam (si veris liceat modo vocibus uti,
> Pace tua, princeps) pensato pondere rerum
> Non tam formosæ rea sit Terdona Papiæ,
> Quam rea Terdonæ formosa Papia tibique.
> Nam præter reliquas, quas aut servire coactas,
> Subdidit, aut captas evertit funditus urbes,
> Aspice quam turpi Lunelli nobile castrum.
> Atque Palatini sedem. fidosque penates
> Verterat illa dolo: comitem, civesque vocabat
> Perfida, colloquio pacis de rebus nabendo [= navando],
> Incautosque viros, et nil hostile tementes
> Fraude mala captos in vincula dura coegit.
> Ipsaque non armis, nec belli jure, sed astu,
> Vel potius subversa dolo castella reliquit.

(Guntheri Cisterciensis *Ligurinus,* III, 62-75, ed. Migne, *Pat. Lat.,* 212, 365).

Sensi rem meam (inquit Terdona) agi, dum paries proximus, Lunellum dico, arderet sub Mediolani confugi alas.   Mediolanum judicas, quòd Cumas legitima occasione destruxerit.   Teipsum non respicis, quae Lunellum Imperiale oppidum, magna & robusta

in these texts that the destruction took place before 1155. Since it is known from several sources that the town was reconstructed by the Milanesi in 1157,[9] Zucchi has supposed that the destruction took place very shortly before 1155. From this conclusion, however, Biscaro dissents, proving by a study of the political conditions in Lombardy at this time that the destruction of Lomello could not have taken place later than 1148 nor earlier than 1112. He conjectures that it occurred probably between the years 1140 and 1148, and more exactly between 1140 and 1145. In this, however, he is apparently wrong, for according to a text in a chronicle of Milan that seems to have been overlooked by all the historians of Lomello, the castle was taken in 1118.[10] On the other hand, some confirmation of Biscaro's conjecture is contained in a gloss to Galvaneo della Fiamma in which the destruction of Lomello is placed among events which took place at the very beginning of Barbarossa's reign before his first descent into Italy, or c. 1146.[11]

In 1164 the emperor decreed that Lomello should never more be rebuilt.[12] This seems to imply that the castle had been again destroyed after its reconstruction by the Milanesi in 1157.

Portalupi states that in 1174 the soldiers of Barbarossa destroyed Lomello as they were marching to the siege of Alessandria. He adds the

equitum manu stipatum, Palatini Comitis tui habitatione inclytum, oppidanis ipsis ad colloquium pacis dolo vocatis, fraudulenterque captis, ad solum usque sine causa prosternere non timueris. (Ottonis Frisingensis, Cap. XIX, ed. Muratori, R. I. S., VIII, 717 c).

[9] Mense Augusto [1157] in proximo quinque Portæ iterum equitaverunt ultra Ticinum tam privatissimè, quòd publicè nesciebatur quò ire vellent, sola Porta Ticinense causa custodiendi domi remanente. Et castrametati sunt ad Lomellum, & reædificaverunt illud castellum, & steterunt ibi per mensem. Et post hæc quinque Portæ regressæ sunt domum, relinquentes ibi bonam custodiam; & reædificaverunt, & custodierunt castellum illud de Lomello per totam hyemem & per totum ver. (Sire Raul, De Rebus Gestis Friderici I, ed. Muratori, R. I. S., VI, 1179).

V. Kal. MCLVII. Mediolanenses reædificaverunt Lomellum. (Excepta Historica, ed. Muratori, R. I. S., I, pt. 2, p. 236). See also Annales Mediolanenses, M. G. H. Script., XVIII, 364, 365; Annales Mediolanenses Breves, ibid., 390.

Igitur Mediolanenses per pontes quos fecerant transmeantes, Lunellum reædificant, totumque penè territorium Papiensium crudeliter depopulantur. (Ottonis Frisingensis, Lib. II, 31, ed. Muratori, R. I. S., VI, 736). Cf. Guntero, V, 519.

[10] 1118. 9 Kal. Novembris indictione 12, die Iovis captum est castrum Lomelli. (Annales Mediolanenses Brevissimi, M. G. H. Script., XVIII, 391).

[11] Glossa. Crotonius in Cronicis: in civitate papiensi comites de Lomello a castro lomellino sic dicti, erant domini in civitate papiensi, et de quolibet nato recipiebant duodecim denarios et plura alia regalia habuerunt. Quodam die Paschatis cum omnes comites venissent Papiam ad festum, cives de Papia clausis ianuis omnes comites interfecerunt, et unus solus transito Ticino evasit. Insuper ceperunt castrum de Lomello et funditus everterunt. Tunc mediolanenses in servitium illius comitis, qui evaserat, burgos civitatis papiensis destruxerunt etc. (Galvanei Flammae, Chron. Maius, ed. Ceruti, 647-648).

[12] Giulini, III, 656.

astounding statement that the church of S. Maria, destroyed at this epoch, was reconstructed with the old materials by Barbarossa, as a penance imposed by the pope, Alexander III.[13] Whence the XVIII century historian derived this account remains a mystery, but the suspicion that he perhaps possessed some semi-reliable sources now lost, arises from two facts. The first is that the existing church of S. Maria shows internal evidence of having been not rebuilt, but repaired, at the end of the XII century. The second is that the tradition still lives at Lomello that the city was destroyed by Barbarossa. A great stucco statue now visible above the vaults of the church is locally called by the name of Barbarossa, and is said to have been erected in remembrance of the reconstruction of the church by the emperor. On the other hand, it is obvious that Portalupi's account, if it possesses a certain basis of truth, is nevertheless entirely erroneous in many of its details. Not one of the many chronicles and historical monuments from which we know even the minutest particulars of the famous descent of Barbarossa on Alessandria, mentions, in any way, Lomello. Indeed, the German army moved against Alessandria from the other side, passing by way of Susa and Asti. Furthermore, it appears quite incredible that the reconstruction of the church of Lomello should have been imposed as a penance by the pope. Such a gentle punishment might have been inflicted by Hildebrand on his friend and supporter, William the Conqueror, but the papacy, in the person of Alexander III, fighting for life or death against the empire in the person of Barbarossa, even after the peace of Venice, was absorbed in questions of an import far too vital to make it conceivable that it should have treated of such a trivial subject with its arch-enemy.

In 1191 Henry IV commanded that Lomello should be no more rebuilt.[14] This seems to imply that the town was destroyed by Barbarossa, but it is not certain that it had ever been rebuilt subsequent to 1164, when a similar order was promulgated by Barbarossa himself.

The church of S. Maria Maggiore is mentioned in a tax-list of 1192.[15] This fact proves that the church was in existence at this epoch, although the castle, and possibly also the town, were in ruins. Indeed, there is not the slightest reason to suppose that the church suffered any complete destruction in the course of the many vicissitudes to which the town and castle were subjected. It was the habit in the Middle Ages to spare scrupulously churches and monasteries even when towns were razed to the ground, and this happened in Lombardy in the destruction of the cities of Como (1127), Lodi Vecchio (1158), Milan (1162), and Castel Seprio (1287). When Isola Comacina was destroyed in 1169, the Comaschi were laid under an interdict because they had burned the churches. The truth seems to be, therefore, that at Lomello

---

[13] 79-84.

[14] Giulini, IV, 60.

[15] *Liber Censuum Romanae Ecclesiae,* ed. Muratori, A. I. M. A., ed. A., XIV, 321.

the church of S. Maria came through all the destructions of the castle and of the city, having suffered only such damage as could easily be repaired without an entire reconstruction of the edifice.

The subsequent vicissitudes of Lomello appear to have left no mark at all upon the architecture of S. Maria. In 1200 and again in 1213, the town was destroyed by the very Milanesi who had built it half a century before.[16] In the XVI, XVII and XVIII centuries the importance of Lomello declined, and the city became too small to support the two collegiate churches, the three monasteries, the two hospitals, the priory, the chapel, and the church of the Knights of Malta, all founded in more prosperous days. In the collegiate church of S. Maria Maggiore, however, was established the Congregazione del SS. Rosario, original documents of which, dating from the middle of the XVIII century, were discovered by Zucchi in the Archivio dello Stato at Milan.[17]

III. The original edifice consisted of a nave nine bays long, two side aisles, slightly projecting transepts, a choir, and three apses (Plate 106), but the building has been much altered. The absidioles were destroyed in 1718, when the main apse was remade and enlarged, as is proved by this date inscribed on its cornice. Traces of the ancient absidioles are, however, still extant. The southern one is largely preserved in the sacristy, and the amortizements of the northern one may still be seen in the east wall of the transept. It was probably also in the XVIII century that the size of the church was materially reduced by erecting a new façade where had originally been the third piers from the west (Plate 106; Plate 109, Fig. 3). The three western bays of the original edifice, thus walled off from the new church, were not destroyed but were allowed to fall into the picturesque state of ruin in which they still exist (Plate 109, Fig. 3, 4; Plate 111, Fig. 2). In the south aisle of these bays were subsequently erected two mortuary chapels, which bear an inscription with the date 1770. In the south-west corner of the old nave, a new campanile was erected to replace the ancient one, the ruins of which may still be seen in the western bay of the southern side aisle (Plate 106; Plate 109, Fig. 1, 2). After having been thus reduced in size, the edifice was subjected to a very thorough restoration, which has hidden— but fortunately not destroyed—the ancient building. The style of these alterations, similar to that of the reconstructions carried out in the early part of the XIX century at S. Simpliciano and S. Calimero of Milan, is pseudo-Lombard (Plate 110, Fig. 3, 4). The nave was covered with a heavy barrel vault. A groin vault was erected over the crossing, and the interior was covered with stucco, gaudily painted in green and gold. Between 1907 and 1909, according to the inscription in the west wall of the church, the building

---

[16] *Annales Placentini Guelfi,* M. G. H., *Script.,* XVIII, 427.

[17] 373.

was still further damaged by the construction of a very ugly northern chapel, and by the addition of paintings quite out of harmony with the simple but imposing lines of the original structure.

The piers[18] anciently all had the same section (Plate 106), which consisted of two semi-columns engaged upon a rectangular core. It is only from certain of these piers, however, that rose the transverse arches by which the nave was originally spanned. This is clear from a study of the three ruined bays existing outside of the present façade (Plate 108; Plate 109, Fig. 3, 4); for in the westernmost pair (Plate 109, Fig. 4) may be plainly seen the springing of a transverse arch. In the second pair, however (Plate 109, Fig. 3), there are traces, not of a transverse arch, but of a pilaster strip continued straight up along the clearstory wall, while in the present façade the old transverse arch, which spanned the nave from the third piers, is still entirely preserved (Plate 109, Fig. 3). Inside the existing church, below the modern vault, are preserved the old transverse arches (Plate 110, Fig. 4), which spring only from every other pier, or from the fifth, seven and ninth of the old edifice (Plate 106; Plate 108), and above the vaults, under the roof, these arches are admirably preserved, together with the coupled windows which pierce the spandrels on either side (Plate 107)—the latter a most unusual feature. These transverse arches evidently supported a pediment wall on which were laid the timbers of the roof (Plate 107). Above the vaults may be seen the pilaster strips which rose from the intermediate piers. These have been destroyed in the eastern double bay, but elsewhere they are preserved to their entire height, and it is clear that they ended beneath the roof quite simply, without even a capital. They were, however, adjusted to the cross-beams of the timber roof by means of consoles and colonnettes of

---

[18] It is interesting to compare with these piers those of the neighbouring church of S. Michele, also at Lomello. Of the history of S. Michele nothing is known beyond the facts recorded by Portalupi (80), that the church had a prevosto and two canons who officiated at feasts, and that it possessed a relic of the true cross acquired in 1370.

The edifice consists of a nave three double bays long, two side aisles, modern chapels, transepts, three apses and a campanile. Over the crossing rises a Lombard cupola. The building has been completely baroccoized, and of the Romanesque structure only the core of the nave (completely covered with plaster), parts of the clearstory wall, the cupola and the apse survive. An intelligent restoration, however, would probably bring to light an important Lombard monument.

The nave had an alternate system, the intermediate piers being cylindrical, the alternate piers having a section like that of the piers of S. Maria Maggiore. It is probable that there were transverse arches. The side-aisle responds consisted of a shaft engaged upon a pilaster strip. The side-aisle vaults are slightly domed. The arched corbel-tables of the apse are grouped two and two, and those of the clearstory walls three and three. The masonry consists of large bricks laid in horizontal courses. Blind arches adorn the cupola. The crypt is filled up so as to be no longer accessible. The capitals seem to have been cubic. It is evident that the design of this church was much influenced by S. Maria Maggiore.

wood which are still preserved. The arrangement of this original and important feature is clearly shown in the drawings (Plate 107; Plate 108).

The side aisles (Plate 110, Fig. 3) were undoubtedly originally covered with groin vaults, somewhat domed, and supplied with wall ribs. This is clear from traces still preserved in the north side aisle of the ruined portion of the church. About the end of the XII or beginning of the XIII century, however, these vaults were reconstructed, at least in great part. This is evident in the eastern bay of both side aisles, where there are at present rib vaults, not domed, but with light diagonals of torus profile. Moreover, in the fourth, fifth, sixth and seventh (counting from the transepts) transverse arches of the south aisle, and in the third, fourth, fifth, sixth and seventh of the north aisle (Plate 110, Fig. 3), pointed arches are introduced. The fifth pair of piers (always counting from the transepts), which were anciently like the others, together with the responds of the side aisles, were at this period remade in their present rectangular form. These two piers, however, are not symmetrical with each other. Within the church the surface of the vaults has been entirely covered with stucco, so that the structure can not be studied (Plate 110, Fig. 3), but in the chapel or storehouse, established in the third bay from the west of the original south aisle, and adjoining the existing façade, the masonry of one of the side-aisle vaults is exposed. This consists of brick ashlar, but is peculiar in that the courses are continued straight across the groin, to be broken at the crowns of the vaults. Similar vaults are found in Gothic monuments, such as, for example, the Porta Ticinese of Milan, a structure which dates from c. 1338, but are almost without analogy among the Romanesque monuments of Lombardy. It is therefore entirely probable that this vault, like those within the church, was reconstructed in the late XII or in the XIII century. The curious part is, however, that the bricks employed in this construction are certainly of the early XI century, which seems to bear out Portalupi's statement that the church was rebuilt after its destruction, with old materials.

The barrel vaults which cover the transepts and choir I suppose to be original, but it is impossible to be certain, since their structure is entirely hidden beneath the stucco. These vaults, like the transverse arches of the nave, are reinforced by no buttresses, and are dependent for their stability upon the strength of the wall (Plate 106).

The edifice possessed no triforium or gallery (Plate 107; Plate 108), but only a simple clearstory, the round-headed windows of which still exist above the modern vault (Plate 110, Fig. 1, 2).

An interesting feature of this church, and one so far as I know without analogy among Lombard edifices, is the fact that the façade formed part of the fortifications. We have not here, strictly speaking, a fortified church like those of which France possesses such excellent examples in the cathedral of Albi, or St.-Pierre of Royat (Puy-de-Dôme), where the edifice was at once church and fortress. At Lomello the church was merely incorporated with the castle, part of the wall of which was formed by the façade. In this respect the monument is entirely analogous to the well-known church of Notre-Dame at Étampes (Eure-et-Loire). Thus it is easy to understand how the castle could have been destroyed without necessarily inflicting injury upon the church. The fact that the façade formed part of the fortifications explains several facts that would otherwise be puzzling. For this reason the façade was set at an angle to the axis of the church, which resulted in the charming irregularities of plan for which the building is notable (Plate 106); for this reason a stairway and a passage were enclosed in the wall of the façade, a motive characteristic of Gothic architecture, and hitherto believed to have found its earliest expression in the abbey churches of Caen. For this reason, perhaps, the architect permitted himself the liberty (taken but very rarely by Lombard builders) of employing arched corbel-tables in the interior of the edifice (Plate 109, Fig. 4).

The masonry consists of bricks, roughly laid (Plate 111, Fig. 3), often obliquely or in herring-bone courses, often with the broad side or the end exposed to view, and separated by broad beds of coarse mortar.

IV. The capitals (Plate 109, Fig. 3, 4) are without carving and of a rudimentary cubic variety.

The transverse arches and clearstory windows are in two orders. In two orders also are the main archivolts on the side of the nave (Plate 108; Plate 109, Fig. 3, 4), but these orders are so disposed that the outer forms a curve slightly higher than the inner. This is, I believe, the earliest example of a motive later employed with such effect in S. Savino of Piacenza, and destined to become characteristic of Italian Gothic.

Along the clearstory walls (Plate 110, Fig. 1, 2), forming a cornice, is a series of arched corbel-tables grouped two and two, and inserted between the windows, which were encircled by a single arched corbel-table. On the side-aisle walls (Plate 110, Fig. 1) and on the transept-ends (Plate 110, Fig. 2), the arched corbel-tables were grouped three and three. The developed arched corbel-tables of the façade were probably added in the XII century.

The cross-hatching on the bricks shows that it was the intention of the builders to cover the edifice with intonaco decorated with frescos. Some traces of these are still extant in the east wall. Above the vault may be seen other signs of intonaco, and a stucco statue, without head.

V. The masonry of Lomello (Plate 111, Fig. 3) is evidently more primitive than that of Sannazzaro Sesia (Plate 201, Fig. 5), a surely dated monument of 1040, or of Lodi Vecchio (Plate 105, Fig. 3), a church which dates from c. 1050, or of Calvenzano (Plate 41, Fig. 2), a monument of c. 1040, or of the campanile of S. Satiro at Milan (Plate 132, Fig. 2), a dated edifice of 1043, or of S. Sepolcro at Milan (Plate 133, Fig. 2), a dated monument of 1030.

The piers of Lomello (Plate 106) seem to be intermediate between those of S. Vincenzo of Galliano (Plate 97), a surely dated monument of 1007, and those of Sannazzaro Sesia (Plate 200), a dated monument of 1040.

The arched corbel-tables grouped two and two (except on the façades of the transepts, where they are grouped three and three) seem more developed than those of Bagnacavallo (Plate 18, Fig. 5), a monument of c. 1000, or of the eastern side of the baptistery of Galliano, erected c. 1015. They are, however, no more advanced than those of S. Antonino of Piacenza (Plate 182, Fig. 5), an authentically dated monument of 1022.

For all these reasons Lomello may be ascribed with confidence to c. 1025.

LOPPIA DI BELLAGIO,[1] S. MARIA

I. The picturesque ruins of S. Maria of Loppia have been published and illustrated by Monti.[2]

II. The nuns of Loppia were transferred to S. Colombano at Como, in 1579.[3]

At the end of the XVI century, the bishop Ninguarda wrote the following description of the church: "The oratory of Santa Maria of Loppia was visited. It is distant a quarter of a mile from the church of S. Giovanni, and was formerly occupied by Benedictine nuns, who were later transferred to the monastery of S. Colombano at Como. It has an ancient chapel, the centre of which is vaulted. The altar, which is still used for services, is surrounded by a railing and steps. Two thirds of the church has a wooden roof, but the central portion is vaulted. There is an ancient ancona painted with the image of the Virgin and many other saints. The campanile has a single bell, and there is a single door in the centre of the edifice."[4]

III. The monument is in a picturesque state of ruin, being entirely overgrown with vines and shrubbery. The church itself, a single-aisled structure with apse, is of little interest, nor does anything of importance

---

1 (Como). The ruins lie about two kilometres to the south-west of Bellagio, on the shore of the lake.

2 475.   3 Tatti, *Martyrologium*, 137.

4 Visitato l'oratorio di santa Maria di Loppia, lontano un quarto di miglio dall'arcipretato, dove altre volte stavano monache dell'ordine di santo Benedetto transferite in Como nel monastero di santo Colombano. Ha una capella antica in mezza volta con un'altare alla forma, consacrato, cinto di cancelli et bradella. Il resto è sofittato per i doi terzi, ma nel mezzo non. Vi è una ancona vecchia pinta in tavola con l'imagine della B. Vergine e di molti altri santi. Ha un campanile con una campana sola et una porta sola nel mezzo. (Ninguarda, ed. Monti, II, 114).

remain in the ruins of the monastic buildings by which it is surrounded. The campanile, however, is a graceful and well preserved monument of the Lombard style. It comprises five stories with windows placed in each face of the four upper ones. The size of these windows is gradually increased toward the top, giving the design an effect of lightness and charm.

The apse vault, which is well preserved, was obviously constructed with solid centering. The masonry consists of stones of irregular sizes and shapes, some roughly squared, others of natural shape, laid in thick beds of mortar of poor quality. The masonry of the campanile consists of squared stones, laid in thinner beds of mortar.

No trace remains of the vault, with which, according to Ninguarda, the central portion of the nave was covered.

IV. The exterior of the side-aisle walls and the apse are without decoration. The campanile has arched corbel-tables.

In the apse may be seen the disappearing remains of Romanesque decoration in fresco, consisting of a fret executed in two shades of blue, red and purple. On the façade are traces of frescos.

V. The masonry of the nave is analogous to, but somewhat more primitive than, that of S. Carpoforo at Como (Plate 60, Fig. 4), an authentically dated monument of 1040. The nave may, consequently, be ascribed to c. 1030. The masonry of the campanile, on the other hand, is analogous to that of S. Giacomo at Como, and may therefore be ascribed to c. 1105.

MADERNO,[1] S. ANDREA

(Plate 112, Fig. 1, 3)

I. Owing to the circumstances that S. Andrea of Maderno is situated within easy walking distance of the great tourist resort of Salò, and that the town itself is well known to historians because of the famous diploma of the commune, now considered false,[2] our monument has received almost disproportionate attention from archæologists. It was first described by the brothers Sacchi.[3] Odorici[4] studied the edifice, which was illustrated also in the *Grande Illustrazione*.[5] In recent years the monument has been the subject of a monograph by Arcioni.

II. Of the history of the edifice nothing is known except that S. Carlo ordered that the crypt should be walled up.[6]

1 (Brescia).   2 Bettoni-Cazzago, 64; Odorici, IV, 95.
3 103.   4 III, 296 f.   5 III, 304.   6 Arcioni, 7.

III.   The church consists of a nave three bays long (Plate 112, Fig. 3), two very narrow side aisles, a choir of a single double bay flanked by side aisles, a modern rectangular apse, and modern chapels on the southern side of the nave.   North of the choir rises a campanile of the XV century.

The nave is at present covered with modern vaults (Plate 112, Fig. 3), as are also the side aisles (Plate 112, Fig. 3).   The modern cupola over the choir (Plate 112, Fig. 3) replaces the original groin vault.   The groin vaults of the side aisles of the choir—these vaults embrace two bays, are very long and narrow, and so highly domed in the longitudinal sense that they resemble barrel vaults—are likewise not original.   It is apparent upon inspection that the edifice has undergone many reconstructions.   The arches of the main arcade were originally semicircular and in two orders, but they were replaced in the Gothic period by pointed arches in one order.   In the Renaissance the church was completely baroccoized.   In modern times, however, the intonaco has been stripped off in places, so that the original masonry (which is still perfectly preserved) can be studied.   It is greatly to be regretted that this method of procedure has not been more generally followed in modern Italian restorations.

The piers of the nave are quatrefoiled, but in the alternate piers the members facing the nave and side aisles are rectangular, while in the intermediate all the members are semicircular.   The side aisles were undoubtedly spanned by transverse arches.   One of these is still preserved in the western bay of the northern side aisle, and it is probable that the corresponding arch in the southern side aisle is also original.   These arches, as may be seen in the western bay of the northern side aisle, were received on rectangular responds, without bases, and with a simple impost moulding for a capital. There was a simple rectangular system, rising from the abaci, and extending along the clearstory wall.   This may well have supported transverse arches spanning the nave, but no certain traces of such are extant.   Corresponding to the westernmost piers, buttresses are erected against the clearstory wall. Similar buttresses are placed at a point corresponding to the piers which separate the nave and choir.   Elsewhere there are no buttresses, even at the east and west angles.   The choir has intermediate supports consisting of columns placed upon high pedestals.   To make way for the organ (Plate 112, Fig. 3), the capital of the column on the north side has been removed, and the two original arches have been replaced by a single great arch as long as the choir.   In the choir, the intermediate columns had no system.

The church has a high clearstory.   There are still visible traces of the original windows, which were obviously intended to serve without glass.   They were widely splayed, and one in the west façade is in several orders, shafted (Plate 112, Fig. 1).

The exterior wall of the southern side aisle is now completely masked by buildings engaged against it.   The masonry of those portions of the edifice which are visible, consists of ashlar of rather variable quality. That of the west façade (Plate 112, Fig. 1), and of the piers, is much better than that of the side aisles. Pilfered Roman blocks, with inscriptions and reliefs, are used as second-hand material. The new stones are of small size, and rather roughly squared. The horizontality of the courses is often broken (Plate 112, Fig. 1), and the mortar-beds are wide, especially in the flanks of the edifice.

IV. The capitals seem to have been strongly influenced by the decorative forms of S. Ambrogio at Milan. They are Corinthianesque, adorned with grotesques (two animals with a single head, which forms the volute, sirens, eagles, etc.) or carved with interlaces, string or leaf patterns. The abaci, which are high, are adorned with grotesques (among others two animals with interlaced tails), interlaces, string or leaf patterns. The bases are Attic, with griffes.

The arched corbel-tables on the east, west and south façades and on the north clearstory, are in two orders, but on the north side-aisle wall they are only in one order. The façade is further ornamented with a great blind arch (Plate 112, Fig. 1). The archivolts of the western portal (Plate 112, Fig. 1) are adorned with grotesques, rinceaux and anthemia, and the jambs have similar motives. This portal is in five orders, moulded and shafted.

The church contains very beautiful frescos, one of which is dated 1499. Other traces of conventional patterns may be earlier, and the red background of two capitals is probably original.

In the triumphal arch are two grotesque carvings.

V. The church in its structure, in the style of its decorations, and in its masonry, shows close analogies with Castell'Arquato (Plate 48, Fig. 2, 4), a surely dated monument of 1117-1122. Maderno may, consequently, be ascribed to c. 1120.

MANTOVA, S. LORENZO

(Plate 112, Fig. 2)

I. This resurrected Lombard edifice was first published in the *Bollettino d'Arte*.[1] For the history of the building, the works of Donesmondi and Bottomi should be consulted. Valuable notices are also contained in the manuscript history of Amadei, preserved in the Archivio Gonzaga at Mantova.[2]

II. The historians of Mantova have repeated one after the other that the church of S. Lorenzo was a pagan temple converted into a Christian

[1] II, Anno 1908, 118.

[2] Amadei Federigo.—*Cronaca Universale della Città di Mantova*, Archivio Gonzaga, Mantova, MS. No. 75, 76.

church in the time of Constantine.[3]   The circular form of the building was
a sufficient basis for such a statement on the part of XVIII century scholars.

The earliest authentic mention of the church dates from the year 1049,
when, according to Volta,[4] the bones of S. Longino were temporarily placed
in the church until the neighbouring edifice of S. Andrea should be completed.

Amadei records a tradition that the church was rebuilt by Matilda.[5]

In 1597 the parish of S. Lorenzo was transferred to S. Andrea, and the
church desecrated, because the noise of the people on the piazza disturbed
the celebration of the offices.[6]   Some remains of the ancient church long
continued visible, however, among others certain frescos and an iron cross.[7]

In the course of time, however, the site of the ancient church came to
be entirely forgotten.   In 1907 the commune of Mantova bought the group
of houses which had been built over the remains of the church, with the
intention of enlarging the piazza.   While these were being demolished,
portions of the ancient church came to light, and it was determined to restore
the edifice.[8]   The reconstruction had just been finished when I visited the
edifice in July, 1913.

[3] Amadei, MS. cit., Vol. I, f. 33; Bottomi, 142.

[4] 69.   [5] MS. cit., I, f. 104.

[6] Notai all'anno 312 lo diroccamento in Mantoua de Tempij profani degl'Idoli,
attesa la conuersione dell'Imperador Costantino, ed all'ora feci menzione di quello
denominato la Rotonda, il quale fu cangiato nella Chiesa dedicata al Martire S. Lorenzo.
Ora nel corrente anno essend' informato il Duca, che gli Uffizj Diuini erano frastornati
dal rumoreggiamento del Popolo, il quale ueniua alla Piazza, presso la Torre
dell'Orologio p[er] comperare le Comestibili (stanbecchè la Porta d'essa Chiesa riferiua
immediatamente sulla Piazza[)]; perciò a fine di togliere una tanta indecenza, fecela
demolire, e così il Titolo di S. Lorenzo, il Fonte Battesimale, e tutte l'altre cose sacre
spettanti alla Parocchia, furono trasferite nella vicina Basilica di S.to Andrea, entro
la prima Cappella d destra in entrando. (MS. cit., II, f. 696).

The same facts are repeated more briefly by Donesmondi (250).   See also
Bottomi (142).

[7] Così pure la Rotonda dedicata a Diana fu conuertita in altra Chiesa, dedicata
al Martire Santo Lorenzo.   Di questa Rotonda uedonsene ancora le uestigia annesse
alla moderna Torre del pubblico Orologio, entro il Recinto del Ghetto Ebraico, ma poi,
come a suo luogo dirò, fu trasferita questa Chiesa, col suo Titolo in quella di S.to
Andrea, e quel Luogo fu fabbricato uerso Piazza dell'Erbe; ma dou'è stata lasciata
memoria Sacra, sovra li Tetti di quelle Case Ebraiche, una Croce eminente di Ferro,
uisibile a nostri giorni, e sul muro esteriore ui si conserva ancora in Pittura stata
rinnouata l'imagine del S.to Martire, come altresi l'altra di S. Longino. (Amadei,
MS. cit., I, f. 33).

. . . ai dì nostri, stando sulla Piazzetta del Ghetto, vedesi ancora un vecchio tetto
sostenuto da pilastroni di pietra, sopra il quale sta innalzata una croce di ferro che
si volle sempre conservare a perpetua memoria di quest'antica chiesa, come verso la
Piazza dell'Erbe, e sulla facciata del Caseggiato che fa parte del Ghetto Ebraico, sotto
i Civici NN. 2797, 2798, 2799, 2800, 2801, 2802 si vedono cinque quadri dipinti a fresco,
rappresentanti S. Andrea, Ap., S. Longino, il martire S. Lorenzo, ed altri due, che
non si ravvisano bene. (Bottomi, 142).

III. The building consists of a circular central nave, a side aisle, a gallery, and an eastern apse in two stories. The second story of the apse, however, is evidently an addition of the Gothic period, since it has a cornice of flat corbel-tables, and cuts across the old round-arched corbel-tables. The nave is covered with a modern dome. The side aisles and gallery have groin vaults trapezoidal in plan. Although the arches of the main arcade are stilted, and the wall arches depressed, the latter, nevertheless, rise to a higher level. The transverse arches, loaded at the crown, reach a level intermediate between that of the arches of the main arcade and that of the wall arches. The groins, broken in plan, intersect at a point higher than the crowns of the transverse arches, but lower than that of the wall arches. In the eastern half of the edifice, the vaults seem to be old; in the western half, they have been restored. The old vaults are, for the most part, covered with intonaco and the remains of frescos, so that the masonry can be studied only in a few places. It is evident, however, that the vaults were constructed of narrow bricks, laid on edge in perfectly regular courses, and separated by rather thick beds of mortar.

The nave and side aisles are separated by eight cylindrical piers of brick and two pilfered columns. There is no system. The arcade of the gallery is supported on columns of a character precisely like those below, except that they are shorter. The side-aisle responds in both stories consist of five rectangular members.

Two stairways in the thickness of the wall give access to the gallery. The outer wall of the gallery is still further lightened by a series of niches, one placed in each bay. The walls are of enormous thickness.

The masonry consists of large, regularly shaped bricks, of a rough surface but not cross-hatched, laid in horizontal courses separated by wide beds of mortar. The windows have been correctly restored as widely splayed, and of one or more unmoulded orders. There are numerous square scaffolding holes (Plate 112, Fig. 2).

[8] The official description of the condition of the ruins at the time they were discovered is as follows: La galleria al piano terra comunicava con la parte centrale a mezzo di 10 arcate delle quali due vennero nei tempi passati demolite insieme con un tratto di muro; questi vani sono superiormente chiusi da un arco molto rialzato. Alcune delle arcate superiori sono scomparse, in corrispondenza al muro sottoposto demolito. La cupola, anni or sono, è caduta. Tutto l'edificio era infine ricoperto da embrici un po' convessi di tipo romano; alcuni di questi embrici, trovati sul tetto, recano la marca di fabbrica. Due porte davano accesso al Tempio: una orientale e una occidentale, alla guisa dei vecchi battisteri; di queste porte rimangono evidenti le traccie decorate a rozzi motivi di foglie policrome. Così rimangono le traccie delle scalette che, nello spessore dei muri esterni, salivano dal piano terreno ai matronei e le traccie delle finestre che illuminavano i matronei stessi. La decorazione delle pareti è molto guasta, si vedono due strati di intonaco dipinto, uno molto vecchio ed uno che può essere attribuito alla prima metà del secolo XVI; sono queste le ultime decorazioni, fatte prima che la chiesa venisse soppressa. (Bollettino d'Arte, Anno 1908, II, 118).

MARENTINO, S. MARIA AI MONTI

IV.   The capitals of the circular piers are cubic, like those of S. Abondio of Como.   The responds are without capitals or bases, and the gallery piers have only a flat stone as a base.   The piers of the lower story have a similar flat stone and one torus moulding.   Otherwise the interior is quite bare of ornament of any kind, except that stone slabs, carved with interlaces, were inlaid on the responds of the gallery.   One of these slabs and half of another are still extant.   Their decoration seems to show the influence of S. Ambrogio.

The exterior (Plate 112, Fig. 2) is adorned with arched corbel-tables in two orders, supported in the lower story on shafts terminating in cubic capitals.   Above the corbel-tables is a saw tooth.   The clearstory cornice has no shafts.

V.   The masonry, the shafts, and the capitals of S. Lorenzo recall the apse of S. Sofia of Padova (Plate 161, Fig. 1, 3), a surely dated edifice of c. 1123, but S. Lorenzo seems somewhat more primitive because of the absence of mouldings, and the simpler and more restful decoration.   The Mantova monument may, consequently, be ascribed to c. 1115, a date not inconsistent with the tradition that it was reconstructed by Matilda.

MARENTINO,[1] CAPPELLA DI S. MARIA AI MONTI AL
CIMITERO

(Plate 113, Fig. 1)

I.   A description of this church was published in *Il Piemonte* under the title *S. Maria di Marentino*.[2]

II.   The earliest reference to the town of Marentino is found in a document of 1164.   The church is mentioned for the first time in 1307.   The frescos of the apse were executed in 1450, as is recorded by an inscription. In 1584 the church still enjoyed the rank of a parish, but must have been already surrounded by a cemetery, since it was used for burials.   At this epoch the baroccoization of the building took place.   The edifice serves now only as chapel for the cemetery.

III.   The chapel consists of a nave of a single aisle and an apse.   The interior has been completely baroccoized, and the half dome of the apse and the eastern portion of the walls have been in great part remade (Plate 113, Fig. 1).   The masonry consists of cross-hatched bricks of regular size, well laid in horizontal courses.   The mortar-beds vary remarkably in width.   In the eastern part of the church a considerable amount of ashlar is introduced (Plate 113, Fig. 1).

1 (Torino).
2 Anno II, No. 2, 16 Gennaio, 1904. This article was signed with the initials A. P.

IV. The northern wall is ornamented with simple arched corbel-tables supported on pilaster strips, except at the east end, where the wall was restored in the XIII century. The apse still retains its shafts and corbels, but the arched corbel-tables themselves have disappeared. The southern flank is adorned with double arched corbel-tables supported on pilaster strips (Plate 113, Fig. 1).

The original windows were widely splayed, intended to serve without glass, and in some cases moulded (Plate 113, Fig. 1). The portal was anciently in three orders, moulded and shafted. This portal is built out, and is covered with a roof of flat tiles. Above it is a biforum and a window in the form of a Greek cross. The façade has pilaster strips but no corbel-tables.

V. The masonry of Marentino is analogous to that of those portions of S. Simpliciano at Milan which were erected c. 1150. Our monument may, consequently, be ascribed to about the same time.

MARIANO,[1] BATTISTERO

(Plate 113, Fig. 2)

I. To the extent of my knowledge, this monument has never been published.

II. About thirty years ago, according to the local tradition, the interior of the edifice was done over like a grotto, with rustication and rough stone-work.

III. The edifice consists of a square central area, from each side of which opens a semicircular niche. The nave is surmounted by an octagonal clearstory (Plate 113, Fig. 2) carried on arched squinches and by a cloistered dome. The edifice is preceded by a Renaissance portico (Plate 113, Fig. 2), and has suffered from many other changes and alterations. The masonry is rough, hardly better than rubble. Bits of brick and uncut stone are laid in courses which are only approximately horizontal.

IV. The interior has an engaged column in each corner. The capitals carry the second order of the archivolts of the niches. Two of these capitals are cubic, one is cubic carved with an interlace, and one has a grotesque head and foliated motives.

The arched corbel-tables of the exterior are grouped two and two or three and three.

V. The capitals of the interior can not be earlier than the XII century. On the other hand, the rough masonry of the edifice suggests that it must

1 (Como).

have been construrcted in the first half of the XI century. In fact, this masonry is almost as rough as that of the baptistery of Galliano (Plate 96, Fig. 1), an edifice of c. 1015. The explanation probably is, that the baptistery of Mariano was first erected c. 1025, but was subsequently remodelled. This reconstruction—which probably took place c. 1100—included the addition of the columns and capitals of the interior, and the reworking of the exterior corbels.

MARNE,[1] S. BARTOLOMEO

I. This monument has never been published.

II. In 1186 the church of S. Bartolomeo of Marne was enumerated among the possessions of the priory of Pontida.[2]

III. Only the apse remains, since the rest of the church was barbarously destroyed about 1907.

IV. This apse is characterized by small arched corbel-tables supported on shafts engaged upon pilaster strips, crude capitals, and windows in several orders, shafted and intended to serve without glass.

V. In style this apse closely resembles S. Tomè at Almenno S. Bartolomeo (Plate 11, Fig. 1), a monument of c. 1140. Since the capitals of Marne, however, seem somewhat more primitive than those of S. Tomè, our church may be ascribed to c. 1130.

MAZZONE,[1] S. MARIA DI NAULA

(Plate 187, Fig. 1, 2)

I. A description of this church and one photograph of the façade were published by Orsenigo.[2]

II. In 1186 S. Maria di Naula enjoyed the rank of pieve, since it is mentioned as such in a bull of Urban III of that date.[3]

In 1255 the town of Naula, or Navola, was abandoned by its inhabitants, who united with the citizens of neighbouring villages to found the fortified town of Serravalle. The ancient church of Naula must, however, have continued to enjoy its former rank, since the *praepositura Naulae* is mentioned in a document of 1440.[4]

---

[1] (Bergamo).   [2] Lupi, II, 1359.
[1] Frazione di Piane di Serravalle Sesia (Novara).
[2] 350.   [3] Orsenigo, 343.   [4] *Ibid.*, 405.

III. The edifice consists of a nave (Plate 187, Fig. 2) four bays long, two side aisles and three apses (Plate 187, Fig. 1). The building is groin-vaulted throughout. The vaults are highly domed and supplied with wall ribs and transverse arches (Plate 187, Fig. 2). The wall ribs, loaded at the crowns, disappear at the springing (Plate 187, Fig. 2). The transverse arches are carried on pilasters, and in some cases are slightly loaded at the crown (Plate 187, Fig. 2). Since the system is uniform, the vaults are all more or less oblong, those of the nave transversely, those of the side aisles longitudinally. In the eastern bay, however, which is longer than the others, the nave compartment is almost square.

The piers all have the same section, and are rectangular with re-entrant angles (Plate 187, Fig. 2). There was originally a clearstory, but this has been walled up.

In the pavement of the choir is inlaid the plan of an earlier apse, nearly as wide as the existing three aisles.

The façade is entirely modern. The widely splayed windows were intended to serve without glass.

The masonry consists of round, uncut stones, mixed with a few cut stones, and some bits of brick (Plate 187, Fig. 1). There is an attempt to maintain horizontal courses.

IV. The exterior is ornamented with arched corbel-tables, very small in size, and supported on broad pilaster strips, placed close together. In twenty instances the arched corbel-tables are grouped three and three. Three times only—and always on the north side—they are grouped four and four.

In addition to later frescos, the apse contains an enthroned Christ, which appears to be part of a much restored work of the Trecento. The apses are still coated with the original intonaco, which bears traces of the ancient decoration in red. This consisted for the most part of conventionalized patterns, founded on the forms of brickwork. Herring-bone motives and triangular zigzags are prominent. The arched corbel-tables have a decoration in fresco which recalls that executed in brick at Sannazzaro Sesia.

V. Compared with Sannazzaro Sesia (Plate 201, Fig. 5), an authentically dated monument of 1040, the masonry of S. Maria di Naula is seen to be much more primitive. S. Maria di Naula may, consequently, be ascribed to c. 1030,[5] a date which agrees well with the character of the corbel-tables.

[5] It is interesting to compare with this church S. Secondo of Magnano (Novara). The edifice lies fifteen minutes' walk to the south-east of the town. The document of 1440, published by Orsenigo (407), speaks of this church, too, as a pieve. The building has been entirely made over, with the exception of the campanile, the apse and the southern absidiole, which date from c. 1040.

MERGOZZO,[1] S. MARTA

(Plate 113, Fig. 3)

I. This monument has never been published.

II. According to an inscription, the belfry was added in 1729.

III. The chapel consists of a nave of a single aisle and an apse. The interior is now vaulted, but was originally roofed in wood. The exterior walls are constructed of ashlar of rather crude quality (Plate 113, Fig. 3). Roughly squared stones are laid in courses which often depart from the horizontal. The mortar-joints are wide, and there are many scaffolding holes. The original windows were intended to serve without glass, but were not widely splayed.

IV. The portal in two orders is shafted and moulded (Plate 113, Fig. 3). The arched corbel-tables are supported on pilaster strips or shafts (Plate 113, Fig. 3).

V. The masonry of Mergozzo (Plate 113, Fig. 3) is superior to that of Garbagnate Monastero (Plate 99, Fig. 5), a monument which dates from c. 1120. Mergozzo may consequently be ascribed to c. 1130.

MIGNANO,[1] ORATORIO

I. This monument has never been published.

II. I know of no documents which illustrate the history of the edifice.

III. Of this ruined chapel only the apse is ancient. This is constructed (including the half dome) entirely of cut stones, regularly laid and well squared, although the joints are wide. The windows, small, and widely splayed, were intended to serve without glass.

IV. The apse is decorated externally with arched corbel-tables—each formed of one stone—shafts and pilaster strips. The capitals are foliated.
On the interior walls are still preserved frescos of the XIV century.

V. The masonry, shafts and corbel-tables are closely analogous to those of Castell'Arquato, an authentically dated monument of 1117-1122. Our chapel may consequently be ascribed to c. 1120.

[1] (Novara).

[1] Frazione di Lugagnano (Piacenza). The monument lies on the left-hand bank of the Arda, two hours' walk from Lugagnano.

LOMBARD ARCHITECTURE

MILAN, CHIESA D'AURONA

(Plate 114, Fig. 1, 2; Plate 115, Fig. 1)

I. The interesting architectural fragments of the destroyed church of Aurona are now gathered together in the Museo Archeologico, situated in the Castello Sforzesco at Milan. For the history of the church the manuscript in the Brera entitled *Monumenta Parthenonum*[1] should be consulted, since it contains XVIII century transcriptions of numerous documents referring to the convent, which are, so far as I know, not accessible elsewhere. The description of the church written by Latuada in 1737 shows that at this time the edifice had been completely modernized.[2] The first account of the discovery of the Romanesque fragments is contained in Ceruti's article on the ancient walls of Milan. This author began to confuse the history of the monastery, a process which was diligently continued by several of his successors. Cattaneo was the first to observe that the fragments were not all of the same epoch. In 1892 appeared a joint monograph by Landriani, Beltrami and De Dartein, published with the purpose of combatting Cattaneo. The work suffers greatly from the disjointed manner in which it was composed, and has contributed little towards an understanding of the complex archæological problems which the fragments present. It contains, however, references to the preceding literature and a bibliography. Far more satisfactory, though perhaps even a little over-critical, is the recent monograph of Testi. In his *Miscellanea*, Ratti has published important documents bearing upon the later history of the church. Observations upon the architecture have been contributed by Sant'Ambrogio.

II. On the abacus of one of the capitals in the museum is the inscription: "Here lies the archbishop Teodoro, who was unjustly condemned."[3] In the chronicle of Goffredo da Bussero or of Filippo da Castel Seprio we read: "In the year of our Lord 725, Teodoro was made archbishop of Milan. He sat fourteen years and lies buried in the monastery of Aurona, with his sister, Aurona."[4] The inedited chronicle of Lampugnano da Legnano states that Teodoro assumed office in 735 and died in 749, and that he was buried in the monastery of Aurona, together with his sister, Aurona, near the altar of

---

[1] Brera MS. AE, XV, 16.

[2] Nè la Chiesa nè il Monastero mostrano a' dì nostri verun segnale dell'antica struttura . . . (Latuada, V, 244).

[3] HIC REQVIES[CI]T DONVS THEODORVS ARHIEPISCOPVS QVI
INIVST[E F]VIT DAMNATVS

[4] Anno dn̄i 725 sedebat Theodoricus Archiepiscopus Mediolanensis sedit annis xiiij et jacet in monasterio Horonae cum sorore sua Horona (*Chronica* detta di Filippo da Castel Seprio, MS. Amb., S. Q. + I, 12, f. 51).

S. Bartolomeo.[5] Galvaneo della Fiamma states in an inedited chronicle of
Vienna that the sister of Teodoro founded the monastery of Aurona, and that
there they were both buried.[6] The same author states in the *Manipulus
Florum:* "Teodoro lies buried in the monastery of Aurona with his sister
Aurona."[7] We also read in two catalogues of the archbishops published by
Muratori, that Teodoro was buried in the monastery of Aurona.[8]

Galvaneo della Fiamma states on the authority of the chronicle of Goffredo
da Bussero that the monastery was founded in the year 740.[9] The same
notice is contained in a manuscript chronicle of the Biblioteca Ambrosiana,
which passes under the name of Filippo da Castel Seprio, although Grazioli
has identified it with the Goffredo da Bussero so frequently cited by Galvaneo.[10]
Another chronicle, however, the *Edificationes Ecclesiarum Mediolani,* assigns
the foundation to the year 744.[11]

The whole question of the exact date of the foundation of the monastery
is, in fact, hopelessly involved. No contemporary documents are extant, and
late chroniclers are notoriously inexact in their chronological references to
early times. Little more can be said than that the monastery was founded
some time in the VIII century, and probably about the year 735.

The convent of Aurona is mentioned in the will of the archbishop Ariberto,
who died in 1045.[12] In 1081 the monastery was destroyed by fire, as we learn
from a diploma of Henry IV. "In the name of the Holy Trinity, three persons
in one God, Henry IV, by divine favour, king: If we succour the churches
dedicated in the name of God and his saints when they are oppressed by

---

[5] Teodorus Mediolanen' archieps xliij. anno dccxxxv. sedit annis xiiij. hic exposuit
egregie officiū matutinale obijt anno dni dccxlviiij Jacet in mon horono cū sorore sua
horona apud altare sci Bertholamei. (*Chronica* di Lampugnano da Legnano, MS.
Amb. H 56 Sup., f. 62).

[6] Isto tpre orona soror Theodori archiēpi fundauit monasterium oronū, ubi ambo
reqescūt. (Galvaneo della Fiamma, *Chronicon,* Vienna MS. No. 3318, Cap. 179, f. 19).

[7] Jacet in Monasterio Horonæ cum suore sua Horona. (CXIII, ed. Muratori,
R. I. S., XI, 597).

[8] Theodorus sedit Ann. XIV. Sepultus in Monasterio Oronæ. (*Ordo antiquus
Episcoporum,* ed. Muratori, R. I. S., I, pt. 1, 229).

Theodorus Episcopus sedit annis XIV. obiit pridie Idus Majas, sepultus est in
Monasterio Olonæ. (*Catalogus Med. Archiep.,* ed. Muratori, IV, 142).

[9] Iacet in Monasterio Horono cum sorore sua Horona: quæ ipsum momaste-
rium [*sic*] ædificavit, Anno Domini septingentesimo quadragesimo: vt dicit Gothofredus
de Bussero. (Galvaneo della Fiamma, *Flos Florum,* cit. Puricelli, 381). Cf. also
Galvanei Flammae, *Chron. Maius,* 542, ed. Ceruti: Eius soror dicta Orona construxit
monasterium Oronum anno Christi DCCXL, secundum Gothofredum de Bussero.

[10] Anno dni 740 factum est monasterium Horanum Mediolano. (*Chronica* detta
di Filippo da Castel Seprio, MS. Amb., S. Q. + I, 12, f. 52).

[11] Anno dni 744 Arona soror Theodori Episcopi fundavit monasterium Oronum
ubi habitant moniales. (MS. Amb., S. Q. + I, 12, f. 70).

[12] Puricelli, 366.

adversity and afflictions, we hope that it will redound to the benefit of our soul and to the advantage of our reign. Therefore we wish it to be known to all the faithful of Christ and ourself that Rolinda, abbess of the monastery of Aurona, together with her entire community besought us as a favour that we should confirm a certain deed of that monastery which has been destroyed by fire."[13]

For the space of seventeen years the documents are silent in regard to our edifice. A famous parchment of the year 1099, however, has given historians much cause for thought: "Anselmo, by the grace of God, archbishop, to Rolinda, abbess of the Monastery of S. [sic] Aurona and to her community, greetings in the name of the Lord. On Tuesday the fifteenth day of March[14] in the *curtis* of the monastery of S. [sic] Aurona in the presence of Armanno, bishop of Brescia, and of the abbot of S. Ambrogio, and of Landolfo the prevosto, and of Alberto of Landriani, notary of the cathedral, and of Anselmo, the archpresbyter of the same church, and of Albino presbyter, and of other clerics, and of Arialdo of Melegnano and of Arderico of Baggio and of Bernardo of Pietra Santa, and of Gariardo Perticaro and of Pagano the judge, and of other noble men, I, Anselmo the archbishop, with my pastoral staff, drew the plan of a chapel in the garden of the monastery of S. [sic] Aurona, within the walls of the city; the said chapel to be built by the said abbess, in whose power and jurisdiction the same chapel and its chaplains must remain together with all the goods which at any time shall come into its possession. I also traced the plan of a cemetery in front of the said chapel on the side of the street which goes to Pusterla and the plan of a house for the chaplains adjoining the said chapel on the south side with entrance on the road to Pusterla. When this had been done in the presence of all the above-mentioned witnesses, with the staff which he held in his hand, Ambrogio son of Giovanni of Andronia, with the consent and approval of those who live near that monastery, renounced in my hand in favour of Rolinda, abbess of the said monastery, all claims that he had against

---

[13] In nomine Sanctæ, et individuæ Trinitatis. Henricus divina favente clementia quartus Rex. Si Ecclesiis Dei, Sanctorumque ejus nomini dedicatis adversitatibus, et tribulationibus oppressis condolebimus, ad remedium animæ nostræ, ad promeritumque nostri Regni pertinere speramus, ideoque notum esse volumus omnibus Christi, nostrisque fidelibus, quomodo Rolinda Abbatissa Oroni Monasterii, cum omni Congregatione sua, nostram clementiam postulavit, quatenus iteraremus scriptum quoddam ejusdem Monasterii, quod igne destructum est, quia carentia ejus, a quodam Castro suo fodrum vi, et injuste requisitum est. . . . Anno Dominicæ Incar. mill. octuagex. primo, indictione quarta, XVIII.—Kal. Maij data, anno autem domni Henrici XXVII, regno vero XXV [*recte* XV]. (Giulini, VII, 69-70).

[14] The year is not given, but it must be 1099, since during the pontificate of Anselmo IV (1097-1101) the fifteenth of March fell on a Tuesday only in this year. That the diploma is of Anselmo IV, and not of any other archbishops of the same name, has been shown by Giulini, II, 666.

her, that is, the church of that monastery and the right to hear there divine offices, and the cemetery and the *curtis,* all of which are situated within the painted portal which gives access to the street, so that they shall do nothing there except by the wish and consent of the said abbess. Wherefore, we, by this deed, give to the above-mentioned abbess all rights which we may have acquired through this renunciation, and we confirm this act with the authority of this our privilege, so that henceforth all may remain in her power and jurisdiction. Beside this we have decreed, with the approval of the clerks whom we have chosen to consider this matter, that none of the chaplains have their domicile in the towers or above the wall of the city between Pusterla and the monastery, lest haply their eyes should be scandalized if they should see the nuns walking through the *curtis* and garden."[15]

The great question raised by this diploma is whether the chapel in the garden, the plan of which was traced by the bishop in 1099, was, or was not, the principal church of the convent, and whether to this chapel should belong all or any of the fragments now in the archæological museum. To my mind, the diploma clearly implies that the new chapel in the garden, *capellam in hortu ejusdem monasterii,* is distinct from the subsequently specified *ecclesiam ejusdem monasterii,* rights to which were renounced into the hands of the bishop by Ambrogio di Giovanni of Adronia. The chapel in question, in my

<hr>

[15] Anselmus gratia Dei Archiepiscopus Rolindæ Abatissæ Monasterii Sanctæ Auronæ, ejusque congregationi in Domino salutem. Die Martis, qui est quintusdecimus dies mensis Martii, in curte Monasterii Sanctæ Auronæ; præsentia Armani Brixiensis Episcopi, et Abbatis Sancti Ambrosii, et Landulfi Præpositi, et Alberti Landrianensis majoris Ecclesiæ Notarii, et Anselmi Archipræsbiteri ejusdem Æcclesiæ, et Albini præsbyteri, et cæterorum Clericorum, et Arialdi de Melegnano, et Arderici de Badaglo, et Bernardi de Petrasancta, et Gariardi Perticarii, et Pagani Judicis, et aliorum nobilium virorum. Ego Anselmus Archiepiscopus fuste pastorali designavi Capellam in hortu ejusdem Monasterii Sanctæ Auronæ, intra murum Civitatis, ædificandam ab ipsa Abatissa, in cujus potestate, et ordinatione eadem Capella, cum rebus sibi quandoque advenientibus et Capellani ejus debent permanere. Cimiterium quoque designavi ante ipsam Capellam a parte via, que vadit per Pusterulam, et domum Capellanorum, justa ipsam Capellam, ex parte meridiei, cum accessu ad viam de Pusterula. Et hoc facto præsentia omnium supradictorum, per fustem, quem sua tenebat manu, Ambrosius Johannis Adroniæ per laudationem et contentum Vicinorum illius monasterii, refutavit in manu mea, ad partem Rolindæ Abatissæ supradicti monasterii, quicquid contra illam causaverant, idest Ecclesiam ejusdem monasterii, ad audiendum ibi divinum officium, et Cimiterium, et curtem, quæ omnia infra portam pictam, supra viam sitam continentur, ut nihil ibi debeant agere, nisi voluntate, et consensu ipsius Abatissæ. Nunc ergo quicquid per hanc refutationem ad Nos pertinet, supradictæ Abatissæ tradimus, et hujus nostri privilegii auctoritate confirmamus, ut exinde in sua maneat potestate, et ordinatione. Præterea statuimus, cum Clericis, quos ad hanc causam definiendam elegimus, ut nullus Capellanorum quodlibet ædifitium habeat in Turribus, vel super Murum civitatis, qui est a Pusterula usque ad monasterium, ne eorum oculi scandalizzentur, cum forte viderent Monachas per curtem, et hortum quandoque deambulantes. (Giulini, VII, 79).

opinion, was undoubtedly the chapel of the cemetery, as is implied by the phrase *cimiterium quoque designavi ante ipsam capellam*. In the XI and XII centuries it was usual for important monasteries to have a mortuary chapel situated in the cemetery and distinct from the church. Such chapels have come down to us at Sagra S. Michele, Piona, and S. Pietro di Civate. Remembering that the convent had been destroyed by fire eighteen years before, in 1081, it is altogether reasonable to suppose that the abbess proceeded first to rebuild the principal church. This having been entirely completed in 1099, work was begun on the chapel.

To which of these constructions, the church rebuilt between 1081 and 1099, or the chapel begun in 1099, belong the fragments in the museum? In the case of two buildings, one built immediately after the other, and both possibly under the direction of the same master-builders, there might well be a confusion of style. However, the fragments of compound piers must have belonged to a church and not to a small chapel such as the cemetery chapels of Sagra S. Michele, Piona, or S. Pietro di Civate. Moreover, it is known that Teodoro was buried in the church, and the inscription on the abacus of one of the columns proves that it came from the building where his body was preserved.

An ancient calendar records that the consecration of the Chiesa d'Aurona took place on February 12.[16] This calendar seems to have been written shortly before 1125, and the dedication referred to must consequently have been that of the new church erected between 1081 and 1099. Now in these years the twelfth of February fell upon a Sunday only twice, that is to say, in the years 1089 and 1095. The first may be excluded as improbable, since it would hardly allow sufficient time after 1081 for the construction of an important edifice. We may, therefore, conclude that the Chiesa d'Aurona was consecrated in 1095.

In the diploma of 1099 there is nothing to indicate that the Chiesa d'Aurona was dependent upon S. Ambrogio.[17] In 1148, however, it was dependent upon that monastery, as appears from a diploma of this date published by Puricelli.[18] A diploma of Barbarossa of 1185[19] confirms to the monastery of S. Ambrogio the possession of the Chiesa d'Aurona, and refers to spurious documents of the Carlovingian era. The Chiesa d'Aurona again

---

[16] Februarius. . . . Prid. Id. Dedicatio S. Mariæ in Monasterio Oronæ. (*Kalendarium Sitonianum*, ed. Muratori, R. I. S., II, pt. 2, 1035). Ordo pro denariorum divisione. . . . In dedicatione ecclesiæ monasterii Horonæ, solidi XVII, cum duobus observatoribus subdiaconibus, custodibus panes II de frumento, et II de secale de cambio, et II libræ de caseo et II staria vini. Veglonibus V panes de secale de cambio, libræ II de caseo, et II staria de vino. (Beroldo, ed. Magistretti, 20). *Ibid.*, 2, the Dedicatio S. Mariæ in Monasterio Oronæ is set down for pridie id. Februarii.

[17] Earlier documents which speak of the convent as dependent upon S. Ambrogio are either entirely spurious, or have been tampered with. See Giulini, I, 310, 342, 384, etc.

[18] 697.   [19] *Ibid.*, 1039.

appears as dependent upon S. Ambrogio in an archiepiscopal decree of 1198.[20]
In a sort of tax-list for 1398, published by Magistretti, appears the entry:
Monasterium Horonum cum Monasterio de Cornate unito secum. . . .

In the XV century the convent of Aurona fell into decline. From a
document of 1472, published by Puricelli,[21] we learn that this church of the
Benedictine order formerly had revenues sufficient to support thirty-five nuns,
but that because of the negligence and bad management of the abbesses, the
possessions of the monastery had been dissipated, and it had been reduced to
such a miserable condition that there was scarcely enough left to support the
abbess and three nuns. The pope Sixtus IV therefore decreed that the
abbatial dignity and the order of St. Benedict be suppressed in the said
monastery of Aurona, and that nuns of the order of S. Agostino should be
introduced from the neighbouring monastery of S. Agnese. This monastery,
known also as S. Agostino in Porta Nuova or S. Maria in Vedano, was
situated directly across the street from the monastery of Aurona, and when the
convents were united, an underground passage beneath the street was built
to connect the two. From documents resumed by Ratti[22] it is evident that
in 1478 the Chiesa d'Aurona was also known as S. Agata.

On November 7, 1594, the nuns of S. Agostino of Porta Nuova sold the
site and building of the monastery of Aurona together with the church of
S. Agata (that is, of Aurona) to the Capucini nuns of S. Barbara. In the
time of Puricelli, who wrote in 1645, these nuns still possessed the church.
This convent was not suppressed until 1782.

In the summer of 1868 the Palazzo dell'Intendenza Militare in the Via
Monte di Pietà was demolished to make room for the new Cassa di Risparmio.
Below the level of the surface and in part employed as building material in
the demolished edifice were found fragments of the Chiesa d'Aurona, which
were gathered together and placed in the Museo Archeologico, at that time
situated in the Brera, but subsequently moved to the Castello Sforzesco.

III, IV. The fragments discovered in 1868 may be separated into five
groups, each of which dates from a different time. These groups, for convenience, I designate by the capital letters A, B, C, D, and E, and shall
describe briefly the fragments belonging to each.

To the first, Group A, belong the remains of nine consoles. Two
(Nos. 651 and 656—Plate 114, Fig. 1) are of large size, the remaining seven
(Nos. 650, 652, 729, 739—Plate 114, Fig. 2,—747?, 750, 751) are much
smaller. There is considerable variation in the technique of the execution
of these consoles, since Nos. 747, 750, 751 and 652 are decidedly inferior to
the others. One, No. 751, still retains part of the iron key by which it was
fastened into the edifice. In addition to the consoles there are extant of

20 *Ibid.*, 1100.   21 381-389.   22 *Del Monaco*, 331.

Group A a fragment of a free-standing capital (No. 690—Plate 114, Fig. 2; Plate 115, Fig. 1), and two stilt-blocks of grey marble, Nos. 657 (Plate 114, Fig. 1) and 707 (Plate 114, Fig. 1), only one face of each of which is finished. There are two fragments of an entablature, Nos. 653 and 665 (Plate 114, Fig. 1), and one of an archivolt, No. 742. No. 706 (Plate 114, Fig. 2) appears to be a door or window jamb, and No. 658 (Plate 114, Fig. 1) is a door jamb of grey marble ornamented with a grape rinceau.

The fragments of Group A are all of marble. The style is distinctly Byzantine and characterized by perforated technique and crisp acanthus leaves. There is, however, strong influence of the Roman decadence, as is shown in the rinceau of the door jamb, No. 706 (Plate 114, Fig. 2). The fragment of the single capital we have (Plate 114, Fig. 2; Plate 115, Fig. 1) is evidently that of a free-standing column, and the fragment of the archivolt (No. 742) indicates that this earliest edifice was a basilica of at least three aisles, separated by a colonnade bearing arches. The church erected in the VIII century was probably built entirely of pilfered fragments taken from some edifice of c. 500. It is to this building that belonged originally the fragments of Group A, which were afterwards utilized to construct the first church of Aurona, c. 735.

A very different style characterizes the fragments of Group B. These include only four pieces: Nos. 686, a colonnette and capital of such small dimensions that they must have belonged to church-furniture of some kind and in all probability to a pergola; No. 693 (Plate 115, Fig. 1), a fragment of an architrave doubtless belonging to the same pergola; No. 676 (Plate 114, Fig. 1) and No. 677 (Plate 114, Fig. 1), small half capitals or possibly two halves of the same capital, not symmetrical with No. 686, but which may possibly have belonged to the same piece of furniture. The execution of these pieces is in the highest degree decadent. The drawing of the volutes is extremely crude and the ornament is merely scratched on the surface, rather than carved. There are no structural fragments belonging to Group B.

The fragments which I classify under Group C probably do not all belong to the same epoch, since they display a certain variation in style among themselves. They all seem to have come from church-furniture. It is reasonable to suppose that the basilica was supplied with new ornaments not all executed at precisely the same time, but within a period of some twenty-five or thirty years from each other. Thus could be explained the variations of technique observable in the fragments of Group C.

The earliest and most interesting fragments of this group belong to a reliquary. They comprise No. 696, part of a free-standing pier ornamented on all four sides, the outer one of which was adorned with free-standing crockets. This pier is only two or three inches in diameter. No. 700 is the lower part of one of the archivolts of the same reliquary, and shows the beginning of the springing of an arch. No. 743 is another bit of one of the archivolts and shows that they, too, were ornamented with crockets. No. 703 (Plate 114, Fig. 2) is a more considerable fragment of the same piece of furniture. It shows characteristic carving, and several letters of an inscription. No. 701 is similar, but more broken. Nos. 732 and 737 also belonged to the same reliquary. Nos. 456 (Plate 114, Fig. 2) and 480 (Plate 114, Fig. 2) are square columns elaborately carved with rinceaux, which served as supports for a ciborio. Nos. 692 (Plate 115, Fig. 1) and 710 (Plate 114, Fig. 2) are fragments of an architrave carved on two opposite sides, and Nos. 697 and 698 may have belonged to the superstructure of this ciborio. Nos. 691, 720, 721, 723, 724 and 774 are all fragments of another architrave which I conjecture belonged to a pergola. Nos. 709 and 725 are fragments of a third architrave ornamented on three sides. Nos. 694 (Plate 115, Fig. 1), 707 (Plate 114, Fig. 2), 711 (Plate 114, Fig. 2) and 715 belonged to a fourth architrave. No. 699 seems to be a bit of vase or lavabo, and No. 660 appears to be a stool. No. 712 is ornamented with a hand and a circle, two heads and a crisp acanthus-leaf motive, very Byzantine in style. Since the back is moulded, it may be part of a door jamb. No. 786, with undercut crockets, appears to belong with none of the other fragments. Nos. 713, 714, and other minor fragments also belong to this group, but are so broken that it is impossible to put them in relationship with each other, or with any of the other fragments. In all the fragments of Group C it is noticeable that there are none (except the door jamb) which belong to structural members, and that all belong to church-furniture, such as a pergola, ciborio, reliquary, stool, etc. They form a most interesting and unique example of the transition from the Carlovingian to the Lombard style of ornament, of the characteristics of both of which they partake. It is for this reason that their style is so perplexing.

The fourth or D Group of fragments consists almost entirely of portions of piers, capitals and bases of the developed Lombard style. The small size of these fragments makes it exceedingly difficult to determine the form of the church from which they come. A typical Lombard basilica, such as S. Ambrogio, for example, contains capitals of many different sizes and types. Those of the intermediate piers differ from those of the alternate piers. The side-aisle responds are alternately heavy and light. The capitals of the vaulting shafts may differ from those of the triumphal arch. Each portal is adorned with capitals different from those of the other portals, and in case the church is supplied with narthex, atrium or gallery, still other capitals are introduced. All Lombard churches, moreover, are characterized by irregularity and asymmetry of construction, so that the capitals of two corresponding members may differ greatly in size, shape and proportion. Owing to these considerations any attempt to reconstruct the Chiesa d'Aurona on the basis of the scanty fragments extant must be based upon mere conjecture.

While fully recognizing the many chances of error, I shall, nevertheless, for the sake of convenience, attempt to classify the fragments belonging to Group D as follows:

(1) Parts belonging to the alternate piers. From the circumstance that the section of the intermediate piers is well established, it is certain that the church must have possessed also alternate piers; but few fragments which can belong to such are extant, and these are so small that it is impossible to determine the section. The capital No. 666 (Plate 114, Fig. 1) in my judgment must have belonged to one of these piers, as well as the abacus No. 741. The latter fragment, since it has two ressauts, corresponds to the section neither of the side-aisle responds nor to that of the intermediate piers. Moreover, it is too high to have belonged to one of the vaulting capitals. Perhaps to the alternate piers belonged also the very large capital, No. 748, the size of which corresponds to no others of which we have fragments.

(2) Intermediate piers. Chance has preserved more pieces belonging to the intermediate piers than to any other portion of the edifice. The extant fragments represent parts of at least three of the minor supports. It is therefore certain that the nave must have been two or more double bays long. The section of these piers was a quatrefoil like certain of the intermediate piers at S. Ambrogio (Plate 116). Nos. 682 (Plate 115, Fig. 1), 683 (Plate 115, Fig. 1), 684 (Plate 115, Fig. 1), 685 (Plate 115, Fig. 1), 686 (Plate 115, Fig. 1), 687 (Plate 115, Fig. 1), 688, 497 (Plate 114, Fig. 2), 704 (Plate 114, Fig. 2), 705 (Plate 114, Fig. 2), 795, 1811, 1793, 703, 468, 718, 1877, 1797, 1796, are all parts of the capitals and abaci of the intermediate piers.

(3) Alternate side-aisle responds. A large group of fragments, obviously belonging to corresponding members, in all probability formed part of the alternate side-aisle responds, since they were engaged in the wall, and are different from the fragments which must be assigned to the intermediate side-aisle responds. They comprise one base (No. 679), and three different half capitals, Nos. 681, 752, 489 (mutilated). These capitals are in size half way between those of the alternate and intermediate piers.

(4) Intermediate side-aisle responds. The fragments of capitals Nos. 733 (Plate 114, Fig. 2) and 745, with their abaci, 734 and 746; 664 (Plate 114, Fig. 1) and the fragment of an abacus, 669, together with the base, No. 485, all appear to have belonged to the intermediate side-aisle responds. Although the section of the latter can not be accurately determined, it is evident that the responds consisted of several members, at least one of which was round.

(5) Half columns engaged on piers in the gallery. To such members must have belonged the large capitals, Nos. 674 and 648; their abaci, Nos. 675 and 674; their shafts, Nos. 1817 and 647; and their bases, Nos. 673 and 646.

(6) Vaulting capitals. The capital, No. 726, and the abaci, Nos. 663,

689, 728 and 731, must have belonged to the vaulting shafts.   The abacus
No. 728 was obviously misclassified by Landriani when he stated that it
belonged to one of the corner responds of the side aisles.   It is evident that
the system included five members, of which the central one was semicircular.

(7) The portals.   The low and symmetrical abaci, Nos. 667, 668, 672
and 730, together with No. 670—part of a sculptured jamb—and 744—part
of a carved archivolt—perhaps belonged to the portals of the basilica.

In addition to the fragments already enumerated, there should be noticed
No. 740 (Plate 114, Fig. 2), which perhaps belonged to one of the alternate
piers, and is still decorated with a fresco; No. 678, a fragment of a sculptured
lamb; Nos. 662 and 671, two symmetrical capitals; 654, another capital;
716 and 738, possibly parts of the same abacus, which may have belonged
to one of the intermediate piers; and many others, the original position of
which in the basilica it is impossible to determine.

Two of the abaci of the intermediate piers bear inscriptions.   The first,
relating to the archbishop Teodoro, has been cited above.   The second bears
the signature of the sculptor Giuliano.[23]

To Group E belongs only the keystone of a XIII century rib vault,
No. 470 (Plate 114, Fig. 2).

V.   The fragments of Group A must have belonged originally to an
edifice of c. 500.   Their similarity to the Byzantine monuments of Ravenna
and Constantinople, erected about this period, is so obvious and striking that
it is singular it has escaped the attention of all the archæologists who have
studied the fragments.   The Byzantine character of the carving is slightly
modified by the survival of a decadent Roman tradition, precisely such as
might be expected to be found in one of the old strongholds of Roman culture
such as Milan.   It is natural to suppose that these fragments come from the
church belonging to the convent founded by Aurona in the VIII century.
The question naturally arises whether Aurona established her nuns in an older
church of the VI century, and contented herself with merely erecting the
monastic buildings, or whether she erected a new church out of fragments
taken from an earlier edifice.   In view of the fact that there is no documentary
evidence that a church existed on this site prior to the time of Aurona, it is
to be presumed that the latter was the case.

Among all the fragments in the Castello Sforzesco, there are none which
can be called original works of the VIII century.   If Group A is two centuries
earlier, Group B must be two centuries later.   The insignificant fragments
belonging to this group seem to have belonged to a pergola.   The style is
decadent in the extreme, and lacks absolutely the crisp, vigorous, imaginative
character of authentic carvings of the VIII century, such as the baptistery
at Cividale (Plate 59, Fig. 3), or the tomb of Bobbio (Plate 24, Fig. 1).

[23]   IVLIANVS: ME: FECIT: SIC: PV[LCRVM]

The volutes are languidly scratched on the surface and inaccurately drawn. The acanthus leaves of flaccid type are lazily and flatly indicated. The splaying of the lower corners of the columns, and the adornment of these surfaces with flat acanthus leaves, recall the capitals of 903 in the crypt of S. Savino at Piacenza (Plate 186, Fig. 2, 3). The execution of the acanthus leaves, on the other hand, is analogous to that of the acanthus leaves in the capital of SS. Felice e Fortunato at Vicenza (Plate 239, Fig. 3), a monument of 975. A careful study, however, will show that the capitals of the Chiesa d'Aurona fall midway between the capitals of S. Savino and those of SS. Felice e Fortunato. We may therefore ascribe them to c. 950.

The fragments of Group C are in the style of the transition from the Carlovingian to the Lombard manner. They show close analogies with the altar front of S. Abondio of Como (Plate 59, Fig. 2) which comes from S. Vincenzo of Galliano, and is a surely dated monument of 1007, and with the carved slab in the cloisters of the cathedral of Aosta (Plate 12, Fig. 1), a monument which dates from c. 1010. This group of fragments may consequently be ascribed to c. 1000.

The fragments of Group D, which are all structural, show a style which is somewhat less advanced than that of S. Savino of Piacenza, an edifice consecrated in 1107. There can, therefore, be no doubt that they belong to the church erected after the fire of 1081, consecrated probably in 1095, and certainly finished before 1099.

The keystone of Group E causes a suspicion that the XI century basilica may have been re-vaulted at the end of the XII or the beginning of the XIII century.

MILAN, CHIESA ROSSA[1]

(Plate 115, Fig. 2)

I. The Chiesa Rossa has been mentioned by Rotta,[2] who gave a translation of the inscription. Fine photogravures were published in the joint work of Fumagalli, Sant'Ambrogio and Beltrami.[3]

II. In the exterior wall, near the portal, is an inscription of the XVIII century, which records that the church was possessed from 1139 to 1303 by Benedictine nuns; that these were succeeded by Dominican nuns, who remained until 1376, and that the church was restored in 1783.

---

[1] Via Leonardo da Vinci, No. 85, on the banks of the Naviglio di Pavia.
[2] *Gite*, 69.
[3] I, 38. Tav. XXXI-XXXIII.

MILAN, CHIESA ROSSA

ECCLESIAM. TIT. S. MARIAE. AD. FONTICVLVM
ANTIQVISSIMAM
A MONIALIBVS. ORD. S. BENEDICTI HEIC. DEGEN
TIBVS RELIGIOSE CVLTAM AB ANNO MCXXXIX
AD ANNVM MCCCIII MONIALES ORD PRAED
S. MARIAE VETERVM MEDIOLANI
CANONICARVM TITVLO SVFFECTAE VSQVE AD
ANNVM MCCCLXXVI
BELLORVM INIVRIA SQVALESCENTEM
PLVSQVE SATIS AMPLAM ET IN IMO
POSITAM
CONTRAHEBANT ELEVABANT ORNABANT
ANNO MDCCLXXXIII

The restoration of 1783 must have been begun at least ten years previously. An inscription records that a tomb was brought from the lower church in 1773. The occasion for this translation must have been the raising of the pavement, and the dividing of the church into two stories.

III. The edifice consists of a single-aisled nave, a narrow barrel-vaulted choir, and an apse. Originally, however, there was a nave of a single aisle and an apse. Subsequently, the existing barrel-vaulted bay was built inside the church. The groin vault of the eastern bay of the nave must, therefore, be a later addition. The present dividing wall inside the church, which forms a sort of narthex, is obviously modern.

The southern wall has been entirely remade. When the Naviglio was built, the level of the road was greatly raised. In consequence it was found necessary in 1773 to raise also the level of the church, which was divided into two stories. The lower of these is now desecrated and used as a series of cellars.

The eastern bay of the nave either was, or was intended to be, vaulted. The wall ribs are still in place. No system is provided for a rib vault, but the rectangular members would have formed logical supports for a groin vault. It may be assumed, consequently, that the builders planned to cover this excessively oblong space with a groin vault.

The northern wall is reinforced externally by salient buttresses (Plate 115, Fig. 2), but these are obviously additions of the XIII century, made to strengthen the new vault.

The ancient masonry consists of fine, regular, cross-hatched bricks, of large size, laid very horizontally in courses separated by mortar-beds of moderate thickness.

IV. The eastern window on the southern side, which may be seen from the garden of the adjoining house, has two little engaged colonnettes of brick, without capitals or bases, and served without glass. The windows of the apse are in three moulded orders. The apse has a cornice of double arched corbel-tables. The façade has a simple cornice of flat corbel-tables and a saw-tooth moulding, but the masonry shows that this was remade in the XIII century. The north side aisle has a cornice of double arched corbel-tables and moulded windows.

V. The style of the Romanesque portions of the edifice confirms the documentary evidence that it was erected in 1139.

MILAN, S. AMBROGIO

(Plate 116; Plate 117, Fig. 2, 4, 5, 6; Plate 118, Fig. 1, 2, 3, 4, 5, 6, 7; Plate 119, Fig. 1, 2, 3, 4; Plate 120, Fig. 1, 2, 3, 4, 5, 6, 7; Plate 121, Fig. 2, 3; Plate 122, Fig. 1, 2, 3; Plate 123, Fig. 1, 2; Plate 124, Fig. 1, 2)

I. Certainly no other Romanesque monument of Italy has excited among archæologists so intense an interest as has the basilica of S. Ambrogio at Milan. In consequence, the bibliography of the monument is an exceedingly long one, and includes not only a vast quantity of monographs and separate articles, but almost every general history of architecture—or even of art—that has been written. It is obviously impossible to mention here any except works of real archæological importance and scientific value.

It is unfortunate that the primary source for the complex and perplexing history of S. Ambrogio has never been published. The original documents regarding the famous strife between the monks and canons are preserved in a modern transcription known as the *Codice della Croce* belonging to the Biblioteca Ambrosiana.[1] Any thoughtful study of the history of the church must begin with this manuscript. The two manuscript chronicles in the same library which pass under the names of Lampugnano de Legnano[2] and Filippo da Castel Seprio[3] contain some notices of value in regard to S. Ambrogio.

The first modern writer to treat of our church in an archæological spirit was Castiglione, who published in 1625 a work in Latin on the antiquities of Milan. He narrated the history of the foundation of the basilica by S. Ambrogio[4] and published the famous diploma of Angiberto referring to the golden altar.[5] He also gave a long description of the Palio d'Oro and of the various relics preserved in the church.[6] The ground thus barely broken by Castiglione yielded rich fruit in the masterly hand of Puricelli, who published

---

[1] The manuscript bears the number D.S.IV.6./I.
[2] No. H 56 Sup. This chronicle was written in 1318 (f. 77).
[3] S. Q. + I, 12.   [4] 127.   [5] 163.   [6] 172 f.

in 1645 in Latin his immortal work on the monuments of the basilica of
S. Ambrogio. So thoroughly did Puricelli explore the rich archives of the
monastery, that his work has ever remained a standard source for all subsequent
writers who have had occasion to deal with the history of S. Ambrogio. His
truly extraordinary penetration, his erudition, his impartiality, and his almost
modern sense of criticism are worthy of the greatest admiration. In addition
to the numerous documents from the archives which he published for the first
time, he called the attention of students to the now world-famous epitaph
of Ansperto, and studied in detail the Palio d'Oro.[7] Unfortunately he did not
have access to the archives of the canons, and his work is thus necessarily
incomplete. Moreover his archæology, as is natural in an author of the XVII
century, is rather naïve. Thus he assigns the atrium to Ansperto, inaugu-
rating an error which has survived to the present day. The Campanile dei
Monaci, for him, was constructed by S. Ambrogio himself. On the other
hand, Puricelli published drawings of the apse mosaic, the ciborio, the Palio
d'Oro, and other parts of the basilica, which are, indeed, extremely crude and
inaccurate, but nevertheless truly remarkable achievements for the time. All
things considered, his work, from an archæological and historical point of
view, is undoubtedly one of the most notable productions of the XVII century.

Five years later Puccinelli published a curious work entitled *Zodiaco della
Chiesa Milanese,* which contains a few important texts on S. Ambrogio. In
1674 there appeared a chronological series of the abbots of S. Ambrogio by
Aresi, a compilation for the most part of little value, but which nevertheless
contains some valuable texts. In the same year (1674) Torre printed his
Ritratto di Milano, which contains an important description of S. Ambrogio,
written before the modern restorations. Torre was the first to assign the
atrium to its correct date. He speaks at length of the traces of fresco in his
time visible, and dwells upon the chapel of SS. Vittore e Satiro, which he
thinks Puricelli is wrong in identifying with the basilica of Fausta.

The earliest writer of the XVIII century to study S. Ambrogio was
Latuada, whose description of Milan, published in 1737, contains a perspective drawing of the monastery of S. Ambrogio, showing the two cloisters
that have now been destroyed.[8] Allegranza wrote in 1757, in Italian, a curious
little book entitled *Spiegazioni e Reflessioni.* This contains a study of the
sarcophagus beneath the pulpit, of which the relief representing Christ and
the Apostles, is strangely misinterpreted by the author as Christ in the Temple
among the Doctors. Allegranza gives a long account of the brazen serpent,
and attempts to establish the authenticity of that relic. He believes that all
the mediæval buildings of Italy may be divided into three classes according
to their artistic merit. The poorer ones are due to the bad taste of the Arabs,
the better ones were constructed by the Goths, the best—like the cathedral

[7] 102 f.   [8] IV, 308.

of Milan—are the work of Germans. In a dissertation upon the portal of S. Ambrogio he expresses the conviction that all Romanesque grotesques are symbolical, and, to prove this assertion, cites a great profusion of texts from the church-fathers. He gives crude and inexact drawings, but still the earliest published, of the portal and atrium of S. Ambrogio, and of various other Romanesque monuments in Milan. He writes, it is true, with no love for mediæval architecture, but is seduced by his love for allegory and his fondness for quoting passages from the fathers into an interest in iconography. He thus prepared the way for more fruitful studies. In 1773 the same author published a collection of Christian inscriptions which is still of value.

From 1760 to 1765 appeared the monumental history of Milan by Giulini. This work, which has deservedly become a classic, contains many illuminating passages on S. Ambrogio. In 1792 Fumagalli published his celebrated work on the antiquities of Milan, defending the monks against the attacks of Sormani, which had been written some time before. The book is frankly controversial in character, but helps to clear up several obscure points in the history of the abbey.

In the XIX century, under the influence of the new ideals of archæological research resulting from increased interest in the Middle Ages, works of a far different character began to be written upon S. Ambrogio, as upon other mediæval monuments of Europe. In 1817 Millin, in his book of travels, included a long description of S. Ambrogio, which is characterized by a new feeling of sympathy towards Romanesque art. Millin has left valuable descriptions of the apse mosaic and of other portions of the edifice as they were before the restoration. In 1824 appeared the important monograph of Ferrario. This work dealt primarily not with the history, but with the architecture, of S. Ambrogio, and is, therefore, the first architectural monograph to be written upon a Lombard church. The work contains the first publication of the inscriptions found in the restoration of 1813 and the first really adequate drawings of the monument to appear. Since the latter were made before the disastrous restorations of the XIX century, they are of great scientific value. The text, in the main, is really a résumé of what had been written by previous historians, and contains little that is new. Ferrario speaks briefly and without sympathy or comprehension of Romanesque architecture, which appears somewhat barbarous to him. The greater portion of the book is devoted to a description of the various accessory monuments of the basilica. Ferrario's plan of the church shows the canonica as supplied with a complete cloister, but it is evident that the plan is an ideal reconstruction. His exterior view of the church shows over the cupola the barocco lantern that has since disappeared, and that of the interior of the church (Plate 119, Fig. 1) shows the pointed transverse arches spanning the nave and the Gothic vaults of the eastern bay, which were destroyed during the restoration. In this view may also be studied the parapets of the gallery, the iron choir-screen, the wall separating the crossing from the side aisle, the barocco panelling of the choir vault and the barocco painting on the pendentives of the cupola, all of which were also removed in the restoration. Ferrario mentions drawings of the XVII century which he had seen, showing that it was planned to destroy the old church of S. Ambrogio and to erect a new one in the barocco style.[9] It is unfortunate that these drawings have disappeared. He publishes also the plan of the monastery, which has since been destroyed. This plan[10] shows the two cloisters of 1498 precisely as they appear in Latuada's perspective. From Ferrario's drawing of the atrium it is evident that in 1824 the vaults were not covered with plaster, so that the brickwork of the soffit was clearly visible. This drawing is of archæological importance, since it makes possible the study of the masonry of the ancient vaults, which has since been hidden from sight. From the drawing of the portal it is evident that the lower story of the narthex was ornamented with painted decoration in 1824 as it is now.

In Pirovano's description of Milan, which appeared in 1826, there is an account of the apse mosaic and of the bacchanale relief in the campanile that drew so much attention on the part of the early observers of the monument.[11] In 1829 appeared the epoch-making work of Cordero, which placed the whole subject of Lombard archæology on a new footing. Cassina, in a sumptuous publication which appeared in 1840, devoted ten superb plates to the illustration of S. Ambrogio. These drawings are of immense value, because they show the condition of the edifice in the first half of the XIX century.[12] Knight[13] has published other important drawings made five years later. In these are clearly shown the Gothic vaults of the eastern bay of the nave, the pointed transverse arches, the iron choir-screen across the pontile, the similar screens separating the nave from the crossing, the screen walls beneath the crossing, the mosaic of the apse, the stone railing of the galleries, the organ on the southern side of the nave, the atrium with the unfinished Campanile dei Canonici and the ciborio. In 1860, at the most acute moment of the struggle for Italian independence, the Austrian, Von Eitelberger, published an excellent monograph upon S. Ambrogio. His study is characterized by erudition, and by a largeness of perspective which is truly extraordinary for the time in which he wrote. It is, however, marred by a pre-conviction that the monument is Carlovingian, and by a political hatred of the Italians which he does not always succeed in disguising.

From 1865 to 1882 De Dartein published his monumental work on Lombard architecture. The place of honour is granted to S. Ambrogio, which is illustrated with a superb series of engravings, certainly the most accurate and most artistic that have ever been made of the monument. These drawings

[9] 35-36.   [10] 35.   [11] 195.   [12] Plates XXV-XXXV.
[13] I, Plate XXIV, XXV, XXVI.

are of special value because they were made at the time of the restoration, when it was possible to take many measurements which otherwise could not have been obtained. De Dartein was also able to correct the restorers in several archæological details. Unfortunately his text is of far less value than his illustrations. His historical notices are taken for the most part at second hand, and he has completely misunderstood the chronology of the monument, following Puricelli and others in assigning the structure to the IX century. In a pamphlet published in 1883 and in another of 1892 the same archæologist repeated the observations already made in his great work, adding little new.

Second in importance only to the drawings of De Dartein are those of De Castro, the second edition of whose illustrations of the principal buildings of Italy appeared in 1870 and seems to be based upon the work of Cassina. In 1875 Romussi published a popular history of the monuments in Milan, which treats at length of the basilica of S. Ambrogio. The book is not a work of profound erudition, but is a well written summary of what was already known about the monument. Romussi followed Puricelli and De Dartein in assigning the atrium to the IX century. A second edition, published in 1893, contains sumptuous illustrations in half-tone. The monograph on S. Ambrogio, by the same author, published in 1897, is also of popular character.

In a guide-book published in 1872 and in a series of articles published in the *Archivio Storico Lombardo* between 1874 and 1877, Mongeri contributed other résumés of the history of the monument, written in a popular style. He, too, assigns the atrium to the IX century, and relates with complacency the progress of the disastrous restoration, of which he records important details, especially in the official *compte rendu* published in 1874. In his work on architectural styles he gives a section and other drawings of S. Ambrogio, evidently made before the restoration and notable for the transverse buttresses shown over the intermediate piers of the nave. In these drawings the Campanile dei Canonici appears still unfinished, or as it was until 1898.

In 1881 Barbier de Montault wrote an important article on the mosaics of Milan, and studied with particular intelligence and care those of S. Ambrogio. Eighteen years later the same author published a study upon the Palio d'Oro, the authenticity of which he does not question.

In 1884 was printed the so-called chronicle of the restoration of S. Ambrogio by Rossi. This in reality consists of a series of private letters written by Rossi (who was the priest in charge of S. Ambrogio at the time of the restoration) to personal friends, and not intended for publication. The book is, however, of great archæological value, since it is the best source for studying the many changes wrought in the basilica at this period. Rossi was in no sense of the word an archæologist, and the light-hearted manner in which he altered the venerable church—destroying portions of it and remaking others according to his fancy—fairly makes the blood of the modern lover of Romanesque art run cold. However, it should be said in justice that Rossi was probably not more stupid nor more ignorant than the government officials who were his rivals in the restoration. The gossipy, but full, account of the chronicle gives an invaluable insight into the inner workings of this never-to-be-sufficiently-regretted reconstruction.

From 1883 to 1889 was published the monumental work of De Fleury on *La Messe*. In this book much space and two not inaccurate plates are devoted to the Palio d'Oro.[14] The apse mosaic is assigned to 1169 on ritualistic grounds,[15] and the ciborio is assigned to the XII century.[16] This expert in iconography, however, makes no attempt to study the subject of the enigmatical sculptures of the ciborio. Finally De Fleury discusses and illustrates the ambo.[17]

In 1888 Cattaneo revolutionized the study of Lombard architecture by showing that the edifices which had been believed to be of the VII, VIII and IX centuries, were, in reality, of the XI and XII. On no monument did he lay greater emphasis than on S. Ambrogio. By subjecting the famous inscription of Ansperto to a critical analysis, he showed that it was by no means proven that the existing atrium was erected in the IX century. Basing himself on a study of the architectural style, he, on the contrary, assigned the atrium to the beginning of the XII century, and the nave and side aisles to the second half of the XI century. Only the apses, the Palio d'Oro, the capitals of the ciborio and the Campanile dei Monaci passed in his critical analysis as genuine works of the IX century. Even the mosaics of the apse and the upper part of the ciborio he believed to have been remade in the XI or XII century. The work of Cattaneo is certainly one of the most important and keen pieces of artistic criticism produced in the XIX century, and deserves to rank with the work of Morelli in another field.

In this following year (1889) appeared two studies of Caffi upon S. Ambrogio, which contain some notices of interest upon the portico of Bramante.

Also in the same year appeared a monograph upon S. Ambrogio by Landriani, the architect in charge of the restoration, who belonged to the old pre-Cattaneo school, and was staunch in his belief that the atrium dated from the IX century. Landriani held that there were three periods of construction anterior to the atrium, viz.: (1) the basilica of Fausta and columns of the nave, which he assigned to the IV century; (2) the three apses and the old campanile, ascribed to the VIII century; (3) the three aisles of the existing basilica, which he believed were erected shortly before the atrium. Subsequently to the atrium were added: (1) the crypt; (2) the new campanile (1128); (3) the cupola, assigned to the XIII century. Landriani's work is

---

[14] I, Plates LX–LXI. [15] I, 75. [16] II, 32, Plate XC.
[17] II, 45, Plate CXCII.

of value because it contains an account of the work executed under his direction, and a plan and description of the early edifice discovered beneath the pavement of the existing structure and no longer accessible. The book is weak, however, from an archæological standpoint, and in his history of the abbey Landriani merely resumes what had been written by previous authors.

In 1893 appeared the first of the series of articles by Sant'Ambrogio, dealing with the church. These articles (fifteen in number) continued to be published in various periodicals and at irregular intervals up to 1910. Sant'Ambrogio fairly out-Cattaneos Cattaneo. He questions the authenticity of the Palio d'Oro, pointing out that the inscription has been much restored. He believes that the basilica was entirely reconstructed in consequence of the earthquake of 1117, and that the nave, the ciborio and the mosaics date from after the disaster of 1196. In the architecture of the church he seeks to trace French influence introduced by the monks and derived from Cluny.

Luca Beltrami has contributed to the literature of S. Ambrogio several articles in which he attempts to confute the chronology of Cattaneo, and support the ascription of the atrium to the IX century. Of greater value is an article which appeared in the *Archivio Storico Lombardo* for 1896, proving that the Campanile dei Canonici, contrary to the generally received opinion, had never been completed.

The elaborate work of Zimmermann on Lombard sculpture appeared in 1897. This author agrees with Cattaneo in accepting as Carlovingian an interlaced panel of the left jamb of the main portal, and also calls the Christ and the eagle of the ambo works of the IX century. The bust of S. Ambrogio in the south aisle he assigns to the XIII century. The ciborio he judges to have been reconstructed after 1196, but he assigns the capitals to the IX century. The altar, he believes, was remade after 1196, but concedes that some enamels of an older altar were employed in its reconstruction.

In 1898 the ranks of the radicals were reinforced by Stiehl, who deduced from a study of the masonry at the intersection of the campanile and the church that the latter was later than the former, and hence built after 1128. In the same year Toschi contributed to *L'Arte* a valuable article entitled "Ambrosiana," in which the writer makes new and important observations of a radical character upon the monument and its history. In 1900 Schmid wrote an article on the history of Carlovingian sculpture which contains important remarks upon the Palio d'Oro. The authenticity of the latter is upheld by comparisons with examples of the goldsmith's art in the IX century in Germany. The ciborio is assigned to the same period. The works of Rotta are of value especially for the more modern history of the monument. In 1901 appeared the well known work of Rivoira on Lombard architecture, which contains an important study of S. Ambrogio.[18] In the main, Rivoira

[18] Ed. 1908, 282 ff.

shows himself to be a follower of Cattaneo, ascribing the nave to the years 1088-1098. A similar view is taken by Venturi in his history of Italian art, of which the volume dealing with Romanesque art was published in 1904. The altar is cited as an authentic monument of the IX century and compared with various ivories of that period.[19] The sculptures of the ciborio are, on the other hand, consigned to the end of the XII century, and are called strongly Byzantine in character. In 1902 Ratti studied the Palio d'Oro in an article contributed to *Rassegna d'Arte*.

By all odds the most important recent contribution to the literature of S. Ambrogio are two articles by Biscaro printed in the *Archivio Storico Lombardo* in 1904-1905. These contain the publication of many new documents of the first importance bearing upon the history of the church. An attempt is made to connect the Adam mentioned in the inscription on the portal with the Adam mentioned in the atrium inscription of 1098. The church is assigned to the first half of the XII century, and it is maintained that in the early XII century the church was without an atrium. Numerous important and inedited documents upon the history of the Palio d'Oro are cited to show that this was almost completely remade after the XI century.

II. S. Ambrogio is said to have constructed four basilicas outside the walls of the city of Milan, viz.: the church of S. Maria and other virgins, subsequently called S. Simpliciano; the church of S. Pietro and the Apostles, now called S. Nazaro; the basilica of SS. Protasio e Gervasio and other martyrs, now known as S. Ambrogio, and the basilica of S. Dionigi.[20] The most authentic proof that the church of SS. Protasio e Gervasio was founded by S. Ambrogio is a letter of the saint to his sister Marcellina: "Since I am accustomed to conceal from your holiness nothing which takes place here in your absence know, dearest sister, that I have found holy martyrs. For when I wished to dedicate the basilica many commenced to speak to me as

---

[19] II, 233.

[20] Puricelli, 2.

Beatus igitur Ambroxius quattuor construxit Ecclesias, inter quas fuit illa, que nunc uere, et proprie Ecclesie Beati Ambrosii apellatur, quia in ea eius sanctum humatum quiescit corpus. que etiam et ex tunc Ambrosiana uocabatur Ecclesia. (Lawyer's brief in suit of 1190, *Codice della Croce*, MS. Amb. D. S. IV, 11/I, 11, f. 56). The construction of the church by S. Ambrogio is referred to very explicitly also on f. 59.

Anno dñi nri yh̄u xp̄i CCCIC. die quarto Aprilis. [S. Ambrogio died] et in ecclia. que' nunc dicitur sancti Ambrosij fuit tumulatus, vbi postea Monasterium ditissimū. et canonicha nobilisa constructa sunt . . . quatuor Deuotas ecclias fundauit, videlicet vnam in honore B. Petri ap̄lor[um] Principis ac omniū ap̄lor[um] que' ecclia hodie vocatur sancti Nazarij in Brolio. Aliā in honore sanctor[um] Protasij et Geruaij. et omnium martyrū que hodie vocat. Sancti Ambrosij. Alia in honorem Sancti Dionisij. et omniū confessor[um]. et Aliam in honore Beate Marie virginis. et omniū virginū: que hodie dicitur Sancti Simpliciani. (*Chronicon*, detto di Filippo da Castel Seprio. MS. Amb. C. S. IV, 18, f. 23 r).

with one mouth, saying: 'Dedicate the basilica just as they do at Rome.'
I replied: 'I shall do so if I find relics of martyrs.' And immediately there
came upon me as it were a certain ardent foreboding. In short, the Lord
granted the grace, and in the presence of the awe-stricken clergy I ordered an
excavation to be made in that place which is in front of the choir-rail of
the basilica of SS. Felice e Nabore. I found the necessary indications; I
summoned those on whom our hands were to be laid. The holy martyrs
commenced to appear to view, and while we stood still silent, the urn was
raised and laid down again near the holy tomb. We found two men of
wonderfully large stature like men of the olden time. The bones were all
intact and there was much blood. A multitude of people gathered there all
those two days. What more should I say? We embalmed (or put sweet-
smelling spices upon?) the bodies, and translated them in due order, and
at evening we came to the basilica of Fausta. There we watched all night
and we laid on hands. On the following day we translated them into the
basilica which they call of Ambrogio. . . . The triumphal victims take
their place in the spot where Christ is the sacrifice. But He who has suffered
for all is placed above the altar; they who have been redeemed by His passion
are below the altar. This place I had predestined for myself. For it is right
that the priest should rest there where he has been accustomed to officiate.
But I yield the place to the right to the holy victims for that position is due
to martyrs. Therefore let us bury the holy relics and let us place them in
a worthy sepulchre, and let us celebrate offices all day long with steadfast
devotion."[21]

[21] Quoniam nihil eorum quæ hic te absente geruntur, sanctitatem tuam celare
soleo, scias etiā dilectissima soror, sanctos martyres a nobis repertos. Nam cum ego
basilicam dedicare uellē, multi tamquā uno ore interpellare cœperunt, dicentes: Sicut
in Romana, sic basilicā dedices. Respondi: Faciam, si martyrū reliquias inuenero.
Statimq. subijt ueluti cuiusdā ardor præsagij. Quid multa? Dominus gratiā dedit,
formidantibus etiam clericis iussi eruderari terram eo loci qui est ante cancellos
sanctorum Felicis atq. Naboris. Inueni signa conuenientia: adhibitis etiā quibus per
nos manus imponenda foret, sic sancti martyres eminere cœperunt, ut adhuc nobis
silentibus arriperetur urna, & sterneretur prona ad locū sancti sepulcri. Inuenimus
miræ magnitudinis uiros duos, vt prisca ætas ferebat. Ossa omnia integra, sanguinis
plurimū. Ingens concursus populi per totum illud biduum. Quid multa? Condiuimus
integra, ad ordinem transtulimus, uespere iam incumbente ad basilicam Faustæ uenimus:
ibi uigiliæ tota nocte, manus impositio. Sequenti die transtulimus ea in basilicam quam
appellant Ambrosianam. . . . Succedant victimæ triumphales in locum vbi Christus
hostia est. Sed ille super altare, qui pro omnibus passus est: isti sub altari, qui illius
redempti sunt passione. Hunc ego locum prædestinaueram mihi. Dignum est enim
vt ibi requiescat sacerdos, vbi offerre consueuit. Sed cedo sacris victimis dexteram
portionem, locus iste martyribus debebatur. Condamus ergo reliquias sacrosanctas, &
dignis ædibus inuehamus, totumq. diem fida deuotione celebremus. (Ambrosius Episcopus Marcellinæ sorori. Epistola, Lib. VII, No. 54, ed. Giovanni Battista Bandinio,
Operum Sancti Ambrosii Tomus Quintus, Romæ, Ex Typographia Dominici Basæ,
1585, 247).

This text of S. Ambrogio is confirmed by three passages of St. Augustine. The first is in a sermon in which the saint states that he was present at Milan at the time that S. Ambrogio discovered the bodies of SS. Protasio and Gervasio.[22] The second occurs in the *Confessions*, immediately after the account of the baptism of the saint and of the Arian prosecution in Milan under Justina: "At that time Thou didst reveal to Thy renowned bishop Ambrogio, in a vision, where were hidden the bodies of the martyrs Protasio and Gervasio. These afterwards were manifested and exhumed and transferred with suitable honours to the basilica of Ambrogio."[23] The third occurs in the *City of God*. "When I was at Milan a blind man miraculously received his sight. Knowledge of this could reach many since the city was large and the emperor was there present at that time, and the act was performed in the presence of a multitude which had assembled to view the bodies of the martyrs Protasio and Gervasio. These bodies had been concealed and were completely unknown, but were revealed to Bishop Ambrogio in a dream and were found."[24]

In the biography of S. Ambrogio written by Paolino in the V century, we read among the events which preceded the death of Maximus and the succession of Theodosius (383): "About the same time the holy martyrs Protasio and Gervasio revealed themselves to Ambrogio. For they were placed in the basilica in which are to-day the bodies of the martyrs Nabore and Felice. . . . There was a certain blind man, Severus by name, who to this day serves God in all sanctity in that very basilica which is called of Ambrogio and to which the bodies of the martyrs were translated. When this blind man touched the garment of the·martyrs, he immediately received his sight."[25] The same facts are also narrated by Gregory of Tours: "In the city of Milan were preserved the victorious bodies of the martyrs Gervasio and Protasio, which had long lain hidden in the grave, as is told in the history

---

[22] Sermo *286 de Sanctis* (alias *de Diversis*, 39), Cap. 5, ed. Migne, *Pat. Lat.*, XXXVIII, 1299.

[23] Tunc memorato antistiti tuo per visum aperuisti, quo loco laterent martyrum corpora Protasii et Gervasii. . . . Cum enim propalata et effossa digno cum honore transferrentur ad Ambrosianam basilicam. . . . (*Confessionum S. Augustini*, Lib. IX, Cap. VII, Sec. 16, ed. Migne, *Pat. Lat.*, XXXII, 770).

[24] Miraculum quod Mediolani factum est, cum illic essemus, quando illuminatus est cæcus, ad multorum notitiam potuit pervenire, quia et grandis est civitas, et ibi erat tunc Imperator, et immenso populo teste res gesta est, concurrente ad corpora martyrum Protasii et Gervasii: quæ cum laterent, et penitus nescirentur, episcopo Ambrosio per somnium revelata reperta sunt. (*De Civitate Dei*, S. Augustini, XX, 8, 2, ed. Migne, *Pat. Lat.*, XLI, 761).

[25] Per idem tempus sancti martyres Protasius et Gervasius se sacerdoti revelaverunt. Erant enim in basilica positi, in qua sunt hodie corpora Naboris et Felicis martyrum. . . . Cæcus etiam Severus nomine, qui nunc usque in eadem basilica quæ dicitur Ambrosiana, in quam martyrum corpora sunt translata, religiose servit; ubi vestem martyrum attigit, statim lumen recepit. (*Vita S. Ambrosii*, auctore Paulino, 14, ed. Migne, *Pat. Lat.*, XIV, 34 .

of their passion. These were revealed to S. Ambrogio and found by him, and buried in the basilica which he himself had built, where miracles were performed by them. . . . For he narrates that when these glorious bodies had been translated into that church while a solemn mass was being celebrated in their honour, a plank fell from the vault and struck the heads of the martyrs, from which flowed a stream of blood."[26]

Of slight value in comparison with these contemporary documents is the notice of Galvaneo della Fiamma: "S. Ambrogio . . . founded . . . a church in honour of the holy martyrs Gervasio and Protasio, twin brothers, and of all the martyrs. This church is now called S. Ambrogio."[27]

The exact date of the translation of the martyrs and the dedication of the basilica is difficult to determine, owing to the confused chronology of the writers of the IV century. According to Puricelli[28] it took place in 387. Fumagalli places it in 386 or 387. Beroldo is therefore in error when he places the death of S. Ambrogio in 382.[29] The authorities are agreed in stating that S. Ambrogio, according to his wish, was buried in the basilica of his name.

It has been supposed by Sormani that S. Ambrogio served for a time as cathedral, but there is no proof of this conjecture. Indeed, Fumagalli has brought forward cogent arguments to prove that the cathedral has always been where it is now.[30] There is no doubt, however, that the church of S. Ambrogio always stood in a peculiar relationship to the bishops of Milan. S. Ambrogio himself states that he was accustomed to officiate there. The archbishop Pietro founded the monastery and the archbishop Angilberto II gave the Palio d'Oro. In the XI and XII centuries the restoration and rebuilding of the church, even its ordinary maintenance, were attended to neither by the canons nor by the monks, but by the superstans who was appointed by the archbishop, and by the archbishop was borne the expense of the restoration of 1196. In the apse was an archiepiscopal throne, and

---

[26] In hac enim urbe beatorum martyrum Gervasi Protasique victricia corpora retenentur, quae diu, sicut ipsa passionis narrat historia, sub fossa latuerunt. Quae beato Ambrosio revelata atque ab eodem reperta, in basilicam, quam ipse proprio aedificavit studio, ostensis miraculis, sunt sepulta. . . . Aiebat enim, quod, quando haec gloriosa corpora translata in eclesia illa fuerunt, dum in honore ipsorum martyrum missarum solemnia celebrarentur, cecidisse e camera tabulam unam, qui inlisa capitibus martyrum, rivum sanguinis elicuerit. (Gregorii Episcopi Turonensis, *Liber in Gloria Martyrum*, 46, ed. Arndt, M. G. H., *Scr. Rer. Mer.*, I, 519).

[27] Beatus verò Ambrosius . . . fundavit . . . Ecclesiam in honorem Sanctorum Gervasii, & Protasii Martyrum & fratum gemellorum, & omnium Martyrum, quae modò dicitur Sancti Ambrosii. (Galvanei Flammae, *Manipulus Florum*, ed. Muratori, R. I. S., XI, 570).

[28] 2.

[29] Nonas Aprilis. Depositio sanctissimi Ambrosii, ubi requiescit, anno dominicae Incarnationis CCC.L.XXXII. indictione X. (Beroldo, ed. Magistretti, 4).

[30] IV, 27.

on either side thrones for the various bishops dependent upon the see of Milan, each with a frescoed effigy and an inscription above.

There has been an unending controversy as to how the basilica was officiated from the V to the VIII century. In subsequent times a bitter feud broke out between the canons and the monks established in the church. Among the chief bones of contention was the right to the offerings made at the high altar of the basilica. To establish their claim to these, the canons contended that from an early time the church had been officiated by a custode and decumani, and that these had subsequently been regularized into a chapter. The canons therefore were the original priests of the basilica and to them belonged the revenues of the high altar. The monks on the other hand bitterly denied all this, contending that the canons had been introduced after the foundation of the monastery. The controversy which broke out as early as the second quarter of the XII century, raged almost without intermission until the end of the XVIII century. Both sides resorted to lawsuits, and even to physical violence and crime.[31] At times these two bodies of priests even waged regular pitched battles against each other, as in the strife connected with the new campanile, described in detail below; and on one occasion the monks actually killed one of the canons.[32] Each side, in order to overreach the other, did not hesitate to resort to open corruption. In 1144 the monks succeeded in bribing the archbishop of Milan, and even attempted to buy up the pope.[33] Both sides had frequent recourse to the expedient of forging false documents and of altering authentic ones.[34] It thus happens that the history of the abbey of S. Ambrogio is hopelessly confused. There is hardly

---

[31] See, for example, the testimony of a witness in the examination of 1200: Inter. Si aliquis ex Monacis vel aliqui iniecit, seu iniecerunt violentia manus in Canonicos et Clericos S. Ambr. vel aliquem eorum. Rx. Quod vidit rixam inter eos sed nescit quid fecerint inter eos, quia statim absentavit se ab eis, et non vidit quod fecerint, verumtamen vidit quendam de nostris, qui tunc eis laborabat, venire cum capite sanguinento ab illa rixa. (*Codice della Croce*, MS. Amb. D. S., IV, 12/I, 12, f. 40). This occurrence was also testified to by several other witnesses. A letter without date of the archbishop of Milan to the pope, Innocent III, mentions that in the church of S. Ambrogio occasione celebrationis officiorum in ipsa ecclesia celebrandorum, discessio foret suborta, idem Monachi et Canonici in iram prouocati, indecenter in eadem Ecclesia rixam perpetrarunt. (*Ibid.*, 6, 229).

[32] cum Monachorum pertinatia non cessaret uerum etiam oblationes inauditis depredationibus auferendo quemdam Sacerdotem Canonicum occidissent. (*Ibid.*, 11, 57).

[33] *Ibid.*, 6, 220, 223-224.

[34] Priuilegium uero Angilberti falsum similiter reprobamus, cum non sit autenticum, uerum etiam cum asserat claues aurei Altaris, ac potestatem, Canonicis [sic—copyist's mistake for *Monachis;* see *Ibid.*, 6, f. 196] ab eiusdem constructore fuisse traditam. Cum enim Monachi olim sicut et nunc Canonicorum iura uiolenti manu semper inuaserint, sicut inauditum, ita etiam incredibile est, quod eisdem Canonicis, quorum deiectioni ex insolentia diuitiarum oportune et inportune instante operam dabant, aliquid umquam de suo iure concesserint. (*Ibid.*, 11, f. 55).

a document anterior to the XII century, the authenticity of which is not open to serious doubt, and which ɪ as not been challenged by one side or the other. To separate the true from the false in this mass of suspicious evidence is impossible. However, a certain amount of truth is probably contained even in the forged documents, where these do not treat directly of the questions at issue. It would far exceed the limits of space at my disposal as well as my ability to give critical analysis to each of the long list of parchments bearing upon the history of S. Ambrogio. In the following pages I shall merely try to select from the documents notices which appear, for one reason or another, to be authentic.

Since so important a basilica as S. Ambrogio obviously could not have been without resident clergy, it is altogether probable that the contention of the canons is correct, and that the basilica was officiated in early times by a custode and decumani.

Undoubtedly false, however, is the donation of confused date purporting to be 742, which mentions a custode of the basilica.[35] The document of 765, referred to by Giulini,[36] is of a similar nature and was doubtless the "deed of the time of Desiderio" brought forward by the canons in the lawsuit of 1144 and called spurious by the monks. A custode of S. Ambrogio is mentioned in another donation of April 13, 776.[37] The document, however, is preserved only in a copy of the XIII century and is hence not above suspicion. Of similarly apocryphal character apparently is still a fourth document of 777 referred to by Giulini.[38]

At the end of the VIII century a monastery was founded in the church of S. Ambrogio. This is recorded in a privilege of 789, conceded by Pietro, archbishop of Milan, to the monastery.[39] The document bears all the earmarks of having been tampered with, but certain parts of it at least are in all probability authentic. It appears that monks had been provisionally established in the basilica as early as 784 or possibly even 783. The privilege of Pietro was soon after confirmed by Charlemagne.[40] The archbishop Pietro who founded the monastery died in the year 806, and was buried at S. Ambrogio. This fact confirms the other evidence that the monastery was really founded by him, and also justifies the inference that at this time the reconstruction of the basilica had not yet begun.

Later writers are unanimous in ascribing the foundation of the monastery to Pietro, and the fact was never seriously questioned even by the canons. The chronicle of Lampugnano de Legnano states that Pietro founded the

[35] Published in *Hist. Pat. Mon.*, XIII, 24. Studied by Puricelli, 10, and by Fumagalli, Dis. XXX. See also Troya, IV, 90.

[36] I, 22. See Troya, V, 329. There is some doubt whether this document refers to our church at all.

[37] *Hist. Pat. Mon.*, XIII, 104.   [38] I, 22.

[39] The document has been published by Puricelli, 18-23.   [40] Puricelli, 43.

monastery of S. Ambrogio,[41] and the chronicle which passes under the name of Filippo da Castel Seprio adds that this event took place in the year 800.[42] These same notices are repeated in the *Edificationes*[43] and by Galvaneo della Fiamma.[44] Therefore, however suspicious we may be of certain details of the privilege of Pietro, the tradition that the monastery was founded by him was current in later times, and I believe is without doubt authentic. I am strengthened in this conviction by observing that the monastery is mentioned in a privilege of Odelberto of 806[45] and in the will of Rotprando of 814,[46] both of which are certainly genuine.

A deed of sale of confused date (826?) mentions a certain Senderario, presbyter and prevosto of the monastery of S. Ambrogio; but this is probably apocryphal,[47] and certainly false is the diploma of Angilberto of 826.[48] The abbot Deusdedit of S. Ambrogio is mentioned in a document of 830.[49] Two diplomas of Lothair I, of 835, confirming the possessions of the monastery, are considered genuine by the editors of the *Historiae Patriae Monumenta*,[50] but I should be inclined to place more reliance in the *Charta Hungarii* of February, 836,[51] which also mentions the monastery. The monastery is referred to in other diplomas of 837[52] and 839.[53]

The archbishop Angilberto II (824-859) erected a golden altar in the church of S. Ambrogio. This fact is proved by several documents, of which the most important is the inscription on the existing Palio d'Oro: "This precious reliquary of pleasing design shines outwardly with glow and splendour of metal, and glitters with inlaid gems, but within it contains sacred bones

---

[41] Petrus Mediolanensis archieps. xlviiij. anno dni dcclxxxviij. sedit annis xvij. mesb' quatuor hic fundauit Monasteriū sci Ambrosij in Mediolano. obijt anno dni dcccv. Jacet ad scū Ambrosiū quod monasteriū est hodie ditius archieps Mediolani. (MS. Amb. H 56 Sup., f. 62).

[42] Anno dñi 800. Petrus Archiepiscopus Mediolani fecit construere monasterium S. Ambrosii Mediolani. (*Chronica* detta di Filippo da Castel Seprio, MS. Amb., S. Q. + I, 12, f. 53).

[43] Anno dni 800 Petrus Archiepiscopus Mediolani construxit monasterium S. Ambrosii Mediolani. (*Edificationes Ecclesiarum Mediolani, ibid.,* 70).

[44] Christi anno DCCLXXXXVII . . . Petrus archiepiscopus mediolanensis sedit annis XVII, mensibus quatuor. Hic fundavit monasterium sancti Ambrosii et largissimis possessionibus dotavit . . . et dicit cronica Gothofredi de Bussero, quod monasterium sancti Ambrosii fuit fundatum anno Domini DCCC. (Galvanei Flammae, *Chron. Maius,* ed. Ceruti, 556).

[45] Puricelli, 53. This document is cited below under S. Vincenzo, p. 665.

[46] *Hist. Pat. Mon.,* XIII, 169.

[47] *Hist. Pat. Mon.,* XIII, 193. The chronological notes are: Hludovicus et Lutharium . . . anni imperii eorum tercidecimo et septimo, duodecimo diae mensis magii, indictione quarta.

[48] *Ibid.,* 643.   [49] *Ibid.,* 205.   [50] XIII, 220, 222.
[51] *Ibid.,* 226.   [52] *Ibid.,* 232.
[53] *Ibid.,* 235. Cf. also the *Breve Firmitatis* of May, 840, *Hist. Pat. Mon.,* XIII, 241.

more precious than any metal. The illustrious and noble prelate Angilberto rejoicing offered to the Lord this work· in honour of S. Ambrogio who lies buried in this church, and he consecrated it in the time in which he was archbishop. Holy Father, look upon and benignly pity thy servant. By Thy mercy, O God, may he achieve the supreme reward."[54]

In addition to the inscription, in the central panel of the altar there is a medallion in which is represented DO|MN|VS| AN|GIL|BER|TV|S, who offers to S̄C̄S̄| AM|BRO|SI|VS the altar and is crowned by him (Plate 122, Fig. 3). Angilberto is represented with a square halo, according to the Byzantine convention which is not found elsewhere in Lombardy. This and many other circumstances might argue that the altar was of Byzantine workmanship, but an adjoining medallion (Plate 122, Fig. 3) shows the smith with Lombard name, Volvinio—VVOL|VI|NI'| MAGIS|T'| PHA|BER—evidently the maker of the altar, crowned by S. Ambrogio— S̄C̄S̄| AM|BRO|SIVS.

Probably no monument in Europe offers greater archæological difficulties or has given rise to more controversy than this golden altar. The obvious and natural interpretation of the inscriptions and of the two reliefs just described seems to prove that the existing altar was given by Angilberto and executed by Wolvinio in the IX century. The style of the sculptures, however, is not that of the IX century, but of a much later epoch. Archæologists consequently have found themselves obliged to choose between the two horns of an exceedingly awkward dilemma. Either they had to show that the sculptures, after all, showed no stylistic peculiarities which are incompatible with their having been executed in the IX century, or else that the inscription itself was false. The result of much controversy, however, has been to show that neither the one nor the other of these alternatives can be accepted. From the most recent studies and especially those of Biscaro it has come to light that the golden altar of S. Ambrogio is in reality something like the famous ship of the Athenians, one part of which after another was renewed until

[54] ÆMICAT ALMA FORIS RVTILOQVE DECORE VENVST[A]
ARCA METALLORVM GEMMIS QVAE COMPTA CORRVSCA[T]
THESAVRO TAMEN HAEC CVNCTO POTIORE METALL[O]
OSSIBVS INTERIVS POLLET DONATA SACRATI[S]
ÆGREGIVS QVOD PRAESVL OPVS SVB HONORE BEAT[I]
INCLITVS *AMBROSII TEMPLO RECVBANTIS IN ISTI*
IPTVLIT ANGILBERTVS OVANS DOMINOQVE DICAVI[T]
TEMPORE QVO NITIDÆ SERVABAT CVLMINA SEDIS
[A]SPICE SVMME PATER FAMVLO MISERERE BENIGNO
TE MISERANTE DEVS DONVM SVBLIME REPORTE[T].

In this inscription, the final letter of each hexameter is the same as the initial letter of the juxtaposed line, and in the original the two are written together as one.

none of the original remained. The Athenian philosophers argued about this ship very much as modern archæologists have about the Palio d'Oro, whether or not it was still the same object.

The numerous restorations and reconstructions of the golden altar in later times will be taken up in their chronological place, and the documentary evidence for each in turn discussed. Suffice it here to anticipate so much as to say, that there is reason to believe one of these reconstructions took place between the years 1126 and 1133, and another subsequent to the collapse of the central cupola in 1196. Now it must be remembered that these two restorations were executed when the strife between the monks and the canons was at its most acute pitch. This strife centered primarily upon the possession of the offerings made at the altar of the basilica, but the real bone of contention was the right to the altar itself. Whichever side could obtain possession of the altar obtained virtually possession of the basilica and precedence over the other clergy. Time and time again in the lawsuits witnesses were examined as to which party held, and which should hold, the keys of the golden altar. In such a state of affairs it will readily be understood that the inscription on the altar was an important piece of evidence carefully watched over by each side. As a matter of fact, the inscription was perfectly neutral, and gave advantage to neither party. Angilberto gave the golden altar, not to the monks or to the canons, but to S. Ambrogio. The restorations carried out in the basilica of S. Ambrogio in the XII century were executed under the direction of the superstans, who was appointed by the archbishop. This official found himself in an extremely delicate position. Any act of restoration which seemed to favour one clergy rather than the other, or which could be interpreted as being in any way partial, immediately involved him in contentions and feuds and not infrequently lawsuits. The superstans was on more than one occasion obliged to wait the decision of litigation before he could proceed even to the most necessary repairs to the basilica. The desire of the superstans and of the archbishop in the XII century seems to have been in general to preserve peace between the two irate clergies, and to maintain an attitude of strict neutrality. Bearing these conditions in mind, we shall find it easy to conjecture what happened to the golden altar. Its reconstruction was determined upon, but the old inscription, with its perfectly neutral declaration that Angilberto gave the altar to S. Ambrogio, was an important document in the then all-absorbing controversy between the monks and the canons. The altar was remade, but the inscription was scrupulously and exactly preserved, and the old relief, representing Angilberto with a square halo, giving the altar to S. Ambrogio, was also reproduced. Moreover, another reason contributed to this retention of the old inscription. Angilberto had donated the gold and silver and gems of which the altar was made. These precious materials constituted the chief value of the altar, and the goldsmith's work was comparatively unimportant. Therefore, when the altar was remade out of the same materials, it was only right to retain out of gratitude to Angilberto the record of his original donation.

Viewed in this light, the Palio d'Oro of S. Ambrogio becomes comprehensible. We understand the presence of an inscription purporting to be of the IX century, combined with reliefs which must be of the XIII century. The inscription of the Palio d'Oro was in no sense a falsification. The superstans of the XII century executed it, not with the intent to deceive modern archæologists, but in a conscientious desire to be just to both canons and monks. The fact, therefore, that Angilberto did give to the basilica a golden altar, is incontestable.

Unlike the inscription on the altar, the famous diploma of Angilberto is a deliberate forgery. This document is extant only in a copy of the XIII century, and was probably fabricated in the XI century. The chronological notes are confused, and the attempts of Giulini[55] to rectify them are completely unsuccessful. In this document we read: "In the name of God, Angilberto, humble archbishop of the holy church of Milan. . . . I long considered whom I ought to invest as abbot of S. Ambrogio . . . and had prayed with my priests for divine guidance. Then, by divine grace, with the consent of our priests, I took Gaudenzio, abbot of the monastery of S. Vincenzo, whom I had ordained abbot there many years before, and appointed him abbot in the monastery of S. Ambrogio . . . Now, moreover, in order that those monks may be strong in the service of God, and may, unhandicapped by want, continually praise and thank Him not only for the preservation of our kings and unconquered emperors, Lodovico and Lotario, but also for the peace of immaculate Mother Church, by this deed I entrust to the care and custody of the above-mentioned abbot Gaudenzio, the church and the altar of wonderful art which I recently constructed there . . . on account of my very great love for the confessor of Christ, Ambrogio."[56]

[55] I, 145-146.

[56] ✠ In Nomine Domini. Angelbertus, Beatæ Mediolanensis Ecclesiæ humilis Archiepiscopus. . . . Cùmquè pro hoc diutiùs, quem Abbatem illius constituere debuissem . . . pro hoc diutiùs cœpissem cogitare, cum meis Sacerdotibus diuinam Clementiam postulando; tunc, Domino fauente, consulentibus etiam Sacerdotibus nostris, abstuli Gaudentium Abbatem Monasterij Sancti Vincentij (quem etiam ego ibi Abbatem iamdudùm ordinaueram) & in præfato Monasterio Sancti Ambrosij Abbatem constitui. . . . Nunc autem, vt ipsi Monachi valeant Deo deseruire, & ei iugiter laudum gratias referre, exclusâ indigentia, tam ob stabilitatem Regum nostrorum, inuictissimorum Imperatorum, Ludouici & Hlotharij, quàm ob pacem immaculatæ Matris Ecclesiæ; per hoc Præceptum confirmo Ecclesiam, & Altare, quod inibi nouiter mirificè ædificaui ob nimium amorem Confessoris Christi Ambrosij, in tutêla & omni custodia suprataxati Gaudentij Abbatis. . . . Anno Domnorum nostrorum, confirmantium hoc, Ludouici & Hlotharij Imperatorum Decimo-octauo & Decimo, Sexto Kalendas Martij, Indictione Decimatertia. (Ed. Puricelli, 80).

MILAN, S. AMBROGIO

The tradition that Angilberto gave the golden altar is repeated by the later chroniclers, Lampugnano de Legnano[57] and Filippo da Castel Seprio,[58] who is probably to be identified with Goffredo da Bussero.[59] The latter adds the date 840. In the second quarter of the XIV century Galvaneo della Fiamma wrote: "Then the archbishop Angilberto . . . caused an altar to be made. About the altar are reliefs of the purest gold with figures and metal reliefs, and it is adorned with many precious stones, and it cost 80,000 pounds or florins of gold. This was done in the year of our Lord 840. The history of the church is as follows: it was founded by S. Ambrogio; Pietro the archbishop established the monastery; afterwards Angilberto caused the golden altar to be erected, and the emperors Otto I and Lothair and the count of Campigono gave to it many possessions."[60]

The same Galvaneo della Fiamma[61] and an anonymous poet of the XIV century[62] narrate a legend in which the construction of the golden altar by Angilberto is said to have taken place in consequence of a miracle. The archbishop opened the tomb of S. Ambrogio, and removed a tooth which he had set in a ring, and always wore as an amulet. One day he lost the tooth, and searched the city for it in vain. It was miraculously revealed to him that the tooth would be found in the place from which it had been taken, and, upon opening the tomb of the saint, the tooth was indeed discovered in its original position.[63]

The monks of S. Ambrogio are mentioned in a document of April 9, 842, and the abbot Gaudenzio in another of August of the same year.[64] Of great importance for the study of the relations of the two clergies of S. Ambrogio is a memorandum of 844 that seems to be without question authentic. It appears that the two bodies together formed what was called the monastery, a fact which need not cause surprise, since there are many instances of

[57] . . . hic [Angilbertus] fecit deaurari altare sci Ambrosij . . . (*Cronaca* de Lampugnano de Legnano. MS. Amb., H 56 Sup., f. 627).

[58] Anno dni 840 Angilbertus fecit deaurari altare S. Ambrosij. (*Chronica* detta di Filippo da Castel Seprio, MS. Amb., S. Q. + I, 12, f. 53).

[59] See Grazioli.

[60] Ex tunc archiepiscopus . . . fieri fecit unum altare; in circuitu altaris sunt spondilia ex auro purissimo cum figuris et celaturis, et lapides pretiosi inserti sunt quamplures, et fuerunt expense LXXX millia librarum sive florenorum auri; et hec acta sunt anno Domini DCCCXL. Ordo istius ecclexie fuit talis: quia beatus Ambroxius eam fundavit, et Petrus archiepiscopus monasterium construxit; postea iste Angibertus altare aureum fabricari fecit, et Otto primus et Lotharius imperator e comes de Campigono possessiones multas addiderunt. (Gal. Flam., *Chron. Maius*, ed. Ceruti, 563).

[61] *Ibid.*, 563.   [62] Ed. Romussi, *Milano*, I, 304.

[63] A bibliography of the various mediæval sources in which the Palio d'Oro is mentioned is given by Puricelli, 90 ff.

[64] *Hist. Pat. Mon.*, XIII, 253, 254.

collegiate churches being designated by the term monastery.[65]   The abbot was in early times the head of both clergies (in this document he is also called custode), and the prevosto was merely his fiscal agent.[66]   From another document of March 2, 862,[67] it is evident that at times at least the prevosto was a monk, and from another of October 17, 852,[68] that the custode was selected from among the secular clergy.   In a document of June, 862,[69] the prevosto again appears as an agent of the abbot.   In another document of 864, the authenticity of which has been much disputed, occurs the phrase: . . . *presbiteris decomanis, qui pro tempore oficiales fuerint in ecclesia beati Christi confessoris Ambrosii.*[70]   If genuine, this diploma establishes the existence of a body of secular clergy at S. Ambrogio in 864.   Some confirmation is lent by another diploma of 867[71] in which reference is made to the *presbiteris oficialis basilice beati Christi confessoris Ambrosii.*   Certainly apocryphal and forged by the monks for use in their lawsuits against the canons is the famous diploma, purporting to be of 866 but with erroneous chronological notes,[72] in which occurs the phrase: *illosque sacerdotes, quos pro sua utilitate ad celebrandum missarum solemnia in eadem ecclesia olim noviter collocaverat.*[73]   In a document of 875 a certain Gardolfo, deacon and monk of S. Ambrogio, is mentioned.[74]   Two years later two *officiales presbyteros* of S. Ambrogio are recorded,[75] and in another document of the same year mention is made of two *presbiteri custodes.*[76]   It is evident therefore that there was more than one custode. Certainly spurious is the privilege of Charles the Fat of March 22, 880.

In the south side aisle of the church near the portal is now placed the stone bearing the famous epitaph of Ansperto: "Here lies Ansperto, the illustrious archbishop of our city.   In his life, in his speech, in his modesty and in his faith, he was ever a follower of the right.   He was generous to the needy, he performed what he had vowed, and was steadfast in his resolutions.   He conscientiously gave back the walls to the city which had been entrusted to him.   He restored the ruined palace of Stilico.   With great labour he rebuilt many sacred edifices; he erected the atrium near and in front of the doors of this basilica.   He then dedicated a church and monastery to S. Satiro, giving all his own estates to the sacred establishment, to maintain forever eight monks to pray to Ambrogio and Satiro in his behalf.   He died

---

[65] For example, the collegiate church of Vezzolano is habitually called a monastery in the documents.

[66] The document is dated: Acto . . . in regno domno Hlutharii anno vigesimo quinto, X diae mense iunio, indictione septima felice. (*Hist. Pat. Mon.*, XIII, 268).

[67] *Ibid.*, 371.   [68] *Ibid.*, 301.   [69] *Ibid.*, 373.

[70] *Hist. Pat. Mon.*, XIII, 388.   [71] *Ibid.*, 407.

[72] Anno domni Hloduvici vigeximo quarto, mense februarii, indictione undecima. Anno dominice incarnationis DCCCLXVI.

[73] *Hist. Pat. Mon.*, XIII, 402.   [74] *Ibid.*, XIII, 444.

[75] *Ibid.*, XIII, 451.   [76] *Ibid.*, 457.

in the year of the Incarnation of our Lord 882 [*i.e.*, A.D. 881] on the seventh of December, the fifteenth indiction. He ruled his diocese thirteen years five months and twelve days. The priest Andrea, moved by his love for the bishop, adorned his tomb with this inscription."[77]

Few historical documents have been subjected to the analysis and critical study that has fallen to the lot of this epitaph of Ansperto. Scholars have much discussed as to why and when he gave back[78] the walls to the city, and as to what is meant by the palace of Stilico.[79] The great crux, however, is the interpretation of the ungrammatical line, *atria vicinas struxit et ante fores*. Does this mean that he constructed the atrium of S. Ambrogio? If so, why the plural? Does not the inscription rather refer to the arcades which documents of the XII century prove existed along the streets leading to S. Ambrogio? Does *vicinas* modify *atria* or *fores?* These are questions it

[77]   HIC IACET ANSPERTVS NRÆ
        CLARISSIMVS VRBIS
        ANTISTES . VITA VOCE PUDORE FIDI
        AEQVI SECTATOR TVRBAE
        PRAELARGVS EGENAE
        EFFECTOR VOTI P[RO]POSITIQ TENAX
        MOENIA SOLLICITVS COM
        MISSAE REDDIDIT VRBI
        DIRVTA RESTITVIT DE STILICHONE DOMV
        QVOT SACRAS AEDES
        QVANTO SVDORE REFECIT
        ATRIA VICINAS STRVX ET ANTE FORES
        TV SCO SATVRO TEPLVQ: DOMVQ. DICAVIT
        DANS SVA SACRATO PDIA CVNCTA LOCO
        VT MONACHOS PASCANT
        AETERNIS OCTO DIEBUS
        AMBROSIV P[RO] SEQ[VE] SATYRVQ. ROGENT
        OBIIT ANNO INCARNATIO
        NIS DNI DCCC.LXXXII
        SEPTIMO IDVS DEC INDIC XV
        REXIT EPISCOPATV SVVM
        ANNIS XIII MEN V DIEB XII
        PSULIS ANDREAS PFATI CAPTVS AMORI
        HOC LÆVITA SIBI CDECORAVIT OPVS

[78] Or should *reddidit* be rendered "restored"?

[79] I cannot forbear to observe in this connection that a certain Stilico *comes* is mentioned in *Vita S. Ambrosii*, auctore Paulino, 34, 43, 50, ed. Migne, *Pat. Lat.*, XIV, 41, 42, 44.

is impossible to answer with certainty. I incline, however, to construe *vicinas* with *atria* and take the latter word as referring to the atrium of S. Ambrogio. "He built the atrium near and before the doors of this church." If this interpretation be accepted we must admit that Ansperto (868-881) did veritably rebuild the atrium. The epitaph is no longer in its original position. Until the middle of the XIX century it was placed to the north of the high altar against one of the pilasters added in the XIII century to support the sustaining arches of the vaults.[80] Obviously, then, even here it could not have been in its original site, although a tomb was found in the pavement below it. In consequence of this, Cattaneo has suspected that the inscription might have been transported from another church. Sant'Ambrogio, as always radical, has even boldly pronounced the epitaph a fabrication of the XII century.[81] There appears, however, no good reason to doubt the authenticity of the inscription, nor to assume that it has not always been placed in the church of S. Ambrogio. The Andrea mentioned in the inscription may well be the same who became archbishop of Milan a score of years later.

In a donation of June 26, 882, mention is made of *viris prebiteris officialis basilice beati Christi confessoris Ambrosii*,[82] and in a *commutatio* of 887 of *presbiteri custodes et officiales ecclesie beati Christi confessoris et episcopi ambrosii*.[83] In these phrases may be traced the gradual development of the secular clergy of the basilica.

A document of 892, the authenticity of which has been disputed but which appears to me genuine, contains a reference to the atrium of S. Ambrogio.[84] In a donation of December 2, 894, mention is again made of the *presbiteris atque officialibus sancti Ambrosii*.[85]

Pietro, elected abbot in 859, died in 900. He was buried in the basilica and his epitaph, published by Puricelli[86] and Mabillon,[87] compares him to St. Benedict and contains the line: *Templa, domos, vites, oleas, pomeria struxit.* The *domos* I believe refers to the monastic buildings, which it is

---

[80] Rossi, 35. The *Codice della Croce*, MS. Amb., D. S. IV, 1, f. 236, gives a copy of the epitaph of Ansperto with the marginal note: Ad sinistram maioris Altaris eiusdem Basilicæ in tabula marmorea haec carmina a pluribus postea edita.

[81] He thinks the lines, *Ambrosium . . . domini*, are restored, and that the inscription originally gave the name, not of Angilberto, but of Anselmo. (*Intorno alla Basilica*, 557).

[82] *Hist. Pat. Mon.*, XIII, 526.   [83] *Ibid.*, XIII, 568.

[84] Situs vero loci ab oriente et meridie suprataxato coheret monasterio, habens ab occidente viam regiam et a septentrione murum et porticum, quibus sacratum munitum est atrium. . . . presenti XI pontificatus nostri anno, seu etiam domini nostri imperatoris Widonis anno II . . . . . Actum est hoc anno ab incarnatione Domini nostri Jhesu Christi octingentesimo nonagesimo tercio, indictione XI. (*Hist. Pat. Mon.*, XIII, 595).

[85] *Ibid.*, XIII, 601.   [86] 268-269.

[87] *Ann. Ben.*, III, 308 ad ann. 900. Is this "la pierre tumulaire de Benoît, premier abbé de ce monastère, vers 785" which Millin (I, 163) says he saw in 1817?

reasonable to suppose were reconstructed by this abbot. What is meant by *templa* I can not conjecture, unless it refers to some of the many churches dependent upon the monastery. There is no evidence to show that the church proper of S. Ambrogio was rebuilt at this time.

A manuscript chronicle in the Biblioteca Ambrosiana contains a notice that the emperor Lothair II (945-950) dedicated the monastery of S. Ambrogio.[88] It is certain that this emperor was in reality buried at S. Ambrogio, but it is impossible that the church, or even the monastic buildings, should have been dedicated by a secular person. The text must, therefore, be corrupt.

A document of January, 955, contains a reference to the secular clergy of the monastery,[89] as does also another of June, 922,[90] while on the other hand the monks appear in a diploma of 942 summarized by Giulini.[91] According to a gloss of Galvaneo della Fiamma, at the time of her coronation (951) the wife of the emperor Otto I gave to the altar of S. Ambrogio a carbuncle of the value of 10 florins of gold.[92] A diploma of Otto I of 952 mentions a chapel[93] of S. Ambrogio dedicated to the saints Maria, Jacopo and Giorgio.[94] A document of June, 964, refers to five *presbiteris, custodes et officiales basilice sancti ambrosii*.[95] A certain *Walperto presbitero de hordine decumanorum sancte mediolanensis ecclesie, officiale basilice beati Christi confessoris Ambrosii* is referred to in a deed of sale of 975[96] and in a will[97] of the same date. In another will of June, 992, mention is made of *presbyteris illis decomanos sanctae mediolanensis ecclesie, officiales ejusdem basilicae sancti Ambrosii*.[98] From an important will of January, 1000, we learn that

[88] Post Vgonem imp[er]auit lotarius secundus qui monasteriū sci Ambrosij dedicauit ubi iacet corpus ipius Jmperatoris. (*Chronica*, MS. Amb., H 56 Sup., f. 86 r).

[89] . . . oficiales fuerint in ecclesia sancti Christi confessoris et episcopi Ambrosii . . . et faciant ipsis presbiteris . . . (*Hist. Pat. Mon.*, XIII, 1037).

[90] . . . illis qui pro tempore oficiales fuerit in basilica beati Christi confessoris et episcopi Ambrosii . . . (*Ibid.*, 857).

[91] I, 491.

[92] Eius uxor dicta Athleyta Agusta relicta condam Lotharii imperatoris, dum coronaretur, donavit altari beati Ambroxii carbunculum, pretii X florenorum auri. (Galvanei Flammae, *Chron. Maius*, ed. Ceruti, 524).

[93] This chapel was probably constructed to contain the body of the emperor, Lothair II (†950).

[94] Capella, que est in honore Beate Marie, et Sancti Jacobi Apostoli, atque Sancti Georgii Martiris, constituta infra . . . . . Beati Ambrosii Ecclesiam, in qua jam dictus Lotharius humatus quiescit, a predicti Monasterii . . . . . luminaria reparentur . . . (Giulini, VII, 38).

[95] *Hist. Pat. Mon.*, XIII, 1188.   [96] *Ibid.*, XIII, 1347.   [97] *Ibid.*, XIII, 1350.

[98] *Ibid.*, XIII, 1529. Cf. also in the will of Landolfo of 997: *presbyteros ille decomanos, oficiales ecclesiarum suorum Nazarii martiris et Ambrosii confessoris.* (*Ibid.*, XIII, 1647). However, in a commutation of 999 the secular priests of S. Ambrogio are called *presbiteris officiales custodes ecclesie beati Christi Confessoris Ambrosii.* (*Ibid.*, XIII, 1701).

the number of secular priests or decumani in the basilica was twelve.[99] However, the two clergies were still occasionally denoted collectively by the word monastery, as is evident from a donation of 1013 analyzed by Giulini.[100]

About the year 1016 the marchese Manfredo gave to the church a quantity of gold with which was made a processional cross.[101] About the same time the archbishop Arnolfo II (998-1018) made a voyage to Constantinople. According to Landolfo Seniore, "he remained with the emperor nearly three months. And having acquired favour in the eyes of the monarch, he requested from the emperor the brazen serpent, which Moses, at the divine command, raised in the desert in the presence of the children of Israel. Because of his merits, his request was granted, and he brought the relic into the church of S. Ambrogio and placed it there."[102] The same notice is repeated in the chronicle which passes under the name of Filippo da Castel Seprio, but the date 1013 is added.[103] Galvaneo della Fiamma also narrates the occurrence.[104] Lampugnano de Legnano, however, states that the brazen serpent was erected, not by Arnolfo, but by his successor, Ariberto (1018-1045).[105]

In 1032 the archbishop Ariberto undertook an investigation of the monasteries of his diocese, and began with S. Ambrogio. Just what changes he wrought in the relationship of the two clergies is not clear, but I suspect that at this time the canons may have been reformed and regularized, though no precise indications of this are to be found in his will dated 1034, by which he left important possessions to different churches of Milan.[106] At all events the canons were certainly regularized before 1038,[107] although even after the

---

[99] presbiteris illis, qui nunc et in antea perpetuis temporibus in eadem basilica sancti Ambrosii ordinati et constituti fuerint, quod esse debent presbiteris illis numeros duodecim . . . (*Ibid.*, XIII, 1713).

[100] II, 59.

[101] Frater verò illius Manfredus Marchio donavit Ecclesiæ auri talenta quam plurima, unde producta est Crux illa pulcherrima, quæ usque hodie præcipuis tantum geritur in diebus. (Arnulphi, *Hist. Med.*, I, XIX, ed. Muratori, R. I. S., IV, 13).

[102] Moratus autem Arnulphus per tres ferè menses apud Imperatorem, gratiâ Regis adeptâ, serpentem æneum, quem Moyses in deserto Divino imperio admonitus coram filiis Israël exaltaverat, Imperatori requisivit, & habere meruit, & veniens in Ecclesia S. Ambrosii ipsum exaltavit. (Landulphi Senioris, *Med. Hist.*, II, 18, ed. Muratori, R. I. S., IV, 81).

[103] Anno 1013 Arnulfus de Arsago Seprii Archiepiscopus Mediolani in Constantinopolim acquisivit quendam serpentem quem posuit ad S. Ambrosium. (*Chronica detta di Filippo da Castel Seprio*, MS. Amb., S. Q. + I, 12, f. 58).

[104] Pro reliquiis autem serpentem æneum, quem Moyses in deserto erexerat, accepit, qui modò in Ecclesia S. Ambrosii erectus conspicitur. (*Manipulus Florum,* Galvanei Flammae, CXXXV, ed. Muratori, R. I. S., XI, 612. Also *Chron. Maius*, ed. Ceruti, 600).

[105] [Heribertus] serpentē eneum in s̄c̄o Ambroxio erexit. (Lampugnano de Legnano, *Chronica*, MS. Amb., H 56 Sup., f. 657).

[106] Puricelli, 367.   [107] Giulini, II, 253.

regularization, they continued to be denoted by the old title *Presbiteris de ordine Decomanorum sancte Mediolanensis Ecclesie, Officiale Basilice beati Christi Confessoris Ambrosii*, in a diploma of 1045 published by Muratori,[108] while in a document of 1046[109] four priests are called *Presbiteris et Officialis Ecclesiæ Beati Christi Confessoris Ambrosii*. In 1052 parallel donations were made to the monks and canons,[110] and the term "canonici" is applied to the chapter for the first time.[111] In 1075 the canons are referred to as a completely regularized body;[112] in 1093 a prevosto of the chapter is mentioned,[113] and in 1095 there is a reference to the house in which the canons lived in common.[114]

In the sixth decade of the XI century broke out the famous civil struggles at Milan which centered about the personality of S. Arialdo. The principal question at issue was the reform of the clergy. S. Arialdo, backed by the pope and the populace, demanded the abolition of simony and of the marriage of priests. It is related in the *Acts* of S. Arialdo that during the bloody disorders which ensued, the reformer went to S. Ambrogio to pray.[115] On May 17, 1067, the body of the saint was laid out in state in the same basilica.[116] The church must, therefore, have been open for worship at this time. From a passage of Landolfo the Younger it is clear that the church was in use in 1093.[117] I therefore suspect that the reconstruction of the nave took place between 1067 and 1093. The new atrium I believe to have been finished before 1098, since an inscription of this date is placed in its west wall. There is, it is true, no absolute proof that the inscription may not have been transported from some other site; but on the other hand there is no particular reason to suppose that it is not in its original position. This inscription is as follows: "In the name of the Holy Trinity, in honour of the Holy Trinity and of the holy martyrs Protasio and Gervasio, it has been decreed by the archbishop Anselmo and by his successors who shall be hereafter, and by the common council of all the citizens, that under pain of excommunication, it shall not be permitted to any man on the day of the festival of those saints, or for three days before or for three days after, to levy the *curtadia*, nor to take oppressive legal action of any kind. They likewise decreed for eight days before the festival, and for eight days after the festival, peace for all men who come to the festival or

---

[108] A. I. M. A., ed. A., IX, 639.

[109] Giulini, VII, 60.

[110] The inscriptions have been published by Giulini, II, 348-349.

[111] See Puricelli, 432.

[112] Giulini, II, 522.

[113] Landulphi Junioris, *Hist. Med.*, I, ed. Muratori, R. I. S., V, 469.

[114] Giulini, VII, 74.

[115] *Acta SS. Arialdi et Erlembaldi*, ed. Migne, *Pat. Lat.*, CXLIII, 1466.

[116] Et sic in sancto die Ascensionis posuimus illum in medio ecclesiæ S. Ambrosii. (*Vitae SS. Arialdi et Erlembaldi*, ed. Migne, *Pat. Lat.*, CXLIII, 1480).

[117] Landulphi Junioris, *Hist. Med.*, I, ed. Muratori, R. I. S., V, 471.

who return from it. Adamo and Pagano applied themselves to procure this good decree in the year of our Lord, 1098."[118]

It is well known that during the Middle Ages it was customary to hold fairs in connection with the feasts of popular saints.[119] It was also not unusual to grant at such times safe-conducts in order that, as it is phrased in a document in the archives of Modena,[120] "debtors might come to the feast of the saint." The *curtadia* was a tax levied on the merchants who sold their goods at a fair.[121]

According to Torre, the atrium of S. Ambrogio was built in the years immediately preceding 1098, and it is possible that he had for this statement some authority other than the inscription we have cited.[122]

Perhaps a further indication that the reconstruction of the basilica was entirely finished about this time is to be found in the fact that in 1098 the revenues of the high altar were assigned to the canons by a synod held under the auspices of the archbishop, Anselmo IV.[123] This decision was the starting point of the strife between the canons and the monks. The judgment of the synod confirmed a previous decree of the pope Urban II, issued in 1096,[124] and was itself, in turn, confirmed by the pope.[125]

Several important notices relating to the church of S. Ambrogio are contained in Landolfo the Younger's account of the trial by fire of Liprando,

[118] ✠ IN NOMINE. SCAE TRINITATIS. AD EI
HONORE. ET. SCOR[UM]. P[RO]TASII. ET. GERVASII. MARTIRV
STA
TVTV E AB ARCHIEPO ANSELMO ET EI POSTEA SVCCESSORIB:
SVB NOE EXCOMVNICATIOIS [ET] COMVNI CONSCILIO TOCI'
CIVITATIS VT NO LICEAT ALICUI HOMI. IN EO[RUM]
FESTIVITATE. [ET]
[PER] DIES TRES ANTEA. [ET] P[ER] TRES POSTEA. CVRTADIAM
TOLLERE. [ET] IN IVS. SI
BI P[RO]PRIV USVRPARE ITERV COFIRMAVERUNT P[ER] OCTO
DIES ANTE FE
STV ET P[ER] OCTO POST FESTV. FIRMAM PACEM OMBVS HOIB:
AD SOLLEMNITATEM. VENIENTIBVS. ET REDEVNTIB'. ADA
[ET] PAGANO HVIC BONO OPE DATIB'. AN. DNI. M.IIC

[119] One is mentioned, for example, in Landulphi Junioris, *Hist. Med.*, 22, ed. Muratori, R. I. S., V, 493.

[120] Published by Dondi, 114.   [121] Romussi, *Milano*, 415.

[122] Dopo trent'anni fù risarcito [l'atrio] ancora dall'Arciuescouo Valuassore Louini, ritornato che si fù dall'acquisto di Terra Santa sotto il Pontificato d'Vrbano Secondo, benche si aui opinione, ch'egli in Constantinopoli facesse vela al Cielo, e soppellito restasse nella Chiesa di Santo Nicolò . . . (Torre, 177).

[123] *Codice della Croce*, MS. Amb. D. S. IV, Vol. III, f. 141.

[124] *Ibid.*, 131.   [125] *Ibid.*, 145.

an event which occurred in 1103. Before his trial, the priest celebrated mass at the high altar of the basilica: "He stood with bare feet upon the marble stone which contains the image of Hercules and is placed at the entrance to the choir. When the clamour of the populace was redoubled, he, though an old man, leaped forward from the stone with the image of Hercules,[126] and . . . followed by the people came into the field before the atrium of S. Ambrogio."[127] It is evident therefore that in the year 1103 the nave and the choir of the basilica were in use, and that the atrium of the church was in existence. This notice therefore confirms the inference we have drawn from the inscription of 1098: that is, that the reconstruction of the church and of the atrium was entirely finished before the close of the XI century.

In 1117 a memorable earthquake occurred in Lombardy which caused the ruin of many churches. It has been supposed by Sant'Ambrogio that our basilica was ruined at this time, and subsequently entirely reconstructed. There is, however, not a particle of evidence to show that such was the case. On the contrary the style of the existing edifice makes it certain that the building was not materially damaged in 1117. Indeed, the fact that the archbishop Giordano (who really died in 1120, although Lampugnano de Legnano places his death in 1117) was buried in the church proves that the edifice could not have been ruined by the earthquake.[128]

The dignity that the basilica enjoyed in the early years of the XII century is proved by a sentence of 1119, in which S. Ambrogio is mentioned as the first of the eleven mother-churches of Milan.[129]

In 1123 the feud between the canons and the monks came to a head. Callistus II confirmed the bull of Urban II, granting the oblations of the altar to the canons.[130] This bull was the occasion of a violent contest on the part of the monks. From the testimony taken, we learn that the canons, in order to keep the peace, had given to the monks half the revenues of the altar, although the entire revenues had been adjudged to them by Urban II. The ultimate decision, virtually confirming the *status quo*, decreed that half the revenues should be given to one clergy and half to the other.[131] The decision

---

[126] The Hercules of the choir is also mentioned by Galvaneo della Fiamma (*Chron. Maius*, ed. Ceruti, 524), and is twice described at length in the *Chronicon Mediolanense*, ed. Cinquini, 13, 14).

[127] Presbytero stante nudis pedibus super lapidem marmoreum, qui in introitu Chori continet Herculis simulacrum . . . Et Presbyter in hoc multiplicato clamore, licèt senex, desuper lapide continente Herculis simulacrum prosiluit, & uno cum populo in campo ante atrium Ecclesiæ Sancti Ambrosii venit. (Landulphi Junioris, *Hist. Med.*, X, ed. Muratori, R. I. S., V, 481).

[128] Lampugnano de Legnano, *Chronica*, MS. Amb., H 56 Sup., f. 66.

[129] Giulini, VII, 85.

[130] *Codice della Croce*, MS. Amb. D. S. IV, Vol. V, f. 176.

[131] *Codice della Croce*, MS. Amb. D. S. IV, Vol. V, f. 156.

also attempted to compromise the question as to which clergy was to officiate at burial services. "Moreover let a bell, of the same size and weight as the one which has been broken by the monks, be returned and placed in the same place within the cloister of the canonica, and let the canons have no other bell or chime except that which is mentioned above."[132]

In Galvaneo della Fiamma we read that the archbishop, Anselmo V da Pusterla (1126-1133), caused a silver altar to be erected in the church of S. Ambrogio.[133] What is meant by the silver altar in this passage? Does the chronicler refer to the famous Palio d'Oro? From the circumstance that much silver is used in the latter, it is probable that he does. The suspicion arises that Galvaneo may have confused the two archbishops, Anselmo and Angilberto. However, he was well aware that a golden altar had been given by Angilberto, since he speaks of it in several passages that we have quoted above.[134] I am therefore inclined to believe that he derived this notice from an authentic source, and that the Palio d'Oro was remade (or at least restored) by Anselmo V between 1126 and 1133. S. Bernardo, according to Puricelli,[135] saw the body of S. Ambrogio in 1130. The body of the saint was not ordinarily accessible, and was preserved beneath the high altar of the basilica. The fact, therefore, that it could be seen in 1130, gives some reason to believe that the Palio d'Oro may have been in restoration at this time. Naturally the altar would be the last thing in the basilica to be renovated. We have seen that there is reason to believe that the nave and the atrium had been rebuilt in the last quarter of the XI century, and we shall presently see that before 1128 the construction of the new campanile had been undertaken. It is therefore entirely reasonable to suppose that the altar was remade at this epoch out of the old materials, and that, for the reasons already stated, the old inscriptions were preserved.

An important document of April 7, 1127, informs us of the existence of a series of arcades along the streets in the neighbourhood of S. Ambrogio, and is important because it offers a possible explanation of the *atria* of the Ansperto epitaph. The document is the will of a certain Waza, deacon in the holy church of Milan, and son of the late Aldo. This ecclesiastic bequeathed to the canons of S. Ambrogio a piece of property on condition that they should keep in repair the roof of the arcade from the church of S. Vitale to its junction with the arcade which led to S. Ambrogio, just as Waza himself

---

[132] Skella verò, quæ a Monachis fracta est, eiusdem ponderis & quantitatis in eodem loco infra claustrum Canonicæ, restituatur & ponatur: & nullam aliam Skellam, uel tintinabulum, habeat nisi illam, quæ superiùs dicta est. (Puricelli, 566).

[133] Anno Domini 1123 [*recte* 1126] vacante Imperio [*sic*], vacante similiter Sede Archiepiscopali, Anselmus de Pusterla factus fuit Archiepiscopus Mediolanensis. Hic fecit fieri Altare argenteum in Ecclesia B. Ambrosii. (Galvanei Flammae, *Manipulus Florum*, CLXIV, ed. Muratori, R. I. S., XI, 630).

[134] Page 549.   [135] 106.

was accustomed to keep it in repair for the benefit of his own soul, and for that of his father Aldo, who was buried under that portico.[136]

In the year 1128, the controversy between the monks and the canons entered upon a new phase. The old question as to which party had the right to ring the bells of the church—a dispute which had before been secondary—now became predominant. A diploma of the archbishop Anselmo dating from this year is one of the most important documents for the history of the edifice: "Anselmo by the grace of God archbishop of the holy church of Milan to Girardo most reverend priest and prevosto of the canonica of S. Ambrogio and to his successors and to the canons of the same chapter who shall live according to canonical discipline hereafter. . . . Since you wish to celebrate, as is your duty, divine service in the church of S. Ambrogio for the people of God, you must summon and assemble that people by the ringing of bells. We will . . . . . that the bell-tower recently founded in that church for your liberty and in great part built, shall remain in your charge, and lest this our act seem to some one unfair or disobliging, we do not invalidate the customary use of the old bell-tower of the same church, but we cordially approve that the abbot and monks shall have charge of it, as has been the custom in the past. Moreover we decree that the canons who are now in the church, or who shall be there in the future, may place bells or chimes in the above-mentioned new campanile, and may ring them, and that, while the bells are ringing the canons may devoutly chant the psalms and the Pater Noster in behalf of the souls of ourselves and all the faithful. . . . Done on the eighteenth day of October, in the year 1128."[137] From the document cited above,[138] it is evident

---

[136] Anno ab incar. dni nri ihu xpi mill. centesimo uigesimo septimo mense aprili indic. quinta. Ego Uuaza diaconus de ordine maiore sancte mediolanensis ecclesie et filius quondam Aldonis etc. . . . Ideo ego . . . uolo et iudico seu per hoc meum iudicatum confirmo, ut camporum petie due iuris mei quas habere uisus sum . . . deueniant in ius et proprietatem ecclesie et canonice beati confessoris Ambrosii ubi eius sanctum requiescit corpus. et faciant canonici ipsius ecclesie post meum decessum uel quocumque die in uita mea dimisero usque in perpetuum de frugibus et censu que ex ipsis campis dns annue dederit ad eorum sumptum et utilitatem quod uoluerint, eo tamen ordine ut ipsi canonici et eorum successores retinere debeant de cohopertorio porticum quod est edificatum ab ecclesia sancti Vitalis usque in capite de arco de illo portico qui uadit ad sanctum Ambrosium, sicut ego qui supra Uuado diaconus solitus sum retinere pro remedio anime mee, et ipsius quondam Aldonis genitoris mei qui iacet subtus ipsum porticum. (Codice della Croce, MS. Amb. D. S. IV, Vol. V, f. 205).

[137] Anselmus Dei gratia Sancte Mediolanensis Ecclesie Archiepiscopus Girardo Reverentissimo Presbitero, et Preposito Canonice Sancti Ambrosii, omnibusque suis Successoribus, et Fratribus in eodem Canonica canonice victuris in perpetuum. . . . Videlicet cum vultis Divinum Officium, prout juris est, in Ecclesia Beati Ambrosii Populo Dei celebrare debeatis ipsum Populum signo Tintinabuli excitare, et convocare. Volumus . . . . . Clocharium noviter in eadem Ecclesia fundatum, et in maxima parte edificatum vestre libertati, vestraque in custodia perseverare. Et ne hec nostra traditio injuriosa, aut inofficiosa alicubi videatur, consuetudinem veteris Clocharii ejusdem Ecclesiae non infirmamus, sed in manibus Abbatis, et Monachorum, prout mos est

that in 1123 the bell-tower had not yet been begun. It is clear, therefore, that the lower part of the structure must have been constructed between 1123 and 1128.[139]

In 1143 the strife between the monks and the canons broke out anew with rather curious developments, as indicated in the following document: ". . . How the dispute between Lord Vifredo, by the grace of God abbot of the monastery of S. Ambrogio, and the monks of that monastery, on the one hand, and . . . . . the prevosto and canons of the same church on the other hand, was submitted by either party under oath through counsel to the consuls of Milan, as the consuls, according to the agreement, directed . . . . . [The prevosto and canons said] that the offerings made at the high altar of S. Ambrogio and at all the other altars and chapels which are in that church ought to belong to the chapter. They likewise said that the new campanile also belonged to the chapter and that they wished to place and keep bells there. To this the abbot and monks replied that all the offerings at the altars and chapels, as is read above, ought to belong to the monastery. But since there had formerly been a controversy between the said monastery and the said chapter concerning the aforesaid offerings and certain other questions, the abbot said that he wished to abide by, and fulfil, the decision rendered when the lawsuit was terminated and finished, and he showed a copy of the deed of that decision. Concerning the campanile and the bells, the monks replied as follows: That that campanile did not belong to the canons, nor did they have a right to place and keep bells there. . . . When they had heard these things . . . the consuls . . . came with both parties to the palace of Lord Robaldo the archbishop of Milan, and into his presence. . . . Immediately thereupon the said Lord Robaldo the archbishop ordered and commanded the said abbot and monks and the prevosto and canons that they should abide by and fulfil the decision of the consuls." The question of the offerings was settled by reiterating the decision of 1123 which, it will be remembered, gave half to each clergy. "Concerning the campanile, however, the above-mentioned Anselmo, the judge, by order of the above-mentioned

permanere laudamus. Canonici vero qui nunc in ipsa sunt Ecclesia, aut inposterum fuerint, decernimus in jam dicto novo Clochario Tintinabulum, seu Cloccas adponere, et sonare, et sonando Psalmos et Dominicam Orationem pro nostrarum, et omnium Fidelium Animarum devote cantare, et psallere. . . . Actum est hoc XV Kal. Novembris, qui fuit Milleximo, Centeximo, vigesimo octavo anno ab Incarnatione Domini nostri Jesu Christi. (Giulini, VII, 92. See also *Codice della Croce*, MS. Amb., D. S. IV, Vol. 5, f. 218).

[138] Page 558.

[139] A puzzling document of which there is a copy in the *Codice della Croce*, V, f. 225, bears the erroneous chronological notes of the year of the Incarnation of Our Lord 1128, the first year of Corrado, king of Italy, and the seventh indiction. Corrado confirms to the canons the oblations of the altar and the *Clocarium novum quod domnus Anselmus archiepiscopus eisdem canonicis tradidit.*

consuls pronounced as follows. That the above-mentioned prevosto and canons from now henceforward, should remain silent and content. Concerning the bells he pronounced that the said abbot should give to the prevosto and canons a bell in the new campanile or in the old campanile, as the abbot should wish, this bell to be one of those of medium size which are now in the campanile, that is, neither one of the largest nor of the smallest. And if the abbot should not wish to give one of his own bells, the prevosto should buy one of the same size and the abbot shall cause it to be placed in one of the campanili as is specified above; and the abbot should have his guardian ring this bell, when the canons send to request this either to the abbot himself or to the monks or give a signal with their little bell at that time in which they are accustomed to celebrate vespers. . . . . All this was done in the palace of the said archbishop in his presence in the middle of the month of June in the year 1143."[140]

[140] Qualiter discordia, quæ erat inter DOMNVM VVIFREDVM, DEI GRATIA ABBATEM MONASTERII SANCTI AMBROSII . . . ET MONACHOS IPSIVS MONASTERII, & ex altera . . . . . ATQUE PRÆPOSITVM SEV CANONICOS EIVSDEM ECCLESIÆ, fuit missa & deposita ab vtraque parte, iure iurando per eorum Aduocatos ex vtraque parte facto in Consulibus Mediolanensibus, sicut ipsi consules eis per Conuenientiam (siue Conuentionem) præciperent. Quæ discordia . . . . . ipse præpositus & Canonici (subintelligendum absque dubio hîc est dicebant). Quòd tota oblatio Altaris Maioris ipsius Sancti Ambrosij, & cæterorum Altarium, seu Oraculorum, quæ sunt infra ambitum ipsius Ecclesiæ, ad ipsam Canonicam pertinere debeat. Ite dicebant, QUOD CLOCARIVM NOVVM AD IPSAM CANONICAM PERTINEBAT, ET CLOCAS PONERE ET HABERE VOLEBANT. . . . Ad hæc ipse Abbas & Monachi respondebant, Quòd tota oblatio ipsorum Altarium, seu Oraculorum, sicut superiùs legitur, ad ipsum Monasterium pertinere debeat. Sed quia quondàm discordia fuit inter ipsum Monasterium & ipsam Canonicam de iamdictis oblationibus, & alijs quampluribus Capitulis; dicebat ipse Abbas, quòd sicut terminata & finita fuit, adtendere & adimplere volebat: & de ipsa Concordia Instrumentum vnum ostendebat. DE CLOCARIO VERO SEV CLOCIS (hoc est, de Turri campanaria, vel aliter Campanili, seu Campanis) ita respondebant: QUOD IPSVM CLOCARIVM AD IPSAM CANONICAM NON PERTINEAT. NEQVE CLOCAS PONERE SEV HABERE LICEAT. . . . His ita auditis . . . IPSI CONSVLES . . . VENERVNT CVM AMBABVS PARTIBVS IN PALATIO DOMNI ROBALDI MEDIOLANENSIS ARCHIEPISCOPI CORAM EIVS PRÆSENTIA. . . . TVNC IBI STATIM IPSE DOMNVS ROBALDVS ARCHIEPISCOPVS IVSSIT ET PRÆCEPIT PRÆDICTO ABBATI ET MONACHIS, ATQVE PRÆPOSITO ET CANONICIS, VT ITA ADTENDERENT ET ADIMPLERENT, SICVT IPSI CONSVLES EIS PRÆCIPERENT. . . . DE CLOCARIO VERO ITA DIXIT IAMDICTVS ANSELMVS IVDEX IVSSIONE PRÆDICTORVM CONSVLVM: VT PRÆDICTVS PRÆPOSITVS ET CANONICI AMODO IN ANTEA PERMANEANT TACITI ET CONTENTI. DE CLOCIS VERO ITA DIXIT: VT PRÆDICTVS ABBAS DAT EIDEM PRÆPOSITO ET CANONICIS VNAM CLOCAM IN CLOCARIO NOVO, SEV VETERI, QVO VOLVERIT IPSE ABBAS, DE ILLIS MEDIOCRIBUS, QVÆ MODO SVNT IN CLOCARIO, id est, neque de maioribus, neque de minoribus. Et si Abbas noluerit eis dare vnam de suis Clocis; Præpositus emat vnam de eadem mensura, & Abbas faciat eam mittere in ipso Clocario, ut supra

The decree of the consuls, far from settling the dispute of the two clergies, simply increased the complications. The defeated party, the canons, promptly appealed from the decision of the lay authorities to the papal legates. Concerning the subsequent progress of the litigation, there are extant the following documents:[141]　(1) Allegations of the canons to the papal legates. The document breaks off unfinished and there is no date, but it must be of the end of 1143, or the beginning of 1144.　(2) The sentence of the legates and of the archbishop in favour of the canons, August, 1144.　(3) Letter of the legates to the pope summarizing their decision, August, 1144.　(4) Letter of the pope to the canons confirming the decision of the legates, October, 1144. (5) Another similar letter covering some points omitted in the first, October 27, 1144.　(6) Letter of the pope to the archbishop confirming his decision, October 27, 1144.　(7) A *concordia* between the monks and canons made in November, 1144.　The oblations are given half to the canons, half to the monks. Restrictions are put upon the use of bells by the canons, whereas the former decisions had given the campanile entirely to this clergy.[142]　It would be a difficult task, and one that is here fortunately not necessary, to trace the history of the case in all its legal subtleties. We need be concerned only with those portions of the legal documents which bear upon the architectural history of the church.

Part of the evidence submitted to the papal delegates is of great importance for our purpose. It is omitted by Puricelli, but has recently been published by Biscaro: "The assertion of the prevosto that he held possession of the keys of the campanile is not at all true, since that officer whom we call the superstans, and who has charge of the construction of the church or of the campanile, had the keys which had been entrusted to his administration by the people of our city. . . . Besides this, the high altar constructed with wonderful art, in which are buried the bodies of the afore-mentioned martyrs and confessor, is under the care and jurisdiction of the abbot of the monastery, as may be read in the diploma of Lord Angilberto, the archbishop of good

legitur. ET FACIAT IPSE ABBAS EAM SONARE SVVM CVSTODEM si requisitus fuerit ipse, uel Monachi per Missum de ipsis Canonicis, seu per signum, quod ipsi Canonici fecerint cum Skella eorū ad illud tempus, quo ipsi Canonici soliti sunt celebrare Vesperas . . . . . FACTVM EST HOC, VT SVPRA, IN DOMO IAMDICTI ARCHIEPISCOPI CORAM EIVS PRÆSENTIA, Anno Dominicæ Incarnationis Millesimo centesimo quadragesimotertio, medio mense Iunij, Indictione sexta . . . (Ed. Puricelli, 668).

[141] *Codice della Croce*, MS. Amb. D. S. IV, 6, ff. 194 f.

[142] CÆTERVM NOVVM CAMPANILE ECCLESIÆ EIVSDEM IN LIBERA PRÆPOSITI ET CANONICORVM POTESTATE IVRE PERPETVO STATVENDO DONAVIMVS: tres QVOQVE CAMPANAS SOLVMMODO IN EODEM CAMPANILI PONERE, ET SECVNDVM PROPRIVM ARBITRIVM CANONICORVM, QUOTIENS EXPEDIERIT, SONARE EISDEM ABSOLVTE CONCESSIMVS. (Ed. Puricelli, 688).

memory, who, as it is known, was the constructor of the above-mentioned marvellous work. . . . And to the assertion of the prevosto that the canonica had been established before the monastery, and had always continued to exist, the abbot replied that the canonica did not exist there at the time the monastery was founded, since it was clearly shown in documents written in the time of King Luitprando that the church was conferred on Fortis the deacon by the archbishop[?]. The prevosto produced a document of the time of Desiderio, king of the Lombards, who it is known ruled later than Luitprando, but this we [*i.e.*, the monks] declare to be false because of the style of the handwriting, the variation in the shape of the letters, and the newness of the parchment, and even if it were free from the suspicion of being spurious, it nevertheless does not mention the canonica, nor say that there were canons there. But even were it proved that the chapter existed at that time, the fact that the Lord Archbishop Pietro built the monastery and gave to the abbot and to his successors jurisdiction and power over the entire church, with all the possessions that belonged to it or should in future be given to it, and made no mention of the canonica, proves that the canonica had been transferred to the monastery. . . . It is only recently that the prevosto Martino and the canons have laid claim to the offerings of the altar and to jurisdiction over the parish and through a decree of Anselmo da Pusterla, have sought to possess the new campanile and have claimed the right to place bells in it."[143]

The reply of the canons was as follows: "First of all, we seek to have restored to us the campanile and bell and those things which we placed in

[143] Quod enim asserit se claves ipsius campanilis habuisse minime verum est. cum ille qui preest operi ipsius ecclesie. seu campanilis. quem superstantem dicimus. commissa sibi a populo nostre civitatis administratione. ipsas claves habebat. . . . Preterea quod altare maius mirabiliter constructum in quo condita sunt corpora predictorum martirum et prefati confessoris. sit sub cura et providentia abbatis eiusdem monasterii. ex lectione precepti dompni Angilberti bone memorie archiepiscopi qui prefati mirifici constructor exstitit. . . . Ad id vero quod prepositus dicit. canonicam ibi ante constructionem monasterii fuisse. eandemque perseverasse. abbas respondet canonicam ibi monasterii constructionis tempore non fuisse. sed ab archiepiscopo per Fortem diaconum eandem ecclesiam detentam fore. ex instrumentis Liutprandi regis tempore confectis. manifeste declaratur. Instrumentum vero quod tempore Desiderii longobardorum regis confectum. quem post Liuprandum fuisse constat. prepositus hostendit. ex scripture qualitate. et signorum varietate. et ipsius membrane novitate. falsum esse redarguimus et si falsi suspicione careret. canonicam tamen seu canonicos ibi fuisse non designat. Sed et si canonicam eo tempore ibi fuisse constaret. ex eo tamen quod predictus reverentissimus dompnus Petrus archiepiscopus monasterium construxit et totius ecclesie rectitudinem et dominationem cum possessionibus ibidem collatis aut conferendis ipsi abbati eiusque successoribus contulit. et canonice nullam mentionem habuit. canonicam in monasterium transtulisse convincitur. . . . Nuper vero Martinus prepositus una cum canonicis super oblatione et parochia campanili quoque novo quod per decretum Anselmi de pusterla sibi vindicabat. ideoque campanas in eo ponere sibi licere asservabat. (*Allegationes iuris* del monastero di S. Ambrogio presentate ai legati apostolici, cardinali Guido ed Ubaldo, nel 1144, printed by Biscaro).

the campanile, since the monks with the authority of the laity [that is, in consequence of the decree of the consuls] broke with violence the door of the campanile and took possession of it. . . . If indeed it be doubted that the canons own that campanile we solemnly affirm that for twelve years and more before the above-mentioned iniquitous decision, and up to the time of that, they possessed it in tranquillity, and of this fact the canons presented proper witnesses to the Lord archbishop. . . . From the argument it is evident that the church of S. Ambrogio which contains the bodies of the holy martyrs Protasio and Gervasio, from the time of its foundation to the establishment of the monastery in the time of Pietro, archbishop of Milan, had *officiales* who possessed jurisdiction over the church, and disposed of its goods as reason dictated. The *officiales* were not monks before the establishment of the monastery. Therefore they were canons, since there is no third class of clergy. From a deed of the time of Desiderio when the monastery had not yet been founded, it is evident that a *commutatio* was made by twelve priests, *officiales* of the above-mentioned church. Since a *commutatio* of the goods of the church was made by these twelve *officiales* it is clearly shown that we were not servants nor paid helpers of the ordinaries, as our opponents are accustomed to claim, but that on the contrary we had power and dominion over the church, since otherwise that *commutatio* would have had to be made by the ordinaries or at least with their consent. This same is clearly demonstrated by other documents of the time of Charlemagne containing deeds made to the canons or by the canons at a time when the monastery had not yet been founded . . . . . That the canonica was not abolished at the time of the foundation of the monastery is clear from deeds made to the canons and by the canons immediately after the foundation of the monastery or in subsequent times, and very frequently at different times during the reigns of Lodovico, Rodolfo, Berengario and other monarchs. Moreover, the lands, the treasure and the vestments which the canons of S. Ambrogio had before the foundation of the monastery, the successors of those canons possess in peace to this day. . . . The prevosto and other canons were formerly ordained by the archbishop. . . . The jurisdiction of the cemetery which it is proved has never been granted to any except those who have jurisdiction over the church itself, the canons still possess freely and in peace, and they appoint at their pleasure guardians and nuns to serve in the church, and the canons hold in their possession the keys of the altar. . . . Moreover we prove the above assertions not only by argument but by documents. It is declared that the canons have jurisdiction over the church in a privilege of Lord Arnolfo, archbishop, in whose times the monks first began to make undue claims, and presumed, contrary to custom, to celebrate divine offices in the above-mentioned church on feast days and Mondays. . . . Moreover we prove that the new campanile belongs to the canons by law and by right—by law, since it is erected in their cemetery, and what has been built upon land belongs to the owner of that land. We show that the campanile and the ground on which it stands belong to the canons by gift and by purchase; by gift, since Lord Anselmo, the archbishop, who had the right to give it both by the authority of the holy church of Milan and by the advice and consent of his brethren the ordinaries, gave the said campanile to the canons. . . . If the monks seek to prove by the privilege of Tadone, on which they lay great stress, that the canons of S. Ambrogio who now are, originated in his time, we show by documents and by logic that this privilege is false. By these documents it is absolutely proved the *officiales* of S. Ambrogio, before the time of Tadone, had the status and dignity of decumani in the above-mentioned church; while the priests introduced in the time of Pietro were never numbered among the decumani. For, from the time of S. Ambrogio the number of decumani in the church of Milan, was ever one hundred; nor was this number ever increased nor diminished; and the above-mentioned canons [of S. Ambrogio], as has been shown, were ever of this body. . . . Moreover what the monks are accustomed to assert, that the new campanile was built with the funds of the monastery, we denounce as false, since the architect of that church constructed it like the rest of the basilica at the expense of both chapters in common."[144]

[144] In primis restitutionem coclarii et campane ac earum rerum que per nos in ipso coclario posita erant petimus, quia monachi auctoritate laicorum ostio coclarii violenter fracto de eodem coclario se intromiserunt. . . . Si vero dubitatur, quod canonici ipsum campanile non tenuissent, in veritate affirmamus quod per duodecim annos et plus ante iam dictam fraudolentam conventionem usque ad ipsam quiete tenuerunt, et ex hoc testes idoneos domino archiepiscopo canonici presentaverunt. . . . De ratione constat, ecclesiam beati Ambrosii sanctissimorum martyrum Protasii et Gervasii corpora continentem a tempore hedificationis sue, usque ad institutionem Monasterii, tempore Petri mediolanensis archiepiscopi factam, officiales habuisse, qui dominium seu regimen ecclesie obtinerent, eiusque bona, prout ratio postulabat, disponerent; monachos officiales ante institutionem monasterii non habuit; canonicos igitur, cum tertium clericorum genus non inveniatur, quod instrumento facto tempore Desiderii cum nondum monasterium institutum esset in quo continetur, per XII predicte ecclesie presbiteros officiales possessionum eiusdem commutatio facta, manifeste probatur. Inde etiam quia per ipsos XII officiales possessionum ecclesie commutatio facta legitur; non eos, sicut pars adversa solet obicere, servientes ordinariorum seu mercenarios fuisse, sed potius dominium, seu regimen ecclesie habuisse, liquido ostenditur, quia si hoc esset, vel per ordinarios principaliter foret ipsa commutatio facta, vel eorum consensu. Hoc idem per alias cartas tempore Caroli, cum nondum monasterium esset, ad partem canonicorum, seu ex parte canonicorum factas certissime demonstratur. . . . Quod destructa non fuit patet per instrumenta statim post hedificationem monasterii ac postea sepissime sub imperatorum diversa tempora Lodoici, Rodulfi et Belengarii aliorumque regum ad partem canonice seu ex parte canonice facta, dum etiam possessiones, thesaurum, pallia, que ante monasterii hedificationem canonici beati Ambrosii habuerant, successores eorum canonici, qui modo sunt, in pace detineant. . . . Prepositus aliique canonici per archiepiscopum olim ordinati sunt. . . . cum cimiterii dominium, quod nunquam aliis invenitur fore concessum nisi eisdem ecclesie dominium obtinentibus, canonici libere ac pacifice teneant, custodes et monachas ad serviendum pro arbitrio suo constituant, claves altaris in sua potestate retineant. . . . Nihilominus autem

This last phrase is significant; other parts of the church had been constructed by the same architect as the campanile and hence not so very long before 1128.

It is worthy of remark that according to the allegations of the canons of 1144, at this time the canons (not the monks) possessed the keys of the golden altar.[145] In a decree of 1147 the archbishop Oberto ruled that the canons must open the golden altar for the monks on the feasts of SS. Gervasio and Protasio and of S. Ambrogio.[146]

If we are to believe several late and not over-trustworthy sources, the fabulous count Alico was buried in the sarcophagus beneath the ambo of S. Ambrogio in 1162.[147]

predicta sicut rationibus, ita et privilegiis comprobamus. Dominium, sive regimen canonicorum esse privilegio d. Arnulfi archiepiscopi declaratur; eius quidem tempore monachi superbire incipientes in festivitatibus ac secundis feriis divina officia in prefata ecclesia contra solitum presumpserunt. . . . Campanile vero novum, de iure et ratione canonicorum esse probamus. De iure quia in eorum cimiterio seu fundo consistit, et quod inedificatur, solo cedit; campanile, seu fundum eius canonicorum esse, donatione et emptione ostendimus; donatione quidem domini Anselmi archiepiscopi qui ius donandi habuit, ac sancte mediolanensis ecclesie auctoritate, nec non assensu et consilio omnium suorum fratrum ordinariorum, predictum campanile canonicis donavit. . . . Si enim privilegio Tadonis cui maxime innituntur, probare contendunt, clericos beati Ambrosii qui modo sunt, eiusdem temporibus originem habuisse, hoc falsum esse, scripto ac ratione ostendimus. . . . Per has quidem cartas necessario comprobatur officiales beati Ambrosii ante tempora Tadonis in predicta ecclesia statum ac dignitatem decumanorum habuisse et presbiteros a Petro abbate Tadonis tempore introductos, in decumanorum numero nequaquam assumptos fuisse. Cum enim a tempore beati Ambrosii decumanorum centenarius numerus, nec augmentatus nec imminutus fuerit, predictis canonicis in eodem numero, sicut ostensum est, perseverantibus. . . . Quod autem solent obicere campanile novum de propriis monasterii stipendiis hedificatum esse, falsum esse asserimus; cum eiusdem ecclesie architectus ipsum, sicut aliam ecclesie fabricam de communi construxerit. (*Allegationes iuris* della canonica di S. Ambrogio, presentate ai legati papali nel 1144, printed by Biscaro). Biscaro interprets the phrase 'de communi,' 'at the expense of the commune.' I prefer, however, the translation given above. For the function of the *ordinarii* in the church of Milan, see Arnulphi, *Hist. Med.*, I, 1, ed. Muratori, R. I. S., IV, 8; Galvanei Flammae, *Manipulus Florum*, ed. Muratori, R. I. S., XI, 570.

[145] Canonici . . . claves Altaris in sua potestate retineant. (*Codice della Croce*, MS. Amb. D. S. IV, 6/I, 6, f. 196). Biscaro interprets this passage as referring to the altar of the cemetery. See above, p. 565, for connection.

[146] *Ibid.*, 276. In 1144 the jurisdiction of the new parish, *ultra muscetam sita* (*Ibid.*, 202), was also disputed. Parochia quoque Canonicorum est, cum Monachorum, sicut prædiximus, iure prohibente, nullatenus esse valeat quia etiam ex quo institui, vel hædificari cępit ipsa Parochia per Presbyteros Ecclesiae Beati Ambrosii a parte illius Canonicæ divina habuit officia. (*Ibid.*, 196).

[147] Tunc instituit unum ducem in civitate, et quidem theutonicus, qui dictus est Alico, factus fuit vicarius super totam Ytaliam, qui post paucos dies obiit, et sepultus in sancto Ambrosio, ubi supra fuit sculptus in cupro deaurato, insuper habens aquilam auream positam sub puplito [*sic*], ubi cantatur epistola. (Galvanei Flammae, *Chron. Maius*, ed. Ceruti, 687).

Guillelmus de Pomo superstes huius eclesie hoc opus et multa alia fieri fecit,

MILAN, S. AMBROGIO

When Milan fell before Barbarossa, the canons, who appear always to have favoured, and to have been favoured by, the government of the commune, went into exile. This fact was testified to by a monk in the lawsuit of 1200.[148] For the five years and six weeks that this exile lasted, the basilica remained in sole charge of the monks, who doubtless took advantage of the opportunity to strengthen their position against the canons in every way possible.[149] The exile began in the middle of March, 1162. On the twentieth of February preceding, there was issued a decision in a fresh controversy between the canons and monks, which shows that the two clergies did not lay aside their internal feuds and dissensions even in the solemn and tragic hours which preceded the destruction of their fatherland. This controversy was between the superstans of S. Ambrogio, Gratiziano Peccora, and his *conversus* on the one side, and the prevosto and canons of S. Ambrogio on the other, in regard to the *modium et uinum, qdam Rigizo qui dicebatur Moxata, iudicauit predicto Labori unde lix erat.*[150]

The canons had not long returned from exile when new disputes arose between them and the monks. A bull of Alexander III, without chronological

hoc est scriptus super nauellum siue monumentum ubi legitur et cantatur supra euangelium et epistolam in eclesia sancti Ambrosij in Mediolani. (*Chronicon Mediolanense,* ed. Cinquini, 21). In nomine Domini. Hoc fuit tempore quod imperator Federicus habuerat civitatem Mediolani. Comes Alico qui erat vicarius dicti imperatoris in civitate Mediolani, quando fuit mortuus, positus in uno nauello, ubi cantatur evangelium et epistola sancti Ambrosij in civitate Mediolani, quod nauellum est super duobus leonibus. Et supra illud nauellum est una aquila, supra quam aquilam cantatur epistolam et euangelium et subter pedes illius aquile est dictus comes Alico intaliatus et sculptus in petra e supra scuniatum auro. Et istud nauellum est regum de Inglexio qui regebant totam Ytaliam et ibi fuit positus dictus comes Alico, occaxione non inveniendi amplius rationem nec ossa nec corpora dictorum regum de Inglexio. (*Ibid.*). Et qui comes Alico quando mortuus fuit, sepultus fuit in eclesia sancti Ambrosij in civitate Mediolani in uno nauello qui fuerat regum de Inglexio et in quo nauello sepulti fuerant septem reges de corona, omnes de Inglexio. Et illa corpora dictorum regum fuerunt extra dictum nauellum posita et dispersa et nescitur ubi deuenisset nec quod sit factum de eis. Et qui transmutauit dictum nauellum et multa remouit et etiam sculpiuit dictum comitem Alico in eodem nauello. Et qui hoc fecit, nominabatur magister Gullielmus de Pomo. Et supra dictum nauellum cantabatur euengelium et epistola in dicta eclesia sancti Ambrosij. (*Ibid.,* 23) . . . Ambrosii Mediolani venerabili ecclesie . . . ubi in sepulcro honorandissimo condam septem regum Anglerie nec non ducum atque comitum ipsius generosissime prolis corpora recondita fuerant supra quod nec non et evangelia usque hodie solempniter decantantur. (*Genealogia comitum Anglerie,* ed. Cinquini, 30).

[148] . . . tempore per quod Mediolanum stetit destructum, in quo non fiebant [a canonicis] alique misse in illa Ecclesia. (*Codice della Croce,* MS. Amb. D. S. IV, 12/I, 12, f. 49).

[149] Mediolanenses enim exierunt de Ciuitate in proximo medio martio et steterunt extra Ciuitatem quinque annis et sex septimanis. (Lawyers' arguments of 1190, *Codice della Croce,* MS. Amb. D. S. IV, 11/I, 11, f. 52).

[150] *Codice della Croce,* MS. Amb., D. S. IV, 9/I, 9, f. 7.

notes, but undoubtedly of 1174, confirms a decision of the bishop of Turin in regard to the unending controversy. The decision practically reiterates the previous decision of 1144, but goes on to rule that the monks should have everything to the south of a line drawn through the middle of the church, the canons everything to the north. This applied, not only to the church itself, but to the cemeteries by which it was surrounded, and the jurisdiction of which was especially disputed. Exceptional rulings, however, were made for the atrium (*cortina*) in front of the church, and the *domum laboris,* which apparently was situated in the cemetery to the west of the basilica.[151]

From a few words of one of the numerous lawsuits between the canons and monks, cited by Puricelli,[152] it is evident that the building of the campanile was interrupted by the dispute over its possession, and that the construction was resumed by the canons only about 1181. At the time of the lawsuit the new work could easily be distinguished from the old by the character of the masonry, and Puricelli remarks that even in his time the break in the masonry was easily distinguishable, as it is, indeed, to-day. This campanile, Beltrami has pointed out, was never finished, and the tradition that its upper part was destroyed at the time the castle was built is not founded upon fact. The belfry never existed, consequently, until it was added by the modern restorers.

From another text in one of the lawsuits we learn that in 1186 the basilica was magnificently adorned for the marriage of Costanza and Federico II. One of the witnesses remarked that it had not been similarly decorated for some time, because the galleries had been filled with the grain of the commune which was there stored.[153]

In 1190 a new judgment was rendered by Milo, archbishop of Milan, in the same controversy. The abbot had sought to enforce "that Pietro the cimiliarca should do or should cause to be done, those things which that cimiliarca himself and his predecessors had been accustomed to do for the abbot and his predecessors, that is, to adorn the pulpit when the monks of that monastery wished to ascend the pulpit to celebrate the divine mysteries, and that they should strip, or cause to be stripped, the altar on Good Friday when the deacon reads in the pulpit *diviserunt vestimenta eius, sortem mittens,* and that he should put out the fire, or should cause it to be put out when

---

[151] Amplius precipimus, ut cimiteria que sunt eidem eccle uersus aquilonem usque ad scm uitalem, uel in claustro canonicorum aut ante scam Mariam que dicitur greca omnifariam sint canonicorum etc. . . . Illud uero cimiterium quod est ante iam dictam ecclam uersus occidentem inter utramque portam circumseptum muris ubi dicitur in cortina, etc. . . . Domum autem laboris que ad iura parrochie canonicis in integrum assignamus, etc. . . . In cimiterio uero quod est extra cortinam uersus occidentem, idem ius seruetur etc. Dat. Anagnie III Idus Februarii. (*Codice della Croce,* MS. Amb. D. S. IV, 9/I, 9, f. 202).

[152] 1067.   [153] Giulini, IV, 23.

the deacon reads *Dominus emisit spiritum,* and that on Holy Saturday he should dress the altar or cause it to be dressed, when the deacon says *ecce iam ignis columna resplendet."* It appears that at this time the cimiliarca held the keys of the wardrobe in which were preserved the church vestments. The abbot goes on to petition that the prevosto should not hinder the cimiliarca or anyone else who had the keys of the wardrobe from adorning the altar with an antependium on the festivals of S. Ambrogio and of SS. Gervasio and Protasio. The cimiliarca, on the other hand, complained that the abbot had failed to furnish him the meal to which he was entitled, because of his services in opening the altar of S. Ambrogio, and on certain other occasions.[154] To appreciate the importance of this dispute, it is necessary to remember that the cimiliarca was a canon. One of the witnesses in the lawsuit speaks contemptuously of that canon who has himself called cimiliarca.[155] An ex-canon testified: *Aperui altare illud.* The fact that the altar was in the possession of the canons at this time and that it was kept closed, is abundantly proved by numerous passages of this document. In the lawyers' brief it is clearly stated that the canons possessed the keys of the altar as well as of *omnium paramentorum.*[156] When the canons returned from exile with the victorious Milanesi, they evidently succeeded in retaliating upon the monks and in obtaining possession of many of the disputed rights in the church. The decision of the lawsuit of 1190 did not affect any vital issues, but was confined to the question of the right of the monks to have the pulpit adorned for them on certain festivals, the right of the canons to be given certain feasts by the monks, and other similar disputes. The decision left the important points essentially *in statu quo,* the altar remaining in the hands of the canons. Nevertheless the canons appealed. It is interesting to note that one of the witnesses in this litigation testified that the pulpit of S. Ambrogio had existed for forty years and more. It therefore must have been erected before 1150.[157]

---

[154] Petebat abbas a jamdicto magistro Petro cymiliarca, ut faceret, uel fieri faceret ea que ipse cymiliarca et predecessores sui sibi et antecessoribus suis facere consueuerant scilicet uestire siue ornare pulpitum quando monachi illius monasterii uolunt pulpitum ascendere ad celebranda diuina misteria, et ut expoliet uel faciat expoliari altare in die ueneris sancti cum diaconus legit in pulpito diuiserunt uestimenta eius sortem mittens, et ignem extinguat uel extingui faciat cum diaconus legit Dns emisit spiritum, et in die Sabbi sancti uestiat uel uestire faciat altare cum diaconus dicit, ecce iam ignis columpna resplendet etc. . . . Iamdictus cymiliarca claues paramentorum ipsius eccle habet. . . . E contra prefatus Petrus cymiliarca postulabat quatinus iamdictus abbas in diebus statutis in quibus ei refectionem prestat propter aperturam altaris sci Ambr. quam illi fieri faciat in mensa iuxta eum faciat sedere ex parte dextra, et ut quinque refectiones, quas se non habuisse dicebat ei prestet. . . . Centesimo monagesimo die Sabbi tercio die marci indic. VIII. (Ms. cit.).

[155] Iussione illius canonici qui fecit se uocare cimiliarca. (*Codice della Croce,* MS. Amb. D. S. IV, 10/I, 10, f. 7).

[156] *Ibid.,* 11, f. 57.   [157] *Ibid.,* 10, f. 7; 11, f. 57.

A document of 1191 implies that the *laborerio* of S. Ambrogio was in the hands of the canons.[158]

About the year 1196 the vault of the eastern bay of the nave where is now the cupola, collapsed. "Under the abbot Ambrogio V (1185-1199), the church of S. Ambrogio in part fell. The restoration was commenced by the archbishop Oberto, 1195-1196, and was completed by Filippo, his successor."[159]

In the *Allegationes Juris*, without date but evidently later than 1190, since the decision of the archbishop Milo of that year is spoken of as iniquitous, and doubtless of c. 1200, occurs the phrase: "On that day the monks do not celebrate divine offices in the church of S. Ambrogio, because of the choir which unfortunately is without roof, but they celebrate the divine offices secretly in the church of S. Maria Greca, which belongs to them and is separated from the church of S. Ambrogio."[160] This fact is confirmed by passages in the lawsuit of the canons and monks of 1200. "Master Guido, monk of the monastery of S. Ambrogio, on Wednesday, the twentieth day of December,[161] was sworn and testified: . . . When the church of S. Ambrogio fell in part, the monks or their agents without the opposition of any one carried part of the stalls into the church of S. Satiro, and the rest they carried to a place near the altar. And when the restoration was finished, they brought back and replaced those stalls in their original position." The thirteenth witness testified: "I have served in the monastery of S. Ambrogio for more than twelve years . . . and when the cupola of the church was being restored I saw the stalls," etc. The choir-stalls, it should be remarked, were the work of Alberto of Paxiliano and were the subject of dispute between the canons and the monks. The fourteenth witness testified: "I saw carried and I myself helped to carry, a part of the stalls into the church of S. Satiro on account of the ruin of the basilica and the works of restoration. And when that restoration had been completed I saw the same stalls carried back by the agents of the monastery," etc. Witnesses in behalf of the monks were asked, "Whether the archbishop appoints the superstans, and, in case the superstans can not rebuild the church, whether the archbishop rebuilds it, and did in fact rebuild it." The first witness answered: "The superstans rebuilds the church with the funds of the archbishop, since the church and whatever the superstans

---

[158] . . . Mainfredus Oculiblanci, et Prepositus de Osinago et Jacobus de Labore Canonici suprascripte Canonice Sancti Ambrosii. (*Codice della Croce*, MS. Amb. D. S. IV, 11/I, 11, f. 72).

[159] Collapsa sub hoc Abbate ex parte Ambrosiana isthæc Basilica, cum ab Oberto primùm Archiepiscopo refici cepisset, à Philippo postmodum Successore absoluta est, & pristinæ integritati restituta. (Aresi, 27).

[160] . . . ea die in ecclesia Beati Ambrosii diuina non celebrant ofitia propter chorum, qui per nimium est in propatulo, imo secrete celebrant diuina ofitia in ecclesia Beate Marie Grece que eorum est et separata ab ecclesia sancti Ambrosii. (*Codice della Croce*, MS. Amb. D. S. IV, 10/I, 10, f. 32).

[161] The twentieth of December did, in fact, fall on a Wednesday in the year 1200.

has belongs to the archbishop." The eleventh witness replied: "I believe that the superstans is the agent of the archbishop, and I believe that if he has sufficient resources he rebuilds the church, but if he has not, the archbishop rebuilds it. And I saw that Archbishop Oberto rebuilt the church, and that Archbishop Filippo finished the restoration which his predecessor had begun." The eighteenth and nineteenth witnesses answered briefly: "The late Lord Oberto, the archbishop, rebuilt the church." The witnesses were then asked, "Whether many stones of the church of S. Ambrogio now are in, and were carried to, the church of S. Satiro when the church was rebuilt." The eleventh witness answered: "Yes, at the command of the superstans." The thirteenth: "Yes, the stones of the pulpit." The fourteenth: "So far as I know, no stones except those of the pulpit were carried into S. Satiro." The witnesses were then asked, "Whether the wall which the archbishop caused to be constructed beneath the cupola, is between the choir and the window, so that the wall shuts off all the light which used to come into the choir from the window." The first answered: "No, but the portico or roof shuts off the light." The seventh answered: "The wall which has been built beneath the cupola makes the choir dark and the portico shuts off the light from the pulpit." The twelfth witness answered: "The wall under the cupola does not shut off all the light, but only a part of it is between the window and the choir."[162]

Another witness in this same lawsuit testified that "the wooden structure which the abbot and the monks had presumed to place in the pulpit was destroyed by an agent of the canons, because it is not the business of the monks

[162] . . . Domnus Guido, Monachus Monasterij Beati Ambrosij, die Mercurij, tertiodecimo Kalendas Ianuarij iuratus dixit. . . . QVANDO ECCLESIA BEATI AMBROSII CECIDIT IN PARTE, tunc Monachi vel nuncij ipsius Monasterij, tulerunt sine contradictione alicuius partem Sedilium in Ecclesiam Sancti Satyri, & alteram partem tulerunt iuxta Altare. Et facto labore (*hoc est, Ecclesiæ in ea parte lapsæ reparatione*) restituerunt & reportauerunt ipsa Sedilia in pristina loca. . . . Duodecim anni sunt & plures, quòd vtor in Monasterio Beati Ambrosij . . . Et tunc QVANDO APTABATVR TIBVRIVS ECCLESIÆ, vidi eadem Sedilia etc. . . . Item vidi, & egomet adiuui portare partem ipsorum Sedilium in Ecclesia Sancti Satyri PROPTER RVINAM ET LABOREM ECCLESIÆ. Et facto labore ipso, vidi eandem partem Sedilium per nuncios ipsius Monasterij reportari etc. . . . Si Dominus Archiepiscopus ponit ibi Superstantem (aliter Superstite) &, si non potest reficere Superstans ille Ecclesiam, si Dominus Archiepiscopus reficit eam & refecit. . . . Superstans reficit de hauere (*hoc est, è facultatibus*) Domini Archiepiscopi; quia Ecclesia, & quantum habet Superstans, est Archiepiscopi. . . . Ego credo, quòd sit ibi Superstes per Dominum Archiepiscopum: & quòd reficiat Ecclesia, sicut potest. Et si non potest; Dominus Archiepiscopus reficit eandem Ecclesiam. Et vidi, QVOD ARCHIEPISCOPVS OBERTVS IPSAM ECCLESIAM FECIT APTARE, ET QVOD DOMINVS PHILIPPVS FECIT OPVS INCŒPTVM PERFICI. . . . QVONDAM DOMINVS OBERTVS ARCHIEPISCOPVS IPSAM REFECIT. . . . Si multi lapides Ecclesiæ Beati Ambrosij sunt & fuerunt portati in Ecclesiam Sancti Satyri, QVANDO REÆDIFICATA FVIT ECCLESIA BEATI AMBROSIJ. . . . Sic, de voluntate Superstitis. . . . Sic, Lapides Pulpiti. . . . Nescio, nisi de lapidibus Pulpiti . . . portali

to repair the pulpit or the church, but of the superstans who is appointed by the archbishop." When he was asked how he knew this he replied: "Because I saw the superstans who is at present in office repair that pulpit when it had been ruined, and I saw him cover that pulpit with scaffolding." Pietro Taverna, a clerk of S. Ambrogio, testified: "Since the monks had presumed to erect a wooden structure in the pulpit, I and Jacopo of the *fabbrica* and certain servants of the canons destroyed it, and before the dawn of day the superstans whose business it was, rebuilt it." Giovanni da San Ciro, a conversus of S. Ambrogio, testified: "I repaired the pulpit for the monks after the canons had destroyed it, but the superstans restored the pulpit as it now is."[163]

This lawsuit of 1200 was in many ways the most important of all those which raged between the monks and the canons. It is perfectly clear that at this time the canons held possession of the altar. The documents contain repeated references to the facts that (1) the altar was kept locked and (2) that the canons held the keys. The abbot and monks did not even venture to attack directly this right of the canons. They drove an opening wedge, however, by petitioning that the altar should be opened whenever the monks requested.[164] They even pushed this wedge a little further in claiming that the jurisdiction of the altar belonged to the cimiliarca, and that the cimiliarca was, or should be, appointed not by the prevosto, but by the archbishop. This really vital issue was masked under a quantity of minor contentions, which chiefly centered in the complaint that, owing to the alterations executed in the church, there was not sufficient light in the choir. Thus the abbot petitioned that all the trees which were back of the apse of the church of S. Ambrogio, should be removed because they obstructed the light for those celebrating the divine offices at the altar.[165] He also claimed that the light was obscured by

in Ecclesiam Sancti Satyri. . . . Si MVRVS, QVI EST SVB TIBVRIO, QVEM FECIT FIERI DOMINVS ARCHIEPISCOPVS est inter Choru̅ & illa̅ fenestram ita quòd ille murus remouet lumen totum, quod consueuit venire in ipsum Chorum ab illa fenestra. . . . Non: immò Lobia, seu tectu̅ illud remouet lumen illud. . . . MVRVS QVI FACTVS EST SVB TIBVRIO præstat obscurationem in Choro, & Lobia ad Pulpitum. . . . No̅ remouet totu̅ lumen; sed PARS IPSIVS MVRI DE TIBVRIO est inter fenestra̅ et Chorum, & non in totu̅ . . . (Puricelli, 1111 ff.).

163 per nuntios canonicorum diruptum fuit hedificium ligneum quod abbas et monaci facere fieri presumpserunt in ipso pulpito, quia ad abbatem vel monacos non pertinet reficere pulpitum vel ecclesiam, sed ad superstitem ecclesie, qui ibi ponitur per d. archiepiscopum. Interr. quo modo scit. R. quia vidi superstitem qui modo est, facere reficere ipsum pulpitum quando diruptum fuit et supra pulpitum facere cohope-rire de cuppis. . . . Quia monaci presumpserunt facere laborem ligneum in pulpito, ego et Jacobus de labore e quidam servitores canonicorum ipsum destruximus, et antequam dies venerit, superstes, cuius officium erat, ipsum reficere fecit. . . . Ego pro monacis ipsum pulpitum aptavi, postea ipsum destruxerunt canonici ecc. quod pulpitum ut modo est, superstes aptare fecit . . . (Cit. Biscaro).

164 MS. cit., Vol. 12, ff. 11, 37.

165 . . . ut remouerant vel remouere faciant omnes arbores quas habent post

wooden frames filled with glass placed in the windows; by a portico erected
on the north side of the church, obscuring the windows towards the canonica;
and by a wall erected between the choir and the side aisles. In reply the
canons stated that they had nothing to do with the reconstruction of the church,
which was superintended by the superstans appointed by the archbishop.
They furthermore stated that the trees behind the apse, the portico over the
north windows, the wall between the choir and the side aisles, and the glass
in the windows, had existed for two hundred and fifty and more years, that is,
in other words, that the church had been rebuilt after the disaster of 1196,
precisely as it had been before.[166] From this important text, therefore, we
learn that the apse had been built more than two hundred and fifty years
before 1200, that is to say, before 950. Witnesses were examined in detail
in regard to the lighting of the church.[167] The documents of this lawsuit
contain several references to the atrium, which is always called *cortina*, and
refer to it as being used for a cemetery.[168]

Biscaro cites also the testimony of the prevosto Martino Corbo, who
testified that he was sixty-six years old, and had been ordained in the apse
because of the wooden scaffolding that was at that time beneath the cupola.
The witness was born in 1134. Biscaro argues that he must have been ordained
about 1150 and that consequently the church must have been in construction
at that time. The argument is specious. There is no reason to suppose that
Martino was ordained before 1196, when, as we know, the cupola was in
construction.

That the pulpit was rebuilt after 1196 is proved not only from several
passages in the records of the lawsuit of 1200-1201 cited above, but from an
inscription on the existing ambo. This states: "Guglielmo de Pomo, superstans of this church, caused this work and many others to be executed."[169]
Guglielmo de Pomo came into office after 1199, since at this date Ottone de

---

tribunal beati Ambrosii quia similiter luminibus obsunt et super altare beati Ambrosii
offitia diuina celebrantibus. (*Ibid.*, 12, f. 11).

[166] . . . quod Superstes reficit Ecclesiam Beati Ambrosii et pulpitum. Item
ponunt quod Superstes ipsi ecclesie ponitur ibi per Dominum Archiepiscopum. (*Codice
della Croce*, MS. Amb. D. S. IV, 12/I, 12, f. 17). . . . Item ponunt, quod fenestre que
sunt in tribunali sancti Ambrosii fuerunt obdurata de uitro et lignis, et quod arbores
que sunt post ipsum tribunal, et presertim murus illa que ibi est modo per quinquaginta
annos et CC amplius ibi fuerat. (*Ibid.*, f. 18).

[167] Inter. Si fenestre que sunt post Altare consueuerunt esse ibi . . . . . de vitro
et lignis. Rx. Quod in parte vidit ibi de vitro et lignis et in parte non. Inter. Si ex
longo tempore retro non consueuerunt inesse arbores ille, uel alie similes, et maxime
mvrus illa, que modo ibi est. Rx. Sic. (*Ibid.*, f. 38-39).

[168] *e.g.*, *ibid.*, f. 40.

[169] ✠ GVILIELMVS : DE POMO : SUPERSTES
      HVI' : ECCLE[SIE] : HOC : OPVS : MVLTAQ; : ALIA :
      FIERI : FECIT : —

Arena was superstans. He was in office in 1204, and continued to be superstans as late as 1212. The pulpit was, therefore, restored after 1199, and it is altogether probable that the superstans awaited the completion of the more necessary repairs to the vaults before beginning work on the church-furniture.[170] Biscaro has conjectured, and I doubt not correctly, that the wooden structure in the ambo referred to by the witnesses in the lawsuit, was a temporary pulpit erected to serve while the stone ambo was being restored.

According to Puricelli[171] the crypt was constructed in 1233, but this statement appears to have been ventured on no better authority than that of the historian Corio, who deduced as much from the escutcheons of his family which were there to be seen as late as the XVI century. Corio's heraldry, however, is not above suspicion of inexactness, and even if it be true that the crypt was restored at this time, it is exceedingly improbable that it was then built anew.

In a fresh lawsuit of 1254 between the monks and the canons there was a dispute as to which of the two chapters must bear the expense of a new restoration of the ambo. The monks claimed that this should be borne by the canons since it had been destroyed by violence through their fault.[172] In the same lawsuit it is mentioned that part of the gold of the Palio d'Oro had been stolen twenty years before, and that the altar was still unrepaired.[173] In 1292 an attempt was made to remedy the bad lighting of the choir complained of a century before, by enlarging the central window of the apse.[174] In 1337 the Palio d'Oro was again damaged.[175] Before this date the western vaults of the nave were being covered with frescos.[176] In 1399 the chapel of San Pietro was in construction.[177] Two years later the abbey was given in commendam, and in 1441 the Benedictine monks were replaced by Cistercians, but in consequence of new disturbances the Benedictines were soon reinstalled.[178] The existing choir-stalls were executed about 1471.[179] In 1478 the lead of the roof of the church, which had been melted, was replaced at an expense of three hundred golden crowns.[180] The northern portico, designed by Bramante,[181] was begun in 1492, but was never completed owing

---

[170] Biscaro conjectures he awaited the decision of the lawsuit of 1200-1201.

[171] *Dis. Naz.*, 562.

[172] Peticiones monachorum, ecc., item quod reficiant [canonici] pulpitum ipsorum culpa destructum vel violatum, cum debeant custodire ecclesiam. (Cit. Biscaro).

[173] Biscaro.   [174] Biscaro.   [175] Biscaro, 73.

[176] me faciente depingi voltas anteriores que sunt penes ianuam mastram que est de arcipresso et quas voltas faciebam depingi ad petitionem domni Venture etc. (Biscaro, *Note e doc. Santa.*, II, 59).

[177] *Arch. Stor. Lomb.*, Anno XXV, 1898, 214.

[178] Puccinelli, 379-380.   [179] Biscaro, *op. cit.*

[180] Ratti, *Misc.*, 124. Biscaro says that this event took place in 1486.

[181] Biscaro.

to the fall of Lodovico Sforza in 1497,[182] although on July 2 of that year stones were ordered from Lago Maggiore for use in the construction.[183] Towards the end of the XVI century the Palio d'Oro was damaged by certain of the canons who attempted to steal some of the precious metal.[184] In 1507 the choir was moved from under the cupola to the apse. At this time was removed a solid wall separating the apse from the nave.[185] In 1589 there was a new theft of a part of the golden altar, but the missing slabs were replaced later by the chapter.[186] In 1630 the atrium was restored by the archbishop Federico Borromeo,[187] and many of the existing capitals date from this epoch. This restoration was altogether an exceptional one for the barocco period, in that a conscientious attempt was made to preserve the style of the ancient architecture. So successful were the restorers in their aim, that at first glance it is not easy to distinguish the capitals remade at this period from the original ones. In 1637 a commission composed of experts on art decided that the ciborio was a work of the IX century, and interpreted the inscription in the apse mosaic: *Angilberto, Karoli Ludovico, fecit Frater Gaudentius*(!).[188] In the XVIII century the Benedictine monks were definitely replaced by the Cistercians,[189] and the archbishop Odescalchi covered the walls of the church with whitewash and stucco. The cupola had already been decorated by S. Carlo. In 1797 the lead was again stripped off the roof.[190] In the following year both the monastery and the chapter were suppressed, but in 1799 the chapter was re-established,[191] and continued in existence until 1866, when it was again suppressed. In 1874 the chapter was re-established.

During the XIX century the basilica was subjected to a long series of so-called archæological restorations, which were disastrous in the highest degree, and which must be studied in detail to comprehend the original architecture of the structure. These restorations began in 1813 when the nave pavement was torn up and remade. Numerous inscriptions, most of which are now placed in the atrium of the church, came to light. The church, however, continued in the main undamaged until 1856, when was begun what eventually amounted to a reconstruction of the edifice. The restoration was at first directed by a commission appointed by the Austrian government and composed of Federico Schmidt (soon succeeded by Giuseppe Pestigalli), Luigi Bisi and Giovanni Brocca. The architect was Roberto Savoia. The first measures taken were to alleviate the humidity by drainage and to examine the foundations and renew them in part. The restorers next proceeded to attempt to rebuild the edifice in the form which they conceived it had in the Lombard period. The guiding spirit in these restorations was that of the parish priest

---

[182] Caffi. In 1566 nine other columns, besides the twelve still in place, were lying in the cloister. (Biscaro).

[183] *Arch. Stor. Lomb., loc. cit.* [184] Biscaro. [185] Latuada, IV, 292.

[186] Biscaro. [187] Torre, 177. [188] Puricelli, 113. [189] Rotta, 118.

[190] Ferrario, 89. [191] *Ibid.*, 30; Forcella, *Chiese*, 656.

Rossi. He it was who obtained from the emperor an annual subsidy for the restoration of the edifice, and his authority often prevailed over that of the government commission, with which he was in frequent conflict. Although actuated by motives which to him doubtless appeared laudable, Rossi regarded the basilica as his own private property which he was at liberty to change or rebuild at the dictates of his personal taste. In 1860 the Italian government superseded the Austrian, but the subsidy for the restoration was continued. In 1865 the most disastrous part of the restoration was completed, but work still continued throughout the XIX century. In the last quarter of the century Landriani obtained entire direction of the restoration, which he carried out in a manner somewhat less barbarous than that of Rossi.

From this restoration the church emerged quite a different structure. The intonaco was stripped off the nave in 1861. In 1864 the principal apse which, according to Rossi, "had lost its original lines, so that it was scarcely possible to restore it even on paper," was rebuilt. The barocco windows were replaced by new ones of Lombard style. The two absidioles which had disappeared were rebuilt on the traces of the original foundations (1864). The transverse arch, erected at the end of the XII century at the eastern end of the choir, to reinforce the vaults, was removed, as was also the wall erected at the same epoch on the south side of the crossing to reinforce the cupola. This is doubtless the wall referred to in the lawsuits of 1201-1203. The ancient transverse arch of the choir was rebuilt and reinforced with chains and tie-rods. In the drawings of De Castro may be seen the vertical wall above the transverse arch of the choir as well as above the other arches of the church. All these have since disappeared. The arches opening on to the side aisles from the gallery, which had been walled up to secure the stability of the edifice, were reopened. A new crypt was built under the altar. The triumphal arch of the choir was remade, as were the vaults and wall of the choir and the vaults of the two eastern bays of the side aisles and of the galleries. "Since the half columns of the triumphal arch had been crushed by the settlement of the masonry from above, it was necessary to remake the arch and the sculptures of the capitals, and to give again to these broken limbs their original stability."

In the restorations of the cupola traces of the ancient Lombard cloistered vault and of its masking wall came to light. The restorers planned at first to erect in place of the barocco cupola which they demolished a rib vault, but this idea was abandoned, and a Lombard cupola erected. At the time of the restoration, Landriani was convinced that this bay was originally covered not by a cupola or a rib vault but by a wooden roof, since the walls appeared to him too thin to support a vault. The form of the cupola with its Renaissance lantern and barocco decorations as it was before the restoration, may be studied in the drawings of De Castro. On the exterior wall of the cupola came to light a painted inscription which Rossi read

MILAN, S. AMBROGIO

```
. . . . . SS. . . . . .
FAB
S. AM C
```

and interpreted

```
SUPERSTES
FABRICAE
S. AMBROSII CURAVIT
```

The eastern gable of the basilica, which rose above the roof and in part hid
the cupola, was demolished. In 1870 the ciborio was raised perpendicularly
to the level of the new pavement. The columns of this ciborio had up to this
date been at a level lower than that of the piers of the church, and its axis
did not correspond with that of the existing basilica. The piers of the church
were restored and especially that one against which the old organ had been
placed was entirely remade. Various pieces of sculpture which have since
disappeared came to light. Among others was one with the inscription:

```
ARDERI
CUS PUER
ME FECIT[192]
```

The eastern vault of the nave had been rebuilt after 1196 with two oblong
rib vaults with pointed arches. In 1866 these vaults, of great archæological
value since among the earliest dated examples of the Gothic style in Italy,
were destroyed, and a new vault like those of the western bays of the nave was
erected. The central vault of the nave was almost entirely reconstructed,[193]
and the western one much restored. The pointed transverse arches, erected
after 1196 to reinforce these vaults, were demolished, together with the piers
which supported them. The vaults of the side aisles were rebuilt rather than
restored. The vaults of the galleries appear to have fared little better. The
foundations of the ancient southern wall, destroyed when the barocco chapels
were made, were discovered, and the wall was in part rebuilt so as to make
the chapels as little conspicuous as possible. The altars of the chapels on the
north side were suppressed, and the chapels themselves remade in pseudo-
Romanesque style. The barocco balustrade of the triforium gallery was
removed, and an iron rail substituted. New windows were opened at the west
end of the gallery.

At the end of the XIX century a new belfry was added to the Campanile
dei Canonici. The second story of the narthex had evidently begun to menace
ruin at an early date. Pointed transverse arches had been added to strengthen
the vault, and two of the arches opening out on the atrium had been walled up.
A heavy cornice had been added to the atrium in 1630. These objectionable
features were all removed, but to avoid the ruin which was threatening, it

[192] Rossi, 168.   [193] Rossi, 183.

was considered necessary to rebuild the vaults and to tie them to the façade by means of chains and rods. The lintels of the north and south portals were remade, but the fragments of the original ones are still preserved in the wall of the atrium. The capitals of the portals were restored but it appears for the most part conscientiously.

Before leaving the subject of the history of S. Ambrogio, a word should be said upon the chapel of S. Satiro. The structure of this oratory is obviously more ancient than that of the present church of S. Ambrogio itself. Moreover, although it is now connected with the church of S. Ambrogio, the chapel of S. Satiro is situated some little distance to the south. In consequence of this, it was conjectured by Puricelli[194] that the chapel is part of the ancient basilica of Fausta, mentioned in the letter of S. Ambrogio cited above.[195] The basilica of Fausta was founded at an early date by a certain Castritiano.[196] It was situated near the church of S. Ambrogio, as is known not only from the letter of the patron saint, but from the mosaic of the apse of S. Ambrogio, in which the two basilicas are represented side by side. Galvaneo della Fiamma, it is true, identified the basilica of Fausta with the church of S. Vitale,[197] and there is nothing to prove that this identification was not correct. The church of S. Satiro was until the XIII century not connected with the basilica of S. Ambrogio.[198] The chapel was restored and probably added to the church by the abbot Guglielmo Cotta.[199]

[194] 235.   [195] Page 540.

[196] Puricelli, 7. Exoratus namque vir sanctissimus [Castricianus] a christiana plebe, duas iterum haud longe a praefata ecclesia, quam ipse olim sacraverat [i.e., Phillipi, first church of Milan], orationis aedes benedixit, ac salutari nomine confirmavit; quarum impensas duo clarissimi apud Caesarem, et apud Christum Philippi filii, nec moribus patris, nec opibus, nec vita honesta degeneres, sumptibus utrimque propriis abundantissime suffecerunt, alteram Portianam, alteramque Faustam suorum cognomento nominum appellantes. (Datiana historia, ed. Biraghi, 40).

[197] Constructo jo templo Saluatoris, faustus filippi filius cõstruxit eccl̄iam fausti in uinea ubi pro xp̄i fide po̅ea fuit int'fectus. Ista ecca d̅r n̅uc sc̄ti vitalis ubi usqm hodie miraculu̅ magnu̅ appet. qa ibi nec aranea, nec auis aliqᵃ po̅t [ha]bitare. (Galvaneo della Fiamma, Cronaca, Vienna MS. 3318, f. 21, Cap. LXXXIX). Ecclesia Faust, id est Sancti Vitalis . . . (Galvanei Flammae, Manipulus Florum, ed. Muratori, R. I. S., XI, 562). This identification is accepted by Torre (185). The church of S. Vitale, demolished by S. Carlo, was, like S. Satiro, situated to the south of S. Ambrogio, "fra la chiesa di S. Valeria e la porta del monastiero di S. Ambrogio," says Villa (52). The position of the church of S. Vitale is also indicated by a will of April 27, 1184. (Ego . . . Petrus Presbiter, et offitialis Ecclesie Sanctorum Martirum Vitalis et Agricole site iusta ecclesiam sancti Ambrosii.—Codice della Croce, MS. Amb. D. S. IV, 10/I, 10, f. 116) and by a deed of sale of April 3, 1185 (ecclesie sancti Vitalis site prope ecclesiam Sancti Ambroxii de Mediolano.—Ibid., 147).

[198] A will of 1022, published by Giulini, VII, 50, contains the phrase: Ob hoc volo . . . ut prædictis casis . . . deveniant in iure et potestatem Ecclesiæ Beati Christi Confessoris Satyri, que est constructa foris, et iuxa Ecclesia Sancti Ambrosii, ubi ejus Sanctum quiescit Corpus . . . and in Landulphi Junioris, Hist. Med., 22, ed. Muratori,

The chapel of S. Satiro suffered more than any other portion of the basilica in the XIX century restorations. The mosaic was restored by Biraghi in a manner which was bitterly complained of by Landriani.[200] Excavations were made to the west of the existing chapel with the result that traces of foundation walls were discovered, justifying the inference that the existing chapel is merely the apse of a small church which formerly existed. The cupola was found to be constructed of hollow terra-cotta cylinders fitted one into the other. The masonry thus resembled that of the cupolas of the churches of Ravenna.[201] The angles of the dome were supported on wooden beams which in the course of centuries had disintegrated, and which it was found necessary to replace by new stone and brick. In 1863 the apse of the chapel was reconstructed. "Finally to omit nothing of note before leaving the subject of this chapel, I shall speak of the altar which we have there erected. In reality it is anything but new, being composed of beautiful slabs of white marble gracefully sculptured in very ancient style and which obviously belonged to an altar. I found them here and there in the walls of the atrium and of the church, and they appeared to me entirely suitable for their present use, so that I did not hesitate to have them fitted together and to supply what was lacking."[202] The apse mosaic of this chapel is entirely modern and an invention of the restorers. The original condition of the mosaics of the cupola and their inscriptions may be studied in the work of Ferrario,[203] who saw them before the restoration.

III.   The basilica of S. Ambrogio comprises portions erected at various dates. Probably the oldest part now visible is the chapel of S. Satiro. This includes at present a single square bay surmounted by a dome. No attempt is made to soften the transition by means of pendentives. To the east is a modern apse erected on the traces of the ancient foundations and below is a crypt. Excavations have shown that the original church comprised three aisles of nearly equal width and extended much farther than the existing edifice to the west. The walls are composed of flat bricks like those of S. Salvatore at Brescia (Plate 35, Fig. 1).

Beneath the existing nave there was discovered in 1813, 1857 and 1869 the foundations of an earlier church the plan of which has been published by Landriani. This church comprised three aisles separated by thirteen pairs of irregularly spaced columns. One of the bases is still visible beneath the ambo, the others have been covered up. The masonry of the foundations, to judge from the description of Landriani,[204] appears to have been of Roman character, and the profile of the bases was symmetrical. The diameter of

R. I. S., V, 493, we read: Sancti Confessores Castus, & Polimius Diacones Sancti Ambrosii, quorum corpora jacent in Ecclesia Sancti Victoris ad Coelum aureum, quæ nunc dicitur Ecclesia Sancti Satyri sita juxta Ecclesiam Sancti Ambrosii.

[199] Ferrario, 174.   [200] 42.   [201] Rossi, 19.   [202] Rossi, 20.

[203] 178 ff.   [204] 26, and Rossi, 13.

these columns was approximately the same as that of the Corinthian column which now stands in the piazza to the north of the atrium, and it is not impossible that this may have come from the basilica.[205] In 1857 there was found not far from the old campanile a fragment of a porphyry column similar to those of the ciborio.[206] It is entirely probable that these fragments and the foundations of the columnar basilica all belonged to the edifice erected by S. Ambrogio at the end of the IV century.

The old Campanile dei Monaci rises to the north of the façade (Plate 120, Fig. 7). It is at present a plain rectangular structure with a belfry of severe simplicity, but such was not the original design.[207] The present upper story with belfry is a modern addition. In the story below on the east and north sides are still visible in the interior colonnettes and traces of ancient coupled windows. The capitals, which are of Corinthian type, and evidently pilfered, are supported on monolithic shafts, probably also pilfered. In the east window there is still preserved a stilt-block without decoration. There were similar coupled windows on the south and west sides, but they are less well preserved. The walls of the campanile, of enormous thickness on the ground floor, are lighter in the upper stories. In them are imbedded wooden chains; wooden lintels are also used for some of the windows. The brickwork (Plate 118, Fig. 4) is very different from that of the rest of the church, the bricks averaging 7 centimetres in thickness; the surface of the wall is not even, some bricks projecting from the surface plane, others receding. The courses are seldom horizontal. The mortar-beds in places are as much as $5\frac{1}{2}$ centimetres in thickness, while the bricks are sometimes as much as 28 centimetres in length. These bricks are not cross-hatched; many herring-bone and vertical courses are inserted.

That the existing choir is older than the nave, there is no room for doubt, and the fact has been admitted by all archæologists who have written on the church. Both in the nave (Plate 119, Fig. 3) and side aisles, the arches and vaults are lower in the choir than in the nave, and the masonry of the two portions of the edifice is entirely different in character. Unfortunately, the absidioles are modern and the choir and apse have been very much restored. The columns of the triumphal arch are in part ancient, and the original bases are still preserved below the existing pavement. The capitals and shafts, like those of the apse arch, however, are modern (Plate 119, Fig. 1, 3). The choir is covered by a barrel vault (Plate 119, Fig. 3), but the character of the masonry can not be studied because the soffit is covered with intonaco and the extrados is of modern concrete. The groin vaults of the side aisles are not

---

[205] This column has stood in its present position at least since the XIV century, as it is mentioned by Galvaneo della Fiamma. (*Chron. Maius*, ed. Ceruti, 524).

[206] Rossi, 18.

[207] Puricelli has published an ancient drawing of this campanile (reproduced by Romussi), but it is so inexact as to be of little service in determining the original form.

domed. These have been remade, but the original form is probably preserved. Although the brick masonry of the apse (Plate 117, Fig. 5) is not quite so rough as that of the old campanile (Plate 118, Fig. 4), the horizontal lines of the masonry are not well maintained, and there are numerous herring-bone and vertical courses. The bricks often seem to be broken and were therefore probably taken, at least in part, from an earlier edifice. Some few are cross-hatched, but these were added in some restoration. The great majority have a fairly smooth and ungrooved outside finish. The size and shape are very irregular, the length of the exposed surface varying from 6 to 30 centimetres and the depth from 6 to 10 centimetres. The mortar-beds average about 2 centimetres.

The main body of the basilica consists of a nave of four double bays (Plate 116), two side aisles surmounted by galleries (Plate 118, Fig. 3), and Renaissance chapels. The side aisles are covered by highly domed groin vaults, the three western bays of the nave by rib vaults, and the eastern bay by an octagonal cloistered vault carried on arched squinches (Plate 119, Fig. 3, 4). It has been supposed that the eastern bay of the nave was originally covered by a rib vault similar to the others in the nave, and certainly there is nothing in the plan of the lower part of the basilica to indicate that the original architects expected to erect a cupola at this point (Plate 116); but in the present state of the edifice it is impossible to determine this question with certainty. At all events in 1196 the vault of this and the bay adjoining to the westward, fell, and a cupola similar to the one erected by the restorers was constructed on the eastern bay and two oblong rib vaults in the bay adjoining to the west. The existing cupola (Plate 117, Fig. 6) seems to be a fairly accurate restoration in which the restorers appear to have followed with intelligence the traces of the original construction. It is greatly to be regretted, however, that, as has been already stated, the Gothic rib vaults of the bay adjoining were destroyed and replaced by the present modern vaults. The rib vault of the second bay from the west is almost entirely modern also, so that only the vault of the western bay preserves its original structure, and even this has been very much restored. Moreover, the extrados has been covered with concrete, and the soffit with intonaco, so that it is impossible to study the masonry. The extrados of all the vaults of the nave is at present supplied with a complicated system of projecting ribs, but these appear to be entirely modern. The vaults of the side aisles and galleries have also been much restored in the few cases in which they have not been entirely remade. The original forms are doubtless preserved, but it is now impossible to determine the character of the masonry.

Although there is no clearstory, the roof of the church at present does not have a continuous slope. This roof in timber is obviously modern. What the original disposition was, it is now impossible to say. Over the transverse arches of the gallery vaults are spur walls. These, it is true, are for the most part modern, but there survive unmistakable traces of the ancient ones, which were probably lower than the existing buttresses and did not project above the roof. Those which abutted against the alternate piers doubtless had the function of strengthening the walls against the thrust of the great vaults of the nave. Spur buttresses, however, were erected not only opposite the alternate but opposite the intermediate piers. They may therefore have also had the function of supporting the roof of the gallery. The ancient roof was without doubt lower than the present one and in all probability of continuous slope. Before the restoration pediment-like walls existed over the transverse arches of the nave vaults. It may therefore well be that originally the roofing lay directly upon the transverse walls erected over the vaults of nave and galleries. It is evident that originally the north wall of the church terminated in a cornice of arched corbel-tables placed at about the level of the summit of the longitudinal ribs of the gallery vaults, since this cornice is still preserved intact in a portion of the original wall still existing west of the Campanile dei Canonici and in a room adjoining the eastern chapel on the north side. Tiles apparently coming from a similar corbel-table destroyed to make a modern skylight, are piled in one of the rooms over the southern chapels.

In a room adjoining the eastern chapel on the northern side may also be seen the original buttresses. They are salient and vigorous and alternately rectangular and prismatic, as shown on De Dartein's plan. At a subsequent epoch, doubtless 1196, these buttresses were made over. The prismatic ones were made rectangular and equal to the others, with which they were connected by heavy arches cutting across the ancient corbel-tables. As thus altered, the buttressing in the nave was analogous to that which still exists in the atrium. The side walls were further reinforced by an ingenious system of internal buttressing. The responds are made alternately heavy and light, corresponding to the alternation of the system (Plate 116).

The system of the nave comprises a separate member to carry each of the vaulting shafts (Plate 116; Plate 118, Fig. 3; Plate 119, Fig. 3, 4). The compound piers show considerable variation in size and section, but always have a separate member to support each of the archivolts which falls upon them (Plate 118, Fig. 2; Plate 119, Fig. 3). From the abaci of the intermediate piers rises a little system which supports an arched corbel-table at the level of the triforium (Plate 118, Fig. 3). The southern porch to the east of the old campanile is ancient. The groin vault is still the original one, and undamaged by modern restorations, since it retains on the soffit frescos of the Renaissance.

The bricks of which the nave was constructed were cross-hatched and laid in courses for the most part horizontal, though considerable herring-bone work is employed. The bricks resemble those of the atrium but are somewhat flatter, running from 4 to 7 centimetres in depth. The masonry beds are also somewhat flatter than those in the atrium, and average about 1½ centimetres.

In the façade is inlaid a piece of checker-board polychromatic masonry, and there are also several similar pieces in the side walls of the church.

The façade (Plate 117, Fig. 2) rises considerably above the vaults and also probably above the line of the original roof. The nave is preceded by a narthex in two stories, of which the lower still preserves its original rib vaults, but the groin and barrel vaults of the upper were entirely remade in the restoration. When the pointed sustaining arches were removed, the two end arches opening to the west were freed of the wall which had encumbered them, and the piers were in great part rebuilt. Above the vaults under the present roof there may be seen in the west wall the traces of ancient arches, two over each of the galleries and eight over the nave. These were all walled up in the Lombard period, possibly at the time that the atrium was constructed.

The atrium consists of a rectangular court, surrounded by groin-vaulted porticoes (Plate 116). It is certain that the church was completely finished before the atrium was constructed, and, indeed, that the atrium is an after-thought and no part of the original plan. The exterior wall of the atrium does not continue the line of the south wall of the church (Plate 118, Fig. 1), but it joins the latter with a clumsy jog in plan awkwardly concealed by a buttress. Moreover, the piers of the atrium are built against the pilaster strips of the old façade which may still be seen underneath, and the roofs cut across the arched corbel-tables of the basilica.

The groin vaults of the atrium are highly domed and supplied with wall ribs. They have, however, almost without exception been restored, and the roof is modern. The piers are quatrefoiled (Plate 116), and resemble the intermediate piers of the nave. From their abaci rises a little system which supports the restored arched corbel-tables of the cornice (Plate 118, Fig. 5; Plate 119, Fig. 2; Plate 120, Fig. 6, 7; Plate 122, Fig. 1). The responds comprise five members (Plate 116).

The exterior wall is reinforced by vigorous rectangular buttresses (Plate 116; Plate 118, Fig. 1, 6). At first glance there appears to be some reason to doubt whether these are contemporary with the atrium, since they seem to have been constructed entirely independently of the wall, and there is always a distinct break in the masonry between the buttresses and the wall. On careful examination, however, it appears that the brickwork is of precisely similar character, and the faces of the buttresses are frequently prolonged inside the wall. The buttresses must therefore be contemporary with the wall. In the west face of the atrium, and in the western bay of the north face, the buttresses are connected by blind arches (Plate 118, Fig. 6). The masonry of the atrium (Plate 118, Fig. 6, 7; Plate 120, Fig. 1) closely resembles that of the church, and consists of bricks with occasional blocks of granite or other stone inserted to form the capitals or bases, or introduced seemingly at haphazard into the masonry of the walls, especially in the lower parts of the buttresses. The bricks are almost invariably cross-hatched, and are of all colours, ranging from a dark yellow to a light red, although the latter shade predominates. They are laid in horizontal or in herring-bone courses. They show great variation of size, the exposed surfaces ranging from 21–65 x 5½– 6½ centimetres. The depth of the bricks averages about 6 centimetres and the mortar-beds about 2 centimetres. The walls are punctuated at frequent intervals with square scaffolding holes.

The Campanile dei Canonici (Plate 120, Fig. 6) dates from three different epochs, as may still be clearly seen in the masonry. The lower portion is of about 1128, the central part of about 1181, and the upper part modern. The masonry of the first is distinctly more advanced than that of the atrium, and there are no herring-bone courses. The masonry of the central part is almost as regular as modern work.

The crypt is certainly more modern than the apse, since it cuts across the bases of the columns of the triumphal arch. It has been entirely denatured during the Renaissance.

IV.   The earlier parts of the basilica contain little pure ornament. The palio of the altar of the chapel of S. Savina (the third chapel from the west on the south side) was part of an early Christian sarcophagus coming from the church of S. Francesco, and possibly represents Pilate washing his hands. The apse mosaic of the chapel of S. Satiro is modern, but the mosaic of the cupola, though restored, is an important monument of the early centuries. It represents the martyr Vittore (VICTOR) in a circular medallion. Below are six full-sized figures representing the saints Protasio (PROTASIVS), Ambrogio (AMBROSIVS), Gervasio (GERVASIVS), Felice (FELIX), Materno (MATERNVS) and Nabore (NAVOR). The inscriptions, thanks to the restorations of Biraghi, have lost all scientific value. The altar, as has been mentioned, is pieced together of various bits of Carlovingian carving, found in different parts of the basilica. In the chapel are several fragments of mosaic and opus sectile which recall those of S. Sabina at Rome.

Of the columnar nave no ornament is extant save the bases, and the column in the piazza, if indeed this latter came from the church. At all events it is certain that the edifice was constructed of pilfered Roman materials.

The apse is adorned externally by a cornice formed of blind niches in two orders surmounted by a saw-tooth moulding (Plate 117, Fig. 5, 6). The outer order of the niches is supported on very thin pilaster strips. The saw-tooth moulding appears to be modern, but may be a correct restoration. The choir is supplied with a cornice formed of arched corbel-tables in two orders, but this can not belong to the original construction. The interior of the apse is adorned with a large mosaic (Plate 119, Fig. 3), which shows Byzantine influence in the confusion of the composition, the hardness of the colours, the Greek inscriptions, the abundance of jewel-like ornament and the stiffness of the figures. It has unfortunately suffered very severely from restoration. In the centre is a seated Christ, bearded, with inscribed halo and bare feet, His right hand raised in benediction, and His left hand holding a book with the inscription: EGO S|VM LUX| MVNDI. Above is a Greek inscription: IC XC O BACHΛEVTIC ΔΩZH [208] On either side are two angels—to the right of Christ the Archangel Michael (XOPA MIXAHIΛ) bearing a crown and a sceptre, to the left Gabriel (XOPA ΓABPIHΛ), also with a rod, bearing the consecrated host on a paten which he holds with a napkin. To the right of the throne stands S[ANCTVS] PROTASIVS[209] bearing a cross; to the left, crowned, and also bearing a cross, is S[ANCTVS] GERVASIVS. Below the throne are three medallions with busts of SCA MARCELINA, S[ANCTVS] SATIRVS, SCA CANDIDA. In either corner is represented a scene depicting a miracle of S. Ambrogio. While celebrating mass at Milan the saint fell asleep at the altar and was transported by angels to Tours in time to celebrate the funeral offices for St. Martin. In the right-hand scene we see S[ANCTVS] ANBROSIVS standing by an altar placed under a ciborio. Near by is the ECLA FAVSTÆ. A deacon seeks to awake the drowsy doctor, while another cleric, who has finished reading the gospel in the ambo, looks on in astonishment. Beyond stand the people. Above are towers symbolizing the city of Milan, as is indicated by the inscription, MEDIOLANVM. The scene is framed by two palms. The symmetrical scene on the other side represents the funeral of St. Martin. The principal personages and the city of Tours are indicated by the inscriptions: TVRONICA, ANBPOCOIC, S[ANCTVS] MARTINVS. Around the lower part of the mosaic are three inscriptions, two of which are modern and added by Rossi.[210] Below this mosaic were formerly frescos of the bishops dependent upon the archiepiscopal see of Milan. During the restorations, some traces of imitation mosaic came to light on the apse arch.[211] It was in all probability on these traces that the present decoration was founded. Other mosaics and frescos were found behind the choir-stalls, and were carried to Rossi's house,[212] but have now disappeared.

In the centre of the apse is still preserved the ancient episcopal throne, said to be the very one of S. Ambrogio. There was a tradition in the Middle Ages that pregnant women could be delivered without pain if they could sit

---

[208] Signifying: Jesus Christ the King of Glory.

[209] The original head of this figure is now in the Museo Archeologico.

[210] The ancient reading of the third has been preserved by Millin (180), who saw it before the restoration:

> Martinus moritur sed vitæ dona meretur
> Tristatur mundus adjubilatque polus
> Mors sua digno bono fertur celebrata Patrono
> Spiritus Ambrosii dum famulatur ibi.

[211] Rossi, 98.   [212] Rossi, 156.

once in this chair.[213] The throne appears to be a typical example of church-furniture of the XII century, and bears the proud inscription:

✚ PRESVL MAGNIFICVS RESIDENS IN SEDE DECORVS
✚ SITV ROMANA VERO QVAE SEDE SECVNDA.

The capitals of the nave of S. Ambrogio (Plate 118, Fig. 2, 3; Plate 119, Fig. 3, 4; Plate 122, Fig. 2) are among the most important examples of Lombard decorative art. Great prominence is given to grotesque features, and a favourite motive is that of two animals having a single head which forms a sort of a volute. Other capitals are ornamented with leaf patterns of Corinthianesque type or with interlaces and rinceaux. It is exceedingly difficult to distinguish any chronological development in these capitals, but those at the east end of the church appear to be slightly earlier than the others. The bases are all of Attic type and supplied with griffes. The archivolts are in two orders and show polychromatic masonry (Plate 118, Fig. 2, 3; Plate 119, Fig. 3, 4; Plate 122, Fig. 2). In some cases, the extrados describes a higher curve than the intrados.

Several of the piers and pilasters are adorned with reliefs of crosses of either the Greek or Latin form. On the jamb of the central portal is a Greek cross with a sort of rope hanging down from it. Symmetrically placed on the other side is a bar. On the second respond from the east in the north gallery of the atrium is a Latin cross 70 centimetres high. There is a similar cross on the second respond from the west in the south side aisle. The decoration of the lower story of the narthex is even richer than that of the church. The portals are in several orders, moulded and covered with the richest decoration. Even the shafts are carved with interlaces. The grotesque elements here run riot. Queer beasts climb up and down the jambs or nestle among the foliage of the rinceaux. Only very occasionally do the figures seem to have any significance. In the central portal is a medallion with the figure of the Lamb, and in another an angel. A capital representing a man among lions and other beasts, holding in one hand a scroll and in the other a staff, may be intended to depict Daniel. Opposite are two flying angels (cherubim?) holding a wheel. To the north of the central portal, a man playing a harp, and a woman dancing seem to be a reminiscence of the Dance of David. Over the door leading from the church into the new campanile is a relief representing the vintage, a decadent Roman sculpture placed in this position in comparatively modern times.

The sculptures of S. Ambrogio were made in great part before the stones were laid. An interesting proof of this is to be found on one of the jambs of the central portal where the inscription, ADAM MAGISTER, is upside down. There is no doubt that this jamb which has been inverted, was made

[213] Puricelli, 282.

to be placed on the other side of the doorway. Adam was doubtless the name of the master who executed this particular jamb.

The church was doubtless originally covered with frescos. On the north side adjoining the choir is still preserved a charming figure called a deaconess. On the alternate pier on the western side is the Madonna, SCA MARIA FILIVS XPS. Below is a haloed bishop, doubtless S. Ambrogio, and a figure, probably a donor, BON'| AMIC'| TAVER|NA. On the soffit of the arch north of the altar are puzzling frescos and grotesques, now unfortunately damaged by the construction of a glass partition. They have been supposed to date from the IX century, but are, notwithstanding their crudity, more probably of the Renaissance. Ferrario,[214] in 1824, saw frescos representing the Seven Sleepers and the four virtues of Peace, Justice, Mercy and Truth, on the west wall. On one of the vaults of the nave there was discovered during the restorations a frescoed sunburst similar to that of S. Babila, that is to say, of the XIV century.[215] The frescos on the alternate piers must have been executed before the sustaining arches were added, shortly after 1196, since they were covered by these. It is, indeed, to this circumstance that the frescos owe their preservation.[216]

The present unsightly frescos of the nave are the work of Landriani, and reproduce others destroyed about the middle of the XIX century. Landriani believed that those destroyed were the ancient ones of the XII century. If his reproduction, however, be even approximately exact, they could not have been older than the XIX century, and were not improbably added in 1813.

In the wall of the narthex are inlaid several sculptures, obviously inferior works of the XIII century. One represents S. Ambrogio, another St. Paul[217] with the Evangelists Mark[218] and Matthew.[219]

Above the famous inscription of Ansperto is a highly coloured terra-cotta bust, dating, I believe, from the early XIII century, since its style is analogous to that of the ciborio. The saint is represented as haloed, and holding in his hands a book with the inscription, SANC|TVS| AM|BRO|SIVS. The border with eggs and darts is unique. Below is the inscription in Gothic characters:

EFFIGIES SANCTI HEC TRACTA EST AB IMAGINE VIVI
AMBROSII PIA, CLARA, HUMILIS, VEN'ANDAQ; CUNCTIS
ERGO GENU FLEXO DICAS O MAXIME DOCTOR
ALME PATRONE DEUM PRO NOBIS IUGITER ORA

[214] 89-90.   [215] Rossi, 27.

[216] Torre (179) speaks of frescos of the atrium which have since disappeared. My friend, Mr. Clement Heaton, informs me that decorative frescos of the façade which he sketched as recently as fifteen years ago have since been destroyed.

[217] Above is the inscription, ✝SCS.P . . . . . ; below the letters . . . . E PSALLENTES D . . . . .

[218] MARCVS EVANGEL . . . . .   [219] MATHEVS EVAG . . . . .

The ciborio (Plate 119, Fig. 3) is supported on four columns with capitals of the IX century (Plate 121, Fig. 3). The upper part in stucco (Plate 121, Fig. 2) is of later date, and consists of a miniature rib vault and four pediment-like gables. In each gable are stucco sculptures which show strong analogies to those of the ciborio of Civate (Plate 57, Fig. 2) and to the western portal at Lodi (Plate 104, Fig. 1). On the front face (Plate 121, Fig. 2) is represented Christ between the saints Peter and Paul. The halo of Christ is decorated with a series of billets, and the inscribed cross is indicated by various colours. Paul, bare-footed and bearded, stands to the right of Christ. To Paul, Christ gives a book, with the inscription:

AC|CIPE| LIB|RVM| SAPI|EN|TIA'

To Peter, at his left, he gives the keys. Both apostles receive the symbols of authority, holding a napkin over their hands. On the south pediment of the ciborio is represented the figure of an archbishop, with halo and book, undoubtedly S. Ambrogio. On either side are two strange figures of bearded men, with round caps. The significance of this much-discussed sculpture seems to be that the two men are the consuls of Milan, typical of the body of the citizens. S. Ambrogio is therefore represented as the patron saint of the city. It will be remembered that during the XII century the canons were closely allied with the government of the commune. On the opposite side of the ciborio is the standing figure of a female saint. Back of her head is a halo and from above descends a dove. This figure is usually identified as a Virgin, but it seems to me more probable that it represents S. Marcellina. On either side of the saint are represented two women, in the same position as the consuls on the opposite face. S. Marcellina, the sister of S. Ambrogio, is, therefore, in all probability here represented as the patroness of the women of Milan, as S. Ambrogio on the opposite face appears as the patron of the men. On the eastern pediment is represented S. Ambrogio standing between the two saints Gervasio and Protasio. Above is the figure of the Holy Spirit. The two martyrs present to the saint two clerics—I think undoubtedly canons—one of whom offers a model of the ciborio. It is evident that we have here to do with the unending dispute between the canons and the monks. The canons erected the ciborio and wished to preserve a record of this fact for use in any future controversy with their rivals. The ciborio, therefore, must have been erected at a time when the jurisdiction of the altar was in the hands of the canons. We have seen that the canons possessed such jurisdiction during the last half of the XII century, with the exception of the short time they were in exile. They possessed it, moreover, in the years immediately following the collapse of the vault in 1196, that is to say, in the years during which both the internal evidence of the style and the external evidence of documents lead us to suppose that the existing ciborio was erected. The ciborio of S. Ambrogio is the work of the same artist who executed the stucco decoration in Civate (Plate 57, Fig. 1, 2, 3, 4, 5) and Cividale (Plate 121, Fig. 4; Plate 57, Fig. 6).

The famous Palio d'Oro (Plate 122, Fig. 3; Plate 123, Fig. 1, 2; Plate 124, Fig. 1, 2) is ornamented with various reliefs of iconographic interest. In the centre of the western face is an oval medallion, with a seated Christ (Plate 123, Fig. 1). About Him are symmetrically disposed the symbols of the four Evangelists[220] and the figures of the twelve apostles (Plate 123, Fig. 1). To the left are the six following reliefs: (1) The Nativity. The Virgin is seated, Joseph raises his arms in prayer, and a shepherd comes running. (2) The Annunciation. The Virgin is seated to the right in an ædicule. The archangel stands before her. (3) The Presentation in the Temple. (4) The Miracle of Cana. (5) The Resurrection of Lazarus. (6) The Transfiguration. On the other side the story of the life of Christ is continued in six other scenes (Plate 123, Fig. 2): (1) The driving of the merchants from the temple. (2) The miracle of the healing of the blind man. (3) The Crucifixion, with John, Mary, the sponge-bearer, Longinus, and two angels. (4) The feast at Emmaus, with the Virgin in the seat of honour. (5) The Resurrection. (6) The Ascension. The last three scenes are barocco. On the ends of the altar are various figures of saints and angels. On one side (Plate 124, Fig. 2) Ambrogio (ABR), Protasio (PRO), Simpliciano (SIPL), Gervasio (GER), eight angels, and four deacon saints. On the other (Plate 124, Fig. 1), Martino (MART), Nabore (NABO), Nazaro (NAZA), Materno (MANV), four unnamed subdeacon saints, and eight angels.

In the centre of the eastern face (Plate 122, Fig. 3) are four medallions, of which the upper two represent the archangels Michael (SCS MICHAEL), and Gabriel (SCS GABRI), the lower two, the reliefs we have already described of S. Ambrogio and Angilberto and of the goldsmith Volvinio crowned by S. Ambrogio. On either side are scenes from the life of S. Ambrogio, all taken, with the exception of the miracle at Tours, from the biography of the saint by Paolino. In many cases the inscriptions are merely condensations of the text of the V century biographer. With the aid of this text, therefore, and of the inscriptions, the scenes are readily identified. (1) VBI EXAM APV PVERI OS COPLEVIT ABROSI. Paolino tells us that when S. Ambrogio was a baby he was one day placed in his cradle in the court-yard of his father's palace, and that he there fell asleep with his mouth open. Suddenly a swarm of bees came and settled about his face, and kept going in and out of his mouth as if it were a hive. The father of the infant boy, who was walking with his mother and sister in the portico, perceived the occurrence, but forbade that the bees should be driven off by the maid who had charge of the baby, being fearful lest the insects should harm the child. With paternal affection, therefore, he awaited the end of the miracle; but the bees

[220]   IO, MR, LV, MA.

flew up in the air and disappeared.[221] (2) VBI ABROSIS EMILIA PETIT
AC LIGURIA. Paolino tells us that after S. Ambrogio had grown up, he
obtained the consular dignity, and was sent to rule the provinces of Lombardy
and Emilia.[222] (3) VBI FVGIENS SPV. SCO. FLANTE REVERTITVR.
Being proclaimed by the people of Milan bishop, S. Ambrogio endeavoured to
escape by various expedients, and finally determined to run away. He left
the city at midnight, and tried to go to Pavia, but at early morning he found
himself back again at the Porta Romana of Milan, for God hindered his
flight.[223] (4) VBI CATHOLICO BAPTIZATVR EPO. When S. Ambrogio
perceived that it was clearly the will of God that he should become bishop
and that he could no longer resist, he postulated that he should be baptized
by none other than by a Catholic bishop.[224] (5) VBI OCTAVO DIE
ORDINATVR EPS. Having been thus baptized, he passed through all the
ecclesiastical degrees, and on the eighth day was ordained bishop.[225] (6) VBI
SUP[ER] ALTARE DORMIENS TVRONIAM PETIT. The legend of
how S. Ambrogio fell asleep at the altar while he was officiating at mass, and
was miraculously transported to Tours, where he officiated at the funeral
of St. Martin, is not found in the life of Paolino, nor in that of Metaphraste.
(7) VBI SEPELIVIT CORPVS BEATI MARTINI. (8) VBI PREDI-
CAT ANGLO LOQ'NTE ABROSIV. Paolino tells us that in those days
there was a certain man who belonged to the heresy of the Arians, a very
bitter disputant, and hard and unconvertible to the Catholic faith. He
happened to be in the church when S. Ambrogio was preaching, and saw, as
he himself afterwards confessed, an angel who whispered into the ears of
the bishop, so that it was evident that the bishop repeated to the people the
words spoken to him by the angel. When he had seen this, he became converted to the faith which he had opposed, and commenced to defend it.[226]

[221] Qui [Ambrosius] infans in area praetorii in cuna positus, cum dormiret aperto
ore, subito examen apum adveniens, faciem ejus atque ora complevit; ita ingrediendi
in os, egrediendique vices frequentarent. (*Vita Sancti Ambrosii*, a Paulino, ed. Migne,
Pat. Lat., XIV, 29 f.).

[222] . . . consularitatis suscepit insignia, ut regeret Liguriam, Aemiliamque pro-
vincias. (*Ibid.*).

[223] Egressusque noctis medio civitatem, cum Ticinum se pergere putaret, mane
ad portam civitatis Mediolanensis, quae Romana dicitur, invenitur. Deus enim . . .
fugam illius impedivit . . . (*Ibid.*).

[224] Cum intelligeret circa se Dei voluntatem, nec se diutius posse resistere, postulavit non si nisi a catholico episcopo baptizari. (*Ibid.*).

[225] Baptizatus itaque fertur omnia ecclesiastica officia implesse, atque octava die
episcopus ordinatus est. (*Ibid.*).

[226] Per idem tempus erat quidam vir de hæresi Arianorum, acerrimus nimium
disputator, et durus atque inconvertibilis ad fidem catholicam. Is constitutus in ecclesia,
tractante episcopo, vidit (ut ipse postmodum loquebatur) angelum ad aures episcopi

MILAN, S. AMBROGIO

(9) VBI PEDE ABROSIVS CALCAT DOLENTI. About the same time, a certain tribune and notary, Nicenzio, was so afflicted with a pain in his feet that he could rarely go out. One time he came to the altar of S. Ambrogio to receive communion, and by accident the saint trod upon him. He cried out with pain, but the saint said to him, "Go, and thou shalt be made whole," nor was he ever afterwards afflicted with pains in his feet.[227] (10) VBI IHVM AD SE VIDET VENIENTE. When his end was near, S. Ambrogio saw Christ coming to him, and smiling at him, and not many days afterwards he died, and from about the eleventh hour until that hour in which he gave up the ghost, he prayed, extending his hands in the form of a cross.[228] (11) VBI AMONIT HONORAT EPS DNI OFF COR. Honorato, bishop of Vercelli, was sleeping in an upper chamber. About the third hour he heard a voice calling him, saying, "Arise, quickly, since he is about to die." Honorato therefore descended and gave to the saint the Viaticum, and after he had swallowed it, S. Ambrogio gave up the ghost.[229] (12) VBI ANIMA IN CELVM DV|CITVR CORPORE IN LECTO POS. The soul of the saint rises to Heaven.[230]

The style of the golden altar has given rise to endless discussion, and the question of its date can not be definitely determined until the monuments of the IX century in gold, ivory and enamel are exhaustively studied. The mobility of the figures, however, the drawing of the wings of the angels, the treatment of the drapery, and numerous other technical details, show such close affinities with the works of sculpture executed in Lombardy in the XII century, that I have little doubt that the altar was then essentially remade.[231]

tractantis loquentem; ut verba angeli populo episcopus renuntiare videretur. Quo viso conversus fidem quam expugnabat coepit ipse defendere. (*Ibid.*).

227 Per idem tempus Nicentius quidam ex tribuno et notario qui ita pedum dolore tenebatur, ut raro in publico videretur; cum ad altare accessisset, ut sacramenta perciperet, calcatusque casu a Sacerdote exclamasset, audivit: Vade et amodo salvus eris. Nec se amplius doluisse pedes. . . . (*Ibid.*).

228 In eodem tamen loco in quo jacebat (sicut referente sancto Bassiano episcopo Laudensis Ecclesiæ, qui ab eodem audierat, didicimus) cum oraret una cum supradicto sacerdote, viderat Dominum Jesum advenisse ad se, et arridentem sibi; nec multos post dies nobis ablatus est. Sed eodem tempore quo migravit ad Dominum, ab hora circiter undecima diei usque ad illam horam, in qua emisit spiritum, expansis manibus in modum crucis oravit. . . . (*Ibid.*).

229 . . . Honoratus etiam sacerdos Ecclesiae Vercellis cum in superioribus domus se ad quiescendum composuisset, tertio vocem vocantis se audivit, dicentisque sibi: Surge, festina, quia modo est recessurus. Qui descendens, obtulit sancto Domini corpus: quo accepto ubi glutivit, emisit spiritum. . . . (*Ibid.*).

230 Corpus ipsius . . . de Ecclesia [majore] levaretur, portandum ad basilicam Ambrosianam, in qua positus est. (*Ibid.*).

231 The influence of ivories, miniatures and goldsmith's work of early times upon the plastic art of later centuries must, however, not be forgotten.

591

The cloissonné enamels however, are probably—at least in great part—fragments of the altar of Angilberto. Several fragments in the Morgan collection, Case J, show close analogy with those of S. Ambrogio. Although ascribed to the XI or XII century, I believe that the Morgan enamels are in reality at least as early as the IX century. A golden crown, said to have belonged to Charlemagne, and preserved at Vienna, shows enamel similar to that of the altar of S. Ambrogio, inserted amid the goldsmith's work.[232]

Modern critics have frequently placed the goldsmith's work of the altar of S. Ambrogio in comparison with the golden altars of Città di Castello and St. Mark's at Venice, and this comparison has rightly given rise to the opinion that the S. Ambrogio Palio must be of the XII century. It gives me pleasure to be able to cite two other golden altars to which that of S. Ambrogio appears even more closely analogous. Both are preserved in the Musée de Cluny at Paris. One, which bears the number 4988, was presented by the emperor Henry II (1004-1112) to the cathedral of Basle. The lettering, the setting of the jewels and the technique of the sculptures are strikingly similar to those of the S. Ambrogio Palio d'Oro. The figures in the Paris altar-front, however, are larger, and the style seems distinctly more primitive. The second altar, even more closely analogous to S. Ambrogio, is without number, but bears the label "Art Allemand (Bord du Rhin) XII siècle," and is exposed in the west gallery, second floor.

The history of the ambo (Plate 122, Fig. 2), broken in 1196 and restored by Guglielmo de Pomo, has already been given. Beneath it is an early Christian sarcophagus of the V century. On the principal face is represented a beardless Christ without halo, holding a book in His hand. Below His feet are a lamb and two very small kneeling figures, which I suppose to be portraits of the persons originally buried in the sarcophagus. On either side are six figures, doubtless representing the apostles. On one end are reliefs of Elijah mounting to Heaven, leaving his cloak to Elisha, and of the Baptism of Christ. On the other end are depicted four standing figures, one of whom carries a book, another a scroll. These are perhaps the four Evangelists. By them is represented the sacrifice of Isaac. Isaac, now headless, with his arms tied behind his back, kneels on an altar. Near by stands Abraham resting his arms on what seems to be a tree. In the background may be seen a mountain with an animal—doubtless intended to be a ram. On the back of this sarcophagus is depicted the Transfiguration, with the twelve apostles. The lid belonged to another sarcophagus. On it is represented a medallion with portraits of the deceased held by two genii. On either side, the three Magi are placed in parallel with the three children of Israel who refused to worship the image which Nebuchadnezzar the king had set up. On the east end is the Nativity, a work of the XIII century in contrast to the other sculptures so

[232] Illustrated by Louandre, I, Plate s.n. IX Siècle.

far described, which are early Christian. The ambo itself is adorned with various sculptures of different dates. The bronze eagle and the figure beneath it I believe to be of the IX century (Plate 122, Fig. 2). On the spandrels and between the sarcophagus and the ambo are many subjects obviously grotesque, and others which appear to have iconographic significance, although they have never been explained. A woman stands between two palm trees, holding one with each hand.[233] To her right is a man with a scythe; to her left, a man seated on the ground, picking a thorn out of his foot. A woman on horse-back with two men and two angels suggests the Flight into Egypt, but there is no child. A grotesque of an ass playing on the harp has been studied by Allegranza,[234] who has sought to read symbolism into the subject. It is, however, purely grotesque or satiric. On the back of the ambo is a relief of the XIII century representing the Last Supper and recalling in style the sculpture of the same subject at Lodi. Owing to lack of space the figures of two apostles have been omitted, which has caused this scene to be misidentified as an Agape. Among the purely grotesque sculptures of the pulpit is one of a pelican with her young, evidently symbolical, since it is labelled PELLICANVS. The pulpit appears to be essentially a monument of the XII century, and it is exceedingly difficult to distinguish the parts remade after the disaster of 1196. However, besides the reliefs already specified, two of the capitals and a lion under one of the bases are certainly of the XIII century.

The capitals of the atrium (Plate 117, Fig. 4; Plate 118, Fig. 5; Plate 119, Fig. 2; Plate 120, Fig. 2, 3, 5; Plate 122, Fig. 1) differ only slightly in character from those of the nave. Grotesque types predominate, but foliage and interlace motives are frequently used. Two capitals are obviously pilfered Corinthian, coming from some Roman edifice. Eagles appear often. There is noticeable a great difference of style between different capitals of the atrium. Those of the west gallery are the richest and most skilfully executed; several with broad, flat leaves seem to foreshadow French Gothic types, but the resemblance is probably accidental, since these capitals are unfinished, and it was undoubtedly intended to carve the leaves with the stiff Byzantinesque foliage of the Lombard style of this period. The capitals of the south gallery are characterized by remarkable vigour, and are doubtless the work of another sculptor. Many of those in the north gallery, on the other hand, were remade in the XVI century. They may be distinguished by their weak execution, and a certain barocco feeling in the forms. Certain capitals of the atrium have the monogram "H" which may indicate that the atrium was erected by the archbishop Arnolfo III (1093-1097).

[233] This relief, the one next to it—representing two birds drinking out of a vase—and the two above the lid on the south side—one of which depicts Adam and Eve—are of the early XIII century.

[234] *Spiegazioni*, 125.

The exterior wall of the atrium is ornamented with arched corbel-tables (Plate 120, Fig. 1). In the north wall several of these corbel-tables are formed of bits of Carlovingian carving used as second-hand material. These were discovered about 1894, and casts were made of them and sent to the Museo Archeologico. In the blind arches of the façade of the atrium are remains of frescos, much faded and probably not of very early date, but sufficient to indicate that the walls were covered with painted decoration. More numerous, and in some cases very ancient, are the traces of frescos on the interior wall. It is probable that the frescos executed in the XII century commenced to fall into bad condition at a comparatively early date and were replaced at various times by later compositions. The unsymmetrical manner in which the later frescos are disposed on the wall, indicates that they are not the result of a carefully thought out and unified scheme of composition, but rather chance embellishments added from time to time. The walls were prepared to receive the frescos by a coating of rough plaster, on top of which was laid one and sometimes two coats of gesso. The cross-hatching of the bricks afforded a key by which the plaster was held in position.

The new campanile (Plate 120, Fig. 6) is adorned with arched corbel-tables supported on pilaster strips and shafts. The cupola (Plate 117, Fig. 6) is characterized by double arched corbel-tables, galleries, polychromatic masonry and other rich ornament. The façade of the crypt is adorned with a richly carved cornice, evidently of the XIII century.

V. It is natural to suppose that the remains of the columnar nave beneath the pavement of the existing edifice belonged to the church erected by S. Ambrogio at the end of the IV century. The chapel of S. Satiro is in the style of the V century. The masonry of the dome is analogous to that of the domes of the churches of Ravenna, and the mosaics are evidently of the same epoch. The fragments of opus sectile are doubtless contemporary. The old campanile, on the other hand, is later. The bricks are not Roman but Lombard in character. The crudeness of the masonry and the absence of decoration indicate the IX century. There are but few examples extant of campaniles or of brickwork of the IX century, and it is consequently difficult to fix with precision the date of this interesting portion of the edifice. It is natural to suppose, however, that it was erected soon after, and in consequence of, the foundation of the monastery (800). To the same epoch belong the Carlovingian carvings in the corbel-tables of the atrium and in the altar of S. Satiro and the bronze eagle and saint of the pulpit. The columns and capitals of the ciborio and the enamels of the Palio d'Oro are without doubt of 840. The choir and apse are usually assigned to the same period, but the quality of the masonry is so different from that of the old campanile that it is impossible to suppose that the two structures were separated by less than a century. The masonry of the apse, as well as its general design and its cornice of blind niches in two orders, recalls S. Eustorgio. I therefore believe that the choir and apse were rebuilt c. 940. This deduction, based upon internal evidence, is completely in accord with the documentary evidence that this part of the monument was built before 950. The nave, on the other hand, is undoubtedly of the last half of the XI century. It appears to be somewhat earlier than the churches of S. Nazaro and S. Stefano, both begun in 1075, and decidedly earlier than the Chiesa d'Aurona, begun in 1095, and S. Savino of Piacenza, consecrated in 1107. In view, therefore, of the historical considerations already noted above, there can be little doubt that the church was begun after 1067, and probably about 1070. The building commenced at the east end, and progressed without interruption until the narthex had been completed. Soon after the atrium was added and must have been completed before 1098. Between 1126 and 1133 and again after 1196, the Palio d'Oro underwent radical restorations, or rather reconstructions, which essentially altered its primitive forms, although the old inscription was retained. Of about the same epoch (c. 1130) is the pulpit, which also was restored and in part remade after the disaster of 1196. The apse mosaic I believe to have been added after the completion of the atrium in 1098 and before the restoration of the Palio d'Oro. The lower part of the Campanile dei Canonici is of 1128, the middle portion of 1181. In 1196 the vaults of the eastern bay of the nave fell, breaking the ciborio, which was rebuilt in its present form. In consequence of the collapse, the vaults in both the third and fourth bays were rebuilt, the former with oblong Gothic vaults, the latter with a cupola resembling the present one.

MILAN, S. BABILA

(Plate 125, Fig. 3)

I. The church of S. Babila was first described in 1627 by Villa, an eyewitness of the baroccoization of the edifice, of which he has left us an important description. This author has also preserved a record of the old ambo, and of the cemetery which formerly existed to the west of the church.[1] In 1674 Torre described in more detail the ambo,[2] which in his time had already been demolished. The notice of Latuada[3] is valuable chiefly for the historical notices. The barocco façade, now destroyed, was described by

[1] 227.

[2] Nel sito, in cui si stà di presente l'Organo alla sinistra mano dell'Altar Maggiore mirauasi vn Pulpito di lauorato marmo bianco, quasi al pari di quello, che osseruaste nella Basilica Ambrogiana (349).

[3] I, 180.

Pirovano, who wrote in 1826.[4] De Dartein studied the edifice, but in his time only two of the ancient capitals were visible.[5] Romussi has also noticed the church.[6] Rivoira[7] has made a careful study of the architecture of the monument, which he has illustrated with three excellent half-tones. De Fabriczy has recently published XVI century drawings of the church, which are of great archæological importance.

II. The historians of Milan are inclined to believe that a certain rather obscure epigram of Ennodio refers to this church. The poem is entitled, "Verses written in another place, that is, in the basilica of the saints, when they had burnt the buildings which were there before, and the church had been rebuilt in its present form." The poem itself may be translated as follows: "Would that the roofs had sooner yielded to the blessed flames, since new splendour comes from damage, since lofty temples to God rise from the ashes, since loss by harmless fire is turned to gain, since the expense of restoration arouses new enthusiasm for religion! Who shall it be who will repair the buildings destroyed by the crackling flames? O Lorenzo, by thy warfare conquer the fire! The sordid earth would have lain hidden in its dark recess, if the cave-like church had preserved its former condition. But after the heavenly Powers sent fortunate flames, ashes brought forth these things to the light of blessed day. Turn hither Thy loving eyes, O Father, who didst predict that all things should be purified by fire and smoke, and instruct those who must be taught by deeds, lest minds ignorant of righteousness stammer vain words."[8]

---

[4] . . . la facciata con pronao ornato di colonne ha due ordini, Dorico il primo, Ionico il secondo (101).

[5] 213.   [6] *Milano*, 351.   [7] 244.

[8] ITEM IN ALIO LOCO FACTOS IN BASILICA SS. QUIA ARSERANT AEDIFICIA QUAE PRIUS IBI FUERANT ET SIC FACTA EST

Vilia tecta prius facibus cessere beatis,
Si splendor per damna venit, si culmina flammis
Consurgunt habitura deum, si perdita crescunt
Ignibus innocuis, si dant dispendia cultum.
Qualis erit reparans crepitantibus usta ruinis?
Laurenti, tua bella gerens incendia vince.
Sordida marcenti latuisset terra recessu,
Si status faciem tenuissent antra vetusti.
Sed postquam superi flammas misere secundas,
Ad lumen cineres traxerunt ista colendum.
Huc oculos converte pios, qui cuncta vapore
Praedicis mundanda, pater, rebusque docendos
Instrue ne verbis titubet mens nescia recti.

(Ennodius XCVII—Carm. 2, 9—ed. Vogel, M. G. H. *Auct. Antiq.*, VII, 120).

Cf. Joel., ii, 30; Act., ii, 19.

MILAN, S. BABILA

That the church of S. Babila formerly bore the title of Concilia Sanctorum or All Saints is expressly stated by Landolfo the Younger, in a passage which will be cited below. Moreover, Beroldo mentions the festival of All Saints as being celebrated at S. Babila with peculiar solemnity.[9] It is therefore probable that our church was burned and restored in the V century.[10]

In early times the basilica was officiated by priests. At what epoch the nuns (who were subsequently transferred to the church of S. Margherita)[11] were introduced, is not altogether clear. Rotta[12] is certainly wrong in believing that this event took place about the middle of the VIII century, since in 1096 there were no nuns, as is proved by an important text of Landolfo the Younger: "At that time (1096) . . . the pope Urban II . . . returned from France to Milan. While in that city he preached from the pulpit of S. Tecla to a great multitude of people of both sexes . . . saying that clerks and priests should not be invested with benefices for money, but should be elected by the parishioners. From these apostolic injunctions a certain clerk, Nazaro, called Muricula, a man of very keen intellect, took wings and flew from his one-story house to the church of SS. Babila e Romano, which was formerly called Concilia Sanctorum, and he did this without royal or ecclesiastical authority; and, since he was backed by the favour of the people who lived near there, he set up his domicile there, and built a new house, and drove out the priest and clerks who had been accustomed to officiate in those churches."[13]

This text of Landolfo makes it clear that at the end of the XI century there were two basilicas, one called S. Babila, and the other S. Romano, which adjoined each other, and formed part of the same establishment. The *Ecclesia Sanctorum Romani et Babilae* is mentioned in a sentence of 1119 as one of chapels dependent upon the mother-churches officiated by decumani.[14] A document of 1148 speaks of the churches of SS. Romano e Babila.[15] The edifice is given the same title in another document of 1149.[16]

---

[9] Kl. Novembris. Festivitas omnium Sanctorum ad s. Babylam. (Beroldo, ed. Magistretti, 12).

[10] Oltrocchi, I, 68.   [11] Giulini, I, 435.   [12] 33.

[13] In isto namque tempore . . . Urbanus Papa . . . de Franzia Mediolanum redivit, in qua civitate cùm ipse Papa staret in pulpito Sanctæ Teglæ immensæ multitudini hominum utriusque sexus prædicavit . . . quòd Clerici, & Sacerdotes per pecuniam in Ecclesias non sunt introducendi, sed per electionem hominum, qui sunt Ecclesiarum vicini, de quibus Apostolicis dictis Clerus iste Nazarius ingenio acutissimus, & Muricula cognominatus pennas assumsit, atque de solario suo ad Ecclesiam Sancti Babilæ, Sanctique Romani, quæ antiquitus dicitur Concilia Sanctorum, sine regali, & sacerdotali auctoritate volavit, & habito favore vulgi illius vicinitatis ibi habitavit, & novum habitaculum ædificavit, expulsis inde Sacerdotibus, & Clericis consuetis deservire ipsis Ecclesiis. (Landulphi Junioris, *Hist. Mediol.*, XXVIII, ed. Muratori, R. I. S., V, 497).

[14] Giulini, VII, 84.

[15] Ego in dei nomine Nazarius presbyter ac primericius ecclesiarum ac presbiterorum Mediolani et offitialis sanctorum Romani et Babille . . . deueniant in manus et potestate presbiterorum iamscriptarum ecclesiarum sanctorum Romani et Babille. . . .

At the end of the XVII century Torre[17] described the church of S. Romano—which, in his day, still existed—as being small (*angusta*), and adjoining (*contigua*) S. Babila.

Nevertheless the two edifices are frequently referred to separately. In Beroldo[18] we find the entry: *XIII K. Decembris S. Romani presbyteri ad ecclesiam suam.* A document of 1145 speaks of S. Babila without referring to S. Romano.[19] In one of the calendars of the Milanese church is the entry: *Januarius . . . IX. Kal. Ss. Babilæ, & trium parvulorum extra portam Orientalem.*[20]

An inscription in the western bay of the southern wall records that a chapel erected in 1344, was restored in 1721.[21]

Another inscription placed close beside the first records the consecration of three altars in the year 1363.[22]

In 1387 the church seems to have been again restored.[23] A document of 1568 mentions that the church was at that time officiated by four rectors, but adds that a chapter had been founded by a legacy.[24] The last part of this text must be an addition made subsequently to 1588, for the chapter was founded in that year, as is recorded by an inscription still extant in the church.[25] The campanile fell in 1575.[26]

Probably in consequence of the foundation of the chapter, a baroccoization of the church was undertaken. Villa, who was present during this restoration,

---

Actum in iamscripta canonica sanctorum Babille et Romani. (*Codice della Croce, MS. Amb., D. S. IV, 6/I, 6, f. 293*).

¹⁶ *Ibid.*, f. 312.   ¹⁷ 349.   ¹⁸ Ed. Magistretti, 13.

¹⁹ . . . et ipsi presbiteri [omnes de Mediolano] faciant omni anno annualem meum ad ecclesiam sancti Babile que est constructa in burgo iamscripte porte orientalis. (*Codice della Croce, MS. Amb., D. S. IV, 6/I, 6, f. 242*).

²⁰ *Kalendarium Sitoniamum,* ed. Muratori, R. I. S., II, pt. 2, 1035.

²¹

D. O. M.

S. MARIÆ DE OSSIBVS

AC SS. BLASIO ET BERNARDO

ÆDEM HANC

A ZONFREDO DE CASTANO

PRÆPOSITO BOLLATI

ET METROP. BASIL. CAN. ORDIN.

PRIDIE NON. MARTIJ 1344

EXCITATAM

PIETAS CONFRATRVM

S. MARIÆ DE OSSIBVS

VETVSTATE LABANTEM

IN HVNC SPLEND. RESTITVIT

IV NON. OC̄BRIS MDCCXXI

states that the core of the old edifice was preserved, but that the church was extended a bay to the westward, and the old choir (which was narrow and too small for the chapter) was razed to the ground (*atterrato*) and a new one erected.[27] This restoration has also been described by Latuada.[28]

From the drawings published by De Fabriczy, it is possible to form a good idea of the architecture of the church as it was before all these alterations. The drawings show the monument a bay shorter than at present. The row of blind arches which exist at present between the gallery and the cornice of the cupola, do not appear in the drawing. The campanile is seen to the south of the church. At the epoch when the drawings were made, a Renaissance chapel had already been added to the south side aisle in the bay over which rises the cupola. In the drawings it is evident that the cupola is later than the church, since its wall cuts across the cornice of the nave. The nave roof is raised above both of the side aisles, but there is no clearstory. The transverse buttresses project above the side-aisle roofs. The original southern absidiole and the apse, destroyed in the barocco period, and now restored in pseudo-Romanesque style, appear in these drawings. A blind arch between the buttresses over the side portal recalls a similar motive in the atrium of S. Ambrogio.

In 1798 the chapter of S. Babila was suppressed,[29] although strangely enough, the church appears in the list of nunneries suppressed in 1810.[30] An

22   A . M CCC L XIII . DIE . VENĪS .
      XXII . MĒSIS . SEPTĒBIS
      [CON]SECTA . FVERVNT .
      ALTARIA . BEATI . BABILLE .
      BTE . MARIE . ET . STI .
      NICOLAI . QM . SITVM . EST
      A MANV . DEXAM . SANCTI
      BABILLE P[ER] FREM . PETRVM
      DE MANANO . EPM . THENE
      DENSAM . ORDNIS . PDICATOR[VM]
      QVI . TVC . GEREBAT . UIC .
      ES . DNI . GVIELMI . DE .
      PVSTERLLA . TVC . ARCHI
      EPI . MEDIOLANI . EXPEN
      P[RO]PRIIS . PSBRI . IACOBI .
      DE . COTTIS . BN . IPIVS
      ECCLEXIE

23 Torre, 348; Latuada, I, 180; Giulini, V, 714.

24 [Ecclia] Babila cú quatuor rectoribus. Errecta in collegiata, ex ligato, quon' dne de . . . . . cú pposito et cancis no . . . . . (*Status Ecclesiae Mediolani 1568 conscriptus* auctore Francisco Castello, MS. Amb., A, 112, Inferiore, f. 441).

inscription still preserved in the edifice, records that the building was restored and the altar consecrated in 1829. At this epoch there was still a chapter of canons.

An archæological restoration of the edifice was begun in 1888,[31] and continued until 1894, under the direction of Cesabianchi. The apse and absidioles, which had been replaced in the barocco period by a modern choir, were rebuilt on the traces of the old foundations. The barocco façade was demolished, and a new one of pseudo-Romanesque style erected. The barocco stucco with which the edifice was entirely covered, was removed and replaced by the present unfortunate decorations in fresco.

III. But little of the original edifice has survived the rebuildings of barocco and modern times. At present, the structure consists of a nave

[25]

HIERONIMAE

MAZENTAE

RELIGIOSISSIMAE MATRONAE

QVAE AVGVSTAM HANC AEDEM

AD DIVINAS QVOTIDIE LAVDES

RITE CONCELEBRANDAS

SACRAQ SOLEMNIA AC PRIVATA

HIC AC ALIBI TVM ANNIVERSARIA

PERFICIENDA

ADDICTIS HONESTIS REDITIBVS

INSIGNI CANONICORVM COLLEGIO

ANNO M D LXXXVIII

AVXIT AC DECORAVIT

SIXTI V PONT MAX

AVCTORITATE

GASPARIS VIC ARCHIEP

OPERA

SVIS PRAETEREA FACVLTATIBVS

INOPES LEVARI DOTARI VIRGINES

PERPLVRAQ ID GENVS EXPLERI

CONSTITVIT

CVRATORES EX EIVS TESTAMENTO

P.

[26] Villa, 226; Torre, 348.

[27] 227.

[28] Anche dopo ne' tempi a noi più vicini fu ristorata, ed abbellita questa Chiesa con accrescimento di un Antiporta sostenuta da Colonne avanti alla Porta di mezzo, ed altri ornamenti nella Facciata, e di dentro per opera del Preosto Alessandro Confalonieri e del Canonico Lecchi, da cui fu fatto fabbricare il Coro, e finalmente d'un Curato cognome Sorbelloni, che fece rifare il Pavimento. (Latuada, I, 180).

[29] Forcella, *Chiese*, 650. [30] *Ibid.* [31] *Arte e Storia*, 25 Agosto, 1888.

(Plate 125, Fig. 3) five bays long, two side aisles, three apses, and chapels. The apses all have half domes, the side aisles are covered with groin vaults, a Lombard cupola rises over the central bay of the nave (Plate 125, Fig. 3), and the other bays of the nave are barrel-vaulted (Plate 125, Fig. 3). The original dispositions, however, were very different. The western bay of the nave, as has been seen, was added in the barocco epoch. The original nave, therefore, was only four bays long, and the cupola rose over the second bay from the west—an extraordinary arrangement. The barrel vaults of the nave have been believed by all archæologists who have studied the monument to be original. The masonry at present can not be examined because the vault surface has been entirely covered with modern frescos. The system, however, comprises three members; or, in the western piers (half of which are presumably old), five members, only the central one of which is at present utilized to carry the transverse arches of the barrel vault. The other two members must certainly have been designed to carry ribs, and in all probability diagonal ribs (Plate 125, Fig. 3). The transverse buttresses over the side aisles have no function with the barrel vault, but were obviously designed to reinforce a rib vault (Plate 125, Fig. 3). The builders therefore intended to cover the nave with cross vaults, and it is entirely probable that such vaults were actually erected, and were replaced by barrel vaults only in the barocco reconstruction. The modern restorers by mistake retained these barocco vaults.

The groin vaults of the side aisles are very oblong in plan and so highly domed in the longitudinal sense, that they appear to be barrel vaults rather than groin vaults. They are supplied with longitudinal ribs and transverse arches in two orders (Plate 125, Fig. 3). The extradoses of the upper order of the transverse arch and of the wall ribs describe a curve slightly more acute than that of the intradoses.

The piers of the nave—with the exception of the westernmost pair, which are modern—are all uniform and of compound section. The bays of the nave are very oblong in plan, being much wider than long. The cupola, added after the completion of the original edifice, doubtless replaced a rib vault. The piers beneath it are no heavier than the others, and are supplied with diagonal shafts, which remained without function when the original rib vault was supplanted by the cupola. Moreover, the cupola cuts across the corbel-tables of the nave, which have been correctly restored, as is proved by the XVI century drawing described above.

The original masonry, but very little of which survives, consists of cross-hatched bricks, with piers and trimmings of stone.

IV.   The capitals are ornamented with refined and minutely executed foliage, which recalls that of S. Pietro in Ciel d'Oro at Pavia (Plate 177, Fig. 1). The grotesque element is distinctly less prominent than at S.

LOMBARD ARCHITECTURE

Ambrogio. The bases, very dryly executed, have an Attic profile, and are peculiar in that the tori and plinths are all placed in the same vertical plane. There are no griffes. The exterior is decorated with cornices formed of arched corbel-tables and saw teeth. The cupola has a gallery. The archivolts of the main arcade are in two unmoulded orders.

V. Both the ornament and structure of S. Babila show close analogies with S. Pietro in Ciel d'Oro of Pavia (Plate 178, Fig. 4). Both edifices were characterized by a uniform system, oblong rib vaults in the nave, and capitals of fine Byzantinesque foliage, of which the abaci were frequently either omitted altogether or very much reduced. S. Pietro in Ciel d'Oro was consecrated in 1132. S. Babila appears somewhat earlier, because its capitals in some respects resemble those of S. Ambrogio more closely than do the capitals of the Pavia edifice. S. Babila may, consequently, be assigned to c. 1120. The cupola is obviously later than the main body of the church, but does not appear to be very much later, since the style of the ornament is similar. It may, therefore, be conjectured that the cupola was added c. 1140.

MILAN, S. CALIMERO

(Plate 125, Fig. 1, 2)

I. Latuada has left an important description of the baroccoization of this church. Otherwise the architecture of the structure has received but scant notice. De Dartein,[1] Romussi, and Rotta[2] have given some description of the apse, which has also been referred to by Rivoira.[3]

II. The basilica of S. Calimero is one of the most venerable of Milan, and is believed to have been founded soon after the death of the saint, who is there buried.[4] S. Calimero, according to Giulini,[5] lived as early as the second century, and suffered martyrdom by being thrown into a well which is still shown as a relic in the crypt of the existing basilica. At all events the basilica was rebuilt by Lorenzo in the V century. This fact is known from an epigram of Ennodio entitled: "Verses written when the basilica of S. Calimero was restored." These lines may be translated: "The free spaces of the lofty temple are like light made captive. The countenance of the church smiles, and is obscured by no cloud. Hither this latest gift of starry Olympus has recently come, brought by the ministry of the priest Lorenzo. This edifice and his life may both be compared to the rays of the sun. Well done, thou restorer of

[1] 214.   [2] Pas., 61.   [3] Passim.
[4] Sanctus Kalimerus sedit Ann. LIII. Depositus est Prid. Kal. Augusti in ecclesia sua. (Ordo antiquus Episcoporum, ed. Muratori, R. I. S., I, pt. 1, 228).
[5] III, 393.

602

ancient buildings! Proceed, thou founder of new edifices, noble in countenance and mind. Under thee as bishop old buildings renew their youth, and a stranger's care supports them when about to fall."[6]

According to Tatti[7] the archbishop Tommaso (†783) gave a golden altar to this basilica. This was stolen by the soldiers of Barbarossa.[8] Giulini[9] states that the church was one of the chapels of the decumani. Subsequently a chapter was established, and this is mentioned in a document of 1152.[10] In a tax-list of 1398, published by Magistretti, it appears that the basilica possessed three canons and two chapels. In a document of 1568, it is stated that the church was officiated by three canons, including the prevosto.[11]

The edifice was baroccoized before 1647.[12] The original dispositions were radically denatured at this period.[13]

In 1891 an archæological restoration was attempted; but so little of the Romanesque edifice was preserved that all attempt to reproduce the original forms had to be abandoned.

III, IV. The existing church is entirely modern, with the exception of the exterior of the apse, and even this has been so much restored that its original character can not be accurately ascertained. The cornice is formed

[6]   VERSUS IN BASILICA SANCTI CALEMERI QUANDO
                        REPARATA EST.

        Libera captivum memuerunt culmina lumen
          Adridet facies nubila nulla gerens.
        Hic nuper astrigeri dos proxima venit Olympi,
          Laurenti vatis ducta ministerio.
        Aedibus et vitae cuius nunc una figura est,
          Ceu solis radiis forma color similis.
        Euge vetustorum reparator, perge, novorum
          Conditor, et vultu clarus et ingenio!
        Abiurant priscam te praesule tecta senectam,
          Advena casuris porrigitur genius.

        (Ennodi CLXXXIII—Carm. 2, 60—ed. Vogel, M. G. H., *Auc. Antiq.*, VII, 158).

[7] I, 828.   [8] Rotta, *Pas.*, 61.   [9] III, 393.   [10] *Ibid.*

[11] [Ecclīa] S. Calimeri cú tribus cancis curatis (*Status Ecclesiae Mediolani 1568 conscriptus* auctore Francesco Castello, MS. Amb., A, 112, Inf., f. 443). *Ibid.*, 541, the names of the prevosto and two canons (name of third omitted) are given, as well as the taxes which they paid.

[12] Torre, 17.

[13] La chiesa fu modernamente rifatta in ordine Dorico, verso la metà del Secolo passato a spese del Canonico Rettore Barbieri, morto nel 1654. . . . Al di fuori fu eretto un Portico, sostenuto da quattro Colonne di vivo sasso, ed introduce per tre Porte nel Tempio formato di una sola nave capace per quattro Cappelle in ogni lato, benchè ve ne sieno solamente tre, servendo il sito da un canto pel Battisterio e nell'altro pel Banco, etc. (Latuada, 22).

of blind niches, surmounted by arched corbel-tables carried on pilaster strips (Plate 125, Fig. 2). The masonry has been much made over (Plate 125, Fig. 1), but the bricks appear analogous to those of the apse of S. Ambrogio. The courses are in general horizontal, but interrupted at intervals by layers of herring-bone masonry.

V. Since the masonry and cornice show close analogies with the apses of S. Ambrogio (Plate 117, Fig. 5) and S. Eustorgio (Plate 127, Fig. 4), the one of which dates from c. 940, and the other from c. 1000, the scanty remains of the apse of S. Calimero may be referred to c. 990. The main body of the church was later rebuilt in great part, for the exterior wall is still supplied with a salient buttress, which can not be earlier than the XII century. At this period the cornice of the apse was also retouched. In the southern wall of the eastern bay, however, some masonry of c. 1000 is still to be seen.

MILAN, S. CELSO

(Plate 125, Fig. 4; Plate 126, Fig. 1, 2, 3)

I. The first to study the history of the monastery of S. Celso was the veteran archæologist Puricelli, who, in his *Dissertatio Nazariana,* investigated the history of the origins of the basilica. Torre's book on Milan, printed in 1674, contains a brief description of the edifice.[1] In the XVIII century the monument attracted the attention of the antiquarian Allegranza, who, in his *Spiegazioni,*[2] studied the sculptures of the portal. Unfortunately he did not describe the architecture of the monument which, in his time, was in a far better state of preservation than it is at present. The description of Latuada,[3] written in 1737, is short but valuable. The historians of Milan, among whom Giulini is pre-eminent, have all of them referred to the church and to the stirring events of which it was the scene. The monograph of Bugati, published in 1782, contains crude drawings of the capitals and important historical notices. In 1817 Millin[4] wrote a short account of the church containing a description of the subjects of the sculptures. Caffi wrote two monographs on the edifice. In the first, published in 1842, he studied especially the earlier history of the monument; in the second (which appeared in 1888) he occupied himself chiefly with its history in modern times. This latter work is of particular value. The drawings of Cassina,[5] published in 1840, should be compared with those of De Castro.[6] Not only the drawings, but the archæological study of De Dartein,[7] merit close study. In 1865 Cavagna Sangiuliani

[1] 80.   [2] 168.   [3] III, 44.   [4] I, 108.   [5] Plates XV-XVI.
[6] II, 48.   [7] 195.

published a monograph upon the church. In recent years Romussi[8] has resumed briefly and tersely what has been written about the edifice by other authors.

II. According to the passion of the saints Nazaro and Celso, after the martyrs had been executed, their bodies were embalmed by religious men, who buried them in their own gardens, presumably situated near the spot where the saints had suffered martyrdom.[9] The existing church of S. Celso stands on the site where the martyrs were buried. It is probable that some sort of an oratory was built over the tomb of the saints at a very early period. At the end of the IV century S. Ambrogio translated the body of S. Nazaro into the church which now bears the name of that martyr, but the body of S. Celso has always remained where it was originally buried. The earliest explicit mention of the church of S. Celso is contained in a litany of the IX century published by Magistretti.

At the end of the X century, the archbishop Landolfo (979-998) established a monastery in the church. So much at least is clear from the series of somewhat confused notices that have come down to us. Of these, the most authoritative is that of Arnolfo: "The bishop, conscious that he had offended the Church by wasting its resources, founded the monastery of the holy martyr Celso to propitiate the clergy and the people."[10] Arnolfo does not state in what year the foundation took place, but in a catalogue of the bishops of Milan we read: "The bishop Landolfo sat for eighteen years, three months, thirteen days. He died on the twenty-second of September, and was buried in the monastery which he himself had recently founded, in the tenth indiction."[11] Now the tenth indiction in the pontificate of Landolfo corresponds only with the years 982 and 997, but since Landolfo died in 998 it is not certain that the indiction cited may not refer to his death rather than to the foundation of the monastery. An inscription formerly placed near the altar of the church, and preserved in a manuscript of Alciati, has been published by Puricelli[12] and by Bugati. It is from the latter that I copy it. "This altar contains the precious body of Celso, whom his pious mother offered to Nazaro at Cimello, that like Nazaro he might attain Heaven, and after death lie forever with Nazaro in the same tomb. But Ambrogio in after years buried

[8] 159.

[9] Eadem itaque nocte aduenientes relligiosi uiri collegerunt corpora eorum: et condita aromatibus in eodem quo decollati fuerant loco posuerunt in propriis hortis. (*Sanctorum Nazarii et Celsi Martyrum Passio*, cit. Mombrizio, ed. 1910, II, 326).

[10] Præterea sentiens se Præsul dispersis facultatibus offendisse Ecclesiam, ut Clerum leniret ac Populum, S. Martyris Celsi fundavit Monasterium, multisque ditavit opibus. (Arnulphi, *Hist. Med.*, I, 10, ed. Muratori, R. I. S., IV, 11).

[11] Landulphus Episcopus sedit annis XVIII. mens. III. diebus XIII. obiit X. Kal. Octubris, sepultus est ad Monasterium S. Celsi, quod ipse noviter ædificavit Indictione X. (*Catalogus Mediolanensis, atque archiepiscoporum*, ed. Muratori, R. I. S., IV, 143).

[12] *Dis. Naz.*, 436.

them separately, carrying Nazaro elsewhere, but leaving Celso. At length, after many centuries, the bishop Landolfo summoned his clergy and the citizens, and in the presence of the people assembled from all quarters, with great joy and with all zeal he translated the body of the martyr, and in the year 976 at his own expense constructed a building suitable for the cult of the saint, and adorned it with marvellous decorations."[13] The date 976 appears to have been added at a later epoch, and is probably inexact, since Landolfo did not become archbishop until 979. A second inscription is similar to the first, but contains some variations. It is also preserved in the manuscript of Alciati, but it has evidently been badly copied, since the first three verses make no sense. I conjecture that they should be restored to read as follows: "We know that this monastery duly consecrated contains the precious (reading *eximium* for *eximiam*) body of Celso the holy martyr, venerated (*veneratum* for *vemeramur*) with such worship as is due to a saint (*iure divinis* for *iuredi* . . . . .). His mother, a most upright woman who lived at Amifico in the district of Cimello, offered Celso to Nazaro, with whom he won the palm of martyrdom, and attained the heavenly sphere. Both together long lay in the same tomb, but afterwards Ambrogio separated the holy bodies, and bore away Nazaro, but left Celso here. After many centuries the bishop Landolfo summoned his clergy and the citizens, and in the presence of the people assembled from all quarters, with great joy and with the praise of all translated the body, and zealously himself built an edifice suitable for the cult of the saint, and adorned it with marvellous decoration. Under the patronage of the martyrs and by the aid of Christ may we attain the heavenly sphere."[14] These inscriptions are very important, since they prove that the church was reconstructed by Landolfo at the time the monastery was founded, but they unfortunately leave us still in the dark regarding the exact year of this foundation. The chronicle of Daniele, according to Giulini,[15] states that the abbey was established in the year 982, which, as we have seen, corresponds with the tenth indiction mentioned in the catalogue of the bishops. The

[13] EXIMIVM HÆC CELSI CORPVS COMPLECITVR ARA
QVEM PIA NAZARIO MATER SVB RVRE CIMELLI
OBTVLIT AD CŒLI PARITER QVI SCANDERET ARCES
MORTE OBITA LONGVM PARITERQVE IACERET IN ÆVVM
AMBROSIVS TANDEM HOS POST SEPARE CONDIDIT AMBOS
NAZARIVM APPORTANS ALIO CELSVMQVE RELINQVENS
SÆCVLA LANDVLFVS DONEC POST PLVRIMA PRÆSVL
VATIBVS ADSCITIS VICINISQVE VNDIQVE TVRBIS
LÆTITIA SVMMA STVDIO ET CERTANTIBVS OMNI
TRANSTVLIT ATQVE LOCVM DIVINIS VSIBVS APTVM
IPSE LIBENS STRVXIT MIROQVE DECORE PARAVIT
P. S. [= propriis sumptibus] ANN. 976

chronicle which passes under the name of Filippo da Castel Seprio, but which is more probably by Goffredo da Bussero,[16] gives the year of the foundation as 981.[17] Calco ascribes the foundation to the year 982.[18] However, as Giulini has pointed out, it is difficult to imagine that Landolfo, in the midst of his struggles with the people of Milan, should have found time or resources to erect monasteries. The statement of Goffredo that the pope imposed as a penance the foundation of the abbey, probably merits no faith. The notice of another late chronicler to the effect that the monastery was founded in the time of the bishop Adelmanno (948-953)[19] suggests a possible solution of the difficulties. If the monastery was founded by Landolfo before he became bishop, this foundation might well have taken place as early as the time of Adelmanno. The tenth indiction corresponds with the year 952, which falls in the episcopate of Adelmanno. But the chronicle in question is not to be relied upon as an historical source.

[14] CÆNOBIVM CLAVSTRVM PRÆSENTIS RITE SACRATVM
EXIMIAM CELSI COMPLECTI MARTYRIS ALMI
NOVIMVS OBSEQVIIS VENERAMVR IVREDI . . . . .
CORPVS QV . . . . . MVLIER SVA NEMPE PROBISSIMA MATER
OBTVLIT ALMIFICO RESIDENS IN RVRE CIMELLI
NAZARIO CELSAM SECVM QVI SVMERE PALMAM
MARTYRIO MERVIT SIMVL AC SVPER ASTRA MIGRAVIT
AMBO NAM LONGVM PARITER IACVERE PER ÆVVM
POST TAMEN AMBROSIVS SECERNENS CORPORA SANCTA
NAZARIVM GESSIT HIC CELSVM RITE RELINQVENS
ANTISTES MVLTVM LANDVLFVS POST QVOQVE SÆCLVM
VATIBVS ACCITIS VICINISQVE VNDIQVE TVRBIS
LÆTITIA SVMMA CVNCTORVM LAVDE SVPERNA
TRANSTVLIT ATQVE LOCVM DIVINIS VSIBVS APTVM
IPSE LIBENS STRVXIT MIROQVE DECORE PARAVIT
QVORVM PRÆSIDIO IVVANTE PER OMNIA CHRISTO
EMPIRII REGIAM PENITVS NOS SCANDERE SVMET.

(Bugati, 112-116).

[15] I, 668.

[16] See the edition by Grazioli.

[17] Anno dn̄i 981. Dn̄us Landulfus de Carcano filius suprascripti dn̄i Ubizioni fecit aedificare monasterium S. Celsi, datum sibi a Papa in poenitentiam. (*Chronica* detta di Filippo da Castel Seprio, MS. Amb., S. Q. + I, 12, f. 58).

[18] Landulphus in emendationem eorum, quæ de Ecclesia auerterat, cœnobium extra vrbem inter Romanam, & Ticinensem portam erexit, in honorem S. Celsi Martyris, amplisq. prædiis ditauit, atq. moriens sepeliri ibidem voluit anno 982. (Calco, Lib. VI, 119).

[19] E in questo tempo [de Adelmanno archiepiscopo] fu edificato lo monasterio de s. Celso in Milano. (*Chron. di Milano*, ed. Lambertenghi, 5).

Another group of chroniclers ascribe the foundation to the last decade of the X century. Galvaneo della Fiamma places it in the year 992,[20] Sigonio refers it to 995[21] and Giulini to 996.[22] In the midst of this conflict of authorities, it is impossible to fix the precise year of the foundation of the monastery with certainty, but there can be no doubt that it was established in the last half of the X century. Neither can there be any doubt that Landolfo was the founder. In addition to the direct evidence to this effect already cited, two facts are significant. The first is that the abbot and the abbey of S. Celso are the beneficiaries under the will of Landolfo, made in 997.[23] The second is that Landolfo was buried in the church, as is stated in several of the texts cited above and in another catalogue of the bishops.[24]

In 1034 the archbishop Ariberto made a bequest to the monastery.[25]

On May 27, 1067, the body of S. Arialdo was buried near, but not in, the church. In the life of the saint we read: "And thus with great glory and ineffable praise the body of S. Arialdo was borne to the monastery of S. Celso. There it was buried in a place entirely suitable, since on one side was the church in which the venerable body of S. Celso is still worshipped, and on the other the church where, as it is said, S. Nazaro formerly long lay buried."[26] The account of Landolfo the Elder is less enthusiastic: "And thus while many doubted, and many rejoiced, and many believed, the body of S. Arialdo was placed on a litter and covered with a pallium. The litter was then raised, and the body, vested, like that of a Levite, with a stole, was buried with great pomp in the monastery of S. Celso in the presence of many people, while the greater litany was chanted. . . . Two years after he had mounted the episcopal

---

[20] Depauperatis itaque cunctis ecclexiis, hic dilapidator archiepiscopus in civitate Mediolani receptus fuit, et conscientia ductus eo quod ecclexias tam turpiter defraudasset, monasterium sancti Celsi construxit anno Domini DCCCCXCII, et post annos sex moriens ibidem tumulatus fuit iuxta hostium, ubi est acqua sancta. (Galvanei Flammae, *Chron. Maius,* ed. Ceruti, 597).

Et Landulphus Archiepiscopus Mediolanensis aspiciens se turpiter Ecclesiam Mediolanensem defraudisse, Monasterium Sancti Celsi construxit. (Galvanei Flammae, *Manipulus Florum,* CXXXII, ed. Muratori, R. I. S., XI, 609).

[21] 298.

[22] I, 668.

[23] *Hist. Pat. Mon.,* XIII, 1647; *Codice della Croce,* MS. Amb., D. S. IV, 2/I, 2, f. 183.

[24] Landulphus sedit Ann. XVIII mens. III. Obiit X. Kal. Aprilis. Sepultus est in Ecclesia Sancti Celsi. (*Ordo antiquus episcoporum,* ed. Muratori, R. I. S., I, pt. 2, 229).

[25] Puricelli, 366.

[26] Et sic cum magna gloria laudeque ineffabili, ad monasterium delatus est S. Celsi. Ibi in locum mirabiliter aptum traditus est sepulturæ, siquidem ex una parte habet ecclesiam, in qua S. Celsi venerabile nunc adoratur corpus; ex altera vero ecclesiam ubi quondam (ut fertur) diu sanctus prelatuit Nazarius. (*Vitæ SS. Arialdi et Erlembadi,* ed. Migne, *Pat. Lat.,* CXLIII, 1481).

throne [that is, in 1097, so the date 1090 written in the margin is incorrect] the archbishop Anselmo learned that the bones and body of Arialdo had been indeed badly buried, and he went in procession with a few clerks to the place, and gathered together such bones as he could find, and deposited them in the church of S. Dionigi."[27] Galvaneo della Fiamma states: "Then the priests vested with their stoles came together in order that they might bury the martyr with every solemnity in the monastery of S. Celso. Anselmo IV, archbishop of Milan, afterwards translated the remains to the church of S. Dionigi."[28]

The monastery is mentioned in a tax-list of 1398 published by Magistretti, and was evidently at this time in a flourishing condition. About the middle of the XV century it was given in commendam.[29] The portal was restored in 1454 by the abbot Carlo, according to an inscription no longer extant but seen and copied by Allegranza c. 1760.[30] In 1549 the pope Paolo III gave the church and the monastery to the canons regular of S. Salvatore.[31] The church was restored at this time, and the façade in especial was much defaced. Another barocco restoration followed in 1651, according to the inscription

Theodorus Cardinalis Princeps Trivultius

MDCLI

which Latuada[32] read on the façade. In 1730 and 1777[33] still further damage was done to the ancient architecture.

From the description of Latuada, written in 1737, we learn that at this epoch there was a piazza in front of the church. Over the western portal

---

[27] Itaque multis dubitantibus, multisque congaudentibus, plurimisque credentibus, tandem pallio superimposito in lectica compositus est, quo assumpto, & quasi Levita cum stola ornato, summis cum Litaniis, magnisque exaltationibus, plurimisque confrequentationibus in Monasterio Sancti Celsi humatum est. . . . Cum enim post biennium [in margine eodem charactere: scilicet MXC] suæ consecrationis Dominus Anselmus Arialdi ossa, & corpus, qualiter malè olim in veritate fuissent humata comperisset, curialiter cum paucis Clericis ad locum tendens, ossa, quae habere potuit, colligens, in Ecclesia S. Dionysii humavit.

[28] Tunc currentes sacerdotes cum stolis et mirabili solemnitate ut martyrem sanctissimum in monasterio sancti Celsi sepeliverunt, cuius ossa Anselmus quartus archiepiscopus mediolanensis ad ecclesiam sancti Dyonisii transtulit . . . (Galvanei Flammae, *Chron. Maius*, ed. Ceruti, 628).

For a more detailed study of the sources of the burial and translation of S. Arialdo, see C. Pellegrini, 'Fonti e memorie storiche di S. Arialdo,' in *Archivio Storico Lombardo*, Anno XXIX, 1902, Vol. XVII, 60.

[29] Caffi.

[30] *Spiegazioni*, 168.

[31] Bugati, 157. Compare also: [Eccla] Celsi, Abbatia, Ecclia data est bnís cancis regularibus nuncupatis schopetinj, ordinis sti Augustinj (*Status ecclesiae Mediolani 1568* conscriptus auctore Francesco Castello, MS. Amb., A, 112, Inf., f. 443). Celsi cancor[um] regularium or sti Augustini ut z. (*Ibid.*, f. 444).

[32] III, 44.

[33] Inscription on west façade.

were sculptures, undoubtedly the same as those which still exist. The church itself was divided into three aisles, and had six arcades on each side. There were altogether six chapels including the choir.[34] Torre's description written in 1674 corroborates Latuada in regard to the number of bays of the nave.[35]

In 1779 the tower was restored, its stairway erected and new bells added.[36] This restoration was followed in 1782 by a translation of the body of the saint.[37] In 1793 the canons of S. Salvatore were suppressed, and the church was desecrated, but in 1795 it was reopened for worship only to be desecrated again by the French troops in 1797. In 1800 it was finally restored to the priests.[38]

In August, 1818, in order to improve the lighting of the neighbouring church of S. Maria, the four western bays of the nave were demolished.[39] A new façade was erected in which, however, the ancient portal was reconstructed. In the south wall of the garden which is in front of the church, the capitals and other architectural fragments of the demolished portions of the structure were gathered together.[40] Other fragments have found their way in considerable number to the archæological museum in the Castello Sforzesco.

About the middle of the XIX century, De Dartein made a careful study of the remains of the ancient church, and collected all the information available as to its condition before its partial destruction. He notes that before 1818 the edifice had been covered with a barocco vault which was then destroyed, and a new vault erected. His authorities for this statement are a drawing

[34] Innanzi alla Chiesa vi ha una Piazza di proporzionata ampiezza. All'ingresso per la Porta maggiore, che conserva alcuni intagli da rozza mano scolpiti, etc. . . . La Chiesa poi è divisa in tre Navi con sei Archi per ogni lato, sostenuti da grossi Pilastri, lavorati in forma di mezze Colonne con Capitelli su l'ordine Corintio. Ha sei Cappelle, computandosi la maggiore . . . (Latuada, III, 44-48).

[35] In tre Naui vedesi la Chiesa compartita con sei Archi per lato sostenuti da poderosi Pilastri fabbricati per entro à mezze Colonne con Capitelli Corintij. (Torre, 80).

[36] In the south wall of the campanile is this inscription:

TVRRIS . RESTAVRATA .

SCALIS . MARMOREIS . ERECTIS .

CAMPANIS . AVCTIS . ET . ADDITIS .

AVREOR . $\overline{\text{MMM}}$.

IMPENSA .

MDCCLXXIX

D. GVLLIELMO . BIVMI . ABBATE .

ET CANONICIS .

[37] Inscription in south wall of church.

[38] Forcella, *Chiese*, 653.

[39] The body of S. Celso was translated out of the church to S. Maria in 1813, according to an inscription in the south wall.

[40] Caffi.

of Canonica which showed the old barrel vault of the nave, and some traces of this vault which he believed to have discovered under the roof. De Dartein was evidently mistaken in thinking that the church was originally roofed in timber. The remains still extant make it evident that it was of the type of Rivolta d'Adda (Plate 195); that is, that the choir was barrel-vaulted, the nave rib-vaulted. If, therefore, the choir vault has been reconstructed—as is in all probability the case—it was undoubtedly along the lines of the original Lombard edifice. De Dartein recognizes that the upper part of the church had been entirely rebuilt: "Il ne subsiste plus du monument lombard que les parties inférieures." He speaks of the restorations executed in 1852, and mentions that the corbels of the arched corbel-tables of the interior of the apse were restored without authority, and that the windows and exterior cornice are entirely modern. Of the groin vaults of the side aisles at least one is ancient. Buttresses were placed against the alternate piers only.[41]

As a result of the studies of De Dartein, the restorers decided to place in the façade of the church a marble plan of the edifice destroyed in 1818.

III. The monument consists at present of a nave of a single double bay (Plate 126, Fig. 2), two side aisles, an apse and a campanile, but the existing nave was originally a choir, and a nave of two double bays extended to the westward. Even the small portion of the original edifice that still survives has been much denatured by barocco restorations, so that it is exceedingly difficult to ascertain the original dispositions. The side aisles are covered with highly domed groin vaults supplied with wall ribs. The nave is barrel-vaulted, and such was undoubtedly the original disposition, although the existing vault appears to have been remade in the barocco period. The system is alternate; from the intermediate piers rise colonnettes which support the transverse arch of the barrel vault. The section of the piers seems to imply clearly that the western bays of the nave were rib-vaulted. The side-aisle responds were alternately heavy and light, of three or five members. There was no gallery, but there may have been a clearstory in the western bays of the nave. The masonry is formed of cross-hatched bricks, wide, but generally of moderate length, laid in horizontal courses separated by mortar-beds of normal thickness. The capitals, bases, piers and trimmings are of stone. The apse is reinforced with heavy buttresses, and the side-aisle walls were originally supplied with similar buttresses.

IV. A number of capitals of S. Celso are still preserved, either in the church itself (Plate 126, Fig. 2), in the garden to the west of it (Plate 125, Fig. 4), or in the Museo Archeologico (Plate 126, Fig. 3). They are all of homogeneous character, and are characterized by a certain coarseness of execution (Plate 126, Fig. 3) which recalls the capitals of S. Giorgio in

[41] De Dartein, 187, Plate XLVI.

Palazzo (Plate 128, Fig. 5). The grotesque element is prominent (Plate 126, Fig. 3). Animals which devour each other, or with their tails or hind legs intertwined, two rams or other animals having a single head which forms the volute, eagles (Plate 126, Fig. 2), sirens, and other typical grotesque motives abound. One capital shows a man holding a tree in his right hand, and in his left the bridle of a saddled horse, the hind leg of which is grasped by another man, who also holds a tree. This sculpture, which not improbably may have a definite content, recalls representations of the month of May in the sculptured calendars. A second capital shows a woman in a niche, a man on either side. A third represents an angel with a book. The abaci are frequently much reduced, but in other cases are ornamented with palmettes, interlaces, rinceaux or vine-patterns. The foliage is very dry and Byzantinesque, with crisp acanthus leaves; much use is made of carved all-over patterns in two planes. The bases are Attic with griffes, the archivolts are in two unmoulded orders.

The apse is adorned externally with a cornice of blind niches in two orders, and internally with an arched corbel-table—the latter an extraordinary feature. The corbels of this, carved with the symbols of the Evangelists, with grotesques and with string-patterns, are modern. The gable line of the eastern wall of the church is still marked by an ancient cornice of arched corbel-tables, but the wall has evidently been raised in modern times. The windows are moulded.

The ancient portal of the west façade is at present quite different in appearance from what it was in the XVIII century, to judge from the engraving published by Giulini. Not only have the barocco adornments disappeared, but the capitals are Romanesque, whereas in Giulini's drawing they appear Gothic. It is evident from an inspection of the stone and the carving, that only the outer capitals of the present portal are ancient, and that the others have been restored (Plate 126, Fig. 1). Whence came the two ancient capitals there is no means of telling, but Giulini's engraving shows that they can not be in their original position. The original capitals were probably of a Corinthianesque type, like those of the Modena portals; which might easily acquire a Gothic-like appearance in the hands of an inaccurate engraver. The sculptured roll-moulding of the archivolt of the existing portal is evidently in part ancient and in part modern. The sculptured architrave clearly once belonged to a wider door, since the scenes at both extremities are cut off and only in part visbile. Below this archivolt are two caryatids, one of which is indecent.

On the archivolt are reliefs depicting the life of the saint. According to the legend, S. Nazaro was baptized at Rome by St. Peter. His mother was a Christian, and he resisted the attempts of his father to initiate him in the mysteries of the pagan religion. Thereupon Nazaro left Rome, and travelled through Italy baptizing. Arrived at Milan, he found Protasio and Gervasio

in prison. Being inspired in a vision by his mother, he next went to Gaul.
Here a certain woman, among the noblest of the city, believed in Christ, and
brought her son Celso to Nazaro. Nero sent and caused Nazaro and Celso to
be arrested and brought to Rome. Here they were ordered to sacrifice to
the idols, but at the prayer of the saints the images collapsed. Thereupon
the emperor ordered the saints to be carried out to sea in a boat, and thrown
overboard, but in vain, since the saints, invoking the cross which they carried,
walked upon the waters.[42] A sudden storm arose, and the sailors were about
to be capsized, but were saved upon being converted and praying to S. Nazaro.
It is evident that the second scene from the right represents the two saints
walking on the water. They are both beardless and haloed, but Nazaro carries
the cross. Further to the left are seen the two sailors who watch the miracle—
or perhaps the storm—with an expression of awe. The storm is indicated
by a demon who blows the sail of the boat. The scene to the right, which
is cut off, and can only be seen in part, possibly represents the entombment
of the saints after their execution, in which case it is out of place. At the
bottom is seen a sarcophagus-like object, over which is suspended a haloed
figure. By the head—which alone is visible—stands a personage, possibly
a cleric. Behind is another taller, only partly to be seen.[43] The legend tells
us that after the saints had reached Genoa by ship, they proceeded to Milan,
where they were again arrested. The third scene of the archivolt represents
the two saints distributing alms to the people of Milan, while a messenger
arrives on horse-back to seize them. The saints are again beardless and
haloed. It is probably Nazaro who distributes the alms to the poor, while
Celso stands with his hands placed in a gesture of dismay, as he sees the good
work so rudely interrupted. The fourth scene shows the two saints still
beardless and haloed, haled by two officers before Anolinus who is crowned
and sits on a throne. The last scene to the left shows the execution of the
saints, but is only in part visible. An executioner strikes off the head of the
kneeling Celso. Behind, Nazaro stands between two palm trees, symbols of
martyrdom, awaiting his turn, with hands clasped in a gesture of prayer and
resignation.[44] Heads are inserted between the arches of the arcade into which
the archivolt is divided, and similar heads appear in the base of one of the
columns to the left.

Considered from the point of view of style, the first thing which strikes
the observer of these sculptures is their crudity. The enormous hands, the

[42] Suscipitur in nauim Nazarius et puer. ad consueta uero arma confugientes signo
crucis muniti (331). . . . et ibat beatus Nazarius cum puero gradiens super aquas
gaudiens et glorificans dominum. (*Sanctorum Nazarii et Celsi Martyrum Passio*, cit.
Mombrizio, ed. 1910, II, 332).

[43] See text cited above, p. 605.

[44] Iussit itaque eos duci extra ciuitatem foras portam romanam in locum qui
dicitur tres moros; et ibi eos decapitauerunt oceulte [*sic*]. . . . (*Ibid.*).

crudely worked eyes, the lack of all artistic feeling, show in a striking manner how wide a gulf separates these reliefs of Milan from contemporary works in Emilia. Nevertheless they are closely connected with the school of Guglielmo, and are not improbably the work of one of his pupils. The boat (Plate 126, Fig. 1) is precisely like the boat in the architrave of the Porta dei Principi (Plate 142, Fig. 4) at Modena, and, indeed, this entire scene, with its wind demon, is evidently inspired by the much freer and far superior relief at Modena. The treatment of the populace of Milan in the third subject (Plate 126, Fig. 1) is entirely similar to the treatment of the figures on either side of the Virgin in the lunette of the northern portal at Borgo S. Donnino (Plate 29, Fig. 5), and the two figures of the officers in the fourth subject show close points of contact with the works of that same sculptor, who also collaborated with Guglielmo in the Porta della Pescheria at Modena (Plate 144, Fig. 8). The two caryatids are of a type introduced by Guglielmo and later taken over by Nicolò. The division of the architrave into arcades by means of spiral-fluted columns in relief, bearing arches, is paralleled in the works of Nicolò at Piacenza (Plate 181, Fig. 1; Plate 182, Fig. 4).

V. The style of the reliefs of the archivolt therefore shows that they are the work of a follower of Guglielmo da Modena, who came strongly under the influence of the two other followers, one of whom worked before 1106 upon the Porta della Pescheria at Modena, and in 1106 at Borgo S. Donnino, the other of whom executed the Porta dei Principi c. 1120. The S. Celso sculptor also shows points of contact with the works of Nicolò at Piacenza begun in 1122. These sculptures may, therefore, well have been executed c. 1125. This ascription of date is confirmed by a study of the architecture. The coarseness of technique in the capitals, we have seen, is analogous to the work at S. Giorgio in Palazzo, an authentically dated monument of 1129. The entire edifice, therefore, may be considered a homogeneous structure of c. 1125.

MILAN, S. EUSTORGIO

(Plate 127, Fig. 1, 2, 8, 4, 5, 6)

I. The problems presented by the church of S. Eustorgio are so peculiarly complicated, that no archæologist has yet had the courage to attempt a complete monograph on the edifice. The literature of the monument is, nevertheless, rich. A photograph of the old façade made before its demolition is preserved in the Castello Sforza, and another print from the same negative may be found in the archives of the parish. This façade was described by Villa[1] in 1627. Somewhat later in the XVII century Puccinelli published a

[1] 283.

valuable collection of the numerous inscriptions which in his days were still to
be seen in the cloister and chapels. The account of Latuada, which appeared
in 1737, contains valuable historical information quoted verbatim from a now
lost manuscript chronicle of S. Eustorgio. Latuada speaks of the piers of
the interior as being of the Corinthian order, and states that there were fifteen
chapels. As he understood the manuscript chronicle, before 1862 the church
had no crypt, and the choir, which extended through the three eastern bays
of the nave, was separated from the latter by a heavy cross-wall or jubé.
This jubé was surmounted by a pulpit. In front of the jubé on the north
side was the chapel of S. Pietro Martire, with the arca of the saint surrounded
by a screen. The principal entrance to the church was on the south side.
On the south side of the western entrance, in the time of Latuada, was an
exterior pulpit of terra-cotta.[2] Pirovano described the church in 1826, and
like Latuada states that the principal entrance was originally on the south
side.[3] In 1841 appeared the monograph of Caffi, containing a valuable
historical notice, and the publication of numerous inscriptions. The same
author wrote another but far less valuable monograph some forty-five years
later. The study of De Dartein is particularly valuable because this
archæologist appears to have been the only competent person present at the
restoration of 1862-1886. De Dartein came to the conclusion that originally
the church had been covered by a wooden roof, and his principal ground for
this opinion was the fact that before the restoration he saw the remains of
a wall rib projecting above the existing vaults of the nave.[4] He believed that
the apse and the eastern bay of the nave and the side aisles, including the
responds, were clearly earlier than the apse, and he gave a description of the
works of exploration carried out in this part of the basilica that will be cited
below. The chronicle of Rotta is a most important source for a study of the
radical changes wrought in the XIX century restoration. The church leapt
into the archæological limelight through the study of Cattaneo, who made of
it one of the corner-stones of his constructive system of archæology. Rivoira,[5]
following in the footsteps of Cattaneo, has published an admirable half-tone
of the apse and a résumé of the architectural features of the monument.

[2] Latuada, III, 231.

[3] In origine aveva la sua fronte verso S. Barnaba con due archi che le servivano
di portico. Nel secolo XIII fu rimodernata ed anche ingrandita. . . . Il campanile,
assai ragguardevole per l'altezza, e per la bella costruzione, fu ultimato nel 1309. . . .
La chiesa ha tre porte corrispondenti alle tre navi dell'interno. . . . Una porta si è
conservata, ove la chiesa aveva l'antica sua facciata; vi si osserva il sepolcro posto in
alto di Federico Maggi. . . . In seguito trovasi la cappella degli stessi Re Magi (153).

[4] Avant que le mur de façade n'eût été reconstruit, ce qui eut lieu de 1863 à 1865,
on voyait sous le toit, contre cette muraille (j'ai fait l'observation en 1861) un ancien
arc formeret plus élevé que les voûtes de la grande nef et paraissant appartenir à
quelque système d'arcs transversaux préexistant à ces voûtes (208).

[5] 211.

The monograph of Nava is of minor importance. In 1911 Biscaro published an important study of the chapel of S. Pietro Martire.

II. According to the ancient Milanese tradition, S. Eustorgio rises near a spot of peculiar veneration, since there St. Barnabas, thought to have been the first bishop of Milan, is said to have erected the first altar and the first baptistery in Lombardy.[6]

According to the legend, S. Eustorgio was sent by the emperor of Constantinople as a legate to Milan. While there he was chosen by the people as their bishop. He returned to Constantinople, where the emperor gave him leave to go to Milan, and also presented him with relics. The saint chose a marble sarcophagus containing the bodies of the three Magi which, with much difficulty, he succeeded in transporting to Milan. Arrived thither, he placed the sarcophagus in a church built in his time in that city. The saint himself, moreover, was buried in the same church which afterwards came to be called by his name.[7] The same events are related in the chronicle which passes under the name of Filippo da Castel Seprio,[8] and in that of Lampugnano de Legnano, the latter of whom, however, adds a beautiful miracle. When the saint, coming from Piacenza, had arrived at a short distance from the city of Milan, one of the cows which was pulling the wagon on which the sarcophagus was carried, was eaten by a wolf, but, at the prayer of the saint, the wolf took the place of the cow he had eaten, and, yoked with the other cow, mildly consented to pull the bodies of the martyrs into the city.[9] Other versions of the story

---

[6] Quanta reuerētia sit habitus locus scti Eustorgii diligens lector auertat, primo qd habitatio p[er] septe annos fuit bti Barnabe apl'i primi archiepi mli ut supra dictū est C. xxxviii. Sedo qd ibi primo fuit situm altare, [et] missa dicta, et sacri ordines celebrati, an qm btus petrus Romā ueisset. Terdo qd ibi fuit pimū baptisteriū. Et pīmus locus baptismatis qui uqm in lombardia fuerit, ut s dictū est C. xlm. Quarto qd ibi fuit īnuabiliū martirum sepultura reuerētie indicibilis. Et hec fcta sūt circa fonte sctm p[er] plures annos an qm in mlo fuerit fcta aliqa ecca. nec dicta missa aliqua. (Galvaneo della Fiamma, *Cronaca*, Vienna Cod. 3318, f. 20, C. lxxxiiij).

[7] . . . arcam marmoream sanctam et sacratissimam sanctorum trium magorum et regum corpora continentem. Hanc autem super eleuatam diuino auxilio comitiua adiutus: tanto proficiscens itinere terra marique multisque laborans uigiliis et orationibus fide plenus ad memoratam urbem usque deduxit. Itaque in celebri loco ubi in diebus suis in honore dei et ipsorum honorabilis est fabricata ecclesia eandem arcam cum sanctorum trium regum corporibus honestissime collocauit: . . . Sepultus est autem beatus Eustorgius in uenerabili sanctorum regum ecclesia; in ipsius honore et nomine postmodum constituta. (Ed. Mombrizio, I, 473 f.).

[8] Huius [S. Eustorgii] tempore triu' Magor[um] Corpora ad ciuitatē Mli deducta sunt: vbi plus qz octingentis Annis in Loco vbi est nuc ecclia sancti Eustorgij fuit frum ordinis p[re]dicator[um] quieuere. (Filippo da Castel Seprio, *Chronica*, MS. Amb., C. S. IV, 18, f. 19).

[9] Beatus Eustorgius nacione grecus Mediolan' archiepus decimus anno dni cccxiij. sedit annis xvij. . . . per mare cum archa marmorea mirabilis magnitudinis usqz Venetias. ac postea contra padi fluenta usqz placetiam p[er]duxit. de placentia vsqz

are slightly different. In one it is S. Eustorgio himself, not the wolf, who takes the place of the deceased cow. When the cortège arrives at Milan and passes the spot where is the present basilica, it is found impossible to move the body farther, in accordance with which divine portent a church is erected on the site to contain the bodies.[10] The critical historians of Milan, however, have shown themselves obdurate towards all this picturesque legend, and insist that the bodies of the Magi were not brought to Milan until a much later time.[11] That S. Eustorgio did, however, found the church, may be safely argued from the circumstances that he was here buried and that the basilica assumed his name.

In a sentence of 1119,[12] S. Eustorgio is mentioned as one of the eleven mother-churches of Milan, and as officiated by decumani. It is entirely probable that the same clergy had existed in the church from a very early period. In 1034 a bequest was made to the church by the archbishop Ariberto.[13] In 1121 a legacy was left to the *labor* of the church.[14] Another legacy given *ad laborem et retinentiam ipsius ecclesiae* was recorded in an inscription without date which came to light in the restoration.[15]

When the army of Barbarossa appeared before Milan in 1159, the relics of the Magi were translated to the church of S. Giorgio, and the basilica of S. Eustorgio was ruined by the Milanesi, that it might not afford protection to the imperial troops. When the emperor took the city, he carried off the relics from S. Giorgio to Cologne. These facts are known from several sources. In the chronicle of William of Newburg, a contemporary though distant authority, we read: "When the Milanesi demolished and destroyed the suburbs

prope Mediolam̄ cum duabus uacis auriga angelo duce p[er]duxit ubi dum uaca pasceretur herbas lupus ipāz iugulauit in loco ubi postea p[er] miraculū Monasterium de Banuacha constructū fuit nam ad p̄ceptum beati eustorgii lupus uace officium gerens usque ad ciuitatē conduxit, beatus uero Eustorgius tantū texaurū xpo et angelo duci recom̄dauit, ut in loco magis secreto conderetur, tunc fusa oratione et ieiunio celebrato, lupus et uaca nullo humano ingenio corpora Magorū in lutum p[er]maximū ingesserut ubi plusqz xv corpora martirum sepulta fuisse creduntur . . . ubi postea ecclam̄ fabricari fecit Beatus Eustorgius anno dni cccxxx. die tertio ante kal̄l octubris. Jacet in eccla fratrū predicatorū in altari maiori. (Lampugnano de Legnano, *Chronica*, MS. Amb., H 56 Sup., 58).

10 Fumagalli, IV, *Dis.* 35.   11 *Ibid.*, 289.

12 Giulini, VII, 85.   13 Puricelli, 366.

14 Anno dominice incar. mill. cent. vigeximo primo Kal. aprilis indict. quartadecima. Ego in dei nomine Ambrosius qui dicor Lagimus . . . confirmo ut statim post meum decessum habeat archiepiscopus etc. . . . et si ipsi mei nepotes non permiserint predictam coniugem meam quiete et pacifice habere et tenere predictum usufructum . . . tunc ipsi vel ipse qui hoc malum fecit perdant predictum iudicatum de iamscripta terra et casis et deueniant ad partem laboris iamscripte ecclesie sancti Eustorgii ad faciendum predictum annuale. Et insuper volo et iudico ut reliqua mobilia . . . presenti die deueniat in iure iamscripti laboris sancti Eustorgii ad retinendum ipsum laborem . . . (*Codice della Croce*, MS. Amb., D. S. IV, Vol. 5, f. 147).

15 Rotta, 23.

of Milan, lest they should prove harmful to the besieged and useful to the besiegers, they demolished for the same reason an ancient and noble monastery situated without the walls of the city, and celebrated for the relics of the saints which it contained. They translated into the city whatever was found in the monastery that was holy and venerable, and especially the bodies of the three Magi, who adored the Infant Saviour with mystic gifts, and thus became the first fruit of the Gentiles to God and the Lamb. And that treasure deposited long before secretly in the church, lay in a place unknown to the monks [sic] and clerks who officiated there, but when the church was destroyed to its foundations, it was found and revealed by manifest tokens . . . The victorious emperor destroyed the city . . . and translated those august relics of the Magi there buried to Germany, to the great grief of the Lombards, and the custody of this treasure now ennobles the city of Cologne."[16] It is from this text of William of Newburg that is derived the notice of Sigonio: "For this reason they demolished the ancient monastery [sic] of S. Eustorgio very venerable because of the many relics of the saints which it contained, and whatever sacred things were in it they brought into the city."[17] In Otto of St.-Blaise we read: "The emperor entered the city with his whole army and carried off an immense amount of very valuable plunder from among the treasures of the churches and other precious things. And he collected from the churches the relics of the saints in which this city was especially rich, and he brought them together with great reverence. Among these relics were found those of the three Magi who, led by the Star, adored Christ in the manger with gifts, and these he gave to Reginald, bishop of Cologne, who had particularly distinguished himself with his troops in the siege, and these relics the venerable bishop translated across the Alps and gave to the church of Cologne."[18] Sire Raoul states: "All the altars were violated. The relics of many saints were carried away. . . . On the tenth day of March, 1164,

[16] Cumque suburbana demolirentur atque diruerent, ne tantum obsessis nociva quantum obsidentibus usui forent, eadem ratione monasterium quoque antiquum et nobile, et sanctorum insigne reliquiis extra moenia destruentes, quicquid in eo sacrum reverendumque repertum est, in urbem transtulerunt: trium præcipue Magorum corpora, qui Salvatoris infantiam mysticis honorando muneribus, facti sunt ex gentibus primitiæ Deo et Agno. Et quidem thesaurus iste, olim in ejusdem ecclesiæ secreto repositus, ipsos quoque monachos clericosque ibidem ministrantes latebat; sed cum usque ad fundamentum destrueretur ipsa ecclesia, repertus et revelatus est cum manifestis indiciis. . . . Victor imperator civitatem evertit; . . . præclaras illas Magorum reliquias ibidem reconditas, Longobardis ægre ferentibus, in regnum Teutonicum transtulit, et thesauri hujus custodia civitatem Coloniam insignivit. (Willelmi Parvi, canonici de Novoburgo, *Historia Rerum Anglicarum* II, 8, ed. Howlett, *Chronicles,* etc., I, 115).

[17] Ea de caussa vetustum monasterium, & sanctorum multorum relliquijs augustissimũ S. Eustorgij euerterunt à fundamentis, & quidquid in eo sacrati erat, transtulerunt in vrbem. (Sigonio, 499, ad ann. 1159).

[18] Ingressus enim Imperator cum toto exercitu, immensa ac ditissima spolia, in Ecclesiasticis thesauris aliisque rebus pretiosis diripuit, Reliquiisque Sanctorum, quibus

Reginald, chamberlain and archbishop of Cologne, took the bodies of the holy martyrs Nabore and Felice and that of the holy confessor, it is said, as well as three other bodies which were deposited in a sarcophagus in the church of S. Eustorgio, and which were said to be the bodies of the three Magi, and he brought them to Cologne."[19]   In Ricobaldo of Ferrara we read: "The bodies of the three Magi, translated in olden times from Persia to Constantinople, and from there to Milan, were carried thence by order of the emperor Barbarossa to Cologne."[20]   Similarly Galvaneo della Fiamma states: "In the time of Constantine the bodies of the three Magi were brought to the city of Milan where they rested more than eight hundred years in the place where is now the monastery of the Dominicans."[21]   Elsewhere in the same *Manipulus Florum* Galvaneo writes: "When the Milanesi heard that the emperor was coming, they feared, as says the chronicle of Leo, lest the bodies of the three Magi should be carried away.   They therefore took those kings from the church of S. Eustorgio, and hid them in the church of S. Giorgio near the campanile because that church was inside the walls."[22]   In Giovanni da Musso we read: "In the year of Christ 1164, the emperor Federico ordered the bodies of the Magi and of three other saints miraculously discovered in S. Eustorgio of Milan to be translated to Cologne."[23]

hæc civitas egregiè nobilitata fuit, per Ecclesias collectis, ac cum magna reverentia asportatis, tres Magos, qui cum muneribus stella duce Christum in cunabulis adoraverunt, inibi inventos, Reginoldo Coloniensi Episcopo, qui in hac obsidione cum sua militia præcipuè claruit, dono dedit: quos venerabilis Pontifex ad cisalpina transferens, Coloniensi Ecclesiæ intulit. (Ottonis de Sancto Blasio, *Chronicon*, XVI, ed. Muratori, R. I. S., VI, 874).

[19] Altaria omnia violata sunt. Sanctorum multorum Reliquiæ exportatæ sunt. . . . Decimo verò die ejusdem mensis Raynaldus Cancellarius, ac Coloniensis Archiepiscopus tulit corpora Sanctorum Martyrum Naboris atque Felicis, & Sancti Confessoris, prout dicebatur; & tria alia corpora, quæ erant condita in archa quæ erat in Ecclesia Beati Eustorgii, & quæ dicebantur esse Magorum trium & exportavit Coloniam. (Sire Raul, *De Rebus Gestis Friderici I*, ed. Muratori, R. I. S., 1187, 1189).

[20] Corpora trium Magorum, olim de Perside in Constantinopolim translata, deinde Mediolanum, inde per hunc Imperatorem in Coloniam Agrippinam translata sunt. (Ricobaldi Ferrariensis, *Compilatio Chronologica*, ed. Muratori, R. I. S., IX, 244).

[21] Cujus tempore trium Magorum corpora ad Civitatem Mediolani conducta sunt, ubi plusquam 800. annis in loco, ubi nunc stat Conventus Fratrum Prædicatorum, quieverunt. (Galvanei Flammæ, *Manipulus Florum*, ed. Muratori, R. I. S., XI, 565).

[22] Audientes ergo Mediolanenses Imperatoris adventum, ut dicit Chronica Leonis, timentes ne trium Magorum Corpora exportarentur, ipsos Reges de Ecclesia S. Eusorgii abstulerunt, & in Ecclesia S. Georgii juxta Campanile absconderunt, quia illa Ecclesia erat intra muros. (Galvanei Flammæ, *Manipulus Florum*, CLXXVIII, ed. Muratori, R. I. S., XI, 636). Anno Domini 1164. [MS. Amb. MCLXIII] Imperator de Alamannia in Italiam rediit, & Archiepiscopo Coloniensi Civitatem Mediolanensem recommendavit, qui XI. die Julii Corpora trium Magorum in Alamanniam de Campanili S. Georgii exportavit. (*Ibid.*, CXCI, ed. M., 644).

[23] Anno Christi MCLXIV. ipse Imperator Fredericus jussit Corpora trium Magorum, & aliorum Sanctorum à S. Eustorgio Mediolani miraculosè elevata trans-

That the Milanesi destroyed the church of S. Eustorgio at the time of the coming of Barbarossa is stated, therefore, only by William of Newburg, although many chroniclers relate the translation of the bodies of the Magi. The statement of the English monk is certainly exaggerated. The church of S. Eustorgio was not destroyed to its foundations in 1159, since many portions of the existing edifice are undoubtedly earlier than this date. However, the monument itself bears witness that it was in part reconstructed after 1164. We may therefore accept as an historical fact that it was ruined, although not completely destroyed, in 1159.

At the end of the XII century there existed in the church a chapter of canons regular. This is first mentioned in a bull of Alexander III, of March 28, 1172,[24] and is again referred to in a bull of Celestine III, of 1194.[25]

It is generally stated by the historians of Milan that the chapter was supplanted by a Dominican monastery in the year 1220.[26] In fact, an inscription of 1578, formerly over the western portal,[27] and now in the second chapel from the east in the northern side aisle, states that the Dominicans were installed by the archbishop, Enrico da Settala, who sat from 1213 to 1230. The same notice is given by Galvaneo della Fiamma.[28] It is probable, however, that Enrico established the Dominicans in the year 1216, as is stated in an inedited text of Lampugnano de Legnano.[29]

The establishment of the Dominicans must have caused a restoration, or, at least, a redecoration of the church, since an altar was consecrated in 1249.[30]

According to Latuada, the monks immediately began to construct the campanile, but works were soon interrupted, and resumed only in 1252. In 1278 the monastery was finished.[31] Work on the campanile was resumed in 1297, and the structure was completed in 1309.[32] Latuada, following a manuscript chronicle, gives a detailed account of the changes wrought in the edifice in the early years of the XIV century. There was made, he says, an enclosure of coupled columns of red marble, shutting off two piers on the

portari Coloniam Alamanniæ. (Johannis de Mussis, *Chronicon Placentinum*, ed. Muratori, R. I. S., XVI, 454).

[24] *Codice della Croce*, MS. Amb., D. S. IV, 9/I, 9, f. 168, 167.

[25] Muratori, A. I. M. A., ed. A., VIII, 69.

[26] See, for example, Latuada, III, 189. Puccinelli, 171, without citing authorities, ascribes the establishment of the Dominican monastery to March, 1220, and in this he is followed by Caffi. On the other hand, Rotta (*Pass.*, 83) assigns the foundation to 1227, similarly without citing authorities.

[27] Puccinelli, *Vita di S. Senatore*, 30-31.

[28] Locum sancti Eustorgii dedit fratribus predicatoribus . . . (Galvanei Flammae, *Chron. Maius*, ed. Ceruti, 768).

[29] . . . et isto anno [1216] predictus dns archiepus dedit ecclam sci Eustorgij frbz p[re]dicatoribz. (Lampugnano de Legnano, *Chronica*, MS. Amb., H 56 Sup., f. 69).

[30] Latuada, *loc. cit.*   [31] Latuada, *loc. cit.;* Caffi, X.

[32] Rotta, 7; Pirovano, 153.

north side of the nave, that is to say, the one next to the choir-screen and the next one adjoining to the westward. Within the enclosure formed by this railing, which was completed in 1312, was erected a chapel paved with black and white marble, finished in 1327. In this chapel was placed the arca of S. Pietro Martire, the work of Giovanni Balducci da Pisa. In 1340 the body of the saint was translated into the arca, and in 1362 there was constructed "towards the garden and the street," that is east of the church, and "in the form of the Pazzi chapel in Florence," the chapel of S. Pietro Martire ad Caput. When the entrance to the church was changed from the south to the west side, the arca of the saint was found to be placed in a dark and unsuitable place, and was consequently translated in 1736 to the chapel ad Caput, east of the church.[33] Latuada also states that the body of the church was vaulted in the time of Gian Galeazzo Visconti (†1402), the columns of the older church, which existed before the establishment of the monastery, being retained.[34] In 1413 Filippo Maria Visconti caused the *pontile* (by which is probably meant the choir-screen placed back of the arca of the saint) and the pulpit to be reconstructed.[35] This choir-screen shut off the three eastern bays from the nave, and continued to divide the church into two parts until 1736. Latuada also states that at the time of the translation of 1340, the church was restored, the capitals and windows altered, and three doors opened in the western façade.[36] In 1420 the large cloister was erected.[37] Latuada's statements in general merit faith, but he was mistaken in thinking that the chapel of S. Pietro Martire was erected in 1362, unless, indeed, it has been rebuilt, since the present structure dates from c. 1441.[38] It was subsequently redecorated in 1577 and in 1591.[39] In 1526 the monastery suffered severely at the hands of the German and Spanish troops who were quartered in it. Among the other restorations carried out in consequence of this damage, as De Dartein has conjectured, was included the addition of a crypt. This was finished in 1537, when the altar was removed to the apse. At this period, the choir, which had formerly been raised only two steps, was raised above the crypt constructed of nine colonnettes taken from the great cloister.[40]

[33] Latuada, III, 218.   [34] This is clearly an error.

[35] . . . Filippo Maria Visconti, terzo Duca di Milano verso l'anno 1413 fece fare la Loggia del Pontile, che era nel mezzo della Chiesa di marmo, sopra del quale era solito di cantarsi l'Epistola.

[36] Nell'occasione della traslazione fu ristorata la Chiesa, ornandola ne' Pilastri coi capitelli d'ordine Corintio; se le introdusse maggiore luce col taglio delle finistre, che prima erano di forma rotonda, e si aprirono le tre Porte, come abbiamo notato, della parte del Cimiterio, che ora introducono alla Chiesa. (Latuada, III, 229).

[37] Latuada, III, 231; Allegranza, *De Sep. Chris.*, 75.

[38] Biscaro.   [39] Caffi, X.

[40] Nell'anno 1537 il Padre Maestro Bernardino Crivelli Inquisitore di Novara fece trasportare l'Altar grande dal mezzo della Cappella, cioè dal mezzo del Santuario d'oggi, al luogo dove or' è stabilito; essendo detta Cappella prima tutta alta due scalini, per la quale dovendosi ire alla Sagrestia, ed al Corpo di San Pietro Martire, se ne scende-

Bianca Maria Visconti Sforza built the western portal, and adorned it with the escutcheon of her son, Galeazzo Maria.[41] In 1561 the new altar of the church was consecrated. Various chapels of the church were restored in 1603, 1621 and 1650. In the early part of the XVIII century the pavement was relaid. In 1730-1731 the chapel of S. Giovanni Evangelista was redecorated, and in 1736 the chapels of the Magi and S. Domenico were restored, and the altar of S. Vincenzo erected. In this same year, as has been seen, the choir-screen and chapel of S. Pietro were removed from the nave, and it was probably at this same time that the church was covered with stucco. The Cappella del Rosario was remade in 1740, and adorned with the statue of the Virgin in 1781. In 1742 the chapel of S. Giuseppe was restored.

In 1798 the monastery was suppressed, giving place to the parochial organization that had been established in 1787. In 1821 the chapel of S. Eugenio was restored, and given the new title of the Crocifisso. About the same time the chapel of S. Ambrogio was destroyed. In the following year the pavement was remade, and the chapel of S. Giobbe, formerly called S. Rosa, was restored. Finally, in 1836, the Cappella dei Brivii was redecorated.[42]

In 1862 began the restoration which was finished only in 1886. From the chronicle of Rotta it is possible to form some idea of the disastrous changes wrought in the edifice at this period. The old façade was demolished in 1863, and an entirely new façade erected. When the old one was torn down, there came to light traces of an exterior narthex in two stories, each of which consisted of three arcades, as at S. Ambrogio.[43] Encouraged by the applause of even such men as Mongeri and Caffi, the indefatigable Rotta proceeded from the destruction of the façade to the renovation of the rest of the basilica. The intonaco was stripped from the nave. "After nine months of tireless hammering" the western bay of the nave with its two side aisles was entirely reconstructed. The same lot befell twelve of the ribs of the nave vault, the existence of which was deduced merely from the abaci of the vaulting capitals. In the side aisles, transverse arches were similarly built beneath the vaults in four bays. The eight piers were restored and the bases and capitals, which had

---

vano doi altri sconciamente, e così ogni cosa riuscì piana &c. il Santuario all'ora fu voltato sopra quelle 9 colonnelle, levate da' quattro angoli del Claustro grande. . . . Sopra di questa Volta fu poi collocato il Coro, come sta oggi, levato dal mezzo della Chiesa, secondo l'antica costumanza, perciochè in fatti n'occupava la metà con que' due Altari, che v'erano inanzi al tramezzo del Pontile sopra di cui si cantava l'Epistola, come si disse di sopra: Il marmo d'esso Pontile parte fu dispensato ne' scalini di esso Altar grande, e parte altrove. Fu questa si fatta opera tanto lodato . . . che fu seguitata poi da molte altre Chiese della Città, cioè di Sant'Ambrogio, Santo Stefano, etc. (Latuada, *loc. cit.*).

[41] *Ibid.*

[42] For a full account of the restorations of the chapel, see Caffi, VI-XII.

[43] 15.

been much damaged, were worked over. The third pier on the north side was entirely remade. Fourteen capitals were also made anew, copied from others which formerly existed in the church.[44] An old fresco was discovered in the half dome of the apse, and destroyed. The same lot seems to have befallen the inscription mentioned above, which is of peculiar interest because it contained the phrase *cementeriv qd est ante ipsa ecla*. On the north side of the high altar, the vault of the side aisle was supplied with ribs, and the same liberty was taken with the first and third bays. The surface of the piers and responds was found to be entirely spoiled, and had to be made over. The organ-gallery at the west end of the church was constructed anew. The frescos of the choir were ruthlessly destroyed. The restorers extended the choir or presbytery a bay to the westward, and lowered it three steps. The windows of the apse were made anew, as was also the cornice of the apse, although some authority was found for this.[45] An imitation mosaic was painted in the half dome of the apse. In the eastern bay were found the foundations and the point of joining of the more ancient and of the Lombard basilica.[46] The high altar was supplied with a new railing, the eastern walls of the side aisles were rebuilt, together with the vaults. The wall over the triumphal arch projecting above the roof was reconstructed, but on traces of the original one, which were discovered. The half dome of the apse was found to be supplied with external ribs. Remains of an ancient apse were discovered in the choir.

In 1893 the capital carved with a centaur (Plate 127, Fig. 5), evidently coming from the basilica, was discovered in the second cloister, and removed to the Musco Archeologico. Three years before, another capital (Plate 127, Fig. 5) found in the piazza in front of the church, had also been obtained by the same museum.

III. In the XII century, the church of S. Eustorgio probably consisted of a nave eight bays long, two side aisles, a choir flanked by side aisles and a single apse, but it has undergone many transformations. The apse (Plate 127, Fig. 6) is unquestionably the oldest part of the existing structure, as is clearly indicated by the style of its masonry (Plate 127, Fig. 4). This, it is true, lost most of its character in the XIX century restoration, but it is still evident that bricks of all sizes and shapes were laid in thick mortar-beds. The courses are approximately horizontal, but much herring-bone work is introduced.

In the crypt a black line inlaid in the pavement indicates the plan of an earlier apse discovered during the restoration. This apse seems to have been

---

[44] 21.   [45] 32.

[46] Come poi già avvene nella nave centrale, così negli ultimi piedritti delle navate minori si scopersero i fondamenti e il punto di congiunzione della antecedente basilica più antica di quella di stile lombardo (34).

semicircular, and to have had a semicircular eastern chapel. If the restorers understood the remains correctly, this fact is of singular archæological importance.

The choir is doubtless contemporary with the apse, although its barrel vault must have been remade at a later epoch, since it describes a curve more acute than that of the apse arch (Plate 127, Fig. 1). Perhaps the choir was originally roofed in wood.

At this point it is necessary to take up the great *crux* of S. Eustorgio, the T-shaped piers, which were described by Cattaneo as having been found imbedded in the easternmost piers (Plate 127, Fig. 2, 3) of the present nave. These piers with their capitals have disappeared without leaving a trace of themselves, and we have only Cattaneo's word for their existence. Rotta, in his elaborate account of the restoration of the church, says nothing about them. De Dartein perhaps refers to them, but his remarks are entirely vague.[47] It is indeed a sad commentary on the intelligence of the XIX century that these remains, of unique importance for the history of Lombard art, were allowed to perish.

The four eastern bays of the nave were originally covered with rib vaults erected on an alternate system (Plate 127, Fig. 1). The alternate piers were compound, the intermediate cylindrical. The capitals of the latter have circular abaci, perhaps the earliest known example of such a feature. From the alternate piers rose a continuous system of three members. The piers also included members to support the archivolts in two unmoulded orders, and the groin and transverse arches of the side-aisle vaults. Above the arches of the main arcade was either a gallery or a clearstory. The side aisles were groin-vaulted. In the eastern bay of the south side aisle one of these ancient vaults still survives. It has wall ribs somewhat oblong in plan, and is highly domed.

The existing vaults have been so much restored in the XIX century that traces of the original clearstory walls have almost entirely disappeared. However, a transverse buttress still intact in the eastern bay of the southern side aisle, makes it evident that in the XII century the church had vaults. On the extrados of one of the vaults there is a fragment of a projecting rib that appears to be old. The north wall of the church has been entirely rebuilt.

In consequence of the ruin of the church in 1159, the original dispositions

---

[47] Il reste à signaler une curieuse particularité mise au jour, en août 1869, par les travaux de restauration. · Entre le dernier support disposé en forme de pilier engagé et le mur circulaire de l'abside, se trouve, de chaque côté de la grande nef, une arcade, autrefois bouchée, soutenue par des piédroits rectangulaires. A cette arcade succède, vers la nef, l'amorce d'un second arc, lequel est brusquement coupé par le pilier cantonné de nervures appartenant aux nefs. Ainsi, le chevet du huitième siècle paraît s'etre continué par un vaisseau du même temps, où deux files d'arcades sur piédroits séparaient simplement la grande nef des bas-côtés. (De Dartein, 209).

were radically changed. The restorers of the third quarter of the XII century appear to have raised the side-aisle vaults to a height almost equal to that of the nave vaults, sacrificing thus the ancient clearstory or gallery.[48] The transverse arches of the side aisle were, however, left at the ancient level (Plate 127, Fig. 1, 3), and very heavily loaded with a wall reaching to the new vault. The ancient alternate rib vaults of the nave were supplanted by new rib vaults erected on a uniform system (Plate 127, Fig. 1). The old intermediate piers were adapted to their new functions by adding above the old capitals new members to support the vaults and archivolts (Plate 127, Fig. 3). In the alternate piers, the shafts were lengthened by inserting new pieces above the old capitals (Plate 127, Fig. 1). The capitals for the new members of both the alternate and intermediate piers were sometimes made anew, or were sometimes old ones taken from some destroyed part of the earlier church, and used as second-hand material. It is the fact that some old capitals were thus used, that makes the archæology of the structure so puzzling.

The four western bays of the nave are entirely different in design from the eastern bays. The section of the piers makes it certain that the builders intended to erect oblong cross vaults on a uniform system. Above the main arches was a gallery or triforium, which is still preserved in the three western bays. These western bays, although distinctly later than the eastern bays, are still earlier than the ruin of 1159, and like the eastern bays were evidently reconstructed in the third quarter of the XII century.

The existing façade is entirely modern. The original façade was preceded by an exterior narthex in two stories, and there may possibly have been even an atrium, since it is known that there was a cemetery to the west of the church.

IV. The capitals of S. Eustorgio are among the most interesting extant examples of Lombard decorative art. They belong to three different epochs. To the first may be assigned those of the original part of the eastern bays of the nave, two now in the Museo Archeologico (Plate 127, Fig. 5), and many used as second-hand material in the later portions of the edifice. These capitals are characterized by an excellence of technique which is not found in other Lombard churches in Milan. They are carved with vine patterns, rinceaux, interlaces or grotesques (Plate 127, Fig. 5). Notable are the cylindrical capitals of the intermediate piers (Plate 127, Fig. 1, 3), which in one capital are whirled, in the others only in part finished, some of the leaves being left uncarved. When separated from the most unfortunate modern restorations, the capitals of this period are seen to be characterized by the fineness and delicacy of the leaf ornament and by restraint in the use of grotesques. To the second epoch belong the capitals of the western portions

---

[48] It is possible, however, that these vaults were not raised until Gothic chapels were added. The existing masonry is obviously of this period.

of the original bays of the nave. They are slightly more advanced in style than those of the first group, although they show far greater predominance of the grotesque element, and are much coarser in execution and less refined. The first group recalls S. Pietro in Ciel d'Oro of Pavia, the second, S. Giorgio in Palazzo of Milan. One—it is the vaulting cap of the fourth pier from the west on the south side, and therefore moved from its original position in the reconstruction of the second half of the XII century—is sculptured with a representation of the miracle of S. Eustorgio related above. To the fourth epoch belong the capitals of those parts of the church remade in the third quarter of the XII century. They show strong French influence in the use of broad, flat leaves, crockets, elaborate mouldings, and other motives distinctly Gothic in character.

The apse is ornamented externally with blind niches (Plate 127, Fig. 4) surmounted by a second order that closely resembles an arched corbel-table. It is almost certain, however, that this feature, as well as the saw-tooth cornice, is a gratuitous addition of the XIX century restorers.

The church still retains notable frescos, notwithstanding that many of the most important ones were destroyed in the restoration. Water-colour copies of the latter, quite valueless scientifically, and mournful records of the noble works of art destroyed, are preserved in the parish archives.

V. The apse and rectangular eastern wall of the southern side aisle, the older portions of the choir, and the T-shaped supports belong to an edifice erected c. 1000. The masonry of the apse (Plate 127, Fig. 4, 6) closely resembles that of the apse of S. Ambrogio at Milan (Plate 117, Fig. 5), which was constructed c. 940, but is slightly more advanced. The T-shaped piers are analogous to those of Bagnacavallo (Plate 18, Fig. 4), an edifice undoubtedly erected c. 1000. As Cattaneo has recognized, they represented an important step in the evolution of the Lombard style, since they are among the earliest attempts made to evolve from the rectangular piers of the Carlovingian epoch supports of organic section adapted to the loads which they must carry. The earlier part of the four eastern bays of the nave is about a century later, and was undoubtedly reconstructed in the first quarter of the XII century. Since the capitals resemble closely those of S. Pietro in Ciel d'Oro of Pavia (compare Plate 127, Fig. 5, with Plate 178, Fig. 1), a surely dated monument of 1132, but seem less advanced in the great predominance of the grotesque element, this portion of the church may be assigned to c. 1120. We have seen, in fact, that a donation was made to the *labor* in 1121, so that it is entirely probable that the church was being reconstructed at this period. It is worthy of remark that cylindrical piers with circular capitals were used for intermediate supports. This is the earliest example of a motive which later became common in Lombard architecture (being used, for example, at Chiaravalle—Plate 55, Fig. 1—an edifice begun in 1136) and which was subsequently adopted by the builders of northern France. The western bays of the nave must have been constructed originally not much later than c. 1120, since the style of the capitals is only slightly more advanced than that of the capitals of the eastern portion of the edifice. On the other hand, the sharp change of plan argues that works must have been interrupted. The uniform system substituted for the alternate system of the earlier portions of the edifice seems to show the influence of S. Pietro in Ciel d'Oro of Pavia (1132). This portion of S. Eustorgio may therefore be ascribed to c. 1135. The parts of the church remodelled after 1162 include the vaults and numerous capitals. The oblong rib vaults, highly domed and with rounded diagonals, are of a Cistercian type that was hardly used in collegiate churches of Lombardy before the third quarter of the XII century. No pointed arches are introduced, and from this and other peculiarities of the style, it may be argued that the reconstruction was completely finished before the year 1185.

MILAN, S. GIORGIO IN PALAZZO

(Plate 128, Fig. 5)

I. The church of S. Giorgio in Palazzo at Milan has been frequently referred to by the historians of that city. Puricelli, Castiglione, Giulini and Allegranza have all collected the texts which refer to the basilica, and have studied the inscriptions of the portal. The two latter published drawings of the portal, made when it was still in its original position in the west façade, and before it had been removed into the court. Latuada wrote an important description of the remains of Romanesque architecture, which in his time were visible in the church.[1] The archæology of the edifice has been discussed by De Dartein[2] and Stiehl.[3]

II. The church of S. Giorgio doubtless owes its epithet 'in Palazzo' to the fact that it was constructed on the site of an ancient Roman palace, architectural fragments of which came to light during the recent restorations and are at present assembled in the court-yard to the north. The basilica

---

[1] Giacchè ragionasi dell'esteriore di questa Chiesa, oltre le antiche memorie della Porta maggiore, testè descritte, avanzano ancora altri indizj della di lei vecchia struttura nella parte inferiore, cioè Pilastri di vivo a mezze collone con capitelli ornati di fiorami e figure, tutte scolpite in simile qualità di sasso, indicando che servissero come a sostenere alcuni archi, che forse ne' secoli trascorsi formavano l'atrio esteriore. . . . In tre Navi è fabbricata, come si accennò questa Chiesa con altrettanti archi per ogni lato sostenuti da Pilastri quadrati, e fatta di nuovo abbellire di stucchi, e pitture da Persone divote. Nell'anno 1589 fu alzato il di lei Pavimento più d'un braccio e rinovato il Coro. . . . Ne' tempi nostri fu di nuovo riabbellita la Chiesa tutta con liscio pavimento ed altri notabili ristori. (Latuada, III, 134-135).

[2] 212.   [3] 8.

itself was founded by the bishop Natale, who, according to Muratori, died c. 741. The foundation is recorded in the epitaph of that bishop, formerly in the church, but now destroyed. This epitaph was copied by Castelli about 1550,[4] and has been published by Muratori: "In this tomb is the venerable body of Natale, the bishop, who was a good man. He was a great honour to his ancestors, for he lived a holy life as pastor, and he ruled his sheep like a father. He founded this church with the aid of Christ, and the king also gave many gifts to the basilica. Wherefore let the priests of the church ever seek to serve the Lord faithfully, and let the dead bishop benefit by their prayers for his sins. He ruled his church fourteen months and died at the age of sixty-two."[5]

The foundation of the basilica is recorded with more or less erroneous variations and embellishments by numerous later chroniclers. Galvaneo della Fiamma states that Natale merely established a chapter of canons in the pre-existing church of S. Giorgio which had been founded by S. Anataleone.[6] Two chronicles transform the name of Natale into Nicolò.[7] Another gives the date as 650 instead of 750.[8] An inedited text of Lampugnano de Legnano places the death of Natale in 764.[9]

---

[4] The *Codice della Croce,* MS. Amb., D. S. IV, I, f. 5, contains a copy of the epitaph, also taken from Castelli. The text is identical, except that in the second line *potens* is read for *bonus.*

[5] MARMORE CONCLUSUM TEGITUR VENERABILE CORPUS
    NATALIS PRÆSUL, QVI FUIT ORBE BONUS
GRANDIS HONOR PATRUM FUERAT NAM PASTOR ET ALMUS
    NOBILITATE VIXIT, REXIT OVESQVE PATER.
CONDIDIT HANC AULAM, CRISTO PRÆSTANTE JUVAMEN.
    REX DEDIT ET RECTE PLURIMA DONA QVOQVE.
UNDE QVEANT VIGILES DOMINO SERVIRE PER ÆVA.
    PROQVE SUIS CULPIS POSSIT HABERE PRECES.
ECCLESIAM REXIT BIS SEPTEM MENSIBUS, ANNOS
    SEXIES ATQVE DECEM QVOQVE DUOBUS HABENS.
                   (Muratori, A. I. M. A., ed. A., XI, 288-289).

[6] Hic in anno Domini DCCL construxit canonicam sancti Georgii in parazo, quam ab antiquo fundaverat beatus Anathaleon. (Galvanei Flammae, *Chron. Maius,* ed. Ceruti, 543).

Natalis sanctus Mediolanensis Archiepiscopus XXXVII. Anno Domini 750. sedit anno I. & mensibus 4. Hic Canonicam Sancti Georgii construxit, ubi etiam dormit in pace. (Galvanei Flammae, *Manipulus Florum,* ed. Muratori, R. I. S., XI, 599).

[7] Anno dni dccL. Nicolaus Archiepus Mli fecit fieri eccliam sancti Georgij Jn pallatio. (*Chronicon,* MS. Amb., C. S. IV, 18, f. 66).

Anno dni 750 Nicolaus Archiepiscopus Mediolani fecit fieri ecclesiam S. Georgii in Palatio. (*Edificationes Ecclesiarum Mediolani,* MS. Amb., S. Q. + I, 12, f. 69).

[8] Anno dni 650 Natalis archiepiscopus Mediolani consecrare fecit Ecclesiam S.

MILAN, S. GIORGIO IN PALAZZO

In a litany probably of the IX century, published by Magistretti, is the entry: *In sco Georgio,* which doubtless refers to our monument.[10] From two documents of 964[11] and a third of 970,[12] we learn that the church was officiated by decumani. Similar notices are contained in documents of January, 988,[13] August, 988,[14] July, 995,[15] and November, 999.[16] A bequest was made to the basilica by the archbishop Ariberto in 1034.[17] In 1043 the church was still officiated by decumani, and there was no chapter, as is evident from a diploma of that date published by Puricelli.[18]

In a sentence of 1119 published by Giulini,[19] S. Giorgio is included in a list of the eleven mother-churches of Milan officiated by decumani.

In 1129 the church was dedicated, doubtless in consequence of a reconstruction. In an ancient calendar of the church is the entry: "On December 15, 1129, the church of S. Giorgio in Palazzo was consecrated, and on the same day died Gibuino, prevosto and primicerio of Milan."[20] The fact that a prevosto is mentioned in this notice indicates that a chapter regular was in existence, and it may well have been in consequence of the foundation of such a chapter that the basilica was rebuilt.

In 1153 the archbishop Oberto decided a controversy between the canons

Georgii in palatio. (*Chronica* detta di Filippo da Castel Seprio, MS. Amb., S. Q. + I, 12, f. 52). Cf. *Cronaca* di Goffredo da Bussero XIII, ed. Grazioli.

9 Beatus Natalis Mediolan' archīeps xliiij. anno d̄ni dccl. sedit mensb'. xiiij. et anno dno. [*sic*] et mensb' duos obijt anno d̄ni dcclxiiij die madij. Jacet in canonica s̄ci Georgij quā fieri fecit. (*Chronica* di Lampugnano de Legnano, MS. Amb., H 56 Sup., f. 61).

10 The other church of S. Giorgio at Milan, according to Galvaneo della Fiamma, was not founded until the end of the X century: Hic Ademarus de Menclotiis [Adelmanno 948-953] construxit ecclexiam s. Georgii ad puteum blanchum, ubi in lapide sculptus est in strata comuni. (Galvanei Flammae, *Chron. Maius*, ed. Ceruti, 583).

11 Waldevertus presbiter de inter decomanos sancte mediolanensis ecclesiae, oficiale ecclesie beati Christi martiri Georgii, que est fundata intra civitate Mediolani prope porta quo clamatur ticinense. . . . (*Hist. Pat. Mon.*, XIII, 1185).

Waldevertus presbiter de inter decomanos sancte mediolanensis ecclesie, oficiale ecclesie beati Christi martiri Georgii, que est fundata intra civitate Mediolani non longe da porta quo clamatur ticinense. . . . (*Ibid.*, 1187).

12 Richardus presbiter de inter decumanos sancte mediolanensis ecclesie, offitiale ecclesie sancti Georgii. . . . (*Ibid.*, 1246).

13 *Ibid.*, 1471.   14 *Ibid.*, 1482.   15 *Ibid.*, 1579.

16 *Ibid.*, 1708.   17 Puricelli, 366.

18 TEUSPRANDUS PRESBYTER DE ORDINE DECUMANORUM SANCTAE MEDIOLANENSIS ECCLESIÆ, OFFICIALIS ECCLESIÆ SANCTI GEORGII, *constructæ intra Ciuitatē Mediolanum ad locu, ubi Palatio dicitur.*

19 VII, 85.

20 Januarii . . . XVIII Kal. MCXXIX. consecrata est Ecclesia Sancti Georgii in Palatio, & obiit Gibuinus Ecclesiæ ejusdem Præpositus, & Primicerius Mediolanensis. (*Excerpta Historica*, ed. Muratori, R. I. S., I, pt. 2, 235).

and the superstans of S. Giorgio.[21]   It appears that the office of superstans had existed at this time in the church for upwards of forty years.

In 1159 the bodies of the three Magi were translated from S. Eustorgio to the campanile of S. Giorgio. "Since the bodies of the Magi were of very great value against hail, tempests, and epilepsy, they were diligently hidden in the campanile of S. Giorgio, where few knew that they were deposited, but if they had not been moved they would not have been carried away to Germany, since the suburbs were always obedient to the emperor, nor was any harm ever done to the suburbs, as is evident in the case of S. Ambrogio and other churches which were outside the walls of the city.   Nor at that time were there Dominicans at S. Eustorgio where the Magi were, since in those days neither the Franciscan nor the Dominican order was in existence. There was another great campanile in the church of S. Giorgio in Palazzo, where, before the city was besieged, the citizens carried the bodies of the three Magi from the church of S. Eustorgio where they had been for eight hundred years. . . . Afterwards the campanile of S. Giorgio in Palazzo was destroyed together with many other edifices. This campanile was very large."[22] In another passage the same Galvaneo states: "There were in Milan two towers which in height surpassed all buildings in Lombardy.   One was the campanile of S. Maria and the other that of S. Giorgio."[23]

[21] The canons complained: quod prefatus Johannes Superstans, ipsius Ecclesie Cimiterium, quod ei non licet, nam ipsius Cimiterii dispositio seu ordinatio ad Prepositum eiusque Fratres liquido spectare dinoscitur, usurpaverat, et ut domus quam in eodem Cimiterio quidam superstans, ut dicebatur, hedificaverat, quia prestat impedimentum, destrueretur, et ostium alterius domus Superstantiæ, quod ad ipsum vergit Cimiterium, clauderetur, intendebat.   Econtra prescriptus Johannes, quoniam, ut cuiusque Ecclesie Superstans, de Ecclesia est, se licite cimiterium posse tenere dicebat, nec domus destruenda, nec ostium claudendum est, quoniam tam ego, quam Predecessores mei per XL annos, et eo amplius hec omnia quiete possideo. . . . Anno millesimo centeximo quinquagesimo tertio, mense Augusto, Indictione prima.   (*Codice della Croce,* MS. Amb., D. S. IV, 8/I, 8, f. 71).

[22] Tum quia valebant contra grandines et tempestates, tum quia succurebant morbo caduco, ideo cum diligentia fuerunt in campanili sancti Georgii absconditi, paucis hoc scientibus.   Quod si non fuissent moti, non fuissent exportati, quia burgi semper obediebant imperatori, nec quicquam mali delatum est burgis, sicut patet de beato Ambroxio et aliis ecclesiis, que erant extra civitatem.   Nec erant in sancto Eustorgio, ubi erant magi, fratres predicatores, quia nundum erant nec fratres predicatores nec fratres minores in mundo.   Erat aliud magnum campanile in ecclesia sancti Georgii in palatio, ubi cives antequam fieret obsidio, portaverunt corpora trium regum de ecclesia sancti Eustorgii, ubi steterant octocentum annis. . . . Tunc destructum fuit campanile sancti Georgii in palatio, quod erat maximum, et plura alia hedifitia. (Galvanei Flammae, *Chron. Maius,* ed. Ceruti, 657, 690).

[23] Duæ verò turres erant in Mediolano sua altitudine omnia ædificia Lombardiæ superantes, scilicet turris, quæ modò dicitur Campanile B. Mariæ. . . . Alia turris erat Campanile S. Georgii.   (Galvanei Flammae, *Manipulus Florum,* CCI, ed. Muratori, R. I. S., XI, 648).

MILAN, S. GIORGIO IN PALAZZO

According to a tax-list of 1398 published by Magistretti, the basilica at that time was officiated by twelve canons, and possessed one dependent chapel. In 1568 there were still twelve canons.[24] In 1798 the chapter was suppressed.[25] The church had already been baroccoized, but in the year 1800 a new façade was erected, and in 1821 the interior was redecorated.[26] In 1889 a new restoration was carried out. A cupola in the barocco style was erected over the centre of the church, and a new campanile added. The façade was again rebuilt, and the ancient Lombard portal moved into the court-yard to the north of the church. In the course of this restoration, several Lombard capitals came to light.[27]

III. The church at present consists of a nave two double bays long, two side aisles, transepts, a choir, an apse, and several chapels, but the edifice has been so entirely denatured that it is impossible to ascertain what were the original dispositions. Of the ancient church, there are now visible only a few fragments gathered together in the court-yard, two capitals serving as holy-water basins, and some remains of the old piers in the east side of the present east piers. It is evident, however, that the Lombard building was erected on an alternate system, and it is to be presumed that the side aisles were groin-vaulted, the nave rib-vaulted. There were no galleries, but there was doubtless a clearstory. The existing transepts, which are entirely modern, perhaps replaced a bay of the original nave, since the remains in the eastern piers give reason to suppose that such a bay formerly existed. Giulini[28] and Latuada saw in the façade traces of arches which apparently belonged to a destroyed atrium.

IV. The capitals of S. Giorgio in Palazzo (Plate 128, Fig. 5) are very crudely executed, and show a square, hard technique that is absolutely different from that of the nearly contemporary capitals in S. Pietro in Ciel d'Oro of Pavia. Grotesque elements enter very largely into the composition. The interlaces and foliage motives are coarse in design and lifeless in execution. It is only in the roll-moulding of the archivolt that there is found a suggestion of the minute and careful ornament characteristic of the Pavia edifice. The much discussed portal appears to be contemporary with the other Romanesque fragments of the church, but it had suffered severely from numerous restorations. It bears two inscriptions. The first, in Latin, is to the following effect: "I am the Door of Life. Enter all, I pray. Through Me shall pass those who seek the joys of heaven. May he who was born from a virgin by no earthly

---

[24] Georgii in Palatio collegiata Curata, cú ppto et Cancis N 12. (*Status Ecclesiae Mediolani*, 1568 conscriptus auctore Francisco Castello, MS. Amb., A, 112, Inf., f. 447). *Ibid.*, f. 538, the names of the prevosto and twelve canons are given and also the taxes they paid.

[25] Forcella, *Chiese*, 655.   [26] *Milano ed il suo Territorio*, II, 362.

[27] *Arte e Storia*, 22 Luglio, 1889.   [28] III, 187-190.

father save those who enter, and direct those who go out."[29]   The second
inscription is in Latin but written in quasi-Greek characters similar to those
employed in the inscription of the contemporary mosaic in the apse of S.
Ambrogio.   The interpretation is much disputed but it seems to mean: Give,
O Lord, the door of Life to those who seek it.[30]

V.   S. Giorgio in Palazzo is an authentically dated monument of 1129,
and as such is of great importance in establishing the chronology of Lombard
architecture.

MILAN, S. NAZARO

(Plate 128, Fig. 1, 2, 3, 4)

I.   In 1674 Torre wrote a brief description of S. Nazaro.[1]   Although
written in 1627, or nearly half a century earlier, the description of Villa is
less important.[2]   The historians of Milan, among whom Giulini and Oltrocchi
deserve especial mention, have all studied the history of our church.   The
monument has been illustrated by Hübsch,[3] who, in his drawings, restored
the apse (Plate 128, Fig. 3) with arched corbel-tables supported on shafts
above the blind arches.   De Dartein[4] has studied the architecture.

II.   In the biography of S. Ambrogio written by Paolino in the V
century is the following passage: "About this time (395) the body of the

[29]   IANVA SVM VITÆ PRECOR OMS INTRO VENITE
          PER ME TRANSIBVNT Q CŒLI GAVDIA QVÆRVNT
          VIRGINE Q NATVS NVLLO DE PATRE CREATVS
          INTRANTES SALVET REDEVNTES IPSE GVBERNET

[30] I give this inscription in Greek and Roman characters since it is impossible to
reproduce the original in type: ΥΙΘΗ ΔΑ ΠΩΡΘΑ ΔΣ Ω QΤΗΡΗΝΘΥΒS ΥΣΘΑ.

[1] Vedesi addesso construtta in ordine Corintio, mà la rozzezza de' Pilastri, e de'
Cappitelli fammi conchiudere, essere stata eretta ne' Tempi delle perdute buone
Arti. . . . Riceuette il secolo passato 1578 questa Basilica per la vigilanza di S. Carlo
qualche visibile ristoramento: in questi suoi bassi archi, che tra tutti ascendono al
numero di dodici sostentitori della volta, rendeuasi oscura, ed occupata, per non hauere
proporzionate finestre, ad introdurre quel chiaro, che le fea d'vopo, perciò egli fecele
ingrandire, dando loro forma quadrata, fasciandole d'ornamenti à stucco, auuertendoui
che le rinnouellate della Cupola furono fatte a' miei tempi, ad istanza di persona pia,
essendoui prima tonde apriture, e di forma assai piccola.   Nel mezzo della Chiesa sotto
la Cupola eraui vn' Altare trà quattro Colonne di Porfido. (Torre, 24-34).
[2] Era tutta questa Basilica coperta di piombo, ma al presente non se ne vede se
non sopra la tribuna, niccia del choro, capella di S. Olderico, & quella della Fioranna,
& il resto tutto è dileguato.   Hà vna gran torre, che serue per le campane, la quale è
coperta di piombo, & sopra vi è il gallo. (Villa, 100).
[3] Plate XLI.   [4] 199.

holy martyr Nazaro which had been placed in a garden outside the city was disinterred and translated by S. Ambrogio to the basilica of the Apostles, which is near the Porta Romana. . . . When the body of the martyr had been disinterred . . . we immediately went with the holy bishop to pray at the tomb of S. Celso the martyr, who was buried in the same garden. We had never known him to pray in that place before this, but it was a sign that the body of a martyr had been revealed to him whenever the holy bishop went to pray at a place to which he had never before gone. . . . Thus the body of the martyr Nazaro was translated to the basilica of the Apostles, where relics of the holy apostles had been deposited long before amid the devout veneration of the faithful."[5]

The account of the translation of the saints as recorded in their lives[6] accords with the account of Paolino, and adds the chronological note, *imperante Theodosio.*

That S. Ambrogio not only translated the relics of S. Nazaro to the church of the Apostles, but also built the basilica, is stated in a breviary of Milan,[7] and in the chronicle of Landolfo the Elder. In the latter we read: "When S. Simpliciano came back from Rome, he brought with him very devoutly, and gave to his holy and most reverend master, Ambrogio, small relics of the Apostles Peter and Paul. In consequence of this, S. Ambrogio with the greatest joy and enthusiasm carefully collected relics of all the other Apostles. When he had acquired these, he founded with due ceremony a worthy basilica, cruciform in plan, situated in the Roman quarter of the city, between the gate that is called 'Romana' and the arch which is called the 'Roman Arch of Triumph.' In this basilica he deposited the relics of all the apostles with the greatest reverence, and the greatest enthusiasm, and in the presence of a mighty multitude of bishops, clerics, laymen, women, youths and old men who came even from the neighbouring cities. To this day the basilica is still called by the name of the Apostles. The verses which S. Ambrogio composed about this church and in honour of S. Nazaro I have heard so often that I know them by heart: 'Ambrogio founded the temple and

---

[5] Quo in tempore sancti Nazarii martyris corpus, quod erat in horto positum extra civitatem, levatum ad basilicam apostolorum quæ est in Romana transtulit. . . . Quo levato corpore martyris . . . statim ad sanctum Celsum martyrem, qui in eodem horto positus est, cum sancto sacerdote ad orationem perreximus. Nunquam tamen illum antea orasse in eodem loco compertum habemus: sed hoc erat signum revelati corporis martyris, si sanctus Sacerdos ad locum, ad quem nunquam antea fuerat, oratum isset. . . . Translatio itaque corpore Martyris ad basilicam Apostolorum ubi pridem sanctorum apostolorum reliquiae summa omnium devotione depositæ fuerant, etc. (*Vita S. Ambrosii*, auctore Paulino, ed. Migne, *Pat. Lat.*, XIV, 40-41).

[6] Cit. Puricelli, *Dis. Naz.*, 252.

[7] In basilica Apostolorum, quæ in Porta Romana à Sancto Ambrosio facta, fuit translatum corpus Sancti Nazarij Martyris, & ibidem positum. (Cit. Puricelli, *op. cit.*, 254).

consecrated it to the Lord in the name of the Apostles, and endowed it with possessions and relics. The temple is cruciform; that is, it has the form of the victory of Christ, because it symbolizes His sacred triumph. In the choir is Nazaro of holy life, and the ground is made exalted by the relics of the martyr. Where the cross raises its sacred head ending in a semicircle is now the head of the temple and the house of Nazaro. He, a victor, earned eternal rest by his piety. The cross was his palm, and the cross is his resting place. Death the stern leveller claspeth all created things (?).' "[8]

It is probably from this source that is derived the account of Galvaneo della Fiamma.[9]

Another inscription, which formerly existed in the pavement of the church, and which is preserved in several copies, is particularly interesting because of the reference to Stilicho (†408): "The curved roofs rise above the hollow niche, and the head of the Holy Cross ends in a semicircle. The founder is exultant that Nazaro, of pure life and blameless character, is buried in this place. The church which Ambrogio first built in the image of the cross of Christ, the faithful wife Serena paved with Lybian marbles in order that she

---

[8] Revertens B. Simplicianus ab Urbe Roma ad B. magistrum, & reverendissimum Ambrosium reliquias particulæ Apostolorum Petri, & Pauli curiosè, summaque devotione ei obtulit. Quo facto B. Ambrosius summo gaudio summaque lætitia omnium aliorum Apostolorum studiosè acquisivit. Quibus adquisitis honestissimam Basilicam ad modum Crucis in Romana parte inter Portam, quam Romanam vocant, & Arcum, qui Romanus Triumphalis dicitur, honorificè condidit, in qua omnium Apostolorum reliquias summa cum diligentia, summoque studio, magnoque cursu Episcoporum, Clericorum, laicorum, mulierum, juvenum, senum vrbium vicinarum apposuit, unde usque hodie Basilica Apostolorum vocatur; At quid idem S. Ambrosius super hanc Ecclesiam dictaverit, & S. Nazarii honorem versificavit ore proprio audiendo cognosco.

> Condidit Ambrosius templum, Dominoq; sacravit
> Nomine Apostolico, munere, reliquiis.
> Forma crucis templū est templū victoria Christi
> Sacra triumphalis signat imago locum.
> In capite est vitæ templi Nazarius almæ.
> Et sublime solum martyris exuviis.
> Crux ubi sacratum caput extulit orbe reflexo
> Moc caput est templum, Nazarioque domus.
> Qui fovet æternam victor pietate quietem,
> Crux cui palma fuit, crux etiam sinus est.
> Tertia sed media mors impedit edita cuncta.

(Landulphi Senioris, *Mediol. Histor.* I, VI, ed. Muratori, R. I. S., IV, 63).

[9] Post hæc Beatissimus Ambrosius Corpus Sancti Nazarii ad Basilicam Beati Petri, quæ fundata fuit in honorem Apostolorum propter eximias reliquias ipsorum transtulit. . . . Beatus verò Ambrosius, dum adhuc in carne viveret, fundavit Ecclesiam in honorem Beati Petri Apostoli, & omnium Apostolorum, quæ modò dicitur Sancti Nazarii. (Galvanei Flammae, *Manipulus Florum,* ed. Muratori, R. I. S., XI, 569-570).

might live to see the joyful day of the return of her spouse Stilicho to his loving children and brothers and relatives."[10]

According to Oltrocchi,[11] Serena gave the pavement in the year 405, but other historians refer this donation to the year 402. At all events, there can be little doubt that the church was constructed by S. Ambrogio before 395, and was completely finished in the early years of the V century.

A diploma of 777 mentions our church under the title of S. Nazaro.[12] The bishop Arderico, who died in 948, was buried in a chapel, which he himself had added to the basilica.[13] Two documents of 992 mention decumani of the church.[14] The archbishop Ariberto left a bequest to the basilica in 1034.[15] Landolfo the Younger mentions a prevosto of the church, so that it is evident that in his time canons regular were already established.[16] Landolfo the Elder mentions a translation of the body of S. Nazaro that took place in the lifetime of S. Arialdo and consequently before 1067.[17]

The basilica of S. Nazaro was destroyed by the fire which swept Milan in the year 1075. Of this fire we know from a number of texts, the most important of which are quoted below[18] in connection with the church of S. Stefano, which was destroyed at the same time.[19]

The reconstruction of the basilica, begun doubtless soon after the fire, must have progressed rapidly. A deed of May, 1082, mentions a priest of

[10]   Qua sinuata cauo consurgunt tecta regressu
     . Sacratæquè Crucis flectitur orbe caput.
     Nazarius vitæ immaculabilis, integer artus,
     Conditor exultat, hunc tumulo esse locum.
     Quem prius Ambrosius signauit imagine Christi,
     Marmoribus Lybicis fida Serena polit
     Coniugis, ut reditu Stiliconis læta fruatur,
     Germanisq; pijs Pignoribus proprijs.

(Puccinelli, 368). Cf. Allegranza, *De Sepulchris Christianis*, Epitaphia, 40.

[11] I, 38.   [12] Giulini, I, 22.

[13] . . . iste [Ardericus] fecit fieri . . . capellam s̄c̄i lini (?) ī ec̄ela s̄c̄i nazarij in qua capella sepultus est. (Lampugnano de Legnano, *Chronica*, MS. Amb., H 56 Sup., f. 63).

[14] *Hist. Pat. Mon.*, XIII, 1537, 1557.   [15] Puricelli, 366.
[16] Landulphi Junioris, *Hist. Med.*, XX, ed. Muratori, R. I. S., V, 491.
[17] Landulphi Senioris, *Hist. Med.*, III, 7, ed. Muratori, R. I. S., IV, 100.
[18] P. 659 f.
[19] The following text of Galvaneo della Fiamma also refers to S. Nazaro: Tunc Herlembaldus Cotta congregans exercitum validum ipsum Archiepiscopum cum tota parte Nobilium in Castelliono obsedit. Et instante hac obsidione ignis mirabilis ferè totam Civitatem combusset, qui propter instantem obsidionem Castri de Castelliono ignis de Castelliono dictus est. Et non solùm Civitas combusta fuit, imò etiam suburbia. Unde Ecclesia Sancti Laurentii, quæ tunc erat extra Civitatem igne illo ferè in cinerem conversa est; similiter & Ecclesia Sancti Nazarii, & Ecclesia Sancti Simpliciani. (Galvanei Flammae, *Manipulus Florum*, CLI, ed. Muratori, R. I. S., XI, 626).

the church who was a decumano, but gives no indication as to the condition of the building at this period.[20]   According to Lampugnano de Legnano[21] and Galvaneo della Fiamma,[22] however, the archbishop, Anselmo III, who died in 1093, was buried in the church, the construction of which must, in consequence, have already been far advanced at this epoch.   It is probable that Anselmo, who was elected in 1086, chose the basilica for his last resting place because he had interested himself especially in its reconstruction.

In 1112 a certain Gisla left a bequest to the *labor* of the church to be continued until such time as the restoration should be completed.[23]   It is therefore evident that at this epoch the reconstruction of the church was not completed, but that the end was within sight.

S. Nazaro was mentioned as one of the eleven churches of Milan officiated by decumani in a sentence of 1119.[24]   Canons regular are mentioned in documents of 1124[25] and 1141,[26] as well as in a tax-list of 1398 published by Magistretti, and in another of 1568, compiled by Castelli.[27]

[20] Aginardo presbiter de ordine Decomanorum sancte Mediolanensis ecclesie et officiale ecclesie Sancti Nazarii, que dicitur a corpo. (Hortzschansky und Perlbach, 71).

[21] *Chronica,* MS. Amb., H 56 Sup., f. 66.

[22] Christi anno MLXXXIII, eminente in Roma Gregorio VII, imperante Henrico tertio gibillino, Anselmus ex capitaneis de Raude factus archiepiscopus sedit annis VII et mensibus V. . . . Sed Cronica archiepiscoporum dicit, quod rediit domum et magnam indulgentiam ecclesie Sancti Sepulcri dedit, cum testimonio omnium cardinalium ecclesie mediolanensis et omnium abatum, et iacet ad sanctum Nazarium. (Galvanei Flammae, *Chron. Maius,* ed. Ceruti, 631-632).

[23] Anno ab incarnatione domini nostri ihesu christi milesimo centesimo duodecimo mense februarii indictione quinta.   Ego gisla uesta et uelamine sanctę religionis induta et relicta qdam amizonis . . . uolo et iudico . . . ut omnis mea portio de omnibus casis et rebus territoriis . . . quas habere uisa sum in loco et fundo sancto paulo qui est prope locum qui dicitur meleso . . . in integrum presenti die et hora deueniat in ius et proprietatem ecclesiarum sanctę dei genitricis marię quę dicitur hyemalis et sancti nazarii quę dicitur ad corpus et sancti stephani quę dicitur ad rotam.   Eo tamen ordine ut iamdicta ecclesia sancti stephani habeat medietatem predictarum. aliam uero medietatem habeant ecclesia sanctę marię et ecclesia sancti nazarii.   Sub ea uidelicet ratione ut duas partes de omni fructu qui exierit annualiter de predicta medietate ipsarum rerum habeant canonici ipsius ecclesię sancti stephani, tertiam uero partem habeat labor eiusdem ecclesię donec restaurata fuerit, post completum uero ipsum laborem ipsam tertiam portionem cum predictis duabus portionibus habeant iamdicti canonici et duas partes de omni fructu et redditu qui exierit annuæ de altera medietate iamscriptarum rerum habeant presbiteri decumani ipsius ecclesię sanctę marię et canonici ipsius ecclesię sancti nazarii, tertiam uero partem habeant ipsę ecclesię donec restauratę fuerint.   Post restaurationem autem earundem ecclesiarum omnes fructu et redditus . . . habeant iamdicti canonici etc. (*Codice della Croce,* MS. Amb., D. S. IV).

[24] Giulini, VII, 85.   [25] *Ibid.,* III, 139.

[26] Bonomi, *Dip. Sti. Bdti.,* Brera MS. AE XV, 33, f. 78.

[27] [Ecclia] S. Nazarij in brolio, Collegiata insignis, cú ppto et sexdecim cancis (*Status ecclesiae Mediolani 1568 conscriptus* auctore Francesco Castello, MS. Amb., A, 112, Inf., f. 443).

The chapel of S. Caterina was added in 1510, and the Cappella Trivulziana in 1518. According to Mezzanotte, the latter is a work of Bramantino. In 1578 the whole structure was baroccoized by S. Carlo Borromeo.[28] In 1579 the restoration was entirely completed, and the relics were translated.[29] In 1830 the basilica was subjected to another disastrous restoration.[30]

III. The church of S. Nazaro as rebuilt after 1075 doubtless preserved the plan of the basilica of S. Ambrogio, and thus are to be explained its somewhat extraordinary dispositions. The edifice consisted of a single-aisled nave (Plate 128, Fig. 4) of two bays, projecting transepts of a single bay ending in semicircular apses, a choir of a single bay (Plate 128, Fig. 4), and an apse (Plate 128, Fig. 3). Many chapels and accessory structures of various kinds have been added in the Renaissance and in modern times.

The rib vaults of the nave (Plate 128, Fig. 4) and of the transepts are the original ones of the XI century. They are supplied with wall ribs of rectangular section, and have heavy diagonals and transverse arches, also rectangular. The web is constructed of bricks, and the vault surface is highly domed. The tiles of the roof are still laid on the extrados of these vaults. The half domes of the choir and transept-ends are probably also the original ones, but have been so completely covered with modern decoration that it is impossible to be certain. Over the crossing (Plate 128, Fig. 4) rose the Lombard cupola, evident traces of which still remain (Plate 128, Fig. 1).

---

[28] Puccinelli, 368. See text of Torre, cited above, p. 632. Morigia (374) says that before this restoration there was a ciborio under the cupola.

[29] Puccinelli, 368.

[30] This restoration is recorded by the following inscription, still extant:

D.O.M.
IN . HONOREM . SS. APOSTOLORVM . ET . NAZARI . MARTYRIS
PATRONOR . CAELESTIVM
AEDEM . A . MAIORIBVS . DICATAM
QVAE . NEC . VALIDO . MVNIMINE . TVTA
NEC . ITERATIS . AEVI . POSTERIORIS . INSTRVCTIONIB . FIRMATA
FATISCEBAT
PRAEPOSITVS . ET . NEOCORI
THOLO . INSTAVRATO . AREA . TESSERIS . ET . SECTILIB. STRATA
AEDICVLIS . REFECTIS . SACRARIO . EXCVLTO
PARIETIBVS . VDO . ILLATIS . ORGANO . IN . APTIOREM . SEDEM .
TRANSVECTO
TRIBVNALIBVS . CONSTITVTIS . SUBSELLARIO . ABSIDIS . ORNATO
INTRA . BIENNIVM . EX . PECVNIA . COLLATITIA
AB . INTERITV . AD . PRISTINAM . DIGNITATEM . REVOCARVNT
AN. M. DCCC.XXX
PETRO . PESTAGALLIO . ARCHITECTO .

Over the choir there is at present a rib vault, but it is impossible to say what was the original disposition here.

The responds (Plate 128, Fig. 4) have all been so completely remade that there remain no data upon which the original section can be determined. It is evident, however, that they must be compound. The eastern and northern apses are reinforced externally by prismatic buttresses (Plate 128, Fig. 3) which must be—at least in part—original.

The masonry is formed of cross-hatched bricks, laid for the most part in horizontal courses. In the cupola (Plate 128, Fig. 1)—which is doubtless later than the rest of the church—these courses are exceedingly regular, and there is a tendency towards polychromatic masonry. The walls of the older portion of the basilica have been repeatedly restored and patched up.

IV. The apse is decorated externally with a row of elongated blind niches (Plate 128, Fig. 3) which doubtless once marked the line of the cornice, but which have become, as it were, drowned in the middle of the wall by the raising of the roof in the barocco period. The cornice of the choir, consisting of a row of arched corbel-tables, is still preserved on the north side (Plate 128, Fig. 3), and traces of the ancient cornices of arched corbel-tables are still extant on the south transept, in the cupola (Plate 128, Fig. 1) and elsewhere. The cupola was furthermore adorned with a row of blind niches in two orders (Plate 128, Fig. 1).

In the north transept may still be seen the carved archivolt of a closed portal (Plate 128, Fig. 2). This is the only fragment of the carved decoration of the Lombard basilica extant. A running ornament of anthemia is interrupted at the keystone by a kneeling lamb holding a cross. The lamb, with extremely elongated body, is crudely executed. The anthemia are more formal and more dry than the carved ornament at S. Ambrogio, with which, nevertheless, they present close analogies.

V. S. Nazaro was begun after the fire of 1075; the main part of the building must have been completed in 1093, although some portions, such as the cupola, were not finished until after 1112.

MILAN, S. SATIRO

(Plate 129; Plate 130; Plate 131, Fig. 2; Plate 132, Fig. 1, 2, 3, 4, 5, 6)

I. The historians of Milan have all touched more or less at length upon the history of the church of S. Satiro and the historical documents which refer to it. Drawings of the·monument have been published by Hübsch[1] and De Castro.[2] Cattaneo was the first to see in the monument an important and

---

[1] Plate XLII.   [2] II, 53 f.

authentically dated example of the style of the IX century. Rivoira[3] and Venturi[4] have followed in his footsteps. Important researches upon the Renaissance reconstruction of the edifice have been contributed by Biscaro and Beltrami.

II. The monastery of S. Satiro was founded by the archbishop Ansperto, who held office from 868 to 881. The most authentic document which establishes this fact is the famous epitaph of the bishop at S. Ambrogio.[5] The foundation is also recorded in a will of the bishop, which, however, has been judged by historians, for excellent reasons, to be spurious.[6] In Galvaneo della Fiamma we read: "In the year of Christ 870 . . . Ansperto of Blassono . . . was made archbishop and sat thirteen years and five months. He constructed

[3] 203.   [4] II, 163.

[5] This inscription has been cited above, pp. 550-551.

[6] See Giulini, I, 301 f. The important phrases of this document are: In nomine Domini Dei, & Salvatoris nostri Jesu Christi. *Karlomannus* divina providentia ordinante *Rex Longobardorum* in Italia Anno Regni ejus Secundo, X. die mensis Septembris, ingrediente Indictione Tertiadecima. Ego in Dei omnipotentis nomine *Anspertus* humilis *Archiepiscopus* sanctae *Mediolanensis Ecclesiae*, & filius bone memorie Albucii de Blassono, qui vixit Lege Longobardorum, presentibus dixi. . . . Et ideo ego, qui supra, Anspertus . . . disponere & ordinare videor. . . . Primis omnium volo et statuo, atque per hunc textum judicati mei confirmo pro amore Dei & Domini nostri Jesu Christi, ut casas illas tam solariatas quam & salas intra hanc Civitatem Mediolani, que fuit domus habitationis mee, ubi ego in propria clausura mea in honorem Dei & Sanctorum Christi Confessorum Satyri, & Silvestri Pape, & beati Ambrosii Episcopi Basilicam a fundamentis edificavi, & illas casas tam solariatas quam & salas, que mihi ex commutatione advenerunt da parte Monasterii Sancti Silvestri, situm Nonantula, que secum ad easdem casas, que fuit domus habitationis mee, tenere videntur cum areas, curtes, hortos, puteos, clausuras, ac pristina omnia una tenentem cum omnibus edificiis inibi constructis, cum finibus & accessionibus suis in integrum, sit Senodochium presenti die obitus mei in elemosinis pauperum, & susceptione peregrinorum, eo ordine sicut hic subter statuero. Et volo ut habeat ipsum Senodochium meum ut ibi debeat pertinere jam dicta Basilica a me inibi constructa cum omnibus quicquid a me, vel a quacunque persona collatum fuerit. In primis volo & statuo idem Senodochium habere & tenere Curtem illam, etc. . . . Illud statuo & confirmo, ut sit Senodochium ipsum a presenti die obitus cum omni integritate sua in jura & potestatem Monasterii Sancti Ambrosii, situm foris muros ipsius Civitatis Mediolani, ubi ejus sanctum Corpus quiescit humatum, in subsidium Fratrum Monachorum ibi Deo deservientium, perpetuis futuris temporibus habendum, & *inibi Cellam Monachorum in sempiternum esse debeat, ubi quotidie octo Monachi Monasterii ipsius Sancti Ambrosii esse debeant, qui in jam dicta Basilica mea & officium & luminaria faciant, & pro me & jam dictis parentibus meis Missas, Vesperum Vigilias, & Matutinam Defunctorum faciant,* & in ipsa Cella regulariter vivant, seu etiam perpetuis temporibus elemosinam . . . dispergant: & ipsi octo Monachi ab Abbate Monasterii semper ordinentur. Et ipsum Senodochium & Cella cum omnibus rebus ibi pertinentibus in integrum, sub ejus Abbatis, qui pro tempore fuerit, potestate & dominio recta sint. Et hoc volo atque confirmo, ut Monachi, qui in eadem Cella ab Abbate suprascripti Monasterii Sancti Ambrosii ordinati fuerint, pascere debeant in ipsum sanctum Senodochium meum per omnes Kalendas pauperes centum. . . . (Ed. Muratori, A. I. M. A., *Dis.* 56, ed. A., XI, 302).

in the city the church of S. Satiro for the monks of S. Ambrogio . . . He also constructed the church of S. Silvestro near the Porta Romana, in the year of our Lord, 873."[7]   The worthy chronicler appears to have made two churches out of one.   The date, 873, which he brings forward, was probably the result of a careless reading of a text which occurs in the chronicle that in the manuscript of the Biblioteca Ambrosiana bears the name Filippo da Castel Seprio, although it has been published by Grazioli under the name of Goffredo da Bussero.   In this we read: "The archbishop Ansperto, in the year 876, constructed the church of the saints Satiro and Silvestro near the Porta Romana."[8]   Another chronicle gives the date of the foundation of the church as 830, but this does not merit faith, since Ansperto did not become archbishop until 868.[9]   Lampugnano de Legnano records the foundation by Ansperto but gives no date.[10]   All things considered, it seems entirely probable that the monastery was founded in the year 876.   It is certain that the church was first built after this, since in the private house of the archbishop there could have been at most a chapel entirely inadequate for the needs of a monastery.

Numerous documents make it evident that the monastery of S. Satiro depended upon S. Ambrogio.[11]

The church of S. Satiro was consecrated in the year 1045 according to the chronicle of Goffredo da Bussero, which passes under the name of Filippo da Castel Seprio.[12]   Galvaneo della Fiamma states that the consecration took place on October 16, 1036.[13]   Lampugnano de Legnano repeats the date of October 16, but mentions no year.   The event, however, is recorded as having

---

[7] Christi anno DCCCLXX . . . Anspertus de Blassono . . . factus archiepiscopus sedit annis XIII et mensibus V; hic construxit in civitate ecclesiam sancti Sathiri fratis beati Ambroxii . . . Item iste archiepiscopus construxit ecclexiam S. Silvestri in porta romana anno domini DCCCLXXIII. (Galvanei Flammae, *Chron. Maius*, ed. Ceruti, 566).

[8] Anno dni 876 . . . Anspertus de Confaloneriis Archiepiscopus Mediolani fecit construi Ecclesiam santis Satiro et Silvestro in Porta Romana. (*Cronaca* detta di Filippo da Castel Seprio, MS. Amb., S. Q. + I, 12, f. 54).

[9] Anno dni 830 Anspertus de Confaloneriis episcopus Mediolani fecit fieri ecclesiam S. Satiri. (*Edificationes ecclesiarum Mediolani*, MS. Amb., S. Q. + I, 12, f. 70).

[10] [Anspertus] fecit ecclm sci satiri in Ciuitate. (Lampugnano de Legnano, *Chronica*, MS. Amb., H 56 Sup., f. 627).

[11] See for example, Puricelli, 465, 997, 1039, 1100; Giulini, I, 607, etc.   Compare also *Hist. Pat. Mon.*, XIII, 1558.

[12] Anno dni 1045 consecrata est Ecclesia Sanctorum Satiri et Silvestri Mediolani. (*Cronaca* detta di Filippo da Castel Seprio, MS. Amb., S. Q. + I, 12, f. 59).   See also Goffredo da Bussero, *Chronica*, ed. Grazioli, 237, and *Chron. Maius*, Galvanei Flammae, ed. Ceruti, 616).

[13] Eodem tempore, scilicet in MXXXVI . . . die XVI octubris ecclesia sancti Satyri in porta romana fuit consecrata. (Galvanei Flammae, *Chron. Maius*, ed. Ceruti, 603).

taken place during the pontificate of Ariberto, 1018-1045.[14] In the *Manipulus Florum*, Galvaneo also states that the consecration was celebrated by Ariberto, but on the eighteenth, not the sixteenth, day of October.[15] If the church was consecrated on the sixteenth of October, as the agreement of Lampugnano de Legnano and the *Chronicon Maius* on this point would lead us to believe, it is impossible that Ariberto celebrated this consecration in 1045, since that arch-bishop died on the sixteenth of January of that year. It is probable, therefore, that we have here one of those examples of mistaken chronology into which the late chronicles of the Middle Ages are so liable to fall when treating of times remote from themselves. The chronicle of the Biblioteca Ambrosiana is earlier, and hence more worthy of faith than is Galvaneo della Fiamma. Moreover, Galvaneo's date of 1036 can not be accepted because, in that year, the sixteenth of October fell on a Saturday, whereas the consecration of churches was regularly celebrated on Sunday. The most probable conjecture is, that the consecration really took place on October 16, 1043, which fell upon a Sunday. The date 1043 was misread or carelessly transcribed as 1045 by Filippo da Castel Seprio, or whoever wrote the chronicle of the Ambrosiana, and was changed into 1036 by Galvaneo della Fiamma.

In the year 1242 there took place in the church a miracle which was the cause of greatly increasing the popularity of the basilica. A certain gambler, overcome by despair, thrust a knife into the image of the Blessed Virgin, which immediately bled.[16]

In 1478 the construction of a new basilica was commenced.[17] Documents studied by Biscaro show that the new edifice was erected on the site of the old church, some parts of which were preserved in the new construction.[18] According to Mongeri[19] this older church had its axis corresponding to that of the present transepts. The reconstruction of the basilica proper seems to have been completed about 1514. About this same time the stucco decoration of the chapel of the Madonna di Pietà was added by Agostino de' Fonduti. In 1888 the chapel of the Madonna di Pietà was restored, but happily no damage seems to have been done either to the original edifice or to the charming XV century decoration.

III. The Cappella della Madonna di Pietà is probably a chapel belonging to the original church erected by Ansperto. Although radically transformed in the period of the early Renaissance, when it was covered with stucco and graceful Bramantesque decorations, it still preserves notable

---

[14] sci satiri eccla consecratur in porta romana die xvj octubr. (Lampugnano de Legnano, *Chronica*, MS. Amb., H 56 Sup., f. 65 r).

[15] Ecclesiam S. Satyri consecravit [Heribertus] die 18 [*sic*] Octobris. (Galvanei Flammae, *Manipulus Florum*, CXXXVII, ed. Muratori, R. I. S., XI, 614).

[16] Cantù, *Milano*, 199.   [17] Biscaro. Others give the date as 1476.

[18] Beltrami.   [19] 215.

portions of the original structure of the third quarter of the IX century. The building was square in plan, and on the middle of each face opened a semi-circular apse (Plate 129). At present the edifice is circular externally, but this is a result of the Renaissance alterations, and it is entirely probable that originally the square plan and the niches were expressed externally. Four columns in the interior supported an octagonal cupola, resting on conical pendentives (Plate 130). The present cupola is of the Renaissance (Plate 132, Fig. 2), but there can be no doubt that a cloistered vault existed originally. The apses are covered with half domes (Plate 130). Above the little square spaces between the columns and corners (Plate 129; Plate 131, Fig. 2) are undomed groin vaults, and barrel vaults at a higher level span the spaces between the four angles (Plate 129; Plate 130; Plate 131, Fig. 2). The walls are completely covered with stucco, so that it is impossible to study the character of the original masonry (Plate 131, Fig. 2; Plate 132, Fig. 2). In a closet which exists in the chapel, however, it is possible to establish the fact that the bricks are not cross-hatched.

The campanile (Plate 132, Fig. 2) is certainly later than the Cappella della Madonna di Pietà, and without doubt belonged to the edifice consecrated in 1043. It is four stories high. The upper two were originally lighted by bifora, and the third from the top by a round-arched window. The masonry is extremely rough. The bricks of enormous size, without cross-hatching, are laid in courses seldom horizontal, and interrupted at frequent intervals, especially in the upper part of the structure, by herring-bone masonry.

IV. The Cappella della Madonna di Pietà retains of its ancient decoration only the columns and the capitals. The two capitals of the free-standing columns to the right as one enters (Plate 131, Fig. 2) were pilfered from some Roman building, probably of the V century. They are a curious mixture of the Corinthian and Composite orders. Of the two free-standing columns on the opposite side, that nearest the entrance (Plate 132, Fig. 6) also appears to have been taken from another edifice. It is of the Corinthian order, and has crisp Byzantinesque acanthus leaves, although the execution is somewhat flaccid. The style appears to be transitional between the Roman and the Byzantine, and the capital may consequently be ascribed to the last years of the V century. The remaining free-standing capital (Plate 132, Fig. 5) is of the IX century, and was evidently executed for its present position. The leaves are dryly and crudely carved in the Carlovingian manner. The inexactly drawn volutes suggest a string-ornament, and in the centre of the principal face is a Greek cross, the arms of which end in a crocket-like motive. There is no undercutting, and the execution is dry and crude. Of the responds, two have pilfered Roman capitals, two capitals Gothic in style, though perhaps not earlier than the XV century, and one has an original capital of the IX century (Plate 132, Fig. 3) not dissimilar in style from that already described. The ancient shafts still exist (Plate 131, Fig. 2), but have been covered with stucco painted to represent marble. The bases, which have been much altered, were probably for the most part either pilfered ancient fragments or imitations of such. In one, the usual central scotia is replaced by a third torus.

The capitals of the campanile (Plate 132, Fig. 1, 4) were evidently not intended for close inspection, and are hence crudely executed. In the second story from the top of the campanile, the original capital and colonnette of the southern biforum have disappeared, having been replaced by a brick pier. The capital of the eastern biforum is of a splayed type and made from an old Roman fragment, with carved ornaments. The capital of the northern biforum (Plate 132, Fig. 1) is of cubic type, but square at the bottom and ornamented with incised lines. The colonnette on which it is supported has a very exaggerated entasis and a spreading base. The capital of the western biforum is nondescript.

In the upper story the capitals of the western and southern bifora (Plate 132, Fig. 4) are of Corinthianesque type, and splendid examples of the style transitional to the Lombard. The capital of the eastern biforum is of cubic type and much weathered. The bell—it can hardly be called a cushion—is low, but the lower part is circular in plan. This capital presents analogies with the capitals of Sannazzaro Sesia (Plate 201, Fig. 6), a surely dated monument of 1040. The capital of the southern biforum consists of a square block, set upon an octagonal shaft.

The ornament of the campanile (Plate 132, Fig. 2) is notable above all for the presence of fully developed arched corbel-tables.

V. The church of S. Satiro offers notable and authentically dated examples of two crucial periods of architectural history. The Cappella della Madonna di Pietà dates from 876, and the campanile from 1043.

MILAN, S. SEPOLCRO

(Plate 133, Fig. 2, 3, 5, 6)

I. Owing to the circumstance that its ancient architectural forms have been very largely destroyed by barocco restorations, the church of S. Sepolcro has attracted but little attention from students of architecture. Clericetti was the first archæologist to study the monument. The numerous drawings of Hübsch[1] are of particular value because made before the restoration. Stiehl's illustrations, consisting of two plans and a photograph, are valuable for the same reason, and that scholar has, in addition, contributed an analysis of the edifice from an archæological standpoint.

[1] Plate XLIV.

Historians, on the other hand, have spoken much of S. Sepolcro. The notice of Calco[2] is probably founded upon documentary evidence that has since been lost. Puricelli worked out the principal facts of the history of the monument. His results were the basis upon which Giulini founded his admirable study.[3] Giulini also published a drawing of the church, which shows the barocco façade and the towers as they were in the XVIII century. The notice of Rotta is of value for the modern history of the monument.

II. "In the name of Christ. Conrad, by the grace of God, emperor, in the ninth year of his reign, on the fourth day of April, the fourth indiction [1036]. I, Benedetto, who am called Rozo, son of Remedio of good memory, who was master of the mint, profess to live according to the law of the Lombards. . . . I wish that the investiture, that I made a few days ago, of my church which I recently built in honour of the Holy Trinity be inalterable, and remain inviolable, just as is read in the deed of that investiture. Only I wish that those three of my near relatives in whose presence that investiture must be made, be Ariprando the subdeacon of the holy church of Milan, the son of Pietro deceased, and Algisio, son of Maurone deceased, and Benedetto, who is also called Rozo, son of Giovanni deceased, all my nephews. Moreover, after my death let each of them elect during his life from amongst his relatives on his father's side, some one to be his successor in this trust, whomever he shall believe most fitted for this task, and let him not demand any payment. And let this be done in this manner perpetually, since such is my will. Done in the city of Milan."[4] This text makes it evident that the church of the Holy Trinity, later called S. Sepolcro, in April, 1036, had been built only a short time. The chronicle ascribed to Goffredo da Bussero states that the foundation took place in this very year,[5] and this notice is quoted by Galvaneo della

[2] 125.   [3] II, 682 f.

[4] IN Christi nomine, CHUNRADUS gratiâ Dei [Im]perator Augustus, Anno Imperij eius nono, quarto die mensis Aprilis, Indictione quarta. EGO BENEDICTUS, QUI ET ROZO, filius bonæ memoriæ Remedij, qui fuit Magister Monetæ, qui professus sum Lege viuere Longobardorum . . . volo, vt illa mea Ordinatio, quam ego ante hos dies per Chartam Iudicati institui, DE ECCLESIA MEA, QUAM EGO NOVITER ÆDIFICAVI, ET EST CONDITA IN HONOREM SANCTÆ TRINITATIS, sit firma, & stabilis permaneat, sicut in ipsa Iudicati legitur Pagina; sed tantum modò, vt ipsi mei tres parentes propinquiores, in quorum præsentia eadem Ordinatio facta esse debet, volo, vt sint Ariprandus Subdiaconus de ordine Sanctæ Ecclesiæ Mediolanensis, filius Quondam Petri: & Algisius, filius Quondam Mauroni: seu itē Benedictus, qui & Rozo, filius Quondam Iohannis: nepotes mei. Post autem meum decessum unus quisque eorum in vita sua eligat de suis parentibus propinquioribus de paterna parte ad hoc ministerium esse successorem sine vllo precio, quem cognouerint vtiliorem ad hoc faciendum, perpetuis temporibus. Quia sic decreuit mea bona volūtas. Actum in Ciuitate Mediolani. (Puricelli, 478).

[5] Anno dn̄i 1036 Benedictus de Cortesella fecit fieri Ecclesiam S. Sepulchri Mediolani. (*Chronica* detta di Filippo da Castel Seprio, MS. Amb., S. Q. + I, 12, f. 59;

Fiamma.[6] The chronicle of Lampugnano de Legnano gives the date July 15, but omits the year.[7] It is certain, however, that Goffredo is in error in ascribing the foundation of the church to the year 1036.   The basilica is mentioned as already existing in 1034, in the will of the archbishop Ariberto.[8] Calco states that the foundation took place in the year 1030, and he seems to have based this statement upon an authentic document, now lost.[9]

The date of July 15 given by Lampugnano de Legnano, and repeated by Galvaneo, was probably derived from the custom observed in later times of celebrating the anniversary of the reconsecration of the church in the year 1100. . This reconsecration took place on July 15. According to one of the ancient Milanese calendars a procession was made annually to the church of S. Sepolcro on this day.[10]

In the third quarter of the XI century, the church of the Trinity was the theatre of important events connected with the reform movement of S. Arialdo. "In those days many clerics began to leave the company of the depraved priests, and followed S. Arialdo. Among these was a certain priest who, moved by the exhortations of the saint, decided to give up a church which he had sinfully bought for a great price. By divine providence, it so happened that the knight, to whom the investiture of this church pertained, was now also converted and a follower of S. Arialdo. And just as he who had bought the church resolved to relinquish it, so the knight chose of his own volition to set free and treat that church as a mistress which, up to this time, he had wickedly oppressed as a servant. Therefore, when many of the faithful had assembled

Goffredo da Bussero, *Chronica,* ed. Grazioli, 237). Magistretti also quotes another text of Goffredo da Bussero: An. 1036 edificata est eccl. S. Sepulcri ad scuriolum Mediol. vz. an. 16 archiepi Dni. Heriberti Mediol.

[6] Eodem tempore, scilicet in MXXXVI, Rozus de Cortesella sive de Canzellariis construxit ecclexiam sancti Sepulchri, ut dicit Gotofredus de Bussero, die XV iulii. (Galvanei Flammae, *Chron. Maius,* ed. Ceruti, 603).

Isto tempore [Heriberti] Eccleia S. Sepulchri per Ronzinum de Cortesella constituitur. . . . (Galvanei Flammae, *Manipulus Florum,* CXXXVII, ed. Muratori, R. I. S., XI, 614).

[7] . . . eccla sci Sepulcri p[er] rozum de Cortexelis edificatur xv Julij. (Lampugnano de Legnano, *Chronica,* MS. Amb., H 56 Sup., f. 65 r).

[8] Puricelli, 366.

[9] Anno quarto Imperij Conradi Benedictus, qui & Rocio vulgo nuncupabatur, cum Ferlenda vxore ædem proprio solo media vrbe struxere in honorem Diuæ Trinitatis, & memoriam locorum, quæ Christus Deus nascendo, moriendoq. & interim baptizatus, excruciatusq. à Iudæis, & nouissimè cælos ascendens sacrauit, singulaq. sacella singulis nominibus distincta diu mansere, donec celebrius vocabulum Sancti Sepulchri inualuit. eius cultui quattuor Canonicos, & octo Monachos adscriptos fuisse lego: licet posterorum neglegētia, illos iam diu desideremus. durat tamen nobilis structura subterraneo specu, pensilibusq. cellis, marmoreo pauimento, & duabus turribus egregia. (Calco, Lib. VI, 125 sub anno 1027).

[10] Julius . . . Idibus. Processio ad S. Sepulcrum. Obiit Ildenatus, qui dicitur Boto. (*Kalendarium Sitonianum,* ed. Muratori, R. I. S., II, pt. 2, 1038).

in the presence of S. Arialdo, the knight received a renunciation from the buyer, and, at the admonition of the man of God, placed the renunciation on the altar, and bade S. Arialdo henceforth to dispose of the church as he knew that God willed. The saint then called three faithful and chaste clerks, and bade them to assume the charge which the knight had placed upon the altar. And when the saint was frequently exhorted to share with these clerks the charge, since his remaining there would be of benefit to many, he replied: 'I shall remain with these priests to instruct them, and to help them in other ways. But lest the word of God, confided to my charge, should suffer impediment under the yoke of some worldly interest, I shall certainly not undertake this charge. I refuse also lest in consequence some harm should befall Azone (Rozo), in whose jurisdiction this church has been constructed, since know that the time is certainly coming in which no one shall be able to live who does not drive me from his borders.' In what way this speech was prophetic the reader will perceive in the sequel. While Arialdo remained in that church he wrought many good works by his words and by his deeds amongst the brethren and the other faithful and unfaithful, and for almost ten years [1057-1067] they requited him with evil for good, such as no one can write nor describe. Amongst other good works he sent a messenger to his home, and withdrew twenty pounds of silver, with which he built a wonderfully contrived house for the priests near the church. . . . Moreover he introduced a certain innovation up to that time in this place entirely unknown, for he caused the choir to be surrounded by a high wall in which was placed a door. Thus the priests, the men, and the women were divided so that they could not see each other. The priests moreover were compelled all to live in the same house. They were not allowed to converse at table, but were obliged instead to listen to the divine scriptures which were assiduously read to them. Moreover while other priests in the morning mumbled rather than sang the sacred offices, Arialdo in the morning when the bell pealed seven times, assembled the brethren, and with great reverence sang the praises due to Omnipotent God, and by word and deed kindled with enthusiasm for the office all the brethren, who might otherwise have been somewhat careless. And just as S. Arialdo was very joyful because he had realized his long and ardent wish, to live in common with the brethren in a church, so many of the faithful were made glad to have a suitable place where they could freely hear the word of God, and take part in the divine mysteries and sacraments. And such a multitude began to flock to the church, not only from the city but also from surrounding towns and castles, that the church, although rather large, was much too small to receive all the people."[11]

[11] 26. In diebus illis quam plurimi clerici cœpere consortium clericorum pravorum relinquere, et B. Arialdo adhærere. Inter quos quidam ex illis sacerdotibus, ipsius exhortatione compunctus, ecclesiam quamdam, quam grandi pretio male emerat, dimittere disposuit. Sed Christo ordinante, Miles, in cujus jure hæc erat, jam de

MILAN, S. SEPOLCRO

In 1099 Jerusalem fell into the hands of the Crusaders. The extraordinary enthusiasm which this event aroused throughout Europe found expression among other ways in numerous churches erected in imitation of the Holy Sepulchre. At Milan, the church of the Trinity was at this time restored and reconsecrated under the title of S. Sepolcro. There is extant a diploma of the archbishop of Milan, Anselmo IV, to the following effect. "I, Anselmo, by the great and abounding grace of God archbishop of the holy mother-church of Milan. . . . Inspired by the great mercy of God which did not allow a city placed on a mountain, that is, the church of S. Sepolcro placed in the midst of this city, longer to remain hidden, but rather made it to be exalted and to rejoice with the sepulchre of Jerusalem in token of victory, we went in procession with our brethren to the church, and consecrated the altar and the

fidelibus, quippe per B. Arialdum edoctus, sicut ille eam deserere disposuerat, qui illam emerat; sic iste suo e jure elegit hanc amittere ut dominam, qui eatenus ipsam nequiter usurparat ut famulam. Convenientibus igitur cum B. Arialdo in unum multis fidelibus, Miles refutationem ab emptore accepit, eamque super altare viri Dei admonitione posuit, et eidem B. Arialdo jussit ut deinceps eam disponeret, secundum quod Deum velle sciret. Qui protinus tres clericos fideles et castos vocavit, et refutationem quam Miles in altare posuerat eos pariter jussit tollere. 27. Cumque idem a pluribus exhortaretur, ut eamdem cum ipsis una sumeret, quatenus ad multorum profectum ibidem manere deberet, ait: Cum ipsis quidem ad eorum instructionem, et cæterorum salutem manebo; verumtamen, ne verbo Dei mihi credito impedimentum sit, sub jugo alicujus terrenæ rei, et ne huic Azoni, in cujus ditione hæc ecclesia est constructa, sub hac occasione aliquod possit damnum inferri, hujus rei sortem nequaquam sumo, quoniam tale tempus scitote procul dubio venturum, in quo nulli vivere liceat, nisi me a suis finibus expellat. Hic quippe sermo quomodo propheticus fuerit, in sequenti lectoris menti luce clarius patebit. Eo namque in eadem ecclesia manente, quanta beneficia tam verbis quam factis, sive ipsis fratribus, sive cæteris tam fidelibus quam infidelibus impenderit, et quanta ab eis pro bonis mala per decem fere annos pertulerit, nemo nec omnia scribere, imo nec valet profecto dicere. Nam protinus legationem in domum paternam misit, et ex ea viginti libras argenti sumpsit, atque juxta eamdem ecclesiam habitaculum mirabiliter aptum ædificavit. . . . Agitur denique res nova et pene ab eodem loco hactenus inscia. Chorus namque alti circumdatione muri concluditur, in quo ostium ponitur: visio clericorum, laicorum ac mulierum, quæ una erat et communis, dividitur; omnes de una arca vivere coguntur, fabulæ ad mensam compescuntur, pro quibus sancta lectio super eam assidue profertur. Cæteri autem clerici mane omnes diei Horas potius murmurabant, quam decantarent; hic vero in die, tacto septies signo, fratribus una congregatis, magna cum veneratione debitam omnipotenti Deo laudem decantabat, atque ad satisfactionem omnes in eodem officio, dum forte delinquerent, dicto et facto provocabat. Porro sicut B. Arialdus lætus nimis est effectus, eo quod ad votum diu nimisque optatum (videlicet, ut cum fratribus ad ecclesiam communiter vivere posset) pervenerat; sic fideles multi læti sunt effecti, pro eo quod aptum locum haberent, ubi Domini verba mente libera audire possent, et divina mysteria ac sacramenta percipere. Cœpit autem tanta illuc ibidem multitudo confluere, non solum de urbe, sed etiam de villis et castellis, quatenus eos nullo modo valeret capere ipsa ecclesia, licet satis esset ampla. Quos tam constanti assiduaque doctrina vir Dei docebat ut plerumque vocem sic amitteret, quatenus ab aliquibus juxta se positis vix audiri posset. (*Sancti Arialdi Vita*, auctore B. Andrea Vallumbrosana,

entire church to the glory of the Holy Sepulchre, and on the altar we celebrated mass."[12]   The archbishop goes on to describe the ceremony of consecration and the anniversary to be celebrated each year in memory of the event, establishing a peace and truce of eight days before and after the festival.   He then accords indulgences to those who shall visit 'this sepulchre made in the true image of the Holy Sepulchre.'[13]   The deed is dated at Milan, July 15, 1100.[14]

The reconsecration of the church in 1100 is also recorded in several chronicles of late date.[15]

ed. Migne, *Patrologiae Cursus Completus,* Series Latina, CXLIII, 1454).   The church is also mentioned in connection with other events that took place during the close of the career of Arialdo.   Quem [B. Arialdum] tollentes in atrium ecclesiæ, quæ dicitur Rozzoni, deveniunt etc.   (*Vitæ SS. Arialdi et Erlembaldi,* ed. Migne, *Pat. Lat.,* CXLIII, 1470). . . . per dies quindecim duo populorum conventicula sunt in urbe vehementia assidue habita; unum scilicet fidelium ad ecclesiam Rozzoni, alterum vero in curia pontificali.   (*Ibid.,* 1472). . . . Levaverunt pariter voces et fustes, omnique plebe commota, in ecclesiam beati viri, quæ canonica nuncupabatur, cum magno impetu irruunt; quidquid inveniunt, diripiunt, domumque destruere incipiunt.   (*Ibid.,* 1466).

[12] IN Nomine Sanctæ sempiternæquè & indiuiduæ Trinitatis, & Sancti Sepulchri Domini nostri Iesu Christi.   EGO ANSELMVS, MAGNA DEI OPITVLANTE CLEMENTIA SANCTÆ MATRIS ECCLESIÆ ARCHIEPISCOPVS MEDIOLANENSIS . . . ne penitùs tamen viderer deditus ignorantiæ, inspiräte summa Dei Clemëtia, quæ Ciuitatem supra montem positam ECCLESIAM SCILICET SANCTI SEPVLCHRI, IN MEDIO HVIVS CIVITATIS SITAM, non est passa diutiùs abscondi; sed eä quasi exaltare fecit & iubilare ad signü victoriæ Ierosolymitani Sepulchri; ad cuius gloriä nos procedentes cum nostris Fratribus ALTARE DOMINO CVM ECCLESIA SIMVL INTERIVS DEDICAVIMVS, & super illud Deo nostro Hostiam laudis obtulimus.   (Puricelli, 481).

[13] AD HOC SEPVLCHRVM, AD EIVS VERAM SIMILITVDINEM FACTVM.   (*Ibid.*).

[14] Actum est hoc omnium Mediolanensium testimonio & confirmatione, Anno ab Incarnatione Domini nostri Iesu Christi Millesimo centesimo, Indictione octaua, Idus Iulij.   (*Ibid.*).

[15] Eodem anno s. m MC Ecclia scti sepulcri p[er] Rozū de Cortesella cōstruit. (Galvaneo della Fiamma, *Chronicon,* Vienna MS. 3318, f. 72, Cap. 246).

Isti cùm pervenissent ultra mare, multis confectis prœliis Civitatem Sanctam sunt aggressi, & finaliter Joannes Rhodensis supradictus, & Petrus de Selvaticis Cives Mediolanenses primò sunt ingressi Civitatem Sanctam anno 1099. die 15. Julii, & anno Domini 1100. supradictus Rozinus ad Civitatem Mediolani reversus Ecclesiam Sancti Sepulcri construxit.   (Galvanei Flammae, *Manipulus Florum,* CXLI, ed. Muratori, R. I. S., XI, 617).

Anno Domini 1100. imperante Conrado [*sic*] adolescente, sedente Crisolano [*sic*] Archiepiscopo Simoniaco, Otto Vicecomes, Joannes Rhodensis, & Rozinus de Cortesela cum aliis Civibus Mediolanensibus ad hanc Civitatem sunt reversi, & fuit mirabile gaudium in terra.   Tunc Ecclesia S. Sepulchri fabricata fuit. ˙ (*Ibid.,* CLIV, ed. M., 627).

Et l'anno MCX Roxo de Cortesella ritornò a Milano e fece costruire la giexa de s. Sepolcro a Milano.   (*Chron. di Milano,* ed. Lambertenghi, 7).   And in the same

MILAN, S. SEPOLCRO

It has been supposed by several authorities that the church of the Trinity was completely reconstructed at the time to which these different texts refer. A little thought however is sufficient to show that this could not have been the case. Only a year elapsed between the fall of Jerusalem and the consecration of the edifice, and out of this year we must allow a not inconsiderable period for the return voyage of the founders, before the alteration of the church could have been begun. The rebuilding of the church therefore could not have occupied more than five or six months. In this period it is obvious that no very radical reconstruction could have taken place. The works, it is true, may have continued somewhat after the consecration of July 15, 1100, but it is certain that at that date the church must have been habitable. We must not be deceived by the assurance of Anselmo that the church is a reproduction of the church of the Holy Sepulchre at Jerusalem. Throughout Europe are to be found many churches which pious authors assure us are exact reproductions of the church of the Holy Sepulchre. Not only, however, do these basilicas bear no particular resemblance to each other, but they are all quite different from the church of the Holy Sepulchre itself. For example, the church of S. Sepolcro at Bologna was believed in the XI century to be an absolutely exact reproduction of the famous shrine of the Holy City, and pious chroniclers assert that S. Petronio brought from Palestine the precise measures of the edifice which he wished to reproduce. As a matter of fact, however, the church is a building of the Lombard style which bears no visible resemblance to the monument it was supposed to imitate. In reality the only feature of the Holy Sepulchre at Jerusalem that seems to have influenced the architecture of shrines in Europe supposed to reproduce it, was the use of a circular instead of a basilican plan. When the Milanesi determined to reconsecrate the church of the Trinity in honour of the Holy Sepulchre, they found themselves already in the possession of a comparatively new and well built basilica. The problem presented itself, how to transform this basilica into an edifice which might pass as an imitation of the church at Jerusalem. It was evidently impossible to transform a basilica into a circular church, which would be the conventional form for such a structure, without entirely demolishing the existing edifice. Accordingly, an easy compromise was effected. The circular form was suggested by erecting new semicircular apses at the transept-ends instead of the flat wall which had previously existed. The structural alterations carried out in the church in the year 1100 were confined to this very simple change. It is possible that new decorations and shrines suitable to the modified character of the church were added to the interior, but of these no traces have survived the barocco centuries.

chronicle (15) we read: Et in questo tempo Oto Visconti, Roxio de Cortesella se ritornarono a Milano con grande allegrezza da Ierusalem, che poi feceno edificare la chiesa di S. Sepolcro in Milano.

In the XII century the church of S. Sepolcro depended upon the monastery of S. Ambrogio, as we learn from diplomas of 1148,[16] 1185,[17] 1193, etc.

In 1188 a lawsuit arose between the heirs of Rozo and the priest Guglielmo, deacon of S. Sepolcro. The inedited document relating to this controversy is of especial interest, because from it we learn that Rozo did not found the church of S. Sepolcro, but rebuilt it, since a chapel of S. Lorenzo pre-existed on the site.[18]

In the XIV century the church was restored and considerably altered, as may be deduced from fragments that came to light in the recent rebuilding. According to a tax-list of 1568, the church in that year was officiated by three canons, and was dependent upon S. Ambrogio.[19]

In the XVIII century the edifice was made over in the barocco style by the cardinal Federigo Borromeo. It suffered even more severely than was usually the case with Lombard buildings remade in that century, so hostile to mediæval art. Indeed, only a few fragments of the original construction were spared.

In 1841 the edifice was again restored.[20] About 1890 an attempt was made to give the church again its Lombard character, but the restorers found so few traces of the ancient construction, that they abandoned the task as hopeless. The two campanili and the façade were rebuilt in a pseudo-Romanesque style. When the intonaco was stripped from the barocco façade, some traces of the bifora in the lower story of the west wall of the side aisles

---

[16] Puricelli, 997.   [17] *Ibid.*, 1039.

[18] The document in question is a sentence of the archbishop of Milan. The heirs of Rozo claim that Guglielmo should be removed: Allegantes, quod in ipsa Ecclesia locum Fundatoris obtineant, et in eadem Juspatronatus debeant habere. . . . E contra praefatus Guilielmus Diaconus se a jamdicta Ecclesia Sancti Sepulchri non esse removendum affirmabat, dicens, ipsum Benedictum qui et Rozo vocabatur, ipsius Ecclesiae Sancti Sepulchri non fuisse Fundatorem, set potius Rehaedificatorem, cum ante ipsius Rozonis tempora ibi ad honorem Beati Laurentii fuerit Ecclesia fundata. . . . Allegabat enim tam se quam antecessores suos ab ipsius Ecclesiae Parochianis, ipsis Actoribus inconsultis, longis retro temporibus in ipsa Ecclesia fuisse electos, et institutos. . . . The decision was: Ipse Dominus archiepiscopus . . . concessit et ordinavit, ut idem Guilielmus ab ipso Archiepiscopo in praedicta Ecclesia Diaconus factus non iure electionis de eo facto sed gratia et benignitate eiusdem Archiepiscopi. . . . Insuper statuit ut praedicti Actores . . . habeant potestatem eligendi in praesenti idoneam personam in ipsa Ecclesia Sancti Sepulchri quae ipsam debeat deservire quem Archiepiscopo Mediolanen. debeant praesentare confirmandum. . . . Anno Dominicae Incarnationis millesimo centesimo octuagesimo octavo vii Kal. Iunii, Indictione VI. (*Codice della Croce*, MS. Amb. D. S., IV, 10/I, 10, f. 228).

[19] Sepulchri cú tribus cancis Hodie congregationis oblator[um] sti Ambrosij. (*Status ecclesiae Mediolani 1568 conscriptus*, auctore Francisco Castello, MS. Amb., A, 112, Inf., f. 446). *Ibid.*, 540, the names of the three canons are given and the taxes they paid. In 1398 there were also three canons, according to a tax-list published by Magistretti.

[20] *Milano e il suo territorio*, II, 350.

were found. There is authority also for the blind arches at the upper part of the west side-aisle walls and the double arched corbel-tables of the central gable. These, however, like the oculus and the great window in the central part of the façade evidently belonged to restorations carried out in the XIV century. The two upper stories of both campanili are either entirely modern or much restored.

III. In the present condition of the church, it is impossible to determine with precision the exact disposition of the Lombard edifice. There was doubtless a western narthex flanked by campanili (Plate 133, Fig. 5), a nave, two side aisles, transepts, a choir, a central cupola and galleries. The original piers have entirely disappeared, and it is impossible to say how the nave was roofed. The edifice was evidently a homogeneous structure with the exception of the transept-ends (Plate 133, Fig. 3) which were added at a later epoch. When the transept-ends were remade, the crypt, which at present extends beneath the entire edifice, may well have been enlarged.

The masonry of the original structure may be seen in the south gallery wall (Plate 133, Fig. 2) and in the lower part of the campanili (Plate 133, Fig. 6). It is formed of rough bricks with occasional blocks of stone inlaid especially at the angles. The bricks vary greatly in size, and the courses depart widely from the horizontal. Layers of herring-bone masonry are inlaid at frequent intervals. The windows of the gallery (Plate 133, Fig. 2), widely splayed, were evidently intended to serve without glass. Quite different in character is the masonry of the transepts (Plate 133, Fig. 3), where the bricks are of more regular shape and laid in more even courses.

IV. The only Lombard ornament extant is to be found in the arched corbel-tables of the exterior. In the lower parts of the campanili (Plate 133, Fig. 6) and in the exterior wall of the galleries (Plate 133, Fig. 2) these corbel-tables are small, but grouped two and two by pilaster strips. In the upper part of the northern campanile we have probably the earliest extant example of fully developed arched corbel-tables.[21] Fully developed also are the later arched corbel-tables of the transept-ends (Plate 133, Fig. 3).

V. The church of S. Sepolcro is an authentically dated monument of 1030, with the exception of the transept-ends which were erected in 1100. It is therefore of great importance for the history of the development of the Lombard style, and it is exceedingly to be regretted that the original forms of the monument can not be more exactly determined. At least enough is extant to prove that early in the second quarter of the XI century the Lombard builders erected a basilica with groin-vaulted galleries. The arched corbel-tables of the exterior, moreover, throw much light upon the history of the evolution of this ornament, so characteristic of the Lombard style.

[21] Those of the southern campanile are modern.

LOMBARD ARCHITECTURE

MILAN, S. SIMPLICIANO

I.   In 1674 the church of S. Simpliciano at Milan was described by Torre.[1]   He speaks of the façade, with the exception of the principal portal, as having been recently restored, and gives a brief description of the edifice which is of great value, because he saw it when it was still in good preservation.[2] Valuable historical notices are contained in the work of Puccinelli, printed in 1650.   In 1737 Latuada published a short description of the edifice.[3]   In the same century Giulini[4] worked out the history of the monastery and published drawings of the façade.   In 1773 Allegranza[5] contributed a fantastic study of the portal.   Millin, writing in 1817, said of the church *ce temple a été tout-à-fait modernisé.*[6]   In 1826 Pirovano wrote a brief description of the interior.[7]

The first of modern archæologists to study the edifice was De Dartein.[8] He was followed by Stiehl, whose analysis, illustrated with drawings and halftones, is certainly the most important contribution to the archæological literature of the monument.   The monograph of Beltrami contains many notices of importance.   The sculptures of the portal have been illustrated by Romussi and studied by Sant'Ambrogio.

II.   It is the constant tradition in the church of Milan that S. Simpliciano was founded by S. Ambrogio.   The earliest text known to me in which this tradition is recorded is the passage in the chronicle which passes under the name of Filippo da Castel Seprio.[9]   It was undoubtedly from this source that Galvaneo della Fiamma derived his information.[10]   Oltrocchi,[11] however,

---

[1] 233.

[2] Mà non più si differisca l'ingresso: osservate ormai la di lui vasta ampiezza e smisurata altezza della sue Volte sostenute da grossi Pilastroni, parte di selce, e parte di pietri cotte, di questi per cadun lato voi ne numerate otto, con altretanti Archi, arriuando sino alla Cupola.   In trè Naui fù disposta la sua antica Architettura, con due altre Naui laterali formando vna Croce (235).

[3] La chiesa . . . si vede, distinta in tre longhissime e del pari alte Navi, fatta in forma di Croce, con otto Pilastroni per ogni lato.   Contansi in essa tredici cappelle, compresavi la Maggiore. . . . l'esteriore Frontispizio del Tempio rimane ancora nell'antica sua primiera forma, a riserva de' finestroni, sostituiti ad altre picciole rotonde finestre, che si chiamavano occhij.   (Latuada, V, 66 f.).

[4] I, 109; III, 191.   [5] *Spiegazioni*, 167.   [6] I, 245.

[7] L'interno della Chiesa è costrutto in tre navi in forma di croce latina con cupola; essa non aveva nella sua prima istituzione che un solo altare sotto la medesima. (Pirovano, 214).

[8] 216.

[9] Cited above under S. Ambrogio of Milan, p. 539.

[10] Beatus verò Ambrosius . . . fundavit . . . Ecclesiam in honorem Beatæ Mariæ Virginis, & omnium Virginum, quæ modò dicitur Sancti Simpliciani.   (Galvanei Flammæ, *Manipulus Florum,* ed. Muratori, R. I. S., XI, 570).

[11] I, 69.

questions whether the basilica may not have been dedicated, not by S. Ambrogio, but by his successor S. Simpliciano. At all events, since the latter was buried in the church, it must have been in existence in the early years of the V century.

The church was rebuilt at the end of the VI century—at least this is the natural inference to draw from the fact that stamped tiles of the epoch of Agilulfo (591-615) were found used as second-hand materials in the roof.[12]

As early as the end of the IX century, the church of S. Simpliciano was connected with that of S. Protasio, but the relations of the two are not altogether clear. Giulini[13] has deduced from the somewhat enigmatical references in numerous documents that at S. Protasio there were originally monks and at S. Simpliciano secular clergy; since the monks, desirous of solitude, wished a church outside of the city, and the canons preferred to be within the walls, an exchange was agreed upon, by which the monks moved to S. Simpliciano and the canons to S. Protasio. The monks, however, continued to claim jurisdiction over the church of S. Protasio. In any case, it is certain that a monastery existed in the church of S. Simpliciano as early as the year 881, since it is mentioned in a bull of this date in which the pope takes the abbot and monks under his apostolic protection.[14] Galvaneo della Fiamma states that the monks of S. Simpliciano came from S. Vittore, but he has probably confused the church of S. Vittore with that of S. Protasio.[15] The monastery of S. Simpliciano is again mentioned in 903,[16] and in the will of the archbishop Ariberto of 1034.[17] A long inscription of 1039 recording a donation to the monastery, misread by Puricelli, has been published by Giulini.[18]

If we are to believe Galvaneo della Fiamma, the church of S. Simpliciano was destroyed by the same fire of 1075 that wiped out the churches of S. Nazaro, S. Stefano, S. Lorenzo, the Cathedral, etc.[19] However, none of the contemporary chroniclers who speak of the fire mention that the church of S. Simpliciano was destroyed, and in view of the fact that the conflagration consumed edifices situated only in the southern and western parts of the city, whereas S. Simpliciano was without the walls to the north-east, there is grave reason to doubt the accuracy of Galvaneo's statement.

[12] Beltrami gives the inscription thus:

✠ G̅L̅. DOM̅N̅ . . . . . AGILVLF

ET ADIWALD. FIER . . . . . AEC P̅R̅

[13] II, 656-657.

[14] Igitur quia te Hadericum venerabilem presbyterum, et abbatem sacrorum monasteriorum, beatorum scilicet Gervasii et Protasii, atque Simpliciani et xenodochii Sanctorum Cosmae et Damiani . . . (Tomassetti, I, 357).

[15] Monasterium sancti Simplitiani primo fuit in ecclexia sancti Victoris ad quercum porte nove, postea fuit translatum ad locum ubi nunc est. (Galvanei Flammae, *Chron. Maius*, ed. Ceruti, 591).

[16] Giulini, VII, 35.   [17] Puricelli, 366.   [18] II, 257 ff.

[19] This text has been cited above, p. 635.

According to Romussi[20] an important bequest was made to the church in the year 1079. It is evident, however, that this notice results from a misreading of the inscription of 1039 mentioned above. In a privilege conceded by Henry IV in 1081,[21] and in another document of 1099[22] the dual monastery of S. Simpliciano and S. Protasio is mentioned.

At the end of the first half of the XII century, there was in existence a *labor* in the basilica. This is first mentioned in the will of a certain Albericio, dated January 27, 1142, and made on the occasion when that worthy was about to set out for the Holy Land.[23] The *labor* is again mentioned in 1147[24] and 1152.[25]

Millin, speaking of the western portal, states that it was built in 1171.[26] I have searched in vain to discover whence came this notice unknown to the historians of Milan. I am inclined, nevertheless, to believe that it merits faith. Millin was an exceptionally well informed and intelligent traveller, and may well have had the notice from some priest or other learned person, who had had access to documents destroyed in the revolution.

There is a legend that at the time of the battle of Legnano (1176) three white doves flew from S. Simpliciano and lit upon the standard of the carroccio of the victorious Lombard League. It has been supposed by Romussi[27] that the basilica was reconstructed in consequence of this miracle, but the text of Millin, cited above, makes it probable that the reconstruction really took place somewhat earlier.

[20] I, 176.

[21] In nomine Sanctæ, et individuæ Trinitatis. Henricus divina favente clementia Quartus Rex. . . . Monasterio Sanctorum Gervasi, et Protasii, seu Simpliciani, et ejusdem Monasterii Abbati, per nostram Regalem auctoritatem, concedimus, ut homines in loco *Trivillio,* qui dicitur *Grasso* etc. . . . Datum XVII, Kal. Maji, Indictione Quarta, anno ab Incarnatione Domini Milleximo LXXXI. Anno autem Domini Henrici XXVII, Regni vero XXV, Mediolani fæliciter. Amen, Amen. (Giulini, VII, 70).

[22] Giulini, I, 321.

[23] Anno ab Incarnatione Domini nostri Ieshu xpi milleximo centeximo quadrageximo secundo, septimo kalendarum februarii, indictione quinta. . . . habeat de facultatibus meis . . . Labor sancti Simpliciani similiter solidos quinque. (Bonnoni, *Diplomatum . . . Claravallis,* MS. Brera AE, XV, 20, f. 211).

[24] Biscaro, *Note e Doc. Sant.,* II, 49. A privilege of this same year, granted by the archbishop Oberto, has been published by Giulini, VII, 109.

[25] This is the bequest made by a certain Guerenzo: Anno ab incarnatione domini nostri ihesu christi mill. centes. quinquagesimo secundo sesto die iunii indictione quintadecima. . . . Canonica sancti Ambrosii ad corpus omni anno fictum ad mensuram Mediol. sicalis et panici modios trex et canonica sancti Kalimeri modios duo et canonica sancti Nazarii de brolio modios duo et . . . monasterium de Cleraualle solidos centum et monasterium de Morimundo libras quinque et labor sancti Simpliciani ad corpus libras trex et labor sancti Victoris ad corpus solidos sexaginta etc. (*Codice della Croce,* MS. Amb., D. S. IV, 8/I, 8, f. 33). Cf. Giulini, III, 394.

[26] Cette porte, ainsi que les petites portes, qui ont été baties en 1171 . . . (I, 245).

[27] 469.

In 1245, according to Puccinelli,[28] or in 1246, according to Giulini,[29] seven altars in the church were dedicated.

The abbey is mentioned in a tax-list of 1398, published by Magistretti. In 1461 it was given in commendam.[30] The monastery was suppressed and united with S. Raffaello.[31] Previously—in 1517, according to Puccinelli[32]—monks of Monte Cassino had been called to officiate it. In consequence of the change of clergy, and perhaps also in part because the upper portion of the campanile had been demolished in 1552, a restoration and enlargement of the basilica was undertaken in 1577.[33] This must have been completed in 1582, since a translation of relics at this period is recorded.[34] In 1783 traces of the foundation of the atrium came to light.[35] The monks who had returned were suppressed anew in 1786, and in 1798 were established in S. Salvatore at Pavia.[36]

In 1813 remains of an old apse were found under the altar.[37] A most disastrous restoration was carried out from 1838 to 1841. No precise account of the changes wrought at this epoch has come down to us, but in the anonymous work entitled *Milano ed il suo Territorio,* written in 1844, are some notices of value.[38] In 1870 the portal was again restored.

III. The interior of the edifice was so completely made over in 1841 that it is now impossible to determine the original forms. From a plan published by Beltrami, and the descriptions cited above, it is possible to draw the inference that the church consisted of an atrium, a nave eight bays long, double side aisles, projecting transepts, a cupola and an apse. The division of the transepts into two equal aisles antedates 1838, but there were until

[28] Già si celebraua la Consecratione di questa basilica il ventesimoprimo giorno del mese di Ottobre, che di poi l'anno 1245, fù ordinato si celebrasse perpetuamente in giorno di Domenica, nel qual anno, e giorno, da Giouanni Buono Vescouo di Cremona furono consecrati in questa Basilica Sette altari: . . . il primo altare lo dedicò a S. Simpliciano etc. . . . (Puccinelli, *Zodiaco. Vita di S. Simpliciano,* 46).

[29] IV, 432.   [30] Puccinelli, *op. cit.,* 100.

[31] [Ecclīa] Simpliciani, suppressa, et Applicata Cura S[ti] Raphaellis, et Ecclesia data est scolaribus p[er] Ill.m D.D. Carolù Carlem intlo Stæ Praxedis Archīepum Mīaensem. (*Status Ecclesiae Mediolani,* 1568 conscriptus auctore Francisco Castello. MS. Amb., A, 112 Inferiore, f. 441).

[32] *Op. cit.,* 81.   [33] Puccinelli, *op. cit.,* 48, 82.

[34] *Ibid.,* 48.   [35] Beltrami, 26.

[36] Original documents published by Forcella.   [37] Beltrami, 26.

[38] Poc' anzi l'architetto Aluisetti restituì all'edifizio il carattere, alterato dai ristauri e dalle aggiunte del 1582; abbattè arditamente quattro piloni che separavano i bracci della croce; levò le irregolarità; al rozzo cartabone dei piloni surrogò capitelli di gesso, imitanti, alquanto più largamente, un vecchio qui trovato; le finestre tornò arcuate che erano state ridotte rettangole. . . . Bel pensiero fu d'aprire verso il coro una celletta a colonne, donde vedasi l'urna de' martiri, e che richiama quella primitiva di cui edificando si scopersero le vestigia. The cupola and apse had been previously restored in classic style by the same architect. (II, 381).

that time four piers, now demolished, by which the side aisles of the nave were carried across the western aisle of the transepts.

The ancient portions of the structure still existing include the exterior of the apse, which, although covered with intonaco, still possesses its original masonry; parts of the cupola and campanile; some portions of the transepts; the responds of the narthex, and the western portal. According to Stiehl, the barrel vaults and the side aisles of the choir are original, but this point is open to question. Stiehl saw the original tiles of the apse roof still in place, and records that they were placed directly on a bed of mortar covering the extrados of the vault. He further studied the structure of this vault, and discovered that its extrados was divided into four parts by projecting ribs (perhaps not original), and that the vault itself was composed of hollow jars similar to those of the chapel of S. Satiro at S. Ambrogio in Milan, and of the churches at Ravenna.

The transepts, although rebuilt in the XIII century, contain some fragments of XII century masonry. They are obviously later than the cupola, since their roof cuts across the latter. Stiehl believed that the church originally had eastern chapels which were later converted into a second aisle of the transept. The upper part of the southern wall is buttressed by a series of blind arches, which recall those of the atrium of S. Ambrogio, but which, apparently, are not ancient. The façade was originally preceded by an atrium, of which the foundations have been discovered, and of which the amortizements still exist in the façade. The masonry of the XII century portions of the edifice consists of enormously large bricks, cross-hatched, laid in courses for the most part nearly horizontal, and separated by mortar-beds of moderate thickness.

IV. The apse is ornamented with pilaster strips and arched corbel-tables. The central portal of the façade is in many orders, richly moulded, and, with spiral-fluted columns. For the bells of the capital are substituted a band of sculpture, except on the outermost face, where are grotesque animals or eagles. The abaci are continuous and adorned with a leaf pattern, but they are cusped into polygonal or semicircular forms, roughly corresponding to the loads. The two side portals are modern, but the responds of the narthex and their capitals are ancient. The capitals are carved with grotesques, rinceaux or foliage of advanced and refined character.

The sculptures of the capitals—unfortunately broken—are peculiar. On the right-hand side are represented five female figures bearing lamps. These must undoubtedly be virgins of the parable in the twenty-fifth chapter of Matthew, but I am inclined to think that they are not foolish virgins, as Sant'Ambrogio would have it, but wise virgins who go to meet the bridegroom with their lamps lighted. The sixth figure, who stands upon the dragon and the serpent, perhaps represents the bridegroom, Christ. On the opposite jamb, in parallel with the wise virgins, are five clerics. Two of these—those furthest to the left—are designated as archbishops by their pallia and hold books. Two others carrying crosses are martyrs, and a third, carrying a book, is probably a sainted cleric. It is evident that these five saints put in parallel with the five wise virgins must be five illustrious examples of sanctity in the church of Milan. The identification of the saints, in the absence of inscriptions, is not an easy matter. The two martyrs might be Gervasio and Protasio; the two archbishops, Simpliciano and Eustorgio; the figure with a book might be S. Arialdo. The archbishop with crosier opposite the bridegroom, and supported by an angel, is probably S. Ambrogio.

In style the sculptures show the survival of the mannerisms characteristic of the school of Milan, much refined and developed, however, and with clear traces of the strong influence of Guglielmo da Modena. They show an important anticipation of Benedetto's work at Borgo S. Donnino (Plate 30, Fig. 3) in the substitution of a continuous frieze of figure subjects for the bells of the capitals.

V. In the present pitiable condition of S. Simpliciano, it is impossible to speak with certainty of the date of the monument. However, it is evident that the fragments of ancient masonry in the campanile, the apse, the cupola, and the transepts all belong to about the middle of the XII century. Since the documents speak of the *labor* of S. Simpliciano between 1142 and 1152, and show that in this period this *labor* was the object of several donations, it is entirely probable that these portions of the edifice were constructed about that time. On the other hand, the central portal and the responds of the west façade are so typical of the style of c. 1170, that it is impossible to doubt Millin's notice that this portal was erected in 1171. The responds are evidently contemporary.

MILAN, S. STEFANO

(Plate 133, Fig. 1, 4)

I. Of the ancient church of S. Stefano, only one capital of the Lombard period survives. This has been described by De Dartein.[1] The historical notices and legends referring to the church have been collected by the antiquarians of Milan, among whom Puricelli, Puccinelli, Villa, Giulini and Romussi[2] deserve especial mention. The description of Torre, written in 1674, makes it clear that the Romanesque basilica was preceded by an atrium.[3]

---

[1] 215.　　[2] 230.

[3] L'Atrio suo, che addesso chiudesi trà diuisi cancelli di marmo nel Frontispizio altre volte veggeuasi trà alte mura con trè Porte. . . . Osservauasi ne' miei primi anni

II. In an epigram of Ennodio we read that the bishop Martiniano, who lived in the V century, erected two basilicas.[4] One of these basilicas was undoubtedly that of S. Stefano, also known in early times as S. Zaccaria. The bishop Martiniano was buried in the church of S. Stefano, as is known from a catalogue of the archbishops of Milan quoted by Oltrocchi.[5] In a calendar published by Muratori there are three entries which are of significance for our study. The first records that on January 2 the festival of S. Martiniano was celebrated in the church of S. Stefano *ad Rotam*. The second, that on the ninth of September was celebrated the anniversary of the dedication of the church of S. Stefano and S. Zaccaria, which is called *ad Rotam*. The third, that on the twenty-fifth of November was celebrated the festival of S. Stefano *ad Rotam*.[6] Giulini[7] also refers to an old martyrology in which it is stated that the church of S. Stefano was formerly called S. Zaccaria and was founded by S. Martiano (*sic*). It is, moreover, known that, until comparatively recent times, the festival of S. Zaccaria was celebrated in the church with peculiar solemnity. In view of all these notices, there can be no doubt that the church of S. Stefano was founded by S. Martiniano in the V century.

In the XII century the church of S. Stefano was given the epithet 'alla porta,' and in modern times it is frequently called 'S. Stefano in Broglio.' The most common name of the church, however, is 'ad rotam.' The explanation of this term has been much discussed. According to the legend, a fierce battle took place between the Catholics and the Arians of Milan, towards the end of the IV century. Many remained dead on the field, and the blood of the true believers mingled with that of the infidels. S. Ambrogio, shocked at such a sacrilege, prayed that the blood of the Catholics might be separated from that of the Arians. His prayer was answered by a miracle. The blood of the Christians instantly separated itself from that of the Arians, and formed itself into the shape of a wheel which rolled to the spot where now stands the church of S. Stefano, and then miraculously dissolved.[8] The legend is at least as old as the XI century, since a stone, apparently of that date, is still

dinanzi alla Porta vn' antico Portico fatto ad Archi veggendosi nelle vecchie pareti laterali anche di presente alcuni vestigij, innestata ritrouandosi marmorea pietra, quale poeticamente faceua noto etc. (Torre, 333).

4   Post geminas sanctis construxit mundior aedes,
      Lumine quas clauso iussit habere diem.
       (CIC Carm. 2, 81, ed. Vogel, M. G. H. *Auct. Antiq.,* VII, 164).

5 I, 79.

6 Januarius . . . B. IV. Non. S. Martiniani ad S. Stephanum ad Rotam. . . . September . . . V. Id. Dedicatio S. Stephani, & Zachariæ, qui dicitur ad Rotam. . . . December . . . VII. Kal. S. Stephani, qui dicitur ad Rotam. . . . (*Kalendarium Sitonianum,* ed. Muratori, R. I. S., II, pt. 2, 1035, 1039, 1041).

7 II, 185 ff.   8 Fumagalli, III, *Dissert.,* 28.

extant in the church and bears the relief of a wheel with the inscription:
Rota Sanguinis Fidelium.[9] Many laboured and far-fetched explanations have
been offered by various scholars to account for the curious legend and for
the name of the church. What I believe to be the true solution, however, is
so simple that it seems not to have occurred to any of the antiquarians who
have studied the question. Ennodio wrote an epigram still extant, entitled
'Concerning the Font of the Baptistery of S. Stefano and the Water which
flowed from the Columns.'[10] From this epigram it is evident that the basilica
was celebrated in the V century for dew which formed upon the columns, and
which was considered miraculous. I therefore conjecture that the church
was designated as 'ad Rorem,' which in the course of centuries became
corrupted to *ad Rotam* and gave rise to the legend narrated above.

In early times the basilica was doubtless officiated by decumani. It
must, therefore, have been one of the most important churches of Milan.
It is a singular fact, however, that the earliest mention of the edifice appears
to be in the will of Archbishop Ariberto, drawn in 1034.[11]

In the year 1075 the church was destroyed in the famous fire which
ravaged the city. This is recorded in an inscription formerly in the basilica,
but destroyed about the middle of the XVI century. Puricelli, knowing that
the inscription was on the point of being broken up, copied it with, as he
assures us, great care and exactness, in order that it might be preserved in
his work for future generations.[12] This inscription states: "The devouring
flames destroyed the former church of which the beauty was surpassed by
no church in the world. For a long time it was the ornament of this city.
Every work of human hands, sooner or later, suffers destruction. The church
was entirely destroyed, but, although ruined, it rises anew from its ashes;
the second church, however, is far from equalling the splendour of the first.
Let the people observe and fear. Sin was the cause of the ruin. Build thyself
first, O man, then shalt thou have power over matter. Be thou the temple
of the Lord; let that temple be pleasing to Him. The year of the Incarnation
of our Lord, 1075, the thirteenth indiction, March 30, Monday."[13] It will
be noticed that this inscription, although dated 1075, was not, in point of

---

[9] This stone is preserved under a bronze grill in the floor of the central nave, near
the western portal, and is not accessible. I have, therefore, been unable to inspect it,
and take the inscription from Fumagalli, III, 291.

[10] DE FONTE BAPTISTERII SANCTI STEFANI ET AQUA QUAE PER
COLUMNAS VENIT. In this epigram occur the lines:

> Sancta per aetherios emanat limpha recessus,
> Eustorgi vatis ducta ministero.

(Epigram CCCLXXIX, Carm. 2, 149, ed. Vogel, M. G. H. *Auct. Antiq.*, VII, 271).

[11] Puricelli, 366.

[12] The inscription was also copied by Torre, 333. See Villa, 115.

fact, erected until some years after that time. The fire took place in 1075, and it is doubtless to this that the date of the inscription refers. The new basilica is spoken of as being already rebuilt, and as being inferior to the one destroyed. Some years, therefore, must have elapsed after the fire before the new church could be completed.

An account of the fire is also given in the history of Arnolfo: "In the year of our Lord 1075, the XIII indiction, four years after the above-mentioned fire [of 1071] on the Monday of Holy Week [i.e., March 30] the unfortunate city again felt the divine wrath, and learned how terrible it is to fall into the hands of the living God. . . . What stronger expression can I use than to say that this second fire was in everything like the first? Nevertheless it was even more cruel, since it burned a greater number of churches and more important ones, amongst others, the admirable summer cathedral of S. Tecla, and the basilicas of S. Nazaro, S. Stefano and many others of which the ruins, I think, will be seen for many years to come. The winter cathedral of S. Maria was also destroyed."[14]

Galvaneo della Fiamma has embellished his account of the fire with a strange bit of unnatural history: "During the siege of the camp of Castiglione, there was a nest of storks on the top of a tower belonging to the della Porta faction and forming part of the Vercelli gate of the city of Milan. A serpent either climbed up to this nest or was carried thither, and killed the young of the storks. When the mother came and saw what had been done, she went and seized with her beak a lighted brand or stick of wood, and threw it upon her nest, and fanning it with her wings, she kindled a great fire. Thus the

[13]   Flamma vorax prisci consumpsit culmina Templi,
         Quod specie formæ nulli cædebat in Orbe;
         Temporibus multis fuerat decus istius Vrbis.
         Omne manufactum recipit post tempora casum.
         Corruit omninò. Collapsum surgit ab imo;
         Sed primi cultum nequit æquiperare secundum.
         Plebs spectando time. Peccatum causa ruinæ.
         Te priùs ædifices: tunc materiale reformes.
         Sis Templum Domini; placet illi fabrica Templi.

Anno Dominicæ Incarnationis Millesimo septuagesimoquinto, Indictione decima-tertia, tertio Kalendas Aprilis, Feria secunda. (Puricelli, 462-463).

[14] Anno humanitatis Dominicæ millesimo septuagesimo quinto, Indictione tertia decima, transactis quatuor à memorato superiùs incendio annis, propinquante sanctissimo Paschæ festo, secundâ videlicet Hebdomadis authenticæ feriâ, miseranda iterum civitas divinam persensit iracundiam, experta quàm sit horrendum incidere in manus Dei viventis. . . . Quid enim dici valet ulteriùs, quàm quòd ignis hic instar fuit per omnia suprataxati alterius? hoc tamen crudelior, quòd multò plures ac majores combussit Ecclesias; illam scilicet æstivam ac mirabilem Sanctæ Virginis Teclæ, Beati quoque Nazarii, necnon Protomartyris Stephani, cæterasque plures, quarum parietinæ annis apparebunt, ut reor, plus mille. Inter quas aliarum mater Sanctæ Dei Genetricis Hyemalis Basilica etc. (Arnulphi, *Hist. Med.,* IV, 8, ed. Muratori, R. I. S., IV, 38).

snake was burned. The fire, however, spread from the tower, and burned three quarters of the city, that is to say, the regions adjacent to the Vercelli, Pavia and Rome gates. At this time the church of S. Lorenzo, which was adorned with mosaics and had an inlaid pavement, was burned. . . . The fire spread towards the Roman gate, and burned the churches of S. Nazaro and S. Stefano ad Rotam, and all the houses between them were destroyed. This fire is called that 'of Castiglione,' because it took place at the time of that siege, or 'of the stork,' because of the stork which kindled it."[15] Finally, the fire of 1075 is recorded in a late chronicle in the vernacular: "In the year 1075 there was another great fire which greatly damaged the city."[16]

It is probable that the rebuilding of S. Stefano was begun immediately after the destruction of the church in 1075. The inscriptions cited above state that the new edifice was inferior to the old one. We may, therefore, conjecture that it was somewhat hastily constructed in the period of poverty and economic exhaustion following the great fire. We know that the church of S. Lorenzo, which was destroyed by the same fire, was rebuilt so quickly and so poorly that twenty-nine years later (or in 1104) it fell into ruin.[17] On the other hand, the finishing touches and final embellishments to S. Stefano must have been delayed for some time. In 1112 Gisla left a bequest to the *labor* until the restoration of the church should be completed.[18] It is probable,

---

[15] Instante supradicta obsidione castri de Castiliono, erat in civitate Mediolani in porta vercellina una turris illorum de la Porta, in cuius summitate erat unus nidus cyconiarum, ad quem cum quidam serpens ascendisset vel delatus fuisset, pullos ciconiarum interfecit. Veniens ciconia et videns quod factum fuerat, abiit et lignum ignitum sive tizonum ore subripiens in nidum suum proiecit, et excutiens alas magnum ignem succendit, et sic serpentem combussit. Ignis autem de turri descendit et succendit civitatis portas tres, scilicet vercellinam, ticinensem et romanam, et tunc ecclesia sancti Laurentii fuit combusta, que erat tota opere musayco ornata, etiam pavimentum fuit tabulatum. Tunc etiam columne XIV, que laminis ereis cum celaturis avium, piscium bestiarum cohoperte erant, ignis calore sunt resolute. Ignis se vergens versus portam romanam, combussit ecclesiam sancti Nazarii et ecclexiam Sancti Stephani ad rotam, et omnes domos interiacentes ignis consumpsit, qui dictus est ignis de Castiliono propter instantem obsidionem castri illius, vel dicitur ignis de ciconia, propter ciconiam que attulit ignem. (Galvanei Flammae, *Chron. Maius*, ed. Ceruti, 625). See also Galvaneo della Fiamma, *Chronica*, Vienna MS. 3318, ca. 245, f. 91.

[16] E l'anno MLXXV fu uno altro grandissimo focho che diede molto grande dampne alla città. (*Chron. di Milano*, ed. Lambertenghi, 15).

Torre adds the following details of the fire of 1075, which he says were taken from a manuscript of Paolo Girolamo Martignoni: Venne però subito redificato, hauutone quasi il comando dal Cielo; per vna pietra ritrouata accaso dopo l'Incendio, le cui incise lettere accennauano il suo rifacimento, ed hannosi memorie fedeli, che vi si adoprassero à tal nuova erezione gli Santi Leone Eremita, e Marino Martire, gli quali affaccendati s'osseruarono in radunare elemosine. (Torre, 334).

Beroldo refers the fire of Castiglione to the year 1121: V. Kal. Mar. Anni Domini M.L.XX.I combustum est Mediolanum ab igne de Castelliono. (Beroldo, ed. Magistretti, 3).

[17] Giulini, II, 737.   [18] See text cited above, under S. Nazaro, p. 636.

therefore, that enough of the church to make it possible to celebrate the offices was completed as quickly as possible after 1075, but that the edifice was entirely finished only some forty years later.

Probably about this time, canons regular were established in the church, since a prevosto is mentioned by Landolfo the Younger.[19] In a sentence of 1119, S. Stefano is mentioned among the eleven mother-churches of Milan officiated by decumani.[20] Two documents of 1125 and 1128 mention a certain Adilla as a recluse of S. Stefano, and her sister Richa, a nun. Both of these females, apparently, resided in the church.[21] In 1398, according to a tax-list published by Magistretti, the church was officiated by six canons, and possessed four subsidiary chapels. In 1568 there were more canons.[22] The chapter was increased by S. Carlo Borromeo in 1577. In 1567 the old basilica was demolished, and a new church was erected in the style of the Renaissance.[23] Some remains of the ancient atrium, however, remained in existence for nearly a century later. In 1642 the ancient campanile collapsed,[24] and a new one was subsequently erected. In 1798 the chapter was suppressed.[25]

III. Of the Lombard edifice there survives only a single respond (Plate 133, Fig. 1), which is at present imbedded in the wall of a house to the south-east of the existing church, and facing upon the piazza. This respond consists of a flat pilaster with two engaged rectangular members to the eastward. It must have belonged to the ancient atrium, the aisles of which, to judge from the section of the respond, were groin-vaulted.

IV. The capital (Plate 133, Fig. 4) is ornamented with an interlaced pattern among the curves of which are two birds.

V. The respond and its capital undoubtedly belonged to the church of S. Stefano reconstructed after the fire of 1075. Since placed in the atrium,

---

[19] Rolucus quoque Praepositus Ecclesiæ sancti Stephani. (Landulphi Junioris, *Hist. Med.*, XX, ed. Muratori, R. I. S., V, 491).

[20] Giulini, VII, 85.

[21] Adille recluse de Sancto Stephano qui dicitur in brolio. et Riche monache que ibi habitat iusta ipsam ecclesiam. . . . (Iudicatum of July, 1125, apud *Codice della Croce*, MS. Amb., D. S. IV, Vol. V, f. 190).

Adilla reclusa de reclussa sancti Stephani qui dicitur ad rotam et Richa monacha socia ipsius Adilliæ etc. (Donation of Sept., 1128, *Codice della Croce*, MS. Amb., D. S. IV, Vol. V, f. 216).

[22] Stephani in Brolio collegiata cú ppto et Cancis IIX [8?]. Prædicta ecclia Sti Stephani, vnita fuit collegiata Sti Ioannis Pontiroli no et Est ecclia ex septem ecclijs. (*Status Ecclesiae Mediolani 1568 conscriptus* auctore Francisco Castello, MS. Amb., A, 112, Inferiore, f. 441-442).

Ibid., 538, are given the names of the prevosto and six canons with the taxes they paid.

[23] Inscription in north side aisle.

[24] Torre, 333.   [25] Forcella, *Chiese*, 649.

however, it may be supposed that they were not one of those portions of the church first built, but that they were, on the contrary, part of the embellishments or secondary constructions which were in progress in the year 1112.

MILAN, S. VINCENZO

(Plate 134; Plate 135, Fig. 1, 2, 3, 4; Plate 136, Fig. 1, 2, 3, 4, 5;
Plate 137, Fig. 1, 2, 3, 4, 5, 6, 7)

I. The church of S. Vincenzo in Prato of Milan has been much discussed by historians and archæologists. In 1625 Castiglione published an important history of the monastery, of which he was abbot. The work deals at length with the many historical problems that the subject presented, and is of great value to the modern archæologist for the elaborate plan and accurate description of the buildings as they existed in the early XVII century. Castiglione studied with great care the details of the problematical Roman temple which he believed to have existed on the site of S. Vincenzo. The historical work of Castiglione was supplemented and completed by the classic publication of Puricelli, printed in 1645. In 1674 Torre published a description of the edifice, of especial importance because it mentions the frescos of the choir, which were undoubtedly the enigmatical restoration executed in 1386.[1] The description written by Latuada in 1737 also speaks of these frescos in the choir, and of the inscription of 1386, which at that time existed *innestata ad una parete della medesima Chiesa*.[2] In the same century, Giulini further elucidated the questions connected with the history of the abbey. In the second half of the XIX century, the agitation for the restoration of the church occasioned the publication of a number of articles of little scientific value, printed, for the most part, in the newspapers of Milan. Of more importance are a group of monographs published about this same time. That of Belgioioso, published in 1868, was the first of these. It is of value for a description of the church as it was before the restoration. In 1872 the Mellas published drawings and another description of the edifice.[3] In 1875 Romussi gave a

[1] Venerabili veramēte sono le pitture à fresco, ma vecchie, che adornano il detto coro, consistendo in più schiere d'Angeli ben coloriti, gli quali tutti stanno adorando il Padre Eterno in varij atteggiamenti, questi cantando, e quegli temporando musicali strumenti. . . . Andiamcene ormai nel sotteraneo Sacrario, à cui vassene per queste due scale laterali alla salita del Maggior' Altare. (Torre, 110).

[2] . . . coro adorno di antiche pitture, che rappresentano l'Eterno Padre adorato da molti Angioli, e Cherubini. Sotto del maggiore Altare giace la Confessione, . . . al quale si discende per due Scale laterali a quella che sopra lo stesso Altare conduce, etc. (Latuada, III, 270).

[3] Una di esse [colonne], la prima a sinistra di chi entra è stata considerevolmente ingrossata con rivestimento di mattoni. . . . L'impalcatura che chiude la parte alta

résumé of the history of the edifice, illustrated in the later edition of this work[4] by a number of excellent half-tones. In 1880 appeared the monograph of Rotta, of little value except for the plan made before restoration. Ten years later, the same author published a chronicle of the restoration of the church, in which is related in detail step by step, and with smug self-complacency, the progress of the stupid and sickening work of destruction. The book is, however, of great value for the data which it contains in regard to the many important portions of the old edifice destroyed and the entirely unwarranted additions made by the restorers. The monograph of Tedeschi, which appeared in 1882, seems to have been written chiefly with a view to urging the destruction of the crypt, a plan which happily was never put into execution. In 1888 appeared the work of Cattaneo, which refers several times to the church of S. Vincenzo,[5] but for once the erudition and intuitive genius of the great archæologist seem to have failed him, for he published a restored capital as an example of the decorative art of the IX century, and was also deceived by the arched corbel-tables added by the restorers. The brief monograph of Caffi, printed in 1889, contains nothing new.

II. The origins of the church and of the monastery of S. Vincenzo are exceedingly obscure. In Landolfo the Elder we read: "After this Desiderio, king of the Lombards, by the mercy of God converted to the Christian religion, built the church and monastery of S. Vincenzo at Milan, for the benefit of his soul, and endowed the same with lands and castles."[6] Landolfo lived three centuries later than the events which he is here recording, and these early chapters of his history are full of many even grotesque errors. Two late manuscript chronicles in the Biblioteca Ambrosiana repeat that S. Vincenzo was founded by Desiderio, and add the year 780.[7] The date 780 is clearly erroneous, since Desiderio ceased to rule in 774.

In Galvaneo della Fiamma is found the same tradition of the foundation by Desiderio, with a more possible date, but complicated by new details: "In the year of Christ 770, Desiderio established the monastery of S. Vincenzo in the city of Milan, near the Porta Ticinese, in the spot where is now the church of S. Sisto. This he endowed so liberally that the monastery of S.

dell'edifizio nasconde tracce della originaria travatura. . . . Il presbitero è considerevolmente rialzato dal piano della chiesa e vi si ascende pei due gradinate che non sembrano originarie.

[4] 260.   [5] 219, 213, etc.

[6] Unde postea Desiderius Rex Longobardorum Dei misericordiâ factus Christianus, inibi S. Vincentii Ecclesiam, & Monachorum Cœnobium pro animæ suæ remedio multis ornando prædiis, & castellis ædificavit. (Landulphi Senioris, *Med. Hist.*, II, 2, ed. Muratori, R. I. S., IV, 70).

[7] The first of these will be cited below under S. Pietro di Civate, Vol. III. The second is: Anno dni dcclxxx Dessiderius Rex. Fecit fieri Monasterium sancti vincentij et sancti Petri de Cliuate. (*Chronicon*, MS. Amb., C. S. IV, 18, f. 667).

Dionigi was founded [by the archbishop Ariberto in the XI century] with goods taken from the endowment of S. Vincenzo."[8] Further on the same author writes: "The monastery of S. Vincenzo was formerly in the church of S. Sisto near the Porta Ticinese, but was subsequently transferred to the spot where it now is."[9] Castiglione cites from Galvaneo still another passage relating to S. Vincenzo: "This church was founded by Desiderio, king of the Lombards, in the year 780 for the everlasting glory of S. Vincenzo, and he endowed it with the sacred relics and venerable remains of that saint."[10]

The tradition that the monastery was founded by Desiderio can be with difficulty reconciled with a diploma of the year 806, in which we read: "Odelberto, by the grace of God . . . . . archbishop of the church of Milan, to Arigauso, abbot of our monastery of S. Ambrogio. . . . Our churches desire to serve with constant devotion Omnipotent God, from whom we have received every benefit which we possess, wherefore . . . . . you, the above-mentioned abbot Arigauso, have sought from us that we grant to you for the days of your life . . . . . the oratory built in our *curtis* of Prata, and dedicated to S. Vincenzo, Levite and martyr of Our Lord Jesus Christ. . . . Therefore we do grant to you Arigauso, abbot, the above-mentioned oratory . . . together with all the possessions which belong to our *curtis* of Prata and to the above-mentioned oratory of S. Vincenzo . . . . . that your fidelity may cause the above-mentioned holy place to be officiated with greater devotion and the feast of the saint to be observed with greater solemnity during the days of your life . . . . . And after your death the above-mentioned *curtis* shall return to the bosom of the holy church of Milan in its entirety, just as we have granted the same to you. . . . The year of our Lord 806."[11]

[8] Et anno Christi DCCLXX in civitate Mediolani ad carubium porte tycinensis, ubi nunc est ecclexia sancti Sixti, monasterium sancti Vicentii construxit, quod amplissimis possessionibus dotavit, in tantum quod ex his monasterium sancti Dionisii fundatum fuit. (Galvanei Flammae, *Chron. Maius,* ed. Ceruti, 547).

[9] Monasterium sancti Vincentii primo fuit in ecclexia sancti Xisti iusta carubium porte tycinensis, et postea fuit translatum ad locum ubi nunc est. (*Ibid.,* 591).

[10] Templum hoc à desiderio Longobardorum rege anno à Salute humano generi restituta, DCCLXXX conditū ad perennē D. Vincentij gloriā, sacrisq; eiusdē Reliquiis, ac cineribus uenerandis addictū.

[11] Odelpertus per Dei gratiam . . . . . Mediolanensis Ecclesiæ Archiepiscopus, Arigauso Abbati Monasterij nostri Sancti Ambrosij. . . . Ecclesiæ nostræ, qui Deo omnipotenti, à quo omnia bona suscipimus quæ habemus, sedola (nempè sedula) deuotione deseruire concupiscunt. Qua de re manifestè . . . . . & quod tu, qui supra, Arigausus Abbas petisti à nobis, vt tibi Oratorium Sancti Vincenti, Leuitæ & Martyris Domini nostri Iesu Christi, ædificatum in Curte nostra Prata . . . . . nomine, diebus vitæ tuæ tibi concedere deueremus (*hoc est* deberemus). . . . Ideoque concedimus tibi Arigauso abbæ ipsum Oratorium . . . . . Curte nostra Prata, siue cum . . . . . Massarijs, aldiones, vel quidquid præsenti die ad prædictam curtem nostram Pratam, vt diximus, & ad ipsum Oratorium Sancti Vincenti pertinere prouantur (nempè probantur) . . . . . aliter tua fidelitas ad prænominatum sanctum locum meliorem ad

665

It is not absolutely certain that the oratory of S. Vincenzo, in the *curtis* of Prata, referred to in this diploma, is to be identified with our S. Vincenzo in Prato, though most of the historians of Milan have so believed. The use of the word *oratorium* which is generally interpreted to mean a chapel of small size is peculiar.[12] Certain it is that the oratory of S. Vincenzo, conceded to Arigauso in 806, could not have been a monastery, since in the diploma no mention is made of monks who officiated there. If therefore this diploma really referred to our S. Vincenzo, as it is altogether probable that it does, it must be that in 806 the monastery was not yet established.

The monastery of S. Vincenzo is mentioned in a diploma purporting to be of 832: "In the name of God, Angilberto, humble archbishop of the holy church of Milan . . . For this reason I long considered . . . whom I ought to appoint as Abbot of S. Ambrogio, praying with my priests for the aid of God. Finally, by the mercy of God and with the advice of our priests, I took Gaudenzio, abbot of the monastery of S. Vincenzo, whom I had ordained as abbot there long before, and I made him abbot in the above-mentioned monastery of S. Ambrogio."[13] The chronological notes of this diploma are erroneous, and many other indications that it is spurious are not lacking. However, the document must have been forged at least as early as the XI or XII century and therefore possesses a certain historical value since it shows that at this time the monastery of S. Vincenzo was believed to have been in existence as early as the IX century. The abbey appears to have been mentioned also in another diploma of the following year, 833, but this has been lost, and it is impossible to judge of its authenticity from the meagre notices that have come down to us.[14]

At all events, the monastery was certainly in existence in the year 870,

deseruiendum deuotionem integram diebus vitæ tuæ magis magisque adimplere festum . . . . . Ea igitur vt statim prædictam Curtem post tuum, qui supra, Arigausi Abbatis obitum, ad iura & gremitū Sanctæ nostræ Mediolanensis Ecclesiæ cum omni integritate sua, vt ipsam tibi concessimus, reuertatur. . . . Anno Domnorum nostrorum Caroli & Pepini Regum hic in Italia Trigesimosecundo & Vigesimoquinto, mense Ianuario, Indictione quartadecima. . . . (Puricelli, 53). The twelfth, not the fourteenth, indiction corresponds with the year 806.

[12] Rotta, *Pas.*, 87, has cited authorities to show that the word *oratorium* may mean a monastic church.

[13] In Nomine Domini, Angelbertus, Beatæ Mediolanensis Ecclesiæ humilis Archiepiscopus. . . . Cùmquè pro hoc diutiùs, quem Abbatem illius constituere debuissem . . . pro hoc diutiùs cœpissem cogitare, cum meis Sacerdotibus diuinam Clementiam postulando; tunc, Domino fauente, consulentibus etiam Sacerdotibus nostris, abstuli Gaudentium Abbatem Monasterij Sancti Vincentij (quem etiam ego ibi Abbatem iamdudùm ordinaueram) & in præfato Monasterio Sancti Ambrosij Abbatem constitui. . . . Anno Domnorum nostrorum, confirmantium hoc, Ludouici & Hlotharij Imperatorum Decimooctauo & Decimo, Sexto Kalendas Martij, Indictione Decimatertia. (Puricelli, 80).

[14] See Giulini, I, 140.

since it is mentioned in the will of Garibaldo, bishop of Bergamo.[15] We may conclude in the light of this text and of the other of 806 cited above that the monastery was founded between the years 806 and 870. Now it is natural to place in connection with the foundation of the monastery the translation of the relics of the saints Quirino and Nicomede into the church of S. Vincenzo, performed, it is almost certain, by the archbishop Angilberto II (824-859).

Lampugnano de Legnano and Galvaneo della Fiamma, it is true, state that these relics were acquired, not by Angilberto, but by Ariberto (1018-1045), who "founded the monastery of S. Dionigi with the blood of S. Vincenzo."[16] This notice is, however, erroneous, since the charter of foundation of S. Dionigi proves, as has been shown by Giulini,[17] that Ariberto founded the latter with his own goods and not with those of S. Vincenzo, and ecclesiastical authorities are almost agreed that the relics of S. Quirino and S. Nicomede were translated to Milan by Angilberto.[18] We may therefore follow Giulini[19] with confidence in assigning the translation of the relics to Angilberto II.

If the plausible conjecture that the relics were translated at the time the monastery was founded, be accepted, we may consequently conclude that the latter event took place between 824 and 859; if the diploma of 833 be

15 In nomine Domini et Salvatoris nostri Jesu Christi. Hludovvicus, Divina hordinante providentia, Imperii eius Deo propitio vigisimo, Marcias, Indictione tertia.—Ego in Dei nomine Garibaldus, licit indignus, Sancte Bergomate Ecclesie Episcopus, et filius b. m. Ursoni, qui vixit legibus Longobardorum p.p. dixi. . . . Et statuo ego Garibaldus Episcopus, ut illa casa massaricia cum rebus omnibus ad eam pertinentibus, que est in fundo Maciaco, et eadem Gariberga, usufructuario nomine, habere dixi, ut post decessum eidem Autelmi, et predicte Gariberge, adque iam dicto Gundelasii Cl. statim deveniat in jura, et potestatem Monasterii Beati Levite, et Martiris Vincentii, quod situm est non lunge ab urbe Mediolanensium, ita ut perpetuis temporibus, in potestatem ejusdem Monasterii persistat, pro remedio anime mee, et jam dicto Autelmi, ut sit in sumto Fratrum Monachorum ibidem Deo famulantium, ut nobis, et parentibus nostris et mercedem, et remedium animabus nostris perveniat. (Giulini, VII, 17).

16 . . . hic [Heribertus] ab̄m sc̄i Vicentij flobotomauit [= plebotomavit] de cuius sanguine nomen sc̄i Dionisij construnxit. . . . hic a p̄pa obtinuit subiectione qui dicebant se exemptos in cuius signū p̄p sibi dedit corpora Sctor[um] quirini nicoēdis et habundij que sunt in p[re]dicto Monasterio. (Lampugnano de Legnano, Chronica, MS. Amb., H 56 Sup., f. 65 r).

Item Monasterii S. Vincentii subjectionem, quod se exceptum dicebat, à Papa obtinuit [Heriberto], in cujus rei testimonium Papa Corpora SS. MM. Quirini, Nicomedis, & Abundii eidem Archiepiscopo Mediolanensi donavit, item prædictum Monasterium S. Vincentii flobotomavit, de cujus sanguine Sancti Dionysii Monasterium construxit. . . . (Galvanei Flammae, Manipulus Florum, ed. Muratori, R. I. S., XI, 614).

17 II, 130.

18 For a discussion of this long and complicated question with full references and citations from the original sources, see Castiglione, 92-94.

19 I, 227.

accepted as authentic, the date of the foundation of the monastery may be still more closely limited between 824 and 833. In the north wall of the church are fragments of an inscription found during the recent restoration of the edifice. The interpretation of these might be difficult were it not for the happy circumstance that Castiglione, who saw the stone before it was broken, has preserved for us an exact copy. With the help of this transcription we read: "Here lies Master Giselberto, the eminent abbot, who founded this monastery and endowed it with many possessions."[20] Although the inscription is unfortunately without date, the character of the letters shows that it must have been carved in the first half of the IX century. It therefore confirms the other evidence that the monastery was founded between the years 824 and 833.

Castiglione[21] has preserved another epitaph of the year 902, which formerly existed in the church.

Galvaneo della Fiamma makes several rather curious statements in regard to events purporting to have occurred in the early XI century: "The archbishop Ariberto of Intimiano (1018-1045) bled the monastery of S. Vincenzo, and founded the monastery of S. Dionigi with its superfluous possessions in the year of Christ 1023, and he strengthened the church of Milan which had long been torn by dissension. By the authority of the Holy See, he reduced to submission two abbots, those of S. Ambrogio and of S. Vincenzo, who had claimed to be exempt from his jurisdiction. In token of this event the pope gave to the archbishop the bodies of the holy martyrs, Quirino, Nicomede, and Abondio, which he buried in the monastery of S. Vincenzo."[22] We have already seen that Ariberto did not translate the relics of Quirino and Nicomede and that he did not bleed the monastery of S. Vincenzo to found that of S. Dionigi. It is entirely probable that the story of the revolts of the two abbots is equally apocryphal. Giulini accepts as authentic only the translation of the relics of Abondio by Ariberto. The statement of Galvaneo in this particular is

[20]   ✠ [HIC CVBAT DOMINVS
            GISELBERTVS] MA[GNIFICVS
            AB]BA[S QⓋI HŌC] C͡OEN[OBIVM]
            PLVRIM[IS BO]NIS [CON]
            ST͡RVX[IT ET] DECOR[AVIT]

                                    (Castiglione, 92).

[21] 21.

[22] Hic archiepiscopus flobotomavit monasterium sancti Vincentii, de cuius superfluis possessionibus fundavit monasterium sancti Dionisii Christi anno MXXIII, et ecclexiam mediolanensem iamdudem laceratam restauravit. Duos abbates, scilicet sancti Ambrosii et sancti Vincentii, qui dicebant se esse exemptos, sibi subiecit auctoritate summi pontificis, in cuius signum papa donavit archiepiscopo corpora santorum martirum Quirini, Nicomedis et Habundii, que in monasterio s. Vincentii tumulavit. (Gal. Flam., *Chron. Maius,* ed. Ceruti, 603).

confirmed by the fact that it is known that the archbishop, before ascending the episcopal throne, buried relics of several saints in the church of S. Vincenzo at Galliano.[23] That Galvaneo is wrong in implying that there was hostility between Ariberto and the monastery of S. Vincenzo, is indicated by the fact that the archbishop left a bequest to the abbey of S. Vincenzo in his will, dated 1034.[24]

The church was restored in 1386, as is known from an inscription formerly over the portal and preserved by Castiglione: "The venerable father, noble, steadfast of soul and pious, brother Beno de' Petroni, of Bernareggio, born of an illustrious family, pure in his morals and life, excelling in the divine office, and formerly abbot of this monastery of S. Vincenzo, which he ruled amid many trials and tribulations for eighteen years and ten months with such diligence, that he left the possessions of the said monastery in good condition and well-ordered—this abbot began the restoration of the church of S. Vincenzo, which, during his incumbency, was falling into ruin because of its age; and he caused the same to be decorated far better than it had been before. Nevertheless, since he was prevented by death from finishing this restoration, in his last days he put the finances of the church in such good order (by gathering together, and laying aside, with immense pains, money for the restoration of the church), that within two months after his death the restoration was finished. He lived in tribulation and he died at a time in which he could have lived quietly and in honour. But then God called him to Himself, and this was peradventure to the benefit of his soul. By the intervention of divine mercy may he rest in peace. Amen. He died in the year 1386, on the fifteenth day of August."[25]

The monastery is mentioned in 1398 in a tax-list published by Magistretti. In the time of the Renaissance it fell into decline, and was given in commendam. According to Rotta[26] the parish was established in the church in

[23] See above, p. 442.   [24] Puricelli, 366.

[25] Venerabilis Pater egregius Constantis animi, & deuotus. Dominus Frater Benus de Petronis de Bernaregio generis nobilitate praeclarus. moribus & vita decoratus. in diuino officio excellentissimus. olim Abbas istius monasterij Sancti Vincentij. cuius gubernationem cum multis tribulationibus & angustia regulauit annis decem octo. mensibus decem. cum magna diligentia. Sic quod bona dicti monasterij reliquit in bouo [sic] statu diligenter conseruata. Hanc ecclesiam S. Vincentij quae tempore suae Abbatiæ vetustate ruerat reparari facere inchoauit. eandem multo plus quam primitus erat decorando. Verum quia eam morte prȩuentus adimplere nequiuit. in vltimis constitutus talem ordinem apposuit. quod de denarijs pro dicta Ecclesia reparanda cum immensis vigilijs per eum addunatis, & conseruatis. Infra duos mēses post eius mortem extitit reparata. Vixit enim in tribulatione decessit in tempore. quo poterat quiete viuere cum honore. Set tunc Deus vocauit eum ad se & forte profuit euis animæ. quæ diuina misericordia interueniente requiescat in pace Amen.

Diem suum enim clausit extremum milleximo trecenteximo octuageximo sexto die quinta decima mensis augusti. (Castiglione, 40).

[26] 8.

the year 1600, but it is mentioned as already existing in a manuscript of 1568 of the Biblioteca Ambrosiana.[27]

From the long description of the monastery written by Castiglione in 1625, and from the plan of the church and surrounding buildings which he published, it is possible to form an accurate and detailed picture of the abbey as it was in the early XVII century. At that time, the city had not yet grown to encroach upon the pleasant fields in which the church was situated. The abbey lay in the midst of smiling meadows, gentle orchards, fruitful vineyards and gardens, irrigated by a network of canals. "Who," asks Castiglione, "can gaze on such beauty without being attracted by it? What beholder does it not entice to love it, and who does not linger to gaze at it even against his will?" To the south-west of the church extended a large area labelled, in Castiglione's plan, a garden (*Viridarium*), at one angle of which was placed the well. To the north-west extended the ample cemetery. To the north-east was the vineyard. Between the vineyard and the garden to the south-east of the basilica was grouped the complex mass of monastic buildings, the kitchen, the large hennery, the reception hall, the store-room, a court, and two rooms designated by the title S. Maria, which were probably chapels. A broad stairway led to the upper story, where were doubtless situated the refectory and dormitory. On Castiglione's plan there is no indication of the campanile, unless the square structure with stairway opposite the western end of the southern side aisle, and labelled stable (*Equile*) be such. In his description he states that the campanile with two bells, one of 1515 and the other of 1623, rose aloft above the roof of the church.[28] It is difficult to see how a campanile could have been erected over any part of the basilica without more substantial supports than appear in Castiglione's plan. On the other hand, it is strange that its lower story should have served for the ignoble purpose of a stable. To the east of the church, between the central apse and the northern absidiole, about a third of the walls of which were masked, was placed a long narrow room serving as sacristy. This had been erected by Baldassare Corio, in 1449, and was lighted by two windows, one to the right and one to the left.

Castiglione writes enthusiastically of the interior of the basilica, which, he says, was large and spacious, and of so charming an aspect as to cause any pious soul to desire to linger. It was characterized by that majesty peculiar to sacred edifices, and which cannot be expressed in words. The three aisles were separated by two rows of nine [*sic*] columns. Any one who sees and carefully examines the epistyles of these columns, he says, will swear without further compulsion that he is at Corinth. He dwells long upon the symbolism

[27] Vincentij in Prato foris, Abbatia et curata. (*Status ecclesiae Mediolani*, 1568 conscriptus auctore Francesco Castello. MS. Amb., A, 112, Inf., f. 447).

[28] Eminet è summo Templi culmine Sacra Turris extructa de More, in qua Campanae duae etc. (43).

of the various portions of the church. He notes that there are nine arches in
the nave arcade on either side, that there are nine windows in the clearstory,
and nine in the side-aisle walls, and that a flight of nine steps led from the
nave to the choir. There were moreover nine doors (he counts probably
two in the west façade, one leading from the chapel of the Virgin to the
monastic buildings, two leading from the choir to the chapels on either side,
one opening into the sacristy, two leading from the nave into the crypt, and
one from the crypt to the chapel of the Virgin) and five chapels (the choir,
the chapels of S. Carlo and the Virgin, the baptistery and the crypt), and
four altars, which, added together, make nine. There are also, he states,
nine 'choirs of angels,' evidently referring to the frescos of the presbytery.
The rounded form of the clearstory windows, and the splaying of the latter,
were not without a mystery, in the eyes of the pious ecclesiastic, who was
well versed in texts of the early church-fathers. The nave was covered with
an open timber roof, with cross- and tie-beams similar to those in use in the
basilicas in Rome. The two side aisles were covered with a timber ceiling
even more imposing than the roof of the nave, although narrower and lower.

In the time of Castiglione, the side aisles of the choir and the absidioles
had been walled off to form chapels, that to the north dedicated to S. Carlo
and that to the south to the Virgin. At the eastern ends of the side aisles
of the nave had been erected semicircular absidioles. I presume that this
change in the original structure had been wrought in 1386. These chapels
must have had their pavement at the same level as that of the nave, since a
flight of steps led from the choir down to the chapel of the Virgin. On the
plan of Castiglione there is no indication of an entrance to the chapel of
S. Carlo. This, however, was probably placed at the eastern end of the
northern side aisle. There were rails before both of the absidioles at the end
of the nave side aisle, and the choir was crossed by two rails, one at the
entrance, the other at the high altar. A flight of steps led from the nave
to the choir, while, on either side of this flight, two others led to the crypt.
In the crypt, beneath the stairway leading to the choir, had been recently
erected a small but venerable shrine of the Holy Sepulchre.

Castiglione gives a long description of the chapel which had been erected
shortly before, near the west end of the northern side aisle, to serve as
baptistery, by Carlo Caraffa, bishop of Aversa. The half dome of the apse
was decorated either with frescos or a mosaic, depicting golden stars inlaid
upon a blue background. The pavement of the choir was in mosaic but was
much mutilated, and had never been completely finished.

Beneath the choir was the crypt, the vault of which was supported by
ten marble columns. This crypt, says Castiglione, was so large that it
resembled a church rather than a chapel. In the central aisle was the altar
in which the bodies of the saints Quirino, Nicomede and Abondio were believed

to be preserved. The façade of the church had only two portals, one opening into the central nave, and one into the northern side aisle.[29]

About 1729 the church was restored and whitewashed.[30]

In 1751 a new campanile was erected. In 1787 the parish was suppressed.[31] The church was desecrated, and in 1798 was turned into a barracks. The roof praised by Castiglione was in part destroyed by fire about this time. In 1810 the edifice was sold at public auction, and eventually passed into the possession of a firm of chemists. To adapt the building to its new use, the nave was divided into two stories, the northern absidiole torn down, and the building damaged in other ways. In the second half of the XIX century an agitation was started to purchase the edifice, restore it and reopen it for worship. This project was carried out, and on the seventh of January, 1885, began the restoration, which continued for four years. When the intonaco and bricks which covered the lunettes above the portals of the west façade were removed, traces of faded Byzantine frescos came to light. As work progressed, many fragments of architecture and inscriptions were discovered. The restorers believed erroneously that the crypt originally extended beneath all three aisles. In consequence, there arose considerable controversy as to the proper manner of restoring this portion of the edifice. A formidable party wished to destroy the crypt altogether. De Rossi prayed in vain for its conservation, and were it not for the happy chance that Landriani succeeded Magni as architect in charge of the restoration, this priceless monument of Carlovingian architecture might well have perished. In the apse were found remains of frescos which the commission considered not worthy of preservation or restoration, and which were destroyed without even being described. The same lot befell the fresco of the dome. In restoring the pavement of the church, several pieces of mosaic came to light, as well as fragments of mica, which had undoubtedly served to glaze the windows. The restorers strengthened the walls with iron chains. When the ceiling was removed, the ancient open timber roof appeared, but it was demolished and a new roof erected in its place. The southern absidiole, which had been torn down in 1751 to make way for the Renaissance campanile, was reconstructed on the traces of the old foundations. Two columns of the nave, crushed by excessive weight, were replaced by new ones,[32] and eight new capitals, in which no attempt was made to reproduce the ancient form, were added. Corbels, which the restorers believed anciently supported an exterior narthex, were removed from the façade. The northern absidiole was next reconstructed, and the upper part

[29] Castiglione, 43-53, et passim.

[30] Verso l'anno 1729 fu ristabilita ed abbianchita tutta la Chiesa. (Latuada, III, 270).

[31] Forcella, Chiese.

[32] One of these columns, encased at a later epoch in bricks, was placed by the restorers in the north side aisle, where it is still preserved.

of the façade, which had been completely destroyed, was built in its present form according to the caprice of the architect, who added the arched corbel-tables and the windows in the shape of a Greek cross, both serious anachronisms. Equally misleading are the arched corbel-tables placed by the restorers on the eastern pediment and on the new absidiole, all of which were added without a shadow of authority.[33] The new campanile was erected in a style which recalls very dimly that of the XII century, and is, of course, entirely a work of the imagination of the restorers. A museum was established in the church during the restorations, and here were placed many fragments of architecture and inscriptions found in various parts of the edifice. In 1890 some of these objects were put in the exterior of the north wall where they may still be seen, although, being placed in a position peculiarly exposed to the weather, they are rapidly disintegrating; but others of great archæological importance have completely disappeared,[34] and I searched in vain to find them. A vast fresco three metres square was discovered in the northern wall. The restorers next proceeded to strengthen the half dome of the apse by covering the extrados with molten metal. The stairway giving access to the choir, the balustrade and the entrance to the crypt were designed by the restorers out of whole cloth, and no attempt was made to reproduce the ancient dispositions, of which Castiglione had left an accurate description. The ancient entrances to the crypt, of great archæological importance, were complacently destroyed to make way for this new construction, which is as valueless artistically as it is historically. At the same epoch, the walls of the crypt were reconstructed, and the baptistery was made over on an entirely new plan. Finally the interior walls were covered with intonaco and decorated with the existing tasteless frescos, which are entirely at variance with the style of the ancient basilica.

III. S. Vincenzo consists of a nave nine bays long, two side aisles, a crypt and three apses (Plate 134). It is entirely roofed in timber, with the exception of the half domes of the apses and the groin vaults, with disappearing ribs, of the crypt. These vaults, however, appear to have been made over. The choir and the crypt occupy the three eastern bays of the nave, and cut across the eastern columns of the main arcade. For this reason, it has been supposed that the crypt is a later addition, and formed no part of the original structure. None of its capitals, however, is later than those of the nave, and while I know of no other example in which a crypt was constructed in precisely this manner, I believe that it is contemporary with the original construction. S. Vincenzo stands on low ground, and the presence of water in the crypt caused considerable annoyance during the recent restoration. This circumstance, perhaps, forced the builders to raise the choir more than they would otherwise have done, so as to avoid depressing unduly the crypt. The important relics here preserved doubtless necessitated that this crypt should

[33] Rotta, 40-41.   [34] *Ibid.*, 42.

be extended beyond the limits of the apse to which confessios of the IX century were generally confined.

In the main arcades of the nave, the archivolts of a single unmoulded order heavily overhang the capitals (Plate 136, Fig. 1).

The windows, especially those of the clearstory, are large (Plate 136, Fig. 1; Plate 135, Fig. 1, 2, 3, 4), and were originally glazed with mica, as has been mentioned. The walls are constructed with brick, with occasional blocks of granite (Plate 135, Fig. 1, 3). These bricks (Plate 137, Fig. 7), except where they have been restored, are without cross-hatching. They are of small and irregular shape, and laid in thick mortar-beds. The courses are, in the main, regular and horizontal, but broken at times by vertical and oblique courses.

IV. The capitals of the nave (Plate 136, Fig. 3, 4, 5) with two exceptions, were pilfered from earlier buildings, but the granite shafts, where they have not been restored, seem to have been made for their present position.[35] The western capital of the northern arcade is of 1885. The next capital to the east, of small size, is evidently pilfered from some Roman edifice of the decadence (Plate 136, Fig. 3). It is much mutilated, and appears to date from the IV century. The next capital is similar, but better preserved. The next has been restored. The fifth is an original capital of the IX century, characterized by the absence of undercutting, and by the curious stiffness of the volutes and petals of the acanthus leaves, which are scratched rather than carved (Plate 136, Fig. 5). This capital has, unfortunately, been much damaged. The remaining three capitals of the northern arcade have all been restored. The western capital of the southern arcade is pilfered Roman. The second one is an original composition of the IX century (Plate 136, Fig. 4); it is of the block or composite type, without volutes, and is very crudely executed. The upper portion describes in plan a curve about half way between a circle and a square. The third, fifth and seventh capitals on this side are pilfered Roman, the fourth, sixth and eighth have been restored.

Of equal interest are the capitals of the crypt. The two westernmost in the northern row of columns are of the decadent Corinthian type; the next one (Plate 137, Fig. 2) is similar, but is even more debased, though this is perhaps due more to careless execution than to late date. These are all of the IX century. The fourth capital is of a Byzantine type, of good proportions, with flaccid but pointed acanthus leaves (Plate 137, Fig. 3). On the centre of two faces is inscribed a Greek cross. This capital is certainly of the second half of the VI century. (Compare the capital of S. Apollinare Nuovo, Ravenna, Plate 137, Fig. 6). The easternmost capital of the northern row (Plate 137, Fig. 1) is of an exactly similar type and

[35] Except the second from the west of the north arcade, part of which, in marble, is pilfered, and the column in the north side aisle, also marble, and also pilfered.

contemporary, but has very strange proportions, being extremely long and slender. It has two rows of slim acanthus leaves. The easternmost capital of the southern row is of decadent Corinthian type, as is the second one, part of the acanthus leaves of which are carved, part not. The third capital is the upper half of a Corinthian capital of very debased style, dating perhaps from the VII century (Plate 136, Fig. 2). The two eastern capitals are modern.

In the exterior of the north wall are collected fragments of capitals (Plate 137, Fig. 5), and slabs belonging to church-furniture of the IX century.

All the arched corbel-tables of the edifice were added in the recent restoration. The apses (Plate 135, Fig. 4) were supplied externally with pilaster strips like those of Agliate, and probably had originally a cornice of blind arches. Those of the central apse are at present in two orders (Plate 137, Fig. 4), but the cornice was very thoroughly restored in 1885. Owing to this circumstance, it is now impossible to say whether such was the original disposition, or whether the cornice was remade in the XI century.

V. The style of S. Vincenzo in Prato is certainly that of the IX century. The masonry (Plate 137, Fig. 7) is analogous to that of the old campanile of S. Ambrogio (Plate 118, Fig. 4), a structure erected in the first quarter of the IX century. Other parts of S. Vincenzo recall S. Pietro of Agliate (third quarter of the IX century). The pilaster strips of the apse are similar in the two structures, and the ground plan is very analogous (Plate 8; Plate 134). However, Agliate appears more advanced, in that the choir and eastern bays of the side aisles are vaulted, whereas, at S. Vincenzo, they are covered with timber. Moreover, the capitals of S. Vincenzo (Plate 136, Fig. 4, 5; Plate 137, Fig. 2, 5) are distinctly cruder and more primitive than those of S. Satiro at Milan (c. 870)—Plate 132, Fig. 3, 5. The style of S. Vincenzo, therefore, is evidently that of the second quarter of the IX century. Now, we have seen that there is reason to believe that the monastery was founded, and relics translated, between 824 and 833. It is consequently entirely probable that the edifice was erected at the same time, or we may say, c. 830. The building, at present, bears few traces of having been restored in 1386. It is probable that the alterations carried out at this epoch were confined to walling off the two chapels on either side of the choir, to frescos, and other additions that have since been destroyed.